수능 1등급 완벽 대비 수능기출

20일 완성 영어 독해

빈칸순삽입 실전

수능 모의고사 전문 출판
입시플라이

수능 영어 1등급
결론은 '빈순삽'

수능에서 영어 1등급을 위한 핵심은 [빈칸 추론·글의 순서·문장 삽입] 유형입니다. 이 세 가지 유형은 8문항으로 전체 45문항 중 18% 밖에 안 되지만, [빈칸 추론·글의 순서·문장 삽입] 유형의 정답 여부로 1등급, 2등급, 3등급이 결정됩니다.

해마다 수능에서 **영어 등급을 결정**하는 대표적 '오답률 1위'는 역시 [빈칸 추론]이며, 그 뒤로 [글의 순서, 문장 삽입]으로 이어지기 때문에 수능 '영어 1등급을 목표'한다면 반드시 이 세 가지 유형을 정복해야 합니다.

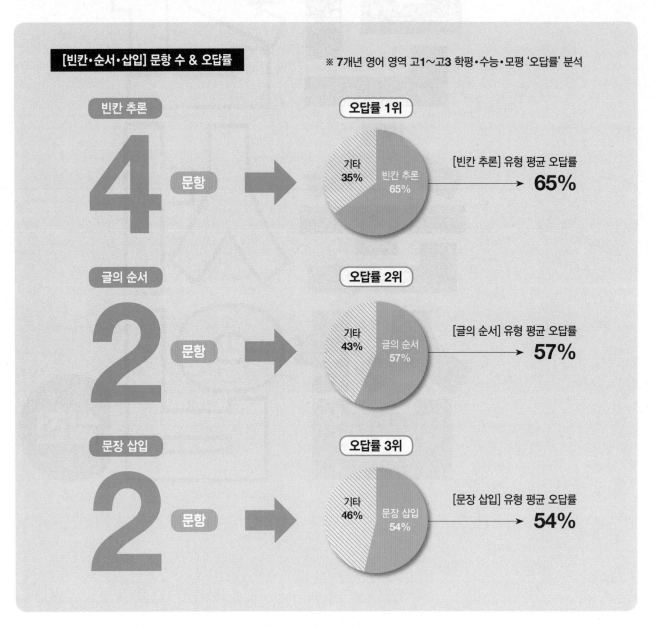

[빈칸·순서·삽입] 문항 수 & 오답률
※ 7개년 영어 영역 고1~고3 학평·수능·모평 '오답률' 분석

빈칸 추론

4 문항 → 오답률 1위

기타 35% / 빈칸 추론 65%

[빈칸 추론] 유형 평균 오답률 → **65%**

글의 순서

2 문항 → 오답률 2위

기타 43% / 글의 순서 57%

[글의 순서] 유형 평균 오답률 → **57%**

문장 삽입

2 문항 → 오답률 3위

기타 46% / 문장 삽입 54%

[문장 삽입] 유형 평균 오답률 → **54%**

※ 오답률 **60%** 이상의 고난도 문제 중 **70%**는 [빈칸·순서·삽입] 유형이며, 최근에는 *[빈칸 추론] 문제뿐 아니라 [글의 순서]와 [문장 삽입] 문제들도 어렵게 출제*된 경우가 많았습니다.

※ 오답률 집계는 기관에 따라 오차가 있을 수 있습니다.

하루 12문제 20분 20일
영어 '1등급' 완성

[빈칸 추론·글의 순서·문장 삽입] 유형의 문제가 모두 어려운 것은 아닙니다. 하루 12문제씩, 20분 학습에는 평이한 문제부터 고난도 2점, 고난도 3점 문항까지 적절히 난이도를 분산 배치해 학습 부담은 낮추고, 효과는 최대한 올릴 수 있도록 '20일 완성'으로 구성했습니다.
[빈칸 추론·글의 순서·문장 삽입] 유형의 문제를 대비하는 **가장 좋은 방법**은 최근 수능에 출제되었던 기출 문제와 학력평가 문제들을 토대로 '다양한 지문의 문제를 풀어보는 것'입니다.

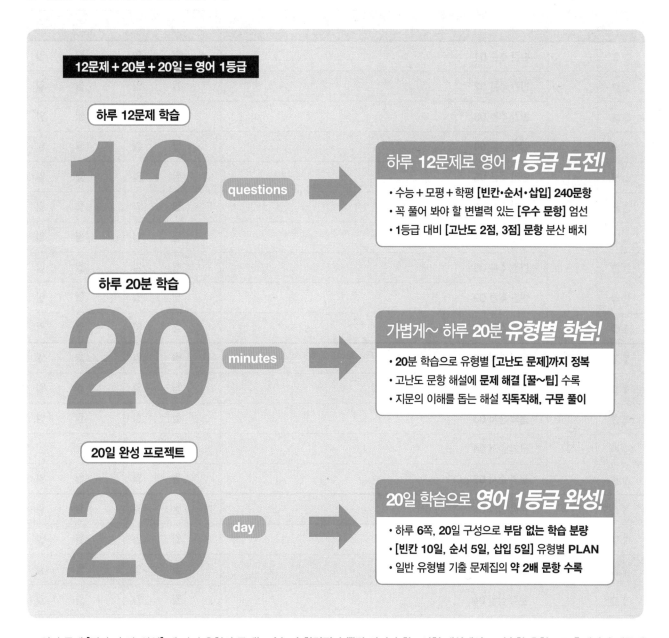

12문제 + 20분 + 20일 = 영어 1등급

하루 12문제 학습

12 questions

하루 12문제로 영어 *1등급 도전!*
- 수능 + 모평 + 학평 [빈칸·순서·삽입] 240문항
- 꼭 풀어 봐야 할 변별력 있는 [우수 문항] 엄선
- 1등급 대비 [고난도 2점, 3점] 문항 분산 배치

하루 20분 학습

20 minutes

가볍게~ 하루 20분 *유형별 학습!*
- 20분 학습으로 유형별 [고난도 문제]까지 정복
- 고난도 문항 해설에 문제 해결 [꿀~팁] 수록
- 지문의 이해를 돕는 해설 직독직해, 구문 풀이

20일 완성 프로젝트

20 day

20일 학습으로 *영어 1등급 완성!*
- 하루 6쪽, 20일 구성으로 부담 없는 학습 분량
- [빈칸 10일, 순서 5일, 삽입 5일] 유형별 PLAN
- 일반 유형별 기출 문제집의 약 2배 문항 수록

※ 영어 독해 [빈칸·순서·삽입] 세 가지 유형의 문제는 *수능과 학력평가* 뿐만 아니라 *학교시험 내신*에서도 비슷한 유형으로 출제되기 때문에 *수능, 내신 모두 영어 1등급*을 위한 필수 유형입니다.

영어 독해 '빈칸·순서·삽입'

20 Day_ planner

- 날짜별로 정해진 **학습 분량**에 맞춰 공부하고 학습 결과를 **기록**합니다.
- **planner**를 이용해 학습 일정을 계획하고 자신의 성적을 체크하면서 **20일 완성**으로 **목표**를 세우세요.
- 학습 분량은 하루 **12문제**로 하시되 자신의 학습 패턴과 상황에 따라 **10일 완성**으로 학습하셔도 좋습니다.

Day	구분	영어 독해 유형	틀린 문제 & 복습해야 할 문제	학습 날짜		복습 날짜	
01	빈칸 추론	빈칸 추론 01		월	일	월	일
02		빈칸 추론 02		월	일	월	일
03		빈칸 추론 03		월	일	월	일
04		빈칸 추론 04		월	일	월	일
05		빈칸 추론 05		월	일	월	일
06		빈칸 추론 06		월	일	월	일
07		빈칸 추론 07		월	일	월	일
08		빈칸 추론 08		월	일	월	일
09		빈칸 추론 09		월	일	월	일
10		빈칸 추론 10		월	일	월	일
11	글의 순서	글의 순서 01		월	일	월	일
12		글의 순서 02		월	일	월	일
13		글의 순서 03		월	일	월	일
14		글의 순서 04		월	일	월	일
15		글의 순서 05		월	일	월	일
16	문장 삽입	문장 삽입 01		월	일	월	일
17		문장 삽입 02		월	일	월	일
18		문장 삽입 03		월	일	월	일
19		문장 삽입 04		월	일	월	일
20		문장 삽입 05		월	일	월	일

영어 독해 '빈칸·순서·삽입'

Contents

빈칸 추론

영어 독해에서 가장 문항수가 많고, 배점이 높아 문항의 난이도 또한 기본으로 높은 게 특징이며, 오답률 1위에 해당할 만큼 까다로운 문제가 많이 출제되고 있습니다. 최근 수능 유형은 주어진 지문이 어려워 해석이 쉽지 않은 경우도 있지만, 선택지에 매력적인 오답이 있어 헷갈리는 1~2문제 때문에 등급이 달라지는 사례가 많았습니다.

▶ 빈칸 추론 유형

> **[31~34] 다음 빈칸에 들어갈 말로 가장 적절한 것을 고르시오.**

영어 영역 31~34번에 해당하는 빈칸 추론은 주어진 제시문을 읽고 그 내용을 이해한 후 빈칸이 포함된 문장과 절 이외의 나머지 부분을 통해 질문에 알맞은 적절한 내용을 빈칸에 완성하는 문제입니다.

중요한 것은 지문의 내용만 묻는 게 아니고 핵심 어구와 절을 완성하는 유형도 있어 빈칸 추론 기출문제 중 고난도 2점, 고난도 3점 문항들을 집중적으로 풀어보고, 지문을 분석하는 논리적 훈련을 통해 고난도 문항에 대한 확실한 대비를 해야 합니다.

 지문 속 표현들을 통해 핵심 내용을 파악 후 선지를 빈칸에 넣고 전후 흐름이 연결 되는지, 빈칸에 들어갈 내용과 잘 통하는지 확인한다.

▶ 빈칸 추론 교재 구성

> **하루 12문항 _ 20분 학습 _ 10일 완성 = 총 120문항**

빈칸 추론은 제시문부터 선지까지 모두 영어로 읽고 답을 해야 하는 부담이 있는 유형입니다. 특히 소재가 정치, 과학, 예술, 철학 등 다양하게 출제되고 있어 **"빈칸이 [전반부, 중반부, 후반부]에 있을 때로 기출 문제를 구분"**하여 학습의 효율성을 높였습니다.

Day 01~02

빈칸이 '전반부'에 있을 때
글의 나머지 내용을 종합해야하는 경우가 많으니 끝까지 쭉 읽고 내용을 파악한다.

Day 03~06

빈칸이 '중반부'에 있을 때
글의 흐름이 하나가 아니고 반전이 있거나 주제를 반박하는 함정이 있으니 주의한다.

Day 07~10

빈칸이 '후반부'에 있을 때
글의 전체 내용을 종합하여 주제문에 자주 등장하는 핵심어 위주로 결론을 완성한다.

PART I
빈칸 추론

Day 01~Day 10

DAY 01

※ 점수 표기가 없는 문항은 모두 2점입니다.

빈칸이 전반부에 있을 때 **빈칸 추론 01**

● 날짜:　월　일　● 시작 시각:　시　분　초

● 목표 시간 : 20분

01

다음 빈칸에 들어갈 말로 가장 적절한 것을 고르시오. [3점]

Much of what we call political risk is in fact _____. This applies to all types of political risks, from civil strife to expropriations to regulatory changes. Political risk, unlike credit or market or operational risk, can be unsystematic and therefore more difficult to address in classic statistical terms. What is the probability that terrorists will attack the United States again? Unlike earthquakes or hurricanes, political actors constantly adapt to overcome the barriers created by risk managers. When corporations structure foreign investments to mitigate risks of expropriations, through international guarantees or legal contracts, host governments seek out new forms of obstruction, such as creeping expropriation or regulatory discrimination, that are very hard and legally costly to prove. Observation of a risk changes the risk itself. There are ways to mitigate high-impact, low-probability events. But analysis of these risks can be as much art as science.

＊expropriation: 몰수　＊＊mitigate: 줄이다

① injustice
② uncertainty
③ circularity
④ contradiction
⑤ miscommunication

02

다음 빈칸에 들어갈 말로 가장 적절한 것을 고르시오.

Learning is *constructive*, not *destructive*. This means we don't _____ mental models — we simply expand upon them. To understand what I mean, think back to your childhood. There was likely a time when you believed in Santa Claus; your mental model accepted him and your predictions accounted for his existence. At some point, however, you came to recognize he was fictitious and you updated your mental model accordingly. At that moment, you didn't suddenly forget everything about Santa Claus. To this day, you can still recognize him, speak of him and embrace young children's belief in him. In other words, you didn't destroy your old mental model, you simply added new information to it. By building upon old mental models we are able to maintain ties to the past, foster a deeper understanding of concepts and develop an ever-expanding pool of information to draw upon in order to continually adapt to an ever-evolving world.

＊fictitious: 가상의

① replace
② imagine
③ predict
④ analyze
⑤ imitate

03

다음 빈칸에 들어갈 말로 가장 적절한 것을 고르시오.

Even as mundane a behavior as watching TV may be a way for some people to _____ _____. To test this idea, Sophia Moskalenko and Steven Heine gave participants false feedback about their test performance, and then seated each one in front of a TV set to watch a video as the next part of the study. When the video came on, showing nature scenes with a musical soundtrack, the experimenter exclaimed that this was the wrong video and went supposedly to get the correct one, leaving the participant alone as the video played. The participants who had received failure feedback watched the video much longer than those who thought they had succeeded. The researchers concluded that distraction through television viewing can effectively relieve the discomfort associated with painful failures or mismatches between the self and self-guides. In contrast, successful participants had little wish to be distracted from their self-related thoughts!

＊mundane: 보통의

① ignore uncomfortable comments from their close peers
② escape painful self-awareness through distraction
③ receive constructive feedback from the media
④ refocus their divided attention to a given task
⑤ engage themselves in intense self-reflection

04

다음 빈칸에 들어갈 말로 가장 적절한 것을 고르시오. [3점]

Theorists of the novel commonly define the genre as a biographical form that came to prominence in the late eighteenth and nineteenth centuries _____ _____ as a replacement for traditional sources of cultural authority. The novel, Georg Lukács argues, "seeks, by giving form, to uncover and construct the concealed totality of life" in the interiorized life story of its heroes. The typical plot of the novel is the protagonist's quest for authority within, therefore, when that authority can no longer be discovered outside. By this accounting, there are no objective goals in novels, only the subjective goal of seeking the law that is necessarily created by the individual. The distinctions between crime and heroism, therefore, or between madness and wisdom, become purely subjective ones in a novel, judged by the quality or complexity of the individual's consciousness.

① to establish the individual character
② to cast doubt on the identity of a criminal
③ to highlight the complex structure of social consciousness
④ to make the objective distinction between crime and heroism
⑤ to develop the inner self of a hero into a collective wisdom

05

다음 빈칸에 들어갈 말로 가장 적절한 것을 고르시오. [3점]

Over a period of time the buildings which housed social, legal, religious, and other rituals evolved into forms that we subsequently have come _____ _____. This is a two-way process; the building provides the physical environment and setting for a particular social ritual such as traveling by train or going to the theater, as well as the symbolic setting. The meaning of buildings evolves and becomes established by experience and we in turn read our experience into buildings. Buildings arouse an empathetic reaction in us through these projected experiences, and the strength of these reactions is determined by our culture, our beliefs, and our expectations. They tell stories, for their form and spatial organization give us hints about how they should be used. Their physical layout encourages some uses and inhibits others; we do not go backstage in a theater unless especially invited. Inside a law court the precise location of those involved in the legal process is an integral part of the design and an essential part of ensuring that the law is upheld.

＊empathetic: 공감할 수 있는

① to identify and relate to a new architectural trend
② to recognize and associate with those buildings' function
③ to define and refine by reflecting cross-cultural interactions
④ to use and change into an integral part of our environment
⑤ to alter and develop for the elimination of their meanings

06

다음 빈칸에 들어갈 말로 가장 적절한 것을 고르시오. [3점]

Scaling up from the small to the large is often accompanied by an evolution from simplicity to complexity while _____. This is familiar in engineering, economics, companies, cities, organisms, and, perhaps most dramatically, evolutionary process. For example, a skyscraper in a large city is a significantly more complex object than a modest family dwelling in a small town, but the underlying principles of construction and design, including questions of mechanics, energy and information distribution, the size of electrical outlets, water faucets, telephones, laptops, doors, etc., all remain approximately the same independent of the size of the building. Similarly, organisms have evolved to have an enormous range of sizes and an extraordinary diversity of morphologies and interactions, which often reflect increasing complexity, yet fundamental building blocks like cells, mitochondria, capillaries, and even leaves do not appreciably change with body size or increasing complexity of the class of systems in which they are embedded.

＊morphology: 형태 ＊＊capillary: 모세관

① maintaining basic elements unchanged or conserved
② optimizing energy use for the structural growth
③ assigning new functions to existing components
④ incorporating foreign items from surroundings
⑤ accelerating the elimination of useless parts

07 1등급 대비 고난도 2점 문제
고3 • 2022학년도 9월 31번

다음 빈칸에 들어갈 말로 가장 적절한 것을 고르시오.

When examining the archaeological record of human culture, one has to consider that it is vastly _____. Many aspects of human culture have what archaeologists describe as low archaeological visibility, meaning they are difficult to identify archaeologically. Archaeologists tend to focus on tangible (or material) aspects of culture: things that can be handled and photographed, such as tools, food, and structures. Reconstructing intangible aspects of culture is more difficult, requiring that one draw more inferences from the tangible. It is relatively easy, for example, for archaeologists to identify and draw inferences about technology and diet from stone tools and food remains. Using the same kinds of physical remains to draw inferences about social systems and what people werethinking about is more difficult. Archaeologists do it, but there are necessarily more inferences involved in getting from physical remains recognized as trash to making interpretations about belief systems.

*archaeological: 고고학의

① outdated　　　　② factual
③ incomplete　　　④ organized
⑤ detailed

08 1등급 대비 고난도 2점 문제
고3 • 2021학년도 6월 32번

다음 빈칸에 들어갈 말로 가장 적절한 것을 고르시오.

One of the great risks of writing is that even the simplest of choices regarding wording or punctuation can sometimes _____ in ways that may seem unfair. For example, look again at the old grammar rule forbidding the splitting of infinitives. After decades of telling students to never split an infinitive (something just done in this sentence), most composition experts now acknowledge that a split infinitive is *not* a grammar crime. Suppose you have written a position paper trying to convince your city council of the need to hire security personnel for the library, and half of the council members — the people you wish to convince — remember their eighth-grade grammar teacher's warning about splitting infinitives. How will they respond when you tell them, in your introduction, that librarians are compelled "to always accompany" visitors to the rare book room because of the threat of damage? How much of their attention have you suddenly lost because of their automatic recollection of what is now a nonrule? It is possible, in other words, to write correctly and still offend your readers' notions of your language competence.

*punctuation: 구두점　**infinitive: 부정사(不定詞)

① reveal your hidden intention
② distort the meaning of the sentence
③ prejudice your audience against you
④ test your audience's reading comprehension
⑤ create fierce debates about your writing topic

09 1등급 대비 고난도 3점 문제 ~~~~~~~ 고3·2023년 4월 34번

다음 빈칸에 들어갈 말로 가장 적절한 것을 고르시오. [3점]

In Hegel's philosophy, even though there is interaction and interrelation between the universal and the individual, _____. For Hegel, individuals are not distinguished in terms of Reason. In *Philosophy of Right* Hegel stresses particularity and universality as follows: "A man, who acts perversely, exhibits particularity. The rational is the highway on which everyone travels, and no one is specially marked." Here, Hegel maintains that individuals can be differentiated from each other in terms of their acts but they are not differentiated with respect to reason. There are specific thoughts, but they are finally resolved into the universal. One might say that Hegel seems to focus on the individual like Aristotle but in reality, he subtly treats the universal as fundamental whereas Aristotle considers the individual as primary substance and universal as secondary substance; in so doing Aristotle emphasizes the universal to be subordinate to the individual in contrast to Hegel.

＊perversely: 별나게

① an individual stands alone apart from the universe
② the universal still has more priority than the individual
③ universal truth cannot be the key to individual problems
④ individuals can't deduce universal principles from reality itself
⑤ every individual should have his or her own particular universe

10 1등급 대비 고난도 3점 문제 ~~~~~~~ 고3·2024학년도 9월 34번

다음 빈칸에 들어갈 말로 가장 적절한 것을 고르시오. [3점]

Prior to photography, _____. While painters have always lifted particular places out of their 'dwelling' and transported them elsewhere, paintings were time-consuming to produce, relatively difficult to transport and one-of-a-kind. The multiplication of photographs especially took place with the introduction of the half-tone plate in the 1880s that made possible the mechanical reproduction of photographs in newspapers, periodicals, books and advertisements. Photography became coupled to consumer capitalism and the globe was now offered 'in limitless quantities, figures, landscapes, events which had not previously been utilised either at all, or only as pictures for one customer'. With capitalism's arrangement of the world as a 'department store', 'the proliferation and circulation of representations ... achieved a spectacular and virtually inescapable global magnitude'. Gradually photographs became cheap mass-produced objects that made the world visible, aesthetic and desirable. Experiences were 'democratised' by translating them into cheap images. Light, small and mass-produced photographs became dynamic vehicles for the spatiotemporal circulation of places.

＊proliferation: 확산　＊＊magnitude: (큰) 규모
＊＊＊aesthetic: 미적인

① paintings alone connected with nature
② painting was the major form of art
③ art held up a mirror to the world
④ desire for travel was not strong
⑤ places did not travel well

11 1등급 대비 고난도 3점 문제 〔고3·2024학년도 수능 34번〕

다음 빈칸에 들어갈 말로 가장 적절한 것을 고르시오. [3점]

Everyone who drives, walks, or swipes a transit card in a city views herself as a transportation expert from the moment she walks out the front door. And how she views the street _____. That's why we find so many well-intentioned and civic-minded citizens arguing past one another. At neighborhood meetings in school auditoriums, and in back rooms at libraries and churches, local residents across the nation gather for often-contentious discussions about transportation proposals that would change a city's streets. And like all politics, all transportation is local and intensely personal. A transit project that could speed travel for tens of thousands of people can be stopped by objections to the loss of a few parking spaces or by the simple fear that the project won't work. It's not a challenge of the data or the traffic engineering or the planning. Public debates about streets are typically rooted in emotional assumptions about how a change will affect a person's commute, ability to park, belief about what is safe and what isn't, or the bottom line of a local business.

＊swipe: 판독기에 통과시키다 ＊＊contentious: 논쟁적인
＊＊＊commute: 통근

① relies heavily on how others see her city's streets
② updates itself with each new public transit policy
③ arises independently of the streets she travels on
④ tracks pretty closely with how she gets around
⑤ ties firmly in with how her city operates

12 1등급 대비 고난도 3점 문제 〔고3·2021학년도 6월 33번〕

다음 빈칸에 들어갈 말로 가장 적절한 것을 고르시오. [3점]

Even when we do something as apparently simple as picking up a screwdriver, our brain automatically _____. We can literally feel things with the end of the screwdriver. When we extend a hand, holding the screwdriver, we automatically take the length of the latter into account. We can probe difficult-to-reach places with its extended end, and comprehend what we are exploring. Furthermore, we instantly regard the screwdriver we are holding as "our" screwdriver, and get possessive about it. We do the same with the much more complex tools we use, in much more complex situations. The cars we pilot instantaneously and automatically become ourselves. Because of this, when someone bangs his fist on our car's hood after we have irritated him at a crosswalk, we take it personally. This is not always reasonable. Nonetheless, without the extension of self into machine, it would be impossible to drive.

＊probe: 탐색하다

① recalls past experiences of utilizing the tool
② recognizes what it can do best without the tool
③ judges which part of our body can best be used
④ perceives what limits the tool's functional utility
⑤ adjusts what it considers body to include the tool

종료 시각	시 분 초	문항 번호	01	02	03	04	05	06	07	08	09	10	11	12
소요 시간	분 초	채점 결과												
초과 시간	분 초	틀린 문항 복습												

DAY 02

※ 점수 표기가 없는 문항은 모두 2점입니다.

빈칸이 전반부에 있을 때 **빈칸 추론 02**

● 날짜 : 　월　일　● 시작 시각 : 　시　분　초

● 목표 시간 : 20분

01

고3 · 2018학년도 9월 31번

다음 빈칸에 들어갈 말로 가장 적절한 것을 고르시오.

One unspoken truth about creativity — it isn't about wild talent so much as it is about ＿＿＿＿＿＿＿＿. To find a few ideas that work, you need to try a lot that don't. It's a pure numbers game. Geniuses don't necessarily have a higher success rate than other creators; they simply do more — and they do a range of different things. They have more successes *and* more failures. That goes for teams and companies too. It's impossible to generate a lot of good ideas without also generating a lot of bad ideas. The thing about creativity is that at the outset, you can't tell which ideas will succeed and which will fail. So the only thing you can do is try to fail faster so that you can move onto the next idea.

＊at the outset: 처음에

① sensitivity
② superiority
③ imagination
④ productivity
⑤ achievement

02

고3 · 2019년 10월 31번

다음 빈칸에 들어갈 말로 가장 적절한 것을 고르시오.

The developmental control that children with certain serious medical problems can exert over their physical activity is relevant to ＿＿＿＿＿＿＿＿. For example, an infant in a crib and a cognitively intact 14-year-old confined to bed due to illness or injury may both be relatively inactive. The adolescent can, however, be expected to have more awareness of and control over movements such as rolling over that might dislodge or otherwise impair the functioning of a medical device such as a breathing tube or feeding tube. Likewise, a 5-year-old and a 25-year-old who have had a cardiac pacemaker implanted may each know that they need to protect the device, but developmental differences in the understanding of risk and causation and in the control of impulses increase the probability of risky behavior by the child, for example, jumping off a porch.

＊dislodge: 떼어 내다　＊＊cardiac pacemaker: 심박 조율기

① device safety
② mental health
③ pain reactions
④ athletic training
⑤ medical diagnoses

03

다음 빈칸에 들어갈 말로 가장 적절한 것을 고르시오.

  Evolutionary biologist Robert Trivers gives an extraordinary example of a case where an animal _____ may be damaging to its evolutionary fitness. When a hare is being chased, it zigzags in a random pattern in an attempt to shake off the pursuer. This technique will be more reliable if it is genuinely random, as it is better for the hare to have no foreknowledge of where it is going to jump next: if it knew where it was going to jump next, its posture might reveal clues to its pursuer. Over time, dogs would learn to anticipate these cues — with fatal consequences for the hare. Those hares with more self-awareness would tend to die out, so most modern hares are probably descended from those that had less self-knowledge. In the same way, humans may be descended from ancestors who were better at the concealment of their true motives. It is not enough to conceal them from others — to be really convincing, you also have to conceal them from yourself.

＊ hare: 산토끼

① disconnecting the link from its circumstance
② having conscious access to its own actions
③ sharpening its own intuitions and instincts
④ relying on its individual prior experiences
⑤ activating its innate survival mechanism

04

다음 빈칸에 들어갈 말로 가장 적절한 것을 고르시오. [3점]

  Enabling animals to _____ is an almost universal function of learning. Most animals innately avoid objects they have not previously encountered. Unfamiliar objects may be dangerous; treating them with caution has survival value. If persisted in, however, such careful behavior could interfere with feeding and other necessary activities to the extent that the benefit of caution would be lost. A turtle that withdraws into its shell at every puff of wind or whenever a cloud casts a shadow would never win races, not even with a lazy rabbit. To overcome this problem, almost all animals habituate to safe stimuli that occur frequently. Confronted by a strange object, an inexperienced animal may freeze or attempt to hide, but if nothing unpleasant happens, sooner or later it will continue its activity. The possibility also exists that an unfamiliar object may be useful, so if it poses no immediate threat, a closer inspection may be worthwhile.

＊ innately: 선천적으로

① weigh the benefits of treating familiar things with care
② plan escape routes after predicting possible attacks
③ overcome repeated feeding failures for survival
④ operate in the presence of harmless stimuli
⑤ monitor the surrounding area regularly

DAY 02

05

다음 빈칸에 들어갈 말로 가장 적절한 것을 고르시오. [3점]

　Like faces, sometimes movement can _____ _____. For example, toys that seem to come alive fascinate children. In my day, one of the popular toys was a piece of finely coiled wire called a "Slinky." It could appear to walk by stretching and lifting up one end over another down an incline, a bit like an acrobatic caterpillar. The attraction of the Slinky on Christmas Day was the lifelike movement it had as it stepped down the stairs before someone trod on it or twisted the spring and ruined it for good. Toys that appear to be alive are curiosities because they challenge how we think inanimate objects and living things should behave. Many toys today exploit this principle to great effect, but be warned: not all babies enjoy objects that suddenly seem lifelike. This anxiety probably reflects their confusion over the question, "Is it alive or what?" Once babies decide that something is alive, they are inclined to see its movements as purposeful.

＊incline: 경사면　＊＊acrobatic: 곡예를 부리는

① fool us into thinking that something has a mind
② help us release and process certain feelings
③ shift our energy and protective mechanisms
④ secretly unlock emotions that words cannot
⑤ create a definite sense of achievement

06

다음 빈칸에 들어갈 말로 가장 적절한 것을 고르시오. [3점]

　Science shows that _____ _____ like gear teeth in a bicycle chain. Rich and novel experiences, like the recollections of the summers of our youth, have lots of new information associated with them. During those hot days, we learned how to swim or traveled to new places or mastered riding a bike without training wheels. The days went by slowly with those adventures. Yet, our adult lives have less novelty and newness, and are full of repeated tasks such as commuting or sending email or doing paperwork. The associated information filed for those chores is smaller, and there is less new footage for the recall part of the brain to draw upon. Our brain interprets these days filled with boring events as shorter, so summers swiftly speed by. Despite our desire for better clocks, our measuring stick of time isn't fixed. We don't measure time with seconds, like our clocks, but by our experiences. For us, time can slow down or time can fly.

＊footage: 장면

① the memory functions of our brain wear out with age
② the richness of experiences relies on intellectual capacity
③ the information storage system in our mind runs restlessly
④ the temporal context of an event pulls our emotions awake
⑤ the size of a memory and our perception of time are coupled

07 1등급 대비 고난도 2점 문제 고3·2022학년도 수능 32번

다음 빈칸에 들어갈 말로 가장 적절한 것을 고르시오.

News, especially in its televised form, is constituted not only by its choice of topics and stories but by its _____. Presentational styles have been subject to a tension between an informational-educational purpose and the need to engage us entertainingly. While current affairs programmes are often 'serious' in tone sticking to the 'rules' of balance, more popular programmes adopt a friendly, lighter, idiom in which we are invited to consider the impact of particular news items from the perspective of the 'average person in the street'. Indeed, contemporary news construction has come to rely on an increased use of faster editing tempos and 'flashier' presentational styles including the use of logos, sound-bites, rapid visual cuts and the 'star quality' of news readers. Popular formats can be said to enhance understanding by engaging an audience unwilling to endure the longer verbal orientation of older news formats. However, they arguably work to reduce understanding by failing to provide the structural contexts for news events.

① coordination with traditional display techniques
② prompt and full coverage of the latest issues
③ educational media contents favoured by producers
④ commitment to long-lasting news standards
⑤ verbal and visual idioms or modes of address

08 1등급 대비 고난도 3점 문제 고3·2022년 4월 31번

다음 빈칸에 들어갈 말로 가장 적절한 것을 고르시오. [3점]

Not only was Eurasia by chance blessed with biological abundance, but the very _____ of the continent greatly promoted the spread of crops between distant regions. When the supercontinent Pangea fragmented, it was torn apart along rifts that just so happened to leave Eurasia as a broad landmass running in an east-west direction — the entire continent stretches more than a third of the way around the world, but mostly within a relatively narrow range of latitudes. As it is the latitude on the Earth that largely determines the climate and length of the growing season, crops domesticated in one part of Eurasia can be transplanted across the continent with only minimal need for adaptation to the new locale. Thus wheat cultivation spread readily from the uplands of Turkey throughout Mesopotamia, to Europe, and all the way round to India, for example. The twin continents of the Americas, by contrast, lie in a north-south direction. Here, the spreading of crops originally domesticated in one region to another led to a much harder process of re-adapting the plant species to different growing conditions.

* fragment: 조각나다 ** rift: 갈라진 틈

① isolation   ② orientation
③ diversity   ④ conservation
⑤ instability

09 [1등급 대비 고난도 3점 문제] 고3·2021학년도 6월 31번

다음 빈칸에 들어갈 말로 가장 적절한 것을 고르시오. [3점]

Research with human runners challenged conventional wisdom and found that the ground-reaction forces at the foot and the shock transmitted up the leg and through the body after impact with the ground _____ as runners moved from extremely compliant to extremely hard running surfaces. As a result, researchers gradually began to believe that runners are subconsciously able to adjust leg stiffness prior to foot strike based on their perceptions of the hardness or stiffness of the surface on which they are running. This view suggests that runners create soft legs that soak up impact forces when they are running on very hard surfaces and stiff legs when they are moving along on yielding terrain. As a result, impact forces passing through the legs are strikingly similar over a wide range of running surface types. Contrary to popular belief, running on concrete is not more damaging to the legs than running on soft sand.

* compliant: 말랑말랑한 ** terrain: 지형

① varied little
② decreased a lot
③ suddenly peaked
④ gradually appeared
⑤ were hardly generated

10 [1등급 대비 고난도 3점 문제] 고3·2022년 10월 34번

다음 빈칸에 들어갈 말로 가장 적절한 것을 고르시오. [3점]

If you are unconvinced that _____ _____, consider the example of the "flying horse." Depictions of galloping horses from prehistoric times up until the mid-1800s typically showed horses' legs splayed while galloping, that is, the front legs reaching far ahead as the hind legs stretched far behind. People just "knew" that's how horses galloped, and that is how they "saw" them galloping. Cavemen *saw* them this way, Aristotle *saw* them this way, and so did Victorian gentry. But all of that ended when, in 1878, Eadweard Muybridge published a set of twelve pictures he had taken of a galloping horse in the space of less than half a second using twelve cameras hooked to wire triggers. Muybridge's photos showed clearly that a horse goes completely airborne in the third step of the gallop with its legs *collected* beneath it, not splayed. It is called the moment of suspension. Now even kids draw horses galloping this way.

* gallop: 질주(하다) ** splay: 벌리다
*** gentry: 상류층

① our beliefs influence how we interpret facts
② what we see is an illusion of our past memories
③ even photographs can lead to a wrong visual perception
④ there is no standard by which we can judge good or bad
⑤ we adhere to our intuition in spite of irresistible evidence

11 1등급 대비 고난도 3점 문제

다음 빈칸에 들어갈 말로 가장 적절한 것을 고르시오. [3점]

Although prices in most retail outlets are set by the retailer, this does not mean that these prices _____ _____. On any particular day we find that all products have a specific price ticket on them. However, this price may be different from day to day or week to week. The price that the farmer gets from the wholesaler is much more flexible from day to day than the price that the retailer charges consumers. If, for example, bad weather leads to a poor potato crop, then the price that supermarkets have to pay to their wholesalers for potatoes will go up and this will be reflected in the prices they mark on potatoes in their stores. Thus, these prices do reflect the interaction of demand and supply in the wider marketplace for potatoes. Although they do not change in the supermarket from hour to hour to reflect local variations in demand and supply, they do change over time to reflect the underlying conditions of the overall production of and demand for the goods in question.

① reflect the principle of demand and supply

② may not change from hour to hour

③ go up due to bad weather

④ do not adjust to market forces over time

⑤ can be changed by the farmer's active role

12 1등급 대비 고난도 3점 문제

다음 빈칸에 들어갈 말로 가장 적절한 것을 고르시오. [3점]

The future of our high-tech goods may lie not in the limitations of our minds, but in _____ _____. In previous eras, such as the Iron Age and the Bronze Age, the discovery of new elements brought forth seemingly unending numbers of new inventions. Now the combinations may truly be unending. We are now witnessing a fundamental shift in our resource demands. At no point in human history have we used *more* elements, in *more* combinations, and in increasingly refined amounts. Our ingenuity will soon outpace our material supplies. This situation comes at a defining moment when the world is struggling to reduce its reliance on fossil fuels. Fortunately, rare metals are key ingredients in green technologies such as electric cars, wind turbines, and solar panels. They help to convert free natural resources like the sun and wind into the power that fuels our lives. But without increasing today's limited supplies, we have no chance of developing the alternative green technologies we need to slow climate change.

＊ ingenuity: 창의력

① our ability to secure the ingredients to produce them

② our effort to make them as eco-friendly as possible

③ the wider distribution of innovative technologies

④ governmental policies not to limit resource supplies

⑤ the constant update and improvement of their functions

학습 Check!

▶ 몰라서 틀린 문항 × 표기   ▶ 헷갈렸거나 찍은 문항 △ 표기   ▶ ×, △ 문항은 다시 풀고 ✔ 표기를 하세요.

종료 시각	시 분 초	문항 번호	01	02	03	04	05	06	07	08	09	10	11	12
소요 시간	분 초	채점 결과												
초과 시간	분 초	틀린 문항 복습												

DAY 03

※ 점수 표기가 없는 문항은 모두 2점입니다.

빈칸이 중반부에 있을 때 **빈칸 추론 03**

● 날짜 :　월　일　● 시작 시각 :　시　분　초　　　　　　　● 목표 시간 : 20분

01

다음 빈칸에 들어갈 말로 가장 적절한 것을 고르시오.

People have always needed to eat, and they always will. Rising emphasis on self-expression values does not put an end to material desires. But prevailing economic orientations are gradually being reshaped. People who work in the knowledge sector continue to seek high salaries, but they place equal or greater emphasis on doing stimulating work and being able to follow their own time schedules. Consumption is becoming progressively less determined by the need for sustenance and the practical use of the goods consumed. People still eat, but a growing component of food's value is determined by its _____ aspects. People pay a premium to eat exotic cuisines that provide an interesting experience or that symbolize a distinctive life-style. The publics of postindustrial societies place growing emphasis on "political consumerism," such as boycotting goods whose production violates ecological or ethical standards. Consumption is less and less a matter of sustenance and more and more a question of life-style — and choice.

* prevail: 우세하다 　** cuisine: 요리

① quantitative 　　② nonmaterial
③ nutritional 　　　④ invariable
⑤ economic

02

다음 빈칸에 들어갈 말로 가장 적절한 것을 고르시오.

Writing lyrics means shaping the meaning of something which, if left as instrumental music, would remain undefined; there is a change of the level of expression. That's one reason why for many songwriters 'lyric' seems to be the hardest word. Picture this scene: a songwriter at the piano, or with a guitar, plays with chords and creates an emotion and atmosphere that is creatively inspiring. Our songwriter invents a melody to go with this mood. Then comes the moment where words are required, and that means getting specific. This sad- or happy-sounding chord progression must now direct its general sadness or happiness to a *particular* human situation. A lyric is the place where the emotional suggestions of pure music are defined as _____ human concerns and events. It's like a piece of translation, from one medium into another. The general musical mood is focused by a lyric into a context, a voice, a human drama.

① concrete 　　　② obscure
③ ethical 　　　　④ unforeseen
⑤ exaggerated

03

다음 빈칸에 들어갈 말로 가장 적절한 것을 고르시오.

Among the most fascinating natural temperature-regulating behaviors are those of social insects such as bees and ants. These insects are able to maintain a nearly constant temperature in their hives or mounds throughout the year. The constancy of these microclimates depends not just on the location and insulation of the habitat, but on _____. When the surrounding temperature increases, the activity in the hive decreases, which decreases the amount of heat generated by insect metabolism. In fact, many animals decrease their activity in the heat and increase it in the cold, and people who are allowed to choose levels of physical activity in hot or cold environments adjust their workload precisely to body temperature. This behavior serves to avoid both hypothermia and hyperthermia.

＊insulation: 단열 ＊＊hypothermia: 저체온(증)

＊＊＊hyperthermia: 고체온(증)

① the activity of the insects in the colony
② the interaction with other species
③ the change in colony population
④ the building materials of the habitat
⑤ the physical development of the inhabitants

04

다음 빈칸에 들어갈 말로 가장 적절한 것을 고르시오.

Animals arguably make art. The male bowerbirds of New Guinea and Australia dedicate huge fractions of their time and energy to creating elaborate structures from twigs, flowers, berries, beetle wings, and even colorful trash. These are the backdrops to their complex mating dances, which include acrobatic moves and even imitations of other species. What's most amazing about the towers and "bowers" they construct is that they aren't stereotyped like a beehive or hummingbird nest. Each one is different. Artistic skill, along with fine craftsbirdship, is rewarded by the females. Many researchers suggest these displays are used by the females to gauge the cognitive abilities of her potential mates, but Darwin thought that she was actually attracted to their beauty. In other words, the bowers _____; they are appreciated by the females for their own sake, much as we appreciate a painting or a bouquet of spring flowers. A 2013 study looked at whether bowerbirds that did better on cognitive tests were more successful at attracting mates. They were not, suggesting whatever the females are looking for, it isn't a straightforward indicator of cognitive ability.

① block any possibility of reproduction
② aren't simply signals of mate quality
③ hardly sustain their forms long enough
④ don't let the mating competition overheat
⑤ can be a direct indicator of aggressiveness

05

다음 빈칸에 들어갈 말로 가장 적절한 것을 고르시오.

With population growth slowing, the strongest force increasing demand for more agricultural production will be *rising incomes*, which are desired by practically all governments and individuals. Although richer people spend smaller proportions of their income on food, in total they consume more food — and richer food, which contributes to various kinds of disease and debilitation. The changes in diet that usually accompany higher incomes will require relatively greater increases in the production of feed grains, rather than food grains, as foods of animal origin partly _____ _____. It takes two to six times more grain to produce food value through animals than to get the equivalent value directly from plants. It is thus quite credible to estimate that in order to meet economic and social needs within the next three to five decades, the world should be producing more than twice as much grain and agricultural products as at present, but in ways that these are accessible to the food-insecure.

*debilitation: 건강 악화

① displace plant-based foods in people's diets
② demand eco-friendly processing systems
③ cause several nutritional imbalances
④ indicate the consumers' higher social status
⑤ play an important role in population growth

06

다음 빈칸에 들어갈 말로 가장 적절한 것을 고르시오. [3점]

An individual characteristic that moderates the relationship with behavior is self-efficacy, or a judgment of one's capability to accomplish a certain level of performance. People who have a high sense of self-efficacy tend to pursue challenging goals that may be outside the reach of the average person. People with a strong sense of self-efficacy, therefore, may be more willing to step outside the culturally prescribed behaviors to attempt tasks or goals for which success is viewed as improbable by the majority of social actors in a setting. For these individuals, _____ _____. For example, Australians tend to endorse the "Tall Poppy Syndrome." This saying suggests that any "poppy" that outgrows the others in a field will get "cut down;" in other words, any overachiever will eventually fail. Interviews and observations suggest that it is the high self-efficacy Australians who step outside this culturally prescribed behavior to actually achieve beyond average.

*self-efficacy: 자기 효능감 **endorse: 지지하다

① self-efficacy is not easy to define
② culture will have little or no impact on behavior
③ setting a goal is important before starting a task
④ high self-efficacy is a typical quality of Australians
⑤ judging the reaction from the community will be hard

07 1등급 대비 고난도 2쩝 문제

다음 빈칸에 들어갈 말로 가장 적절한 것을 고르시오.

"What's in a name? That which we call a rose, by any other name would smell as sweet." This thought of Shakespeare's points up a difference between roses and, say, paintings. Natural objects, such as roses, are not _____. They are not taken as vehicles of meanings and messages. They belong to no tradition, strictly speaking have no style, and are not understood within a framework of culture and convention. Rather, they are sensed and savored relatively directly, without intellectual mediation, and so what they are called, either individually or collectively, has little bearing on our experience of them. What a work of art is titled, on the other hand, has a significant effect on the aesthetic face it presents and on the qualities we correctly perceive in it. A painting of a rose, by a name other than the one it has, might very well smell different, aesthetically speaking. The painting titled *Rose of Summer* and an indiscernible painting titled *Vermillion Womanhood* are physically, but also semantically and aesthetically, distinct objects of art.

* savor: 음미하다 ** indiscernible: 식별하기 어려운
*** semantically: 의미적으로

① changed   ② classified
③ preserved   ④ controlled
⑤ interpreted

08 1등급 대비 고난도 2쩝 문제

다음 빈칸에 들어갈 말로 가장 적절한 것을 고르시오.

Infants' preference for looking at new things is so strong that psychologists began to realize that they could use it as a test of infants' visual discrimination, and even their *memory*. Could an infant tell the difference between two similar images? Between two similar shades of the same color? Could an infant recall having seen something an hour, a day, a week ago? _____ _____ held the answer. If the infant's gaze lingered, it suggested that the infant could tell that a similar image was nonetheless different in some way. If the infant, after a week without seeing an image, didn't look at it much when it was shown again, the infant must be able at some level to *remember* having seen it the week before. In most cases, the results revealed that infants were more cognitively capable earlier than had been previously assumed. The visual novelty drive became, indeed, one of the most powerful tools in psychologists' toolkit, unlocking a host of deeper insights into the capacities of the infant mind.

① Memory distortion in infancy
② Undeveloped vision of newborns
③ The preference for social interaction
④ The inbuilt attraction to novel images
⑤ Infants' communication skills with parents

09 1등급 대비 고난도 3점 문제
고3 · 2021년 3월 31번

다음 빈칸에 들어갈 말로 가장 적절한 것을 고르시오. [3점]

People unknowingly sabotage their own work when they withhold help or information from others or try to undermine them lest they become more successful or get more credit than "me." _____ is alien to the ego, except when there is a secondary motive. The ego doesn't know that the more you include others, the more smoothly things flow and the more easily things come to you. When you give little or no help to others or put obstacles in their path, the universe — in the form of people and circumstances — gives little or no help to you because you have cut yourself off from the whole. The ego's unconscious core feeling of "not enough" causes it to react to someone else's success as if that success had taken something away from "me." It doesn't know that your resentment of another person's success curtails your own chances of success. In order to attract success, you need to welcome it wherever you see it.

＊sabotage: 방해하다　＊＊curtail: 줄이다

① Patience
② Rationality
③ Independence
④ Competition
⑤ Cooperation

10 1등급 대비 고난도 3점 문제
고3 · 2024학년도 수능 33번

다음 빈칸에 들어갈 말로 가장 적절한 것을 고르시오. [3점]

There have been psychological studies in which subjects were shown photographs of people's faces and asked to identify the expression or state of mind evinced. The results are invariably very mixed. In the 17th century the French painter and theorist Charles Le Brun drew a series of faces illustrating the various emotions that painters could be called upon to represent. What is striking about them is that _____ _____. What is missing in all this is any setting or context to make the emotion determinate. We must know who this person is, who these other people are, what their relationship is, what is at stake in the scene, and the like. In real life as well as in painting we do not come across just faces; we encounter people in particular situations and our understanding of people cannot somehow be precipitated and held isolated from the social and human circumstances in which they, and we, live and breathe and have our being.

＊evince: (감정 따위를) 분명히 나타내다　＊＊precipitate: 촉발하다

① all of them could be matched consistently with their intended emotions
② every one of them was illustrated with photographic precision
③ each of them definitively displayed its own social narrative
④ most of them would be seen as representing unique characteristics
⑤ any number of them could be substituted for one another without loss

11 1등급 대비 고난도 3점 문제   고3 · 2022학년도 9월 33번

다음 빈칸에 들어갈 말로 가장 적절한 것을 고르시오. [3점]

It is important to recognise the interdependence between individual, culturally formed actions and the state of cultural integration. People work within the forms provided by the cultural patterns that they have internalised, however contradictory these may be. Ideas are worked out as logical implications or consequences of other accepted ideas, and it is in this way that cultural innovations and discoveries are possible. New ideas are discovered through logical reasoning, but such discoveries are inherent in and integral to the conceptual system and are made possible only because of the acceptance of its premises. For example, the discoveries of new prime numbers are 'real' consequences of the particular number system employed. Thus, cultural ideas show 'advances' and 'developments' because they _____ _____. The cumulative work of many individuals produces a corpus of knowledge within which certain 'discoveries' become possible or more likely. Such discoveries are 'ripe' and could not have occurred earlier and are also likely to be made simultaneously by numbers of individuals.

      ＊corpus: 집적(集積)   ＊＊simultaneously: 동시에

① are outgrowths of previous ideas
② stem from abstract reasoning ability
③ form the basis of cultural universalism
④ emerge between people of the same age
⑤ promote individuals' innovative thinking

12 1등급 대비 고난도 3점 문제   고3 · 2023학년도 6월 33번

다음 빈칸에 들어갈 말로 가장 적절한 것을 고르시오. [3점]

Manufacturers design their innovation processes around the way they think the process works. The vast majority of manufacturers still think that product development and service development are always done by manufacturers, and that their job is always to find a need and fill it rather than to sometimes find and commercialize an innovation that _____. Accordingly, manufacturers have set up market-research departments to explore the needs of users in the target market, product-development groups to think up suitable products to address those needs, and so forth. The needs and prototype solutions of lead users — if encountered at all — are typically rejected as outliers of no interest. Indeed, when lead users' innovations do enter a firm's product line — and they have been shown to be the actual source of many major innovations for many firms — they typically arrive with a lag and by an unusual and unsystematic route.

      ＊lag: 지연

① lead users tended to overlook
② lead users have already developed
③ lead users encountered in the market
④ other firms frequently put into use
⑤ both users and firms have valued

▶ 몰라서 틀린 문항 ✕ 표기   ▶ 헷갈렸거나 찍은 문항 △ 표기   ▶ ✕, △ 문항은 다시 풀고 ✔ 표기를 하세요.

종료 시각	시	분	초	문항 번호	01	02	03	04	05	06	07	08	09	10	11	12
소요 시간		분	초	채점 결과												
초과 시간		분	초	틀린 문항 복습												

DAY 04

※ 점수 표기가 없는 문항은 모두 **2점**입니다.

빈칸이 중반부에 있을 때 **빈칸 추론 04**

● 날짜 :   월   일   ● 시작 시각 :   시   분   초

● 목표 시간 : 20분

01

다음 빈칸에 들어갈 말로 가장 적절한 것을 고르시오.

There is a difference between a newsworthy event and news. A newsworthy event will not necessarily become news, just as news is often about an event that is not, in itself, newsworthy. We can define news as an event that is recorded in the news media, regardless of whether it is about a newsworthy event. The very fact of its transmission means that it is regarded as news, even if we struggle to understand why that particular story has been selected from all the other events happening at the same time that have been ignored. News selection is _____ so not all events seen as newsworthy by some people will make it to the news. All journalists are familiar with the scenario where they are approached by someone with the words 'I've got a great story for you'. For them, it is a major news event, but for the journalist it might be something to ignore.

① subjective
② passive
③ straightforward
④ consistent
⑤ crucial

02

다음 빈칸에 들어갈 말로 가장 적절한 것을 고르시오.

In labor-sharing groups, people contribute labor to other people on a regular basis (for seasonal agricultural work such as harvesting) or on an irregular basis (in the event of a crisis such as the need to rebuild a barn damaged by fire). Labor sharing groups are part of what has been called a "moral economy" since no one keeps formal records on how much any family puts in or takes out. Instead, accounting is _____. The group has a sense of moral community based on years of trust and sharing. In a certain community of North America, labor sharing is a major economic factor of social cohesion. When a family needs a new barn or faces repair work that requires group labor, a barn-raising party is called. Many families show up to help. Adult men provide manual labor, and adult women provide food for the event. Later, when another family needs help, they call on the same people.

＊cohesion: 응집성

① legally established
② regularly reported
③ socially regulated
④ manually calculated
⑤ carefully documented

03

다음 빈칸에 들어갈 말로 가장 적절한 것을 고르시오.

A musical score within any film can add an additional layer to the film text, which goes beyond simply imitating the action viewed. In films that tell of futuristic worlds, composers, much like sound designers, have added freedom to create a world that is unknown and new to the viewer. However, unlike sound designers, composers often shy away from creating unique pieces that reflect these new worlds and often present musical scores that possess familiar structures and cadences. While it is possible that this may interfere with creativity and a sense of space and time, it in fact _____. Through recognizable scores, visions of the future or a galaxy far, far away can be placed within a recognizable context. Such familiarity allows the viewer to be placed in a comfortable space so that the film may then lead the viewer to what is an unfamiliar, but acceptable vision of a world different from their own.

＊score: 악보　＊＊cadence: (율동적인) 박자

① frees the plot of its familiarity
② aids in viewer access to the film
③ adds to an exotic musical experience
④ orients audiences to the film's theme
⑤ inspires viewers to think more deeply

04

다음 빈칸에 들어갈 말로 가장 적절한 것을 고르시오.

Jeffrey A. Rodgers, a vice president of a big company, was once taught the simple idea of pausing to refresh. It began when Jeff realized that as he drove home from work each evening his mind was still focused on work-related projects. We all know this feeling. We may have left the office physically, but we are very much still there mentally, as our minds get caught in the endless loop of replaying the events of today and worrying about all the things we need to get done the following day. So now, as he gets to the door of his house, he applies what he calls "the pause that refreshes." He stops for just a moment. He closes his eyes. He breathes in and out once: deeply and slowly. As he exhales, he _____. This allows him to walk through the front door to his family with more singleness of purpose. It supports the sentiment attributed to Lao Tzu: "In work, do what you enjoy. In family life, be completely present."

＊loop: 루프(반복 실행되는 일련의 명령)

① lets the work issues fall away
② makes plans for tomorrow's work
③ retraces the projects not completed yet
④ feels emotionally and physically exhausted
⑤ reflects on the achievements he made that day

05

다음 빈칸에 들어갈 말로 가장 적절한 것을 고르시오.

Through recent decades academic archaeologists have been urged to conduct their research and excavations according to hypothesis-testing procedures. It has been argued that we should construct our general theories, deduce testable propositions and prove or disprove them against the sampled data. In fact, the application of this 'scientific method' often ran into difficulties. The data have a tendency to lead to unexpected questions, problems and issues. Thus, archaeologists claiming to follow hypothesis-testing procedures found themselves having to create a fiction. In practice, their work and theoretical conclusions partly developed _____. In other words, they already knew the data when they decided upon an interpretation. But in presenting their work they rewrote the script, placing the theory first and claiming to have tested it against data which they discovered, as in an experiment under laboratory conditions.

＊excavation: 발굴 ＊＊deduce: 추론하다

① from the data which they had discovered
② from comparisons of data in other fields
③ to explore more sites for their future studies
④ by supposing possible theoretical frameworks
⑤ by observing the hypothesis-testing procedures

06

다음 빈칸에 들어갈 말로 가장 적절한 것을 고르시오. [3점]

Gordon Allport argued that history records many individuals who were not content with an existence that offered them little variety, a lack of psychic tension, and minimal challenge. Allport considers it normal to be pulled forward by a vision of the future that awakened within persons their drive to _____ _____. He suggests that people possess a need to invent motives and purposes that would consume their inner energies. Similarly, Erich Fromm proposed a need on the part of humans to rise above the roles of passive creatures in an accidental if not random world. To him, humans are driven to transcend the state of merely having been created; instead, humans seek to become the creators, the active shapers of their own destiny. Rising above the passive and accidental nature of existence, humans generate their own purposes and thereby provide themselves with a true basis of freedom.

＊transcend: 초월하다

① alter the course of their lives
② possess more than other people
③ suppress their negative emotions
④ sacrifice themselves for noble causes
⑤ show admiration for supernatural power

07 1등급 대비 고난도 2점 문제

다음 빈칸에 들어갈 말로 가장 적절한 것을 고르시오.

The role of science can sometimes be overstated, with its advocates slipping into scientism. Scientism is the view that the scientific description of reality is the only truth there is. With the advance of science, there has been a tendency to slip into scientism, and assume that any factual claim can be authenticated if and only if the term 'scientific' can correctly be ascribed to it. The consequence is that non-scientific approaches to reality — and that can include all the arts, religion, and personal, emotional and value-laden ways of encountering the world — may become labelled as merely subjective, and therefore of little _____ in terms of describing the way the world is. The philosophy of science seeks to avoid crude scientism and get a balanced view on what the scientific method can and cannot achieve.

* ascribe: 속하는 것으로 생각하다 ** crude: 투박한

① question
② account
③ controversy
④ variation
⑤ bias

08 1등급 대비 고난도 2점 문제

다음 빈칸에 들어갈 말로 가장 적절한 것을 고르시오.

Ecological health depends on keeping the surface of the earth rich in humus and minerals so that it can provide a foundation for healthy plant and animal life. The situation is disrupted if the soil loses these raw materials or if _____. When man goes beneath the surface of the earth and drags out minerals or other compounds that did not evolve as part of this system, then problems follow. The mining of lead and cadmium are examples of this. Petroleum is also a substance that has been dug out of the bowels of the earth and introduced into the surface ecology by man. Though it is formed from plant matter, the highly reduced carbon compounds that result are often toxic to living protoplasm. In some cases this is true of even very tiny amounts, as in the case of "polychlorinated biphenyls," a petroleum product which can cause cancer.

* humus: 부식토, 부엽토 ** protoplasm: 원형질

① the number of plants on it increases too rapidly
② it stops providing enough nourishment for humans
③ climate change transforms its chemical components
④ alien species prevail and deplete resources around it
⑤ great quantities of contaminants are introduced into it

09 1등급 대비 고난도 3점 문제

다음 빈칸에 들어갈 말로 가장 적절한 것을 고르시오. [3점]

Development can get very complicated and fanciful. A fugue by Johann Sebastian Bach illustrates how far this process could go, when a single melodic line, sometimes just a handful of notes, was all that the composer needed to create a brilliant work containing lots of intricate development within a coherent structure. Ludwig van Beethoven's famous Fifth Symphony provides an exceptional example of how much mileage a classical composer can get out of a few notes and a simple rhythmic tapping. The opening da-da-da-DUM that everyone has heard somewhere or another _____ _____ throughout not only the opening movement, but the remaining three movements, like a kind of motto or a connective thread. Just as we don't always see the intricate brushwork that goes into the creation of a painting, we may not always notice how Beethoven keeps finding fresh uses for his motto or how he develops his material into a large, cohesive statement. But a lot of the enjoyment we get from that mighty symphony stems from the inventiveness behind it, the impressive development of musical ideas.

＊intricate: 복잡한　＊＊coherent: 통일성 있는

① makes the composer's musical ideas contradictory
② appears in an incredible variety of ways
③ provides extensive musical knowledge creatively
④ remains fairly calm within the structure
⑤ becomes deeply associated with one's own enjoyment

10 1등급 대비 고난도 3점 문제

다음 빈칸에 들어갈 말로 가장 적절한 것을 고르시오. [3점]

Externalization is the foundation from which many narrative conversations are built. This requires a particular shift in the use of language. Often externalizing conversations involve tracing the influence of the problem in a child's life over time and how the problem has disempowered the child by limiting his ability to see things in a different light. The counsellor helps the child to change by deconstructing old stories and reconstructing preferred stories about himself and his life. To help the child to develop a new story, the counsellor and child search for times when the problem has not influenced the child or the child's life and focus on the different ways the child thought, felt and behaved. These _____ help the child create a new and preferred story. As a new and preferred story begins to emerge, it is important to assist the child to hold on to, or stay connected to, the new story.

① exceptions to the problem story
② distances from the alternative story
③ problems that originate from the counsellor
④ efforts to combine old and new experiences
⑤ methods of linking the child's stories to another's

11 *1등급* 대비 고난도 *3점* 문제   고3 • 2021학년도 9월 34번

다음 빈칸에 들어갈 말로 가장 적절한 것을 고르시오. [3점]

Protopia is a state of becoming, rather than a destination. It is a process. In the protopian mode, things are better today than they were yesterday, although only a little better. It is incremental improvement or mild progress. The "pro" in protopian stems from the notions of process and progress. This subtle progress is not dramatic, not exciting. It is easy to miss because a protopia generates almost as many new problems as new benefits. The problems of today were caused by yesterday's technological successes, and the technological solutions to today's problems will cause the problems of tomorrow. This circular expansion of both problems and solutions _____. Ever since the Enlightenment and the invention of science, we've managed to create a tiny bit more than we've destroyed each year. But that few percent positive difference is compounded over decades into what we might call civilization. Its benefits never star in movies.

* incremental: 증가의 ** compound: 조합하다

① conceals the limits of innovations at the present time
② makes it difficult to predict the future with confidence
③ motivates us to quickly achieve a protopian civilization
④ hides a steady accumulation of small net benefits over time
⑤ produces a considerable change in technological successes

12 *1등급* 대비 고난도 *3점* 문제   고3 • 2018학년도 6월 34번

다음 빈칸에 들어갈 말로 가장 적절한 것을 고르시오. [3점]

Since life began in the oceans, most life, including freshwater life, has a chemical composition more like the ocean than fresh water. It appears that most freshwater life did not originate in fresh water, but is secondarily adapted, having passed from ocean to land and then back again to fresh water. As improbable as this may seem, the bodily fluids of aquatic animals show a strong similarity to oceans, and indeed, most studies of ion balance in freshwater physiology document the complex regulatory mechanisms by which fish, amphibians and invertebrates attempt to _____. It is these sorts of unexpected complexities and apparent contradictions that make ecology so interesting. The idea of a fish in a freshwater lake struggling to accumulate salts inside its body to mimic the ocean reminds one of the other great contradiction of the biosphere: plants are bathed in an atmosphere composed of roughly three-quarters nitrogen, yet their growth is frequently restricted by lack of nitrogen.

* amphibian: 양서류 ** invertebrate: 무척추동물

① maintain an inner ocean in spite of surrounding fresh water
② attain ion balance by removing salts from inside their body
③ return to the ocean to escape from their natural enemies
④ rebuild their external environment to obtain resources
⑤ change their physiology in accord with their surroundings

DAY 04

학습 Check!   ▶ 몰라서 틀린 문항 ✕ 표기 ▶ 헷갈렸거나 찍은 문항 △ 표기 ▶ ✕, △ 문항은 다시 풀고 ✔ 표기를 하세요.

종료 시각	시 분 초	문항 번호	01	02	03	04	05	06	07	08	09	10	11	12
소요 시간	분 초	채점 결과												
초과 시간	분 초	틀린 문항 복습												

DAY 05

※ 점수 표기가 없는 문항은 모두 2점입니다.

빈칸이 중반부에 있을 때 **빈칸 추론 05**

● 날짜 :　월　일　● 시작 시각 :　시　분　초

● 목표 시간 : 20분

01

고3 · 2023년 10월 31번

다음 빈칸에 들어갈 말로 가장 적절한 것을 고르시오.

There's reason to worry that an eyes-on-the-prize mentality could be a mistake. Lots of research shows that we tend to be over-confident about how easy it is to be self-disciplined. This is why so many of us optimistically buy expensive gym memberships when paying per-visit fees would be cheaper, register for online classes we'll never complete, and purchase family-size chips on discount to trim our monthly snack budget, only to consume every last crumb in a single sitting. We think "future me" will be able to make good choices, but too often "present me" gives in to temptation. People have a remarkable ability to _____ their own failures. Even when we flounder again and again, many of us manage to maintain a rosy optimism about our ability to do better next time rather than learning from our past mistakes. We cling to fresh starts and other reasons to stay upbeat, which may help us get out of bed in the morning but can prevent us from approaching change in the smartest possible way.

＊crumb: 부스러기　＊＊flounder: 실패하다
＊＊＊upbeat: 낙관적인

① criticize　　　　② remind
③ ignore　　　　④ detect
⑤ overestimate

02

고3 · 2023학년도 9월 32번

다음 빈칸에 들어갈 말로 가장 적절한 것을 고르시오.

Fans feel for feeling's own sake. They make meanings beyond what seems to be on offer. They build identities and experiences, and make artistic creations of their own to share with others. A person can be an individual fan, feeling an "idealized connection with a star, strong feelings of memory and nostalgia," and engaging in activities like "collecting to develop a sense of self." But, more often, individual experiences are embedded in social contexts where other people with shared attachments socialize around the object of their affections. Much of the pleasure of fandom _____ _____. In their diaries, Bostonians of the 1800s described being part of the crowds at concerts as part of the pleasure of attendance. A compelling argument can be made that what fans love is less the object of their fandom than the attachments to (and differentiations from) one another that those affections afford.

＊embed: 끼워 넣다　＊＊compelling: 강력한

① is enhanced by collaborations between global stars
② results from frequent personal contact with a star
③ deepens as fans age together with their idols
④ comes from being connected to other fans
⑤ is heightened by stars' media appearances

03

다음 빈칸에 들어갈 말로 가장 적절한 것을 고르시오.

Interest in extremely long periods of time sets geology and astronomy apart from other sciences. Geologists think in terms of billions of years for the age of Earth and its oldest rocks — numbers that, like the national debt, are not easily comprehended. Nevertheless, the _____ are important for environmental geologists because they provide a way to measure human impacts on the natural world. For example, we would like to know the rate of natural soil formation from solid rock to determine whether topsoil erosion from agriculture is too great. Likewise, understanding how climate has changed over millions of years is vital to properly assess current global warming trends. Clues to past environmental change are well preserved in many different kinds of rocks.

① time scales of geological activity
② global patterns in species diversity
③ regional differences in time perception
④ statistical methods for climate projections
⑤ criticisms of geological period classifications

04

다음 빈칸에 들어갈 말로 가장 적절한 것을 고르시오.

Some of the most insightful work on information seeking emphasizes "strategic self-ignorance," understood as "the use of ignorance as an excuse to engage excessively in pleasurable activities that may be harmful to one's future self." The idea here is that if people are present-biased, they might avoid information that would _____ — perhaps because it would produce guilt or shame, perhaps because it would suggest an aggregate trade-off that would counsel against engaging in such activities. St. Augustine famously said, "God give me chastity — tomorrow." Present-biased agents think: "Please let me know the risks — tomorrow." Whenever people are thinking about engaging in an activity with short-term benefits but long-term costs, they might prefer to delay receipt of important information. The same point might hold about information that could make people sad or mad: "Please tell me what I need to know — tomorrow."

＊aggregate: 합계의 ＊＊chastity: 정결

① highlight the value of preferred activities
② make current activities less attractive
③ cut their attachment to past activities
④ enable them to enjoy more activities
⑤ potentially become known to others

05

다음 빈칸에 들어갈 말로 가장 적절한 것을 고르시오.

The Swiss psychologist Jean Piaget frequently analyzed children's conception of time via their ability to compare or estimate the time taken by pairs of events. In a typical experiment, two toy cars were shown running synchronously on parallel tracks, _____ _____. The children were then asked to judge whether the cars had run for the same time and to justify their judgment. Preschoolers and young school-age children confuse temporal and spatial dimensions: Starting times are judged by starting points, stopping times by stopping points and durations by distance, though each of these errors does not necessitate the others. Hence, a child may claim that the cars started and stopped running together (correct) and that the car which stopped further ahead, ran for more time (incorrect).

* synchronously: 같은 시간에

① one running faster and stopping further down the track
② both stopping at the same point further than expected
③ one keeping the same speed as the other to the end
④ both alternating their speed but arriving at the same end
⑤ both slowing their speed and reaching the identical spot

06

다음 빈칸에 들어갈 말로 가장 적절한 것을 고르시오. [3점]

The narratives that people create to understand their landscapes come to be viewed as marketable entities and a source of income for residents. Landscapes with a strong place identity have an advantage in marketing to tourists, as it is relatively easy to compartmentalize and market their narratives. Such places may have disadvantages as well, however. If place identity is tied to a particular industry, local residents may feel strongly attached to the definitions of place that stem from involvement in that industry, and they may _____ _____ in favor of one based on a tourism industry. People rooted in landscape may feel strong connections to other community members and may resent the invasion of outsiders who they believe are different and challenge their common identity. Finally, local residents may feel that this process reduces their identities to mere commercial transactions, and they may believe they sacrifice what is unique and special about their place.

* entity: 실재   ** compartmentalize: 구획하다
*** transaction: 거래

① resist losing that identity
② stop persisting with the old tie
③ tolerate the shift of that industry
④ alienate themselves from that place
⑤ refuse the advantage of that industry

07 1등급 대비 고난도 2점 문제

고3·2021학년도 수능 31번

다음 빈칸에 들어갈 말로 가장 적절한 것을 고르시오.

In the classic model of the Sumerian economy, the temple functioned as an administrative authority governing commodity production, collection, and redistribution. The discovery of administrative tablets from the temple complexes at Uruk suggests that token use and consequently writing evolved as a tool of centralized economic governance. Given the lack of archaeological evidence from Uruk-period domestic sites, it is not clear whether individuals also used the system for _____. For that matter, it is not clear how widespread literacy was at its beginnings. The use of identifiable symbols and pictograms on the early tablets is consistent with administrators needing a lexicon that was mutually intelligible by literate and nonliterate parties. As cuneiform script became more abstract, literacy must have become increasingly important to ensure one understood what he or she had agreed to.

＊archaeological: 고고학적인　＊＊lexicon: 어휘 목록
＊＊＊cuneiform script: 쐐기 문자

① religious events
② personal agreements
③ communal responsibilities
④ historical records
⑤ power shifts

08 1등급 대비 고난도 2점 문제

고3·2023학년도 6월 32번

다음 빈칸에 들어갈 말로 가장 적절한 것을 고르시오.

The critic who wants to write about literature from a formalist perspective must first be a close and careful reader who examines all the elements of a text individually and questions how they come together to create a work of art. Such a reader, who respects the autonomy of a work, achieves an understanding of it by _____. Instead of examining historical periods, author biographies, or literary styles, for example, he or she will approach a text with the assumption that it is a self-contained entity and that he or she is looking for the governing principles that allow the text to reveal itself. For example, the correspondences between the characters in James Joyce's short story "Araby" and the people he knew personally may be interesting, but for the formalist they are less relevant to understanding how the story creates meaning than are other kinds of information that the story contains within itself.

＊entity: 실체

① putting himself or herself both inside and outside it
② finding a middle ground between it and the world
③ searching for historical realities revealed within it
④ looking inside it, not outside it or beyond it
⑤ exploring its characters' cultural relevance

DAY 05

09 1등급 대비 고난도 3점 문제

다음 빈칸에 들어갈 말로 가장 적절한 것을 고르시오. [3점]

The entrance to a honeybee colony, often referred to as the dancefloor, is a market place for information about the state of the colony and the environment outside the hive. Studying interactions on the dancefloor provides us with a number of illustrative examples of how individuals changing their own behavior in response to local information _____. For example, upon returning to their hive honeybees that have collected water search out a receiver bee to unload their water to within the hive. If this search time is short then the returning bee is more likely to perform a waggle dance to recruit others to the water source. Conversely, if this search time is long then the bee is more likely to give up collecting water. Since receiver bees will only accept water if they require it, either for themselves or to pass on to other bees and brood, this unloading time is correlated with the colony's overall need of water. Thus the individual water forager's response to unloading time (up or down) regulates water collection in response to the colony's need.

＊brood: 애벌레　＊＊forager: 조달자

① allow the colony to regulate its workforce
② search for water sources by measuring distance
③ decrease the colony's workload when necessary
④ divide tasks according to their respective talents
⑤ train workers to acquire basic communication patterns

10 1등급 대비 고난도 3점 문제

다음 빈칸에 들어갈 말로 가장 적절한 것을 고르시오. [3점]

The history of perspective in Western painting matters because of what it reveals for the art of living. Just as most artists conform to the stylistic conventions of the era into which they are born, we similarly conform to prevailing social conventions about how to live. These unwritten rules typically include getting married and having children, owning your own home and having a mortgage, having a regular job and commuting to work, and flying abroad for holidays. For some people these are realities, for others they remain aspirations. It is common to _____. At this point in Western history, they are amongst the dominant conventions that most of us have accepted with little questioning, much as Vermeer and other Dutch baroque painters of the seventeenth century accepted linear perspective without question. It is difficult to see beyond the limitations of the culture that has shaped our ways of looking at the world and at ourselves. We are trapped in the perspective of our own time.

＊mortgage: 담보 대출

① distinguish them from ideas and wishes
② feel social pressure to comply with them
③ apply them to create inspirational artworks
④ ignore them on account of their complexity
⑤ have an objection to being controlled by them

11 1등급 대비 고난도 3점 문제

다음 빈칸에 들어갈 말로 가장 적절한 것을 고르시오. [3점]

The human species is unique in its ability to expand its functionality by inventing new cultural tools. Writing, arithmetic, science — all are recent inventions. Our brains did not have enough time to evolve for them, but I reason that they were made possible because _____ _____. When we learn to read, we recycle a specific region of our visual system known as the visual word-form area, enabling us to recognize strings of letters and connect them to language areas. Likewise, when we learn Arabic numerals we build a circuit to quickly convert those shapes into quantities — a fast connection from bilateral visual areas to the parietal quantity area. Even an invention as elementary as finger-counting changes our cognitive abilities dramatically. Amazonian people who have not invented counting are unable to make exact calculations as simple as, say, 6 − 2. This "cultural recycling" implies that the functional architecture of the human brain results from a complex mixture of biological and cultural constraints.

* bilateral: 양측의 ** parietal: 정수리(부분)의

*** constraint: 제약

① our brains put a limit on cultural diversity
② we can mobilize our old areas in novel ways
③ cultural tools stabilize our brain functionality
④ our brain regions operate in an isolated manner
⑤ we cannot adapt ourselves to natural challenges

12 1등급 대비 고난도 3점 문제

다음 빈칸에 들어갈 말로 가장 적절한 것을 고르시오. [3점]

The revolution's victorious party can claim to have resolved the fundamental anomalies of the old paradigm and to have renewed the prospects for successful research governed by shared assumptions. Indeed, the new community typically rewrites the textbooks, and retells its own history, to reflect this point of view. But from the standpoint of the losers, or even of those who look on impartially, such rewritings might seem to mark change without any genuine claim to progress, because there is no neutral standard by which to assess the merits of the change. The resulting body of knowledge is in any case not cumulative, since much of what was previously known (or merely believed) had to be excluded without ever having been conclusively refuted. One likewise cannot plausibly talk about revolutionary reconstitutions of science as aiming toward truth, for similarly, there can be no _____. The available justification of scientific knowledge after revolutions, couched in new terms according to newly instituted standards, may well be sufficient, but perhaps only because these standards and terms are now inevitably our own.

* anomaly: 변칙, 이례 ** refute: 반박하다

*** plausibly: 그럴듯하게

① official connection between scientists and policy makers
② impartial formulation of standards for its assessment
③ incomplete terms to describe the reconstitutions
④ easy process to learn about new scientific theories
⑤ strong belief that scientific progress benefits everyone

학습 Check!

▶ 몰라서 틀린 문항 × 표기 ▶ 헷갈렸거나 찍은 문항 △ 표기 ▶ ×, △ 문항은 다시 풀고 ✔ 표기를 하세요.

종료 시각	시	분	초	문항 번호	01	02	03	04	05	06	07	08	09	10	11	12
소요 시간		분	초	채점 결과												
초과 시간		분	초	틀린 문항 복습												

DAY 06

※ 점수 표기가 없는 문항은 모두 2점입니다.

빈칸이 중반부에 있을 때　**빈칸 추론 06**

● 날짜 :　　월　　일　● 시작 시각 :　　시　　분　　초

● 목표 시간 : 20분

01

고3 · 2024학년도 9월 31번

다음 빈칸에 들어갈 말로 가장 적절한 것을 고르시오.

　In the post-World War II years after 1945, unparalleled economic growth fueled a building boom and a massive migration from the central cities to the new suburban areas. The suburbs were far more dependent on the automobile, signaling the shift from primary dependence on public transportation to private cars. Soon this led to the construction of better highways and freeways and the decline and even loss of public transportation. With all of these changes came a ＿＿＿＿＿＿ of leisure. As more people owned their own homes, with more space inside and lovely yards outside, their recreation and leisure time was increasingly centered around the home or, at most, the neighborhood. One major activity of this home-based leisure was watching television. No longer did one have to ride the trolly to the theater to watch a movie; similar entertainment was available for free and more conveniently from television.

＊unparalleled: 유례없는

① downfall
② uniformity
③ restoration
④ privatization
⑤ customization

02

고3 · 2021년 4월 31번

다음 빈칸에 들어갈 말로 가장 적절한 것을 고르시오.

　Contrary to popular opinion, woodpeckers don't restrict themselves to rotten trees, and they often start construction in healthy trees. Just like us, woodpeckers want the place where they bring up their families to be solid and durable. Even though the birds are well equipped to hammer away at healthy wood, it would be too much for them to complete the job all at once. And that's why they take a months-long break after making a hole that may be only an inch or two deep, hoping fungi will pitch in. As far as the fungi are concerned, this is the invitation they have been waiting for, because usually they can't get past the bark. In this case, the fungi quickly move into the opening and begin to break down the wood. What the tree sees as a coordinated attack, the woodpecker sees as a(n) ＿＿＿＿＿＿＿＿＿＿＿＿＿. After a while, the wood fibers are so soft that it's much easier for the woodpecker to enlarge the hole.

＊fungi: fungus(균류)의 복수형

① division of labor
② act of sympathy
③ process of negotiation
④ competition for habitat
⑤ defense from predators

03

Minorities tend not to have much power or status and may even be dismissed as troublemakers, extremists or simply 'weirdos'. How, then, do they ever have any influence over the majority? The social psychologist Serge Moscovici claims that the answer lies in their *behavioural style*, i.e. the *way* _____ _____. The crucial factor in the success of the suffragette movement was that its supporters were *consistent* in their views, and this created a considerable degree of social influence. Minorities that are active and organised, who support and defend their position *consistently*, can create social conflict, doubt and uncertainty among members of the majority, and ultimately this may lead to social change. Such change has often occurred because a minority has converted others to its point of view. Without the influence of minorities, we would have no innovation, no social change. Many of what we now regard as 'major' social movements (e.g. Christianity, trade unionism or feminism) were originally due to the influence of an outspoken minority.

＊dismiss: 일축하다　＊＊weirdo: 별난 사람
＊＊＊suffragette: 여성 참정권론자

① the minority gets its point across
② the minority tones down its voice
③ the majority cultivates the minority
④ the majority brings about social change
⑤ the minority cooperates with the majority

04

다음 빈칸에 들어갈 말로 가장 적절한 것을 고르시오.

Choosing similar friends can have a rationale. Assessing the survivability of an environment can be risky (if an environment turns out to be deadly, for instance, it might be too late by the time you found out), so humans have evolved the desire to associate with similar individuals as a way to perform this function efficiently. This is especially useful to a species that lives in so many different sorts of environments. However, the carrying capacity of a given environment _____. If resources are very limited, the individuals who live in a particular place cannot all do the exact same thing (for example, if there are few trees, people cannot all live in tree houses, or if mangoes are in short supply, people cannot all live solely on a diet of mangoes). A rational strategy would therefore sometimes be to *avoid* similar members of one's species.

① exceeds the expected demands of a community
② is decreased by diverse means of survival
③ places a limit on this strategy
④ makes the world suitable for individuals
⑤ prevents social ties to dissimilar members

DAY 06

05

다음 빈칸에 들어갈 말로 가장 적절한 것을 고르시오. [3점]

If the nature of a thing is such that when removed from the environment in which it naturally occurs it alters radically, you will not glean an accurate account of it by examining it within laboratory conditions. If you are only accustomed to seeing it operate within such an artificialarena, you may not even recognize it when it is functioning in its normal context. Indeed, if you ever spot it in that environment you may think it is something else. Similarly, if you believe that leadership only takes the form of heroic men metaphorically charging in on white horses to save the day, you may neglect the many acts which _____ _____. You may fail to see the importance of the grooms who care for the horses, the messengers who bring attention to the crisis or the role played by those cheering from the sidelines. You may miss the fact that without troops supporting them, any claims to leading on the part of these heroes would be rather hollow.

* glean: 찾아내다

① alter the powers of local authorities
② contribute to their ability to be there
③ compel them to conceal their identity
④ impose their sacrifice and commitment
⑤ prevent them from realizing their potential

06

다음 빈칸에 들어갈 말로 가장 적절한 것을 고르시오. [3점]

Elinor Ostrom found that there are several factors critical to bringing about stable institutional solutions to the problem of the commons. She pointed out, for instance, that the actors affected by the rules for the use and care of resources must have the right to _____ _____. For that reason, the people who monitor and control the behavior of users should also be users and/or have been given a mandate by all users. This is a significant insight, as it shows that prospects are poor for a centrally directed solution to the problem of the commons coming from a state power in comparison with a local solution for which users assume personal responsibility. Ostrom also emphasizes the importance of democratic decision processes and that all users must be given access to local forums for solving problems and conflicts among themselves. Political institutions at central, regional, and local levels must allow users to devise their own regulations and independently ensure observance.

* commons: 공유지 ** mandate: 위임

① participate in decisions to change the rules
② claim individual ownership of the resources
③ use those resources to maximize their profits
④ demand free access to the communal resources
⑤ request proper distribution based on their merits

07 1등급 대비 고난도 2편 문제

다음 빈칸에 들어갈 말로 가장 적절한 것을 고르시오.

A connection with ancestors, especially remote ones, is useful for getting a wide-angled, philosophical view of life. Whereas our immediate ancestors are notably skilled at helping us with the "little pictures," namely the particular, the trees — say, a problem with a boss — our remote ones are best for seeing the "Big Picture," namely the general, the forest — say, the meaning of our job. As modern people rush around blowing small problems out of proportion, thus contributing to a global anxiety epidemic, ancestral spirits have a broader perspective that can _____. When it comes to a trivial problem, for example, they'll just tell us, "This too will pass." They appreciate how rapidly and often things change. According to American anthropologist Richard Katz, for instance, Fijians say that from the ancestral viewpoint whatever looks unfortunate may turn out to be fortunate after all: "What may seem to be a horrible outcome ... is seen in another light by the ancestors." The ancestors, it might be said, keep their heads when everyone around them is losing theirs.

* epidemic: 확산 ** anthropologist: 인류학자

① calm the disquieted soul
② boost cooperation in the community
③ make us stick to the specific details
④ result in a waste of time
⑤ complicate situations

08 1등급 대비 고난도 3편 문제

다음 빈칸에 들어갈 말로 가장 적절한 것을 고르시오. [3점]

Innate behaviors used for finding food, such as grazing, scavenging, or hunting, are more dependent on learning than behaviors used to consume food. Mating, nesting, eating, and prey-killing behaviors tend to be governed more by instinct. The greater dependence on learning to find food makes animals in the wild _____. Behaviors used to kill or consume food can be the same in any environment. Ernst Mayr, an evolutionary biologist, called these different behavioral systems "open" or "closed" to the effects of experience. A lion hunting her prey is an example of an open system. The hunting female lion recognizes her prey from a distance and approaches it carefully. Charles Herrick, a neurobiologist, wrote, "the details of the hunt vary every time she hunts. Therefore no combination of simple reflex arcs laid down in the nervous system will be adequate to meet the infinite variations of the requirements for obtaining food."

* scavenge: 동물의 사체를 찾아 다니다
** reflex arc: 반사궁(충격이 통과하여 반사를 형성하는 신경 경로)

① less cooperative with others in their community
② less focused on monitoring predators' approaches
③ more intelligent to build their natural surroundings
④ more sensitive to visual information than any other stimuli
⑤ more flexible and able to adapt to a variety of environments

DAY 06

09 1등급 대비 고난도 3점 문제
고3 · 2020학년도 수능 34번

다음 빈칸에 들어갈 말로 가장 적절한 것을 고르시오. [3점]

There have been many attempts to define what music is in terms of the specific attributes of musical sounds. The famous nineteenth-century critic Eduard Hanslick regarded 'the measurable tone' as 'the primary and essential condition of all music'. Musical sounds, he was saying, can be distinguished from those of nature by the fact that they involve the use of fixed pitches, whereas virtually all natural sounds consist of constantly fluctuating frequencies. And a number of twentieth-century writers have assumed, like Hanslick, that fixed pitches are among the defining features of music. Now it is true that in most of the world's musical cultures, pitches are _____. However, this is a generalization about music and not a definition of it, for it is easy to put forward counter-examples. Japanese *shakuhachi* music and the *sanjo* music of Korea, for instance, fluctuate constantly around the notional pitches in terms of which the music is organized.

① not so much artificially fixed as naturally fluctuating
② not only fixed, but organized into a series of discrete steps
③ hardly considered a primary compositional element of music
④ highly diverse and complicated, and thus are immeasurable
⑤ a vehicle for carrying unique and various cultural features

10 1등급 대비 고난도 3점 문제
고3 · 2020학년도 6월 34번

다음 빈칸에 들어갈 말로 가장 적절한 것을 고르시오. [3점]

Not all Golden Rules are alike; two kinds emerged over time. The negative version instructs restraint; the positive encourages intervention. One sets a baseline of at least not causing harm; the other points toward aspirational or idealized beneficent behavior. While examples of these rules abound, too many to list exhaustively, let these versions suffice for our purpose here: "What is hateful to you do not do to another" and "Love another as yourself." Both versions insist on caring for others, whether through acts of omission, such as not injuring, or through acts of commission, by actively intervening. Yet while these Golden Rules encourage an agent to care for an other, they _____. The purposeful displacement of concern away from the ego nonetheless remains partly self-referential. Both the negative and the positive versions invoke the ego as the fundamental measure against which behaviors are to be evaluated.

＊ an other: 타자(他者)

① do not lead the self to act on concerns for others
② reveal inner contradiction between the two versions
③ fail to serve as a guide when faced with a moral dilemma
④ do not require abandoning self-concern altogether
⑤ hardly consider the benefits of social interactions

11 1등급 대비 고난도 3점 문제

다음 빈칸에 들어갈 말로 가장 적절한 것을 고르시오. [3점]

In the less developed world, the percentage of the population involved in agriculture is declining, but at the same time, those remaining in agriculture are not benefiting from technological advances. The typical scenario in the less developed world is one in which a very few commercial agriculturalists are technologically advanced while the vast majority are incapable of competing. Indeed, this vast majority _____ _____ because of larger global causes. As an example, in Kenya, farmers are actively encouraged to grow export crops such as tea and coffee at the expense of basic food production. The result is that a staple crop, such as maize, is not being produced in a sufficient amount. The essential argument here is that the capitalist mode of production is affecting peasant production in the less developed world in such a way as to limit the production of staple foods, thus causing a food problem.

* staple: 주요한 ** maize: 옥수수
*** peasant: 소농(小農)

① have lost control over their own production
② have turned to technology for food production
③ have challenged the capitalist mode of production
④ have reduced their involvement in growing cash crops
⑤ have regained their competitiveness in the world market

12 1등급 대비 고난도 3점 문제

다음 빈칸에 들어갈 말로 가장 적절한 것을 고르시오. [3점]

To make plans for the future, the brain must have an ability to take certain elements of prior experiences and reconfigure them in a way that does not copy any actual past experience or present reality exactly. To accomplish that, the organism must go beyond the mere ability to form internal representations, the models of the world outside. It must acquire the ability to _____ . We can argue that tool-making, one of the fundamental distinguishing features of primate cognition, depends on this ability, since a tool does not exist in a ready-made form in the natural environment and has to be imagined in order to be made. The neural machinery for creating and holding 'images of the future' was a necessary prerequisite for tool-making, and thus for launching human civilization.

① mirror accurate images of the world outside
② manipulate and transform these models
③ visualize the present reality as it is
④ bring the models back from memory
⑤ identify and reproduce past experiences faithfully

학습 Check!   ▶ 몰라서 틀린 문항 × 표기 ▶ 헷갈렸거나 찍은 문항 △ 표기 ▶ ×, △ 문항은 다시 풀고 ✔ 표기를 하세요.

종료 시각	시 분 초	문항 번호	01	02	03	04	05	06	07	08	09	10	11	12
소요 시간	분 초	채점 결과												
초과 시간	분 초	틀린 문항 복습												

DAY 07

※ 점수 표기가 없는 문항은 모두 2점입니다.

빈칸이 후반부에 있을 때 **빈칸 추론 07**

● 날짜 :　　월　　일　●시작 시각 :　　시　　분　　초

● 목표 시간 : 20분

01

고3・2022학년도 수능 31번

다음 빈칸에 들어갈 말로 가장 적절한 것을 고르시오.

Humour involves not just practical disengagement but cognitive disengagement. As long as something is funny, we are for the moment not concerned with whether it is real or fictional, true or false. This is why we give considerable leeway to people telling funny stories. If they are getting extra laughs by exaggerating the silliness of a situation or even by making up a few details, we are happy to grant them comic licence, a kind of poetic licence. Indeed, someone listening to a funny story who tries to correct the teller — 'No, he didn't spill the spaghetti on the keyboard and the monitor, just on the keyboard' — will probably be told by the other listeners to stop interrupting. The creator of humour is putting ideas into people's heads for the pleasure those ideas will bring, not to provide _____ information.

＊cognitive: 인식의　＊＊leeway: 여지

① accurate
② detailed
③ useful
④ additional
⑤ alternative

02

고3・2023년 4월 31번

다음 빈칸에 들어갈 말로 가장 적절한 것을 고르시오.

Although a balance or harmony between partners clearly develops over time in a relationship, it is also a factor in initial attraction and interest in a partner. That is, to the extent that two people share similar verbal and nonverbal habits in a first meeting, they will be more comfortable with one another. For example, fast-paced individuals talk and move quickly and are more expressive, whereas slow-paced individuals have a different tempo and are less expressive. Initial interactions between people at opposite ends of such a continuum may be more difficult than those between similar types. In the case of contrasting styles, individuals may be less interested in pursuing a relationship than if they were similar in interaction styles. Individuals with similar styles, however, are more comfortable and find that they just seem to "click" with one another. Thus, _____ may provide a selection filter for the initiation of a relationship.

① information deficit
② cultural adaptability
③ meaning negotiation
④ behavioral coordination
⑤ unconditional acceptance

03

다음 빈칸에 들어갈 말로 가장 적절한 것을 고르시오.

Many people create and share pictures and videos on the Internet. The difficulty is finding what you want. Typically, people want to search using words (rather than, say, example sketches). Because most pictures don't come with words attached, it is natural to try and build tagging systems that tag images with relevant words. The underlying machinery is straightforward — we apply image classification and object detection methods and tag the image with the output words. But tags aren't _____. It matters who is doing what, and tags don't capture this. For example, tagging a picture of a cat in the street with the object categories "cat", "street", "trash can" and "fish bones" leaves out the information that the cat is pulling the fish bones out of an open trash can on the street.

① a set of words that allow users to identify an individual object
② a comprehensive description of what is happening in an image
③ a reliable resource for categorizing information by pictures
④ a primary means of organizing a sequential order of words
⑤ a useful filter for sorting similar but not identical images

04

다음 빈칸에 들어갈 말로 가장 적절한 것을 고르시오.

The quest for knowledge in the material world is a never-ending pursuit, but the quest does not mean that a thoroughly schooled person is an educated person or that an educated person is a wise person. We are too often blinded by our ignorance of our ignorance, and our pursuit of knowledge is no guarantee of wisdom. Hence, we are prone to becoming the blind leading the blind because our overemphasis on competition in nearly everything makes looking good more important than being good. The resultant fear of being thought a fool and criticized therefore is one of greatest enemies of true learning. Although our ignorance is undeniably vast, it is from the vastness of this selfsame ignorance that our sense of wonder grows. But, when we do not know we are ignorant, we do not know enough to even question, let alone investigate, our ignorance. No one can teach another person anything. All one can do with and for someone else is to facilitate learning by helping the person to _____.

* prone to: ~하기 쉬운 ** selfsame: 똑같은

① find their role in teamwork
② learn from others' successes and failures
③ make the most of technology for learning
④ obtain knowledge from wonderful experts
⑤ discover the wonder of their ignorance

05

다음 빈칸에 들어갈 말로 가장 적절한 것을 고르시오. [3점]

Thanks to newly developed neuroimaging technology, we now have access to the specific brain changes that occur during learning. Even though all of our brains contain the same basic structures, our neural networks are as unique as our fingerprints. The latest developmental neuroscience research has shown that the brain is much more malleable throughout life than previously assumed; it develops in response to its own processes, to its immediate and distant "environments," and to its past and current situations. The brain seeks to create meaning through establishing or refining existing neural networks. When we learn a new fact or skill, our neurons communicate to form networks of connected information. Using this knowledge or skill results in structural changes to allow similar future impulses to travel more quickly and efficiently than others. High-activity synaptic connections are stabilized and strengthened, while connections with relatively low use are weakened and eventually pruned. In this way, our brains are _____.

＊malleable: 순응성이 있는　＊＊prune: 잘라 내다

① sculpted by our own history of experiences
② designed to maintain their initial structures
③ geared toward strengthening recent memories
④ twinned with the development of other organs
⑤ portrayed as the seat of logical and creative thinking

06

다음 빈칸에 들어갈 말로 가장 적절한 것을 고르시오. [3점]

Modern psychological theory states that the process of understanding is a matter of construction, not reproduction, which means that the process of understanding takes the form of the interpretation of data coming from the outside and generated by our mind. For example, the perception of a moving object as a car is based on an interpretation of incoming data within the framework of our knowledge of the world. While the interpretation of simple objects is usually an uncontrolled process, the interpretation of more complex phenomena, such as interpersonal situations, usually requires active attention and thought. Psychological studies indicate that it is knowledge possessed by the individual that determines which stimuli become the focus of that individual's attention, what significance he or she assigns to these stimuli, and how they are combined into a larger whole. This subjective world, interpreted in a particular way, is for us the "objective" world; we cannot know any world other than _____.

① the reality placed upon us through social conventions
② the one we know as a result of our own interpretations
③ the world of images not filtered by our perceptual frame
④ the external world independent of our own interpretations
⑤ the physical universe our own interpretations fail to explain

07 1등급 대비 고난도 2점 문제

다음 빈칸에 들어갈 말로 가장 적절한 것을 고르시오.

Young contemporary artists who employ digital technologies in their practice rarely make reference to computers. For example, Wade Guyton, an abstractionist who uses a word processing program and inkjet printers, does not call himself a computer artist. Moreover, some critics, who admire his work, are little concerned about his extensive use of computers in the art-making process. This is a marked contrast from three decades ago when artists who utilized computers were labeled by critics — often disapprovingly — as computer artists. For the present generation of artists, the computer, or more appropriately, the laptop, is one in a collection of integrated, portable digital technologies that link their social and working life. With tablets and cell phones surpassing personal computers in Internet usage, and as slim digital devices resemble nothing like the room-sized mainframes and bulky desktop computers of previous decades, it now appears that the computer artist is finally _____.

① awake
② influential
③ distinct
④ troublesome
⑤ extinct

08 1등급 대비 고난도 2점 문제

다음 빈칸에 들어갈 말로 가장 적절한 것을 고르시오.

In the health area, the concern with use after "purchase" is as critical as and even more critical than the concern with the purchase itself. The person who is sold on and goes through disease screening procedures but does not follow through with medical treatment for a diagnosed condition, is as much of a failure as a person who did not avail himself of the screening program to begin with. The obese individual who has been successfully sold on going on a medically prescribed diet but is lured back to his candy jar and apple pie after one week, is as much of a failure as if he never had been sold on the need to lose and control his weight. The most challenging, most difficult, most perplexing problem is not how to sell people on health-supportive practices, not even how to get them to initiate such practices. We have been fairly successful with these. It is to persuade and help them _____.

① to discover the blind spot
② to stick with new practices
③ to build a sense of security
④ to avoid unnecessary treatment
⑤ to come up with novel solutions

09 1등급 대비 고난도 2점 문제

다음 빈칸에 들어갈 말로 가장 적절한 것을 고르시오.

Imagine there are two habitats, a rich one containing a lot of resources and a poor one containing few, and that there is no territoriality or fighting, so each individual is free to exploit the habitat in which it can achieve the higher pay-off, measured as rate of consumption of resource. With no competitors, an individual would simply go to the better of the two habitats and this is what we assume the first arrivals will do. But what about the later arrivals? As more competitors occupy the rich habitat, the resource will be depleted, and so less profitable for further newcomers. Eventually a point will be reached where the next arrivals will do better by occupying the poorer quality habitat where, although the resource is in shorter supply, there will be less competition. Thereafter, the two habitats should be filled so that the profitability for an individual is the same in each one. In other words, competitors should adjust their distribution in relation to habitat quality so that each individual _____

_____.

① fails to find adequate resources in time

② invades the other habitat to get more resources

③ enjoys the same rate of acquisition of resources

④ needs to gather resources faster than newcomers

⑤ is more attracted to the rich habitat than the poor one

10 1등급 대비 고난도 3점 문제

다음 빈칸에 들어갈 말로 가장 적절한 것을 고르시오. [3점]

In *A Theory of Adaptation*, Linda Hutcheon argues that "An adaptation is not vampiric: it does not draw the life-blood from its source and leave it dying or dead, nor is it paler than the adapted work. It may, on the contrary, keep that prior work alive, giving it an afterlife it would never have had otherwise." Hutcheon's refusal to see adaptation as "vampiric" is particularly inspiring for those of us who do work on adaptations. The idea of an "afterlife" of texts, of seeing what comes before as an inspiration for what comes now, is, by its very definition, keeping works "alive." Adaptations for young adults, in particular, have the added benefit of engaging the young adult reader with both then and now, past and present — functioning as both "monuments" to history and the "flesh" of the reader's lived experience. While this is true for adaptations in general, it is especially important for those written with young adults in mind. Such adaptations _____ that might otherwise come across as old-fashioned or irrelevant.

① allow young readers to make personal connections with texts

② are nothing more than the combination of different styles

③ break familiar patterns of the ancient heroic stories

④ give a new spotlight to various literary theories

⑤ encourage young writers to make plots original

11 1등급 대비 고난도 3점 문제

다음 빈칸에 들어갈 말로 가장 적절한 것을 고르시오. [3점]

There was nothing modern about the idea of men making women's clothes — we saw them doing it for centuries in the past. In the old days, however, the client was always primary and her tailor was an obscure craftsman, perhaps talented but perhaps not. She had her own ideas like any patron, there were no fashion plates, and the tailor was simply at her service, perhaps with helpful suggestions about what others were wearing. Beginning in the late nineteenth century, with the hugely successful rise of the artistic male couturier, it was the designer who became celebrated, and the client elevated by his inspired attention. In a climate of admiration for male artists and their female creations, the dress-designer first flourished as the same sort of creator. Instead of the old rule that dressmaking is a craft, _____ _____ was invented that had not been there before.

* obscure: 무명의 ** patron: 후원자
*** couturier: 고급 여성복 디자이너

① a profitable industry driving fast fashion
② a widespread respect for marketing skills
③ a public institution preserving traditional designs
④ a modern connection between dress-design and art
⑤ an efficient system for producing affordable clothing

12 1등급 대비 고난도 3점 문제

다음 빈칸에 들어갈 말로 가장 적절한 것을 고르시오. [3점]

Emma Brindley has investigated the responses of European robins to the songs of neighbors and strangers. Despite the large and complex song repertoire of European robins, they were able to discriminate between the songs of neighbors and strangers. When they heard a tape recording of a stranger, they began to sing sooner, sang more songs, and overlapped their songs with the playback more often than they did on hearing a neighbor's song. As Brindley suggests, the overlapping of song may be an aggressive response. However, this difference in responding to neighbor versus stranger occurred only when the neighbor's song was played by a loudspeaker placed at the boundary between that neighbor's territory and the territory of the bird being tested. If the same neighbor's song was played at another boundary, one separating the territory of the test subject from another neighbor, it was treated as the call of a stranger. Not only does this result demonstrate that _____, but it also shows that the choice of songs used in playback experiments is highly important.

* robin: 울새 ** territory: 영역

① variety and complexity characterize the robins' songs
② song volume affects the robins' aggressive behavior
③ the robins' poor territorial sense is a key to survival
④ the robins associate locality with familiar songs
⑤ the robins are less responsive to recorded songs

DAY 07

학습 Check!

▶ 몰라서 틀린 문항 × 표기 ▶ 헷갈렸거나 찍은 문항 △ 표기 ▶ ×, △ 문항은 다시 풀고 ✔ 표기를 하세요.

종료 시각	시 분 초	문항 번호	01	02	03	04	05	06	07	08	09	10	11	12
소요 시간	분 초	채점 결과												
초과 시간	분 초	틀린 문항 복습												

DAY 08

※ 점수 표기가 없는 문항은 모두 2점입니다.

빈칸이 후반부에 있을 때

빈칸 추론 08

● 날짜 :   월   일 ● 시작 시각 :   시   분   초

● 목표 시간 : 20분

01

고3 • 2020학년도 6월 31번

다음 빈칸에 들어갈 말로 가장 적절한 것을 고르시오.

Some people have defined wildlife damage management as the science and management of overabundant species, but this definition is too narrow. All wildlife species act in ways that harm human interests. Thus, all species cause wildlife damage, not just overabundant ones. One interesting example of this involves endangered peregrine falcons in California, which prey on another endangered species, the California least tern. Certainly, we would not consider peregrine falcons as being overabundant, but we wish that they would not feed on an endangered species. In this case, one of the negative values associated with a peregrine falcon population is that its predation reduces the population of another endangered species. The goal of wildlife damage management in this case would be to stop the falcons from eating the terns without _____ the falcons.

 * peregrine falcon: 송골매 ** least tern: 작은 제비갈매기

① cloning
② harming
③ training
④ overfeeding
⑤ domesticating

02

고3 • 2023년 3월 32번

다음 빈칸에 들어갈 말로 가장 적절한 것을 고르시오.

Lewis-Williams believes that the religious view of hunter groups was a contract between the hunter and the hunted. 'The powers of the underworld allowed people to kill animals, provided people responded in certain ritual ways, such as taking fragments of animals into the caves and inserting them into the "membrane".' This is borne out in the San. Like other shamanistic societies, they have admiring practices between human hunters and their prey, suffused with taboos derived from extensive natural knowledge. These practices suggest that honouring may be one method of softening the disquiet of killing. It should be said that this disquiet needn't arise because there is something fundamentally wrong with a human killing another animal, but simply because we are aware of doing the killing. And perhaps, too, because in some sense we 'know' what we are killing. We make sound guesses that the pain and desire for life we feel — our worlds of experience — have a counterpart in the animal we kill. As predators, this can create problems for us. One way to smooth those edges, then, is to _____.

 * membrane: 지하 세계로 통하는 바위 표면
 ** suffused with: ~로 가득 찬

① view that prey with respect
② domesticate those animals
③ develop tools for hunting
④ avoid supernatural beliefs
⑤ worship our ancestors' spirits

03

다음 빈칸에 들어갈 말로 가장 적절한 것을 고르시오. [3점]

Concepts of nature are always cultural statements. This may not strike Europeans as much of an insight, for Europe's landscape is so much of a blend. But in the new worlds — 'new' at least to Europeans — the distinction appeared much clearer not only to European settlers and visitors but also to their descendants. For that reason, they had the fond conceit of primeval nature uncontrolled by human associations which could later find expression in an admiration for wilderness. Ecological relationships certainly have their own logic and in this sense 'nature' can be seen to have a self-regulating but not necessarily stable dynamic independent of human intervention. But the context for ecological interactions _____. We may not determine how or what a lion eats but we certainly can regulate where the lion feeds.

* conceit: 생각   ** primeval: 원시(시대)의
*** ecological: 생태학의

① has supported new environment-friendly policies
② has increasingly been set by humanity
③ inspires creative cultural practices
④ changes too frequently to be regulated
⑤ has been affected by various natural conditions

04

다음 빈칸에 들어갈 말로 가장 적절한 것을 고르시오. [3점]

Since human beings are at once both similar and different, they should be treated equally because of both. Such a view, which grounds equality not in human uniformity but in the interplay of uniformity and difference, builds difference into the very concept of equality, breaks the traditional equation of equality with similarity, and is immune to monist distortion. Once the basis of equality changes so does its content. Equality involves equal freedom or opportunity to be different, and treating human beings equally requires us to take into account both their similarities and differences. When the latter are not relevant, equality entails uniform or identical treatment; when they are, it requires differential treatment. Equal rights do not mean identical rights, for individuals with different cultural backgrounds and needs might _____ _____ in respect of whatever happens to be the content of their rights. Equality involves not just rejection of irrelevant differences as is commonly argued, but also full recognition of legitimate and relevant ones.

* monist: 일원론의   ** entail: 내포하다

① require different rights to enjoy equality
② abandon their own freedom for equality
③ welcome the identical perception of inequality
④ accept their place in the social structure more easily
⑤ reject relevant differences to gain full understanding

05

다음 빈칸에 들어갈 말로 가장 적절한 것을 고르시오.

Plants are genius chemists. They rely on their ability to manufacture chemical compounds for every single aspect of their survival. A plant with juicy leaves can't run away to avoid being eaten. It relies on its own chemical defenses to kill microbes, deter pests, or poison would-be predators. Plants also need to reproduce. They can't impress a potential mate with a fancy dance, a victory in horn-to-horn combat, or a well-constructed nest like animals do. Since plants need to attract pollinators to accomplish reproduction, they've evolved intoxicating scents, sweet nectar, and pheromones that send signals that bees and butterflies can't resist. When you consider that plants solve almost all of their problems by making chemicals, and that there are nearly 400,000 species of plants on Earth, it's no wonder that the plant kingdom is _____ _____.

① a factory that continuously generates clean air

② a source for a dazzling array of useful substances

③ a silent battlefield in which plants fight for sunshine

④ a significant habitat for microorganisms at a global scale

⑤ a document that describes the primitive state of the earth

06

다음 빈칸에 들어갈 말로 가장 적절한 것을 고르시오. [3점]

If one looks at the Oxford definition, one gets the sense that post-truth is not so much a claim that truth *does not exist* as that *facts are subordinate to our political point of view*. The Oxford definition focuses on "*what*" post-truth is: the idea that feelings sometimes matter more than facts. But just as important is the next question, which is *why* this ever occurs. Someone does not argue against an obvious or easily confirmable fact for no reason; he or she does so when it is to his or her advantage. When a person's beliefs are threatened by an "inconvenient fact," sometimes it is preferable to challenge the fact. This can happen at either a conscious or unconscious level (since sometimes the person we are seeking to convince is ourselves), but the point is that this sort of post-truth relationship to facts occurs only when we are seeking to assert something _____.

* subordinate: 종속하는

① to hold back our mixed feelings

② that balances our views on politics

③ that leads us to give way to others in need

④ to carry the constant value of absolute truth

⑤ that is more important to us than the truth itself

07 1등급 대비 고난도 2점 문제 〔고3·2023학년도 수능 31번〕

다음 빈칸에 들어갈 말로 가장 적절한 것을 고르시오.

There is something deeply paradoxical about the professional status of sports journalism, especially in the medium of print. In discharging their usual responsibilities of description and commentary, reporters' accounts of sports events are eagerly consulted by sports fans, while in their broader journalistic role of covering sport in its many forms, sports journalists are among the most visible of all contemporary writers. The ruminations of the elite class of 'celebrity' sports journalists are much sought after by the major newspapers, their lucrative contracts being the envy of colleagues in other 'disciplines' of journalism. Yet sports journalists do not have a standing in their profession that corresponds to the size of their readerships or of their pay packets, with the old saying (now reaching the status of cliché) that sport is the 'toy department of the news media' still readily to hand as a dismissal of the worth of what sports journalists do. This reluctance to take sports journalism seriously produces the paradoxical outcome that sports newspaper writers are much read but little _____.

* discharge: 이행하다 ** rumination: 생각
*** lucrative: 돈을 많이 버는

① paid ② admired
③ censored ④ challenged
⑤ discussed

08 1등급 대비 고난도 2점 문제 〔고3·2022년 3월 31번〕

다음 빈칸에 들어갈 말로 가장 적절한 것을 고르시오.

In the Indian language of pali, *mettā* means benevolence, kindness or tenderness. It is one of the most important ideas in Buddhism. Buddhism recommends a daily ritual meditation (known as *mettā bhāvanā*) to foster this attitude. The meditation begins with a call to think carefully every morning of an individual with whom one tends to get irritated or to whom one feels aggressive or cold and — in place of one's normal hostile impulses — to rehearse kindly messages like 'I hope you will find peace' or 'I wish you to be free from suffering'. This practice can be extended outwards ultimately to include pretty much everyone on Earth. The background assumption is that, with the right stimulus, our feelings towards people are not fixed and unalterable, but open to deliberate change and improvement. _____ is a learnable skill, and we need to direct it as much towards those we are tempted to dismiss and detest as to those we love.

① Creativity ② Relaxation
③ Compassion ④ Justification
⑤ Empowerment

DAY 08

09 1등급 대비 고난도 3점 문제

다음 빈칸에 들어갈 말로 가장 적절한 것을 고르시오. [3점]

Whatever their differences, scientists and artists begin with the same question: *can you and I see the same thing the same way? If so, how?* The scientific thinker looks for features of the thing that can be stripped of subjectivity — ideally, those aspects that can be quantified and whose values will thus never change from one observer to the next. In this way, he arrives at a reality independent of all observers. The artist, on the other hand, relies on the strength of her artistry to effect a marriage between her own subjectivity and that of her readers. To a scientific thinker, this must sound like magical thinking: *you're saying you will imagine something so hard it'll pop into someone else's head exactly the way you envision it?* The artist has sought the opposite of the scientist's observer-independent reality. She creates a reality dependent upon observers, indeed a reality in which _____ in order for it to exist at all.

① human beings must participate
② objectivity should be maintained
③ science and art need to harmonize
④ readers remain distanced from the arts
⑤ she is disengaged from her own subjectivity

10 1등급 대비 고난도 3점 문제

다음 빈칸에 들어갈 말로 가장 적절한 것을 고르시오. [3점]

The ideal sound quality varies a lot in step with technological and cultural changes. Consider, for instance, the development of new digital audio formats such as MP3 and AAC. Various media feed us daily with data-compressed audio, and some people rarely experience CD-quality (that is, *technical* quality) audio. This tendency could lead to a new generation of listeners with other sound quality preferences. Research by Stanford University professor Jonathan Berger adds fuel to this thesis. Berger tested first-year university students' preferences for MP3s annually for ten years. He reports that each year more and more students come to prefer MP3s to CD-quality audio. These findings indicate that listeners gradually become accustomed to data-compressed formats and change their listening preferences accordingly. The point is that while technical improvements strive toward increased sound quality in a technical sense (e.g., higher resolution and greater bit rate), listeners' expectations do not necessarily follow the same path. As a result, "improved" *technical* digital sound quality may in some cases lead to a(n) _____ _____ .

* compress: 압축하다

① decrease in the perceptual worth of the sound
② failure to understand the original function of music
③ realization of more sophisticated musical inspiration
④ agreement on ideal sound quality across generations
⑤ revival of listeners' preference for CD-quality audio

11 1등급 대비 고난도 3점 문제

다음 빈칸에 들어갈 말로 가장 적절한 것을 고르시오. [3점]

Precision and determinacy are a necessary requirement for all meaningful scientific debate, and progress in the sciences is, to a large extent, the ongoing process of achieving ever greater precision. But historical representation puts a premium on a proliferation of representations, hence not on the refinement of one representation but on the production of an ever more varied set of representations. Historical insight is not a matter of a continuous "narrowing down" of previous options, not of an approximation of the truth, but, on the contrary, is an "explosion" of possible points of view. It therefore aims at the unmasking of previous illusions of determinacy and precision by the production of new and alternative representations, rather than at achieving truth by a careful analysis of what was right and wrong in those previous representations. And from this perspective, the development of historical insight may indeed be regarded by the outsider as a process of creating ever more confusion, a continuous questioning of _____, rather than, as in the sciences, an ever greater approximation to the truth.

＊proliferation: 증식

① criteria for evaluating historical representations
② certainty and precision seemingly achieved already
③ possibilities of alternative interpretations of an event
④ coexistence of multiple viewpoints in historical writing
⑤ correctness and reliability of historical evidence collected

12 1등급 대비 고난도 3점 문제

다음 빈칸에 들어갈 말로 가장 적절한 것을 고르시오. [3점]

One of the criticisms of Stoicism by modern translators and teachers is the amount of repetition. Marcus Aurelius, for example, has been dismissed by academics as not being original because his writing resembles that of other, earlier Stoics. This criticism misses the point. Even before Marcus's time, Seneca was well aware that there was a lot of borrowing and overlap among the philosophers. That's because real philosophers weren't concerned with authorship, but only what worked. More important, they believed that what was said mattered less than what was done. And this is true now as it was then. You're welcome to take all of the words of the great philosophers and use them to your own liking (they're dead; they don't mind). Feel free to make adjustments and improvements as you like. Adapt them to the real conditions of the real world. The way to prove that you truly understand what you speak and write, that you truly are original, is to _____.

＊Stoicism: 스토아 철학

① put them into practice
② keep your writings to yourself
③ combine oral and written traditions
④ compare philosophical theories
⑤ avoid borrowing them

DAY 08

DAY 09

※ 점수 표기가 없는 문항은 모두 2점입니다.

빈칸이 후반부에 있을 때 **빈칸 추론 09**

● 날짜: 월 일 ● 시작 시각: 시 분 초

● 목표 시간 : 20분

01

고3・2019학년도 수능 31번

다음 빈칸에 들어갈 말로 가장 적절한 것을 고르시오.

Finkenauer and Rimé investigated the memory of the unexpected death of Belgium's King Baudouin in 1993 in a large sample of Belgian citizens. The data revealed that the news of the king's death had been widely socially shared. By talking about the event, people gradually constructed a social narrative and a collective memory of the emotional event. At the same time, they consolidated their own memory of the personal circumstances in which the event took place, an effect known as "flashbulb memory." The more an event is socially shared, the more it will be fixed in people's minds. Social sharing may in this way help to counteract some natural tendency people may have. Naturally, people should be driven to "forget" undesirable events. Thus, someone who just heard a piece of bad news often tends initially to deny what happened. The _____ social sharing of the bad news contributes to realism.

＊consolidate: 공고히 하다

① biased
② illegal
③ repetitive
④ temporary
⑤ rational

02

고3・2023학년도 9월 31번

다음 빈칸에 들어갈 말로 가장 적절한 것을 고르시오.

More than just *having* territories, animals also *partition* them. And this insight turned out to be particularly useful for zoo husbandry. An animal's territory has an internal arrangement that Heini Hediger compared to the inside of a person's house. Most of us assign separate functions to separate rooms, but even if you look at a one-room house you will find the same internal specialization. In a cabin or a mud hut, or even a Mesolithic cave from 30,000 years ago, this part is for cooking, that part is for sleeping; this part is for making tools and weaving, that part is for waste. We keep _____. To a varying extent, other animals do the same. A part of an animal's territory is for eating, a part for sleeping, a part for swimming or wallowing, a part may be set aside for waste, depending on the species of animal.

＊husbandry: 관리

① an interest in close neighbors
② a neat functional organization
③ a stock of emergency supplies
④ a distance from potential rivals
⑤ a strictly observed daily routine

03

다음 빈칸에 들어갈 말로 가장 적절한 것을 고르시오.

When you are born, your neocortex knows almost nothing. It doesn't know any words, what buildings are like, how to use a computer, or what a door is and how it moves on hinges. It has to learn countless things. The overall structure of the neocortex is not random. Its size, the number of regions it has, and how they are connected together is largely determined by our genes. For example, genes determine what parts of the neocortex are connected to the eyes, what other parts are connected to the ears, and how those parts connect to each other. Therefore, we can say that the neocortex is structured at birth to see, hear, and even learn language. But it is also true that the neocortex doesn't know what it will see, what it will hear, and what specific languages it might learn. We can think of the neocortex as starting life _____ but knowing nothing in particular. Through experience, it learns a rich and complicated model of the world.

＊neocortex: (대뇌의) 신피질

① having some built-in assumptions about the world
② causing conflicts between genes and environments
③ being able to efficiently reprocess prior knowledge
④ controlling the structure and processing power of the brain
⑤ fighting persistently against the determined world of genes

04

다음 빈칸에 들어갈 말로 가장 적절한 것을 고르시오. [3점]

A large part of what we see is what we expect to see. This explains why we "see" faces and figures in a flickering campfire, or in moving clouds. This is why Leonardo da Vinci advised artists to discover their motifs by staring at patches on a blank wall. A fire provides a constant flickering change in visual information that never integrates into anything solid and thereby allows the brain to engage in a play of hypotheses. On the other hand, the wall does not present us with very much in the way of visual clues, and so the brain begins to make more and more hypotheses and desperately searches for confirmation. A crack in the wall looks a little like the profile of a nose and suddenly a whole face appears, or a leaping horse, or a dancing figure. In cases like these the brain's visual strategies are _____.

＊flicker: 흔들리다

① ignoring distracting information unrelated to visual clues
② projecting images from within the mind out onto the world
③ categorizing objects into groups either real or imagined
④ strengthening connections between objects in the real world
⑤ removing the broken or missing parts of an original image

DAY 09

05

다음 빈칸에 들어갈 말로 가장 적절한 것을 고르시오. [3점]

Politics cannot be suppressed, whichever policy process is employed and however sensitive and respectful of differences it might be. In other words, there is no end to politics. It is wrong to think that proper institutions, knowledge, methods of consultation, or participatory mechanisms can make disagreement go away. Theories of all sorts promote the view that there are ways by which disagreement can be processed or managed so as to make it disappear. The assumption behind those theories is that disagreement is wrong and consensus is the desirable state of things. In fact, consensus rarely comes without some forms of subtle coercion and the absence of fear in expressing a disagreement is a source of genuine freedom. Debates cause disagreements to evolve, often for the better, but a positively evolving debate does not have to equal a reduction in disagreement. The suppression of disagreement should never be made into a goal in political deliberation. A defense is required against any suggestion that _____.

* consensus: 합의 ** coercion: 강압

① political development results from the freedom of speech
② political disagreement is not the normal state of things
③ politics should not restrict any form of difference
④ freedom could be achieved only through tolerance
⑤ suppression could never be a desirable tool in politics

06

다음 빈칸에 들어갈 말로 가장 적절한 것을 고르시오. [3점]

The empiricist philosopher John Locke argued that when the human being was first born, the mind was simply a blank slate — a *tabula rasa* — waiting to be written on by experience. Locke believed that our experience shapes who we are and who we become — and therefore he also believed that, given different experiences, human beings would have different characters. The influence of these ideas was profound, particularly for the new colonies in America, for example, because these were conscious attempts to make a new start and to form a new society. The new society was to operate on a different basis from that of European culture, which was based on the feudal system in which people's place in society was almost entirely determined by birth, and which therefore tended to emphasize innate characteristics. Locke's emphasis on the importance of experience in forming the human being provided

_____.

* empiricist: 경험주의자 ** slate: 석판
*** feudal: 봉건 제도의

① foundations for reinforcing ties between European and colonial societies
② new opportunities for European societies to value their tradition
③ an optimistic framework for those trying to form a different society
④ an example of the role that nature plays in building character
⑤ an access to expertise in the areas of philosophy and science

07 [1등급 대비 고난도 2점 문제]   고3 · 2020학년도 9월 31번

다음 빈칸에 들어갈 말로 가장 적절한 것을 고르시오.

When you begin to tell a story again that you have retold many times, what you retrieve from memory is the index to the story itself. That index can be embellished in a variety of ways. Over time, even the embellishments become standardized. An old man's story that he has told hundreds of times shows little variation, and any variation that does exist becomes part of the story itself, regardless of its origin. People add details to their stories that may or may not have occurred. They are recalling indexes and reconstructing details. If at some point they add a nice detail, not really certain of its validity, telling the story with that same detail a few more times will ensure its permanent place in the story index. In other words, the stories we tell time and again are _____ to the memory we have of the events that the story relates.

* retrieve: 회수하다   ** embellish: 윤색하다

① identical   ② beneficial
③ alien   ④ prior
⑤ neutral

08 [1등급 대비 고난도 2점 문제]   고3 · 2021년 4월 32번

다음 빈칸에 들어갈 말로 가장 적절한 것을 고르시오.

The urban environment is generally designed so as not to make contact with our skin. We do not push through bushes on our way to school or work. Roads and sidewalks are kept clear of obstacles. Only once in a while are we reminded of the materiality of the environment, as when we feel the brush of an unexpected tree branch or nearly fall over a curb. Most of our time is not even spent outside. "Outside" is often just a space we go through to get "inside." Our time is largely spent indoors, where architecture and design collude to provide an environment as lacking as possible in tactile stimulation. In the modern university or office building, floors and walls are flat and smooth, corridors are clear, the air is still, the temperature is neutral, and elevators carry one effortlessly from one level to another. It is commonly assumed that we are best served by our tactile environment when _____.

* collude: 결탁하다

① we accept its harsh elements
② we scarcely notice its presence
③ it does not hinder social interactions
④ we experience it using all the senses
⑤ its design reflects the natural environment

09 1등급 대비 고난도 3편 문제 고3·2022년 3월 32번

다음 빈칸에 들어갈 말로 가장 적절한 것을 고르시오. [3점]

When trying to understand the role of the sun in ancient journeys, the sources become fewer and the journeys less well known. Herodotus writes about an exploratory voyage commissioned by the ancient Egyptian King Necho II in about 600 BC. Necho II reportedly ordered a Phoenician expedition to sail clockwise around Africa, starting at the Red Sea and returning to the mouth of the Nile. They were gone for three years. Herodotus writes that the Phoenicians, upon returning from their heroic expedition, reported that after sailing south and then turning west, they found the sun was on their right, the opposite direction to where they were used to seeing it or expecting it to be. Contemporary astronomical science was simply not strong enough to fabricate such an accurate, fundamental and yet prosaic detail of where the sun would be after sailing past the equator and into the southern hemisphere. It is this that leads many of today's historians to conclude that the journey _____.

* fabricate: 꾸며 내다, 만들어 내다 ** prosaic: 평범한

① must have taken place
② was not reported at all
③ was not worth the time
④ should have been planned better
⑤ could be stopped at any moment

10 1등급 대비 고난도 3편 문제 고3·2024학년도 6월 34번

다음 빈칸에 들어갈 말로 가장 적절한 것을 고르시오. [3점]

One of the common themes of the Western philosophical tradition is the distinction between sensual perceptions and rational knowledge. Since Plato, the supremacy of rational reason is based on the assertion that it is able to extract true knowledge from experience. As the discussion in the *Republic* helps to explain, perceptions are inherently unreliable and misleading because the senses are subject to errors and illusions. Only the rational discourse has the tools to overcome illusions and to point towards true knowledge. For instance, perception suggests that a figure in the distance is smaller than it really is. Yet, the application of logical reasoning will reveal that the figure only appears small because it obeys the laws of geometrical perspective. Nevertheless, even after the perspectival correction is applied and reason concludes that perception is misleading, the figure still *appears* small, and the truth of the matter is revealed _____.

* discourse: 담화 ** geometrical: 기하학의

① as the outcome of blindly following sensual experience
② by moving away from the idea of perfect representation
③ beyond the limit of where rational knowledge can approach
④ through a variety of experiences rather than logical reasoning
⑤ not in the perception of the figure but in its rational representation

11 1등급 대비 고난도 3점 문제
고3·2021학년도 수능 34번

다음 빈칸에 들어갈 말로 가장 적절한 것을 고르시오. [3점]

Successful integration of an educational technology is marked by that technology being regarded by users as an unobtrusive facilitator of learning, instruction, or performance. When the focus shifts from the technology being used to the educational purpose that technology serves, then that technology is becoming a comfortable and trusted element, and can be regarded as being successfully integrated. Few people give a second thought to the use of a ball-point pen although the mechanisms involved vary — some use a twist mechanism and some use a push button on top, and there are other variations as well. Personal computers have reached a similar level of familiarity for a great many users, but certainly not for all. New and emerging technologies often introduce both fascination and frustration with users. As long as _____ in promoting learning, instruction, or performance, then one ought not to conclude that the technology has been successfully integrated — at least for that user.

* unobtrusive: 눈에 띄지 않는

① the user successfully achieves familiarity with the technology

② the user's focus is on the technology itself rather than its use

③ the user continues to employ outdated educational techniques

④ the user involuntarily gets used to the misuse of the technology

⑤ the user's preference for interaction with other users persists

12 1등급 대비 고난도 3점 문제
고3·2018학년도 수능 34번

다음 빈칸에 들어갈 말로 가장 적절한 것을 고르시오. [3점]

Over the past 60 years, as mechanical processes have replicated behaviors and talents we thought were unique to humans, we've had to change our minds about what sets us apart. As we invent more species of AI, we will be forced to surrender more of what is supposedly unique about humans. Each step of surrender — we are not the only mind that can play chess, fly a plane, make music, or invent a mathematical law — will be painful and sad. We'll spend the next three decades — indeed, perhaps the next century — in a permanent identity crisis, continually asking ourselves what humans are good for. If we aren't unique toolmakers, or artists, or moral ethicists, then what, if anything, makes us special? In the grandest irony of all, the greatest benefit of an everyday, utilitarian AI will not be increased productivity or an economics of abundance or a new way of doing science — although all those will happen. The greatest benefit of the arrival of artificial intelligence is that _____ .

* replicate: 복제하다

① AIs will help define humanity

② humans could also be like AIs

③ humans will be liberated from hard labor

④ AIs could lead us in resolving moral dilemmas

⑤ AIs could compensate for a decline in human intelligence

DAY 09

DAY 10

※ 점수 표기가 없는 문항은 모두 **2점**입니다.

빈칸이 후반부에 있을 때　**빈칸 추론 10**

● 날짜 :　　월　　일　● 시작 시각 :　　시　　분　　초　　　　　　　　　● 목표 시간 : 20분

01

다음 빈칸에 들어갈 말로 가장 적절한 것을 고르시오. [3점]

The creativity that children possess needs to be cultivated throughout their development. Research suggests that overstructuring the child's environment may actually limit creative and academic development. This is a central problem with much of science instruction. The exercises or activities are devised to eliminate different options and to focus on predetermined results. The answers are structured to fit the course assessments, and the wonder of science is lost along with cognitive intrigue. We define cognitive intrigue as the wonder that stimulates and intrinsically motivates an individual to voluntarily engage in an activity. The loss of cognitive intrigue may be initiated by the sole use of play items with predetermined conclusions and reinforced by rote instruction in school. This is exemplified by toys, games, and lessons that are a(n) _____ in and of themselves and require little of the individual other than to master the planned objective.

＊rote: 기계적인 암기

① end
② input
③ puzzle
④ interest
⑤ alternative

02

다음 빈칸에 들어갈 말로 가장 적절한 것을 고르시오.

Over the last decade the attention given to how children learn to read has foregrounded the nature of *textuality*, and of the different, interrelated ways in which readers of all ages make texts mean. 'Reading' now applies to a greater number of representational forms than at any time in the past: pictures, maps, screens, design graphics and photographs are all regarded as text. In addition to the innovations made possible in picture books by new printing processes, design features also predominate in other kinds, such as books of poetry and information texts. Thus, reading becomes a more complicated kind of interpretation than it was when children's attention was focused on the printed text, with sketches or pictures as an adjunct. Children now learn from a picture book that words and illustrations complement and enhance each other. Reading is not simply _____. Even in the easiest texts, what a sentence 'says' is often not what it means.

＊adjunct: 부속물

① knowledge acquisition
② word recognition
③ imaginative play
④ subjective interpretation
⑤ image mapping

03

다음 빈칸에 들어갈 말로 가장 적절한 것을 고르시오.

People have always wanted to be around other people and to learn from them. Cities have long been dynamos of social possibility, foundries of art, music, and fashion. Slang, or, if you prefer, "lexical innovation," has always started in cities — an outgrowth of all those different people so frequently exposed to one another. It spreads outward, in a manner not unlike trans-missible disease, which itself typically "takes off" in cities. If, as the noted linguist Leonard Bloomfield argued, the way a person talks is a "composite result of what he has heard before," then language innovation would happen where the most people heard and talked to the most other people. Cities drive taste change because they _____, who not surprisingly are often the creative people cities seem to attract. Media, ever more global, ever more far-reaching, spread language faster to more people.

* foundry: 주물 공장 ** lexical: 어휘의

① provide rich source materials for artists
② offer the greatest exposure to other people
③ cause cultural conflicts among users of slang
④ present ideal research environments to linguists
⑤ reduce the social mobility of ambitious outsiders

04

다음 빈칸에 들어갈 말로 가장 적절한 것을 고르시오. [3점]

Imagine some mutation appears which makes animals spontaneously die at the age of 50. This is unambiguously disadvantageous — but only very slightly so. More than 99 per cent of animals carrying this mutation will never experience its ill effects because they will die before it has a chance to act. This means that it's pretty likely to remain in the population — not because it's good, but because the 'force of natural selection' at such advanced ages is not strong enough to get rid of it. Conversely, if a mutation killed the animals at two years, striking them down when many could reasonably expect to still be alive and producing children, evolution would get rid of it very promptly: animals with the mutation would soon be outcompeted by those fortunate enough not to have it, because the force of natural selection is powerful in the years up to and including reproductive age. Thus, problematic mutations can accumulate, just so long as _____.

* mutation: 돌연변이

① the force of natural selection increases as animals get older
② their accumulation is largely due to their evolutionary benefits
③ evolution operates by suppressing reproductive success of animals
④ animals can promptly compensate for the decline in their abilities
⑤ they only affect animals after they're old enough to have reproduced

05

다음 빈칸에 들어갈 말로 가장 적절한 것을 고르시오. [3점]

The way we perceive the colors of the rainbow, and the universe in general, is influenced by the words we use to describe them. This is not limited to visual perception but also applies to smell, taste, touch, our perception of time and countless other human experiences. A wine or Scotch connoisseur, for example, has a much richer vocabulary at their disposal to describe the fullness, finish, flavors and aroma of the drink, which in turn improves their ability to recognize and remember subtle differences of which a non-expert may be unaware. Similarly, a chef or perfumer has at their disposal labels for flavors and smells that allow them to perceive, differentiate among, prepare and remember subtle variations. The labels that we have at our disposal influence how we see the world around us. Regardless of where you place the limits of linguistic effects on cognition, there is evidence that at least some of the things that we perceive and remember differ depending on _____.

* connoisseur: (예술품·음식·음악의) 감정가   ** cognition: 인식

① where we purchase them
② how expensive they are
③ what labels we use
④ how persuasive ads are
⑤ who makes the products

06

다음 빈칸에 들어갈 말로 가장 적절한 것을 고르시오. [3점]

Apocalypse Now, a film produced and directed by Francis Ford Coppola, gained widespread popularity, and for good reason. The film is an adaptation of Joseph Conrad's novel *Heart of Darkness*, which is set in the African Congo at the end of the 19th century. Unlike the original novel, *Apocalypse Now* is set in Vietnam and Cambodia during the Vietnam War. The setting, time period, dialogue and other incidental details are changed but the fundamental narrative and themes of *Apocalypse Now* are the same as those of *Heart of Darkness*. Both describe a physical journey, reflecting the central character's mental and spiritual journey, down a river to confront the deranged Kurtz character, who represents the worst aspects of civilisation. By giving *Apocalypse Now* a setting that was contemporary at the time of its release, audiences were able to experience and identify with its themes more easily than they would have if the film had been _____.

* deranged: 제정신이 아닌

① a literal adaptation of the novel
② a source of inspiration for the novel
③ a faithful depiction of the Vietnam War
④ a vivid dramatisation of a psychological journey
⑤ a critical interpretation of contemporary civilisation

07 1등급 대비 고난도 2점 문제　　고3·2022학년도 6월 31번

다음 빈칸에 들어갈 말로 가장 적절한 것을 고르시오.

The growth of academic disciplines and sub-disciplines, such as art history or palaeontology, and of particular figures such as the art critic, helped produce principles and practices for selecting and organizing what was worthy of keeping, though it remained a struggle. Moreover, as museums and universities drew further apart toward the end of the nineteenth century, and as the idea of objects as a highly valued route to knowing the world went into decline, collecting began to lose its status as a worthy intellectual pursuit, especially in the sciences. The really interesting and important aspects of science were increasingly those invisible to the naked eye, and the classification of things collected no longer promised to produce cutting-edge knowledge. The term "butterfly collecting" could come to be used with the adjective "mere" to indicate a pursuit of _____ academic status.

* palaeontology: 고생물학　** adjective: 형용사

① competitive　　② novel
③ secondary　　④ reliable
⑤ unconditional

08 1등급 대비 고난도 2점 문제　　고3·2021학년도 9월 32번

다음 빈칸에 들어갈 말로 가장 적절한 것을 고르시오.

Genetic engineering followed by cloning to distribute many identical animals or plants is sometimes seen as a threat to the diversity of nature. However, humans have been replacing diverse natural habitats with artificial monoculture for millennia. Most natural habitats in the advanced nations have already been replaced with some form of artificial environment based on mass production or repetition. The real threat to biodiversity is surely the need to convert ever more of our planet into production zones to feed the ever-increasing human population. The cloning and transgenic alteration of domestic animals makes little difference to the overall situation. Conversely, the renewed interest in genetics has led to a growing awareness that there are many wild plants and animals with interesting or useful genetic properties that could be used for a variety of as-yet-unknown purposes. This has led in turn to a realization that _____ _____ because they may harbor tomorrow's drugs against cancer, malaria, or obesity.

* monoculture: 단일 경작

① ecological systems are genetically programmed
② we should avoid destroying natural ecosystems
③ we need to stop creating genetically modified organisms
④ artificial organisms can survive in natural environments
⑤ living things adapt themselves to their physical environments

DAY 10

09 1등급 대비 고난도 3점 문제
고3 · 2023학년도 9월 34번

다음 빈칸에 들어갈 말로 가장 적절한 것을 고르시오. [3점]

In trying to explain how different disciplines attempt to understand autobiographical memory the literary critic Daniel Albright said, "Psychology is a garden, literature is a wilderness." He meant, I believe, that psychology seeks to make patterns, find regularity, and ultimately impose order on human experience and behavior. Writers, by contrast, dive into the unruly, untamed depths of human experiences. What he said about understanding memory can be extended to our questions about young children's minds. If we psychologists are too bent on identifying the orderly pattern, the regularities of children's minds, we may miss an essential and pervasive characteristic of our topic: the child's more unruly and imaginative ways of talking and thinking. It is not only the developed writer or literary scholar who seems drawn toward a somewhat wild and idiosyncratic way of thinking; young children are as well. The psychologist interested in young children may have to _____ in order to get a good picture of how children think.

* unruly: 제멋대로 구는 ** pervasive: 널리 퍼져 있는
*** idiosyncratic: 색다른

① venture a little more often into the wilderness
② help them recall their most precious memories
③ better understand the challenges of parental duty
④ disregard the key characteristics of children's fiction
⑤ standardize the paths of their psychological development

10 1등급 대비 고난도 3점 문제
고3 · 2022년 10월 33번

다음 빈칸에 들어갈 말로 가장 적절한 것을 고르시오. [3점]

Magical thinking, intellectual insecurity, and confirmation bias are all powerful barriers to scientific discovery; they blocked the eyes of generations of astronomers before Copernicus. But as twenty-first-century researchers have discovered, these three barriers can all be destroyed with a simple teaching trick: transporting our brain to an environment outside our own. That environment can be a nature preserve many miles from our home, or a computer-simulated Mars, or any other space that our ego doesn't associate directly with our health, social status, and material success. In that environment, our ego will be less inclined to take the failure of its predictions personally. Certainly, our ego may feel a little upset that its guesses about the nature preserve or Mars were wrong, but it was never really that invested in the guesses to begin with. Why should it care too much about things that have no bearing on its own fame or well-being? So, in that happy state of apathy, our ego is less likely to get data manipulative, mentally threatened, or magically minded, leaving the rest of our brain free to _____.

* apathy: 무관심

① do away with irregularity and seek harmony
② justify errors by reorganizing remaining data
③ build barriers to avoid intellectual insecurity
④ abandon failed hypotheses and venture new ones
⑤ manipulate the surroundings and support existing ideas

11 1등급 대비 고난도 3점 문제 고3·2020학년도 9월 34번

다음 빈칸에 들어갈 말로 가장 적절한 것을 고르시오. [3점]

The debates between social and cultural anthropologists concern not the differences between the concepts but the analytical priority: which should come first, the social chicken or the cultural egg? British anthropology emphasizes the social. It assumes that social institutions determine culture and that universal domains of society (such as kinship, economy, politics, and religion) are represented by specific institutions (such as the family, subsistence farming, the British Parliament, and the Church of England) which can be compared cross-culturally. American anthropology emphasizes the cultural. It assumes that culture shapes social institutions by providing the shared beliefs, the core values, the communicative tools, and so on that make social life possible. It does not assume that there are universal social domains, preferring instead to discover domains empirically as aspects of each society's own classificatory schemes — in other words, its culture. And it rejects the notion that any social institution can be understood _____.

* anthropology: 인류학 ** subsistence farming: 자급 농업
*** empirically: 경험적으로

① in relation to its cultural origin
② in isolation from its own context
③ regardless of personal preferences
④ without considering its economic roots
⑤ on the basis of British-American relations

12 1등급 대비 고난도 3점 문제 고3·2019학년도 수능 33번

다음 빈칸에 들어갈 말로 가장 적절한 것을 고르시오. [3점]

Heritage is concerned with the ways in which very selective material artefacts, mythologies, memories and traditions become resources for the present. The contents, interpretations and representations of the resource are selected according to the demands of the present; an imagined past provides resources for a heritage that is to be passed onto an imagined future. It follows too that the meanings and functions of memory and tradition are defined in the present. Further, heritage is more concerned with meanings than material artefacts. It is the former that give value, either cultural or financial, to the latter and explain why they have been selected from the near infinity of the past. In turn, they may later be discarded as the demands of present societies change, or even, as is presently occurring in the former Eastern Europe, when pasts have to be reinvented to reflect new presents. Thus heritage is _____.

① a collection of memories and traditions of a society
② as much about forgetting as remembering the past
③ neither concerned with the present nor the future
④ a mirror reflecting the artefacts of the past
⑤ about preserving universal cultural values

DAY 10

▶ 몰라서 틀린 문항 ✕ 표기 ▶ 헷갈렸거나 찍은 문항 △ 표기 ▶ ✕, △ 문항은 다시 풀고 ✔ 표기를 하세요.

종료 시각	시 분 초	문항 번호	01	02	03	04	05	06	07	08	09	10	11	12
소요 시간	분 초	채점 결과												
초과 시간	분 초	틀린 문항 복습												

글의 순서

최근 수능에서는 **글의 순서가 빈칸 추론 못지않게 어렵고 까다롭게 출제된** 경우가 많았습니다. 실제 **수능과 내신 1~2등급을 받는 수험생들도 글의 순서 문제를 어려워하는 경향이** 있습니다. 영어 영역에서 1등급을 목표한다면 반드시 글의 순서 2문항도 확실한 대비를 해야 합니다.

▶ 글의 순서 유형

> **[36~37]** 주어진 글 다음에 이어질 글의 순서로 가장 적절한 것을 고르시오.

영어 영역 **36~37번에 해당하는 글의 순서는 주어진 한 문단의 글과 이어지는 나머지 (A), (B), (C) 세 문단의 연결고리를 찾아 논리적으로 순서를 정하는 문제입니다.**

글의 순서는 해석을 기본으로 하기 때문에 **어법과 구문에 대한 실력이 있어야하며, A글과 B글이 연결되는 근거를 찾아서 단락들을 연결하는 것이므로 연결고리가 되는 대명사나 연결사, 지시어가 가리키는 것을 잘 파악**해야 합니다. 특히 연결고리의 단서가 주어지지 않는 고난도 문제에 대한 대응력도 키워야합니다.

> **꿀팁!** 수능에 자주 출제되는 연결사를 익히고, 순서를 연결 한 후 전체 글을 다시 읽으며 흐름이 처음부터 끝까지 잘 이어지는지 확인한다.

▶ 글의 순서 교재 구성

> **하루 12문항 _ 20분 학습 _ 5일 완성 = 총 60문항**

글의 순서는 주어진 글부터 (A), (B), (C) 문단이 순차적으로 자연스럽게 연결고리를 찾을 수 있는 문항의 경우 정답률이 높습니다. 하지만 **주어진 글 뒤에 어떤 단락이 와야 하는지 명확하지 않은 경우가 있는데 기출문제를 통해서 단락을 연결하는 연습과 전체적인 흐름을 확인하는 훈련**을 할 수 있도록 했습니다.

소재를 파악하자

주어진 글을 어떻게 연결할지 고민하지 말고, 일단 **글을 읽고 정확히 어떤 내용에 관한 글인지를 소재를 파악**한다.

단서가 핵심이다

this, that, it 등 지시어가 가리키는 것과 문장 간의 연결 고리가 되는 **대명사, 연결사 및 부사구를 단서로 활용**한다.

결정 NO, 임시 OK

예를 들어 **주어진 글과 (B), (C)가 순서라고 생각이 들어도 바로 결정하지 말고, 임시적으로 연결만 해 놓은 다음 글의 전체적인 흐름을 다시 한 번 확인한 후 결정하는 습관**을 길러야한다.

2020

PART Ⅱ
글의 순서

Day 11~Day 15

DAY 11

※ 점수 표기가 없는 문항은 모두 **2점**입니다.

글의 순서 01

● 날짜 :　월　일 ● 시작 시각 :　시　분　초

● 목표 시간 : 20분

01

고3 · 2023학년도 수능 36번

주어진 글 다음에 이어질 글의 순서로 가장 적절한 것을 고르시오.

A fascinating species of water flea exhibits a kind of flexibility that evolutionary biologists call *adaptive plasticity*.

(A) That's a clever trick, because producing spines and a helmet is costly, in terms of energy, and conserving energy is essential for an organism's ability to survive and reproduce. The water flea only expends the energy needed to produce spines and a helmet when it needs to.

(B) If the baby water flea is developing into an adult in water that includes the chemical signatures of creatures that prey on water fleas, it develops a helmet and spines to defend itself against predators. If the water around it doesn't include the chemical signatures of predators, the water flea doesn't develop these protective devices.

(C) So it may well be that this plasticity is an adaptation: a trait that came to exist in a species because it contributed to reproductive fitness. There are many cases, across many species, of adaptive plasticity. Plasticity is conducive to fitness if there is sufficient variation in the environment.

＊spine: 가시 돌기 ＊＊conducive: 도움되는

① (A) − (C) − (B)　　② (B) − (A) − (C)
③ (B) − (C) − (A)　　④ (C) − (A) − (B)
⑤ (C) − (B) − (A)

02

고3 · 2021학년도 6월 36번

주어진 글 다음에 이어질 글의 순서로 가장 적절한 것을 고르시오.

Studies of people struggling with major health problems show that the majority of respondents report they derived benefits from their adversity. Stressful events sometimes force people to develop new skills, reevaluate priorities, learn new insights, and acquire new strengths.

(A) High levels of adversity predicted poor mental health, as expected, but people who had faced intermediate levels of adversity were healthier than those who experienced little adversity, suggesting that moderate amounts of stress can foster resilience. A follow-up study found a similar link between the amount of lifetime adversity and subjects' responses to laboratory stressors.

(B) Intermediate levels of adversity were predictive of the greatest resilience. Thus, having to deal with a moderate amount of stress may build resilience in the face of future stress.

(C) In other words, the adaptation process initiated by stress can lead to personal changes for the better. One study that measured participants' exposure to thirty-seven major negative events found a curvilinear relationship between lifetime adversity and mental health.

＊resilience: 회복력

① (A) − (C) − (B)　　② (B) − (A) − (C)
③ (B) − (C) − (A)　　④ (C) − (A) − (B)
⑤ (C) − (B) − (A)

03

주어진 글 다음에 이어질 글의 순서로 가장 적절한 것을 고르시오.

Aristotle explains that the Good for human beings consists in *eudaimoniā* (a Greek word combining *eu* meaning "good" with *daimon* meaning "spirit," and most often translated as "happiness").

(A) It depends only on knowledge of human nature and other worldly and social realities. For him it is the study of human nature and worldly existence that will disclose the relevant meaning of the notion of *eudaimoniā*.

(B) Some people say it is worldly enjoyment while others say it is eternal salvation. Aristotle's theory will turn out to be "naturalistic" in that it does not depend on any theological or metaphysical knowledge. It does not depend on knowledge of God or of metaphysical and universal moral norms.

(C) Whereas he had argued in a purely formal way that the Good was that to which we all aim, he now gives a more substantive answer: that this universal human goal is happiness. However, he is quick to point out that this conclusion is still somewhat formal since different people have different views about what happiness is.

* salvation: 구원   ** theological: 신학의
*** substantive: 실질적인

① (A) − (C) − (B) ② (B) − (A) − (C)
③ (B) − (C) − (A) ④ (C) − (A) − (B)
⑤ (C) − (B) − (A)

04

주어진 글 다음에 이어질 글의 순서로 가장 적절한 것을 고르시오.

The objective of battle, to "throw" the enemy and to make him defenseless, may temporarily blind commanders and even strategists to the larger purpose of war. War is never an isolated act, nor is it ever only one decision.

(A) To be political, a political entity or a representative of a political entity, whatever its constitutional form, has to have an intention, a will. That intention has to be clearly expressed.

(B) In the real world, war's larger purpose is always a political purpose. It transcends the use of force. This insight was famously captured by Clausewitz's most famous phrase, "War is a mere continuation of politics by other means."

(C) And one side's will has to be transmitted to the enemy at some point during the confrontation (it does not have to be publicly communicated). A violent act and its larger political intention must also be attributed to one side at some point during the confrontation. History does not know of acts of war without eventual attribution.

* entity: 실체   ** transcend: 초월하다

① (A) − (C) − (B) ② (B) − (A) − (C)
③ (B) − (C) − (A) ④ (C) − (A) − (B)
⑤ (C) − (B) − (A)

05

주어진 글 다음에 이어질 글의 순서로 가장 적절한 것을 고르시오.
[3점]

Birds use many techniques to save energy when they are flying, most of which are tricks to stay aloft without flapping.

(A) When it reaches the top, the bird bends its wings and glides in the direction it wants to travel, searching for the next thermal. All soaring birds take advantage of thermals, but some species, like the Broad-winged Hawk, are specialists and in the right conditions can travel hundreds of miles with almost no flapping.

(B) Riding updrafts to gain altitude is one of the most conspicuous. Bare ground such as fields or parking lots absorbs more heat from the sun, and as air near the ground warms up it rises.

(C) This creates a column of rising warm air — a *thermal* — reaching hundreds or even thousands of feet high. A soaring bird can sense the air movement and fly in circles to stay in the column. It simply fans its wings and tail and lets the rising air carry it up like an elevator.

＊aloft: 높이　＊＊thermal: 상승 온난 기류
＊＊＊conspicuous: 뚜렷한

① (A) − (C) − (B)　　② (B) − (A) − (C)
③ (B) − (C) − (A)　　④ (C) − (A) − (B)
⑤ (C) − (B) − (A)

06

주어진 글 다음에 이어질 글의 순서로 가장 적절한 것을 고르시오.
[3점]

Culture operates in ways we can consciously consider and discuss but also in ways of which we are far less cognizant.

(A) In some cases, however, we are far less aware of why we believe a certain claim to be true, or how we are to explain why certain social realities exist. Ideas about the social world become part of our worldview without our necessarily being aware of the source of the particular idea or that we even hold the idea at all.

(B) When we have to offer an account of our actions, we consciously understand which excuses might prove acceptable, given the particular circumstances we find ourselves in. In such situations, we use cultural ideas as we would use a particular tool.

(C) We select the cultural notion as we would select a screwdriver: certain jobs call for a Phillips head while others require an Allen wrench. Whichever idea we insert into the conversation to justify our actions, the point is that our motives are discursively available to us. They are not hidden.

＊cognizant: 인식하는　＊＊discursively: 만연하게

① (A) − (C) − (B)　　② (B) − (A) − (C)
③ (B) − (C) − (A)　　④ (C) − (A) − (B)
⑤ (C) − (B) − (A)

07

주어진 글 다음에 이어질 글의 순서로 가장 적절한 것을 고르시오.
[3점]

In economics, there is a principle known as the *sunk cost fallacy*. The idea is that when you are invested and have ownership in something, you overvalue that thing.

(A) Sometimes, the smartest thing a person can do is quit. Although this is true, it has also become a tired and played-out argument. Sunk cost doesn't always have to be a bad thing.

(B) This leads people to continue on paths or pursuits that should clearly be abandoned. For example, people often remain in terrible relationships simply because they've invested a great deal of themselves into them. Or someone may continue pouring money into a business that is clearly a bad idea in the market.

(C) Actually, you can leverage this human tendency to your benefit. Like someone invests a great deal of money in a personal trainer to ensure they follow through on their commitment, you, too, can invest a great deal up front to ensure you stay on the path you want to be on.

* leverage: 이용하다

① (A) − (C) − (B) 　② (B) − (A) − (C)
③ (B) − (C) − (A) 　④ (C) − (A) − (B)
⑤ (C) − (B) − (A)

08

주어진 글 다음에 이어질 글의 순서로 가장 적절한 것을 고르시오.
[3점]

It raises much less reactance to tell people what to do than to tell them what not to do. Therefore, advocating action should lead to higher compliance than prohibiting action.

(A) This is a prescription that is rife with danger, failing to provide an implementation rule and raising reactance. Much better is to say, "To help make sure that other people provide answers as useful as yours have been, when people ask you about this study, please tell them that you and another person answered some questions about each other."

(B) For example, researchers have a choice of how to debrief research participants in an experiment involving some deception or omission of information. Often researchers attempt to commit the participant to silence, saying "Please don't tell other potential participants that feedback from the other person was false."

(C) Similarly, I once saw a delightful and unusual example of this principle at work in an art gallery. A fragile acrylic sculpture had a sign at the base saying, "Please touch with your eyes." The command was clear, yet created much less reactance in me than "Don't touch!" would have.

* reactance: 저항 ** rife: 가득한
*** debrief: 비밀[기밀] 준수 의무를 지우다[부여하다]

① (A) − (C) − (B) 　② (B) − (A) − (C)
③ (B) − (C) − (A) 　④ (C) − (A) − (B)
⑤ (C) − (B) − (A)

09 1등급 대비 고난도 2편 문제

주어진 글 다음에 이어질 글의 순서로 가장 적절한 것을 고르시오.

> Anger and empathy — like matter and antimatter — can't exist in the same place at the same time. Let one in, and you have to let the other one go. So when you shift a blamer into empathy, you stop the person's angry ranting dead in its tracks.

(A) The relief from no longer feeling "fear or hatred" toward the blamer spontaneously triggers a tremendous rush of gratitude and — miraculously — the person's quiet rage turns into forgiveness and, beyond that, a willingness to work toward solutions.

(B) Suddenly and unexpectedly, however, the blamer knows just how sad, angry, scared, or lonely the defender feels and spontaneously turns into an ally. When the defender feels understood by the blamer and that they are on the same side, there's nothing to defend against. The defender's wall, and with it his unspoken rage and frustration, disappears.

(C) And what about the person who's on the defensive? Initially, this human punching bag is frustrated because no matter what he or she is trying to mirror outward the ignorant blamer is blind to it. As a result, the person who's under attack is usually in a state of quiet, barely controlled rage.

＊rant: 폭언하다 ＊＊spontaneously: 자연스럽게

① (A) − (C) − (B) ② (B) − (A) − (C)
③ (B) − (C) − (A) ④ (C) − (A) − (B)
⑤ (C) − (B) − (A)

10 1등급 대비 고난도 2편 문제

주어진 글 다음에 이어질 글의 순서로 가장 적절한 것을 고르시오.

> Negotiation can be defined as an attempt to explore and reconcile conflicting positions in order to reach an acceptable outcome.

(A) Areas of difference can and do frequently remain, and will perhaps be the subject of future negotiations, or indeed remain irreconcilable. In those instances in which the parties have highly antagonistic or polarised relations, the process is likely to be dominated by the exposition, very often in public, of the areas of conflict.

(B) In these and sometimes other forms of negotiation, negotiation serves functions other than reconciling conflicting interests. These will include delay, publicity, diverting attention or seeking intelligence about the other party and its negotiating position.

(C) Whatever the nature of the outcome, which may actually favour one party more than another, the purpose of negotiation is the identification of areas of common interest and conflict. In this sense, depending on the intentions of the parties, the areas of common interest may be clarified, refined and given negotiated form and substance.

＊reconcile: 화해시키다 ＊＊antagonistic: 적대적인
＊＊＊exposition: 설명

① (A) − (C) − (B) ② (B) − (A) − (C)
③ (B) − (C) − (A) ④ (C) − (A) − (B)
⑤ (C) − (B) − (A)

11 [1등급 대비 고난도 3점 문제]

주어진 글 다음에 이어질 글의 순서로 가장 적절한 것을 고르시오. [3점]

Plants show finely tuned adaptive responses when nutrients are limiting. Gardeners may recognize yellow leaves as a sign of poor nutrition and the need for fertilizer.

(A) In contrast, plants with a history of nutrient abundance are risk averse and save energy. At all developmental stages, plants respond to environmental changes or unevenness so as to be able to use their energy for growth, survival, and reproduction, while limiting damage and nonproductive uses of their valuable energy.

(B) Research in this area has shown that plants are constantly aware of their position in the environment, in terms of both space and time. Plants that have experienced variable nutrient availability in the past tend to exhibit risk-taking behaviors, such as spending energy on root lengthening instead of leaf production.

(C) But if a plant does not have a caretaker to provide supplemental minerals, it can proliferate or lengthen its roots and develop root hairs to allow foraging in more distant soil patches. Plants can also use their memory to respond to histories of temporal or spatial variation in nutrient or resource availability.

＊nutrient: 영양소 ＊＊fertilizer: 비료
＊＊＊forage: 구하러 다니다

① (A) − (C) − (B)　　② (B) − (A) − (C)
③ (B) − (C) − (A)　　④ (C) − (A) − (B)
⑤ (C) − (B) − (A)

12 [1등급 대비 고난도 3점 문제]

주어진 글 다음에 이어질 글의 순서로 가장 적절한 것을 고르시오. [3점]

Living in dispersal correlates with a shocking retreat from public life, according to extensive analysis of the Social Capital Community Benchmark Survey of nearly thirty thousand people begun in 2000. It is hard to pinpoint the origin of this retreat.

(A) Meanwhile, the architectures of sprawl inhibit political activity that requires face-to-face interaction. It is not that sprawl makes political activity impossible, but by privatizing gathering space and dispersing human activity, sprawl makes political gathering less likely.

(B) These are both possible, but evidence suggests that the spatial landscape matters. Sociologists point out that the suburbs have done an efficient job of sorting people into communities where they will be surrounded by people of the same socioeconomic status.

(C) It may be because people in the dispersed city have invested so heavily in private comfort that they feel insulated from the problems of the rest of the world. It may be that sprawl has attracted people who are naturally less interested in engaging with the world, socially or politically.

＊sprawl: 스프롤(무질서하게 뻗어 나간 도시 외곽 지역)

① (A) − (C) − (B)　　② (B) − (A) − (C)
③ (B) − (C) − (A)　　④ (C) − (A) − (B)
⑤ (C) − (B) − (A)

DAY 12

※ 점수 표기가 없는 문항은 모두 2점입니다.

글의 순서 02

● 날짜 : 　월　일　● 시작 시각 : 　시　분　초

● 목표 시간 : 20분

01

고3·2024학년도 9월 36번

주어진 글 다음에 이어질 글의 순서로 가장 적절한 것을 고르시오.

The intuitive ability to classify and generalize is undoubtedly a useful feature of life and research, but it carries a high cost, such as in our tendency to stereotype generalizations about people and situations.

(A) Intuitively and quickly, we mentally sort things into groups based on what we perceive the differences between them to be, and that is the basis for stereotyping. Only afterwards do we examine (or not examine) more evidence of how things are differentiated, and the degree and significance of the variations.

(B) Our brain performs these tasks efficiently and automatically, usually without our awareness. The real danger of stereotypes is not their inaccuracy, but their lack of flexibility and their tendency to be preserved, even when we have enough time to stop and consider.

(C) For most people, the word stereotype arouses negative connotations: it implies a negative bias. But, in fact, stereotypes do not differ in principle from all other generalizations; generalizations about groups of people are not necessarily always negative.

＊intuitive: 직관적인　＊＊connotation: 함축

① (A) − (C) − (B)　　② (B) − (A) − (C)
③ (B) − (C) − (A)　　④ (C) − (A) − (B)
⑤ (C) − (B) − (A)

02

고3·2020학년도 6월 36번

주어진 글 다음에 이어질 글의 순서로 가장 적절한 것을 고르시오.

Notation was more than a practical method for preserving an expanding repertoire of music.

(A) Written notes freeze the music rather than allowing it to develop in the hands of individuals, and it discourages improvisation. Partly because of notation, modern classical performance lacks the depth of nuance that is part of aural tradition. Before notation arrived, in all history music was largely carried on as an aural tradition.

(B) It changed the nature of the art itself. To write something down means that people far away in space and time can re-create it. At the same time, there are downsides.

(C) Most world music is still basically aural, including sophisticated musical traditions such as Indian and Balinese. Most jazz musicians can read music but often don't bother, and their art is much involved with improvisation. Many modern pop musicians, one example being Paul McCartney, can't read music at all.

＊improvisation: 즉흥 연주　＊＊aural: 청각의

① (A) − (C) − (B)　　② (B) − (A) − (C)
③ (B) − (C) − (A)　　④ (C) − (A) − (B)
⑤ (C) − (B) − (A)

03

주어진 글 다음에 이어질 글의 순서로 가장 적절한 것을 고르시오.

The Earth formed from rocky and metallic fragments during the construction of the solar system — debris that was swept up by an initial nucleus and attracted together into a single body by the force of gravity.

(A) This increasing gravity, combined with the timeless radioactive decay of elements like uranium and thorium, caused the new Earth to heat up. The internal temperature and pressure were high enough for many compounds to break down or melt, releasing their water and gases.

(B) The original materials were cold as outer space and dry as dust; whatever water and gases they contained were locked inside individual fragments as chemical compounds. As the fragments joined, the Earth's gravity increased, attracting larger and larger objects to impact the Earth.

(C) Even solid material could begin to move and flow under such conditions. Separation by density began, and the Earth started to organize into its present layered structure. The heaviest metals sank to the center; the lightest materials migrated outward.

① (A) − (C) − (B)　　② (B) − (A) − (C)
③ (B) − (C) − (A)　　④ (C) − (A) − (B)
⑤ (C) − (B) − (A)

04

주어진 글 다음에 이어질 글의 순서로 가장 적절한 것을 고르시오.

One common strategy and use of passive misdirection in the digital world comes through the use of repetition.

(A) This action is repeated over and over to navigate their web browsers to the desired web page or action until it becomes an almost immediate, reflexive action. Malicious online actors take advantage of this behavior to distract the user from carefully examining the details of the web page that might tip off the user that there is something amiss about the website.

(B) The website is designed to focus the user's attention on the action the malicious actor wants them to take (e.g., click a link) and to draw their attention away from any details that might suggest to the user that the website is not what it appears to be on the surface.

(C) This digital misdirection strategy relies on the fact that online users utilizing web browsers to visit websites have quickly learned that the most basic ubiquitous navigational action is to click on a link or button presented to them on a website.

① (A) − (C) − (B)　　② (B) − (A) − (C)
③ (B) − (C) − (A)　　④ (C) − (A) − (B)
⑤ (C) − (B) − (A)

05

주어진 글 다음에 이어질 글의 순서로 가장 적절한 것을 고르시오.
[3점]

A large body of research in decision science has indicated that one attribute that is regularly substituted for an explicit assessment of decision costs and benefits is an affective valuation of the prospect at hand.

(A) People were willing to pay almost as much to avoid a 1 percent probability of receiving a shock as they were to pay to avoid a 99 percent probability of receiving a shock. Clearly the affective reaction to the thought of receiving a shock was overwhelming the subjects' ability to evaluate the probabilities associated.

(B) This is often a very rational attribute to substitute — affect does convey useful signals as to the costs and benefits of outcomes. A problem sometimes arises, however, when affective valuation is not supplemented by any analytic processing and adjustment at all.

(C) For example, sole reliance on affective valuation can make people insensitive to probabilities and to quantitative features of the outcome that should effect decisions. One study demonstrated that people's evaluation of a situation where they might receive a shock is insensitive to the probability of receiving the shock because their thinking is swamped by affective evaluation of the situation.

＊swamp: 압도하다

① (A) − (C) − (B) 　② (B) − (A) − (C)
③ (B) − (C) − (A) 　④ (C) − (A) − (B)
⑤ (C) − (B) − (A)

06

주어진 글 다음에 이어질 글의 순서로 가장 적절한 것을 고르시오.
[3점]

In spite of the likeness between the fictional and real world, the fictional world deviates from the real one in one important respect.

(A) The author has selected the content according to his own worldview and his own conception of relevance, in an attempt to be neutral and objective or convey a subjective view on the world. Whatever the motives, the author's subjective conception of the world stands between the reader and the original, untouched world on which the story is based.

(B) Because of the inner qualities with which the individual is endowed through heritage and environment, the mind functions as a filter; every outside impression that passes through it is filtered and interpreted. However, the world the reader encounters in literature is already processed and filtered by another consciousness.

(C) The existing world faced by the individual is in principle an infinite chaos of events and details before it is organized by a human mind. This chaos only gets processed and modified when perceived by a human mind.

＊deviate: 벗어나다 ＊＊endow: 부여하다
＊＊＊heritage: 유산

① (A) − (C) − (B) 　② (B) − (A) − (C)
③ (B) − (C) − (A) 　④ (C) − (A) − (B)
⑤ (C) − (B) − (A)

07

주어진 글 다음에 이어질 글의 순서로 가장 적절한 것을 고르시오. [3점]

Promoting attractive images of one's country is not new, but the conditions for trying to create soft power have changed dramatically in recent years. For one thing, nearly half the countries in the world are now democracies.

(A) Technological advances have led to a dramatic reduction in the cost of processing and transmitting information. The result is an explosion of information, and that has produced a "paradox of plenty." Plentiful information leads to scarcity of attention.

(B) In such circumstances, diplomacy aimed at public opinion can become as important to outcomes as traditional classified diplomatic communications among leaders. Information creates power, and today a much larger part of the world's population has access to that power.

(C) When people are overwhelmed with the volume of information confronting them, they have difficulty knowing what to focus on. Attention, rather than information, becomes the scarce resource, and those who can distinguish valuable information from background clutter gain power.

＊clutter: 혼란

① (A) − (C) − (B)　　② (B) − (A) − (C)
③ (B) − (C) − (A)　　④ (C) − (A) − (B)
⑤ (C) − (B) − (A)

08

주어진 글 다음에 이어질 글의 순서로 가장 적절한 것을 고르시오. [3점]

There's a direct counterpart to pop music in the classical song, more commonly called an "art song," which does not focus on the development of melodic material.

(A) But the pop song will rarely be sung and played exactly as written; the singer is apt to embellish that vocal line to give it a "styling," just as the accompanist will fill out the piano part to make it more interesting and personal. The performers might change the original tempo and mood completely.

(B) Both the pop song and the art song tend to follow tried-and-true structural patterns. And both will be published in the same way — with a vocal line and a basic piano part written out underneath.

(C) You won't find such extremes of approach by the performers of songs by Franz Schubert or Richard Strauss. These will be performed note for note because both the vocal and piano parts have been painstakingly written down by the composer with an ear for how each relates to the other.

＊embellish: 꾸미다　＊＊tried-and-true: 유효성이 증명된

① (A) − (C) − (B)　　② (B) − (A) − (C)
③ (B) − (C) − (A)　　④ (C) − (A) − (B)
⑤ (C) − (B) − (A)

09 1등급 대비 고난도 2점 문제
고3·2022학년도 6월 36번

주어진 글 다음에 이어질 글의 순서로 가장 적절한 것을 고르시오.

> Spatial reference points are larger than themselves. This isn't really a paradox: landmarks are themselves, but they also define neighborhoods around themselves.

(A) In a paradigm that has been repeated on many campuses, researchers first collect a list of campus landmarks from students. Then they ask another group of students to estimate the distances between pairs of locations, some to landmarks, some to ordinary buildings on campus.

(B) This asymmetry of distance estimates violates the most elementary principles of Euclidean distance, that the distance from A to B must be the same as the distance from B to A. Judgments of distance, then, are not necessarily coherent.

(C) The remarkable finding is that distances from an ordinary location to a landmark are judged shorter than distances from a landmark to an ordinary location. So, people would judge the distance from Pierre's house to the Eiffel Tower to be shorter than the distance from the Eiffel Tower to Pierre's house. Like black holes, landmarks seem to pull ordinary locations toward themselves, but ordinary places do not.

＊asymmetry: 비대칭

① (A) − (C) − (B) ② (B) − (A) − (C)
③ (B) − (C) − (A) ④ (C) − (A) − (B)
⑤ (C) − (B) − (A)

10 1등급 대비 고난도 3점 문제
고3·2022년 4월 37번

주어진 글 다음에 이어질 글의 순서로 가장 적절한 것을 고르시오. [3점]

> Both ancient farmers and foragers suffered seasonal food shortages. During these periods children and adults alike would go to bed hungry some days and everyone would lose fat and muscle.

(A) Typically, in complex ecosystems when weather one year proves unsuitable for one set of plant species, it almost inevitably suits others. But in farming societies when harvests fail as a result of, for example, a sustained drought, then catastrophe emerges.

(B) This is firstly because foragers tended to live well within the natural limits imposed by their environments, and secondly because where farmers typically relied on one or two staple crops, foragers in even the harshest environments relied on dozens of different food sources and so were usually able to adjust their diets to align with an ecosystem's own dynamic responses to changing conditions.

(C) But over longer periods of time farming societies were far more likely to suffer severe, existentially threatening famines than foragers. Foraging may be much less productive and generate far lower energy yields than farming but it is also much less risky.

＊forager: 수렵 채집인 ＊＊catastrophe: 참사
＊＊＊staple: 주요한

① (A) − (C) − (B) ② (B) − (A) − (C)
③ (B) − (C) − (A) ④ (C) − (A) − (B)
⑤ (C) − (B) − (A)

11 1등급 대비 고난도 3점 문제

주어진 글 다음에 이어질 글의 순서로 가장 적절한 것을 고르시오.

[3점]

A sovereign state is usually defined as one whose citizens are free to determine their own affairs without interference from any agency beyond its territorial borders.

(A) No citizen could be a full member of the community so long as she was tied to ancestral traditions with which the community might wish to break — the problem of Antigone in Sophocles' tragedy. Sovereignty and citizenship thus require not only borders in space, but also borders in time.

(B) Sovereignty and citizenship require freedom from the past at least as much as freedom from contemporary powers. No state could be sovereign if its inhabitants lacked the ability to change a course of action adopted by their forefathers in the past, or even one to which they once committed themselves.

(C) But freedom in space (and limits on its territorial extent) is merely one characteristic of sovereignty. Freedom in time (and limits on its temporal extent) is equally important and probably more fundamental.

＊sovereign: 주권의 ＊＊territorial: 영토의

① (A) − (C) − (B)   ② (B) − (A) − (C)
③ (B) − (C) − (A)   ④ (C) − (A) − (B)
⑤ (C) − (B) − (A)

12 1등급 대비 고난도 3점 문제

주어진 글 다음에 이어질 글의 순서로 가장 적절한 것을 고르시오.

[3점]

Experts have identified a large number of measures that promote energy efficiency. Unfortunately many of them are not cost effective. This is a fundamental requirement for energy efficiency investment from an economic perspective.

(A) And this has direct repercussions at the individual level: households can reduce the cost of electricity and gas bills, and improve their health and comfort, while companies can increase their competitiveness and their productivity. Finally, the market for energy efficiency could contribute to the economy through job and firms creation.

(B) There are significant externalities to take into account and there are also macroeconomic effects. For instance, at the aggregate level, improving the level of national energy efficiency has positive effects on macroeconomic issues such as energy dependence, climate change, health, national competitiveness and reducing fuel poverty.

(C) However, the calculation of such cost effectiveness is not easy: it is not simply a case of looking at private costs and comparing them to the reductions achieved.

＊repercussion: 반향, 영향 ＊＊aggregate: 집합의

① (A) − (C) − (B)   ② (B) − (A) − (C)
③ (B) − (C) − (A)   ④ (C) − (A) − (B)
⑤ (C) − (B) − (A)

학습 Check!

▶ 몰라서 틀린 문항 × 표기 ▶ 헷갈렸거나 찍은 문항 △ 표기 ▶ ×, △ 문항은 다시 풀고 ✔ 표기를 하세요.

종료 시각	시	분	초	문항 번호	01	02	03	04	05	06	07	08	09	10	11	12
소요 시간		분	초	채점 결과												
초과 시간		분	초	틀린 문항 복습												

DAY 13

※ 점수 표기가 없는 문항은 모두 **2점**입니다.

글의 순서 03

● 날짜 :　　월　　일　● 시작 시각 :　　시　　분　　초

● 목표 시간 : 20분

01

주어진 글 다음에 이어질 글의 순서로 가장 적절한 것을 고르시오.

The growing complexity of computer software has direct implications for our global safety and security, particularly as the physical objects upon which we depend — things like cars, airplanes, bridges, tunnels, and implantable medical devices — transform themselves into computer code.

(A) As all this code grows in size and complexity, so too do the number of errors and software bugs. According to a study by Carnegie Mellon University, commercial software typically has twenty to thirty bugs for every thousand lines of code — 50 million lines of code means 1 million to 1.5 million potential errors to be exploited.

(B) This is the basis for all malware attacks that take advantage of these computer bugs to get the code to do something it was not originally intended to do. As computer code grows more elaborate, software bugs flourish and security suffers, with increasing consequences for society at large.

(C) Physical things are increasingly becoming information technologies. Cars are "computers we ride in," and airplanes are nothing more than "flying Solaris boxes attached to bucketfuls of industrial control systems."

＊exploit: 활용하다

① (A) − (C) − (B)　　② (B) − (A) − (C)
③ (B) − (C) − (A)　　④ (C) − (A) − (B)
⑤ (C) − (B) − (A)

02

주어진 글 다음에 이어질 글의 순서로 가장 적절한 것을 고르시오.

In the fifth century *B.C.E.*, the Greek philosopher Protagoras pronounced, "Man is the measure of all things." In other words, we feel entitled to ask the world, "What good are you?"

(A) Abilities said to "make us human" — empathy, communication, grief, toolmaking, and so on — all exist to varying degrees among other minds sharing the world with us. Animals with backbones (fishes, amphibians, reptiles, birds, and mammals) all share the same basic skeleton, organs, nervous systems, hormones, and behaviors.

(B) We assume that we are the world's standard, that all things should be compared to us. Such an assumption makes us overlook a lot.

(C) Just as different models of automobiles each have an engine, drive train, four wheels, doors, and seats, we differ mainly in terms of our outside contours and a few internal tweaks. But like naive car buyers, most people see only animals' varied exteriors.

＊contour: 윤곽, 외형　＊＊tweak: 조정, 개조

① (A) − (C) − (B)　　② (B) − (A) − (C)
③ (B) − (C) − (A)　　④ (C) − (A) − (B)
⑤ (C) − (B) − (A)

03

고3 · 2023년 7월 36번

주어진 글 다음에 이어질 글의 순서로 가장 적절한 것을 고르시오.

The desire to see and interact with animals, shaped as it is by popular culture, can be a motivating factor for travel, but negative perceptions of certain animals can perform an entirely opposite role in discouraging people from visiting some destinations.

(A) For example, there are a variety of t-shirt and tea towel designs which celebrate the dangerous animals that can be encountered in Australia. This is a whimsical reconfiguration of the perceived threat that these animals pose to some tourists considering travel to this country.

(B) The harmful effects of animals on tourism experiences has been the subject of analysis in a small number of studies, but deaths or injuries caused by animals to tourists are tiny in comparison to other causes such as drowning and vehicular accidents.

(C) Nevertheless, the possibility that they might encounter a dangerous animal such as shark or snake or catch a disease such as malaria is sufficient to stop at least some tourists from visiting destinations where such threats exist. Sometimes this fear is turned into a marketing opportunity.

＊whimsical: 기발한　＊＊reconfiguration: 재구성

① (A) − (C) − (B)　　② (B) − (A) − (C)
③ (B) − (C) − (A)　　④ (C) − (A) − (B)
⑤ (C) − (B) − (A)

04

고3 · 2022년 4월 36번

주어진 글 다음에 이어질 글의 순서로 가장 적절한 것을 고르시오.

What are some characteristics of cities that must be maintained even if the population decreases? If this question can be answered, a new city model can be proposed based on the concept. Here, we focus on productivity and diversity as characteristics of cities.

(A) Given that gold mining cities and coal mining cities have risen and fallen, their vulnerability is obvious. A city where various people gather in various industries is secure against social changes. The same is true in the natural world, and the importance of biodiversity is essential for the sustainability of the species.

(B) This is because ensuring productivity and diversity is the driving force for sustainability. For example, if there is a place to work, people gather and work there, and the population gradually accumulates to form a city. However, the industrial structure that depends on a single industry is vulnerable to social changes.

(C) The same is true in cities. In a society where people of all ages and income levels live together, and diverse industries coexist while depending on each other, cities will continue to exist overcoming environmental changes such as population decline.

① (A) − (C) − (B)　　② (B) − (A) − (C)
③ (B) − (C) − (A)　　④ (C) − (A) − (B)
⑤ (C) − (B) − (A)

05

주어진 글 다음에 이어질 글의 순서로 가장 적절한 것을 고르시오.
[3점]

> A classic positive-sum game in economic life is the trading of surpluses.

(A) One infrastructure that allows efficient exchange is transportation, which makes it possible for producers to trade their surpluses even when they are separated by distance. Another is money, interest, and middlemen, which allow producers to exchange many kinds of surpluses with many other producers at many points in time.

(B) If a farmer has more grain than he can eat, and a herder has more milk than he can drink, both of them come out ahead if they trade some wheat for some milk. As they say, everybody wins. Of course, an exchange at a single moment in time only pays when there is a division of labor.

(C) There would be no point in one farmer giving a bushel of wheat to another farmer and receiving a bushel of wheat in return. A fundamental insight of modern economics is that the key to the creation of wealth is a division of labor, in which specialists learn to produce a commodity with increasing cost-effectiveness and have the means to exchange their specialized products efficiently.

① (A) − (C) − (B)　　② (B) − (A) − (C)
③ (B) − (C) − (A)　　④ (C) − (A) − (B)
⑤ (C) − (B) − (A)

06

주어진 글 다음에 이어질 글의 순서로 가장 적절한 것을 고르시오.
[3점]

> Traditionally, Kuhn claims, the primary goal of historians of science was 'to clarify and deepen an understanding of *contemporary* scientific methods or concepts by displaying their evolution'.

(A) Some discoveries seem to entail numerous phases and discoverers, none of which can be identified as definitive. Furthermore, the evaluation of past discoveries and discoverers according to present-day standards does not allow us to see how significant they may have been in their own day.

(B) This entailed relating the progressive accumulation of breakthroughs and discoveries. Only that which survived in some form in the present was considered relevant. In the mid-1950s, however, a number of faults in this view of history became apparent. Closer analysis of scientific discoveries, for instance, led historians to ask whether the dates of discoveries and their discoverers can be identified precisely.

(C) Nor does the traditional view recognise the role that non-intellectual factors, especially institutional and socio-economic ones, play in scientific developments. Most importantly, however, the traditional historian of science seems blind to the fact that the concepts, questions and standards that they use to frame the past are themselves subject to historical change.

① (A) − (C) − (B)　　② (B) − (A) − (C)
③ (B) − (C) − (A)　　④ (C) − (A) − (B)
⑤ (C) − (B) − (A)

07

주어진 글 다음에 이어질 글의 순서로 가장 적절한 것을 고르시오.
[3점]

> Most of us have a general, rational sense of what to eat and when — there is no shortage of information on the subject.

(A) *Emotional eating* is a popular term used to describe eating that is influenced by emotions, both positive and negative. Feelings may affect various aspects of your eating, including your motivation to eat, your food choices, where and with whom you eat, and the speed at which you eat. Most overeating is prompted by feelings rather than physical hunger.

(B) Yet there is often a disconnect between what we know and what we do. We may have the facts, but decisions also involve our feelings. Many people who struggle with difficult emotions also struggle with eating problems.

(C) Individuals who struggle with obesity tend to eat in response to emotions. However, people who eat for emotional reasons are not necessarily overweight. People of any size may try to escape an emotional experience by preoccupying themselves with eating or by obsessing over their shape and weight.

* obsess: 강박감을 갖다

① (A) − (C) − (B) ② (B) − (A) − (C)
③ (B) − (C) − (A) ④ (C) − (A) − (B)
⑤ (C) − (B) − (A)

08

주어진 글 다음에 이어질 글의 순서로 가장 적절한 것을 고르시오.
[3점]

> Today the term artist is used to refer to a broad range of creative individuals across the globe from both past and present. This rather general usage erroneously suggests that the concept or word "artist" existed in original contexts.

(A) Inventions, ideas, and discoveries have been credited to the persons who originated them. This view is also at the core of the definition of an "artist." Artists are perceived to establish a strong bond with their art to the point of combining into one "entity."

(B) In contrast to the diversity it is applied to, the meaning of this term continues to be mostly based on Western views and values. Since the fifteenth century, this tradition has been concerned with recognizing individual achievements.

(C) Art history has reinforced this oneness: A painting by Pablo Picasso is called "a Picasso." This union between artists and their work has determined the essential qualities of an artist: originality, authorship, and authenticity.

* authenticity: 진정함, 확실성

① (A) − (C) − (B) ② (B) − (A) − (C)
③ (B) − (C) − (A) ④ (C) − (A) − (B)
⑤ (C) − (B) − (A)

09 1등급 대비 고난도 2점 문제 고3·2022학년도 9월 36번

주어진 글 다음에 이어질 글의 순서로 가장 적절한 것을 고르시오.

> Green products involve, in many cases, higher ingredient costs than those of mainstream products.

(A) They'd rather put money and time into known, profitable, high-volume products that serve populous customer segments than into risky, less-profitable, low-volume products that may serve current noncustomers. Given that choice, these companies may choose to leave the green segment of the market to small niche competitors.

(B) Even if the green product succeeds, it may cannibalize the company's higher-profit mainstream offerings. Given such downsides, companies serving mainstream consumers with successful mainstream products face what seems like an obvious investment decision.

(C) Furthermore, the restrictive ingredient lists and design criteria that are typical of such products may make green products inferior to mainstream products on core performance dimensions (e.g., less effective cleansers). In turn, the higher costs and lower performance of some products attract only a small portion of the customer base, leading to lower economies of scale in procurement, manufacturing, and distribution.

* segment: 조각 ** cannibalize: 잡아먹다
*** procurement: 조달

① (A) − (C) − (B) ② (B) − (A) − (C)
③ (B) − (C) − (A) ④ (C) − (A) − (B)
⑤ (C) − (B) − (A)

10 1등급 대비 고난도 3점 문제 고3·2023년 4월 37번

주어진 글 다음에 이어질 글의 순서로 가장 적절한 것을 고르시오.
[3점]

> Representation is control. The power to represent the world is the power to represent us in it or it in us, for the final stage of representing merges the representor and the represented into one. Imperializing cultures produce great works of art (great representations) which can be put to work intellectually as armies and trading houses work militarily and economically.

(A) That is because unless we can control the world intellectually by maps we cannot control it militarily or economically. Mercator, Molière, Columbus and Captain Cook imperialized in different ways, but they all imperialized, and ultimately the effectiveness of one depended upon and supported the effectiveness of all the others.

(B) Similarly the US form of contemporary colonization, which involves occupying economies and political parties rather than physical territories, is accompanied by the power of both Hollywood and the satellite to represent the world to and for the US.

(C) Shakespeare, Jane Austen and maps were as important to English Imperial power as was the East India Company, the British army and the churches of England. It is no coincidence that modern Europe, the Europe of colonization, was also the Europe of "great art," and no coincidence either that it was the Europe of great map makers.

① (A) − (C) − (B) ② (B) − (A) − (C)
③ (B) − (C) − (A) ④ (C) − (A) − (B)
⑤ (C) − (B) − (A)

11 1등급 대비 고난도 3점 문제 　　　고3·2022년 10월 37번

주어진 글 다음에 이어질 글의 순서로 가장 적절한 것을 고르시오. [3점]

Bipedalism, upright walking, started a chain of enormous evolutionary adjustments. It liberated hominin arms for carrying weapons and for taking food to group sites instead of consuming it on the spot. But bipedalism was necessary to trigger hand dexterity and tool use.

(A) This creates the ability to use each digit independently in the complex manipulations required for tool use. But without bipedalism it would be impossible to use the trunk for leverage in accelerating the hand during toolmaking and tool use.

(B) Hashimoto and co-workers concluded that adaptations underlying tool use evolved independently of those required for human bipedalism because in both humans and monkeys, each finger is represented separately in the primary sensorimotor cortex, just as the fingers are physically separated in the hand.

(C) Bipedalism also freed the mouth and teeth to develop a more complex call system as the prerequisite of language. These developments required larger brains whose energy cost eventually reached three times the level for chimpanzees, accounting for up to one-sixth of the total basal metabolic rate.

＊hominin: 호미닌(인간의 조상으로 분류되는 종족)
＊＊dexterity: (손)재주　＊＊＊sensorimotor cortex: 감각 운동 피질

① (A) − (C) − (B)　　② (B) − (A) − (C)
③ (B) − (C) − (A)　　④ (C) − (A) − (B)
⑤ (C) − (B) − (A)

12 1등급 대비 고난도 3점 문제 　　　고3·2019학년도 수능 37번

주어진 글 다음에 이어질 글의 순서로 가장 적절한 것을 고르시오. [3점]

Clearly, schematic knowledge helps you — guiding your understanding and enabling you to reconstruct things you cannot remember.

(A) Likewise, if there are things you can't recall, your schemata will fill in the gaps with knowledge about what's typical in that situation. As a result, a reliance on schemata will inevitably make the world seem more "normal" than it really is and will make the past seem more "regular" than it actually was.

(B) Any reliance on schematic knowledge, therefore, will be shaped by this information about what's "normal." Thus, if there are things you don't notice while viewing a situation or event, your schemata will lead you to fill in these "gaps" with knowledge about what's normally in place in that setting.

(C) But schematic knowledge can also hurt you, promoting errors in perception and memory. Moreover, the *types* of errors produced by schemata are quite predictable: Bear in mind that schemata summarize the broad pattern of your experience, and so they tell you, in essence, what's typical or ordinary in a given situation.

① (A) − (C) − (B)　　② (B) − (A) − (C)
③ (B) − (C) − (A)　　④ (C) − (A) − (B)
⑤ (C) − (B) − (A)

DAY 14

※ 점수 표기가 없는 문항은 모두 **2점**입니다.

글의 순서 04

● 날짜 :　월　일　● 시작 시각 :　시　분　초

● 목표 시간 : 20분

01

고3 · 2023학년도 9월 36번

주어진 글 다음에 이어질 글의 순서로 가장 적절한 것을 고르시오.

When two natural bodies of water stand at different levels, building a canal between them presents a complicated engineering problem.

(A) Then the upper gates open and the ship passes through. For downstream passage, the process works the opposite way. The ship enters the lock from the upper level, and water is pumped from the lock until the ship is in line with the lower level.

(B) When a vessel is going upstream, the upper gates stay closed as the ship enters the lock at the lower water level. The downstream gates are then closed and more water is pumped into the basin. The rising water lifts the vessel to the level of the upper body of water.

(C) To make up for the difference in level, engineers build one or more water "steps," called locks, that carry ships or boats up or down between the two levels. A lock is an artificial water basin. It has a long rectangular shape with concrete walls and a pair of gates at each end.

＊rectangular: 직사각형의

① (A) − (C) − (B)
② (B) − (A) − (C)
③ (B) − (C) − (A)
④ (C) − (A) − (B)
⑤ (C) − (B) − (A)

02

고3 · 2020학년도 9월 37번

주어진 글 다음에 이어질 글의 순서로 가장 적절한 것을 고르시오.
[3점]

Because a main goal of science is to discover lawful relationships, science assumes that what is being investigated is lawful. For example, the chemist assumes that chemical reactions are lawful, and the physicist assumes that the physical world is lawful.

(A) The determinist, then, assumes that everything that occurs is a function of a finite number of causes and that, if these causes were known, an event could be predicted with complete accuracy. However, knowing *all* causes of an event is not necessary; the determinist simply assumes that they exist and that as more causes are known, predictions become more accurate.

(B) The assumption that what is being studied can be understood in terms of causal laws is called determinism. Richard Taylor defined determinism as the philosophical doctrine that "states that for everything that ever happens there are conditions such that, given them, nothing else could happen."

(C) For example, almost everyone would agree that the weather is a function of a finite number of variables such as sunspots, high-altitude jet streams, and barometric pressure; yet weather forecasts are always probabilistic because many of these variables change constantly, and others are simply unknown.

＊altitude: 고도(高度)　＊＊barometric: 기압의

① (A) − (C) − (B)
② (B) − (A) − (C)
③ (B) − (C) − (A)
④ (C) − (A) − (B)
⑤ (C) − (B) − (A)

03

주어진 글 다음에 이어질 글의 순서로 가장 적절한 것을 고르시오.

> Humans are unique in the realm of living beings in knowing there is a future. If people experience worry and hope, it is because they realize the future exists, that it can be better or worse, and that the outcome depends to some extent on them.

(A) That is why we so often have a poor relationship with the future and are either more fearful than we need to be or allow ourselves to hope against all evidence; we worry excessively or not enough; we fail to predict the future or to shape it as much as we are able.

(B) The future, on the other hand, must be imagined in advance and, for that very reason, is always uncertain. Getting along with the future is not an easy task, nor is it one in which instinct prevents us from blunders.

(C) But having this knowledge does not imply that they know what to do with it. People often repress their awareness of the future because thinking about it distorts the comfort of the now, which tends to be more powerful than the future because it is present and because it is certain.

* blunder: 큰 실수

① (A) − (C) − (B) ② (B) − (A) − (C)
③ (B) − (C) − (A) ④ (C) − (A) − (B)
⑤ (C) − (B) − (A)

04

주어진 글 다음에 이어질 글의 순서로 가장 적절한 것을 고르시오.

> Forget-me-nots can conquer new territory because they have an army of tiny allies: ants. It's not that ants are particularly fond of flowers — at least, they are not attracted by their aesthetic qualities.

(A) This fat-and sugar-rich treat is like chips and chocolate to an ant. The tiny creatures quickly carry the seeds back to their nest, where the colony is waiting eagerly in the tunnels for the calorie boost. The tasty treat is bitten off and the seed itself is discarded.

(B) Ants are motivated by their desire to eat them, and their interest is triggered when forget-me-nots form their seeds. The seeds are designed to make an ant's mouth water, for attached to the outside is a structure called an elaiosome, which looks like a tiny bit of cake.

(C) Along come the trash collectors in the form of worker ants, which dispose of the seeds in the neighborhood — carrying them up to 200 feet away from home base. Wild strawberries and other plants also benefit from this distribution service: ants are nature's gardeners, as it were.

* forget-me-not: 물망초

① (A) − (C) − (B) ② (B) − (A) − (C)
③ (B) − (C) − (A) ④ (C) − (A) − (B)
⑤ (C) − (B) − (A)

05

주어진 글 다음에 이어질 글의 순서로 가장 적절한 것을 고르시오.
[3점]

> Darwin saw blushing as uniquely human, representing an involuntary physical reaction caused by embarrassment and self-consciousness in a social environment.

(A) Maybe our brief loss of face benefits the long-term cohesion of the group. Interestingly, if someone blushes after making a social mistake, they are viewed in a more favourable light than those who don't blush.

(B) If we feel awkward, embarrassed or ashamed when we are alone, we don't blush; it seems to be caused by our concern about what others are thinking of us. Studies have confirmed that simply being told you are blushing brings it on. We feel as though others can see through our skin and into our mind.

(C) However, while we sometimes want to disappear when we involuntarily go bright red, psychologists argue that blushing actually serves a positive social purpose. When we blush, it's a signal to others that we recognize that a social norm has been broken; it is an apology for a faux pas.

＊faux pas: 실수

① (A) − (C) − (B)　　② (B) − (A) − (C)
③ (B) − (C) − (A)　　④ (C) − (A) − (B)
⑤ (C) − (B) − (A)

06

주어진 글 다음에 이어질 글의 순서로 가장 적절한 것을 고르시오.
[3점]

> Evolution works to maximize the number of descendants that an animal leaves behind. Where the risk of death from fishing increases as an animal grows, evolution favors those that grow slowly, mature younger and smaller, and reproduce earlier.

(A) Surely these adaptations are good news for species hard-pressed by excessive fishing? Not exactly. Young fish produce many fewer eggs than large-bodied animals, and many industrial fisheries are now so intensive that few animals survive more than a couple of years beyond the age of maturity.

(B) This is exactly what we now see in the wild. Cod in Canada's Gulf of St. Lawrence begin to reproduce at around four today; forty years ago they had to wait until six or seven to reach maturity. Sole in the North Sea mature at half the body weight they did in 1950.

(C) Together this means there are fewer eggs and larvae to secure future generations. In some cases the amount of young produced today is a hundred or even a thousand times less than in the past, putting the survival of species, and the fisheries dependent on them, at grave risk.

① (A) − (C) − (B)　　② (B) − (A) − (C)
③ (B) − (C) − (A)　　④ (C) − (A) − (B)
⑤ (C) − (B) − (A)

07

주어진 글 다음에 이어질 글의 순서로 가장 적절한 것을 고르시오.
[3점]

> In the course of acquiring a language, children are exposed to only a finite set of utterances. Yet they come to use and understand an infinite set of sentences.

(A) Yet, they all arrive a pretty much the same grammar. The input that children get is haphazard in the sense that caretakers do not talk to their children to illustrate a particular point of grammar. Yet, all children develop systematic knowledge of a language.

(B) Thus, despite the severe limitations and variation in the input children receive, and also in their personal circumstances, they all develop a rich and uniform system of linguistic knowledge. The knowledge attained goes beyond the input in various ways.

(C) This has been referred to as the creative aspect of language use. This 'creativity' does not refer to the ability to write poetry or novels but rather the ability to produce and understand an unlimited set of new sentences never spoken or heard previously. The precise linguistic input children receive differs from child to child; no two children are exposed to exactly the same set of utterances.

* haphazard: 무작위적인, 되는 대로의

① (A) − (C) − (B) ② (B) − (A) − (C)
③ (B) − (C) − (A) ④ (C) − (A) − (B)
⑤ (C) − (B) − (A)

08

주어진 글 다음에 이어질 글의 순서로 가장 적절한 것을 고르시오.
[3점]

> It can be difficult to decide the place of fine art, such as oil paintings, watercolours, sketches or sculptures, in an archival institution.

(A) The best archival decisions about art do not focus on territoriality (this object belongs in my institution even though I do not have the resources to care for it) or on questions of monetary value or prestige (this object raises the cultural standing of my institution). The best decisions focus on what evidential value exists and what is best for the item.

(B) But art can also carry aesthetic value, which elevates the job of evaluation into another realm. Aesthetic value and the notion of artistic beauty are important considerations, but they are not what motivates archival preservation in the first instance.

(C) Art can serve as documentary evidence, especially when the items were produced before photography became common. Sketches of soldiers on a battlefield, paintings of English country villages or portraits of Dutch townspeople can provide the only visual evidence of a long-ago place, person or time.

* archival: 기록(보관소)의 ** prestige: 명성, 위신
*** realm: 영역

① (A) − (C) − (B) ② (B) − (A) − (C)
③ (B) − (C) − (A) ④ (C) − (A) − (B)
⑤ (C) − (B) − (A)

09 1등급 대비 고난도 2점 문제

주어진 글 다음에 이어질 글의 순서로 가장 적절한 것을 고르시오.

> Shakespeare wrote, "What's in a name? That which we call a rose by any other name would smell as sweet."

(A) Take the word *bridge*. In German, *bridge* (die brücke) is a feminine noun; in Spanish, *bridge* (el puente) is a masculine noun. Boroditsky found that when asked to describe a bridge, native German speakers used words like *beautiful, elegant, slender*. When native Spanish speakers were asked the same question, they used words like *strong, sturdy, towering*.

(B) According to Stanford University psychology professor Lera Boroditsky, that's not necessarily so. Focusing on the grammatical gender differences between German and Spanish, Boroditsky's work indicates that the gender our language assigns to a given noun influences us to subconsciously give that noun characteristics of the grammatical gender.

(C) This worked the other way around as well. The word *key* is masculine in German and feminine in Spanish. When asked to describe a key, native German speakers used words like *jagged, heavy, hard, metal*. Spanish speakers used words like *intricate, golden, lovely*.

* jagged: 뾰족뾰족한 ** intricate: 정교한

① (A) − (C) − (B)   ② (B) − (A) − (C)
③ (B) − (C) − (A)   ④ (C) − (A) − (B)
⑤ (C) − (B) − (A)

10 1등급 대비 고난도 3점 문제

주어진 글 다음에 이어질 글의 순서로 가장 적절한 것을 고르시오.
[3점]

> A firm is deciding whether to invest in shipbuilding. If it can produce at sufficiently large scale, it knows the venture will be profitable.

(A) There is a "good" outcome, in which both types of investments are made, and both the shipyard and the steelmakers end up profitable and happy. Equilibrium is reached. Then there is a "bad" outcome, in which neither type of investment is made. This second outcome also is an equilibrium because the decisions not to invest reinforce each other.

(B) Assume that shipyards are the only potential customers of steel. Steel producers figure they'll make money if there's a shipyard to buy their steel, but not otherwise. Now we have two possible outcomes — what economists call "multiple equilibria."

(C) But one key input is low-cost steel, and it must be produced nearby. The company's decision boils down to this: if there is a steel factory close by, invest in shipbuilding; otherwise, don't invest. Now consider the thinking of potential steel investors in the region.

* equilibrium: 균형

① (A) − (C) − (B)   ② (B) − (A) − (C)
③ (B) − (C) − (A)   ④ (C) − (A) − (B)
⑤ (C) − (B) − (A)

11 1등급 대비 고난도 3점 문제　　고3·2024학년도 수능 37번

주어진 글 다음에 이어질 글의 순서로 가장 적절한 것을 고르시오.
[3점]

Norms emerge in groups as a result of people conforming to the behavior of others. Thus, the start of a norm occurs when one person acts in a particular manner in a particular situation because she thinks she ought to.

(A) Thus, she may prescribe the behavior to them by uttering the norm statement in a prescriptive manner. Alternately, she may communicate that conformity is desired in other ways, such as by gesturing. In addition, she may threaten to sanction them for not behaving as she wishes. This will cause some to conform to her wishes and act as she acts.

(B) But some others will not need to have the behavior prescribed to them. They will observe the regularity of behavior and decide on their own that they ought to conform. They may do so for either rational or moral reasons.

(C) Others may then conform to this behavior for a number of reasons. The person who performed the initial action may think that others ought to behave as she behaves in situations of this sort.

＊sanction: 제재를 가하다

① (A) − (C) − (B)　　② (B) − (A) − (C)
③ (B) − (C) − (A)　　④ (C) − (A) − (B)
⑤ (C) − (B) − (A)

12 1등급 대비 고난도 3점 문제　　고3·2018학년도 수능 37번

주어진 글 다음에 이어질 글의 순서로 가장 적절한 것을 고르시오.
[3점]

To modern man disease is a biological phenomenon that concerns him only as an individual and has no moral implications. When he contracts influenza, he never attributes this event to his behavior toward the tax collector or his mother-in-law.

(A) Sometimes they may not strike the guilty person himself, but rather one of his relatives or tribesmen, to whom responsibility is extended. Disease, action that might produce disease, and recovery from disease are, therefore, of vital concern to the whole primitive community.

(B) Disease, as a sanction against social misbehavior, becomes one of the most important pillars of order in such societies. It takes over, in many cases, the role played by policemen, judges, and priests in modern society.

(C) Among primitives, because of their supernaturalistic theories, the prevailing moral point of view gives a deeper meaning to disease. The gods who send disease are usually angered by the moral offences of the individual.

＊sanction: 제재

① (A) − (C) − (B)　　② (B) − (A) − (C)
③ (B) − (C) − (A)　　④ (C) − (A) − (B)
⑤ (C) − (B) − (A)

DAY 14

DAY 15

※ 점수 표기가 없는 문항은 모두 2점입니다.

글의 순서 05

● 날짜 : 　월　일　● 시작 시각 : 　시　분　초

● 목표 시간 : 20분

01

고3・2022학년도 수능 36번

주어진 글 다음에 이어질 글의 순서로 가장 적절한 것을 고르시오.

According to the market response model, it is increasing prices that drive providers to search for new sources, innovators to substitute, consumers to conserve, and alternatives to emerge.

(A) Many examples of such "green taxes" exist. Facing landfill costs, labor expenses, and related costs in the provision of garbage disposal, for example, some cities have required households to dispose of all waste in special trash bags, purchased by consumers themselves, and often costing a dollar or more each.

(B) Taxing certain goods or services, and so increasing prices, should result in either decreased use of these resources or creative innovation of new sources or options. The money raised through the tax can be used directly by the government either to supply services or to search for alternatives.

(C) The results have been greatly increased recycling and more careful attention by consumers to packaging and waste. By internalizing the costs of trash to consumers, there has been an observed decrease in the flow of garbage from households.

① (A) – (C) – (B)　② (B) – (A) – (C)
③ (B) – (C) – (A)　④ (C) – (A) – (B)
⑤ (C) – (B) – (A)

02

고3・2019학년도 9월 37번

주어진 글 다음에 이어질 글의 순서로 가장 적절한 것을 고르시오.

Ever since the first scientific opinion polls revealed that most Americans are at best poorly informed about politics, analysts have asked whether citizens are equipped to play the role democracy assigns them.

(A) Such factors, however, can explain only the misinformation that has always been with us. The sharp rise in misinformation in recent years has a different source: our media. "They are making us dumb," says one observer. When fact bends to fiction, the predictable result is political distrust and polarization.

(B) It's the difference between ignorance and irrationality. Whatever else one might conclude about self-government, it's at risk when citizens don't know what they're talking about. Our misinformation owes partly to psychological factors, including our tendency to see the world in ways that suit our desires.

(C) However, there is something worse than an inadequately informed public, and that's a misinformed public. It's one thing when citizens don't know something, and realize it, which has always been a problem. It's another thing when citizens don't know something, but think they know it, which is the new problem.

＊poll: 여론 조사

① (A) – (C) – (B)　② (B) – (A) – (C)
③ (B) – (C) – (A)　④ (C) – (A) – (B)
⑤ (C) – (B) – (A)

03

주어진 글 다음에 이어질 글의 순서로 가장 적절한 것을 고르시오.

The fossil record provides evidence of evolution. The story the fossils tell is one of change. Creatures existed in the past that are no longer with us. Sequential changes are found in many fossils showing the change of certain features over time from a common ancestor, as in the case of the horse.

(A) If multicelled organisms were indeed found to have evolved before single-celled organisms, then the theory of evolution would be rejected. A good scientific theory always allows for the possibility of rejection. The fact that we have not found such a case in countless examinations of the fossil record strengthens the case for evolutionary theory.

(B) The fossil record supports this prediction — multicelled organisms are found in layers of earth millions of years after the first appearance of single-celled organisms. Note that the possibility always remains that the opposite could be found.

(C) Apart from demonstrating that evolution did occur, the fossil record also provides tests of the predictions made from evolutionary theory. For example, the theory predicts that single-celled organisms evolved before multicelled organisms.

① (A) − (C) − (B) ② (B) − (A) − (C)
③ (B) − (C) − (A) ④ (C) − (A) − (B)
⑤ (C) − (B) − (A)

04

주어진 글 다음에 이어질 글의 순서로 가장 적절한 것을 고르시오.

A carbon sink is a natural feature that absorbs or stores more carbon than it releases.

(A) Carbon sinks have been able to absorb about half of this excess CO_2, and the world's oceans have done the major part of that job. They absorb about one-fourth of humans' industrial carbon emissions, doing half the work of all Earth's carbon sinks combined.

(B) Its mass of plants and other organic material absorb and store tons of carbon. However, the planet's major carbon sink is its oceans. Since the Industrial Revolution began in the eighteenth century, CO_2 released during industrial processes has greatly increased the proportion of carbon in the atmosphere.

(C) The value of carbon sinks is that they can help create equilibrium in the atmosphere by removing excess CO_2. One example of a carbon sink is a large forest.

＊equilibrium: 평형 상태

① (A) − (C) − (B) ② (B) − (A) − (C)
③ (B) − (C) − (A) ④ (C) − (A) − (B)
⑤ (C) − (B) − (A)

05

주어진 글 다음에 이어질 글의 순서로 가장 적절한 것을 고르시오.

It has been said that eye movements are windows into the mind, because where people look reveals what environmental information they are attending to. However, there is more to attention than just moving the eyes to look at objects.

(A) You may have had this experience if you have been reading a book and then suddenly become aware that although you were moving your eyes across the page and "reading" the words, you had no idea what you had just read.

(B) Even though you were *looking* at the words, you apparently were not *paying attention*. There is a mental aspect of attention that involves processing that can occur independently of eye movements.

(C) We can pay attention to things that are not directly in our line of vision, as evidenced by the basketball player who dribbles down court while paying attention to a teammate off to the side, just before she throws a perfect pass without looking. We can also look directly at something without paying attention to it.

① (A) − (C) − (B)　　② (B) − (A) − (C)
③ (B) − (C) − (A)　　④ (C) − (A) − (B)
⑤ (C) − (B) − (A)

06

주어진 글 다음에 이어질 글의 순서로 가장 적절한 것을 고르시오.
[3점]

When a young child sees clouds moving across the sky, the clouds may seem alive and independent, perhaps dangerous. But if one sees clouds as fleecy lambs, a metaphorical chain begins to neutralize the fear.

(A) "Cloud movement" becomes differentiated from the kind of movement that makes things alive, because the clouds move only if they are "pushed" by the wind, and what can't move without a push from the outside is not alive.

(B) The cloud may still be thought of as alive, but it is no longer terrifying. Repression and neutralization through metaphor are possible strategies, but there is another. Faced with the moving clouds, the child can theorize about their movement in such a way that the clouds cease to be alive.

(C) Children develop theoretical constructs that separate the motion of clouds from the motion of people and animals so that eventually the fear of living clouds disappears. If things seem uncomfortably on the border between the alive and the not-alive, use logic to redefine the boundaries so that things fall more comfortably into place. If it scares you, make a theory.

＊fleecy: 털이 많은　＊＊repression: 억제

① (A) − (C) − (B)　　② (B) − (A) − (C)
③ (B) − (C) − (A)　　④ (C) − (A) − (B)
⑤ (C) − (B) − (A)

07

주어진 글 다음에 이어질 글의 순서로 가장 적절한 것을 고르시오.
[3점]

Marshall McLuhan, among others, noted that clothes are people's extended skin, wheels extended feet, camera and telescopes extended eyes. Our technological creations are great extrapolations of the bodies that our genes build.

(A) The blueprints for our shells spring from our minds, which may spontaneously create something none of our ancestors ever made or even imagined. If technology is an extension of humans, it is not an extension of our genes but of our minds. Technology is therefore the extended body for ideas.

(B) In this way, we can think of technology as our extended body. During the industrial age it was easy to see the world this way. Steam-powered shovels, locomotives, television, and the levers and gears of engineers were a fabulous exoskeleton that turned man into superman.

(C) A closer look reveals the flaw in this analogy: The extended costume of animals is the result of their genes. They inherit the basic blueprints of what they make. Humans don't.

* extrapolation: 연장(延長) ** exoskeleton: 외골격

*** flaw: 결함

① (A) − (C) − (B)　　② (B) − (A) − (C)
③ (B) − (C) − (A)　　④ (C) − (A) − (B)
⑤ (C) − (B) − (A)

08

주어진 글 다음에 이어질 글의 순서로 가장 적절한 것을 고르시오.
[3점]

Recently, a number of commercial ventures have been launched that offer social robots as personal home assistants, perhaps eventually to rival existing smart-home assistants.

(A) They might be motorized and can track the user around the room, giving the impression of being aware of the people in the environment. Although personal robotic assistants provide services similar to those of smart-home assistants, their social presence offers an opportunity that is unique to social robots.

(B) Personal robotic assistants are devices that have no physical manipulation or locomotion capabilities. Instead, they have a distinct social presence and have visual features suggestive of their ability to interact socially, such as eyes, ears, or a mouth.

(C) For instance, in addition to playing music, a social personal assistant robot would express its engagement with the music so that users would feel like they are listening to the music together with the robot. These robots can be used as surveillance devices, act as communicative intermediates, engage in richer games, tell stories, or be used to provide encouragement or incentives.

* locomotion: 이동　** surveillance: 감시

① (A) − (C) − (B)　　② (B) − (A) − (C)
③ (B) − (C) − (A)　　④ (C) − (A) − (B)
⑤ (C) − (B) − (A)

09

주어진 글 다음에 이어질 글의 순서로 가장 적절한 것을 고르시오. [3점]

> Our perception always involves some imagination. It is more similar to painting than to photography. And, according to the confirmation effect, we blindly trust the reality we construct.

(A) You will see that the majority of us are quite ignorant about what lies around us. This is not so puzzling. The most extraordinary fact is that we completely disregard this ignorance.

(B) This is best witnessed in visual illusions, which we perceive with full confidence, as if there were no doubt that we are portraying reality faithfully. One interesting way of discovering this — in a simple game that can be played at any moment — is the following.

(C) Whenever you are with another person, ask him or her to close their eyes, and start asking questions about what is nearby — not very particular details but the most striking elements of the scene. What is the color of the wall? Is there a table in the room? Does that man have a beard?

① (A) – (C) – (B)　　② (B) – (A) – (C)
③ (B) – (C) – (A)　　④ (C) – (A) – (B)
⑤ (C) – (B) – (A)

10 1등급 대비 고난도 2점 문제

주어진 글 다음에 이어질 글의 순서로 가장 적절한 것을 고르시오.

> In a process called *seeding*, you need to have a time frame in mind. Start telling your family how you feel about your current job. Tell them how you get frustrated and bored with this job.

(A) These stories will make them realise that you are meant to follow your passion. At times they need to be surprised with your small achievements, which could be some additional skills you acquired, or some awards you won in your field of passion.

(B) Discuss this almost twice a week. Then start doing work related to your passion on the side and let them see and experience how happy you are while doing this. Find a way to get your family and friends involved in your passion. The more they see you doing your passion, the more they connect with you emotionally.

(C) Tell them stories of how you are inspired by the passion and how it makes a difference not only to you but also to others. Give examples of how someone living a similar passion started his or her life and today how he or she is living happily.

① (A) – (C) – (B)　　② (B) – (A) – (C)
③ (B) – (C) – (A)　　④ (C) – (A) – (B)
⑤ (C) – (B) – (A)

11 1등급 대비 고난도 3점 문제

고3·2021학년도 6월 37번

주어진 글 다음에 이어질 글의 순서로 가장 적절한 것을 고르시오.
[3점]

The fruit ripening process brings about the softening of cell walls, sweetening and the production of chemicals that give colour and flavour. The process is induced by the production of a plant hormone called ethylene.

(A) If ripening could be slowed down by interfering with ethylene production or with the processes that respond to ethylene, fruit could be left on the plant until it was ripe and full of flavour but would still be in good condition when it arrived at the supermarket shelf.

(B) In some countries they are then sprayed with ethylene before sale to the consumer to induce ripening. However, fruit picked before it is ripe has less flavour than fruit picked ripe from the plant. Biotechnologists therefore saw an opportunity in delaying the ripening and softening process in fruit.

(C) The problem for growers and retailers is that ripening is followed sometimes quite rapidly by deterioration and decay and the product becomes worthless. Tomatoes and other fruits are, therefore, usually picked and transported when they are unripe.

＊deterioration: (품질의) 저하

① (A) − (C) − (B)　　② (B) − (A) − (C)
③ (B) − (C) − (A)　　④ (C) − (A) − (B)
⑤ (C) − (B) − (A)

12 1등급 대비 고난도 3점 문제

고3·2023학년도 수능 37번

주어진 글 다음에 이어질 글의 순서로 가장 적절한 것을 고르시오.
[3점]

The most commonly known form of results-based pricing is a practice called *contingency pricing*, used by lawyers.

(A) Therefore, only an outcome in the client's favor is compensated. From the client's point of view, the pricing makes sense in part because most clients in these cases are unfamiliar with and possibly intimidated by law firms. Their biggest fears are high fees for a case that may take years to settle.

(B) By using contingency pricing, clients are ensured that they pay no fees until they receive a settlement. In these and other instances of contingency pricing, the economic value of the service is hard to determine before the service, and providers develop a price that allows them to share the risks and rewards of delivering value to the buyer.

(C) Contingency pricing is the major way that personal injury and certain consumer cases are billed. In this approach, lawyers do not receive fees or payment until the case is settled, when they are paid a percentage of the money that the client receives.

＊intimidate: 위협하다

① (A) − (C) − (B)　　② (B) − (A) − (C)
③ (B) − (C) − (A)　　④ (C) − (A) − (B)
⑤ (C) − (B) − (A)

학습 Check!　▶ 몰라서 틀린 문항 × 표기　▶ 헷갈렸거나 찍은 문항 △ 표기　▶ ×, △ 문항은 다시 풀고 ✔ 표기를 하세요.

종료 시각	시	분	초	문항 번호	01	02	03	04	05	06	07	08	09	10	11	12
소요 시간		분	초	채점 결과												
초과 시간		분	초	틀린 문항 복습												

문장 삽입

수능 영어 **문장 삽입**에서 무엇보다 중요한 것은 연결사를 정확히 알고 이해를 하는 것입니다. 단순히 뜻만 알고 있는 것이 아니고, 연결사 앞 문장과 뒤에 나오는 문장이 어떤 관계에 있는지를 **추론**할 수 있어야합니다.

영어 영역 1등급을 위한 '오답 3대장' 중 마지막 관문인 '문장 삽입'을 반드시 정복해 목표를 이루시기를 바랍니다.

▶ 문장 삽입 유형

> **[38~39]** 글의 흐름으로 보아 주어진 문장이 들어가기에 가장 적절한 곳을 고르시오.

영어 영역 **38~39번**에 해당하는 **문장 삽입**은 연결어 등의 단서를 이용해 주어진 한 문장을 끼워 넣어 논리적인 흐름에 맞게 만드는 문제입니다.

글을 쭉 읽으며 문장 사이의 대비가 자연스럽지 않거나 연결이 어색한 문장들 사이에 주어진 문장을 그 사이에 넣어 흐름이 매끄러운지 확인하는 훈련을 해야 하며, 충분한 연습이 가능하도록 기출문제를 수록했습니다.

> 갑자기 흐름이 끊겨서 어색한 곳을 찾아내 주어진 문장을 알맞은 위치에 넣고, 전 후 흐름이 자연스럽게 이어졌는지 확인한다.

▶ 문장 삽입 교재 구성

> **하루 12문항 _ 20분 학습 _ 5일 완성 = 총 60문항**

문장 삽입은 앞 문장에는 등장하지 않았던 어구가 갑자기 나오거나 문맥상 원인이 주어지지 않았는데 결과가 갑자기 등장한다면, 또는 글의 흐름이 아무 연결어 없이 완전히 전환되거나 화재가 넘어가는 부분이 정답일 수 있습니다. **일관성**을 유지하는 주제를 파악하여 '주어진 문장의 위치를 찾는 연습'이 영어 '1등급으로 향하는 실력'이 됩니다.

단서에 유의하자

한정사(such, both…), 대명사, 지시어, 정관사, 대동사, 연결어, 시간 흐름 등의 단서에 유의해서 해석한다.

흐름을 파악하자

글의 전반부가 부정이고 후반으로 갈수록 긍정이라면 삽입 문장은 역접이 시작하는 부분일 가능성이 높다.

논리의 비약을 찾자

주어진 문장에서 논리적 흐름이 이상한 곳과 글에서 내용상의 단절되는 부분을 찾으면 쉽게 답을 찾을 수 있다.

2020 하루 20분 20일 완성

PART Ⅲ
문장 삽입

Day 16~Day 20

DAY 16

※ 점수 표기가 없는 문항은 모두 2점입니다.

문장 삽입 01

● 날짜 :   월   일 ● 시작 시각 :   시   분   초

● 목표 시간 : 20분

01

고3 · 2022학년도 9월 38번

글의 흐름으로 보아, 주어진 문장이 들어가기에 가장 적절한 곳을 고르시오.

It was not until relatively recent times that scientists came to understand the relationships between the structural elements of materials and their properties.

The earliest humans had access to only a very limited number of materials, those that occur naturally: stone, wood, clay, skins, and so on. (①) With time, they discovered techniques for producing materials that had properties superior to those of the natural ones; these new materials included pottery and various metals. (②) Furthermore, it was discovered that the properties of a material could be altered by heat treatments and by the addition of other substances. (③) At this point, materials utilization was totally a selection process that involved deciding from a given, rather limited set of materials, the one best suited for an application based on its characteristics. (④) This knowledge, acquired over approximately the past 100 years, has empowered them to fashion, to a large degree, the characteristics of materials. (⑤) Thus, tens of thousands of different materials have evolved with rather specialized characteristics that meet the needs of our modern and complex society, including metals, plastics, glasses, and fibers.

02

고3 · 2023학년도 수능 38번

글의 흐름으로 보아, 주어진 문장이 들어가기에 가장 적절한 곳을 고르시오.

There's a reason for that: traditionally, park designers attempted to create such a feeling by planting tall trees at park boundaries, building stone walls, and constructing other means of partition.

Parks take the shape demanded by the cultural concerns of their time. Once parks are in place, they are no inert stage — their purposes and meanings are made and remade by planners and by park users. Moments of park creation are particularly telling, however, for they reveal and actualize ideas about nature and its relationship to urban society. (①) Indeed, what distinguishes a park from the broader category of public space is the representation of nature that parks are meant to embody. (②) Public spaces include parks, concrete plazas, sidewalks, even indoor atriums. (③) Parks typically have trees, grass, and other plants as their central features. (④) When entering a city park, people often imagine a sharp separation from streets, cars, and buildings. (⑤) What's behind this idea is not only landscape architects' desire to design aesthetically suggestive park spaces, but a much longer history of Western thought that envisions cities and nature as antithetical spaces and oppositional forces.

＊ aesthetically: 미적으로 ＊＊ antithetical: 대조적인

03

글의 흐름으로 보아, 주어진 문장이 들어가기에 가장 적절한 곳을 고르시오.

> But many signals, as they are passed from generation to generation by whatever means, go through changes that make them either more elaborate or simply different.

Many of the ritualized displays performed by animals look so bizarre to us that we wonder how they came about. (①) Most of the various forms of signaling that are used by different species of animals have not arisen afresh in each separate species. (②) As one species evolves into another, particular forms of signaling may be passed on, owing to the effects of both genes and learning or experience. (③) Some signals have significance across many species, and so remain much the same over generations and in a number of species. (④) If we examine closely related species, we can often see slight variations in a particular display and we can piece together an explanation for the spread of the display across species. (⑤) Some very elaborate displays may have begun as simpler versions of the same behavioral pattern that became more elaborate as they developed and were passed on from generation to generation.

＊bizarre: 기이한

04

글의 흐름으로 보아, 주어진 문장이 들어가기에 가장 적절한 곳을 고르시오.

> Thus, individuals of many resident species, confronted with the fitness benefits of control over a productive breeding site, may be forced to balance costs in the form of lower nonbreeding survivorship by remaining in the specific habitat where highest breeding success occurs.

Resident-bird habitat selection is seemingly a straightforward process in which a young dispersing individual moves until it finds a place where it can compete successfully to satisfy its needs. (①) Initially, these needs include only food and shelter. (②) However, eventually, the young must locate, identify, and settle in a habitat that satisfies not only survivorship but reproductive needs as well. (③) In some cases, the habitat that provides the best opportunity for survival may not be the same habitat as the one that provides for highest reproductive capacity because of requirements specific to the reproductive period. (④) Migrants, however, are free to choose the optimal habitat for survival during the nonbreeding season and for reproduction during the breeding season. (⑤) Thus, habitat selection during these different periods can be quite different for migrants as opposed to residents, even among closely related species.

＊disperse: 흩어지다　＊＊optimal: 최적의

05

글의 흐름으로 보아, 주어진 문장이 들어가기에 가장 적절한 곳을 고르시오. [3점]

> Charred bones or even carbon deposits from an ancient campfire can be informative documents to people who know how to read them.

The evolutionary history of a species or a disease is like any other kind of history. (①) There is no experiment, in the usual sense, that we can do now to decide how long ago our ancestors first started to use fires for cooking or other purposes and what subsequent evolutionary effects that change may have had. (②) History can be investigated only by examining the records it has left. (③) Likewise, the chemical structure of proteins and DNA may be read to reveal relationships among now strikingly different organisms. (④) Until a time machine is invented, we will not be able to go back and watch the evolution of major traits, but we can nonetheless reconstruct prehistoric events by the records they left in fossils, carbon traces, structures, and behavioral tendencies, as well as protein and DNA structures. (⑤) Even when we cannot reconstruct the history of a trait, we can often still be confident that it was shaped by natural selection.

＊charred: (탄화로) 까맣게 된

06

글의 흐름으로 보아, 주어진 문장이 들어가기에 가장 적절한 곳을 고르시오. [3점]

> At the next step in the argument, however, the analogy breaks down.

Misprints in a book or in any written message usually have a negative impact on the content, sometimes (literally) fatally. (①) The displacement of a comma, for instance, may be a matter of life and death. (②) Similarly most mutations have harmful consequences for the organism in which they occur, meaning that they reduce its reproductive fitness. (③) Occasionally, however, a mutation may occur that increases the fitness of the organism, just as an accidental failure to reproduce the text of the first edition might provide more accurate or updated information. (④) A favorable mutation is going to be more heavily represented in the next generation, since the organism in which it occurred will have more offspring and mutations are transmitted to the offspring. (⑤) By contrast, there is no mechanism by which a book that accidentally corrects the mistakes of the first edition will tend to sell better.

＊analogy: 유사 ＊＊mutation: 돌연변이

07

글의 흐름으로 보아, 주어진 문장이 들어가기에 가장 적절한 곳을 고르시오. [3점]

> This is why it is difficult to wake up from or scream out during a nightmare.

Most dreaming occurs during REM sleep. (①) REM stands for Rapid Eye Movement, a stage of sleep discovered by Professor Nathaniel Kleitman at the University of Chicago in 1958. (②) Along with a medical student, Eugene Aserinsky, he noted that when people are sleeping, they exhibit rapid eye movement, as if they were "looking" at something. (③) Ongoing research by Kleitman and Aserinsky concluded that it was during this period of rapid eye movement that people dream, yet their minds are as active as someone who is awake. (④) Interestingly enough, studies have found that along with rapid eye movement, our heart rates increase and our respiration is also elevated — yet our bodies do not move and are basically paralyzed due to a nerve center in the brain that keeps our bodies motionless besides some occasional twitches and jerks. (⑤) To sum it up, during the REM dream state, your mind is busy but your body is at rest.

* twitch: 씰룩거림

08

1등급 대비 고난도 2점 문제

글의 흐름으로 보아, 주어진 문장이 들어가기에 가장 적절한 곳을 고르시오.

> Because the manipulation of digitally converted sounds meant the reprogramming of binary information, editing operations could be performed with millisecond precision.

The shift from analog to digital technology significantly influenced how music was produced. First and foremost, the digitization of sounds — that is, their conversion into numbers — enabled music makers to undo what was done. (①) One could, in other words, twist and bend sounds toward something new without sacrificing the original version. (②) This "undo" ability made mistakes considerably less momentous, sparking the creative process and encouraging a generally more experimental mindset. (③) In addition, digitally converted sounds could be manipulated simply by programming digital messages rather than using physical tools, simplifying the editing process significantly. (④) For example, while editing once involved razor blades to physically cut and splice audiotapes, it now involved the cursor and mouse-click of the computer-based sequencer program, which was obviously less time consuming. (⑤) This microlevel access at once made it easier to conceal any traces of manipulations (such as joining tracks in silent spots) and introduced new possibilities for manipulating sounds in audible and experimental ways.

* binary: 2진법의 ** splice: 합쳐 잇다

09 1등급 대비 고난도 2점 문제 　　고3 · 2019학년도 6월 38번

글의 흐름으로 보아, 주어진 문장이 들어가기에 가장 적절한 곳을 고르시오.

> There is a considerable difference as to whether people watch a film about the Himalayas on television and become excited by the 'untouched nature' of the majestic mountain peaks, or whether they get up and go on a trek to Nepal.

Tourism takes place simultaneously in the realm of the imagination and that of the physical world. In contrast to literature or film, it leads to 'real', tangible worlds, while nevertheless remaining tied to the sphere of fantasies, dreams, wishes — and myth. It thereby allows the ritual enactment of mythological ideas. (①) Even in the latter case, they remain, at least partly, in an imaginary world. (②) They experience moments that they have already seen at home in books, brochures and films. (③) Their notions of untouched nature and friendly, innocent indigenous people will probably be confirmed. (④) But now this confirmation is anchored in a physical experience. (⑤) The myth is thus transmitted in a much more powerful way than by television, movies or books.

* indigenous: 토착의

10 1등급 대비 고난도 3점 문제 　　고3 · 2024학년도 6월 39번

글의 흐름으로 보아, 주어진 문장이 들어가기에 가장 적절한 곳을 고르시오. [3점]

> As a result, they are fit and grow better, but they aren't particularly long-lived.

When trees grow together, nutrients and water can be optimally divided among them all so that each tree can grow into the best tree it can be. If you "help" individual trees by getting rid of their supposed competition, the remaining trees are bereft. They send messages out to their neighbors unsuccessfully, because nothing remains but stumps. Every tree now grows on its own, giving rise to great differences in productivity. (①) Some individuals photosynthesize like mad until sugar positively bubbles along their trunk. (②) This is because a tree can be only as strong as the forest that surrounds it. (③) And there are now a lot of losers in the forest. (④) Weaker members, who would once have been supported by the stronger ones, suddenly fall behind. (⑤) Whether the reason for their decline is their location and lack of nutrients, a passing sickness, or genetic makeup, they now fall prey to insects and fungi.

* bereft: 잃은　** stump: 그루터기
*** photosynthesize: 광합성하다

11 1등급 대비 고난도 3점 문제

고3·2023년 10월 38번

글의 흐름으로 보아, 주어진 문장이 들어가기에 가장 적절한 곳을 고르시오. [3점]

> But when students were given "worked-examples" (such as pre-solved problems) placed between problems to solve, studying the worked-examples freed up cognitive resources that allowed students to see the key features of the problem and to analyze the steps and reasons behind problem-solving moves.

How can we help students manage cognitive load as they learn to perform complex tasks? One method that has proved effective in research studies is to support some aspects of a complex task while students perform the entire task. (①) For example, Swelter and Cooper demonstrated this with students learning to solve problems in a variety of quantitative fields from statistics to physics. (②) They found that when students were given typical word problems, it was possible for them to solve the problems without actually learning much. (③) This is because the problems themselves were sufficiently demanding that students had no cognitive resources available to learn from what they did. (④) The researchers found this improved students' performance on subsequent problem solving. (⑤) This result, called the *worked-example effect*, is one example of a process called *scaffolding*, by which instructors temporarily relieve some of the cognitive load so that students can focus on particular dimensions of learning.

＊ word problem: 문장제(이야기 형식으로 제시된 문제)

＊＊ scaffolding: 발판 놓기

12 1등급 대비 고난도 3점 문제

고3·2019학년도 9월 39번

글의 흐름으로 보아, 주어진 문장이 들어가기에 가장 적절한 곳을 고르시오. [3점]

> We become entrusted to teach culturally appropriate behaviors, values, attitudes, skills, and information about the world.

Erikson believes that when we reach the adult years, several physical, social, and psychological stimuli trigger a sense of *generativity*. A central component of this attitude is the desire to care for others. (①) For the majority of people, parenthood is perhaps the most obvious and convenient opportunity to fulfill this desire. (②) Erikson believes that another distinguishing feature of adulthood is the emergence of an inborn desire to teach. (③) We become aware of this desire when the event of being physically capable of reproducing is joined with the events of participating in a committed relationship, the establishment of an adult pattern of living, and the assumption of job responsibilities. (④) According to Erikson, by becoming parents we learn that we have the need to be needed by others who depend on our knowledge, protection, and guidance. (⑤) By assuming the responsibilities of being primary caregivers to children through their long years of physical and social growth, we concretely express what Erikson believes to be an inborn desire to teach.

DAY 16

▶ 몰라서 틀린 문항 × 표기 ▶ 헷갈렸거나 찍은 문항 △ 표기 ▶ ×, △ 문항은 다시 풀고 ✔ 표기를 하세요.

종료 시각	시 분 초	문항 번호	01	02	03	04	05	06	07	08	09	10	11	12
소요 시간	분 초	채점 결과												
초과 시간	분 초	틀린 문항 복습												

DAY 17

※ 점수 표기가 없는 문항은 모두 **2점**입니다.

문장 삽입 02

● 날짜 :　　월　　일　● 시작 시각 :　　시　　분　　초　　　　　　　　● 목표 시간 : **20분**

01

고3 · 2024학년도 6월 38번

글의 흐름으로 보아, 주어진 문장이 들어가기에 가장 적절한 곳을 고르시오.

> Instead, much like the young child learning how to play 'nicely', the apprentice scientist gains his or her understanding of the moral values inherent in the role by absorption from their colleagues — socialization.

As particular practices are repeated over time and become more widely shared, the values that they embody are reinforced and reproduced and we speak of them as becoming 'institutionalized'. (①) In some cases, this institutionalization has a formal face to it, with rules and protocols written down, and specialized roles created to ensure that procedures are followed correctly. (②) The main institutions of state — parliament, courts, police and so on — along with certain of the professions, exhibit this formal character. (③) Other social institutions, perhaps the majority, are not like this; science is an example. (④) Although scientists are trained in the substantive content of their discipline, they are not formally instructed in 'how to be a good scientist'. (⑤) We think that these values, along with the values that inform many of the professions, are under threat, just as the value of the professions themselves is under threat.

*apprentice: 도제, 견습　**inherent: 내재된

02

고3 · 2022학년도 6월 38번

글의 흐름으로 보아, 주어진 문장이 들어가기에 가장 적절한 곳을 고르시오.

> A problem, however, is that supervisors often work in locations apart from their employees and therefore are not able to observe their subordinates' performance.

In most organizations, the employee's immediate supervisor evaluates the employee's performance. (①) This is because the supervisor is responsible for the employee's performance, providing supervision, handing out assignments, and developing the employee. (②) Should supervisors rate employees on performance dimensions they cannot observe? (③) To eliminate this dilemma, more and more organizations are implementing assessments referred to as *360-degree evaluations*. (④) Employees are rated not only by their supervisors but by coworkers, clients or citizens, professionals in other agencies with whom they work, and subordinates. (⑤) The reason for this approach is that often coworkers and clients or citizens have a greater opportunity to observe an employee's performance and are in a better position to evaluate many performance dimensions.

*subordinate: 부하 직원

03

고3 · 2022년 10월 38번

글의 흐름으로 보아, 주어진 문장이 들어가기에 가장 적절한 곳을 고르시오.

> However, after all the available materials on the Earth's surface, mostly iron, had combined with the free oxygen, it began to appear in the atmosphere in sizable quantities.

Water molecules circulate through the atmosphere as a result of evaporation. (①) As water molecules rise high up in the atmosphere, they may split up into their constituent chemical elements, hydrogen and oxygen, under the influence of sunlight. (②) Whereas the much heavier oxygen either remains in the atmosphere or is captured on the Earth's surface, the hydrogen tends to escape into space, because it is so light that Earth's gravity cannot retain it. (③) As long as there was little or no free oxygen in the atmosphere that could capture hydrogen before it escaped into the cosmos, this process would have continued unhindered. (④) As soon as this happened, the free oxygen would have captured most of the free hydrogen by forming water molecules again, thus slowing down the loss of hydrogen. (⑤) Over the course of time, this process would have helped to retain water on Earth, while it also contributed to the emergence of oxygen in the atmosphere.

04

고3 · 2019학년도 수능 38번

글의 흐름으로 보아, 주어진 문장이 들어가기에 가장 적절한 곳을 고르시오.

> The advent of literacy and the creation of handwritten scrolls and, eventually, handwritten books strengthened the ability of large and complex ideas to spread with high fidelity.

The printing press boosted the power of ideas to copy themselves. Prior to low-cost printing, ideas could and did spread by word of mouth. While this was tremendously powerful, it limited the complexity of the ideas that could be propagated to those that a single person could remember. (①) It also added a certain amount of guaranteed error. (②) The spread of ideas by word of mouth was equivalent to a game of telephone on a global scale. (③) But the incredible amount of time required to copy a scroll or book by hand limited the speed with which information could spread this way. (④) A well-trained monk could transcribe around four pages of text per day. (⑤) A printing press could copy information thousands of times faster, allowing knowledge to spread far more quickly, with full fidelity, than ever before.

* fidelity: 충실 ** propagate: 전파하다

05

글의 흐름으로 보아, 주어진 문장이 들어가기에 가장 적절한 곳을 고르시오. [3점]

> It may be easier to reach an agreement when settlement terms don't have to be implemented until months in the future.

Negotiators should try to find ways to slice a large issue into smaller pieces, known as using *salami tactics*. (①) Issues that can be expressed in quantitative, measurable units are easy to slice. (②) For example, compensation demands can be divided into cents-per-hour increments or lease rates can be quoted as dollars per square foot. (③) When working to fractionate issues of principle or precedent, parties may use the time horizon (when the principle goes into effect or how long it will last) as a way to fractionate the issue. (④) Another approach is to vary the number of ways that the principle may be applied. (⑤) For example, a company may devise a family emergency leave plan that allows employees the opportunity to be away from the company for a period of no longer than three hours, and no more than once a month, for illness in the employee's immediate family.

* increment: 증가 ** fractionate: 세분하다

06

글의 흐름으로 보아, 주어진 문장이 들어가기에 가장 적절한 곳을 고르시오. [3점]

> Rather, it evolved naturally as certain devices were found in practice to be both workable and useful.

Film has no grammar. (①) There are, however, some vaguely defined rules of usage in cinematic language, and the syntax of film — its systematic arrangement — orders these rules and indicates relationships among them. (②) As with written and spoken languages, it is important to remember that the syntax of film is a result of its usage, not a determinant of it. (③) There is nothing preordained about film syntax. (④) Like the syntax of written and spoken language, the syntax of film is an organic development, descriptive rather than prescriptive, and it has changed considerably over the years. (⑤) "Hollywood Grammar" may sound laughable now, but during the thirties, forties, and early fifties it was an accurate model of the way Hollywood films were constructed.

* preordained: 미리 정해진

07

글의 흐름으로 보아, 주어진 문장이 들어가기에 가장 적절한 곳을 고르시오. [3점]

> By a fortunate coincidence, elements and materials that we use in large amounts need less natural concentration than those that we use in small amounts.

Ore deposits represent work that nature does for us. (①) For instance, Earth's crust contains an average of about 55 ppm (parts per million) of copper, whereas copper ore deposits must contain about 5,000 ppm (0.5%) copper before we can mine them. (②) Thus, geologic processes need to concentrate the average copper content of the crust by about 100 times to make a copper ore deposit that we can use. (③) We then use industrial processes to convert copper ore into pure copper metal, an increase of about 200 times. (④) Thus, we are likely to have larger deposits of mineral commodities that we use in large amounts. (⑤) As long as energy costs remain high, the relation between work that we can afford to do and work that we expect nature to do will control the lower limit of natural concentrations that we can exploit, and this puts very real limits on our global mineral resources.

＊ore deposit: 광상(광물이 집적된 곳)　＊＊Earth's crust: 지각(地殼)

＊＊＊copper: 구리

08 1등급 대비 고난도 2점 문제

글의 흐름으로 보아, 주어진 문장이 들어가기에 가장 적절한 곳을 고르시오.

> Yes, some contests are seen as world class, such as identification of the Higgs particle or the development of high temperature superconductors.

Science is sometimes described as a winner-take-all contest, meaning that there are no rewards for being second or third. This is an extreme view of the nature of scientific contests. (①) Even those who describe scientific contests in such a way note that it is a somewhat inaccurate description, given that replication and verification have social value and are common in science. (②) It is also inaccurate to the extent that it suggests that only a handful of contests exist. (③) But many other contests have multiple parts, and the number of such contests may be increasing. (④) By way of example, for many years it was thought that there would be "one" cure for cancer, but it is now realized that cancer takes multiple forms and that multiple approaches are needed to provide a cure. (⑤) There won't be one winner — there will be many.

＊replication: 반복　＊＊verification: 입증

DAY 17

09 1등급 대비 고난도 2편 문제   고3·2019학년도 6월 39번

글의 흐름으로 보아, 주어진 문장이 들어가기에 가장 적절한 곳을 고르시오.

> There are also clinical cases that show the flip side of this coin.

Humans can tell lies with their faces. Although some are specifically trained to detect lies from facial expressions, the average person is often misled into believing false and manipulated facial emotions. One reason for this is that we are "two-faced." By this I mean that we have two different neural systems that manipulate our facial muscles. (①) One neural system is under voluntary control and the other works under involuntary control. (②) There are reported cases of individuals who have damaged the neural system that controls voluntary expressions. (③) They still have facial expressions, but are incapable of producing deceitful ones. (④) The emotion that you see is the emotion they are feeling, since they have lost the needed voluntary control to produce false facial expressions. (⑤) These people have injured the system that controls their involuntary expressions, so that the only changes in their demeanor you will see are actually willed expressions.

* demeanor: 태도, 표정

10 1등급 대비 고난도 3편 문제   고3·2023학년도 9월 39번

글의 흐름으로 보아, 주어진 문장이 들어가기에 가장 적절한 곳을 고르시오. [3점]

> On top of the hurdles introduced in accessing his or her money, if a suspected fraud is detected, the account holder has to deal with the phone call asking if he or she made the suspicious transactions.

Each new wave of technology is intended to enhance user convenience, as well as improve security, but sometimes these do not necessarily go hand-in-hand. For example, the transition from magnetic stripe to embedded chip slightly slowed down transactions, sometimes frustrating customers in a hurry. (①) Make a service too burdensome, and the potential customer will go elsewhere. (②) This obstacle applies at several levels. (③) Passwords, double-key identification, and biometrics such as fingerprint-, iris-, and voice recognition are all ways of keeping the account details hidden from potential fraudsters, of keeping your data dark. (④) But they all inevitably add a burden to the use of the account. (⑤) This is all useful at some level — indeed, it can be reassuring knowing that your bank is keeping alert to protect you — but it becomes tiresome if too many such calls are received.

* fraud: 사기

11 1등급 대비 고난도 3점 문제
고3·2020학년도 수능 39번

글의 흐름으로 보아, 주어진 문장이 들어가기에 가장 적절한 곳을 고르시오. [3점]

> Still, it is arguable that advertisers worry rather too much about this problem, as advertising in other media has always been fragmented.

The fragmentation of television audiences during recent decades, which has happened throughout the globe as new channels have been launched everywhere, has caused advertisers much concern. (①) Advertisers look back nostalgically to the years when a single spot transmission would be seen by the majority of the population at one fell swoop. (②) This made the television advertising of mass consumer products relatively straightforward — not to say easy — whereas today it is necessary for advertisers to build up coverage of their target markets over time, by advertising on a host of channels with separate audiences. (③) Moreover, advertisers gain considerable benefits from the price competition between the numerous broadcasting stations. (④) And television remains much the fastest way to build up public awareness of a new brand or a new campaign. (⑤) Seldom does a new brand or new campaign that solely uses other media, without using television, reach high levels of public awareness very quickly.

* fragment: 조각내다 ** at one fell swoop: 단번에, 일거에

12 1등급 대비 고난도 3점 문제
고3·2021학년도 6월 38번

글의 흐름으로 보아, 주어진 문장이 들어가기에 가장 적절한 곳을 고르시오. [3점]

> Compounding the difficulty, now more than ever, is what ergonomists call information overload, where a leader is overrun with inputs — via e-mails, meetings, and phone calls — that only distract and confuse her thinking.

Clarity is often a difficult thing for a leader to obtain. Concerns of the present tend to seem larger than potentially greater concerns that lie farther away. (①) Some decisions by their nature present great complexity, whose many variables must come together a certain way for the leader to succeed. (②) Alternatively, the leader's information might be only fragmentary, which might cause her to fill in the gaps with assumptions — sometimes without recognizing them as such. (③) And the merits of a leader's most important decisions, by their nature, typically are not clear-cut. (④) Instead those decisions involve a process of assigning weights to competing interests, and then determining, based upon some criterion, which one predominates. (⑤) The result is one of judgment, of shades of gray; like saying that Beethoven is a better composer than Brahms.

* ergonomist: 인간 공학자 ** fragmentary: 단편적인

DAY 17

학습 Check!

▶ 몰라서 틀린 문항 ✕ 표기 ▶ 헷갈렸거나 찍은 문항 △ 표기 ▶ ✕, △ 문항은 다시 풀고 ✔ 표기를 하세요.

종료 시각	시 분 초	문항 번호	01	02	03	04	05	06	07	08	09	10	11	12
소요 시간	분 초	채점 결과												
초과 시간	분 초	틀린 문항 복습												

DAY 18

※ 점수 표기가 없는 문항은 모두 2점입니다.

문장 삽입 03

● 날짜 :　　월　　일　　● 시작 시각 :　　시　　분　　초

● 목표 시간 : 20분

01

글의 흐름으로 보아, 주어진 문장이 들어가기에 가장 적절한 곳을 고르시오.

> Also, it has become difficult for companies to develop new pesticides, even those that can have major beneficial effects and few negative effects.

Simply maintaining yields at current levels often requires new cultivars and management methods, since pests and diseases continue to evolve, and aspects of the chemical, physical, and social environment can change over several decades. (①) In the 1960s, many people considered pesticides to be mainly beneficial to mankind. (②) Developing new, broadly effective, and persistent pesticides often was considered to be the best way to control pests on crop plants. (③) Since that time, it has become apparent that broadly effective pesticides can have harmful effects on beneficial insects, which can negate their effects in controlling pests, and that persistent pesticides can damage non-target organisms in the ecosystem, such as birds and people. (④) Very high costs are involved in following all of the procedures needed to gain government approval for new pesticides. (⑤) Consequently, more consideration is being given to other ways to manage pests, such as incorporating greater resistance to pests into cultivars by breeding and using other biological control methods.

* pesticide: 살충제　** cultivar: 품종
*** breed: 개량하다

02

글의 흐름으로 보아, 주어진 문장이 들어가기에 가장 적절한 곳을 고르시오.

> However, within British society not everybody would see football as 'their' game.

If we look at contemporary British 'culture' we will probably quickly conclude that sport is an important part of the culture. In other words, it is something that many people in the society share and value. (①) In addition, we would also probably conclude that the most 'important' sport within British culture is football. (②) We would 'know' this from the evidence that on a daily basis there is a significant amount of 'cultural' activity all focused on football in terms of the amount of people who play it, watch it, read about it and talk about it. (③) It could be argued from looking at their 'cultural' activities and habits, that people from a middle-class background seem to prefer rugby over football, or that more women play netball than football. (④) Equally, if you went to the USA and were talking about 'football', most people would assume you were talking about American football rather than soccer. (⑤) From this we can conclude that different cultures produce different ways of understanding, or evaluating, human activities such as sport.

03

글의 흐름으로 보아, 주어진 문장이 들어가기에 가장 적절한 곳을 고르시오.

> In order to make some sense of this, an average wind direction over an hour is sometimes calculated, or sometimes the direction that the wind blew from the most during the hour is recorded.

Wind direction is usually measured through the use of a simple vane. (①) This is simply a paddle of some sort mounted on a spindle; when it catches the wind, it turns so that the wind passes by without obstruction. (②) The direction is recorded, but if you ever have a chance to watch a wind vane on a breezy day, you will notice that there is a lot of variation in the direction of wind flow — *a lot*! (③) Sometimes the wind can blow from virtually every direction within a minute or two. (④) Either way, it is a generalization, and it's important to remember that there can be a lot of variation in the data. (⑤) It's also important to remember that the data recorded at a weather station give an indication of conditions prevailing in an area but will not be exactly the same as the conditions at a landscape some distance from the weather station.

* vane: 풍향계 ** spindle: 회전축

04

글의 흐름으로 보아, 주어진 문장이 들어가기에 가장 적절한 곳을 고르시오.

> Experiments show that rats display an immediate liking for salt the first time they experience a salt deficiency.

Both humans and rats have evolved taste preferences for *sweet* foods, which provide rich sources of calories. A study of food preferences among the Hadza hunter-gatherers of Tanzania found that honey was the most highly preferred food item, an item that has the highest caloric value. (①) Human newborn infants also show a strong preference for sweet liquids. (②) Both humans and rats dislike *bitter* and *sour* foods, which tend to contain toxins. (③) They also adaptively adjust their eating behavior in response to deficits in water, calories, and salt. (④) They likewise increase their intake of sweets and water when their energy and fluids become depleted. (⑤) These appear to be specific evolved mechanisms, designed to deal with the adaptive problem of food selection, and coordinate consumption patterns with physical needs.

* deficiency: 결핍 ** deplete: 고갈시키다

05

고3 · 2022년 3월 39번

글의 흐름으로 보아, 주어진 문장이 들어가기에 가장 적절한 곳을 고르시오. [3점]

> If the goal is to figure out how best to cover a set curriculum — to fill students with facts — then it might seem appropriate to try to maximize time on task, such as by assigning homework.

Carole Ames, dean of the college of education at Michigan State University, points out that it isn't "quantitative changes in behavior" (such as requiring students to spend more hours in front of books or worksheets) that help children to learn better. (①) Rather, it's "qualitative changes in the ways students view themselves in relation to the task, engage in the process of learning, and then respond to the learning activities and situation." (②) In turn, these attitudes and responses on the part of students emerge from the way teachers think about learning and, as a result, the ways they've organized their classrooms. (③) But that's unlikely to have a positive effect on the critical variables that Ames identifies. (④) Perhaps it makes sense to see education as being less about how much the teacher covers and more about what the students can be helped to discover. (⑤) More time won't do a thing to bring about that shift.

06

고3 · 2020학년도 6월 39번

글의 흐름으로 보아, 주어진 문장이 들어가기에 가장 적절한 곳을 고르시오. [3점]

> That puts you each near a focus, a special point at which the sound of your voice gets focused as it reflects off the passageway's curved walls and ceiling.

Whispering galleries are remarkable acoustic spaces found beneath certain domes or curved ceilings. A famous one is located outside a well-known restaurant in New York City's Grand Central Station. (①) It's a fun place to take a date: the two of you can exchange romantic words while you're forty feet apart and separated by a busy passageway. (②) You'll hear each other clearly, but the passersby won't hear a word you're saying. (③) To produce this effect, the two of you should stand at diagonally opposite corners of the space, facing the wall. (④) Ordinarily, the sound waves you produce travel in all directions and bounce off the walls at different times and places, scrambling them so much that they are inaudible when they arrive at the ear of a listener forty feet away. (⑤) But when you whisper at a *focus*, the reflected waves all arrive at the *same* time at the other focus, thus reinforcing one another and allowing your words to be heard.

* acoustic: 음향의 ** diagonally: 대각선으로

07

글의 흐름으로 보아, 주어진 문장이 들어가기에 가장 적절한 곳을 고르시오. [3점]

> Note that copyright covers the expression of an idea and not the idea itself.

Designers draw on their experience of design when approaching a new project. This includes the use of previous designs that they know work — both designs that they have created themselves and those that others have created. (①) Others' creations often spark inspiration that also leads to new ideas and innovation. (②) This is well known and understood. (③) However, the expression of an idea is protected by copyright, and people who infringe on that copyright can be taken to court and prosecuted. (④) This means, for example, that while there are numerous smartphones all with similar functionality, this does not represent an infringement of copyright as the idea has been expressed in different ways and it is the expression that has been copyrighted. (⑤) Copyright is free and is automatically invested in the author, for instance, the writer of a book or a programmer who develops a program, unless they sign the copyright over to someone else.

* infringe: 침해하다   ** prosecute: 기소하다

08 1등급 대비 고난도 2점 문제

글의 흐름으로 보아, 주어진 문장이 들어가기에 가장 적절한 곳을 고르시오.

> In particular, they define a group as two or more people who interact with, and exert mutual influences on, each other.

In everyday life, we tend to see any collection of people as a group. (①) However, social psychologists use this term more precisely. (②) It is this sense of mutual interaction or inter-dependence for a common purpose which distinguishes the members of a group from a mere aggregation of individuals. (③) For example, as Kenneth Hodge observed, a collection of people who happen to go for a swim after work on the same day each week does not, strictly speaking, constitute a group because these swimmers do not interact with each other in a structured manner. (④) By contrast, a squad of young competitive swimmers who train every morning before going to school *is* a group because they not only share a common objective (training for competition) but also interact with each other in formal ways (e.g., by warming up together beforehand). (⑤) It is this sense of people coming together to achieve a common objective that defines a "team".

* exert: 발휘하다   ** aggregation: 집합

09 1등급 대비 고난도 2점 문제

글의 흐름으로 보아, 주어진 문장이 들어가기에 가장 적절한 곳을 고르시오.

> The net effect of this was that, although customers benefited, the banks lost out as their costs increased but the total number of customers stayed the same.

In mature markets, breakthroughs that lead to a major change in competitive positions and to the growth of the market are rare. (①) Because of this, competition becomes a zero sum game in which one organization can only win at the expense of others. (②) However, where the degree of competition is particularly intense a zero sum game can quickly become a negative sum game, in that everyone in the market is faced with additional costs. (③) As an example of this, when one of the major high street banks in Britain tried to gain a competitive advantage by opening on Saturday mornings, it attracted a number of new customers who found the traditional Monday-Friday bank opening hours to be a constraint. (④) However, faced with a loss of customers, the competition responded by opening on Saturdays as well. (⑤) In essence, this proved to be a negative sum game.

10 1등급 대비 고난도 3점 문제

글의 흐름으로 보아, 주어진 문장이 들어가기에 가장 적절한 곳을 고르시오. [3점]

> To understand how human societies operate, it is therefore not sufficient to only look at their DNA, their molecular mechanisms and the influences from the outside world.

A meaningful level of complexity in our history consists of culture: information stored in nerve and brain cells or in human records of various kinds. The species that has developed this capacity the most is, of course, humankind. (①) In terms of total body weight, our species currently makes up about 0.005 per cent of all planetary biomass. (②) If all life combined were only a paint chip, all human beings today would jointly amount to no more than a tiny colony of bacteria sitting on that flake. (③) Yet through their combined efforts humans have learned to control a considerable portion of the terrestrial biomass, today perhaps as much as between 25 and 40 percent of it. (④) In other words, thanks to its culture this tiny colony of microorganisms residing on a paint chip has gained control over a considerable portion of that flake. (⑤) We also need to study the cultural information that humans have been using for shaping their own lives as well as considerable portions of the rest of nature.

11 1등급 대비 고난도 3점 문제 고3 · 2021년 4월 39번

글의 흐름으로 보아, 주어진 문장이 들어가기에 가장 적절한 곳을 고르시오. [3점]

> In this analogy, the microbes of mathematics are the earliest topics: numbers, shapes, and word problems.

The era of unicellular life lasted for about three and half billion years, dominating most of the Earth's history. But around half a billion years ago, during the Cambrian explosion, a diversity of multicellular life including major animal groups emerged in short period. Similarly, calculus was the Cambrian explosion for mathematics. (①) Once it arrived, an amazing diversity of mathematical fields began to evolve. (②) Their lineage is visible in their calculus-based names, in adjectives like *differential* and *integral* and *analytic*, as in differential geometry, integral equations, and analytic number theory. (③) These advanced branches of mathematics are like the many branches and species of multicellular life. (④) Like unicellular organisms, they dominated the mathematical scene for most of its history. (⑤) But after the Cambrian explosion of calculus three hundred and fifty years ago, new mathematical life forms began to flourish, and they altered the landscape around them.

* microbe: 미생물 ** calculus: 미적법
*** lineage: 계보

12 1등급 대비 고난도 3점 문제 고3 · 2020학년도 9월 39번

글의 흐름으로 보아, 주어진 문장이 들어가기에 가장 적절한 곳을 고르시오. [3점]

> So, there was a social pressure for art to come up with some vocation that both distinguished it from science and, at the same time, made it equal in stature to science.

Representational theories of art treat the work of the artist as similar to that of the scientist. Both, so to speak, are involved in describing the external world. (①) But by the nineteenth century, any comparison between the scientist and the artist was bound to make the artist look like a poor relation in terms of making discoveries about the world or holding a mirror up to nature. (②) Here, science clearly had the edge. (③) The notion that art specialized in the expression of the emotions was particularly attractive in this light. (④) It rendered unto science its own — the exploration of the objective world — while saving something comparably important for art to do — to explore the inner world of feeling. (⑤) If science held the mirror up to nature, art turned a mirror at the self and its experiences.

* vocation: 소명 ** stature: 수준
*** render: 주다

학습 Check!   ▶ 몰라서 틀린 문항 × 표기 ▶ 헷갈렸거나 찍은 문항 △ 표기 ▶ ×, △ 문항은 다시 풀고 ✔ 표기를 하세요.

종료 시각	시 분 초	문항 번호	01	02	03	04	05	06	07	08	09	10	11	12
소요 시간	분 초	채점 결과												
초과 시간	분 초	틀린 문항 복습												

DAY 19

※ 점수 표기가 없는 문항은 모두 **2점**입니다.

문장 삽입 04

● 날짜 : 　월　일　● 시작 시각 : 　시　분　초　　　　　　　● 목표 시간 : 20분

01

고3 · 2023년 7월 38번

글의 흐름으로 보아, 주어진 문장이 들어가기에 가장 적절한 곳을 고르시오.

> The result was that we don't always buy what we like best, but when things have to happen quickly, we tend to go for the product that catches our eye the most.

Often time, or lack of time, plays an important role in the purchase of everyday products. Milica Milosavljevic and his coworkers conducted an experiment looking at the relationship between visual salience and the decision to purchase. (①) They showed subjects 15 different food items on fMRI, such as those we find in a candy vending machine at the train station, that is, bars, chips, fruity items, etc. (②) These were rated by the subjects on a scale of 1 – 15 according to "favorite snack" to "don't like at all." (③) They were then presented in varying brightness and time, with subjects always having to make a choice between two products. (④) If we are also distracted because we are talking to someone, on the phone, or our thoughts are elsewhere at the moment, our actual preference for a product falls further into the background and visual conspicuousness comes to the fore. (⑤) Colors play an important role in this.

*salience: 두드러짐　**fMRI: 기능적 자기 공명 영상
***conspicuousness: 눈에 잘 띔

02

고3 · 2021학년도 9월 38번

글의 흐름으로 보아, 주어진 문장이 들어가기에 가장 적절한 곳을 고르시오.

> As long as you do not run out of copies before completing this process, you will know that you have a sufficient number to go around.

We sometimes solve number problems almost without realizing it. (①) For example, suppose you are conducting a meeting and you want to ensure that everyone there has a copy of the agenda. (②) You can deal with this by labelling each copy of the handout in turn with the initials of each of those present. (③) You have then solved this problem without resorting to arithmetic and without explicit counting. (④) There are numbers at work for us here all the same and they allow precise comparison of one collection with another, even though the members that make up the collections could have entirely different characters, as is the case here, where one set is a collection of people, while the other consists of pieces of paper. (⑤) What numbers allow us to do is to compare the relative size of one set with another.

*arithmetic: 산수

03

글의 흐름으로 보아, 주어진 문장이 들어가기에 가장 적절한 곳을 고르시오.

> Rather, happiness is often found in those moments we are most vulnerable, alone or in pain.

We seek out feel-good experiences, always on the lookout for the next holiday, purchase or culinary experience. This approach to happiness is relatively recent; it depends on our capacity both to pad our lives with material pleasures and to feel that we can control our suffering. (①) Painkillers, as we know them today, are a relatively recent invention and access to material comfort is now within reach of a much larger proportion of the world's population. (②) These technological and economic advances have had significant cultural implications, leading us to see our negative experiences as a problem and maximizing our positive experiences as the answer. (③) Yet, through this we have forgotten that being happy in life is not just about pleasure. (④) Comfort, contentment and satisfaction have never been the elixir of happiness. (⑤) Happiness is there, on the edges of these experiences, and when we get a glimpse of *that* kind of happiness it is powerful, transcendent and compelling.

* culinary: 요리의 ** elixir: 특효약
*** transcendent: 뛰어난

04

글의 흐름으로 보아, 주어진 문장이 들어가기에 가장 적절한 곳을 고르시오.

> It is postulated that such contamination may result from airborne transport from remote power plants or municipal incinerators.

An incident in Japan in the 1950s alerted the world to the potential problems of organic mercury in fish. Factories were discharging mercury into the waters of Minamata Bay, which also harbored a commercial fishing industry. Mercury was being bioaccumulated in the fish tissue and severe mercury poisoning occurred in many people who consumed the fish. (①) The disabling neurological symptoms were subsequently called Minamata disease. (②) Control over direct discharge of mercury from industrial operations is clearly needed for prevention. (③) However, it is now recognized that traces of mercury can appear in lakes far removed from any such industrial discharge. (④) Strictly controlled emission standards for such sources are needed to minimize this problem. (⑤) Fish advisories have been issued for many lakes in the United States; these recommend limits on the number of times per month particular species of fish should be consumed.

* postulate: 가정하다 ** incinerator: 소각로

05

글의 흐름으로 보아, 주어진 문장이 들어가기에 가장 적절한 곳을 고르시오. [3점]

> In the case of specialists such as art critics, a deeper familiarity with materials and techniques is often useful in reaching an informed judgement about a work.

Acknowledging the making of artworks does not require a detailed, technical knowledge of, say, how painters mix different kinds of paint, or how an image editing tool works. (①) All that is required is a general sense of a significant difference between working with paints and working with an imaging application. (②) This sense might involve a basic familiarity with paints and paintbrushes as well as a basic familiarity with how we use computers, perhaps including how we use consumer imaging apps. (③) This is because every kind of artistic material or tool comes with its own challenges and affordances for artistic creation. (④) Critics are often interested in the ways artists exploit different kinds of materials and tools for particular artistic effect. (⑤) They are also interested in the success of an artist's attempt — embodied in the artwork itself — to push the limits of what can be achieved with certain materials and tools.

* affordance: 행위유발성   ** exploit: 활용하다

06

글의 흐름으로 보아, 주어진 문장이 들어가기에 가장 적절한 곳을 고르시오. [3점]

> However, human reasoning is still notoriously prone to confusion and error when causal questions become sufficiently complex, such as when it comes to assessing the impact of policy interventions across society.

Going beyond very simple algorithms, some AI-based tools hold out the promise of supporting better causal and probabilistic reasoning in complex domains. (①) Humans have a natural ability to build causal models of the world — that is, to explain *why* things happen — that AI systems still largely lack. (②) For example, while a doctor can explain to a patient why a treatment works, referring to the changes it causes in the body, a modern machine-learning system could only tell you that patients who are given this treatment tend, on average, to get better. (③) In these cases, supporting human reasoning with more structured AI-based tools may be helpful. (④) Researchers have been exploring the use of Bayesian Networks — an AI technology that can be used to map out the causal relationships between events, and to represent degrees of uncertainty around different areas — for decision support, such as to enable more accurate risk assessment. (⑤) These may be particularly useful for assessing the threat of novel or rare threats, where little historical data is available, such as the risk of terrorist attacks and new ecological disasters.

* notoriously: 악명 높게도

07

글의 흐름으로 보아, 주어진 문장이 들어가기에 가장 적절한 곳을 고르시오. [3점]

> At the same time, the lack of knowledge proved to be important for stabilizing political and social order.

Power and knowledge, as well as ignorance, are interconnected in a productive and constitutive relationship. (①) Rulers know that power cannot be executed without knowledge — mortality tables, tax data, and the like are crucial to running an effective public administration — and conquerors have understood that information is essential for dominating a territory. (②) Since the twentieth century, Western societies have defined themselves as knowledge societies, where knowledge is essential for social organization and productivity. (③) For instance, secrets were essential to creating legitimacy in the early modern period, when individuals believed the world was created and ruled by divine power. (④) By concealing the circumstances of their decisions, rulers cultivated a special aura that set them apart from ordinary people and made them seem more like unknowable gods. (⑤) The complementary relationship between knowledge and ignorance is perhaps most exposed in transitional societies seeking to first disrupt and then stabilize social and political order.

08 1등급 대비 고난도 2펌 문제

글의 흐름으로 보아, 주어진 문장이 들어가기에 가장 적절한 곳을 고르시오.

> Retraining current employees for new positions within the company will also greatly reduce their fear of being laid off.

Introduction of robots into factories, while employment of human workers is being reduced, creates worry and fear. (①) It is the responsibility of management to prevent or, at least, to ease these fears. (②) For example, robots could be introduced only in new plants rather than replacing humans in existing assembly lines. (③) Workers should be included in the planning for new factories or the introduction of robots into existing plants, so they can participate in the process. (④) It may be that robots are needed to reduce manufacturing costs so that the company remains competitive, but planning for such cost reductions should be done jointly by labor and management. (⑤) Since robots are particularly good at highly repetitive simple motions, the replaced human workers should be moved to positions where judgment and decisions beyond the abilities of robots are required.

DAY 19

09 1등급 대비 고난도 2점 문제

글의 흐름으로 보아, 주어진 문장이 들어가기에 가장 적절한 곳을 고르시오.

> Jacques Derrida argues that instead of one line between Man on the one side and Animal on the other, there is a multiple and heterogeneous border; beyond the edge of the "so-called human," we find a heterogeneous plurality of the living.

Language, and the word "animal," deceives us. The word "animal" categorizes all non-human animals and distances humans from other animals. (①) Seeing all other animals as one group in contrast to humans reinforces anthropocentrism, which contributes to the legitimization of practices in which other animals are used for human benefit. (②) To account for this multitude, using the word "animot" has been proposed. (③) In speech it refers to the plural, the multiplicity of animals, which is necessary because there is no one "animal." (④) The "mot" in "animot" refers to the act of naming and the risks involved in drawing a distinction between human and animal by the human. (⑤) It reminds us of the fact that it is a word for animals, not a reference to an existing group of animals.

10 1등급 대비 고난도 3점 문제

글의 흐름으로 보아, 주어진 문장이 들어가기에 가장 적절한 곳을 고르시오. [3점]

> This makes sense from the perspective of information reliability.

The dynamics of collective detection have an interesting feature. Which cue(s) do individuals use as evidence of predator attack? In some cases, when an individual detects a predator, its best response is to seek shelter. (①) Departure from the group may signal danger to nonvigilant animals and cause what appears to be a coordinated flushing of prey from the area. (②) Studies on dark-eyed juncos (a type of bird) support the view that nonvigilant animals attend to departures of individual group mates but that the departure of multiple individuals causes a greater escape response in the nonvigilant individuals. (③) If one group member departs, it might have done so for a number of reasons that have little to do with predation threat. (④) If nonvigilant animals escaped each time a single member left the group, they would frequently respond when there was no predator (a false alarm). (⑤) On the other hand, when several individuals depart the group at the same time, a true threat is much more likely to be present.

* predator: 포식자 ** vigilant: 경계하는
*** flushing: 날아오름

11 1등급 대비 고난도 3점 문제 고3·2022학년도 9월 39번

글의 흐름으로 보아, 주어진 문장이 들어가기에 가장 적절한 곳을 고르시오. [3점]

> Personal stories connect with larger narratives to generate new identities.

The growing complexity of the social dynamics determining food choices makes the job of marketers and advertisers increasingly more difficult. (①) In the past, mass production allowed for accessibility and affordability of products, as well as their wide distribution, and was accepted as a sign of progress. (②) Nowadays it is increasingly replaced by the fragmentation of consumers among smaller and smaller segments that are supposed to reflect personal preferences. (③) Everybody feels different and special and expects products serving his or her inclinations. (④) In reality, these supposedly individual preferences end up overlapping with emerging, temporary, always changing, almost tribal formations solidifying around cultural sensibilities, social identifications, political sensibilities, and dietary and health concerns. (⑤) These consumer communities go beyond national boundaries, feeding on global and widely shared repositories of ideas, images, and practices.

* fragmentation: 파편화 ** repository: 저장소

12 1등급 대비 고난도 3점 문제 고3·2018학년도 9월 39번

글의 흐름으로 보아, 주어진 문장이 들어가기에 가장 적절한 곳을 고르시오. [3점]

> But it is no light matter to quickly and correctly pen a long and complicated composition.

There are many instances of rapid work on the part of the great composers; and their facility and quickness of composition causes great wonder and admiration. (①) But our admiration is often misdirected. (②) When we hear of some of the speedy writing of great works by Mozart or Mendelssohn, we might think that this speed was of the composing power as well as of pen, but, in fact, such was seldom the case. (③) These great musicians generally did their composition mentally without reference to pen or piano, and simply postponed the unpleasant manual labor of committing their music to paper until it became absolutely necessary. (④) Then they got credit for incredible rapidity of composition. (⑤) One has only to copy a piece of music or to try to put into notes some piece of music previously memorized, to realize this.

DAY 19

학습 Check!

▶ 몰라서 틀린 문항 × 표기   ▶ 헷갈렸거나 찍은 문항 △ 표기   ▶ ×, △ 문항은 다시 풀고 ✔ 표기를 하세요.

종료 시각	시 분 초	문항 번호	01	02	03	04	05	06	07	08	09	10	11	12
소요 시간	분 초	채점 결과												
초과 시간	분 초	틀린 문항 복습												

[Day 19] 문장 삽입 04 125

DAY 20

※ 점수 표기가 없는 문항은 모두 **2점**입니다.

문장 삽입 05

● 날짜 :   월   일 ● 시작 시각 :   시   분   초

● 목표 시간 : 20분

01

고3 · 2023년 10월 39번

글의 흐름으로 보아, 주어진 문장이 들어가기에 가장 적절한 곳을 고르시오.

> In contrast, the other major advocate of utilitarianism, John Stuart Mill, argued for a more qualitative approach, assuming that there can be different subjective levels of pleasure.

Utilitarian ethics argues that all action should be directed toward achieving the greatest total amount of happiness for the largest number of people. (①) Utilitarian ethics assumes that all actions can be evaluated in terms of their moral worth, and so the desirability of an action is determined by its resulting hedonistic consequences. (②) This is a consequentialist creed, assuming that the moral value and desirability of an action can be determined from its likely outcomes. (③) Jeremy Bentham suggested that the value of hedonistic outcomes can be quantitatively assessed, so that the value of consequent pleasure can be derived by multiplying its intensity and its duration. (④) Higher-quality pleasures are more desirable than lower-quality pleasures. (⑤) Less sophisticated creatures (like pigs!) have an easier acces s to the simpler pleasures, but more sophisticated creatures like humans have the capacity to access higher pleasures and should be motivated to seek those.

* utilitarianism: 공리주의 ** hedonistic: 쾌락적인

*** creed: 신조

02

고3 · 2021학년도 6월 39번

글의 흐름으로 보아, 주어진 문장이 들어가기에 가장 적절한 곳을 고르시오.

> When the team painted fireflies' light organs dark, a new set of bats took twice as long to learn to avoid them.

Fireflies don't just light up their behinds to attract mates, they also glow to tell bats not to eat them. This twist in the tale of the trait that gives fireflies their name was discovered by Jesse Barber and his colleagues. The glow's warning role benefits both fireflies and bats, because these insects taste disgusting to the mammals. (①) When swallowed, chemicals released by fireflies cause bats to throw them back up. (②) The team placed eight bats in a dark room with three or four fireflies plus three times as many tasty insects, including beetles and moths, for four days. (③) During the first night, all the bats captured at least one firefly. (④) But by the fourth night, most bats had learned to avoid fireflies and catch all the other prey instead. (⑤) It had long been thought that firefly bioluminescence mainly acted as a mating signal, but the new finding explains why firefly larvae also glow despite being immature for mating.

* bioluminescence: 생물 발광(發光)

** larvae: larva(애벌레)의 복수형

03

글의 흐름으로 보아, 주어진 문장이 들어가기에 가장 적절한 곳을 고르시오.

> The field of international politics is, however, dominated by states and other powerful actors (such as multinational corporations) that have priorities other than human rights.

There is obviously a wide gap between the promises of the Universal Declaration of Human Rights in 1948 and the real world of human-rights violations. In so far as we sympathize with the victims, we may criticize the UN and its member governments for failing to keep their promises. (①) However, we cannot understand the gap between human-rights ideals and the real world of human-rights violations by sympathy or by legal analysis. (②) Rather, it requires investigation by the various social sciences of the causes of social conflict and political oppression, and of the interaction between national and international politics. (③) The UN introduced the concept of human rights into international law and politics. (④) It is a leading feature of the human-rights field that the governments of the world proclaim human rights but have a highly variable record of implementing them. (⑤) We must understand why this is so.

* oppression: 억압

04

글의 흐름으로 보아, 주어진 문장이 들어가기에 가장 적절한 곳을 고르시오.

> Moreover, more than half of Americans age 18 and older derive benefits from various transfer programs, while paying little or no personal income tax.

Both the budget deficit and federal debt have soared during the recent financial crisis and recession. (①) During 2009 – 2010, nearly 40 percent of federal expenditures were financed by borrowing. (②) The huge recent federal deficits have pushed the federal debt to levels not seen since the years immediately following World War II. (③) The rapid growth of baby-boomer retirees in the decade immediately ahead will mean higher spending levels and larger and larger deficits for both Social Security and Medicare. (④) All of these factors are going to make it extremely difficult to slow the growth of federal spending and keep the debt from ballooning out of control. (⑤) Projections indicate that the net federal debt will rise to 90 percent of GDP by 2019, and many believe it will be even higher unless constructive action is taken soon.

* deficit: 부족, 결손 ** federal: 연방의
*** soar: 급등하다, 치솟다

05

고3·2022학년도 수능 39번

글의 흐름으로 보아, 주어진 문장이 들어가기에 가장 적절한 곳을 고르시오. [3점]

> As long as the irrealism of the silent black and white film predominated, one could not take filmic fantasies for representations of reality.

Cinema is valuable not for its ability to make visible the hidden outlines of our reality, but for its ability to reveal what reality itself veils — the dimension of fantasy. (①) This is why, to a person, the first great theorists of film decried the introduction of sound and other technical innovations (such as color) that pushed film in the direction of realism. (②) Since cinema was an entirely fantasmatic art, these innovations were completely unnecessary. (③) And what's worse, they could do nothing but turn filmmakers and audiences away from the fantasmatic dimension of cinema, potentially transforming film into a mere delivery device for representations of reality. (④) But sound and color threatened to create just such an illusion, thereby destroying the very essence of film art. (⑤) As Rudolf Arnheim puts it, "The creative power of the artist can only come into play where reality and the medium of representation do not coincide."

* decry: 공공연히 비난하다 ** fantasmatic: 환상의

06

고3·2023년 4월 39번

글의 흐름으로 보아, 주어진 문장이 들어가기에 가장 적절한 곳을 고르시오. [3점]

> Indeed, in the Middle Ages in Europe, calculating by hand and eye was sometimes seen as producing a rather shabby sort of knowledge, inferior to that of abstract thought.

Babylonian astronomers created detailed records of celestial movements in the heavens, using the resulting tables to sieve out irregularities and, with them, the favour of the gods. (①) This was the seed of what we now call the scientific method — a demonstration that accurate observations of the world could be used to forecast its future. (②) The importance of measurement in this sort of cosmic comprehension did not develop smoothly over the centuries. (③) The suspicion was due to the influence of ancient Greeks in the era's scholasticism, particularly Plato and Aristotle, who stressed that the material world was one of unceasing change and instability. (④) They emphasized that reality was best understood by reference to immaterial qualities, be they Platonic forms or Aristotelian causes. (⑤) It would take the revelations of the scientific revolution to fully displace these instincts, with observations of the night sky once again proving decisive.

* celestial: 천체의 ** sieve: 거르다

07

글의 흐름으로 보아, 주어진 문장이 들어가기에 가장 적절한 곳을 고르시오. [3점]

> Human beings discovered this art thousands of years ago, and they have invented several devices to make it easier and faster.

In fiber processing the word 'spinning' means two quite different things. (①) One is the formation of individual fibers by squeezing a liquid through one or more small openings in a nozzle called a spinneret and letting it harden. (②) Spiders and silkworms have been spinning fibers in this way for millions of years, but chemists and engineers learned the procedure from them only about a century ago. (③) In the other kind of spinning — sometimes called throwing to prevent confusion with the first kind — two or more fibers are twisted together to form a thread. (④) The ancient distaff and spindle are examples that were replaced by the spinning wheel in the Middle Ages. (⑤) Later came the spinning jenny, the water frame, and Crompton's mule — spinning machines that became symbols of the Industrial Revolution.

* distaff and spindle: 실을 감는 막대와 추

08 1등급 대비 고난도 2편 문제

글의 흐름으로 보아, 주어진 문장이 들어가기에 가장 적절한 곳을 고르시오.

> However, while our resources come with histories of meanings, *how they come to mean* at a particular communicative moment is always open to negotiation.

The linguistic resources we choose to use do not come to us as empty forms ready to be filled with our personal intentions; rather, they come to us with meanings already embedded within them. (①) These meanings, however, are not derived from some universal, logical set of principles; rather, as with their shapes, they are built up over time from their past uses in particular contexts by particular groups of participants in the accomplishment of particular goals that, in turn, are shaped by myriad cultural, historical and institutional forces. (②) The linguistic resources we choose to use at particular communicative moments come to these moments with their conventionalized histories of meaning. (③) It is their conventionality that binds us to some degree to particular ways of realizing our collective history. (④) Thus, in our individual uses of our linguistic resources we accomplish two actions simultaneously. (⑤) We create their typical — historical — contexts of use and at the same time we position ourselves in relation to these contexts.

* myriad: 무수히 많은

09 1등급 대비 고난도 2점 문제

고3 · 2021학년도 수능 38번

글의 흐름으로 보아, 주어진 문장이 들어가기에 가장 적절한 곳을 고르시오.

> I have still not exactly pinpointed Maddy's character since wickedness takes many forms.

Imagine I tell you that Maddy is bad. Perhaps you infer from my intonation, or the context in which we are talking, that I mean morally bad. Additionally, you will probably infer that I am disapproving of Maddy, or saying that I think you should disapprove of her, or similar, given typical linguistic conventions and assuming I am sincere. (①) However, you might not get a more detailed sense of the particular sorts of way in which Maddy is bad, her typical character traits, and the like, since people can be bad in many ways. (②) In contrast, if I say that Maddy is wicked, then you get more of a sense of her typical actions and attitudes to others. (③) The word 'wicked' is more specific than 'bad'. (④) But there is more detail nevertheless, perhaps a stronger connotation of the sort of person Maddy is. (⑤) In addition, and again assuming typical linguistic conventions, you should also get a sense that I am disapproving of Maddy, or saying that you should disapprove of her, or similar, assuming that we are still discussing her moral character.

* connotation: 함축

10 1등급 대비 고난도 2점 문제

고3 · 2021년 4월 38번

글의 흐름으로 보아, 주어진 문장이 들어가기에 가장 적절한 곳을 고르시오.

> Under such circumstances, recycling previously composed music was the only way to make it more durable.

In the classical period of European music, much musical material was *de facto* considered common property. (①) When Antonio Vivaldi presented in Venice his opera *Rosmira fedele*, the score was actually a pastiche in which, among his own ideas, musicologists later identified ideas by George Frederic Handel, Giovanni Battista Pergolesi and Johann Adolph Hasse, among others. (②) As far as recycling of segments of music initially written for other occasions into new pieces is concerned, it needs to be observed how today composers are discouraged from doing so for a number of reasons. (③) A practical one is that each new piece is sure to remain available, in score or as an audio file. (④) In the 18th century, on the contrary, once the particular occasion for performing a new piece was over, it became almost impossible to ever hear it again. (⑤) And if new pieces also contained ideas from other composers, that would re-enforce European musical traditions by increasing the circulation of melodies and harmonic patterns people loved to hear.

* *de facto*: 사실상 ** pastiche: 혼성곡(混成曲)
*** segment: 부분

11 1등급 대비 고난도 3점 문제

글의 흐름으로 보아, 주어진 문장이 들어가기에 가장 적절한 곳을 고르시오. [3점]

> This is particularly true since one aspect of sleep is decreased responsiveness to the environment.

The role that sleep plays in evolution is still under study. (①) One possibility is that it is an advantageous adaptive state of decreased metabolism for an animal when there are no more pressing activities. (②) This seems true for deeper states of inactivity such as hibernation during the winter when there are few food supplies, and a high metabolic cost to maintaining adequate temperature. (③) It may be true in daily situations as well, for instance for a prey species to avoid predators after dark. (④) On the other hand, the apparent universality of sleep, and the observation that mammals such as cetaceans have developed such highly complex mechanisms to preserve sleep on at least one side of the brain at a time, suggests that sleep additionally provides some vital service(s) for the organism. (⑤) If sleep is universal even when this potential price must be paid, the implication may be that it has important functions that cannot be obtained just by quiet, wakeful resting.

＊metabolism: 신진대사 ＊＊mammal: 포유동물

12 1등급 대비 고난도 3점 문제

글의 흐름으로 보아, 주어진 문장이 들어가기에 가장 적절한 곳을 고르시오. [3점]

> A round hill rising above a plain, therefore, would appear on the map as a set of concentric circles, the largest at the base and the smallest near the top.

A major challenge for map-makers is the depiction of hills and valleys, slopes and flatlands collectively called the *topography*. This can be done in various ways. One is to create an image of sunlight and shadow so that wrinkles of the topography are alternately lit and shaded, creating a visual representation of the shape of the land. (①) Another, technically more accurate way is to draw contour lines. (②) A contour line connects all points that lie at the same elevation. (③) When the contour lines are positioned closely together, the hill's slope is steep; if they lie farther apart, the slope is gentler. (④) Contour lines can represent scarps, hollows, and valleys of the local topography. (⑤) At a glance, they reveal whether the relief in the mapped area is great or small: a "busy" contour map means lots of high relief.

＊concentric: 중심이 같은 ＊＊scarp: 가파른 비탈
＊＊＊relief: (토지의) 고저, 기복

DAY 20

MEMO

PART I · 빈칸 추론 [Day 01~Day 10]

Day 01   빈칸 추론 01

01 ② 02 ① 03 ② 04 ① 05 ② 06 ① 07 ③ 08 ③ 09 ② 10 ⑤
11 ④ 12 ⑤

Day 02   빈칸 추론 02

01 ④ 02 ① 03 ② 04 ④ 05 ① 06 ⑤ 07 ⑤ 08 ② 09 ① 10 ①
11 ④ 12 ①

Day 03   빈칸 추론 03

01 ② 02 ① 03 ① 04 ② 05 ① 06 ② 07 ⑤ 08 ④ 09 ⑤ 10 ⑤
11 ① 12 ②

Day 04   빈칸 추론 04

01 ① 02 ③ 03 ② 04 ① 05 ① 06 ① 07 ② 08 ⑤ 09 ② 10 ①
11 ④ 12 ①

Day 05   빈칸 추론 05

01 ③ 02 ④ 03 ① 04 ② 05 ① 06 ① 07 ② 08 ④ 09 ① 10 ②
11 ② 12 ②

Day 06   빈칸 추론 06

01 ④ 02 ① 03 ① 04 ③ 05 ② 06 ① 07 ① 08 ⑤ 09 ② 10 ④
11 ① 12 ②

Day 07   빈칸 추론 07

01 ① 02 ④ 03 ② 04 ⑤ 05 ① 06 ② 07 ⑤ 08 ② 09 ③ 10 ①
11 ④ 12 ④

Day 08   빈칸 추론 08

01 ② 02 ① 03 ② 04 ① 05 ② 06 ⑤ 07 ⑤ 08 ③ 09 ① 10 ①
11 ② 12 ①

Day 09   빈칸 추론 09

01 ③ 02 ② 03 ① 04 ② 05 ② 06 ③ 07 ① 08 ② 09 ① 10 ⑤
11 ② 12 ①

Day 10   빈칸 추론 10

01 ① 02 ② 03 ② 04 ⑤ 05 ③ 06 ① 07 ③ 08 ② 09 ① 10 ④
11 ② 12 ②

PART II · 글의 순서 [Day 11~Day 15]

Day 11   글의 순서 01

01 ② 02 ④ 03 ⑤ 04 ② 05 ③ 06 ③ 07 ② 08 ② 09 ⑤ 10 ④
11 ⑤ 12 ⑤

Day 12   글의 순서 02

01 ④ 02 ② 03 ② 04 ④ 05 ③ 06 ⑤ 07 ② 08 ② 09 ① 10 ⑤
11 ⑤ 12 ⑤

Day 13   글의 순서 03

01 ④ 02 ② 03 ③ 04 ② 05 ③ 06 ② 07 ② 08 ② 09 ⑤ 10 ④
11 ② 12 ⑤

Day 14   글의 순서 04

01 ⑤ 02 ② 03 ⑤ 04 ② 05 ③ 06 ② 07 ④ 08 ⑤ 09 ② 10 ⑤
11 ④ 12 ④

Day 15   글의 순서 05

01 ② 02 ⑤ 03 ⑤ 04 ⑤ 05 ④ 06 ② 07 ③ 08 ② 09 ③ 10 ③
11 ⑤ 12 ④

PART III · 문장 삽입 [Day 16~Day 20]

Day 16   문장 삽입 01

01 ④ 02 ⑤ 03 ④ 04 ④ 05 ③ 06 ④ 07 ⑤ 08 ⑤ 09 ① 10 ②
11 ④ 12 ⑤

Day 17   문장 삽입 02

01 ⑤ 02 ② 03 ④ 04 ③ 05 ④ 06 ④ 07 ④ 08 ③ 09 ⑤ 10 ⑤
11 ③ 12 ②

Day 18   문장 삽입 03

01 ④ 02 ③ 03 ④ 04 ④ 05 ③ 06 ④ 07 ④ 08 ② 09 ⑤ 10 ⑤
11 ④ 12 ③

Day 19   문장 삽입 04

01 ④ 02 ③ 03 ⑤ 04 ④ 05 ③ 06 ③ 07 ③ 08 ⑤ 09 ② 10 ③
11 ⑤ 12 ⑤

Day 20   문장 삽입 05

01 ④ 02 ⑤ 03 ④ 04 ④ 05 ④ 06 ③ 07 ④ 08 ④ 09 ④ 10 ⑤
11 ⑤ 12 ③

SPEED 정답 체크   영어 독해 | 빈칸 순서 삽입 [실전]

PART I · 빈칸 추론 [Day 01~Day 10]

PART II · 글의 순서 [Day 11~Day 15]

PART III · 문장 삽입 [Day 16~Day 20]

20일 완성 영어독해
빈칸 순서 삽입 실전
해설편

Contents

REAL ORIGINAL

수록된 정답률은 실제와 차이가 있을
수 있습니다. 문제 난도를 파악하는데
참고용으로 활용하시기 바랍니다.

DAY 01 — 빈칸 추론 01

01 ②	02 ①	03 ②	04 ①	05 ②
06 ①	07 ③	08 ③	09 ②	10 ⑤
11 ④	12 ⑤			

---

01 정치적 리스크의 불확실성 — 정답률 53% | 정답 ②

다음 빈칸에 들어갈 말로 가장 적절한 것을 고르시오. [3점]

① injustice - 불평등   ✓ uncertainty - 불확실성
③ circularity - 순환 논리   ④ contradiction - 모순
⑤ miscommunication - 의사소통 오류

Much of what we call political risk / is in fact uncertainty.
우리가 정치적 리스크라고 부르는 것의 많은 부분은 / 사실 불확실성이다.

This applies to all types of political risks, / from civil strife to expropriations to regulatory changes.
이것은 모든 유형의 정치적 리스크에 적용된다. / 내란에서부터 몰수, 규제상의 변화에 이르기까지

Political risk, / unlike credit or market or operational risk, / can be unsystematic / and therefore more difficult / to address in classic statistical terms.
정치적 리스크는 / 신용, 시장 또는 운영 리스크와는 달리 / 비체계적이고, / 그래서 더 어려울 수 있다. / 전형적인 통계적 관점에서 처리하기가

What is the probability / that terrorists will attack the United States again?
확률은 얼마나 되는가? / 테러리스트들이 미국을 다시 공격할

Unlike earthquakes or hurricanes, / political actors constantly adapt / to overcome the barriers / created by risk managers.
지진이나 허리케인과는 달리, / 정치 행위자들은 끊임없이 적응한다. / 장벽을 넘어서기 위해 / 리스크 관리자들이 만든

When corporations structure foreign investments / to mitigate risks of expropriations, / through international guarantees or legal contracts, / host governments seek out new forms of obstruction, / such as creeping expropriation or regulatory discrimination, / that are very hard and legally costly to prove.
기업이 해외 투자를 체계화할 때, / 몰수의 리스크를 줄이기 위해 / 국제적 보증이나 법적 계약을 통해 / 소재국 정부는 새로운 형태의 방해를 모색한다. / 은밀히 진행되는 몰수나 규제상의 차별과 같은, / 증명하기 매우 힘들고 법적으로 비용이 많이 드는

Observation of a risk / changes the risk itself.
리스크에 대한 관찰은 / 리스크 자체를 바꾼다.

There are ways / to mitigate high-impact, low-probability events.
방법들이 있다. / 충격이 크지만 확률은 낮은 사건들을 줄이는

But / analysis of these risks / can be as much art as science.
그러나 / 이러한 리스크에 대한 분석은 / 과학인 만큼이나 예술일 수 있다.

우리가 정치적 리스크라고 부르는 것의 많은 부분은 사실 불확실성이다. 이것은 내란에서부터 몰수, 규제상의 변화에 이르기까지 모든 유형의 정치적 리스크에 적용된다. 신용, 시장 또는 운영 리스크와는 달리 정치적 리스크는 비체계적이고, 그래서 전형적인 통계적 관점에서 처리하기가 더 어려울 수 있다. 테러리스트들이 미국을 다시 공격할 확률은 얼마나 되는가? 지진이나 허리케인과는 달리, 정치 행위자들은 리스크 관리자들이 만든 장벽을 넘어서기 위해 끊임없이 적응한다. 기업들이 몰수의 리스크를 줄이기 위해 국제적 보증이나 법적 계약을 통해 해외 투자를 체계화할 때, (사업) 소재국 정부는 은밀히 진행되는 몰수나 규제상의 차별과 같은, 증명하기 매우 힘들고 법적으로 비용이 많이 드는 새로운 형태의 방해를 모색한다. 리스크를 관찰하면 리스크 자체가 변한다. 충격이 크지만 확률은 낮은 사건들을 줄이는 방법들이 있다. 그러나 이러한 리스크에 대한 분석은 과학인 만큼이나 예술일 수 있다.

Why? 왜 정답일까?

정치적 리스크는 전형적인 통계 처리가 어려울 만큼 비체계적이며(Political risk ~ can be unsystematic and therefore more difficult to address in classic statistical terms.) 끊임없이 변한다는 내용으로 보아, 빈칸에 들어갈 말로 가장 적절한 것은 ② '불확실성'이다.

- apply ⓥ 적용되다
- expropriation ⓝ 몰수
- unsystematic ⓐ 비체계적인
- statistical ⓐ 통계적인
- earthquake ⓝ 지진
- adapt to ~에 적응하다
- civil strife 내란
- operational ⓐ 운영상의
- address ⓥ 처리하다
- probability ⓝ 확률, 가능성
- constantly ⓐⓓ 지속적으로
- barrier ⓝ 장벽

- mitigate ⓥ 줄이다
- legal contract 법적 계약
- obstruction ⓝ 방해
- regulatory ⓐ 규제의
- observation ⓝ 관찰
- uncertainty ⓝ 불확실성
- contradiction ⓝ 모순
- guarantee ⓝ 보증 ⓥ 보장하다
- seek out ~을 모색하다
- creeping ⓐ 서서히 진행되는
- discrimination ⓝ 차별
- injustice ⓝ 불평등, 부당함
- circularity ⓝ 순환 논리

구문 풀이

1행 Much of what we call political risk is in fact uncertainty.
주어(부분 + of + 전체)   동사(단수)

---

02 기존의 정신적 모델을 기반으로 확장되는 학습 — 정답률 69% | 정답 ①

다음 빈칸에 들어갈 말로 가장 적절한 것을 고르시오.

✓ replace - 교체하지   ② imagine - 상상하지
③ predict - 예측하지   ④ analyze - 분석하지
⑤ imitate - 모방하지

Learning is *constructive*, not *destructive*.
학습은 *파괴적*이지 않고 *건설적*이다.

This means we don't replace mental models / — we simply expand upon them.
이것은 우리가 정신적 모델을 교체하지 않는다는 뜻이다. / 우리는 단지 그것을 기반으로 확장한다.

To understand what I mean, / think back to your childhood.
내 말 뜻을 이해하려면, / 여러분의 어린 시절을 회상해보라.

There was likely a time / when you believed in Santa Claus; / your mental model accepted him / and your predictions accounted for his existence.
때가 있었을 것이다. / 여러분이 산타클로스를 믿었던 / 여러분의 정신적 모델은 그를 받아들였고 / 여러분의 예측은 그의 존재를 설명했다.

At some point, however, / you came to recognize he was fictitious / and you updated your mental model accordingly.
하지만 어느 순간, / 여러분은 그가 가상이라는 것을 인식하게 되었고 / 그에 따라 여러분의 정신적 모델을 갱신했다.

At that moment, / you didn't suddenly forget everything about Santa Claus.
그 순간, / 여러분이 산타클로스에 관한 전부를 잊어버린 것은 아니다.

To this day, / you can still recognize him, / speak of him / and embrace young children's belief in him.
오늘날까지도, / 여러분은 여전히 그를 인식하고, / 그에 대해 말하고, / 그에 대한 어린아이들의 믿음을 받아들일 수 있다.

In other words, / you didn't destroy your old mental model, / you simply added new information to it.
다시 말해, / 여러분은 이전의 정신적 모델을 파괴한 것이 아니라, / 거기에 단지 새로운 정보를 추가했을 뿐이다.

By building upon old mental models / we are able to maintain ties to the past, / foster a deeper understanding of concepts / and develop an ever-expanding pool of information / to draw upon in order to continually adapt to an ever-evolving world.
이전의 정신적 모델을 기반으로 하여 / 우리는 과거와의 연결을 유지할 수 있고, / 개념에 대한 더 깊은 이해를 촉진할 수 있으며, / 계속 확장되는 정보 저장소를 개발할 수 있다. / 끊임없이 진화하는 세계에 계속해서 적응하기 위해 활용할

학습은 *파괴적*이지 않고 *건설적*이다. 이것은 우리가 정신적 모델을 교체하지 않는다는 뜻이다. 우리는 단지 그것을 기반으로 확장한다. 내 말 뜻을 이해하려면, 여러분의 어린 시절을 회상해보라. 여러분이 산타클로스를 믿었던 때가 있었을 것이다. 여러분의 정신적 모델은 그를 받아들였고 여러분의 예측은 그의 존재를 설명했다. 하지만 어느 순간, 여러분은 그가 가상이라는 것을 인식하게 되었고 그에 따라 여러분의 정신적 모델을 갱신했다. 그 순간 여러분이 산타클로스에 관한 전부를 잊어버린 것은 아니다. 오늘날까지도, 여러분은 여전히 그를 인식하고, 그에 대해 말하고, 그에 대한 어린아이들의 믿음을 받아들일 수 있다. 다시 말해, 여러분은 이전의 정신적 모델을 파괴한 것이 아니라, 거기에 단지 새로운 정보를 추가했을 뿐이다. 이전의 정신적 모델을 기반으로 하여 우리는 과거와의 연결을 유지할 수 있고, 개념에 대한 더 깊은 이해를 촉진할 수 있으며, 끊임없이 진화하는 세계에 계속해서 적응하기 위해 활용할 계속 확장되는 정보 저장소를 개발할 수 있다.

Why? 왜 정답일까?

우리는 이미 형성된 정신적 모델을 '파괴하지(destroy)' 않고 단지 그것을 기반으로 확장해 나가면서 세계에 적응해 나간다는 내용이다. 따라서 빈칸에 들어갈 말로 가장 적절한 것은 '파괴한다'는 내용을 가장 가깝게 재진술한 ① '교체하지'이다.

- constructive ⓐ 건설적인
- account for ~을 설명하다
- fictitious ⓐ 가상의
- destructive ⓐ 파괴적인
- existence ⓝ 존재
- embrace ⓥ 수용하다

- **foster** ⓥ 촉진하다
- **continually** [ad] 지속적으로
- **analyze** ⓥ 분석하다
- **draw upon** ~을 이용하다
- **replace** ⓥ 교체하다

구문 풀이

15행 By building upon old mental models we are able to maintain
~함으로써 　　　　　　　　　　　　　　동사원형1
ties to the past, foster a deeper understanding of concepts and
동사원형2
develop an ever-expanding pool of information to draw upon
동사원형3 　　　　　　　　　　　　　　　↳형용사적 용법
in order to continually adapt to an ever-evolving world.
~하기 위해서

---

03 주의를 딴 데로 돌려 고통스러운 상황을 벗어나기 　　정답률 54% | 정답 ②

다음 빈칸에 들어갈 말로 가장 적절한 것을 고르시오.

① ignore uncomfortable comments from their close peers
　가까운 동료의 불편한 지적을 무시하는
✔ escape painful self-awareness through distraction
　주의를 딴 데로 돌려 고통스러운 자각에서 벗어나는
③ receive constructive feedback from the media
　미디어에서 건설적인 피드백을 받는
④ refocus their divided attention to a given task
　분산된 집중력을 주어진 과업에 다시 집중시키는
⑤ engage themselves in intense self-reflection
　강렬한 자기반성에 참여하는

Even as mundane a behavior as watching TV / may be a way for some people / to escape painful self-awareness through distraction.
TV를 보는 것처럼 평범한 행동일지라도 / 어떤 사람들에게는 방법이 될 수 있다. / 주의를 딴 데로 돌려 고통스러운 자각에서 벗어나는

To test this idea, / Sophia Moskalenko and Steven Heine / gave participants false feedback about their test performance, / and then seated each one in front of a TV set / to watch a video / as the next part of the study.
이 생각을 검증하기 위해, / Sophia Moskalenko와 Steven Heine은 / 참가자들에게 시험 성적에 관한 거짓 피드백을 주었고, / 그런 다음 각각을 TV 앞에 앉혀 / 비디오를 시청하게 했다. / 연구의 다음 부분으로

When the video came on, / showing nature scenes with a musical soundtrack, / the experimenter exclaimed / that this was the wrong video / and went supposedly to get the correct one, / leaving the participant alone as the video played.
비디오가 나오자, / 음악 사운드트랙과 함께 자연의 장면을 보여 주는 / 실험자는 소리쳤고, / 이것이 잘못된 비디오라고 / 아마도 제대로 된 것을 가지러 가면서, / 참가자를 비디오가 재생될 때 홀로 남겨두었다.

The participants who had received failure feedback / watched the video much longer / than those who thought they had succeeded.
실패라는 피드백을 받았던 참가자들은 / 훨씬 더 오래 비디오를 시청했다. / 자신이 성공했다고 생각하는 참가자들보다

The researchers concluded / that distraction through television viewing / can effectively relieve the discomfort / associated with painful failures / or mismatches between the self and self-guides.
연구자들은 결론지었다. / 텔레비전 시청을 통해 주의를 딴 데로 돌리는 것이 / 불편함을 효과적으로 완화할 수 있다고 / 고통스러운 실패와 연관된 / 또는 자아와 자아에 관한 지침 사이의 불일치와

In contrast, / successful participants had little wish / to be distracted from their self-related thoughts!
이와 대조적으로, / 성공한 참가자들은 거의 바라지 않았다! / 자기 자신과 관련된 생각에서 주의가 딴 데로 돌려지기를

TV를 보는 것처럼 평범한 행동일지라도 어떤 사람들이 주의를 딴 데로 돌려 고통스러운 자각에서 벗어나는 방법이 될 수 있다. 이 생각을 검증하기 위해, Sophia Moskalenko와 Steven Heine은 참가자들에게 시험 성적에 관한 거짓 피드백을 주었고, 그런 다음 연구의 다음 부분으로 각각 TV 앞에 앉아 비디오를 시청하게 했다. 음악 사운드트랙과 함께 자연의 장면을 보여 주는 비디오가 나오자, 실험자는 이것이 잘못된 비디오라고 소리쳤고, 아마도 제대로 된 것을 가지러 가면서, 참가자를 비디오가 재생될 때 홀로 남겨두었다. (시험 성적에 관하여) 실패라는 피드백을 받았던 참가자들은 자신이 성공했다고 생각하는 참가자들보다 훨씬 더 오래 비디오를 시청했다. 연구자들은 텔레비전 시청을 통해 주의를 딴 데로 돌리는 것이 고통스러운 실패나 자아와 자아에 관한 지침 사이의 불일치와 연관된 불편함을 효과적으로 완화할 수 있다고 결론지었다. 이와 대조적으로, 성공한 참가자들은 자기 자신과 관련된 생각에서 주의가 딴 데로 돌려지기를 거의 바라지 않았다!

Why? 왜 정답일까?

연구를 소개한 글이므로 결과에 주목한다. 'The researchers concluded ~' 문장에서 시험 성적에 대해 좋지 못한 피드백을 받았던 참가자들은 TV 시청을 통해 주의를 환기하여 실패의 고통이나 불편함을 완화하려 했다는 결과가 제시된다. 이를 근거로 볼

때, 빈칸에 들어갈 말로 가장 적절한 것은 ② '주의를 딴 데로 돌려 고통스러운 자각에서 벗어나는'이다.

- **exclaim** ⓥ 외치다, 소리치다
- **distraction** ⓝ 주의를 딴 데로 돌리는 것
- **discomfort** ⓝ 불편함
- **ignore** ⓥ 무시하다
- **constructive** ⓐ 건설적인
- **intense** ⓐ 강렬한
- **supposedly** [ad] 추정상, 아마
- **effectively** [ad] 효과적으로
- **mismatch** ⓝ 부조화, 불일치
- **self-awareness** ⓝ 자각
- **engage A in B** A를 B에 관여시키다

구문 풀이

1행 Even as mundane a behavior as watching TV may be
　　　　　주어(as+형+as+a/an+명: 그렇게나 ~한 …이) 　동사
a way (for some people to escape painful self-awareness through
보어 　　의미상 주어 　　　형용사적 용법
distraction).

---

04 소설 줄거리의 특징 　　정답률 34% | 정답 ①

다음 빈칸에 들어갈 말로 가장 적절한 것을 고르시오. [3점]

✔ to establish the individual character
　개인적 특성을 확립하기 위해
② to cast doubt on the identity of a criminal
　범죄자의 신원을 의심하기 위해
③ to highlight the complex structure of social consciousness
　사회적 의식의 복잡한 구조를 강조하기 위해
④ to make the objective distinction between crime and heroism
　범죄와 영웅주의 간의 객관적인 구별을 하기 위해
⑤ to develop the inner self of a hero into a collective wisdom
　영웅의 내면적 자아를 집단적인 지혜로 발전시키기 위해

Theorists of the novel commonly define the genre as a biographical form / that came to prominence in the late eighteenth and nineteenth centuries / to establish the individual character / as a replacement for traditional sources of cultural authority.
소설의 이론가들은 공통으로 그 장르를 전기 형식으로 규정한다. / 18세기 말과 19세기에 두드러졌던 / 개인적 특성을 확립하기 위해 / 문화적 권위의 전통적 원천에 대한 대체물로서

The novel, / Georg Lukács argues, / "seeks, by giving form, / to uncover and construct the concealed totality of life" / in the interiorized life story of its heroes.
소설은 / Georg Lukács는 주장한다. / "형식을 제공함으로써 / 삶의 숨겨진 전체를 드러내어 구성하고자 한다." / 라고 / 주인공들의 내면화된 인생 이야기에서

The typical plot of the novel / is the protagonist's quest for authority within, / therefore, / when that authority can no longer be discovered outside.
소설의 전형적인 줄거리는 / 주인공이 내부에서 하는 권위 탐구이다. / 따라서 / 그 권위를 더는 외부에서 찾을 수 없을 때 일어나는

By this accounting, / there are no objective goals in novels, / only the subjective goal of seeking the law / that is necessarily created by the individual.
이 설명에 의하면 / 소설에 객관적 목표는 없으며, / 법칙을 찾는 주관적 목표만 있을 뿐이다. / 반드시 개인에 의해 만들어지는

The distinctions between crime and heroism, / therefore, / or between madness and wisdom, / become purely subjective ones in a novel, / judged by the quality or complexity / of the individual's consciousness.
범죄와 영웅주의, / 따라서 / 혹은 광기와 지혜의 차이는 / 소설에서는 전적으로 주관적인 것이 되고, / 특성이나 복잡성에 의해 판단된다. / 개인적 의식의

소설의 이론가들은 공통으로 그 장르를, 문화적 권위의 전통적 원천에 대한 대체물로서 개인적 특성을 확립하기 위해 18세기 말과 19세기에 두드러졌던 전기 형식으로 규정한다. 소설은 "형식을 제공함으로써" 주인공들의 내면화된 인생 이야기에서 "삶의 숨겨진 전체를 드러내어 구성하고자 한다."라고 Georg Lukács는 주장한다. 따라서 소설의 전형적인 줄거리는 그 권위를 더는 외부에서 찾을 수 없을 때 일어나는, 주인공이 내부에서 하는 권위 탐구이다. 이 설명에 의하면 소설에 객관적 목표는 없으며, 반드시 개인에 의해 만들어지는 법칙을 찾는 주관적 목표만 있을 뿐이다. 따라서 범죄와 영웅주의, 혹은 광기와 지혜의 차이는 소설에서는 전적으로 주관적인 것이 되고, 개인적 의식의 특성이나 복잡성에 의해 판단된다.

Why? 왜 정답일까?

소설에서는 객관적인 목표가 있다기보다 주인공 개인이 만든 법칙을 찾는 주관적 목표가 있을 뿐이며(~ there are no objective goals in novels, only the subjective goal of seeking the law that is necessarily created by the individual.), 개인의 특성이나 복잡성에 의해 많은 요소가 판단된다(~ judged by the quality or complexity of the individual's consciousness.)는 내용을 설명한 글이다. 따라서 빈칸에 들어갈 말로 가장 적절한 것은 ① '개인적 특성을 확립하기 위해'이다.

- **prominence** ⓝ 두드러짐, 탁월, 현저함
- **interiorize** ⓥ (감정 등을) 내면화하다
- **cast doubt on** ~을 의심하다
- **replacement** ⓝ 대체물, 대체
- **protagonist** ⓝ (연극·영화·책 속의) 주인공
- **highlight** ⓥ 강조하다

구문 풀이

10행 By this accounting, there are no objective goals in novels,
주어 「not A + (but) only B : A가 아니라 B뿐이다」
only the subjective goal of seeking the law [that is necessarily
동명사   ↖ 주격 관계대명사
created by the individual].

---

05 건물의 기능과 의미 | 정답률 48% | 정답 ②

다음 빈칸에 들어갈 말로 가장 적절한 것을 고르시오. [3점]

① to identify and relate to a new architectural trend
확인하고 새로운 건축의 추세를 관련지을 수 있는
☑ to recognize and associate with those buildings' function
그런 건물의 기능과 결부시키고 인식한
③ to define and refine by reflecting cross-cultural interactions
문화 간 상호작용을 반영하면서 정의하고 개선할 수 있는
④ to use and change into an integral part of our environment
우리 환경의 필수적인 부분으로 사용하고 변화시킬 수 있는
⑤ to alter and develop for the elimination of their meanings
그것의 의미를 없애기 위해 변경하고 발전할 수 있는

Over a period of time / the buildings which housed social, legal, religious,
and other rituals / evolved into forms / that we subsequently have come to
recognize and associate with those buildings' function.
일정 시간을 넘어 오면서 / 사회적, 법적, 종교적인, 그리고 다른 의식에 필요한 장소를 제공한 건물은 / 형태로 발전했다. / 우리가 나중에 그런 건물의 기능과 결부시키고 인식한

This is a two-way process; / the building provides the physical environment
and setting / for a particular social ritual / such as traveling by train or going
to the theater, / as well as the symbolic setting.
이는 쌍방향의 절차이다. / 건물은 물리적인 환경과 장소를 제공한다. / 특정한 사회적 의식을 위한 / 기차로 여행을 하거나 극장에 가는 것과 같은 / 상징적인 장소뿐만 아니라

The meaning of buildings evolves and becomes established by experience /
and we in turn read our experience into buildings.
건물의 의미는 경험으로 인해서 발전하고 수립되며 / 우리는 차례로 우리의 경험을 건물에 입힌다.

Buildings arouse an empathetic reaction in us / through these projected
experiences, / and the strength of these reactions is determined / by our
culture, our beliefs, and our expectations.
건물은 우리 안에 공감할 수 있는 반응을 불러일으키고 / 이런 투영된 경험을 통해 / 이 반응의 세기는 결정된다. / 우리의 문화, 신념, 기대로

They tell stories, / for their form and spatial organization give us hints /
about how they should be used.
그것은 이야기를 들려준다. / 형태와 공간 구성이 힌트를 우리에게 주기 때문에 / 그것들이 어떻게 사용되어야 하는지에 관한

Their physical layout encourages some uses and inhibits others; / we do not
go backstage in a theater / unless especially invited.
그것의 물리적인 설계는 일정한 사용을 권장하고 다른 사용을 억제한다. / 우리는 극장의 무대 뒤로 가지 않는다. / 특별하게 초대받지 않는다면

Inside a law court / the precise location of those involved in the legal process
/ is an integral part of the design / and an essential part of ensuring that the
law is upheld.
법정 안에서 / 법적인 절차와 관련된 사람들의 정확한 위치는 / 설계를 하는 데 필수적인 부분이고 / 법 준수를 확실히 할 수 있는 필수적인 부분이다.

일정 시간을 넘어 오면서 사회적, 법적, 종교적인, 그리고 다른 의식에 필요한 장소를 제공한 건물은 우리가 나중에 그런 건물의 기능과 결부시키고 인식한 형태로 발전했다. 이는 쌍방향의 절차이다. 건물은 상징적인 장소뿐만 아니라 기차로 여행을 하거나 극장에 가는 것과 같은 특정한 사회적 의식을 위한 물리적인 환경과 장소를 제공한다. 건물의 의미는 경험으로 인해서 발전하고 수립되며 우리는 차례로 우리의 경험을 건물에 입힌다. 건물은 이런 투영된 경험을 통해 우리 안에 공감할 수 있는 반응을 불러일으키고 이 반응의 세기는 우리의 문화, 신념, 기대로 결정된다. 그것은 형태와 공간 구성이 어떻게 사용되어야 하는지에 관한 힌트를 우리에게 주기 때문에 이야기를 들려준다. 그것의 물리적인 설계는 일정한 사용을 권장하고 다른 사용을 억제한다. 우리는 특별하게 초대받지 않는다면 극장의 무대 뒤로 가지 않는다. 법정 안에서 법적인 절차와 관련된 사람들의 정확한 위치는 설계를 하는 데 필수적인 부분이고 법 준수를 확실히 할 수 있는 필수적인 부분이다.

Why? 왜 정답일까?

'~ the building provides the physical environment and setting for a
particular social ritual ~'에서 건물은 특정한 사회적 행위가 수행될 배경을 제공한다고 말하는데, 이어지는 'The meaning of buildings ~ becomes established

---

by experience and we in turn read our experience into buildings.'에서는 그 행위의 경험이 쌓일수록 건물이 그 경험의 의미를 덧입게 된다고 말한다. 이는 건물의 기능적인 의미가 시간이 지날수록 강화되면서 건물이 그 기능과 '일체화된' 것처럼 여겨진다는 뜻을 비유적으로 나타낸다. 따라서 빈칸에 들어갈 말로 가장 적절한 것은 ② '그런 건물의 기능과 결부시키고 인식한'이다.

- **house** ⓥ ~에 장소를 제공하다
- **evolve into** ~로 진화하다(발달하다)
- **symbolic** ⓐ 상징적인, 상징하는
- **arouse** ⓥ 불러일으키다
- **inhibit** ⓥ 억제하다
- **religious** ⓐ 종교적인
- **subsequently** ⓐⓓ 따라서
- **establish** ⓥ 설립(수립)하다
- **spatial** ⓐ 공간의

구문 풀이

4행 This is a two-way process; the building provides [the physical
주어1 동사1   주어2   동사2
environment and setting / for a particular social ritual / such as
traveling by train or going to the theater], as well as [the symbolic
[B] + as well as + [A] : A뿐만 아니라 B도
setting].

---

06 기본 요소의 변화 없이 이루어지는 규모의 진화 | 정답률 47% | 정답 ①

다음 빈칸에 들어갈 말로 가장 적절한 것을 고르시오. [3점]

☑ maintaining basic elements unchanged or conserved
기본적인 요소가 변하지 않거나 보존되도록 유지하면서
② optimizing energy use for the structural growth
구조적 성장을 위해 에너지 사용을 최적화하면서
③ assigning new functions to existing components
기존 구성 요소에 새 기능을 부여하면서
④ incorporating foreign items from surroundings
주변에서 얻은 이질적인 물품을 포함시키면서
⑤ accelerating the elimination of useless parts
쓸모없는 부품의 제거를 가속화하면서

Scaling up from the small to the large / is often accompanied / by an
evolution from simplicity to complexity / while maintaining basic elements
unchanged or conserved.
작은 것에서 큰 것으로 규모가 커지는 것에는 / 흔히 수반된다. / 단순함에서 복잡함으로의 진화가 / 기본적인 요소가 변하지 않거나 보존되도록 유지하면서

This is familiar in engineering, economics, companies, cities, organisms, /
and, perhaps most dramatically, evolutionary process.
이것은 공학, 경제학, 회사, 도시, 유기체에 흔하다. / 그리고 어쩌면 가장 극적으로는 진화 과정에서

For example, a skyscraper in a large city / is a significantly more complex
object / than a modest family dwelling in a small town, / but the underlying
principles of construction and design, / including questions of mechanics,
energy and information distribution, the size of electrical outlets, water
faucets, telephones, laptops, doors, etc., / all remain approximately the same
/ independent of the size of the building.
예를 들어, 대도시의 고층 건물은 / 상당히 더 복잡한 물체이지만, / 소도시의 보통 가정집보다 / 건축과 디자인의 기본 원리는 / 역학의 문제, 에너지와 정보의 분배, 전기 콘센트, 수도꼭지, 전화기, 노트북 컴퓨터, 문 등의 크기를 포함한 / 모두 거의 똑같이 유지된다. / 건물의 규모와 상관없이

Similarly, organisms have evolved / to have an enormous range of sizes / and
an extraordinary diversity of morphologies and interactions, / which often
reflect increasing complexity, / yet fundamental building blocks / like cells,
mitochondria, capillaries, and even leaves / do not appreciably change / with
body size or increasing complexity of the class of systems / in which they
are embedded.
마찬가지로, 유기체는 진화했는데, / 대단히 다양한 크기와 / 놀랄 만큼 다양한 형태와 상호 작용을 가지도록 / 그것은 흔히 증가하는 복잡성을 반영하지만, / 근본적인 구성 요소는 / 세포, 미토콘드리아, 모세관, 그리고 심지어 나뭇잎과 같은 / 눈에 띄게 변하지는 않는다. / 몸체의 크기, 혹은 체계 부류의 복잡함이 증가함에 따라 / 그것들이 속한

작은 것에서 큰 것으로 규모가 커지는 것은 기본적인 요소가 변하지 않거나 보존되도록 유지하면서 흔히 단순함에서 복잡함으로의 진화를 수반한다. 이것은 공학, 경제학, 회사, 도시, 유기체, 그리고 어쩌면 가장 극적으로는 진화 과정에서 흔하다. 예를 들어, 대도시의 고층 건물은 소도시의 보통 가정집보다 상당히 더 복잡한 물체이지만, 역학의 문제, 에너지와 정보의 분배, 전기 콘센트, 수도꼭지, 전화기, 노트북 컴퓨터, 문 등의 크기를 포함한 건축과 디자인의 기본 원리는 모두 건물의 규모와 상관없이 거의 똑같이 유지된다. 마찬가지로, 유기체는 대단히 다양한 크기와 놀랄 만큼 다양한 형태와 상호 작용을 가지도록 진화했는데, 그것은 흔히 증가하는 복잡성을 반영하지만, 세포, 미토콘드리아, 모세관, 그리고 심지어 나뭇잎과 같은 근본적인 구성 요소는 몸체의 크기, 혹은 그것들이 속한 체계 부류의 복잡함이 증가함에 따라 눈에 띄게 변하지는 않는다.

Why? 왜 정답일까?

For example 이후로 작은 규모에서 큰 규모로 진화한 건축 및 디자인과 유기체의 예를 들어, 이들이 아무리 복잡해졌다 해도 기본적인 원리나 구성 요소는 작은 것과 거의 똑같이 유지되거나 눈에 띄게 변화하지 않았다고 설명하고 있다. 따라서 빈칸에 들어갈 말로 가장 적절한 것은 ① '기본적인 요소가 변하지 않거나 보존되도록 유지하면서'이다.

- scale up ⓥ (규모를) 키우다, 확대하다
- skyscraper ⓝ 고층 건물
- modest ⓐ 보통의, 대단하지 않은
- underlying ⓐ 근본적인
- distribution ⓝ 분배
- independent of ~와 상관없이
- fundamental ⓐ 근본적인
- appreciably ⓐ𝖽 눈에 띄게
- optimize ⓥ 최적화하다
- incorporate ⓥ 포함시키다
- accompany ⓥ 수반하다, 동반하다
- significantly ⓐ𝖽 상당히
- dwelling ⓝ 주택
- mechanics ⓝ 역학
- approximately ⓐ𝖽 거의, 대략
- extraordinary ⓐ 놀라운, 대단한
- building block ⓝ 구성 요소
- embedded in ~에 박힌
- assign ⓥ 부여하다, 할당하다
- accelerate ⓥ 가속화하다

구문 풀이

13행 Similarly, organisms have evolved to have an enormous
주어1　동사1(현재완료)　부사적 용법(~하도록)
range of sizes and an extraordinary diversity of morphologies and
interactions, which often reflect increasing complexity, yet
계속적 용법
fundamental building blocks (like cells, mitochondria, capillaries,
주어2　　　( ) : 전명구
and even leaves) do not appreciably change with body size or
동사2(자동사)
increasing complexity of the class of systems [in which they are
선행사　　「전치사＋관·대」
embedded].

★★★ 1등급 대비 고난도 2점 문제

| 07 | 고고학적 기록의 불완전성 | 정답률 37% | 정답 ③ |

다음 빈칸에 들어갈 말로 가장 적절한 것을 고르시오.

① outdated – 구식이다
② factual – 사실에 기반을 둔다
✓ incomplete – 불완전하다
④ organized – 체계적이다
⑤ detailed – 상세하다

When examining the archaeological record of human culture, / one has to consider / that it is vastly incomplete.
인류 문화의 고고 기록을 살펴볼 때, / 우리는 고려해야 한다, / 그것이 엄청나게 불완전하다는 것을

Many aspects of human culture have / what archaeologists describe as low archaeological visibility, / meaning they are difficult to identify archaeologically.
인류 문화의 많은 측면은 지니고 있는데, / 고고학자들이 낮은 고고학적 가시성이라고 말하는 것을 / 그것들이 고고학적으로 식별하기 어렵다는 것을 의미한다.

Archaeologists tend to focus on tangible (or material) aspects of culture: / things that can be handled and photographed, / such as tools, food, and structures.
고고학자들은 문화의 유형적인 (혹은 물질적인) 측면에 초점을 맞추는 경향이 있다. / 즉 다루고 사진을 찍을 수 있는 것들 / 도구, 음식, 구조물처럼

Reconstructing intangible aspects of culture / is more difficult, / requiring that one draw more inferences from the tangible.
문화의 무형적 측면을 재구성하는 것은 / 더 어려워서, / 우리는 유형적인 것에서 더 많은 추론을 끌어내야 한다.

It is relatively easy, / for example, / for archaeologists to identify and draw inferences / about technology and diet / from stone tools and food remains.
비교적 쉽다, / 예를 들어, / 고고학자들이 식별하고 추론을 도출하기는 / 기술과 식습관에 관해 / 석기와 음식 유물로부터

Using the same kinds of physical remains / to draw inferences / about social systems / and what people were thinking about / is more difficult.
같은 종류의 물질적인 유물을 사용하는 것은 / 추론을 도출하려고 / 사회 체계와 사람들이 무엇을 생각하고 있었는지에 관한 / 더 어렵다.

Archaeologists do it, / but there are necessarily more inferences / involved in getting / from physical remains recognized as trash / to making interpretations about belief systems.
고고학자들은 그렇게 하지만, / 더 많은 추론이 필연적으로 있어야 한다. / 도달하는 것과 관련된 / 쓸모없는 것으로 인식되는 물리적 유물로부터 / 신념 체계에 관한 해석에

인류 문화의 고고학 기록을 살펴볼 때, 우리는 그것이 엄청나게 불완전하다는 것을 고려해야 한다. 인류 문화의 많은 측면은 고고학자들이 낮은 고고학적 가시성이라고 말하는 것을 지니고 있는데, 이것은 그것들이 고고학적으로 식별하기 어렵다는 것을 의미한다. 고고학자들은 문화의 유형적인 (혹은 물질적)

측면, 즉 도구, 음식, 구조물처럼 다루고 사진을 찍을 수 있는 것들에 초점을 맞추는 경향이 있다. 문화의 무형적 측면을 재구성하는 것은 더 어려워서, 우리는 유형적인 것에서 더 많은 추론을 끌어내야 한다. 예를 들어, 고고학자들이 석기와 음식 유물로부터 기술과 식습관을 식별하고 그것에 관한 추론을 도출하기는 비교적 쉽다. 같은 종류의 물질적인 유물을 사용하여 사회 체계와 사람들이 무엇을 생각하고 있었는지에 관한 추론을 도출하는 것은 더 어렵다. 고고학자들은 그렇게 하지만, 쓸모없는 것으로 인식되는 물리적 유물로부터 신념 체계에 관한 해석에 도달하는 것과 관련된 더 많은 추론이 필연적으로 있어야 한다.

Why? 왜 정답일까?

두 번째 문장에서 인류 문화는 고고학적으로 식별되기 어려운 특성을 지니고 있다고 언급한 후, 문화의 무형적 측면을 재구성하기 위해서는 유형적인 것으로부터 필연적으로 추론을 가미할 수밖에 없고, 이 과정은 몹시 어렵다는 내용이 이어지고 있다. 이를 근거로 볼 때, 빈칸에 들어갈 말로 가장 적절한 것은 고고학적 기록의 부족한 점을 시사할 수 있는 ③ '불완전하다'이다.

- examine ⓥ 조사[검토]하다
- vastly ⓐ𝖽 대단히
- identify ⓥ 식별하다
- intangible ⓐ 무형적인
- relatively ⓐ𝖽 비교적, 상대적으로
- interpretation ⓝ 해석, 이해
- factual ⓐ 사실에 기반을 둔
- consider ⓥ 고려하다, 여기다
- visibility ⓝ 가시성
- tangible ⓐ 유형적인, 만질 수 있는
- draw an inference 추론하다
- necessarily ⓐ𝖽 필연적으로
- outdated ⓐ 구식인
- incomplete ⓐ 불완전한

구문 풀이

8행 Reconstructing intangible aspects of culture is more difficult,
→ 분사구문(요구 동사)
requiring that one (should) draw more inferences from the tangible.
접속사　주어　동사

★★ 문제 해결 꿀~팁 ★★

▶ 많이 틀린 이유는?
이 글은 고고학적 증거의 특성을 설명하고 있다. 고고학에서 주로 다루는 증거는 형태가 있고 물질적이라는 설명으로 보아, 언뜻 보면 ②와 같이 고고학적 증거는 '사실적'이라는 결론이 적합해 보인다. 하지만 글 후반부를 읽어보면 증거의 유형적 특성으로 인해 무형의 문화를 재구성하는 데에는 '어려움'이 따른다고 했다. 따라서 빈칸에는 단순히 고고학적 증거가 '사실적'이라고 언급하는 대신 증거의 한계를 지적해줄 수 있는 말이 들어가야 함을 알 수 있다.

▶ 문제 해결 방법은?
고고학적 증거를 가지고 문화를 연구하는 과정에는 필연적으로 '추론'이 들어간다는 빈칸 뒤 내용으로 보아, 유형의 증거만으로는 무형의 문화를 다 알기 '부족하다'라는 말이 빈칸에 들어가야 한다.

★★★ 1등급 대비 고난도 2점 문제

| 08 | 필자에 대한 편견을 형성할 수 있는 글쓰기 | 정답률 31% | 정답 ③ |

다음 빈칸에 들어갈 말로 가장 적절한 것을 고르시오.

① reveal your hidden intention
여러분의 숨겨진 의도를 드러낼
② distort the meaning of the sentence
문장의 의미를 왜곡할
✓ prejudice your audience against you
독자가 여러분에 대해 편견을 갖게 할
④ test your audience's reading comprehension
독자의 독해력을 시험할
⑤ create fierce debates about your writing topic
여러분의 작문 주제에 관한 열띤 논쟁을 만들어 낼

One of the great risks of writing is / that even the simplest of choices / regarding wording or punctuation / can sometimes prejudice your audience against you / in ways that may seem unfair.
글쓰기의 가장 큰 위험 중 하나는 / 가장 사소한 선택조차 / 단어 선택이나 구두점과 관련한 / 때때로 독자가 여러분에 대해 편견을 갖게 할 수 있다는 것이다. / 부당해 보일 수 있는 방식으로

For example, look again at the old grammar rule / forbidding the splitting of infinitives.
예를 들어 옛날 문법 규칙을 다시 보라. / 부정사를 분리하는 것을 금지하는

After decades of telling students / to never split an infinitive / (something just done in this sentence), / most composition experts now acknowledge / that a split infinitive is *not* a grammar crime.
학생들에게 수십 년 동안 말한 후에, / 부정사 분리를 절대 하지 말라고 / (지금 바로 이 문장에서 행해진 것) / 지금 대부분의 작문 전문가들은 인정한다. / 분리된 부정사가 문법적으로 끔찍한 일이 *아니라*는 점을

Suppose you have written a position paper / trying to convince your city council of the need / to hire security personnel for the library, / and half of the council members / — the people you wish to convince — / remember their eighth-grade grammar teacher's warning / about splitting infinitives.
여러분이 의견서를 작성했다고 하자. / 시의회에 필요를 납득시키려고 하는 / 도서관을 위한 보안 요원을 고용할 / 그리고 시의회 의원 중 절반이 / 여러분이 납득시키고 싶어 하는 사람들인 / 자신들의 8학년 문법 교사가 경고한 내용을 기억한다고 / 부정사를 분리하는 것에 대해

How will they respond / when you tell them, in your introduction, / that librarians are compelled "to always accompany" visitors / to the rare book room / because of the threat of damage?
그들은 어떻게 반응할까? / 여러분이 도입부에서 그들에게 말할 때 / 도서관 사서는 방문객과 '동행을 항상 해야' 한다고 / 희귀 서적 자료실에 / 공공기물 손상의 위험 때문에

How much of their attention have you suddenly lost / because of their automatic recollection / of what is now a nonrule?
여러분이 그들의 관심을 얼마나 많이 갑작스럽게 잃었는가? / 그들이 자동으로 떠올린 것 때문에 / 지금은 규칙이 아닌 것을

It is possible, in other words, / to write correctly / and still offend your readers' notions of your language competence.
다른 말로 하면, 가능하다. / 올바르게 글을 쓰면서도 / 여러분의 언어 능력에 대한 독자의 생각에 불쾌감을 주는 것이

글쓰기의 가장 큰 위험 중 하나는 단어 선택이나 구두점과 관련한 가장 사소한 선택조차 부당해 보일 수 있는 방식으로 때때로 독자가 여러분에 대해 편견을 갖게 할 수 있다는 것이다. 예를 들어 부정사를 분리하는 것을 금지하는 옛날 문법 규칙을 다시 보라. 학생들에게 부정사 분리를 절대 하지 말라고(지금 바로 이 문장에서 행해진 것) 수십 년 동안 말한 후에, 지금 대부분의 작문 전문가들은 분리된 부정사가 문법적으로 끔찍한 일이 *아니라*는 점을 인정한다. 여러분이 시의회에 도서관을 위한 보안 요원을 고용할 필요를 납득시키려고 하는 의견서를 작성했고, 여러분이 납득시키고 싶어 하는 사람들인 시의회 의원 중 절반이 자신들의 8학년 문법 교사가 부정사를 분리하는 것에 대해 경고한 내용을 기억한다고 하자. 여러분이 도입부에서, 공공기물 손상의 위험 때문에 도서관 사서는 희귀 서적 자료실에 방문객과 '동행을 항상 해야' 한다고 할 때 그들은 어떻게 반응할까? 지금은 규칙이 아닌 것을 그들이 자동으로 떠올린 것 때문에 여러분이 그들의 관심을 얼마나 많이 갑작스럽게 잃었는가? 다른 말로 하면, 올바르게 글을 쓰면서도 여러분의 언어 능력에 대한 독자의 생각에 불쾌감을 주는 것이 가능하다.

Why? 왜 정답일까?

부정사의 to와 동사원형 사이에 부사를 끼워넣지 말아야 한다는 옛 문법 규칙(분리부정사 금지 규칙)의 예를 들어, 현재로서는 그러한 규칙이 통용된다고 할지라도 과거에 그것이 불가능하다고 배웠던 사람들에 의해 필자의 언어 능력에 대한 편견이 생겨날 수 있다는 내용을 다룬 글이다. 마지막 문장인 'It is possible, in other words, to write correctly and still offend your readers' notions of your language competence.'에서 예시의 결론을 잘 제시한다. 따라서 빈칸에 들어갈 말로 가장 적절한 것은 글쓰기에서의 사소한 선택들이 필자에 대한 독자의 인상에 부정적인 영향을 미칠 수 있다는 내용을 완성하는 ③ '독자가 여러분에 대해 편견을 갖게 할'이다.

- unfair ⓐ 부당한
- composition ⓝ 작문
- convince A of B A에게 B를 납득시키다
- introduction ⓝ 도입
- accompany ⓥ 동반하다
- competence ⓝ 능력
- prejudice ⓥ 편견을 갖게 하다 ⓝ 편견
- splitting ⓝ 분리
- acknowledge ⓥ 인정하다
- personnel ⓝ 직원
- compel ⓥ 강제하다
- recollection ⓝ 기억, 회상
- distort ⓥ 왜곡시키다
- comprehension ⓝ 이해

구문 풀이

9행 Suppose you have written a position paper trying to
   주어1   동사1
convince your city council of the need to hire security personnel for
「convince + A + of + B : A에게 B를 납득시키다」
the library, and half of the council members — the people [you wish
                        주어2   동격(=주어2)
to convince] — remember their eighth-grade grammar teacher's
                동사2(복수)   목적어2
warning about splitting infinitives.

★★ 문제 해결 꿀~팁 ★★

▶ 많이 틀린 이유는?
마지막 문장에 따르면 독자들은 필자의 글쓰기에 기초해 필자(의 언어 능력)에 대한 인상을 형성한다고 한다. 하지만 ②는 필자가 글쓰기 과정에서 선택한 단어나 구두점 등이 '문장의 의미 자체를 왜곡할 수 있다'는 뜻이므로 글의 내용과 맞지 않다.

▶ 문제 해결 방법은?
예시가 구체적이고 생소할수록 빈칸의 답은 지문의 큰 흐름만 파악하면 도출되는 경우가 많다. 이 문제에서도 문법 규칙의 세부적인 내용을 이해하려고 애쓰기보다 결론 문장을 주의 깊게 읽는 것이 좋다.

★★★ 1등급 대비 고난도 3점 문제

09 개별자에 비해 보편자를 강조한 헤겔   정답률 38% | 정답 ②

다음 빈칸에 들어갈 말로 가장 적절한 것을 고르시오. [3점]
① an individual stands alone apart from the universe
   개별자는 우주에서 동떨어져 혼자 서 있다
✓ the universal still has more priority than the individual
   보편자는 여전히 개별자보다 더 많은 우위를 갖는다
③ universal truth cannot be the key to individual problems
   보편적 진리는 개인적 문제의 핵심이 될 수 없다
④ individuals can't deduce universal principles from reality itself
   개별자들은 실제 그 자체로부터 보편적 원리를 추론할 수 없다
⑤ every individual should have his or her own particular universe
   모든 개별자는 자기만의 특별한 우주를 지녀야 한다

In Hegel's philosophy, / even though there is interaction and interrelation / between the universal and the individual, / the universal still has more priority than the individual.
헤겔의 철학에서 / 비록 상호 작용과 상호 관계가 있긴 하지만 / 보편자와 개별자 사이에 / 보편자는 여전히 개별자보다 더 많은 우위를 갖는다.

For Hegel, / individuals are not distinguished in terms of Reason.
헤겔에게 / 개인은 '이성'의 관점에서는 구별되지 않는다.

In *Philosophy of Right* / Hegel stresses particularity and universality as follows: / "A man, who acts perversely, / exhibits particularity. / The rational is the highway / on which everyone travels, / and no one is specially marked."
*Philosophy of Right*에서 / 헤겔은 다음과 같이 특수성과 보편성을 강조한다. / '사람은 별나게 행동하며 / 특수성을 보여 준다. / 이성적인 것은 고속 도로이며, / 모든 사람이 이동하는 / 아무도 특별하게 두드러지지 않는다.'

Here, / Hegel maintains / that individuals can be differentiated from each other / in terms of their acts / but they are not differentiated with respect to reason.
여기서 / 헤겔은 주장한다. / 개인이 서로 구별될 수 있지만, / 행동의 관점에서는 / 그들이 이성의 측면에서는 구별되지 않는다고

There are specific thoughts, / but they are finally resolved into the universal.
특수한 생각은 존재하기는 하지만 / 결국 그것은 보편자로 귀착된다.

One might say / that Hegel seems to focus on the individual like Aristotle / but in reality, / he subtly treats the universal as fundamental / whereas Aristotle considers the individual as primary substance / and universal as secondary substance; / in so doing / Aristotle emphasizes the universal to be subordinate to the individual / in contrast to Hegel.
혹자는 말할 수도 있다 / 헤겔이 아리스토텔레스처럼 개별자에만 초점을 맞춘 것 같다고 / 하지만 실로 / 헤겔은 미묘하게 보편자를 근본적인 것으로 다룬다. / 아리스토텔레스가 개별자를 제일(第一) 실체로 여기고 / 보편자를 제이(第二) 실체로 여긴 반면 / 그렇게 하여 / 아리스토텔레스는 보편자가 개별자에게 종속된다고 강조하는 것과는 달리, / 헤겔과는 대조적으로

헤겔의 철학에서 비록 보편자와 개별자 사이에 상호 작용과 상호 관계가 있긴 하지만 보편자는 여전히 개별자보다 더 많은 우위를 갖는다. 헤겔에게 개인은 '이성'의 관점에서는 구별되지 않는다. *Philosophy of Right*에서 헤겔은 다음과 같이 특수성과 보편성을 강조한다. '사람은 별나게 행동하며 특수성을 보여 준다. 이성적인 것은 모든 사람이 이동하는 고속 도로이며, 아무도 특별하게 두드러지지 않는다.' 여기서 헤겔은 개인이 행동의 관점에서는 서로 구별될 수 있지만, 이성의 측면에서는 구별되지 않는다고 주장한다. 특수한 생각은 존재하기는 하지만 결국 보편자로 귀착된다. 혹자는 헤겔이 아리스토텔레스처럼 개별자에만 초점을 맞춘 것 같다고 말할 수도 있지만, 아리스토텔레스가 개별자를 제일(第一) 실체로, 보편자를 제이(第二) 실체로 여기고, 그렇게 하여 헤겔과는 대조적으로 보편자가 개별자에게 종속된다고 강조하는 것과는 달리, 헤겔은 실로 미묘하게 보편자를 근본적인 것으로 다룬다.

Why? 왜 정답일까?

글 전체에 걸쳐 헤겔은 (개별자가 아닌) 보편자를 근본적인 것으로 여겼다(he subtly treats the universal as fundamental)는 내용이 반복 제시된다. 따라서 빈칸에 들어갈 말로 가장 적절한 것은 ② '보편자는 여전히 개별자보다 더 많은 우위를 갖는다(the universal still has more priority than the individual)'이다.

- universal ⓝ 보편적인 것 ⓐ 보편적인
- universality ⓝ 보편성
- particularity ⓝ 특수성
- as follows 다음과 같이

- perversely @ 별나게
- differentiate ⓥ 구별하다
- subtly @ 미묘하게
- be subordinate to ~에 종속되다
- deduce ⓥ 추론하다, 연역하다
- marked @ 두드러진
- resolve into (차츰) ~로 바뀌다
- substance ⓝ 실체, 본질, 물질
- apart from ~에서 동떨어진

구문 풀이

13행 One might say that Hegel seems to focus on the individual like Aristotle but in reality, he subtly treats the universal as fundamental whereas Aristotle considers the individual as primary
접속사(~한 반면에) 「consider A1 as B1 +
substance and universal as secondary substance; in so doing
and + A2 as B2 : A1을 B1로, A2를 B2로 여기다」 그렇게 함으로써
Aristotle emphasizes the universal to be subordinate to the individual in contrast to Hegel.
~와는 대조적으로

★★ 문제 해결 꿀~팁 ★★

▶ 많이 틀린 이유는?
추상적인 철학 개념을 다루고 있어 난이도가 높은 문제이다. 특히 ③처럼 주제와 반대되는 선택지를 고르지 않도록 주의하자.

▶ 문제 해결 방법은?
첫 문장에 제시되듯 글의 내용은 '헤겔'의 철학을 파악하는 것이다. 특히 '아리스토텔레스'의 철학을 함께 제시하는 마지막 문장에서 두 학자의 주장을 혼동하지 않아야 한다.

★★★ 1등급 대비 고난도 3점 문제

10 사진술 이전과 이후 정답률 20% | 정답 ⑤

다음 빈칸에 들어갈 말로 가장 적절한 것을 고르시오. [3점]

① paintings alone connected with nature – 그림만이 자연과 연관되었다
② painting was the major form of art – 그림은 예술의 주요한 형식이었다
③ art held up a mirror to the world – 예술은 세상을 비추는 거울을 떠받쳤다
④ desire for travel was not strong – 여행을 위한 욕구가 강하지 않았다
✓ places did not travel well – 장소들이 잘 이동하지 않았다

Prior to photography, / places did not travel well.
사진이 나오기 전에는, / 장소들이 잘 이동하지 않았다.

While painters have always lifted particular places out of their 'dwelling' / and transported them elsewhere, / paintings were time-consuming to produce, / relatively difficult to transport / and one-of-a-kind.
화가들이 항상 특정한 장소를 그것의 '거주지'에서 벗어나게 해 / 다른 곳으로 이동시켜 왔기는 해도, / 그림은 제작에 시간이 많이 들었으며, / 운반이 비교적 어려웠고, / 단품 수주 생산이었다.

The multiplication of photographs especially took place / with the introduction of the half-tone plate in the 1880s / that made possible the mechanical reproduction of photographs / in newspapers, periodicals, books and advertisements.
사진의 증가는 특히 이루어졌다. / 1880년대 하프톤 판의 도입으로 / 사진의 기계적인 복제를 가능하게 했던 / 신문, 정기간행물, 책, 그리고 광고에서

Photography became coupled to consumer capitalism / and the globe was now offered 'in limitless quantities, / figures, landscapes, events / which had not previously been utilised either at all, / or only as pictures for one customer'.
사진은 소비자 자본주의와 결합하게 되었고, / 세상은 '이제 무한한 양으로 제공받았다. / 인물, 풍경, 사건들을 / 이전에는 전혀 사용된 적이 없거나 / 단 한 명의 고객을 위한 그림으로만 (사용되었던)'

With capitalism's arrangement of the world as a 'department store', / 'the proliferation and circulation of representations ... / achieved a spectacular and virtually inescapable global magnitude'.
자본주의가 세계를 '백화점'으로 정리함에 따라, / '표현물의 확산과 유통은… / 극적이고 사실상 피할 수 없는 세계적 규모를 달성했다'

Gradually photographs became cheap mass-produced objects / that made the world visible, aesthetic and desirable.
점차 사진은 값싼 대량 생산품이 되었다. / 세계를 가시적이고, 미적이며, 탐나게 만드는

Experiences were 'democratised' / by translating them into cheap images.
경험들은 '대중화'되었다. / 그것을 저렴한 이미지로 바꾸어

Light, small and mass-produced photographs / became dynamic vehicles for the spatiotemporal circulation of places.
가볍고 작고 대량으로 제작된 사진은 / 장소의 시공간적 순환을 위한 역동적인 수단이 되었다.

사진이 나오기 전에는, 장소들이 잘 이동하지 않았다. 화가들이 항상 특정한 장소를 그것의 '거주지'에서 벗어나게 해 다른 곳으로 이동시켜 왔기는 해도,

---

그림은 제작에 시간이 많이 들었으며, 운반이 비교적 어려웠고, 단품 수주 생산이었다. 사진의 증가는 특히 신문, 정기간행물, 책, 그리고 광고에서 사진의 기계적인 복제를 가능하게 했던 1880년대 하프톤 판의 도입으로 이루어졌다. 사진은 소비자 자본주의와 결합하게 되었고, 세상은 이제 '이전에는 전혀 사용된 적이 없거나 단 한 명의 고객을 위한 그림으로만 사용되었던 인물, 풍경, 사건들을 무한한 양으로 제공받았다'. 자본주의가 세계를 '백화점'으로 정리함에 따라, '표현물의 확산과 유통은… 극적이고 사실상 피할 수 없는 세계적 규모를 달성했다'. 점차 사진은 세계를 가시적이고, 미적이며, 탐나게 만드는 값싼 대량 생산품이 되었다. 경험들은 그것을 저렴한 이미지로 바꾸어 '대중화'되었다. 가볍고 작고 대량으로 제작된 사진은 장소의 시공간적 순환을 위한 역동적인 수단이 되었다.

Why? 왜 정답일까?

사진이 출현하고 세계가 이미지의 '백화점'이 되면서 표현의 확산과 유통은 극적으로 증가했고, 장소의 시공간적 순환이 일어나게 되었다고 한다. 첫 문장은 장소의 이미지가 하나씩 어렵게 생산되던(paintings were time-consuming to produce, relatively difficult to transport and one-of-a-kind.) 사진 출현 이전의 상황을 묘사하고 있으므로, 빈칸에 들어갈 말로 가장 적절한 것은 ⑤ '장소들이 잘 이동하지 않았다'이다.

- lift out of ~에서 들어올리다
- time-consuming @ 시간이 많이 걸리는
- multiplication ⓝ 증가
- periodical ⓝ 정기 간행물
- globe ⓝ 세계, 지구
- previously @ 이전에
- proliferation ⓝ 확산
- representation ⓝ 표현(물)
- virtually @ 사실상, 거의
- magnitude ⓝ (큰) 규모
- democratise ⓥ 대중화하다, 민주화하다
- dwelling ⓝ 거주지, 주택
- one-of-a-kind @ 단품 수주의, 독특한
- reproduction ⓝ 재생
- capitalism ⓝ 자본주의
- landscape ⓝ 풍경
- arrangement ⓝ 정리, 배열
- circulation ⓝ 순환, 유통
- spectacular @ 장관의
- inescapable @ 피할 수 없는
- aesthetic @ 미적인
- spatiotemporal @ 시공간적인

구문 풀이

5행 The multiplication of photographs especially took place with the introduction of the half-tone plate in the 1880s [that made
5형식 동사
possible the mechanical reproduction of photographs in newspapers,
목적격 보어 목적어(길어서 보어 뒤로 빠짐)
periodicals, books and advertisements].

★★ 문제 해결 꿀~팁 ★★

▶ 많이 틀린 이유는?
단순히 사진 또는 예술이 '주류'였던 사실을 비교하는 내용이 아니므로 ②는 답으로 적절하지 않다. 사진 이전에는 이미지가 하나씩 제작되고 소비되었지만, 사진 이후로는 이미지가 무한히 만들어지고 소비될 수 있었다는 내용을 충분히 담아낸 선택지가 필요하다.

▶ 문제 해결 방법은?
⑤의 did not travel well을 문자 그대로의 의미로 받아들이면 오답처럼 보인다. 하지만 여기서 '이동'은 사진을 통해 장소의 이미지가 활발히 확산되는 과정을 이른다.

★★★ 1등급 대비 고난도 3점 문제

11 각 개인과 밀접히 연관되는 교통 정답률 24% | 정답 ④

다음 빈칸에 들어갈 말로 가장 적절한 것을 고르시오. [3점]

① relies heavily on how others see her city's streets
다른 사람이 그 사람의 도시 도로를 어떻게 보느냐에 크게 의존한다
② updates itself with each new public transit policy
각각의 새로운 대중교통 정책에 맞춰 자체로 업데이트된다
③ arises independently of the streets she travels on
그 사람이 이동하는 도로와 관계없이 발생한다
✓ tracks pretty closely with how she gets around
그 사람이 돌아다니는 방식과 매우 밀접하게 일치한다
⑤ ties firmly in with how her city operates
그 사람의 도시가 운영되는 방식과 긴밀하게 연계되어 있다

Everyone who drives, walks, or swipes a transit card in a city / views herself as a transportation expert / from the moment she walks out the front door.
도시에서 운전하거나 걷거나 교통 카드를 판독기에 통과시키는 모든 사람은 / 본인을 교통 전문가로 여긴다 / 현관문을 나서는 순간부터

And how she views the street / tracks pretty closely with how she gets around.
그리고 그 사람이 도로를 바라보는 방식은 / 그 사람이 돌아다니는 방식과 매우 밀접하게 일치한다.

That's why we find / so many well-intentioned and civic-minded citizens / arguing past one another.
그런 이유로 우리는 보게 된다. / 선의의 시민 의식을 가진 매우 많은 사람이 / 서로를 지나치며 언쟁하는 것을

At neighborhood meetings in school auditoriums, / and in back rooms at libraries and churches, / local residents across the nation / gather for often-contentious discussions / about transportation proposals / that would change a city's streets.
학교 강당에서 열리는 주민 회의에서, / 도서관과 교회의 뒷방에서, / 전국의 지역 주민들이 / 모여서 흔히 논쟁적인 토론을 벌인다. / 교통 제안에 대해 / 도시의 거리를 바꿀

And like all politics, / all transportation is local and intensely personal.
그리고 모든 정치와 마찬가지로, / 모든 교통은 지역적이고 지극히 개인적이다.

A transit project / that could speed travel for tens of thousands of people / can be stopped / by objections to the loss of a few parking spaces / or by the simple fear that the project won't work.
교통 프로젝트는 / 수만 명의 이동 속도를 높일 수 있는 / 중단될 수 있다. / 주차 공간 몇 개가 없어지는 데 대한 반대나, / 프로젝트가 무용할 것이라는 단순한 두려움 때문에

It's not a challenge of the data or the traffic engineering or the planning.
그것은 데이터나 교통 공학 또는 계획의 과제가 아니다.

Public debates about streets / are typically rooted in emotional assumptions / about how a change will affect a person's commute, / ability to park, / belief about what is safe and what isn't, / or the bottom line of a local business.
도로에 대한 대중 토론은 / 보통 감정적인 추정에 뿌리를 두고 있다. / 변화가 개인의 통근에 어떤 영향을 미칠지에 대한 / 주차 능력, / 안전한 것과 안전하지 않은 것에 대한 믿음, / 또는 지역 사업체의 순익에

도시에서 운전하거나 걷거나 교통 카드를 판독기에 통과시키는 모든 사람은 현관문을 나서는 순간부터 본인을 교통 전문가로 여긴다. 그리고 그 사람이 도로를 바라보는 방식은 그 사람이 돌아다니는 방식과 매우 밀접하게 일치한다. 그런 이유로, 우리는 선의의 시민 의식을 가진 매우 많은 사람이 서로를 지나치며 언쟁하는 것을 보게 된다. 학교 강당에서 열리는 주민 회의에서, 도서관과 교회의 뒷방에서, 전국의 지역 주민들이 모여 도시의 거리를 바꿀 교통 제안에 대해 흔히 논쟁적인 토론을 벌인다. 그리고 모든 정치와 마찬가지로, 모든 교통은 지역적이고 지극히 개인적이다. 수만 명의 이동 속도를 높일 수 있는 교통 프로젝트는 주차 공간 몇 개가 없어지는 데 대한 반대나, 프로젝트가 무용할 것이라는 단순한 두려움 때문에 중단될 수 있다. 그것은 데이터나 교통 공학 또는 계획의 과제가 아니다. 도로에 대한 대중 토론은 보통 변화가 개인의 통근, 주차 능력, 안전한 것과 안전하지 않은 것에 대한 믿음, 또는 지역 사업체의 순익에 어떤 영향을 미칠지에 대한 감정적인 추정에 뿌리를 두고 있다.

Why? 왜 정답일까?

모든 교통은 지역적이고 대단히 개인적이며(~ like all politics, all transportation is local and intensely personal.), 교통에 대한 대중 토론은 개인의 감정적 추정에 근거하기 마련(Public debates about streets are typically rooted in emotional assumptions ~)이라는 내용이다. 이러한 글의 주제로 미루어 보아, 빈칸에 들어갈 말로 가장 적절한 것은 ④ '그 사람이 돌아다니는 방식과 매우 밀접하게 일치한다'이다.

- swipe ⓥ 판독기에 통과시키다
- transportation ⓝ 교통, 운송
- civic-minded ⓐ 시민 의식을 가진
- well-intentioned ⓐ 선의의
- resident ⓝ 주민
- contentious ⓐ 논쟁적인
- intensely ⓐ 지극히, 몹시
- tens of thousands of 수만의
- parking space 주차 공간
- dabate ⓝ 논쟁
- commute ⓝ 통근
- rely on ~에 의존하다
- independently of ~와 별개로
- closely ⓐ 밀접하게

- transit card 교통 카드
- expert ⓝ 전문가
- neighborhood meeting 반상회
- auditorium ⓝ 강당
- gather ⓥ 모이다
- politics ⓝ 정치
- personal ⓐ 개인적인
- objection ⓝ 반대, 이의
- engineering ⓝ 공학
- be rooted in ~에 근원을 두다
- bottom line 순익, 최종 결산 결과
- arise ⓥ 발생하다
- track with ~와 일치하다
- firmly ⓐ 확고하게

구문 풀이

1행 Everyone [who drives, walks, or swipes a transit card in a
주어 ┊ 주격 관·대
city] views herself as a transportation expert from the moment she
「view+A+as+B: A를 B로 여기다」
walks out the front door.

★★ 문제 해결 꿀~팁 ★★

▶ 많이 틀린 이유는?
글에서 교통 정책을 둘러싼 토론이나 이의 제기 상황을 이야기하는 것으로 볼 때 역

시 '정책'을 언급하는 ②가 자연스러워 보일 수 있다. 하지만 ②를 빈칸에 넣으면, 교통이 개인 시각에 영향을 받는다는 글의 핵심 내용과는 반대로, 개인의 시각이 교통 정책에 영향을 받아 바뀐다는 모순된 진술이 된다.

▶ 문제 해결 방법은?
local and intensely personal이라는 핵심 어구와 가장 맥락이 통하는 선택지를 찾는 것이 포인트이다.

★★★ 1등급 대비 고난도 3점 문제

12 도구를 신체의 일부처럼 느끼고 행동하는 인간 정답률 38% | 정답 ⑤

다음 빈칸에 들어갈 말로 가장 적절한 것을 고르시오. [3점]

① recalls past experiences of utilizing the tool
그 도구를 활용했던 지난 경험을 떠올린다
② recognizes what it can do best without the tool
그 도구 없이 그것이 가장 잘할 수 있는 것을 인식한다
③ judges which part of our body can best be used
우리 신체의 어느 부분이 가장 잘 활용될 수 있는지 판단한다
④ perceives what limits the tool's functional utility
무엇이 그 도구의 기능적 효용을 제한하는지를 인식한다
✓⑤ adjusts what it considers body to include the tool
그것이 신체라고 간주하는 것에 도구를 포함시키도록 조정한다

Even when we do something as apparently simple / as picking up a screwdriver, / our brain automatically adjusts / what it considers body / to include the tool.
우리가 겉으로 보기에 간단한 일을 할 때조차도, / 나사돌리개를 집는 것만큼 / 우리의 뇌는 무의식적으로 조정한다. / 그것이 신체라고 간주하는 것을 / 도구를 포함시키도록

We can literally feel things / with the end of the screwdriver.
우리는 말 그대로 사물을 느낄 수 있다. / 나사돌리개의 끝부분으로

When we extend a hand, holding the screwdriver, / we automatically take the length of the latter into account.
우리가 손을 뻗어 나사돌리개를 들고 있을 때, / 우리는 무의식적으로 후자의 길이를 계산에 넣는다.

We can probe difficult-to-reach places with its extended end, / and comprehend what we are exploring.
우리는 그것의 확장된 끝을 가지고 도달하기 어려운 곳을 탐색할 수 있고, / 우리가 탐색하고 있는 것을 이해할 수 있다.

Furthermore, / we instantly regard the screwdriver we are holding / as "our" screwdriver, / and get possessive about it.
게다가, / 우리는 즉시 우리가 들고 있는 나사돌리개를 간주하고, / '자신의' 나사돌리개로 / 그것에 대해 소유욕을 갖게 된다.

We do the same / with the much more complex tools we use, / in much more complex situations.
우리는 똑같이 한다. / 우리가 사용하는 훨씬 더 복잡한 도구를 두고 / 훨씬 더 복잡한 상황에서도

The cars we pilot / instantaneously and automatically become ourselves.
우리가 조종하는 자동차는 / 순간적이면서도 무의식적으로 우리 자신이 된다.

Because of this, / when someone bangs his fist on our car's hood / after we have irritated him at a crosswalk, / we take it personally.
이것 때문에 / 누군가가 우리 자동차의 덮개를 주먹으로 칠 때, / 우리가 건널목에서 그 사람을 짜증 나게 한 후에, / 우리는 그것을 자신의 일로 받아들인다.

This is not always reasonable.
이것은 항상 합리적인 것은 아니다.

Nonetheless, without the extension of self into machine, / it would be impossible to drive.
그렇더라도, 자신을 기계까지로 확장하지 않으면 / 운전하는 것은 불가능할 것이다.

우리가 나사돌리개를 집는 것만큼 겉으로 보기에 간단한 일을 할 때조차도, 우리의 뇌는 무의식적으로 그것이 신체라고 간주하는 것에 도구를 포함시키도록 조정한다. 우리는 말 그대로 나사돌리개의 끝부분으로 사물을 느낄 수 있다. 손을 뻗어서 나사돌리개를 들고 있을 때, 우리는 무의식적으로 후자(나사돌리개)의 길이를 계산에 넣는다. 우리는 그것의 확장된 끝을 가지고 도달하기 어려운 곳을 탐색할 수 있고, 우리가 탐색하고 있는 것을 이해할 수 있다. 게다가, 우리는 즉시 우리가 들고 있는 나사돌리개를 '자신의' 나사돌리개로 간주하고, 그것에 대해 소유욕을 갖게 된다. 우리는 훨씬 더 복잡한 상황에서도 우리가 사용하는 훨씬 더 복잡한 도구를 두고도 똑같이 한다. 우리가 조종하는 자동차는 순간적이면서도 무의식적으로 우리 자신이 된다. 이것 때문에 우리가 건널목에서 누군가를 짜증 나게 한 후에, 그 사람이 우리 자동차의 덮개를 주먹으로 칠 때, 우리는 그것을 자신의 일로 받아들인다. 이것은 항상 합리적인 것은 아니다. 그렇더라도, 자신을 기계까지로 확장하지 않으면 운전하는 것은 불가능할 것이다.

Why? 왜 정답일까?

우리는 도구를 사용할 때 도구가 신체의 일부인 것처럼 생각한다는 내용을 다룬 글이다.

특히 'We can literally feel things with the end of the screwdriver.'와 'The cars we pilot instantaneously and automatically become ourselves.'에서 나사돌리개와 자동차의 예를 들어 도구를 무의식적으로 '일체화'시키는 인간의 경향성에 관해 잘 설명한다. 따라서 빈칸에 들어갈 말로 가장 적절한 것은 ⑤ '그것이 신체라고 간주하는 것에 도구를 포함시키도록 조정한다'이다.

- **apparently** [ad] 겉으로 보기에, 분명히
- **take into account** [V] ~을 고려하다
- **possessive** [a] 소유욕이 강한
- **irritate** [V] 짜증나게 하다
- **automatically** [ad] 무의식적으로
- **extended** [a] 확장된
- **instantaneously** [ad] 순간적으로
- **functional** [a] 기능적인

구문 풀이

1행 Even when we do something as apparently simple as picking
심지어 ~할 때조차 「as + 원급 + as : ~만큼 …한」
up a screwdriver, our brain automatically adjusts what it considers
주어 / 동사 / 목적어(명사절)
body to include the tool.
~하도록

★★ 문제 해결 꿀~팁 ★★

▶ 많이 틀린 이유는?
인간은 도구를 사용할 때 그 도구를 신체의 일부처럼 여긴다는 추상적인 내용을 다룬 글이다. ①은 인간이 도구를 쓸 때 그 도구를 사용했던 '과거의 경험을 떠올린다'는 내용인데, 이는 주제와 관련이 없다.

▶ 문제 해결 방법은?
주제문인 첫 문장을 완성하는 빈칸 문제로, 글의 다른 부분에서 요약된 결론이 제시되지 않아 예시를 다 읽어야 한다. '~ we instantly regard the screwdriver we are holding as "our" screwdriver ~'와 'The cars we pilot instantaneously and automatically become ourselves.' 등 공통된 내용을 말하는 표현에 주목한다.

---

01 ④	02 ①	03 ②	04 ④	05 ①
06 ⑤	07 ⑤	08 ②	09 ①	10 ①
11 ④	12 ①			

01 많은 시도를 통해 나오는 창의성 　 정답률 41% | 정답 ④

다음 빈칸에 들어갈 말로 가장 적절한 것을 고르시오.

① sensitivity – 민감성
② superiority – 우월성
③ imagination – 상상력
✓ productivity – 생산성
⑤ achievement – 성취

One unspoken truth about creativity / — it isn't about wild talent / so much as it is about productivity.
창의성에 관해 입 밖에 내지 않는 진실 중 하나는, / 그것이 아주 특이한 재능보다는 / 생산성과 관련이 있다는 점이다.

To find a few ideas that work, / you need to try a lot that don't.
쓸모 있는 몇 가지 아이디어를 발견하기 위해서는 / 쓸모 있지 않은 많은 것들을 시도할 필요가 있다.

It's a pure numbers game.
이는 순전히 숫자 게임이다.

Geniuses don't necessarily have a higher success rate than other creators; / they simply do more — / and they do a range of different things.
천재들이 반드시 다른 창조자들보다 성공률이 높은 게 아니다. / 이들은 그저 더 많이 하고, / 여러 가지 다양한 것들을 해 본다.

They have more successes *and* more failures.
이들은 성공도 더 많이 *하고* 실패도 더 많이 한다.

That goes for teams and companies too.
이는 팀과 회사에도 적용된다.

It's impossible to generate a lot of good ideas / without also generating a lot of bad ideas.
많은 좋은 아이디어를 창출하는 것이 불가능하다. / 많은 형편없는 생각을 만들어내 보지 않고는

The thing about creativity is / that at the outset, / you can't tell which ideas will succeed and which will fail.
창의성에 대해 중요한 것은, / 처음부터 / 어떤 아이디어가 성공하고 어떤 것이 실패할지 구별할 수 없다는 것이다.

So the only thing you can do is try to fail faster / so that you can move onto the next idea.
따라서 할 수 있는 유일한 것은 더 빨리 실패해 보는 것이다. / 다음 아이디어로 넘어갈 수 있도록

창의성에 관해 입 밖에 내지 않는 진실 중 하나는, 그것이 아주 특이한 재능보다는 생산성과 관련이 있다는 점이다. 쓸모 있는 몇 가지 아이디어를 발견하기 위해서는 쓸모 있지 않은 많은 것들을 시도할 필요가 있다. 이는 순전히 숫자 게임이다. 천재들이 반드시 다른 창조자들보다 성공률이 높은 게 아니다. 이들은 그저 더 많이 하고, 여러 가지 다양한 것들을 해 본다. 이들은 성공도 더 많이 하고 실패도 더 많이 한다. 이는 팀과 회사에도 적용된다. 많은 형편없는 생각을 만들어내 보지 않고는 많은 좋은 아이디어를 창출하는 것이 불가능하다. 창의성에 대해 중요한 것은, 처음부터 어떤 아이디어가 성공하고 어떤 것이 실패할지 구별할 수 없다는 것이다. 따라서 할 수 있는 유일한 것은 다음 아이디어로 넘어갈 수 있도록 더 빨리 실패해 보는 것이다.

Why? 왜 정답일까?

'To find a few ideas that work, you need to try a lot that don't.'에서 쓸모 있는 생각을 발견하기 위해서는 쓸모없는 생각도 많이 시도해 봐야 한다고 하고, 이어지는 세 문장에서는 천재들의 예를 통해 이들도 아이디어를 모두 처음부터 성공시키는 것이 아니라 많은 시도를 하면서 실패도 더 많이 하고 성공도 더 많이 하게 되는 것이라고 이야기한다. 마지막 문장인 'So the only thing you can do is try to fail faster so that you can move onto the next idea.'에서도 다음 아이디어로 빨리 넘어가도록 일단 시도해보는 것의 중요성을 말하므로, 빈칸에 들어갈 말로 가장 적절한 것은 '많은 시도, 생산'을 요약하여 나타낸 ④ '생산성'이다.

- **unspoken** [a] 입 밖에 내지 않는
- **pure** [a] 순수한, 순전한
- **success rate** 성공률
- **go for** ~에 해당되다
- **at the outset** 처음에(는)
- **superiority** [n] 우월성
- **talent** [n] 재능
- **not necessarily** 반드시 ~ 아닌
- **simply** [ad] 그저, 단순히
- **generate** [V] 만들어내다, 창출하다
- **sensitivity** [n] 민감성

구문 풀이

10행 The thing about creativity is [that (at the outset), you can't
<u>주어</u> <u>동사</u> <u>접속사(~것)</u>
tell which ideas will succeed and which will fail].
<u>의문사절1</u> <u>의문사절2</u>

---

understanding of risk and causation) and (in the control of impulses)
( ) : 전명구(주어 수식)
increase the probability of risky behavior by the child, for example,
<u>동사2</u> <u>목적어</u>
jumping off a porch.

---

02 | 의학적 문제가 있는 아이들의 행동 제어력 | 정답률 51% | 정답 ①

다음 빈칸에 들어갈 말로 가장 적절한 것을 고르시오.

☑ device safety – 기기 안전
② mental health – 정신 건강
③ pain reactions – 통증 반응
④ athletic training – 운동 훈련
⑤ medical diagnoses – 의학적 진단

The developmental control / that children with certain serious medical
problems / can exert over their physical activity / is relevant to device safety.
발달상의 제어 능력은 / 어떤 심각한 의학적 문제가 있는 아이들이 / 자신의 신체 활동에 대해 발휘할 수 있는 /
기기 안전과 관련이 있다.

For example, an infant in a crib / and a cognitively intact 14-year-old /
confined to bed due to illness or injury / may both be relatively inactive.
예를 들어, 아기 침대 안의 아기와 / 인지적으로 온전한 14세 아이는 / 질병이나 부상으로 인해 침대에 누워 있어
야만 하는 / 둘 다 비교적 움직이지 못할 수 있다.

The adolescent can, however, be expected / to have more awareness of and
control over movements / such as rolling over / that might dislodge or
otherwise impair the functioning of a medical device / such as a breathing
tube or feeding tube.
그러나 그 청소년은 기대될 수 있다. / 동작에 대해 더 잘 알고 있고 그것을 더 잘 조절할 것으로 / (몸) 뒤집기와
같은 / 의료 기기를 떼어 내거나 그렇지 않으면 그 기능을 손상시킬 수도 있는 / 호흡관이나 영양관과 같은

Likewise, a 5-year-old and a 25-year-old / who have had a cardiac
pacemaker implanted / may each know / that they need to protect the device,
/ but developmental differences / in the understanding of risk and causation /
and in the control of impulses / increase the probability of risky behavior by
the child, / for example, jumping off a porch.
마찬가지로, 5세와 25세의 사람은 / 심박 조율기를 이식받은 / 각각 알고 있을 수는 있지만, / 그들이 그 기기를
보호해야 한다는 것을 / 발달상의 차이가, / 위험과 인과 관계에 대한 이해 / 그리고 충동 조절에서의 / 어린이에
의한 위험한 행동의 가능성을 증가시킨다. / 예를 들자면, 현관에서 뛰어내리는 것과 같은

어떤 심각한 의학적 문제가 있는 아이들이 자신의 신체 활동에 대해 발휘할 수
있는 발달상의 제어 능력은 기기 안전과 관련이 있다. 예를 들어, 아기 침대 안
의 아기와 질병이나 부상으로 인해 침대에 누워 있어야만 하는 인지적으로 온
전한 14세 아이는 둘 다 비교적 움직이지 못할 수 있다. 그러나 그 청소년은 호
흡관이나 영양관과 같은 의료 기기를 떼어 내거나 그렇지 않으면 그 기능을 손
상시킬 수도 있는 (몸) 뒤집기와 같은 동작에 대해 더 잘 알고 있고 그것을 더
잘 조절할 것으로 기대될 수 있다. 마찬가지로, 심박 조율기를 이식받은 5세와
25세의 사람은 각각 그들이 그 기기를 보호해야 한다는 것을 알고 있을 수는
있지만, 위험과 인과 관계에 대한 이해 및 충동 조절에서 발달상의 차이가, 예
를 들자면 현관에서 뛰어내리는 것과 같은 어린이의 위험한 행동의 가능성을
증가시킨다.

Why? 왜 정답일까?

의학적 문제가 있는 어린이들은 비슷한 상황에 있는 청소년이나 어른에 비해 기기를 떼
어내거나 손상시킬 수 있는 행동을 잘 통제하거나 조절하지 못하기에 위험한 행동을 할
가능성이 높다는 내용을 두 가지 예시로 보여준 글이다. 따라서 예시의 내용을 일반화하
는 빈칸에 들어갈 말로 가장 적절한 것은 아이들의 행동 제어력이 '기기를 보호하는 것'과
관련이 있다는 의미를 완성하는 ① '기기 안전'이다.

- exert ⓥ 발휘하다
- crib ⓝ (난간이 있는) 유아용 침대
- intact ⓐ 온전한
- inactive ⓐ 활동하지 않는
- otherwise ⓐⓓ 그렇지 않으면
- functioning ⓝ 기능
- causation ⓝ 인과 관계, 야기
- probability ⓝ 가능성
- relevant to ~와 관련된
- cognitively ⓐⓓ 인지적으로
- confined to ~에 틀어박힌
- adolescent ⓝ 청소년
- impair ⓥ 손상시키다
- implant ⓥ 이식하다, 심다
- impulse ⓝ 충동
- diagnosis ⓝ 진단

구문 풀이

10행 Likewise, a 5-year-old and a 25-year-old [who have had
<u>주어1(선행사)</u> <u>주격 관·대 복수 동사</u>
a cardiac pacemaker implanted] may each know that they need
<u>동사1</u> <u>접속사(~것)</u>
to protect the device, but developmental differences (in the
<u>주어2</u>

---

03 | 행동에 대한 의식과 진화적 적합성 | 정답률 43% | 정답 ②

다음 빈칸에 들어갈 말로 가장 적절한 것을 고르시오.

① disconnecting the link from its circumstance
상황과의 연결고리를 단절하는
☑ having conscious access to its own actions
자기 자신의 행동에 의식적인 접근을 하는
③ sharpening its own intuitions and instincts
자신만의 직관과 본능을 연마하는
④ relying on its individual prior experiences
자신의 이전 경험에 의존하는
⑤ activating its innate survival mechanism
타고난 생존 기제를 발동시키는

Evolutionary biologist Robert Trivers / gives an extraordinary example of a
case / where an animal having conscious access to its own actions / may be
damaging to its evolutionary fitness.
진화 생물학자 Robert Trivers는 / 탁월한 사례를 제시한다. / 자기 자신의 행동에 의식적인 접근을 하는 동물이
/ 자신의 진화적 적합성에 해를 줄 수 있다는

When a hare is being chased, / it zigzags in a random pattern / in an attempt
to shake off the pursuer.
산토끼가 쫓기고 있을 때, / 그것은 무작위 방식으로 지그재그로 나아간다. / 추격자를 떨쳐 내기 위한 시도로

This technique will be more reliable / if it is genuinely random, / as it is
better / for the hare to have no foreknowledge / of where it is going to jump
next: / if it knew where it was going to jump next, / its posture might reveal
clues to its pursuer.
이 기술은 좀 더 믿을 만할 것이다. / 그 기술이 정말로 무작위라면 / 더 좋기 때문에, / 산토끼가 미리 알지 못하
는 것이 / 다음에 자신이 어디로 뛰어오를 것인지를 / 만약 산토끼가 다음에 자신이 어디로 뛰어오를지 안다면, /
그것의 자세가 자신의 추격자에게 단서를 드러낼지도 모른다.

Over time, dogs would learn to anticipate these cues / — with fatal
consequences for the hare.
시간이 지나, 개들이 이러한 신호들을 예상하는 것을 배우게 될 것이고, / 이는 산토끼에게 치명적인 결과를 가져
올 것이다.

Those hares with more self-awareness / would tend to die out, / so most
modern hares are probably descended from those / that had less self-
knowledge.
좀 더 자기 인식을 하는 그런 산토끼들이 / 멸종되는 경향이 있을 것이므로, / 오늘날의 산토끼들 대부분은 산토끼
들의 후손일 것이다. / 아마도 자각을 덜 했던

In the same way, humans may be descended from ancestors / who were
better at the concealment of their true motives.
마찬가지로, 인간들은 조상들의 후손일지도 모른다. / 자신의 진짜 동기들을 숨기는 것을 더 잘했던

It is not enough to conceal them from others / — to be really convincing, /
you also have to conceal them from yourself.
그것들을 다른 사람들한테 숨기는 것은 충분치 않으며, / 확실히 설득력이 있으려면 / 여러분 자신한테도 그것들
을 숨겨야 한다.

진화 생물학자 Robert Trivers는 자기 자신의 행동에 의식적인 접근을 하는 동
물이 자신의 진화적 적합성에 해를 줄 수 있다는 탁월한 사례를 제시한다. 산
토끼가 쫓기고 있을 때, 그것은 추격자를 떨쳐 내기 위한 시도로 무작위 방식
으로 지그재그로 나아간다. 산토끼가 다음에 자신이 어디로 뛰어오를 것인지
를 미리 알지 못하는 것이 더 좋기 때문에, 그 기술이 정말로 무작위라면 이것
은 좀 더 믿을 만할 것이다. 만약 산토끼가 다음에 자신이 어디로 뛰어오를지
안다면, 그것의 자세가 자신의 추격자에게 단서를 드러낼지도 모른다. 시간이
지나, 개들이 이러한 신호들을 예상하는 것을 배우게 될 것이고, 이는 산토끼
에게 치명적인 결과를 가져올 것이다. 좀 더 자기 인식을 하는 그런 산토끼들
이 멸종되는 경향이 있을 것이므로, 오늘날의 산토끼들 대부분은 아마도 자각
을 덜 했던 산토끼들의 후손일 것이다. 마찬가지로, 인간들은 자신의 진짜 동
기들을 숨기는 것을 더 잘했던 조상들의 후손일지도 모른다. 그것들을 다른 사
람들한테 숨기는 것은 충분치 않으며, 확실히 (행동에) 설득력이 있으려면 여
러분 자신한테도 그것들을 숨겨야 한다.

Why? 왜 정답일까?

'~ if it knew where it was going to jump next, its posture might reveal
clues to its pursuer. ~ Those hares with more self-awareness would
tend to die out, so most modern hares are probably descended from
those that had less self-knowledge.'에서 자신의 행동을 더 잘 자각하는 산토끼
는 자신이 다음에 어디로 향할 것인지를 미리 알고 있어 자세 등으로 추격자에게 힌트를

줄 수 있고, 그리하여 더 멸종될 가능성이 높다고 설명하고 있다. 이를 토대로 '자신의 행동을 더 잘 자각하고 있는 것'이 진화적으로는 더 해가 된다는 결론을 내릴 수 있으므로, 빈칸에 들어갈 말로 가장 적절한 것은 ② '자기 자신의 행동에 의식적인 접근을 하는'이다.

● evolutionary ⓐ 진화적인	● extraordinary ⓐ 탁월한
● fitness ⓝ 적합성	● chase ⓥ 쫓다
● in an attempt to ~하기 위한 시도로	● shake off ⓥ 떨쳐내다
● genuinely [ad] 정말로	● foreknowledge ⓝ 미리 앎, 예측
● anticipate ⓥ 예상하다	● fatal ⓐ 치명적인
● consequence ⓝ 결과	● self-awareness ⓝ 자기 인식
● die out ⓥ 멸종하다	● be descended from ⓥ ~의 자손이다
● concealment ⓝ 숨김, 은폐	● convincing ⓐ 설득력 있는
● disconnect ⓥ 단절하다	● sharpen ⓥ (기술 등을) 연마하다
● activate ⓥ 발동시키다, 활성화하다	● innate ⓐ 타고난

구문 풀이

6행 This technique will be more reliable if it is genuinely random,
└~ 때문에   미래시제   조건 접속사└현재시제
as it is better for the hare to have no foreknowledge of where it is
└가주어   의미상 주어   진주어   의문부사
going to jump next: if it knew where it was going to jump next,
                                 「if + 주어 + 과거 동사 ~
its posture might reveal clues to its pursuer.
주어 + 조동사 과거형 + 동사원형 … : 가정법 과거(현재 사실의 반대 가정)」

---

04 무해한 자극 앞에서 움직임을 계속하는 동물   정답률 38% | 정답 ④

다음 빈칸에 들어갈 말로 가장 적절한 것을 고르시오. [3점]

① weigh the benefits of treating familiar things with care
익숙한 것을 조심해서 다루는 것의 이점을 따져 볼
② plan escape routes after predicting possible attacks
공격 가능성을 예측한 후에 퇴로를 계획할
③ overcome repeated feeding failures for survival
생존을 위해 반복된 먹이 섭취의 실패를 극복할
✓④ operate in the presence of harmless stimuli
무해한 자극 앞에서 움직일
⑤ monitor the surrounding area regularly
주변 지역을 정기적으로 모니터할

Enabling animals to <u>operate in the presence of harmless stimuli</u> / is an almost universal function of learning.
동물이 무해한 자극 앞에서 움직일 수 있게 하는 것은 / 학습의 거의 보편적인 기능이다.
Most animals innately avoid objects / they have not previously encountered.
대부분의 동물은 선천적으로 대상을 피한다. / 그들이 이전에 마주치지 않은
Unfamiliar objects may be dangerous; / treating them with caution has survival value.
익숙하지 않은 대상은 위험할 수 있으므로, / 그것을 조심해서 다루는 것은 생존가(生存價)를 갖는다.
If persisted in, however, / such careful behavior could interfere / with feeding and other necessary activities / to the extent that the benefit of caution would be lost.
그러나 그러한 신중한 행동이 지속된다면, / 그 행동은 방해할 수도 있다. / 먹이 섭취와 다른 필요한 활동을 / 조심해서 얻는 이익이 소실될 정도로
A turtle / that withdraws into its shell at every puff of wind / or whenever a cloud casts a shadow / would never win races, / not even with a lazy rabbit.
거북은 / 바람이 조금 불 때마다 등껍질 속으로 움츠리는 / 또는 구름이 그림자를 드리울 때마다 / 경주를 결코 이기지 못할 것이다. / 게으른 토끼와의 경주라도
To overcome this problem, / almost all animals habituate to safe stimuli / that occur frequently.
이 문제를 극복하기 위해, / 거의 모든 동물은 안전한 자극에 익숙해져 있다. / 자주 발생하는
Confronted by a strange object, / an inexperienced animal may freeze or attempt to hide, / but if nothing unpleasant happens, / sooner or later it will continue its activity.
낯선 대상에 직면하면, / 경험이 없는 동물은 얼어붙거나 숨으려고 할 수도 있지만, / 불쾌한 일이 일어나지 않으면 / 그것은 머잖아 활동을 계속할 것이다.
The possibility also exists / that an unfamiliar object may be useful, / so if it poses no immediate threat, / a closer inspection may be worthwhile.
가능성도 있으므로, / 익숙하지 않은 대상이 유용할 / 그것이 즉각적인 위험을 주지 않는다면, / 더 자세히 살펴보는 것이 가치가 있을 수도 있다.

동물이 무해한 자극 앞에서 움직일 수 있게 하는 것은 학습의 거의 보편적인 기능이다. 대부분의 동물은 선천적으로 이전에 마주치지 않은 대상을 피한다. 익숙하지 않은 대상은 위험할 수 있으므로, 그것을 조심해서 다루는 것은 생존가(生存價)를 갖는다. 그러나 그러한 신중한 행동이 지속된다면, 그 행동은 조심해서 얻는 이익이 소실될 정도로 먹이 섭취와 다른 필요한 활동을 방해할 수도 있다. 바람이 조금 불 때마다, 또는 구름이 그림자를 드리울 때마다 등껍질 속으로 움츠리는 거북은 게으른 토끼와의 경주라도 결코 이기지 못할 것이다.

이 문제를 극복하기 위해, 거의 모든 동물은 자주 발생하는 안전한 자극에 익숙해져 있다. 낯선 대상에 직면하면, 경험이 없는 동물은 얼어붙거나 숨으려고 할 수도 있지만, 불쾌한 일이 일어나지 않으면 그것은 머잖아 활동을 계속할 것이다. 익숙하지 않은 대상이 유용할 가능성도 있으므로, 그것이 즉각적인 위협을 주지 않는다면, 더 자세히 살펴보는 것이 가치가 있을 수도 있다.

Why? 왜 정답일까?

'To overcome this problem, ~' 이하로 동물은 모든 상황에서 위험을 피하려다 먹이를 못 찾게 되는 지경에 이르지 않기 위해 자주 발생하는 안전한 자극에 대한 익숙함을 키우며, 낯선 대상을 마주친 상황에서도 불쾌한 일이 뒤따르지 않는 한 하던 일을 지속한다는 내용이 이어지고 있다. 따라서 빈칸에 들어갈 말로 가장 적절한 것은 동물의 이러한 행동 경향을 잘 요약한 ④ '무해한 자극 앞에서 움직일'이다.

● universal ⓐ 보편적인	● encounter ⓥ 마주치다
● unfamiliar ⓐ 친숙하지 않은	● caution ⓝ 주의
● persist ⓥ 지속하다	● interfere with ~을 방해하다
● withdraw ⓥ 물러나다, 철수하다	● cast ⓥ 드리우다, 던지다
● overcome ⓥ 극복하다	● habituate to ~에 길들이다
● inexperienced ⓐ 미숙한	● pose a threat 위협을 가하다
● immediate ⓐ 즉각적인, 당면한	● inspection ⓝ 조사
● weigh ⓥ 따져보다, 저울질하다	● harmless ⓐ 무해한

구문 풀이

5행 If (it is) persisted in, however, such careful behavior
접속사└ 생략   과거분사구   주어
could interfere with feeding and other necessary activities to the
동사구   목적어1   목적어2
extent {that the benefit of caution would be lost}. [ ] : 동격(= the extent)

---

05 살아 있는 듯한 움직임으로 인해 드는 생각   정답률 52% | 정답 ①

다음 빈칸에 들어갈 말로 가장 적절한 것을 고르시오. [3점]

✓① fool us into thinking that something has a mind
어떤 것이 생각을 가지고 있다고 믿도록 우리를 속일
② help us release and process certain feelings
우리가 어떤 감정을 표출하고 처리하는 데 도움을 줄
③ shift our energy and protective mechanisms
우리의 에너지와 방어기제를 바꿀
④ secretly unlock emotions that words cannot
말이 드러내지 못하는 감정을 은밀히 드러낼
⑤ create a definite sense of achievement
확실한 성취감을 자아낼

Like faces, / sometimes movement can <u>fool us</u> / <u>into thinking that something has a mind</u>.
얼굴과 마찬가지로, / 움직임은 간혹 우리를 속일 수 있다. / 어떤 것이 생각을 가지고 있다고 믿도록
For example, / toys that seem to come alive / fascinate children.
예를 들어, / 살아 움직이는 것처럼 보이는 장난감은 / 아이들을 매료시킨다.
In my day, / one of the popular toys / was a piece of finely coiled wire / called a "Slinky."
내가 어렸을 적 / 인기 있던 장난감 중 하나는 / 촘촘하게 나선형으로 감긴 뭉치의 철사였다. / 'Slinky'라는
It could appear to walk / by stretching and lifting up one end over another / down an incline, / a bit like an acrobatic caterpillar.
이것은 걷는 것처럼 보일 수 있는데, / 한쪽 끝을 늘리면서 다른 쪽 끝 위로 들어 올려서 / 경사면 아래로 / 애벌레가 곡예를 부리는 것과 약간 비슷하다.
The attraction of the Slinky on Christmas Day / was the lifelike movement it had / as it stepped down the stairs / before someone trod on it / or twisted the spring and ruined it for good.
크리스마스 날 Slinky의 매력은 / 그것이 지녔던 생동감 있는 움직임이었다. / 그것이 계단을 내려갈 때 / 누군가가 밟기 전까지 / 또는 스프링을 비틀어 영원히 망가뜨리기
Toys that appear to be alive / are curiosities / because they challenge / how we think inanimate objects and living things should behave.
살아 있는 듯 보이는 장난감은 / 진기한 물건이다. / 그것들이 거스르기 때문에 / 우리가 생각하는 무생물과 생물의 행동 방식을
Many toys today exploit this principle to great effect, / but be warned: / not all babies enjoy objects / that suddenly seem lifelike.
오늘날 많은 장난감이 이 원리를 이용해 큰 효과를 내려고 하지만 / 주의해야 하는데, / 모든 아기가 물건을 좋아하는 것은 아니다. / 갑자기 살아 있는 것처럼 보이는
This anxiety probably reflects their confusion over the question, / "Is it alive or what?"
이러한 불안감은 아마도 질문에 대한 그들의 혼란을 나타낸다. / "저게 살아있는 거야 뭐야?"라는
Once babies decide that something is alive, / they are inclined to see its movements as purposeful.
일단 아기는 무언가가 살아 있다고 판단하면, / 그들은 그것의 움직임을 의도적인 것으로 보는 경향이 있다.

표정과 마찬가지로, 움직임은 간혹 어떤 것이 생각을 가지고 있다고 믿도록 우

리를 속일 수 있다. 예를 들어, 살아 움직이는 것처럼 보이는 장난감은 아이들을 매료시킨다. 내가 어렸을 적 인기 있던 장난감 중 하나는 'Slinky'라는 촘촘하게 나선형으로 감긴 한 뭉치의 철사였다. 이것은 한쪽 끝을 늘리면서 다른 쪽 끝 위로 들어 올려서 경사면 아래로 걷는 것처럼 보일 수 있는데, 애벌레가 곡예를 부리는 것과 약간 비슷하다. 크리스마스 날 Slinky의 매력은 누군가가 밟거나 스프링을 비틀어 영원히 망가뜨리기 전까지 그것이 계단을 내려올 때 보인 생동감 있는 움직임이었다. 살아 있는 듯 보이는 장난감은 우리가 생각하는 무생물과 생물의 행동 방식을 거스르기 때문에 진기한 물건이다. 오늘날 많은 장난감이 이 원리를 이용해 큰 효과를 내려고 하지만 주의해야 하는데, 모든 아기가 갑자기 살아 있는 것처럼 보이는 물건을 좋아하는 것은 아니다. 이러한 불안감은 아마도 "저게 살아있는 거야 뭐야?"라는 질문에 대한 그들의 혼란을 나타낸다. 일단 무언가가 살아 있다고 판단하면, 아기는 그것의 움직임을 의도적인 것으로 보는 경향이 있다.

Why? 왜 정답일까?

마지막 문장에서 아이들은 무언가가 살아있다고 믿으면 그것의 움직임을 의도적인 것으로 생각한다고 했다(Once babies decide that something is alive, they are inclined to see its movements as purposeful.). 이는 실제로 무생물인 대상이 살아있다고 여겨지면 그것이 생각과 의도를 갖는 주체라고 여기게 되는 인지적 경향을 설명한 것이다. 따라서 빈칸에 들어갈 말로 가장 적절한 것은 ① '어떤 것이 생각을 가지고 있다고 믿도록 우리를 속일'이다.

- **fascinate** ⓥ 매료시키다
- **caterpillar** ⓝ 애벌레
- **for good** 영원히
- **exploit** ⓥ 이용하다
- **purposeful** ⓐ 의도적인
- **unlock** ⓥ 드러내다, 열다
- **finely** ⓐ 미세하게
- **trod on** ~을 발로 밟다
- **inanimate** ⓐ 무생물의
- **be inclined to** ~하는 경향이 있다
- **fool A into B** A를 속여 B하게 하다

구문 풀이

7행 The attraction of the Slinky on Christmas Day was
주어(단수) / 동사
the lifelike movement [it had] as it stepped down the stairs before
보어(선행사) / 접속사(~할 때) / 접속사(~하기 전에)
someone trod on it or twisted the spring and ruined it for good.
동사1 / 동사2 / 동사3

---

06 경험과 기억에 따라 다르게 느껴지는 시간의 흐름 정답률 40% | 정답 ⑤

다음 빈칸에 들어갈 말로 가장 적절한 것을 고르시오. [3점]

① the memory functions of our brain wear out with age
우리 뇌의 기억 기능이 나이가 들면서 마모된다
② the richness of experiences relies on intellectual capacity
경험의 풍부함은 지능에 의존한다
③ the information storage system in our mind runs restlessly
뇌 속의 정보 저장 체계가 쉴새없이 작동한다
④ the temporal context of an event pulls our emotions awake
사건의 시간적 맥락이 우리의 감정을 깨운다
✓ ⑤ the size of a memory and our perception of time are coupled
기억의 양과 시간에 대한 우리의 인식이 연결되어 있다

Science shows / that the size of a memory and our perception of time are coupled / like gear teeth in a bicycle chain.
과학은 보여 준다. / 기억의 양과 시간에 대한 우리의 인식이 연결되어 있다는 것을 / 자전거 체인의 톱니처럼

Rich and novel experiences, / like the recollections of the summers of our youth, / have lots of new information associated with them.
다채롭고 새로운 경험들은 / 우리의 어린 시절 여름날의 기억과 같은 / 그것들과 관련된 많은 새로운 정보를 가지고 있다.

During those hot days, / we learned how to swim / or traveled to new places / or mastered riding a bike without training wheels.
그 뜨거운 날 동안 / 우리는 수영하는 법을 배웠거나 / 새로운 장소로 여행을 갔거나 / 보조 바퀴 없이 자전거를 타는 것을 완벽히 익혔다.

The days went by slowly with those adventures.
그날들은 그러한 모험들로 천천히 흘러갔다.

Yet, our adult lives have less novelty and newness, / and are full of repeated tasks / such as commuting or sending email or doing paperwork.
그러나 성년기의 우리 삶은 새로움과 생소함이 더 적고 / 반복되는 일로 가득 차 있다. / 통근하거나 이메일을 보내거나 서류 작업을 하는 것 같은

The associated information filed for those chores / is smaller, / and there is less new footage / for the recall part of the brain to draw upon.
그러한 지루한 일에 대해 보관된 관련 정보는 / 더 적고 / 새로운 장면이 더 적다. / 두뇌의 기억 부분이 이용할 수 있는

Our brain interprets these days filled with boring events as shorter, / so summers swiftly speed by.
우리의 두뇌는 지루한 일로 채워진 이러한 날들을 더 짧다고 이해하며 / 따라서 여름날이 빠르게 지나간다.

Despite our desire for better clocks, / our measuring stick of time isn't fixed.
더 나은 시계를 향한 우리의 바람에도 불구하고 / 우리의 시간 측정 잣대는 고정되어 있지 않다.

We don't measure time with seconds, like our clocks, / but by our experiences.
우리는 우리의 시계처럼 시간을 초로 측정하는 것이 아니라 / 우리의 경험으로 측정한다.

For us, time can slow down or time can fly.
우리에게 시간은 느려질 수도 있고 빠르게 흘러갈 수도 있다.

과학은 자전거 체인의 톱니처럼 기억의 양과 시간에 대한 우리의 인식이 연결되어 있다는 것을 보여 준다. 우리의 어린 시절 여름날의 기억과 같은 다채롭고 새로운 경험들은 그것들과 관련된 많은 새로운 정보를 가지고 있다. 그 뜨거운 날 동안 우리는 수영하는 법을 배웠거나 새로운 장소로 여행을 갔거나 보조 바퀴 없이 자전거를 타는 것을 완벽히 익혔다. 그날들은 그러한 모험들로 천천히 흘러갔다. 그러나 성년기의 우리 삶은 새로움과 생소함이 더 적고 통근하거나 이메일을 보내거나 서류 작업을 하는 것 같은 반복되는 일로 가득 차 있다. 그러한 지루한 일에 대해 보관된 관련 정보는 더 적고 두뇌의 기억 부분이 이용할 수 있는 새로운 장면이 더 적다. 우리의 두뇌는 지루한 일로 채워진 이러한 날들을 더 짧다고 이해하며 따라서 여름날이 빠르게 지나간다. 더 나은 시계를 향한 우리의 바람에도 불구하고 우리의 시간 측정 잣대는 고정되어 있지 않다. 우리는 시계처럼 시간을 초로 측정하는 것이 아니라 우리의 경험으로 측정한다. 우리에게 시간은 느려질 수도 있고 빠르게 흘러갈 수도 있다.

Why? 왜 정답일까?

빈칸 뒤에 따르면 새롭고 다채로운 일들이 가득했던 어린 시절에는 시간이 천천히 흐르지만, 성년기에 접어들어 일상이 반복되는 일로 채워지면 시간은 더 빨리 흐른다. 그리하여 마지막 두 문장(We don't measure time with seconds, like our clocks, but by our experiences. For us, time can slow down or time can fly.)에서는 우리가 시간을 고정된 잣대로 측정하지 않고 '경험'에 따라 그 흐름을 판단하기 때문에 시간이 느려질 수도 있고 빨라질 수도 있다고 결론내린다. 이에 근거할 때, 빈칸에 들어갈 말로 가장 적절한 것은 우리의 시간 흐름이 우리의 경험이나 기억과 연동되어 있다는 의미를 완성하는 ⑤ '기억의 양과 시간에 대한 우리의 인식이 연결되어 있다'이다.

- **gear tooth** 톱니
- **recollection** ⓝ 기억, 추억
- **draw upon** ~을 이용하다, ~에 의지하다
- **swiftly** ⓐ 빠르게
- **wear out** 마모되다
- **restlessly** ⓐ 쉴새없이
- **novel** ⓐ 새로운
- **commuting** ⓝ 통근
- **interpret A as B** A를 B로 해석하다
- **fixed** ⓐ 고정된
- **with age** 나이가 들면서, 늙어감에 따라
- **temporal** ⓐ 시간적인

구문 풀이

2행 Rich and novel experiences, (like the recollections of the
주어 / 전치사(~처럼)
summers of our youth), have lots of new information associated
( ): 삽입구 / 동사(복수) / 목적어 / 과거분사
with them.

★★★ 1등급 대비 고난도 2점 문제

07 뉴스의 표현 방식 정답률 33% | 정답 ⑤

다음 빈칸에 들어갈 말로 가장 적절한 것을 고르시오.

① coordination with traditional display techniques
전통적인 표현 기법과의 조화
② prompt and full coverage of the latest issues
최신 이슈에 대한 신속하고도 완전한 취재
③ educational media contents favoured by producers
제작자가 선호하는 교육용 매체 내용
④ commitment to long-lasting news standards
오래도록 지속하는 뉴스 기준에 대한 전념
✓ ⑤ verbal and visual idioms or modes of address
언어적, 시각적 표현 양식이나 전달 방식

News, especially in its televised form, / is constituted / not only by its choice of topics and stories / but by its verbal and visual idioms or modes of address.
뉴스, 특히 텔레비전으로 방송되는 형태는 / 구성된다. / 그것이 선택하는 주제와 이야기뿐만 아니라 / 그것의 언어적, 시각적 표현 양식이나 전달 방식에 의해서도

Presentational styles have been subject to a tension / between an informational-educational purpose / and the need to engage us entertainingly.
표현 방식은 긴장 상태에 영향을 받아 왔다. / 정보 제공 및 교육적 목적과 / 재미있게 우리의 주의를 끌 필요성 사이의

While current affairs programmes are often 'serious' in tone / sticking to the 'rules' of balance, / more popular programmes adopt a friendly, lighter, idiom / in which we are invited / to consider the impact of particular news items / from the perspective of the 'average person in the street'.

시사 프로그램들이 흔히 어조가 '진지하지만', / 균형이라는 '규칙'을 고수하면서 / 더 대중적인 프로그램들은 친근하고 더 가벼운 표현 양식을 채택하는데 / 그 표현 양식에서 우리는 요청된다 / 특정 뉴스 기사의 영향을 고려해보게 / '거리에서 만나는 보통 사람'의 관점에서

Indeed, / contemporary news construction / has come to rely on an increased use / of faster editing tempos and 'flashier' presentational styles / including the use of logos, / sound-bites, / rapid visual cuts / and the 'star quality' of news readers.

사실, / 현대의 뉴스 구성은 / 더 많은 이용에 의존하게 되었다. / 더 빠른 편집 속도와 '더 현란한' 표현 방식의 / 로고의 이용을 포함한 / 짤막한 방송용 어구, / 빠른 시각적 편집 화면, / 그리고 뉴스 독자의 '스타성'을

Popular formats can be said to enhance understanding / by engaging an audience / unwilling to endure the longer verbal orientation of older news formats.

대중적인 구성은 이해를 높였다고 할 수 있다. / 시청자의 주의를 끌어서 / 장황한 언어를 지향하는 오래된 뉴스 구성 방식을 견딜 의사가 없는

However, / they arguably work to reduce understanding / by failing to provide the structural contexts for news events.

하지만, / 그것은 아마 틀림없이 이해를 감소시키는 효과가 있다. / 뉴스 사건에 관한 구조적 맥락을 제공하지 못하여

뉴스, 특히 텔레비전으로 방송되는 형태는 그것이 선택하는 주제와 이야기뿐만 아니라 그것의 언어적, 시각적 표현 양식이나 전달 방식에 의해서도 구성된다. 표현 방식은 정보 제공 및 교육적 목적과 재미있게 우리의 주의를 끌 필요성 사이의 긴장 상태에 영향을 받아 왔다. 시사 프로그램들이 흔히 균형이라는 '규칙'을 고수하면서 어조가 '진지하지만', 더 대중적인 프로그램들은 친근하고 더 가벼운 표현 양식을 채택하는데 그 표현 양식에서 우리는 '거리에서 만나는 보통 사람'의 관점에서 특정 뉴스 기사의 영향을 고려해보게 요청된다. 사실, 현대의 뉴스 구성은 로고, 짤막한 방송용 어구, 빠른 시각적 편집 화면, 그리고 뉴스 독자의 '스타성'을 이용하는 것을 포함한 더 빠른 편집 속도와 '더 현란한' 표현 방식을 더 많이 이용하는 것에 의존하게 되었다. 대중적인 구성은 장황한 언어를 지향하는 오래된 뉴스 구성 방식을 견딜 의사가 없는 시청자의 주의를 끌어서 이해를 높였다고 할 수 있다. 하지만 그것은 뉴스 사건에 관한 구조적 맥락을 제공하지 못하여 아마 틀림없이 이해를 감소시키는 효과가 있다.

Why? 왜 정답일까?

빈칸 문장에서 텔레비전으로 방송되는 뉴스는 주제나 내용 뿐 아니라 '빈칸'으로도 구성된다고 하는데, 바로 다음 문장에서 '표현 방식(Presentational styles)'을 언급하고 있다. 글의 나머지 부분에서도 현대의 뉴스가 어구, 화면 구성 등 '표현 양식' 면에서 더 가볍고 현란한 방식을 채택한다는 내용이 주를 이룬다. 따라서 빈칸에 들어갈 말로 가장 적절한 것은 ⑤ '언어적, 시각적 표현 양식이나 전달 방식'이다.

- constitute ⓥ 구성하다
- entertainingly ⓐⓓ 재미있게, 유쾌하게
- contemporary ⓐ 현대의
- enhance ⓥ 높이다, 향상시키다
- endure ⓥ 견디다
- arguably ⓐⓓ 거의 틀림없이
- commitment ⓝ 전념, 헌신
- subject to ~에 영향 받는
- stick to ~을 고수하다
- rely on ~에 의지하다
- unwilling to ~할 의사가 없는
- orientation ⓝ 지향
- prompt ⓐ 신속한

구문 풀이

6행 While current affairs programmes are often 'serious' in tone
　　　　접속사(~한 반면)
sticking to the 'rules' of balance, more popular programmes adopt
a friendly, lighter, idiom [in which we are invited to consider the
　　　　　　　　　　　　선행사　　=where　　　　　~하도록 요청받다
impact of particular news items from the perspective of the 'average
person in the street'].

★★ 문제 해결 꿀~팁 ★★

▶ **많이 틀린 이유는?**

'~ an audience unwilling to endure the longer verbal orientation of older news formats.'에서 뉴스 시청자들은 장황한 언어를 사용하는 '옛날(older)' 뉴스 방식을 견디지 못한다고 했다. 따라서 글에 따르면 오늘날 뉴스는 뉴스의 내용뿐 아니라 더 '재미있고 가벼운' 전달 방식에도 초점을 맞추고 있다. 이를 근거로 볼 때, 뉴스가 '전통적(traditional)' 전달 방식과의 조화를 도모한다는 의미의 ①은 글의 흐름과 정반대된다.

▶ **문제 해결 방법은?**

빈칸 뒤에 바로 Presentational styles라는 키워드가 등장하며 뉴스의 '전달 방식'을 주요하게 다루는 것으로 보아, '방식(modes)'이라는 단어를 그대로 포함한 ⑤가 답으로 가장 적절하다.

---

08 대륙 방향에 따른 농작물 확산　　　정답률 29% | 정답 ②

다음 빈칸에 들어갈 말로 가장 적절한 것을 고르시오. [3점]

① isolation – 고립　　　　　✓ orientation – 방향
③ diversity – 다양성　　　　④ conservation – 보존
⑤ instability – 불안정성

Not only was Eurasia by chance / blessed with biological abundance, / but the very orientation of the continent / greatly promoted the spread of crops between distant regions.

유라시아는 우연히 ~했을 뿐만 아니라 / 생물학적 풍부함으로 축복받았을 / 그 대륙의 방향이야말로 / 멀리 떨어진 지역 간의 농작물들의 확산을 크게 촉진시켰다.

When the supercontinent Pangea fragmented, / it was torn apart along rifts / that just so happened to leave Eurasia as a broad landmass / running in an east-west direction / — the entire continent stretches / more than a third of the way around the world, / but mostly within a relatively narrow range of latitudes.

초대륙 판게아가 조각났을 때, / 그것은 갈라진 틈을 따라 분열되었다. / 유라시아를 넓은 땅덩어리로 우연히 남겨두었던 / 동서 방향으로 가로지르는 / 그 전체 대륙은 뻗어있다 / 세계를 둘러싼 거리의 3분의 1 이상, / 하지만 대부분 상대적으로 좁은 위도의 범위 내에서

As it is the latitude on the Earth / that largely determines the climate and length of the growing season, / crops domesticated in one part of Eurasia / can be transplanted across the continent / with only minimal need for adaptation to the new locale.

바로 지구의 위도가 / 기후와 성장 계절의 길이를 주로 결정하기 때문에, / 유라시아의 한 지역에서 재배된 농작물들은 / 대륙을 가로질러 이식될 수 있다. / 새로운 장소에의 적응에 대한 단지 최소한의 필요만 지닌 채

Thus wheat cultivation spread readily / from the uplands of Turkey / throughout Mesopotamia, to Europe, / and all the way round to India, / for example.

그러므로 밀 재배는 손쉽게 퍼져나갔다. / 터키의 고지대로부터 / 메소포타미아 전역, 유럽으로, / 그리고 인도에 이르기까지 / 예를 들어

The twin continents of the Americas, / by contrast, / lie in a north-south direction.

아메리카의 한 쌍의 대륙은 / 대조적으로 / 남북 방향으로 놓여 있다.

Here, / the spreading of crops / originally domesticated in one region / to another / led to a much harder process of re-adapting the plant species / to different growing conditions.

이곳에서는 / 농작물들이 퍼지는 것은 / 한 지역에서 본래 재배된 / 또 다른 지역으로 / 식물종을 재적응시키는 훨씬 더 어려운 과정을 야기했다. / 다른 성장 환경에

유라시아는 우연히 생물학적 풍부함으로 축복받았을 뿐만 아니라, 그 대륙의 방향이야말로 멀리 떨어진 지역 간의 농작물들의 확산을 크게 촉진시켰다. 초대륙 판게아가 조각났을 때, 그것은 유라시아를 동서 방향으로 가로지르는 넓은 땅덩어리로 우연히 남겨두었던 갈라진 틈을 따라 분열되었다. 그 전체 대륙은 세계를 둘러싼 거리의 3분의 1 이상, 하지만 대부분 상대적으로 좁은 위도의 범위 내에서 뻗어있다. 바로 지구의 위도가 기후와 성장 계절의 길이를 주로 결정하기 때문에, 유라시아의 한 지역에서 재배된 농작물들은 새로운 장소에 적응할 필요성이 오로지 최소인 채로 대륙을 가로질러 이식될 수 있다. 그러므로 예를 들어 밀 재배는 터키의 고지대로부터 메소포타미아 전역, 유럽으로, 그리고 인도에 이르기까지 손쉽게 퍼져나갔다. 대조적으로 아메리카의 한 쌍의 대륙은 남북 방향으로 놓여 있다. 이곳에서는 한 지역에서 본래 재배된 농작물들이 또 다른 지역으로 퍼지는 것은 식물종을 다른 성장 환경에 재적응시키는 훨씬 더 어려운 과정을 야기했다.

Why? 왜 정답일까?

남북 방향으로 뻗은 아메리카 대륙과는 달리, 유라시아는 동서 방향으로 뻗어 있어(Eurasia as a broad landmass running in an east-west direction) 같은 위도에서 자라는 농작물이 쉽게 대륙 전역에 퍼질 수 있다는 내용의 글이다. 따라서 빈칸에 들어갈 말로 가장 적절한 것은 ② '방향'이다.

- by chance 우연히, 뜻밖에
- abundance ⓝ 풍부함
- promote ⓥ 촉진하다
- crop ⓝ 농작물
- region ⓝ 지방, 지역
- fragment ⓥ 조각나다
- rift ⓝ 갈라진 틈
- landmass ⓝ 땅덩어리
- stretch ⓥ 뻗어 있다
- narrow ⓐ 좁은
- latitude ⓝ 위도
- biological ⓐ 생물학의
- continent ⓝ 대륙
- spread ⓝ 확산
- distant ⓐ 먼, (멀리) 떨어져 있는
- supercontinent ⓝ 초대륙
- tear apart 분열시키다, 떼어놓다
- broad ⓐ (폭이) 넓은
- direction ⓝ 방향
- relatively ⓐⓓ 상대적으로, 비교적
- range ⓝ 범위
- climate ⓝ 기후

DAY 02

- growing season (식물의) 성장 시기
- transplant ⓥ 이식하다
- locale ⓝ 장소, 현장
- readily [ad] 손쉽게
- by contrast 그에 반해서, 그와 대조적으로
- originally [ad] 원래, 본래
- isolation ⓝ 고립
- instability ⓝ 불안정
- domesticate ⓥ (작물을) 재배하다
- minimal ⓐ 아주 적은, 최소의
- cultivation ⓝ 재배, 경작
- upland ⓝ 고지대
- lie ⓥ 놓여 있다
- process ⓝ 과정
- orientation ⓝ 방향

구문 풀이

1행 Not only was Eurasia by chance blessed with biological
「부정어구＋be＋주어＋과거분사 : 도치 구문」
abundance, but the very orientation of the continent greatly promoted
the spread of crops between distant regions.

★★ 문제 해결 꿀~팁 ★★

▶ 많이 틀린 이유는?
biological abundance, the spread of crops 등 키워드만 얼핏 보면 '생물
다양성, 작물 종류' 등에 관한 글처럼 보이지만, 유라시아 대륙이 '동서'로 뻗어서 지
니는 이점을 설명하는 것이 핵심이다. 따라서 ③ '다양성'은 주제와 거리가 멀다.

▶ 문제 해결 방법은?
가로로 넓은 유라시아 대륙과 비교되는 대상이 세로로 길게 뻗은 아메리카 양 대륙임
을 고려하면 대륙의 '방향'에 초점을 둔 글임을 쉽게 파악할 수 있다.

★★★ 1등급 대비 고난도 3점 문제

09 지표면에 따라 조절되는 다리의 경직도   정답률 32% | 정답 ①

다음 빈칸에 들어갈 말로 가장 적절한 것을 고르시오. [3점]

✔ varied little – 거의 달라지지 않았다
② decreased a lot – 많이 감소했다
③ suddenly peaked – 갑자기 최고조에 달했다
④ gradually appeared – 점차 나타났다
⑤ were hardly generated – 거의 발생되지 않았다

Research with human runners / challenged conventional wisdom / and found
/ that the ground-reaction forces at the foot / and the shock transmitted up
the leg and through the body / after impact with the ground / varied little / as
runners moved from extremely compliant / to extremely hard running
surfaces.
달리는 사람에 관한 연구는 / 사회적 통념에 이의를 제기하여 / 알아냈다 / 발에 작용하는 지면 반발력과 / 다리
위로 몸을 통해 전달되는 충격은 / 지면과의 충격 이후에 / 거의 달라지지 않았다는 것을 / 달리는 사람이 매우
말랑말랑한 지표면에서 / 매우 단단한 지표면으로 옮겨갔을 때

As a result, / researchers gradually began to believe / that runners are
subconsciously able to adjust leg stiffness / prior to foot strike / based on
their perceptions / of the hardness or stiffness of the surface / on which they
are running.
결과적으로 / 연구자들은 점차 믿기 시작했다. / 달리는 사람은 다리의 경직도를 잠재의식 차원에서 조정할 수
있다고 / 발이 땅에 닿기 전에 / 자신의 인식을 바탕으로 / 지표면의 경도나 경직도에 대한 / 자신이 달리고 있는

This view suggests / that runners create soft legs / that soak up impact forces
/ when they are running on very hard surfaces / and stiff legs / when they are
moving along on yielding terrain.
이 견해는 제시한다. / 달리는 사람은 푹신한 다리를 만들고 / 충격력을 흡수하는 / 그들이 매우 단단한 지표면에
서 달리고 있을 때는 / 그리고 단단한 다리를 만든다고 / 그들이 물렁한 지형에서 움직일 때는

As a result, impact forces passing through the legs / are strikingly similar /
over a wide range of running surface types.
그 결과 다리를 통해 전해지는 충격력은 / 놀랄 만큼 비슷하다. / 아주 다양한 지표면 유형에 걸쳐서

Contrary to popular belief, / running on concrete / is not more damaging to
the legs / than running on soft sand.
통념과는 반대로, / 콘크리트 위를 달리는 것은 / 다리에 더 해롭지는 않다. / 푹신한 모래 위를 달리는 것보다

달리는 사람에 관한 연구는 사회적 통념에 이의를 제기하여 발에 작용하는 지
면 반발력과 발이 지면에 부딪히고 난 후에 다리 위로 몸을 통해 전달되는 충
격은 달리는 사람이 매우 말랑말랑한 지표면에서 매우 단단한 지표면으로 옮
겨갔을 때 거의 달라지지 않았다는 것을 알아냈다. 결과적으로 연구자들은 점
차 달리는 사람은 자신이 달리고 있는 지표면의 경도나 경직도에 대한 자신의
인식을 바탕으로 발이 땅에 닿기 전에 다리의 경직도를 잠재의식 차원에서 조
정할 수 있다고 믿기 시작했다. 이 견해에 따르면, 달리는 사람은 매우 단단한
지표면에서 달리고 있을 때는 충격력을 흡수하는 푹신한 다리를 만들고 물렁
한 지형에서 움직일 때는 단단한 다리를 만든다. 그 결과 다리를 통해 전해지

는 충격력은 아주 다양한 지표면 유형에 걸쳐서 놀랄 만큼 비슷하다. 통념과는
반대로, 콘크리트 위를 달리는 것은 푹신한 모래 위를 달리는 것보다 다리에
더 해롭지는 않다.

Why? 왜 정답일까?

'As a result, impact forces passing through the legs are strikingly
similar over a wide range of running surface types.'에서 물렁한 표면이든
단단한 표면이든 상관없이 다리를 통해 몸에 전달되는 충격은 비슷하다고 하므로, 빈칸
에 들어갈 말로 가장 적절한 것은 ① '거의 달라지지 않았다'이다.

- transmit ⓥ 전달하다
- extremely [ad] 극도로
- stiffness ⓝ 경직도, 뻣뻣함
- soak up ⓥ ~을 흡수하다
- strikingly [ad] 놀랄 만큼
- impact ⓝ 충격, 영향
- gradually [ad] 점차
- perception ⓝ 인식
- yielding ⓐ 유연한
- damaging ⓐ 해로운

구문 풀이

1행 Research with human runners challenged conventional
동사1
wisdom and found that the ground-reaction forces at the foot and
동사2 접속사(~것) 주어1
the shock [transmitted up the leg and through the body after impact
주어2 과거분사
with the ground] varied little as runners moved from extremely
동사 부사 접속사(~할 때) 「from＋A＋
compliant (surfaces) to extremely hard running surfaces.
to＋B : A에서 B로」

★★ 문제 해결 꿀~팁 ★★

▶ 많이 틀린 이유는?
마지막 두 문장에 따르면 어느 표면에서 달리든 다리에 가해지는 힘은 비슷하며, 더
딱딱한 바닥에서 달린다고 다리에 더 무리가 가지는 않는다고 한다. ⑤는 다리에 가
해지는 힘이 '거의 발생되지 않는다'는 의미인데, 글에서 힘의 발생 자체를 부정하지
는 않았다. ②, ③은 표면에 따라 다리가 받는 힘이 '달라진다'는 의미를 나타내므로
주제와 상충된다.

▶ 문제 해결 방법은?
글이 '연구'를 소개하며 시작되므로 후반부에 주제가 있다. 중반부의 예시는 가볍게
훑고 결론에서 답의 근거를 찾도록 한다.

★★★ 1등급 대비 고난도 3점 문제

10 우리의 사실 해석에 영향을 미치는 우리의 믿음   정답률 38% | 정답 ①

다음 빈칸에 들어갈 말로 가장 적절한 것을 고르시오. [3점]

✔ our beliefs influence how we interpret facts
우리의 믿음이 우리가 사실을 해석하는 방식에 영향을 미친다
② what we see is an illusion of our past memories
우리가 보는 것은 우리 과거 경험의 환상이다
③ even photographs can lead to a wrong visual perception
심지어 사진도 잘못된 시각 인식을 초래할 수 있다
④ there is no standard by which we can judge good or bad
우리가 옳고 그름을 판단할 수 있는 기준은 없다
⑤ we adhere to our intuition in spite of irresistible evidence
우리는 반박할 수 없는 증거에도 불구하고 직관을 고수한다

If you are unconvinced / that our beliefs influence how we interpret facts, /
consider the example of the "flying horse."
만약 여러분이 확신하지 못한다면, / 우리의 믿음이 우리가 사실을 해석하는 방식에 영향을 미친다는 것을 / '날고
있는 말'의 사례를 생각해보라.

Depictions of galloping horses / from prehistoric times up until the mid-
1800s / typically showed horses' legs splayed / while galloping, / that is, the
front legs reaching far ahead / as the hind legs stretched far behind.
질주하는 말의 묘사는 / 선사 시대부터 1800년대 중반까지 / 말의 다리가 벌어져 있는 것을 전형적으로 보여 주
었다. / 질주하는 동안 / 즉 앞다리를 멀리 앞으로 내딛는 모습을 / 뒷다리를 뒤로 멀리 뻗은 채

People just "knew" / that's how horses galloped, / and that is how they "saw"
them galloping.
사람들은 그저 '알고 있었고', / 그것이 말이 질주하는 방식이라고 / 그리고 그것은 그들이 말이 질주하는 것을
'본' 방식이었다.

Cavemen *saw* them this way, / Aristotle *saw* them this way, / and so did
Victorian gentry.
동굴 거주인들도 그것들을 이런 식으로 보았고, / 아리스토텔레스도 보았고, / 빅토리아 시대의 상류층도 그랬다.

But all of that ended / when, in 1878, Eadweard Muybridge published a set
of twelve
pictures / he had taken of a galloping horse in the space of less than half a
second / using twelve cameras hooked to wire triggers.

그러나 그 모든 것은 끝이 났다. / 1878년 Eadweard Muybridge가 일련의 사진 열두 장을 공개했을 때 / 그가 0.5초도 안 되는 사이에 질주하는 말을 찍은 / 와이어 트리거에 연결된 열두 대의 카메라를 사용하여

Muybridge's photos showed clearly / that a horse goes completely airborne / in the third step of the gallop / with its legs *collected* beneath it, / not splayed.
Muybridge의 사진은 분명히 보여 주었다. / 말이 완전히 공중에 뜬 채 가는 것을 / 질주의 세 번째 스텝에서 / 그 말의 다리가 *모아진* 상태로 / 벌어지지 않고

It is called the moment of suspension.
그것은 부유의 순간이라고 불린다.

Now even kids draw horses galloping this way.
지금은 아이들도 이런 식으로 질주하는 말을 그린다.

만약 여러분이 우리의 믿음이 우리가 사실을 해석하는 방식에 영향을 미친다는 것을 확신하지 못한다면, '날고 있는 말'의 사례를 생각해보라. 선사 시대부터 1800년대 중반까지 질주하는 말의 묘사는 질주하는 동안 말의 다리가 벌어져 있는 것을, 즉 뒷다리를 뒤로 멀리 뻗은 채 앞다리를 멀리 앞으로 내딛는 모습을 전형적으로 보여 준다. 그것이 그들이 말이 그렇게 질주한다고 그저 '알고 있었고', 말이 그렇게 질주하는 것을 '보았다'. 동굴 거주인들도 그것들을 이런 식으로 보았고, 아리스토텔레스도 보았고, 빅토리아 시대의 상류층도 그랬다. 그러나 그 모든 것은 1878년 Eadweard Muybridge가 와이어 트리거에 연결된 열두 대의 카메라를 사용하여 0.5초도 안 되는 사이에 질주하는 말을 찍은 일련의 사진 열두 장을 공개했을 때 끝이 났다. Muybridge의 사진은 말이 보통 질주의 세 번째 스텝에서 그 말 다리가 벌어지지 않고 *모아진* 상태로 완전히 공중에 뜬 채 가는 것을 분명히 보여 주었다. 그것은 부유의 순간이라고 불린다. 지금은 아이들도 이런 식으로 질주하는 말을 그린다.

Why? 왜 정답일까?

빈칸 뒤의 예시를 바탕으로 추론한 결론을 빈칸에 넣어야 하는 문제이다. 예시에 따르면, 과거에 사람들은 질주하는 말의 다리가 앞뒤로 벌어진다고 믿고 그렇게 '보았다'고 믿었으나, 실제로 달리는 말을 촬영했을 때 다리가 모아진다는 것을 알게 되었다고 한다. 즉, 사람들은 현상을 있는 그대로 알기보다 자신이 믿는 대로 보았다는 것이 핵심 내용이므로, 빈칸에 들어갈 말로 가장 적절한 것은 ① '우리의 믿음이 우리가 사실을 해석하는 방식에 영향을 미친다'이다.

- unconvinced ⓐ 확신하지 않는
- gallop ⓝ 질주 ⓥ 질주하다
- splay ⓥ 벌리다
- caveman ⓝ 동굴 거주인
- hook ⓥ 연결하다
- completely ⓐⓓ 완전히
- collect ⓥ 모으다
- interpret ⓥ 해석하다
- perception ⓝ 지각
- intuition ⓝ 직관
- irresistible ⓐ 저항할 수 없는
- depiction ⓝ 묘사
- prehistoric ⓐ 선사 시대의
- stretch ⓥ 뻗다
- gentry ⓝ 상류층
- trigger ⓝ 트리거, 방아쇠
- airborne ⓐ 하늘에 떠 있는
- suspension ⓝ (공중에) 부유(한 상태)
- illusion ⓝ 환상
- adhere to ~을 고수하다
- in spite of ~에도 불구하고

구문 풀이

10행 But all of that ended when, in 1878, Eadweard Muybridge
      접속사(~할 때)
published a set of twelve pictures [(that) he had taken of a galloping
              선행사   목적격 관·대 주어 동사
horse in the space of less than half a second using twelve cameras
                                              분사구문(~해서)
hooked to wire triggers].

★★ 문제 해결 꿀~팁 ★★

▶ 많이 틀린 이유는?
예시의 결론을 완성하는 빈칸 문제이다. 예시 내용은 과거에 사람들이 말이 뛰는 모습을 '믿는 대로 봤다' 나중에서야 실제와 달랐음을 깨닫게 되었다는 내용인데, 이는 '과거 경험(의 환상)'과는 관련이 없다. 따라서 **past memories**라는 엉뚱한 키워드가 포함된 ②는 답으로 적절하지 않다.

▶ 문제 해결 방법은?
과거 내용이 많이 나온다고 해서 **past**를 키워드로 오해하면 안 된다. 핵심은 실제 사실과 다른 내용을 사람들이 '본다고 착각했었다'는 것이다.

★★★ 1등급 대비 고난도 3점 문제

11 소매점에서의 가격 결정   정답률 29% | 정답 ④

다음 빈칸에 들어갈 말로 가장 적절한 것을 고르시오. [3점]

① reflect the principle of demand and supply
   수요와 공급의 원칙을 반영한다

② may not change from hour to hour
   시간마다 달라지지 않을 수도 있다
③ go up due to bad weather
   나쁜 날씨로 인해 올라간다
✓④ do not adjust to market forces over time
   시간이 지나면서 시장의 힘에 조정되지 않는다
⑤ can be changed by the farmer's active role
   농부의 적극적인 역할로 인해 바뀔 수 있다

Although prices in most retail outlets are set by the retailer, / this does not mean / that these prices do not adjust to market force over time.
대부분의 소매점에서 가격은 소매상에 의해 결정되지만, / 이 말은 의미하지는 않는다. / 이런 가격이 시간이 지나면서 시장의 힘에 조정되지 않는다는 것을

On any particular day / we find / that all products have a specific price ticket on them.
그 어느 특정한 날에도 / 우리는 안다. / 모든 제품에 명확한 가격표가 붙어 있다는 것을

However, / this price may be different / from day to day or week to week.
그러나 / 이 가격은 다를 수 있다. / 날마다 또는 주마다

The price / that the farmer gets from the wholesaler / is much more flexible from day to day / than the price / that the retailer charges consumers.
가격은 / 도매상에게서 농부가 받는 / 그날그날 훨씬 더 유동적이다. / 가격보다 / 소매상이 소비자에게 부과하는

If, for example, bad weather leads to a poor potato crop, / then the price that supermarkets have to pay / to their wholesalers for potatoes / will go up / and this will be reflected in the prices / they mark on potatoes in their stores.
예를 들어, 악천후가 감자의 흉작을 초래한다면, / 슈퍼마켓이 지급해야 하는 가격은 / 감자에 대해 도매상에게 / 상승할 것이다. / 이것은 가격에 반영될 것이다. / 그들이 자기 가게의 감자에 매기는

Thus, / these prices do reflect the interaction of demand and supply / in the wider marketplace for potatoes.
따라서 / 이 가격은 수요와 공급의 상호 작용을 정말로 반영하는 것이다. / 더 광범위한 감자 시장의

Although they do not change in the supermarket from hour to hour / to reflect local variations in demand and supply, / they do change over time / to reflect the underlying conditions / of the overall production of and demand / for the goods in question.
그 가격이 슈퍼마켓에서 시간마다 바뀌지는 않지만, / 수요와 공급의 지역적 변동을 반영하기 위해 / 그 가격은 시간이 지나면서 정말로 바뀐다. / 기저 상황을 반영하기 위해 / 전체적인 생산과 수요의 / 문제되는 상품의

대부분의 소매점에서 가격은 소매상에 의해 결정되지만, 이 말은 이런 가격이 시간이 지나면서 시장의 힘에 조정되지 않는다는 것을 의미하지는 않는다. 그 어느 특정한 날에도 우리는 모든 제품에 명확한 가격표가 붙어 있다는 것을 안다. 그러나 이 가격은 날마다 또는 주마다 다를 수 있다. 도매상에게서 농부가 받는 가격은 소매상이 소비자에게 부과하는 가격보다 그날그날 훨씬 더 유동적이다. 예를 들어, 악천후가 감자의 흉작을 초래한다면, 감자에 대해 슈퍼마켓이 도매상에게 지급해야 하는 가격은 상승할 것이고, 이것은 그들이 자기 가게의 감자에 매기는 가격에 반영될 것이다. 따라서 이 가격은 더 광범위한 감자 시장의 수요와 공급의 상호 작용을 정말로 반영하는 것이다. 그 가격이 수요와 공급의 지역적 변동을 반영하기 위해 슈퍼마켓에서 시간마다 바뀌지는 않지만, 그 가격은 문제되는 상품의 전체적인 생산과 수요의 기저 상황을 반영하기 위해 시간이 지나면서 정말로 바뀐다.

Why? 왜 정답일까?

예시 앞뒤의 'However, this price may be different from day to day or week to week.'와 '~ they do change over time to reflect the underlying conditions of the overall production of and demand for the goods in question.'에서 상품의 소매가는 소매상에 의해 결정되기는 하지만 해당 상품의 생산과 수요와 관련된 기저 상황을 반영하기 위해 시간에 따라 달라질 수 있음을 이야기한다. 이때 빈칸 문장은 전체적으로 '~을 의미하지는 않는다'와 같이 해석되므로, 빈칸 안에는 주제와 반대되는 내용이 들어가야 주제에 부합하는 문장이 완성된다. 따라서 빈칸에 들어갈 말로 가장 적절한 것은 ④ '시간이 지나면서 시장의 힘에 조정되지 않는다'이다.

- retail ⓝ 소매, 유통 ⓐ 소매의
- wholesaler ⓝ 도매상
- reflect ⓥ 반영하다
- underlying ⓐ 기저의
- in question 문제의, 논의되고 있는
- adjust ⓥ 조정[조절]하다
- specific ⓐ 특정한, 구체적인
- charge ⓥ (요금·값을) 청구하다 ⓝ 요금
- variation ⓝ 변동, 변화
- overall ⓐ 전반적인, 전체적인
- supply ⓥ 공급하다 ⓝ 공급
- force ⓝ 힘, 영향력

구문 풀이

1행 Although they do not change in the supermarket from
      양보 접속사
hour to hour to reflect local variations in demand and supply, /
              ~하기 위해
they do change over time to reflect the underlying conditions of
      동사 강조
the overall production of and demand for the goods in question.
      ~의 전반적인 생산   ~의 수요   of/for의 공통 목적어

★★ **문제 해결 꿀~팁** ★★

▶ **많이 틀린 이유는?**
전체적인 주제는 '비록 소매가가 매 시간 바뀌는 않을지 몰라도 제품의 수요 및 공급에 관한 기저 상황을 반영하여 시간에 따라 바뀐다'는 것인데, 빈칸 문장에 **not**이 있으므로 주제와 반대되는 말을 빈칸에 넣어야 한다. ①을 넣으면 '수요와 공급의 법칙을 반영한다는 뜻은 아니다'라는 의미가 되므로 주제와 어긋난다. ② 또한 '시간마다 달라지지 않을 수도 있다'라는 말이 주제와 합하므로 빈칸 문장에 넣어서 읽어보면 주제와 반대되는 뜻이 완성된다.

▶ **문제 해결 방법은?**
빈칸 문제에서 선택지가 헷갈리는 경우에는 선택지를 빈칸에 넣고 전체 문장을 해석한 뒤, 이 해석이 주제와 맞는지를 검토한다.

★★★ 1등급 대비 고난도 3점 문제

12 친환경 기술 개발을 위한 자원 공급을 늘릴 필요성 정답률 46% | 정답 ①

다음 빈칸에 들어갈 말로 가장 적절한 것을 고르시오. [3점]

✓① our ability to secure the ingredients to produce them
그것을 생산하기 위한 재료를 확보할 수 있는 우리의 능력
② our effort to make them as eco-friendly as possible
그것을 가능한 한 친환경적이게 만들고자 하는 우리의 노력
③ the wider distribution of innovative technologies
혁신 기술의 더 광범위한 보급
④ governmental policies not to limit resource supplies
자원 공급을 제한하지 않는 정부 정책
⑤ the constant update and improvement of their functions
그 기능의 지속적인 업데이트와 개선

The future of our high-tech goods may lie / not in the limitations of our minds, / but in our ability to secure the ingredients to produce them.
첨단 기술 제품의 미래는 있는 것이 아니라, / 우리 생각의 제한점에 / 그것을 생산하기 위한 재료를 확보할 수 있는 우리의 능력에 있을지도 모른다.

In previous eras, such as the Iron Age and the Bronze Age, / the discovery of new elements / brought forth seemingly unending numbers of new inventions.
철기와 청동기와 같은 이전 시대에, / 새로운 원소의 발견은 / 끝이 없을 것 같은 무수한 새로운 발명품을 낳았다.

Now the combinations may truly be unending.
이제 그 조합은 진정 끝이 없을 수도 있다.

We are now witnessing a fundamental shift / in our resource demands.
우리는 이제 근본적인 변화를 목격하고 있다. / 자원 수요에 있어서

At no point in human history / have we used *more* elements, / in *more* combinations, and in increasingly refined amounts.
인류 역사의 어느 지점에서도, / 우리는 (지금보다) 더 *많은* 원소를 사용한 적은 없었다. / 더 *많은* 조합으로, 그리고 점차 정밀한 양으로

Our ingenuity will soon outpace our material supplies.
우리의 창의력은 우리의 물질 공급을 곧 앞지를 것이다.

This situation comes at a defining moment / when the world is struggling to reduce its reliance on fossil fuels.
이 상황은 결정적인 순간에 온다. / 세계가 화석연료에 대한 의존을 줄이고자 분투하고 있는

Fortunately, rare metals are key ingredients in green technologies / such as electric cars, wind turbines, and solar panels.
다행히, 희귀한 금속들이 친환경 기술의 핵심 재료이다. / 전기 자동차, 풍력 발전용 터빈, 태양 전지판과 같은

They help to convert free natural resources / like the sun and wind / into the power that fuels our lives.
그것들은 천연 자유재를 전환하는 데 도움을 준다. / 태양과 바람과 같은 / 우리의 생활에 연료를 공급하는 동력으로

But without increasing today's limited supplies, / we have no chance of developing the alternative green technologies / we need to slow climate change.
하지만 오늘날의 제한된 공급을 늘리지 않고는, / 우리는 친환경 대체 기술을 개발할 가망이 없다. / 기후 변화를 늦추기 위해 우리가 필요로 하는

첨단 기술 제품의 미래는 우리 생각의 제한점에 있는 것이 아니라, 그것을 생산하기 위한 재료를 확보할 수 있는 우리의 능력에 있을지도 모른다. 철기와 청동기와 같은 이전 시대에, 새로운 원소의 발견은 끝이 없을 것 같은 무수한 새로운 발명품을 낳았다. 이제 그 조합은 진정 끝이 없을 수도 있다. 우리는 이제 자원 수요에 있어서 근본적인 변화를 목격하고 있다. 인류 역사의 어느 지점에서도, 우리는 (지금보다) 더 *많은* 조합으로, 그리고 점차 정밀한 양으로, 더 *많은* 원소를 사용한 적은 없었다. 우리의 창의력은 우리의 물질 공급을 곧 앞지를 것이다. 이 상황은 세계가 화석연료에 대한 의존을 줄이고자 분투하고 있는 결정적인 순간에 온다. 다행히, 희귀한 금속들이 전기 자동차, 풍력 발전용 터빈, 태양 전지판과 같은 친환경 기술의 핵심 재료이다. 그것들은 태양과 바람과 같은 천연 자유재를 우리의 생활에 연료를 공급하는 동력으로 전환하

는 데 도움을 준다. 하지만 오늘날의 제한된 공급을 늘리지 않고는, 우리는 기후 변화를 늦추기 위해 우리가 필요로 하는 친환경 대체 기술을 개발할 가망이 없다.

Why? 왜 정답일까?

글 중반에서 우리의 창의력은 우리의 물질 공급을 곧 앞지르게 될 것이라고 언급한 후, 마지막 문장에서 오늘날의 제한된 공급량을 늘리지 않고서는 우리가 화석연료에 대한 의존을 줄이고자 개발하려 하는 친환경 대체 기술을 개발할 수 없다(But without increasing today's limited supplies, we have no chance of developing the alternative green technologies we need to slow climate change.)고 전망하고 있다. 따라서 빈칸에 들어갈 말로 가장 적절한 것은 충분한 자원 공급량의 확보가 중요함을 뜻하는 ① '그것을 생산하기 위한 재료를 확보할 수 있는 우리의 능력'이다.

- limitation ⓝ 한계
- element ⓝ 원소
- refined ⓐ 정밀한
- outpace ⓥ 앞지르다
- reliance ⓝ 의존
- alternative ⓐ 대체의
- distribution ⓝ 분배
- era ⓝ 시대
- witness ⓥ 목격하다
- ingenuity ⓝ 창의력
- struggle ⓥ 분투하다
- convert ⓥ 전환하다
- secure ⓥ 확보하다
- constant ⓐ 끊임없는

구문 풀이

8행 At no point in human history have we used *more* elements,
「부정어구 + have + 주어 + 과거분사 : 도치 구문」
in *more* combinations, and in increasingly refined amounts.

★★ **문제 해결 꿀~팁** ★★

▶ **많이 틀린 이유는?**
에너지 기술을 소재로 한 글로 첫 문장인 주제문을 완성하는 빈칸 문제이다. 최다 오답인 ②의 경우 지문의 키워드인 '친환경'을 포함하고 있지만, 본문의 또 다른 키워드인 '자원'을 포함하고 있지 않아 오답이다.

▶ **문제 해결 방법은?**
글에 But이 나오면 중요한 내용은 뒤에 나온다. 이 지문 또한 마지막 문장의 But 뒤로 '제한된 공급' 때문에 신기술 개발이 어렵다고 지적하는 것으로 볼 때, '공급=자원'에 관한 언급이 빈칸에 들어가야 함을 알 수 있다.

DAY 03 · 빈칸 추론 03

01 ②	02 ①	03 ①	04 ②	05 ①
06 ②	07 ⑤	08 ④	09 ⑤	10 ⑤
11 ①	12 ②			

DAY 03

---

01 소비의 목적 변화
정답률 44% | 정답 ②

다음 빈칸에 들어갈 말로 가장 적절한 것을 고르시오.

① quantitative – 양적인
✓ nonmaterial – 비물질적인
③ nutritional – 영양의
④ invariable – 불변의
⑤ economic – 경제적인

People have always needed to eat, / and they always will.
사람들은 항상 먹을 것이 필요했으며, / 또 항상 그럴 것이다.

Rising emphasis on self-expression values / does not put an end to material desires.
자기표현 가치에 관한 늘어나는 강조가 / 물질적 욕구를 끝내지는 않는다.

But / prevailing economic orientations are gradually being reshaped.
하지만 / 우세한 경제적 방향성이 서서히 재형성되고 있다.

People who work in the knowledge sector / continue to seek high salaries, / but they place equal or greater emphasis / on doing stimulating work / and being able to follow their own time schedules.
지식 부문에서 일하는 사람들은 / 계속 높은 급료를 추구하지만, / 그들은 그 이상의 중점을 둔다. / 아주 즐거운 일을 하고 / 자기 시간 계획을 따를 수 있는 것에

Consumption is becoming progressively less determined / by the need for sustenance / and the practical use of the goods consumed.
소비는 점진적으로 결정되는 경우가 덜해진다. / 생존에 대한 필요와 / 소비되는 재화의 실용적 사용으로

People still eat, / but a growing component of food's value / is determined by its nonmaterial aspects.
사람들은 여전히 먹지만, / 음식 가치의 점점 더 많은 구성 요소는 / 그것의 비물질적인 측면에 의해 결정된다.

People pay a premium / to eat exotic cuisines / that provide an interesting experience / or that symbolize a distinctive life-style.
사람들은 추가 금액을 낸다. / 이국적인 요리를 먹으려고 / 흥미로운 경험을 제공하거나 / 독특한 생활 방식을 상징하는

The publics of postindustrial societies / place growing emphasis on "political consumerism," / such as boycotting goods whose production violates ecological or ethical standards.
탈공업화 사회의 대중은 / '정치적 소비주의'에 점점 더 많은 중점을 둔다. / 상품을 구매하기를 거부하는 것 같은 / 그것의 생산이 생태적 또는 윤리적 기준을 위반하는

Consumption is less and less a matter of sustenance / and more and more a question of life-style / — and choice.
소비는 생존의 문제로는 점점 덜 여겨지고, / 점점 더 생활 양식의 문제가 되고 있다. / 즉 선택

사람들은 항상 먹을 것이 필요했으며, 또 항상 그럴 것이다. 자기표현 가치에 관한 늘어나는 강조가 물질적 욕구를 끝내지는 않는다. 하지만 우세한 경제적 방향성이 서서히 재형성되고 있다. 지식 부문에서 일하는 사람들은 계속 높은 급료를 추구하지만, 그들은 아주 즐거운 일을 하고 자기 시간 계획을 따를 수 있는 것에 그 이상의 중점을 둔다. 소비는 점진적으로 생존에 대한 필요와 소비되는 재화의 실용적 사용으로 결정되는 경우가 덜해진다. 사람들은 여전히 먹지만, 음식 가치의 구성 요소는 점점 더 그것의 비물질적인 측면에 의해 결정된다. 사람들은 흥미로운 경험을 제공하거나 독특한 생활 방식을 상징하는 이국적인 요리를 먹으려고 추가 금액을 낸다. 탈공업화 사회의 대중은 '정치적 소비주의'에 점점 더 많은 중점을 두며, 생산이 생태적 또는 윤리적 기준을 위반하는 상품 구매를 거부하는 등의 행위를 한다. 소비는 생존의 문제로는 점점 덜 여겨지고, 점점 더 생활 양식, 즉 선택의 문제가 되고 있다.

Why? 왜 정답일까?

탈산업화 사회에서 소비는 생존의 문제보다는 생활 양식과 선택의 문제로 여겨지고 있다(Consumption is less and less a matter of sustenance and more and more a question of life-style — and choice.)는 내용이다. 빈칸 뒤에서 사람들이 이국적인 요리를 '경험'하는 것을 중시하고, 생태 또는 윤리적 가치를 위해 특정 물품 구매를 반대하는 등 '물질적이지 않은', 생활 양식적 측면에 의해 소비 행동을 결정하는 사례를 든다. 따라서 빈칸에 들어갈 말로 가장 적절한 것은 ② '비물질적인'이다.

- **emphasis** ⓝ 강조, 역점
- **put an end to** ~을 끝내다
- **self-expression** 자기 표현
- **desire** ⓝ 욕구, 욕망

- **prevail** ⓥ 우세하다
- **gradually** ⓐⓓ 점차
- **seek** ⓥ 추구하다
- **place** ⓥ 두다, 놓다
- **stimulating** ⓐ 아주 즐거운, 자극이 되는
- **progressively** ⓐⓓ 계속해서
- **component** ⓝ 구성 요소
- **exotic** ⓐ 이국적인
- **symbolize** ⓥ 상징하다
- **postindustrial** ⓐ 탈공업화의
- **boycott** ⓥ 불매하다
- **ecological** ⓐ 생태적인
- **orientation** ⓝ 방향, 지향
- **reshape** ⓥ 재형성하다
- **salary** ⓝ 급료
- **equal** ⓐ 똑같은
- **consumption** ⓝ 소비
- **sustenance** ⓝ 생명 유지, 지속
- **premium** ⓝ 추가 금액, 할증금
- **cuisine** ⓝ 요리
- **distinctive** ⓐ 독특한
- **consumerism** ⓝ 소비주의
- **violate** ⓥ 위반하다

구문 풀이

5행 People [who work in the knowledge sector] continue to seek
주어   주격 관계대명사   동사(복수)
high salaries, but they place equal or greater emphasis on doing
전치사 동명사1
stimulating work and being able to follow their own time schedules.
동명사2

---

02 음악의 의미를 구체화하는 가사
정답률 50% | 정답 ①

다음 빈칸에 들어갈 말로 가장 적절한 것을 고르시오.

✓ concrete – 구체적인
② obscure – 모호한
③ ethical – 윤리적인
④ unforeseen – 예견되지 않은
⑤ exaggerated – 과장된

Writing lyrics means shaping the meaning of something / which, if left as instrumental music, / would remain undefined; / there is a change of the level of expression.
가사를 쓰는 것은 무언가의 의미를 만드는 것을 의미한다. / 만약 기악곡으로 남겨진다면 / 막연한 채로 있을 / 표현 수준의 변화가 생긴다.

That's one reason / why for many songwriters / 'lyric' seems to be the hardest word.
그것이 한 가지 이유이다. / 곡을 쓰는 많은 사람들에게 / '가사'가 가장 어려운 말처럼 보이는

Picture this scene: / a songwriter at the piano, or with a guitar, / plays with chords / and creates an emotion and atmosphere / that is creatively inspiring.
이런 장면을 상상해 보라. / 곡을 쓰는 사람이 피아노나 기타로 / 코드를 활용하여 / 감정과 분위기를 만들어 낸다. / 독창적으로 영감을 불러일으키는

Our songwriter invents a melody to go with this mood.
곡을 쓰는 사람은 이 분위기에 잘 어울리는 멜로디를 만들어 낸다.

Then comes the moment / where words are required, / and that means getting specific.
그런 다음 순간이 오고, / 가사가 필요한 / 이는 곧 특정화됨을 의미한다.

This sad- or happy-sounding chord progression / must now direct its general sadness or happiness / to a *particular* human situation.
슬프거나 행복하게 들리는 이 코드의 진행은 / 이제 일반적인 슬픔이나 행복을 향하게 해야 한다. / 특정한 인간적 상황으로

A lyric is the place / where the emotional suggestions of pure music / are defined as concrete human concerns and events.
가사는 부분이다. / 순전히 음악만 있는 정서적 연상들이 / 구체적인 인간의 관심사와 사건으로 한정되는

It's like a piece of translation, / from one medium into another.
그것은 마치 한 편의 번역 작품과도 같다. / 한 매체에서 다른 매체로 바뀐

The general musical mood is focused by a lyric / into a context, a voice, a human drama.
막연한 음악적 분위기는 가사에 의해 초점이 맞춰진다. / 하나의 맥락, 하나의 목소리, 하나의 인간 드라마로

가사를 쓰는 것은 만약 기악곡으로 남겨진다면 막연한 채로 있을 무언가의 의미를 만드는 것을 의미한다. (그리하여) 표현 수준의 변화가 생긴다. 그것이 곡을 쓰는 많은 사람들에게 '가사'가 가장 어려운 말처럼 보이는 이유 중 하나이다. 이런 장면을 상상해 보라. 곡을 쓰는 사람이 피아노나 기타로 코드를 활용하여 독창적으로 영감을 불러일으키는 감정과 분위기를 만들어 낸다. 곡을 쓰는 사람은 이 분위기에 잘 어울리는 멜로디를 만들어 낸다. 그런 다음 가사가 필요한 순간이 오고, 이는 곧 특정화됨을 의미한다. 슬프거나 행복하게 들리는 이 코드의 진행은 이제 일반적인 슬픔이나 행복을 특정한 인간적 상황으로 향하게 해야 한다. 가사는 (가사 없이) 순전히 음악만 있는 정서적 연상들이 구체적인 인간의 관심사와 사건으로 한정되는 부분이다. 그것은 마치 한 매체에서 다른 매체로 바뀐 한 편의 번역 작품과도 같다. 막연한 음악적 분위기는 가사에 의해 하나의 맥락, 하나의 목소리, 하나의 인간 드라마로 초점이 맞춰진다.

Why? 왜 정답일까?

첫 문장과 마지막 문장에서 가사 쓰기를 통해 음악에 의미가 부여되며(Writing lyrics

[문제편 p.021]

means shaping the meaning of something ~), 막연한 분위기가 '하나의' 맥락, 목소리, 드라마로 집중될 수 있다(The general musical mood is focused by a lyric into a context, a voice, a human drama.)고 한다. 즉 가사를 쓰는 작업은 멜로디만 있는 곡의 막연하고 특정되지 않은 의미를 '한정시켜' 준다는 의미로서 빈칸에 들어갈 말로 가장 적절한 것은 ① '구체적인'이다.

- **undefined** ⓐ 막연한, 규정되지 않은
- **progression** ⓝ 진행, 진전
- **translation** ⓝ 번역, 이해
- **obscure** ⓐ 모호한
- **specific** ⓐ 구체적인
- **direct A to B** A를 B로 향하게 하다
- **concrete** ⓐ 구체적인
- **unforeseen** ⓐ 예견되지 않은

구문 풀이

1행 Writing lyrics means shaping the meaning of something
　　　　　　　　　　　　　　　　　　　　　　　　선행사
[which, (if left as instrumental music), would remain undefined];
주격 관·대　　（ ）: 삽입구(분사구문)
there is a change of the level of expression.

---

03 사회적 곤충들의 체온 조절 행동　　정답률 62% | 정답 ①

다음 빈칸에 들어갈 말로 가장 적절한 것을 고르시오.

✓① the activity of the insects in the colony – 군체 내에서 하는 이 곤충들의 활동
② the interaction with other species – 다른 종들과의 상호작용
③ the change in colony population – 군체 내의 개체 수 변화
④ the building materials of the habitat – 서식지의 건축 재료
⑤ the physical development of the inhabitants – 서식 동물들의 신체적 발달

Among the most fascinating natural temperature-regulating behaviors / are those of social insects / such as bees and ants.
가장 흥미로운 자연의 체온 조절 행동 중에는 / 사회적 곤충들의 행동이 있다. / 벌과 개미와 같은
These insects / are able to maintain a nearly constant temperature / in their hives or mounds / throughout the year.
이 곤충들은 / 거의 일정한 온도를 유지할 수 있다. / 자신들의 벌집이나 개미탑에서 / 일 년 내내
The constancy of these microclimates depends / not just on the location and insulation of the habitat, / but on the activity of the insects in the colony.
이러한 미기후의 지속성은 달려 있다. / 서식지의 위치와 단열뿐만 아니라, / 군체 내에서 하는 이 곤충들의 활동에도
When the surrounding temperature increases, / the activity in the hive decreases, / which decreases the amount of heat / generated by insect metabolism.
주변 온도가 올라가면, / 벌집 안에서의 활동은 줄어드는데, / 이는 열의 양을 감소시킨다. / 곤충의 신진대사에 의해 발생하는
In fact, / many animals decrease their activity in the heat / and increase it in the cold, / and people who are allowed to choose levels of physical activity / in hot or cold environments / adjust their workload / precisely to body temperature.
사실상, / 많은 동물은 더위 속에서는 자신들의 활동을 줄이고 / 추위 속에서는 활동을 늘리며, / 신체적 활동 수준을 선택할 수 있는 인간은 / 덥거나 추운 환경에서 / 자신들의 작업량을 조절한다. / 정확하게 체온에 맞추어
This behavior / serves to avoid both hypothermia and hyperthermia.
이러한 행동은 / 저체온증과 고체온증을 둘 다 피하는 데 도움이 된다.

가장 흥미로운 자연의 체온 조절 행동 중에는 벌과 개미와 같은 사회적 곤충들의 행동이 있다. 이 곤충들은 일 년 내내 자신들의 벌집이나 개미탑에서 거의 일정한 온도를 유지할 수 있다. 이러한 미기후의 지속성은 서식지의 위치와 단열뿐만 아니라, 군체 내에서 하는 이 곤충들의 활동에도 달려 있다. 주변 온도가 올라가면, 벌집 안에서의 활동은 줄어드는데, 이는 곤충의 신진대사에 의해 발생하는 열의 양을 감소시킨다. 사실상, 많은 동물은 더위 속에서는 자신들의 활동을 줄이고 추위 속에서는 활동을 늘리며, 덥거나 추운 환경에서 신체적 활동 수준을 선택할 수 있는 인간은 자신들의 작업량을 정확하게 체온에 맞추어 조절한다. 이러한 행동은 저체온증과 고체온증을 둘 다 피하는 데 도움이 된다.

Why? 왜 정답일까?

첫 문장에서 사회적 곤충들의 체온 조절 활동(natural temperature-regulating behaviors ~ of social insects)을 화제로 제시한 데 이어, 빈칸 뒤의 문장에서는 온도가 올라갈 때 벌집 안에서의 활동을 줄이는 벌들의 예를 들고 있다. 즉 이 글의 핵심은 군체 내 개체들이 군체에서의 활동량을 통제하여 체온을 조절하는 경우를 설명하는 것이므로, 빈칸에 들어갈 말로 가장 적절한 것은 ① '군체 내에서 하는 이 곤충들의 활동'이다.

- **fascinating** ⓐ 흥미로운, 매력적인
- **constant** ⓐ 일정한, 변함없는
- **microclimate** ⓝ 미기후
- **regulate** ⓥ 조절하다, 통제하다
- **mound** ⓝ 더미, 무더기, 돌무더기, 언덕
- **metabolism** ⓝ 신진대사

018 영어 독해 [빈칸·순서·삽입] – 실전

- **precisely** ad 정확히
- **population** ⓝ (전체) 인구 수
- **colony** ⓝ 군체, 집단, 부락, 식민지
- **inhabitant** ⓝ 서식 동물, 거주민

구문 풀이

1행 Among the most fascinating natural temperature-regulating
「among the + 최상급 + 복수명사: 가장 ~한 것들 중에」
behaviors are those of social insects such as bees and ants.
　　　　　동사(복수) ←　　→ 주어(= behaviors)

---

04 아름다움 그 자체로 인정받는 바우어　　정답률 55% | 정답 ②

다음 빈칸에 들어갈 말로 가장 적절한 것을 고르시오.

① block any possibility of reproduction
　번식의 가능성을 아예 차단한다
✓② aren't simply signals of mate quality
　단순히 짝의 자질에 대한 신호인 것은 아니다
③ hardly sustain their forms long enough
　거의 자기 형태를 충분히 오래 유지하지 못한다
④ don't let the mating competition overheat
　짝짓기 경쟁이 과열되게 두지 않는다
⑤ can be a direct indicator of aggressiveness
　공격성의 직접적 지표가 될 수 있다

Animals arguably make art.
동물은 거의 틀림없이 예술을 만든다.
The male bowerbirds of New Guinea and Australia / dedicate huge fractions of their time and energy / to creating elaborate structures / from twigs, flowers, berries, beetle wings, and even colorful trash.
뉴기니와 오스트레일리아의 수컷 바우어새는 / 자기 시간과 에너지의 큰 부분을 바친다. / 정교한 구조물을 만드는 데 / 나뭇가지, 꽃, 딸기류, 딱정벌레 날개, 그리고 심지어 다채로운 잡동사니로부터
These are the backdrops to their complex mating dances, / which include acrobatic moves and even imitations of other species.
이것들은 그들의 복잡한 짝짓기 춤을 위한 배경이며 / 그 춤은 곡예 동작과 심지어 다른 종들의 모방까지 포함한다.
What's most amazing / about the towers and "bowers" they construct / is / that they aren't stereotyped like a beehive or hummingbird nest.
가장 놀라운 점은 / 바우어새가 지은 탑과 '바우어'에 관해 / ~이다. / 이것이 벌집이나 벌새 둥지처럼 정형화되어 있지 않다는 것
Each one is different.
각각은 다르다.
Artistic skill, / along with fine craftsbirdship, / is rewarded by the females.
예술적 기술은 / 새의 정교한 장인정신과 함께 / 암컷에 의해 보상받는다.
Many researchers suggest / these displays are used by the females / to gauge the cognitive abilities of her potential mates, / but Darwin thought / that she was actually attracted to their *beauty*.
많은 연구자들은 말하지만, / 이 과시가 암컷들에 의해 이용된다고 / 자기 잠재적 짝의 인지적 능력을 측정하려고 / 다원은 생각했다. / 암컷이 실제로 그것의 *아름다움*에 끌렸다고
In other words, / the bowers aren't simply signals of mate quality; / they are appreciated by the females for their own sake, / much as we appreciate a painting or a bouquet of spring flowers.
다시 말해, / 바우어는 단순히 짝의 자질에 대한 신호인 것은 아니다. / 그것은 암컷들에게 그 자체로 감상된다. / 우리가 그림이나 봄꽃 한 다발을 감상하는 것처럼
A 2013 study looked at / whether bowerbirds that did better on cognitive tests / were more successful at attracting mates.
2013년의 한 연구는 ~을 살펴보았다. / 인지 검사에서 더 잘했던 바우어새가 / 짝을 유혹하는 데 더 성공적이었는지를
They were not, / suggesting / whatever the females are looking for, / it isn't a straightforward indicator of cognitive ability.
그들은 그렇지 않았다 / 이것은 시사한다. / 암컷이 찾는 것이 무엇이든, / 그것이 인지 능력의 직접적인 지표는 아니라는 것을

동물은 거의 틀림없이 예술을 만든다. 뉴기니와 오스트레일리아의 수컷 바우어새는 나뭇가지, 꽃, 딸기류, 딱정벌레 날개, 그리고 심지어 다채로운 잡동사니로부터 정교한 구조물을 만드는 데 자기 시간과 에너지의 큰 부분을 바친다. 이것들은 그들의 복잡한 짝짓기 춤을 위한 배경이며 그 춤은 곡예 동작과 심지어 다른 종들의 모방까지 포함한다. 바우어새가 지은 탑과 '바우어'의 가장 놀라운 점은 이것이 벌집이나 벌새 둥지처럼 정형화되어 있지 않다는 것이다. 각각은 다르다. 새의 정교한 장인정신과 함께 예술적 기술은 암컷에 의해 보상받는다. 많은 연구자들은 이 과시가 암컷들이 자기 잠재적 짝의 인지적 능력을 측정하려고 이용하는 것이라 말하지만, 다원은 암컷이 실제로 그것의 *아름다움*에 끌렸다고 생각했다. 다시 말해, 바우어는 단순히 짝의 자질에 대한 신호인 것은 아니다. 그것은 우리가 그림이나 봄꽃 한 다발을 감상하는 것처럼 암컷들에게 그 자체로 감상된다. 2013년의 한 연구는 인지 검사에서 더 잘했던 바우어새가 짝을 유혹하는 데 더 성공적이었는지를 살펴보았다. 그렇지 않았고, 이것은 암컷이 찾는 것이 무엇이든, 그것이 인지 능력의 직접적인 지표는 아니라는 것을 시사한다.

Why? 왜 정답일까?

빈칸 문장 앞뒤에서 수컷 바우어새가 지은 바우어는 단지 그 수컷이 좋은 짝이 될 만한 자질을 지녔다는 것을 보여주는 데 그치지 않고, 그 자체의 아름다움을 지니고 있어 감상의 대상이 된다(attracted to their *beauty* / appreciated by the females for their own sake)고 한다. 따라서 빈칸에 들어갈 말로 가장 적절한 것은 ② '단순히 짝의 자질에 대한 신호인 것은 아니다(aren't simply signals of mate quality)'이다.

- **arguably** [ad] 거의 틀림없이
- **hugeous** ⓐ 거대한
- **elaborate** ⓐ 정교한 ⓥ 자세히 말하다
- **backdrop** ⓝ 배경, 환경
- **beehive** ⓝ 벌집
- **gauge** ⓥ 측정하다
- **reproduction** ⓝ 번식, 재생
- **dedicate** ⓥ 바치다, 헌신하다
- **fraction** ⓝ 부분
- **twig** ⓝ (나무의) 잔가지
- **acrobatic** ⓐ 곡예의
- **hummingbird** ⓝ 벌새
- **straightforward** ⓐ 직접적인, 간단한
- **aggressiveness** ⓝ 공격성

구문 풀이

7행 [What's most amazing about the towers and "bowers"
[　]: 명사절 주어
they construct] is that they aren't stereotyped like a beehive or
동사(단수)　접속사(~것)　　　　전치사(~처럼)
hummingbird nest.

---

05 소득 증가와 식단 변화　　정답률 47% | 정답 ①

다음 빈칸에 들어갈 말로 가장 적절한 것을 고르시오.

✔ displace plant-based foods in people's diets
사람들의 식단에서 식물에 기반한 식품을 대체하기
② demand eco-friendly processing systems
친환경적인 가공 시스템을 요구하기
③ cause several nutritional imbalances
여러 가지 영양 불균형을 유발하기
④ indicate the consumers' higher social status
소비자의 더 높은 사회적 지위를 나타내기
⑤ play an important role in population growth
인구 증가에서 중요한 역할을 하기

With population growth slowing, / the strongest force / increasing demand for more agricultural production / will be *rising incomes*, / which are desired by practically all governments and individuals.
인구 증가가 둔화됨에 따라, / 가장 강력한 힘은 / 더 많은 농업 생산에 대한 수요를 증가시키는 / 높아지는 소득일 것인데, / 그것은 거의 모든 정부와 개인이 원하는 바이다.

Although richer people spend smaller proportions of their income on food, / in total they consume more food — and richer food, / which contributes to various kinds of disease and debilitation.
비록 더 부유한 사람들이 소득에서 더 낮은 비율을 음식에 소비하지만, / 그들은 통틀어 더 많은 음식 그리고 더 기름진 음식을 섭취하는데, / 그것은 다양한 종류의 질병과 건강 악화의 원인이 된다.

The changes in diet / that usually accompany higher incomes / will require relatively greater increases / in the production of feed grains, rather than food grains, / as foods of animal origin / partly displace plant-based foods in people's diets.
식단의 변화는 / 보통 더 높은 소득에 수반하는 / 상대적으로 더 큰 증가를 요구할 것인데, / 식용 곡물보다는 사료용 곡물의 생산에서 / 그 이유는 동물성 식품이 / 부분적으로 사람들의 식단에서 식물에 기반한 식품을 대체하기 때문이다.

It takes two to six times more grain / to produce food value through animals / than to get the equivalent value directly from plants.
2배에서 6배 더 많은 곡물이 필요하다. / 동물을 통해 영양가를 생산하려면 / 식물에서 직접 그와 동등한 영양가를 얻을 때보다

It is thus quite credible to estimate / that in order to meet economic and social needs / within the next three to five decades, / the world should be producing / more than twice as much grain and agricultural products / as at present, / but in ways that these are accessible to the food-insecure.
따라서 추정하는 것은 꽤 설득력이 있다. / 경제적 그리고 사회적 요구를 충족시키기 위해서는 / 향후 30년에서 50년 이내에 / 세계가 생산해야 하는데 / 2배가 넘는 곡물과 농산물을 / 현재보다 / 그러면서도 식량이 부족한 사람들도 이것들을 얻을 수 있는 방식으로 해야 한다고

인구 증가가 둔화됨에 따라, 더 많은 농업 생산에 대한 수요를 증가시키는 가장 강력한 힘은 높아지는 소득일 것인데, 그것은 거의 모든 정부와 개인이 원하는 바이다. 비록 더 부유한 사람들이 소득에서 더 낮은 비율을 음식에 소비하지만, 그들은 통틀어 더 많은 음식 그리고 더 기름진 음식을 섭취하는데, 그것은 다양한 종류의 질병과 건강 악화의 원인이 된다. 보통 더 높은 소득에 수반하는 식단의 변화는 식용 곡물보다는 사료용 곡물의 생산에서 상대적으로 더 큰 증가를 요구할 것인데, 그 이유는 동물성 식품이 부분적으로 사람들의 식단에서 식물에 기반한 식품을 대체하기 때문이다. 동물을 통해 영양가를 생산하려면 식물에서 직접 그와 동등한 영양가를 얻을 때보다 2배에서 6배 더 많은 곡물이 필요하다. 따라서 향후 30년에서 50년 이내에 경제적 그리고 사회

적 요구를 충족시키기 위해서는 세계가 현재보다 2배가 넘는 곡물과 농산물을 생산해야 하는데 그러면서도 식량이 부족한 사람들도 이것들을 얻을 수 있는 방식으로 해야 한다고 추정하는 것은 꽤 설득력이 있다.

Why? 왜 정답일까?

소득이 높아짐에 따라 사람들은 더 기름진 음식을 섭취하므로(~ in total they consume more food — and richer food, ~), 이에 맞추어 동물성 식품을 만들어내는 데 필요한 사료용 곡물과 농작물 생산이 비약적으로 늘어나야 한다고 설명하는 글이다. 따라서 빈칸에 들어갈 말로 가장 적절한 것은 ① '사람들의 식단에서 식물에 기반한 식품을 대체하기'이다.

- **agricultural** ⓐ 농업의
- **feed grain** 사료용 곡물
- **credible** ⓐ 설득력 있는, 믿을 만한
- **food-insecure** 식량이 부족한
- **processing** ⓝ (식품 등의) 가공, 처리
- **practically** [ad] 거의, 실질적으로
- **equivalent** ⓐ 동등한
- **accessible to** ~에 접근 가능한
- **plant-based** 식물에 기반한
- **imbalance** ⓝ 불균형

구문 풀이

1행 With population growth slowing, the strongest force
「with + 명사 + 분사: ~한 채로」　　　주어
[increasing demand for more agricultural production] will be
현재분사　　　　　　　　　　　　　　동사
rising incomes, which are desired by practically all governments
보어(선행사)　계속적 용법
and individuals.

---

06 자기 효능감이 높은 이들의 특징　　정답률 35% | 정답 ②

다음 빈칸에 들어갈 말로 가장 적절한 것을 고르시오. [3점]

① self-efficacy is not easy to define
자기 효능감은 정의내리기 쉽지 않다
✔ culture will have little or no impact on behavior
문화는 행동에 거의 혹은 전혀 영향을 주지 않을 것이다
③ setting a goal is important before starting a task
목표를 설정하는 것은 일을 시작하기 전에 중요하다
④ high self-efficacy is a typical quality of Australians
높은 자기 효능감은 호주들의 전형적 특징이다
⑤ judging the reaction from the community will be hard
공동체의 반응을 판단하기는 어려울 것이다

An individual characteristic / that moderates the relationship with behavior / is self-efficacy, / or a judgment of one's capability / to accomplish a certain level of performance.
개인적인 특징은 / 행동과의 관계를 조정하는 / 자기 효능감, / 즉 자신의 능력에 대한 판단이다. / 특정한 수준의 성과를 달성하는

People who have a high sense of self-efficacy / tend to pursue challenging goals / that may be outside the reach of the average person.
높은 자기 효능감을 가진 사람들은 / 도전적인 목표를 추구하는 경향이 있다. / 평균적인 사람들의 범위 밖에 있을 수도 있는

People with a strong sense of self-efficacy, therefore, / may be more willing to step / outside the culturally prescribed behaviors / to attempt tasks or goals for / which success is viewed as improbable / by the majority of social actors in a setting.
그러므로 강한 자기 효능감을 가진 사람들은 / 더 기꺼이 발을 디디려 할 수도 있다. / 문화적으로 규정된 행동 밖으로 / 일이나 목표를 시도하기 위해 / 성공할 법하지 않다고 여기는 / 어떤 환경의 사회적인 행위자들 대다수가

For these individuals, / culture will have little or no impact on behavior.
이런 사람들에게, / 문화는 행동에 거의 혹은 전혀 영향을 주지 않을 것이다.

For example, / Australians tend to endorse the "Tall Poppy Syndrome."
예를 들어, / 호주 사람들은 '키 큰 양귀비 증후군'을 지지하는 경향이 있다.

This saying suggests / that any "poppy" that outgrows the others in a field / will get "cut down;" / in other words, / any overachiever will eventually fail.
이 격언은 보여 준다. / 밭에서 다른 것들보다 더 자라는 어떤 '양귀비'이든 / '잘리게' 된다는 것, / 다시 말해 / 기대 이상의 성공을 거두는 사람은 누구든지 결국 실패하리라는 것을

Interviews and observations suggest / that it is the high self-efficacy Australians / who step outside this culturally prescribed behavior / to actually achieve beyond average.
면접과 관찰에서는 보여준다. / 바로 높은 자기 효능감을 가진 호주 사람들임을 / 이 문화적으로 규정된 행동을 벗어나는 사람들이 / 표준 이상을 실제로 성취하기 위해

행동과의 관계를 조정하는 개인적인 특징은 자기 효능감, 즉 특정한 수준의 성과를 달성하는 자신의 능력에 대한 판단이다. 높은 자기 효능감을 가진 사람들은 평균적인 사람들의 범위 밖에 있을 수도 있는 도전적인 목표를 추구하는 경향이 있다. 그러므로 강한 자기 효능감을 가진 사람들은 어떤 환경의 사회적인 행위자들 대다수가 성공할 법하지 않다고 여기는 일이나 목표를 시도하기 위해 문화적으로 규정된 행동 밖으로 더 기꺼이 발을 디디려 할 수도 있다. 이런 사람들에게, 문화는 행동에 거의 혹은 전혀 영향을 주지 않을 것이다. 예를 들

어 호주 사람들은 '키 큰 양귀비 증후군'을 지지하는 경향이 있다. 이 격언은 밭에서 다른 것들보다 더 자라는 어떤 '양귀비'이든 '잘리게' 된다는 것, 다시 말해 기대 이상의 성공을 거두는 사람은 누구든지 결국 실패하리라는 것을 보여준다. 면접과 관찰에서는 표준 이상을 실제로 성취하기 위해 이 문화적으로 규정된 행동을 벗어나는 사람들이 바로 높은 자기 효능감을 가진 호주 사람들임을 보여준다.

Why? 왜 정답일까?

표준 이상을 성취해내는, 자기 효능감이 높은 사람들의 경우 문화적으로 규정된 행동의 범위를 벗어나는 경향이 있고(~ the high self-efficacy Australians who step outside this culturally prescribed behavior to actually achieve beyond average) 바로 이러한 특징이 그들의 높은 성취를 이끌어 낸다는 결론을 담은 글이다. 따라서 빈칸에 들어갈 말로 가장 적절한 것은 ② '문화는 행동에 거의 혹은 전혀 영향을 주지 않을 것이다'이다.

- **characteristic** ⓝ 특징, 특성
- **challenging** ⓐ 어려운, 도전적인
- **improbable** ⓐ 있을 법하지 않은
- **moderate** ⓥ 조정하다
- **prescribe** ⓥ 규정하다, 처방하다
- **outgrow** ⓥ ~보다 더 크게 자라다

구문 풀이

6행 People with a strong sense of self-efficacy, therefore, [주어] may be more willing to step outside the culturally prescribed [동사(기꺼이 ~하다)] behaviors / to attempt tasks or goals [for which success is viewed as [~하기 위해] [선행사] [「전치사＋관계대명사」] [~로 여겨지다] improbable by the majority of social actors in a setting]. [보어(형용사)]

★★★ 1등급 대비 고난도 2점 문제

07 자연물과 예술 작품의 이름 또는 제목의 의미 | 정답률 38% | 정답 ⑤

다음 빈칸에 들어갈 말로 가장 적절한 것을 고르시오.

① changed – 바뀌지
② classified – 분류되지
③ preserved – 보존되지
④ controlled – 통제되지
✓ interpreted – 해석되지

"What's in a name? / That which we call a rose, / by any other name / would smell as sweet."
"이름에는 무엇이 들어있나요? / 우리가 장미라고 부르는 것은 / 다른 어떤 이름으로 부른다 해도 / 향기는 똑같이 달콤할 거예요.

This thought of Shakespeare's points up a difference / between roses and, say, paintings.
셰익스피어의 이 생각은 차이를 강조한다. / 장미와 이를테면 그림의

Natural objects, such as roses, are not interpreted.
장미와 같은 자연물은 해석되지 않는다.

They are not taken as vehicles of meanings and messages.
그것들은 의미와 메시지의 매개체로 받아들여지지 않는다.

They belong to no tradition, / strictly speaking have no style, / and are not understood within a framework of culture and convention.
그것들은 어떤 전통에도 속하지 않고, / 엄밀히 말하면 양식이 없으며, / 문화와 관습의 틀 안에서 이해되지 않는다.

Rather, they are sensed and savored relatively directly, / without intellectual mediation, / and so what they are called, / either individually or collectively, / has little bearing on our experience of them.
오히려 그것들은 비교적 직접적으로 감지되고 음미되며, / 지적인 매개 없이 / 따라서 그것들이 불리는 이름은 / 개별적으로든 집합적으로든, / 그것들에 대한 우리의 경험과는 거의 관계가 없다.

What a work of art is titled, / on the other hand, / has a significant effect / on the aesthetic face it presents / and on the qualities we correctly perceive in it.
미술 작품에 붙여지는 제목은 / 반면에 / 상당한 영향을 미친다. / 그것이 제시하는 미학적 측면과 / 그 속에서 우리가 올바르게 인지하는 특징에

A painting of a rose, / by a name other than the one it has, / might very well smell different, / aesthetically speaking.
장미 한 송이의 그림은 / 그것이 가지고 있는 이름과는 다른 이름으로 불리는 / 아마 향기가 다를 것이다. / 미학적으로 말하면

The painting titled *Rose of Summer* and an indiscernible painting titled *Vermillion Womanhood* / are physically, but also semantically and aesthetically, distinct objects of art.
*Rose of Summer*라는 제목의 그림과 (그것과) 분간하기 어려운 *Vermillion Womanhood*라는 제목의 그림은 / 물리적으로, 또한 의미적으로나 미학적으로도 별개의 미술품이다.

"이름에는 무엇이 들어있나요? 우리가 장미라고 부르는 것은 다른 어떤 이름으로 부른다 해도 향기는 똑같이 달콤할 거예요." 셰익스피어의 이 생각은 장

미와 이를테면 그림의 차이를 강조한다. 장미와 같은 자연물은 해석되지 않는다. 그것들은 의미와 메시지의 매개체로 받아들여지지 않는다. 그것들은 어떤 전통에도 속하지 않고, 엄밀히 말하면 양식이 없으며, 문화와 관습의 틀 안에서 이해되지 않는다. 오히려 그것들은 지적인 매개 없이 비교적 직접적으로 감지되고 음미되며, 따라서 개별적으로든 집합적으로든, 그것들이 불리는 이름은 그것들에 대한 우리의 경험과는 거의 관계가 없다. 반면에 미술 작품에 붙여지는 제목은 그것이 제시하는 미학적 측면과 그 속에서 우리가 올바르게 인지하는 특징에 상당한 영향을 미친다. 가지고 있는 이름(장미)과는 다른 이름으로 불리는 장미 한 송이의 그림은 미학적으로 말하면 아마 향기가 다를 것이다. *Rose of Summer*라는 제목의 그림과 그것과 분간하기 어려운 *Vermillion Womanhood*라는 제목의 그림은 물리적으로, 또한 의미적으로나 미학적으로도 별개의 미술품이다.

Why? 왜 정답일까?

자연물과 예술 작품에 있어 이름이나 제목이 갖는 의미가 다르다는 내용의 글이다. 장미와 같은 자연물은 이름에 상관없이 그 자체로 이해될 수 있지만, 'What a work of art is titled, on the other hand, has a significant effect on the aesthetic face it presents and on the qualities we correctly perceive in it.'에서 언급하듯이 자연물을 묘사한 예술 작품은 그 제목에 따라 특징이 다르게 이해될 수 있다는 것이다. 이에 근거할 때, 자연물에 관해 언급하는 빈칸에 들어갈 말로 가장 적절한 것은 자연물이 이름에 따라 '이해되거나 인식되지' 않는다는 의미를 완성하는 ⑤ '해석되지'이다.

- **vehicle** ⓝ 매개체, 수단
- **relatively** ⓐⓓ 비교적
- **collectively** ⓐⓓ 집단적으로
- **aesthetic** ⓐ 미학의
- **physically** ⓐⓓ 물리적으로
- **interpret** ⓥ 해석하다, 이해하다
- **strictly speaking** 엄밀히 말하면
- **mediation** ⓝ 매개
- **significant** ⓐ 상당한
- **perceive** ⓥ 인지하다
- **classify** ⓥ 분류하다

구문 풀이

8행 Rather, they are sensed and savored relatively directly, [주어1] [동사1] without intellectual mediation, and so what they are called, [주어2(~것)] either individually or collectively, has little bearing on our experience 「either＋A＋or＋B : A이든 B이든」 [동사구2(~와 관계가 거의 없다)] of them.

★★ 문제 해결 꿀~팁 ★★

▶ **많이 틀린 이유는?**
장미가 장미로 불리지 않더라도 장미꽃 자체는 그대로 경험될 수 있지만, 장미를 그린 그림은 제목이 어떻게 붙여지는가에 따라 다르게 경험될 수 있다는 내용의 글이다. 이는 장미 자체가 '변하거나 바뀐다'는 내용과는 무관하므로 ①은 빈칸에 적합하지 않다. 또한 글에서 장미 등 자연물을 '분류하는' 내용 또한 다루지 않으므로 ②도 답으로 적절하지 않다.

▶ **문제 해결 방법은?**
여기서 정답인 ⑤ interpreted는 예술 작품의 경우에서 알 수 있듯이 '(이름에 따라 다르게) 해석되다, 경험되다'의 의미를 나타낸다.

★★★ 1등급 대비 고난도 2점 문제

08 새로운 시각 정보를 선호하는 유아 | 정답률 43% | 정답 ④

다음 빈칸에 들어갈 말로 가장 적절한 것을 고르시오.

① Memory distortion in infancy – 유아기의 기억 왜곡
② Undeveloped vision of newborns – 신생아의 덜 발달된 시력
③ The preference for social interaction – 사회적 상호작용에 대한 선호
✓ The inbuilt attraction to novel images – 새로운 이미지를 향한 내재된 끌림
⑤ Infants' communication skills with parents – 유아가 부모와 의사소통하는 기술

Infants' preference for looking at new things / is so strong / that psychologists began to realize / that they could use it / as a test of infants' visual discrimination, / and even their *memory*.
유아는 새로운 것을 보려는 선호가 / 너무 강해서 / 심리학자들은 깨닫기 시작했다. / 그들이 그것을 사용할 수 있음을 / 유아들의 시각적 식별에 관한 테스트로 / 심지어는 그들의 *기억*에 관한

Could an infant tell the difference between two similar images?
유아가 두 개의 비슷한 이미지 간의 차이를 알 수 있을까?

Between two similar shades of the same color?
같은 색의 비슷한 두 음영 간의 차이는?

Could an infant recall having seen something / an hour, a day, a week ago?
무언가를 봤다는 것을 유아가 떠올릴 수 있을까? / 한 시간 전, 하루 전, 일주일 전에

The inbuilt attraction to novel images / held the answer.
새로운 이미지를 향한 내재된 끌림이 / 해답을 쥐었다.

If the infant's gaze lingered, / it suggested / that the infant could tell / that a similar image was nonetheless different in some way.
만약 유아의 시선이 계속 머물렀다면, / 그것은 암시했다. / 그 유아가 알 수 있다는 것을 / 비슷한 이미지가 그래도 어떤 식으로든 다르다는 것

If the infant, / after a week without seeing an image, / didn't look at it much / when it was shown again, / the infant must be able at some level to *remember* / having seen it the week before.
만일 그 유아가, / 이미지를 보지 않고 일주일 후에, / 그것을 별로 보지 않았다면, / 그 이미지가 다시 보였을 때 / 그 유아는 어느 정도는 틀림없이 *기억*할 수 있다. / 일주일 전에 그것을 보았다고

In most cases, / the results revealed / that infants were more cognitively capable / earlier than had been previously assumed.
대부분 경우에 / 그 결과는 드러냈다. / 유아가 더 일찍 인지적으로 유능했다는 것을 / 이전에 추정되었던 것보다

The visual novelty drive became, / indeed, / one of the most powerful tools in psychologists' toolkit, / unlocking a host of deeper insights / into the capacities of the infant mind.
시각적으로 새로운 것에 대한 욕구는, / 실로, / 심리학자의 도구 모음 중 가장 강력한 도구 중 하나가 되었다. / 많은 더 깊은 통찰력을 드러내며, / 유아의 정신 능력에 대한

유아는 새로운 것을 보려는 선호가 너무 강해서 심리학자들은 그것을 유아들의 시각적 식별과 심지어는 그들의 기억에 관한 테스트로 사용할 수 있음을 깨닫기 시작했다. 유아가 두 개의 비슷한 이미지 간의 차이를 알 수 있을까? 같은 색의 비슷한 두 색조 간의 차이는? 유아는 한 시간 전, 하루 전, 일주일 전에 무언가를 봤다는 것을 떠올릴 수 있을까? 새로운 이미지를 향한 내재된 끌림이 해답을 쥐었다. 만약 유아의 시선이 계속 머물렀다면, 그것은 비슷한 이미지가 그래도 어떤 식으로든 다르다는 것을 그 유아가 알 수 있다는 것을 암시했다. 만일 이미지를 보지 않고 일주일 후에 그 이미지가 다시 보였을 때 그 유아가 그것을 별로 보지 않았다면, 그 유아는 일주일 전에 그것을 보았다고 어느 정도는 틀림없이 *기억*할 수 있다. 대부분 경우에 그 결과는 이전에 추정되었던 것보다 유아가 더 일찍 인지적으로 유능했다는 것을 드러냈다. 실로, 시각적으로 새로운 것에 대한 욕구는 유아의 정신 능력에 대한 많은 더 깊은 통찰력을 드러내며, 심리학자의 도구 모음 중 가장 강력한 도구 중 하나가 되었다.

Why? 왜 정답일까?

첫 문장(Infants' preference for looking at new things)과 마지막 문장(The visual novelty drive)에서 공통적으로 유아가 새로운 시각 정보에 더 관심을 보인다는 점이 심리학 연구에 많은 도움이 되었다고 하므로, 핵심 소재를 나타내는 빈칸에 들어갈 말로 가장 적절한 것은 ④ '새로운 이미지를 향한 내재된 끌림'이다.

- infant ⑥ 유아, 젖먹이, 아기
- psychologist ⑥ 심리학자
- discrimination ⑥ 차이, 구별, 차별
- similar ⓐ 비슷한, 유사한
- gaze ⑥ 응시, 바라봄
- nonetheless ⓪ 그래도, 그렇기는 하지만
- reveal ⓥ 드러내다
- capable ⓐ 유능한
- assume ⓥ 가정하다
- drive ⑥ 충동, 욕구
- toolkit ⑥ 도구 모음
- insight ⑥ 통찰력
- infancy ⑥ 유아기
- inbuilt ⓐ 내재된

- preference ⑥ 선호
- realize ⓥ 깨닫다, 알아차리다
- tell the difference 차이를 알다
- recall ⓥ 기억하다, 회상하다
- linger ⓥ (오래) 남다, 계속되다
- some way 어떤 방식
- cognitively ⓪ 인지적으로
- previous ⓐ 이전의
- novelty ⑥ 새로움
- indeed ⓪ 사실, 실은
- unlock ⓥ 드러내다, (열쇠로) 열다
- distortion ⑥ 왜곡
- newborn ⑥ 신생아
- attraction ⑥ 끌림

구문 풀이

1행 Infants' preference for looking at new things is so strong that
「so ~ that … : 너무 ~해서 …하다」
psychologists began to realize {that they could use it as a test of
{ }: 명사절(to realize의 목적어) └→ 전치사(~로서)
infants' visual discrimination, and even their *memory*}.

★★ 문제 해결 꿀~팁 ★★

▶ 많이 틀린 이유는?
아이들이 '새로운' 것을 더 오래 응시하는 경향이 있다는 점을 토대로 아이들의 '기억'에 관해 연구할 수 있다는 내용이므로, 유아들이 기억을 '왜곡한다'는 내용의 ①은 오답이다.

▶ 문제 해결 방법은?
첫 문장에 제시된 일반적 진술을 토대로 빈칸 뒤의 예시를 이해하고, 이를 토대로 다

시 일반적 진술인 빈칸을 완성하는 문제이다. 즉, 첫 문장의 핵심 소재가 곧 빈칸에 들어갈 말이다.

★★★ 1등급 대비 고난도 3점 문제

09 성공 가능성을 더 높여주는 협력   정답률 42% | 정답 ⑤

다음 빈칸에 들어갈 말로 가장 적절한 것을 고르시오. [3점]

① Patience - 인내   ② Rationality - 합리성
③ Independence - 자립   ④ Competition - 경쟁
✓ Cooperation - 협력

People unknowingly sabotage their own work / when they withhold help or information from others / or try to undermine them / lest they become more successful or get more credit than "me."
사람들은 자신도 모르게 자신의 일을 방해하게 된다. / 그들이 다른 사람들에게 도움이나 정보를 주지 않으려 하거나, / 그들을 깎아 내리려 할 때, / 다른 사람들이 '나'보다 더 성공하거나 더 많은 명성을 얻지 못하도록

Cooperation is alien to the ego, / except when there is a secondary motive.
협력은 자아에게 용납되지 않는다. / 부차적인 동기가 있는 경우를 제외하고는

The ego doesn't know / that the more you include others, / the more smoothly things flow / and the more easily things come to you.
자아는 알지 못한다. / 여러분이 다른 사람들을 더 많이 포함할수록, / 일이 더 순조롭게 흘러가고, / 자신에게 더 쉽게 다가온다는 것을

When you give little or no help to others / or put obstacles in their path, / the universe / — in the form of people and circumstances — / gives little or no help to you / because you have cut yourself off from the whole.
여러분이 다른 사람들에게 거의 혹은 전혀 도움을 주지 않거나 / 그들의 길을 방해할 때 / 우주는, / 사람과 상황의 모습으로, / 여러분에게 거의 혹은 전혀 도움을 주지 않는데, / 이것은 여러분이 전체로부터 자신을 단절시켰기 때문이다.

The ego's unconscious core feeling of "not enough" / causes it to react to someone else's success / as if that success had taken something away from "me."
'충분하지 않다'라는 자아의 무의식적인 핵심 감정은 / 자아가 다른 사람의 성공에 대해 반응하게 한다. / 마치 그 성공이 '나'로부터 무언가를 빼앗아 간 것처럼

It doesn't know / that your resentment of another person's success / curtails your own chances of success.
자아는 알지 못한다. / 여러분이 다른 사람의 성공에 대한 여러분의 분개는 / 여러분 자신의 성공 기회가 줄어들게 한다는 것을

In order to attract success, / you need to welcome it wherever you see it.
성공을 끌어들이려면 / 여러분은 그것을 어디서 보든지 그것을 기꺼이 받아들여야 한다.

사람들은 다른 사람들에게 도움이나 정보를 주지 않으려 하거나, 다른 사람들이 '나'보다 더 성공하거나 더 많은 명성을 얻지 못하도록 그들을 깎아 내리려 할 때, 자신도 모르게 자신의 일을 방해하게 된다. 협력은 부차적인 동기가 있는 경우를 제외하고는 자아에게 용납되지 않는다. 다른 사람들을 더 많이 포함할수록, 일이 더 순조롭게 흘러가고, 자신에게 더 쉽게 다가온다는 것을 자아는 알지 못한다. 다른 사람들에게 거의 혹은 전혀 도움을 주지 않거나 그들의 길을 방해할 때, 우주는 사람과 상황의 모습으로 여러분에게 거의 혹은 전혀 도움을 주지 않는데, 이것은 여러분이 전체로부터 자신을 단절시켰기 때문이다. '충분하지 않다'라는 자아의 무의식적인 핵심 감정으로 인해 자아는 다른 사람의 성공에 대해 마치 그 성공이 '나'로부터 무언가를 빼앗아 간 것처럼 반응한다. 자아는 다른 사람의 성공에 대해 여러분이 분개하면 여러분 자신의 성공 기회가 줄어든다는 것을 알지 못한다. 성공을 끌어들이려면 그것을 어디서 보든지 그것을 기꺼이 받아들여야 한다.

Why? 왜 정답일까?

'The ego doesn't know that the more you include others, the more smoothly things flow and the more easily things come to you.'에서 자아는 다른 사람을 더 많이 포함할수록 일이 더 순조롭게 진행된다는 사실을 모른다고 한다. 따라서 빈칸에 들어갈 말로 가장 적절한 것은 '타인을 포함하는 것'을 한 단어로 나타낸 ⑤ '협력'이다.

- unknowingly ⓪ 자신도 모르게
- undermine ⓥ 약화시키다
- get credit 공로를 인정받다
- ego ⑥ 자아
- smoothly ⓪ 순조롭게
- circumstances ⑥ 환경, 상황
- core ⑥ 핵심
- patience ⑥ 인내

- withhold ⓥ 주지 않다
- lest ⓪ ~하지 않도록
- alien to ~에 맞지 않는, 이질적인
- secondary ⓐ 부차적인
- obstacle ⑥ 장애물
- unconscious ⓐ 무의식적인
- resentment ⑥ 억울함, 분개

구문 풀이

6행 People unknowingly sabotage their own work when they
　　　　　　　　　　　　　　　　　　　　　　접속새(~할 때)
withhold help or information from others or try to **undermine** them
동사1　　　　　　　　　　　　　　　　　　　　　　동사2
lest they (should) become more successful or **get** more credit than
「lest + 주어 + (should) 동사원형 : ~하지 않도록」
"me."

★★ 문제 해결 꿀~팁 ★★

▶ 많이 틀린 이유는?
우리의 자아는 성공을 위해 협력보다는 단절과 고립을 선택하지만, 사실 성공에는 협력이 더 주요하게 작용한다는 내용의 글로, 마지막 두 문장이 주제를 잘 제시한다. 최다 오답인 ③을 빈칸에 넣어서 읽으면 '자립'이 자아에게 생소한 것이라는 의미가 완성되는데, 이는 주제와 상반된다.

▶ 문제 해결 방법은?
빈칸 뒤의 'the + 비교급 ~, the + 비교급 …(~할수록 더 …하다' 구문을 통해 글의 주제를 파악했다면, 빈칸이 포함된 문장을 주의 깊게 읽어야 한다. 자아가 성공을 위해 마땅히 취해야 하지만 '생소하게' 여기는 대상이 빈칸에 들어갈 말이다.

★★★ 1등급 대비 고난도 3점 문제

10 평정심 유지에 도움이 되는 먼 조상들의 시각　　정답률 16% | 정답 ⑤

다음 빈칸에 들어갈 말로 가장 적절한 것을 고르시오. [3점]

① all of them could be matched consistently with their intended emotions
　모든 얼굴 그림이 의도된 감정과 일관되게 매칭될 수 있었다
② every one of them was illustrated with photographic precision
　모든 얼굴 그림이 사진처럼 정밀하게 그려졌다
③ each of them definitively displayed its own social narrative
　각 얼굴 그림이 그 그림 자체의 사회적 이야기를 명확하게 보여주었다
④ most of them would be seen as representing unique characteristics
　얼굴 그림 대부분이 고유한 특징을 나타낸다고 여겨질 것이다
✔ any number of them could be substituted for one another without loss
　어떤 수의 얼굴 그림이든 손실 없이 서로 대체될 수 있었다

There have been psychological studies / in which subjects were shown photographs of people's faces / and asked to identify the expression or state of mind evinced.
심리학 연구가 이루어져 왔다. / 피실험자에게 사람들의 얼굴 사진을 보여주고 / 분명히 나타나는 표정이나 마음 상태를 파악하도록 요청하는

The results are invariably very mixed.
그 결과는 언제나 매우 엇갈린다.

In the 17th century / the French painter and theorist Charles Le Brun / drew a series of faces / illustrating the various emotions / that painters could be called upon to represent.
17세기에 / 프랑스의 화가이자 이론가인 Charles Le Brun은 / 일련의 얼굴 그림을 그렸다. / 다양한 감정을 분명히 보여주는 / 화가가 표현해 달라고 요청받을 수 있는

What is striking about them / is / that any number of them could be substituted for one another without loss.
이 그림들에서 놀라운 점은 / ~이다. / 어떤 수의 얼굴 그림이든 손실 없이 서로 대체될 수 있었다는 것

What is missing in all this / is any setting or context / to make the emotion determinate.
이 모든 것에서 빠진 것은 / 어떤 환경이나 맥락이다. / 감정을 확정적인 것으로 만드는

We must know / who this person is, / who these other people are, / what their relationship is, / what is at stake in the scene, / and the like.
우리는 알아야 한다. / 이 사람이 누구인지, / 이 다른 사람들이 누구인지, / 그들은 어떤 관계인지, / 그 장면에서 관건이 무엇인지, / 그리고 기타 등등

In real life as well as in painting / we do not come across just faces; / we encounter people in particular situations / and our understanding of people cannot somehow be precipitated and held / isolated from the social and human circumstances / in which they, and we, live and breathe and have our being.
그림에서뿐만 아니라 실생활에서도 / 우리는 단지 얼굴만 우연히 마주치는 것이 아니다. / 우리는 사람들을 특정 상황 속에서 마주치며, / 사람들에 대한 우리의 이해는 어떤 식으로도 촉발되고 보유될 수 없다. / 사회적, 인간적 상황으로부터 괴리된 채로는 / 그들과 우리가 살아 숨 쉬고 존재하는

피실험자에게 사람들의 얼굴 사진을 보여주고 분명히 나타나는 표정이나 마음 상태를 파악하도록 요청하는 심리학 연구가 이루어져 왔다. 그 결과는 언제나 매우 엇갈린다. 17세기에 프랑스의 화가이자 이론가인 Charles Le Brun은 화가가 표현해 달라고 요청받을 수 있는 다양한 감정을 분명히 보여주는 일련의 얼굴 그림을 그렸다. 이 그림들에서 놀라운 점은 어떤 수의 얼굴 그림이든 손실 없이 서로 대체될 수 있었다는 것이다. 이 모든 것에서 빠진 것은

감정을 확정적인 것으로 만드는 어떤 환경이나 맥락이다. 우리는 이 사람이 누구인지, 이 다른 사람들이 누구인지, 그들은 어떤 관계인지, 그 장면에서 관건이 무엇인지 등을 알아야 한다. 그림에서뿐만 아니라 실생활에서도 우리는 단지 얼굴만 우연히 마주치는 것이 아니다. 우리는 사람들을 특정 상황 속에서 마주치며, 사람들에 대한 우리의 이해는 그들과 우리가 살아 숨 쉬고 존재하는 사회적, 인간적 상황으로부터 괴리된 채로는 어떤 식으로도 촉발되고 보유될 수 없다.

Why? 왜 정답일까?

이 글의 요지는 얼굴에 나타난 감정을 이해하기 위해서는 환경이나 맥락 정보가 중요하다(we encounter people in particular situations and our understanding of people cannot somehow be precipitated and held isolated from the social and human circumstances)는 것이다. 하지만 빈칸 문장에서 언급되는 얼굴 표정 그림은 상황에 관한 정보를 담고 있지 않아서(What is missing in all this is any setting or context to make the emotion determinate.) 감정이 '제대로 특정될 수 없었다'는 내용이 빈칸에 적합하다. 따라서 빈칸에 들어갈 말로 가장 적절한 것은 ⑤ '어떤 수의 얼굴 그림이든 손실 없이 서로 대체될 수 있었다'이다.

- **psychological** ⓐ 심리학의
- **expression** ⓝ 표정, 표현
- **evince** ⓥ (감정 따위를) 분명히 나타내다
- **mixed** ⓐ 엇갈린, 혼합된
- **illustrate** ⓥ 분명히 보여주다, 그려 넣다
- **determinate** ⓐ 확정적인, 확실한
- **at stake** 관건이 되는, 성패를 좌우하는
- **come across** ~을 우연히 마주치다
- **somehow** ⓐd 어떻게든
- **isolated** ⓐ 분리된, 고립된
- **substitute** ⓥ 대체하다
- **precision** ⓝ 정확성
- **subject** ⓝ 피실험자
- **state of mind** 마음 상태
- **invariably** ⓐd 언제나, 변함없이
- **theorist** ⓝ 이론가
- **call upon** 요청하다
- **striking** ⓐ 놀라운
- **and the like** 기타 등등 비슷한 것
- **encounter** ⓥ 마주치다, 맞닥뜨리다
- **precipitate** ⓥ 촉발하다
- **circumstance** ⓝ 상황
- **consistently** ⓐd 일관되게
- **definitively** ⓐd 명확하게, 결정적으로

구문 풀이

7행 What is striking about them is that any number of them
　　　주어(명사절 : ~것)　　동사(단수)　　　　　　「A +
could be substituted for one another without loss.
be substituted for + B : A가 B로 대체되다」

★★ 문제 해결 꿀~팁 ★★

▶ 많이 틀린 이유는?
주제를 잘 파악해도 선택지의 의미를 알지 못해 틀리기 쉬운 문제다. 우선, 글에서 감정을 잘 이해하려면 맥락과 환경이 있어야 한다고 하는데, 예시에 언급된 감정 그림에는 맥락이 '빠져' 있었다고 한다. 이 경우에는 감정이 확정적으로 규정되기 어려울 것이기 때문에, ①과 같이 '그림이 의도된 감정 그대로 이해되었다'는 설명은 흐름상 오히려 모순된다.

▶ 문제 해결 방법은?
⑤의 어떤 그림이든 '손실 없이 그대로 대체될 수 있었다'는 말은, 어느 감정 그림이든 맥락이 없어 '어느 하나로 확정될 수 없었기 때문에' 서로 대체되어도 무방했다는 의미이다.

★★★ 1등급 대비 고난도 3점 문제

11 기존의 개념 체계에서 비롯되는 새로운 사상　　정답률 35% | 정답 ①

다음 빈칸에 들어갈 말로 가장 적절한 것을 고르시오. [3점]

✔ are outgrowths of previous ideas – 이전 사상의 결과물이기
② stem from abstract reasoning ability – 추상적 추론 능력에서 비롯되기
③ form the basis of cultural universalism – 문화적 보편성의 토대를 형성하기
④ emerge between people of the same age – 같은 시대의 사람들 사이에서 출현하기
⑤ promote individuals' innovative thinking – 개인들의 혁신적 사고를 촉진하기

It is important to recognise the interdependence / between individual, culturally formed actions / and the state of cultural integration.
상호의존성을 인식하는 것은 중요하다. / 개별적이고 문화적으로 형성된 행동과 / 문화적 통합의 상태 사이의

People work within the forms / provided by the cultural patterns / that they have internalised, / however contradictory these may be.
사람들은 형태 내에서 일한다. / 문화적 패턴에 의해 제공되는 / 자신이 내면화한 / 이것들이 아무리 모순되더라도

Ideas are worked out / as logical implications or consequences of other accepted ideas, / and it is in this way / that cultural innovations and discoveries are possible.

사상은 도출되고, / 다른 수용된 사상의 논리적 영향이나 결과로 / 바로 이러한 방식으로 / 문화적 혁신과 발견이 가능하다.

New ideas are discovered through logical reasoning, / but such discoveries are / inherent in and integral to the conceptual system / and are made possible / only because of the acceptance of its premises.
새로운 사상은 논리적 추론을 통해 발견되지만, / 그러한 발견은 / 개념 체계에 내재 및 내장되어 있고, / 가능해진다. / 오직 그 전제를 수용하기 때문에

For example, / the discoveries of new prime numbers / are 'real' consequences / of the particular number system employed.
예를 들어, / 새로운 소수의 발견은 / '실제' 결과이다. / 사용되고 있는 특정 숫자 체계의

Thus, cultural ideas show 'advances' and 'developments' / because they are outgrowths of previous ideas.
따라서, 문화적 사상은 '진보'와 '발전'을 보여 준다. / 그것들이 이전 사상의 결과물이기 때문에

The cumulative work of many individuals / produces a corpus of knowledge / within which certain 'discoveries' become possible or more likely.
많은 개인의 축적된 작업은 / 집적된 지식을 생산한다. / 특정 '발견'이 가능해지거나 가능성이 높아지는

Such discoveries are 'ripe' / and could not have occurred earlier / and are also likely to be made simultaneously / by numbers of individuals.
그러한 발견은 '알맞게 익었고', / 더 일찍 발생할 수 없었을 것이며, / 또한 동시에 이루어질 가능성이 있다. / 다수의 개인에 의해

개별적이고 문화적으로 형성된 행동과 문화적 통합의 상태 사이의 상호의존성을 인식하는 것은 중요하다. 사람들은 아무리 모순되더라도 자신이 내면화한 문화적 패턴에 의해 제공되는 형태 내에서 일한다. 사상은 다른 수용된 사상의 논리적 영향이나 결과로 도출되고, 바로 이러한 방식으로 문화적 혁신과 발견이 가능하다. 새로운 사상은 논리적 추론을 통해 발견되지만, 그러한 발견은 개념 체계에 내재 및 (일부로서) 내장되어 있고, 오직 그 전제를 수용하기 때문에 가능해진다. 예를 들어, 새로운 소수의 발견은 사용되고 있는 특정 숫자 체계의 '실제' 결과이다. 따라서, 문화적 사상은 이전 사상의 결과물이기 때문에 '진보'와 '발전'을 보여 준다. 많은 개인의 축적된 작업은 특정 '발견'이 가능해지거나 가능성이 높아지는 집적된 지식을 생산한다. 그러한 발견은 (이루어지기에) '알맞게 익었고', 더 일찍 발생할 수 없었을 것이며, 또한 다수의 개인에 의해 동시에 이루어질 가능성이 있다.

Why? 왜 정답일까?

'New ideas are discovered through logical reasoning, but such discoveries are inherent in and integral to the conceptual system ~' 에서 새로운 사상은 논리적 추론을 통해 발전하지만 이미 이러한 발견은 기존의 개념 체계에 내재되어 있으며, 기존 체계의 전제를 수용하기 때문에 발전할 수 있는 것이라고 했다. 즉 새로운 사상이라 할지라도 기존 것에서 비롯된다는 것이 글의 주제이므로, 빈칸에 들어갈 말로 가장 적절한 것은 ① '이전 사상의 결과물이기'이다.

- **interdependence** ⓝ 상호의존성
- **internalise** ⓥ 내면화하다
- **implication** ⓝ 영향, 함축
- **inherent** ⓐ 내재하는
- **acceptance** ⓝ 수용
- **prime number** (수학) 소수(素數)
- **ripe** ⓐ 다 익은
- **abstract** ⓐ 추상적인
- **integration** ⓝ 통합
- **contradictory** ⓐ 모순되는
- **consequence** ⓝ 결과
- **integral** ⓐ (~에 일부로 들어가) 내장된
- **premise** ⓝ 전제
- **cumulative** ⓐ 누적되는
- **outgrowth** ⓝ ~에서 자란 것, 결과물
- **emerge** ⓥ 생겨나다, 나타나다

구문 풀이

17행 The cumulative work of many individuals produces
　　　　　　주어　　　　　　　　　　　　　　동사(단수)
a corpus of knowledge [within which certain 'discoveries' become
　목적어(선행사)　　　　　　　「전치사＋관·대」
possible or more likely].

★★ 문제 해결 꿀~팁 ★★

▶ 많이 틀린 이유는?
글에서 '혁신, 발전, 진보' 등이 많이 언급되기에 언뜻 보면 마찬가지로 '혁신적 사고'를 언급하는 ⑤가 답으로 적합해 보인다. 하지만 단어보다는 흐름에 집중해야 정확한 답을 고를 수 있다.

▶ 문제 해결 방법은?
글의 요점이 제시되는 빈칸 앞 내용에 따르면 새로운 사상은 이미 있었던(accepted) 사상의 논리적 결과물이라고 했다. 그래서 마지막 두 문장에 따르면 사실상 사람들이 축적해 왔던 작업이 적절한 시점에 새로운 결과물처럼 튀어나오는 것이며, 같은 발견이 여러 사람에 의해 동시다발적으로 이루어질 수도 있다는 것이다. 이러한 흐름으로 볼 때, 이전 사상과 새로운 사상의 연결고리를 시사할 수 있는 말이 빈칸에 들어가야 한다.

---

12 제조업자들로부터 외면당하는 리드 유저의 혁신　　정답률 33% | 정답 ②

다음 빈칸에 들어갈 말로 가장 적절한 것을 고르시오. [3점]

① lead users tended to overlook – 리드 유저가 간과하는 경향이 있던
② lead users have already developed – 리드 유저가 이미 개발한 ✓
③ lead users encountered in the market – 리드 유저가 시장에서 마주친
④ other firms frequently put into use – 다른 회사들이 자주 실행한
⑤ both users and firms have valued – 사용자와 회사 둘 다 가치 있게 여긴

Manufacturers design their innovation processes / around the way they think the process works.
제조업자들은 자신의 혁신 과정을 설계한다. / 그들이 생각하기에 혁신 과정이 작동되는 방식에 맞춰

The vast majority of manufacturers still think / that product development and service development / are always done by manufacturers, / and that their job is always to find a need and fill it / rather than to sometimes find and commercialize an innovation / that lead users have already developed.
제조업자의 대다수는 여전히 생각한다. / 제품 개발과 서비스 개발은 / 항상 제조업자들에 의해 이루어지며, / 자신들의 일은 항상 필요를 발견하고 그것을 채우는 것이라고 / 가끔 혁신을 발견하고 상업화하기보다는 / 리드 유저가 이미 개발한

Accordingly, / manufacturers have set up market-research departments / to explore the needs of users in the target market, / product-development groups / to think up suitable products to address those needs, and so forth.
그래서, / 제조업자들은 시장 연구 부서를 설치했다. / 핵심 대상 시장 사용자들의 필요를 탐구하기 위한 / 제품 개발 집단 / 그러한 필요에 대처하기에 적절한 제품, 그리고 기타 등등을 고안하기 위한

The needs and prototype solutions of lead users / — if encountered at all — / are typically rejected as outliers of no interest.
리드유저의 필요와 시제품 해결책은 / 만일 정말 마주치기라도 한다면 / 대체로 전혀 흥미롭지 않은 아웃라이어로 거부된다.

Indeed, / when lead users' innovations do enter a firm's product line / — and they have been shown / to be the actual source of many major innovations for many firms — / they typically arrive with a lag / and by an unusual and unsystematic route.
정말로, / 리드유저의 혁신이 그 회사의 제품 라인에 정말로 편입될 때 / 그리고 이는 알려졌다 / 많은 회사의 여러 주요 혁신의 실질적인 원천이 되는 것으로 / 그것은 대체로 지연 후에 도착한다. / 그리고 이례적이고 비체계적인 경로를 통해

제조업자들은 자신들이 생각하기에 혁신 과정이 작동되는 방식에 맞춰 그 과정을 설계한다. 제조업자의 대다수는 제품 개발과 서비스 개발은 항상 제조업자들에 의해 이루어지며, 자신들의 일은 가끔 리드 유저(시장 경향을 선도하는 사용자)가 이미 개발한 혁신을 발견하고 상업화하기보다는 항상 필요를 발견하고 그것을 채우는 것이라고 여전히 생각한다. 그래서, 제조업자들은 핵심 대상 시장 사용자들의 필요를 탐구하기 위한 시장 연구 부서, 그러한 필요에 대처하기에 적절한 제품을 고안하기 위한 제품 개발 집단 및 기타 등등을 설치했다. 리드 유저의 필요와 시제품 해결책은, 만일 정말 마주치기라도 한다면, 대체로 전혀 흥미롭지 않은 아웃라이어(해당 범위에서 많이 벗어나는 것)로 거부된다. 정말로, 리드 유저의 혁신이 그 회사의 제품 라인에 정말로 편입될 때 — 이는 많은 회사의 여러 주요 혁신의 실질적인 원천이 되는 것으로 알려졌는데 — 그것은 대체로 지연 후에 이례적이고 비체계적인 경로를 통해 도착한다.

Why? 왜 정답일까?

제조업자가 생각하는 혁신은 여전히 수요를 찾아 그에 맞추는 과정으로 이해될 뿐, 리드 유저가 이미 해낸 생각을 적극 반영하는 과정과는 거리가 있다는 내용의 글이다. 'The needs and prototype solutions of lead users ~ are typically rejected as outliers of no interest.'에서 리드 유저의 혁신적인 생각은 전혀 흥미롭지 않은 것으로 치부당하기 쉽다고 언급하는 것으로 보아, 빈칸에 들어갈 말로 가장 적절한 것은 이들이 '이미 생각해낸' 것들이 뒷전으로 밀리기 쉽다는 의미를 완성하는 ② '리드 유저가 이미 개발한'이다.

- **manufacturer** ⓝ 제조업자
- **the vast majority of** ~의 대다수
- **accordingly** 〔ad〕 그에 따라
- **address** ⓥ 대처하다, 다루다
- **encounter** ⓥ 마주하다
- **actual** ⓐ 현실의, 실제의, 사실상의
- **unsystematic** ⓐ 비체계적인
- **tend** ⓥ 경향이 있다
- **innovation** ⓝ 혁신
- **commercialize** ⓥ 상업화하다
- **suitable** ⓐ 적합한
- **prototype** ⓝ 시제품, 견본
- **outlier** ⓝ 관련 없는 것, 범위를 벗어난 것
- **firm** ⓝ 회사
- **route** ⓝ 길, 경로

DAY 03

11행 The needs and prototype solutions of lead users —
　　　　　　　　　　　　　　　주어
(if encountered at all) — are typically rejected as outliers of no interest.
( ): 삽입구(they are 생략)　　　　　동사(수동태)　　　「of + 추상명사」: 형용사 역할

★★ 문제 해결 꿀~팁 ★★

▶ 많이 틀린 이유는?
이 글은 리드유저가 제품을 선도적으로 사용하는 과정에서 내놓는 해결책이 실제 제조업자들의 혁신에 도움이 된다는 내용이다. ③은 본문에 나온 표현(if encountered at all)을 반복하여 언뜻 답처럼 보이지만, 리드유저들이 제안하는 변화가 '이미 그들이 시장에서 마주했던' 변화라는 의미이므로 핵심 내용과 무관하다.

▶ 문제 해결 방법은?
제조업자들은 리드유저의 '선제적인 시제품 해결책(prototype solutions)'을 흔히 거절하지만, 실제로 이 아이디어는 회사에 다른 경로로 도달해 혁신의 실제적 근원이 될 때가 많다는 것이 빈칸 뒤의 요지이다. 이를 근거로 할 때, 이들 리드유저가 '이미 제안한' 아이디어를 채택하기보다는 제조업자 본인들이 뭔가 해보려 한다는 것이 빈칸 문장의 내용일 것이다.

---

01 ①	02 ③	03 ②	04 ①	05 ①
06 ①	07 ②	08 ⑤	09 ②	10 ①
11 ④	12 ①			

---

01 뉴스 선정의 주관성　　　　　정답률 60% | 정답 ①

다음 빈칸에 들어갈 말로 가장 적절한 것을 고르시오.

✔ subjective – 주관적　　　　② passive – 수동적인
③ straightforward – 간단한　　④ consistent – 일관적인
⑤ crucial – 중요한

There is a difference / between a newsworthy event and news.
차이가 있다. / 뉴스 가치가 있는 사건과 뉴스 간에는
A newsworthy event will not necessarily become news, / just as news is often about an event / that is not, in itself, newsworthy.
뉴스 가치가 있는 사건이 반드시 뉴스가 되는 않을 것이다. / 사건에 관한 뉴스가 종종 있듯이, / 그 자체로는 뉴스 가치가 없는
We can define news as an event / that is recorded in the news media, / regardless of whether it is about a newsworthy event.
우리는 뉴스를 사건이라고 규정할 수 있다. / 뉴스 매체에 기록된 / 그것이 뉴스 가치가 있는 사건에 대한 것인지와 상관없이
The very fact of its transmission means / that it is regarded as news, / even if we struggle to understand / why that particular story has been selected from all the other events / happening at the same time that have been ignored.
그것의 전송이라는 바로 그 사실이 의미한다. / 그것이 뉴스로 간주됨을 / 비록 우리가 이해하려고 몹시 애쓸지라도, / 다른 모든 일들 중에서 그 특정 이야기가 선정된 이유를 / 같은 시기에 발생하였지만 선정되지 못한
News selection is subjective / so not all events seen as newsworthy by some people / will make it to the news.
뉴스 선정은 주관적이어서 / 일부 사람들에게 뉴스 가치가 있어 보이는 모든 사건이 / 뉴스가 되지는 않는다.
All journalists are familiar with the scenario / where they are approached by someone with the words / 'I've got a great story for you'.
모든 기자들은 시나리오에 익숙하다. / 누군가가 말과 함께 접근하는 / '너한테 해줄 엄청난 이야기가 있어'라는
For them, / it is a major news event, / but for the journalist it might be something to ignore.
그들에게는 / 그것이 주요한 뉴스 사건이지만, / 기자에게는 그것이 무시할 만한 것일 수도 있다.

뉴스 가치가 있는 사건과 뉴스 간에는 차이가 있다. 그 자체로는 뉴스 가치가 없는 사건에 관한 뉴스가 종종 있듯이, 뉴스 가치가 있는 사건이 반드시 뉴스가 되는 않을 것이다. 우리는 그것이 뉴스 가치가 있는 사건에 대한 것인지와 상관없이, 뉴스를 뉴스 매체에 기록된 사건이라고 규정할 수 있다. 비록 같은 시기에 발생하였지만 무시돼 버린 다른 모든 일들 중에서 그 특정 이야기가 선정된 이유를 우리가 이해하려고 몹시 애쓸지라도, 그것의 전송이라는 바로 그 사실이 그것이 뉴스로 간주됨을 의미한다. 뉴스 선정은 주관적이어서 일부 사람들에게 뉴스 가치가 있어 보이는 모든 사건이 뉴스가 되지는 않는다. 모든 기자들은 누군가가 '너한테 해줄 엄청난 이야기가 있어'라는 말로 접근하는 시나리오(상황)에 익숙하다. 그들에게는 그것이 주요한 뉴스 사건이지만, 기자에게는 그것이 무시할 만한 것일 수도 있다.

Why? 왜 정답일까?

첫 두 문장과 빈칸 바로 뒤에서 어떤 사람들에게 뉴스 가치가 있는 사건이어도 그것이 꼭 뉴스가 되는 것은 아니라고(~ not all events seen as newsworthy by some people will make it to the news.) 한다. 이는 뉴스 선정이 '사람에 따라' 달리 이루어질 수 있다는 의미이므로, 빈칸에 들어갈 말로 가장 적절한 것은 ① '주관적'이다.

- newsworthy ⓐ 뉴스 가치가 있는
- record ⓥ 기록하다
- transmission ⓝ 전송
- particular ⓐ 특정한
- familiar with ~에 익숙한
- subjective ⓐ 주관적인
- define ⓥ 정의하다
- regardless of ~와 상관없이
- struggle to ~하려고 노력하다
- ignore ⓥ 무시하다
- approach ⓥ 접근하다
- straightforward ⓐ 쉬운, 단순한

2행 A newsworthy event will not necessarily become news, just as
　　　　　　　　　　　　　　　　　　　　　　　접속사(~와 마찬가지로)
news is often about an event [that is not, (in itself), newsworthy].
　　　　　　　　　　선행사　　주격 관·대　( ): 삽입구

02 노동력 공유 체계
정답률 54% | 정답 ③

다음 빈칸에 들어갈 말로 가장 적절한 것을 고르시오.

① legally established – 법적으로 확립된다
② regularly reported – 정기적으로 보고된다
☑ socially regulated – 사회적으로 규제된다
④ manually calculated – 수동으로 계산된다
⑤ carefully documented – 신중하게 문서화된다

In labor-sharing groups, / people contribute labor to other people / on a
regular basis / (for seasonal agricultural work such as harvesting) / or on an
irregular basis / (in the event of a crisis / such as the need to rebuild a barn
damaged by fire).
노동력 공유 집단에서 / 사람들은 다른 사람들에게 노동력을 제공한다. / 정기적으로 / (수확과 같은 계절적
인 농사일을 위해) / 혹은 비정기적으로 / (위기 상황 발생 시 / 화재로 손상된 헛간을 다시 지어야 하는 것
과 같은)

Labor sharing groups / are part of what has been called a "moral economy" /
since no one keeps formal records / on how much any family puts in or takes
out.
노동력 공유 집단은 / '도덕적 경제'라고 불린 것의 일부다. / 아무도 공식적인 기록을 남기지 않으므로 / 어떤 가
족이 얼마나 많이 투입하고 얼마나 많이 가져갔는지에 대해

Instead, accounting is socially regulated.
대신에, 정산은 사회적으로 규제된다.

The group has a sense of moral community / based on years of trust and
sharing.
그 집단은 도덕적 공동체 의식을 지닌다. / 다년간의 신뢰와 나눔을 바탕으로 하는

In a certain community of North America, / labor sharing is a major
economic factor of social cohesion.
북미의 특정 지역 사회에서는 / 노동력 공유가 사회적 응집성의 주요 경제적 요소이다.

When a family needs a new barn / or faces repair work / that requires group
labor, / a barn-raising party is called.
한 가족이 새 헛간이 필요하거나, / 수리 작업에 직면할 때, / 단체 노동력을 필요로 하는 / 헛간 조성 모임이 소
집된다.

Many families show up to help.
여러 가족이 도우러 온다.

Adult men provide manual labor, / and adult women provide food for the
event.
성인 남성은 육체노동을 제공하고, / 성인 여성은 행사를 위한 음식을 제공한다.

Later, / when another family needs help, / they call on the same people.
나중에, / 다른 가족이 도움이 필요할 때 / 그들은 똑같은 사람에게 부탁한다.

동력 공유 집단에서 사람들은 정기적으로(수확과 같은 계절적인 농사일을 위
해) 혹은 비정기적으로(화재로 손상된 헛간을 다시 지어야 하는 것과 같은 위
기 상황 발생 시) 다른 사람들에게 노동력을 제공한다. 아무도 어떤 가족이 얼
마나 많이 투입하고 얼마나 많이 가져갔는지에 대해 공식적인 기록을 남기지
않으므로, 노동력 공유 집단은 '도덕적 경제'라고 불린 것의 일부다. 대신에,
정산은 사회적으로 규제된다. 그 집단은 다년간의 신뢰와 나눔을 바탕으로 하
는 도덕적 공동체 의식을 지닌다. 북미의 특정 지역 사회에서는 노동력 공유가
사회적 응집성의 주요 경제적 요소이다. 한 가족이 새 헛간이 필요하거나, 단
체 노동력을 필요로 하는 수리 작업에 직면할 때, 헛간 조성 모임이 소집된다.
여러 가족이 도우러 온다. 성인 남성은 육체노동을 제공하고, 성인 여성은 행
사를 위한 음식을 제공한다. 나중에, 다른 가족이 도움이 필요할 때 그들은 똑
같은 사람들에게 부탁한다.

Why? 왜 정답일까?

빈칸 뒤에서 북미 어느 지역의 예를 통해, 노동력 공유 집단은 다년간의 신뢰와 나눔을
바탕으로 한 도덕적 공동체에서 한 집에서 일이 필요하면 부르고, 대가로 음식을 나눠 먹
고, 다음 번에 다른 집에서 일손을 필요로 하면 또 똑같은 이들이 동원되는 식이라고 한
다. 결국 정산이 공동체 안에서 '사회적으로' 이뤄졌다는 결론이 적합하므로, 빈칸에 들어
갈 말로 가장 적절한 것은 ③ '사회적으로 규제된다'이다.

- **labor** ⓝ 노동력
- **on a regular basis** 정기적으로
- **agricultural** ⓐ 농업의
- **irregular** ⓐ 비정기적인
- **barn** ⓝ 헛간
- **formal** ⓐ 공식적인
- **accounting** ⓝ 정산, 회계
- **community** ⓝ 공동체, 지역사회
- **cohesion** ⓝ 응집성
- **call on** ~에게 부탁하다, 시키다
- **document** ⓥ 문서화하다
- **contribute** ⓥ 기여하다, 기증하다
- **seasonal** ⓐ 계절적인
- **harvesting** ⓝ 수확
- **rebuild** ⓥ 다시 짓다
- **moral** ⓐ 도덕적인
- **put in** ~을 투입하다
- **trust** ⓝ 신뢰
- **factor** ⓝ 요인
- **manual** ⓐ 손으로 하는, 육체 노동의
- **regulate** ⓥ 규제하다

구문 풀이

5행 Labor sharing groups are part of {what has been called
　　　　　　　　　　　　　　　　　　　　　　　현재완료 수동태
a "moral economy"} since no one keeps formal records on [how much
　　보어　　　　　　　접속사(~ 때문에)　　　　　　　　　　전치사 의문부사(얼마나)
any family puts in or takes out].

---

03 영화 속에서 음악의 역할
정답률 42% | 정답 ②

다음 빈칸에 들어갈 말로 가장 적절한 것을 고르시오.

① frees the plot of its familiarity – 줄거리에서 친숙함을 없앤다
☑ aids in viewer access to the film – 관객이 영화에 접근하는 데 도움이 된다
③ adds to an exotic musical experience – 이국적인 음악 경험을 더해준다
④ orients audiences to the film's theme – 관객이 영화의 주제 쪽으로 향하게 한다
⑤ inspires viewers to think more deeply – 관객이 더 깊이 생각하도록 자극을 준다

A musical score within any film / can add an additional layer to the film text,
/ which goes beyond simply imitating the action viewed.
어떤 영화 속에서든 악보는 / 영화 텍스트에 추가적인 층을 추가할 수 있는데, / 이것은 보이는 연기를 단순히 흉
내 내기를 넘어선다.

In films / that tell of futuristic worlds, / composers, much like sound
designers, / have added freedom to create a world / that is unknown and new
to the viewer.
미래 세계에 관해 말하는 영화에서, / 작곡가는 꼭 사운드 디자이너처럼 / 자유를 추가해서 세계를 창조해 왔다.
/ 관객에게 알려지지 않은 새로운

However, / unlike sound designers, / composers often shy away from
creating unique pieces / that reflect these new worlds / and often present
musical scores / that possess familiar structures and cadences.
그러나 / 사운드 디자이너와 달리, / 작곡가는 흔히 독특한 곡을 만들어 내기를 피하고, / 이러한 새로운 세계를
반영하는 / 흔히 악보를 제시한다. / 익숙한 구조와 박자를 가진

While it is possible / that this may interfere with creativity and a sense of
space and time, / it in fact aids in viewer access to the film.
가능성이 있지만, / 이것이 창의성과 시공간 감각을 저해할 / 사실 그것은 관객이 영화에 접근하는 데 도움이
된다.

Through recognizable scores, / visions of the future or a galaxy far, far away
/ can be placed within a recognizable context.
쉽게 파악되는 악보를 통해 / 미래나 멀고 먼 은하계에 대한 비전이 / 쉽게 파악되는 맥락 안에 놓일 수 있다.

Such familiarity allows the viewer / to be placed in a comfortable space / so
that the film may then lead the viewer / to what is an unfamiliar, but
acceptable vision of a world / different from their own.
그러한 친숙함은 관객이 ~하게 하고 / 편안한 공간에 놓일 수 있게 / 그러면 영화는 관객을 안내할 수 있을 것
이다. / 세계에 관한 낯설지만 받아들일 수 있는 비전으로 / 자신들의 세계와는 다른

어떤 영화 속에서든 악보는 영화 텍스트에 추가적인 층을 추가할 수 있는데,
이것은 보이는 연기를 단순히 흉내 내기를 넘어선다. 미래 세계에 관해 말하는
영화에서, 작곡가는 꼭 사운드 디자이너처럼, 자유를 추가해서 관객에게 알려
지지 않은 새로운 세계를 창조해 왔다. 그러나 사운드 디자이너와 달리, 작곡
가는 흔히 이러한 새로운 세계를 반영하는 독특한 곡을 만들어 내기를 피하고,
흔히 익숙한 구조와 박자를 가진 악보를 제시한다. 이는 창의성과 시공간 감각
을 저해할 가능성이 있지만, 사실 그것은 관객이 영화에 접근하는 데 도움이
된다. 미래나 멀고 먼 은하계에 대한 비전이 쉽게 파악되는 악보를 통해 쉽게
파악되는 맥락 안에 놓일 수 있다. 그러한 친숙함을 통해 관객은 편안한 공간
에 놓이게 되고, 그러면 영화는 관객을 자신들의 세계와는 다른 세계에 관한
낯설지만 받아들일 수 있는 비전으로 안내할 수 있을 것이다.

Why? 왜 정답일까?

빈칸 뒤에서 친숙한 악보가 영화 속 낯선 세계나 비전을 쉽게 이해하는 데 도움을 주고
관객에게 편안함을 준다(Through recognizable scores, visions ~ can be
placed within a recognizable context.)는 내용이 전개되는 것으로 보아, 빈칸에
들어갈 말로 가장 적절한 것은 ② '관객이 영화에 접근하는 데 도움이 된다'이다.

- **score** ⓝ 악보
- **go beyond** ~을 넘어서다
- **composer** ⓝ 작곡가
- **unknown** ⓐ 미지의
- **shy away from** ~을 피하다
- **structure** ⓝ 구조
- **cadence** ⓝ (율동적인) 박자
- **interfere with** ~을 방해하다
- **galaxy** ⓝ 은하계
- **layer** ⓝ 층
- **futuristic** ⓐ 미래의
- **add A to B** A를 B에 더하다
- **unlike** prep ~와는 달리
- **unique** ⓐ 독특한
- **familiar** ⓐ 친숙한
- **reflect** ⓥ 반영하다
- **recognizable** ⓐ 쉽게 파악되는
- **acceptable** ⓐ 받아들일 수 있는

● free A of B A에서 B를 없애다 ● aid ⓥ 돕다
● exotic ⓐ 이국적인

구문 풀이

14행 Such familiarity allows the viewer to be placed in a
「allow+목적어+to부정사 : ~이 …하게 하다」
comfortable space so that the film may then lead the viewer to
접속사(~하도록)
{what is an unfamiliar, but acceptable vision of a world different from
관계대명사(~것) 형용사구
their own}.

---

04 일과 휴식의 분리 정답률 68% | 정답 ①

다음 빈칸에 들어갈 말로 가장 적절한 것을 고르시오.

✓ lets the work issues fall away
일과 관련된 문제를 서서히 사라지게 한다
② makes plans for tomorrow's work
내일 업무에 대한 계획을 세운다
③ retraces the projects not completed yet
아직 완수되지 않은 프로젝트를 되짚어본다
④ feels emotionally and physically exhausted
정서적으로나 신체적으로나 지쳤음을 느낀다
⑤ reflects on the achievements he made that day
그가 그날 이룬 성취를 되돌아본다

Jeffrey A. Rodgers, a vice president of a big company, / was once taught the simple idea of pausing to refresh.
한 대기업의 부사장인 Jeffrey A. Rodgers는 / 예전에 원기 회복을 위해 잠시 멈춘다는 간단한 아이디어를 배웠다.

It began / when Jeff realized / that as he drove home from work each evening / his mind was still focused on work-related projects.
그것은 시작되었다. / Jeff가 깨달았을 때 / 그가 매일 저녁 직장에서 집으로 차를 몰고 가던 중 / 자신의 마음이 여전히 업무 관련 프로젝트에 집중되어 있다는 것을

We all know this feeling.
우리는 모두 이 기분을 안다.

We may have left the office physically, / but we are very much still there mentally, / as our minds get caught in the endless loop / of replaying the events of today / and worrying about all the things / we need to get done the following day.
우리는 육체적으로는 사무실을 떠났을지 모르지만, / 우리는 정신적으로는 매우 많이 아직 그곳에 있는데, / 왜냐하면 우리의 마음이 끝없는 루프에 사로잡혀 있기 때문이다. / 오늘의 사건들을 재생하고 / 모든 일에 대해 걱정하는 / 우리가 이튿날 처리해야 할 필요가 있는

So now, as he gets to the door of his house, / he applies what he calls "the pause that refreshes."
그래서 지금, 그는 집 문 앞에 이르러, / 그는 자칭 '원기를 회복하게 하는 멈춤'을 적용한다.

He stops for just a moment.
그는 아주 잠깐 멈춘다.

He closes his eyes.
그는 눈을 감는다.

He breathes in and out once: deeply and slowly.
그는 한 번, 깊게 그리고 천천히 숨을 들이쉬고 내쉰다.

As he exhales, / he lets the work issues fall away.
그가 숨을 내쉬면서 / 그는 일과 관련된 문제를 서서히 사라지게 한다.

This allows him to walk through the front door to his family / with more singleness of purpose.
이렇게 하고 나면 그는 현관문을 통해 그의 가족에게 걸어갈 수 있게 된다. / 한 가지 목표에 더 몰두하면서

It supports the sentiment attributed to Lao Tzu:
그것은 노자가 말한 것으로 여겨지는 다음과 같은 정서를 뒷받침한다:

"In work, do what you enjoy.
"직장에서는 당신이 즐기는 것을 하라.

In family life, be completely present."
가정생활에서는 온전히 참여하라."

한 대기업의 부사장인 Jeffrey A. Rodgers는 예전에 원기 회복을 위해 잠시 멈추는 간단한 아이디어를 배웠다. 그것은 Jeff가 매일 저녁 직장에서 집으로 차를 몰고 가던 중 자신의 마음이 여전히 업무 관련 프로젝트에 집중되어 있다는 것을 깨달았을 때 시작되었다. 우리는 모두 이 기분을 안다. 우리는 육체적으로는 사무실을 떠났을지 모르지만, 정신적으로는 매우 많이 아직 그곳에 있는데, 왜냐하면 우리의 마음이 오늘의 사건들을 재생하고 이튿날 처리해야 할 필요가 있는 모든 일에 대해 걱정하는 끝없는 루프에 사로잡혀 있기 때문이다. 그래서 지금, 집 문 앞에 이르러, 그는 자칭 '원기를 회복하게 하는 멈춤'을 적용한다. 그는 아주 잠깐 멈춘다. 그는 눈을 감는다. 그는 한 번, 깊게 천천히 숨을 들이쉬고 내쉰다. 숨을 내쉬면서 그는 일과 관련된 문제를 서서히 사라지게 한다. 이렇게 하고 나면 그는 한 가지 목표에 더 몰두하면서 현관문을 통해

그의 가족에게 걸어갈 수 있게 된다. 그것은 노자가 말한 것으로 여겨지는 다음과 같은 정서를 뒷받침한다. "직장에서는 당신이 즐기는 것을 하라. 가정생활에서는 온전히 참여하라."

Why? 왜 정답일까?

'In work, do what you enjoy. In family life, be completely present.'에서 직장에서는 일을 즐기며 하되 집에 와서는 가정생활에 온전히 집중하라고 언급하는 것으로 보아, 빈칸에 들어갈 말로 가장 적절한 것은 퇴근 후에는 원기 회복에 도움이 되도록 일에 관한 생각을 하지 않는다는 의미의 ① '일과 관련된 문제를 서서히 사라지게 한다'이다.

● physically ⓐⓓ 물리적으로 ● endless ⓐ 끝이 없는, 무한의
● exhale ⓥ 내쉬다 ● singleness ⓝ 일심전력
● attribute A to B A를 B의 것으로 보다 ● completely ⓐⓓ 완전히
● fall away 서서히 줄어들다 ● retrace ⓥ 되짚어보다
● reflect on ~을 되돌아보다, 반추하다

구문 풀이

5행 We may have left the office physically, but we are very much
~했을지도 모른다(과거에 대한 약한 추측)
still there mentally, as our minds get caught in the endless loop of
접속사(~하기 때문에) 전치사
replaying the events of today and worrying about all the things [we
동명사1 동명사2 선행사
need to get done the following day].

---

05 고고학 연구에서의 과학적 방법 정답률 51% | 정답 ①

다음 빈칸에 들어갈 말로 가장 적절한 것을 고르시오.

✓ from the data which they had discovered
자신들이 발견했던 자료에서
② from comparisons of data in other fields
다른 분야의 데이터와의 비교로부터
③ to explore more sites for their future studies
향후 연구를 위한 더 많은 현장을 탐색하기 위해서
④ by supposing possible theoretical frameworks
가능한 이론적인 틀을 가정함으로써
⑤ by observing the hypothesis-testing procedures
가설 검증 절차를 준수함으로써

Through recent decades / academic archaeologists have been urged / to conduct their research and excavations / according to hypothesis-testing procedures.
최근 몇 십 년 동안 내내 / 학계의 고고학자들은 촉구 받아 왔다. / 연구와 발굴을 수행하라고 / 가설 검증 절차에 따라

It has been argued / that we should construct our general theories, / deduce testable propositions / and prove or disprove them against the sampled data.
주장되어 왔다. / 우리가 일반적인 이론을 구축하고, / 검증할 수 있는 명제를 추론하며, / 그것을 표본 자료와 비교하여 증명하거나 논박해야 한다고

In fact, the application of this 'scientific method' / often ran into difficulties.
사실 이런 '과학적 방법'의 적용은 / 자주 어려움에 봉착했다.

The data have a tendency / to lead to unexpected questions, problems and issues.
자료는 경향이 있다. / 예상치 못한 질문, 문제 그리고 쟁점으로 이어지는

Thus, archaeologists claiming to follow hypothesis-testing procedures / found themselves having to create a fiction.
따라서 가설 검증 절차를 따를 것을 주장하는 고고학자들은 / 가공의 이야기를 써야하는 자기 자신을 발견했다.

In practice, / their work and theoretical conclusions partly developed / from the data which they had discovered.
실제로는, / 그들의 연구물과 이론적 결론이 부분적으로 비롯되었다. / 자신들이 발견했던 자료에서

In other words, they already knew the data / when they decided upon an interpretation.
다시 말해서, 그들은 이미 그 자료를 알고 있었다. / 그들이 어떤 해석으로 결정할 때

But in presenting their work / they rewrote the script, / placing the theory first / and claiming to have tested it against data, / which they discovered, / as in an experiment under laboratory conditions.
그러나 연구물을 발표할 때, / 그들은 대본을 다시 작성했다. / 이론을 앞세우고 / 그것을 자료와 비교하여 검증했다고 주장하면서 / 자신들이 발견한 / 실험실 조건에서의 실험에서처럼

최근 몇 십 년 동안 내내 학계의 고고학자들은 가설 검증 절차에 따라 연구와 발굴을 수행하라고 촉구받아 왔다. 우리가 일반적인 이론을 구축하고, 검증할 수 있는 명제를 추론하며, 그것을 표본 자료와 비교하여 증명하거나 논박해야 한다고 주장되어 왔다. 사실 이런 '과학적 방법'의 적용은 자주 어려움에 봉착했다. 자료는 예상치 못한 질문, 문제 그리고 쟁점으로 이어지는 경향이 있다. 따라서 가설 검증 절차를 따를 것을 주장하는 고고학자들은 가공의 이야기를

써야하는 자기 자신을 발견했다. 실제로는, 그들의 연구물과 이론적 결론이 부분적으로 자신들이 발견했던 자료에서 비롯되었다. 다시 말해서, 그들이 어떤 해석으로 결정할 때 그들은 이미 그 자료를 알고 있었다. 그러나 연구물을 발표할 때, 그들은 실험실 조건에서의 실험에서처럼 이론을 앞세우고 그것을 자신들이 발견한 자료와 비교하여 검증했다고 주장하면서 대본을 다시 작성했다.

Why? 왜 정답일까?

과학적 연구 방법이 고고학 연구에 적용되는 과정에서 생겨난 한계를 주로 설명한 글이다. 빈칸 앞의 두 문장에서 연구 데이터가 때때로 예상치 못한 질문거리나 쟁점을 낳았기에 고고학자들은 때때로 이야기를 지어내야 했다는 내용을 언급한 데 이어, 빈칸 뒤의 두 문장에서는 이들이 마치 실험실에서 이론을 먼저 세우고 이를 검증할 자료를 나중에 발견한 것처럼 꾸몄지만 사실은 자료 내용을 먼저 알고 그에 들어맞는 해석이나 이론을 세운 것임을 설명하고 있다. 특히 '~ they already knew the data when they decided upon an interpretation.'를 근거로 볼 때, 빈칸에 들어갈 말로 가장 적절한 것은 ① '자신들이 발견했던 자료에서'이다.

- archaeologist ⓝ 고고학자
- hypothesis-testing procedure 가설 검증 절차
- construct ⓥ 구성하다
- disprove ⓥ 논박하다, 틀렸음을 입증하다
- run into ~을 우연히 마주치다
- procedure ⓝ 절차
- proposition ⓝ 명제
- application ⓝ 적용
- theoretical ⓐ 이론적인
- observe ⓥ (법률, 규칙 등을) 준수하다

구문 풀이

9행 Thus, archaeologists [claiming to follow hypothesis-testing procedures] found themselves having to create a fiction.
주어 / 현재분사 / 동사 / 목적어 / 목적격 보어(현재분사)

06 자신만의 목적과 운명을 만들어 가려는 인간   정답률 45% | 정답 ①

다음 빈칸에 들어갈 말로 가장 적절한 것을 고르시오. [3점]

✔① alter the course of their lives – 자기 삶의 행로를 바꾸려는
② possess more than other people – 다른 사람들보다 더 많이 소유하려는
③ suppress their negative emotions – 자신의 부정적인 감정을 억누르려는
④ sacrifice themselves for noble causes – 숭고한 대의명분을 위해 자신을 희생하려는
⑤ show admiration for supernatural power – 초자연적인 힘에 대해 존경심을 보이려는

Gordon Allport argued / that history records many individuals / who were not content with an existence / that offered them / little variety, a lack of psychic tension, and minimal challenge.
Gordon Allport는 주장했다. / 역사가 많은 개개인을 기록하고 있다고 / 생활에 만족하지 못한 / 그들에게 제공하는 / 다양성이 거의 없고 심적 긴장이 결핍되어 있으며 최소한의 도전만을

Allport considers it normal / to be pulled forward by a vision of the future / that awakened within persons their drive / to alter the course of their lives.
Allport는 정상이라고 여긴다. / 미래에 대한 통찰력에 의해 앞으로 나아가게 되는 것을 / 인간의 내면에서 욕구를 일깨운 / 자기 삶의 행로를 바꾸려는

He suggests / that people possess a need to invent motives and purposes / that would consume their inner energies.
그는 말한다. / 사람들이 동기와 목적을 만들어 내려는 욕구를 지니고 있다고 / 그들의 내면의 에너지를 다 쓸

Similarly, / Erich Fromm proposed a need / on the part of humans / to rise above the roles of passive creatures / in an accidental if not random world.
마찬가지로 / Erich Fromm은 욕구를 제시했다. / 인간에게 있는 / 수동적인 피조물의 역할을 넘어서고 싶은 / 마구잡이는 아니더라도 우연한 세계에서

To him, / humans are driven / to transcend the state of merely having been created; / instead, / humans seek to become the creators, / the active shapers of their own destiny.
그에게, / 인간은 이끌리지만, / 단지 창조된 상태를 넘어서도록 / 대신에 / 인간은 창조자가 되려고 노력하는 존재이다. / 즉 자신의 운명을 만드는 적극적인 행위자

Rising above the passive and accidental nature of existence, / humans generate their own purposes / and thereby provide themselves with a true basis of freedom.
존재의 수동적이고 우연한 본질을 넘어서서, / 인간은 자신만의 목적을 만들어 내고, / 그렇게 함으로써 자신에게 자유의 진정한 토대를 제공한다.

Gordon Allport는 다양성이 거의 없고 심적 긴장이 결핍되어 있으며 최소한의 도전만을 제공하는 생활에 만족하지 못한 많은 개개인을 역사가 기록하고 있다고 주장했다. Allport는 인간의 내면에서 자기 삶의 행로를 바꾸려는 욕구를 일깨운 미래에 대한 통찰력에 의해 앞으로 나아가게 되는 것이 정상이라고 여긴다. 그는 사람들이 내면의 에너지를 다 쓸 동기와 목적을 만들어 내려는 욕구를 지니고 있다고 말한다. 마찬가지로 Erich Fromm은 인간에게는 마구잡이

는 아니더라도 우연한 세계에서 수동적인 피조물의 역할을 넘어서고 싶은 욕구가 있다고 제시했다. 그에게, 인간은 단지 창조된 상태를 넘어서도록 이끌리지만, 대신에 창조자, 즉 자신의 운명을 만드는 적극적인 행위자가 되려고 노력하는 존재이다. 존재의 수동적이고 우연한 본질을 넘어서서, 인간은 자신만의 목적을 만들어 내고, 그렇게 함으로써 자신에게 자유의 진정한 토대를 제공한다.

Why? 왜 정답일까?

마지막 두 문장에서 인간은 수동적 피조물의 역할을 넘어 자신의 운명과 목적을 만들려는 적극적 행위자가 되기 위해 노력한다(~ humans are driven to transcend the state of merely having been created; instead, humans seek to become the creators, the active shapers of their own destiny.)고 언급하는 것으로 볼 때, 빈칸에 들어갈 말로 가장 적절한 것은 이를 비유적으로 나타낸 ① '자기 삶의 행로를 바꾸려는'이다.

- content with ~에 만족한
- variety ⓝ 다양성, 변화
- minimal ⓐ 최소한의
- drive ⓝ 욕구, 이끌다
- consume ⓥ 다 쓰다, 소비하다
- passive ⓐ 수동적인
- accidental ⓐ 우연한
- merely ⓐⓓ 단지, 그저, 다만
- generate ⓥ 만들어내다
- sacrifice ⓥ 희생하다
- existence ⓝ 존재
- psychic ⓐ 정신의, 마음의
- awaken ⓥ 일깨우다, 자각시키다
- motive ⓝ 동기
- rise above ~을 넘어서다
- creature ⓝ 피조물, 창조물
- transcend ⓥ 초월하다, 능가하다
- destiny ⓝ 운명
- suppress ⓥ 억누르다
- noble ⓐ 고귀한, 숭고한

구문 풀이

4행 Allport considers it normal to be pulled forward by a vision
동사 / 목적격 보어 / 진목적어(~것) / 가목적어 / 선행사
of the future [that awakened (within persons) their drive to alter the
동사 / 목적어 / 형용사적 용법
course of their lives].

★★★ 1등급 대비 고난도 2점 문제

07 과학만능주의와 과학 철학   정답률 40% | 정답 ②

다음 빈칸에 들어갈 말로 가장 적절한 것을 고르시오.

① question – 의문
✔② account – 중요
③ controversy – 논쟁
④ variation – 변화
⑤ bias – 편견

The role of science can sometimes be overstated, / with its advocates slipping into scientism.
과학의 역할은 때때로 과장될 수 있고, / 그것의 옹호자들은 과학만능주의에 빠져든다.

Scientism is the view / that the scientific description of reality / is the only truth there is.
과학만능주의는 견해이다. / 현실에 대한 과학적 기술만이 / 존재하는 유일한 진실이라는

With the advance of science, / there has been a tendency to slip into scientism, / and assume that any factual claim can be authenticated / if and only if the term 'scientific' can correctly be ascribed to it.
과학의 발전과 함께, / 과학만능주의에 빠져드는 경향이 있어 왔다. / 사실에 입각한 어떤 주장이든 진짜로 입증될 수 있다고 가정하는 / '과학적'이라는 용어가 정확하게 그것에 속하는 것으로 생각될 수 있는 경우에 그리고 오직 그런 경우에만

The consequence is / that non-scientific approaches to reality / — and that can include all the arts, / religion, / and personal, emotional and value-laden ways of encountering the world — / may become labelled as merely subjective, / and therefore of little account / in terms of describing the way the world is.
그 결과, / 현실에 대한 비과학적 접근 방식은 / 그런데 그것에는 모든 예술, / 종교, / 그리고 세상을 접하는 개인적, 감정적, 가치 판단적인 방식이 포함될 수 있다 / 주관적인 것에 불과하고, / 따라서 거의 중요하지 않은 것으로 분류될지도 모른다. / 세상이 존재하는 방식을 기술하는 것의 관점에서

The philosophy of science seeks to avoid crude scientism / and get a balanced view / on what the scientific method can and cannot achieve.
과학 철학은 투박한 과학만능주의를 피하고 / 균형 잡힌 시각을 가지려고 노력한다. / 과학적 방법이 성취할 수 있는 것과 성취할 수 없는 것에 대한

과학의 역할은 때때로 과장될 수 있고, 그것의 옹호자들은 과학만능주의에 빠져든다. 과학만능주의는 현실에 대한 과학적 기술만이 존재하는 유일한 진실이라는 견해이다. 과학의 발전과 함께, 과학만능주의에 빠져들어 '과학적'이라는 용어가 정확하게 그것에 속하는 것으로 생각될 수 있는 경우에 그리고 오직 그런 경우에만 사실에 입각한 어떤 주장이든 진짜로 입증될 수 있다고 가정하

DAY 04

는 경향이 있어 왔다. 그 결과, 현실에 대한 비과학적 접근 방식은—그런데 그것에는 모든 예술, 종교, 그리고 세상을 접하는 개인적, 감정적, 가치 판단적인 방식이 포함될 수 있다—주관적인 것에 불과하고, 따라서 세상이 존재하는 방식을 기술하는 것의 관점에서 거의 중요하지 않은 것으로 분류될지도 모른다. 과학 철학은 투박한 과학만능주의를 피하고 과학적 방법이 성취할 수 있는 것과 성취할 수 없는 것에 대한 균형 잡힌 시각을 가지려고 노력한다.

Why? 왜 정답일까?

과학만능주의에서 나타날 수 있는 오류와 이를 바로잡기 위한 과학 철학의 노력에 관해 기술한 글이다. 'Scientism is the view that the scientific description of reality is the only truth there is.'에서 과학만능주의란 현상에 관한 과학적 기술만을 진실로 취급하는 견해라고 설명하는 것으로 볼 때, 빈칸 문장에서 언급하는 비과학적인 접근 방식은 과학만능주의에 따르면 주관적이며 '중요하지 않은' 대상으로 치부될 것임을 추론할 수 있다. 따라서 빈칸에 들어갈 말로 가장 적절한 것은 ② '중요'이다.

- **overstate** ⓥ 과장하다
- **slip into** ~으로 빠져들다
- **description** ⓝ 기술, 묘사
- **authenticate** ⓥ 진짜임을 증명하다
- **consequence** ⓝ 결과
- **encounter** ⓥ 접하다, 마주치다
- **subjective** ⓐ 주관적인
- **advocate** ⓝ 지지자
- **scientism** ⓝ 과학만능주의
- **factual** ⓐ 사실에 입각한
- **correctly** ⓐ 정확하게
- **value-laden** ⓐ 가치 판단적인
- **merely** ⓐ 단지
- **of little account** 거의 중요하지 않은

구문 풀이

8행 The consequence is {that non-scientific approaches to
　　　　　주어　　　　동사 접속사　　　　　　┌A+
reality — (and that can include all the arts, religion, and personal,
( ): 주어 보충 설명
emotional and value-laden ways of encountering the world) —
may become labelled as merely subjective, and therefore of little
　　　　　be labelled + as + B + and C : A가 B하고 C한 것으로 분류되다
account in terms of describing the way [the world is]}.
　　　　　　　　　　　　　　　└ { }: 전체 문장 보어

★★ 문제 해결 꿀~팁 ★★

▶ 많이 틀린 이유는?
EBS 연계문항이지만 내용이 추상적이고 빈칸의 단어가 내용적인 키워드가 아니라는 점에서 난이도가 높다. 또한 답인 account가 '계좌, 설명' 등이 아닌 '중요성'이라는 의미로 쓰였다는 점도 수험생들의 혼란을 가중시켰을 여지가 있다.

▶ 문제 해결 방법은?
과학만능주의의 개념을 토대로 빈칸이 포함된 문장을 꼼꼼하게 독해한 후, 선택지의 단어를 빈칸에 하나씩 대입하며 오답을 소거하도록 한다.

★★★ 1등급 대비 고난도 2점 문제

08 생태 건강과 지표면 상태　　　정답률 25% | 정답 ⑤

다음 빈칸에 들어갈 말로 가장 적절한 것을 고르시오.

① the number of plants on it increases too rapidly
토양 위 식물 수가 너무 빨리 증가하면
② it stops providing enough nourishment for humans
토양이 인류에게 충분한 영양을 제공하기를 멈추면
③ climate change transforms its chemical components
기후 변화가 토양의 화학 성분을 바꾸면
④ alien species prevail and deplete resources around it
외래종이 번창하고 토양 주변 자원을 고갈시키면
✓⑤ great quantities of contaminants are introduced into it
다량의 오염 물질이 토양에 유입되면

Ecological health depends on / keeping the surface of the earth rich in humus and minerals / so that it can provide a foundation for healthy plant and animal life.
생태 건강은 ~에 달려 있다. / 지표면을 부식토와 광물이 풍부한 상태로 유지하는 것 / 그것이 동물물의 건강한 삶을 위한 토대를 제공할 수 있도록

The situation is disrupted / if the soil loses these raw materials / or if great quantities of contaminants are introduced into it.
그 상황은 붕괴된다. / 토양이 이러한 원료를 잃거나 / 다량의 오염 물질이 토양에 유입되면

When man goes beneath the surface of the earth / and drags out minerals or other compounds / that did not evolve as part of this system, / then problems follow.
인간이 지표면 아래로 가서, / 광물이나 다른 화합물을 끄집어내면, / 이 시스템의 일부로 변하지 않은 / 문제가 뒤따른다.

The mining of lead and cadmium / are examples of this.
납과 카드뮴의 채굴이 / 이것의 예이다.

Petroleum is also a substance / that has been dug out of the bowels of the earth / and introduced into the surface ecology / by man.
석유 또한 물질이다. / 지구의 내부에서 채굴되어 / 지표 생태계에 유입된 / 인간에 의해

Though it is formed from plant matter, / the highly reduced carbon compounds that result / are often toxic to living protoplasm.
비록 석유가 식물로부터 형성되지만, / 그로 인해 생기는 고도로 환원된 탄소 화합물은 / 살아 있는 원형질에 유독한 경우가 많다.

In some cases this is true of even very tiny amounts, / as in the case of "polychlorinated biphenyls," / a petroleum product which can cause cancer.
몇몇 경우에는 심지어 매우 적은 양일 때도 그렇다. / '폴리염화 바이페닐'의 경우에서처럼, / 암을 유발할 수 있는 석유 생성 물질인

생태 건강은 지표면이 동식물의 건강한 삶을 위한 토대를 제공할 수 있도록 지표면을 부식토와 광물이 풍부한 상태로 유지하는 데 달려 있다. 토양이 이러한 원료를 잃거나 다량의 오염 물질이 토양에 유입되면 그 상황은 붕괴된다. 인간이 지표면 아래로 가서, 이 시스템의 일부로 변하지 않은 광물이나 다른 화합물을 끄집어내면, 문제가 뒤따른다. 납과 카드뮴의 채굴이 이것의 예이다. 석유 또한 인간에 의해 지구의 내부에서 채굴되어 지표 생태계에 유입된 물질이다. 비록 석유가 식물로부터 형성되지만, 그로 인해 생기는 고도로 환원된 탄소 화합물은 살아 있는 원형질에 유독한 경우가 많다. 암을 유발할 수 있는 석유 생성 물질인 '폴리염화 바이페닐'의 경우에서처럼, 몇몇 경우에는 심지어 매우 적은 양일 때도 그렇다.

Why? 왜 정답일까?

인간이 지표 밑으로 내려가 광물이나 화합물을 끄집어 내오면 그것이 지표 위 생태계에 유독하게 작용할 수 있다(When man goes beneath the surface of the earth and drags out minerals or other compounds that did not evolve as part of this system, then problems follow.)는 내용으로 보아, 빈칸에 들어갈 말로 가장 적절한 것은 ⑤ '다량의 오염 물질이 토양에 유입되면'이다.

- **ecological** ⓐ 생태의
- **surface** ⓝ 지표, 표면
- **humus** ⓝ 부식토, 부엽토
- **so that** ~하기 위해
- **disrupt** ⓥ 파괴하다, 지장을 주다
- **beneath** prep ~ 아래로
- **compound** ⓝ 화합물
- **lead** ⓝ 납
- **substance** ⓝ 물질
- **bowel** ⓝ ~의 가장 깊은 곳, 내부
- **protoplasm** ⓝ 원형질
- **tiny** ⓐ 아주 작은
- **nourishment** ⓝ 영양
- **prevail** ⓥ 우세하다
- **depend on** ~에 달려 있다
- **rich** ⓐ 풍부한
- **mineral** ⓝ 광물
- **foundation** ⓝ 기반, 토대
- **raw material** 원재료
- **drag out** 끄집어내다
- **mining** ⓝ 채굴
- **petroleum** ⓝ 석유
- **dig out of** ~에서 파내다
- **toxic** ⓐ 유독한
- **true of** ~에 해당하는
- **the number of** ~의 수
- **chemical component** 화학 성분

구문 풀이

14행 In some cases this is true of even very tiny amounts,
as in the case of "polychlorinated biphenyls," a petroleum product
~의 경우와 마찬가지로　　　　　동격(= "polychlorinated biphenyls")
[which can cause cancer].

★★ 문제 해결 꿀~팁 ★★

▶ 많이 틀린 이유는?
첫 문장에 rich in humus and minerals, a foundation for healthy plant and animal life 등의 표현이 나오므로 '영양분 공급'을 언급하는 ②가 답처럼 보일 수 있다. 하지만, 빈칸 내용을 뒷받침하는 석유의 예시에 '영양분 공급 (중단)'에 관한 내용은 없다. 오히려 이 물질이 토양에 유입됐을 때 생명체에 '유독한' 경우가 있음을 지적하는 것이 예시의 핵심이다.

▶ 문제 해결 방법은?
예시 부분에서 주제를 추론해 빈칸을 채워야 한다. 석유에 관한 내용을 보면, 원래 땅속에 있다가 외부 생태계에 유입된 물질로 간혹 생명체에 '유독한(toxic)' 경우가 있다고 한다. 이를 정답 선택지에서는 contaminants라는 표현으로 바꾸었다.

★★★ 1등급 대비 고난도 3점 문제

09 음악의 전개부 구성　　　정답률 32% | 정답 ②

다음 빈칸에 들어갈 말로 가장 적절한 것을 고르시오. [3점]

① makes the composer's musical ideas contradictory
작곡가의 음악적 아이디어를 모순되게 만든다

✔ **appears in an incredible variety of ways**
엄청나게 다양한 방식으로 나타난다
③ provides extensive musical knowledge creatively
광범위한 음악적 지식을 창의적으로 제공한다
④ remains fairly calm within the structure
구조 내에서 상당히 조용하게 남아 있다
⑤ becomes deeply associated with one's own enjoyment
사람들의 즐거움과 깊이 관련된다

Development can get very complicated and fanciful.
전개부는 매우 복잡하고 별날 수가 있다.

A fugue by Johann Sebastian Bach illustrates / how far this process could go, / when a single melodic line, sometimes just a handful of notes, / was all that the composer needed to create a brilliant work / containing lots of intricate development within a coherent structure.
Johann Sebastian Bach의 푸가는 보여준다. / 이 과정이 어디까지 갈 수 있는지를 / 멜로디 라인 하나, 때로는 단 몇 개의 음만이 / 작곡가가 수작을 창작하는 데 필요한 전부였을 때 / 일관성 있는 구조 내에서 여러 복잡한 전개부가 포함된

Ludwig van Beethoven's famous Fifth Symphony / provides an exceptional example / of how much mileage a classical composer can get / out of a few notes and a simple rhythmic tapping.
루드비히 반 베토벤의 유명한 5번 교향곡은 / 우수한 예시를 제공한다. / 클래식 작곡가가 얼마나 많은 이익을 얻어낼 수 있는지에 대해 / 음 몇 개와 규칙적으로 반복되는 박자로부터

The opening da-da-da-DUM / that everyone has heard somewhere or another / appears in an incredible variety of ways / throughout not only the opening movement, / but the remaining three movements, / like a kind of motto or a connective thread.
시작부의 다-다-다-덤은 / 모든 사람들이 어디선가 들어본 / 엄청나게 다양한 방식으로 나타난다. / 시작 악장뿐만 아니라 / 나머지 3악장 내내 / 일종의 반복 악구나 연결 끈처럼

Just as we don't always see the intricate brushwork / that goes into the creation of a painting, / we may not always notice / how Beethoven keeps finding fresh uses for his motto / or how he develops his material into a large, cohesive statement.
우리가 복잡한 붓놀림을 항상 볼 수 있지 않듯이, / 그림 작품 하나를 완성하는 데 들인 / 우리는 항상 알아보지는 못할 수도 있다. / Beethoven이 반복 악구를 어떻게 계속 새롭게 사용해낼 방법을 찾는지 / 또는 제재를 거대하고 응집력 있는 진술로 어떻게 전개하는지

But / a lot of the enjoyment / we get from that mighty symphony / stems from the inventiveness behind it, / the impressive development of musical ideas.
그러나 / 즐거움의 많은 부분은 / 그 강력한 교향곡에서 우리가 얻는 / 그 이면의 독창성에서 비롯된다. / 즉 음악적 아이디어의 인상적인 전개에서

전개부는 매우 복잡하고 별날 수가 있다. 요한 세바스찬 바흐의 푸가는 작곡가가 일관성 있는 구조 내에서 여러 복잡한 전개부가 포함된 수작을 창작하는 데 멜로디 라인 하나, 때로는 단 몇 개의 음만이 필요했을 때, 이 과정이 어디까지 갈 수 있는지를 보여준다. 루드비히 반 베토벤의 유명한 5번 교향곡은 음 몇 개와 리드미컬한 간단한 박자로 클래식 작곡가가 얼마나 많은 이익을 얻어낼 수 있는지에 대해 우수한 예시를 제공한다. 모든 사람들이 어디선가 들어본 시작부의 다-다-다-덤은 일종의 반복 악구나 연결 끈처럼, 시작 악장뿐만 아니라 나머지 3악장 내내 엄청나게 다양한 방식으로 나타난다. 우리가 그림 작품 하나를 완성하는 데 들인 복잡한 붓놀림을 항상 볼 수 있지 않듯이, 베토벤이 반복 악구를 어떻게 계속 새롭게 사용할 방법을 찾아내는지나 제재를 거대하고 응집력 있는 진술로 어떻게 전개하는지를 항상 알아보지는 못할 수도 있다. 그러나 그 강력한 교향곡에서 우리가 얻는 즐거움의 많은 부분은 그 이면의 독창성, 즉 음악적 아이디어의 인상적인 전개에서 비롯된다.

Why? 왜 정답일까?

베토벤의 5번 교향곡을 예로 들어, 음 몇 개와 단순한 박자 구조를 계속 새롭게 활용하고 변주하여(how Beethoven keeps finding fresh uses ~ cohesive statement) 인상적인 전개부를 만들어가는 방식을 설명한 글이다. 따라서 빈칸에 들어갈 말로 가장 적절한 것은 ② '엄청나게 다양한 방식으로 나타난다'이다.

● development ⓝ 전개부	● complicated ⓐ 복잡한
● fanciful ⓐ 별난, 기발한	● illustrate ⓥ 보여주다
● a handful of 소수의	● note ⓝ 음표
● composer ⓝ 작곡가	● brilliant ⓐ 훌륭한
● intricate ⓐ 복잡한	● coherent ⓐ 통일성 있는
● structure ⓝ 구조	● exceptional ⓐ 우수한, 이례적인
● mileage ⓝ 이익	● tapping ⓝ 박자, 두드림
● movement ⓝ 악장	● motto ⓝ 반복 악구
● connective ⓐ 연결하는	● thread ⓝ 실, 끈
● brushwork ⓝ (화가의) 화법, 붓놀림	● material ⓝ 제재
● cohesive ⓐ 응집력 있는, 단결된	● mighty ⓐ 강력한
● stem from ~에서 나오다	● inventiveness ⓝ 독창적임
● contradictory ⓐ 모순되는	

구문 풀이

15행 Just as we don't always see the intricate brushwork [that
접속사(~와 마찬가지로)
goes into the creation of a painting], we may not always notice
{how Beethoven keeps finding fresh uses for his motto} or {how he
{ } : 간접의문문(notice의 목적어)
develops his material into a large, cohesive statement}.

★★ 문제 해결 꿀~팁 ★★

▶ 많이 틀린 이유는?
이 글은 음악의 전개부가 어떻게 '복잡하고 별난지' 설명하고 있다. 재료는 소수의 음표나 리듬에 불과해도 이것을 '어떻게 계속 새롭게 사용할지' 계속 보여주는 것이 곧 전개부라는 것이다. 오답 선택지 중, ①의 키워드는 '악상의 모순'인데, '음과 리듬의 새로운 사용'을 '모순'이라고 보기는 어렵다.

▶ 문제 해결 방법은?
글 내용이 예시 위주로 전개되고 문제 또한 복잡하므로 독해하기 어려울 수 있다. 하지만 예시를 정리하는 마지막 두 문장의 fresh uses와 inventiveness만 제대로 포착하면 바로 ②의 incredible variety와 연결할 수 있다.

★★★ 1등급 대비 고난도 3점 문제

10 상담에서 문제 해결에 도움을 주는 외재화   정답률 30% | 정답 ①

다음 빈칸에 들어갈 말로 가장 적절한 것을 고르시오. [3점]

✔ exceptions to the problem story
문제 이야기에 대한 예외들
② distances from the alternative story
대안이 되는 이야기와의 거리
③ problems that originate from the counsellor
상담사로부터 나온 문제들
④ efforts to combine old and new experiences
옛 경험과 새로운 경험을 결합하려는 노력
⑤ methods of linking the child's stories to another's
한 아이의 이야기를 다른 아이의 이야기와 연결시키는 방법

Externalization is the foundation / from which many narrative conversations are built.
외재화는 토대이다. / 많은 이야기식 대화가 이루어지는

This requires a particular shift in the use of language.
이는 언어의 사용에 있어 특별한 전환을 요구한다.

Often externalizing conversations / involve tracing the influence of the problem in a child's life over time / and how the problem has disempowered the child / by limiting his ability to see things in a different light.
외재화하는 대화에는, / 시간이 흐르며 문제가 아이의 삶에 미친 영향력을 추적하는 것이 포함되는 경우가 흔하다. / 그리고 그 문제가 아이로부터 힘을 빼앗아 왔던 방식 / 아이가 다른 시각에서 상황을 보는 능력을 제한하여

The counsellor helps the child to change / by deconstructing old stories / and reconstructing preferred stories / about himself and his life.
상담사는 아이가 변화하는 것을 도와준다. / 아이가 오래된 이야기를 해체하고 / 선호되는 이야기를 재구성하여 / 자기 자신과 삶에 관한

To help the child to develop a new story, / the counsellor and child search for times / when the problem has not influenced the child or the child's life / and focus on the different ways / the child thought, felt and behaved.
아이가 새로운 이야기를 전개하는 것을 돕기 위해, / 상담사와 아이는 시간을 찾아내어, / 문제가 아이와 아이의 삶에 영향을 미치지 않았던 / 다양한 방식에 초점을 둔다. / 아이가 생각하고 느끼고 행동했던

These exceptions to the problem story / help the child create a new and preferred story.
문제 이야기에 대한 이런 예외들이 / 아이가 새로운 선호되는 이야기를 만들어 내는 데 도움을 준다.

As a new and preferred story begins to emerge, / it is important to assist the child / to hold on to, or stay connected to, the new story.
새로운 선호되는 이야기가 나오기 시작할 때, / 아이를 도와주는 것이 중요하다. / 그 새로운 이야기를 붙들고 있도록, 즉 계속 그 이야기에 연결되어 있도록

외재화는 많은 이야기식 대화가 이루어지는 토대이다. 이는 언어의 사용에 있어 특별한 전환을 요구한다. 외재화하는 대화에는, 시간이 흐르며 문제가 아이의 삶에 미친 영향력과, 그 문제가 아이가 다른 시각에서 상황을 보는 능력을 제한하여 아이로부터 힘을 빼앗아 왔던 방식을 추적하는 것이 포함되는 경우가 흔하다. 상담사는 아이가 자기 자신과 삶에 관한 오래된 이야기를 해체하고 선호되는 이야기를 재구성하여 아이가 변화하는 것을 도와준다. 아이가 새로운 이야기를 전개하는 것을 돕기 위해, 상담사와 아이는 문제가 아이와 아이의 삶에 영향을 미치지 않았던 시간을 찾아내어, 아이가 다르게 생각하고 느끼고 행동했던 방식에 초점을 둔다. 문제 이야기에 대한 이런 예외들이 아이가 새로운 선호되는 이야기를 만들어 내는 데 도움을 준다. 새로운 선호되는 이야기가

나오기 시작할 때, 아이가 그 새로운 이야기를 붙들고 있도록, 즉 계속 그 이야기에 연결되어 있도록 도와주는 것이 중요하다.

Why? 왜 정답일까?

글의 전반부에서 상담사는 아이가 자기 자신과 자기 삶에 대한 해묵은 이야기를 재구성하고 새로운 이야기를 구성하게 함으로써 아이가 변화하는 것을 도울 수 있다고 말한 데 이어, 'To help the child to develop a new story, the counsellor and child search for times when the problem has not influenced the child or the child's life and focus on the different ways the child thought, felt and behaved.'에서는 새로운 이야기를 구성하는 데 도움을 줄 구체적인 방안을 제시한다. 즉 문제가 아이의 삶에 영향력을 미치지 '않던' 시절의 이야기로 돌아가 그때 아이가 생각하고 느끼고 행동했던 방식에 집중하면 새로운 이야기가 전개될 수 있다는 것인데, 이는 결국 '문제' 입장에서 생각하면 문제가 적용되지 않는 '예외' 상황을 생각하게 하는 것과 관련이 있다. 따라서 빈칸에 들어갈 말로 가장 적절한 것은 ① '문제 이야기에 대한 예외들'이다.

- externalization ⑩ 외재화
- narrative ⓐ 이야기의, 서술식의
- built ⓐ ~으로 만들어진
- involve ⓥ 관련되다, 포함하다
- disempower ⓥ ~의 영향력을 뺏다
- light ⑩ 관점, 견지
- reconstruct ⓥ 재구성하다
- exception ⑩ 예외, 제외
- hold on to ~을 붙잡다, ~에 매달리다
- foundation ⑩ 기초, 기반, 토대
- conversation ⑩ 대화, 회화
- shift ⑩ 전환
- trace ⓥ 추적하다
- limit ⑩ 제한, 한계
- deconstruct ⓥ 해체하다
- behave ⓥ 행동하다
- emerge ⓥ 나오다, 드러나다
- connected to ~에 연결된

구문 풀이

10행 To help the child to develop a new story, / the counsellor
부사적 용법(~하기 위해)   목적격 보어(= develop)
and child search for times [when the problem has not influenced the
동사1(~을 찾다)   관계부사
child or the child's life] and focus on the different ways [the child
동사2(~에 집중하다)   (how 생략)
thought, felt and behaved].

★★ 문제 해결 꿀~팁 ★★

▶ 많이 틀린 이유는?

아이를 상담할 때 '외재화' 과정을 통해서, 아이가 안고 있는 문제 '밖'의 이야기를 생각하게 하고 다시 자신에 대한 이야기를 구성할 수 있도록 도와 상담의 효과를 높이라는 조언을 담은 글이다. '상담'이라는 맥락이 글의 중반부까지 등장하지 않은 채 서두에는 '외재화'라는 추상적인 개념만 제시되기 때문에 흐름 및 주제를 파악하기가 쉽지 않은 문제이다. 오답으로 ④, ⑤가 많이 나왔는데 이는 지문에 나온 키워드를 포함하기는 하지만 지문과 무관한 내용을 담고 있다.

▶ 문제 해결 방법은?

지문의 내용은 옛 이야기(문제 상황과 관련된 이야기)를 새로운 이야기로 교체해 주라는 것인데 ④는 두 이야기를 '결합하라'는 내용을 담고 있어 포인트가 어긋난다. ⑤의 경우 'link'라는 단어가 지문과 연관성이 있어 보이나 'another's'에 오류가 있다. 이는 '한 아이의 이야기를 다른 아이의 이야기와 연결시켜 주라'는 뜻인데 지문에서 여러 아이를 한꺼번에 상담하거나 치료하는 상황이 등장하지 않는다.

★★★ 1등급 대비 고난도 3점 문제

11 프로토피아로 설명하는 인간 진보의 역사   정답률 34% | 정답 ④

다음 빈칸에 들어갈 말로 가장 적절한 것을 고르시오. [3점]

① conceals the limits of innovations at the present time
현재의 혁신의 한계를 감춘다
② makes it difficult to predict the future with confidence
자신감 있게 미래를 예측하는 것을 어렵게 만든다
③ motivates us to quickly achieve a protopian civilization
우리가 프로토피아적인 문명을 빨리 이루도록 동기를 부여한다
④ hides a steady accumulation of small net benefits over time
시간이 지남에 따른 작은 순이익의 꾸준한 축적을 보이지 않게 한다
⑤ produces a considerable change in technological successes
기술적 성공에서 상당한 변화를 만든다

Protopia is a state of becoming, / rather than a destination.
프로토피아는 생성의 상태이다. / 목적지라기보다는

It is a process.
그것은 과정이다.

In the protopian mode, / things are better today than they were yesterday, / although only a little better.
프로토피아적인 방식에서는 / 어제보다 오늘 상황이 더 낫다. / 비록 그저 약간 더 나아졌을 뿐이라도

It is incremental improvement or mild progress.
그것은 점진적인 개선이나 가벼운 진보이다.

The "pro" in protopian / stems from the notions of process and progress.
프로토피아적이라는 말에서 '프로'는 / 과정과 진보라는 개념에서 비롯된다.

This subtle progress is not dramatic, not exciting.
이 미묘한 진보는 극적이지도 않고 자극적이지도 않다.

It is easy to miss / because a protopia generates / almost as many new problems as new benefits.
그것을 놓치기 쉽다. / 프로토피아는 발생시키기 때문에 / 거의 새로운 이점만큼 많은 새로운 문제를

The problems of today were caused / by yesterday's technological successes, / and the technological solutions to today's problems / will cause the problems of tomorrow.
오늘의 문제는 야기된 것이고, / 어제의 기술적 성공에 의해 / 오늘의 문제에 대한 기술적 해결책은 / 내일의 문제를 유발할 것이다.

This circular expansion of both problems and solutions / hides a steady accumulation of small net benefits over time.
문제와 해결책 둘 다의 이런 순환적 팽창은 / 시간이 지남에 따른 작은 순이익의 꾸준한 축적을 보이지 않게 한다.

Ever since the Enlightenment and the invention of science, / we've managed to create a tiny bit more / than we've destroyed each year.
계몽주의와 과학의 발명 이래로 줄곧, / 우리는 조금 더 많은 것을 만들어냈다. / 우리가 매년 파괴해 온 것보다

But that few percent positive difference / is compounded over decades / into what we might call civilization.
그러나 그 작은 몇 퍼센트의 긍정적인 차이는 / 수십 년에 걸쳐 조합된다. / 우리가 문명이라고 부를지도 모르는 것으로

Its benefits never star in movies.
그것의 장점은 영화에서 주연을 맡는 법이 없다.

프로토피아는 목적지라기보다는 생성의 상태이다. 그것은 과정이다. 프로토피아적인 방식에서는 어제보다 오늘, 비록 그저 약간 더 나아졌을 뿐이라도, 상황이 더 낫다. 그것은 점진적인 개선이나 가벼운 진보이다. 프로토피아적이라는 말에서 '프로'는 과정과 진보라는 개념에서 비롯된다. 이 미묘한 진보는 극적이지도 않고 자극적이지도 않다. 프로토피아는 거의 새로운 이점만큼 많은 새로운 문제를 발생시키기 때문에 그것을 놓치기 쉽다. 오늘의 문제는 어제의 기술적 성공이 가져온 것이고, 오늘의 문제에 대한 기술적 해결책은 내일의 문제를 유발할 것이다. 문제와 해결책 둘 다의 이런 순환적 팽창은 시간이 지남에 따른 작은 순이익의 꾸준한 축적을 보이지 않게 한다. 계몽주의와 과학의 발명 이래로 줄곧, 우리는 매년 파괴해 온 것보다 조금 더 많은 것을 만들어냈다. 그러나 그 작은 몇 퍼센트의 긍정적인 차이는 수십 년에 걸쳐 우리가 문명이라고 부를지도 모르는 것으로 조합된다. 그것의 장점은 영화에서 주연을 맡는 법이 없다.

Why? 왜 정답일까?

글에 따르면 프로토피아란 점진적이고 가벼운 개선의 상태나 과정을 이르는 말로, 발전이 이룩되더라도 그만큼의 새로운 문제가 파생되기 때문에 발전이나 진보가 눈에 띄게 드러나지 않는 상황과 연관되어 있다(It is easy to miss because a protopia generates almost as many new problems as new benefits. The problems of today were caused by yesterday's technological successes, and the technological solutions to today's problems will cause the problems of tomorrow.). 글의 마지막 두 문장에서도 진보는 꾸준히 수십 년간 쌓여 우리가 문명이라 부르는 것으로 조합될 뿐 영화의 주연처럼 전면에 도드라지는 법이 없다는 부연 설명을 제시하고 있다. 따라서 빈칸에 들어갈 말로 가장 적절한 것은 ④ '시간이 지남에 따른 작은 순이익의 꾸준한 축적을 보이지 않게 한다'이다.

- becoming (철학에서) 생성
- subtle ⓐ 미묘한
- technological ⓐ 기술적인
- expansion ⑩ 확장
- conceal ⓥ 감추다
- accumulation ⑩ 축적
- improvement ⑩ 개선, 향상
- generate ⓥ 발생시키다, 만들어내다
- circular ⓐ 순환적인
- star in ⓥ ~에서 주연을 맡다
- steady ⓐ 꾸준한
- considerable ⓐ 상당한

구문 풀이

7행 It is easy to miss because a protopia generates almost
= This subtle progress(to miss의 의미상 목적어)
as many new problems as new benefits.
「as + 원급 + as : ~만큼 …한」

★★ 문제 해결 꿀~팁 ★★

▶ 많이 틀린 이유는?

빈칸 앞뒤 내용으로 미루어볼 때, 이 글은 오늘의 발전이나 진보가 과거의 문제에 대한 해결책을 제시하는 동시에 미래에 해결해야 할 새로운 문제를 낳기 때문에 오랜 시간이 흐른 뒤에야 긍정적인 차이로 나타나게 된다는 내용을 다루고 있다. 본문에

'미래 예측'에 관한 내용은 없으므로 ②는 빈칸에 부적절하다. 또한 'This subtle progress is not dramatic, not exciting.'에서 진보는 미묘하며 극적이지도 자극적이지도 않다고 서술하는 것으로 보아 '현저한, 상당한' 변화를 언급하는 ⑤도 답으로 적합하지 않다.

▶ 문제 해결 방법은?
Protopia라는 낯선 용어에 얽매이기보다는, 이를 설명하는 progress에 집중하여 글을 읽도록 한다.

★★★ 1등급 대비 고난도 3점 문제

12 바닷물과 유사한 생명체의 체액 성분　　　정답률 37% | 정답 ①

다음 빈칸에 들어갈 말로 가장 적절한 것을 고르시오. [3점]

✓① maintain an inner ocean in spite of surrounding fresh water
주변이 민물임에도 불구하고 체내의 바다 상태를 유지하려고
② attain ion balance by removing salts from inside their body
몸 안에서 소금을 없애 이온 균형을 달성하려고
③ return to the ocean to escape from their natural enemies
천적에서 도망쳐 바다로 돌아가려고
④ rebuild their external environment to obtain resources
자원을 획득하고자 외부 환경을 다시 구축하려고
⑤ change their physiology in accord with their surroundings
주변 환경에 맞춰 생리 상태를 바꾸려고

Since life began in the oceans, / most life, including freshwater life, / has a chemical composition / more like the ocean than fresh water.
생명체는 바다에서 시작되었기 때문에, / 민물 생물을 포함하여 대부분의 생물은 / 화학 성분을 지니고 있다. / 민물보다는 대양과 비슷한

It appears / that most freshwater life did not originate in fresh water, / but is secondarily adapted, / having passed from ocean to land / and then back again to fresh water.
보인다. / 대부분의 민물 생명체는 민물에서 근원하지 않았고, / 종국에 적응한 것으로 / 바다에서 뭍으로 왔다가 / 다시 민물로 돌아가면서

As improbable as this may seem, / the bodily fluids of aquatic animals / show a strong similarity to oceans, / and indeed, / most studies of ion balance in freshwater physiology / document the complex regulatory mechanisms / by which fish, amphibians and invertebrates attempt to maintain an inner ocean / in spite of surrounding fresh water.
있을 법해 보이지 않을지라도, / 수중 동물의 체액은 / 바닷물과 강한 유사성을 보이고, / 실제로 / 민물 생리의 이온 균형에 대한 대부분의 연구에서는 / 복잡한 조절 기제에 대해서 자세히 기술한다. / 물고기와 양서류, 무척추동물이 체내의 바다 상태를 유지하려고 시도하는 / 주변이 민물임에도 불구하고

It is these sorts of unexpected complexities and apparent contradictions / that make ecology so interesting.
이런 예기치 못한 복잡성과 명백한 모순이다. / 생태학을 그토록 흥미롭게 만드는 것은

The idea / of a fish in a freshwater lake / struggling to accumulate salts inside its body / to mimic the ocean / reminds one of the other great contradiction of the biosphere: / plants are bathed in an atmosphere / composed of roughly three-quarters nitrogen, / yet their growth is frequently restricted by lack of nitrogen.
개념은 / 민물 호수에 사는 물고기가 / 자기 몸 안에 소금을 쌓으려고 노력한다는 / 바닷물을 닮고자 / 생물권의 다른 위대한 모순들 가운데 하나를 상기시킨다. / 식물은 대기로 몸을 적시고 있음에도 불구하고, / 질소로 대략 4분의 3 정도 구성되어 있는 / 식물의 성장은 질소 결핍으로 빈번히 제한된다.

생명체는 바다에서 시작되었기 때문에, 민물 생물을 포함하여 대부분의 생물은 민물보다는 대양과 비슷한 화학 성분을 지니고 있다. 대부분의 민물 생명체는 민물에서 근원하지 않았고, 바다에서 뭍으로 왔다가 다시 민물로 돌아가면서 종국에 적응한 것으로 보인다. 있을 법해 보이지 않을지라도, 수중 동물의 체액은 바닷물과 강한 유사성을 보이고, 실제로 민물 생리의 이온 균형에 대한 대부분의 연구에서는 물고기와 양서류, 무척추동물이 주변이 민물임에도 불구하고 체내의 바다 상태를 유지하려고 시도하는 복잡한 조절 기제에 대해서 자세히 기술한다. 생태학을 그토록 흥미롭게 만드는 것은 이런 예기치 못한 복잡성과 명백한 모순이다. 민물 호수에 사는 물고기가 바닷물을 닮고자 자기 몸 안에 소금을 쌓으려고 노력한다는 개념은 생물권의 다른 위대한 모순들 가운데 하나를 상기시킨다. 식물은 질소로 대략 4분의 3 정도 구성되어 있는 대기로 몸을 적시고 있음에도 불구하고, 식물의 성장은 질소 결핍으로 빈번히 제한된다.

Why? 왜 정답일까?

'Since life began in the oceans, most life, including freshwater life, has a chemical composition more like the ocean than fresh water.'에서 생명체는 본디 바다에 근원을 두므로 바닷물과 유사한 체액 성분을 지니고 있다고 이야기하고, 'The idea of a fish in a freshwater lake struggling to accumulate salts

---

inside its body to mimic the ocean ~'에서도 민물에 사는 물고기가 몸 내부에서는 바닷물 상태를 닮으려고 애쓰고 있다는 사실을 되짚어 이야기한다. 따라서 빈칸에 들어갈 말로 가장 적절한 것은 ① '주변이 민물임에도 불구하고 체내의 바다 상태를 유지하려고'이다.

- composition ⓝ 성분, 구성
- secondarily ⓐⓓ 종국에는, 2차적으로
- bodily fluid 체액
- amphibian ⓝ 양서류
- biosphere ⓝ 생물권
- lack ⓝ 결핍, 결여, 부족
- originate in ~에서 기원하다
- improbable ⓐ 있을법하지 않은
- physiology ⓝ 생리
- invertebrate ⓝ 무척추동물
- nitrogen ⓝ 질소

구문 풀이

6행 As improbable as this may seem, the bodily fluids of aquatic
문두의 원급비교 : 양보구문(~일지라도)　　주어1
animals show a strong similarity to oceans, / and indeed, most studies
동사1(복수)　~에 대한 유사성　접속부사(실제로, 사실)　주어2
of ion balance in freshwater physiology document the complex
동사2(복수)
regulatory mechanisms [by which fish, amphibians and invertebrates
전치사 + 관계대명사
attempt to maintain an inner ocean / in spite of surrounding fresh
~하려고 시도하다　~에도 불구하고
water].

★★ 문제 해결 꿀~팁 ★★

▶ 많이 틀린 이유는?
정답 선택지에 함축적인 표현이 나와서 이를 제대로 이해하지 못하면 오답을 고르게 되는 문제였다. '체내의 바다 상태'라는 말이 결국 본문의 '체액 구성이 바닷물과 비슷한 것'과 같음을 파악하여야 한다.

▶ 문제 해결 방법은?
③, ④는 본문 내용과 비교적 무관하나 ②, ⑤는 주제와 반대되는 내용에 가까운데, 몸 안에서 소금을 '없앤다'는 내용의 ②는 체액을 바닷물과 비슷한 상태, 즉 적절한 염분을 머금은 상태로 유지하려 하는 생물의 습성을 정반대로 기술한 것이다. ⑤ 또한 민물에 사는 물고기가 주변 환경인 '민물'의 상황에 맞추어 생리 상태를 바꾼다고 하면 바닷물과 정반대로 '염분이 없는 민물의' 상태를 닮으려고 노력한다는 뜻을 나타낸다는 점에서 주제와 상반된다.

DAY 05 　　빈칸 추론 05

01 ③	02 ④	03 ①	04 ②	05 ①
06 ①	07 ②	08 ④	09 ①	10 ②
11 ②	12 ②			

01　과거의 실수를 무시하고 미래를 낙관하는 우리들　정답률 62% | 정답 ③

다음 빈칸에 들어갈 말로 가장 적절한 것을 고르시오.

① criticize – 비판하는
② remind – 상기하는
✓ ignore – 무시하는
④ detect – 감지하는
⑤ overestimate – 과대평가하는

There's reason to worry / that an eyes-on-the-prize mentality could be a mistake.
우려할 이유가 있다. / 자기 목표에 몰두하는 사고방식은 실수일 수 있다고

Lots of research shows / that we tend to be over-confident / about how easy it is to be self-disciplined.
많은 연구에 따르면, / 우리는 과신하는 경향이 있다. / 자기 수양을 하기가 얼마나 쉬운지에 관해서

This is why so many of us optimistically buy expensive gym memberships / when paying per-visit fees would be cheaper, / register for online classes / we'll never complete, / and purchase family-size chips on discount / to trim our monthly snack budget, / only to consume every last crumb in a single sitting.
이것이 우리 중 매우 많은 사람이 낙관적으로 값비싼 체육관 회원권을 사는 이유이다. / 방문당 이용료를 내는 것이 더 저렴할 텐데도 / 온라인 강좌에 등록하는 (이유) / 우리가 다 끝내지도 못할 / 그리고 할인하는 대형 과자를 사서 / 한 달 치 간식 예산을 줄이기 위해 / 결국 앉은 자리에서 한 번에 마지막 부스러기까지 다 먹는 (이유)

We think "future me" will be able to make good choices, / but too often "present me" gives in to temptation.
우리는 '미래의 내'가 좋은 선택을 할 수 있을 거라고 생각하지만, / 너무나 자주 '현재의 나'는 유혹에 굴복한다.

People have a remarkable ability / to ignore their own failures.
사람들에게는 놀라운 능력이 있다. / 자기 실패를 무시하는

Even when we flounder again and again, / many of us manage to maintain a rosy optimism / about our ability to do better next time / rather than learning from our past mistakes.
우리가 거듭 실패할 때조차 / 우리 중 많은 사람은 장밋빛 낙관주의를 용케 유지한다. / 다음에는 더 잘할 거라는 우리의 능력에 관해 / 과거의 실수로부터 배우기보다는

We cling to fresh starts and other reasons to stay upbeat, / which may help us get out of bed in the morning / but can prevent us from approaching change / in the smartest possible way.
우리는 새로운 시작과 낙관적인 태도를 유지할 다른 이유에 매달리고, / 이것은 아침에 우리가 침대에서 일어나는 데 도움이 될지는 모르지만 / 우리가 변화에 다가가지 못하게 막을 수 있다. / 할 수 있는 가장 영리한 방식으로

자기 목표에 몰두하는 사고방식은 실수일 수 있다고 우려할 이유가 있다. 많은 연구에 따르면, 우리는 자기 수양을 하기가 얼마나 쉬운지에 관해서 과신하는 경향이 있다. 이것이 우리 중 매우 많은 사람이 낙관적으로 방문당 이용료를 내는 것이 더 저렴할 텐데도 값비싼 체육관 회원권을 사고, 다 끝내지도 못할 온라인 강좌에 등록하며, 한 달 치 간식 예산을 줄이기 위해 할인하는 대형 과자를 사서 결국 앉은 자리에서 한 번에 마지막 부스러기까지 다 먹는 이유다. 우리는 '미래의 내'가 좋은 선택을 할 수 있을 거라고 생각하지만, 너무나 자주 '현재의 나'는 유혹에 굴복한다. 사람들에게는 자기 실패를 무시하는 놀라운 능력이 있다. 거듭 실패할 때조차 우리 중 많은 사람은 과거의 실수로부터 배우기보다는 다음에는 더 잘할 거라는 우리의 능력에 관해 장밋빛 낙관주의를 용케 유지한다. 우리는 새로운 시작과 낙관적인 태도를 유지할 다른 이유에 매달리고, 이것은 아침에 우리가 침대에서 일어나는 데 도움이 될지는 모르지만 할 수 있는 가장 영리한 방식으로 우리가 변화에 다가가지 못하게 막을 수 있다.

Why?　왜 정답일까?

사람들은 과거의 실수로부터 배우기보다는 앞으로 더 잘할 수 있다고 낙관하는 경우가 많다(~ many of us manage to maintain a rosy optimism about our ability to do better next time rather than learning from our past mistakes.)는 내용이다. 따라서 빈칸에 들어갈 말로 가장 적절한 것은 자기 실패를 '잘 깨닫지 못한다'는 의미의 ③ '무시하는'이다.

● eyes-on-the-prize ⓐ 목표에 몰두하는　● over-confident ⓐ 과신하는
● self-disciplined ⓐ 자기 수양이 된　● optimistically ⓐⓓ 낙관적으로

● trim ⓥ 줄이다, 잘라내다, 다듬다
● give in to ~에 굴복하다
● flounder ⓥ 실패하다
● rosy ⓐ 장밋빛의
● upbeat ⓐ 낙관적인
● overestimate ⓥ 과대평가하다
● crumb ⓝ 부스러기
● temptation ⓝ 유혹
● manage to 가까스로 ~하다
● cling to ~에 집착하다
● detect ⓥ 감지하다

구문 풀이

4행 This is why so many of us optimistically buy expensive gym
　　　이 이유로 ~하다　　　　　　　　　　　　　　동사1
memberships (when paying per-visit fees would be cheaper), register
　　　　　　　　　동명사구 주어　　　동사　　　　　　동사2
for online classes [we'll never complete], and purchase family-size
　　　　　　　　　　　　　　　　　　　　동사3
chips on discount to trim our monthly snack budget, only to consume
　　　　　　　　　　　　　　　　　　　　　　결국 ~하다(결과)
every last crumb in a single sitting.

02　팬덤의 대상보다도 더 중요한 팬들 간의 교류　정답률 58% | 정답 ④

다음 빈칸에 들어갈 말로 가장 적절한 것을 고르시오.

① is enhanced by collaborations between global stars
　세계적인 스타들 간의 협업으로 고양된다
② results from frequent personal contact with a star
　스타와 자주 개인적인 연락을 나누는 데서 기인한다
③ deepens as fans age together with their idols
　팬이 그들의 우상과 함께 나이 들수록 깊어진다
✓ comes from being connected to other fans
　다른 팬들과 관계를 맺는 데서 온다
⑤ is heightened by stars' media appearances
　스타가 미디어에 등장함으로써 고양된다

Fans feel for feeling's own sake.
팬은 감정 그 자체를 느낀다.

They make meanings / beyond what seems to be on offer.
그들은 의미를 만든다. / 제공된다고 보이는 것을 넘어서는

They build identities and experiences, / and make artistic creations of their own / to share with others.
그들은 정체성과 경험을 만들고, / 자신의 예술적 창작물을 만든다. / 다른 사람들과 공유하려

A person can be an individual fan, / feeling an "idealized connection with a star, / strong feelings of memory and nostalgia," / and engaging in activities / like "collecting to develop a sense of self."
한 사람은 개인적인 팬이 되어, / '어떤 스타와 이상적인 관계'를 느끼며, / 즉 '기억과 향수의 강한 감정' / 활동을 할 수 있다. / '자아감 형성을 위해 수집하기'와 같은

But, more often, / individual experiences are embedded in social contexts / where other people with shared attachments / socialize around the object of their affections.
그러나 더 흔히 / 개인적인 경험은 사회적인 상황에 끼워 넣어져 있다. / 애착을 공유하는 다른 사람들이 / 애정의 대상을 중심으로 교제하는

Much of the pleasure of fandom / comes from being connected to other fans.
팬덤의 많은 즐거움은 / 다른 팬들과 관계를 맺는 데서 온다.

In their diaries, / Bostonians of the 1800s / described being part of the crowds at concerts / as part of the pleasure of attendance.
그들의 일기에 / 1800년대의 보스턴 사람들은 / 콘서트에 모인 군중의 일부가 되는 것을 묘사했다. / 참석하는 즐거움의 일부라고

A compelling argument can be made / that what fans love is less the object of their fandom / than the attachments to (and differentiations from) one another / that those affections afford.
강력한 주장이 제기될 수 있다. / 팬이 사랑하는 것은 팬덤의 대상이라기보다 / 서로에 대한 애착(그리고 서로 간의 차이)이라는 / 그 애정이 제공하는

팬은 감정 그 자체를 느낀다. 그들은 제공된다고 보이는 것을 넘어서는 의미를 만든다. 그들은 정체성과 경험을 만들고, 자신의 예술적 창작물을 만들어 다른 사람들과 공유한다. 한 사람은 개인적인 팬이 되어, '어떤 스타와 이상적인 관계, 기억과 향수의 강한 감정'을 느끼며, '자아감 형성을 위해 수집하기' 등의 활동을 할 수 있다. 그러나 더 흔히 개인적인 경험은 애착을 공유하는 다른 사람들이 애정의 대상을 중심으로 교제하는 사회적인 상황에 끼워 넣어져 있다. 팬덤의 많은 즐거움은 다른 팬들과 관계를 맺는 데서 온다. 1800년대의 보스턴 사람들은 콘서트에 모인 군중의 일부가 되는 것이 참석하는 즐거움의 일부라고 일기에 묘사했다. 팬이 사랑하는 것은 팬덤의 대상이라기보다 그 애정이 제공하는 서로에 대한 애착(그리고 서로 간의 차이)이라는 강력한 주장이 제기될 수 있다.

Why?　왜 정답일까?

팬으로서의 개인적 경험은 팬덤을 공유하는 다른 사람들과의 사회적 상황과 맞물려 있다(~ individual experiences are embedded in social contexts where

---

other people with shared attachments socialize ~)는 빈칸 앞의 내용으로 보아, 빈칸에 들어갈 말로 가장 적절한 것은 ④ '다른 팬들과 관계를 맺는 데서 온다'이다.

- for one's own sake 그 자체로
- artistic ⓐ 예술적인
- nostalgia ⓝ 향수
- sense of self 자아 관념
- attachment ⓝ 애착
- affection ⓝ 애정
- describe ⓥ 기술하다, 묘사하다
- attendance ⓝ 참석
- argument ⓝ 주장, 논거
- afford ⓥ (격식) 주다, 제공하다
- collaboration ⓝ 협업, 협력
- heighten ⓥ 고양시키다

- identity ⓝ 정체성
- idealize ⓥ 이상화하다
- collect ⓥ 모으다, 수집하다
- embed ⓥ 끼워 넣다
- socialize ⓥ 교제하다, 사회화하다
- fandom ⓝ 팬덤
- part of ~의 일부
- compelling ⓐ 강력한
- differentiation ⓝ 차이
- enhance ⓥ 고양시키다, 강화하다
- conflict ⓝ 갈등

구문 풀이

15행 A compelling argument can be made [that what fans love is
주어 / 동사(수동태) / [ ]: 주어 동격
less the object of their fandom than the attachments to (and
「less + A + than + B」: A라기보다 B인」
differentiations from) one another that those affections afford].

03 긴 시간의 관점에서 이해되는 지질학   정답률 56% | 정답 ①

다음 빈칸에 들어갈 말로 가장 적절한 것을 고르시오.

✓ time scales of geological activity – 지질학적 활동의 시간적 척도
② global patterns in species diversity – 종 다양성의 세계적 패턴
③ regional differences in time perception – 시간 지각에 있어 지역적 차이
④ statistical methods for climate projections – 기후 예측을 위한 통계적 방법
⑤ criticisms of geological period classifications – 지질학적 시기 분류에 대한 비판

Interest in extremely long periods of time / sets geology and astronomy apart / from other sciences.
지극히 긴 시간에 대한 관심은 / 지질학 및 천문학을 구별짓는다. / 타 과학 분야로부터

Geologists think / in terms of billions of years / for the age of Earth and its oldest rocks / — numbers that, like the national debt, are not easily comprehended.
지질학자들은 사고하는데, / 수십억 년의 관점에서 / 지구 및 가장 오래된 암석의 나이에 관하여 / 이는 마치 국가 부채처럼 쉽게 이해되지 않는 숫자이다.

Nevertheless, / the time scales of geological activity / are important for environmental geologists / because they provide a way / to measure human impacts on the natural world.
그럼에도 불구하고, / 지질학적 활동의 시간적 척도는 / 환경 지질학자들에게 중요한데 / 그것들이 한 가지 방법을 제공해주기 때문이다. / 자연 세계에 대한 인간의 영향력을 측정하는

For example, / we would like to know the rate of natural soil formation from solid rock / to determine whether topsoil erosion from agriculture is too great.
예를 들어, / 우리는 단단한 암석으로부터 자연적으로 토양이 형성되는 과정의 속도를 알아야 한다. / 농업으로 인한 표토 침식이 너무 심했는지 알아내기 위해.

Likewise, / understanding how climate has changed over millions of years / is vital / to properly assess current global warming trends.
마찬가지로, / 수백만 년 동안 기후가 어떻게 변해왔는가를 아는 것은 / 필수적이다. / 현재의 지구 온난화 추세를 적절히 가늠하는 데

Clues to past environmental change / are well preserved / in many different kinds of rocks.
과거의 환경 변화에 대한 단서는 / 잘 보존되어 있다. / 많은 종류의 암석들에

지극히 긴 시간에 대한 관심은 타 과학 분야로부터 지질학 및 천문학을 구별짓는다. 지질학자들은 지구 및 가장 오래된 암석의 나이에 관하여 수십억 년의 관점에서 사고하는데, 이는 마치 국가 부채처럼 쉽게 이해되지 않는 숫자이다. 그럼에도 불구하고, 지질학적 활동의 시간적 척도는 환경 지질학자들에게 중요한데 자연 세계에 대한 인간의 영향력을 측정하는 한 가지 방법을 제공해주기 때문이다. 예를 들어, 우리는 농업으로 인한 표토 침식이 너무 심했는지 알아내기 위해, 단단한 암석으로부터 자연적으로 토양이 형성되는 과정의 속도를 알아야 한다. 마찬가지로, 수백만 년 동안 기후가 어떻게 변해왔는가를 아는 것은 현재의 지구 온난화 추세를 적절히 가늠하는 데 필수적이다. 과거의 환경 변화에 대한 단서는 많은 종류의 암석들에 잘 보존되어 있다.

Why? 왜 정답일까?

'Interest in extremely long periods of time sets geology and astronomy apart from other sciences. Geologists think in terms of billions of

years for the age of Earth and its oldest rocks ~'에서 다른 과학 분야와는 달리 지질학은 '긴 시간'에 관심을 두는 분야임을 이야기하며 지질학적 현상을 오랜 시간의 관점에서 바라볼 필요가 있음을 암시한다. 따라서 빈칸에 들어갈 말로 가장 적절한 것은 ① '지질학적 활동의 시간적 척도'이다.

- extremely ⓐⓓ 지극히, 극도로
- set apart ~을 구별하다
- national debt 국가 부채
- nevertheless ⓐⓓ 그럼에도 불구하고
- impact ⓝ 영향, 충격
- soil ⓝ 토양, 흙
- topsoil ⓝ 표토
- agriculture ⓝ 농업
- vital ⓐ 필수적인, 아주 중요한
- assess ⓥ 가늠하다
- preserve ⓥ 보존하다
- activity ⓝ 활동
- regional ⓐ 지역의
- criticism ⓝ 비판, 비난

- geology ⓝ 지질학
- astronomy ⓝ 천문학
- comprehend ⓥ 이해하다
- measure ⓥ 측정하다
- rate ⓝ 속도
- formation ⓝ 형성
- erosion ⓝ 침식
- likewise ⓐⓓ 마찬가지로
- properly ⓐⓓ 제대로, 적절히
- clue ⓝ 단서
- scale ⓝ 규모, 범위
- diversity ⓝ 다양성
- projection ⓝ 예상, 추정
- classification ⓝ 분류

구문 풀이

2행 Geologists think in terms of billions of years for the age of
~의 관점에서
Earth and its oldest rocks — numbers [that, (like the national debt),
= Earth's / billions를 부연 / 주격 관계대명사 전명구(~처럼)
are not easily comprehended].

04 전략적 자기 무지   정답률 47% | 정답 ②

다음 빈칸에 들어갈 말로 가장 적절한 것을 고르시오.

① highlight the value of preferred activities – 선호되는 활동의 가치를 강조할
✓ make current activities less attractive – 현재의 활동을 덜 매력적으로 만들
③ cut their attachment to past activities – 과거 활동에 대한 자신의 애착을 끊을
④ enable them to enjoy more activities – 자신들로 하여금 더 많은 활동을 즐기게 해줄
⑤ potentially become known to others – 다른 사람들에게 잠재적으로 알려지게 될

Some of the most insightful work on information seeking / emphasizes "strategic self-ignorance," / understood as "the use of ignorance as an excuse / to engage excessively in pleasurable activities / that may be harmful to one's future self."
정보 탐색에 관한 가장 통찰력 있는 연구 중 일부는 / '전략적 자기 무지'를 강조하는데, / 이는 '무지를 핑계로 이용하는 것'으로 이해된다. / '즐거운 활동을 과도하게 할 / 자신의 미래 자아에 해로울 수도 있는'

The idea here is / that if people are present-biased, / they might avoid information / that would make current activities less attractive / — perhaps because it would produce guilt or shame, / perhaps because it would suggest an aggregate trade-off / that would counsel against engaging in such activities.
여기서의 생각은 / 만약 사람들이 현재에 편향되어 있다면, / 정보를 피할 수도 있다는 것인데 / 현재의 활동을 덜 매력적으로 만들 / 아마도 그것이 죄책감이나 수치심을 유발할 것이고, / 총체적 절충을 제안할 것이기 때문일 것이다. / 그러한 활동을 하지 말라고 충고할

St. Augustine famously said, / "God give me chastity — tomorrow."
성 아우구스티누스는 유명한 말을 했다, / "하나님 제게 정결을 내일 주시옵소서."라는

Present-biased agents think: / "Please let me know the risks — tomorrow."
현재에 편향되어 있는 행위자들은 생각한다. / "제가 위험을 내일 알게 해주세요."라고

Whenever people are thinking about engaging in an activity / with short-term benefits but long-term costs, / they might prefer to delay receipt of important information.
사람들이 활동을 하려고 생각하고 있을 때마다, / 단기적인 혜택은 있지만 장기적인 대가가 있는 / 그들은 중요한 정보의 수신을 미루는 것을 선호할 수도 있다.

The same point might hold about information / that could make people sad or mad: / "Please tell me what I need to know — tomorrow."
정보에 관해서도 똑같은 점이 있을 수 있다. / 사람들을 슬프게 하거나 화나게 할 수 있는 / "제가 알아야 할 것을 내일 말해 주세요."라고

정보 탐색에 관한 가장 통찰력 있는 연구 중 일부는 '전략적 자기 무지'를 강조하는데, 이는 '자신의 미래 자아에 해로울 수도 있는 즐거운 활동을 과도하게 할 핑계로 무지를 이용하는 것'으로 이해된다. 여기서의 생각은 만약 사람들이 현재에 편향되어 있다면, 현재의 활동을 덜 매력적으로 만들 정보를 피할 수도 있다는 것인데, 아마도 그것이 죄책감이나 수치심을 유발할 것이고, 그러한 활동을 하지 말라고 충고할 총체적 절충을 제안할 것이기 때문일 것이다. 성 아우구스티누스는 "하나님 제게 정결을 내일 주시옵소서."라는 유명한 말을 했다. 현재에 편향되어 있는 행위자들은 "제가 위험을 내일 알게 해주세요."라고

생각한다. 사람들이 단기적인 혜택은 있지만 장기적인 대가가 있는 활동을 하려고 생각하고 있을 때마다, 그들은 중요한 정보의 수신을 미루는 것을 선호할 수도 있다. 사람들을 슬프게 하거나 화나게 할 수 있는 정보에 관해서도 똑같은 점이 있을 수 있다. "제가 알아야 할 것을 내일 말해 주세요."

Why? 왜 정답일까?

'Whenever people are thinking about engaging in an activity with short-term benefits but long-term costs, they might prefer to delay receipt of important information.'에서 단기적으로는 이득이 되지만 장기적으로는 대가가 따르는 행동을 할 때 사람들은 '중요한' 정보 입수를 미룰 수도 있다고 언급하고 있다. 여기서 중요한 정보란 '~ perhaps because it would produce guilt or shame, because it would suggest an aggregate trade-off that would counsel against engaging in such activities.'에 따르면 그러한 행동을 하려는 것에 대해 수치심이나 죄책감이 들게 하여 활동에 참여하지 못하게 만들 수 있는 정보를 가리킨다. 따라서 빈칸에 들어갈 말로 가장 적절한 것은 ② '현재의 활동을 덜 매력적으로 만들'이다.

- insightful ⓐ 통찰력 있는
- strategic ⓐ 전략적인
- excessively ⓐ 과도하게
- harmful ⓐ 해로운
- delay ⓥ 미루다
- attachment ⓝ 애착

- emphasize ⓥ 강조하다
- ignorance ⓝ 무지
- pleasurable ⓐ 즐거운
- guilt ⓝ 죄책감
- highlight ⓥ 강조하다

구문 풀이

1행 Some of the most insightful work on information seeking
주어
emphasizes "strategic self-ignorance," (which is) understood as
동사(단수)   목적어(선행사)   생략
"the use of ignorance as an excuse to engage excessively in
전치사(~로서)   형용사적 용법
pleasurable activities [that may be harmful to one's future self]."
선행사   주격 관계대명사

05 아이들의 시간 개념   정답률 63% | 정답 ①

다음 빈칸에 들어갈 말로 가장 적절한 것을 고르시오.

✔ one running faster and stopping further down the track
한 대가 더 빠르게 달려 선로를 따라 더 먼 곳에서 멈췄다
② both stopping at the same point further than expected
두 대 모두 예상보다 더 먼 곳의 같은 지점에서 멈췄다
③ one keeping the same speed as the other to the end
한 차는 다른 차와 끝까지 같은 속도를 유지했다
④ both alternating their speed but arriving at the same end
두 대 모두 번갈아 속도를 바꿨지만 같은 목표에 도착했다
⑤ both slowing their speed and reaching the identical spot
두 대 모두 속도를 늦춰 동일한 지점에 도착했다

The Swiss psychologist Jean Piaget / frequently analyzed children's conception of time / via their ability to compare or estimate the time / taken by pairs of events.
스위스의 심리학자 Jean Piaget는 / 아이들의 시간 개념을 자주 분석했다. / 시간을 비교하거나 추정하는 그들의 능력을 통해 / 짝 지은 사건에 소요되는

In a typical experiment, / two toy cars were shown running synchronously on parallel tracks, / one running faster and stopping further down the track.
한 대표적인 실험에서 / 두 대의 장난감 자동차가 같은 시간에 평행 선로에서 달리고 있는 것을 보여 주었는데, / 한 대가 더 빠르게 달려 선로를 따라 더 먼 곳에서 멈췄다.

The children were then asked to judge / whether the cars had run for the same time / and to justify their judgment.
그리고 나서 아이들은 판단하라고 요청을 받았다. / 그 자동차들이 같은 시간 동안 달렸는지의 여부를 / 그리고 자신들의 판단이 옳다는 것을 설명해 보라는

Preschoolers and young school-age children / confuse temporal and spatial dimensions:
미취학 아동과 어린 학령기 아동은 / 시간 차원과 공간 차원을 혼동한다.

Starting times are judged by starting points, / stopping times by stopping points / and durations by distance, / though each of these errors does not necessitate the others.
시작 시각은 시작 지점에 의해, / 정지 시각은 정지 지점에 의해, / 그리고 지속 시간은 거리에 의해 판단되는데, / 그렇기는 하나 이 오류들 각각이 나머지 오류 모두를 필연적으로 동반하지는 않는다.

Hence, a child may claim / that the cars started and stopped running together (correct) / and that the car which stopped further ahead, / ran for more time (incorrect).
따라서 아이는 주장할 수도 있다. / 그 자동차들이 동시에 달리기 시작해서 동시에 달리는 것을 멈췄고(맞는 내용이다), / 앞쪽 더 먼 곳에 멈춘 자동차가 / 더 오랜 시간 동안 달렸다(틀린 내용이다)고

스위스의 심리학자 Jean Piaget는 짝 지은 사건에 소요되는 시간을 비교하거나 추정하는 아이들의 능력을 통해 그들의 시간 개념을 자주 분석했다. 한 대표적인 실험에서 두 대의 장난감 자동차가 같은 시간에 평행 선로에서 달리고 있는 것을 보여 주었는데, 한 대가 더 빠르게 달려 선로를 따라 더 먼 곳에서 멈췄다. 그리고 나서 아이들은 그 자동차들이 같은 시간 동안 달렸는지의 여부를 판단하고 자신들의 판단이 옳다는 것을 설명해 보라는 요청을 받았다. 미취학 아동과 어린 학령기 아동은 시간 차원과 공간 차원을 혼동한다. 시작 시각은 시작 지점에 의해, 정지 시각은 정지 지점에 의해, 그리고 지속 시간은 거리에 의해 판단되는데, 그렇기는 하나 이 오류들 각각이 나머지 오류 모두를 필연적으로 동반하지는 않는다. 따라서 아이는 그 자동차들이 동시에 달리기 시작해서 동시에 달리는 것을 멈췄고(맞는 내용이다), 앞쪽 더 먼 곳에 멈춘 자동차가 더 오랜 시간 동안 달렸다(틀린 내용이다)고 주장할 수도 있다.

Why? 왜 정답일까?

아이들의 시간 개념에 관한 Piaget의 실험을 설명한 글이다. 'Preschoolers and young school-age children confuse temporal and spatial dimensions: ~'에서 아이들은 시간 차원과 공간 차원을 혼동하여, 시작 시각은 공간상의 시작 지점, 정지 시각은 공간상의 정지 지점, 지속 시간은 거리로 판단하는 경향이 있다고 설명한다. 그리하여 마지막 문장에서는 아이들이 두 차가 동시에 달리기 시작하여 멈추었다고 제대로 파악할 수도 있지만 더 먼 곳에 정차한 자동차가 달린 시간도 더 길다고 오해할 수도 있다는 결과를 제시한다. 이러한 결과가 도출되기 위해서는 똑같은 시간을 달린 자동차 두 대 중 한 대가 더 멀리 나아가 공간상의 차이가 나타났어야 하므로, 빈칸에 들어갈 말로 가장 적절한 것은 ① '한 대가 더 빠르게 달려 선로를 따라 더 먼 곳에서 멈췄다'이다.

- frequently ⓐ 자주
- compare ⓥ 비교하다
- parallel ⓐ 평행한
- preschooler ⓝ 미취학 아동
- confuse ⓥ 혼동하다
- spatial ⓐ 공간의
- necessitate ⓥ 필연적으로 동반하다

- conception ⓝ 개념
- estimate ⓥ 추정하다
- judgment ⓝ 판단
- school-age 학령기의
- temporal ⓐ 시간의
- distance ⓝ 거리
- alternating ⓐ 교차의

구문 풀이

10행 Starting times are judged by starting points, stopping times
주어1   동사1   주어2
(are judged) by stopping points and durations (are judged) by
동사2(생략)   주어3 동사3(생략)
distance, though each of these errors does not necessitate the
양보 접속사
others.

06 장소 정체성이 강한 장소를 마케팅하는 것   정답률 42% | 정답 ①

다음 빈칸에 들어갈 말로 가장 적절한 것을 고르시오. [3점]

✔ resist losing that identity – 그 정체성을 잃게 되는 것을 반대할
② stop persisting with the old tie – 오랜 유대를 고집하는 것을 그만둘
③ tolerate the shift of that industry – 그 산업의 전환을 용인할
④ alienate themselves from that place – 그 장소로부터 그들 자신을 분리할
⑤ refuse the advantage of that industry – 그 산업의 이점을 거부할

The narratives that people create to understand their landscapes / come to be viewed as marketable entities / and a source of income for residents.
사람들이 풍경을 이해하기 위해 만들어 내는 이야기는 / 시장성이 높은 실재이자 / 주민들의 소득원으로 여겨지게 된다.

Landscapes with a strong place identity / have an advantage in marketing to tourists, / as it is relatively easy / to compartmentalize and market their narratives.
장소 정체성이 강한 풍경은 / 관광객들에게 마케팅하는 데 이점이 있다. / 비교적 쉽기 때문에, / 그 장소의 이야기를 구획하고 광고하기가

Such places may have disadvantages as well, however.
하지만 그런 장소는 단점 또한 지니고 있을 수 있다.

If place identity is tied to a particular industry, / local residents may feel strongly attached to the definitions of place / that stem from involvement in that industry, / and they may resist losing that identity / in favor of one based on a tourism industry.
만약 장소 정체성이 어떤 특정 산업과 묶여 있다면, / 지역 주민들은 장소적 정의에 강한 애착을 느낄 수 있고, / 그 산업과의 관련으로 인해 생기는 / 그 정체성을 잃게 되는 것을 반대할 수 있다. / 관광 산업을 기반으로 하는 정체성을 지지하느라

People rooted in landscape / may feel strong connections to other community members / and may resent the invasion of outsiders / who they believe are different and challenge their common identity.

풍경에 뿌리를 둔 사람들은 / 공동체의 다른 일원들과 강한 유대감을 느낄 수 있으며, / 외부인의 침입에 분개할 수도 있다. / 자신들과는 다르며 공통된 정체성에 도전한다고 여겨지는

Finally, local residents may feel / that this process reduces their identities to mere commercial transactions, / and they may believe / they sacrifice what is unique and special about their place.

결국, 지역 주민은 느낄 수도 있으며, / 이 과정이 자신들의 정체성이 단순한 상거래로 격하시킨다고 / 그들은 믿을 수도 있다. / 자신들의 장소에 관한 독특하고 특별한 것을 희생하게 된다고

사람들이 풍경을 이해하기 위해 만들어 내는 이야기는 시장성이 높은 실재이자 주민들의 소득원으로 여겨지게 된다. 장소 정체성이 강한 풍경은 그 장소의 이야기를 구획하고 광고하기가 비교적 쉽기 때문에, 관광객들에게 마케팅하기에 이점이 있다. 하지만 그런 장소는 단점 또한 지니고 있을 수 있다. 만약 장소 정체성이 어떤 특정 산업과 묶여 있다면, 지역 주민들은 그 산업과의 관련으로 인해 생기는 장소적 정의에 강한 애착을 느낄 수 있고, 관광 산업을 기반으로 하는 정체성을 지지하느라 그 정체성을 잃게 되는 것을 반대할 수 있다. 풍경에 뿌리를 둔 사람들은 공동체의 다른 일원들과 강한 유대감을 느낄 수 있으며, 자신과는 다르며 공통된 정체성에 도전한다고 여겨지는 외부인이 몰려드는 데 분개할 수도 있다. 결국, 지역 주민들은 이 과정으로 인해 자신들의 정체성이 단순한 상거래로 격하된다고 느낄 수도 있으며, 자신들의 장소에 관한 독특하고 특별한 것을 희생하게 된다고 믿을 수도 있다.

Why? 왜 정답일까?

장소의 강한 정체성이 장소 마케팅에 도움이 되는지 여부를 'Such places may have disadvantages as well, however.' 앞뒤로 대조하며 설명한 글이다. 이 문장 앞에서는 강한 장소 정체성이 스토리를 구성하기 좋아 마케팅하기가 보다 쉽다는 내용을, 뒤에서는 도리어 그 강한 정체성이 내부인으로 하여금 외부인에 대한 반발을 갖게 만들어 마케팅 진행(관광 사업 추진)에 반대를 표명하게 만들 수 있다는 내용을 다룬다. 빈칸 뒤의 두 문장에서 장소 정체성에 애착이 있는 사람들은 자신들과 다른 외부인의 침입에 분개할 수 있으며(~ may resent the invasion of outsiders who they believe are different ~) 자신들의 고유한 정체성이 '희생된다'고 느낄 수 있음(~ they may believe they sacrifice what is unique and special about their place.)을 말하므로, 빈칸에 들어갈 말로 가장 적절한 것은 ① '그 정체성을 잃게 되는 것을 반대할'이다.

- **be viewed as** ~로 보이다, ~로 여겨지다
- **entity** ⓝ 실재, 독립체
- **be tied to** ~와 연결되다, ~와 관련되다
- **involvement** ⓝ 관련, 관여, 연루
- **resent** ⓥ 분개하다, 화를 내다
- **marketable** ⓐ 시장성이 높은
- **compartmentalize** ⓥ 구획하다
- **attached to** ~에 애착을 느끼는
- **rooted in** ~에 뿌리를 둔
- **sacrifice** ⓥ 희생하다

구문 풀이

12행 People [rooted in landscape] may feel strong connections to other community members / and may resent the invasion of outsiders [who (they believe) are different and challenge their common identity].
( ) : 삽입절

★★★ 1등급 대비 고난도 2점 문제

07 수메르 시대의 문자 사용　　정답률 46% | 정답 ②

다음 빈칸에 들어갈 말로 가장 적절한 것을 고르시오.

① religious events – 종교 행사
✓ personal agreements – 사적인 합의
③ communal responsibilities – 공동 책임
④ historical records – 역사적 기록
⑤ power shifts – 권력 이동

In the classic model of the Sumerian economy, / the temple functioned as an administrative authority / governing commodity production, collection, and redistribution.

수메르 경제의 전형적 모델에서 / 사원은 행정 당국으로서 기능했다. / 상품의 생산, 수집, 그리고 재분배를 관장하는

The discovery of administrative tablets / from the temple complexes at Uruk / suggests / that token use and consequently writing / evolved as a tool of centralized economic governance.

행정용 (점토)판의 발견은 / Uruk의 사원 단지에서 나온 / 시사한다. / 상징의 사용, 그리고 결과적으로 글자가 중앙 집권화된 경제 지배의 도구로 발달했음을

Given the lack of archaeological evidence / from Uruk-period domestic sites, / it is not clear / whether individuals also used the system for personal agreements.

고고학적 증거가 없다는 것을 고려하면, / Uruk 시기 가정집의 터에서 나온 / 명확하지 않다. / 개인이 또한 사적인 합의를 위해 그 체계를 사용했는지는

For that matter, / it is not clear / how widespread literacy was at its beginnings.

그 문제와 관련하여, / 명확하지 않다. 읽고 쓰는 능력이 초기에 얼마나 널리 퍼져 있었는지

The use of identifiable symbols and pictograms / on the early tablets / is consistent with administrators needing a lexicon / that was mutually intelligible by literate and nonliterate parties.

인식 가능한 기호와 그림 문자의 사용은 / 초기의 판에서의 / 행정가들이 어휘 목록을 필요로 했던 것과 일치한다. / 읽고 쓸 줄 아는 측과 읽고 쓸 수 없는 측이 서로 이해할 수 있는

As cuneiform script became more abstract, / literacy must have become increasingly important / to ensure / one understood what he or she had agreed to.

쐐기 문자가 더욱 추상적이 되면서, / 읽고 쓰는 능력이 점점 더 중요해졌음이 틀림없다. / 확실히 하기 위해 / 자신이 합의했던 것을 이해하고 있다는 것을

수메르 경제의 전형적 모델에서 사원은 상품의 생산, 수집, 그리고 재분배를 관장하는 행정 당국으로서 기능했다. Uruk의 사원 단지에서 나온 행정용 (점토)판의 발견은 상징의 사용, 그리고 결과적으로 글자가 중앙 집권화된 경제 지배의 도구로 발달했음을 시사한다. Uruk 시기 가정집의 터에서 나온 고고학적 증거가 없다는 것을 고려하면, 개인들이 또한 사적인 합의를 위해 그 체계를 사용했는지는 명확하지 않다. 그 문제와 관련하여, 읽고 쓰는 능력이 초기에 얼마나 널리 퍼져 있었는지 명확하지 않다. 초기의 판에서의 인식 가능한 기호와 그림 문자의 사용은 행정가들이 읽고 쓸 줄 아는 측과 읽고 쓸 수 없는 측이 서로 이해할 수 있는 어휘 목록을 필요로 했던 것과 일치한다. 쐐기 문자가 더욱 추상적이 되면서, 읽고 쓰는 능력이 자신이 합의했던 것을 이해하고 있다는 것을 확실히 하기 위해 점점 더 중요해졌음이 틀림없다.

Why? 왜 정답일까?

빈칸 앞에서 문자 도입 초기에 문자는 경제 지배 도구로서 활용되었다고 언급한 데 이어, 빈칸 바로 뒤의 문장에서는 문자를 읽고 쓰는 능력이 대중들 사이에 얼마나 퍼져 있었는지는 분명하지 않다고 했다. 이를 근거로 볼 때, 빈칸 문장은 공적 환경이 아닌 '사적' 환경에서 문자 체계가 사용되었는지는 명확하지 않다는 의미여야 함을 알 수 있다. 따라서 빈칸에 들어갈 말로 가장 적절한 것은 ② '사적인 합의'이다.

- **administrative** ⓐ 행정의, 관리의
- **commodity** ⓝ 상품, 물품
- **token** ⓝ 상징, 대용화폐
- **domestic** ⓐ 가정의, 국내의
- **pictogram** ⓝ 그림 문자
- **mutually** ⓐⓓ 서로, 상호 간에
- **nonliterate** ⓐ 읽고 쓸 수 없는
- **authority** ⓝ 당국, 권위, 권한
- **redistribution** ⓝ 재분배, 재배포
- **governance** ⓝ 지배, 관리
- **identifiable** ⓐ 인식 가능한
- **consistent with** ~와 일치하는
- **intelligible** ⓐ (쉽게) 이해할 수 있는
- **abstract** ⓐ 추상적인

구문 풀이

15행 As cuneiform script became more abstract, literacy must have become increasingly important to ensure (that) one understood what he or she had agreed to.

★★ 문제 해결 꿀~팁 ★★

▶ 많이 틀린 이유는?

이 글은 수메르 경제에서 문자가 처음에 중앙 집권화된 지배의 수단으로 활용되다가 이후에 개인들 간의 합의 수단으로 발전했을 것이라는 내용을 중점적으로 다루고 있으며, '역사 기록' 자체를 중요하게 언급하지는 않는다. 따라서 ④는 정답이 아니다.

▶ 문제 해결 방법은?

빈칸 앞뒤로 흐름이 반전된다. 빈칸 앞에서는 문자가 경제 지배의 도구로 활용되었다는 이야기가 주를 이루지만, 빈칸 뒤에서는 문자와 읽고 쓰는 능력의 발달을 연관시켜 개인들 간에 문자가 어떻게 보급되었을지를 추론하고 있다. 따라서 빈칸에는 '개인들'과 관련된 내용이 들어가야 흐름 전환이 알맞게 일어난다.

★★★ 1등급 대비 고난도 2점 문제

08 형식주의적 문학 비평　　정답률 41% | 정답 ④

다음 빈칸에 들어갈 말로 가장 적절한 것을 고르시오.

① putting himself or herself both inside and outside it
자기 자신을 작품 안팎 모두에 놓음
② finding a middle ground between it and the world
작품과 세상 사이에 중간 위치를 찾음

③ searching for historical realities revealed within it
작품 안에 드러난 역사적인 사실을 찾아봄
✓ looking inside it, not outside it or beyond it
작품의 외부나 작품 너머가 아니라 작품 내부를 들여다봄
⑤ exploring its characters' cultural relevance
작품 속 등장인물들의 문화적 연관성을 탐구함

The critic / who wants to write about literature from a formalist perspective / must first be a close and careful reader / who examines all the elements of a text individually / and questions how they come together to create a work of art.
비평가는 / 형식주의 관점에서 문학에 관해 쓰고자 하는 / 먼저 면밀하고도 주의 깊은 독자가 되어야 한다. / 글의 모든 요소를 개별적으로 검토하고 / 그것들이 모여 예술 작품을 만드는 방식에 대해 질문하는
Such a reader, / who respects the autonomy of a work, / achieves an understanding of it / by looking inside it, not outside it or beyond it.
그러한 독자는 / 작품의 자율성을 존중하는 / 그러한 독자는 / 작품에 대한 이해를 달성한다. / 작품의 외부나 작품 너머가 아니라 작품 내부를 들여다봄으로써
Instead of examining historical periods, author biographies, or literary styles, / for example, / he or she will approach a text / with the assumption that it is a self-contained entity / and that he or she is looking for the governing principles / that allow the text to reveal itself.
역사상의 시대, 작가의 전기, 또는 문학적 양식을 검토하는 대신, / 예를 들어, / 그 사람은 글에 접근할 것이다. / 글이 자족적인 실체라는 추정으로 / 그리고 자신은 지배적인 원칙을 찾고 있다는 / 그 글이 스스로를 드러내도록 해 주는
For example, / the correspondences / between the characters in James Joyce's short story "Araby" / and the people he knew personally / may be interesting, / but for the formalist / they are less relevant to understanding how the story creates meaning / than are other kinds of information / that the story contains within itself.
예를 들어, / 관련성은 / James Joyce의 단편 소설인 'Araby' 속 등장인물들과 / 그가 개인적으로 알았던 사람들과의 / 흥미로울 수도 있겠지만, / 형식주의자에게 / 그것들은 그 이야기가 의미를 만들어내는 방식을 이해하는 데 덜 연관되어 있다. / 다른 종류의 정보가 그런 것보다 / 그 이야기가 그 안에 포함하고 있는

형식주의의 관점에서 문학에 관해 쓰고자 하는 비평가는 먼저 글의 모든 요소를 개별적으로 검토하고 그것들이 모여 예술 작품을 만드는 방식에 대해 질문하는 면밀하고도 주의 깊은 독자가 되어야 한다. 작품의 자율성을 존중하는 그러한 독자는 작품의 외부나 작품 너머가 아니라 작품 내부를 들여다봄으로써 작품에 대한 이해를 달성한다. 예를 들어, 역사상의 시대, 작가의 전기, 또는 문학적 양식을 검토하는 대신, 그 사람은 글이 자족적인 실체이며, 자신은 그 글이 스스로를 드러내도록 해 주는 지배적인 원칙을 찾고 있다는 추정으로 글에 접근할 것이다. 예를 들어, James Joyce의 단편 소설인 'Araby' 속 등장인물들과 그가 개인적으로 알았던 사람들과의 관련성은 흥미로울 수도 있겠지만, 형식주의자에게 그것들은 이야기가 의미를 만들어내는 방식을 이해하는 데 있어 그 이야기 속에 포함된 다른 종류의 정보보다 관련성이 덜하다.

Why? 왜 정답일까?
형식주의적 관점에서 문학에 접근하는 사람들은 글을 그 자체로 이해될 수 있는 자족적 실체로 보고(~ it is a self-contained entity and that he or she is looking for the governing principles that allow the text to reveal itself), 작품 외적인 정보보다도 작품 안에서 이야기가 만들어지는 방식(how the story creates meaning ~ within itself) 자체에 초점을 둔다고 한다. 따라서 빈칸에 들어갈 말로 가장 적절한 것은 ④ '작품의 외부나 작품 너머가 아니라 작품 내부를 들여다봄'이다.

- critic ⓝ 비평가
- formalist ⓝ 형식주의
- careful ⓐ 주의 깊은
- respect ⓥ 존중하다
- historical ⓐ 역사적인
- biography ⓝ 생애, 전기
- assumption ⓝ 가정, 추정
- entity ⓝ 실체
- reveal ⓥ 드러내다
- relevant ⓐ 관련된
- literature ⓝ 문학
- close ⓐ 철저한, 면밀한
- element ⓝ 요소
- autonomy ⓝ 자율성
- author ⓝ 작가
- literary ⓐ 문학의
- self-contained ⓐ 자족적인, 자립적인
- governing ⓐ 지배적인
- correspondence ⓝ (~ 사이의) 관련성

구문 풀이

12행 For example, the correspondences (between the characters
                                         주어1
in James Joyce's short story "Araby" and the people [he knew
                                       주어2
personally]) may be interesting, but (for the formalist) they are
                               동사   주격 보어   부사구
less relevant to understanding {how the story creates meaning}
비교급 형용사(덜 ~한)   { }: 간접의문문
than are other kinds of information [that the story contains within
「than+대동사+주어: 도치 구문」   목적격 관·대
itself].

▶ 많이 틀린 이유는?
형식주의적 문학 비평에서는 작품 외적 요소보다 텍스트 그 자체가 주는 정보에 집중하는 것이 글의 핵심 내용이다. ①의 경우, 독자가 작품 '외부와 내부에' 모두 있어 봐야 한다는 의미이므로 주제에 어긋난다. ③은 '역사적 실체'를 찾으라는 뜻인데, 역사적 실체는 작품 외적 정보에 해당하므로 주제와 모순된다.
▶ 문제 해결 방법은?
빈칸 뒤의 historical periods, author biographies, or literary styles와 a self-contained entity는 문맥상 서로 반대되는 소재다. 전자는 작품 '외적' 요소의 예로, 작품 그 자체에 집중하지 않고 다른 정보를 끌어들이는 상황과 관련돼 있다. 반면, a self-contained entity는 작품이 '그 자체로 충족적'이라고 여기는 것이다. 즉 작품 '내적' 정보만으로 충분하다는 견해와 관련 있다.

★★★ 1등급 대비 고난도 3점 문제

09 꿀벌 군집이 노동력을 조절하는 방식   정답률 43% | 정답 ①

다음 빈칸에 들어갈 말로 가장 적절한 것을 고르시오. [3점]
✓ allow the colony to regulate its workforce
군집이 노동력을 조절할 수 있게 하는지
② search for water sources by measuring distance
거리를 측정하여 물이 있는 곳을 찾는지
③ decrease the colony's workload when necessary
필요할 때 군집의 작업 부담을 줄이는지
④ divide tasks according to their respective talents
각자의 재능에 따라 일을 나누는지
⑤ train workers to acquire basic communication patterns
일벌들이 기본적인 의사소통 패턴을 습득하도록 훈련시키는지

The entrance to a honeybee colony, / often referred to as the dancefloor, / is a market place for information / about the state of the colony / and the environment outside the hive.
꿀벌 군집의 입구는 / 흔히 댄스 플로어라고 불리는 / 정보를 교환하기 위한 시장이다. / 군집의 상태에 관한 / 그리고 벌집 밖의 환경에 관한
Studying interactions on the dancefloor / provides us / with a number of illustrative examples / of how individuals / changing their own behavior in response to local information / allow the colony to regulate its workforce.
댄스 플로어에서의 상호 작용을 연구하는 것은 / 우리에게 제공한다. / 많은 분명한 예들을 / 개체들이 어떻게 / 지역적 정보에 반응하여 행동을 바꾸는 / 군집이 노동력을 조절할 수 있게 하는지에 대한
For example, / upon returning to their hive / honeybees that have collected water / search out a receiver bee / to unload their water to within the hive.
예를 들어, / 자신들의 벌집으로 돌아오자마자 / 물을 가져온 꿀벌들은 / 수신자 벌을 찾는다. / 벌집 안에 물을 내려놓기 위해
If this search time is short / then the returning bee is more likely to perform a waggle dance / to recruit others to the water source.
만약 이 찾는 시간이 짧으면, / 그 돌아오는 벌은 8자 춤을 출 가능성이 더 크다. / 물이 있는 곳으로 데려갈 다른 벌들을 모집하기 위해
Conversely, / if this search time is long / then the bee is more likely to give up collecting water.
반대로, / 이 찾는 시간이 길면 / 그러면 그 벌은 물을 가지러 가는 것을 포기할 가능성이 더 크다.
Since receiver bees will only accept water / if they require it, / either for themselves / or to pass on to other bees and brood, / this unloading time is correlated / with the colony's overall need of water.
물을 받는 벌들은 오로지 물을 받을 것이므로, / 그들이 물이 필요할 경우에만 / 자신들을 위해서 / 혹은 다른 벌들과 애벌레들에게 전해주기 위해서, / 이러한 물을 넘겨주는 시간은 상관관계가 있다. / 군집의 전반적인 물 수요와
Thus / the individual water forager's response to unloading time / (up or down) / regulates water collection / in response to the colony's need.
따라서 / 물을 넘겨주는 시간에 대한 개별적인 물 조달자의 반응은 / (시간이 늘어나든 혹은 줄어들든 간에) / 물 수집을 조절한다. / 군집의 수요에 맞춰서

흔히 댄스 플로어라고 불리는 꿀벌 군집의 입구는 군집의 상태와 벌집 밖의 환경에 관한 정보를 교환하기 위한 시장이다. 댄스 플로어에서의 상호 작용을 연구하는 것은 우리에게 지역적 정보에 반응하여 행동을 바꾸는 개체들이 어떻게 군집이 노동력을 조절할 수 있게 하는지에 대한 많은 분명한 예들을 제공한다. 예를 들어, 물을 가져온 꿀벌들은 자신들의 벌집으로 돌아오자마자 물을 받아 벌집 안에 내려놓아줄 수신자 벌을 찾는다. 만약 이 (물을 받을 벌을) 찾는 시간이 짧으면, 그 돌아오는 벌은 물이 있는 곳으로 데려갈 다른 벌들을 모집하기 위해 8자 춤을 출 가능성이 더 크다. 반대로, 이 찾는 시간이 길면 그 벌은 물을 가지러 가는 것을 포기할 가능성이 더 크다. 물을 받는 벌들은 자신들을 위해서든 다른 벌들과 애벌레들에게 전해주기 위해서든, 물이 필요할 때만 물을 받을 것이므로, 이러한 물을 넘겨주는 시간은 군집의 전반적인 물 수

요와 상관관계가 있다. 따라서 (시간이 늘어나든 혹은 줄어들든 간에) 물을 넘겨주는 시간에 대한 개별적인 물 조달자의 반응은 군집의 수요에 맞춰서 물 수집을 조절한다.

Why? 왜 정답일까?

마지막 두 문장에서 벌이 군집 내 다른 벌에게 물을 넘겨주는 데 걸리는 시간은 군집 내 전반적인 물 수요와 관련이 있으며, 물을 수집하는 벌은 결국 군집의 수요에 맞춰 수집 활동을 조절하게 된다고 한다. 따라서 빈칸에 들어갈 말로 가장 적절한 것은 ① '군집이 노동력을 조절할 수 있게 하는지(allow the colony to regulate its workforce)'이다.

- entrance ⓝ 입구
- state ⓝ 상태
- interaction ⓝ 상호작용
- a number of 많은
- in response to ~에 대응하여
- unload ⓥ (짐을) 내리다
- recruit ⓥ 모집하다
- pass on to ~로 전하다
- be correlated with ~와 상관관계가 있다
- forager ⓝ 조달자
- divide ⓥ 나누다
- refer to A as B A를 B라고 부르다
- hive ⓝ 벌집, 벌떼
- provide A with B A에게 B를 제공하다
- illustrative ⓐ 분명히 보여주는
- local ⓐ 지엽적인
- waggle dance (꿀벌이 추는) 8자 춤
- give up ~을 포기하다
- brood ⓝ 애벌레
- overall ⓐ 전반적인
- workforce ⓝ 노동력
- respective ⓐ 각각의

구문 풀이

15행 Since receiver bees will only accept water if they require it,
접속사(~ 때문에)
either for themselves or to pass on to other bees and brood, this
「either+A+ or+B : A 또는 B」
unloading time is correlated with the colony's overall need of water.

★★ 문제 해결 꿀~팁 ★★

▶ 많이 틀린 이유는?
예시에 따르면 물을 받아줄 벌을 찾는 시간이 얼마 들지 않으면, 물을 구해온 벌은 다시 물을 수집하러 갈 벌들을 추가로 모집한다고 한다. 이런 경우 물 수집 작업에 대한 부담은 줄지 않고 오히려 '커진' 것이므로, '줄어드는' 경우만을 언급하는 ③은 답으로 적절하지 않다.

▶ 문제 해결 방법은?
예시의 일반화에 주의해야 한다. 군집 내 벌들이 물을 얼마나 금방 받아가는지로 물에 대한 수요를 파악하고, 그에 따라 추가로 벌을 동원할지 아니면 작업을 그만둘지 결정한다는 것은 '벌집 내 노동력을 어떻게 활용할지' 결정한다는 의미와 같다.

★★★ 1등급 대비 고난도 3점 문제

10 자기 시대의 사회적 관습에 갇히는 우리들 정답률 39% | 정답 ②

다음 빈칸에 들어갈 말로 가장 적절한 것을 고르시오. [3점]
① distinguish them from ideas and wishes
그것을 생각 및 바람과 구분하는
✓ feel social pressure to comply with them
그것에 순응해야 한다는 사회적 압박을 느끼는
③ apply them to create inspirational artworks
영감을 주는 예술품을 만들기 위해 그것을 적용하는
④ ignore them on account of their complexity
복잡함 때문에 그것을 무시하는
⑤ have an objection to being controlled by them
그것에 의해 통제되기를 거부하는

The history of perspective in Western painting / matters / because of what it reveals for the art of living.
서양화에서 원근법의 역사는 / 중요하다. / 그것이 삶의 기술에 대해 드러내는 것 때문에
Just as most artists / conform to the stylistic conventions of the era / into which they are born, / we similarly conform to prevailing social conventions / about how to live.
대부분의 예술가가 / 시대의 양식적 관습에 순응하듯이 / 자신이 태어나는 / 우리도 지배적인 사회적 관습에 비슷하게 순응한다. / 어떻게 살아야 하는지에 대한
These unwritten rules typically include / getting married and having children, / owning your own home and having a mortgage, / having a regular job and commuting to work, / and flying abroad for holidays.
이러한 불문율은 일반적으로 포함한다. / 결혼해서 아이를 갖는 것, / 자기 집을 소유하고 담보 대출을 받는 것, / 일정한 직업을 갖고 통근하는 것, / 휴가를 위해 비행기로 해외에 가는 것
For some people these are realities, / for others they remain aspirations.
어떤 사람들에게는 이것이 현실이고, / 다른 사람들에게는 염원으로 남는다.
It is common / to feel social pressure to comply with them.
일반적이다. / 그것에 순응해야 한다는 사회적 압박을 느끼는 것

At this point in Western history, / they are amongst the dominant conventions / that most of us have accepted with little questioning, / much as Vermeer and other Dutch baroque painters of the seventeenth century / accepted linear perspective without question.
서구 역사의 현시점에서, / 그것은 지배적인 관습 중 하나이다. / 우리 대부분이 거의 의문 없이 받아들여 온 / 17세기 Vermeer와 다른 네덜란드 바로크 화가들이 / 선형 원근법을 문제없이 받아들였던 것처럼
It is difficult / to see beyond the limitations of the culture / that has shaped our ways of looking at the world and at ourselves.
어렵다. / 문화의 한계 그 너머를 보는 것 / 세상과 자신을 바라보는 우리의 방식을 형성해 온
We are trapped in the perspective of our own time.
우리는 우리 시대의 관점에 갇혀 있다.

서양화에서 원근법의 역사는 그것이 삶의 기술에 대해 드러내는 것 때문에 중요하다. 대부분의 예술가가 자신이 태어나는 시대의 양식적 관습에 순응하듯이, 우리도 어떻게 살아야 하는지에 대한 지배적인 사회적 관습에 비슷하게 순응한다. 이러한 불문율에는 일반적으로 결혼해서 아이를 갖는 것, 자기 집을 소유하고 담보 대출을 받는 것, 일정한 직업을 갖고 통근하는 것, 휴가를 위해 비행기로 해외에 가는 것이 포함된다. 어떤 사람들에게는 이것이 현실이고, 다른 사람들에게는 염원으로 남는다. 그것에 순응해야 한다는 사회적 압박을 느끼는 것은 일반적이다. 17세기 Vermeer와 다른 네덜란드 바로크 화가들이 선형 원근법을 문제없이 받아들였던 것처럼, 서구 역사의 현시점에서, 그것은 우리 대부분이 거의 의문 없이 받아들여 온 지배적인 관습 중 하나이다. 세상과 자신을 바라보는 우리의 방식을 형성해 온 문화의 한계 그 너머를 보는 어렵다. 우리는 우리 시대의 관점에 갇혀 있다.

Why? 왜 정답일까?

화가들이 자기 시대의 예술적 관습을 받아들이듯이 우리는 우리 시대적 관습에 갇혀 그 한계 너머를 보기 어려워한다(conform to prevailing social conventions)는 내용의 글이다. 따라서 빈칸에 들어갈 말로 가장 적절한 것은 ② '그것에 순응해야 한다는 사회적 압박을 느끼는'이다.

- perspective ⓝ (그림) 원근법
- stylistic ⓐ 양식의
- unwritten ⓐ 불문의, 성문화되지 않은
- mortgage ⓝ 대출
- aspiration ⓝ 열망, 염원
- Dutch ⓐ 네덜란드의
- limitation ⓝ 한계
- distinguish A from B A와 B를 구별하다
- inspirational ⓐ 영감을 주는
- conform to ~에 순응하다
- prevailing ⓐ 지배적인, 우세한
- typically ⓐ 보통, 일반적으로
- commute ⓥ 통근하다
- dominant ⓐ 지배적인
- linear ⓐ 선형의
- be trapped in ~에 갇혀 있다
- pressure ⓝ 압박, 압력
- on account of ~ 때문에

구문 풀이

1행 The history of perspective in Western painting matters
주어 동사(단수)
because of {what it reveals for the art of living}. { } : because of의 목적어
전치사(~ 때문에)

★★ 문제 해결 꿀~팁 ★★

▶ 많이 틀린 이유는?
앞에서 예술에 관해 언급되므로 artworks가 포함된 ③이 답으로 적절해 보일 수 있다. 하지만, 예술가들이 원근법 등 시대의 주요 화풍을 아무 의심 없이 받아들였다는 설명은 우리가 사회적 관습을 받아들이는 방식도 마찬가지라는 주제를 뒷받침하기 위한 비유이다. 따라서 '예술 작품'에 관한 내용은 주제로 볼 수 없다.

▶ 문제 해결 방법은?
두 번째 문장은 「just as A, B(A와 마찬가지로 B하다)」 형태로, A는 비유, B는 주제에 해당한다. 즉 '~ we similarly conform to prevailing social conventions about how to live.'와 결론인 'We are trapped in the perspective of our own time.'이 주제를 나타내고, 이 주제와 같은 진술이 빈칸에 들어가야 한다.

★★★ 1등급 대비 고난도 3점 문제

11 문화적 재활용 정답률 29% | 정답 ②

다음 빈칸에 들어갈 말로 가장 적절한 것을 고르시오. [3점]
① our brains put a limit on cultural diversity
우리 뇌는 문화적 다양성에 제한을 두기
✓ we can mobilize our old areas in novel ways
우리가 우리의 오래된 영역들을 새로운 방식으로 동원할 수 있기
③ cultural tools stabilize our brain functionality
문화적 도구는 우리 뇌의 기능성을 안정화하기
④ our brain regions operate in an isolated manner
우리 뇌 영역들은 고립된 방식으로 작동하기

⑤ we cannot adapt ourselves to natural challenges
우리는 자연의 도전과제에 적응할 수 없기

The human species is unique / in its ability to expand its functionality / by inventing new cultural tools.
인간은 독특하다. / 자신의 기능성을 확장하는 능력에 있어서 / 새로운 문화적 도구를 발명하여

Writing, arithmetic, science / — all are recent inventions.
쓰기, 산수, 과학, / 이 모든 것은 최근에 발명된 것이다.

Our brains did not have enough time / to evolve for them, / but I reason / that they were made possible / because we can mobilize our old areas in novel ways.
우리의 뇌가 충분한 시간이 없었으나, / 그것들을 위해 진화할 / 나는 추론한다. / 그것들이 가능하게 되었으리라고 / 우리가 우리의 오래된 영역들을 새로운 방식으로 동원할 수 있기 때문에

When we learn to read, / we recycle a specific region of our visual system / known as the visual word-form area, / enabling us to recognize strings of letters / and connect them to language areas.
우리가 읽는 것을 배울 때, / 우리는 우리의 시각 시스템의 특정 영역을 재활용하는데, / 시각적인 단어–형태 영역이라고 알려진 / 이것이 우리가 일련의 문자를 인식하고 / 그것들을 언어 영역에 연결할 수 있게 해 준다.

Likewise, / when we learn Arabic numerals / we build a circuit / to quickly convert those shapes into quantities / — a fast connection / from bilateral visual areas to the parietal quantity area.
마찬가지로, / 우리가 아라비아 숫자를 배울 때 / 우리는 회로를 만드는데, / 그러한 모양들을 빠르게 수량으로 변환하는 / 이것은 빠르게 연결하는 것이다. / 양측의 시각 영역을 정수리 부분의 수량 영역과

Even an invention as elementary as finger-counting / changes our cognitive abilities dramatically.
손가락으로 헤아리기와 같은 기본적인 발명조차 / 우리의 인지 능력을 극적으로 변화시킨다.

Amazonian people who have not invented counting / are unable to make exact calculations / as simple as, say, 6 – 2.
수를 세는 것을 발명하지 않았던 아마존 사람들은, / 정확하게 계산할 수 없다. / 예를 들어, 6 빼기 2처럼 간단한 것을

This "cultural recycling" implies / that the functional architecture of the human brain / results from a complex mixture / of biological and cultural constraints.
이러한 '문화적 재활용'은 암시한다. / 인간의 두뇌의 기능적 구조가 / 복잡한 혼합물로부터 생겨난 것임을 / 생물학적, 문화적 제약의

인간은 새로운 문화적 도구를 발명하여 자신의 기능성을 확장하는 능력에 있어서 독특하다. 쓰기, 산수, 과학, 이 모든 것은 최근에 발명된 것이다. 우리의 뇌가 그것들을 위해 진화할 충분한 시간이 없었으나, 우리가 우리의 오래된 영역들을 새로운 방식으로 동원할 수 있기 때문에 그것들이 가능하게 되었으리라고 나는 추론한다. 우리가 읽는 것을 배울 때, 우리는 시각적인 단어–형태 영역이라고 알려진 우리의 시각 시스템의 특정 영역을 재활용하는데, 이것이 우리가 일련의 문자를 인식하고 그것들을 언어 영역에 연결할 수 있게 해 준다. 마찬가지로, 우리가 아라비아 숫자를 배울 때 우리는 그러한 모양들을 빠르게 수량으로 변환하는 회로를 만드는데, 이것은 양측의 시각 영역을 정수리 부분의 수량 영역과 빠르게 연결하는 것이다. 손가락으로 헤아리기와 같은 기본적인 발명조차도 우리의 인지 능력을 극적으로 변화시킨다. 수를 세는 것을 발명하지 않았던 아마존 사람들은, 예를 들어, 6 빼기 2처럼 간단한 것을 정확하게 계산할 수 없다. 이러한 '문화적 재활용'은 인간의 두뇌의 기능적 구조가 생물학적, 문화적 제약의 복잡한 혼합물로부터 생겨난 것임을 암시한다.

Why? 왜 정답일까?

빈칸 뒤의 예시에서 인간은 읽기나 숫자를 배우는 과정에서 앞서 활용했던 영역을 '재활용'하여 인지 기능을 확장해 나간다는 내용을 다루고, 마지막 문장에서 이를 'cultural recycling'이라는 용어로 정리하고 있다. 따라서 빈칸에 들어갈 말로 가장 적절한 것은 이 용어를 풀어 쓴 ② '우리가 우리의 오래된 영역들을 새로운 방식으로 동원할 수 있기'이다.

● expand ⓥ 확장하다	● functionality ⓝ 기능성
● arithmetic ⓝ 산수, 연산	● reason ⓥ 추론하다
● numeral ⓝ 숫자, 수사	● circuit ⓝ 회로
● bilateral ⓐ 양측(쪽)의	● parietal ⓐ 정수리 (부분)의
● cognitive ⓐ 인지적인	● imply ⓥ 암시하다
● architecture ⓝ 구조, 건축	● constraint ⓝ 제약, 제한, 통제
● put a limit on ～에 제한을 두다	● mobilize ⓥ 동원하다, 집결시키다
● stabilize ⓥ 안정화하다, 안정시키다	● isolated ⓐ 고립된

구문 풀이

3행 Our brains did not have enough time to evolve for them, /
　　　　　　　　　　　　　　　　～하기에 충분한 …
but I reason {that they were made possible because we can mobilize
　　　　　　　{ } 명사절　5형식의 수동태(가능하게 되다)　～이기 때문에
our old areas in novel ways}.

▶ 많이 틀린 이유는?
새로운 것을 발명하고 이해하는 데 기존의 자원을 활용한다는 내용 자체는 크게 낯설지 않지만 예시가 복잡하고 구문이 까다로워 속독하고 이해하기에 많은 어려움이 따르는 지문이다. 최다 오답인 ①은 지문에서 언급된 적 없는 'cultural diversity' 개념을 포함하고 있어 주제와 무관하다.

▶ 문제 해결 방법은?
빈칸이 주제 부분에 있으므로 뒤에 나오는 예시에서 힌트를 얻어야 한다. 'we recycle a specific region of our visual system', 'build a circuit to quickly convert those shapes into quantities', 'cultural recycling' 등은 크게 보아 오래된 인지 자원을 새롭게 활용하여 기능을 확장하는 예로 볼 수 있는데 이 의미를 그대로 나타낸 것이 ②이다.

★★★ 1등급 대비 고난도 3점 문제

12 과학 혁명을 공명정대하게 평가할 기준의 부재　정답률 38% | 정답 ②

다음 빈칸에 들어갈 말로 가장 적절한 것을 고르시오. [3점]

① official connection between scientists and policy makers
　과학자들과 정책 입안자들 간의 공식적 연결
✓ impartial formulation of standards for its assessment
　과학의 평가를 위한 기준의 공정한 공식화
③ incomplete terms to describe the reconstitutions
　재구성을 설명하는 불완전한 용어
④ easy process to learn about new scientific theories
　새로운 과학 이론에 관해 학습하는 쉬운 과정
⑤ strong belief that scientific progress benefits everyone
　과학적 진보가 모두에게 이익이 된다는 강한 신념

The revolution's victorious party can claim / to have resolved the fundamental anomalies of the old paradigm / and to have renewed the prospects for successful research / governed by shared assumptions.
혁명의 승리파는 주장할 수 있다. / 낡은 패러다임의 근본적인 변칙을 해결했고, / 성공적인 연구의 전망을 새롭게 했다고 / 공유된 가정에 의해 좌우된

Indeed, / the new community typically rewrites the textbooks, / and retells its own history, / to reflect this point of view.
실제로, / 새로운 공동체는 보통 교과서를 다시 쓰고, / 자신의 역사를 다시 이야기한다. / 이러한 관점을 반영하기 위해

But from the standpoint of the losers, / or even of those who look on impartially, / such rewritings might seem to mark change / without any genuine claim to progress, / because there is no neutral standard / by which to assess the merits of the change.
그러나 패배자들의 관점에서 / 또는 심지어 공정하게 보는 사람들 / 이런 재작성은 변화를 나타내는 것처럼 보일 수 있는데 / 진보에 대한 진정한 주장 없이 / 왜냐하면 중립적인 기준이 없기 때문이다. / 그 변화의 장점을 평가할 수 있는

The resulting body of knowledge / is in any case not cumulative, / since much of what was previously known (or merely believed) / had to be excluded / without ever having been conclusively refuted.
그 결과적인 지식의 체계는 / 어떠한 경우에도 누적되지 않는데 / 왜냐하면 이전에 알려졌던 것(또는 단순히 믿어진 것)의 많은 부분이 / 배제되어야 했던 까닭이다. / 한 번도 확실하게 반박된 적 없는 채로

One likewise cannot plausibly talk / about revolutionary reconstitutions of science / as aiming toward truth, / for similarly, / there can be no impartial formulation of standards for its assessment.
우리는 마찬가지로 설득력 있게 말할 수 없는데, / 과학의 혁명적 재구성에 관해 / (그것이) 진리를 지향하는 것이라고 / 왜냐하면 유사하게도 / 과학의 평가를 위한 기준의 공정한 공식화가 있을 수 없기 때문이다.

The available justification of scientific knowledge after revolutions, / couched in new terms / according to newly instituted standards, / may well be sufficient, / but perhaps only because these standards and terms are now inevitably our own.
혁명 이후의 과학 지식의 유효한 정당화는 / 새로운 용어로 표현된 / 새로 도입된 기준에 따라 / 충분할 것 같지만, / 단지 아마도 이런 기준과 용어가 이제 불가피하게 우리 것이기 때문일 것이다.

혁명의 승리파는 낡은 패러다임의 근본적인 변칙을 해결했고, 공유된 가정에 의해 좌우된 성공적인 연구의 전망을 새롭게 했다고 주장할 수 있다. 실제로, 새로운 공동체는 이러한 관점을 반영하기 위해 보통 교과서를 다시 쓰고, 자신의 역사를 다시 이야기한다. 그러나 패배자들이나, 심지어 공정하게 보는 사람들의 관점에서조차, 이런 재작성은 진보에 대한 진정한 주장 없이 변화를 나타내는 것처럼 보일 수 있는데, 왜냐하면 그 변화의 장점을 평가할 수 있는 중립적인 기준이 없기 때문이다. 그 결과적인 지식의 체계는 어떠한 경우에도 누적되지 않는데, 이전에 알려졌던 것(또는 단순히 믿어진 것)의 많은 부분이 한 번도 확실하게 반박된 적 없는 채로 배제되어야 했던 까닭이다. 마찬가지로, 우리는 과학의 혁명적 재구성이 진리 지향이라고 설득력 있게 말할 수 없는데,

왜냐하면 마찬가지로 과학의 평가를 위한 기준의 공정한 공식화가 있을 수 없기 때문이다. 새로 도입된 기준에 따라 새로운 용어로 표현된 혁명 이후의 과학 지식의 유효한 정당화는 충분할 것 같지만, 그건 단지 아마도 이런 기준과 용어가 이제 불가피하게도 우리 것이기 때문일 것이다.

Why? 왜 정답일까?

역사는 승리자의 기준에서 작성되므로 혁명을 중립적으로 평가할 기준이 없다(~ there is no neutral standard by which to assess the merits of the change.)는 설명 뒤로, 과학에 같은 내용이 적용되고 있다. 즉 과학 혁명 이후에도 이 혁명을 평가할 '객관적이고 중립된' 기준이 없다는 의미가 되도록, 빈칸에 들어갈 말로 가장 적절한 것은 ② '과학의 평가를 위한 기준의 공정한 공식화'이다.

- revolution ⓝ 혁명
- party ⓝ 정당, 이해 당사자
- anomaly ⓝ 변칙, 이례
- prospect ⓝ 전망, 가능성
- standpoint ⓝ 관점
- genuine ⓐ 진정한
- assess ⓥ 평가하다
- exclude ⓥ 배제하다
- plausibly ⓐⓓ 그럴듯하게
- justification ⓝ 타당한 설명[이유], 정당화
- institute ⓥ 도입하다, 시작하다
- formulation ⓝ 공식화
- victorious ⓐ 승리한
- resolve ⓥ 해결하다
- renew ⓥ 새롭게 하다
- assumption ⓝ 가정
- impartially ⓐⓓ 편견 없이, 공명정대하게
- progress ⓝ 진보, 진전
- cumulative ⓐ 누적되는
- refute ⓥ 반박하다
- reconstitution ⓝ 재구성
- couched in (특정한 방식으로) 표현된
- may well 아마 ~일 것이다
- incomplete ⓐ 불완전한

구문 풀이

1행 The revolution's victorious party can claim to have resolved
완료부정사1(can claim보다 이전 시제를 나타냄)
the fundamental anomalies of the old paradigm and to have renewed
완료부정사2
the prospects for successful research governed by shared
assumptions.

★★ 문제 해결 꿀~팁 ★★

▶ 많이 틀린 이유는?
빈칸 문장의 문맥으로 보아 '있을 수 없는' 것을 골라야 하므로 ③은 답으로 부적절하다. '혁명적 재구성을 설명하기에 불충분한 단어가 존재할 수 없다'는 말은 결국 혁명적 재구성을 제대로 설명하는 말이 '존재한다'는 의미로 읽힐 수 있기 때문이다. 이는 글의 주제와 맞지 않다.

▶ 문제 해결 방법은?
역사의 예를 과학에 '적용'하는 문제이다. 역사적으로 혁명의 이점을 평가할 수 있는 객관적 기준이 없다(no neutral standard by which to assess the merits of the change)는 지적이 나온 것으로 보아, 과학에서도 동일한 지적이 나와야 한다.

DAY 06 | 빈칸 추론 06

01 2차 세계 대전 후 여가의 양상 　　정답률 51% | 정답 ④

다음 빈칸에 들어갈 말로 가장 적절한 것을 고르시오.

① downfall - 몰락
② uniformity - 획일성
③ restoration - 회복
✔ privatization - 사유화
⑤ customization - 맞춤화

In the post-World War II years after 1945, / unparalleled economic growth / fueled a building boom and a massive migration / from the central cities to the new suburban areas.
1945년 이후 제2차 세계대전 이후 시절에 / 유례없는 경제 성장은 / 건축 붐과 대규모 이주를 부추겼다. / 중심 도시에서 새로운 교외 지역으로의

The suburbs were far more dependent on the automobile, / signaling the shift / from primary dependence on public transportation / to private cars.
교외 지역은 자동차에 훨씬 더 많이 의존했고, / 전환을 알렸다. / 대중교통에 대한 주된 의존으로부터 / 자가용으로의

Soon this led to the construction of better highways and freeways / and the decline and even loss of public transportation.
이것은 곧 더 나은 고속도로와 초고속도로의 건설로 이어졌다. / 그리고 대중교통의 감소, 심지어 쇠퇴로

With all of these changes / came a privatization of leisure.
이러한 모든 변화와 함께 / 여가의 사유화가 이루어졌다.

As more people owned their own homes, / with more space inside and lovely yards outside, / their recreation and leisure time / was increasingly centered around the home / or, at most, the neighborhood.
더 많은 사람이 자기 집을 갖게 되면서 / 내부 공간은 더 넓어지고 외부 정원은 더 아름다운 / 그들의 휴양과 여가 시간은 / 점점 더 집에 집중되었다. / 기껏해야 이웃

One major activity of this home-based leisure / was watching television.
가정에 기반을 둔 이런 여가의 한 가지 주요 활동은 / TV를 보는 것이었다.

No longer / did one have to ride the trolly to the theater / to watch a movie; / similar entertainment was available / for free and more conveniently / from television.
더 이상 없었다 / 전차를 타고 극장까지 갈 필요가 / 영화를 보려고 / 유사한 오락(물)이 이용 가능해졌다. / 무료로 더 편리하게 / 텔레비전을 통해

1945년 이후 제2차 세계대전 이후 시절에 유례없는 경제 성장은 건축 붐과 중심 도시에서 새로운 교외 지역으로의 대규모 이주를 부추겼다. 교외 지역은 자동차에 훨씬 더 많이 의존했고, 대중교통에 주로 의존하던 것에서 자가용으로의 전환을 알렸다. 이것은 곧 더 나은 고속도로와 초고속도로의 건설과 대중교통의 감소, 심지어 쇠퇴로 이어졌다. 이러한 모든 변화와 함께 여가의 사유화가 이루어졌다. 더 많은 사람이 내부 공간은 더 넓어지고 외부 정원은 더 아름다운 자기 집을 갖게 되면서 그들의 휴양과 여가 시간은 점점 더 집, 기껏해야 이웃에 집중되었다. 가정에 기반을 둔 이런 여가의 한 가지 주요 활동은 TV를 보는 것이었다. 더 이상 전차를 타고 극장까지 영화를 보러 갈 필요가 없었고, 유사한 오락(물)이 텔레비전을 통해 무료로 더 편리하게 이용 가능해졌다.

Why? 왜 정답일까?

3차 대전 이후의 엄청난 경제 성장과 함께 집 안에서 즐기는 여가 시간(home-based leisure)이 늘어났다는 내용이므로, 빈칸에 들어갈 말로 가장 적절한 것은 ④ '사유화'이다.

- fuel ⓥ 부추기다
- suburban ⓐ 교외의
- decline ⓝ 감소
- home-based ⓐ 집에 기반을 둔
- conveniently ⓐⓓ 편하게
- uniformity ⓝ 획일성
- privatization ⓝ 사유화, 민영화
- massive ⓐ 대규모의
- public transportation 대중교통
- at most 기껏해야
- trolly ⓝ 전차, 카트
- downfall ⓝ 몰락
- restoration ⓝ 회복, 복구
- customization ⓝ 맞춤화

구문 풀이

14행 No longer did one have to ride the trolly to the theater to
「도치 구문 : 부정어구＋did＋주어＋동사원형」
watch a movie; similar entertainment was available for free and
more conveniently from television.

02 균류 때문에 나무에 구멍을 쉽게 내는 딱따구리 정답률 42% | 정답 ①

다음 빈칸에 들어갈 말로 가장 적절한 것을 고르시오.

✔ division of labor – 분업
② act of sympathy – 연민의 행동
③ process of negotiation – 합의의 과정
④ competition for habitat – 서식지를 위한 경쟁
⑤ defense from predators – 포식자로부터의 방어

Contrary to popular opinion, / woodpeckers don't restrict themselves to rotten trees, / and they often start construction in healthy trees.
통념과 달리 / 딱따구리들은 썩은 나무에 국한되지 않고 / 그것들은 대개 건강한 나무에서 공사를 시작한다.

Just like us, / woodpeckers want the place / where they bring up their families / to be solid and durable.
우리와 마찬가지로 / 딱따구리들은 장소를 원한다. / 그것들이 자신의 가족을 양육하는 곳이 / 견고하고 내구성이기를

Even though the birds are well equipped / to hammer away at healthy wood, / it would be too much / for them to complete the job all at once.
비록 그 새들이 능력을 잘 갖추고 있다 할지라도 / 건강한 나무를 끊임없이 두드려 대는 / 너무 과한 일일 것이다. / 그것들이 그 일을 한꺼번에 완수하는 것은

And that's why they take a months-long break / after making a hole / that may be only an inch or two deep, / hoping fungi will pitch in.
그래서 그것들은 몇 달간의 휴식을 취하며 / 구멍을 만든 후 / 단지 1에서 2인치 깊이일 수 있는 / 균류가 협력하기를 바란다.

As far as the fungi are concerned, / this is the invitation they have been waiting for, / because usually they can't get past the bark.
균류에 관한 한 / 이것은 그것들이 기다려 온 초대장인데 / 왜냐하면 대개 그것들은 나무껍질을 통과하지 못하기 때문이다.

In this case, / the fungi quickly move into the opening / and begin to break down the wood.
이 경우에 / 균류는 재빠르게 그 구멍 안으로 들어가 / 나무를 분해하기 시작한다.

What the tree sees as a coordinated attack, / the woodpecker sees as a division of labor.
나무가 합동 공격으로 여기는 것을 / 딱따구리는 분업으로 여긴다.

After a while, the wood fibers are so soft / that it's much easier / for the woodpecker to enlarge the hole.
얼마 후에 나무 섬유가 매우 연해져서 / 훨씬 쉬워진다. / 딱따구리가 그 구멍을 확대하는 것이

통념과 달리 딱따구리들은 썩은 나무에 국한되지 않고 대개 건강한 나무에서 공사를 시작한다. 우리와 마찬가지로 딱따구리들은 자신의 가족을 양육하는 장소가 견고하고 내구성이 있기를 원한다. 비록 그 새들이 건강한 나무를 끊임없이 두드려 대는 능력을 잘 갖추고 있다 할지라도 그 일을 한꺼번에 완수하는 것은 너무 과한 일일 것이다. 그래서 그것들은 단지 1에서 2인치 깊이일 수 있는 구멍을 만든 후 몇 달간의 휴식을 취하며 균류가 협력하기를 바란다. 균류에 관한 한 이것은 기다려 온 초대장인데, 왜냐하면 대개 그것들은 나무껍질을 통과하지 못하기 때문이다. 이 경우에 균류는 재빠르게 그 구멍 안으로 들어가 나무를 분해하기 시작한다. 나무가 합동 공격으로 여기는 것을 딱따구리는 분업으로 여긴다. 얼마 후에 나무 섬유가 매우 연해져서 딱따구리가 그 구멍을 확대하는 것이 훨씬 쉬워진다.

Why? 왜 정답일까?

'And that's why they take a months-long break after making a hole that may be only an inch or two deep, hoping fungi will pitch in.'에서 딱따구리는 건강한 나무를 어느 정도 두드려 놓은 뒤에는 몇 달간 쉬면서 균류가 협력해 오기를 기다린다고 언급한다. 이어지는 내용에 따르면 균류는 평소에는 나무 껍질을 통과하지 못하지만 딱따구리가 구멍을 내놓으면 이 구멍으로 침투하여 나무를 분해할 수 있고, 이에 따라 딱따구리가 구멍을 넓혀가는 과정이 쉬워진다고 한다. 이러한 설명으로 볼 때, 딱따구리는 균류와 나무에 구멍을 내는 작업을 '나누어서' 진행하는 것으로 이해할 수 있으므로, 빈칸에 들어갈 말로 가장 적절한 것은 ① '분업'이다.

- woodpecker ⓝ 딱따구리
- construction ⓝ 공사, 구성
- durable ⓐ 내구성이 있는
- pitch in 협력하다, 일에 본격적으로 착수하다
- enlarge ⓥ 확대하다
- sympathy ⓝ 연민, 동정

- restrict A to B A를 B에 국한시키다
- solid ⓐ 튼튼한, 견고한
- hammer away at ~을 두드리다
- bark ⓝ 나무껍질
- division of labor 분업
- predator ⓝ 포식자

구문 풀이

13행 What the tree sees as a coordinated attack, the woodpecker
　　　　　　목적어(~것)　　　　　　　　　　　　　주어
sees as a division of labor.
동사　전치사(~로서)

---

03 소수 집단이 사회에 영향력을 행사하는 방식 정답률 61% | 정답 ①

다음 빈칸에 들어갈 말로 가장 적절한 것을 고르시오.

✔ the minority gets its point across – 소수 집단이 자기네 의견을 이해시키는
② the minority tones down its voice – 소수 집단이 자기 목소리를 낮추는
③ the majority cultivates the minority – 다수 집단이 소수 집단을 교화하는
④ the majority brings about social change – 다수 집단이 사회 변화를 초래하는
⑤ the minority cooperates with the majority – 소수 집단이 다수 집단과 협력하는

Minorities tend not to have much power or status / and may even be dismissed / as troublemakers, extremists or simply 'weirdos'.
소수 집단은 많은 힘이나 지위를 가지고 있지 않은 경향이 있고 / 심지어 일축될 수도 있다. / 말썽꾼, 극단주의자, 또는 단순히 '별난 사람'으로

How, then, do they ever have any influence / over the majority?
그렇다면 대체 그들은 어떻게 영향력을 행사하는가? / 다수 집단에 대한

The social psychologist Serge Moscovici claims / that the answer lies in their *behavioural style*, / i.e. the *way* the minority gets its point across.
사회 심리학자 Serge Moscovici는 주장한다. / 그 답이 그들의 *행동 양식*, / 즉 소수 집단이 자기네 의견을 이해시키는 *방식*에 있다고

The crucial factor in the success of the suffragette movement / was that its supporters were *consistent* in their views, / and this created a considerable degree of social influence.
여성 참정권 운동이 성공을 거둔 중대한 요인은 / 지지자들이 자기 관점 안에서 *일관적*이었다는 것이었는데, / 이것이 상당한 정도의 사회적 영향력을 행사하였다.

Minorities that are active and organised, / who support and defend their position *consistently*, / can create social conflict, doubt and uncertainty / among members of the majority, / and ultimately this may lead to social change.
활동적이고 조직적인 소수 집단이 / 자신들의 입장을 *일관되게* 옹호하고 방어하는 / 사회적 갈등, 의심, 그리고 반신반의하는 마음을 만들어 낼 수 있고, / 다수 집단의 구성원 사이에 / 궁극적으로 이것이 사회 변화를 가져올 수도 있다.

Such change has often occurred / because a minority has converted others / to its point of view.
그러한 변화가 흔히 일어난 까닭은 / 소수 집단이 다른 사람들을 바꿔 놓았기 때문이다. / 자신의 관점으로

Without the influence of minorities, / we would have no innovation, no social change.
소수 집단의 영향 없이는 / 우리에게 어떤 혁신, 어떤 사회 변화도 없을 것이다.

Many of what we now regard as 'major' social movements / (e.g. Christianity, trade unionism or feminism) / were originally due to the influence / of an outspoken minority.
우리가 현재 '주요' 사회 운동으로 여기는 많은 것이 / (예를 들어, 기독교 사상, 노동조합 운동, 또는 남녀평등주의) / 본래는 영향력 때문에 생겨났다. / 거침없이 말하는 소수 집단의

소수 집단은 많은 힘이나 지위를 가지고 있지 않은 경향이 있고 심지어 말썽꾼, 극단주의자, 또는 단순히 '별난 사람'으로 일축될 수도 있다. 그렇다면 대체 그들은 어떻게 다수 집단에 대한 영향력을 행사하는가? 사회 심리학자 Serge Moscovici는 그 답이 그들의 행동 양식, 즉 소수 집단이 자기네 의견을 이해시키는 *방식*에 있다고 주장한다. 여성 참정권 운동이 성공을 거둔 중대한 요인은 지지자들이 자기 관점 안에서 *일관적*이었다는 것이었는데, 이것이 상당한 정도의 사회적 영향력을 행사하였다. 자신들의 입장을 *일관되게* 옹호하고 방어하는 활동적이고 조직적인 소수 집단이 다수 집단의 구성원 사이에 사회적 갈등, 의심, 그리고 반신반의하는 마음을 만들어 낼 수 있고, 궁극적으로 이것이 사회 변화를 가져올 수도 있다. 그러한 변화가 흔히 일어난 까닭은 소수 집단이 다른 사람들을 자신의 관점으로 바꿔 놓았기 때문이다. 소수 집단의 영향 없이는 우리에게 어떤 혁신, 어떤 사회 변화도 없을 것이다. 우리가 현재 '주요' 사회 운동(예를 들어, 기독교 사상, 노동조합 운동, 또는 남녀평등주의)으로 여기는 많은 것이 본래는 거침없이 말하는 소수 집단의 영향력 때문에 생겨났다.

Why? 왜 정답일까?

'Such change has often occurred because a minority has converted others to its point of view.'에서 소수 집단이 다수 집단에 영향을 미치고 나아가 사회 변화를 이끌어내는 이유는 소수 집단이 타인을 그들의 관점으로 바꾸었기 때문임을 이야기하므로, 빈칸에 들어갈 말로 가장 적절한 것은 ① '소수 집단이 자기네 의견을 이해시키는'이다.

- extremist ⓝ 극단주의자, 과격파
- considerable ⓐ 상당한
- unionism ⓝ 노동조합 운동
- get across ~을 이해시키다
- bring about ~을 초래하다, 야기하다

- have influence over ~에 영향을 미치다
- convert A to B A를 B로 변화시키다
- outspoken ⓐ 거침없이 말하는
- cultivate ⓥ 교화하다, 계발하다

구문 풀이

10행 Minorities [that are active and organised, who support and
주어1 　관계대명사1 　　　 주격 관계대명사2
defend their position consistently], can create social conflict, doubt
동사1 　 목적어
and uncertainty among members of the majority, / and ultimately
this may lead to social change.
주어2 　동사2

---

04 비슷한 구성원보다 다른 구성원을 선택하는 이유　정답률 50% | 정답 ③

다음 빈칸에 들어갈 말로 가장 적절한 것을 고르시오.

① exceeds the expected demands of a community
　공동체의 예상 수요를 초과한다
② is decreased by diverse means of survival
　다양한 생존 수단에 의해 감소된다
✓③ places a limit on this strategy
　이 전략에 제한을 둔다
④ makes the world suitable for individuals
　세상을 개인들에게 적합하게 만든다
⑤ prevents social ties to dissimilar members
　비슷하지 않은 구성원과의 사회적 연대를 막는다

Choosing similar friends can have a rationale.
비슷한 친구를 선택하는 것은 논리적 근거를 가질 수 있다.
Assessing the survivability of an environment / can be risky / (if an
environment turns out to be deadly, for instance, / it might be too late by the
time you found out), / so humans have evolved the desire / to associate with
similar individuals / as a way to perform this function efficiently.
어떤 환경에서의 생존 가능성을 평가하는 것은 / 위험할 수 있어서, / (예컨대 어떤 환경이 치명적인 것으로 판명
되면, / 그 사실을 알 때쯤에는 너무 늦을 수도 있다) / 인간은 욕구를 진화시켜 왔다. / 유사한 개인들과 함께하
고자 하는 / 이 기능을 효율적으로 수행하기 위한 한 방법으로
This is especially useful to a species / that lives in so many different sorts of
environments.
이것은 종에게 특히 유용하다. / 매우 다양한 종류의 환경에 사는
However, / the carrying capacity of a given environment / places a limit on
this strategy.
그러나 / 주어진 환경의 수용 능력은 / 이 전략에 제한을 둔다.
If resources are very limited, / the individuals who live in a particular place /
cannot all do the exact same thing / (for example, if there are few trees, /
people cannot all live in tree houses, / or if mangoes are in short supply, /
people cannot all live solely on a diet of mangoes).
자원이 매우 한정되어 있다면, / 특정 장소에 사는 개인이 / 모두 똑같은 것을 할 수는 없다. / (예를 들어, 나무가
거의 없다면, / 사람들이 모두 나무집에 살 수는 없으며, / 또는 망고의 공급이 부족하면, / 사람들이 모두 망고를
먹고만 살 수는 없다)
A rational strategy / would therefore sometimes be / to *avoid* similar
members of one's species.
합리적인 전략은 / 그러므로 때때로 ~일 것이다. / 자신의 종의 비슷한 구성원을 *피하는* 일

비슷한 친구를 선택하는 것은 논리적 근거를 가질 수 있다. 어떤 환경에서의
생존 가능성을 평가하는 것은 위험할 수 있어서(예컨대 어떤 환경이 치명적인
것으로 판명되면, 그 사실을 알 때쯤에는 너무 늦을 수도 있다), 인간은 이 기
능을 효율적으로 수행하기 위한 한 방법으로 유사한 개인들과 함께하고자 하
는 욕구를 진화시켜 왔다. 이것은 매우 다양한 종류의 환경에 사는 종에게 특
히 유용하다. 그러나 주어진 환경의 수용 능력은 이 전략에 제한을 둔다. 자원
이 매우 한정되어 있다면, 특정 장소에 사는 개인이 모두 똑같은 것을 할 수는
없다(예를 들어, 나무가 거의 없다면, 사람들이 모두 나무집에 살 수는 없으며,
또는 망고의 공급이 부족하면, 사람들이 모두 망고를 먹고만 살 수는 없다). 그
러므로 합리적인 전략은 때때로 자신의 종의 비슷한 구성원을 *피하는* 일일 것
이다.

Why? 왜 정답일까?

빈칸 문장의 **However**를 기점으로 글의 흐름이 반전된다. **However** 앞에서 인간이
자신과 비슷한 사람들을 가까이 하려는 욕구를 진화시켜온 배경을 설명한 데 반해,
However 뒤에서는 이러한 전략이 자원이 한정된 환경에서는 실행되기 어려운 이유를
언급하며 비슷한 무리를 '피하는' 전략이 도리어 효과적임을 설명하고 있다. 따라서 빈칸
에 들어갈 말로 가장 적절한 것은 비슷한 친구를 찾는 전략을 **this strategy**로 받으며
이것에 한계가 있음을 지적하는 ③ '이 전략에 제한을 둔다'이다.

- **rationale** ⓝ 논리적 근거, 이유
- **survivability** ⓝ 생존 가능성
- **carrying capacity** 수용 능력, 적재량
- **solely** ⓐⓓ 오로지
- **means** ⓝ 수단, 방법
- **assess** ⓥ 평가하다
- **associate with** ~와 함께하다
- **in short supply** 공급이 부족한
- **diverse** ⓐ 다양한
- **suitable** ⓐ 적합한, 적절한

구문 풀이

2행 Assessing the survivability of an environment can be risky
주어1 　　　　　　　　　　　　　　　 동사1 보어
(if an environment turns out to be deadly, for instance, it might be
접속사(~라면) 　　　　　　　 비인칭 주어 　 동사
too late by the time you found out), so humans have evolved
접속사(~할 무렵에) 　　　　　　 주어2 　 동사2
the desire to associate with similar individuals as a way to perform
목적어 　 형용사적 용법 　　　 전치사(~로서) 명사구 　형용사적 용법
this function efficiently.

---

05 사물의 본질에 대한 인식　정답률 45% | 정답 ②

다음 빈칸에 들어갈 말로 가장 적절한 것을 고르시오. [3점]

① alter the powers of local authorities – 지역 당국의 권한을 변경하는
✓② contribute to their ability to be there – 그들이 그곳에 있을 수 있는 데 이바지하는
③ compel them to conceal their identity – 그들이 정체성을 숨기도록 강제하는
④ impose their sacrifice and commitment – 그들의 희생과 헌신을 강요하는
⑤ prevent them from realizing their potential – 그들이 잠재력을 실현하지 못하게 하는

If the nature of a thing is such / that when removed from the environment /
in which it naturally occurs / it alters radically, / you will not glean an
accurate account of it / by examining it within laboratory conditions.
사물의 본질이 그런 것이라면, / 환경으로부터 동떨어져 있을 때 / 그것이 자연스럽게 발생하는 / 그것이 근본적
으로 변하는 / 여러분은 그 본질에 대한 정확한 설명을 찾아내지 못할 것이다. / 실험실 환경 안에서 조사하는 것
으로
If you are only accustomed to seeing it operate / within such an artificial arena, /
you may not even recognize it / when it is functioning in its normal context.
여러분이 그것이 작동하는 것을 보는 것에만 익숙하다면, / 그런 인위적인 영역 안에서 / 여러분은 그것을 인식
조차 못할 수도 있다. / 여러분이 그것이 정상적인 상황에서 작동하고 있을 때
Indeed, if you ever spot it in that environment / you may think it is
something else.
사실, 여러분이 그러한 환경에서 그것을 발견한다 해도 / 여러분은 그것을 무언가 다른 것으로 여길지도 모른다.
Similarly, / if you believe / that leadership only takes the form of heroic men
/ metaphorically charging in on white horses to save the day, / you may
neglect the many acts / which contribute to their ability to be there.
마찬가지로, / 만약 여러분이 믿는다면, / 리더십이 그저 영웅적인 사람의 모습을 취한다고 / 은유적으로 말해서
백마를 타고 돌진하여 궁지에서 벗어나게 하는 / 여러분은 많은 행동들을 간과할 수도 있다. / 그들이 그곳에 있
을 수 있는 데 이바지하는
You may fail to see the importance / of the grooms who care for the horses, /
the messengers who bring attention to the crisis / or the role played by those
cheering from the sidelines.
여러분은 중요성을 못 볼 수도 있다. / 말을 돌보는 마부들의 / 위기에 주의를 기울이게 하는 전령들의 / 혹은 옆
에서 응원하는 사람들이 하는 역할의
You may miss the fact / that without troops supporting them, / any claims to
leading on the part of these heroes / would be rather hollow.
여러분은 사실을 깨닫지 못할 수도 있다. / 그들을 지원하는 군대가 없으면 / 이 영웅들의 편에 서야 한다는 그
어떤 주장도 / 상당히 공허할 것이라는

사물의 본질이 자연스럽게 발생하는 환경으로부터 동떨어져 있을 때 근본적으
로 변하는 그런 것이라면, 여러분은 실험실 환경 안에서 조사하는 것으로 그
본질에 대한 정확한 설명을 찾아내지 못할 것이다. 그것이 그런 인위적인 영역
안에서 작동하는 것을 보는 것에만 익숙하다면, 그것이 정상적인 상황에서 작
동하고 있을 때 그것을 인식조차 못할 수도 있다. 사실, 그러한 환경에서 그것
을 발견한다 해도 여러분은 그것을 무언가 다른 것으로 여길지도 모른다. 마찬
가지로, 만약 리더십이 그저 은유적으로 말해서 백마를 타고 돌진하여 궁지에
서 벗어나게 하는 영웅적인 사람의 모습을 취한다고 믿는다면, 여러분은 그들
이 그곳에 있을 수 있는 데 이바지하는 많은 행동들을 간과할 수도 있다. 말을
돌보는 마부들, 위기에 주의를 기울이게 하는 전령들, 혹은 옆에서 응원하는
사람들이 하는 역할의 중요성을 못 볼 수도 있다. 이 영웅들의 편에 서야 한다
는 그 어떤 주장도 그들을 지원하는 군대가 없으면 상당히 공허할 것이라는 사
실을 깨닫지 못할 수도 있다.

Why? 왜 정답일까?

마지막 두 문장에서 리더를 영웅적인 인물로만 생각한다면 그 리더를 리더로 만들어주는
존재들, 즉 마부와 전령, 옆에서 응원해주는 사람들, 지원군 등의 역할이 중요하다는 것을
깨닫지 못할 수도 있다고 언급한다. 이로 미루어볼 때, 빈칸이 포함된 문장은 영웅이라는
상에만 몰두하고 있으면 그 영웅의 위치에 도달하게끔 도와주는 사람들의 존재를 간과할
수 있다는 의미가 되어야 한다. 따라서 빈칸에 들어갈 말로 가장 적절한 것은 ② '그들이
그곳에 있을 수 있는 데 이바지하는'이다.

- removed from ~로부터 동떨어진
- accurate ⓐ 정확한
- artificial ⓐ 인공적인
- metaphorically ⓐ 은유적으로
- save the day 궁지에서 벗어나다
- crisis ⓝ 위기
- compel ⓥ 강제하다
- commitment ⓝ 헌신, 약속

- radically ⓐ 근본적으로
- be accustomed to ~에 익숙해지다
- take the form of ~의 형태를 취하다
- charge in on ~에 돌진하다
- neglect ⓥ 간과하다, 무시하다
- hollow ⓐ 빈, 공허한
- sacrifice ⓝ 희생

구문 풀이

1행 If the nature of a thing is │such that │when removed from
접속사(조건)   현재시제   「such that : ~한 그런 것, (너무) ~해서 …하다」 접속사 분사구문
the environment [in which it naturally occurs] it alters radically, you
선행사
will not glean an accurate account of it by examining it within
미래시제   ~함으로써
laboratory conditions.

---

06 공유지 문제 해결을 위해 이용자를 참여시키기   정답률 47% | 정답 ①

다음 빈칸에 들어갈 말로 가장 적절한 것을 고르시오. [3점]

✓① participate in decisions to change the rules
    규칙을 변경하는 결정에 참여할
② claim individual ownership of the resources
    자원에 대한 개인의 소유권을 주장할
③ use those resources to maximize their profits
    자신의 이익을 최대화하기 위해 그 자원을 이용할
④ demand free access to the communal resources
    공동 자원에 대한 자유로운 이용 권한을 요구할
⑤ request proper distribution based on their merits
    자신의 공로를 바탕으로 적당한 분배를 요청할

Elinor Ostrom found / that there are several factors / critical to bringing
about stable institutional solutions / to the problem of the commons.
Elinor Ostrom은 알게 되었다. / 몇 가지 요인이 있음을 / 안정적인 제도적 해결책을 가져오는 데 중요한 /
공유지 문제에 대한
She pointed out, for instance, / that the actors / affected by the rules for the
use and care of resources / must have the right / to participate in decisions to
change the rules.
예를 들어, 그녀는 지적했다. / 행위자들이 / 자원의 이용 및 관리 규칙의 영향을 받는 / 권리를 가져야 한다고 /
규칙을 변경하는 결정에 참여할
For that reason, / the people who monitor and control the behavior of users /
should also be users / and / or have been given a mandate by all users.
그러한 이유로, / 이용자의 행동을 감시하고 통제하는 사람은 / 또한 이용자이다 / 그리고/또는 모든 이용자에
의한 위임을 받았어야 한다.
This is a significant insight, / as it shows that prospects are poor / for a
centrally directed solution / to the problem of the commons / coming from a
state power / in comparison with a local solution / for which users assume
personal responsibility.
이것은 중요한 통찰인데, / 전망이 열악하다는 것을 보여주기 때문이다. / 중앙 (정부) 지향적 해결책의 / 공유지
문제에 대한 / 국가 권력에서 나오는 / 지역적인 해결책에 비해 / 이용자가 개인적 책임을 지는
Ostrom also emphasizes the importance of democratic decision processes /
and that all users must be given access to local forums / for solving problems
and conflicts among themselves.
Ostrom은 또한 민주적 의사결정 과정의 중요성을 강조한다. / 그리고 모든 이용자에게 지역 포럼에 참여할 권한
이 주어져야 한다고 / 그들 사이의 문제와 갈등을 해결하기 위한
Political institutions at central, regional, and local levels / must allow users /
to devise their own regulations / and independently ensure observance.
중앙, 지방 및 지역 차원의 정치 기관들은 / 이용자가 ~하도록 해야 한다. / 자체 규정을 고안하고 / 독립적으로
준수할 수 있도록

Elinor Ostrom은 공유지 문제에 대한 안정적인 제도적 해결책을 가져오는 데
중요한 몇 가지 요인이 있음을 알게 되었다. 예를 들어, 그녀는 자원의 이용 및
관리 규칙의 영향을 받는 행위자에게 규칙을 변경하는 결정에 참여할 권리가
있어야 한다고 지적했다. 그러한 이유로 이용자의 행동을 감시하고 통제하는
사람 또한 이용자이고/이거나 모든 이용자에 의한 위임을 받았어야 한다. 이것
은 중요한 통찰인데, 이용자가 개인적 책임을 지는 지역적인 해결책에 비해 국
가 권력에서 나오는 공유지 문제에 대한 중앙 (정부) 지향적 해결책의 전망이
열악하다는 것을 보여주기 때문이다. Ostrom은 또한 민주적 의사결정 과정의
중요성과 모든 이용자에게 그들 사이의 문제와 갈등을 해결하기 위한 지역 포
럼에 참여할 권한이 주어져야 한다고 강조한다. 중앙, 지방 및 지역 차원의 정
치 기관들은 이용자가 자체 규정을 고안하고 독립적으로 준수할 수 있도록 해
야 한다.

Why? 왜 정답일까?

마지막 문장에서 정치 기관은 이용자가 자체적으로 규정을 고안하고 준수할 수 있게 해

야 한다(~ must allow users to devise their own regulations and
independently ensure observance.)고 언급하는 것으로 보아, 빈칸 또한 행위자
가 직접 규칙을 '고안하는' 것에 관한 설명이어야 한다. 따라서 빈칸에 들어갈 말로 가장
적절한 것은 ① '규칙을 변경하는 결정에 참여할'이다.

- stable ⓐ 안정된
- significant ⓐ 중요한
- in comparison with ~에 비해
- give access to ~에 접근을 허가하다
- observance ⓝ 준수
- distribution ⓝ 분배

- institutional ⓐ 제도적인
- prospect ⓝ 전망
- emphasize ⓥ 강조하다
- devise ⓥ 고안하다
- maximize ⓥ 최대화하다

구문 풀이

9행 This is a significant insight, as it shows that prospects are
접속사(~이기 때문에)   접속사(~것)
poor for a centrally directed solution to the problem of the commons
                꾸밈 받는 명사   전명구
coming from a state power in comparison with a local solution [for
현재분사구(a ~ solution 수식)   ~에 비해   선행사
which users assume personal responsibility].

★★★ **1등급 대비 고난도 2점 문제**

07 평정심 유지에 도움이 되는 먼 조상들의 시각   정답률 44% | 정답 ①

다음 빈칸에 들어갈 말로 가장 적절한 것을 고르시오.

✓① calm the disquieted soul – 불안한 영혼을 진정시킬
② boost cooperation in the community – 공동체의 협력을 증진시킬
③ make us stick to the specific details – 우리가 특정 세부사항을 고수하게 할
④ result in a waste of time – 시간 낭비로 이어질
⑤ complicate situations – 상황을 복잡하게 만들

A connection with ancestors, / especially remote ones, / is useful for getting
a wide-angled, philosophical view of life.
조상들과의 관계, / 특히 먼 조상들과의 관계는 / 삶에 대한 폭넓은 철학적 관점을 얻는 데 유용하다.
Whereas our immediate ancestors are notably skilled / at helping us with the
"little pictures," / namely the particular, the trees — say, a problem with a
boss — / our remote ones are best for seeing the "Big Picture," / namely the
general, the forest — say, the meaning of our job.
우리의 직계 조상들은 특히 능숙하지만, / '작은 그림'을 도와주는 데 / 즉 세부적인 것, 나무들 / 가령 상사와의
문제 / 우리의 먼 조상들은 '큰 그림'을 보는 데 가장 알맞다. / 즉 일반적인 것, 숲 / 가령 직업의 의미 같은 것
As modern people rush around blowing small problems out of proportion, /
thus contributing to a global anxiety epidemic, / ancestral spirits have a
broader perspective / that can calm the disquieted soul.
현대인들이 바쁘게 작은 문제를 어울리지 않게 부풀려서 / 세계적인 불안 확산의 원인이 될 때, / 조상들은 더
넓은 시야가 있다. / 불안한 영혼을 진정시킬 수 있는
When it comes to a trivial problem, / for example, / they'll just tell us, "This
too will pass."
사소한 문제에 관한 한, / 예를 들어, / 그들은 그저 우리에게 "이 또한 지나갈 것이다."라고 말할 것이다.
They appreciate / how rapidly and often things change.
그들은 이해한다. / 상황이 얼마나 빨리 그리고 자주 변하는지를
According to American anthropologist Richard Katz, / for instance, / Fijians
say / that from the ancestral viewpoint / whatever looks unfortunate / may
turn out to be fortunate after all: / "What may seem to be a horrible outcome
/ ... is seen in another light by the ancestors."
미국 인류학자 Richard Katz에 따르면 / 예를 들어, / 피지 사람들은 말한다. / 조상의 관점에서 볼 때, / 불운해
보이는 무엇이든 / 결국은 운 좋은 것으로 판명될 수 있다고 / "끔찍한 결과로 보일지도 모르는 것은 … 조상들
에게는 또 다른 관점으로 보인다."
The ancestors, / it might be said, / keep their heads / when everyone around
them is losing theirs.
조상들은 / ~라고 할 수 있다. / 그들의 평정심을 유지한다고 / 주변의 모든 사람이 평정심을 잃고 있을 때도

조상들과의 관계, 특히 먼 조상들과의 관계는 삶에 대한 폭넓은 철학적 관점을
얻는 데 유용하다. 우리의 직계 조상들은 '작은 그림', 즉 세부적인 것, 나무들
(가령 상사와의 문제)을 도와주는 데 특히 능숙하지만, 우리의 먼 조상들은 '큰
그림', 즉 일반적인 것, 숲(가령 직업의 의미 같은 것)을 보는 데 가장 알맞다.
현대인들이 바쁘게 작은 문제를 어울리지 않게 부풀려서 세계적인 불안 확산
의 원인이 될 때, 조상들은 불안한 영혼을 진정시킬 수 있는 더 넓은 시야가 있
다. 예를 들어, 사소한 문제에 관한 한, 그들은 그저 우리에게 "이 또한 지나갈
것이다."라고 말할 것이다. 그들은 상황이 얼마나 빨리 그리고 자주 변하는지
를 이해한다. 예를 들어, 미국 인류학자 Richard Katz에 따르면 피지 사람들은
조상의 관점에서 볼 때, 불운해 보이는 무엇이든 결국은 운 좋은 것으로 판명
될 수 있다고 말한다. "끔찍한 결과로 보일지도 모르는 것은 … 조상들에게는

또 다른 관점으로 보인다." 조상들은 주변의 모든 사람이 평정심을 잃고 있을 때도 그들의 평정심을 유지한다고 할 수 있다.

Why? 왜 정답일까?

먼 옛날 조상들의 시각은 우리가 세부사항이 아닌 큰 그림을 보게 해주며(our remote ones are best for seeing the "Big Picture," namely the general, the forest), 그렇기에 평정심을 유지하는 데 도움이 될 수 있다(The ancestors, it might be said, keep their heads when everyone around them is losing theirs.)는 내용이다. 따라서 빈칸에 들어갈 말로 가장 적절한 것은 ① '불안한 영혼을 진정시킬'이다.

- wide-angled ⓐ 폭넓은
- notably [ad] 특히, 현저히
- blow A out of proportion A를 지나치게 부풀리다
- epidemic ⓝ (급속한) 확산, 전염(병)
- ancestral ⓐ 조상의
- trivial ⓐ 사소한
- anthropologist ⓝ 인류학자
- horrible ⓐ 무서운, 끔찍한
- outcome ⓝ 결과
- disquiet ⓥ 불안하게 하다, 동요시키다
- stick to ~을 고수하다
- complicate ⓥ 복잡하게 하다

구문 풀이

14행 According to American anthropologist Richard Katz, for instance, Fijians say that from the ancestral viewpoint {whatever
복합관계대명사(= anything that)
looks unfortunate} may turn out to be fortunate after all: ~
~한 것으로 판명되다

★★ 문제 해결 꿀~팁 ★★

▶ 많이 틀린 이유는?
글을 피상적으로 이해하거나 소재를 올바르게 파악하지 못하면 '조상'이라는 키워드에서 '협력', '공동체' 등을 연상하여 ②를 고르기 쉽다. 지문 내용보다 사전 지식이나 고정 관념에 의존해 답을 고르지 않도록 유의하자.

▶ 문제 해결 방법은?
빈칸 뒤의 '이 또한 지나간다'는 인용구는 작은 변화에 일희일비할 필요 없이 내면의 평화를 지키라는 의미로 주로 사용된다. 또한 빈칸 앞에도 나무보다 '숲'을 보게 해준다는 일반적인 비유가 사용되는데, 이 역시 작은 것보다는 '큰 그림'에 집중하고 사소한 문제나 변화에 좌우되지 않게 해준다는 의미이다.

★★★ 1등급 대비 고난도 3점 문제

08 학습과 환경에 좌우되는 먹이 찾기 행동 정답률 43% | 정답 ⑤

다음 빈칸에 들어갈 말로 가장 적절한 것을 고르시오. [3점]

① less cooperative with others in their community
공동체 안의 다른 개체들과 덜 협력하게
② less focused on monitoring predators' approaches
포식자의 접근을 관찰하는 데 덜 집중하게
③ more intelligent to build their natural surroundings
자연 환경을 지을 수 있도록 더 똑똑하게
④ more sensitive to visual information than any other stimuli
다른 어떤 자극보다 시각적 자극에 더 민감하게
✔ more flexible and able to adapt to a variety of environments
더 유연하고도 다양한 환경에 적응할 수 있게

Innate behaviors used for finding food, / such as grazing, scavenging, or hunting, / are more dependent on learning / than behaviors used to consume food.
먹이를 찾는 데 사용되는 타고난 행동은 / 풀 뜯어 먹기, 동물 사체 찾기, 또는 사냥하기처럼, / 학습에 더 의존적이다. / 음식을 먹는 데 사용되는 행동보다

Mating, nesting, eating, and prey-killing behaviors / tend to be governed / more by instinct.
짝짓기, 둥지 틀기, 먹기, 그리고 먹이를 죽이는 행동은 / 지배되는 경향이 있다. / 본능에 의해서 더 많이

The greater dependence on learning to find food / makes animals in the wild / more flexible and able to adapt to a variety of environments.
먹이를 찾기 위해 학습에 더 크게 의존하는 것은 / 야생의 동물들을 만든다. / 더 유연하고도 다양한 환경에 적응할 수 있게

Behaviors used to kill or consume food / can be the same in any environment.
먹이를 죽이거나 먹기 위해 사용되는 행동은 / 어떤 환경에서도 동일할 수 있다.

Ernst Mayr, an evolutionary biologist, / called these different behavioral systems / "open" or "closed" to the effects of experience.
진화 생물학자인 Ernst Mayr는 / 이러한 다른 행동 체계들을 칭했다. / 경험의 영향에 '개방적' 또는 '폐쇄적'이라고

A lion hunting her prey / is an example of an open system.
사냥감을 사냥하는 사자는 / 개방적 체계의 한 예이다.

The hunting female lion / recognizes her prey from a distance / and approaches it carefully.
사냥하는 암사자는 / 멀리서 먹이를 알아보고 / 조심스럽게 접근한다.

Charles Herrick, a neurobiologist, wrote, / "the details of the hunt vary / every time she hunts. / Therefore / no combination of simple reflex arcs / laid down in the nervous system / will be adequate / to meet the infinite variations of the requirements for obtaining food."
신경 생물학자인 Charles Herrick은 썼다. / "사냥할 때의 세부사항은 다르다. / 사자가 사냥할 때마다 / 따라서 / 단순한 반사궁들의 어떤 조합도 / 신경계에 있는 / 충분하지 않을 것이다. / 먹이를 획득하기 위한 무한한 요건 변화를 충족시키기에"

풀 뜯어 먹기, 동물 사체 찾기, 또는 사냥하기처럼, 먹이를 찾는 데 사용되는 타고난 행동은 음식을 먹는 데 사용되는 행동보다 학습에 더 의존적이다. 짝짓기, 둥지 틀기, 먹기, 그리고 먹이를 죽이는 행동은 본능에 더 지배되는 경향이 있다. 먹이를 찾기 위해 학습에 더 크게 의존하는 것은 야생의 동물들을 더 유연하고도 다양한 환경에 적응할 수 있게 만든다. 먹이를 죽이거나 먹기 위해 사용되는 행동은 어떤 환경에서도 동일할 수 있다. 진화 생물학자인 Ernst Mayr는 이러한 다른 행동 체계들이 경험의 영향에 대해 '개방적' 또는 '폐쇄적'이라고 칭했다. 사냥감을 사냥하는 사자는 개방적 체계의 한 예이다. 사냥하는 암사자는 멀리서 먹이를 알아보고 조심스럽게 접근한다. 신경 생물학자인 Charles Herrick은 "사냥할 때의 세부사항은 사냥할 때마다 다르다. 따라서 신경계에 있는 단순한 반사궁들의 어떤 조합도 먹이를 획득하기 위한 무한한 요건 변화를 충족시키기에 충분하지 않을 것이다."라고 썼다.

Why? 왜 정답일까?

글 후반부에서, 사냥 시 세부사항은 사냥을 할 때마다 달라지며(the details of the hunt vary every time she hunts), 이 때문에 사냥 행위는 '개방적(open)' 체계로 볼 수 있다고 했다. 빈칸에는 이를 요약한 결론이 들어가야 하므로, 답으로 가장 적절한 것은 ⑤ '더 유연하고도 다양한 환경에 적응할 수 있게'이다.

- innate ⓐ 타고난
- graze ⓥ 풀을 뜯다
- scavenge ⓥ 동물의 사체를 찾아 다니다
- consume ⓥ 먹다, 섭취하다, 소비하다
- instinct ⓝ 본능
- neurobiologist ⓝ 신경 과학자
- combination ⓝ 조합, 결합
- reflex arc 반사궁
- nervous system 신경 체계
- infinite ⓐ 무한한

구문 풀이

16행 Therefore no combination of simple reflex arcs laid down in
주어　수식　과거분사구
the nervous system will be adequate to meet the infinite variations
동사　주격 보어　부사적 용법(형용사 수식)
of the requirements for obtaining food.
전치사　동명사

★★ 문제 해결 꿀~팁 ★★

▶ 많이 틀린 이유는?
암사자의 사냥을 예로 들어, 먹이 찾기 행동은 학습과 환경에 크게 좌우되는 행동임을 설명하는 글이다. 환경이라는 핵심어만 보고 ③을 답으로 고르면 안 된다. '환경을 직접 구축한다'는 내용은 주제와 무관하기 때문이다.

▶ 문제 해결 방법은?
맨 마지막 문장의 meet the infinite variations of the requirements for obtaining food가 정답인 ⑤의 'adapt to a variety of environments'와 같은 의미이다.

★★★ 1등급 대비 고난도 3점 문제

09 악음의 속성에 따른 음악의 정의 정답률 43% | 정답 ②

다음 빈칸에 들어갈 말로 가장 적절한 것을 고르시오. [3점]

① not so much artificially fixed as naturally fluctuating
인위적으로 고정되어 있기 보다는 자연적으로 변동하고
✔ not only fixed, but organized into a series of discrete steps
고정되어 있을 뿐만 아니라 연속된 별개의 음정으로 조직되어
③ hardly considered a primary compositional element of music
음악의 주된 구성 요소로 거의 여겨지지 않고
④ highly diverse and complicated, and thus are immeasurable
매우 다양하고 복잡하고, 그래서 측정될 수 없는
⑤ a vehicle for carrying unique and various cultural features
독특하고 다양한 문화적 특징을 전달하는 수단

There have been many attempts / to define what music is / in terms of the specific attributes of musical sounds.
많은 시도가 있었다. / 음악이 무엇인가를 정의하고자 하는 / 악음(樂音)의 특정 속성이라는 관점에서

The famous nineteenth-century critic Eduard Hanslick / regarded 'the measurable tone' / as 'the primary and essential condition of all music'.
19세기의 유명 평론가인 Eduard Hanslick은 / '측정할 수 있는 음조'를 간주했다. / '모든 음악의 주요하고 본질적인 조건'으로

Musical sounds, he was saying, / can be distinguished from those of nature / by the fact that they involve the use of fixed pitches, / whereas virtually all natural sounds consist of constantly fluctuating frequencies.
그가 말하기를 음악은 / 자연의 소리와 구별될 수 있다. / 고정된 음 높이 사용을 수반한다는 사실로 인해 / 자연의 거의 모든 소리가 지속적으로 변동하는 주파수로 구성되어 있는 것에 반해

And a number of twentieth-century writers have assumed, like Hanslick, / that fixed pitches are among the defining features of music.
그리고 20세기의 많은 작곡가들은 Hanslick과 마찬가지로 추정했다. / 고정된 음 높이가 음악의 결정적인 특징 중 하나라고

Now it is true / that in most of the world's musical cultures, / pitches are not only fixed, / but organized into a series of discrete steps.
이제, 사실이다 / 세계의 대부분의 음악 문화에서 / 음 높이는 고정되어 있을 뿐만 아니라 / 연속된 별개의 음정으로 조직되어 있는 것은

However, this is a generalization about music / and not a definition of it, / for it is easy to put forward counter-examples.
하지만 이것은 음악에 관한 일반화이지 / 그것에 관한 정의는 아닌데, / 왜냐하면 반례를 제기하는 것이 쉽기 때문이다.

Japanese *shakuhachi* music and the *sanjo* music of Korea, for instance, / fluctuate constantly around the notional pitches / in terms of which the music is organized.
예를 들어, 일본의 *샤쿠하치* 음악과 한국의 산조 음악은 / 관념상의 음 높이 주위에서 끊임없이 변한다. / 그 음악이 구성된

악음(樂音)의 특정 속성이라는 관점에서 음악이 무엇인가를 정의하고자 하는 많은 시도가 있었다. 19세기의 유명 평론가인 Eduard Hanslick은 '측정할 수 있는 음조'를 '모든 음악의 주요하고 본질적인 조건'으로 간주했다. 그가 말하기를 악음은 자연의 거의 모든 소리가 지속적으로 변동하는 주파수로 구성되어 있는 것에 반해 고정된 음 높이 사용을 수반한다는 사실로 인해 자연의 소리와 구별될 수 있다. 그리고 20세기의 많은 작곡가들은 Hanslick과 마찬가지로 고정된 음 높이가 음악의 결정적인 특징 중 하나라고 추정했다. 이제, 세계의 대부분의 음악 문화에서 음 높이는 고정되어 있을 뿐만 아니라 연속된 별개의 음정으로 조직되어 있다는 것은 사실이다. 하지만 이것은 음악에 관한 일반화이지 그것에 관한 정의는 아닌데, 왜냐하면 반례를 제기하는 것이 쉽기 때문이다. 예를 들어, 일본의 샤쿠하치 음악과 한국의 산조 음악은 그 음악이 구성된 관념상의 음 높이 주위에서 끊임없이 변한다.

Why? 왜 정답일까?

악음의 특성에 따라 음악을 정의하는 것에 관해 설명한 글이다. 빈칸 앞의 두 문장(Musical sounds, ~ involve the use of fixed pitches, ~ / ~ fixed pitches are among the defining features of music.)에서 악음은 계속해서 주파수가 변하는 자연의 소리와는 달리 고정된 음 높이를 사용하는 결정적인 특징이 있음을 언급한다. 이에 근거할 때, 빈칸에 들어갈 말로 가장 적절한 것은 '고정된 음 높이'라는 내용을 포함한 ② '고정되어 있을 뿐만 아니라 연속된 별개의 음정으로 조직되어'이다.

- **attempt** ⓝ 시도
- **attribute** ⓝ 특성
- **primary** ⓐ 주요한
- **virtually** ⓐ 사실상
- **frequency** ⓝ 주파수
- **generalization** ⓝ 일반화
- **artificially** ⓐ 인위적으로
- **step** ⓝ 음정
- **immeasurable** ⓐ 헤아릴[측정할] 수 없는
- **define** ⓥ 정의하다
- **measurable** ⓐ 측정할 수 있는
- **involve** ⓥ 포함시키다
- **fluctuate** ⓥ 변동하다
- **feature** ⓝ 특징
- **notional** ⓐ 관념상의
- **discrete** ⓐ 별개의
- **compositional** ⓐ 구성의

구문 풀이

5행 Musical sounds, (he was saying), can be distinguished from
　　　주어　　　( ): 삽입절　　　동사(조동사 수동태)
those of nature by the fact {that they involve the use of fixed pitches},
　　　　　　　　　　　　└─{ }: 동격
whereas virtually all natural sounds consist of constantly fluctuating
접속사(~하는 반면에)
frequencies.

★★ 문제 해결 꿀~팁 ★★

▶ 많이 틀린 이유는?

악음의 속성에 기초한 음악의 개념 정의를 소재로 다룬 글로 내용이 상당히 추상적이다. 최다 오답인 ①의 경우 악음이 '인위적으로 고정되어' 있지 않고 '자연적으로 변동'한다고 언급하는데, 이는 앞 내용과 정반대되는 설명이다.

▶ 문제 해결 방법은?

글에 However가 나오지만 빈칸은 이보다 앞에 나오므로, 답에 대한 근거 또한 However 뒤가 아닌 앞을 읽어 찾아야 한다. 즉 앞에서 일관되게 악음은 고정된 음 높이를 사용한다는 언급이 나오므로 빈칸 또한 '고정된' 음에 관한 언급을 포함해야 한다.

★★★ 1등급 대비 고난도 3점 문제

10 황금률의 긍정적·부정적 버전　　정답률 26% | 정답 ④

다음 빈칸에 들어갈 말로 가장 적절한 것을 고르시오. [3점]

① do not lead the self to act on concerns for others
　자로 하여금 다른 사람들을 염려하여 행동하게 하지 않는다
② reveal inner contradiction between the two versions
　두 버전 사이의 내적 모순을 드러낸다
③ fail to serve as a guide when faced with a moral dilemma
　도덕적 딜레마에 직면했을 때 지침으로서의 역할을 하지 못한다
④ do not require abandoning self-concern altogether ✓
　자신에 대해 마음 쓰는 것을 완전히 그만두도록 요구하지는 않는다
⑤ hardly consider the benefits of social interactions
　사회적 상호 작용의 이점을 거의 고려하지 않는다

Not all Golden Rules are alike; / two kinds emerged over time.
모든 황금률이 다 같은 것은 아니다. / 시간이 지나면서 두 종류가 나타났다.

The negative version instructs restraint; / the positive encourages intervention.
부정적인 버전은 자제를 지시하고, / 긍정적인 버전은 개입을 장려한다.

One sets a baseline of at least not causing harm; / the other points toward aspirational or idealized beneficent behavior.
하나는 최소한 해를 끼치지 않는 기준선을 설정하고, / 다른 하나는 염원하거나 이상화된 선행을 베푸는 행위를 가리킨다.

While examples of these rules abound, / too many to list exhaustively, / let these versions suffice for our purpose here: / "What is hateful to you do not do to another" / and "Love another as yourself."
이러한 규칙의 예는 많고, / 너무 많아서 남김없이 열거할 수 없을 정도지만, / 여기서는 우리의 목적을 위해 이 버전들로 충분한 것으로 하자. / "자신이 싫은 것은 다른 사람에게 행하지 말라."와 / "다른 사람을 자신처럼 사랑하라."라는

Both versions insist on caring for others, / whether through acts of omission, such as not injuring, / or through acts of commission, / by actively intervening.
이 두 버전은 모두 다른 사람을 배려할 것을 주장한다. / 해치지 않는 것과 같은 부작위를 통해서든, / 아니면 작위를 통해서든, / 적극적 개입에 의한

Yet while these Golden Rules encourage an agent to care for an other, / they do not require abandoning self-concern altogether.
그러나 이러한 황금률은 행위자에게 타자를 배려하도록 권장하는 반면, / 자신에 대해 마음 쓰는 것을 완전히 그만두도록 요구하지는 않는다.

The purposeful displacement of concern away from the ego / nonetheless remains partly self-referential.
의도적으로 관심을 자아로부터 멀어지도록 옮긴다 해도 / 부분적으로는 자신을 가리키는 상태로 남아 있다.

Both the negative and the positive versions / invoke the ego as the fundamental measure / against which behaviors are to be evaluated.
부정적인 버전과 긍정적인 버전은 둘 다 / 본질적인 척도로서 자아를 언급한다. / 행동 평가의 기준이 되는

모든 황금률이 다 같은 것은 아니다. 시간이 지나면서 두 종류가 나타났다. 부정적인 버전은 자제를 지시하고, 긍정적인 버전은 개입을 장려한다. 하나는 최소한 해를 끼치지 않는 기준선을 설정하고, 다른 하나는 염원하거나 이상화된 선행을 베푸는 행위를 가리킨다. 이러한 규칙의 예는 많고, 너무 많아서 남김없이 열거할 수 없을 정도지만, 여기서는 우리의 목적을 위해 "자신이 싫은 것은 다른 사람에게 행하지 말라."와 "다른 사람을 자신처럼 사랑하라."라는 이 버전들로 충분한 것으로 하자. 해치지 않는 것과 같은 부작위를 통해서든, 아니면 적극적 개입에 의한 작위를 통해서든, 이 두 버전은 모두 다른 사람을 배려할 것을 주장한다. 그러나 이러한 황금률은 행위자에게 타자를 배려하도록 권장하는 반면, 자신에 대해 마음 쓰는 것을 완전히 그만두도록 요구하지는 않는다. 의도적으로 관심을 자아로부터 멀어지도록 옮긴다 해도 부분적으로는 자신을 가리키는 상태로 남아 있다. 부정적인 버전과 긍정적인 버전은 둘 다 행동 평가의 기준이 되는 본질적인 척도로서 자아를 언급한다.

Why? 왜 정답일까?

빈칸 뒤의 두 문장에서 다른 사람을 배려하는 것과 관련된 황금률의 긍정적 버전과 부정적 버전 모두 부분적으로는 자아를 향하며 행동 평가의 본질적인 척도로서 자아를 기준 삼고 있다고 하므로(The purposeful displacement of concern away from the ego nonetheless remains partly self-referential. Both the negative and the positive versions invoke the ego as the fundamental measure against which behaviors are to be evaluated.), 빈칸에 들어갈 말로 가장 적절한 것은 마찬가지로 자아에 대한 고려를 언급하고 있는 ④ '자신에 대해 마음 쓰는 것을 완전히 그만두도록 요구하지는 않는다'이다.

- golden rule 황금률
- intervention ⓝ 개입
- idealized ⓐ 이상화된
- abound ⓥ 아주 많다
- omission ⓝ 부작위
- displacement 옮김, 이동
- invoke ⓥ 언급하다, (근거, 이유 등을) 들다
- evaluate ⓥ 평가하다
- restraint ⓝ 자제, 제한
- aspirational ⓐ 염원하는
- beneficent ⓐ 유익한, 선을 베푸는
- exhaustively ⓐⓓ 남김없이, 철저하게
- commission ⓝ 작위
- self-referential 자기 지시적인
- fundamental ⓐ 기본적인
- act on ~에 따라 행동하다

구문 풀이

5행 「too ~ to … : 너무 ~해서 …할 수 없다」
While examples of these rules abound, too many to list exhaustively, let these versions suffice for our purpose here: / "What is hateful to you do not do to another" and "Love another as yourself."

★★ 문제 해결 꿀~팁 ★★

▶ 많이 틀린 이유는?
타인을 배려할 것을 권하는 황금률이라고 할지라도 결국에는 자아에 대한 고려를 완전히 배제하지는 않는다는 추상적인 내용을 다룬 글이다. ①의 경우 황금률이 자아로 하여금 남을 배려하게 하지 않는다는 뜻으로서 주제와 상반된다. ②는 황금률의 두 가지 버전, 즉 부정적 버전(~을 하지 말라)과 긍정적 버전(~을 하라) 간에 내적 모순이 있다는 뜻을 나타내는데, 두 버전 간의 모순에 관해서는 글에서 다루지 않았다.

▶ 문제 해결 방법은?
빈칸 뒤의 두 문장에서 가장 중요한 단어는 self-referential과 the ego이므로, 마찬가지로 자아에 대한 고려를 긍정하는 선택지를 답으로 찾는다.

★★★ 1등급 대비 고난도 3점 문제

11 저개발 지역의 소작농들이 당면한 위기 　정답률 44% | 정답 ①

다음 빈칸에 들어갈 말로 가장 적절한 것을 고르시오. [3점]

✔ have lost control over their own production
　자신들의 생산에 대한 통제력을 잃게 되었다
② have turned to technology for food production
　식량 생산을 위해 기술에 의존하게 되었다
③ have challenged the capitalist mode of production
　자본주의적 생산 방식에 맞섰다
④ have reduced their involvement in growing cash crops
　환금 작물 재배로의 참여를 줄였다
⑤ have regained their competitiveness in the world market
　세계 시장에서 경쟁력을 되찾았다

In the less developed world, / the percentage of the population involved in agriculture / is declining, / but at the same time, those remaining in agriculture / are not benefiting from technological advances.
저개발 세계에서, / 농업에 종사하는 인구 비율은 / 감소하고 있지만, / 동시에 계속 농업에 종사하는 사람들은 / 기술 발전의 혜택을 입지 못하게 되었다.

The typical scenario in the less developed world / is one in which a very few commercial agriculturalists are technologically advanced / while the vast majority are incapable of competing.
저개발 세계의 전형적인 시나리오는 / 아주 소수의 상업적 농업 경영인들이 기술적으로 발전해 있는 것이다. / 대다수는 이와 경쟁할 수 없는 반면에

Indeed, this vast majority have lost control over their own production / because of larger global causes.
사실, 이 대다수는 자신들의 생산에 대한 통제력을 잃게 되었다. / 더 큰 세계적인 원인으로 인해

As an example, in Kenya, / farmers are actively encouraged to grow export crops / such as tea and coffee / at the expense of basic food production.
한 가지 예로 케냐에서, / 농부들은 수출 작물을 재배하도록 적극 독려된다. / 차와 커피 같은 / 기초식품 생산을 희생해가며

The result is / that a staple crop, such as maize, / is not being produced in a sufficient amount.
그 결과는 / 옥수수와 같은 주요 작물은 / 충분한 양으로 생산되지 못하고 있다는 것이다.

The essential argument here is / that the capitalist mode of production is affecting peasant production / in the less developed world / in such a way as to limit the production of staple foods, / thus causing a food problem.
여기서 본질적인 논점은 / 자본주의적 생산 방식이 소작농의 생산에 영향을 끼쳐 / 저개발 세계의 / 주요 식품의 생산을 제한하는 식으로 / 식량 문제를 일으키고 있다는 것이다.

저개발 세계에서, 농업에 종사하는 인구 비율은 감소하고 있지만, 동시에 계속 농업에 종사하는 사람들은 기술 발전의 혜택을 입지 못하고 있다. 저개발 세계의 전형적인 시나리오는 아주 소수의 상업적 농업 경영인들이 기술적으로 발전해 있는 반면에 대다수는 이와 경쟁할 수 없다는 것이다. 사실, 이 대다수는 더 큰 세계적인 원인으로 인해 자신들의 생산에 대한 통제력을 잃게 되었다. 한 가지 예로 케냐에서, 농부들은 기초식품 생산을 희생해가며 차와 커피 같은 수출 작물을 재배하도록 적극 독려된다. 결과적으로 옥수수와 같은 주요 작물은 충분한 양으로 생산되지 못하고 있다. 여기서 본질적인 논점은 자본주의적 생산 방식이 주요 식품의 생산을 제한하는 식으로 저개발 세계 소작농의 생산에 영향을 끼쳐 식량 문제를 일으키고 있다는 것이다.

Why? 왜 정답일까?
저개발 지역의 소작농들이 상업적 농업인과의 기술 격차뿐 아니라 자본주의적 생산 방식의 여파로 인하여 작물 재배에 대한 통제권을 잃고 식량 위기를 겪고 있다는 내용을 다룬 글이다. 빈칸 뒤의 두 문장에서 케냐의 예를 통해 농부들이 나라에 돈을 벌어다줄 수출 작물을 재배하도록 권장 받으면서 막상 주요 작물을 충분히 재배하지 못하게 되었다는 내용을 설명하는데, 마지막 문장인 '~ the capitalist mode of production is affecting peasant production in the less developed world in such a way as to limit the production of staple foods ~'에서는 예시의 내용을 '자본주의적 생산 방식이 주요 식품의 생산을 제한한다'라는 말로 정리하였다. 이는 결국 자본을 위한 생산을 중시하면서 소작농들이 작물 재배에 대한 결정권 및 통제력을 잃어버렸다는 말로 바꿀 수 있으므로, 빈칸에 들어갈 말로 가장 적절한 것은 ① '자신들의 생산에 대한 통제력을 잃게 되었다'이다.

- decline ⓥ 감소하다, 줄다
- typical ⓐ 전형적인
- encourage ⓥ 권장하다, 독려하다
- sufficient ⓐ 충분한
- peasant ⓝ 소작농, 소농
- benefit from ~로부터 이익을 보다
- commercial ⓐ 상업적인
- staple crop 주요 작물, 곡물
- affect ⓥ ~에 영향을 미치다

구문 풀이

4행 The typical scenario in the less developed world is one
부정대명사(a scenario)
[in which a very few commercial agriculturalists are technologically
전치사+관계대명사
advanced / while the vast majority are incapable of competing].
~하는 반면에　~할 수 없다　동명사

★★ 문제 해결 꿀~팁 ★★

▶ 많이 틀린 이유는?
자본주의적 생산 방식에 의하여 저개발 지역 소농들이 식량 대신 환금 작물을 생산하고 이에 따른 식량 위기 상황에 직면했다는 내용을 담은 글이다. 빈칸의 앞보다는 뒤에 주목할 때 '재배에 대한 주체적 통제권을 뺏기고' (선진국의) 수요를 맞추기 위한 작물을 주로 재배하게 되었다는 의미로서 ①을 답으로 고를 수 있다. 최다 오답은 ③이었는데 이는 자본주의적 생산 방식에 '저항한다'는 뜻이므로 정답 또는 주제와 반대되는 내용을 나타낸다.

▶ 문제 해결 방법은?
이 글은 어떤 주장이나 개념을 제시한다기보다는 흐름에 따라 어떤 일이 일어난 이유와 결과를 전개하고 있다. 따라서 답의 근거로 삼을 특정 부분에만 집중하여 읽기보다는 전체적인 맥락을 살피며 내용의 맥을 잡아야 풀이를 정확하게 할 수 있다.

★★★ 1등급 대비 고난도 3점 문제

12 인간 고유의 재구성 능력 　정답률 36% | 정답 ②

다음 빈칸에 들어갈 말로 가장 적절한 것을 고르시오. [3점]

① mirror accurate images of the world outside
　외부 세계의 정확한 이미지를 반영하는
✔ manipulate and transform these models
　이 모델을 조작하고 변형시키는
③ visualize the present reality as it is
　현재의 현실을 있는 그대로 시각화하는
④ bring the models back from memory
　기억에서 모델을 꺼내오는
⑤ identify and reproduce past experiences faithfully
　과거 경험을 확인하고 충실하게 복제해 내는

To make plans for the future, / the brain must have an ability / to take certain elements of prior experiences / and reconfigure them / in a way that does not copy any actual past experience or present reality exactly.
미래 계획을 세우기 위해, / 뇌는 능력이 필요하다. / 사전 경험의 특정한 요소를 취해서 / 그 경험을 재구성하는 / 그 어떤 실제적인 과거 경험이나 현재 현실을 그대로 베끼지 않는 방식으로

To accomplish that, / the organism must go beyond the mere ability / to form internal representations, the models of the world outside.
이를 성취하기 위해서는, / 유기체는 단순한 능력을 뛰어넘어야 한다. / 내적 표상, 즉 외부 세계의 모델을 구성하는

It must acquire the ability / to manipulate and transform these models.
뇌는 능력을 습득해야 한다. / 이 모델을 조작하고 변형시키는

We can argue / that tool-making, / one of the fundamental distinguishing features of primate cognition, / depends on this ability, / since a tool does not exist in a ready-made form in the natural environment / and has to be imagined in order to be made.
주장할 수 있는데, / 도구 제작이 / 영장류의 인지력에 있어 기본적인 고유 특징 중 하나인 / 이 능력에 달려 있다고 / 어떤 도구는 자연 환경에 미리 제작된 상태로 존재하지 않으며, / 만들어지기 위해서 상상되어야 하기 때문이다.

The neural machinery / for creating and holding 'images of the future' / was a necessary prerequisite / for tool-making, / and thus for launching human civilization.
신경 기제는 / '미래의 이미지'를 만들어내고 보존하는 / 필수적인 선행 조건이었다. / 도구 제작을 위해, 그리하여 인간 문명이 시작되기 위한

미래 계획을 세우기 위해, 뇌는 사전 경험의 특정한 요소를 취해서 그 어떤 실제적인 과거 경험이나 현재 현실을 그대로 베끼지 않는 방식으로 그 경험을 재구성하는 능력이 필요하다. 이를 성취하기 위해서는, 유기체는 내적 표상, 즉 외부 세계의 모델을 구성하는 단순한 능력을 뛰어넘어야 한다. 뇌는 이 모델을 조작하고 변형시키는 능력을 습득해야 한다. 영장류의 인지력에 있어 기본적인 고유 특징 중 하나인 도구 제작이 이 능력에 달려 있다고 주장할 수 있는데, 어떤 도구는 자연 환경에 미리 제작된 상태로 존재하지 않으며, 만들어지기 위해서 상상되어야 하기 때문이다. '미래의 이미지'를 만들어내고 보존하는 신경 기제는 도구 제작을 위해, 그리하여 인간 문명이 시작되기 위한 필수적인 선행 조건이었다.

Why? 왜 정답일까?

첫 문장인 'To make plans for the future, the brain must have an ability to take certain elements of prior experiences and reconfigure them in a way that does not copy any actual past experience or present reality exactly.'에서 인간의 뇌는 미래의 계획을 세우기 위해 과거나 현재의 실체를 그대로 베껴내지 않고 '재구성하는' 능력이 필요하다고 말하므로, 빈칸에 들어갈 말로 가장 적절한 것은 ② '이 모델을 조작하고 변형시키는'이다.

- **prior** ⓐ 사전의, 이전의
- **accomplish** ⓥ 성취하다, 얻다
- **primate** ⓐ 영장류의 ⓝ 영장류
- **ready-made** 미리 만들어진, 기성품의
- **civilization** ⓝ 문명
- **reconfigure** ⓥ 재구성하다, 변경하다
- **representation** ⓝ 표상, 나타낸 것
- **cognition** ⓝ 인지(력)
- **prerequisite** ⓝ 선행 조건, 전제 조건

구문 풀이

1행 To make plans for the future, the brain must have an
(부사적 용법(~하기 위해, ~하려면))
ability [to take certain elements of prior experiences and reconfigure
(형용사적 용법1) (to 생략) (형용사적 용법2)
them in a way {that does not copy any actual past experience or
(~한 방식으로) (주격 관·대) (a way에 수 일치(단수))
present reality exactly}].

★★ 문제 해결 꿀~팁 ★★

▶ 많이 틀린 이유는?
추상적인 지문이지만 주제가 무엇인지만을 정확히 파악한다면 비교적 쉽게 풀리는 문제이다. 첫 번째 문장에서 '경험을 재구성'하는 능력이 중요하다고 강조하였으므로, 'reconfingure'를 'manipulate and transform'으로 바꾼 ②를 고르는 것이 적절하다. ①, ③의 경우 현실을 '있는 그대로' 본뜨거나 시각화한다는 내용을 담고 있는데 이는 '재구성'이라는 말과 반대되는 표현이다.

▶ 문제 해결 방법은?
흔히 빈칸은 주제 부분에 나오는 것이 가장 정석적인데 이와 함께 선택지에는 주제를 아예 반대로 뒤집은 내용이 나온다. 이 문제에서도 '주제' 부분에 빈칸이 있고 매력적인 오답인 ①, ③이 주제와 정확히 반대되는 내용을 말하여 풀이에 혼동을 유발한다. 항상 내용의 주된 줄기를 잡고 주제문에 포함된 핵심 어휘나 표현이 선택지에서 어떻게 바뀌어 등장하는가에 집중하여 문제를 해결하는 습관을 들이도록 한다.

---

01 ①	02 ④	03 ②	04 ⑤	05 ①
06 ②	07 ⑤	08 ②	09 ③	10 ①
11 ④	12 ④			

01 인식의 이탈을 허용하는 유머 | 정답률 58% | 정답 ①

다음 빈칸에 들어갈 말로 가장 적절한 것을 고르시오.

✓ ① accurate - 정확한
② detailed - 상세한
③ useful - 유용한
④ additional - 부가적인
⑤ alternative - 대안적인

Humour involves / not just practical disengagement / but cognitive disengagement.
유머는 포함한다. / 실제적인 이탈뿐만 아니라 / 인식의 이탈을

As long as something is funny, / we are for the moment not concerned / with whether it is real or fictional, true or false.
어떤 것이 재미있다면, / 우리는 잠깐 관심을 두지 않는다. / 그것이 진짜인지 허구인지, 진실인지 거짓인지에 관해

This is why we give considerable leeway / to people telling funny stories.
이것이 우리가 상당한 여지를 주는 이유이다. / 재미있는 이야기를 하는 사람들에게

If they are getting extra laughs / by exaggerating the silliness of a situation / or even by making up a few details, / we are happy to grant them comic licence, a kind of poetic licence.
만약 그들이 추가 웃음을 얻고 있다면, / 상황의 어리석음을 과장하거나 / 심지어 몇 가지 세부 사항을 꾸며서라도 / 우리는 그들에게 기꺼이 희극적 파격, 일종의 시적 파격을 허락한다.

Indeed, / someone listening to a funny story / who tries to correct the teller / — 'No, he didn't spill the spaghetti on the keyboard and the monitor, / just on the keyboard' — / will probably be told by the other listeners / to stop interrupting.
실제로, / 재미있는 이야기를 듣고 있는 누군가가 / 말하는 사람을 바로잡으려고 하면 / '아니야, 그는 스파게티를 키보드와 모니터에 쏟은 것이 아니라 / 키보드에만 쏟았어.'라며 / 그는 아마 듣고 있는 다른 사람들에게서 말을 들을 것이다. / 방해하지 말라는

The creator of humour is putting ideas into people's heads / for the pleasure those ideas will bring, / not to provide accurate information.
유머를 만드는 사람은 사람들의 머릿속에 생각을 집어넣고 있는데, / 그 생각이 가져올 재미를 위해서이지 / 정확한 정보를 제공하기 위해서가 아니다.

유머는 실제적인 이탈뿐만 아니라 인식의 이탈을 포함한다. 어떤 것이 재미있다면, 우리는 잠깐 그것이 진짜인지 허구인지, 진실인지 거짓인지에 관해 관심을 두지 않는다. 이것이 우리가 재미있는 이야기를 하는 사람들에게 상당한 여지를 주는 이유이다. 만약 그들이 상황의 어리석음을 과장하거나 심지어 몇 가지 세부 사항을 꾸며서라도 추가 웃음을 얻고 있다면, 우리는 그들에게 기꺼이 희극적 파격, 일종의 시적 파격을 허락한다. 실제로, 재미있는 이야기를 듣고 있는 누군가가 '아니야, 그는 스파게티를 키보드와 모니터에 쏟은 것이 아니라 키보드에만 쏟았어.'라며 말하는 사람을 바로잡으려고 하면 그는 아마 듣고 있는 다른 사람들에게서 방해하지 말라는 말을 들을 것이다. 유머를 만드는 사람은 사람들의 머릿속에 생각을 집어넣고 있는데, 그 생각이 가져올 재미를 위해서이지 정확한 정보를 제공하기 위해서가 아니다.

Why? 왜 정답일까?

첫 두 문장에서 유머는 인식의 이탈을 허용하므로 우리가 어떤 대상을 재미있다고 느낀다면 그 대상이 진실인지 거짓인지는 잠시나마 관심에서 벗어난다고 언급한다. 이어서 예시를 드는 'Indeed, someone listening to a funny story ~'에 따르면 재미있는 이야기를 듣던 중 사실과 다른 부분을 바로잡으려는 사람은 다른 사람들로부터 방해하지 말라는 말을 들을 가능성이 크다고 한다. 이를 근거로 보아, 유머에서 중요한 부분은 '사실적인' 정보 전달이 아니라는 것을 유추할 수 있으므로, 빈칸에 들어갈 말로 가장 적절한 것은 ① '정확한'이다.

- **disengagement** ⓝ 이탈, 해방
- **fictional** ⓐ 허구의
- **exaggerate** ⓥ 과장하다
- **make up** 만들어내다, 꾸며내다
- **licence** ⓝ (창작상의) 파격, 허용
- **spill** ⓥ 쏟다, 흘리다
- **accurate** ⓐ 정확한
- **be concerned with** ~에 관심을 두다
- **considerable** ⓐ 상당한
- **silliness** ⓝ 어리석음, 우둔한 짓
- **grant** ⓥ 주다, 부여하다
- **poetic** ⓐ 시적인
- **interrupt** ⓥ 방해하다, 끼어들다
- **alternative** ⓐ 대안의

구문 풀이

2행 As long as something is funny, we are (for the moment)
접속사(~하는 한)　　　　　동사2 ( ): 삽입구
not concerned with whether it is real or fictional, true or false.
~에 관심을 갖지 않는　접속사(A이든 B이든)

구문 풀이

4행 That is, to the extent that two people share similar verbal
~할 정도까지
and nonverbal habits in a first meeting, they will be more comfortable
with one another.

02　비슷한 사람들끼리 더 쉽게 시작되는 관계　　정답률 56% | 정답 ④

다음 빈칸에 들어갈 말로 가장 적절한 것을 고르시오.

① information deficit – 정보 부족
② cultural adaptability – 문화적 적응력
③ meaning negotiation – 의미 협상
✔ behavioral coordination – 행동의 조화
⑤ unconditional acceptance – 무조건적 수용

Although a balance or harmony between partners / clearly develops over time in a relationship, / it is also a factor / in initial attraction and interest in a partner.
비록 파트너 사이의 균형이나 조화는 / 관계에서 시간이 지남에 따라 분명히 발전하지만 / 이것은 요인이기도 하다. / 파트너에 대한 초기 매력과 관심에 있어

That is, / to the extent / that two people share similar verbal and nonverbal habits in a first meeting, / they will be more comfortable with one another.
즉, / 정도만큼 / 두 사람이 첫 만남에서 비슷한 언어적 및 비언어적 습관을 공유하는 / 그들은 서로 더 편안할 것이다.

For example, / fast-paced individuals talk and move quickly / and are more expressive, / whereas slow-paced individuals have a different tempo / and are less expressive.
예를 들어, / 속도가 빠른 사람들은 빠르게 말을 하고 움직이며 / 더 표현하는 반면, / 속도가 느린 사람들은 속도가 다르며 / 덜 표현한다.

Initial interactions / between people at opposite ends of such a continuum / may be more difficult / than those between similar types.
초기 상호 작용은 / 이러한 연속체의 반대쪽 끝에 있는 사람들 간의 / 더 어려울 수 있다. / 유사한 유형들 간의 상호 작용보다

In the case of contrasting styles, / individuals may be less interested in pursuing a relationship / than if they were similar in interaction styles.
대비되는 유형인 경우, / 사람들은 관계 추구에 관심을 덜 보일 수 있다. / 그들이 상호 작용 유형 면에서 비슷한 경우보다

Individuals with similar styles, / however, / are more comfortable / and find that they just seem to "click" with one another.
비슷한 유형의 사람들은 / 그러나 / 더 편안하고, / 그야말로 서로 '즉시 마음이 통하는' 것 같다고 느낀다.

Thus, / behavioral coordination may provide a selection filter / for the initiation of a relationship.
따라서 / 행동의 조화는 선택 필터를 제공할 수 있다. / 관계의 시작을 위한

파트너 사이의 균형이나 조화는 관계에서 시간이 지남에 따라 분명히 발전하지만, 이것은 파트너에 대한 초기 매력과 관심의 요인이기도 하다. 즉, 두 사람은 첫 만남에서 비슷한 언어적 및 비언어적 습관을 공유하는 정도만큼 서로 더 편안할 것이다. 예를 들어, 속도가 빠른 사람들은 빠르게 말을 하고 움직이며 더 표현하는 반면, 속도가 느린 사람들은 속도가 다르며 덜 표현한다. 이러한 연속체의 반대쪽 끝에 있는 사람들 간의 초기 상호 작용은 유사한 유형보다 더 어려울 수 있다. 대비되는 유형인 경우 사람들은 상호 작용 유형이 비슷한 경우보다 관계 추구에 관심을 덜 보일 수 있다. 그러나 비슷한 유형의 사람들은 더 편안하고, 그야말로 서로 '즉시 마음이 통하는' 것 같다고 느낀다. 따라서 행동의 조화는 관계의 시작을 위한 선택 필터를 제공할 수 있다.

Why? 왜 정답일까?

첫 문장에서 사람들은 비슷하면 처음에 서로 매력을 느끼기 쉽다고 이야기한다(Although a balance or harmony between partners clearly develops over time in a relationship, it is also a factor in initial attraction and interest in a partner.). 따라서 빈칸에 들어갈 말로 가장 적절한 것은 a balance or harmony와 같은 의미인 ④ '행동의 조화(behavioral coordination)'이다.

- **clearly** ⓐ 명백하게
- **verbal** ⓐ 언어적인
- **one another** 서로
- **expressive** ⓐ 표현적인, 잘 표현하는
- **continuum** ⓝ 연속체
- **click** ⓥ 잘 통하다, 맞다
- **deficit** ⓝ 부족, 적자
- **negotiation** ⓝ 협상, 타협
- **unconditional** ⓐ 무조건적인
- **attraction** ⓝ 끌림, 매력
- **nonverbal** ⓐ 비언어적인
- **fast-paced** ⓐ 속도가 빠른
- **opposite** ⓐ 정반대의
- **contrasting** ⓐ 대비되는
- **initiation** ⓝ 시작
- **adaptability** ⓝ 적응력
- **coordination** ⓝ 조화

03　키워드 중심의 태그 시스템이 갖는 한계　　정답률 47% | 정답 ②

다음 빈칸에 들어갈 말로 가장 적절한 것을 고르시오.

① a set of words that allow users to identify an individual object
　사용자가 각각의 사물을 식별할 수 있게 하는 일련의 단어
✔ a comprehensive description of what is happening in an image
　이미지에서 일어나고 있는 일에 대한 포괄적인 설명
③ a reliable resource for categorizing information by pictures
　사진으로 정보를 분류할 수 있는 믿을 만한 자원
④ a primary means of organizing a sequential order of words
　단어의 순차적 순서를 구성하는 주요 수단
⑤ a useful filter for sorting similar but not identical images
　유사하지만 똑같지는 않은 이미지를 분류하는 데 유용한 필터

Many people create and share pictures and videos on the Internet.
많은 사람이 사진과 영상을 만들어 인터넷에 공유한다.

The difficulty is finding what you want.
어려운 점은 여러분이 원하는 것을 찾는 것이다.

Typically, / people want to search using words / (rather than, say, example sketches).
일반적으로 / 사람들은 단어를 사용하여 검색하기를 원한다. / (예시 스케치 같은 것이 아니라)

Because most pictures don't come with words attached, / it is natural / to try and build tagging systems / that tag images with relevant words.
대부분의 사진에는 단어가 첨부되어 있지 않기 때문에, / 당연하다. / 태그 시스템을 써보고 만들어가는 것은 / 이미지에 관련 단어를 태그하는

The underlying machinery is straightforward / — we apply image classification and object detection methods / and tag the image with the output words.
기본적인 시스템은 간단하다 / 우리는 이미지 분류와 개체 감지 방법을 적용하고 / 출력된 단어로 이미지를 태그한다.

But tags aren't a comprehensive description / of what is happening in an image.
하지만 태그는 포괄적인 설명이 아니다. / 이미지에서 일어나고 있는 일에 대한

It matters who is doing what, / and tags don't capture this.
누가 무엇을 하고 있는지가 중요한데, / 태그는 이것을 포착하지 못한다.

For example, / tagging a picture of a cat in the street / with the object categories "cat", "street", "trash can" and "fish bones" / leaves out the information / that the cat is pulling the fish bones / out of an open trash can on the street.
예를 들어, / 거리에 있는 고양이의 사진을 태그하는 것은 / '고양이', '거리', '쓰레기통', '생선 뼈'라는 개체 범주로 / 정보를 빠뜨리게 된다. / 그 고양이가 생선 뼈를 빼내고 있다는 / 거리에 있는 열린 쓰레기통에서

많은 사람이 사진과 영상을 만들어 인터넷에 공유한다. 어려운 점은 여러분이 원하는 것을 찾는 것이다. 일반적으로 사람들은 (예시 스케치 같은 것이 아니라) 단어를 사용하여 검색하기를 원한다. 대부분의 사진에는 단어가 첨부되어 있지 않기 때문에, 이미지에 관련 단어를 태그하는 태그 시스템을 써보고 만들어가는 것은 당연하다. 기본적인 시스템은 간단한데, 이미지 분류와 개체 감지 방법을 적용하고 출력된 단어로 이미지를 태그한다. 하지만 태그는 이미지에서 일어나고 있는 일에 대한 포괄적인 설명이 아니다. 누가 무엇을 하고 있는지가 중요한데, 태그는 이것을 포착하지 못한다. 예를 들어, 거리에 있는 고양이의 사진을 '고양이', '거리', '쓰레기통', '생선 뼈'라는 개체 범주로 태그하는 것은 그 고양이가 거리에 있는 열린 쓰레기통에서 생선 뼈를 빼내고 있다는 정보를 빠뜨리게 된다.

Why? 왜 정답일까?

마지막 문장의 예시는 키워드 중심의 태그 시스템이 이미지 속의 상황을 묘사하지 못한다는 것을 보여준다. 즉 단어 중심으로 나열할 뿐, 어떤 행위가 일어나고 있는지 설명하지 못한다는(It matters who is doing what, and tags don't capture this.) 의미가 되도록 빈칸에 들어갈 말로 가장 적절한 것은 ② '이미지에서 일어나고 있는 일에 대한 포괄적인 설명'이다.

- **attached** ⓐ 부착된, 첨부된
- **relevant** ⓐ 관련 있는, 적절한
- **classification** ⓝ 분류
- **leave out** 빠뜨리다
- **identify** ⓥ 식별하다
- **sequential** ⓐ 순차적인
- **tag** ⓥ 태그를 달다, 꼬리표를 붙이다
- **straightforward** ⓐ 쉬운, 간단한
- **detection** ⓝ 감지
- **pull out of** ~에서 꺼내다
- **comprehensive** ⓐ 광범위한

DAY 07

구문 풀이

11행 For example, tagging a picture of a cat in the street with the
　　　　　　　　　동명사구 주어
object categories "cat", "street", "trash can" and "fish bones"
leaves out the information {that the cat is pulling the fish bones out
동사(단수)　　　목적어　　　　　{ }: 동격(= the information)
of an open trash can on the street}.

---

04 우리 자신의 무지 인식하기　　　정답률 60% | 정답 ⑤

다음 빈칸에 들어갈 말로 가장 적절한 것을 고르시오.

① find their role in teamwork – 팀워크에서 자기 역할을 찾도록
② learn from others' successes and failures – 다른 사람의 성공과 실패로부터 배우도록
③ make the most of technology for learning – 학습을 위해 기술을 최대한 활용하도록
④ obtain knowledge from wonderful experts – 멋진 전문가들로부터 지식을 얻도록
✔ discover the wonder of their ignorance – 자신의 무지함의 경이로움을 알게 되도록

The quest for knowledge in the material world / is a never-ending pursuit, / but the quest does not mean / that a thoroughly schooled person is an educated person / or that an educated person is a wise person.
물질적인 세계에서 지식 탐구는 / 끝없는 추구이지만, / 그 탐구는 의미하지는 않는다. / 온전하게 학교 교육을 받은 사람이 배운 사람이라거나 / 배운 사람이 현명한 사람이라는 것을

We are too often blinded / by our ignorance of our ignorance, / and our pursuit of knowledge is no guarantee of wisdom.
우리는 너무 자주 눈이 멀며, / 우리의 무지함에 대한 우리의 무지로 / 우리의 지식 추구가 현명함을 보장하는 것은 아니다.

Hence, / we are prone to / becoming the blind leading the blind / because our overemphasis on competition in nearly everything / makes looking good more important / than being good.
그래서 / 우리는 ~하기 쉽다. / 앞 못 보는 사람들을 이끄는 앞 못 보는 사람이 되기 / 왜냐하면 거의 모든 것에서 경쟁에 대한 우리의 과도한 강조는 / 훌륭해 보이는 것을 더 중요하게 만들기 때문에 / 훌륭한 것보다

The resultant fear / of being thought a fool and criticized / therefore is one of greatest enemies of true learning.
그 결과로 생기는 두려움은 / 바보라고 여겨져 비판받는 것에 대한 / 그렇기 때문에 진정한 배움의 가장 큰 적 중 하나이다.

Although our ignorance is undeniably vast, / it is from the vastness of this selfsame ignorance / that our sense of wonder grows.
우리의 무지함은 부인할 수 없을 정도로 크지만, / 다름 아닌 이 똑같은 무지함의 광대함으로부터이다. / 우리의 경이감이 자라는 것은

But, / when we do not know we are ignorant, / we do not know enough to even question, / let alone investigate, / our ignorance.
하지만, / 우리가 무지하다는 것을 우리가 모를 때, / 우리는 심지어 의문을 품을 만큼도 알지 못한다. / 조사하기는커녕 / 우리의 무지를

No one can teach another person anything.
그 누구도 타인에게 아무것도 가르쳐주지 못한다.

All one can do with and for someone else / is to facilitate learning / by helping the person to discover the wonder of their ignorance.
우리가 다른 누군가와 함께, 그리고 그 사람을 위해 해줄 수 있는 것이라고는 / 배움을 촉진하는 것뿐이다. / 그 사람이 자신의 무지함의 경이로움을 알게 되도록 도와서

물질적인 세계에서 지식 탐구는 끝없는 추구이지만, 그 탐구는 온전하게 학교 교육을 받은 사람이 배운 사람이라거나 배운 사람이 현명한 사람이라는 뜻은 아니다. 우리의 무지함에 대한 무지로 우리는 너무 자주 눈이 멀며, 우리의 지식 추구가 현명함을 보장하는 것은 아니다. 그래서 거의 모든 것에서 경쟁에 대한 우리의 과도한 강조는 훌륭해 보이는 것을 (실제) 훌륭한 것보다 더 중요하게 만들기 때문에, 우리는 앞 못 보는 사람들을 이끄는 (마찬가지로) 앞 못 보는 사람이 되기 쉽다. 그 결과로 생기는, 바보라고 여겨져 비판받는 것에 대한 두려움은 그렇기 때문에 진정한 배움의 가장 큰 적 중 하나이다. 우리의 무지함은 부인할 수 없을 정도로 크지만, 우리의 경이감이 자라는 것은 다름 아닌 이 똑같은 무지함의 광대함으로부터이다. 하지만, 우리가 무지하다는 것을 우리가 모를 때, 우리는 우리의 무지를 조사하기는커녕 심지어 의문을 품을 만큼도 알지 못한다. 그 누구도 타인에게 아무것도 가르쳐주지 못한다. 우리가 다른 누군가와 함께, 그리고 그 사람을 위해 해줄 수 있는 것이라고는 그 사람이 자신의 무지함의 경이로움을 알게 되도록 도와서 배움을 촉진하는 것뿐이다.

Why? 왜 정답일까?

글 중반부에서 진정한 배움의 적은 자신이 모르고 있다는 그 사실을 모르는 것이며, 우리는 놀랍도록 무지하지만 바로 이 무지로부터 경이로움이 이룩된다(~ it is from the vastness of this selfsame ignorance that our sense of wonder grows.)고 한다. 이는 무지에 대한 깨달음이 즉 진정한 배움으로 나아갈 수 있는 '경이로운' 출발

점이 된다는 의미이다. 이때 빈칸 앞의 두 문장에서는 다시 우리가 스스로의 무지를 모른다는 점을 언급한다. 우리는 우리 자신의 무지도 의심하고 조사할 만큼 제대로 알고 있지 못하며, 따라서 남을 '가르칠' 상황도 안 된다는 설명이 나온다. 이를 근거로 할 때, 우리가 타인이 진정한 배움으로 나가게 도와주기 위해 해줄 수 있는 일이라고는 그 사람이 '직접 자신의 무지를 깨닫게' 도와주는 것이라는 결론을 내릴 수 있다. 따라서 빈칸에 들어갈 말로 가장 적절한 것은 ⑤ '자신의 무지함의 경이로움을 알게 되도록(discover the wonder of their ignorance)'이다.

- **thoroughly** [ad] 철저히
- **prone to** ~하기 쉬운
- **resultant** [a] 그 결과로 생기는
- **vast** [a] 광대한, 큰
- **let alone** ~하기는커녕, ~은 말할 것도 없이
- **make the most of** ~을 최대한 활용하다
- **ignorance** [n] 무지
- **overemphasis** [n] 과도한 강조
- **undeniably** [ad] 부인할 수 없을 정도로
- **selfsame** [a] 똑같은
- **facilitate** [v] 촉진하다

구문 풀이

6행 Hence, we are prone to becoming the blind leading the blind
　　　　　　　　　　　~하기 쉽다　　동명사(전치사 to의 목적어)
because our overemphasis (on competition in nearly everything)
접속사　　　　주어
makes looking good more important than being good.
동사　　　목적어　　　　목적격 보어

---

05 경험에 따라 발달하는 뇌　　　정답률 48% | 정답 ①

다음 빈칸에 들어갈 말로 가장 적절한 것을 고르시오. [3점]

✔ sculpted by our own history of experiences
　우리 자신의 경험 이력에 의해 만들어진
② designed to maintain their initial structures
　그것의 최초의 구조를 유지하도록 설계된다
③ geared toward strengthening recent memories
　최근의 기억을 강화하도록 조정된다
④ twinned with the development of other organs
　다른 기관의 발달과 밀접하게 연결된다
⑤ portrayed as the seat of logical and creative thinking
　논리적이고 창의적인 사고가 일어나는 장소로 그려진다

Thanks to newly developed neuroimaging technology, / we now have access to the specific brain changes / that occur during learning.
새롭게 개발된 신경 촬영 기술 덕분에, / 우리는 이제 특정한 뇌 변화에 접근할 수 있게 되었다. / 학습 중에 일어나는

Even though all of our brains contain the same basic structures, / our neural networks are as unique as our fingerprints.
모든 뇌는 같은 기본 구조를 가지고 있음에도 불구하고, / 우리의 신경망은 우리의 지문만큼이나 독특하다.

The latest developmental neuroscience research has shown / that the brain is much more malleable throughout life / than previously assumed; / it develops in response to its own processes, / to its immediate and distant "environments," / and to its past and current situations.
가장 최신의 발달 신경 과학 연구는 보여 주는데, / 뇌가 평생 동안 훨씬 더 순응성이 있다는 것을 / 이전에 가정된 것보다도 / 뇌는 자기만의 처리 과정에 반응하여 발달한다. / 자신에게 인접한 '환경'과 멀리 떨어진 '환경'에, / 그리고 자신의 과거와 현재의 상황에

The brain seeks to create meaning / through establishing or refining existing neural networks.
뇌는 의미를 창조하려 한다. / 기존의 신경망을 확립하거나 개선하여

When we learn a new fact or skill, / our neurons communicate to form networks of connected information.
우리가 새로운 사실이나 기술을 배울 때, / 우리의 뉴런들은 연결된 정보망을 형성하기 위해 소통한다.

Using this knowledge or skill / results in structural changes / to allow similar future impulses / to travel more quickly and efficiently than others.
이러한 지식이나 기술을 사용하는 것은 / 구조적 변화를 가져온다. / 앞으로 유사한 자극이 ~하게 하는 / 다른 것들보다 더 빠르고 효율적으로 이동할 수 있게

High-activity synaptic connections are stabilized and strengthened, / while connections with relatively low use are weakened and eventually pruned.
고활동성 시냅스 연결이 안정화되고 강화된다. / 상대적으로 적게 사용되는 연결은 약해져서 결국에는 잘리는 반면

In this way, / our brains are sculpted by our own history of experiences.
이런 식으로, / 우리의 뇌는 우리 자신의 경험 이력에 의해 만들어진다.

새롭게 개발된 신경 촬영 기술 덕분에, 우리는 이제 학습 중에 일어나는 특정한 뇌 변화에 접근할 수 있게 되었다. 모든 뇌는 같은 기본 구조를 가지고 있음에도 불구하고, 우리의 신경망은 우리의 지문만큼이나 독특하다. 가장 최신의 발달 신경 과학 연구는 이전에 가정된 것보다도 뇌가 평생 동안 훨씬 더 순응성이 있다는 것을 보여 주는데, 뇌는 자기만의 처리 과정에, 자신에게 인접한 '환경'과 멀리 떨어진 '환경'에, 자신의 과거와 현재의 상황에 반응하여 발달한다. 뇌는 기존의 신경망을 확립하거나 개선하여 의미를 창조하려고 한다. 우리가 새로운 사실이나 기술을 배울 때, 우리의 뉴런들은 연결된 정보망을 형성하

기 위해 소통한다. 이러한 지식이나 기술을 사용하는 것은 앞으로 유사한 자극이 다른 것들보다 더 빠르고 효율적으로 이동할 수 있게 하는 구조적 변화를 가져온다. 고활동성 시냅스 연결이 안정화되고 강화되는 반면에, 상대적으로 적게 사용되는 연결은 약해져서 결국에는 잘린다. 이런 식으로, 우리의 뇌는 우리 자신의 경험 이력에 의해 만들어진다.

Why? 왜 정답일까?

세 번째 문장과 네 번째 문장에서 뇌는 특유의 처리 과정과 환경과 과거 및 현재 상황에 맞추어 발달하며, 기존의 신경망을 확립하거나 개선하는 방식으로 의미를 창조한다(The brain seeks to create meaning through establishing or refining existing neural networks)고 설명하고 있다. 이를 근거로 볼 때, 뇌가 지문만큼이나 고유해지는 이유는 결국 우리 각자의 경험이 반영되기 때문이라는 결론을 내릴 수 있다. 따라서 빈칸에 들어갈 말로 가장 적절한 것은 ① '우리 자신의 경험 이력에 의해 만들어진다'이다.

- **neural** ⓐ 신경의
- **previously** [ad] 이전에
- **establish** ⓥ 확립하다
- **existing** ⓐ 기존의
- **stabilize** ⓥ 안정화하다
- **geared A toward B** A를 B에 맞춰 조정하다
- **neuroscience** ⓝ 신경 과학
- **immediate** ⓐ 즉각적인, 당면한
- **refine** ⓥ 개선하다
- **impulse** ⓝ 자극
- **sculpt** ⓥ 조각하다, 형상을 만들다

구문 풀이

5행 The latest developmental neuroscience research `has shown`
주어1 동사1
that the brain is much more malleable throughout life than previously
접속사(~것) 비교급 강조(훨씬) 보어(비교급 형용사)
assumed; it develops in response to its own processes, (in response)
주어2 동사2 ~에 반응하여 생략
to its immediate and distant "environments," and (in response) to its
생략
past and current situations.

---

06 정보의 해석으로 구성되는 인간의 주관적 세계 | 정답률 46% | 정답 ②

다음 빈칸에 들어갈 말로 가장 적절한 것을 고르시오. [3점]

① the reality placed upon us through social conventions
사회적 관습을 통해 우리에게 자리 잡은 현실
✔② the one we know as a result of our own interpretations
우리 자신의 해석의 결과로 알고 있는 세계
③ the world of images not filtered by our perceptual frame
우리의 인지적 틀을 통해 걸러지지 않은 이미지의 세계
④ the external world independent of our own interpretations
우리 자신의 해석과는 별개인 외부 세계
⑤ the physical universe our own interpretations fail to explain
우리 자신의 해석이 설명하지 못하는 물리적 우주

Modern psychological theory states / that the process of understanding is a matter of construction, not reproduction, / which means that the process of understanding takes the form of the interpretation of data / coming from the outside and generated by our mind.
현대의 심리학 이론에서 말하는데, / 이해의 과정은 재생이 아니라 구성의 문제라고 / 그것은 이해의 과정이 정보를 해석하는 형태를 취한다는 말이다. / 외부로부터 들어오고 우리 마음에서 생성되는

For example, / the perception of a moving object as a car / is based on an interpretation of incoming data / within the framework of our knowledge of the world.
예를 들어, / 움직이는 물체를 차라고 인식하는 것은 / 들어오는 정보를 해석하는 데 근거한다. / 세상에 대한 우리의 지식이라는 틀 안에서

While the interpretation of simple objects is usually an uncontrolled process, / the interpretation of more complex phenomena, / such as interpersonal situations, / usually requires active attention and thought.
간단한 물체의 해석은 대개 통제되지 않는 과정이지만, / 더 복잡한 현상에 대한 해석은 / 대인 관계 상황 같은 / 대개 적극적인 주의 집중과 사고를 필요로 한다.

Psychological studies indicate / that it is knowledge possessed by the individual / that determines / which stimuli become the focus of that individual's attention, / what significance he or she assigns to these stimuli, / and how they are combined into a larger whole.
심리학 연구에서는 보여준다. / 바로 그 개인이 소유하고 있는 지식이라는 점을 / 결정하는 것은 / 어떤 자극이 개인의 주의에 초점이 되는지, / 그 사람이 이 자극에 어떤 의미를 부여하는지, / 그리고 그 자극들이 어떻게 결합되어 더 커다란 전체를 이루는지를

This subjective world, / interpreted in a particular way, / is for us the "objective" world; / we cannot know any world / other than the one / we know as a result of our own interpretations.
이 주관적 세계는 / 특정한 방식으로 해석되는 / 우리에게 있어 '객관적인' 세계인데, / 우리는 그 어떤 세계도 알 수 없다. / 세계 외에는 / 우리 자신의 해석의 결과로 알고 있는

현대의 심리학 이론에서 이해의 과정은 재생이 아니라 구성의 문제라고 말하는데, 그것은 이해의 과정이 외부로부터 들어오고 우리 마음에서 생성되는 정보를 해석하는 형태를 취한다는 말이다. 예를 들어 움직이는 물체를 차라고 인식하는 것은 세상에 대한 우리의 지식이라는 틀 안에서, 들어오는 정보를 해석하는 데 근거한다. 간단한 물체의 해석은 대개 통제되지 않는 과정이지만, 대인 관계 상황 같은 더 복잡한 현상에 대한 해석은 대개 적극적인 주의 집중과 사고를 필요로 한다. 심리학 연구에서는 어떤 자극이 개인의 주의에 초점이 되는지, 그 사람이 이 자극에 어떤 의미를 부여하는지, 그리고 그 자극들이 어떻게 결합되어 더 커다란 전체를 이루는지를 결정하는 것은 바로 그 개인이 소유하고 있는 지식이라는 점을 보여준다. 특정한 방식으로 해석되는 이 주관적 세계는 우리에게 있어 '객관적인' 세계인데, 우리는 우리 자신의 해석의 결과로 알고 있는 세계 외에는 그 어떤 세계도 알 수 없다.

Why? 왜 정답일까?

'~ the process of understanding is a matter of construction, not reproduction, which means that the process of understanding takes the form of the interpretation of data coming from the outside and generated by our mind.'에서 현대 심리학에 따르면 인간은 외부의 정보를 그대로 재생하기보다 마음속에서 해석하여 구성한다고 하는데, 이는 인간이 인지하는 세계가 '주관적'일 수밖에 없다는 의미를 나타낸다. 따라서 빈칸에 들어갈 말로 가장 적절한 것은 ② '우리 자신의 해석의 결과로 알고 있는 세계'이다.

- **construction** ⓝ 구성, 이해
- **generate** ⓥ 생성하다, 만들어내다
- **uncontrolled** ⓐ 통제되지 않는
- **assign** ⓥ 부여하다, 할당하다
- **independent of** ~와는 별개인, 독립적인
- **interpretation** ⓝ 해석, 이해, 설명
- **perception** ⓝ 인식, 인지
- **phenomenon** ⓝ 현상
- **subjective** ⓐ 주관적인

구문 풀이

1행 Modern psychological theory states {that the process of understanding is a matter of construction, not reproduction}, which
{ }: 명사절(선행사) 계속적 용법
means that the process of understanding takes the form of the
~의 형태를 취하다
interpretation of data [coming from the outside and generated by
분사구1 분사구2
our mind].

★★★ 1등급 대비 고난도 2점 문제

07 컴퓨터 아티스트의 소멸 | 정답률 31% | 정답 ⑤

다음 빈칸에 들어갈 말로 가장 적절한 것을 고르시오.

① awake – 깨어 있는
② influential – 영향력 있는
③ distinct – 뚜렷이 다른
④ troublesome – 골칫거리인
✔⑤ extinct – 소멸한

Young contemporary artists / who employ digital technologies in their practice / rarely make reference to computers.
젊은 현대 미술가들은 / 작업에 디지털 기술을 이용하는 / 컴퓨터를 거의 언급하지 않는다.

For example, / Wade Guyton, / an abstractionist who uses a word processing program and inkjet printers, / does not call himself a computer artist.
예를 들어, / Wade Guyton은 / 워드 프로세싱 프로그램과 잉크젯식 프린터를 사용하는 추상파 화가인 / 자신을 컴퓨터 아티스트라고 부르지 않는다.

Moreover, / some critics, / who admire his work, / are little concerned about his extensive use of computers / in the art-making process.
게다가, / 몇몇 비평가들은 / 그의 작품을 높이 평가하는 / 그의 광범위한 컴퓨터 사용에 관해 거의 신경 쓰지 않는다. / 예술 창작 과정에서

This is a marked contrast from three decades ago / when artists who utilized computers were labeled by critics / — often disapprovingly — / as computer artists.
이것은 30년 전과 뚜렷이 대조된다. / 컴퓨터를 활용하는 미술가들이 비평가들에 의해 명명되었던 / 흔히 못마땅하게 / 컴퓨터 아티스트라고

For the present generation of artists, / the computer, or more appropriately, the laptop, / is one in a collection of integrated, portable digital technologies / that link their social and working life.
현 세대의 미술가들에게 / 컴퓨터, 혹은 더욱 적절히는 휴대용 컴퓨터는 / 일련의 통합되고 휴대 가능한 디지털 기술 중 하나이다. / 그들의 사회 생활과 직업 생활을 연결하는

With tablets and cell phones surpassing personal computers in Internet usage, / and as slim digital devices resemble nothing / like the room-sized mainframes and bulky desktop computers of previous decades, / it now appears / that the computer artist is finally extinct.

DAY 07

인터넷 사용에서 태블릿 컴퓨터와 휴대 전화가 개인용 컴퓨터를 능가하는 상황에서, / 얇은 디지털 기기들이 전혀 닮지 않았으므로, / 수십 년 전의 방 크기의 중앙 컴퓨터와 부피가 큰 탁상용 컴퓨터와 / 오늘날에는 ~한 것으로 보인다. / 컴퓨터 아티스트가 결국 소멸한

작업에 디지털 기술을 이용하는 젊은 현대 미술가들은 컴퓨터를 거의 언급하지 않는다. 예를 들어, 워드 프로세싱 프로그램과 잉크젯식 프린터를 사용하는 추상파 화가인 Wade Guyton은 자신을 컴퓨터 아티스트라고 부르지 않는다. 게다가, 그의 작품을 높이 평가하는 몇몇 비평가들은 그가 예술 창작 과정에서 광범위하게 컴퓨터를 사용한다는 점에 관해 거의 신경 쓰지 않는다. 이것은 컴퓨터를 활용하는 미술가들을 비평가들이 흔히 못마땅하게 컴퓨터 아티스트라고 명명했던 30년 전과 뚜렷이 대조된다. 현 세대의 미술가들에게 컴퓨터, 혹은 더욱 적절히는 휴대용 컴퓨터는 그들의 사회 생활과 직업 생활을 연결하는 일련의 통합되고 휴대 가능한 디지털 기술 중 하나이다. 인터넷 사용에서 태블릿 컴퓨터와 휴대 전화가 개인용 컴퓨터를 능가하는 상황에서, 얇은 디지털 기기들이 수십 년 전 방만큼 컸던 중앙 컴퓨터와 부피 큰 탁상용 컴퓨터와 전혀 닮지 않았으므로, 오늘날에는 컴퓨터 아티스트가 결국 소멸한 것으로 보인다.

Why? 왜 정답일까?

오늘날 컴퓨터는 젊은 현대 미술가들이 이용할 수 있는 여러 디지털 기기 중 하나로 전락했으며, 그 입지를 점점 잃어가는 추세라고 한다. 이에 따라 젊은 미술가들은 자신을 컴퓨터 아티스트라고 잘 정의하지 않는다(~ rarely make reference to computers)고 한다. 따라서 빈칸에 들어갈 말로 가장 적절한 것은 ⑤ '소멸한'이다.

- **contemporary** ⓐ 현대의
- **rarely** [ad] 좀처럼 ~하지 않는
- **abstractionist** ⓝ 추상파 화가
- **admire** ⓥ 높이 평가하다
- **label** ⓥ 명명하다, 이름을 붙이다
- **generation** ⓝ 세대
- **integrated** ⓐ 통합된
- **surpass** ⓥ 능가하다
- **mainframe** ⓝ 중앙 컴퓨터
- **previous** ⓐ 이전의
- **distinct** ⓐ 뚜렷이 다른
- **extinct** ⓐ 소멸한
- **employ** ⓥ 이용하다
- **make reference to** ~을 언급하다
- **inkjet** ⓝ 잉크젯식
- **marked** ⓐ 두드러진, 눈에 띄는
- **disapprovingly** [ad] 못마땅하게
- **appropriately** [ad] 적절히
- **portable** ⓐ 휴대 가능한, 들고 다닐 수 있는
- **resemble** ⓥ ~을 닮다
- **bulky** ⓐ 부피가 큰
- **influential** ⓐ 영향력 있는
- **troublesome** ⓐ 골칫거리인

구문 풀이

14행 {With tablets and cell phones surpassing personal computers
{ }: with부사구문(with + 명사 + 분사: ~이 …한 채로)
in Internet usage}, and {as slim digital devices resemble nothing like
{ }: 부사절(~하므로)
the room-sized mainframes and bulky desktop computers of previous
decades}, it now appears that the computer artist is finally extinct.
~한 것 같다

★★ 문제 해결 꿀~팁 ★★

▶ 많이 틀린 이유는?
글 서두에서 오늘날 아티스트들은 스스로를 '컴퓨터 아티스트'라고 정의하는 경우가 드물다고 했는데, ②는 컴퓨터 아티스트가 '영향력이 있다'는 의미이므로 주제와 모순된다.

▶ 문제 해결 방법은?
예시 앞의 첫 문장 뒤는 전부 부연 설명이다. 흐름을 뒤집는 역접 연결어도 없으므로, '요즘 아티스트들은 컴퓨터와 멀어져 있다'는 주제에 맞게 빈칸을 완성한다.

★★★ 1등급 대비 고난도 2점 문제

08 건강 분야의 중요 쟁점   정답률 41% | 정답 ②

다음 빈칸에 들어갈 말로 가장 적절한 것을 고르시오.

① to discover the blind spot – 맹점을 발견하도록
✓ to stick with new practices – 새로운 습관을 끝까지 지키도록
③ to build a sense of security – 안정감을 쌓아나가도록
④ to avoid unnecessary treatment – 불필요한 치료를 피하도록
⑤ to come up with novel solutions – 새로운 해결책을 떠올리도록

In the health area, / the concern with use after "purchase" / is as critical as / and even more critical / than the concern with the purchase itself.
건강 분야에서는 / '구매' 후 사용에 대한 우려가 / 못지않게 중요하고, / 그리고 훨씬 더 중요하다. / 구매 자체에 대한 우려보다

The person / who is sold on and goes through disease screening procedures / but does not follow through with medical treatment for a diagnosed

condition, / is as much of a failure / as a person / who did not avail himself of the screening program to begin with.
사람은 / 질병 검진 절차를 납득하여 그 절차를 거치지만 / 진단받은 질환에 대한 의학적 치료를 끝까지 하지 않는 / 큰 실패자이다. / 사람 못지 않은 / 애초에 검진 프로그램을 이용하지 않은

The obese individual / who has been successfully sold on / going on a medically prescribed diet / but is lured back to his candy jar and apple pie after one week, / is as much of a failure / as if he never had been sold on the need / to lose and control his weight.
비만인 사람은 / 성공적으로 납득했으나 / 의학적으로 처방된 다이어트를 하겠다고 / 일주일 후에 유혹에 빠져 다시 사탕이 든 병과 애플파이에 손대는 / 큰 실패자이다. / 그가 아예 필요성을 받아들이지 않은 경우와 다름없는 / 자신의 체중을 감량하고 조절할

The most challenging, most difficult, most perplexing problem / is not how to sell people on health-supportive practices, / not even how to get them to initiate such practices.
가장 까다롭고, 가장 어렵고, 가장 복잡한 문제는 / 어떻게 사람들에게 건강에 도움을 주는 습관을 받아들이게 하는가가 아니다. / 심지어 어떻게 그들에게 그러한 습관을 시작하게 하는가도

We have been fairly successful with these.
우리는 이것들에 상당히 성공적이었다.

It is to persuade and help them to stick with new practices.
문제는 그들이 새로운 습관을 끝까지 지키도록 설득하고 돕는 것이다.

건강 분야에서는 '구매' 후 사용에 대한 우려가 구매 자체에 대한 우려 못지않게, 그리고 훨씬 더 중요하다. 질병 검진 절차를 납득하여 그 절차를 거치지만 진단받은 질환에 대한 의학적 치료를 끝까지 하지 않는 사람은 애초에 검진 프로그램을 이용하지 않은 사람 못지않은 실패자이다. 의학적으로 처방된 다이어트를 하겠다고 성공적으로 납득했으나 일주일 후에 유혹에 빠져 다시 사탕이 든 병과 애플파이에 손대는 비만인 사람은 아예 자신의 체중 감량과 조절의 필요성을 받아들이지 않은 경우와 다름없는 실패자이다. 가장 까다롭고, 가장 어렵고, 가장 복잡한 문제는 어떻게 사람들에게 건강에 도움을 주는 습관을 받아들이게 하는가가 아니며, 심지어 어떻게 그들에게 그러한 습관을 시작하게 하는가도 아니다. 우리는 이것들에 상당히 성공적이었다. 문제는 그들이 새로운 습관을 끝까지 지키도록 설득하고 돕는 것이다.

Why? 왜 정답일까?

첫 문장에서 건강 분야에서는 구매 자체보다도 구매 후 사용에 대한 우려가 더 중요하다고 한다(In the health area, the concern with use after "purchase" is as critical as and even more critical than the concern with the purchase itself.). 또한 이어지는 예시에서 질병을 진단 받은 후 치료를 끝까지 이어가지 못하는 사람이나 과체중을 인지한 후 의학적으로 처방된 다이어트를 끝까지 따르지 못하는 사람은 애초에 진단이나 인지가 없었던 사람이나 다름없음을 언급하며, 결국 중요한 것은 새로운 변화를 받아들이고 유지하는 것임을 설명하고 있다. 따라서 빈칸에 들어갈 말로 가장 적절한 것은 ② '새로운 습관을 끝까지 지키도록'이다.

- **sell on** ~을 납득시키다
- **diagnose** ⓥ 진단하다
- **obese** ⓐ 비만인
- **lure** ⓥ 유혹하다, 꾀다
- **perplexing** ⓐ 복잡한
- **blind spot** 맹점
- **novel** ⓐ 새로운
- **disease screening** 질병 검사
- **avail oneself of** ~을 이용하다
- **prescribe** ⓥ 처방하다
- **challenging** ⓐ 까다로운
- **initiate** ⓥ 시작하다
- **stick with** ~을 계속하다

구문 풀이

3행 The person [who is sold on and goes through disease
주어(선행사)   주격 관·대
screening procedures but does not follow through with medical
treatment for a diagnosed condition], is as much of a failure as
동사(단수) ←   「as + 원급 + as : ~만큼 …한」
a person [who did not avail himself of the screening program to
선행사   주격 관·대
begin with].

★★ 문제 해결 꿀~팁 ★★

▶ 많이 틀린 이유는?
건강 문제를 해결하기 위해 치료법을 '구입'했다면 끝까지 사용하는 것이 중요하다는 내용의 글로, 예시에서 질병이나 비만 때문에 의학적으로 '필요한' 치료나 요법을 처방받았음에도 끝까지 따르지 못해 문제가 되는 경우를 언급하고 있다.
최다 오답인 ④는 '불필요한 치료를 피하게' 만드는 것이 어렵다는 의미이므로 예시와 상충한다.

▶ 문제 해결 방법은?
첫 문장의 use after "purchase"가 정답인 ②의 stick with new practices와 같은 말이다.

★★★ 1등급 대비 고난도 2점 문제

09 자원 양이 다른 개체의 수익성이 같아지는 과정
정답률 41% | 정답 ③

다음 빈칸에 들어갈 말로 가장 적절한 것을 고르시오.

① fails to find adequate resources in time
제때 적당량의 자원을 찾지 못하게 된다
② invades the other habitat to get more resources
더 많은 자원을 얻기 위해 다른 쪽 서식지를 침범한다
✓③ enjoys the same rate of acquisition of resources
같은 비율의 자원 획득을 누리게 된다
④ needs to gather resources faster than newcomers
새로 온 개체보다 더 빨리 자원을 모을 필요가 있다
⑤ is more attracted to the rich habitat than the poor one
자원이 부족한 서식지보다 풍부한 서식지에 더 끌린다

Imagine there are two habitats, / a rich one containing a lot of resources / and a poor one containing few, / and that there is no territoriality or fighting, / so each individual is free to exploit the habitat / in which it can achieve the higher pay-off, / measured as rate of consumption of resource.
두 서식지가 있다고 상상해 보라. / 많은 자원을 보유한 풍족한 서식지와 / 자원을 거의 보유하지 못한 부족한 서식지, / 그리고 영토권이나 싸움이 없어서 / 각 개체가 서식지를 자유롭게 이용할 수 있다고 / 그것이 더 높은 이익을 얻을 수 있는 / 자원 소비율로 측정되는

With no competitors, / an individual would simply go to the better of the two habitats / and this is what we assume the first arrivals will do.
경쟁자가 없다면, / 한 개체는 단순히 두 서식지 중 더 나은 곳으로 갈 것이고, / 이것은 처음 도착한 개체들이 할 것이라고 우리가 가정하는 것이다.

But what about the later arrivals?
하지만 더 늦게 도착하는 개체는 어떨까?

As more competitors occupy the rich habitat, / the resource will be depleted, / and so less profitable for further newcomers.
더 많은 경쟁자들이 풍족한 서식지를 차지함에 따라, / 자원이 고갈될 것이고, / 추가로 오는 개체들은 수익성이 낮아질 것이다.

Eventually a point will be reached / where the next arrivals will do better / by occupying the poorer quality habitat / where, although the resource is in shorter supply, / there will be less competition.
결국 지점에 이르게 될 것이다. / 그다음에 도착하는 개체들이 더 잘 살 수 있는 / 질이 더 낮은 서식지를 차지함으로써 / 자원의 양은 부족하지만 / 경쟁이 덜한

Thereafter, / the two habitats should be filled / so that the profitability for an individual / is the same in each one.
그 후에, / 두 서식지는 채워지게 될 것이고 / 그 결과 개체의 수익성은 / 각각의 서식지에서 같아질 것이다.

In other words, / competitors should adjust their distribution / in relation to habitat quality / so that each individual enjoys the same rate of acquisition of resources.
다시 말해, / 경쟁자는 자신의 분배를 틀림없이 조정하고, / 서식지 질과 관련해 / 그 결과 각 개체가 같은 비율의 자원 획득을 누리게 된다.

많은 자원을 보유한 풍족한 서식지와 자원을 거의 보유하지 못한 부족한 서식지, 이렇게 두 서식지가 있고, 영토권이나 싸움이 없어서 각 개체가 자원 소비율로 측정되는 더 높은 이익을 얻을 수 있는 서식지를 자유롭게 이용할 수 있다고 상상해 보라. 경쟁자가 없다면, 한 개체는 단순히 두 서식지 중 더 나은 곳으로 갈 것이고, 이것은 처음 도착한 개체들이 할 행동으로 여겨지는 것이다. 하지만 더 늦게 도착하는 개체는 어떨까? 더 많은 경쟁자들이 풍족한 서식지를 차지함에 따라, 자원이 고갈될 것이고, 추가로 오는 개체들은 수익성이 낮아질 것이다. 결국 자원의 양은 부족하지만 경쟁이 덜한 질이 더 낮은 서식지를 차지함으로써 그다음에 도착하는 개체들이 더 잘 살 수 있는 지점에 이르게 될 것이다. 그 후에, 두 서식지는 (개체들로) 채워지게 될 것이고 그 결과 개체의 수익성은 각각의 서식지에서 같아질 것이다. 다시 말해, 경쟁자는 서식지 질과 관련해 자신의 분배를 틀림없이 조정하고, 그 결과 각 개체가 같은 비율의 자원 획득을 누리게 된다.

Why? 왜 정답일까?

글에 따르면 자원 보유량이 많고 적은 두 서식지가 있을 때 먼저 온 개체는 자원이 많은 서식지를 우선 차지하는데, 그에 따라 자원이 고갈되어 가면서 뒤에 온 개체는 초기 자원이 적지만 경쟁이 덜한 서식지를 택하는 것이 이득일 수 있다고 한다. 결과적으로 두 서식지에 사는 개체의 수익성은 같아진다(~ the profitability for an individual is the same in each one.)는 설명으로 보아, 빈칸에 들어갈 말로 가장 적절한 것은 ③ '같은 비율의 자원 획득을 누리게 된다'이다.

● habitat ⑪ 서식지		● resource ⑪ 자원	
● territoriality ⑪ 영토권, 세력권		● exploit ⓥ 이용하다	
● payoff ⑪ 이익, 보상		● consumption ⑪ 소비	
● competitor ⑪ 경쟁자		● arrival ⑪ 도착	
● occupy ⓥ 차지하다, 점유하다		● deplete ⓥ 고갈하다	
● profitable ⓐ 수익성 있는		● newcomer ⑪ 새로 온 사람	
● profitability ⑪ 수익성		● adjust ⓥ 조정하다	

● distribution ⑪ 분배	● in relation to ~에 관련해
● adequate ⓐ 적당한, 충분한	● invade ⓥ 침입하다
● acquisition ⑪ 획득, 습득	● gather ⓥ 모으다
● attract ⓥ (주의·흥미 등을) 끌다, 끌어당기다	

구문 풀이

1행 Imagine {(that) there are two habitats, a rich one containing
접속사(생략)　　　　　　명사구1　현재분사구1
a lot of resources and a poor one containing few}, and {that there is
명사구2　　　　현재분사구2
no territoriality or fighting, so each individual is free to exploit
the habitat [in which it can achieve the higher pay-off, measured as
선행사　　=where
rate of consumption of resource]}.
{ } : 명사절(Imagine의 목적어)

★★ 문제 해결 꿀~팁 ★★

▶ 많이 틀린 이유는?
자원을 더 얻기 위해 상대편 서식지를 '침입한다'는 내용은 글 어디에도 언급되지 않으므로 ②는 답으로 적절하지 않다. 내부에서 자원 경쟁이 치열하다 보면 '밖으로 나갈 것이라는' 추론은 배경 지식에 의존한 발상이다.

▶ 문제 해결 방법은?
In other words 앞의 the profitability ~ is the same'을 명사구로 쓴 것이 바로 'the same rate of acquisition 'of resources'이다.

★★★ 1등급 대비 고난도 3점 문제

10 각색 작품의 의의
정답률 36% | 정답 ①

다음 빈칸에 들어갈 말로 가장 적절한 것을 고르시오. [3점]

✓① allow young readers to make personal connections with texts
어린 독자들이 텍스트와 개인적인 관계를 맺게 해 준다
② are nothing more than the combination of different styles
다양한 양식의 혼합에 지나지 않는다
③ break familiar patterns of the ancient heroic stories
고대 영웅 이야기의 익숙한 패턴을 깬다
④ give a new spotlight to various literary theories
다양한 문학 이야기에 새로운 스포트라이트를 비추다
⑤ encourage young writers to make plots original
젊은 작가들이 플롯을 독창적으로 만들도록 부추긴다

In *A Theory of Adaptation*, / Linda Hutcheon argues / that "An adaptation is not vampiric: / it does not draw the life-blood from its source / and leave it dying or dead, / nor is it paler than the adapted work. / It may, on the contrary, / keep that prior work alive, / giving it an afterlife / it would never have had otherwise."
*A Theory of Adaptation*에서 / Linda Hutcheon은 주장한다. / "각색 작품은 흡혈귀 같지 않다. / 이것은 원전에서 생명의 피를 빨아들이지 않는다 / 그리고 원전을 죽어 가게 하거나 죽은 상태로 내버려 두지 (않는다) / 또한 각색 당한 작품보다 더 창백하지도 않다. / 오히려 이것은 / 이전의 작품을 계속 살아 있게 하면서, / 그것을 내세를 준다. / 그렇지 않았더라면 그것이 결코 살지 못했을"이라고

Hutcheon's refusal to see adaptation as "vampiric" / is particularly inspiring for those of us / who do work on adaptations.
각색을 '흡혈귀 같다'라고 여기지 않겠다는 Hutcheon의 거부는 / 우리 같은 사람들에게 특히 고무적이다. / 각색 작품을 쓰는

The idea of an "afterlife" of texts, / of seeing what comes before / as an inspiration for what comes now, / is, by its very definition, / keeping works "alive."
텍스트의 '내세', / 즉 먼저 있는 것을 여기는 생각은 / 현재 생기는 것을 위한 영감으로 / 바로 그 정의로 볼 때 / 작품을 계속 '살아 있게' 한다.

Adaptations for young adults, in particular, / have the added benefit of engaging the young adult reader / with both then and now, past and present / — functioning as both "monuments" to history / and the "flesh" of the reader's lived experience.
특히 청소년을 위한 각색 작품은 / 청소년 독자에게 관계를 맺게 하는 추가적인 이점을 가진다. / 그때와 지금, 과거와도 현재와도 모두 / 즉 역사의 '기념비'로 기능하는 / 그리고 독자의 산 경험의 '살'로도 모두

While this is true for adaptations in general, / it is especially important / for those written with young adults in mind.
이것이 각색 작품 전반에 해당하긴 하지만, / 특히 중요하다. / 청소년을 염두에 두고 쓰인 각색 작품에

Such adaptations / that allow young readers / to make personal connections with texts / might otherwise come across / as old-fashioned or irrelevant.
그런 각색 작품은 / 어린 독자들이 ~하게 해 주는 / 텍스트와 개인적인 관계를 맺게 / 그러지 않았다면 보일 수 있었을 것이다. / 구식이거나 무관한 것으로

*A Theory of Adaptation*에서 Linda Hutcheon은 "각색 작품은 흡혈귀 같지 않다. 이것은 원전에서 생명의 피를 빨아들여 원전을 죽어 가게 하거나 (이미) 죽은 상태로 내버려 두지 않으며, 또한 각색 당한 작품(원전)보다 더 창백하지도 않

DAY 07

다. 오히려 이것은 이전의 작품을 계속 살아 있게 하면서, 각색되지 않았더라면 그것이 결코 살지 못했을 내세를 그것에 준다."라고 주장한다. 각색을 '흡혈귀 같다'라고 여기지 않겠다는 Hutcheon의 거부는 각색 작품을 쓰는 우리 같은 사람들에게 특히 고무적이다. 텍스트의 '내세', 즉 먼저 있는 것을 현재 생기는 것을 위한 영감으로 여기는 생각은 바로 그 정의로 볼 때 작품을 계속 '살아 있게' 한다. 특히 청소년을 위한 각색 작품은 청소년 독자에게 그때와 지금, 과거와도 현재와도 모두 관계를 맺게 하는, 즉 역사의 '기념비'와 독자의 산 경험의 '살'로 기능하는 추가적인 이점을 가진다. 이것이 각색 작품 전반에 해당하기는 하지만, 청소년을 염두에 두고 쓰인 각색 작품에 특히 중요하다. 그런 각색 작품은 어린 독자들이 그러지 않았다면 구식이거나 무관한 것으로 보일 수 있었을 텍스트와 개인적인 관계를 맺게 해 준다.

Why? 왜 정답일까?

글 초반부에서 인용구를 들어 각색 작품의 의의를 설명하고 있다. 각색 작품은 원전을 퇴색시키거나 원전보다 못하지 않으며, 오히려 원전이 '다시' 오래 살아남을 수 있도록 한다는 데서 나름의 가치를 갖는다는 것이다. 특히 'Adaptations for young adults ~' 부터는 특히 청소년 대상의 각색 작품에서 그렇다고 언급한다. 청소년을 위한 각색 작품은 청소년이 원작의 시대인 과거와 그들이 사는 현재와 모두 관계를 맺도록(engaging the young adult reader with both then and now, past and present) 도와준다는 내용으로 보아, 빈칸에 들어갈 말로 가장 적절한 것은 ① '어린 독자들이 텍스트와 개인적인 관계를 맺게 해 준다(allow young readers to make personal connections with texts)'이다.

- **adaptation** ⓝ (작품의) 각색
- **on the contrary** 대조적으로
- **otherwise** [ad] 그러지 않으면
- **inspiring** ⓐ 고무적인, 영감을 주는
- **engage A with B** A와 B가 맞물리게 하다
- **flesh** ⓝ 살, 피부
- **old-fashioned** ⓐ 구식의
- **nothing more than** 단지 ~인
- **original** ⓐ 독창적인
- **pale** ⓐ 창백한
- **afterlife** ⓝ 내세, 다음 생, 사후 세계
- **refusal** ⓝ 거부, 거절
- **definition** ⓝ 정의, 의미
- **monument** ⓝ 기념비
- **come across as** ~라는 인상을 주다
- **irrelevant** ⓐ 무관한
- **literary** ⓐ 문학적인

구문 풀이

2행 ~ it does not draw the life-blood from its source and
동사1
(does not) leave it dying or dead, nor is it paler than the adapted work.
동사2 목적어 목적격 보어 「nor + 동사 + 주어 : ~도 않다」

★★ 문제 해결 꿀~팁 ★★

▶ 많이 틀린 이유는?
각색 작품은 청소년들이 원전을 쉽게 이해하는 데 도움이 될 수 있다는 내용이다. ②는 각색 작품이 '여러 스타일을 혼합'한 것에 지나지 않는다는 의미인데, 이는 각색 작품의 의의보다는 한계를 부각한 설명이다. ③의 경우, 글에서 영웅 이야기의 '패턴'에 관해 언급한 바 없으며, 각색의 대상을 '고대 영웅 이야기'로 한정 짓지도 않아 오답이다.
▶ 문제 해결 방법은?
keeping works "alive."와 the "flesh" of the reader's lived experience 가 중요한 표현이다. 둘 다 텍스트가 '현재에도 생생한 의미를 갖는' 상황을 설명한다.

★★★ 1등급 대비 고난도 3점 문제

11 여성복을 제작하는 남성 디자이너의 입지 향상   정답률 46% | 정답 ④

다음 빈칸에 들어갈 말로 가장 적절한 것을 고르시오. [3점]

① a profitable industry driving fast fashion
패스트 패션을 주도하는 수익성 있는 산업
② a widespread respect for marketing skills
마케팅 기술에 대한 광범위한 존중
③ a public institution preserving traditional designs
전통 디자인을 보존하는 공공 기관
✓④ a modern connection between dress-design and art
의상 디자인과 예술 사이의 현대적 연결
⑤ an efficient system for producing affordable clothing
적정 가격의 의류를 생산하기 위한 효율적인 체계

There was nothing modern / about the idea of men making women's clothes / — we saw them doing it for centuries in the past.
전혀 현대적인 게 없다 / 남자가 여자 옷을 만든다는 생각에 관해서는 / 우리는 과거 여러 세기에 걸쳐 이것이 이뤄지는 것을 보았다.
In the old days, however, / the client was always primary / and her tailor was an obscure craftsman, / perhaps talented but perhaps not.
하지만 옛 시절에는 / 항상 고객 위주였고, / 여성 고객의 재단사는 무명의 장인이었다. / 아마 재능이 있었을 것이지만 없었을지도 모르는

She had her own ideas like any patron, / there were no fashion plates, / and the tailor was simply at her service, / perhaps with helpful suggestions / about what others were wearing.
여성 고객은 여느 후원자와 마찬가지로 자기만의 생각이 있었고, / 유행복의 본은 없었으며, / 재단사는 그저 그녀의 생각에 따랐다. / 아마도 유용한 제안을 하면서 / 다른 사람들의 복장에 관한
Beginning in the late nineteenth century, / with the hugely successful rise of the artistic male couturier, / it was the designer who became celebrated, / and the client elevated by his inspired attention.
19세기 후반부터, / 예술적인 남성 고급 여성복 디자이너들이 매우 성공적으로 부흥함에 따라, / 유명해진 것은 바로 디자이너였고, / 고객은 그의 영감 어린 관심에 의해 치켜세워졌다.
In a climate of admiration for male artists and their female creations, / the dress-designer first flourished / as the same sort of creator.
남성 예술가와 여성을 위한 그들의 작품에 대한 찬탄의 분위기 속에서, / 의상 디자이너는 번영했다. / 처음으로 같은 창작자로서
Instead of the old rule / that dressmaking is a craft, / was a modern connection between dress-design and art invented / that had not been there before.
옛 규칙 대신에, / 의상 제작은 공예에 불과하다는 / 의상 디자인과 예술 사이의 현대적 연결이 만들어졌다. / 예전에는 없던

남자가 여자 옷을 만든다는 생각은 전혀 현대적이지 않으며, 우리는 과거 여러 세기에 걸쳐 이것이 이뤄지는 것을 보았다. 하지만 옛 시절에는 항상 고객 위주였고, 여성 고객의 재단사는 아마 재능이 있었을 것이지만 없었을지도 모르는 무명의 장인이었다. 여느 후원자와 마찬가지로 여성 고객은 자기만의 생각이 있었고, 유행복의 본은 없었으며, 재단사는 아마도 다른 사람들의 복장에 관한 유용한 제안을 하면서 그저 그녀의 생각에 따랐다. 19세기 후반부터, 예술적인 남성 고급 여성복 디자이너들이 매우 성공적으로 부흥함에 따라, 유명해진 것은 바로 디자이너였고, 고객은 그의 영감 어린 관심에 의해 치켜세워졌다. 남성 예술가와 여성을 위한 그들의 작품에 대한 찬탄의 분위기 속에서, 의상 디자이너는 처음으로 (예술가와) 같은 창작자로서 번영했다. 의상 제작은 공예에 불과하다는 옛 규칙 대신에, 예전에는 없던 의상 디자이너와 예술 사이의 현대적 연결이 만들어졌다.

Why? 왜 정답일까?

여성복을 만드는 사람이 무명의 장인에서 예술가적 지위를 확립한 디자이너로 넘어오게 되었다는 내용의 글이다. 빈칸 앞의 두 문장에서, 19세기 후반부터 여성복을 만드는 남성 디자이너가 예술가와 같은 창작자 입지를 인정받게 되었다(In a climate of admiration for male artists and their female creations, the dress-designer first flourished as the same sort of creator.)는 점이 언급되는 것으로 볼 때, 빈칸에 들어갈 말로 가장 적절한 것은 ④ '의상 디자인과 예술 사이의 현대적 연결'이다.

- **primary** ⓐ 주요한
- **obscure** ⓐ 무명의
- **talented** ⓐ 재능 있는
- **fashion plate** 유행복의 본
- **suggestion** ⓝ 제안
- **couturier** ⓝ 고급 여성복 디자이너
- **inspire** ⓥ 영감을 주다
- **flourish** ⓥ 번영하다
- **widespread** ⓐ 널리 퍼진
- **institution** ⓝ 기관, 제도
- **tailor** ⓝ 재단사
- **craftsman** ⓝ 장인
- **patron** ⓝ 후원자
- **at one's service** ~의 마음대로 하는
- **rise** ⓝ 부상, 부흥
- **elevate** ⓥ 고양시키다
- **admiration** ⓝ 감탄, 존경, 찬탄
- **profitable** ⓐ 수익성 있는
- **respect** ⓝ 존경
- **affordable** ⓐ (가격이) 적당한, 적정한

구문 풀이

14행 Instead of the old rule that dressmaking is a craft,
a modern connection between dress-design and art was invented
주어 동사
[that had not been there before].
[ ] : 주어 수식

★★ 문제 해결 꿀~팁 ★★

▶ 많이 틀린 이유는?
패션 디자인이 언제부터 예술과 연관되기 시작했는지 설명하는 글이다. ①~③의 경우 글에서 언급되지 않은 소재를 포함하고 있는데, '수익성, 패스트 패션', '마케팅 기술', '전통 디자인' 등이 무관한 소재에 해당한다. ⑤는 '효율적인 생산 체계'에 관해서 언급하는데, 비록 글에서 사람에 의한 의상 제작을 다루기는 하지만 생산의 '체계'나 '효율성'을 다루지는 않으므로 답으로 부적합하다.
▶ 문제 해결 방법은?
'~ the dress-designer first flourished as the same sort of creator.' 에서 '디자이너가 예술적 창작자로 인정받기 시작했다'는 내용만 파악해도 답은 쉽게 나온다.

★★★ 1등급 대비 고난도 3점 문제

12 장소에 따라 노래를 달리 인식하는 울새   정답률 34% | 정답 ④

다음 빈칸에 들어갈 말로 가장 적절한 것을 고르시오. [3점]

① variety and complexity characterize the robins' songs
다양성과 복잡성이 울새 노래의 특징이다
② song volume affects the robins' aggressive behavior
노래의 크기가 울새의 공격적 행동에 영향을 미친다
③ the robins' poor territorial sense is a key to survival
울새의 부족한 영역 감각이 생존의 열쇠이다
✓④ the robins associate locality with familiar songs
울새가 장소를 친숙한 노래와 연관시킨다
⑤ the robins are less responsive to recorded songs
울새는 녹음된 노래에 대해서는 덜 반응한다

Emma Brindley / has investigated the responses of European robins / to the songs of neighbors and strangers.
Emma Brindley는 / 유럽 울새의 반응을 조사해 왔다. / 이웃 새와 낯선 새의 노래에 대한

Despite the large and complex song repertoire of European robins, / they were able to discriminate / between the songs of neighbors and strangers.
유럽 울새의 많고 복잡한 노래 목록에도 불구하고, / 그것은 구별할 수 있었다. / 이웃 새와 낯선 새의 노래를

When they heard a tape recording of a stranger, / they began to sing sooner, / sang more songs, / and overlapped their songs with the playback more often / than they did on hearing a neighbor's song.
그것이 테이프 녹음된 낯선 새의 소리를 들었을 때, / 그것은 금방 노래를 부르기 시작했고, / 더 많은 노래를 불렀으며, / 자기 노래를 재생된 노래와 더 자주 겹치게 불렀다. / 그것이 이웃 새의 노래를 들었을 때 그랬던 것보다

As Brindley suggests, / the overlapping of song may be an aggressive response.
Brindley가 언급하듯이, / 노래를 겹치게 부르는 것은 공격적인 반응일 수도 있다.

However, / this difference in responding to neighbor versus stranger / occurred / only when the neighbor's song was played by a loudspeaker / placed at the boundary / between that neighbor's territory and the territory of the bird being tested.
그러나 / 이웃 새와 낯선 새에 대한 반응의 이러한 차이는 / 발생했다. / 확성기로 이웃 새의 노래를 틀었을 때만 / 경계에 놓인 / 이웃 새의 영역과 실험 대상인 새의 영역 사이의

If the same neighbor's song was played at another boundary, / one separating the territory of the test subject from another neighbor, / it was treated as the call of a stranger.
같은 이웃 새의 노래를 다른 경계에서 틀었을 경우, / 즉 실험 대상의 영역을 또 다른 이웃 새의 영역과 분리해 주는 경계 / 그것은 낯선 새의 울음으로 취급되었다.

Not only does this result demonstrate / that the robins associate locality with familiar songs, / but it also shows / that the choice of songs used in playback experiments / is highly important.
이 결과는 입증할 뿐만 아니라, / 울새가 장소를 친숙한 노래와 연관시킨다는 것을 / 그것은 또한 보여 준다. / 재생 실험에 사용되는 노래의 선택이 / 매우 중요하다는 것을

Emma Brindley는 이웃 새와 낯선 새의 노래에 유럽 울새가 보이는 반응을 조사해 왔다. 유럽 울새의 많고 복잡한 노래 목록에도 불구하고, 그것은 이웃 새와 낯선 새의 노래를 구별할 수 있었다. 테이프 녹음된 낯선 새의 소리를 들었을 때, 그것은 이웃 새의 노래를 들었을 때 그랬던 것보다 더 금방 노래를 부르기 시작했고, 더 많은 노래를 불렀으며, 자기 노래를 재생된 노래와 더 자주 겹치게 불렀다. Brindley가 언급하듯이, 노래를 겹치게 부르는 것은 공격적인 반응일 수도 있다. 그러나 이웃 새와 낯선 새에 대한 반응의 이러한 차이는 이웃 새의 영역과 실험 대상인 새의 영역 사이의 경계에 놓인 확성기로 이웃 새의 노래를 틀었을 때만 발생했다. 같은 이웃 새의 노래를 다른 경계, 즉 실험 대상의 영역을 또 다른 이웃 새의 영역과 분리해 주는 경계에서 틀었을 경우, 그것은 낯선 새의 울음으로 취급되었다. 이 결과는 울새가 장소를 친숙한 노래와 연관시킨다는 것을 입증할 뿐만 아니라, 또한 (녹음 소리) 재생 실험에 사용되는 노래의 선택이 매우 중요하다는 것을 보여 준다.

Why? 왜 정답일까?

However 이후로 제시되는 결과에 따르면 울새가 이웃 새와 낯선 새의 노래에 다른 반응을 보이는 것은 노래를 틀어주는 '위치'가 어디인지와 관련되어 있다고 한다. 같은 이웃 새의 노래도 다른 경계 지점에서 틀면 낯선 새의 노래로 간주한다는 내용으로 보아, 빈칸에 들어갈 말로 가장 적절한 것은 ④ '울새가 장소를 친숙한 노래와 연관시킨다'이다.

- **investigate** ⓥ 조사하다
- **discriminate** ⓥ 구별하다
- **overlap** ⓥ 겹치다, 포개다
- **suggest** ⓥ 말하다, (뜻을) 비치다
- **versus** prep ~에 비해
- **separate** ⓥ 분리시키다
- **treat** ⓥ 대하다
- **characterize** ⓥ 특징 짓다
- **repertoire** ⓝ (한 사람이 할 수 있는) 모든 것
- **recording** ⓝ 녹음
- **playback** ⓝ 재생
- **aggressive** ⓐ 공격적인
- **loudspeaker** ⓝ 확성기
- **subject** ⓝ 대상
- **demonstrate** ⓥ 입증하다, 보여주다

구문 풀이

18행 Not only does this result demonstrate that the robins
「부정어구＋조동사＋주어＋동사원형 : 도치 구문」
associate locality with familiar songs, but it also shows that the
「not only＋A＋but (also)＋B : A뿐만 아니라 B도」
choice of songs used in playback experiments is highly important.

★★ 문제 해결 꿀~팁 ★★

▶ 많이 틀린 이유는?

유럽 울새의 소리 구별 능력에 관한 글로, 실험 내용을 잘 이해하여 올바른 결론을 도출해야 한다. 최다 오답인 ②는 노랫소리의 크기가 울새의 공격적 행동에 영향을 미친다는 의미인데, 글에서 소리 크기는 중요하게 언급되지 않았다. 또한 ①은 울새의 노래가 다양하고 복잡한 특징을 갖고 있다는 내용인데 글에서 울새의 노래 특징에 관해서는 언급되지 않았다.

▶ 문제 해결 방법은?

However로 시작하는 문장에 따르면, 유럽 울새가 이웃 새의 소리를 알아들을 수 있는지는 이웃 새의 소리를 '어느 경계 지점에서' 틀어주는가와 관련이 있었다. 따라서 빈칸에도 '장소'에 관한 언급이 있어야 한다.

DAY 07

DAY 08 　　빈칸 추론 08

01 ②	02 ①	03 ②	04 ①	05 ②
06 ⑤	07 ②	08 ③	09 ①	10 ①
11 ②	12 ①			

01 　야생 동물 피해 관리의 정의 　　정답률 56% | 정답 ②

다음 빈칸에 들어갈 말로 가장 적절한 것을 고르시오.

① cloning - 복제하지
✔ harming - 해를 끼치지
③ training - 훈련시키지
④ overfeeding - 먹이를 너무 많이 주지
⑤ domesticating - 길들이지

Some people have defined wildlife damage management / as the science and management of overabundant species, / but this definition is too narrow.
어떤 사람들은 야생 동물 피해 관리를 정의했지만, / 과잉 종들에 대한 과학과 관리로 / 이 정의는 너무 좁다.

All wildlife species act in ways / that harm human interests.
모든 야생 동물 종들은 방식으로 행동한다. / 인간의 이익에 해를 끼치는

Thus, all species cause wildlife damage, / not just overabundant ones.
따라서 모든 종이 야생 동물 피해를 야기한다. / 단지 과잉 종뿐만 아니라

One interesting example of this / involves endangered peregrine falcons in California, / which prey on another endangered species, / the California least tern.
이것의 흥미로운 한 사례는 / 캘리포니아의 멸종 위기에 처한 송골매인데, / 그것들은 또 다른 멸종 위기 종을 먹이로 한다. / 캘리포니아 작은 제비갈매기라는

Certainly, we would not consider peregrine falcons / as being overabundant, / but we wish that they would not feed on an endangered species.
분명히 우리는 송골매를 생각하지 않겠지만, / 과잉이라고 / 우리는 그것들이 멸종 위기에 처한 종들을 먹고 살지 않기를 바란다.

In this case, one of the negative values / associated with a peregrine falcon population / is that its predation reduces the population of another endangered species.
이런 경우에, 부정적인 가치들 중 하나는 / 송골매 개체 수와 관련된 / 그것의 포식이 또 다른 멸종 위기 종들의 개체 수를 감소시킨다는 것이다.

The goal of wildlife damage management in this case / would be to stop the falcons from eating the terns / without harming the falcons.
이런 경우에 야생 동물 피해 관리의 목표는 / 송골매가 작은 제비갈매기를 잡아먹지 못하게 하는 것일 것이다. / 송골매에 해를 끼치지 않으면서

어떤 사람들은 야생 동물 피해 관리를 과잉 종들에 대한 과학과 관리로 정의했지만, 이 정의는 너무 좁다. 모든 야생 동물 종들은 인간의 이익에 해를 끼치는 방식으로 행동한다. 따라서 단지 과잉 종뿐만 아니라 모든 종이 야생 동물 피해를 야기한다. 이것의 흥미로운 한 사례는 캘리포니아의 멸종 위기에 처한 송골매인데, 그것들은 캘리포니아 작은 제비갈매기라는 또 다른 멸종 위기 종을 먹이로 한다. 분명히 우리는 송골매를 과잉이라고 생각하지 않겠지만, 우리는 그것들이 멸종 위기에 처한 종들을 먹고 살지 않기를 바란다. 이런 경우에, 송골매 개체 수와 관련된 부정적인 가치들 중 하나는 그것의 포식이 또 다른 멸종 위기 종들의 개체 수를 감소시킨다는 것이다. 이런 경우에 야생 동물 피해 관리의 목표는 송골매에 해를 끼치지 않으면서 송골매가 작은 제비갈매기를 잡아먹지 못하게 하는 것일 것이다.

Why? 왜 정답일까?

빈칸 앞의 두 문장에서 송골매가 멸종 위기에 처한 작은 제비갈매기를 잡아먹고 살면 작은 제비갈매기 종의 개체 수가 감소하는 부정적 결과가 나타나기에 송골매가 과잉 개체는 아니지만 야생 동물 피해 관리의 대상이 될 수 있음을 설명하고 있다(Certainly, we would not consider peregrine falcons as being overabundant, but we wish that they would not feed on an endangered species.). 이를 근거로 볼 때, 야생 동물 피해 관리의 목표는 송골매와 작은 제비갈매기 모두가 적절한 개체 수를 유지하도록 관리하는 것이리라는 점을 유추할 수 있다. 따라서 빈칸에 들어갈 말로 가장 적절한 것은 ② '해를 끼치지'이다.

- **wildlife** ⓝ 야생 생물
- **definition** ⓝ 정의, 의미
- **involve** ⓥ 포함하다, 수반하다
- **prey on** ~을 먹이로 하다
- **predation** ⓝ 포식
- **train** ⓥ 교육[훈련]시키다
- **domesticate** ⓥ 길들이다, 사육하다
- **overabundant** ⓐ 과잉의
- **narrow** ⓥ 좁다
- **endangered** ⓐ 멸종 위기에 처한
- **feed on** ~을 먹고 살다
- **clone** ⓥ 복제하다
- **overfeed** ⓥ 너무 많이 먹이다[주다]

구문 풀이

11행 In this case, one of the negative values [associated with a peregrine falcon population] is {that its predation reduces the population of another endangered species}.
주어 / 과거분사(~와 연관된) / 동사 / { }: 주격 보어

02 　사냥감을 존중하는 관습 　　정답률 48% | 정답 ①

다음 빈칸에 들어갈 말로 가장 적절한 것을 고르시오.

✔ view that prey with respect - 그 먹이를 존중하며 바라보는
② domesticate those animals - 그 동물들을 길들이는
③ develop tools for hunting - 사냥 도구를 개발하는
④ avoid supernatural beliefs - 초자연적 믿음을 피하는
⑤ worship our ancestors' spirits - 우리 조상의 영혼을 경배하는

Lewis-Williams believes / that the religious view of hunter groups / was a contract between the hunter and the hunted.
Lewis-Williams는 믿는다. / 사냥 집단이 가진 종교관은 / 사냥꾼과 사냥감 간의 계약이었다고

'The powers of the underworld / allowed people to kill animals, / provided people responded in certain ritual ways, / such as taking fragments of animals into the caves / and inserting them into the "membrane".'
'지하 세계의 신들은 / 사람들에게 동물을 살생해도 된다고 허용했다. / 사람들이 특정한 의식으로 대응한다는 조건으로 / 동물의 작은 조각을 동굴로 가지고 들어가 / '지하 세계로 통하는 바위 표면' 속에 넣는 것과 같은.'

This is borne out in the San.
이것은 San족에서 유지된다.

Like other shamanistic societies, / they have admiring practices / between human hunters and their prey, / suffused with taboos / derived from extensive natural knowledge.
다른 무속 사회처럼, / 그들에게는 존중하는 관습이 있는데, / 사냥하는 인간과 먹이 간에 / 이것은 금기로 가득 차 있다. / 광범위한 자연 지식에서 유래한

These practices suggest / that honouring may be one method of softening the disquiet of killing.
이런 관습들은 보여준다. / 경의를 표하는 것이 살생의 불안을 경감하는 한 가지 수단일 수도 있음을

It should be said / that this disquiet needn't arise / because there is something fundamentally wrong / with a human killing another animal, / but simply because we are aware of doing the killing.
말할 수 있다. / 이런 불안은 일어날 필요가 있는 게 아니라, / 근본적으로 잘못된 무언가가 있기 때문에 / 인간이 다른 동물을 죽이는 데 / 그저 우리가 죽인다는 것을 의식하고 있기 때문에 일어나야 한다고

And perhaps, too, / because in some sense / we 'know' what we are killing.
그리고 또한 어쩌면 / 어떤 의미로는 / 우리가 무엇을 죽이는지를 '알기' 때문일 수도 있다.

We make sound guesses / that the pain and desire for life we feel / — our worlds of experience — / have a counterpart in the animal we kill.
우리는 타당하게 추측한다. / 우리가 느끼는 고통과 살고자 하는 욕망에 / (즉 우리의 경험 세계) / 우리가 죽이는 동물에게 똑같은 것이 있다고

As predators, / this can create problems for us.
포식자로서 볼 때 / 이것은 우리에게 문제를 만들어 낼 수 있다.

One way to smooth those edges, then, / is to view that prey with respect.
그렇다면, 그런 문제를 완화하는 한 가지 방법은 / 그 먹이를 존중하며 바라보는 것이다.

Lewis-Williams는 사냥 집단이 가진 종교관은 사냥꾼과 사냥감 간의 계약이었다고 믿는다. '지하 세계의 신들은 사람들에게 동물을 살생해도 된다고 허용했는데, 사람들이 동물 (몸)의 작은 조각을 동굴로 가지고 들어가 '지하 세계로 통하는 바위 표면' 속에 넣는 것과 같은 특정한 의식으로 대응한다는 조건으로 그렇게 했다.' 이것은 San족에서 유지된다. 다른 무속 사회처럼, 그들에게는 사냥하는 인간과 먹이 간 존중하는 관습이 있는데, 이것은 광범위한 자연 지식에서 유래한 금기로 가득 차 있다. 이런 관습들은 경의를 표하는 것이 살생의 불안을 경감하는 한 가지 수단일 수도 있음을 보여준다. 이런 불안은 인간이 다른 동물을 죽이는 데 근본적으로 잘못된 무언가가 있기 때문이 아니라, 그저 우리가 죽인다는 것을 의식하고 있기 때문에 일어날 필요가 있다고 말할 수 있다. 그리고 또한 어쩌면 어떤 의미로는 우리가 무엇을 죽이는지를 '알기' 때문일 수도 있다. 우리는 우리가 죽이는 동물에게 우리가 느끼는 고통과 살고자 하는 욕망(즉 우리의 경험 세계)과 같은 것이 있다고 타당하게 추측한다. 포식자로서 볼 때 이것은 우리에게 문제를 만들어 낼 수 있다. 그렇다면, 그런 문제를 완화하는 한 가지 방법은 그 먹이를 존중하며 바라보는 것이다.

Why? 왜 정답일까?

먹잇감을 살생하는 행위와 그 대상을 의식하는 인간이 먹잇감을 존중하며(honouring) 바라보는 관습을 발전시켰다는 내용이다. 후반부에 그 이유가 제시되는데, 삶에 대한 욕망과 고통을 느낄 줄 아는 인간은 동물 또한 이를 비슷하게 느낄 것으로 추측하기 때문에

그 먹이에 '존중을 표하는' 방식으로 살생 행위의 불안을 해소하려 한다는 것이다. 따라서 빈칸에 들어갈 말로 가장 적절한 것은 ① '그 먹이를 존중하며 바라보는(view that prey with respect)'이다.

- **contract** ⓝ 계약
- **ritual** ⓐ 의식적인
- **membrane** ⓝ 지하 세계로 통하는 바위 표면
- **shamanistic** ⓐ 주술적인
- **derive from** ~로부터 유래하다
- **disquiet** ⓝ 불안, 동요
- **domesticate** ⓥ 길들이다, 가축으로 만들다
- **provided** ⓒⓞⓝⓙ ~한다는 조건으로
- **fragment** ⓝ (작은) 조각
- **bear out** 지탱하다, 유지되다, 근거가 되다
- **suffused with** ~로 가득 찬
- **extensive** ⓐ 광범위한
- **counterpart** ⓝ 대응물, 동등한 것
- **worship** ⓥ 경배하다

12행 It should be said [that this disquiet needn't arise because
가주어   ┌not because+A+
there is something fundamentally wrong with a human killing another
animal, but simply because we are aware of doing the killing].
but+because+B : A 때문이 아니라 B 때문인,   [ ] : 진주어

---

03 점점 인류의 영향을 받는 자연   정답률 38% | 정답 ②

다음 빈칸에 들어갈 말로 가장 적절한 것을 고르시오. [3점]

① has supported new environment-friendly policies
새로운 친환경적인 정책을 지지해 왔다
② has increasingly been set by humanity ✓
점점 더 인류에 의해 설정되어 왔다
③ inspires creative cultural practices
창의적인 문화적 관행을 고취한다
④ changes too frequently to be regulated
너무 자주 바뀌어 규제할 수 없다
⑤ has been affected by various natural conditions
다양한 자연 조건의 영향을 받아 왔다

Concepts of nature are always cultural statements.
자연에 대한 개념은 항상 문화적 진술이다.

This may not strike Europeans as much of an insight, / for Europe's landscape is so much of a blend.
이것은 유럽인들에게 대단한 통찰이라는 인상을 주지 않을 수도 있는데, / 왜냐하면 유럽의 풍경은 너무나 많이 혼합되어 있기 때문이다.

But in the new worlds / — 'new' at least to Europeans — / the distinction appeared much clearer / not only to European settlers and visitors / but also to their descendants.
그러나 새로운 세계에서, / 적어도 유럽인들에게는 '새로운' / 그 차이는 훨씬 더 분명해 보였다. / 유럽 정착민과 방문객뿐만 아니라 / 그들의 후손에게도

For that reason, / they had the fond conceit of primeval nature / uncontrolled by human associations / which could later find expression in an admiration for wilderness.
그런 이유 때문에, / 그들은 원시 자연이라는 허황된 생각을 가졌다. / 인간과의 연관으로 통제되지 않는 / 후에 황야에 대한 감탄에서 표현을 찾을 수 있었던

Ecological relationships certainly have their own logic / and in this sense 'nature' can be seen / to have a self-regulating but not necessarily stable dynamic / independent of human intervention.
생태학적 관계는 확실히 그 나름의 논리를 가지고 있었고, / 이런 의미에서 '자연'은 여겨질 수 있다. / 자율적이지만 반드시 안정적이지는 않은 역동성을 가지고 있다고 / 인간의 개입과 무관하게

But the context for ecological interactions / has increasingly been set by humanity.
그러나 생태학적 상호작용의 환경은 / 점점 더 인류에 의해 설정되어 왔다.

We may not determine how or what a lion eats / but we certainly can regulate where the lion feeds.
우리는 사자가 어떻게 또는 무엇을 먹는지는 정하지 못할 수도 있지만, / 사자가 어디에서 먹이를 먹을지는 확실히 규제할 수 있다.

자연에 대한 개념은 항상 문화적 진술이다. 이것은 유럽인들에게 대단한 통찰이라는 인상을 주지 않을 수도 있는데, 왜냐하면 유럽의 풍경은 너무나 많이 혼합되어 있기 때문이다. 그러나 새로운 — 적어도 유럽인들에게는 '새로운' — 세계에서, 그 차이는 유럽 정착민과 방문객뿐만 아니라 그들의 후손에게도 훨씬 더 분명해 보였다. 그런 이유 때문에, 그들은 후에 황야에 대한 감탄에서 표현을 찾을 수 있었던, 인간과의 연관으로 통제되지 않는 원시 자연이라는 허황된 생각을 가졌다. 생태학적 관계는 확실히 그 나름의 논리를 가지고 있었고, 이런 의미에서 '자연'은 인간의 개입과 무관하게, 자율적이지만 반드시 안정적이지는 않은 역동성을 가지고 있다고 볼 수 있다. 그러나 생태학적 상호작용의 환경은 점점 더 인류에 의해 설정되어 왔다. 우리는 사자가 어떻게 또는 무엇을 먹는지는 정하지 못할 수도 있지만, 사자가 어디에서 먹이를 먹을지는 확실히 규제할 수 있다.

앞에서 자연은 인간의 개입과 무관하게 자율적인 역동성을 지닌 것으로 이해되었다고 언급한 데 이어, 빈칸이 있는 문장에서는 But으로 흐름을 반전시키고 있다. 즉 인간이 생태 환경 설정에 점점 관여해왔다는 설명이 빈칸에 들어가야 한다. 실제로 빈칸 뒤에서 인간은 사자가 먹이를 어떤 식으로 먹고, 어느 먹이를 먹을지까지는 통제할 수 없지만, '어디에서' 먹는지는 확실히 통제할 수 있다는 예시가 나온다. 따라서 빈칸에 들어갈 말로 가장 적절한 것은 ② '점점 더 인류에 의해 설정되어 왔다'이다.

- **strike as** ~와 같은 인상을 주다
- **blend** ⓝ 혼합 ⓥ 섞이다, 혼합하다
- **descendant** ⓝ 후손
- **admiration** ⓝ 감탄
- **self-regulating** ⓐ 스스로 규제하는
- **independent of** ~와는 무관하게
- **humanity** ⓝ 인류
- **landscape** ⓝ 풍경
- **distinction** ⓝ 구별
- **fond** ⓐ (명사 앞에서) 허황된
- **wilderness** ⓝ 황무지, 황야
- **stable** ⓐ 안정적인
- **intervention** ⓝ 개입, 간섭

6행 For that reason, they had the fond conceit of primeval nature
선행사
uncontrolled by human associations [which could later find expression
과거분사   주격 관계대명사
in an admiration for wilderness].

---

04 평등의 진정한 의미   정답률 48% | 정답 ①

다음 빈칸에 들어갈 말로 가장 적절한 것을 고르시오. [3점]

① require different rights to enjoy equality ✓
평등을 누릴 수 있게 각기 다른 권리를 요구할
② abandon their own freedom for equality
평등을 위해 자신의 자유를 포기할
③ welcome the identical perception of inequality
불평등에 관한 동일한 인식을 기꺼이 받아들일
④ accept their place in the social structure more easily
사회 구조에서 자신의 위치를 더 쉽게 받아들일
⑤ reject relevant differences to gain full understanding
온전한 이해를 얻기 위해 타당한 차이점을 거부할

Since human beings are at once both similar and different, / they should be treated equally because of both.
인간은 동시에 비슷하기도 하고 다르기도 해서 / 그들은 둘 다로 인해 동등하게 대우받아야 한다.

Such a view, / which grounds equality not in human uniformity / but in the interplay of uniformity and difference, / builds difference into the very concept of equality, / breaks the traditional equation of equality with similarity, / and is immune to monist distortion.
그러한 견해는 / 평등의 기초를 인간의 획일성이 아니라 / 획일성과 차이의 상호작용에 두는 / 평등이라는 바로 그 개념에 차이를 포함시키고, / 전통적으로 평등을 유사성과 동일시하는 것을 깨뜨리며, / 일원론적 왜곡에 영향을 받지 않는다.

Once the basis of equality changes / so does its content.
일단 평등의 기초가 바뀌면 / 그 내용도 바뀐다.

Equality involves equal freedom or opportunity to be different, / and treating human beings equally requires us / to take into account both their similarities and differences.
평등은 서로 다를 수 있는 동등한 자유나 기회를 포함하고, / 인간을 동등하게 취급하는 것은 우리에게 요구한다. / 우리가 그들의 유사성과 차이점을 둘 다 고려하도록

When the latter are not relevant, / equality entails uniform or identical treatment; / when they are, / it requires differential treatment.
후자(차이점)가 타당하지 않을 때 / 평등은 균일하거나 똑같은 대우를 내포하고, / 차이점이 타당할 때 / 그것은 차등적인 대우를 필요로 한다.

Equal rights do not mean identical rights, / for individuals with different cultural backgrounds and needs / might require different rights / to enjoy equality / in respect of whatever happens to be the content of their rights.
평등한 권리는 똑같은 권리를 의미하지 않는데, / 서로 다른 문화적 배경과 요구를 가진 개인이 / 각기 다른 권리를 요구할지도 모르기 때문이다. / 평등을 누릴 수 있게 / 우연히 그들의 권리의 내용이 되는 어떤 것이든 그것에 관해서

Equality involves / not just rejection of irrelevant differences / as is commonly argued, / but also full recognition of legitimate and relevant ones.
평등은 포함한다. / 타당하지 않은 차이에 대한 거부뿐만 아니라 / 흔히 주장되듯이 / 합법적이고 타당한 차이들에 대한 완전한 인정도

인간은 동시에 비슷하기도 하고 다르기도 해서 둘 다로 인해 동등하게 대우받아야 한다. 평등의 기초를 인간의 획일성이 아니라 획일성과 차이의 상호작용에 두는 그러한 견해는 평등이라는 바로 그 개념에 차이를 포함시키고, 전통적으로 평등을 유사성과 동일시하는 것을 깨뜨리며, 일원론적 왜곡에 영향을 받지 않는다. 일단 평등의 기초가 바뀌면 그 내용도 바뀐다. 평등은 서로 다를 수

있는 동등한 자유나 기회를 포함하고, 인간을 동등하게 취급하는 것은 우리가 그들의 유사성과 차이점을 둘 다 고려하도록 요구한다. 후자(차이점)가 타당하지 않을 때 평등은 균일하거나 똑같은 대우를 내포하고, 차이점이 타당할 때 그것은 차등적인 대우를 필요로 한다. 평등한 권리는 똑같은 권리를 의미하지 않는데, 서로 다른 문화적 배경과 요구를 가진 개인들이 우연히 그들의 권리의 내용이 되는 어떤 것이든 그것에 관해서 평등을 누릴 수 있게 각기 다른 권리를 요구할지도 모르기 때문이다. 평등은 흔히 주장되듯이 타당하지 않은 차이들에 대한 거부뿐만 아니라 합법적이고 타당한 차이들에 대한 완전한 인정도 포함한다.

Why? 왜 정답일까?

인간은 비슷한 동시에 서로 다른 존재이기에 유사성에 기반하여 모두를 똑같이 대우하는 데 초점을 둘 것이 아니라, 타당한 차이를 인정하고 그 차이에 맞게 대하는 것이 진정한 평등임을 설명한 글이다. 빈칸이 포함된 문장의 앞부분에서 평등은 똑같은 권리를 의미하지 않는다고 언급한 데 이어 마지막 문장에서도 합법적인 차이에 대한 완전한 인정이 평등에 포함될 수 있다고 설명하고 있다(Equality involves ~ full recognition of legitimate and relevant ones.). 이를 근거로 볼 때, 빈칸에는 서로 다른 배경과 요구를 지닌 개인들이 이 차이를 고려하여 '서로 다른 권리를 주장함으로써' 평등을 실현하려 할 수 있다는 내용이 들어가야 한다. 따라서 빈칸에 들어갈 말로 가장 적절한 것은 ① '평등을 누릴 수 있게 각기 다른 권리를 요구할'이다.

- **ground in** ⓥ ~에 기초를 두다
- **interplay** ⓝ 상호작용
- **immune to** ~에 영향을 받지 않는
- **take into account** ⓥ ~을 고려하다
- **in respect of** ~에 관해서
- **abandon** ⓥ 포기하다, 버리다
- **uniformity** ⓝ 획일성
- **equation** ⓝ 동일시, 등식, 방정식
- **distortion** ⓝ 왜곡
- **differential** ⓐ 차등을 두는
- **legitimate** ⓐ 합법적인

구문 풀이

3행 Such a view, which grounds equality not in human uniformity
주어 / 계속적 용법(주어 보충) / 「not + A + but + B : A가 아니라 B인」
but in the interplay of uniformity and difference, builds difference
동사1
into the very concept of equality, breaks the traditional equation of
바로 그(명사 수식) / 동사2
equality with similarity, and is immune to monist distortion.
동사3

---

05 화학 물질의 보고인 식물   정답률 51% | 정답 ②

다음 빈칸에 들어갈 말로 가장 적절한 것을 고르시오.

① a factory that continuously generates clean air
계속해서 깨끗한 공기를 만들어내는 공장
✓② a source for a dazzling array of useful substances
놀랍도록 많은 유용한 물질의 공급원
③ a silent battlefield in which plants fight for sunshine
식물들이 햇빛을 위해 싸우는 침묵의 전쟁터
④ a significant habitat for microorganisms at a global scale
전 세계 미생물의 중요한 서식지
⑤ a document that describes the primitive state of the earth
지구의 원시 상태를 기술해주는 문서

Plants are genius chemists.
식물은 천재적인 화학자다.

They rely on their ability / to manufacture chemical compounds / for every single aspect of their survival.
그것들은 능력에 의존한다. / 화학적 혼합물을 제조하는 / 생존의 모든 측면 하나하나에 대해

A plant with juicy leaves / can't run away to avoid being eaten.
즙이 많은 잎을 가진 식물이 / 먹히는 것을 피하려고 달아날 수는 없다.

It relies on its own chemical defenses / to kill microbes, deter pests, or poison would-be predators.
그것은 자체의 화학적 방어 수단에 의존해 / 세균을 죽이거나, 해충을 저지하거나, 잠재적 포식자를 독살한다.

Plants also need to reproduce.
식물은 또한 번식도 해야 한다.

They can't impress a potential mate / with a fancy dance, / a victory in horn-to-horn combat, / or a well-constructed nest / like animals do.
식물은 잠재적 짝을 감동시킬 수 없다. / 화려한 춤이나 / 뿔 대 뿔 결투에서의 승리, / 혹은 잘 지어진 둥지로 / 동물이 하듯이

Since plants need to attract pollinators / to accomplish reproduction, / they've evolved intoxicating scents, sweet nectar, and pheromones / that send signals / that bees and butterflies can't resist.
식물은 꽃가루 매개자를 끌어들여야 하기 때문에, / 번식을 완수하기 위해서는 / 식물은 취하게 하는 향기, 달콤한 화밀, 그리고 페로몬을 진화시켜 왔다. / 신호를 보내는 / 벌과 나비가 저항할 수 없는

When you consider / that plants solve almost all of their problems / by making chemicals, / and that there are nearly 400,000 species of plants on

---

Earth, / it's no wonder / that the plant kingdom is a source / for a dazzling array of useful substances.
여러분이 고려해 볼 때, / 식물이 거의 모든 문제를 해결한다는 것과 / 화학 물질을 만들어 / 지구상에 거의 40만 종의 식물이 있다는 것을 / 전혀 놀랍지 않다. / 식물 왕국은 공급원이라는 것이 / 놀랍도록 많은 유용한 물질의

식물은 천재적인 화학자다. 그것들은 생존의 모든 측면 하나하나를 화학적 혼합물을 제조하는 능력에 의존한다. 즙이 많은 잎을 가진 식물이 먹히는 것을 피하려고 달아날 수는 없다. 그것은 자체의 화학적 방어 수단에 의존해 세균을 죽이거나, 해충을 저지하거나, 잠재적 포식자를 독살한다. 식물은 또한 번식도 해야 한다. 식물은 동물처럼 화려한 춤이나 뿔 대 뿔 결투에서의 승리, 혹은 잘 지어진 둥지로 잠재적인 짝을 감동시킬 수 없다. 번식을 완수하기 위해서는 꽃가루 매개자를 끌어들여야 하기 때문에, 식물은 취하게 하는 향기, 달콤한 화밀, 그리고 벌과 나비가 저항할 수 없는 신호를 보내는 페로몬을 진화시켜 왔다. 식물이 거의 모든 문제를 화학 물질을 만들어 해결한다는 것과 지구상에 거의 40만 종의 식물이 있다는 것을 고려해 볼 때, 식물 왕국은 놀랍도록 많은 유용한 물질의 공급원이라는 것이 전혀 놀랍지 않다.

Why? 왜 정답일까?

빈칸 앞의 종속절인 'When you consider that plants solve almost all of their problems by making chemicals, and that there are nearly 400,000 species of plants on Earth, ~'에서 지구상에 40만 종 가까운 식물이 있는데, 이것들은 모두 자신에게 필요한 화학 물질을 만들어 사용한다고 한다. 이를 근거로, 식물은 아주 많은 물질의 공급원 역할을 할 것이라는 결론을 추론할 수 있다. 따라서 빈칸에 들어갈 말로 가장 적절한 것은 ② '놀랍도록 많은 유용한 물질의 공급원'이다.

- **genius** ⓝ 천재
- **compound** ⓝ 화합물, 혼합물
- **deter** ⓥ 저지하다, 단념시키다
- **reproduce** ⓥ 번식하다, 재생하다
- **pollinator** ⓝ 꽃가루 매개자
- **intoxicate** ⓥ 도취시키다
- **dazzling** ⓐ 휘황찬란한, 눈부신
- **significant** ⓐ 중요한
- **manufacture** ⓥ 만들어내다, 제조하다
- **microbe** ⓝ 미생물
- **predator** ⓝ 포식자
- **combat** ⓝ 전투, 싸움
- **accomplish** ⓥ 완수하다, 성취하다
- **an array of** 다수의
- **substance** ⓝ 물질
- **primitive** ⓐ 원시의

구문 풀이

7행 They can't impress a potential mate with a fancy dance,
전치사 / 명사구1
a victory in horn-to-horn combat, or a well-constructed nest like
명사구2 / 명사구3 / ~처럼
animals do.
= impress

---

06 탈진실이 일어나는 이유   정답률 47% | 정답 ⑤

다음 빈칸에 들어갈 말로 가장 적절한 것을 고르시오. [3점]

① to hold back our mixed feelings
우리의 혼재된 감정을 억누름
② that balances our views on politics
정치에 관한 우리의 견해들의 균형을 잡는
③ that leads us to give way to others in need
우리가 어려운 처지의 타인에게 양보하게 하는
④ to carry the constant value of absolute truth
절대적 진리의 변치 않는 가치를 지님
✓⑤ that is more important to us than the truth itself
진실 그 자체보다 우리에게 더 중요한

If one looks at the Oxford definition, / one gets the sense / that post-truth is not so much a claim / that truth *does not exist* / as that *facts are subordinate to our political point of view.*
Oxford 사전의 정의를 보면, / 우리는 알게 된다. / 탈진실이란 주장이 아니라, / 진실이 *존재하지 않는다는* / *사실이 우리의 정치적 관점에 종속되어 있다는* 주장임을

The Oxford definition focuses on "*what*" post-truth is: / the idea that feelings sometimes matter more than facts.
Oxford 사전의 정의는 탈진실이란 '*무엇인가*'에 초점을 둔다. / 즉 때로는 감정이 사실보다 더 중요하다는 생각에

But just as important is the next question, / which is *why* this ever occurs.
하지만 그다음 질문은 그에 못지않게 중요한데, / 그것은 도대체 *왜* 이런 일이 일어나는가이다.

Someone does not argue against an obvious or easily confirmable fact / for no reason; / he or she does so / when it is to his or her advantage.
어떤 사람은 분명하거나 쉽게 확인할 수 있는 사실에 반대하는 게 아니며, / 아무런 이유 없이 / 그 사람은 그렇게 한다. / 그렇게 하는 것이 자신의 이익에 부합할 때

When a person's beliefs are threatened by an "inconvenient fact," / sometimes it is preferable to challenge the fact.
어떤 사람의 믿음이 '불편한 사실'에 의해 위협받을 때, / 때로는 그 사실에 이의를 제기하는 것이 선호된다.

This can happen at either a conscious or unconscious level / (since sometimes the person we are seeking to convince / is ourselves), / but the point is / that this sort of post-truth relationship to facts occurs / only when we are seeking to assert something / <u>that is more important to us than the truth itself.</u>

이것은 의식적인 수준이나 무의식적인 수준에서 일어날 수 있지만, / (때로는 우리가 납득시키려고 추구하는 사람이 / 우리 자신이기 때문에) / 핵심은 / 사실에 대한 이러한 종류의 탈진실적 관계가 일어난다는 것이다. / 우리가 어떤 것을 주장하려고 할 때에만 / 진실 그 자체보다 우리에게 더 중요한

Oxford 사전의 정의를 보면, 탈진실이란 진실이 존재하지 않는다는 주장이 아니라, *사실이 우리의 정치적 관점에 종속되어 있다*는 주장임을 알게 된다. Oxford 사전의 정의는 탈진실이란 '*무엇인가*', 즉 때로는 감정이 사실보다 더 중요하다는 생각에 초점을 둔다. 하지만 그다음 질문은 그에 못지않게 중요한데, 그것은 도대체 *왜* 이런 일이 일어나는가이다. 어떤 사람은 아무런 이유 없이 분명하거나 쉽게 확인할 수 있는 사실에 반대하는 게 아니며, 그렇게 하는 것이 자신의 이익에 부합할 때 그렇게 한다. 어떤 사람의 믿음이 '불편한 사실'에 의해 위협받을 때, 때로는 그 사실에 이의를 제기하는 것이 선호된다. 이것은 (때로는 우리가 납득시키려고 추구하는 사람이 우리 자신이기 때문에) 의식적인 수준이나 무의식적인 수준에서 일어날 수 있지만, 핵심은 사실에 대한 이러한 종류의 탈진실적 관계가 우리가 <u>진실 그 자체보다 우리에게 더 중요한</u> 어떤 것을 주장하려고 할 때에만 일어난다는 것이다.

Why? 왜 정답일까?

'∼ he or she does so when it is to his or her advantage.'에서 탈진실 현상, 즉 사실이 개인의 정치적 관점에 종속되는 현상이 일어나는 까닭은 그것이 그 개인의 이익에 부합하기 때문임을 설명한다. 따라서 빈칸에 들어갈 말로 가장 적절한 것은 사실보다도 개인의 이익이 중시된다는 의미를 나타낸 ⑤ '진실 그 자체보다 우리에게 더 중요한'이다.

- **definition** ⓝ 정의, 의미
- **argue against** ∼에 반대하다
- **hold back** 억누르다
- **in need** 어려운 처지의
- **post-truth** 탈진실
- **to one's advantage** ∼에게 이득이 되는
- **give way to** ∼에 못 이기다, 양보하다

구문 풀이

> **12행** This <u>can happen</u> at either a conscious or unconscious level
> 　　　　　　　자동사　　　　　「either+A or+B : A, B 둘 중 하나」
> (since sometimes the person [we are seeking to convince] is
> 　∼이기 때문에
> ourselves), / but the point is that this sort of post-truth relationship
> 　　　　　　　　　　　　　핵심은 ∼이다　　　　　　주어
> to facts occurs only when we are seeking to assert something
> 자동사　　오로지 ∼할 때에만
> [that is more important to us than the truth itself].
> 주격 관계대명사　　　　　　　↳ 강조

★★★ 1등급 대비 고난도 2점 문제

07 스포츠 저널리스트의 전문성 입지	정답률 43% | 정답 ②

다음 빈칸에 들어갈 말로 가장 적절한 것을 고르오.

① paid – 돈을 받지　　　　　✔ admired – 존경받지
③ censored – 검열되지　　　　④ challenged – 의문이 제기되지
⑤ discussed – 논의되지

There is something deeply paradoxical / about the professional status of sports journalism, / especially in the medium of print.
매우 역설적인 것이 있다. / 스포츠 저널리즘의 전문적 지위에 관해서, / 특히 인쇄 매체에서

In discharging their usual responsibilities of description and commentary, / reporters' accounts of sports events / are eagerly consulted by sports fans, / while in their broader journalistic role of covering sport in its many forms, / sports journalists are among the most visible of all contemporary writers.
설명하고 논평하는 통상적인 직무를 이행할 때, / 스포츠 경기에 관한 기자들의 설명은 / 스포츠 팬들에 의해 열심히 참고되는 한편, / 여러 형식으로 스포츠를 취재하는 더 폭넓은 저널리스트의 역할을 수행하는 데 있어, / 스포츠 저널리스트는 동시대의 모든 작가 중에서 가장 눈에 띄는 이들 가운데 있다.

The ruminations of the elite class of 'celebrity' sports journalists / are much sought after by the major newspapers, / their lucrative contracts being the envy of colleagues / in other 'disciplines' of journalism.
'유명인급' 스포츠 저널리스트 중 엘리트 계층의 생각은 / 주요 신문사들이 많이 원하고, / 이들의 돈을 많이 버는 계약은 동료들의 선망 대상이 된다. / 저널리즘의 다른 '부문'에 있는

Yet sports journalists do not have a standing in their profession / that corresponds to the size of their readerships or of their pay packets, / with the old saying (now reaching the status of cliché) / that sport is the 'toy department of the news media' / still readily to hand / as a dismissal of the worth of what sports journalists do.

그러나 스포츠 저널리스트는 전문직 지위를 누리지 못한다. / 독자 수나 급여 액수의 크기에 상응하는 / (이제는 상투적인 문구의 입지에 이른) 옛말과 더불어, / 스포츠는 '뉴스 매체의 장난감 부서'라는 / 여전히 쉽게 건네지는 / 이들이 하는 일의 가치를 묵살하는 말로

This reluctance to take sports journalism / seriously produces the paradoxical outcome / that sports newspaper writers are much read but little admired.
이렇게 스포츠 저널리즘을 진지하게 여기기를 꺼리는 것은 / 진정 역설적인 결과를 낳는다. / 스포츠 신문 작가들이 많이 읽히면서도 거의 존경받지 못하는

스포츠 저널리즘의 전문적 지위에 관해서, 특히 인쇄 매체에서 매우 역설적인 것이 있다. 설명하고 논평하는 통상적인 직무를 이행할 때, 스포츠 경기에 관한 기자들의 설명은 스포츠 팬들에 의해 열심히 참고되는 한편, 여러 형식으로 스포츠를 취재하는 더 폭넓은 저널리스트의 역할을 수행하는 데 있어, 스포츠 저널리스트는 동시대의 모든 작가 중에서 가장 눈에 띄는 이들 가운데 있다. '유명인급' 스포츠 저널리스트 중 엘리트 계층의 생각은 주요 신문사들이 많이 원하고, 이들의 돈을 많이 버는 계약은 저널리즘의 다른 '부문'에 있는 동료들의 선망 대상이 된다. 그러나 스포츠 저널리스트는 이들이 하는 일의 가치를 묵살하는 말로 여전히 쉽게 건네지는 '뉴스 매체의 장난감 부서'라는 (이제는 상투적인 문구의 입지에 이른) 옛말과 더불어, 독자 수나 급여 액수의 크기에 상응하는 전문직 지위를 누리지 못한다. 이렇게 스포츠 저널리즘을 진지하게 여기기를 꺼리는 것은 스포츠 신문 작가들이 많이 읽히면서도 거의 존경받지 못하는 역설적인 결과를 낳는다.

Why? 왜 정답일까?

스포츠 저널리스트들은 스포츠 취재에 있어 가장 많이 주목받고 큰 수익을 올리며, 이들의 기사 또한 스포츠 팬들에게 널리 읽히지만, 전문성 부분에서는 이 모든 것에 상응하는 입지를 누리지 못한다(Yet sports journalists do not have a standing in their profession ∼)는 내용의 글이다. 따라서 빈칸에 들어갈 말로 가장 적절한 것은 ② '존경받지(admired)'이다.

- **paradoxical** ⓐ 역설적인
- **medium** ⓝ 매체
- **responsibility** ⓝ 직무, 맡은 일, 책임
- **account** ⓝ 설명, 해석, 이야기
- **cover** ⓥ 보도하다, 취재하다, 다루다
- **contemporary** ⓐ 동시대의, 현대의
- **celebrity** ⓝ 유명 인사
- **lucrative** ⓐ 돈을 많이 버는, 수익성 있는
- **envy** ⓝ 부러움
- **standing** ⓝ 입지, 자리
- **readership** ⓝ 독자 수
- **cliché** ⓝ 상투적인 말
- **dismissal** ⓝ 무시, 묵살
- **take seriously** 진지하게 여기다
- **status** ⓝ 입지
- **discharge** ⓥ 이행하다
- **description** ⓝ 묘사
- **eagerly** ⓐⓓ 열정적으로
- **visible** ⓐ 눈에 띄는, (잘) 보이는
- **rumination** ⓝ 생각
- **seek after** ∼을 구하다, 찾다, 원하다
- **contract** ⓝ 계약
- **discipline** ⓝ 부문, 분야
- **correspond to** ∼에 상응하다
- **pay packet** 급여 액수
- **department** ⓝ 부서
- **reluctance** ⓝ (∼하기를) 꺼림, 마지못해 함
- **admire** ⓥ 존경하다

구문 풀이

> **8행** The ruminations of the elite class of 'celebrity' sports
> journalists are much sought after by the major newspapers,
> 　　　　　　　　　　　　구동사 seek after의 수동태
> their lucrative contracts being the envy of colleagues in other
> 　　의미상 주어　　　　　　　분사구문
> 'disciplines' of journalism.

★★ 문제 해결 꿀~팁 ★★

▶ 많이 틀린 이유는?
오답 중 특히 ①은 본문의 'a standing ∼ that corresponds to the size of ∼ their pay packets'과 반대되는 내용이다. 스포츠 기자들이 그들의 '급여'에 걸맞는 입지를 인정받지 못한다고 했는데 이들의 '급여가 적다'는 의미를 나타내는 **paid**가 정답일 수는 없다.

▶ 문제 해결 방법은?
Yet sports journalists do not have a standing in their profession이 결정적인 힌트이다. '전문성에 있어 입지가 없다'는 것은 이들이 자기 직업에 마땅히 받아야 할 '존중'이나 '인정'을 충분히 받지 못하고 있다는 의미이다. 빈칸 앞의 little(거의 ∼않다)이 부정어임을 염두에 둔다.

★★★ 1등급 대비 고난도 2점 문제

08 연민의 학습	정답률 26% | 정답 ③

다음 빈칸에 들어갈 말로 가장 적절한 것을 고르오.

① Creativity – 창의성　　　　② Relaxation – 이완

✔ Compassion – 연민   ④ Justification – 정당화
⑤ Empowerment – 권한 부여

In the Indian language of pali, / *mettā* means benevolence, kindness or tenderness.
인도 팔리어에서 / *mettā*는 자비심, 친절, 혹은 다정함을 의미한다.
It is one of the most important ideas in Buddhism.
그것은 불교에서 가장 중요한 관념 중 하나다.
Buddhism recommends a daily ritual meditation / (known as *mettā bhāvanā*) / to foster this attitude.
불교에서는 매일 의례적으로 하는 명상을 권한다. / (*mettā bhāvanā*로 알려진) / 이러한 태도를 기르기 위해
The meditation begins with a call / to think carefully every morning of an individual / with whom one tends to get irritated / or to whom one feels aggressive or cold / and — in place of one's normal hostile impulses — / to rehearse kindly messages / like 'I hope you will find peace' or 'I wish you to be free from suffering'.
명상은 요구로 시작한다. / 어떤 한 사람을 매일 아침 사려 깊게 생각하라는 / 짜증이 나게 하는 경향이 있는 / 또는 공격적인 혹은 냉담한 기분이 들게 하는 / 그리고 평소의 적대적인 충동 대신 / 친절한 메시지를 기꺼이 연습하라는 / '나는 당신이 평안을 찾길 바랍니다.' 또는 '나는 당신이 고통에서 벗어나기를 기원합니다.'와 같은
This practice can be extended outwards / ultimately to include pretty much everyone on Earth.
이 수행은 밖으로 확장되어 / 결국 지상의 거의 모든 사람을 포함할 수 있다.
The background assumption is / that, with the right stimulus, / our feelings towards people are not fixed and unalterable, / but open to deliberate change and improvement.
그 배경이 되는 가정은 ~이다. / 적절한 자극으로 / 사람들을 향한 우리의 감정이 고정되어 바뀔 수 없는 게 아니라 / 의도적인 변화와 개선의 여지가 있다는 것
Compassion is a learnable skill, / and we need to direct it / as much towards those / we are tempted to dismiss and detest / as to those we love.
연민은 배울 수 있는 기술이며, / 우리는 이것을 향하게 할 필요가 있다. / 사람을 향해서도 / 우리가 무시하고 혐오하고 싶은 마음이 생기는 / 우리가 사랑하는 사람에게만큼이나

인도 팔리어에서 *mettā*는 자비심, 친절, 혹은 다정함을 의미한다. 그것은 불교에서 가장 중요한 관념 중 하나다. 불교에서는 이러한 태도를 기르기 위해 매일 의례적으로 하는 (*mettā bhāvanā*로 알려진) 명상을 권한다. 명상은 짜증이 나게 하거나, 공격적인 혹은 냉담한 기분이 들게 하는 경향이 있는 어떤 한 사람을 매일 아침 사려 깊게 생각하고, 평소의 적대적인 충동 대신 '나는 당신이 평안을 찾길 바랍니다.' 또는 '나는 당신이 고통에서 벗어나기를 기원합니다.'와 같은 친절한 메시지를 기꺼이 연습하라는 요구로 시작한다. 이 수행은 밖으로 확장되어 결국 지상의 거의 모든 사람을 포함할 수 있다. 그 배경이 되는 가정은 사람들을 향한 우리의 감정이 고정되어 바뀔 수 없는 게 아니라 적절한 자극으로 의도적인 변화와 개선의 여지가 있다는 것이다. 연민은 배울 수 있는 기술이며, 우리가 사랑하는 사람에게만큼이나 우리가 무시하고 혐오하고 싶은 마음이 생기는 사람에게도 이것을 향하게 할 필요가 있다.

Why? 왜 정답일까?

첫 문장의 '자비심, 친절, 다정함(benevolence, kindness or tenderness)'이 키워드다. 불교에서는 이러한 마음을 기를 수 있도록 수행자들에게 평소 짜증이나 적대감을 느끼는 사람들에 대해 마음의 평화를 빌어주도록 권한다는 내용으로 보아, 빈칸에 들어갈 말로 가장 적절한 것은 ③ '연민'이다.

- benevolence ⓝ 자비
- tenderness ⓝ 다정함
- recommend ⓥ 권하다, 추천하다
- meditation ⓝ 명상
- attitude ⓝ 태도, 마음가짐
- tend ⓥ (~하는) 경향이 있다
- hostile ⓐ 적대적인
- rehearse ⓥ 연습하다
- extend ⓥ 확장하다
- stimulus ⓝ 자극
- deliberate ⓐ 의도적인, 계획적인
- be tempted to ~할 생각이 나다
- detest ⓥ 혐오하다
- kindness ⓝ 친절, 다정함
- Buddhism ⓝ 불교
- ritual ⓐ 의례적인
- foster ⓥ 기르다
- individual ⓝ 개인의
- irritated ⓐ 짜증이 난
- impulse ⓝ 충동
- suffering ⓝ 고통
- assumption ⓝ 가정
- unalterable ⓐ 바뀔 수 없는
- improvement ⓝ 개선
- dismiss ⓥ 무시하다, 일축하다
- compassion ⓝ 연민, 동정

구문 풀이

5행 The meditation begins with a call to think (carefully every
　　　　　　　　　　　　　　　형용사적 용법1　( ) : 부사구
morning) of an individual [with whom one tends to get irritated] or
　　　　선행사　　　　[ ] : 형용사절(an individual 수식)
[to whom one feels aggressive or cold] and — in place of one's
normal hostile impulses — to rehearse kindly messages like 'I hope
　　　　　　　　　　　　　　형용사적 용법2
you will find peace' or 'I wish you to be free from suffering'.

▶ 많이 틀린 이유는?
글에 명상(meditation)이라는 소재가 등장하므로 얼핏 보면 마음챙김, 휴식 등에 관한 내용으로 보여 ②를 고르기 쉽다. 하지만 명상을 하면서 어떤 말을 되뇌이는가가 중요하다.
▶ 문제 해결 방법은?
예시를 통해 힌트를 얻도록 한다. 우리를 화나거나 괴롭게 하는 사람들에 대해 평안해지라고('I hope you will find peace', 'I wish you to be free from suffering') 기도해주는 것은 '자비, 친절, 연민'을 그들에게 베푸는 것과 다름없다.

★★★ 1등급 대비 고난도 3점 문제

09　과학자와 예술가가 지향하는 현실　정답률 28% | 정답 ①

다음 빈칸에 들어갈 말로 가장 적절한 것을 고르시오. [3점]
✔ human beings must participate – 인간들이 참여해야만 하는
② objectivity should be maintained – 객관성이 유지되어야 하는
③ science and art need to harmonize – 과학과 예술이 조화를 이룰 필요가 있는
④ readers remain distanced from the arts – 독자가 예술로부터 떨어진 채로 있는
⑤ she is disengaged from her own subjectivity – 예술가가 자신의 주관성에서 벗어난

Whatever their differences, / scientists and artists begin with the same question: / *can you and I see the same thing the same way? / If so, how?*
과학자와 예술가의 차이점이 무엇이든, / 그들은 똑같은 질문으로 시작한다. / 당신과 내가 똑같은 것을 똑같은 방식으로 볼 수 있을까? / 만약 그렇다면 어떻게?
The scientific thinker looks for features of the thing / that can be stripped of subjectivity / — ideally, those aspects / that can be quantified / and whose values will thus never change from one observer to the next.
과학적 사고를 하는 사람은 사물의 특징을 찾는다. / 주관성이 박탈될 수 있는 / 즉 이상적으로는 그런 측면 / 정량화될 수 있고 / 그래서 그것의 가치가 관찰자마다 전혀 달라지지 않을
In this way, / he arrives at a reality / independent of all observers.
이런 식으로, / 그 사람은 현실에 도달한다. / 모든 관찰자로부터 독립적인
The artist, / on the other hand, / relies on the strength of her artistry / to effect a marriage / between her own subjectivity and that of her readers.
예술가는 / 다른 한편, / 자신의 예술가적 솜씨의 힘에 의지한다. / 결합을 이루기 위해 / 자기 자신의 주관성과 자기 독자의 주관성 간의
To a scientific thinker, / this must sound like magical thinking: / *you're saying you will imagine something so hard / it'll pop into someone else's head / exactly the way you envision it?*
과학적 사고를 하는 사람에게, / 이것은 틀림없이 마술적인 사고처럼 들릴 것이다. / 당신이 뭔가를 매우 열심히 상상한 나머지 / 다른 누군가의 머릿속에 그것이 떠오를 것이라는 말인가? / 당신이 그것을 머릿속으로 그린 그대로
The artist has sought the opposite of the scientist's observer-independent reality.
예술가는 과학자의 관찰자 독립적 현실과 정반대인 것을 추구해 왔다.
She creates a reality / dependent upon observers, / indeed a reality / in which human beings must participate / in order for it to exist at all.
예술가는 현실을 만들어 낸다. / 관찰자에게 의존하는 / 다시 말해 현실 / 인간들이 참여해야만 하는 / 그것이 존재할 수라도 있으려면

과학자와 예술가의 차이점이 무엇이든, 그들은 똑같은 질문, 즉 *당신과 내가 똑같은 것을 똑같은 방식으로 볼 수 있을까? 만약 그렇다면 어떻게?*라는 질문으로 시작한다. 과학적 사고를 하는 사람은 주관성이 박탈될 수 있는 사물의 특징, 즉 이상적으로는 정량화될 수 있고 그래서 그것의 가치가 관찰자마다 전혀 달라지지 않는 그런 측면을 찾는다. 이런 식으로, 그 사람은 모든 관찰자로부터 독립적인 현실에 도달한다. 다른 한편, 예술가는 자기 자신의 주관성과 자기 독자의 주관성 간의 결합을 이루기 위해 자신의 예술가적 솜씨의 힘에 의지한다. 과학적 사고를 하는 사람에게, 이것은 틀림없이 마술적인 사고처럼 들릴 것이다. 즉 당신이 뭔가를 매우 열심히 상상한 나머지 당신이 그것을 머릿속으로 그린 그대로 다른 누군가의 머릿속에 그것이 떠오를 것이라는 말인가? 예술가는 과학자의 관찰자 독립적 현실과 정반대인 것을 추구해 왔다. 예술가는 관찰자에게 의존하는 현실, 다시 말해 그것이 존재할 수라도 있으려면 인간들이 참여해야만 하는 현실을 만들어 낸다.

Why? 왜 정답일까?

과학과 예술은 모두 '대상을 똑같은 눈으로 볼 수 있을지'라는 질문으로 출발하지만, 과학은 객관성으로 향하고 예술은 주관적 시각의 결합을 추구한다는 내용이다. 특히 마지막 두 문장에서, 과학은 관찰자 독립적, 즉 관찰자와 누구든지 상관없는 '객관적' 현실을 추구하지만, 예술가는 '관찰자에 의존하는' 현실(a reality dependent upon observers)을 만들어낸다고 하는데, 이는 관찰자가 '함께' 예술가의 현실 만들기에 동

참한다는 의미로 볼 수 있다. 따라서 빈칸에 들어갈 말로 가장 적절한 것은 ① '인간들이 참여해야만 하는'이다.

- **begin with** ~로 시작하다
- **subjectivity** ⓝ 주관성
- **quantify** ⓥ 정량화하다
- **strength** ⓝ 힘, 강점
- **effect** ⓥ (어떤 결과를) 가져오다
- **pop into one's head** ~에게 불현듯 떠오르다
- **envision** ⓥ (머릿속에) 그리다
- **exist** ⓥ 존재하다
- **be disengaged from** ~에서 벗어나다
- **be stripped of** ~을 빼앗다
- **aspect** ⓝ 측면
- **on the other hand** 반면에
- **artistry** ⓝ 예술적 솜씨
- **magical** ⓐ 마법 같은
- **opposite** ⓝ 정반대
- **harmonize** ⓥ 조화되다

구문 풀이

1행 Whatever their differences (are), scientists and artists begin
복합관계대명사(무엇이 ~하든 간에)   생략
with the same question: *can you and I see the same thing the same*
동격(= the same question)
way? If so, how?

★★ 문제 해결 꿀~팁 ★★

▶ 많이 틀린 이유는?
똑같은 질문에 대해 과학과 예술이 답하는 방식이 다르므로, 둘을 구별하는 것이 핵심이다. ②의 '객관성'은 과학과 관련된 키워드인데, 빈칸에는 예술과 관련된 내용을 넣어야 한다.

▶ 문제 해결 방법은?
과학은 관찰자마다 달라지지 않은 객관적 특징을 찾지만, 예술은 '예술가와 관찰자의 주관적 시각을 서로 통합하는' 데 중점을 두고, '관찰자에 따라 달라지는' 현실을 구현한다고 한다. 이는 결국 관찰자가 예술적 실체 구축의 일부가 된다는 의미와 같다.

★★★ 1등급 대비 고난도 3점 문제

| 10 | 이상적인 음질에 대한 판단 | 정답률 24% | 정답 ① |

다음 빈칸에 들어갈 말로 가장 적절한 것을 고르시오. [3점]

✓① decrease in the perceptual worth of the sound
그 소리의 인지적 가치 저하
② failure to understand the original function of music
음악의 본래 기능을 이해하지 못하는 것
③ realization of more sophisticated musical inspiration
더 정교한 음악적 영감의 실현
④ agreement on ideal sound quality across generations
이상적 음질에 대한 세대 간의 합의
⑤ revival of listeners' preference for CD-quality audio
CD 음질 오디오에 대한 청자 선호의 부활

The ideal sound quality varies a lot / in step with technological and cultural changes.
이상적인 음질은 많이 달라진다. / 기술적 및 문화적 변화에 발맞춰
Consider, for instance, / the development of new digital audio formats / such as MP3 and AAC.
예를 들어, 생각해 보라. / 새로운 디지털 오디오 포맷들의 발달을 / MP3와 AAC와 같은
Various media feed us daily with data-compressed audio, / and some people rarely experience CD-quality (that is, *technical* quality) audio.
다양한 매체가 매일 우리에게 압축된 데이터 오디오를 제공하며 / 어떤 사람들은 좀처럼 CD 음질(즉, *기술적으로 우수한 음질*)의 오디오를 경험하지 못한다.
This tendency could lead to a new generation of listeners / with other sound quality preferences.
이런 추세가 새로운 청자 세대를 이끌어 낼 수도 있다. / 다른 음질 선호도를 지닌
Research by Stanford University professor Jonathan Berger / adds fuel to this thesis.
Stanford 대학 교수인 Jonathan Berger의 연구가 / 이 논지에 불을 지핀다.
Berger tested first-year university students' preferences for MP3s / annually for ten years.
Berger는 대학교 1학년 학생들의 MP3에 대한 선호도를 측정했다. / 10년 동안 매년
He reports / that each year more and more students / come to prefer MP3s to CD-quality audio.
그는 말한다. / 매년 점점 더 많은 학생들이 / CD 음질 오디오보다 MP3를 선호하게 된다고
These findings indicate / that listeners gradually become accustomed to data-compressed formats / and change their listening preferences accordingly.
이러한 발견들은 보여 준다. / 청자들이 점차 압축된 데이터 포맷에 익숙해지며, / 그에 맞춰 그들의 듣기 선호도를 바꾼다는 것을
The point is / that while technical improvents strive toward increased sound quality / in a technical sense (e.g., higher resolution and greater bit rate), / listeners' expectations do not necessarily follow the same path.

핵심은 / 기술적 향상이 높아진 음질을 얻으려고 애쓰는 반면에, / (예를 들어, 더 높은 선명도와 더 큰 비트 전송률 같은) 기술적 의미에서 / 청자들의 기대는 반드시 같은 길을 따르는 것은 아니라는 점이다.

As a result, / "improved" *technical* digital sound quality / may in some cases lead to a decrease / in the perceptual worth of the sound.
결과적으로 / '향상된' 기술적으로 우수한 디지털 음질이 / 어떤 경우에는 저하를 초래할 수도 있다. / 그 소리의 인지적 가치에 있어서의

이상적인 음질은 기술적 및 문화적 변화에 발맞춰 많이 달라진다. 예를 들어, MP3와 AAC와 같은 새로운 디지털 오디오 포맷들의 발달을 생각해 보라. 다양한 매체가 매일 우리에게 압축된 데이터 오디오를 제공하며 어떤 사람들은 좀처럼 CD 음질(즉, 기술적으로 우수한 음질)의 오디오를 경험하지 못한다. 이런 추세가 다른 음질 선호도를 지닌 새로운 청자 세대를 이끌어 낼 수도 있다. Stanford 대학 교수인 Jonathan Berger의 연구가 이 논지에 불을 지핀다. Berger는 10년 동안 매년 대학교 1학년 학생들의 MP3에 대한 선호도를 측정했다. 그는 매년 점점 더 많은 학생들이 CD 음질 오디오보다 MP3를 선호하게 된다고 말한다. 이러한 발견들은 청자들이 점차 압축된 데이터 포맷에 익숙해지며, 그에 맞춰 그들의 듣기 선호도를 바꾼다는 것을 보여 준다. 핵심은 기술적 향상이 (예를 들어, 더 높은 선명도와 더 큰 비트 전송률 같은) 기술적 의미에서 높아진 음질을 얻으려고 애쓰는 반면에, 청자들의 기대는 반드시 같은 길을 따르는 것은 아니라는 점이다. 결과적으로 어떤 경우에는 '향상된' 기술적으로 우수한 디지털 음질이 그 소리의 인지적 가치 저하를 초래할 수도 있다.

Why? 왜 정답일까?

'The point is that while technical improvements strive toward increased sound quality in a technical sense ~, listeners' expectations do not necessarily follow the same path.'에서 기술은 최고의 음질을 추구하지만 청자들은 반드시 같은 방향을 지향하지는 않는다고 했다. 즉 과거 CD에 비해 음질 면에서 더 떨어지는 다양한 디지털 음원에 익숙해져 있는 현대의 청자들은 반드시 기술적으로 최상의 음질만을 추구하지는 않는다는 것이다. 따라서 빈칸에 들어갈 말로 가장 적절한 것은 기술적으로 더 우수한 디지털 음원을 듣더라도 오히려 그 음질에 대한 평가는 더 떨어질 수 있다는 의미를 완성하는 ① '그 소리의 인지적 가치 저하'이다.

- **in step with** 발맞추어, 보조를 맞추어
- **add fuel to** ~에 불을 지피다
- **accustomed to** ~에 익숙한
- **strive toward** ~을 얻으려고 노력하다
- **perceptual** ⓐ 지각의, 인지의
- **preference** ⓝ 선호
- **gradually** ⓐⓓ 점차
- **accordingly** ⓐⓓ 그에 따라
- **resolution** ⓝ 선명도, 해상도
- **sophisticated** ⓐ 정교한, 세련된

구문 풀이

16행 The point is that (while technical improvements strive toward
주어   동사   접속사(~것) 접속사(~한 반면에)
increased sound quality in a technical sense (e.g., higher resolution
and greater bit rate)), listeners' expectations do not necessarily follow
( ):부사절   주어   동사구
the same path.

★★ 문제 해결 꿀~팁 ★★

▶ 많이 틀린 이유는?
음질에 대한 소비자의 판단이라는 생소한 소재에 관한 글이다. 음질이 아무리 기술적으로 우수한 수준에 이르더라도, 압축된 음원 질에 익숙해져 있는 소비자들은 좋은 음질에 크게 반응하지 않을 수도 있다는 내용이 주를 이룬다. 세대 간 합의 또는 차이에 대해서는 주요하게 언급되지 않으므로 ④는 답으로 부적절하다. ⑤는 소비자들이 CD 음질, 즉 최고급 음질에 대한 선호를 다시 보일 것이라는 내용인데, 빈칸 앞에 따르면 소비자들의 기대는 기술적 향상과 같은 방향이 '아닐' 수도 있다고 한다. 이는 소비자들이 반드시 기술적 향상을 원하지는 않을 수도 있다는 의미이므로, CD 음질에 대한 소비자 선호가 부활될 것이라는 의미의 ⑤는 주제와 상충한다.

▶ 문제 해결 방법은?
'~ listeners' expectations do not necessarily follow the same path.'에서 the same path는 맥락상 'strive toward increased sound quality'를 가리킨다. 즉 소비자의 기대는 '음질 향상을 위한 노력'과 일치하지 않을 수도 있다는 것이 글의 핵심 내용이다.

★★★ 1등급 대비 고난도 3점 문제

| 11 | 역사적 진술의 특징 | 정답률 28% | 정답 ② |

다음 빈칸에 들어갈 말로 가장 적절한 것을 고르시오. [3점]

① criteria for evaluating historical representations
역사적 진술을 평가하는 기준

DAY 08

✓ certainty and precision seemingly achieved already
이미 획득한 것처럼 보이는 확실성과 정확성
③ possibilities of alternative interpretations of an event
어떤 사건에 대한 대안적 해석의 가능성
④ coexistence of multiple viewpoints in historical writing
역사 저술에서 다수의 관점 공존
⑤ correctness and reliability of historical evidence collected
수집된 역사적 증거의 정확성과 신뢰성

Precision and determinacy are a necessary requirement / for all meaningful scientific debate, / and progress in the sciences is, to a large extent, / the ongoing process of achieving ever greater precision.
정확성과 확정성은 필요조건이며, / 모든 의미 있는 과학 토론을 위한 / 과학에서의 발전은 상당 부분, / 훨씬 더 높은 정확성을 달성하는 계속 진행 중인 과정이다.

But / historical representation / puts a premium on a proliferation of representations, / hence not on the refinement of one representation / but on the production of an ever more varied set of representations.
그러나 / 역사적 진술은 / 진술의 증식을 중요시한다. / 그러므로 한 가지 진술의 정제가 아닌, / 훨씬 더 다양한 진술 집합의 생성에

Historical insight is not a matter / of a continuous "narrowing down" of previous options, / not of an approximation of the truth, / but, on the contrary, is an "explosion" of possible points of view.
역사적 통찰은 문제가 아니라 / 이전에 선택한 것들을 지속적으로 '좁혀 가는' 것의 / 즉 진리에 근접해가는 것의 / 반대로 가능한 관점들의 '폭발적 증가'이다.

It therefore aims / at the unmasking of previous illusions of determinacy and precision / by the production of new and alternative representations, / rather than at achieving truth / by a careful analysis of what was right and wrong / in those previous representations.
그러므로 그것은 목표로 한다. / 확정성과 정확성에 대한 이전의 환상의 정체를 드러내는 것 / 새롭고 대안적인 진술의 생성에 의해 / 진리를 획득하는 것이 아니라, / 무엇이 옳고 틀렸는지에 대한 신중한 분석에 의해 / 이전의 진술에서

And from this perspective, / the development of historical insight / may indeed be regarded by the outsider / as a process of creating ever more confusion, / a continuous questioning of certainty and precision / seemingly achieved already, / rather than, / as in the sciences, / an ever greater approximation to the truth.
그리고 이러한 관점에서 보면, / 역사적 통찰의 발전은 / 외부인에게는 진정 여겨질 수도 있다. / 훨씬 더 큰 혼란을 만들어내는 과정으로 / 즉 확실성과 정확성에 대한 지속적인 의문 제기로 / 이미 획득한 것처럼 보이는 / ~하기보다는 / 과학에서처럼 / 진리에 훨씬 더 많이 근접해가기

정확성과 확정성은 모든 의미 있는 과학 토론을 위한 필요조건이며, 과학에서의 발전은 상당 부분, 훨씬 더 높은 정확성을 달성하는 계속 진행 중인 과정이다. 그러나 역사적 진술은 진술의 증식을 중요시하는데, 이는 한 가지 진술의 정제가 아닌, 훨씬 더 다양한 진술 집합의 생성에 중요성을 두는 것이다. 역사적 통찰은 이전에 선택한 것들을 지속적으로 '좁혀 가는' 것의 문제, 즉 진리에 근접해가는 문제가 아니라, 반대로 가능한 관점들의 '폭발적 증가'이다. 그러므로 그것은 이전의 진술에서 무엇이 옳고 틀렸는지에 대한 신중한 분석에 의해 진리를 획득하는 것이 아니라, 새롭고 대안적인 진술의 생성에 의해 확정성과 정확성에 대해 이전에 가진 환상의 정체를 드러내는 것을 목표로 한다. 그리고 이러한 관점에서 보면, 역사적 통찰의 발전은 외부인에게는 과학에서처럼 진리에 훨씬 더 많이 근접해가기보다는 훨씬 더 큰 혼란을 만들어내는 과정, 즉 이미 획득한 것처럼 보이는 확실성과 정확성에 대한 지속적인 의문 제기로 진정 여겨질 수도 있다.

Why? 왜 정답일까?

과학적 진술은 정확성과 확정성을 향해 나아가지만 역사적 진술은 진술의 증식을 추구하므로, 이전에 논의된 진술의 범위를 계속해서 좁혀가기보다는 다른 관점을 찾는 것을 중요시한다는 내용의 글이다. 'It therefore aims at the unmasking of previous illusions of determinacy and precision ~'에서 그리하여 역사적 토론에서는 이전의 진술이 지녔던 정확성과 확정성의 '환상'을 또 다른 진술로 밝히는 것이 목표가 된다고 했다. 이를 근거로 보아, 빈칸을 포함한 마지막 문장은 '이미 정확하고 확정적이라고 여겨졌던' 진술이 계속해서 시험대에 오르며 더 큰 혼란을 만들어내는 것처럼 보일 수도 있다는 결론이 되어야 자연스럽다. 따라서 빈칸에 들어갈 말로 가장 적절한 것은 ② '이미 획득한 것처럼 보이는 확실성과 정확성'이다.

● precision ⓝ 정확성	● determinacy ⓝ 확정성
● meaningful ⓐ 의미 있는, 중요한	● progress ⓝ 발전, 진보
● to a large extent 상당 부분	● ongoing ⓐ 진행 중인
● representation ⓝ 진술, 표현	● put a premium on ~에 중요성을 두다
● refinement ⓝ 정제, 정련	● varied ⓐ 다양한
● continuous ⓐ 계속되는, 지속적인	● narrow down 좁히다, 줄이다
● approximation ⓝ 근접	● explosion ⓝ 폭발(적 증가)
● unmask ⓥ 정체를 밝히다, 가면을 벗기다	● confusion ⓝ 혼란, 혼동
● criterion ⓝ 기준	● coexistence ⓝ 공존

구문 풀이

12행 It therefore aims {at the unmasking of previous illusions of determinacy and precision by the production of new and alternative representations}, rather than {at achieving truth by a careful analysis
{A} + rather than + {B} : {B}라기보다 {A}인
of what was right and wrong in those previous representations}.
의문사(무엇)

★★ 문제 해결 꿀~팁 ★★

▶ 많이 틀린 이유는?
정확성과 확정성이라는 두 가지 키워드와 관련해 과학적 진술과 역사적 진술의 특성을 설명한 글로, 내용뿐 아니라 구문과 단어도 까다로워 이해하기가 쉽지 않다. 최다 오답인 ①의 경우 역사적 진술을 평가하는 '기준'을 언급하고 있는데, 글에서 진술에 대한 평가가 이루어지는 상황과 그 기준에 관해서는 제시되지 않았다.

▶ 문제 해결 방법은?
글에 따르면 과학적 진술은 정확성과 확정성으로 나아가기 위해 기존 진술의 범위를 계속 '좁혀 나가지만', 역사적 진술은 기존과 다른 진술의 등장과 대안의 '폭발적 증가'를 허용한다. 즉 기존 진술의 정확성과 확정성을 강화하거나 발전시키면서 계속해서 같은 흐름의 논의를 진행하기보다는, 기존 진술의 '정확성에 대한 환상을 깨고 (unmasking of previous illusions of determinacy and precision)' 다른 관점의 가능성을 탐색하는 것이 역사적 논의라는 것이다.

★★★ 1등급 대비 고난도 3점 문제

12 철학자들의 말을 행동으로 옮겨보기   정답률 42% | 정답 ①

다음 빈칸에 들어갈 말로 가장 적절한 것을 고르시오. [3점]

✓ put them into practice - 그것들을 실행에 옮기는
② keep your writings to yourself - 여러분의 글을 혼자 간직하는
③ combine oral and written traditions - 말과 글로 된 전통을 결합하는
④ compare philosophical theories - 철학 이론을 비교하는
⑤ avoid borrowing them - 그것들을 차용하기를 피하는

One of the criticisms of Stoicism / by modern translators and teachers / is the amount of repetition.
스토아 철학에 대한 비판 중 하나는 / 현대 번역가들과 교사들에 의한 / 반복의 정도이다.

Marcus Aurelius, for example, / has been dismissed by academics / as not being original / because his writing resembles that of other, earlier Stoics.
예를 들어, Marcus Aurelius는 / 학자들에게 무시당했다. / 독창적이지 않다고 / 그의 글이 다른 앞선 스토아 철학자들의 글과 닮았기 때문에

This criticism misses the point.
이러한 비판은 핵심을 놓친다.

Even before Marcus's time, / Seneca was well aware / that there was a lot of borrowing and overlap among the philosophers.
Marcus 시대 이전에도 / Seneca는 잘 알고 있었다. / 철학자들 사이에 많은 차용과 중복이 있다는 것을

That's because real philosophers weren't concerned with authorship, / but only what worked.
그것은 진정한 철학자들이 원저자라는 것에 관심을 두지 않고 / 오직 효과가 있는 것에만 관심을 두었기 때문이다.

More important, / they believed / that what was said mattered less / than what was done.
더 중요한 것은, / 그들이 믿었다는 점이다. / 말로 한 것이 덜 중요하다고 / 행동으로 한 것보다

And this is true now as it was then.
그리고 이것은 그때처럼 지금도 사실이다.

You're welcome to take all of the words of the great philosophers / and use them to your own liking / (they're dead; they don't mind).
여러분은 위대한 철학자들의 모든 말을 가져다가 / 여러분의 취향에 맞게 사용해도 된다 / (그들은 죽었으니 개의치 않는다).

Feel free to make adjustments and improvements / as you like.
맘껏 수정하고 개선하라. / 여러분이 원하는 대로

Adapt them to the real conditions of the real world.
그것을 실제 세계의 실제 여건에 맞게 적용하라.

The way to prove / that you truly understand what you speak and write, / that you truly are original, / is to put them into practice.
증명하는 방법은 / 여러분이 직접 말하고 쓴 것을 진짜로 이해하고 있다는 것, / 자신이 진정으로 독창적임을 / 그것들을 실행에 옮기는 것이다.

현대 번역가들과 교사들이 스토아 철학을 비판하는 것 중 하나는 반복의 정도이다. 예를 들어, Marcus Aurelius는 그의 글이 다른 앞선 스토아 철학자들의 글과 닮았기 때문에 독창적이지 않다고 학자들에게 무시당했다. 이러한 비판은 핵심을 놓친다. Marcus 시대 이전에도 Seneca는 철학자들 사이에 많은 차

용과 중복이 있다는 것을 잘 알고 있었다. 그것은 진정한 철학자들이 원저라는 것에 관심을 두지 않고 오직 효과가 있는 것에만 관심을 두었기 때문이다. 더 중요한 것은, 그들은 말로 한 것이 행동으로 한 것보다 덜 중요하다고 믿었다는 점이다. 그리고 이것은 그때처럼 지금도 사실이다. 원한다면 위대한 철학자들의 모든 말을 가져다가 자신의 취향에 맞게 사용해도 된다(그들은 죽었으니 개의치 않는다). 원하는 대로 맘껏 수정하고 개선하라. 그것을 실제 세계의 실제 여건에 맞게 적용하라. 여러분이 직접 말하고 쓴 것을 진짜로 이해하고 있다는 것, 자신이 진정으로 독창적임을 증명하는 방법은 그것들을 실행에 옮기는 것이다.

Why? 왜 정답일까?

철학자들의 말을 현실에 맞게 수정하고 적용하고 사용해보라(You're welcome to take all of the words of the great philosophers and use them to your own liking ~. / Adapt them to the real conditions of the real world.)는 내용이므로, 빈칸에 들어갈 말로 가장 적절한 것은 ① '그것들을 실행에 옮기는'이다.

- translator ⓝ 번역가
- overlap ⓝ 중복 ⓥ 겹치다
- authorship ⓝ (원)저자
- adjustment ⓝ 조정, 수정, 적응
- put A into practice A를 실천하다
- dismiss ⓥ 묵살하다, 무시하다
- concerned with ~에 관심을 둔
- to one's own liking ~이 좋을 대로
- improvement ⓝ 개선, 향상

구문 풀이

2행 Marcus Aurelius, for example, has been dismissed by
　　　　　　　　　　　　　　　　　　　　　　현재완료 수동태
academics as not being original because his writing resembles
　　　　　　　　　　동명사의 부정(not + 동명사)
that of other, earlier Stoics.
지시대명사(= writing)

★★ 문제 해결 꿀~팁 ★★

▶ 많이 틀린 이유는?
다른 철학자들의 주장과 비슷한 글을 써서 비판을 받았다는 사례를 보고 ②와 같이 '글을 혼자 간직해야 한다'는 결론을 내리면 안 된다.

▶ 문제 해결 방법은?
글에 명령문이 나온다면 글의 요지와 직결된다. 즉 'Feel free to ~. Adapt ~.'가 정답의 결정적 근거이다.

DAY 09　　　빈칸 추론 09

01 ③	02 ②	03 ①	04 ②	05 ②
06 ③	07 ①	08 ②	09 ①	10 ⑤
11 ②	12 ①			

01 기억의 사회적 공유　　　　　정답률 54% | 정답 ③

다음 빈칸에 들어갈 말로 가장 적절한 것을 고르시오.

① biased – 편향된
② illegal – 불법적인
✓ repetitive – 반복되는
④ temporary – 일시적인
⑤ rational – 합리적인

Finkenauer and Rimé investigated the memory / of the unexpected death of Belgium's King Baudouin in 1993 / in a large sample of Belgian citizens.
Finkenauer와 Rimé는 기억을 조사했다. / 1993년 벨기에 왕 Baudouin의 예기치 못한 죽음에 대한 / 표본으로 추출된 많은 벨기에 시민들을 대상으로

The data revealed / that the news of the king's death / had been widely socially shared.
그 자료는 나타냈다. / 왕의 죽음에 대한 소식이 / 널리 사회적으로 공유되었다는 것을

By talking about the event, / people gradually constructed / a social narrative and a collective memory / of the emotional event.
그 사건에 관해 이야기함으로써 / 사람들은 서서히 구축했다. / 사회적 이야기와 집단 기억을 / 그 감정적 사건의

At the same time, / they consolidated their own memory of the personal circumstances / in which the event took place, / an effect known as "flashbulb memory."
동시에 / 그들은 개인적 상황에 대한 자신들의 기억을 공고히 했는데, / 그 사건이 발생했던 / 그것은 '섬광 기억'으로 알려진 효과이다.

The more an event is socially shared, / the more it will be fixed in people's minds.
한 사건이 사회적으로 더 많이 공유되면 될수록, / 그것은 사람들 마음속에 더 많이 고착될 것이다.

Social sharing may in this way help / to counteract some natural tendency / people may have.
사회적 공유는 이런 식으로 도움이 될 수도 있다. / 어떤 자연적인 성향을 중화시키는 데 / 사람들이 갖고 있을 수 있는

Naturally, / people should be driven / to "forget" undesirable events.
자연스럽게 / 사람들은 이끌릴 것이다. / 바람직하지 않은 사건을 '잊도록'

Thus, / someone who just heard a piece of bad news / often tends initially to deny what happened.
그래서 / 방금 어떤 나쁜 소식을 들은 어떤 사람은 / 발생한 일을 처음에는 흔히 부인하고 싶어 한다.

The repetitive social sharing of the bad news / contributes to realism.
나쁜 소식의 반복되는 사회적 공유는 / 현실성에 기여한다.

Finkenauer와 Rimé는 표본으로 추출된 많은 벨기에 시민들을 대상으로 1993년 벨기에 왕 Baudouin의 예기치 못한 죽음에 대한 기억을 조사했다. 그 자료는 왕의 죽음에 대한 소식이 널리 사회적으로 공유되었다는 것을 나타냈다. 그 사건에 관해 이야기함으로써 사람들은 서서히 그 감정적 사건의 사회적 이야기와 집단 기억을 구축했다. 동시에 그들은 그 사건이 발생했던 개인적 상황에 대한 자신들의 기억을 공고히 했는데, 그것은 '섬광 기억'으로 알려진 효과이다. 한 사건이 사회적으로 더 많이 공유되면 될수록, 그것은 사람들 마음속에 더 많이 고착될 것이다. 사회적 공유는 이런 식으로 사람들이 갖고 있을 수 있는 어떤 자연적인 성향을 중화시키는 데 도움이 될 수도 있다. 자연스럽게 사람들은 바람직하지 않은 사건을 '잊도록' 이끌릴 것이다. 그래서 방금 어떤 나쁜 소식을 들은 어떤 사람은 발생한 일을 처음에는 흔히 부인하고 싶어 한다. 나쁜 소식의 반복되는 사회적 공유는 현실성에 기여한다.

Why? 왜 정답일까?

'The more an event is socially shared, the more it will be fixed in people's minds.'에서 한 사건에 대한 기억은 더 많이 공유될수록 더 공고해진다고 이야기하므로, 빈칸에 들어갈 말로 가장 적절한 것은 ③ '반복되는'이다.

- unexpected ⓐ 예기치 못한
- gradually ⓐd 서서히
- at the same time 동시에
- flashbulb memory ⓝ 섬광 기억
- tendency ⓝ 성향, 경향
- undesirable ⓐ 바람직하지 않은
- deny ⓥ 부인하다, 부정하다
- reveal ⓥ 드러내다, 밝히다
- narrative ⓝ 이야기
- consolidate ⓥ 굳히다, 공고히 하다
- counteract ⓥ 중화시키다, 대항하다
- naturally ⓐd 당연히, 자연스럽게
- initially ⓐd 처음에
- contribute to ~에 기여하다

- realism ⓝ 현실성, 현실주의
- biased ⓐ 편향된
- temporary ⓐ 일시적인

구문 풀이

7행 At the same time, they consolidated their own memory of the personal circumstances [in which the event took place], (which is) an effect [known as "flashbulb memory."]

(선행사 / =where / 자동사 / 생략(계속적 용법) / ~라고 알려진)

02 공간을 기능별로 분화하는 동물의 특성

정답률 65% | 정답 ②

다음 빈칸에 들어갈 말로 가장 적절한 것을 고르시오.

① an interest in close neighbors – 가까운 이웃에 대한 관심
② a neat functional organization – 정돈된 기능적 체계
③ a stock of emergency supplies – 비상 용품의 비축량
④ a distance from potential rivals – 잠재적 경쟁자로부터의 거리
⑤ a strictly observed daily routine – 엄격하게 지켜지는 일상

More than just *having* territories, / animals also *partition* them.
그저 영역을 *갖는* 것을 넘어서 / 동물은 영역을 *분할하기도* 한다.
And this insight turned out / to be particularly useful for zoo husbandry.
그리고 이러한 통찰은 밝혀졌다. / 동물원 관리에 특히 유용한 것으로
An animal's territory has an internal arrangement / that Heini Hediger compared to the inside of a person's house.
동물의 영역에는 내부 배치가 있다. / Heini Hediger가 사람의 집 내부에 비유한
Most of us assign separate functions to separate rooms, / but even if you look at a one-room house / you will find the same internal specialization.
우리 대부분은 방마다 별도의 기능을 할당하지만, / 여러분이 원룸 주택을 살펴봐도 / 여러분은 내부의 동일한 분화를 발견할 것이다.
In a cabin or a mud hut, / or even a Mesolithic cave from 30,000 years ago, / this part is for cooking, / that part is for sleeping; / this part is for making tools and weaving, / that part is for waste.
오두막이나 진흙 오두막 안에 / 혹은 심지어 3만년 전의 중석기 시대의 동굴 안에도, / 이 부분은 요리를 위한 곳이고, / 저 부분은 잠을 자기 위한 곳이며, / 이 부분은 도구 제작과 직조를 위한 곳이고, / 저 부분은 폐기물을 위한 곳이다.
We keep a neat functional organization.
우리는 정돈된 기능적 체계를 유지한다.
To a varying extent, / other animals do the same.
다양한 정도로, / 다른 동물들도 같은 행동을 한다.
A part of an animal's territory is for eating, / a part for sleeping, / a part for swimming or wallowing, / a part may be set aside for waste, / depending on the species of animal.
동물의 영역 중 일부는 먹기 위한 곳이고, / 일부는 잠을 자기 위한 곳이며, / 일부는 헤엄치거나 뒹굴기 위한 곳이고, / 일부는 폐기물을 위해 남겨두는 부분이 있을 수 있다. / 동물의 종에 따라

동물은 그저 영역을 *갖는* 것을 넘어서 영역을 *분할하기도* 한다. 그리고 이러한 통찰은 동물원 관리에 특히 유용한 것으로 밝혀졌다. 동물의 영역에는 Heini Hediger가 사람의 집 내부에 비유한 내부 배치가 있다. 우리 대부분은 방마다 별도의 기능을 할당하지만, 원룸 주택을 살펴봐도 (집) 내부의 동일한 분화를 발견할 것이다. 오두막이나 진흙 오두막, 혹은 심지어 3만년 전의 중석기 시대의 동굴 안에도, 이 부분은 요리를 위한 곳이고, 저 부분은 잠을 자기 위한 곳이며, 이 부분은 도구 제작과 직조를 위한 곳이고, 저 부분은 폐기물을 위한 곳이라는 구분이 있다. 우리는 정돈된 기능적 체계를 유지한다. 다양한 정도로, 다른 동물들도 같은 행동을 한다. 동물의 종에 따라, 동물의 영역 중 일부는 먹기 위한 곳이고, 일부는 잠을 자기 위한 곳이며, 일부는 헤엄치거나 뒹굴기 위한 곳이고, 일부는 폐기물을 위해 남겨두는 부분이 있을 수 있다.

Why? 왜 정답일까?

첫 문장에서 동물은 영역을 분화하는(*partition*) 습성이 있다고 언급한 뒤, 사람이 사는 공간과 동물의 거주 공간을 예로 들어 영역별로 특정한 기능이 부여되어 있음을 설명하고 있다. 따라서 빈칸에 들어갈 말로 가장 적절한 것은 이 기능별로 '분화'된 체계를 다른 말로 표현한 ② '정돈된 기능적 체계'이다.

- territory ⓝ 영역, 영토
- partition ⓥ 분할하다
- insight ⓝ 통찰력
- useful ⓐ 유용한
- husbandry ⓝ 관리
- internal ⓐ 내부의
- arrangement ⓝ 배치
- compare ⓥ 비유하다, 비교하다
- separate ⓐ 별개의 ⓥ 분리하다
- function ⓝ 기능
- specialization ⓝ 분화, 전문화
- cabin ⓝ 오두막
- hut ⓝ 오두막
- Mesolithic ⓐ 중석기의
- weave ⓥ (직물을) 짜다
- waste ⓝ 폐기물, 쓰레기
- wallow ⓥ 뒹굴다
- set aside ~을 떼어두다, 따로 마련하다
- depending on ~에 따라
- neat ⓐ 정돈된, 단정한
- strictly ad 엄격하게
- daily routine 일상

구문 풀이

12행 A part of an animal's territory is for eating, a part (is) for sleeping, a part (is) for swimming or wallowing, a part may be set aside for waste, depending on the species of animal.

(생략(중복) / ~에 따라)

03 신피질의 특징

정답률 39% | 정답 ①

다음 빈칸에 들어갈 말로 가장 적절한 것을 고르시오.

① having some built-in assumptions about the world
세상에 대한 어떤 내재된 가정을 가졌지만
② causing conflicts between genes and environments
유전자와 환경 사이의 갈등을 일으키지만
③ being able to efficiently reprocess prior knowledge
효율적으로 사전 지식을 재처리할 수 있지만
④ controlling the structure and processing power of the brain
뇌의 구조와 처리 능력을 통제하지만
⑤ fighting persistently against the determined world of genes
결정되어 있는 유전자의 세계와 끊임없이 싸우지만

When you are born, / your neocortex knows almost nothing.
여러분이 태어날 때, / 여러분의 신피질은 거의 아무것도 모른다.
It doesn't know any words, / what buildings are like, / how to use a computer, / or what a door is and how it moves on hinges.
그것은 어떠한 단어도 알지 못한다. / 건물이 어떤지, / 컴퓨터를 어떻게 사용하는지, / 혹은 문이 무엇이며 경첩에서 어떻게 움직이는지를
It has to learn countless things.
그것은 무수한 것을 배워야 한다.
The overall structure of the neocortex / is not random.
신피질의 전체적인 구조는 / 무작위가 아니다.
Its size, / the number of regions it has, / and how they are connected together / is largely determined by our genes.
신피질의 크기, / 신피질에 있는 영역의 수, / 그리고 어떻게 그 영역들이 함께 연결되어 있는지는 / 우리의 유전자에 의해 주로 결정된다.
For example, / genes determine / what parts of the neocortex are connected to the eyes, / what other parts are connected to the ears, / and how those parts connect to each other.
예를 들어, / 유전자는 결정한다. / 신피질의 어떤 부분들이 눈과 연결되어 있는지, / 어떤 다른 부분들이 귀와 연결되어 있는지, / 그리고 어떻게 그 부분들이 서로 연결되는지를
Therefore, / we can say / that the neocortex is structured at birth / to see, hear, and even learn language.
그러므로 / 우리는 말할 수 있다. / 신피질은 태어날 때 구조화되어 있다고 / 보고 듣고 심지어 언어를 배울 수 있도록
But it is also true / that the neocortex doesn't know / what it will see, / what it will hear, / and what specific languages it might learn.
하지만 또한 사실이다. / 신피질은 모른다는 것 / 무엇을 볼지, / 무엇을 들을지, / 그리고 어떤 특정한 언어를 배울지
We can think of the neocortex as starting life / having some built-in assumptions about the world / but knowing nothing in particular.
우리는 신피질이 생을 시작한다고 생각할 수 있다. / 세상에 대한 어떤 내재된 가정을 가졌지만 / 특별히 아는 것은 없이
Through experience, / it learns a rich and complicated model of the world.
경험을 통해 / 그것은 풍부하고 복잡한 세상 모형을 배운다.

여러분이 태어날 때, 여러분의 신피질은 거의 아무것도 모른다. 그것은 어떠한 단어도, 건물이 어떤지, 컴퓨터를 어떻게 사용하는지, 혹은 문이 무엇이며 경첩에서 어떻게 움직이는지를 알지 못한다. 그것은 무수한 것을 배워야 한다. 신피질의 전체적인 구조는 무작위가 아니다. 신피질의 크기, 신피질에 있는 영역의 수, 그리고 어떻게 그 영역들이 함께 연결되어 있는지는 우리의 유전자에 의해 주로 결정된다. 예를 들어, 유전자는 신피질의 어떤 부분들이 눈과 연결되어 있는지, 어떤 다른 부분들이 귀와 연결되어 있는지, 그리고 어떻게 그 부분들이 서로 연결되는지를 결정한다. 그러므로 우리는 신피질은 태어날 때 보고 듣고 심지어 언어를 배울 수 있도록 구조화되어 있다고 말할 수 있다. 하지만 신피질은 무엇을 볼지, 무엇을 들을지, 그리고 어떤 특정한 언어를 배울지 모른다는 것 또한 사실이다. 우리는 신피질이 세상에 대한 어떤 내재된 가정을 가졌지만 특별히 아는 것은 없이 생을 시작한다고 생각할 수 있다. 경험을 통해 그것은 풍부하고 복잡한 세상 모형을 배운다.

Why? 왜 정답일까?

빈칸 앞에서 신피질의 구조는 무작위적이지 않고 유전자에 의해 대체로 결정되어 있기

에, 태어날 때부터 보고 듣고 언어를 배워나갈 수 있는 상태라고 한다(~ the neocortex is structured at birth to see, hear, and even learn language.). 따라서 빈칸에 들어갈 말로 가장 적절한 것은 신피질이 아주 구체적인 단계까지는 아니더라도 기본적으로 구조화되어 있다는 의미를 다르게 표현한 ① '세상에 대한 어떤 내재된 가정을 가졌지만'이다.

- **neocortex** ⓝ (두뇌의) 신피질
- **countless** ⓐ 무수히 많은
- **structure** ⓝ 구조
- **gene** ⓝ 유전자
- **specific** ⓐ 특정한
- **complicated** ⓐ 복잡한
- **assumption** ⓝ 가정, 추정
- **reprocess** ⓥ 재처리하다
- **persistently** [ad] 끊임없이

- **hinge** ⓝ (문의) 경첩
- **overall** ⓐ 종합적인, 전체의
- **largely** [ad] 주로
- **connect** ⓥ 연결하다
- **particular** ⓐ 특별한
- **built-in** ⓐ 내장된
- **efficiently** [ad] 효율적으로
- **prior** ⓐ 사전의

구문 풀이

8행 For example, genes determine {what parts of the neocortex
　　　　　　　　　　　　　　　　동사
are connected to the eyes}, {what other parts are connected to the
　　　　　　　　　　　　　{A}, {B}, and {C} : 간접의문문 병렬구조
ears}, and {how those parts connect to each other}.

---

04 우리가 기대하는 것을 보게 하는 우리의 뇌　　정답률 44% | 정답 ②

다음 빈칸에 들어갈 말로 가장 적절한 것을 고르시오. [3점]

① ignoring distracting information unrelated to visual clues
　시각적 단서와 관련이 없는, 정신을 산만하게 하는 정보를 무시하는 것
✓ projecting images from within the mind out onto the world
　마음속으로부터의 이미지를 세계로 투영하는 것
③ categorizing objects into groups either real or imagined
　사물을 실제이거나 상상한 집단으로 (범주화하여) 분류하는 것
④ strengthening connections between objects in the real world
　실제 세계의 사물들 간의 관련성을 강화하는 것
⑤ removing the broken or missing parts of an original image
　원래의 상(像)에서 부서지거나 유실된 부분을 제거하는 것

A large part of what we see / is what we expect to see.
우리가 보는 것의 많은 부분은 / 우리가 볼 것이라 기대하는 것이다.
This explains why we "see" faces and figures / in a flickering campfire, or in moving clouds.
이것은 왜 우리가 얼굴과 형상을 '보는'지 설명해준다. / 흔들리는 모닥불이나 움직이는 구름 속에서
This is why Leonardo da Vinci advised artists to discover their motifs / by staring at patches on a blank wall.
이것이 레오나르도 다 빈치가 화가들에게 그들의 모티프를 찾으라고 권한 이유다. / 빈 벽의 부분들을 응시함으로써
A fire provides a constant flickering change in visual information / that never integrates into anything solid / and thereby allows the brain to engage in a play of hypotheses.
불은 시각 정보에 있어 지속적으로 흔들리는 변화를 제공하고, / (형태가) 확실한 어떤 것에도 절대 통합되지 않는 / 그렇게 함으로써 뇌가 가설 놀이에 참여할 수 있게 한다.
On the other hand, / the wall does not present us with very much / in the way of visual clues, / and so the brain begins to make more and more hypotheses / and desperately searches for confirmation.
반면에, / 벽은 우리에게 그다지 많이 주지는 않고, / 시각적인 단서의 방식으로 / 그래서 뇌는 점점 더 많은 가설을 세우기 시작하고 / 필사적으로 확인을 모색한다.
A crack in the wall / looks a little like the profile of a nose / and suddenly a whole face appears, / or a leaping horse, or a dancing figure.
벽에 난 금이 / 코의 옆모습과 약간 닮아 / 갑자기 얼굴 전체가 나타나기도 한다. / 또는 도약하는 말, 또는 춤추는 형상이
In cases like these / the brain's visual strategies are / projecting images from within the mind out onto the world.
이와 같은 경우에 / 뇌의 시각적 전략은 / 마음속으로부터의 이미지를 세계로 투영하는 것이다.

우리가 보는 것의 많은 부분은 우리가 볼 것이라 기대하는 것이다. 이것은 왜 우리가 흔들리는 모닥불이나 움직이는 구름 속에서 얼굴과 형상을 '보는'지 설명해준다. 이것이 레오나르도 다 빈치가 화가들에게 빈 벽의 부분들을 응시함으로써 그들의 모티프를 찾으라고 권한 이유다. 불은 (형태가) 확실한 어떤 것에도 절대 통합되지 않는 시각 정보에 있어 지속적으로 흔들리는 변화를 제공하고, 그렇게 함으로써 뇌가 가설 놀이에 참여할 수 있게 한다. 반면에, 벽은 우리에게 시각적인 단서라고 할 만한 것을 그다지 많이 주지는 않고, 그래서 뇌는 점점 더 많은 가설을 세우기 시작하고 필사적으로 확인을 모색한다. 벽에 난 금이 코의 옆모습과 약간 닮아 갑자기 얼굴 전체가 나타나거나, 도약하는 말 또는 춤추는 형상이 나타나기도 한다. 이와 같은 경우에 뇌의 시각적 전략은 마음속으로부터의 이미지를 세계로 투영하는 것이다.

Why? 왜 정답일까?

첫 문장인 'A large part of what we see is what we expect to see.'에서 우리가 보는 것은 결국 우리가 보기를 기대하는 것이라는 주제를 제시한다. 이를 레오나르도 다 빈치가 언급한 빈 벽의 예에 적용하면, 시각적 정보가 많이 없는 빈 벽에서 인간이 갖가지 형상을 목도하는 것은 그들이 마음속으로 기대한 바가 뇌에 의해 투영되어 나타나기 때문임을 추론할 수 있다. 따라서 빈칸에 들어갈 말로 가장 적절한 것은 ② '마음속으로부터의 이미지를 세계로 투영하는 것'이다.

- **constant** ⓐ 지속적인
- **hypothesis** ⓝ 가설
- **desperately** [ad] 필사적으로
- **distracting** ⓐ 정신을 산만하게 하는
- **strengthen** ⓥ 강화하다

- **integrate** ⓥ 통합되다
- **present** ⓥ 주다, 제시하다
- **confirmation** ⓝ 확인
- **unrelated to** ~와 관계없는

구문 풀이

5행 A fire provides a constant flickering change in visual
　　　　　　　　　　　동사1　　　　　　　　　　　　　선행사(불가산명사)
information [that never integrates into anything solid] and thereby
　　　　　　주격 관·대　　　동사(단수)
allows the brain to engage in a play of hypotheses.
동사2 「allow+목적어+to부정사 : ~이 …하게 해주다」

---

05 정치 과정에서 다른 의견을 억압하면 안 되는 이유　　정답률 42% | 정답 ②

다음 빈칸에 들어갈 말로 가장 적절한 것을 고르시오. [3점]

① political development results from the freedom of speech
　정치적 발전은 언론의 자유에서 나온다는
✓ political disagreement is not the normal state of things
　정치적 갈등이 정상적 상태가 아니라는
③ politics should not restrict any form of difference
　정치는 그 어떤 형태의 차이도 제한해서는 안 된다는
④ freedom could be achieved only through tolerance
　자유는 관용을 통해서만 성취된다는
⑤ suppression could never be a desirable tool in politics
　억압은 정치에서 결코 바람직한 도구가 될 수 없다는

Politics cannot be suppressed, / whichever policy process is employed / and however sensitive and respectful of differences it might be.
정치적 견해는 억압될 수 없다. / 어떤 정치 과정이 이용되든, / 그 과정이 얼마나 민감하고 차이를 얼마나 존중하든
In other words, / there is no end to politics.
다시 말해서, / 정치적 견해에는 끝이 없다.
It is wrong to think / that proper institutions, knowledge, methods of consultation, or participatory mechanisms / can make disagreement go away.
생각하는 것은 잘못된 것이다. / 적절한 기관이나 지식, 협의 과정, 또는 참여 기제가 / 의견의 불일치를 없앨 수 있다고
Theories of all sorts promote the view / that there are ways / by which disagreement can be processed or managed / so as to make it disappear.
모든 종류의 이론은 견해를 조장한다. / 방법이 있다는 / 불일치를 처리하고 다룰 수 있는 / 의견 불일치가 사라지게 하기 위하여
The assumption behind those theories is / that disagreement is wrong / and consensus is the desirable state of things.
그런 이론들 뒤에 숨겨진 가정은 / 불일치가 틀린 것이고 / 합의란 만물의 바람직한 상태라는 것이다.
In fact, / consensus rarely comes / without some forms of subtle coercion / and the absence of fear in expressing a disagreement / is a source of genuine freedom.
사실은, / 합의란 좀처럼 이루어지지 않으며, / 어떤 형태로든 미묘한 강요 없이는 / 다른 의견을 표하는 데 두려움이 없는 것은 / 진정한 자유의 원천이다.
Debates cause disagreements to evolve, / often for the better, / but a positively evolving debate / does not have to equal a reduction in disagreement.
논쟁은 갈등이 발전하게 만드는데, / 때때로 보다 나은 쪽으로 / 긍정적으로 발전하는 논쟁이 / 불일치의 감소와 동일시될 필요는 없다.
The suppression of disagreement / should never be made into a goal / in political deliberation.
다른 의견의 억압은 / 결코 목표가 되어서는 안 된다. / 정치적 숙고의
A defense is required against any suggestion / that political disagreement is not the normal state of things.
그 어떤 제안에도 맞서는 항변이 필요하다. / 정치적 갈등이 정상적 상태가 아니라는

어떤 정치 과정이 이용되든, 그 과정이 얼마나 민감하고 차이를 얼마나 존중하든, 정치적 견해는 억압될 수 없다. 다시 말해서, 정치적 견해에는 끝이 없다. 적절한 기관이나 지식, 협의 과정, 또는 참여 기제가 의견의 불일치를 없앨 수 있다고 생각하는 것은 잘못된 것이다. 모든 종류의 이론은 의견 불일치가 사라지게 하기 위하여 불일치를 처리하고 다룰 수 있는 방법이 있다는 견해를 조장

한다. 그런 이론들 뒤에 숨겨진 가정은 불일치가 틀린 것이고 합의란 만물의 바람직한 상태라는 것이다. 사실은, 합의란 어떤 형태로든 미묘한 강요 없이는 좀처럼 이루어지지 않으며, 다른 의견을 표하는 데 두려움이 없는 것은 진정한 자유의 원천이다. 논쟁은 갈등이 때때로 보다 나은 쪽으로 발전하게 만드는데, 긍정적으로 발전하는 논쟁이 불일치의 감소와 동일시될 필요는 없다. 다른 의견의 억압은 결코 정치적 숙고의 목표가 되어서는 안 된다. 정치적 갈등이 정상적 상태가 아니라는 그 어떤 제안에도 맞서는 항변이 필요하다.

Why? 왜 정답일까?

'It is wrong to think that proper institutions, knowledge, methods of consultation, or participatory mechanisms can make disagreement go away.'와 'The suppression of disagreement should never be made into a goal in political deliberation.'에서 적절한 방법으로 정치 과정 내 의견의 불일치를 줄이거나 없애겠다고 생각하는 것은 잘못된 것이며 합의를 위해 다른 의견을 억압하는 것은 정치적 숙고 과정의 목표가 될 수 없음을 이야기한다. 이때 빈칸 문장은 '~한 견해에는 항변해야 한다'는 내용이므로, 빈칸 부분에는 '불일치를 나쁘게 보지 말라'는 주제 대신 '불일치를 나쁘게 본다'는 내용이 들어가야 이러한 견해에 항변을 할 수 있어야 한다는 맥락이 성립한다. 따라서 빈칸에 들어갈 말로 가장 적절한 것은 ② '정치적 갈등이 정상적 상태가 아니라'이다.

- **suppress** ⓥ 억압하다, 억누르다
- **proper** ⓐ 적절한
- **mechanism** ⓝ 기제
- **consensus** ⓝ 합의, 의견 일치
- **coercion** ⓝ 강요
- **employ** ⓥ 이용하다, 사용하다
- **institution** ⓝ 기관, 제도
- **process** ⓥ 처리하다
- **subtle** ⓐ 미묘한, 감지하기 힘든
- **deliberation** ⓝ 숙고, 숙의

구문 풀이

1행 Politics cannot be suppressed, (whichever policy process is
　　　　조동사 수동태　　　　　　복합관계형용사(어떤 ~이든)
employed) and (however sensitive and respectful of differences it
복합관계부사(아무리 ~이든)　　　　　　~을 존중하는
might be). ( ) : 부사절

---

06 새로운 식민지의 이념적 기초가 된 Locke의 사상　정답률 41% | 정답 ③

다음 빈칸에 들어갈 말로 가장 적절한 것을 고르시오. [3점]

① foundations for reinforcing ties between European and colonial societies
유럽 사회와 식민 사회 간의 연결고리를 강조하는 기반
② new opportunities for European societies to value their tradition
유럽 사회가 그들의 전통을 중시할 새로운 기회
✓③ an optimistic framework for those trying to form a different society
다른 사회를 형성하려는 사람들에게 낙관적인 틀
④ an example of the role that nature plays in building character
천성이 성격 형성에 행하는 역할의 예시
⑤ an access to expertise in the areas of philosophy and science
철학 및 과학 분야의 전문 지식에 대한 접근

The empiricist philosopher John Locke argued / that when the human being was first born, / the mind was simply a blank slate — a *tabula rasa* — / waiting to be written on by experience.
경험주의 철학자 John Locke는 주장했다. / 인간이 처음 태어났을 때, / 그 마음은 그저 빈 석판 — 백지 상태의 마음 — 이었다고 / 경험에 의해 기록되기를 기다리는

Locke believed / that our experience shapes / who we are and who we become — / and therefore he also believed / that, given different experiences, / human beings would have different characters.
Locke는 믿었고, / 우리의 경험이 형성한다고 / 우리가 누구이고 어떤 사람이 되어 갈지를 / 그래서 그는 또한 믿었다. / 다른 경험이 주어지면 / 인간은 다른 성격을 가지게 되리라고

The influence of these ideas was profound, / particularly for the new colonies in America, for example, / because these were conscious attempts / to make a new start and to form a new society.
이런 생각의 영향은 크게 나타났는데, / 가령 특히 미대륙의 새로운 식민지에서 / 왜냐하면 이들 식민지는 의식적인 시도였기 때문이었다. / 새로운 시작을 하고 새로운 사회를 형성하려는

The new society / was to operate on a different basis / from that of European culture, / which was based on the feudal system / in which people's place in society was almost entirely determined by birth, / and which therefore tended to emphasize innate characteristics.
새로운 사회는 / 기반에서 작동될 것이었는데, / 유럽 문화의 기반과는 다른 / 유럽 문화는 봉건 제도에 기반을 두었고, / 사람들의 사회적 지위가 거의 전적으로 출생에 의해 결정되는 / 따라서 그것은 선천적인 특성을 강조하는 경향이 있었다.

Locke's emphasis on the importance of experience / in forming the human being / provided an optimistic framework for those / trying to form a different society.
경험이 갖는 중요성에 대한 Locke의 강조는 / 인간의 형성에서의 / 사람들에게 낙관적인 틀을 제공했다. / 다른 사회를 형성하려는

경험주의 철학자 John Locke는 인간이 처음 태어났을 때, 그 마음은 경험에 의해 기록되기를 기다리는 그저 빈 석판 — 백지 상태의 마음 — 이었다고 주장했다. Locke는 우리의 경험이 우리가 누구이고 어떤 사람이 되어 갈지를 형성한다고 믿었고, 그래서 그는 또한 인간은 다른 경험이 주어지면 다른 성격을 가지게 되리라고 믿었다. 이런 생각의 영향은 가령 특히 미대륙의 새로운 식민지에서 크게 나타났는데, 왜냐하면 이들 식민지는 새로운 시작을 하고 새로운 사회를 형성하려는 의식적인 시도였기 때문이었다. 새로운 사회는 유럽 문화의 기반과는 다른 기반에서 작동될 것이었는데, 유럽 문화는 사람들의 사회적 지위가 거의 전적으로 출생에 의해 결정되는 봉건 제도에 기반을 두었고, 따라서 그것은 선천적인 특성을 강조하는 경향이 있었다. 인간의 형성에서 경험이 갖는 중요성에 대한 Locke의 강조는 다른 사회를 형성하려는 사람들에게 낙관적인 틀을 제공했다.

Why? 왜 정답일까?

John Locke의 백지 상태 가설이 초기 식민지의 이념적 배경으로 작용했다는 내용이다. 선도 악도 타고나지 않은 인간이 어떤 경험을 하는가에 따라 아예 다른 성격을 구축할 수 있다는 주장은 선천적 특성보다 '후천적 경험'을 강조하는 것이었고, 이것은 출신 성분을 중시했던 유럽 봉건주의 사상과는 대척점에 있었기에 새로 태동하는 식민지 사회에 힘이 되었다(The influence of these ideas was profound ~ in America)는 것이다. 따라서 빈칸에 들어갈 말로 가장 적절한 것은 ③ '다른 사회를 형성하려는 사람들에게 낙관적인 틀(an optimistic framework for those trying to form a different society)'이다.

- **empiricist** ⓝ 경험주의자
- **tabula rasa** 백지 상태
- **colony** ⓝ 식민지
- **emphasize** ⓥ 강조하다
- **foundation** ⓝ 기반, 근본
- **expertise** ⓝ 전문 지식
- **slate** ⓝ 석판
- **profound** ⓐ 심오한, (영향이) 큰
- **feudal** ⓐ 봉건 제도의
- **innate** ⓐ 타고난, 선천적인
- **reinforce** ⓥ 강조하다, 강화하다, 증강하다

구문 풀이

11행 The new society was to operate on a different basis from
　　　　　　　　　　　　　　　　　지시대명사(= the basis)
that of European culture, which was based on the feudal system
　　　선행사　　　　　　　　계속적 용법　　　　　　선행사
[in which people's place in society was almost entirely determined by birth], and [which therefore tended to emphasize innate characteristics]. [ ] : the feudal system 수식

★★★ 1등급 대비 고난도 2점 문제

07 세부 사항에 대한 기억　정답률 35% | 정답 ①

다음 빈칸에 들어갈 말로 가장 적절한 것을 고르시오.

✓① identical – 동일하다
② beneficial – 이롭다
③ alien – 맞지 않다
④ prior – 우선하다
⑤ neutral – 중립적이다

When you begin to tell a story again / that you have retold many times, / what you retrieve from memory / is the index to the story itself.
당신이 이야기를 다시 하기 시작할 때, / 당신이 여러 번 반복하여 말했던 / 기억에서 불러오는 것은 / 이야기 자체에 대한 지표이다.

That index can be embellished in a variety of ways.
그 지표는 다양한 방식으로 윤색될 수 있다.

Over time, even the embellishments become standardized.
시간이 흐르면서, 그 윤색된 것들조차도 표준화된다.

An old man's story that he has told hundreds of times / shows little variation, / and any variation that does exist / becomes part of the story itself, / regardless of its origin.
한 노인이 수백 번 말한 이야기는 / 변형을 거의 보이지 않으며, / 어떤 변형이든 실제로 존재하는 것이면 / 이야기 자체의 일부가 된다. / 그것의 기원에 관계없이

People add details to their stories / that may or may not have occurred.
사람들은 세부 사항을 자신들의 이야기에 덧붙인다. / 일어났을 수도, 또는 일어나지 않았을 수도 있는

They are recalling indexes and reconstructing details.
그들은 지표들을 기억해 내고 세부 사항들을 재구성하고 있는 것이다.

If at some point they add a nice detail, / not really certain of its validity, / telling the story with that same detail a few more times / will ensure its permanent place in the story index.
만약, 어떤 시점에 그들이 어떤 멋진 세부 사항을 덧붙이고, / 그것의 타당성에 대해 정말로 확신하지 못한 채 / 동일한 그 세부 사항과 함께 몇 번 더 그 이야기를 말하는 것은 / 이야기 지표에서 영구적인 위치를 확보할 것이다.

In other words, the stories we tell time and again / are identical to the memory / we have of the events that the story relates.

다시 말해 우리가 되풀이해서 말하는 이야기는 / 기억과 동일하다. / 그 이야기가 전달하는 사건들에 대해 우리가 가지고 있는

여러 번 반복하여 말했던 이야기를 다시 하기 시작할 때, 기억에서 불러오는 것은 이야기 자체에 대한 지표이다. 그 지표는 다양한 방식으로 윤색될 수 있다. 시간이 흐르면서, 그 윤색된 것들조차도 표준화된다. 한 노인이 수백 번 말한 이야기는 변형을 거의 보이지 않으며, 어떤 변형이든 실제로 존재하는 것이면 그것의 기원에 관계없이 이야기 자체의 일부가 된다. 사람들은 일어났을 수도, 또는 일어나지 않았을 수도 있는 세부 사항을 자신들의 이야기에 덧붙인다. 그들은 지표들을 기억해 내고 세부 사항들을 재구성하고 있는 것이다. 만약, 어떤 시점에 그들이 어떤 멋진 세부 사항의 타당성에 대해 정말로 확신하지 못한 채 그것을 덧붙이고, 동일한 그 세부 사항과 함께 몇 번 더 그 이야기를 말하다보면 그것은 이야기 지표에서 영구적인 위치를 확보할 것이다. 다시 말해 우리가 되풀이해서 말하는 이야기는 그 이야기가 전달하는 사건들에 대해 우리가 가지고 있는 기억과 동일하다.

Why? 왜 정답일까?

우리는 어떤 이야기를 기억할 때 이야기의 모든 세부 사항이 아닌 지표를 기억하는 것이며, 세부 사항은 지표에 맞게 재구성되는데, 시간이 흐르며 반복적으로 언급된 세부 사항은 기원에 관계없이 이야기의 일부가 되며(~ any variation that does exist becomes part of the story itself, ~), 즉 이야기 지표에서 영구적인 입지를 확보하게 된다(~ ensure its permanent place in the story index.)는 내용의 글이다. 다시 말해 어떤 세부 사항이 실제로 일어났는지 여부에 상관없이 이야기를 재구성하는 데 반복적으로 포함되다 보면 기억의 일부가 된다는 내용이 핵심이므로, 빈칸에 들어갈 말로 가장 적절한 것은 ① '동일하다'이다.

- standardize ⓥ 표준화하다
- regardless of ~에 관계없이
- validity ⓝ 타당성
- relate ⓥ 이야기하다, 말하다, 관련시키다
- alien to ~에 맞지 않는
- variation ⓝ 변형, 변주
- certain of ~을 확신하는
- ensure ⓥ 확보하다
- identical to ~와 동일한
- prior to ~에 우선하는

구문 풀이

5행 An old man's story [that he has told hundreds of times]
　　　　　주어1　　　　　　목적격 관계대명사
shows little variation, and any variation [that does exist] becomes
동사1　　　　　　　　　　　주어2　　주격 관·대　동사 강조　동사2
part of the story itself, regardless of its origin.
　　강조　　　　　　　　　~에 관계없이

★★ 문제 해결 꿀~팁 ★★

▶ 많이 틀린 이유는?
기억을 소재로 한 추상적인 내용의 글이다. 빈칸 앞의 내용을 요약하면 어떤 세부 사항이 실제 일어나지 않았더라도 반복적으로 언급되다보면 기억의 일부가 될 수 있다는 것이다. 빈칸 문장의 'the stories we tell time and again'은 '우리가 세부 사항을 붙여 타인에게 전달하는 이야기'를 가리키므로, 이것이 결국 기억과 '동일한' 입지를 갖게 된다는 의미로서 빈칸에는 ①이 적절하다. ②는 기억에 '이롭다'는 표현이 지문의 내용과 무관하며, ③은 주제와 반대된다.

▶ 문제 해결 방법은?
빈칸 문장이 In other words로 시작하는 것으로 볼 때, 빈칸 앞의 문장과 빈칸이 포함된 문장은 서로 같은 내용을 말할 것이다. 따라서 바로 앞의 문장을 주의 깊게 읽도록 한다.

★★★ 1등급 대비 고난도 2점 문제

08 촉각적 자극이 없도록 설계되는 도시 환경　　정답률 36% | 정답 ②

다음 빈칸에 들어갈 말로 가장 적절한 것을 고르시오.

① we accept its harsh elements – 우리가 그것의 너무 강렬한 요소를 받아들일
✔ we scarcely notice its presence – 우리가 그 존재를 거의 알아차리지 않을
③ it does not hinder social interactions – 그것이 사회적 상호 작용을 방해하지 않을
④ we experience it using all the senses – 우리가 그것을 온 감각으로 경험할
⑤ its design reflects the natural environment – 그것의 설계가 자연 환경을 반영할

The urban environment is generally designed / so as not to make contact with our skin.
도시 환경은 일반적으로 설계된다. / 우리의 피부와 접촉하지 않도록
We do not push through bushes / on our way to school or work.
우리는 덤불을 통과하지 않는다. / 우리가 학교 혹은 직장에 가는 길에

Roads and sidewalks are kept clear of obstacles.
길과 보도는 장애물이 없도록 유지된다.
Only once in a while / are we reminded of the materiality of the environment, / as when we feel the brush of an unexpected tree branch / or nearly fall over a curb.
오직 이따금 한 번씩 / 우리는 환경의 물질성에 대해 떠올리게 된다. / 우리가 예상치 못한 나뭇가지의 스침을 느끼거나 / 연석에 거의 넘어질 뻔할 때처럼
Most of our time is not even spent outside.
우리 시간의 대부분은 심지어 밖에서 소비되지 않는다.
"Outside" is often just a space / we go through to get "inside."
보통 '외부'는 단지 공간일 뿐이다. / 우리가 '내부'에 가기 위해 거쳐 가는
Our time is largely spent indoors, / where architecture and design collude to provide an environment / as lacking as possible in tactile stimulation.
우리의 시간은 주로 실내에서 소비되는데, / 여기서 건축술과 설계는 환경을 제공하기 위해 결탁한다. / 최대한 촉각적 자극이 결여된
In the modern university or office building, / floors and walls are flat and smooth, / corridors are clear, / the air is still, / the temperature is neutral, / and elevators carry one effortlessly from one level to another.
현대의 대학 혹은 사무실 건물에서 / 바닥과 벽은 평평하고 매끈하며 / 복도는 깨끗하고 공기는 바람 한 점 없으며 / 온도는 중간이고 / 승강기는 사람을 한 층에서 다른 층으로 수월하게 실어 나른다.
It is commonly assumed / that we are best served by our tactile environment / when we scarcely notice its presence.
흔히 여겨진다. / 우리는 촉각 환경에 의해 최고의 편의를 제공받는다고 / 우리가 그 존재를 거의 알아차리지 않을 때

도시 환경은 일반적으로 우리의 피부와 접촉하지 않도록 설계된다. 우리는 우리가 학교 혹은 직장에 가는 길에 덤불을 통과하지 않는다. 길과 보도는 장애물이 없도록 유지된다. 우리가 예상치 못한 나뭇가지의 스침을 느끼거나 연석에 거의 넘어질 뻔할 때처럼 우리는 오직 이따금 한 번씩 환경의 물질성에 대해 떠올리게 된다. 우리 시간의 대부분은 심지어 밖에서 소비되지 않는다. 보통 '외부'는 단지 우리가 '내부'에 가기 위해 거쳐 가는 공간일 뿐이다. 우리의 시간은 주로 실내에서 소비되는데, 여기서 건축술과 설계는 최대한 촉각적 자극이 결여된 환경을 제공하기 위해 결탁한다. 현대의 대학 혹은 사무실 건물에서 바닥과 벽은 평평하고 매끈하며 복도는 깨끗하고 공기는 바람 한 점 없으며 온도는 중간이고 승강기는 사람을 한 층에서 다른 층으로 수월하게 실어 나른다. 우리가 그 존재를 거의 알아차리지 않을 때 우리는 촉각 환경에 의해 최고의 편의를 제공받는다고 흔히 여겨진다.

Why? 왜 정답일까?

'The urban environment is generally designed so as not to make contact with our skin.'에서 도시 환경은 보통 인간의 피부에 닿지 않게 설계된다고 언급하는 것으로 보아, 빈칸에도 인간이 환경을 촉각으로 거의 느낄 일이 없다는 내용이 들어가야 한다. 따라서 빈칸에 들어갈 말로 가장 적절한 것은 ② '우리가 그 존재를 거의 알아차리지 않을'이다.

- make contact with ~와 접촉하다
- obstacle ⓝ 장애물
- unexpected ⓐ 예기치 못한
- curb ⓝ (도로의) 연석
- tactile ⓐ 촉각의
- neutral ⓐ 중립적인
- harsh ⓐ (손상을 입힐 정도로) 너무 강한
- hinder ⓥ 방해하다
- keep clear of ~에서 떨어져 있다
- materiality ⓝ 물질성, 유형성
- branch ⓝ 나뭇가지
- architecture ⓝ 건축
- stimulation ⓝ 자극
- effortlessly ⓐⓓ 쉽게
- scarcely ⓐⓓ 거의 ~않다

구문 풀이

4행 Only once in a while are we reminded of the materiality of
　　　　　「only＋부사구＋be＋주어＋과거분사 : 도치 구문」
the environment, as when we feel the brush of an unexpected tree
　　　　　　　　　~할 때처럼　　　동사1
branch or nearly fall over a curb.
　　　　　　동사2

★★ 문제 해결 꿀~팁 ★★

▶ 많이 틀린 이유는?
도시 환경의 특성을 설명하는 지문이다. 글 처음과 중간에 따르면 도시 환경과 건축물은 인간에게 가급적 촉각적 자극을 주지 않도록 설계된다고 한다. 최다 오답인 ⑤는 촉각 환경이 '자연 환경을 반영하여' 설계된다는 의미인데, 글에서 자연 환경은 언급되지 않는다.

▶ 문제 해결 방법은?
글 처음과 중간에서 '촉각적 자극이 거의 없는 환경'에 관해 반복적으로 언급하므로, 이와 관련된 표현을 답으로 골라야 한다.

DAY 09

★★★ 1등급 대비 고난도 3점 문제

09 태양 위치의 진술로 알 수 있는 고대 여행의 증거   정답률 32% | 정답 ①

다음 빈칸에 들어갈 말로 가장 적절한 것을 고르시오. [3점]

☑ ① must have taken place – 이루어졌음이 틀림없다
② was not reported at all – 전혀 보고되지 않았다
③ was not worth the time – 시간을 들일 가치가 없었다
④ should have been planned better – 더 잘 계획되었어야만 했다
⑤ could be stopped at any moment – 언제고 중단될 수 있었다

When trying to understand the role of the sun / in ancient journeys, / the sources become fewer / and the journeys less well known.
태양의 역할을 이해하려고 할 때, / 고대 여행에서 / 자료는 더 적어지고 / 알려진 여행은 더 적어진다.

Herodotus writes about an exploratory voyage / commissioned by the ancient Egyptian King Necho II / in about 600 BC.
Herodotus는 탐험 항해에 대해 기록한다. / 고대 이집트 왕 Necho 2세가 의뢰한 / 기원전 600년경

Necho II reportedly ordered a Phoenician expedition / to sail clockwise around Africa, / starting at the Red Sea / and returning to the mouth of the Nile.
전해 오는 바에 따르면 Necho 2세는 페니키아 원정대에게 명령했다 / 아프리카 주위를 시계 방향으로 항해하라고 / 홍해에서 출발해 / 나일강 하구로 돌아오도록

They were gone for three years.
그들은 3년간 나가 있었다.

Herodotus writes / that the Phoenicians, / upon returning from their heroic expedition, / reported / that after sailing south and then turning west, / they found the sun was on their right, / the opposite direction / to where they were used to seeing it or expecting it to be.
Herodotus는 기록한다. / 페니키아인들이 / 영웅적인 탐험을 마치고 돌아오자마자 / 보고했다고 / 남쪽으로 항해를 한 다음 서쪽으로 방향을 바꾼 후에 / 그들은 태양이 자신들의 오른편에 있는 것을 발견했노라고 / 정반대 방향인, / 자신들이 늘 보았거나 떠 있으리라고 으레 예상했던 곳과는

Contemporary astronomical science / was simply not strong enough / to fabricate such an accurate, fundamental and yet prosaic detail / of where the sun would be / after sailing past the equator and into the southern hemisphere.
당시의 천문 과학은 / 결코 충분히 뛰어나지 않았다. / 그렇게 정확하고 기초적이지만 평범한 세부 사항을 꾸며낼 만큼 / 태양이 어디에 있을지에 대해 / 적도를 지나 남반구로 항해한 후

It is this / that leads many of today's historians / to conclude that the journey must have taken place.
바로 이 때문이다. / 오늘날의 역사가 중 많은 이들이 ~하게 되는 것이 / 그 여행이 이루어졌음이 틀림없다고 결론 짓게

고대 여행에서 태양의 역할을 이해하려고 할 때, 자료는 더 적어지고 알려진 여행은 더 적어진다. Herodotus는 기원전 600년경 고대 이집트 왕 Necho 2세가 의뢰한 탐험 항해에 대해 기록한다. 전해 오는 바에 따르면 Necho 2세는 페니키아 원정대에게 홍해에서 출발해 나일강 하구로 돌아오도록, 아프리카 주위를 시계 방향으로 항해하라고 명령했다고 한다. 그들은 3년간 (원정을) 나가 있었다. Herodotus는 페니키아인들이 영웅적인 탐험을 마치고 돌아와, 남쪽으로 항해를 한 다음 서쪽으로 방향을 바꾼 후에 태양이 자신들의 오른편에 있는 것을 발견했노라고 보고했다고 기록하는데, 이는 그들이 늘 보았거나 떠 있으리라고 으레 예상했던 곳과는 정반대 방향이었다. 당시의 천문 과학은 적도를 지나 남반구로 항해한 후 태양이 어디에 있을지에 대해 그렇게 정확하고 기초적이지만 평범한 세부 사항을 꾸며 낼 만큼 결코 충분히 뛰어나지 않았다. 오늘날의 역사가 중 많은 이들이 그 여행이 이루어졌음이 틀림없다고 결론을 내리게 되는 것이 바로 이 때문이다.

Why? 왜 정답일까?

'Contemporary astronomical science ~' 문장에서 당대 천문 과학은 태양의 위치와 관련한 세부적인 사항을 꾸며낼 만큼 정교하지 않았다는 설명으로 보아, '실제로 여행을 했기에' 태양 위치에 대해 구체적으로 말할 수 있었을 것이라는 결론이 뒤따라야 한다. 따라서 빈칸에 들어갈 말로 가장 적절한 것은 ① '이루어졌음이 틀림없다'이다.

- role ⓝ 역할
- source ⓝ 출처, 자료
- voyage deliberate 항해
- reportedly ⓐⓓ 전해 오는 바에 따르면
- clockwise ⓐⓓ 시계 방향으로
- heroic ⓐ 영웅적인
- opposite ⓐ 반대편의, 맞은편의
- contemporary ⓐ 당대의, 동시대의
- strong ⓐ 뛰어난, 설득력 있는
- accurate ⓐ 정확한
- journey ⓝ 여행
- exploratory ⓐ 탐험의
- commission ⓥ 의뢰하다
- expedition ⓝ 원정(대), 탐험
- Phoenician ⓐ 페니키아(사람)의
- sailing ⓝ 항해
- direction ⓝ 방향
- astronomical ⓐ 천문학의
- fabricate ⓥ 지어내다, 꾸며내다
- fundamental ⓐ 기초적인

- prosaic ⓐ 평범한
- southern hemisphere 남반구
- equator ⓝ 적도
- conclude ⓥ 결론을 내리다

구문 풀이

8행 Herodotus writes that the Phoenicians, (upon returning from their heroic expedition), reported that after sailing south and then turning west, they found the sun was on their right, the opposite direction to (the place) [where they were used to seeing it or expecting it to be].

★★ 문제 해결 꿀~팁 ★★

▶ 많이 틀린 이유는?

태양의 위치가 적도를 지나 변한다는 것을 알아냈던 고대 여행에 관한 글이다. 중반부의 'Herodotus writes that the Phoenicians, ~ reported ~'에서 '보고한' 내용이 언급되는 것으로 보아 여행 자체가 '보고되지 않았다'는 의미의 ②는 부적절하다.

▶ 문제 해결 방법은?

결론에 충실하면 쉽게 풀린다. 여행이 있었던 당시에는 과학이 정교하게 발달하지 않아 태양의 위치에 관해 지어내기가 어려웠을 것이라는 내용을 통해, 여행이 '실제로 일어났을' 수밖에 없다는 추론이 가능해진다.

★★★ 1등급 대비 고난도 3점 문제

10 서양 철학에서 더 우위로 여겨지는 합리적 지식   정답률 29% | 정답 ⑤

다음 빈칸에 들어갈 말로 가장 적절한 것을 고르시오. [3점]

① as the outcome of blindly following sensual experience
감각적인 경험을 맹목적으로 따르는 것의 결과로
② by moving away from the idea of perfect representation
완벽한 재현이라는 생각에서 벗어남으로써
③ beyond the limit of where rational knowledge can approach
합리적 지식이 접근할 수 있는 곳의 한계 너머에
④ through a variety of experiences rather than logical reasoning
논리적 추론이 아닌 다양한 경험을 통해
☑ ⑤ not in the perception of the figure but in its rational representation
형체의 지각이 아니라 그 합리적 재현에서

One of the common themes of the Western philosophical tradition / is the distinction / between sensual perceptions and rational knowledge.
서양의 철학적 전통의 공통된 주제 중 하나는 / 구별이다. / 감각적 지각과 합리적 지식 사이의

Since Plato, / the supremacy of rational reason is based on the assertion / that it is able to extract true knowledge from experience.
플라톤 이래로, / 합리적 이성의 우월성은 주장에 근거한다. / 이성으로 경험에서 참된 지식을 얻어낼 수 있다는

As the discussion in the *Republic* helps to explain, / perceptions are inherently unreliable and misleading / because the senses are subject to errors and illusions.
*Republic*에서의 논의가 설명에 도움이 되듯이, / 지각은 본질적으로 신뢰할 수 없고 오해의 소지가 있다. / 감각은 오류와 착각의 영향을 받기 때문에

Only the rational discourse / has the tools to overcome illusions / and to point towards true knowledge.
오직 합리적 담론만이 / 착각을 극복하는 도구를 가지고 있다. / 그리고 참된 지식을 가리키는

For instance, / perception suggests / that a figure in the distance is smaller / than it really is.
예를 들어, / 지각은 보여준다. / 멀리 있는 어떤 형체가 더 작다는 것을 / 실제 그런 것보다

Yet, / the application of logical reasoning will reveal / that the figure only appears small / because it obeys the laws of geometrical perspective.
하지만, / 논리적 추론을 적용하면 드러날 것이다. / 그 형체는 작게 보일 뿐이라는 것이 / 그것이 기하학적 원근법을 따르기 때문에

Nevertheless, / even after the perspectival correction is applied / and reason concludes that perception is misleading, / the figure still *appears* small, / and the truth of the matter is revealed / not in the perception of the figure / but in its rational representation.
그럼에도 불구하고, / 원근 보정을 적용한 후에도 / 그리고 이성이 지각이 오해의 소지가 있다는 결론을 내린 (후에도) / 그 형체는 여전히 작게 *보이고*, / 문제의 진실은 드러난다. / 형체의 지각이 아니라 / 그것의 합리적 재현에서

서양의 철학적 전통의 공통된 주제 중 하나는 감각적 지각과 합리적 지식 사이의 구별이다. 플라톤 이래로, 합리적 이성의 우월성은 이성으로 경험에서 참된 지식을 얻어낼 수 있다는 주장에 근거한다. (플라톤의 저서인) *Republic*에서의 논의가 설명에 도움이 되듯이, 감각은 오류와 착각의 영향을 받기 때문에 지각은 본질적으로 신뢰할 수 없고 오해의 소지가 있다. 오직 합리적 담론만이 착

각을 극복하고 참된 지식을 가리키는 도구를 가지고 있다. 예를 들어, 지각은 멀리 있는 어떤 형체가 실제보다 더 작다는 것을 보여준다. 하지만, 논리적 추론을 적용하면 그 형체는 기하학적 원근법을 따르기 때문에 작게 보일 뿐이라는 것이 드러날 것이다. 그럼에도 불구하고, 원근 보정을 적용하여 이성이 지각이 오해의 소지가 있다는 결론을 내린 후에도, 그 형체는 여전히 작게 *보이*고, 문제의 진실은 형체의 지각이 아니라 그 합리적 재현에서 드러난다.

Why? 왜 정답일까?

감각에 바탕을 둔 지각은 오류를 내포하므로 본질적으로 신뢰할 수 없지만, 합리적 지식은 오류나 착각을 극복하게 해주기 때문에 참된 지식을 가리킨다는 내용이다. 예시에서 어떤 형체가 실제보다 작아 보이는 경우 원근 보정을 이용하면 그저 작아 '보일 뿐' 실제는 보이는 것과 다르다는 것을 알 수 있다고 한다. 즉 감각에 의한 지각은 한계가 있고, 실체를 보려면 '합리적 이성'을 동원해야 한다는 것이 글의 결론이므로, 빈칸에 들어갈 말로 가장 적절한 것은 ⑤ '형체의 지각이 아니라 그 합리적 재현에서'이다.

- theme ⓝ 주제
- tradition ⓝ 전통
- sensual ⓐ 감각적인
- supremacy ⓝ 우월성
- assertion ⓝ 주장
- republic ⓝ 공화국, 국가
- unreliable ⓐ 신뢰할 수 없는
- be subject to ~의 영향을 받다
- discourse ⓝ 담론
- application ⓝ 적용, 응용
- reveal ⓥ 드러내다
- geometrical ⓐ 기하학적인
- correction ⓝ 보정, 정정, 수정
- representation ⓝ 재현
- philosophical ⓐ 철학적인
- distinction ⓝ 구별
- perception ⓝ 지각, 인식
- be based on ~에 바탕을 두다
- extract ⓥ 추출하다
- inherently ⓐⓓ 본질적으로
- misleading ⓐ 오해의 소지가 있는
- illusion ⓝ 환상, 착각
- figure ⓝ 형체, 숫자, 인물
- logical ⓐ 논리적인
- obey ⓥ 따르다, 복종하다
- perspective ⓝ 원근법, 시각
- truth ⓝ 진실

구문 풀이

3행 Since Plato, the supremacy of rational reason is based on the
전치사(~ 이래로)
assertion [that it is able to extract true knowledge from experience].
가주어   진주어   [ ] : 동격(= the assertion)

★★ 문제 해결 꿀~팁 ★★

▶ 많이 틀린 이유는?
지각은 한계가 있으나 이성은 그 한계를 극복하게 해준다는 내용이다. ①, ③, ④가 모두 주제와 반대되는데, ①과 ④는 '경험 또는 감각'과 관련된 내용이고, ③은 감각이 아닌 '이성에 한계'가 있다고 말하기 때문이다.

▶ 문제 해결 방법은?
지각(sensual perceptions = experience = perception)은 오해와 착각에 취약하고, 합리적 지식(rational knowledge = rational representation)은 참된 지식이라는 내용으로 보아, ⑤가 답으로 적절하다.

★★★ 1등급 대비 고난도 3점 문제

11 교육 기술의 통합 조건   정답률 38% | 정답 ②

다음 빈칸에 들어갈 말로 가장 적절한 것을 고르시오. [3점]

① the user successfully achieves familiarity with the technology
사용자가 성공적으로 그 기술에 대한 친숙함을 얻는
✔ the user's focus is on the technology itself rather than its use
사용자의 초점이 기술의 사용이 아니라 기술 그 자체에 맞춰져 있는
③ the user continues to employ outdated educational techniques
사용자가 구식의 교육 기술을 계속 사용하는
④ the user involuntarily gets used to the misuse of the technology
사용자가 무의식적으로 그 기술의 오용에 익숙해지는
⑤ the user's preference for interaction with other users persists
다른 사용자와의 상호작용에 대한 사용자의 선호가 지속하는

Successful integration of an educational technology / is marked by that technology being regarded by users / as an unobtrusive facilitator of learning, instruction, or performance.
교육 기술의 성공적인 통합은 / 그 기술이 사용자에 의해 여겨지는 것으로 나타난다. / 학습이나 교육, 또는 수행의 눈에 띄지 않는 촉진자로

When the focus shifts / from the technology being used / to the educational purpose that technology serves, / then that technology is becoming a comfortable and trusted element, / and can be regarded as being successfully integrated.
초점이 옮겨갈 때, / 사용되고 있는 기술에서 / 기술이 이바지하는 교육적 목적으로 / 그 기술은 편안하고 신뢰할 수 있는 요소가 되고 있으며, / 성공적으로 통합되고 있다고 여겨질 수 있다.

Few people give a second thought to the use of a ball-point pen / although the mechanisms involved vary / — some use a twist mechanism / and some use a push button on top, / and there are other variations as well.
볼펜 사용법에 대해 재고하는 사람들은 거의 없다 / 그 구조가 다양하지만, / (볼펜 중) 어떤 것들은 돌리는 방법을 사용하고, / 또 어떤 것들은 위에 달린 누름단추를 사용하며, / 그리고 다른 변형된 방법들도 있다

Personal computers have reached a similar level of familiarity / for a great many users, / but certainly not for all.
개인용 컴퓨터는 (볼펜과) 비슷한 수준의 친숙함에 도달했지만, / 아주 많은 사용자들에게 / 분명 모두에게 그렇지는 않다.

New and emerging technologies / often introduce both fascination and frustration with users.
새롭고 떠오르는 기술은 / 흔히 사용자들에게 매력과 좌절감을 동시에 경험하게 한다.

As long as in the user's focus is on the technology itself / rather than its use / promoting learning, instruction, or performance, / then one ought not to conclude / that the technology has been successfully integrated / — at least for that user.
사용자의 초점이 기술 그 자체에 맞춰져 있는 한, / 기술의 사용이 아니라 / 학습, 교육 또는 수행을 촉진하는 데 있어서 / 우리는 결론을 내려서는 안 된다 / 그 기술이 성공적으로 통합되었다는 / 적어도 그 사용자에게는

교육 기술의 성공적인 통합은 그 기술이 사용자에 의해 학습이나 교육, 또는 수행의 눈에 띄지 않는 촉진자로 여겨지는 것으로 나타난다. 사용되고 있는 기술에서 기술이 이바지하는 교육적 목적으로 초점이 옮겨갈 때, 그 기술은 편안하고 신뢰할 수 있는 요소가 되고 있으며, 성공적으로 통합되고 있다고 여겨질 수 있다. (볼펜들 중) 어떤 것들은 돌리는 방법을 사용하고, 또 어떤 것들은 위에 달린 누름단추를 사용하며, 그리고 다른 변형된 방법들도 있을 정도로 그 구조가 다양하지만, 볼펜 사용법에 대해 재고하는 사람들은 거의 없다. 개인용 컴퓨터는 아주 많은 사용자들에게 (볼펜과) 비슷한 수준의 친숙함에 도달했지만, 분명 모두에게 그렇지는 않다. 새롭고 떠오르는 기술은 흔히 사용자들에게 매력과 좌절감을 동시에 경험하게 한다. 학습, 교육 또는 수행을 촉진하는 데 있어서 사용자의 초점이 기술의 사용이 아니라 기술 그 자체에 맞춰져 있는 한, 적어도 그 사용자에게는 그 기술이 성공적으로 통합되었다는 결론을 내려서는 안 된다.

Why? 왜 정답일까?

'When the focus shifts from the technology being used to the educational purpose that technology serves, then that technology is becoming a comfortable and trusted element, and can be regarded as being successfully integrated.'에서 교육 기술이 교육 및 학습과 성공적으로 통합되었다고 여겨지기 위해서는 사용자의 초점이 기술 자체가 아니라 기술로 인해 달성되는 목적으로 옮겨가 있어야 한다고 했다. 이를 근거로 추론해볼 때, 빈칸 문장에서 언급되듯이 기술이 성공적 통합을 이루지 못한 경우에는 아직 사용자의 초점이 목적으로 옮겨가지 못하고 기술 그 자체에 머무르고 있을 것임을 알 수 있다. 따라서 빈칸에 들어갈 말로 가장 적절한 것은 ② '사용자의 초점이 기술의 사용이 아니라 기술 그 자체에 맞춰져 있는'이다.

- integration ⓝ 통합
- give a second thought to ~을 재고하다
- variation ⓝ 변형, 변화
- emerging ⓐ 떠오르는, 신흥의
- frustration ⓝ 좌절
- outdated ⓐ 구식의
- facilitator ⓝ 촉진자
- mechanism ⓝ 구조, 기제
- familiarity ⓝ 친숙함
- fascination ⓝ 매력
- promote ⓥ 촉진하다
- involuntarily ⓐⓓ 무의식적으로

구문 풀이

8행 Few people give a second thought to the use of a ball-point
부정 주어(~한 사람은 거의 없다)   동사구
pen although the mechanisms involved vary — some use a twist
접속사(~일지라도)   주어   ┗과거분사┛ 동사
mechanism and some use a push button on top, and there are other
「some ~ other … : 일부는 ~하고, 다른 일부는 …하다」
variations as well.

★★ 문제 해결 꿀~팁 ★★

▶ 많이 틀린 이유는?
빈칸 뒤의 절의 술어가 ought not to conclude인 것으로 보아 빈칸에는 '교육 기술이 제대로 통합되지 못한 상황'에 관한 말이 들어가야 한다. ①은 기술 사용자가 기술을 친숙해 한다는 뜻이므로, 통합에 '실패'한 상황보다는 '성공'한 상황에 어울리는 설명이다.

▶ 문제 해결 방법은?
지문 내용이 추상적이고 복잡할수록 답의 근거는 쉽게 제시된다. 이 문제 또한 주제문인 두 번째 문장을 정확히 읽고, 빈칸 문장 술어에 not이 있다는 점만 주의하여 주제와 반대되는 선택지를 찾으면 어렵지 않게 해결할 수 있다.

DAY 09

★★★ 1등급 대비 고난도 3점 문제

12 인간성 정의에 도움을 주는 인공 지능　정답률 45% | 정답 ①

다음 빈칸에 들어갈 말로 가장 적절한 것을 고르시오. [3점]

☑ AIs will help define humanity
　AI가 인간성을 정의하는 데 도움을 줄 것이라는
② humans could also be like AIs
　사람도 AI와 같아질 수 있다는
③ humans will be liberated from hard labor
　사람은 힘든 노동으로부터 해방될 것이라는
④ AIs could lead us in resolving moral dilemmas
　AI는 도덕적 딜레마 해결에서 우리를 이끌 수 있다는
⑤ AIs could compensate for a decline in human intelligence
　AI는 인간의 지능 감퇴를 보완해줄 수 있다는

Over the past 60 years, / as mechanical processes have replicated behaviors and talents / we thought were unique to humans, / we've had to change our minds about what sets us apart.
지난 60년 동안 / 기계식 공정이 행동과 재능을 복제해왔기 때문에, / 우리가 생각하기에 인간에게만 있는 / 우리는 우리를 다르게 만드는 것에 관한 생각을 바꿔야만 했다.

As we invent more species of AI, / we will be forced to surrender more / of what is supposedly unique about humans.
더 많은 종의 AI를 발명하면서, / 우리는 더 많은 것을 내줘야만 할 것이다. / 아마도 인간에게만 있는 것 중

Each step of surrender / — we are not the only mind / that can play chess, fly a plane, make music, or invent a mathematical law — / will be painful and sad.
매번 내주는 일은 / (우리가 유일한 존재가 아니라는 것) / 체스를 둘 줄 알거나, 비행기를 날릴 줄 알거나, 음악을 만들거나, 아니면 수학 법칙을 발명할 줄 아는 / 고통스럽고 슬플 것이다.

We'll spend the next three decades — indeed, perhaps the next century — / in a permanent identity crisis, / continually asking ourselves what humans are good for.
우리는 앞으로 다가올 30년(사실, 어쩌면 앞으로 다가올 한 세기)을 보내며, / 영속적인 정체성 위기 속에서 / 계속 스스로에게 인간이 무슨 소용이 있는지를 질문하게 될 것이다.

If we aren't unique toolmakers, or artists, or moral ethicists, / then what, if anything, makes us special?
우리가 유일한 도구 제작자나 예술가, 또는 도덕 윤리학자가 아니라면, / 도대체 무엇이 우리를 특별하게 만드는가?

In the grandest irony of all, / the greatest benefit of an everyday, utilitarian AI / will not be increased productivity / or an economics of abundance / or a new way of doing science / — although all those will happen.
가장 아이러니하게도, / 일상적이고도 실용적인 AI의 가장 큰 이점은, / 생산성 증가나 / 풍요의 경제학, 혹은 과학을 행하는 새로운 방식이 아닐 것이다. / 비록 이 모든 일이 일어난다 할지라도

The greatest benefit of the arrival of artificial intelligence is / that AIs will help define humanity.
인공 지능의 도래가 주는 가장 큰 이점은 / AI가 인간성을 정의하는 데 도움을 줄 것이라는 점이다.

―――

지난 60년 동안 기계식 공정이 우리가 생각하기에 인간에게만 있는 행동과 재능을 복제해왔기 때문에, 우리는 우리를 다르게 만드는 것에 관한 생각을 바꿔야만 했다. 더 많은 종의 AI(인공지능)를 발명하면서, 우리는 아마도 인간에게만 있는 것 중 더 많은 것을 내줘야만 할 것이다. 매번 내주는 일(우리가 체스를 둘 줄 알거나, 비행기를 날릴 줄 알거나, 음악을 만들거나, 아니면 수학 법칙을 발명할 줄 아는 유일한 존재가 아니라는 것)은 고통스럽고 슬플 것이다. 우리는 앞으로 다가올 30년(사실, 어쩌면 앞으로 다가올 한 세기)을 영속적인 정체성 위기 속에서 보내며, 계속 스스로에게 인간이 무슨 소용이 있는지를 질문하게 될 것이다. 우리가 유일한 도구 제작자나 예술가, 또는 도덕 윤리학자가 아니라면, 도대체 무엇이 우리를 특별하게 만드는가? 가장 아이러니하게도, 일상적이고도 실용적인 AI의 가장 큰 이점은, 비록 이 모든 일이 일어난다 할지라도, 생산성 증가나 풍요의 경제학, 혹은 과학을 행하는 새로운 방식이 아닐 것이다. 인공 지능의 도래가 주는 가장 큰 이점은 AI가 인간성을 정의하는 데 도움을 줄 것이라는 점이다.

Why? 왜 정답일까?

기존에 인간에게만 있는 것이라고 생각해 왔던 것들을 기계식 공정이 복제해내고 정교한 AI가 만들어지게 되면서 인간의 고유성에 대한 문제의식이 커지게 되었는데, '아이러니하게도' 여기에 AI가 도움을 줄 수 있다는 내용을 다룬 글이다. 따라서 빈칸에 들어갈 말로 가장 적절한 것은 ① 'AI가 인간성을 정의하는 데 도움을 줄 것이라는'이다.

- **mechanical** ⓐ 기계(상)의, 기계적인
- **set apart** 다르게 하다, 구별시키다
- **supposedly** ⓐd 아마
- **indeed** ⓐd 정말로, 사실은
- **continually** ⓐd 계속해서, 지속적으로
- **moral** ⓐ 도덕의
- **utilitarian** ⓐ 실용적인, 공리주의의
- **abundance** ⓝ 풍요
- **replicate** ⓥ 복제하다
- **surrender** ⓥ 내어주다, 항복하다
- **mathematical** ⓐ 수학의
- **permanent** ⓐ 영속적인, 영구적인
- **toolmaker** ⓝ 연장 제작자[수리공]
- **ethicist** ⓝ 윤리학자
- **economics** ⓝ 경제학
- **artificial intelligence** 인공 지능

- **liberate** ⓥ 해방시키다, 자유롭게 하다
- **resolve** ⓥ 해결하다
- **compensate for** ~을 보완하다, 보상하다
- **labor** ⓝ 노동
- **dilemma** ⓝ 딜레마, 어려운 문제
- **intelligence** ⓝ 지능, 정보

구문 풀이

1행 Over the past 60 years, as mechanical processes
　　　기간 부사구　　　　接続詞(~ 때문에)
have replicated behaviors and talents (we thought) were unique to
　현재완료　　　　　　　　　　　└(주격 관계대명사 생략)
humans, / we've had to change our minds about [what sets us apart].

★★ 문제 해결 꿀~팁 ★★

▶ 많이 틀린 이유는?
답과 바로 대응될만한 표현이 지문에 등장하지 않고 '유추'를 통해 답을 찾아야 했다는 점에서 난이도가 높은 문항이었다.
오답률은 대동소이했는데 이는 매력적인 오답 선택지가 있었다기보다는, 지문의 내용 자체를 파악하는 데 어려움을 느낀 수험생이 많았다는 사실을 보여준다.

▶ 문제 해결 방법은?
'AI'라는 핵심 소재와 첫 문장에서 제시한 '인간성의 정의'가 어떤 식으로 연관이 되어야 하는지를 능동적으로 유추해보도록 한다.
AI는 정교화되면서 인간의 많은 행위를 따라하게 되고, 이에 따라 인간은 과연 AI와 인간을 구별해주는 특성이 무엇일지 고민하게 된다는 내용이 나오는데, 여기서 '아이러니하게도'라는 말이 등장하여 흐름을 반전시킨다. 이는 AI가 인간의 정체성 고민을 '촉발'시키는 존재였지만 동시에 '해결'을 해 주기도 한다는 '역설적인' 내용을 설명하기 위해 등장한 부사어이다.

DAY 10 빈칸 추론 10

01 ①	02 ②	03 ②	04 ⑤	05 ③
06 ①	07 ③	08 ②	09 ①	10 ④
11 ②	12 ②			

구문 풀이

15행 This is exemplified by toys, games, and lessons [that are an
　　주어　　　　동사　　　　　　　　　　선행사　　　　　주격 관계대명사
end in and of themselves and require little of the individual other than
　　　　　　　　　　　　　　　　　　　　　　　　　　　　～이외에는
to master the planned objective].
과거분사

---

01 아이들이 지닌 인지적 호기심　정답률 35% | 정답 ①

다음 빈칸에 들어갈 말로 가장 적절한 것을 고르시오. [3점]

☑ end – 목적　　　　　　　② input – 투입
③ puzzle – 퍼즐　　　　　　④ interest – 흥미
⑤ alternative – 대안

The creativity that children possess / needs to be cultivated throughout their development.
아이들이 지닌 창의성은 / 그들이 성장하는 동안 함양되어야 한다.

Research suggests / that overstructuring the child's environment / may actually limit creative and academic development.
어떤 연구는 시사한다. / 아이의 환경을 과도하게 구조화하는 것이 / 사실은 창의적이고 학문적인 발달을 제한할지도 모른다는 것을

This is a central problem with much of science instruction.
이것은 과학 교육의 많은 부분에서 가장 중요한 문제이다.

The exercises or activities are devised to eliminate different options / and to focus on predetermined results.
연습이나 활동은 다양한 선택권을 없애도록 고안된다. / 그리고 미리 정해진 결과에 집중하도록

The answers are structured to fit the course assessments, / and the wonder of science is lost along with cognitive intrigue.
정답은 수업의 평가에 맞게 구조화되고 / 과학의 경이로움은 인지적인 호기심과 함께 잃게 된다.

We define cognitive intrigue as the wonder / that stimulates and intrinsically motivates an individual / to voluntarily engage in an activity.
우리는 인지적 호기심을 경이로움으로 정의한다. / 한 개인을 자극하고 본질적으로 동기를 부여하는 / 어떤 활동에 자의적으로 참여할 수 있게

The loss of cognitive intrigue may be initiated / by the sole use of play items with predetermined conclusions / and reinforced by rote instruction in school.
인지적인 호기심의 상실은 시작되고 / 미리 정해진 결론을 가지고 놀이 품목을 한 가지 방식으로 사용하면서 / 학교에서 기계적으로 암기하는 교육을 통해 강화될 수 있다.

This is exemplified by toys, games, and lessons / that are an end in and of themselves / and require little of the individual / other than to master the planned objective.
이것은 장난감, 게임, 그리고 수업에서 전형적인 사례를 보여준다. / 그 자체로 목적이 되고 / 개인에게 거의 아무것도 요구하지 않는 / 계획된 목표를 통달하는 것 외에

아이들이 지닌 창의성은 그들이 성장하는 동안 함양되어야 한다. 어떤 연구는 아이의 환경을 과도하게 구조화하는 것이 사실은 창의적이고 학문적인 발달을 제한할지도 모른다는 것을 시사한다. 이것은 과학 교육의 많은 부분에서 가장 중요한 문제이다. 연습이나 활동은 다양한 선택권을 없애고 미리 정해진 결과에 집중하도록 고안된다. 정답은 수업의 평가에 맞게 구조화되고 과학의 경이로움은 인지적인 호기심과 함께 잃게 된다. 우리는 인지적 호기심을 한 개인이 어떤 활동에 자의적으로 참여할 수 있게 자극하고 본질적으로 동기를 부여하는 경이로움으로 정의한다. 인지적인 호기심의 상실은 미리 정해진 결론을 가지고 놀이 품목을 한 가지 방식으로 사용하면서 시작되고 학교에서 기계적으로 암기하는 교육을 통해 강화될 수 있다. 이것은 그 자체로 목적이 되고 계획된 목표를 통달하는 것 외에 개인에게 거의 아무것도 요구하지 않는 장난감, 게임, 그리고 수업에서 전형적인 사례를 보여준다.

Why? 왜 정답일까?

아이의 환경을 지나치게 구조화하는 것이 오히려 아이의 창의력 발달을 제한할 수 있다는 내용을 다룬 글이다. 'The loss of cognitive intrigue may be initiated by the sole use of play items with predetermined conclusions ~'에서 놀이 품목을 '미리 결정된 단 하나의' 방식으로 사용하게 되면서 아이의 인지적인 호기심이 상실되기 시작할 수 있음을 지적하는데, 이는 놀거나 배우는 방식이 '정해진 결론'을 위해 짜여져 그 자체로 '목적'처럼 기능하고 마는 상황이 일어났음을 뜻한다. 따라서 빈칸에 들어갈 말로 가장 적절한 것은 ① '목적'이다.

- **cultivate** ⓥ 육성하다, 기르다
- **overstructure** ⓥ 지나치게 구조화하다
- **cognitive** ⓐ 인식의, 인지의
- **engage in** ~에 참여하다
- **development** ⓝ 발달, 성장, 개발
- **instruction** ⓝ 교육
- **intrigue** ⓥ (호기심을) 불러일으키다
- **reinforce** ⓥ 강화하다, 보강하다

---

02 텍스트성의 확장으로 인한 읽기의 대상 확대　정답률 70% | 정답 ②

다음 빈칸에 들어갈 말로 가장 적절한 것을 고르시오.

① knowledge acquisition – 지식 습득
☑ word recognition – 단어 인식
③ imaginative play – 창의적인 놀이
④ subjective interpretation – 주관적인 해석
⑤ image mapping – 이미지 맵핑

Over the last decade / the attention given to how children learn to read / has foregrounded the nature of *textuality*, / and of the different, interrelated ways / in which readers of all ages make texts mean.
지난 10년 동안 / 어린이가 읽기를 배우는 방법에 관한 관심은 / 텍스트성의 본질을 전면으로 불러왔다. / 그리고 여러 상호 연관된 방식의 본질을 / 모든 연령대의 독자가 텍스트에 의미를 부여하는

'Reading' now applies to a greater number of representational forms / than at any time in the past: / pictures, maps, screens, design graphics and photographs / are all regarded as text.
'읽기'는 이제 훨씬 더 많은 표현 형식에 적용되어서, / 과거 그 어느 시대보다 / 그림, 지도, 화면, 디자인 그래픽, 사진이 / 모두 텍스트로 여겨진다.

In addition to the innovations / made possible in picture books by new printing processes, / design features also predominate in other kinds, / such as books of poetry and information texts.
혁신에 더해, / 새로운 인쇄 공정으로 그림책에서 가능해진 / 다른 종류에서도 디자인적 특징이 두드러진다. / 시집이나 정보 텍스트와 같은

Thus, / reading becomes a more complicated kind of interpretation / than it was / when children's attention was focused on the printed text, / with sketches or pictures as an adjunct.
이처럼, / 읽기는 더 복잡한 종류의 해석이 된다. / 그것이 그랬던 것보다 / 어린이들의 주의 집중이 인쇄된 텍스트에 집중되던 때 / 스케치나 그림이 부속물로 있고

Children now learn from a picture book / that words and illustrations complement and enhance each other.
이제 어린이들은 그림책을 통해 배운다. / 글과 삽화가 서로를 보완하고 향상시킨다는 것을

Reading is not simply word recognition.
읽기는 단순히 단어 인식이 아니다.

Even in the easiest texts, / what a sentence 'says' is often not what it means.
아무리 쉬운 텍스트에서도 / 흔히 문장이 '말하는' 바가 곧 그 문장의 의미인 것은 아니다.

지난 10년 동안 어린이가 읽기를 배우는 방법에 관한 관심은 *텍스트성*의 본질, 그리고 모든 나이의 독자가 텍스트에 의미를 부여하는 여러 상호 연관된 방식의 본질을 전면으로 불러왔다. '읽기'는 이제 과거 그 어느 시대보다 훨씬 더 많은 표현 형식에 적용되어서, 그림, 지도, 화면, 디자인 그래픽, 사진이 모두 텍스트로 여겨진다. 새로운 인쇄 공정으로 그림책에서 가능해진 혁신에 더해, 시집이나 정보 텍스트와 같은 다른 종류에서도 디자인적 특징이 두드러진다. 이처럼, 읽기는 어린이들의 주의 집중이 인쇄된 텍스트에 집중되고 스케치나 그림이 부속물일 때보다 더 복잡한 종류의 해석이 된다. 이제 어린이들은 그림책을 통해 글과 삽화가 서로를 보완하고 향상시킨다는 것을 배운다. 읽기는 단순히 단어 인식이 아니다. 아무리 쉬운 텍스트에서도 흔히 문장이 '말하는' 바가 곧 그 문장의 의미인 것은 아니다.

Why? 왜 정답일까?

읽기의 범주가 글뿐만 아니라 그림, 지도, 그래픽, 사진 등까지 다양하게 아우르게 되면서('Reading' now applies to a greater number of representational forms ~ pictures, maps, screens, design graphics and photographs are all regarded as text.) 단순히 '문장을 있는 그대로 읽는 것'이 읽기로 여겨지지 않게 되었다(what a sentence 'says' is often not what it means)는 내용이다. 따라서 빈칸에 들어갈 말로 가장 적절한 것은 ② '단어 인식'이다.

- **foreground** ⓥ 전면에 내세우다
- **interrelated** ⓐ 상호 연관된
- **representational** ⓐ 표현의, 나타내는
- **in addition to** ~에 더해
- **poetry** ⓝ 시, 운문
- **interpretation** ⓝ 이해, 해석
- **textuality** ⓝ 텍스트성
- **apply to** ~에 적용되다
- **be regarded as** ~로 간주되다
- **predominate** ⓥ 두드러지다, 지배적이다
- **complicated** ⓐ 복잡한
- **adjunct** ⓝ 부속물

DAY 10

[문제편 p.063]

- illustration ⓝ 삽화
- enhance ⓥ 향상하다
- recognition ⓝ 인식, 식별
- complement ⓥ 보완하다
- acquisition ⓝ 습득
- subjective ⓐ 주관적인

구문 풀이

1행 Over the last decade the attention (given to how children learn to read) has foregrounded the nature of *textuality*, and of the different, interrelated ways [in which readers of all ages make texts mean].

기간 부사구 / 주어 / 과거분사 / 동사(현재완료) / 선행사 / 「전치사+관·대」

03 도시에서 어휘 혁신이 일어날 수 있는 이유

정답률 62% | 정답 ②

다음 빈칸에 들어갈 말로 가장 적절한 것을 고르시오.

① provide rich source materials for artists
예술가들에게 풍부한 원재료를 공급하기
✔ offer the greatest exposure to other people
다른 사람들과의 가장 많은 접촉을 제공하기
③ cause cultural conflicts among users of slang
속어 사용자들 사이에서 문화 갈등을 초래하기
④ present ideal research environments to linguists
언어학자들에게 이상적인 연구 환경을 제공하기
⑤ reduce the social mobility of ambitious outsiders
야심에 찬 외부인의 사회 이동을 줄이기

People have always wanted / to be around other people / and to learn from them.
사람들은 항상 원해 왔다. / 다른 사람들 주위에 머무르며 / 그들로부터 배우기를
Cities have long been dynamos of social possibility, / foundries of art, music, and fashion.
도시는 오랫동안 사회적 가능성의 발전기였다. / 즉 예술, 음악, 패션의 주물 공장
Slang, or, if you prefer, "lexical innovation," / has always started in cities / — an outgrowth of all those different people / so frequently exposed to one another.
속어, 또는 여러분이 선호한다면 '어휘의 혁신'은 / 늘 도시에서 시작되었는데, / 그 모든 별의별 사람의 결과물이다. / 그렇게도 빈번히 서로에게 접촉한
It spreads outward, / in a manner not unlike transmissible disease, / which itself typically "takes off" in cities.
그것은 외부로 퍼져나가는데, / 전염성 질병과 다르지 않은 방식으로 / 그 전염성 질병 자체도 보통 도시에서 '이륙한다.'
If, as the noted linguist Leonard Bloomfield argued, / the way a person talks / is a "composite result of what he has heard before," / then language innovation would happen / where the most people heard and talked to the most other people.
만일, 저명한 언어학자 Leonard Bloomfield가 주장하듯이, / 사람이 말하는 방식이 / '전에 들었던 것을 합성한 결과물'이라면, / 언어 혁신은 일어날 것이다. / 가장 많은 사람이 가장 많은 다른 사람의 말을 듣고 가장 많은 다른 사람에게 말한 곳에서
Cities drive taste change / because they offer the greatest exposure to other people, / who not surprisingly are often the creative people / cities seem to attract.
도시는 취향 변화를 이끄는데, / 다른 사람들과의 가장 많은 접촉을 제공한다는 점에서 / 그들은 놀랄 것도 없이 흔히 창의적인 사람들이다. / 도시가 끌어들이는 듯 보이는
Media, / ever more global, ever more far-reaching, / spread language faster to more people.
미디어는 / 그 어느 때보다 더 전방위적이고, 그 어느 때보다 더 멀리까지 미치는 / 언어를 더 빨리 더 많은 사람에게 퍼뜨린다.

사람들은 항상 다른 사람들 주위에 머무르며 그들로부터 배우기를 원해 왔다. 도시는 오랫동안 사회적 가능성의 발전기, 즉 예술, 음악, 패션의 주물 공장이었다. 속어, 또는 여러분이 선호한다면 '어휘의 혁신'은 늘 도시에서 시작되었는데, 그 모든 별의별 사람이 그렇게도 빈번히 서로에게 접촉한 결과물이다. 그것은 전염성 질병과 다르지 않은 방식으로 외부로 퍼져나가는데, 그 전염성 질병 자체도 보통 도시에서 '이륙한다.' 저명한 언어학자 Leonard Bloomfield가 주장하듯이, 사람이 말하는 방식이 '전에 들었던 것을 합성한 결과물'이라면, 언어 혁신은 가장 많은 사람이 가장 많은 다른 사람의 말을 듣고 가장 많은 다른 사람에게 말한 곳에서 일어날 것이다. 도시는 다른 사람들과의 가장 많은 접촉을 제공한다는 점에서 취향 변화를 이끄는데, 그들은 놀랄 것도 없이 흔히 도시가 끌어들이는 듯 보이는 창의적인 사람들이다. 그 어느 때보다 더 전방위적이고, 그 어느 때보다 더 멀리까지 미치는 미디어는 언어를 더 빨리 더 많은 사람에게 퍼뜨린다.

Why? 왜 정답일까?

빈칸 문장 앞에서 언어 혁신은 가장 많은 사람들이 가장 많은 타인과 소통할 수 있는 (~ the most people heard and talked to the most other people.) 공간에서 일어날 것이라고 한다. 이를 근거로 볼 때, 빈칸에도 도시에 '사람들이 많기 때문에' 변화가 일어날 수 있다는 내용이 들어가야 한다. 따라서 빈칸에 들어갈 말로 가장 적절한 것은 ② '다른 사람들과의 가장 많은 접촉을 제공한다(offer the greatest exposure to other people)'이다.

- learn from ~로부터 배우다
- foundry ⓝ 주물 공장
- lexical ⓐ 어휘의
- be exposed to ~에 노출되다
- one another 서로
- outward ad 밖으로
- take off 이륙하다
- drive ⓥ 이끌다, 추진하다
- mobility ⓝ 이동(성)
- dynamo ⓝ 발전기
- slang ⓝ 속어
- outgrowth ⓝ 결과물
- frequently ad 자주, 빈번히
- spread ⓥ 퍼지다
- transmissible ⓐ 전염되는
- composite ⓐ 합성의 ⓝ 합성물
- far-reaching ⓐ 광범위한
- ambitious ⓐ 야심에 찬

구문 풀이

8행 If, (as the noted linguist Leonard Bloomfield argued), the way a person talks is a "composite result of what he has heard before," then language innovation would happen where the most people heard and talked to the most other people.

접속사(조건) / ( ): 삽입절 / 주어 / 관계부사절(how 생략) / 동사 / ~한 곳에서

04 돌연변이의 지속

정답률 24% | 정답 ⑤

다음 빈칸에 들어갈 말로 가장 적절한 것을 고르시오. [3점]

① the force of natural selection increases as animals get older
자연 선택의 힘은 동물이 나이가 들수록 커지는
② their accumulation is largely due to their evolutionary benefits
그것의 축적이 주로 진화적 이득 때문인
③ evolution operates by suppressing reproductive success of animals
진화가 동물의 번식 성공을 억제하여 작용하는
④ animals can promptly compensate for the decline in their abilities
동물들이 자신의 능력 감소를 즉시 상쇄할 수 있는
✔ they only affect animals after they're old enough to have reproduced
동물들이 이미 번식했을 만큼 나이가 충분히 든 후에야 겨우 동물에게 영향을 미치는

Imagine some mutation appears / which makes animals / spontaneously die at the age of 50.
어떤 돌연변이가 나타난다고 상상해 보라. / 동물들을 만드는 / 50살의 나이에 저절로 죽게
This is unambiguously disadvantageous / — but only very slightly so.
이것은 분명히 불리하지만 / 아주 약간 그러하다.
More than 99 per cent of animals / carrying this mutation / will never experience its ill effects / because they will die before it has a chance to act.
99퍼센트 이상의 동물들은 / 이 돌연변이를 지닌 / 결코 그것의 부작용을 경험하지 못할 것이다. / 돌연변이가 작용할 기회를 갖기 전에 죽을 것이기 때문에
This means / that it's pretty likely to remain in the population / — not because it's good, / but because the 'force of natural selection' at such advanced ages / is not strong enough to get rid of it.
이는 의미하는데, / 그것이 개체군에 남아 있을 가능성이 꽤 있다는 것을 / 그것이 좋아서가 아니라, / 그러한 고령에 '자연 선택의 힘'이 / 그것을 없앨 만큼 충분히 강하지 않기 때문이다.
Conversely, / if a mutation killed the animals at two years, / striking them down / when many could reasonably expect / to still be alive and producing children, / evolution would get rid of it very promptly: / animals with the mutation would soon be outcompeted / by those fortunate enough not to have it, / because the force of natural selection is powerful / in the years up to and including reproductive age.
반대로, / 만약 한 돌연변이가 2살에 동물들을 죽게 하고, / 목숨을 앗아 간다면, / 다수가 마땅히 예상할 수 있을 때 / 여전히 살아서 새끼를 낳을 것이라 / 진화는 그것을 매우 신속하게 제거할 것이다. / 그 돌연변이가 있는 동물들은 곧 경쟁에서 뒤처지게 될 것인데, / 돌연변이가 없을 만큼 운이 좋은 동물에 의해 / 왜냐하면 자연 선택의 힘이 강력하기 때문이다. / 번식 연령을 포함해서 그 연령에 이르기까지 여러 해 동안
Thus, / problematic mutations can accumulate, / just so long as they only affect animals / after they're old enough to have reproduced.
그러므로 / 문제가 되는 돌연변이들은 축적될 수 있다. / 그것이 겨우 동물에게 영향을 미치는 한 / 그들이 이미 번식했을 만큼 나이가 충분히 든 후에야

동물들이 50살의 나이에 저절로 죽게 만드는 어떤 돌연변이가 나타난다고 상상해 보라. 이것은 분명히 불리하지만, 아주 약간만 그러하다. 이 돌연변이를 지닌 99퍼센트 이상의 동물들은 돌연변이가 작용할 기회를 갖기 전에 죽을 것이기 때문에 결코 그것의 부작용을 경험하지 못할 것이다. 이는 그것이 개체군에 남아 있을 가능성이 꽤 있다는 것을 의미하는데, 그것이 좋아서가 아니라, 그러한 고령에 '자연 선택의 힘'이 그것을 없앨 만큼 충분히 강하지 않기 때문이다. 반대로, 만약 한 돌연변이가 2살에 동물들을 죽게 하고, 다수가 여전히 살아서 새끼를 낳을 것이라 마땅히 예상할 수 있을 때 목숨을 앗아 간다면, 진

화는 그것을 매우 신속하게 제거할 것이다. 그 돌연변이가 있는 동물들은 돌연변이가 없을 만큼 운이 좋은 동물에 의해 곧 경쟁에서 뒤처지게 될 것인데, 왜냐하면 번식 연령을 포함해서 그 연령에 이르기까지 여러 해 동안 자연 선택의 힘이 강력하기 때문이다. 그러므로 문제가 되는 돌연변이들은 동물들이 이미 번식했을 만큼 나이가 충분히 든 후에야 겨우 동물에게 영향을 미치는 한, 축적될 수 있다.

Why? 왜 정답일까?

어렸을 때 혹은 번식 연령 이전에 나타나는 돌연변이는 자연 선택에 의해 제거될 가능성이 높지만, 번식기 이후 나이가 많이 들었을 때 작용하는 돌연변이는 그럴 가능성이 낮다(~ the 'force of natural selection' at such advanced ages is not strong enough to get rid of it.)는 내용의 글이다. 따라서 빈칸에 들어갈 말로 가장 적절한 것은 ⑤ '동물들이 이미 번식했을 만큼 나이가 충분히 든 후에야 겨우 동물에게 영향을 미치는'이다.

- mutation ⓝ 돌연변이
- spontaneously [ad] 저절로, 자발적으로
- disadvantageous ⓐ 불리한
- pretty [ad] 어느 정도, 꽤
- population ⓝ (전체) 개체 수
- advanced ⓐ (발달 단계상) 후기의
- conversely [ad] 반대로
- evolution ⓝ 진화
- reproductive ⓐ 번식의
- suppress ⓥ 억제하다
- appear ⓥ 나타나다
- unambiguously [ad] 분명히
- slightly [ad] 약간
- remain ⓥ 남아 있다
- natural selection 자연 선택
- get rid of ~을 제거하다
- expect ⓥ 예상하다
- promptly [ad] 즉시
- accumulate ⓥ 축적하다
- compensate for ~을 상쇄하다, 보상하다

구문 풀이

> **9행** Conversely, if a mutation killed the animals at two years,
> 「if + 주어 + 과거 동사 ~」
> striking them down when many could reasonably expect to still be
> 분사구문
> alive and producing children, evolution would get rid of it very
> 주어1 + 조동사 과거형1 + 동사원형1 ~
> promptly: animals with the mutation would soon be outcompeted
> 주어2 + 조동사 과거형 + 동사원형 2 ~ 「가정법 과거」
> by those fortunate enough not to have it, because the force of natural
> = animals   형용사구
> selection is powerful in the years up to and including reproductive age.

---

05 사용하는 말(라벨)에 영향을 받는 우리의 세계관 정답률 65% | 정답 ③

다음 빈칸에 들어갈 말로 가장 적절한 것을 고르시오. [3점]

① where we purchase them – 우리가 그것을 어디서 구매하느냐
② how expensive they are – 그것이 얼마나 비싸냐
✔ what labels we use – 우리가 무슨 라벨을 사용하느냐
④ how persuasive ads are – 광고가 얼마나 설득력 있느냐
⑤ who makes the products – 누가 제품을 만드냐

The way we perceive the colors of the rainbow, / and the universe in general, / is influenced by the words / we use to describe them.
우리가 무지개의 색깔을 인식하는 방식은 / 그리고 일반적으로 우주를 / 말에 영향을 받는다. / 그것을 묘사하고자 우리가 사용하는

This is not limited to visual perception / but also applies to smell, taste, touch, our perception of time / and countless other human experiences.
이것은 시각적인 인식에 국한되는 것이 아니라 / 후각, 미각, 촉각, 시간에 대한 우리의 인식에도 적용된다. / 그리고 수많은 여타 인간의 경험에도

A wine or Scotch connoisseur, for example, / has a much richer vocabulary at their disposal / to describe the fullness, finish, flavors and aroma of the drink, / which in turn improves their ability / to recognize and remember subtle differences / of which a non-expert may be unaware.
예를 들어 와인이나 스카치위스키 감정가는 / 훨씬 더 풍부한 어휘를 마음대로 사용하고, / 그 음료의 풍부함, 끝맛, 맛과 향을 묘사하는 데 / 이것은 결국 그들의 능력을 향상시킨다. / 미묘한 차이를 인식하고 기억하는 / 비전문가라면 모를 수 있는

Similarly, / a chef or perfumer has at their disposal labels for flavors and smells / that allow them / to perceive, differentiate among, prepare and remember subtle variations.
마찬가지로 / 요리사나 조향사는 맛과 향에 대한 라벨을 마음대로 사용한다. / 그들이 ~할 수 있게 해주는 / 미묘한 차이를 인지하고 구별하며 준비하고 기억할

The labels that we have at our disposal / influence / how we see the world around us.
우리가 마음대로 사용하는 라벨이 / 영향을 준다. / 우리가 주변의 세상을 보는 방식에

Regardless of where you place the limits of linguistic effects on cognition, / there is evidence / that at least some of the things / that we perceive and

remember / differ depending on what labels we use.
인식에 미치는 언어적 영향의 한계를 어디에 두느냐와 상관없이 / 증거가 있다. / 적어도 대상 중 일부는 / 우리가 인식하고 기억하는 / 우리가 무슨 라벨을 사용하느냐에 따라 달라진다는

우리가 무지개의 색깔, 그리고 일반적으로 우주를 인식하는 방식은 그것을 묘사하고자 우리가 사용하는 말에 영향을 받는다. 이것은 시각적인 인식에 국한되는 것이 아니라 후각, 미각, 촉각, 시간에 대한 우리의 인식, 수많은 여타 인간의 경험에도 적용된다. 예를 들어 와인이나 스카치위스키 감정가는 그 음료의 풍부함, 끝맛, 맛과 향을 묘사하는 데 훨씬 더 풍부한 어휘를 마음대로 사용하고, 이것은 결국 비전문가라면 모를 수 있는 미묘한 차이를 인식하고 기억하는 그들의 능력을 향상시킨다. 마찬가지로 요리사나 조향사는 미묘한 차이를 인지하고 구별하며 준비하고 기억할 수 있게 해 주는, 맛과 향에 대한 라벨을 마음대로 사용한다. 우리가 마음대로 사용하는 라벨이 우리가 주변의 세상을 보는 방식에 영향을 준다. 인식에 미치는 언어적 영향의 한계를 어디에 두느냐와 상관없이 적어도 우리가 인식하고 기억하는 것의 일부는 우리가 무슨 라벨을 사용하느냐에 따라 달라진다는 증거가 있다.

Why? 왜 정답일까?

우리가 어떤 단어, 즉 '라벨'을 사용하는가에 따라 우리가 세상을 인지하는 방식에 영향이 갈 수 있다(The labels that we have at our disposal influence how we see the world around us.)는 내용이므로, 빈칸에 들어갈 말로 가장 적절한 것은 ③ '우리가 무슨 라벨을 사용하느냐'이다.

- countless ⓐ 수없이 많은
- at one's disposal ~의 마음대로 사용하는
- in turn 결국
- unaware ⓐ 모르는
- variation ⓝ 차이, 변형
- linguistic ⓐ 언어적인
- connoisseur ⓝ 감정가
- flavor ⓝ 풍미
- subtle ⓐ 미묘한
- perfumer ⓝ 조향사
- regardless of ~와 상관없이
- cognition ⓝ 인식

구문 풀이

> **5행** A wine or Scotch connoisseur, for example, has a much richer vocabulary at their disposal to describe the fullness, finish,
> 부사적 용법(~하기 위해)
> flavors and aroma of the drink, which in turn improves their ability
> 계속적 용법(= and it)
> to recognize and remember subtle differences [of which a non-expert
> 형용사적 용법   선행사   「전치사 + 관·대」
> may be unaware].

---

06 영화 *Apocalypse Now*와 원작과의 비교 정답률 63% | 정답 ①

다음 빈칸에 들어갈 말로 가장 적절한 것을 고르시오. [3점]

✔ a literal adaptation of the novel
소설을 있는 그대로 각색한 것
② a source of inspiration for the novel
소설에 대한 영감의 근원
③ a faithful depiction of the Vietnam War
베트남 전쟁에 대한 충실한 묘사
④ a vivid dramatisation of a psychological journey
심리적 여정의 생생한 극화
⑤ a critical interpretation of contemporary civilisation
현대 문명에 대한 비판적인 해석

Apocalypse Now, a film produced and directed by Francis Ford Coppola, / gained widespread popularity, and for good reason.
Francis Ford Coppola가 제작하고 감독한 영화인 *Apocalypse Now*는 / 폭넓은 인기를 얻었는데, 그럴 만한 이유가 있었다.

The film is an adaptation / of Joseph Conrad's novel *Heart of Darkness*, / which is set in the African Congo at the end of the 19th century.
그 영화는 각색인데, / Joseph Conrad의 소설 *Heart of Darkness*의 / 이 소설은 19세기 말 아프리카의 콩고를 배경으로 한다.

Unlike the original novel, / *Apocalypse Now* is set in Vietnam and Cambodia / during the Vietnam War.
원작 소설과는 달리 / *Apocalypse Now*는 베트남과 캄보디아를 배경으로 한다. / 베트남 전쟁 당시의

The setting, time period, dialogue and other incidental details / are changed / but the fundamental narrative and themes of *Apocalypse Now* / are the same as those of *Heart of Darkness*.
배경, 시기, 대화 및 기타 부수적 세부 사항은 / 바뀌어 있지만, / *Apocalypse Now*의 기본적인 줄거리와 주제는 / *Heart of Darkness*와 같다.

Both describe a physical journey, / reflecting the central character's mental and spiritual journey, / down a river to confront the deranged Kurtz character, / who represents the worst aspects of civilisation.
둘 다 물리적 여정을 묘사하는데, / 이는 주인공의 정신적 여정과 영적 여정을 반영한 것이며, / 제정신이 아닌 Kurtz라는 인물에 맞서려고 강을 따라 내려가는 / Kurtz는 문명의 가장 나쁜 단면을 대표한다.

DAY 10

By giving *Apocalypse Now* / a setting that was contemporary at the time of its release, / audiences were able to experience and identify with its themes more easily / than they would have / if the film had been a literal adaptation of the novel.
*Apocalypse Now*에 제공함으로써, / 영화 개봉 당시와 같은 시대적 배경을 / 더 쉽게 영화의 주제를 접하고 영화와 동질감을 느낄 수 있었다. / 그들이 그랬을 것보다 / 관객들은 영화가 소설을 있는 그대로 각색한 것이었다면

Francis Ford Coppola가 제작하고 감독한 영화인 *Apocalypse Now*는 폭넓은 인기를 얻었는데, 그럴만한 이유가 있었다. 그 영화는 Joseph Conrad의 소설 *Heart of Darkness*를 각색한 것인데, 이 소설은 19세기 말 아프리카의 콩고를 배경으로 한다. 원작 소설과는 달리 *Apocalypse Now*는 베트남 전쟁 당시의 베트남과 캄보디아를 배경으로 한다. 배경, 시기, 대화 및 기타 부수적 세부 사항은 바뀌어 있지만, *Apocalypse Now*의 기본적인 줄거리와 주제는 *Heart of Darkness*와 같다. 둘 다 물리적 여정을 묘사하는데, 이는 제정신이 아닌 Kurtz라는 인물에 맞서려고 강을 따라 내려가는, 주인공의 정신적 여정과 영적 여정을 반영한 것이며, Kurtz는 문명의 가장 나쁜 단면을 대표한다. *Apocalypse Now*에 영화 개봉 당시와 같은 시대적 배경을 제공함으로써, 관객들은 영화가 소설을 있는 그대로 각색한 것이었다면 그러했을 것보다 더 쉽게 영화의 주제를 접하고 영화와 동질감을 느낄 수 있었다.

Why? 왜 정답일까?

글에 따르면 영화 *Apocalypse Now*는 소설 *Heart of Darkness*를 각색하여 만든 영화이지만 배경, 시기, 대화, 기타 세부 사항 면에서 변화를 시도했는데, 마지막 문장에 따르면 이는 관객으로 하여금 영화의 주제를 더 쉽게 접하고 영화에 동질감을 느끼게 하기 위한 장치였다. 원작에 '변화를 주어 각색한 것'은 원작을 '그대로 각색한 것'과 비교해야 적절하므로, 빈칸에 들어갈 말로 가장 적절한 것은 ① '소설을 있는 그대로 각색한 것'이다.

- **widespread** ⓐ 널리 퍼진, 만연한
- **unlike** [prep] ~와는 달리
- **fundamental** ⓐ 기본적인
- **describe** ⓥ 묘사하다
- **spiritual** ⓐ 영적인, 영혼의
- **deranged** ⓐ 미친, 혼란된
- **aspect** ⓝ 양상, 측면
- **contemporary** ⓐ 현대의, 동시대의
- **identify with** ~과 동일시하다
- **inspiration** ⓝ 영감
- **depiction** ⓝ 묘사

- **adaptation** ⓝ 각색, 적응
- **incidental** ⓐ 부수적인, ~에 따르기 마련인
- **narrative** ⓝ 줄거리, 묘사
- **mental** ⓐ 마음의, 정신의
- **confront** ⓥ 대면하다
- **represent** ⓥ 대표하다
- **civilisation** ⓝ 문명
- **release** ⓝ 개봉, 발표
- **literal** ⓐ (어구의 뜻이) 문자 그대로의
- **faithful** ⓐ 충실한
- **interpretation** ⓝ 해석

구문 풀이

10행 Both describe a physical journey, [reflecting the central character's mental and spiritual journey, down a river to confront the deranged Kurtz character], {who represents the worst aspects of civilisation}.
[ ] : a physical journey 부연
선행사 / 주격 관계대명사

★★★ 1등급 대비 고난도 2펌 문제

07   수집의 입지 약화   정답률 22% | 정답 ③

다음 빈칸에 들어갈 말로 가장 적절한 것을 고르시오.

① competitive – 경쟁력 있는
② novel – 새로운
✓ secondary – 부차적인
④ reliable – 신뢰할 만한
⑤ unconditional – 무조건적인

The growth of academic disciplines / and sub-disciplines, such as art history or palaeontology, / and of particular figures such as the art critic, / helped produce principles and practices / for selecting and organizing what was worthy of keeping, / though it remained a struggle.
학과의 성장과 / 미술사학이나 고생물학과 같은 하위 학과의 (성장), / 그리고 미술평론가와 같은 특정 인물의 (성장은) / 원칙과 관행의 도출에 도움이 되었다. / 지킬 가치가 있는 것을 선택하고 정리하기 위한 / 비록 그것이 힘든 일로 남게 되었지만

Moreover, / as museums and universities drew further apart / toward the end of the nineteenth century, / and as the idea of objects / as a highly valued route to knowing the world / went into decline, / collecting began to lose its status / as a worthy intellectual pursuit, / especially in the sciences.
게다가, / 박물관과 대학이 서로 더욱 멀어지고, / 19세기 말엽에 / 대상 개념이 / 세상을 알게 되는 매우 가치 있는 경로로서의 / 쇠퇴하면서, / 수집은 지위를 잃기 시작했다. / 가치 있는 지적 활동으로서의 / 특히 과학에서

The really interesting and important aspects of science / were increasingly

---

those invisible to the naked eye, / and the classification of things collected / no longer promised to produce cutting-edge knowledge.
과학의 참으로 흥미롭고 중요한 측면은 / 점점 더 육안에 보이지 않는 것들이었고, / 수집된 것들에 대한 분류는 / 더 이상 최첨단의 지식을 생산할 가망이 없었다.

The term "butterfly collecting" could come to be used / with the adjective "mere" / to indicate a pursuit of secondary academic status.
'나비 채집'이라는 용어는 사용될 수 있었다. / '한낱'이라는 형용사와 / 부차적인 학문적 지위의 추구를 나타내기 위해

학과의 성장과 미술사학이나 고생물학과 같은 하위 학과의 성장, 그리고 미술평론가와 같은 특정 인물의 성장은 비록 힘든 일로 남게 되었지만 지킬 가치가 있는 것을 선택하고 정리하기 위한 원칙과 관행을 도출하는 데 도움이 되었다. 게다가, 19세기 말엽에 박물관과 대학이 서로 더욱 멀어지고, 세상을 알게 되는 매우 가치 있는 경로로서의 대상 개념이 쇠퇴하면서, 수집은 특히 과학에서 가치 있는 지적 활동으로서의 지위를 잃기 시작했다. 과학의 참으로 흥미롭고 중요한 측면은 점점 더 육안에 보이지 않는 것들이었고, 수집된 것들에 대한 분류는 더 이상 최첨단의 지식을 생산할 가망이 없었다. '나비 채집'이라는 용어는 '한낱(mere)'이라는 형용사와 사용되어 부차적인 학문적 지위의 추구를 나타낼 수 있었다.

Why? 왜 정답일까?

과학 연구에서 수집의 비중과 입지가 약화되었다(~ collecting began to lose its status as a worthy intellectual pursuit, especially in the sciences. / ~ the classification of things collected no longer promised to produce cutting-edge knowledge.)는 내용으로 보아, 빈칸에 들어갈 말로 가장 적절한 것은 ③ '부차적인'이다.

- **discipline** ⓝ 분야
- **struggle** ⓝ 힘든 일, 투쟁
- **go into decline** 쇠퇴하다
- **invisible** ⓐ 눈에 보이지 않는
- **cutting-edge** ⓐ 최첨단의
- **novel** ⓐ 새로운
- **unconditional** ⓐ 무조건적인

- **be worthy of** ~할 가치가 있다
- **draw apart** ~와 떨어지다
- **intellectual** ⓐ 지적인
- **classification** ⓝ 분류
- **mere** ⓐ 한낱 (~에 불과한), 단지 ~한
- **secondary** ⓐ 부차적인

구문 풀이

1행 The growth of academic disciplines and sub-disciplines,
주어 / 수식어구1
such as art history or palaeontology, and of particular figures such
수식어구2
as the art critic, helped produce principles and practices for selecting
동사 / 목적어(원형부정사)
and organizing what was worthy of keeping, though it remained a
관계대명사(~것) / 접속사(비록 ~이지만)
struggle.

★★ 문제 해결 꿀~팁 ★★

▶ 많이 틀린 이유는?
수집의 학문적 지위라는 낯선 소재에 관한 글로, 19세기 말 이후로 수집 활동이 새로운 지식 생산에 기여할 가망이 없다고 여겨지면서 가치 있는 지적 활동으로서의 지위를 잃기 시작했다는 내용이 주를 이루고 있다. ②는 수집 활동이 '참신하게' 받아들여졌다는 의미를 완성하므로 맥락상 부적절하고, ④ 또한 수집 활동이 '믿을 만하게' 여겨졌다는 뜻을 나타내므로 흐름상 적절하지 않다.

▶ 문제 해결 방법은?
Moreover 이하에 따르면 눈에 보이는 것보다도 보이지 않는 것들의 학문적 중요성이 부각되면서 수집 활동의 입지가 약화되었다고 하므로, 이 약해진 지위를 한 단어로 나타낼 수 있는 형용사를 답으로 골라야 한다.

★★★ 1등급 대비 고난도 2펌 문제

08   생물 다양성에 대한 인식을 돕는 유전 공학   정답률 32% | 정답 ②

다음 빈칸에 들어갈 말로 가장 적절한 것을 고르시오.

① ecological systems are genetically programmed
생태계는 유전적으로 프로그램되어 있다
✓ we should avoid destroying natural ecosystems
우리가 자연 생태계를 파괴하는 것을 피해야 한다
③ we need to stop creating genetically modified organisms
우리가 유전자 변형 유기체를 만드는 것을 중단할 필요가 있다
④ artificial organisms can survive in natural environments
인위적인 유기체는 자연환경에서 생존할 수 있다
⑤ living things adapt themselves to their physical environments
살아있는 것들은 자신의 물리적 환경에 적응한다

Genetic engineering followed by cloning / to distribute many identical animals or plants / is sometimes seen as a threat to the diversity of nature.
복제로 이어지는 유전 공학은 / 많은 똑같은 동물이나 식물을 퍼뜨리기 위한 / 때로 자연의 다양성에 대한 위협으로 여겨진다.

However, / humans have been replacing diverse natural habitats / with artificial monoculture / for millennia.
그러나 / 인간은 다양한 자연 서식지를 대체해 오고 있다. / 인위적인 단일 경작으로 / 수천 년 동안

Most natural habitats in the advanced nations / have already been replaced / with some form of artificial environment / based on mass production or repetition.
선진국 자연 서식지의 대부분은 / 이미 대체되었다. / 어떤 형태의 인위적인 환경으로 / 대량 생산 또는 반복에 기반을 둔

The real threat to biodiversity / is surely the need to convert ever more of our planet into production zones / to feed the ever-increasing human population.
생물 다양성에 대한 진정한 위협은 / 지구의 더욱 많은 부분을 생산지대로 전환해야 할 필요성임이 확실하다. / 계속 늘어나는 인구에 식량을 공급하기 위해서

The cloning and transgenic alteration of domestic animals / makes little difference to the overall situation.
가축의 복제와 이식 유전자에 의한 변형은 / 전반적인 상황에 거의 변화를 주지 않는다.

Conversely, / the renewed interest in genetics / has led to a growing awareness / that there are many wild plants and animals with interesting or useful genetic properties / that could be used for a variety of as-yet-unknown purposes.
반대로, / 유전학에 관한 새로워진 관심은 / 인식을 점점 키웠다. / 흥미롭거나 유용한 유전 특성을 가진 많은 야생 동식물이 있다는 / 아직 알려지지 않은 다양한 목적을 위해서 이용될 수 있는

This has led in turn to a realization / that we should avoid destroying natural ecosystems / because they may harbor tomorrow's drugs against cancer, malaria, or obesity.
이것은 결국 깨닫게 해 주었다. / 우리가 자연 생태계를 파괴하는 것을 피해야 한다는 것을 / 자연 생태계가 암, 말라리아 또는 비만을 치료하는 미래의 약을 품고 있을 수도 있기 때문에

많은 똑같은 동물이나 식물을 퍼뜨리기 위한 복제로 이어지는 유전 공학은 때때로 자연의 다양성에 대한 위협으로 여겨진다. 그러나 인간은 수천 년 동안 인위적인 단일 경작으로 다양한 자연 서식지를 대체해 오고 있다. 선진국 자연 서식지의 대부분은 대량 생산 또는 반복에 기반을 둔 어떤 형태의 인위적인 환경으로 이미 대체되었다. 생물 다양성에 대한 진정한 위협은 계속 늘어나는 인구에 식량을 공급하기 위해서 지구의 더욱더 많은 부분을 생산지대로 전환해야 할 필요성임이 확실하다. 가축의 복제와 이식 유전자에 의한 변형은 전반적인 상황에 거의 변화를 주지 않는다. 반대로, 유전학에 관한 새로워진 관심은 아직 알려지지 않은 다양한 목적을 위해서 이용될 수 있는 흥미롭거나 유용한 유전 특성을 가진 많은 야생 동식물이 있다는 인식을 점점 키웠다. 이것은 결국 자연 생태계가 암, 말라리아 또는 비만을 치료하는 미래의 약을 품고 있을 수도 있기 때문에 우리가 자연 생태계를 파괴하는 것을 피해야 한다는 것을 깨닫게 해 주었다.

Why? 왜 정답일까?

첫 문장에서 유전 공학의 발전은 흔히 생물 다양성에 대한 위협으로 인식된다는 통념을 제시한 후 이를 반박한 글이다. 특히 'Conversely, the renewed interest in genetics has led to a growing awareness that there are many wild plants and animals with interesting or useful genetic properties that could be used for a variety of as-yet-unknown purposes.'에서는 유전학에 대한 관심이 커지면서 오히려 인간은 아직 알려지지 못한 유용한 생물 종들이 있음을 인식하게 된다고 설명하는 것으로 볼 때, 빈칸에는 유전 공학이 발전함에 따라 '생물 다양성에 대한 사람들의 인식이 높아질 수 있다'는 내용이 들어가야 한다. 따라서 빈칸에 들어갈 말로 가장 적절한 것은 '생물 다양성 보존'을 '생태계 파괴 방지'라는 말로 바꾸어 표현한 ② '우리가 자연 생태계를 파괴하는 것을 피해야 한다'이다.

- genetic ⓐ 유전학의, 유전적인
- distribute ⓥ 퍼뜨리다, 분배하다
- artificial ⓐ 인위적인
- mass production ⓝ 대량 생산
- convert ⓥ 바꾸다, 전환하다
- transgenic ⓐ 이식 유전자를 가진
- property ⓝ 특성
- harbor ⓥ (계획이나 생각을) 품다
- clone ⓥ 복제하다
- identical ⓐ 똑같은, 동일한
- millennia ⓝ 천년
- biodiversity ⓝ 생물 다양성
- ever-increasing ⓐ 계속 늘어나는
- alteration ⓝ 변형
- as-yet-unknown ⓐ 아직 알려지지 않은
- obesity ⓝ 비만

구문 풀이

13행 Conversely, the renewed interest in genetics has led to a growing awareness that there are many wild plants and animals with interesting or useful genetic properties [that could be used for a variety of as-yet-unknown purposes].

[문제편 p.066]

★★ 문제 해결 꿀~팁 ★★

▶ 많이 틀린 이유는?
이 글은 통념과는 달리 유전 공학이 발전하면 사람들이 여태까지 미지의 영역 안에 있었던 다양한 생물군에 대해 알게 되면서 오히려 생물 다양성의 가치에 대한 인식을 높일 수 있다는 내용을 다루고 있다. ③은 '유전자 변형 생물의 생산 중단'을 언급하고 있는데, 이는 유전 공학 기술을 부정적으로 보는 시각과 더 관련되어 있어 답으로 적절치 않다. ④의 '인공 유기체의 생존'에 관해서는 글에서 언급되지 않았다.

▶ 문제 해결 방법은?
Conversely 이하로 필자의 핵심 주장이 전개된다. 유전 공학의 발전은 도리어 다양한 생물에 대한 관심을 일깨운다는 내용으로 볼 때, 사람들이 '다양한 생물 종을 보존해야 한다 = 생태계 파괴를 멈춰야 한다'는 결론에 이르게 된다는 내용이 이어져야 한다.

★★★ 1등급 대비 고난도 3점 문제

09 심리학자가 아이들을 연구할 때 가져야 할 태도   정답률 47% | 정답 ①

다음 빈칸에 들어갈 말로 가장 적절한 것을 고르시오. [3점]

✔① venture a little more often into the wilderness
위험을 무릅쓰고 조금 더 자주 황무지로 들어서야
② help them recall their most precious memories
그들이 자신의 가장 소중한 기억을 떠올리도록 도와야
③ better understand the challenges of parental duty
부모의 의무라는 난제를 더 잘 이해해야
④ disregard the key characteristics of children's fiction
아동 소설의 핵심 특징을 무시해야
⑤ standardize the paths of their psychological development
그들의 심리발달 경로를 표준화해야

In trying to explain / how different disciplines attempt to understand autobiographical memory / the literary critic Daniel Albright said, / "Psychology is a garden, literature is a wilderness."
설명하려고 노력할 때, / 서로 다른 학문이 자전적 기억을 어떻게 이해하려고 하는지 / 문학평론가 Daniel Albright는 말했다. / '심리학은 정원이고, 문학은 황무지이다.'라고

He meant, / I believe, / that psychology seeks to make patterns, / find regularity, / and ultimately impose order on human experience and behavior.
그는 의미했다. / 내가 믿기로, / 심리학은 패턴을 만들고, / 규칙성을 찾으며, / 궁극적으로 인간의 경험과 행동에 질서를 부여하고자 한다는 것

Writers, / by contrast, / dive into the unruly, untamed depths of human experiences.
작가는 / 반면에, / 제멋대로 굴고 길들여지지 않은 인간 경험의 깊이를 파고든다.

What he said about understanding memory / can be extended to our questions / about young children's minds.
그가 기억의 이해에 관해 말한 것은 / 우리의 질문으로 확장될 수 있다. / 어린아이의 마음에 관한

If we psychologists are too bent on identifying the orderly pattern, / the regularities of children's minds, / we may miss an essential and pervasive characteristic of our topic: / the child's more unruly and imaginative ways of talking and thinking.
만약 우리 심리학자들이 질서 있는 패턴을 밝히는 데 너무 열중한다면, / 즉 아이 마음의 규칙성을 / 우리는 우리 주제의 본질적이고 널리 퍼져 있는 특성을 놓칠 수도 있다. / 즉 더 제멋대로이고 상상력이 풍부한 아이의 말하기 및 사고방식

It is not only the developed writer or literary scholar / who seems drawn toward a somewhat wild and idiosyncratic way of thinking; / young children are as well.
비단 성숙한 작가나 문학 연구가뿐만이 아니라, / 다소 거칠고 색다른 사고방식에 끌리는 것처럼 보이는 것은 / 어린아이도 역시 그렇다.

The psychologist interested in young children / may have to venture a little more often into the wilderness / in order to get a good picture of how children think.
어린아이에게 관심이 있는 심리학자는 / 위험을 무릅쓰고 조금 더 자주 황무지로 들어서야 할지도 모른다. / 아이의 사고방식을 잘 이해하기 위해

서로 다른 학문이 자전적 기억을 어떻게 이해하려고 하는지 설명하려고 노력할 때, 문학평론가 Daniel Albright는 '심리학은 정원이고, 문학은 황무지이다.'라고 말했다. 내가 믿기로, 그의 말은 심리학은 패턴을 만들고, 규칙성을 찾으며, 궁극적으로 인간의 경험과 행동에 질서를 부여하고자 한다는 뜻이었다. 반면에, 작가는 제멋대로 굴고 길들여지지 않은 인간 경험의 깊이를 파고든다. 그가 기억의 이해에 관해 말한 것은 어린아이의 마음에 관한 우리의 질문으로 확장될 수 있다. 만약 우리 심리학자들이 질서 있는 패턴, 즉 아이 마음의 규칙성을 밝히는 데 너무 열중한다면, 우리는 우리 주제의 본질적이고 널리 퍼져 있는 특성, 즉 더 제멋대로이고 상상력이 풍부한 아이의 말하기 및 사고방식을 놓칠 수도 있다. 다소 거칠고 색다른 사고방식에 끌리는 것처럼 보이는 것은 비단 성숙한 작가나 문학 연구가뿐만이 아니라, 어린아이도 역시 그렇다. 어린

아이에게 관심이 있는 심리학자는 아이의 사고방식을 잘 이해하기 위해 **위험을 무릅쓰고 조금 더 자주 황무지로 들어서야** 할지도 모른다.

Why? 왜 정답일까?

첫 세 문장에 따르면 심리학은 마치 정원 가꾸기처럼 규칙성을 밝히는 한편, 문학은 마치 황무지를 탐구하듯 정형화할 수 없는 인간의 경험을 파고든다고 한다. 글의 중반부 이후에서는 이것을 아이들의 마음을 연구하는 데 적용해볼 때, 심리학자로서 패턴과 규칙을 찾는 데 열중하기보다 문학가처럼 자유로운 탐구를 추구할 필요가 있다고 한다. 따라서 빈칸에 들어갈 말로 가장 적절한 것은 ① '위험을 무릅쓰고 조금 더 자주 황무지로 들어서야'이다.

- **discipline** ⓝ 학문 분야
- **autobiographical** ⓐ 자전적인
- **critic** ⓝ 비평가
- **regularity** ⓝ 규칙성
- **impose** ⓥ 부과하다, 부여하다
- **by contrast** 반대로, 대조적으로
- **unruly** ⓐ 제멋대로 구는
- **extend** ⓥ 확장하다
- **identify** ⓥ 식별하다, 알아내다
- **pervasive** ⓐ 널리 퍼져 있는
- **somewhat** ⓐⓓ 다소
- **venture into** 위험을 감수하고 ~로 들어가다
- **precious** ⓐ 소중한
- **standardize** ⓥ 표준화하다
- **attempt** ⓥ 노력하다, 시도하다
- **literary** ⓐ 문학의
- **wilderness** ⓝ 황무지
- **ultimately** ⓐⓓ 궁극적으로
- **order** ⓝ 질서
- **dive into** ~로 뛰어들다
- **untamed** ⓐ 길들여지지 않은
- **bent on** ~에 열중하는
- **essential** ⓐ 본질적인
- **characteristic** ⓝ 특징, 특성
- **idiosyncratic** ⓐ 색다른
- **recall** ⓥ 회상하다, 떠올리다
- **disregard** ⓥ 무시하다

구문 풀이

> **10행** If we psychologists are too bent on identifying the orderly pattern, the regularities of children's minds, we may miss an essential and pervasive characteristic of our topic: the child's more unruly and imaginative ways of talking and thinking.
> (동격 표시)

★★ 문제 해결 꿀~팁 ★★

▶ 많이 틀린 이유는?

글 초반부에 언급되는 '문학'이 마치 글의 핵심 소재인 것처럼 보이지만, 실제로 이 글은 문학 연구에 관한 글이 아니다. '아동 심리'를 탐구하는 데 있어 문학의 연구 방식을 참고할 수 있다는 글일 뿐, '아동 문학'이나 그 특징은 언급되지 않는다. 따라서 ④는 답으로 부적절하다.

▶ 문제 해결 방법은?

정답에 비유적인 표현이 나와서 쉽게 고르기 어렵다. 하지만, 첫 문장에서 '심리학 = 정원', '문학 = 황무지'라는 등식을 잘 확인하고, 'What he said ~' 이하로 이 등식이 반박된다는 것을 확인하면 정답을 찾을 수 있다. '정원 가꾸기'처럼 보이는 아동 심리 연구가 사실은 문학과 마찬가지로 '황무지 탐구'와 같다는 것이 요지임을 파악하도록 한다.

★★★ 1등급 대비 고난도 3점 문제

| 10 | 인지적 장벽의 극복 방법 | 정답률 27% | 정답 ④ |

다음 빈칸에 들어갈 말로 가장 적절한 것을 고르시오. [3점]

① do away with irregularity and seek harmony
　불규칙성을 버리고 조화를 추구하게
② justify errors by reorganizing remaining data
　남아있는 데이터를 재조직하여 실수를 정당화하게
③ build barriers to avoid intellectual insecurity
　지적 불안을 피하기 위해 장벽을 세우게
✓④ abandon failed hypotheses and venture new ones
　실패한 가설을 버리고 새로운 가설을 과감히 시도하게
⑤ manipulate the surroundings and support existing ideas
　환경을 조작하고 기존의 관념을 지지하게

Magical thinking, intellectual insecurity, and confirmation bias / are all powerful barriers to scientific discovery; / they blocked the eyes of generations of astronomers before Copernicus.
주술적 사고, 지적 불안, 그리고 확증 편향은 / 모두 과학적 발견에 대한 강력한 장벽이며, / 그것들은 코페르니쿠스 이전 여러 세대 천문학자들의 눈을 가렸다.

But as twenty-first-century researchers have discovered, / these three barriers can all be destroyed with a simple teaching trick: / transporting our brain to an environment outside our own.
그러나 21세기 연구자들이 발견했듯이, / 이 세 가지 장벽은 모두 간단한 교수 기법으로 무너뜨릴 수 있다. / 즉 우리의 뇌를 우리 자신 밖의 환경으로 이동시키는 것

That environment can be a nature preserve / many miles from our home, / or

a computer-simulated Mars, / or any other space / that our ego doesn't associate directly / with our health, social status, and material success.
그 환경은 자연 보호 구역이 될 수 있다. / 우리의 집으로부터 몇 마일 떨어진 / 혹은 컴퓨터로 시뮬레이션한 화성이나, / 다른 어떤 공간 / 우리의 자아가 직접 연관짓지 않는 / 우리의 건강, 사회적 지위, 그리고 물질적 성공과

In that environment, / our ego will be less inclined / to take the failure of its predictions personally.
그런 환경에서, / 우리의 자아는 경향이 덜할 것이다. / 자기 예측이 틀린 것에 기분 상하는

Certainly, / our ego may feel a little upset / that its guesses about the nature preserve or Mars / were wrong, / but it was never really that invested in the guesses / to begin with.
분명히, / 우리의 자아는 약간 언짢은 느낌이 들 수도 있다 / 그 자연 보호 구역이나 화성에 대한 자기 추측이 틀렸다는 것에 / 하지만 그것은 결코 그 추측에 실제로 그다지 관여를 하지 않았다. / 애초에

Why should it care too much about things / that have no bearing on its own fame or well-being?
대상에 대해 자아가 왜 지나치게 크게 관심을 두겠는가? / 자신의 명성이나 행복과는 관계가 없는

So, / in that happy state of apathy, / our ego is less likely / to get data manipulative, mentally threatened, or magically minded, / leaving the rest of our brain / free to abandon failed hypotheses and venture new ones.
그래서 / 그런 행복한 무관심 상태에서 / 우리의 자아는 ~할 가능성이 더 작아져서, / 데이터를 조작하거나, 정신적으로 위협받거나, 주술적으로 생각하게 될 / 우리 뇌의 나머지 부분이 ~하게 둔다. / 자유롭게 실패한 가설을 버리고 새로운 가설을 과감히 시도하게

주술적 사고, 지적 불안, 그리고 확증 편향은 모두 과학적 발견에 대한 강력한 장벽이며, 그것들은 코페르니쿠스 이전 여러 세대 천문학자들의 눈을 가렸다. 그러나 21세기 연구자들이 발견했듯이, 이 세 가지 장벽은 모두 간단한 교수 기법으로 무너뜨릴 수 있는데, 그것은 우리의 뇌를 우리 자신 밖의 환경으로 이동시키는 것이다. 그 환경은 우리의 집으로부터 몇 마일 떨어진 자연 보호 구역이나, 컴퓨터로 시뮬레이션한 화성이나, 우리의 자아가 우리의 건강, 사회적 지위, 그리고 물질적 성공과 직접 연관짓지 않는 다른 어떤 공간도 될 수 있다. 그런 환경에서, 우리의 자아는 자기 예측이 틀린 것에 기분 상하는 경향이 덜할 것이다. 분명히, 우리의 자아는 그 자연 보호 구역이나 화성에 대한 자기 추측이 틀렸다는 것에 약간 언짢은 느낌이 들 수도 있지만, 애초에 결코 그 추측에 실제로 그다지 관여를 하지 않았다. 자신의 명성이나 행복과는 관계가 없는 것들에 대해 자아가 왜 크게 관심을 두겠는가? 그래서 그런 행복한 무관심 상태에서 우리의 자아는 데이터를 조작하거나, 정신적으로 위협받거나, 주술적으로 생각하게 될 가능성이 더 작아져서, 우리 뇌의 나머지 부분이 자유롭게 실패한 가설을 버리고 새로운 가설을 과감히 시도하게 둔다.

Why? 왜 정답일까?

우리가 틀린 예측을 버리지 않고 고수하게 만드는 갖가지 인지적 편향을 무력화시키려면 우리 뇌를 자아와 분리된 환경으로 이동시키면 된다(~ these three barriers can all be destroyed with a simple teaching trick: transporting our brain to an environment outside our own.)는 내용의 글이다. 이런 인지적 편향이 영향을 발휘하지 않는 곳에서는 우리 자아가 틀린 가설에 기분이 덜 상하고, 위험도 덜 느끼게 되어서 '인지 편향을 극복할 수 있다'는 것이 글의 결론으로 적합하다. 따라서 빈칸에 들어갈 말로 가장 적절한 것은 ④ '실패한 가설을 버리고 새로운 가설을 과감히 시도하게'이다.

- **insecurity** ⓝ 불안정
- **astronomer** ⓝ 천문학자
- **preserve** ⓝ 보호 구역
- **associate A with B** A와 B를 연관 짓다
- **be inclined to** ~하는 경향이 있다
- **personally** ⓐⓓ 개인적으로
- **apathy** ⓝ 무관심
- **manipulative** ⓐ 조작하는
- **the rest of** ~의 나머지
- **do away with** ~을 없애다
- **justify** ⓥ 정당화하다
- **confirmation bias** 확증 편향
- **destroy** ⓥ 파괴하다
- **simulate** ⓥ 시뮬레이션하다, 모의 실험하다
- **social status** 사회적 지위
- **prediction** ⓝ 예측
- **have no bearing on** ~와 관계가 없다
- **be likely to** ~할 가능성이 있다
- **mentally** ⓐⓓ 정신적으로
- **free to** 자유롭게 ~하는
- **irregularity** ⓝ 불규칙성
- **abandon** ⓥ 버리다, 포기하다

구문 풀이

> **13행** Certainly, our ego may feel a little upset that its guesses (about the nature preserve or Mars) were wrong, but it was never really that invested in the guesses to begin with.
> (감각동사 / 주격 보어 / 접속사 / 주어 / 동사(복수) / 부사(그렇게))

★★ 문제 해결 꿀~팁 ★★

▶ 많이 틀린 이유는?

원래 있던 환경 밖으로 자꾸 나가다 보면 우리 뇌가 '틀리는' 것을 두려워하지 않게 될 것이라는 내용이다. 이는 '지적 불안 상태를 피하지 않고 맞아들이는' 상황인데, ③의 경우 지적 불안을 '피하는' 방법을 이야기하므로 주제와 정반대된다.

- **concern** ⓥ ~에 관한 것이다
- **emphasize** ⓥ 강조하다
- **cross-culturally** 비교 문화적으로
- **in isolation from** ~와 분리되어
- **analytical** ⓐ 분석적인
- **kinship** ⓝ 친족 관계, 연대감
- **in relation to** ~에 관하여
- **on the basis of** ~을 기반으로

구문 풀이

> **15행** ＝ American anthropology
> It does not assume that there are universal social domains,
> 접속사(~것)
> preferring instead to discover domains empirically as aspects of each
> 분사구문 　　　　　 목적어 　　　　　 전치사(~로서)
> society's own classificatory schemes — in other words, its culture.
> 　　　　　　　　　　　　　　　　 동격

★★ 문제 해결 꿀~팁 ★★

▶ **많이 틀린 이유는?**
미국 인류학과 영국 인류학의 관점 차이를 이해한 뒤 빈칸을 완성하는 문제이다. 빈칸 앞의 두 문장에서 미국의 인류학은 문화를 중시하며 사회를 문화의 맥락 안에서 이해하려 한다는 설명이 나오는 것으로 볼 때, '사회를 맥락과 분리시켜 이해할 수 있다는 견해를 거부한다'라는 문장을 완성하기에 적절한 선택지는 ②이다. ①이 들어가면 전체 문장이 '사회를 문화적 기원과 연결시켜 이해할 수 있다는 견해를 거부한다'라는 의미를 나타낸다. 즉 주제와 반대되는 의미가 완성되는 것이다.

▶ **문제 해결 방법은?**
빈칸 앞에 나오는 동사 **rejects**가 부정의 의미를 내포하므로, 빈칸 문장이 주제를 나타내기 위해서는 빈칸에 주제와 반대되는 내용이 들어가야 함에 유의한다.

★★★ 1등급 대비 고난도 3점 문제

11　　사회와 문화의 관계　　　　정답률 32% | 정답 ②

다음 빈칸에 들어갈 말로 가장 적절한 것을 고르시오. [3점]

① in relation to its cultural origin - 그것의 문화적 기원과 관련하여
✔ in isolation from its own context - 그것 자체의 상황으로부터 분리되어
③ regardless of personal preferences - 개인적인 선호와 상관없이
④ without considering its economic roots - 그것의 경제적 뿌리를 고려하지 않고서
⑤ on the basis of British-American relations - 영국과 미국 사이의 관계를 기반으로

The debates between social and cultural anthropologists / concern not the differences between the concepts / but the analytical priority: / which should come first, / the social chicken or the cultural egg?
사회 인류학자와 문화 인류학자 사이의 논쟁은 / 개념들 간의 차이에 관한 것이 아니라 / 분석적 우선순위에 관한 것으로, / 즉 어느 것이 먼저냐는 것이다 / 사회적인 닭과 문화적인 달걀 중에

British anthropology emphasizes the social.
영국의 인류학은 사회적인 것을 강조한다.

It assumes that social institutions determine culture / and that universal domains of society / (such as kinship, economy, politics, and religion) / are represented by specific institutions / (such as the family, subsistence farming, the British Parliament, and the Church of England) / which can be compared cross-culturally.
그것은 사회 제도가 문화를 결정하고 / 사회의 보편적인 영역이 / (예를 들면, 친족 관계, 경제, 정치, 그리고 종교) / 구체적인 제도로 표현된다고 가정한다. / (예를 들면, 가족, 자급 농업, 영국 의회, 그리고 영국 국교회) / 서로 다른 문화 간에 비교될 수 있는

American anthropology emphasizes the cultural.
미국의 인류학은 문화적인 것을 강조한다.

It assumes / that culture shapes social institutions / by providing the shared beliefs, the core values, the communicative tools, and so on / that make social life possible.
그것은 가정한다, / 문화가 사회 제도를 형성한다고 / 공유된 믿음, 핵심적 가치관, 의사소통 도구 등등을 제공함으로써 / 사회생활을 가능하게 하는

It does not assume that there are universal social domains, / preferring instead to discover domains empirically / as aspects of / each society's own classificatory schemes — in other words, its culture.
그것은 보편적인 사회적 영역이 있다고 가정하지 않고 / 그 대신 영역들을 경험적으로 발견하는 것을 선호한다. / 측면으로서의 / 각각의 사회 나름의 분류안 / 즉 문화

And it rejects the notion / that any social institution can be understood / in isolation from its own context.
그리고 그것은 개념을 거부한다. / 어떤 사회 제도가 이해될 수 있다는 / 그것 자체의 상황으로부터 분리되어

사회 인류학자와 문화 인류학자 사이의 논쟁은 개념들 간의 차이에 관한 것이 아니라 분석적 우선순위에 관한 것으로, 즉 사회적인 닭이 먼저냐, 문화적인 달걀이 먼저냐는 것이다. 영국의 인류학은 사회적인 것을 강조한다. 그것은 사회 제도가 문화를 결정하고 사회의 보편적인 영역(예를 들면, 친족 관계, 경제, 정치, 그리고 종교)이 서로 다른 문화 간에 비교될 수 있는 구체적인 제도(예를 들면, 가족, 자급 농업, 영국 의회, 그리고 영국 국교회)로 표현된다고 가정한다. 미국의 인류학은 문화적인 것을 강조한다. 그것은 문화가 사회생활을 가능하게 하는 공유된 믿음, 핵심적 가치관, 의사소통 도구 등등을 제공함으로써 사회 제도를 형성한다고 가정한다. 그것은 보편적인 사회적 영역이 있다고 가정하지 않고 그 대신 각각의 사회 나름의 분류안, 즉 문화 측면으로서의 영역들을 경험적으로 발견하는 것을 선호한다. 그리고 그것은 어떤 사회 제도가 <u>그것 자체의 상황으로부터 분리되어</u> 이해될 수 있다는 개념을 거부한다.

Why? 왜 정답일까?

사회와 문화의 관계에 대한 영국 인류학과 미국 인류학의 관점을 비교한 글로, 빈칸은 문화를 강조하는 미국의 인류학을 설명하는 부분에 있다. 빈칸 앞의 두 문장에서 미국 인류학의 관점에 따르면 문화가 사회 제도를 형성하며, 사회적 영역은 보편적으로 존재하기보다 각 문화의 측면으로서 발견될 수 있다(It does not assume that there are universal social domains, preferring instead to discover domains empirically as aspects of ~ its culture.)고 한다. 따라서 빈칸에 들어갈 말로 가장 적절한 것은 사회 제도가 문화, 즉 개별 사회 특유의 상황과 밀접 관련이 있다는 의미를 완성하는 ② '그것 자체의 상황으로부터 분리되어'이다.

★★★ 1등급 대비 고난도 3점 문제

12　　현재와 밀접히 관련되어 있는 문화유산　　정답률 29% | 정답 ②

다음 빈칸에 들어갈 말로 가장 적절한 것을 고르시오. [3점]

① a collection of memories and traditions of a society
　한 사회의 기억과 전통의 모음
✔ as much about forgetting as remembering the past
　과거를 기억하는 것만큼 과거를 잊는 데 관한 것
③ neither concerned with the present nor the future
　현재와도 미래와도 연관이 없는
④ a mirror reflecting the artefacts of the past
　과거의 인공물을 반영하고 있는 거울
⑤ about preserving universal cultural values
　보편적인 문화적 가치를 보존하는 데 관한 것

Heritage is concerned with the ways / in which very selective material artefacts, mythologies, memories and traditions / become resources for the present.
문화유산은 방식과 관련이 있다. / 매우 선별적인 물질적 인공물, 신화, 기억, 그리고 전통이 / 현재를 위한 자원이 되는

The contents, interpretations and representations of the resource / are selected / according to the demands of the present; / an imagined past provides resources for a heritage / that is to be passed onto an imagined future.
그 자원의 내용, 해석, 표현은 / 선택되며, / 현재의 요구에 따라 / 상상된 과거는 유산을 위한 자원을 제공한다. / 상상된 미래로 전해질 수 있는

It follows too / that the meanings and functions of memory and tradition / are defined in the present.
그것은 또한 말이 된다. / 기억과 전통의 의미와 기능들이 / 현재에 와서 정의된다는

Further, / heritage is more concerned with meanings / than material artefacts.
게다가, / 유산은 의미와 더 많이 관련된다. / 물질적 인공물보다

It is the former / that give value, either cultural or financial, / to the latter / and explain / why they have been selected / from the near infinity of the past.
바로 전자(의미)이다. / 문화적 또는 재정적 가치를 부여하고 / 후자(인공물)에 / 설명해 주는 것은 / 왜 그것들이 선택되었는지 / 거의 무한하게 많은 과거의 것들로부터

In turn, / they may later be discarded / as the demands of present societies change, / or even, as is presently occurring in the former Eastern Europe, / when pasts have to be reinvented / to reflect new presents.
결국, / 그것들은 나중에 버려질 수도 있다. / 현재 사회의 요구가 변화함에 따라, / 혹은 심지어, 구 동유럽에서 현재 일어나고 있는 것처럼, / 과거가 재창조되어야 할 때, / 새로운 현재를 반영하기 위해서

Thus heritage is as much about forgetting / as remembering the past.
따라서 유산은 과거를 잊는 데 관한 것이다. / 과거를 기억하는 것만큼

문화유산은 매우 선별적인 물질적 인공물, 신화, 기억, 그리고 전통이 현재를 위한 자원이 되는 방식과 관련이 있다. 그 자원의 내용, 해석, 표현은 현재의 요구에 따라 선택되며, 상상된 과거는 상상된 미래로 전해질 수 있는 유산을 위한 자원을 제공한다. 그것은 또한 기억과 전통의 의미와 기능들이 현재에 와서 정의된다는 말이 된다. 게다가, 유산은 물질적 인공물보다 의미와 더 많이

관련된다. 후자(인공물)에 문화적 또는 재정적 가치를 부여하고 거의 무한하게 많은 과거의 것들로부터 왜 그것들이 선택되었는지 설명해 주는 것은 바로 전자(의미)이다. 결국, 현재 사회의 요구가 변화함에 따라, 혹은 심지어, 구 동유럽에서 현재 일어나고 있는 것처럼, 새로운 현재를 반영하기 위해서 과거가 재창조되어야 할 때, 그것들은 나중에 버려질 수도 있다. 따라서 유산은 과거를 기억하는 것만큼 과거를 잊는 데 관한 것이다.

Why? 왜 정답일까?

'~ the meanings and functions of memory and tradition are defined in the present.'에서 문화유산의 의미와 기능은 현재에 와서 정의된다고 말한 데 이어, 'In turn, they may later be discarded as the demands of present societies change, ~ when pasts have to be reinvented to reflect new presents.'에서는 새로이 변화한 현재를 반영하기 위한 과정에서 이미 선택되었던 문화유산이 버려질 수도 있음을 이야기한다. 이는 문화유산이 절대불변의 가치를 갖는다기보다는 현재의 필요에 의해 유동적으로 정의된다는 뜻이므로, 빈칸에 들어갈 말로 가장 적절한 것은 ② '과거를 기억하는 것만큼 과거를 잊는 데 관한 것'이다.

- **heritage** ⓝ 유산
- **artefact** ⓝ 인공물, 가공품
- **interpretation** ⓝ 해석, 이해, 설명
- **it follows that** 결과적으로 ~하다
- **discard** ⓥ 버리다, 폐기하다
- **universal** ⓐ 보편적인
- **selective** ⓐ 선별적인, 조심해서 고르는
- **mythology** ⓝ 신화
- **pass A onto B** A를 B에게 넘겨주다
- **infinity** ⓝ 무한성, 무한대
- **reinvent** ⓥ 재창조하다

구문 풀이

11행 It is **the former** that give value, [either cultural or financial],
「it is ~ that …: 강조 구문」 동사1
to **the latter** and **explain** {why they have been selected from the near
동사2 현재완료 수동태
infinity of the past}.
{ } : 목적어(의문사절)

★★ 문제 해결 꿀~팁 ★★

▶ 많이 틀린 이유는?
문화유산은 고정된 것이 아니고 현재의 필요에 따라 유산이 될 수도 있고 그렇지 않을 수도 있다는 추상적인 내용을 다룬 글이다. 최다 오답인 ①은 유산을 과거의 기억 또는 전통과 동일시되는 개념으로 보고 있는데, 이는 지문의 주제보다는 유산에 대한 통념이나 상식과 더 연관되어 있다.

▶ 문제 해결 방법은?
본문의 'they may later be discarded'와 ②의 'much about forgetting'은 서로 같은 맥락이다. 즉 이는 시대가 변하고 과거를 재구성할 필요가 생기면 한때 유산으로 여겨졌던 것을 버리고 그 과거를 '잊기로' 결정할 수 있다는 의미를 나타낸다.

DAY 11   글의 순서 01

01 ②	02 ④	03 ⑤	04 ②	05 ③
06 ③	07 ②	08 ②	09 ⑤	10 ④
11 ⑤	12 ⑤			

01   적응적 가소성   정답률 57% | 정답 ②

주어진 글 다음에 이어질 글의 순서로 가장 적절한 것을 고르시오.

① (A) − (C) − (B)   ✓② (B) − (A) − (C)
③ (B) − (C) − (A)   ④ (C) − (A) − (B)
⑤ (C) − (B) − (A)

A fascinating species of water flea / exhibits a kind of flexibility / that evolutionary biologists call *adaptive plasticity*.
물벼룩이라는 매혹적인 종은 / 일종의 유연성을 보여 준다. / 진화생물학자들이 *적응적 가소성*이라고 부르는

(B) If the baby water flea is developing into an adult in water / that includes the chemical signatures of creatures / that prey on water fleas, / it develops a helmet and spines / to defend itself against predators.
만일 새끼 물벼룩이 물에서 성체로 발달하고 있으면, / 생물의 화학적인 특징을 포함하는 / 물벼룩을 잡아먹고 사는 / 그것은 머리 투구와 가시 돌기를 발달시킨다. / 자신을 포식자로부터 지키기 위해

If the water around it / doesn't include the chemical signatures of predators, / the water flea doesn't develop these protective devices.
만일 주변의 물이 / 포식자의 화학적인 특징을 포함하지 않으면, / 그 물벼룩은 이러한 보호 장치를 발달시키지 않는다.

(A) That's a clever trick, / because producing spines and a helmet is costly, / in terms of energy, / and conserving energy is essential / for an organism's ability to survive and reproduce.
이것은 영리한 묘책인데, / 가시 돌기와 머리 투구를 만드는 것은 비용이 많이 들고, / 에너지 면에서 / 에너지를 보존하는 것은 핵심적이기 때문이다. / 살아남고 생식하는 유기체의 능력을 위해

The water flea only expends the energy / needed to produce spines and a helmet / when it needs to.
물벼룩은 오직 에너지를 소모한다. / 가시 돌기와 머리 투구를 만드는 데 필요한 / 그것이 필요할 때만

(C) So it may well be / that this plasticity is an adaptation: / a trait that came to exist in a species / because it contributed to reproductive fitness.
그러므로 아마 ~일 것이다. / 이러한 가소성은 적응일 / 즉 생물 종에 존재하게 된 특징 / 그것이 생식의 적합성에 이바지하기 때문에

There are many cases, / across many species, / of adaptive plasticity.
많은 사례가 있다. / 많은 종에 걸쳐 / 적응적 가소성의

Plasticity is conducive to fitness / if there is sufficient variation in the environment.
가소성은 적합성에 도움이 된다. / 환경에 충분한 차이가 있을 때

물벼룩이라는 매혹적인 종은 진화생물학자들이 *적응적 가소성*이라고 부르는 일종의 유연성을 보여 준다.

(B) 만일 새끼 물벼룩이 물벼룩을 잡아먹고 사는 생물의 화학적인 (고유한) 특징을 포함하는 물에서 성체로 발달하고 있으면, 그것은 자신을 포식자로부터 지키기 위해 머리 투구와 가시 돌기를 발달시킨다. 만일 주변의 물이 포식자의 화학적인 특징을 포함하지 않으면, 그 물벼룩은 이러한 보호 장치를 발달시키지 않는다.

(A) 이것은 영리한 묘책인데, 에너지 면에서 가시 돌기와 머리 투구를 만드는 것은 비용이 많이 들고, 에너지를 보존하는 것은 살아남고 생식하는 유기체의 능력을 위해 핵심적이기 때문이다. 물벼룩은 오직 필요할 때만 가시 돌기와 머리 투구를 만드는 데 필요한 에너지를 소모한다.

(C) 그러므로 이러한 가소성은 아마 적응일 텐데, 즉 그것은 생식의 적합성에 이바지하기 때문에 생물 종에 존재하게 된 특징이다. 많은 종에 걸쳐 적응적 가소성의 많은 사례가 있다. 가소성은 환경에 충분한 차이가 있을 때 적합성에 도움이 된다.

Why? 왜 정답일까?

물벼룩이 적응적 가소성을 보여주는 예시라고 언급하는 주어진 글 뒤로, 물벼룩이 환경에 따라 가시 돌기와 머리 투구를 발달시킬지 결정한다고 설명하는 (B), '이것'이 영리한 묘책인 이유를 설명하는 (A), So로 시작하며 결론을 내리는 (C)가 차례로 연결되어야 한다. 따라서 글의 순서로 가장 적절한 것은 ② '(B) − (A) − (C)'이다.

- **fascinating** ⓐ 매력적인
- **species** ⓝ (생물) 종

- evolutionary ⓐ 진화의
- adaptive ⓐ 적응의, 적응할 수 있는
- clever ⓐ 영리한
- costly ⓐ 비용이 많이 드는
- conserve ⓥ 보존하다
- reproduce ⓥ 번식하다, 재생하다
- expend ⓥ (시간, 에너지, 비용 등을) 쓰다
- signature ⓝ 특징
- defend against ~로부터 보호하다
- may well 아마 ~일 것이다
- fitness ⓝ 적합성
- variation ⓝ 차이, 변주

- biologist ⓝ 생물학자
- plasticity ⓝ 가소성
- spine ⓝ 가시 돌기
- in terms of ~의 면에서
- essential ⓐ 필수적인
- flea ⓝ 벼룩
- chemical ⓐ 화학적인
- prey on ~을 먹고 살다
- protective ⓐ 보호하는
- adaptation ⓝ 적응
- conducive ⓐ 도움이 되는

구문 풀이

7행 The water flea only expends the energy needed to produce spines and a helmet when it needs to.

대부정사(= to produce spines and a helmet)

---

02 적당한 스트레스가 초래하는 긍정적 결과   정답률 62% | 정답 ④

주어진 글 다음에 이어질 글의 순서로 가장 적절한 것을 고르시오.
① (A) – (C) – (B)
② (B) – (A) – (C)
③ (B) – (C) – (A)
✔④ (C) – (A) – (B)
⑤ (C) – (B) – (A)

Studies of people / struggling with major health problems / show / that the majority of respondents report / they derived benefits from their adversity.
사람들에 대한 연구는 / 중대한 건강 문제를 해결하려고 노력하는 / 보여준다. / 대다수의 응답자가 보고한다는 것을 / 자신이 겪은 역경에서 이익을 얻었다고

Stressful events sometimes force people / to develop new skills, / reevaluate priorities, / learn new insights, / and acquire new strengths.
스트레스를 주는 사건들은 때때로 사람들에게 ~하게 한다. / 새로운 기술을 개발하고, / 우선순위를 재평가하고, / 새로운 통찰을 배우고 / 새로운 강점을 얻게

(C) In other words, / the adaptation process initiated by stress / can lead to personal changes for the better.
다시 말해, / 스트레스에 의해 시작된 적응 과정은 / 더 나은 쪽으로의 개인적 변화를 가져올 수 있다.

One study / that measured participants' exposure to thirty-seven major negative events / found a curvilinear relationship / between lifetime adversity and mental health.
한 연구는 / 참가자들의 서른일곱 가지 주요 부정적인 사건 경험을 측정한 / 곡선 관계를 발견했다. / 생애에서 겪은 역경과 정신 건강 사이의

(A) High levels of adversity / predicted poor mental health, as expected, / but people who had faced intermediate levels of adversity / were healthier than those / who experienced little adversity, / suggesting that moderate amounts of stress can foster resilience.
높은 수준의 역경은 / 예상대로 나쁜 정신 건강을 예측했지만, / 중간 수준의 역경에 직면했던 사람들은 / 사람들보다 더 건강했는데, / 역경을 거의 경험하지 않았던 / 이것은 적당한 양의 스트레스가 회복력을 촉진할 수 있음을 보여준다.

A follow-up study found a similar link / between the amount of lifetime adversity / and subjects' responses to laboratory stressors.
후속 연구는 비슷한 관계를 발견했다. / 생애에서 겪은 역경의 양과 / 실험 중 주어진 스트레스 요인에 대한 피실험자들의 반응 사이에서

(B) Intermediate levels of adversity / were predictive of the greatest resilience.
중간 수준의 역경이 / 가장 큰 회복력을 예측했다.

Thus, having to deal with a moderate amount of stress / may build resilience in the face of future stress.
따라서 적당한 양의 스트레스를 해결해야 하는 것은 / 미래에 스트레스를 직면할 때의 회복력을 기를 수도 있다.

중대한 건강 문제를 해결하려고 노력하는 사람들에 대한 연구는 대다수의 응답자가 자신이 겪은 역경에서 이익을 얻었다고 보고한다는 것을 보여준다. 스트레스를 주는 사건들은 때때로 사람들이 새로운 기술을 개발하고, 우선순위를 재평가하고, 새로운 통찰을 배우고 새로운 강점을 얻게 한다.

(C) 다시 말해, 스트레스에 의해 시작된 적응 과정은 더 나은 쪽으로의 개인적 변화를 가져올 수 있다. 참가자들의 서른일곱 가지 주요 부정적인 사건 경험을 측정한 한 연구는 생애에서 겪은 역경과 정신 건강 사이의 곡선 관계를 발견했다.

(A) 높은 수준의 역경은 예상대로 나쁜 정신 건강을 예측했지만, 중간 수준의 역경에 직면했던 사람들은 역경을 거의 경험하지 않았던 사람들보다 더 건강했는데, 이것은 적당한 양의 스트레스가 회복력을 촉진할 수 있음을

보여준다. 후속 연구는 생애에서 겪은 역경의 양과 실험 중 주어진 스트레스 요인에 대한 피실험자들의 반응 사이에서 비슷한 관계를 발견했다.

(B) 중간 수준의 역경이 가장 큰 회복력을 예측했다. 따라서 적당한 양의 스트레스를 해결해야 하는 것은 미래에 스트레스를 직면할 때의 회복력을 기를 수도 있다.

Why? 왜 정답일까?

사람들이 역경에서 도리어 이익을 얻을 수 있다는 내용을 제시하는 주어진 글 뒤에는, In other words 뒤로 스트레스에 의해 시작되는 적응 과정이 긍정적인 개인적 변화를 가져올 수 있다고 풀어서 설명하는 (C)가 먼저 연결된다. 이어서 (A)는 (C)의 후반부에서 처음 언급된 역경과 정신 건강에 관한 연구를 서술하고, (B)는 후속 연구, 즉 역경의 양과 스트레스 회복력을 연관시킨 연구에 관해 부연한다. 따라서 글의 순서로 가장 적절한 것은 ④ '(C) – (A) – (B)'이다.

- adversity ⓝ 역경
- acquire ⓥ 얻다, 습득하다
- foster ⓥ 촉진하다, 키우다
- adaptation ⓝ 적응
- curvilinear ⓐ 곡선의

- reevaluate ⓥ 재평가하다
- moderate ⓐ 중간의, 온건한
- predictive of ~을 예측하는
- initiate ⓥ 착수시키다

구문 풀이

7행 High levels of adversity predicted poor mental health, as
주어1   동사1
expected, but people [who had faced intermediate levels of adversity]
주어2   과거완료
were healthier than those [who experienced little adversity], suggesting
동사2   선행사   분사구문
that moderate amounts of stress can foster resilience.
접속사(~것)   「비교급+than : 더 ~한/하게」

---

03 선과 행복   정답률 38% | 정답 ⑤

주어진 글 다음에 이어질 글의 순서로 가장 적절한 것을 고르시오.
① (A) – (C) – (B)
② (B) – (A) – (C)
③ (B) – (C) – (A)
④ (C) – (A) – (B)
✔⑤ (C) – (B) – (A)

Aristotle explains / that the Good for human beings consists in *eudaimoniā* / (a Greek word / combining *eu* meaning "good" with *daimon* meaning "spirit," / and most often translated as "happiness").
아리스토텔레스는 설명한다. / 인간을 위한 '선'은 *eudaimoniā*에 있다고 / (그리스어 단어인 / '좋다'라는 의미인 *eu*와 '영혼'이라는 의미의 *daimon*을 결합하는, / '행복'이라고 가장 흔히 번역되는

(C) Whereas he had argued in a purely formal way / that the Good was that to which we all aim, / he now gives a more substantive answer: / that this universal human goal is happiness.
그는 순전히 형식적으로 주장했지만, / '선'은 우리 모두가 목표로 하는 것이라고 / 그는 이제는 더 실질적인 답을 준다. / 이 보편적인 인간의 목표는 행복이라는 것

However, / he is quick to point out / that this conclusion is still somewhat formal / since different people have different views / about what happiness is.
하지만, / 그는 재빨리 지적하기를, / 결론이 여전히 다소 형식적이라고 한다. / 사람마다 서로 견해가 다르기에 / 행복이 무엇인지에 관해

(B) Some people say it is worldly enjoyment / while others say it is eternal salvation.
어떤 사람들은 이것을 세속적 쾌락이라고 말하지만, / 다른 사람들은 이것을 영원한 구원이라고 말한다.

Aristotle's theory will turn out to be "naturalistic" / in that it does not depend on any theological or metaphysical knowledge.
아리스토텔레스의 이론은 '자연적'이라고 판명될 것이다. / 그것이 어떤 신학이나 형이상학 지식에도 의존하지 않는다는 점에서

It does not depend on knowledge of God / or of metaphysical and universal moral norms.
그것은 신에 대한 지식에 의존하지 않는다. / 혹은 형이상학적, 보편적 도덕 규범에 관한

(A) It depends only / on knowledge of human nature and other worldly and social realities.
그것은 오직 의존한다. / 인간 본성과 여타의 세속적이고 사회적인 현실에 관한 지식에만

For him / it is the study of human nature and worldly existence / that will disclose the relevant meaning of the notion of *eudaimoniā*.
그에게 / 바로 인간 본성과 세속적 존재에 대한 연구이다. / *eudaimoniā*라는 개념의 적절한 의미를 밝혀줄 것은

아리스토텔레스는 인간을 위한 '선'은 *eudaimoniā*('좋다'라는 의미인 *eu*와 '영혼'이라는 의미의 *daimon*을 결합하여, '행복'이라고 가장 흔히 번역되는 그리스어 단어)에 있다고 설명한다.

(C) 그는 순전히 형식적으로 '선'은 우리 모두가 목표로 하는 것이라고 주장했지만, 그는 이제는 더 실질적인 답을 준다. 이 보편적인 인간의 목표는 행복이라는 것이다. 하지만, 그는 재빨리 지적하기를, 사람마다 행복이 무엇인지에 관해 서로 견해가 다르기에 결론이 여전히 다소 형식적이라고 한다.

(B) 어떤 사람들은 이것을 세속적 쾌락이라고 말하지만, 다른 사람들은 이것을 영원한 구원이라고 말한다. 아리스토텔레스의 이론은 어떤 신학이나 형이상학 지식에도 의존하지 않는다는 점에서 '자연적'이라고 판명될 것이다. 그것은 신에 대한 지식이나 형이상학적, 보편적 도덕 규범에 관한 지식에 의존하지 않는다.

(A) 그것은 오직 인간 본성과 여타의 세속적이고 사회적인 현실에 대한 지식에만 의존한다. 그에게 *eudaimonia*라는 개념의 적절한 의미를 밝혀줄 것은 바로 인간 본성과 세속적 존재에 대한 연구이다.

Why? 왜 정답일까?

주어진 글에서 아리스토텔레스가 해석한 '선' 개념을 언급한다. **(C)**는 아리스토텔레스를 he로 받아, 그가 보편적 인간의 목표는 행복이라고 말했고, 사람마다 행복이 무엇인가에 대한 견해는 다 다르기에 그러한 견해가 형식적일 수 있다고 지적했다고 서술한다. 이어서 **(B)**는 행복을 세속적 쾌락으로 보는 일부 사람들(Some people)이 있는가 하면, 영원한 구원으로 보는 사람들(others)도 있다고 보충 설명한다. 한편 **(B)** 말미에서는 아리스토텔레스의 이론으로 다시 돌아가, 이것이 형이상학적 지식에 의존하지 않는다고 언급하는데, **(A)**에서는 그 대신 이 이론이 인간 본성과 현실에 대한 지식에 의존한다고 설명한다. **(B)** 마지막의 'It does not depend on ~'와 **(A)** 초반의 'It depends only on ~'이 크게 보아 not A (but) B 형태로 대구를 이루는 구조이다. 따라서 글의 순서로 가장 적절한 것은 ⑤ '**(C) − (B) − (A)**'이다.

- **translate** ⓥ 번역하다
- **disclose** ⓥ 폭로하다
- **notion** ⓝ 관념
- **salvation** ⓝ 구원
- **theological** ⓐ 신학의
- **whereas** [conj] ~한 반면에
- **substantive** ⓐ 실질적인
- **worldly** ⓐ 세속적인
- **relevant** ⓐ 관련된, 적절한
- **eternal** ⓐ 영원한
- **naturalistic** ⓐ 자연적인
- **metaphysical** ⓐ 형이상학적인
- **formal** ⓐ 형식적인, 공식적인

구문 풀이

11행 Aristotle's theory will turn out to be "naturalistic" in that it
　　　　　　　　　　　　 2형식 동사　　　 주격 보어　 ~라는 점에서
does not depend on any theological or metaphysical knowledge.

---

04 전쟁의 정치적 목적　　　　　　정답률 70% | 정답 ②

주어진 글 다음에 이어질 글의 순서로 가장 적절한 것을 고르시오.

① (A) − (C) − (B)　　　　✔ (B) − (A) − (C)
③ (B) − (C) − (A)　　　　④ (C) − (A) − (B)
⑤ (C) − (B) − (A)

The objective of battle, / to "throw" the enemy and to make him defenseless, / may temporarily blind commanders and even strategists / to the larger purpose of war.
전투의 목표, 즉 적군을 '격멸하고' 무방비 상태로 만드는 것은 / 일시적으로 지휘관과 심지어 전략가까지도 보지 못하게 할 수도 있다. / 전쟁의 더 큰 목적을

War is never an isolated act, / nor is it ever only one decision.
전쟁은 결코 고립된 행위가 아니며, / 또한 결코 단 하나의 결정도 아니다.

(B) In the real world, / war's larger purpose is always a political purpose.
현실 세계에서 / 전쟁의 더 큰 목적은 항상 정치적 목적이다.

It transcends the use of force.
그것은 물리력의 사용을 초월한다.

This insight was famously captured by Clausewitz's most famous phrase, / "War is a mere continuation of politics by other means."
이 통찰은 Clausewitz의 가장 유명한 한마디에 의해 멋지게 포착되었다. / "전쟁은 다른 수단으로 단지 정치를 계속하는 것에 불과하다."

(A) To be political, / a political entity or a representative of a political entity, / whatever its constitutional form, / has to have an intention, a will.
정치적이 되려면, / 정치적 실체나 정치적 실체의 대표자는 / 체제상의 형태가 무엇이든지 / 의도, 즉 의지가 있어야 한다.

That intention has to be clearly expressed.
그 의도는 분명히 표현되어야 한다.

(C) And one side's will has to be transmitted to the enemy / at some point during the confrontation / (it does not have to be publicly communicated).
그리고 한쪽의 의지는 적에게 전달되어야 한다. / 대치하는 동안 어느 시점에 / (그것이 공개적으로 전달될 필요는 없다)

A violent act and its larger political intention / must also be attributed to one side / at some point during the confrontation.
폭력 행위와 그것의 더 큰 정치적 의도도 / 또한 한쪽의 탓으로 돌려져야 한다. / 대치하는 동안 어느 시점에

History does not know of acts of war without eventual attribution.
역사는 궁극적인 귀인이 없는 전쟁 행위에 대해 알지 못한다.

전투의 목표, 즉 적군을 '격멸하고' 무방비 상태로 만드는 것은 일시적으로 지휘관과 심지어 전략가까지도 전쟁의 더 큰 목적을 보지 못하게 할 수도 있다. 전쟁은 결코 고립된 행위가 아니며, 또한 결코 단 하나의 결정도 아니다.

(B) 현실 세계에서 전쟁의 더 큰 목적은 항상 정치적 목적이다. 그것은 물리력의 사용을 초월한다. 이 통찰은 "전쟁은 다른 수단으로 단지 정치를 계속하는 것에 불과하다."라고 한 Clausewitz의 가장 유명한 한마디에 의해 멋지게 포착되었다.

(A) 정치적이 되려면, 체제상의 형태가 무엇이든지 정치적 실체나 정치적 실체의 대표자는 의도, 즉 의지가 있어야 한다. 그 의도는 분명히 표현되어야 한다.

(C) 그리고 한쪽의 의지는 대치하는 동안 어느 시점에 적에게 전달되어야 한다 (그것이 공개적으로 전달될 필요는 없다). 폭력 행위와 그것의 더 큰 정치적 의도 또한 대치하는 동안 어느 시점에 한쪽의 탓으로 돌려져야 한다. 역사상 궁극적인 귀인이 없는 전쟁 행위는 없다.

Why? 왜 정답일까?

전쟁은 결코 목적과 동떨어진 행위가 아니라는 내용의 주어진 글 뒤에는, 전쟁 뒤에 항상 정치적 목적이 있음을 언급하는 **(B)**, 전쟁이 정치적이기 위해서는 분명히 표현된 의도 또는 의지가 있어야 한다는 내용의 **(A)**, 어느 한쪽의 의도나 의지는 다른 쪽에 반드시 전달되어야 한다는 설명을 추가하는 **(C)**가 차례로 연결되어야 한다. 따라서 글의 순서로 가장 적절한 것은 ② '**(B) − (A) − (C)**'이다.

- **objective** ⓝ 목표
- **commander** ⓝ 지휘관
- **isolated** ⓐ 고립된
- **constitutional** ⓐ 체제상의, 구성상의
- **will** ⓝ 의지
- **continuation** [ad] 계속
- **confrontation** ⓝ 대치, 대결
- **A be attributed to B** A가 B의 탓으로 돌려지다
- **temporarily** [ad] 일시적으로
- **strategist** ⓝ 전략가
- **representative** ⓝ 대표자
- **intention** ⓝ 의도, 의사
- **capture** ⓥ 포착하다
- **transmit** ⓥ 전달하다, 전수하다

구문 풀이

6행 To be political, a political entity or a representative of a political
　　　 부사적 용법(목적)　　　　　　　　　　　 주어
entity, whatever its constitutional form, has to have an intention,
　　　 복합관계대명사(~이 무엇이든 간에)　　　 동사구　　　 목적어
a will.
목적어 동격

---

05 새들이 비행 시 에너지를 아끼는 방법　　　　정답률 62% | 정답 ③

주어진 글 다음에 이어질 글의 순서로 가장 적절한 것을 고르시오. [3점]

① (A) − (C) − (B)　　　　② (B) − (A) − (C)
✔ (B) − (C) − (A)　　　　④ (C) − (A) − (B)
⑤ (C) − (B) − (A)

Birds use many techniques to save energy / when they are flying, / most of which are tricks / to stay aloft without flapping.
새들은 에너지를 절약하기 위해 많은 기술들을 사용하는데, / 그것들이 날 때 / 그중 대부분은 요령이다. / 날갯짓을 하지 않고 높이 머무르기 위한

(B) Riding updrafts to gain altitude / is one of the most conspicuous.
고도를 확보하기 위해 상승 기류를 타는 것이 / 가장 뚜렷한 요령 중 하나이다.

Bare ground such as fields or parking lots / absorbs more heat from the sun, / and as air near the ground warms up / it rises.
들판이나 주차장과 같은 텅 빈 지면은 / 태양으로부터 더 많은 열을 흡수하고, / 지면 근처의 공기가 따뜻해지면서 / 그것은 상승한다.

(C) This creates a column of rising warm air / — a *thermal* — / reaching hundreds or even thousands of feet high.
이는 따뜻한 상승 공기 기둥을 형성한다. / 즉 상승 온난 기류 / 수백 혹은 심지어 수천 피트 높이에 이르는

A soaring bird can sense the air movement / and fly in circles to stay in the column.
날아오르는 새는 이 공기 움직임을 감지할 수 있고 / 그 기둥에 머무르기 위해 원을 그리며 날 수 있다.

It simply fans its wings and tail / and lets the rising air carry it up like an elevator.

그것은 단순히 그 날개와 꼬리를 펴서 / 상승하는 공기가 엘리베이터처럼 자신을 들어 올리도록 한다.

(A) When it reaches the top, / the bird bends its wings / and glides in the direction it wants to travel, / searching for the next thermal.

그것이 최고점에 도달했을 때 / 그 새는 날개를 구부려서 / 자신이 이동하고 싶은 방향으로 활공하며 / 다음 상승 온난 기류를 탐색한다.

All soaring birds take advantage of thermals, / but some species, like the Broad-winged Hawk, / are specialists / and in the right conditions can travel hundreds of miles / with almost no flapping.

모든 날아오르는 새들은 상승 온난 기류를 이용하지만, / 넓적날개말똥가리와 같은 몇몇 종들은 / 전문가여서 / 적절한 조건에서는 수백 마일을 이동할 수 있다. / 거의 날갯짓을 하지 않고

새들은 날 때 에너지를 절약하기 위해 많은 기술들을 사용하는데, 그중 대부분은 날갯짓을 하지 않고 높이 머무르기 위한 요령이다.

(B) 고도를 확보하기 위해 상승 기류를 타는 것이 가장 뚜렷한 요령 중 하나이다. 들판이나 주차장과 같은 텅 빈 지면은 태양으로부터 더 많은 열을 흡수하고, 지면 근처의 공기는 따뜻해지면서 상승한다.

(C) 이는 수백 혹은 심지어 수천 피트 높이에 이르는 따뜻한 상승 공기 기둥, 즉 상승 온난 기류를 형성한다. 날아오르는 새는 이 공기 움직임을 감지할 수 있고 그 기둥에 머무르기 위해 원을 그리며 날 수 있다. 그것은 단순히 그 날개와 꼬리를 펴서 상승하는 공기가 엘리베이터처럼 자신을 들어 올리도록 한다.

(A) 최고점에 도달했을 때 그 새는 날개를 구부려서 자신이 이동하고 싶은 방향으로 활공하며 다음 상승 온난 기류를 탐색한다. 모든 날아오르는 새들은 상승 온난 기류를 이용하지만, 넓적날개말똥가리와 같은 몇몇 종들은 전문가여서 적절한 조건에서는 거의 날갯짓을 하지 않고 수백 마일을 이동할 수 있다.

Why? 왜 정답일까?

새들은 날갯짓을 하지 않고도 높이 떠 있기 위해 다양한 기술을 사용한다고 언급한 주어진 글 뒤에는, 그러한 요령 중 하나가 상승 기류를 타는 것임을 언급하는 (B)가 먼저 연결된다. (C)는 (B)의 후반부에 이어 텅 빈 지면에서 따뜻한 공기의 상승 기류가 형성되는 과정을 설명한다. (A)는 (C)의 후반부에 이어, 날아오르는 새들이 상승 기류를 감지하고 나서 이 기류를 타고 최고점까지 올라 자신이 목표하는 방향을 향해 간다는 내용을 서술한다. 따라서 글의 순서로 가장 적절한 것은 ③ '(B) – (C) – (A)'이다.

- **flap** ⓥ 퍼덕거리다
- **soar** ⓥ 솟아오르다
- **specialist** ⓝ 전문가
- **altitude** ⓝ 고도
- **column** ⓝ 기둥
- **glide** ⓥ 활공하다, 미끄러지듯 가다
- **take advantage of** ~을 이용하다
- **updraft** ⓝ 상승 기류
- **absorb** ⓥ 흡수하다

구문 풀이

1행 Birds use many techniques to save energy when they are
<u>선행사</u> <u>부사적 용법</u>
flying, most of which are tricks to stay aloft without flapping.
<u>계속적 용법</u> <u>동사(복수)</u> <u>형용사적 용법</u>

---

06 의식과 무의식에서 모두 작용하는 문화   정답률 51% | 정답 ③

주어진 글 다음에 이어질 글의 순서로 가장 적절한 것을 고르시오. [3점]
① (A) – (C) – (B)
② (B) – (A) – (C)
✓③ (B) – (C) – (A)
④ (C) – (A) – (B)
⑤ (C) – (B) – (A)

Culture operates / in ways we can consciously consider and discuss / but also in ways of which we are far less cognizant.

문화는 작동한다. / 우리가 의식적으로 고려하고 논의할 수 있는 방식뿐만 아니라 / 또한 우리가 훨씬 덜 인식하는 방식으로

(B) When we have to offer an account of our actions, / we consciously understand / which excuses might prove acceptable, / given the particular circumstances / we find ourselves in.

우리가 우리의 행동을 설명해야 할 때, / 우리는 의식적으로 이해한다. / 어떤 변명이 용인될 수도 있는지를 / 특정한 상황을 고려할 때 / 우리가 처한

In such situations, / we use cultural ideas / as we would use a particular tool.

그런 상황에서 / 우리는 문화적 관념을 사용한다. / 우리가 마치 특정한 도구를 사용하듯이

(C) We select the cultural notion / as we would select a screwdriver: / certain jobs call for a Phillips head / while others require an Allen wrench.

우리는 문화적 개념을 선택한다. / 우리가 스크루드라이버를 선택하는 것처럼 / 어떤 일에는 십자 드라이버 헤드가 있으면 되지만 / 다른 일에는 육각 렌치가 있어야 한다.

Whichever idea we insert into the conversation / to justify our actions, / the point is / that our motives are discursively available to us. // They are not hidden.

우리가 대화에 어떤 생각을 집어넣든, / 우리의 행동을 정당화하기 위해 / 요점은 ~이다. / 우리가 동기를 만연하게 이용할 수 있다는 것 // 그것들은 숨겨져 있지 않다.

(A) In some cases, however, / we are far less aware of / why we believe a certain claim to be true, / or how we are to explain why certain social realities exist.

하지만 어떤 경우에는, / 우리는 훨씬 더 모른다. / 우리가 왜 어떤 주장을 사실이라고 믿는지, / 또는 우리가 어떤 사회적 현실이 존재하는 이유를 어떻게 설명할 것인지를

Ideas about the social world / become part of our worldview / without our necessarily being aware of the source of the particular idea / or that we even hold the idea at all.

사회적 세계에 대한 관념은 / 우리 세계관의 일부가 된다. / 우리가 특정한 관념의 출처를 꼭 알지 못한 상태에서도 / 혹은 우리가 심지어 그런 관념을 갖고 있다는 것조차

문화는 우리가 의식적으로 고려하고 논의할 수 있는 방식뿐만 아니라 우리가 훨씬 덜 인식하는 방식으로도 작동한다.

(B) 우리의 행동을 설명해야 할 때, 우리는 우리가 처한 특정한 상황에서 어떤 변명이 용인된다고 판명될 수도 있는지를 의식적으로 이해한다. 그런 상황에서 우리는 마치 특정한 도구를 사용하듯이 문화적 관념을 사용한다.

(C) 우리는 스크루드라이버를 선택하는 것처럼 문화적 개념을 선택한다. 어떤 일에는 십자 드라이버 헤드가 있으면 되지만 다른 일에는 육각 렌치가 있어야 한다. 우리의 행동을 정당화하기 위해 대화에 어떤 생각을 집어넣든, 요점은 우리가 동기를 만연하게 이용할 수 있다는 것이다. 그것들은 숨겨져 있지 않다.

(A) 하지만 어떤 경우에는, 우리는 우리가 왜 어떤 주장을 사실이라고 믿는지, 또는 어떤 사회적 현실이 존재하는 이유를 어떻게 설명할 것인지를 훨씬 더 모른다. 사회적 세계에 대한 관념은 우리가 특정한 관념의 출처를 꼭 알지 못하거나, 심지어 그런 관념을 갖고 있다는 것조차 꼭 알고 있지 못한 상태에서도 우리 세계관의 일부가 된다.

Why? 왜 정답일까?

문화는 우리의 의식 또는 무의식 수준에서 모두 작용할 수 있다는 주어진 글 뒤로, 우리가 의식적으로 문화적 개념을 이해하고 선택할 수 있는 경우를 언급하는 (B)가 먼저 이어진다. 특히 (B)의 후반부에 우리는 마치 상황에 맞는 '도구를 고르듯이' 문화적 개념을 선택한다는 내용이 나오는데, (C)의 초반부는 '스크루드라이버, 십자 드라이버, 육각 렌치' 등 세부적인 도구의 이름을 열거하며 비유를 심화하고 있다. 마지막으로 (A)는 무의식 수준에서 문화 개념이 작동하는 경우를 설명한다. 따라서 글의 순서로 가장 적절한 것은 ③ '(B) – (C) – (A)'이다.

- **consciously** ⓐⓓ 의식적으로
- **aware of** ~을 알고 있는
- **worldview** ⓝ 세계관
- **account** ⓝ 설명
- **acceptable** ⓐ 용인될 수 있는
- **notion** ⓝ 관념
- **justify** ⓥ 정당화하다
- **discursively** ⓐⓓ 만연하게
- **cognizant** ⓐ 인식하는
- **claim** ⓝ 주장
- **source** ⓝ 출처, 근원
- **excuse** ⓝ 변명
- **circumstance** ⓝ 상황
- **insert** ⓥ 집어넣다, 삽입하다
- **motive** ⓝ 동기
- **available** ⓐ 이용 가능한

구문 풀이

18행 Whichever idea we insert into the conversation to justify our
<u>복합관계형용사(어떤 ~이든지)</u>
actions, the point is that our motives are discursively available to us.

---

07 경제학의 매몰 비용 오류   정답률 42% | 정답 ②

주어진 글 다음에 이어질 글의 순서로 가장 적절한 것을 고르시오. [3점]
① (A) – (C) – (B)
✓② (B) – (A) – (C)
③ (B) – (C) – (A)
④ (C) – (A) – (B)
⑤ (C) – (B) – (A)

In economics, / there is a principle / known as the *sunk cost fallacy*.

경제학에서 / 원리가 있다. / 매몰 비용 오류라고 알려진

The idea is that / when you are invested and have ownership in something, / you overvalue that thing.

이 개념은 ~하다는 것이다. / 여러분이 어떤 것에 투자하고 소유권을 가지면, / 여러분이 그것을 지나치게 중시한다는

(B) This leads people to continue on paths or pursuits / that should clearly be abandoned.
이것은 사람들이 경로를 계속 따르거나 추구를 계속하게 한다. / 분명히 그만두어야 하는

For example, / people often remain in terrible relationships / simply because they've invested a great deal of themselves into them.
예를 들어, / 사람들은 자주 끔찍한 연애를 지속한다. / 그저 자신의 많은 것을 투입했다는 이유로

Or someone may continue pouring money into a business / that is clearly a bad idea in the market.
또는, 누군가는 사업에 계속 돈을 쏟아부을지도 모른다. / 시장에서 분명히 나쁜 아이디어인

(A) Sometimes, / the smartest thing a person can do / is quit.
때로는, / 사람들이 할 수 있는 가장 현명한 일은 / 중지하는 것이다.

Although this is true, / it has also become a tired and played-out argument.
이것이 진실이더라도, / 그것은 또한 식상하고 효력이 떨어진 주장이 될 수 있다.

Sunk cost doesn't always have to be a bad thing.
매몰 비용이 언제나 나쁜 것이 틀림없는 것은 아니다.

(C) Actually, / you can leverage this human tendency to your benefit.
실제로, / 여러분은 이 인간적인 경향을 여러분에게 득이 되도록 이용할 수 있다.

Like someone invests a great deal of money in a personal trainer / to ensure they follow through on their commitment, / you, too, can invest a great deal up front / to ensure you stay on the path you want to be on.
많은 돈을 개인 트레이너에 투자하는 사람처럼, / 확실히 자기 약속을 끝까지 완수하기 위해 / 여러분 또한 선불로 많은 돈을 투자할 수 있다. / 자신이 있고 싶은 길에 확실히 있기 위해

경제학에서 매몰 비용 오류라고 알려진 원리가 있다. 여러분이 어떤 것에 투자하고 소유권을 가지면, 그것을 지나치게 중요하게 여긴다는 개념이다.

(B) 이것은 사람들이 분명히 그만두어야 하는 경로를 계속 따르거나 추구하게 한다. 예를 들어, 사람들은 그저 자신의 많은 것을 투입했다는 이유로 자주 끔찍한 연애를 지속한다. 또는, 누군가는 시장에서 분명히 나쁜 아이디어인 사업에 계속 돈을 쏟아부을지도 모른다.

(A) 때로는 사람들이 할 수 있는 가장 현명한 일은 중지하는 것이다. 이것이 진실이더라도, 그것은 또한 식상하고 효력이 떨어진 주장이 될 수 있다. 매몰 비용이 언제나 틀림없이 나쁜 것은 아니다.

(C) 실제로, 여러분은 이 인간적인 경향을 여러분에게 득이 되도록 이용할 수 있다. 확실히 자기 약속을 끝까지 완수하기 위해 많은 돈을 개인 트레이너에게 투자하는 사람처럼, 여러분 또한 자신이 있고 싶은 길에 확실히 있기 위해 선불로 많은 돈을 투자할 수 있다.

Why? 왜 정답일까?

'매몰 비용 오류'라는 개념을 소개하는 주어진 글 뒤로, 이로 인한 부작용을 열거하는 (B), 부작용을 막으려면 추가 비용 투입을 멈춰야 하지만 매몰 비용이 항상 나쁘지는 않을 수 있다는 언급으로 흐름을 반전하는 (A), 어떻게 하면 매몰 비용을 유리하게 이용할 수 있는지 열거하는 (C)가 차례로 이어져야 한다. 따라서 글의 순서로 가장 적절한 것은 ② '(B) – (A) – (C)'이다.

- principle ⓝ 원리
- fallacy ⓝ 오류
- ownership ⓝ 소유권
- smart ⓐ 현명한
- played-out ⓐ 효력이 다 떨어진
- pursuit ⓝ 일, 추구
- relationship ⓝ 연애
- pour ⓥ 쏟아 붓다
- tendency ⓝ 성향, 경향
- follow through on ~을 완수하다
- sunk cost 매몰 비용
- invest ⓥ 투자하다
- overvalue ⓥ 지나치게 중시하다
- quit ⓥ 중지하다 ⓝ 단념, 포기
- argument ⓝ 주장
- abandon ⓥ 포기하다, 버리다
- continue ⓥ 계속하다
- leverage ⓥ 이용하다
- to one's benefit ~에게 유리하게
- up front 선불로

구문 풀이

17행 Like someone invests a great deal of money in a personal
전치사(접속사처럼 쓰임)
trainer to ensure they follow through on their commitment, you, too,
부사적 용법(~하기 위해)   부사적 용법(~하기 위해)   주어
can invest a great deal up front to ensure (that) you stay on the path
동사구   접속사(생략)   선행사
[you want to be on].

08 하지 말아야 할 행동보다 해야 할 행동 말하기 정답률 56% | 정답 ②

주어진 글 다음에 이어질 글의 순서로 가장 적절한 것을 고르시오. [3점]

① (A) – (C) – (B) ✔(B) – (A) – (C)
③ (B) – (C) – (A) ④ (C) – (A) – (B)
⑤ (C) – (B) – (A)

It raises much less reactance / to tell people what to do / than to tell them what not to do.
훨씬 더 적은 저항을 일으킨다. / 사람들에게 해야 할 것을 말하는 것이 / 그들에게 하지 말아야 할 것을 말하기보다

Therefore, / advocating action should lead to higher compliance / than prohibiting action.
그러므로 / 행동을 지지하는 것은 더 높은 승낙의 결과를 가져올 것이다. / 행동을 금지하는 것보다

(B) For example, / researchers have a choice / of how to debrief research participants / in an experiment / involving some deception or omission of information.
예를 들어 / 연구자들은 선택의 여지가 있다. / 연구 참여자들에게 비밀 준수 의무를 지우는 방법에 대한 / 실험에서 / 정보의 어떤 속임이나 생략과 관련한

Often researchers attempt to commit the participant to silence, / saying "Please don't tell other potential participants / that feedback from the other person was false."
연구자들은 흔히 참여자에게 비밀엄수의 의무를 지우려고 시도한다. / "다른 잠재적 참여자들에게 말하지 마세요." 라고 말하여 / "상대방이 준 피드백이 거짓이었다고"

(A) This is a prescription / that is rife with danger, / failing to provide an implementation rule and raising reactance.
이는 지시이다. / 위험으로 가득한 / 실행 규칙을 제공하지 못하고 저항을 높이는

Much better is to say, / "To help make sure that other people provide answers / as useful as yours have been, / when people ask you about this study, / please tell them / that you and another person answered some questions about each other."
훨씬 더 좋은 것은 말하는 것이다. / "다른 사람들이 응답을 제공하도록 돕기 위해, / 당신의 응답만큼 유용한 / 사람들이 이 연구에 대해 당신에게 질문하면, / 그들에게 말해주세요. / 당신과 다른 사람이 서로에 대한 몇 가지 질문에 답했다고"

(C) Similarly, / I once saw a delightful and unusual example / of this principle at work in an art gallery.
마찬가지로, / 나는 이전에 즐겁고 특이한 사례를 보았다. / 미술관에서 이 원칙이 작동하고 있는

A fragile acrylic sculpture had a sign at the base / saying, "Please touch with your eyes."
깨지기 쉬운 아크릴 조각품 밑면에 팻말이 있었다. / "눈으로 만져주세요"라는

The command was clear, / yet created much less reactance in me / than "Don't touch!" would have.
그 지시는 명확했지만, / 나에게는 훨씬 더 적은 저항을 만들어 냈다. / "손대지 마세요!"가 그랬을 보다

사람들에게 하지 말아야 할 것을 말하기보다 해야 할 것을 말하는 것이 훨씬 더 적은 저항을 일으킨다. 그러므로 행동을 지지하는 것은 행동을 금지하는 것보다 더 높은 승낙의 결과를 가져올 것이다.

(B) 예를 들어 연구자들은 정보의 어떤 속임이나 생략과 관련한 실험에서 연구 참여자들에게 비밀 준수 의무를 지우는 방법에 대한 선택의 여지가 있다. 연구자들은 흔히 "다른 잠재적 참여자들에게 상대방이 준 피드백이 거짓이었다고 말하지 마세요."라고 말하여 참여자에게 비밀엄수의 의무를 지우려고 시도한다.

(A) 이는 실행 규칙을 제공하지 못하고 저항을 높이는 위험으로 가득한 지시이다. 훨씬 더 좋은 것은, "다른 사람들이 당신의 응답만큼 유용한 응답을 제공하도록 돕기 위해, 사람들이 이 연구에 대해 당신에게 질문하면, 당신과 다른 사람이 서로에 대한 몇 가지 질문에 답했다고 말해주세요."라고 말하는 것이다.

(C) 마찬가지로, 나는 이전에 미술관에서 이 원칙이 작동하고 있는 즐겁고 특이한 사례를 보았다. 깨지기 쉬운 아크릴 조각품 밑면에 "눈으로 만져주세요"라는 팻말이 있었다. 그 지시는 명확했지만, 나에게는 "손대지 마세요!"보다 훨씬 더 적은 저항을 만들어 냈다.

Why? 왜 정답일까?

하지 말아야 할 행동보다 해야 할 행동에 관해 말해주는 것이 저항을 덜 불러일으킨다는 일반적인 내용 뒤로, 연구자들이 참가자들에게 하지 말아야 할 것을 말해주는 상황을 예로 드는 (B), 대신에 해야 할 것을 지시하는 것이 좋다고 제안하는 (A), 미술관에서 필자가 비슷한 사례를 보았다는 내용의 (C)가 차례로 이어지는 것이 자연스럽다. 따라서 글의 순서로 가장 적절한 것은 ② '(B) – (A) – (C)'이다.

- reactance ⓝ 저항
- compliance ⓝ 승낙, 순응
- prescription ⓝ 지시, 처방
- implementation ⓝ 실행, 시행
- experiment ⓝ 실험
- omission ⓝ 생략
- potential ⓐ 잠재적인
- principle ⓝ 원칙
- sculpture ⓝ 조각품
- advocate ⓥ 지지하다, 옹호하다
- prohibit ⓥ 금지하다
- rife ⓐ 가득한
- debrief ⓥ 비밀 준수 의무를 지우다
- deception ⓝ 속임, 기만
- attempt ⓥ 시도하다
- delightful ⓐ 기쁜
- fragile ⓐ 깨지기 쉬운, 손상되기 쉬운

구문 풀이

7행 Much better is to say, "To help make sure {that other people
　　　　보어(도치)　동사　주어　　목적(~하기 위해서)　　접속사
provide answers as useful as yours have been}, when people ask
　　　　　　　= your answers　　　　　접속사(~할 때)
you about this study, please tell them that you and another person
　　　　　　　　　　　　　명령문(~하라)
answered some questions about each other."

★★★ 1등급 대비 고난도 2점 문제

09 공감으로 인한 분노의 해소　　　　정답률 36% | 정답 ⑤

주어진 글 다음에 이어질 글의 순서로 가장 적절한 것을 고르시오.

① (A) — (C) — (B)　　　② (B) — (A) — (C)
③ (B) — (C) — (A)　　　④ (C) — (A) — (B)
✓⑤ (C) — (B) — (A)

Anger and empathy / — like matter and antimatter — / can't exist in the same place at the same time.
분노와 공감은 / 물질과 반물질처럼 / 같은 시간, 같은 장소에 존재할 수 없다.

Let one in, / and you have to let the other one go.
하나를 들여보내라 / 그러면 여러분은 다른 하나를 내보내야 한다.

So when you shift a blamer into empathy, / you stop the person's angry ranting dead in its tracks.
따라서 여러분이 비난자를 공감 속으로 이동시킬 때, / 여러분은 그 사람의 분노에 찬 폭언을 즉시 멈추게 한다.

(C) And what about the person / who's on the defensive?
그렇다면 사람은 어떤가? / 방어하는 쪽에 있는

Initially, / this human punching bag is frustrated / because no matter what he or she is trying to mirror outward / the ignorant blamer is blind to it.
처음에 / 이 인간 펀칭백은 좌절한다. / 자신이 그 무엇을 밖으로 잘 보여 주려 애써도 / 그 무지한 비난자가 그것을 보지 못하므로

As a result, / the person who's under attack / is usually in a state of quiet, barely controlled rage.
그 결과 / 공격당하는 사람은 / 대체로 간신히 통제되고 있는 조용한 분노 상태에 있게 된다.

(B) Suddenly and unexpectedly, however, / the blamer knows / just how sad, angry, scared, or lonely the defender feels / and spontaneously turns into an ally.
그러나 갑자기 뜻밖에도 / 그 비난자는 알게 되고, / 방어자가 정말 얼마나 슬프거나 화가 나거나 겁먹었거나 외로운지를 / 자연스럽게 동맹자로 바뀐다.

When the defender feels understood by the blamer / and that they are on the same side, / there's nothing to defend against.
방어자가 자신이 비난자에 의해 이해받고 있으며, / 그들이 서로가 같은 편이라고 느낄 때, / 맞서서 방어할 것은 아무것도 없다.

The defender's wall, / and with it / his unspoken rage and frustration, / disappears.
방어자의 벽, / 그리고 그것과 함께 / 입 밖에 내지 못한 그의 분노와 좌절이 / 사라진다.

(A) The relief / from no longer feeling "fear or hatred" / toward the blamer / spontaneously triggers a tremendous rush of gratitude /
and — miraculously — / the person's quiet rage turns into forgiveness / and, beyond that, a willingness to work toward solutions.
안도감은 / 더는 '두려움이나 증오'를 느끼지 않게 되는 데서 오는 / 비난자에 대해 / 엄청난 고마움이 물밀 듯이 자연스럽게 밀려오게 하고, / 그리고 기적적으로 / 그 사람의 조용한 분노는 용서로 바뀐다. / 그리고 그것을 넘어 해결을 향해 기꺼이 노력하고자 하는 의지로

분노와 공감은 물질과 반물질처럼 같은 시간, 같은 장소에 존재할 수 없다. 하나를 들여보내면 다른 하나는 내보내야 한다. 따라서 비난하는 사람을 공감 속으로 이동시킬 때, 여러분은 그 사람의 분노에 찬 폭언을 즉시 멈추게 한다.

(C) 그렇다면 방어하는 쪽의 사람은 어떤가? 처음에 이 인간 펀칭백은 자신이 그 무엇을 밖으로 잘 보여 주려 애써도 그 무지한 비난하는 사람이 그것을 보지 못하므로 좌절한다. 그 결과 공격당하는 사람은 대체로 간신히 통제되고 있는 조용한 분노 상태에 있게 된다.

(B) 그러나 갑자기 뜻밖에도 그 비난하는 사람은 방어하는 사람이 정말 얼마나 슬픈지, 얼마나 화가 나 있는지, 얼마나 겁먹었는지, 또는 얼마나 외로운지를 알게 되고, 자연스럽게 동맹자로 바뀐다. 방어하는 사람이 비난하는 사람에 의해 이해받고 있다고 느끼며 서로가 같은 편이라고 느낄 때, 맞서서 방어할 것은 아무것도 없다. 방어하는 사람의 벽, 그리고 벽과 함께 입 밖에 내지 못한 그의 분노와 좌절이 사라진다.

(A) 비난하는 사람에 대해 더는 '두려움이나 증오'를 느끼지 않게 됨으로써 오

는 안도감으로 인해 엄청난 고마움이 물밀 듯이 자연스럽게 밀려오고, 기적적으로 그 사람의 조용한 분노는 용서로, 그리고 그것을 넘어 해결을 향해 기꺼이 노력하고자 하는 의지로 바뀐다.

Why? 왜 정답일까?

분노와 공감은 하나의 시공간 안에 있을 수 없다는 일반론과 함께 비난하는 사람의 입장을 언급하는 주어진 글 뒤로, 방어하는 사람의 입장이 어떤지 설명하는 (C)가 이어진다. 이어서 (B)에서는 분노를 기준으로 반대되는 입장에 있던 비난하는 사람과 방어하는 사람이 공감으로 묶이는 과정을 설명하고, (A)는 그 결과를 서술한다. 따라서 글의 순서로 가장 적절한 것은 ⑤ '(C) – (B) – (A)'이다.

- empathy ⓝ 공감
- blamer ⓝ 비난하는 사람
- relief ⓝ 안도(감)
- spontaneously ⓐⓓ 자연스럽게
- tremendous ⓐ 엄청난
- gratitude ⓝ 감사
- rage ⓝ 분노
- willingness ⓝ 기꺼이 ~하려는 마음
- scared ⓐ 겁먹은
- ally ⓝ 동맹(자)
- frustration ⓝ 좌절
- defensive ⓐ 방어의, 수비의
- frustrate ⓥ 좌절하다, 꺾이다, 실망하다
- barely ⓐⓓ 가까스로, 거의 ~않다
- matter ⓝ 물질
- in one's tracks 즉시
- hatred ⓝ 미움, 증오
- trigger ⓥ 유발하다
- rush ⓝ 북받침, 쇄도
- miraculously ⓐⓓ 기적적으로
- forgiveness ⓝ 용서
- unexpectedly ⓐⓓ 뜻밖에
- defender ⓝ 방어자
- defend against ~에 대해 방어하다
- disappear ⓥ 사라지다
- initially ⓐⓓ 처음에
- mirror ⓥ (거울처럼) 잘 보여 주다, 반영하다

구문 풀이

6행 The relief from no longer feeling "fear or hatred" toward the
　　　　　주어1
blamer spontaneously triggers a tremendous rush of gratitude and
　　　　　　　　　　　동사1(단수)
— miraculously — the person's quiet rage turns into forgiveness and,
　　　　　　　　　　　　주어2　　　　　동사2
(beyond that), a willingness to work toward solutions.
( ) : 부사구

★★ 문제 해결 꿀~팁 ★★

▶ 많이 틀린 이유는?
언뜻 보면 주어진 글의 a blamer와 (B)의 the blamer가 연결되는 것처럼 보이지만, (B)의 however 때문에 흐름이 매끄럽지 않다. 주어진 글의 마지막 문장은 비난하는 사람에게 공감하게 되면 비난이 중단된다는 의미인데, (B)의 첫 문장은 동일한 내용을 역접의 however와 함께 제시하고 있다. however 앞뒤로 똑같은 내용이 연결될 수는 없으므로, 둘 사이에 다른 단락이 있어야 함을 파악할 수 있다.

▶ 문제 해결 방법은?
주어진 글에서 공감이 비난하는 사람의 비난을 중단시킬 수 있다는 일반적인 내용 뒤로, (C)에서 비난하는 사람의 반대편에 있는, 방어하는 사람을 언급했다가, 다시 (B)에서 비난하는 사람에 관한 내용으로 돌아오는 흐름이다.

★★★ 1등급 대비 고난도 2점 문제

10 협상의 정의와 다양한 형태　　　　정답률 35% | 정답 ④

주어진 글 다음에 이어질 글의 순서로 가장 적절한 것을 고르시오.

① (A) — (C) — (B)　　　② (B) — (A) — (C)
③ (B) — (C) — (A)　　　✓④ (C) — (A) — (B)
⑤ (C) — (B) — (A)

Negotiation can be defined / as an attempt to explore and reconcile conflicting positions / in order to reach an acceptable outcome.
협상은 정의될 수 있다. / 상충하는 입장을 탐색하고 화해시키려는 시도라고 / 수용할 수 있는 결과에 도달하기 위해

(C) Whatever the nature of the outcome, / which may actually favour one party more than another, / the purpose of negotiation / is the identification of areas of common interest and conflict.
그 결과의 성격이 어떻든 간에 / 다른 당사자보다 어느 한쪽에 실제로 유리할 수도 있는 / 협상의 목적은 / 공통의 이익과 갈등의 영역을 밝히는 것이다.

In this sense, / depending on the intentions of the parties, / the areas of common interest / may be clarified, refined and given negotiated form and substance.
이러한 의미에서 / 당사자들의 의도에 따라 / 공통의 이익 영역은 / 명확해지고, 정제되며, 협의가 이뤄진 형식과 실체가 주어질 수 있다.

(A) Areas of difference can and do frequently remain, / and will perhaps be the subject of future negotiations, / or indeed remain irreconcilable.
이견이 있는 영역은 남을 수 있고, 실제로 자주 남으며, / 아마도 향후 협상의 주제가 되거나 / 실제로 화해할 수 없는 상태로 남게 될 것이다.

In those instances / in which the parties have highly antagonistic or polarised relations, / the process is likely to be dominated by the exposition, / very often in public, / of the areas of conflict.
그런 경우 / 당사자들이 매우 적대적이거나 양극화된 관계를 맺고 있는 / 그 과정은 설명에 의해 지배될 가능성이 있다. / 흔히 공개적인 / 갈등 영역에 관한

(B) In these and sometimes other forms of negotiation, / negotiation serves functions / other than reconciling conflicting interests.
이런 협상과 혹은 간혹 다른 형태의 협상에서, / 협상은 기능을 수행한다. / 상충하는 이익을 화해시키는 것이 아닌

These will include / delay, publicity, diverting attention or seeking intelligence / about the other party and its negotiating position.
여기에는 포함되기 마련이다. / 지연, 홍보, 주의 분산, 혹은 정보를 구하는 것이 / 상대방과 그쪽이 협상 중인 입장에 관한

협상은 수용할 수 있는 결과에 도달하기 위해 상충하는 입장을 탐색하고 화해시키려는 시도라고 정의될 수 있다.

(C) 그 결과의 성격이 어떻든 간에(다른 당사자보다 어느 한쪽에 실제로 유리할 수도 있다), 협상의 목적은 공통의 이익과 갈등의 영역을 밝히는 것이다. 이러한 의미에서 당사자들의 의도에 따라 공통의 이익 영역은 명확해지고, 정제되며, 협의가 이뤄진 형식과 실체가 주어질 수 있다.

(A) 이견이 있는 영역은 남을 수 있고, 실제로 자주 남으며, 아마도 향후 협상의 주제가 되거나 실제로 화해할 수 없는 상태로 남게 될 것이다. 당사자들이 매우 적대적이거나 양극화된 관계를 맺고 있는 경우, 그 과정은 갈등 영역에 관한 설명, 흔히 공개적인 설명에 의해 지배될 가능성이 있다.

(B) 이런 협상과 혹은 간혹 다른 형태의 협상에서, 협상은 상충하는 이익을 화해시키는 것이 아닌 기능을 수행한다. 여기에는 지연, 홍보, 주의 분산, 혹은 상대방과 그쪽이 협상 중인 입장의 정보를 구하는 것이 포함되기 마련이다.

Why? 왜 정답일까?

주어진 글에서 협상은 상충하는 과정을 화해시키려는 시도로 정의된다고 한다. (C)는 결과에 상관없이 협상을 통해 공통의 이익 및 갈등 영역이 밝혀진다는 내용으로 주어진 글을 뒷받침한다. 이어서 (A)는 협상 이후 이견이 남거나 화해하지 못하는 경우도 흔하다며 당사자가 서로 적대적인 관계일 때를 예로 들고, (B)는 (A)에 언급된 상황 등등을 고려할 때 협상의 결과가 꼭 화해는 아닐 수도 있다는 전체적 결론으로 나아간다. 따라서 글의 순서로 가장 적절한 것은 ④ '(C) – (A) – (B)'이다.

- negotiation ⓝ 협상
- reconcile ⓥ 화해시키다
- outcome ⓝ 결과
- irreconcilable ⓐ 화해할 수 없는
- polarise ⓥ 양극화를 초래하다
- exposition ⓝ 설명
- divert ⓥ 방향을 바꾸게 하다
- intelligence ⓝ 정보, 기밀
- intention ⓝ 의도
- refine ⓥ 정제하다, 다듬다
- attempt ⓝ 시도, 노력 ⓥ 시도하다
- conflicting ⓐ 상충하는
- frequently ⓐⓓ 자주
- antagonistic ⓐ 적대적인
- dominate ⓥ 지배하다
- publicity ⓝ 홍보
- seek ⓥ 추구하다
- the other party 상대방
- clarify ⓥ 명확하게 하다
- substance ⓝ 실체

구문 풀이

16행 Whatever the nature of the outcome (is), which may actually
복합관계대명사(~하든 간에) | 계속적 용법(the nature of the outcome 설명) | 생략
favour one party more than another, the purpose of negotiation is the identification of areas of common interest and conflict.

★★ 문제 해결 꿀~팁 ★★

▶ 많이 틀린 이유는?
(A), (B), (C) 중 어느 것도 연결어로 시작되지 않으므로 전형적인 패턴으로는 풀기 어려운 순서 문제이다. 이 경우 모든 단락을 최대한 다 읽고, 내용적인 연결고리를 잘 찾아야 한다.
▶ 문제 해결 방법은?
주어진 글을 상술하는 단락이 곧 (C)임을 이해해야 한다. 즉 주어진 글에서 협상이란 상충하는 이해 관계를 조율하는 시도로 규정된다고 짧게 언급한 내용을, (C)에서는 '어느 한쪽에 유리한 결과가 발생할 수도 있지만, 어쨌든 공통된 이익 영역과 갈등 영역을 밝히는 것이 곧 협상'이라고 구체적으로 설명하는 것이다. 주어진 글에서 (B)의 these와 연결될 만한 여러 가지 상황을 언급하지 않기 때문에 (B)를 가장 먼저 배치할 수 없다.

★★★ 1등급 대비 고난도 3점 문제

11 식물의 적응 반응 정답률 35% | 정답 ⑤

주어진 글 다음에 이어질 글의 순서로 가장 적절한 것을 고르시오. [3점]
① (A) – (C) – (B) ② (B) – (A) – (C)
③ (B) – (C) – (A) ④ (C) – (A) – (B)
✓ (C) – (B) – (A)

Plants show finely tuned adaptive responses / when nutrients are limiting.
식물은 미세하게 조정된 적응 반응을 보인다. / 영양분이 제한적일 때

Gardeners may recognize yellow leaves / as a sign of poor nutrition and the need for fertilizer.
정원사는 노란 잎을 인식할 수도 있다. / 영양 부족과 비료가 필요하다는 신호로

(C) But if a plant does not have a caretaker / to provide supplemental minerals, / it can proliferate or lengthen its roots and develop root hairs / to allow foraging in more distant soil patches.
그러나 식물에 보충하는 관리자가 없다면, / 미네랄을 공급해 줄 / 식물은 뿌리를 증식하거나, 더 길게 늘리고 뿌리털을 발달시킬 수 있다. / (양분을) 더 먼 토양에서 구하러 다니려고

Plants can also use their memory / to respond to histories of temporal or spatial variation / in nutrient or resource availability.
또한 식물은 자신의 기억을 사용할 수 있다. / 시간적 또는 공간적 변화의 역사에 대응하기 위해 / 영양 혹은 자원 가용성에서의

(B) Research in this area has shown / that plants are constantly aware of their position in the environment, / in terms of both space and time.
이 분야의 연구는 보여주었다. / 식물은 환경 속 자기 위치를 지속해서 인식한다는 것을 / 공간 및 시간 둘 다에 있어

Plants that have experienced variable nutrient availability in the past / tend to exhibit risk-taking behaviors, / such as spending energy on root lengthening / instead of leaf production.
과거에 영양소의 이용 가능성을 다양하게 경험한 식물은 / 위험을 감수하는 행동을 보이는 경향이 있다. / 뿌리 길이를 연장하는 데 에너지를 소비하는 등 / 잎 생산 대신

(A) In contrast, / plants with a history of nutrient abundance / are risk averse and save energy.
반대로, / 영양분이 풍부했던 이력을 가진 식물은 / 위험을 회피하고 에너지를 절약한다.

At all developmental stages, / plants respond to environmental changes or unevenness / so as to be able to use their energy / for growth, survival, and reproduction, / while limiting damage and nonproductive uses of their valuable energy.
모든 발달 단계에서 / 식물은 환경 변화나 불균형에 반응한다. / 에너지를 사용할 수 있도록 / 성장, 생존, 번식을 위해 / 귀중한 에너지의 손상과 비생산적인 사용을 제한하는 한편

식물은 영양분이 제한적일 때 미세하게 조정된 적응 반응을 보인다. 정원사는 노란 잎을 영양 부족과 비료가 필요하다는 신호로 인식할 수도 있다.

(C) 그러나 식물에 보충하는 미네랄을 공급해 줄 관리자가 없다면, 식물은 뿌리를 증식하거나 더 길게 늘리고 뿌리털을 발달시켜 (양분을) 더 먼 토양에서 구하러 다닐 수 있다. 또한, 식물은 자신의 기억을 사용해 영양 혹은 자원 가용성의 시간적 또는 공간적 변화의 역사에 대응할 수 있다.

(B) 이 분야의 연구는 식물은 공간 및 시간 둘 다에 있어 환경 속 자기 위치를 지속해서 인식한다는 것을 보여주었다. 과거에 영양소의 이용 가능성을 다양하게 경험한 식물은 잎 생산 대신 뿌리 길이를 연장하는 데 에너지를 소비하는 등 위험을 감수하는 행동을 보이는 경향이 있다.

(A) 반대로, 영양분이 풍부했던 이력을 가진 식물은 위험을 회피하고 에너지를 절약한다. 모든 발달 단계에서 식물은 성장, 생존, 번식에 에너지를 사용할 수 있도록 환경 변화나 불균형에 반응하는 동시에, 귀중한 에너지의 손상과 비생산적인 사용을 제한한다.

Why? 왜 정답일까?

식물의 적응 반응에 관해 설명하는 글이다. 주어진 글 마지막 문장에서 정원사가 있는 환경을 언급하는데, (C)는 관리자가 없는 경우를 대비해서 설명한다. 이어서 (B)는 다양한 영양 환경을 경험한 식물이 더 위험을 감수한다는 내용인데, (A)는 이와 반대로(In contrast) 영양이 풍부한 환경을 경험해본 식물이 위험을 회피한다는 내용을 제시한다. 따라서 글의 순서로 가장 적절한 것은 ④ '(C) – (B) – (A)'이다.

- finely tuned 미세 조정된
- nutrition ⓝ 영양소
- abundance ⓝ 풍부
- unevenness ⓝ 불균형
- constantly ⓐⓓ 계속
- proliferate ⓥ 증식하다
- patch ⓝ (작은) 땅
- adaptive ⓐ 적응적인
- fertilizer ⓝ 비료
- risk averse 위험을 회피하는
- nonproductive ⓐ 비생산적인
- supplemental ⓐ 보충하는
- forage ⓥ (먹이를) 구하러 다니다

구문 풀이

14행 Plants [that have experienced variable nutrient availability
주어
in the past] tend to exhibit risk-taking behaviors, such as
동사(복수)
spending energy on root lengthening instead of leaf production.
「spend+A+on+B : A를 B에 소비하다」

★★ 문제 해결 꿀~팁 ★★

▶ 많이 틀린 이유는?
Research로 시작하는 (B)가 주어진 글에 대한 예시처럼 보인다. 하지만 (B)를 먼저 배치하면 주어진 글에서 왜 '정원사가 있는 환경'을 언급하고, (C)에서 '관리자가 없는 환경'을 언급하는지 알 수 없게 되어버린다.
▶ 문제 해결 방법은?
주어진 글의 '정원사가 있는 환경'과 (C)의 '관리할 사람이 없는 환경'이 But 앞뒤로 대비된다는 것을 파악한다. (B)는 (C) 마지막 문장의 내용을 연구의 사례로 뒷받침한다. 또한, (B)의 '위험을 감수하는 식물'과 (A)의 '위험을 피하는 식물'이 In contrast 앞뒤로 적절한 대비 관계를 형성한다.

★★★ 1등급 대비 고난도 3점 문제

12 공적 생활로부터 사람들이 멀어지는 원인   정답률 33% | 정답 ⑤

주어진 글 다음에 이어질 글의 순서로 가장 적절한 것을 고르시오. [3점]
① (A) − (C) − (B)
② (B) − (A) − (C)
③ (B) − (C) − (A)
④ (C) − (A) − (B)
☑ (C) − (B) − (A)

Living in dispersal / correlates with a shocking retreat from public life, / according to extensive analysis of the Social Capital Community Benchmark Survey / of nearly thirty thousand people / begun in 2000.
흩어져 생활하는 것은 / 공적 생활로부터 놀라울 정도로 멀어지는 것과 관련이 있다고 한다. / 사회 자본 공동체 기준 조사의 광범위한 분석에 따르면, / 거의 3만 명을 대상으로 한 / 2000년에 시작된

It is hard / to pinpoint the origin of this retreat.
어렵다. / 이렇게 멀어지는 것의 원인을 정확히 집어내는 것은

(C) It may be because / people in the dispersed city / have invested so heavily in private comfort / that they feel insulated from the problems of the rest of the world.
그것은 아마도 ~때문일 수 있다. / 분산된 도시에 사는 사람들이 / 사적 편안함에 너무 많이 투자를 해서 / 나머지 세상의 문제들로부터 차단되었다고 느끼기

It may be / that sprawl has attracted people / who are naturally less interested in engaging with the world, / socially or politically.
~였을 수도 있다. / 스프롤이 사람들을 끌어들였을 / 세상일에 관여하는 데 원래 관심이 적은 / 사회적으로 또는 정치적으로

(B) These are both possible, / but evidence suggests / that the spatial landscape matters.
이 두 가지가 모두 가능하지만, / 증거가 말해 준다. / 공간적 상황이 중요하다는 점을

Sociologists point out / that the suburbs have done an efficient job of sorting people into communities / where they will be surrounded by people of the same socioeconomic status.
사회학자들은 지적한다. / 교외 지역이 사람들을 지역 사회로 나누어 놓는 일을 효율적으로 해 왔음을 / 그들이 같은 사회경제적 지위에 있는 사람들 가운데서 살게 될

(A) Meanwhile, / the architectures of sprawl inhibit political activity / that requires face-to-face interaction.
한편, / 스프롤의 구조는 정치 활동을 억제한다. / 대면 상호 작용이 필요한

It is not that sprawl makes political activity impossible, / but by privatizing gathering space and dispersing human activity, / sprawl makes political gathering less likely.
스프롤이 정치 활동을 불가능하게 만들지는 않지만, / 모임 공간을 사유화하고 인간의 활동을 분산시킴으로써, / 스프롤은 정치 모임을 덜 가능하게 만든다.

2000년에 시작된 거의 3만 명을 대상으로 한 사회 자본 공동체 기준 조사(Social Capital Community Benchmark Survey)의 광범위한 분석에 따르면, 흩어져 생활하는 것은 공적 생활로부터 놀라울 정도로 멀어지는 것과 관련이 있다고 한다. 이렇게 멀어지는 것의 원인을 정확히 집어내는 것은 어렵다.

(C) 그것은 아마도 분산된 도시에 사는 사람들이 사적 편안함에 너무 많은 투자를 해서 나머지 세상의 문제들로부터 차단되었다고 느끼기 때문일 수 있다. 스프롤이 사회적으로 또는 정치적으로 세상일에 관여하는 데 원래 관심이 적은 사람들을 끌어들였을 수도 있다.

(B) 이 두 가지가 모두 가능하지만, 공간적 상황이 중요하다는 점을 증거가 말해 준다. 사회학자들은 교외 지역이 사람들을 같은 사회경제적 지위에 있는 사람들 가운데서 살게 할 지역 사회로 나누어 놓는 일을 효율적으로 해 왔음을 지적한다.

(A) 한편, 스프롤의 구조는 대면 상호 작용이 필요한 정치 활동을 억제한다. 스프롤이 정치 활동을 불가능하게 만들지는 않지만, 모임 공간을 사유화하고 인간의 활동을 분산시킴으로써, 스프롤은 정치 모임을 덜 가능하게 만든다.

Why? 왜 정답일까?

주어진 글에서 흩어져 생활하다 보면 공적인 생활과 멀어지게 되고, 그 원인을 정확히 진단하기는 어렵다고 한다. 이에 이어 (C)는 '아마도' 가능한 이유로서 분산된 도시에 사는 사람들이 사적 편안함을 우선시하여 세상 문제로부터 차단된 기분을 느끼기 때문이거나 스프롤 때문일 수 있다는 두 가지 이유를 언급한다. (B)는 (C)에서 언급된 이유를 These로 가리키며 두 설명이 모두 가능하지만 증거에 따르면 공간적 상황, 즉 스프롤의 역할이 더 크게 작용하기 때문인 것 같다는 설명을 이어 간다. 마지막으로 (A)는 (B)에 Meanwhile로 연결되며 스프롤의 작용에 대한 추가적인 설명을 덧붙이고 있다. 따라서 글의 순서로 가장 적절한 것은 ⑤ '(C) − (B) − (A)'이다.

- **dispersal** ⑩ 분산
- **retreat** ⑩ 멀어짐, 후퇴
- **architecture** ⑩ 구조, 건축
- **privatize** ⓥ 사유화하다, 민영화하다
- **socioeconomic** ⓐ 사회경제적인
- **engage with** ~에 관여하다
- **correlate with** ~와 관련이 있다
- **pinpoint** ⓥ 이유를 정확히 집어내다
- **inhibit** ⓥ 억제하다
- **suburb** ⑩ 교외
- **insulated from** ~로부터 차단된

구문 풀이

17행 It may be because people in the dispersed city have
접속사(이유)
invested so heavily in private comfort that they feel insulated from
「so ~ that … : 너무 ~해서 …하다」
the problems of the rest of the world.

★★ 문제 해결 꿀~팁 ★★

▶ 많이 틀린 이유는?
(B)의 'These ~ both ~'로 미루어 보아 바로 앞 단락에서 어떤 대상에 관한 두 가지 설명이나 선택 사항을 언급해야 한다. 하지만 주어진 글이나 (A)에는 '두 가지'로 요약할 수 있는 내용이 나오지 않는다.
▶ 문제 해결 방법은?
(C)에서 'It may be ~'로 시작하는 두 문장을 통해 주어진 글에서 언급한 the origin of this retreat에 관한 두 가지 가능성을 제시하고 있다. 이 두 가능성과 연결되는 지시어가 (B)의 'These ~ both ~'이다.

DAY 12 글의 순서 02

01 ④	02 ②	03 ②	04 ④	05 ③
06 ⑤	07 ②	08 ②	09 ①	10 ⑤
11 ⑤	12 ⑤			

01 대상을 분류하고 일반화하는 인간의 능력 정답률 49% | 정답 ④

주어진 글 다음에 이어질 글의 순서로 가장 적절한 것을 고르시오.
① (A) – (C) – (B)　　　② (B) – (A) – (C)
③ (B) – (C) – (A)　　　✔(C) – (A) – (B)
⑤ (C) – (B) – (A)

The intuitive ability to classify and generalize / is undoubtedly a useful feature of life and research, / but it carries a high cost, / such as in our tendency / to stereotype generalizations about people and situations.
분류하고 일반화하는 직관적인 능력은 / 분명 생활과 연구에 유용한 특징이지만 / 그것은 많은 대가를 수반한다. / 가령 우리의 경향 / 사람과 상황에 대해 일반화를 고착시키는

(C) For most people, / the word stereotype arouses negative connotations: / it implies a negative bias.
사람들 대부분에게 / 고정 관념이라는 단어는 부정적인 함축을 불러일으킨다 / 즉 그것은 부정적인 편견을 암시한다.

But, in fact, / stereotypes do not differ in principle from all other generalizations; / generalizations about groups of people / are not necessarily always negative.
하지만 사실 / 고정 관념은 원칙적으로 모든 다른 일반화와 다르지 않으며, / 집단에 대한 사람들의 일반화가 / 반드시 꼭 부정적인 것은 아니다.

(A) Intuitively and quickly, / we mentally sort things into groups / based on what we perceive the differences between them to be, / and that is the basis for stereotyping.
직관적이고도 신속하게, / 우리는 머릿속에서 사물을 그룹으로 분류하며, / 우리가 그들끼리 차이가 있다고 생각하는 것에 근거해 / 그리고 그것이 고정관념의 기초이다.

Only afterwards / do we examine (or not examine) more evidence / of how things are differentiated, / and the degree and significance of the variations.
그 후에 비로소 / 우리는 더 많은 증거를 조사한다(혹은 조사하지 않는다). / 사물이 어떻게 차별화되는지 / 그리고 그 차이의 정도와 중요성에 대한

(B) Our brain performs these tasks efficiently and automatically, / usually without our awareness.
우리의 뇌는 이런 일을 효율적이고 자동으로 수행한다. / 대개 우리가 인식하지 못하는 사이에

The real danger of stereotypes is not their inaccuracy, / but their lack of flexibility and their tendency to be preserved, / even when we have enough time to stop and consider.
고정 관념이 진정 위험한 것은 그것의 부정확함이 아니라, / 그것의 유연성 부족과 유지되려는 경향이다. / 우리가 곰곰이 생각할 시간이 충분할 때조차

분류하고 일반화하는 직관적인 능력은 분명 생활과 연구에 유용한 특징이지만 많은 대가를 수반하는데, 가령 우리가 사람과 상황에 대해 일반화를 고착시키는 경향 등이 그 예이다.

(C) 사람들 대부분에게 고정 관념이라는 단어는 부정적인 함축을 불러일으킨다. 즉 그것은 부정적인 편견을 암시한다. 하지만 사실 고정 관념은 원칙적으로 모든 다른 일반화와 다르지 않으며, 집단에 대한 사람들의 일반화가 반드시 꼭 부정적인 것은 아니다.

(A) 직관적이고도 신속하게, 우리는 사물끼리 차이가 있다고 생각하는 것에 근거해 머릿속에서 그들을 그룹으로 분류하며, 그것이 고정관념의 기초이다. 그 후에 비로소 우리는 사물이 어떻게 차별화되는지, 그리고 그 차이의 정도와 중요성에 대한 더 많은 증거를 조사한다(혹은 조사하지 않는다).

(B) 우리의 뇌는 대개 우리가 인식하지 못하는 사이에 이런 일을 효율적이고 자동으로 수행한다. 고정 관념이 진정 위험한 것은 그것의 부정확함이 아니라, 그것의 유연성 부족과 유지되려는 경향인데, 이는 우리가 곰곰이 생각할 시간이 충분할 때조차 그렇다.

Why? 왜 정답일까?

분류하고 일반화하는 능력이 '대가'를 낳는다는 주어진 글 뒤로 (C)가 연결되어 고정 관념이 항상 나빠지는 않다고 설명한다. (A)에서는 고정 관념이 어떻게 만들어지는지 보충 설명하고, (B)는 고정 관념이 '진짜' 위험할 때가 언제인지 구체화한다. 따라서 글의 순서로 가장 적절한 것은 ④ '(C) – (A) – (B)'이다.

- intuitive ⓐ 직관적인
- feature ⓝ 특징
- stereotype ⓥ 고정 관념으로 만들다
- intuitively ⓐⓓ 직관적으로
- differentiate ⓥ 구별하다, 차별화하다
- inaccuracy ⓝ 부정확함
- arouse ⓥ 불러일으키다
- imply ⓥ 시사하다
- in principle 원칙적으로
- undoubtedly ⓐⓓ 의심의 여지 없이
- tendency ⓝ 경향
- generalization ⓝ 일반화
- examine ⓥ 조사하다
- automatically ⓐⓓ 자동으로
- preserve ⓥ 보존하다
- connotation ⓝ 함축
- bias ⓝ 편견

구문 풀이

9행 Only afterwards do we examine (or not examine) more
「도치 구문 : only 부사구 + do + 주어 + 동사원형」
evidence of [how things are differentiated], and the degree and
의문사절(of의 목적어1)　　　　명사구(of의 목적어2)
significance of the variations.

02 악보 표기법의 등장으로 인한 음악 예술의 변화 정답률 50% | 정답 ②

주어진 글 다음에 이어질 글의 순서로 가장 적절한 것을 고르시오.
① (A) – (C) – (B)　　　✔(B) – (A) – (C)
③ (B) – (C) – (A)　　　④ (C) – (A) – (B)
⑤ (C) – (B) – (A)

Notation was more than a practical method / for preserving an expanding repertoire of music.
악보 표기법은 실용적인 방법 이상이었다. / 음악의 확장되는 레퍼토리를 보존하기 위한

(B) It changed the nature of the art itself.
그것은 그 예술 자체의 본성을 바꾸었다.

To write something down means / that people far away in space and time / can re-create it.
뭔가를 적는다는 것은 의미한다. / 공간과 시간 면에서 멀리 떨어져 있는 사람들이 / 그것을 재창조할 수 있다는 것을

At the same time, there are downsides.
동시에 단점이 있다.

(A) Written notes freeze the music / rather than allowing it to develop in the hands of individuals, / and it discourages improvisation.
악보로 쓰인 음은 그 음악을 굳어지게 하며, / 그 음악이 개인들의 손에서 발전하도록 허용하기보다는 / 즉흥 연주를 억제한다.

Partly because of notation, / modern classical performance lacks the depth of nuance / that is part of aural tradition.
부분적으로 악보 표기 때문에 / 현대의 고전 음악 공연은 뉘앙스의 깊이가 부족하다. / 청각 전승 방식의 일부인

Before notation arrived, in all history / music was largely carried on as an aural tradition.
악보 표기법이 등장하기 전에, 역사를 통틀어 / 음악은 대체로 청각 전승 방식으로 계속되었다.

(C) Most world music is still basically aural, / including sophisticated musical traditions such as Indian and Balinese.
대부분의 세계 음악은 여전히 기본적으로 청각적이다. / 인도 음악과 발리 음악과 같이 정교한 음악적인 전통을 포함하여

Most jazz musicians / can read music but often don't bother, / and their art is much involved with improvisation.
재즈 음악가 대부분은 / 악보를 읽을 수 있지만 흔히 신경 쓰지 않으며, / 그들의 예술은 즉흥 연주와 많은 연관을 맺고 있다.

Many modern pop musicians, one example being Paul McCartney, / can't read music at all.
많은 현대 대중 음악가들은, Paul McCartney가 한 사례인데, / 악보를 전혀 읽지 못한다.

악보 표기법은 음악의 확장되는 레퍼토리를 보존하기 위한 실용적인 방법 이상이었다.

(B) 그것은 그 예술 자체의 본성을 바꾸었다. 뭔가를 적는다는 것은 공간과 시간 면에서 멀리 떨어져 있는 사람들이 그것을 재창조할 수 있다는 것을 의미한다. 동시에 단점이 있다.

(A) 악보로 쓰인 음은 그 음악이 개인들의 손에서 발전하도록 허용하기보다는 그 음악을 굳어지게 하며, 즉흥 연주를 억제한다. 부분적으로 악보 표기 때문에 현대의 고전 음악 공연은 청각 전승 방식의 일부인 뉘앙스의 깊이가 부족하다. 악보 표기법이 등장하기 전에, 역사를 통틀어 음악은 대체로 청각 전승 방식으로 계속되었다.

(C) 인도 음악과 발리 음악과 같이 정교한 음악적인 전통을 포함하여 대부분의 세계 음악은 여전히 기본적으로 청각적이다. 재즈 음악가 대부분은 악보를 읽을 수 있지만 흔히 신경 쓰지 않으며, 그들의 예술은 즉흥 연주와 많은 연관을 맺고 있다. 많은 현대 대중 음악가들은, Paul McCartney가 한 사례인데, 악보를 전혀 읽지 못한다.

Why? 왜 정답일까?

악보 표기법을 화제로 언급하는 주어진 글 뒤에는, 악보 표기법이 음악의 본성을 바꾸었지만 한편으로 한계를 지녔다는 내용의 **(B)**, 악보 표기가 시작되면서 기존의 청각 전승 방식이 지속될 수 없었다는 내용의 **(A)**, 전 세계의 음악이 기본적으로는 청각적임을 부언하는 내용의 **(C)**가 차례로 이어져야 한다. 따라서 글의 순서로 가장 적절한 것은 ② '**(B)** – **(A)** – **(C)**'이다.

- **notation** ⓝ (수학, 과학, 음악 등의) 표기법
- **in the hands of** ~의 수중에 있는
- **lack** ⓥ 부족하다, ~이 없다
- **sophisticated** ⓐ 정교한, 세련된
- **practical** ⓐ 실용적인
- **discourage** ⓥ 막다, 좌절시키다
- **downside** ⓝ 불리한 면, 단점

구문 풀이

18행 Many modern pop musicians, one example being Paul
<u>주어</u> <u>의미상 주어</u> <u>분사구문</u>
McCartney, can't read music at all.
<u>동사</u>

---

03 지구의 생성 과정   정답률 58% | 정답 ②

주어진 글 다음에 이어질 글의 순서로 가장 적절한 것을 고르시오.

① (A) – (C) – (B)   ✔ (B) – (A) – (C)
③ (B) – (C) – (A)   ④ (C) – (A) – (B)
⑤ (C) – (B) – (A)

The Earth formed from rocky and metallic fragments / during the construction of the solar system / — debris that was swept up by an initial nucleus / and attracted together into a single body / by the force of gravity.
지구는 암석과 금속 조각들로부터 만들어졌는데, / 태양계의 형성 도중 / 이는 초기 핵에 의해 휩쓸린 파편들이다. / 그리고 끌려 함께 하나의 덩어리가 된 / 중력의 힘으로

(B) The original materials were cold as outer space / and dry as dust; / whatever water and gases they contained / were locked inside individual fragments / as chemical compounds.
원래 물질들은 우주 공간처럼 차갑고, / 먼지처럼 건조했는데, / 여기 포함된 물과 가스는 무엇이든지 / 개별 조각 안에 갇혀 있었다. / 화학 혼합물로서

As the fragments joined, / the Earth's gravity increased, / attracting larger and larger objects / to impact the Earth.
그 조각들이 모이면서 / 지구의 중력이 증가했고, / 이것은 점점 더 큰 물체들을 끌어당겨 / 지구에 충돌하게 했다.

(A) This increasing gravity, / combined with the timeless radioactive decay of elements / like uranium and thorium, / caused the new Earth to heat up.
이러한 중력의 증가는 / 원소의 끝없는 방사선 붕괴와 결합해 / 우라늄과 토륨과 같은 / 새로운 지구가 가열되게 했다.

The internal temperature and pressure / were high enough / for many compounds to break down or melt, / releasing their water and gases.
내부 온도와 압력은 / 충분히 높았고, / 많은 혼합물이 분해되거나 녹을 정도로 / 물과 가스를 방출했다.

(C) Even solid material / could begin to move / and flow under such conditions.
심지어 고체 물질도 / 그러한 상태에서 움직이고 / 흐르기 시작할 수 있었다.

Separation by density began, / and the Earth started to organize into its present layered structure.
밀도에 의한 분리가 시작되었고, / 지구는 현재의 지층 구조로 구성되기 시작했다.

The heaviest metals sank to the center; / the lightest materials migrated outward.
가장 무거운 금속은 중심부로 가라앉았고, / 가장 가벼운 물질은 바깥으로 이동했다.

지구는 태양계의 형성 도중 암석과 금속 조각들로부터 만들어졌는데, 이는 초기 핵에 의해 휩쓸리고 중력의 힘으로 끌려와 하나의 덩어리가 된 파편들이다.

(B) 원래 물질들은 우주 공간처럼 차갑고 먼지처럼 건조했는데, 여기 포함된 물과 가스는 무엇이든지 화학 혼합물로서 개별 조각 안에 갇혀 있었다. 그 조각들이 모이면서 지구의 중력이 증가했고, 이것은 점점 더 큰 물체들을 끌어당겨 지구에 충돌하게 했다.

(A) 이러한 중력의 증가는 우라늄과 토륨과 같은 원소의 끝없는 방사선 붕괴와 결합해 새로운 지구가 가열되게 했다. 내부 온도와 압력은 많은 혼합물이 분해되거나 녹을 정도로 충분히 높았고, 물과 가스를 방출했다.

(C) 심지어 고체 물질도 그러한 상태에서 움직이고 흐르기 시작할 수 있었다. 밀도에 의한 분리가 시작되었고, 지구는 현재의 지층 구조로 구성되기 시작했다. 가장 무거운 금속은 중심부로 가라앉았고, 가장 가벼운 물질은 바깥으로 이동했다.

Why? 왜 정답일까?

초기 지구의 형성 과정을 설명한 글로, 먼저 주어진 글은 지구가 암석과 금속 조각으로부

터 만들어졌고 이 조각들은 중력의 힘으로 끌려왔다는 내용을 제시한다. 이어서 **(B)**는 이 조각들이 모이면서 지구의 중력이 커졌다는 내용을, **(A)**는 중력의 증가로 인해 지구가 가열되어 혼합물이 녹기 시작했다는 내용을 다룬다. 마지막으로 **(C)**는 **(A)**의 결과로 고체도 움직여 흐를 수 있었으며, 물질이 이동하면서 현재의 지층 구조가 만들어졌다는 내용으로 글을 마무리한다. 따라서 글의 순서로 가장 적절한 것은 ② '**(B)** – **(A)** – **(C)**'이다.

- **metallic** ⓐ 금속의
- **sweep up** 휩쓸다
- **timeless** ⓐ 끝없는, 변치 않는
- **decay** 붕괴, 부패
- **melt** ⓥ 녹다
- **density** ⓝ 밀도
- **debris** ⓝ 잔해, 파편
- **nucleus** ⓝ 핵
- **radioactive** ⓐ 방사성의
- **compound** ⓝ 화합물
- **separation** ⓝ 분리
- **sink** ⓥ 가라앉다

구문 풀이

7행 The internal temperature and pressure were high enough for many compounds to break down or melt, releasing
「형/부 + enough + 의미상 주어 + to부정사 : ~이 … 할 만큼 충분히 ~한」
their water and gases.

---

04 디지털 환경에서 시선을 돌리게 만드는 전략   정답률 44% | 정답 ④

주어진 글 다음에 이어질 글의 순서로 가장 적절한 것을 고르시오.

① (A) – (C) – (B)   ② (B) – (A) – (C)
③ (B) – (C) – (A)   ✔ (C) – (A) – (B)
⑤ (C) – (B) – (A)

One common strategy and use of passive misdirection / in the digital world / comes through the use of repetition.
인식하지 못한 채 시선을 다른 곳으로 돌리게 하는 것에 대한 한 가지 흔한 전략과 사용은 / 디지털 세계에서 / 반복을 이용하여 이루어진다.

(C) This digital misdirection strategy relies on the fact / that online users utilizing web browsers to visit websites / have quickly learned / that the most basic ubiquitous navigational action / is to click on a link or button / presented to them on a website.
디지털상에서 시선을 다른 곳으로 돌리게 하는 이 전략은 사실에 의존한다. / 웹 사이트를 방문하기 위하여 웹 브라우저를 사용하는 온라인 사용자가 / 바로 배웠다는 / 가장 기본적이고 어디에서나 하는 탐색 동작이 / 링크나 버튼을 클릭하는 것이라는 것을 / 웹 사이트에서 그들에게 제시되는

(A) This action is repeated over and over / to navigate their web browsers / to the desired web page or action / until it becomes an almost immediate, reflexive action.
이 동작은 여러 번 되풀이하여 반복된다. / 웹 브라우저를 조종해 가기 위해, / 원하는 웹 페이지나 동작으로 / 그것이 거의 즉각적이고 반사적인 동작으로 바뀔 때까지

Malicious online actors take advantage of this behavior / to distract the user / from carefully examining the details of the web page / that might tip off the user / that there is something amiss about the website.
악의적인 온라인 행위자들은 이 행동을 이용한다. / 사용자의 관심을 다른 곳으로 돌리기 위해 / 웹 페이지의 세부 사항을 주의 깊게 검토하지 못하도록 / 사용자에게 귀띔해 주는 / 이들이 웹 사이트에 어떤 잘못된 것이 있다고

(B) The website is designed / to focus the user's attention on the action / the malicious actor wants them to take / (e.g., click a link) / and to draw their attention away from any details / that might suggest to the user / that the website is not what it appears to be on the surface.
그 웹 사이트는 설계된다. / 행동에 사용자의 관심을 집중시키고 / 악의적인 행위자가 그들이 수행하기를 원하는 / (예를 들어, 링크를 클릭하는 것) / 세부 사항으로부터 주의를 다른 곳으로 돌리도록 / 사용자에게 암시할 수 있는 / 웹 사이트가 겉으로 보이는 것과 다르다는 것을

디지털 세계에서 인식하지 못한 채 시선을 다른 곳으로 돌리게 하는 것에 대한 한 가지 흔한 전략과 사용은 반복을 이용하여 이루어진다.

(C) 디지털상에서 시선을 다른 곳으로 돌리게 하는 이 전략은 웹 사이트를 방문하기 위하여 웹 브라우저를 사용하는 온라인 사용자가 가장 기본적이고 어디에서나 하는 탐색 동작이 웹 사이트에서 그들에게 제시되는 링크나 버튼을 클릭하는 것임을 바로 배웠다는 사실에 의존한다.

(A) 이 동작은 원하는 웹 페이지나 동작으로 웹 브라우저를 조종해 가기 위해, 그것이 거의 즉각적이고 반사적인 동작으로 바뀔 때까지 여러 번 되풀이하여 반복된다. 악의적인 온라인 행위자들은 이 행동을 이용해 사용자의 관심을 다른 곳으로 돌려 이들이 웹 사이트에 어떤 잘못된 것이 있다고 사용자에게 귀띔해 주는 웹 페이지의 세부 사항을 주의 깊게 검토하지 못하게 한다.

(B) 그 웹 사이트는 악의적인 행위자가 사용자들이 수행하기를 원하는 행동에 사용자의 관심을 집중시키고(예를 들어, 링크를 클릭하는 것) 사용자에게 웹 사이트가 겉으로 보이는 것과 다르다는 것을 암시할 수 있는 세부 사항으로부터 주의를 다른 곳으로 돌리도록 설계된다.

Why? 왜 정답일까?

디지털 환경에서 시선을 무의식적으로 돌리게 만드는 전략에 관해 언급하는 주어진 글 뒤로, 이 전략은 클릭 동작과 관련되어 있음을 설명하는 (C), 클릭 동작의 반복성을 설명한 뒤, 악의적인 사이트에서 이를 악용한다는 내용으로 넘어가는 (A), 이들 사이트의 의도에 관해 보충 설명하는 (B)가 차례로 이어져야 자연스럽다. 따라서 글의 순서로 가장 적절한 것은 ④ '(C) – (A) – (B)'이다.

- **passive** ⓐ 소극적인, 시키는 대로 하는
- **repetition** ⓝ 반복
- **immediate** ⓐ 즉각적인
- **malicious** ⓐ 악의적인
- **tip off** ~에게 제보하다, 귀띔하다
- **ubiquitous** ⓐ 어디에나 하는
- **misdirection** ⓝ 잘못된 지시, 그릇된 방향
- **over and over** 여러 번 되풀이하여
- **reflexive** ⓐ 반사적인
- **distract** ⓥ 마음을 다른 곳으로 돌리다
- **amiss** ⓐ 잘못된

구문 풀이

7행 Malicious online actors take advantage of this behavior
to distract the user from carefully examining the details of the web
(목적(~하기 위해서))   (선행사)
page [that might tip off the user that there is something amiss about
(주격 관·대)   (접속사(~것))   (-thing + 형용사(~한 것))
the website].

---

05 의사 결정에서의 감정적 평가 | 정답률 46% | 정답 ③

주어진 글 다음에 이어질 글의 순서로 가장 적절한 것을 고르시오. [3점]

① (A) – (C) – (B) ② (B) – (A) – (C)
✓(B) – (C) – (A) ④ (C) – (A) – (B)
⑤ (C) – (B) – (A)

A large body of research in decision science / has indicated / that one attribute that is regularly substituted / for an explicit assessment of decision costs and benefits / is an affective valuation of the prospect at hand.
의사 결정 과학에 대한 많은 연구에서는 / 보여주었다. / 대신해서 자주 쓰이는 한 가지 속성은 / 의사 결정 비용과 편익에 대한 명시적인 평가를 / 당면한 가능성에 대한 감정적 평가라고 한다.

(B) This is often a very rational attribute to substitute — / affect does convey useful signals / as to the costs and benefits of outcomes.
이것은 대체하기에 매우 합리적인 속성인 경우가 흔하다. / 감정은 정말로 유용한 신호를 전달하기 때문이다. / 결과의 비용과 편익에 대한

A problem sometimes arises, / however, / when affective valuation is not supplemented / by any analytic processing and adjustment at all.
때로 문제가 발생하기도 한다. / 그러나 / 감정적 평가가 전혀 보완되지 않으면 / 그 어떤 분석적 처리와 조정으로도

(C) For example, / sole reliance on affective valuation / can make people insensitive / to probabilities and to quantitative features of the outcome / that should effect decisions.
예를 들어, / 오로지 감정적 평가에만 의존하는 것은 / 사람들이 둔감하게 할 수 있다. / 결과의 확률 및 양적 특징에 / 의사 결정을 초래할

One study demonstrated / that people's evaluation of a situation / where they might receive a shock / is insensitive to the probability of receiving the shock / because their thinking is swamped by affective evaluation of the situation.
한 연구는 보여주었다. / 상황에 대한 사람들의 평가가 / 감전될지도 모르는 / 감전될 확률에 둔감한데, / 그들의 사고가 그 상황에 대한 감정적 평가에 압도되기 때문이라는 것을

(A) People were willing to pay almost as much / to avoid a 1 percent probability of receiving a shock / as they were to pay / to avoid a 99 percent probability of receiving a shock.
사람들은 거의 맞먹는 정도를 지불할 의향을 보였다. / 1퍼센트의 감전 확률을 피할 목적으로 / 그들이 기꺼이 지불할 만큼과 / 99퍼센트의 감전 확률을 피하고자

Clearly / the affective reaction to the thought of receiving a shock / was overwhelming the subjects' ability / to evaluate the probabilities associated.
분명히, / 감전된다는 생각에 대한 감정적 반응이 / 피실험자들의 능력을 압도하고 있었다. / 관련된 확률을 평가하는

의사 결정 과학에 대한 많은 연구에서 보여주기를, 의사 결정 비용과 편익에 대한 명시적인 평가를 대신해 자주 쓰이는 한 가지 속성은 당면한 가능성에 대한 감정적 평가라고 한다.

(B) 이것은 대체하기에 매우 합리적인 속성인 경우가 흔하다. 감정은 정말로 결과의 비용과 편익에 대한 유용한 신호를 전달하기 때문이다. 그러나 감정적 평가가 그 어떤 분석적 처리와 조정으로도 전혀 보완되지 않으면, 때로 문제가 발생하기도 한다.

(C) 예를 들어, 오로지 감정적 평가에만 의존하는 것은 의사 결정을 초래할 결과의 확률 및 양적 특징에 사람들이 둔감해지게 할 수 있다. 한 연구는 감전될지도 모르는 상황에 대한 사람들의 평가가 감전될 확률에 둔감한데,

---

그들의 사고가 그 상황에 대한 감정적 평가에 압도되기 때문이라는 것을 보여주었다.

(A) 사람들은 1퍼센트의 감전 확률을 피할 목적으로 99퍼센트의 감전 확률을 피하고자 기꺼이 지불할 대가와 거의 맞먹는 정도를 지불할 의향을 보였다. 분명히, 감전된다는 생각에 대한 감정적 반응이 (감전과) 관련된 확률을 평가하는 피실험자들의 능력을 압도하고 있었다.

Why? 왜 정답일까?

주어진 글은 의사 결정 과정 도중 비용–편익에 대한 명시적 분석 대신 감정적 평가가 흔히 개입된다는 내용이다. (B)는 '감정적 평가'를 This로 언급하며, 이것은 실제로 의사 결정에 유용하게 작용하기도 하지만 문제를 낳기도 한다고 설명한다. (C)에서는 '문제' 상황의 예를 들기 시작하고(For example), (A)는 예시를 마무리한다. 따라서 글의 순서로 가장 적절한 것은 ③ '(B) – (C) – (A)'이다.

- **a body of** 많은
- **substitute A for B** A를 B로 대체하다
- **prospect** ⓝ 가능성
- **probability** ⓝ 확률, 개연성
- **supplement** ⓥ 보충하다
- **sole** ⓐ 전적인, 단 하나의
- **quantitative** ⓐ 양적인
- **attribute** ⓝ 특성, 속성
- **valuation** ⓝ 평가, 가치 판단
- **be willing to** ~할 의향을 보이다
- **overwhelming** ⓐ 압도적인, 너무도 강렬한
- **analytic** ⓐ 분석적인
- **insensitive to** ~에 둔감한
- **swamp** ⓥ 압도하다

구문 풀이

6행 People were willing to pay almost as much to avoid a
「as + 원급 + as : ~만큼 …한」
1 percent probability of receiving a shock as they were to pay to
(대동사(= were willing))
avoid a 99 percent probability of receiving a shock.

---

06 허구 세계와 현실 세계의 차이 | 정답률 61% | 정답 ⑤

주어진 글 다음에 이어질 글의 순서로 가장 적절한 것을 고르시오. [3점]

① (A) – (C) – (B) ② (B) – (A) – (C)
③ (B) – (C) – (A) ④ (C) – (A) – (B)
✓(C) – (B) – (A)

In spite of the likeness / between the fictional and real world, / the fictional world deviates from the real one / in one important respect.
유사성에도 불구하고 / 허구의 세계와 현실의 세계 사이의 / 허구의 세계는 현실 세계로부터 벗어난다. / 하나의 중요한 측면에서

(C) The existing world faced by the individual / is in principle an infinite chaos of events and details / before it is organized by a human mind.
개인이 직면한 기존의 세계는 / 이론상으로는 사건들과 세부 사항들의 무한한 혼돈 상태이다. / 인간의 정신에 의해 조직되기 전에는

This chaos only gets processed and modified / when perceived by a human mind.
이 혼돈 상태는 오로지 처리되고 수정된다. / 인간의 정신에 의해 인식될 때만이

(B) Because of the inner qualities / with which the individual is endowed / through heritage and environment, / the mind functions as a filter; / every outside impression / that passes through it / is filtered and interpreted.
내적 특성 때문에 / 개인이 부여받은 / 유산과 환경을 통해 / 그러한 정신은 여과기 역할을 한다. / 모든 외부의 인상이 / 그것을 통과하는 / 걸러지고 해석된다.

However, / the world the reader encounters in literature / is already processed and filtered by another consciousness.
그러나 / 문학에서 독자가 접하는 세계는 / 이미 또 다른 의식에 의해 처리되고 여과되어 있다.

(A) The author has selected the content / according to his own worldview and his own conception of relevance, / in an attempt to be neutral and objective / or convey a subjective view on the world.
작가는 내용을 선정했다. / 자신의 세계관과 적절성에 대한 자신의 개념에 따라 / 중립적이고 객관적이려는 노력에서 / 또는 세계에 대한 주관적인 견해를 전달하려는

Whatever the motives, / the author's subjective conception of the world / stands between the reader and the original, untouched world / on which the story is based.
동기가 무엇이든, / 세계에 대한 작가의 주관적인 개념이 / 독자와 원래의 손대지 않은 세계 사이에 존재한다. / 이야기의 기초가 되는

허구의 세계와 현실의 세계 사이의 유사성에도 불구하고 허구의 세계는 하나의 중요한 측면에서 현실 세계로부터 벗어난다.

(C) 개인이 직면한 기존의 세계는 이론상으로는 인간의 정신에 의해 조직되기 전에는 사건들과 세부 사항들의 무한한 혼돈 상태이다. 이 혼돈 상태는 인간의 정신에 의해 인식될 때만이 처리되고 수정된다.

(B) 개인이 유산과 환경을 통해 부여받은 내적 특성 때문에 그러한 정신은 그것을 통과하는 모든 외부의 인상이 걸러지고 해석되는 여과기 역할을 한다. 그러나 문학에서 독자가 접하는 세계는 이미 또 다른 의식에 의해 처리되고 여과되어 있다.

(A) 작가는 중립적이고 객관적이 되고자, 또는 세계에 대한 주관적인 견해를 전달하고자 자신의 세계관과 적절성에 대한 자신의 개념에 따라 내용을 선정했다. 동기가 무엇이든, 세계에 대한 작가의 주관적인 개념이 독자와 이야기의 기초가 되는 원래의 손대지 않은 세계 사이에 존재한다.

Why? 왜 정답일까?

주어진 글에서 허구 세계는 현실과 비슷하기는 하지만 현실과 다른 한 가지 중요한 측면이 있다는 일반론을 제시한 데 이어, (C)는 먼저 개인이 직면하는 현실 세계의 특징을 설명한다. (C)에 따르면 개인이 마주하는 세계는 개인의 정신 속에서 정리되기 전까지는 혼돈 상태인데, (B)의 초반부는 이 '정신'이 바로 외부 현상을 거르고 해석하는 여과기 같은 역할을 한다고 설명한다. 하지만 (B)의 후반부에서 문학적 허구 세계의 경우 이미 한 번의 여과를 거쳐 있다는 내용으로 흐름을 반전시킨 후, (A)에서는 이 세계가 이미 작가의 정신 속에서 걸러진 세계이기에 현실 세계와 다를 수밖에 없다고 설명한다. 따라서 글의 순서로 가장 적절한 것은 ⑤ '(C) – (B) – (A)'이다.

- **likeness** ⓝ 유사성
- **relevance** ⓝ 적절성
- **neutral** ⓐ 중립적인
- **objective** ⓐ 객관적인
- **subjective** ⓐ 주관적인
- **interpret** ⓥ 해석하다
- **encounter** ⓥ 마주하다
- **in principle** 이론상으로, 원칙적으로

구문 풀이

7행 Whatever the motives, the author's subjective conception
복합관계대명사(무엇이 ~이든 간에) 주어
of the world stands between the reader and the original, untouched
동사(단수) 「between + A + and + B : A와 B 사이에」
world [on which the story is based].

07 정보의 양 증가가 정보 권력에 미치는 영향 정답률 44% | 정답 ②

주어진 글 다음에 이어질 글의 순서로 가장 적절한 것을 고르시오. [3점]
① (A) – (C) – (B) ✔ (B) – (A) – (C)
③ (B) – (C) – (A) ④ (C) – (A) – (B)
⑤ (C) – (B) – (A)

Promoting attractive images of one's country / is not new, / but the conditions for trying to create soft power / have changed dramatically in recent years.
자국의 매력적인 이미지를 홍보하는 것이 / 새로운 것은 아니지만, / 소프트파워를 창출하려는 노력을 위한 환경은 / 최근 몇 년 동안에 크게 바뀌었다.

For one thing, / nearly half the countries in the world / are now democracies.
한 예로, / 전 세계 국가의 거의 절반이 / 현재 민주 국가이다.

(B) In such circumstances, / diplomacy aimed at public opinion / can become as important to outcomes / as traditional classified diplomatic communications among leaders.
그러한 상황에서는 / 대중의 의견을 목표로 한 외교가 / 결과에 중요할 수 있다. / 지도자들 사이의 전통적인 비밀 외교 소통만큼이나

Information creates power, / and today / a much larger part of the world's population / has access to that power.
정보는 권력을 창출하는데, / 오늘날에는 / 세계 인구의 훨씬 더 많은 부분이 / 그 권력에 접근할 수 있다.

(A) Technological advances / have led to a dramatic reduction / in the cost of processing and transmitting information.
기술적인 발전은 / 극적인 감소를 가져왔다. / 정보의 처리와 전달 비용의

The result is an explosion of information, / and that has produced a "paradox of plenty."
그 결과로 정보가 폭발적으로 증가하게 되었고, / 그로 인해 '풍요의 역설'이 생겨났다.

Plentiful information / leads to scarcity of attention.
풍요로운 정보는 / 주의력 부족을 초래한다.

(C) When people are overwhelmed / with the volume of information confronting them, / they have difficulty knowing what to focus on.
압도당할 때, / 자신들이 직면해 있는 정보의 양에 / 사람들은 무엇에 초점을 두어야 할지 알기 어렵다.

Attention, rather than information, / becomes the scarce resource, / and those who can distinguish valuable information from background clutter / gain power.
정보가 아니라 주의력이 / 부족 자원이 되고, / 배후의 혼란으로부터 가치 있는 정보를 식별해 낼 수 있는 사람이 / 권력을 얻는다.

자국의 매력적인 이미지를 홍보하는 것이 새로운 것은 아니지만, 소프트파워를 창출하려는 노력을 위한 환경은 최근 몇 년 동안에 크게 바뀌었다. 한 예로 전 세계 국가의 거의 절반이 현재 민주 국가이다.

(B) 그러한 상황에서는 대중의 의견을 목표로 한 외교가 지도자들 사이의 전통적인 비밀 외교 소통만큼이나 결과에 중요할 수 있다. 정보는 권력을 창출하는데, 오늘날에는 세계 인구의 훨씬 더 많은 부분이 그 권력에 접근할 수 있다.

(A) 기술적인 발전은 정보의 처리와 전달 비용의 극적인 감소를 가져왔다. 그 결과로 정보가 폭발적으로 증가하게 되었고, 그로 인해 '풍요의 역설'이 생겨났다. 풍요로운 정보는 주의력 부족을 초래한다.

(C) 자신들이 직면해 있는 정보의 양에 압도당할 때, 사람들은 무엇에 초점을 두어야 할지 알기 어렵다. 정보가 아니라 주의력이 부족 자원이 되고, 배후의 혼란으로부터 가치 있는 정보를 식별해 낼 수 있는 사람이 권력을 얻는다.

Why? 왜 정답일까?

소프트파워를 창출하려는 노력을 위한 환경이 최근 크게 변화하여 많은 국가가 민주화되었다는 내용을 다룬 주어진 글 뒤에는, 이러한 민주 국가에서는 많은 사람들이 정보로 창출되는 권력에 접근할 수 있다는 내용의 (B), 더불어 정보의 양이 폭발적으로 증가하면서 주의력 부족이 야기되었다는 내용의 (A), 그리하여 오늘날에는 가치 있는 정보를 알아보는 주의력과 식별 능력을 가진 이들이 권력을 얻게 된다는 내용의 (C)가 차례로 이어지는 것이 자연스럽다. 따라서 글의 순서로 가장 적절한 것은 ② '(B) – (A) – (C)'이다.

- **promote** ⓥ 홍보하다, 촉진하다
- **dramatically** ⓐⓓ 크게, 극적으로
- **explosion** ⓝ 폭발적 증가, 폭발, 폭파
- **scarcity** ⓝ 부족
- **diplomacy** ⓝ 외교
- **classified** ⓐ 비밀의, 분류된
- **have access to** ~에 접근할 수 있다
- **confront** ⓥ 직면하다
- **distinguish** ⓥ 식별하다, 구별하다

구문 풀이

19행 Attention, rather than information, becomes the scarce
주어1 「A + rather than + B : B라기보다 A」 동사1
resource, / and those [who can distinguish valuable information from
주어2 「distinguish + A + from + B : A와 B를 구별하다」
background clutter] gain power.
동사2

08 대중음악과 예술가곡의 차이점 정답률 54% | 정답 ②

주어진 글 다음에 이어질 글의 순서로 가장 적절한 것을 고르시오. [3점]
① (A) – (C) – (B) ✔ (B) – (A) – (C)
③ (B) – (C) – (A) ④ (C) – (A) – (B)
⑤ (C) – (B) – (A)

There's a direct counterpart to pop music in the classical song, / more commonly called an "art song," / which does not focus on the development of melodic material.
고전 성악에는 대중음악에 직접 상응하는 것이 있어, / 더 일반적으로 '예술가곡'이라 불리는데, / 이는 멜로디 내용의 전개에 초점을 맞추지 않는다.

(B) Both the pop song and the art song / tend to follow tried-and-true structural patterns.
대중음악과 예술가곡 모두 / 유효성이 입증된 구조적 패턴을 따르는 경향이 있다.

And both will be published in the same way / — with a vocal line and a basic piano part written out underneath.
그리고 두 장르도 모두 동일한 방식으로 출판되기 마련이다. / 노래 선율과 그 아래에 간단한 피아노 선율이 적힌

(A) But the pop song will rarely be sung and played / exactly as written; / the singer is apt to embellish that vocal line / to give it a "styling," / just as the accompanist will fill out the piano part / to make it more interesting and personal.
그러나 대중음악은 좀처럼 불리거나 연주되지 않는데, / 쓰인 대로 정확히 / 가수 또한 노래 라인을 꾸며 넣어 / '스타일링'을 하는 경향이 있기 때문이다. / 반주자가 피아노 파트를 더 채워 넣어 / 더 흥미롭고 독특하게 만드는 것과 마찬가지로

The performers / might change the original tempo and mood / completely.
공연자들은 / 원래의 박자와 분위기를 바꿀 수도 있다. / 완전히

(C) You won't find such extremes of approach / by the performers of songs / by Franz Schubert or Richard Strauss.
이러한 극단적인 접근법을 찾지 못할 것이다. / 노래의 연주자에게서는 / 프란츠 슈베르트나 리하르트 슈트라우스가 쓴

These will be performed note for note / because both the vocal and piano parts / have been painstakingly written down / by the composer / with an ear for how each relates to the other.
이런 곡들은 한 음 한 음 연주되는데, / 노래와 피아노 파트가 모두, / 공들여 쓰였기 때문이다. / 작곡가에 의해 / 각각이 서로 어떤 관련을 맺는지를 아는

고전 성악에는 대중음악에 직접 상응하는 것이 있어, 더 일반적으로 '예술가곡'이라 불리는데, 이는 멜로디 내용의 전개에 초점을 맞추지 않는다.

(B) 대중음악과 예술가곡 모두 유효성이 입증된 구조적 패턴을 따르는 경향이 있다. 그리고 두 장르는 모두 노래 선율과 그 아래에 간단한 피아노 선율이 적힌, 동일한 방식으로 출판되기 마련이다.

(A) 그러나 대중음악은 좀처럼 쓰인 대로 정확히 불리거나 연주되지 않는데, 반주자가 피아노 파트를 더 채워 넣어 더 흥미롭고 독특하게 만드는 것과 마찬가지로, 가수 또한 노래 라인을 꾸며 넣어 '스타일링'을 하는 경향이 있기 때문이다. 공연자들은 원래의 박자와 분위기를 완전히 바꿀 수도 있다.

(C) 프란츠 슈베르트나 리하르트 슈트라우스가 쓴 노래의 연주자에게서는 이러한 극단적인 접근법을 찾지 못할 것이다. 이런 곡들은 한 음 한 음 연주되는데, 노래와 피아노 파트가 모두, 각각이 서로 어떤 관련을 맺는지를 아는 작곡가에 의해 공들여 쓰였기 때문이다.

Why? 왜 정답일까?

고전 예술가곡이 오늘날의 대중음악에 대응될 수 있다고 말한 주어진 글 뒤에는, 두 장르 모두 특정한 패턴을 따르며 노래 파트와 피아노 파트로 나누어 쓰이는 공통점이 있다고 말한 (B), '그러나' 대중음악의 경우 연주자 개인의 스타일링이 가미될 수 있다는 내용의 (A), 예술가곡의 경우 한 음 한 음이 정확히 연주된다는 내용의 (C)가 차례로 이어지는 것이 자연스럽다. 따라서 주어진 글 다음에 이어질 글의 순서로 가장 적절한 것은 ② '(B) – (A) – (C)'이다.

- **counterpart** ⓝ 상응물, 대응물
- **development** ⓝ 전개, 발전
- **underneath** prep 아래에
- **relate to** ~와 관련을 맺다, ~와 연관되다
- **focus on** ~에 초점을 맞추다
- **structural** ⓐ 구조적인, 구성적인
- **painstakingly** ⓐ 공들여, 힘들여

구문 풀이

5행 But the pop song will rarely be sung and played exactly
└접속사(~대로, ~듯이)
as written; / the singer is apt to embellish that vocal line to give it a
└(it is 생략) ~하는 경향이 있다 지시형용사(그, 그런)
"styling," / just as the accompanist will fill out the piano part to make
접속사(마치 ~처럼) 부사적 용법
it more interesting and personal.
to make의 목적격 보어(형용사)

★★★ 1등급 대비 고난도 2점 문제

09 랜드마크의 특성 정답률 25% | 정답 ①

주어진 글 다음에 이어질 글의 순서로 가장 적절한 것을 고르시오.

☑ (A) – (C) – (B) ② (B) – (A) – (C)
③ (B) – (C) – (A) ④ (C) – (A) – (B)
⑤ (C) – (B) – (A)

Spatial reference points are larger than themselves.
공간 기준점은 기준점 이상이다.

This isn't really a paradox: / landmarks are themselves, / but they also define neighborhoods around themselves.
이것은 그다지 역설적이지 않은데, / 랜드마크는 랜드마크이기도 하지만 / 또한 자기 자신 주변 지역을 규정하기도 한다.

(A) In a paradigm / that has been repeated on many campuses, / researchers first collect a list of campus landmarks from students.
한 전형적인 예에서, / 많은 대학 캠퍼스에서 반복되어 온 / 연구원들은 우선 학생들에게서 캠퍼스 랜드마크의 목록을 수집한다.

Then they ask another group of students / to estimate the distances between pairs of locations, / some to landmarks, / some to ordinary buildings / on campus.
그런 다음, 그들은 다른 학생 집단에게 요청한다. / 쌍으로 이루어진 장소 사이의 거리를 추정하라고 / 몇몇은 랜드마크까지, / 몇몇은 평범한 건물까지의 거리를 / 캠퍼스의

(C) The remarkable finding is / that distances from an ordinary location to a landmark / are judged shorter / than distances from a landmark to an ordinary location.
주목할 만한 결과는 / 평범한 장소에서 랜드마크까지의 거리가 / 더 짧다고 추정된다는 것이다. / 랜드마크에서 평범한 장소까지의 거리보다

So, / people would judge / the distance from Pierre's house to the Eiffel Tower / to be shorter / than the distance from the Eiffel Tower to Pierre's house.
그래서 / 사람들은 추정할 것이다. / Pierre의 집에서 에펠탑까지의 거리가 / 더 짧다고 / 에펠탑에서 Pierre의 집까지의 거리보다

Like black holes, / landmarks seem to pull ordinary locations toward themselves, / but ordinary places do not.

블랙홀처럼, / 랜드마크는 평범한 장소를 자기 쪽으로 끌어당기는 것처럼 보이지만, / 평범한 장소들은 그렇지 않다.

(B) This asymmetry of distance estimates / violates the most elementary principles of Euclidean distance, / that the distance from A to B / must be the same as the distance from B to A.
거리 추정에 관한 이 비대칭은 / 가장 기초적인 유클리드 거리 법칙에 위배된다. / A에서부터 B까지의 거리가 / B에서부터 A까지의 거리와 같아야 한다는

Judgments of distance, then, / are not necessarily coherent.
그렇다면, 거리에 관한 추정은 / 반드시 일관성이 있는 것은 아니다.

공간 기준점은 기준점 이상이다. 이것은 그다지 역설적이지 않은데, 랜드마크는 랜드마크이기도 하지만 또한 자기 자신 주변 지역을 (자신의 범위로) 규정하기도 한다.

(A) 많은 대학 캠퍼스에서 반복되어 온 한 전형적인 예에서, 연구원들은 우선 학생들에게서 캠퍼스 랜드마크의 목록을 수집한다. 그런 다음, 그들은 다른 학생 집단에게 쌍으로 이루어진 장소 사이의 거리를 추정하라고 요청하는데, 몇몇은 (평범한 건물로부터) 캠퍼스의 랜드마크까지, 몇몇은 (랜드마크로부터) 평범한 건물까지의 거리를 추정하게 한다.

(C) 주목할 만한 결과는 평범한 장소에서 랜드마크까지의 거리가 랜드마크에서 평범한 장소까지의 거리보다 더 짧다고 추정된다는 것이다. 그래서 사람들은 Pierre의 집에서 에펠탑까지의 거리가 에펠탑에서 Pierre의 집까지의 거리보다 더 짧다고 추정할 것이다. 블랙홀처럼, 랜드마크는 평범한 장소를 자기 쪽으로 끌어당기는 것처럼 보이지만, 평범한 장소들은 그렇지 않다.

(B) 거리 추정에 관한 이 비대칭은 A에서부터 B까지의 거리가 B에서부터 A까지의 거리와 같아야 한다는 가장 기초적인 유클리드 거리 법칙에 위배된다. 그렇다면, 거리에 관한 추정은 반드시 일관성이 있는 것은 아니다.

Why? 왜 정답일까?

공간 기준점은 단순한 기준점 이상이라는 내용의 주어진 글 뒤로, (A)에서는 대학 캠퍼스 랜드마크와 평범한 다른 건물 간의 거리를 추정해보게 했던 실험 내용을 소개한다. 이어서 (C)는 '주목할 만한 결과' 내용을 소개한다. (B)는 (C)에서 언급된 결과를 토대로 거리에 관한 추정에 항상 일관성이 있지는 않다는 일반적인 결론을 도출한다. 따라서 글의 순서로 가장 적절한 것은 ① '(A) – (C) – (B)'이다.

- **spatial** ⓐ 공간적인
- **landmark** ⓝ 랜드마크, 주요 지형지물
- **paradigm** ⓝ 전형적인 예
- **violate** ⓥ 위배되다, 위반하다
- **coherent** ⓐ 일관된
- **reference** ⓝ 기준, 준거, 참고
- **define** ⓥ 규정하다
- **estimate** ⓥ 추정하다 ⓝ 추정치
- **elementary** ⓐ 기본적인
- **remarkable** ⓐ 주목할 만한

구문 풀이

10행 This asymmetry of distance estimates violates
주어 동사(단수)
the most elementary principles of Euclidean distance, {that the
목적어
distance from A to B must be the same as the distance from B to A}.
{ } : 목적어 동격

★★ 문제 해결 꿀~팁 ★★

▶ **많이 틀린 이유는?**
지시사 힌트를 적극 활용해야 하는 순서 문제이다. (C)를 보면 **This asymmetry**라는 단어로 시작하는데, 이는 앞에 '비대칭'이라는 말로 요약될 수 있는 내용이 나온다는 신호이다. 주어진 글은 '비대칭'으로 볼 만한 내용이 없고 랜드마크라는 핵심 소재만을 언급하며 끝나므로 이 뒤에 바로 (C)를 연결하기에는 적절하지 않다.

▶ **문제 해결 방법은?**
주어진 글에서 랜드마크의 특징이라는 핵심 소재를 언급하고 이를 잘 보여주는 실험을 이어서 소개하는 글이다. 따라서 실험의 예(In a paradigm)를 들겠다는 말로 시작하는 (A)가 가장 먼저 나오고, 실험의 결과(The remarkable finding)를 제시하는 (C)가 이어진 후, (C)의 내용을 This asymmetry로 요약하며 최종 결론을 도출하는 (B)가 마지막으로 연결되는 것이 가장 자연스럽다.

★★★ 1등급 대비 고난도 3점 문제

10 수렵 사회보다 농경 사회에서 기근이 심각했던 이유 정답률 37% | 정답 ⑤

주어진 글 다음에 이어질 글의 순서로 가장 적절한 것을 고르시오. [3점]

① (A) – (C) – (B) ② (B) – (A) – (C)
③ (B) – (C) – (A) ④ (C) – (A) – (B)
☑ (C) – (B) – (A)

Both ancient farmers and foragers / suffered seasonal food shortages.
고대 농부와 수렵 채집인 모두 / 계절에 따른 식량 부족을 겪었다.

During these periods / children and adults alike / would go to bed hungry some days / and everyone would lose fat and muscle.
이 기간에 / 어린이와 어른 모두 / 어떤 날에는 배가 고픈 채 잠자리에 들었을 것이며 / 모두가 지방과 근육을 잃었을 것이다.

(C) But over longer periods of time / farming societies were far more likely / to suffer severe, existentially threatening famines / than foragers.
그러나 더 오랜 기간에 걸쳐, / 농경 사회는 ~할 가능성이 훨씬 더 컸다. / 심각하고 존재적으로 위협적인 기근에 시달릴 / 수렵 채집인보다

Foraging may be much less productive / and generate far lower energy yields / than farming / but it is also much less risky.
수렵 채집이 훨씬 덜 생산적이고 / 훨씬 더 낮은 에너지 생산량을 발생시킬지 모르지만 / 농업보다 / 그것은 또한 훨씬 덜 위험하다.

(B) This is firstly because foragers tended to live well within the natural limits / imposed by their environments, / and secondly because where farmers typically relied on one or two staple crops, / foragers in even the harshest environments / relied on dozens of different food sources / and so were usually able to adjust their diets / to align with an ecosystem's own dynamic responses / to changing conditions.
이는 첫째로 수렵 채집인이 자연적 한계 내에서 잘 사는 경향이 있었기 때문이고 / 자신들의 환경에 의해 부과된 / 둘째로 농부는 보통 한두 가지 주요한 작물에 의존했던 상황에서 / 정말로 가장 가혹한 환경에 있던 수렵 채집인은 / 수십 가지의 다른 식량원에 의존했고 / 그래서 보통 식단을 조정할 수 있었기 때문이다 / 생태계 자체의 역동적인 반응에 맞추기 위해 / 변화하는 상황에 대한

(A) Typically, / in complex ecosystems / when weather one year proves unsuitable / for one set of plant species, / it almost inevitably suits others.
일반적으로 / 복잡한 생태계에서 / 한 해 날씨가 적합하지 않다고 판명될 때, / 한 집단의 식물종에게 / 그것은 거의 필연적으로 다른 것들에게 적합하다.

But in farming societies / when harvests fail / as a result of, for example, a sustained drought, / then catastrophe emerges.
그러나 농업 사회에서 / 수확이 실패한다면 / 가령 지속적인 가뭄의 결과로 / 참사가 일어난다.

고대 농부와 수렵 채집인 모두 계절에 따른 식량 부족을 겪었다. 이 기간에 어린이와 어른 모두 어떤 날에는 배가 고픈 채 잠자리에 들었을 것이며 모두가 지방과 근육을 잃었을 것이다.

(C) 그러나 더 오랜 기간에 걸쳐, 농경 사회는 수렵 채집인보다 심각하고 존재적으로 위협적인 기근에 시달릴 가능성이 훨씬 더 컸다. 수렵 채집이 농업보다 훨씬 덜 생산적이고 훨씬 더 낮은 에너지 생산량을 발생시킬지 모르지만 그것은 또한 훨씬 덜 위험하다.

(B) 이는 첫째로 수렵 채집인이 환경에 의해 부과된 자연적 한계 내에서 잘 사는 경향이 있었기 때문이고, 둘째로 농부는 보통 한두 가지 주요한 작물에 의존했던 상황에서, 정말로 가장 가혹한 환경에 있던 수렵 채집인은 수십 가지의 다른 식량원에 의존했고, 그래서 변화하는 상황에 대한 생태계 자체의 역동적인 반응에 맞추기 위해 보통 식단을 조정할 수 있었기 때문이다.

(A) 일반적으로 복잡한 생태계에서 한 해 날씨가 한 집단의 식물종에게 적합하지 않다고 판명될 때, 그것은 거의 필연적으로 다른 것들에게 적합하다. 그러나 농업 사회에서 가령 지속적인 가뭄의 결과로 수확이 실패한다면 참사가 일어난다.

Why? 왜 정답일까?

농업 사회와 수렵 채집 사회에서의 식량 부족을 화제로 언급하는 주어진 글 뒤로, 농경 사회가 더 취약하고 수렵 사회가 덜 위험하다고 설명하는 (C), 그 이유를 두 가지 드는 (B), 이유에 대한 설명을 마무리하는 (A)가 차례로 이어져야 한다. 따라서 글의 순서로 가장 적절한 것은 ⑤ '(C) – (B) – (A)'이다.

● **ancient** ⓐ 고대의	● **forager** ⓝ 수렵 채집인
● **suffer** ⓥ 겪다	● **seasonal** ⓐ 계절적인
● **shortage** ⓝ 부족	● **A and B alike** A와 B 둘 다
● **fat** ⓝ 지방	● **muscle** ⓝ 근육
● **complex** ⓐ 복잡한	● **ecosystem** ⓝ 생태계
● **prove** ⓥ 판명되다	● **unsuitable** ⓐ 부적합한
● **inevitably** ad 필연적으로	● **suit** ⓥ 적합하다
● **fail** ⓥ 실패하다	● **result** ⓝ 결과, 결실
● **sustained** ⓐ 지속된	● **drought** ⓝ 가뭄
● **catastrophe** ⓝ 참사, 재앙	● **emerge** ⓥ (곤란·문제 등이) 일어나다
● **tend** ⓥ 경향이 있다	● **limit** ⓝ 한계
● **impose** ⓥ 부과하다	● **rely** ⓥ 의지하다
● **staple** ⓐ 주된, 주요한	● **align with** ~에 맞추다
● **severe** ⓐ 심각한	● **existentially** ad 존재적으로
● **threatening** ⓐ 위협적인	● **famine** ⓝ 기근
● **generate** ⓥ 만들어내다	● **yield** ⓝ 산출량
● **risky** ⓐ 위험한	

구문 풀이

10행 This is firstly {because foragers tended to live well within
접속사1
the natural limits imposed by their environments}, and secondly
과거분사
{because (where farmers typically relied on one or two staple crops),
접속사2 ( ): 부사절(~한 상황에서)
foragers in even the harshest environments relied on dozens of
주어 동사구1
different food sources and so were usually able to adjust their diets
동사구2
to align with an ecosystem's own dynamic responses to changing
conditions}.

★★ 문제 해결 꿀~팁 ★★

▶ 많이 틀린 이유는?
주어진 글 뒤에 바로 (B)를 연결하면 This의 의미가 명확하지 않다. (B)의 firstly because와 secondly because를 읽어보면 수렵채집인이 농경인보다 환경적 제약에 더 잘 맞춰 살았고, 식량원도 더 다양했다는 내용인데, 주어진 글은 '둘 다' 식량 부족을 겪었다는 공통점에 관해서만 언급하므로 흐름상 (B)와 연결되지 않는다.

▶ 문제 해결 방법은?
일반적으로 글은 일반적 진술에서 구체적 진술로 흐른다. 주어진 글에서 수렵채집인과 농경인이 겪은 식량 부족을 화제로 언급한 후, 농경인의 식량 부족이 더 심각한 결과를 불러왔다는 설명으로 논의를 좁히는 (C), firstly because와 secondly because로 이유를 열거하는 (B), 내용을 마무리하는 (A)가 차례로 연결되어야 논리적 흐름이 자연스럽다.

★★★ 1등급 대비 고난도 3점 문제

11 주권과 시민권을 정의하는 데 필요한 것   정답률 28% | 정답 ⑤

주어진 글 다음에 이어질 글의 순서로 가장 적절한 것을 고르시오. [3점]
① (A) – (C) – (B)   ② (B) – (A) – (C)
③ (B) – (C) – (A)   ④ (C) – (A) – (B)
✔ (C) – (B) – (A)

A sovereign state is usually defined as one / whose citizens are free to determine their own affairs / without interference from any agency / beyond its territorial borders.
주권 국가는 국가라고 정의된다. / 보통 그 시민들이 자신들의 일을 스스로 결정할 자유가 있는 / 그 어떤 기관으로부터도 간섭받지 않고 / 국경 너머의

(C) But freedom in space (and limits on its territorial extent) / is merely one characteristic of sovereignty.
하지만 공간적 자유는 (그리고 영토 범위의 제한은) / 단지 주권의 한 가지 특징일 뿐이다.

Freedom in time (and limits on its temporal extent) / is equally important and probably more fundamental.
시간적 자유가 (그리고 시간적 범위에 대한 제한이) / 마찬가지로 중요하며 어쩌면 더 근본적이다.

(B) Sovereignty and citizenship require freedom from the past / at least as much as freedom from contemporary powers.
주권과 시민권은 과거로부터의 자유를 필요로 한다. / 최소한 동시대 권력으로부터의 자유만큼이나

No state could be sovereign / if its inhabitants lacked the ability to change a course of action / adopted by their forefathers in the past, / or even one to which they once committed themselves.
그 어떤 국가도 주권적일 수 없을 것이다. / 국민들이 행동 방침을 바꿀 능력이 없다면 / 과거에 그들의 조상들에 의해 채택된 / 또는 한때 그들이 전념했던 행동 방침조차

(A) No citizen could be a full member of the community / so long as she was tied to ancestral traditions / with which the community might wish to break / — the problem of Antigone in Sophocles' tragedy.
어떤 시민도 그 공동체의 완전한 구성원이 될 수 없을 것인데, / 선조의 전통에 묶여 있는 한 / 공동체가 단절하기를 원할 수 있는 / 이것은 Sophocles의 비극에서 Antigone의 문제이기도 하다.

Sovereignty and citizenship / thus require not only borders in space, / but also borders in time.
주권과 시민권은 / 따라서 공간의 경계뿐만 아니라 / 시간의 경계 또한 필요로 한다.

주권 국가는 보통 그 시민들이 국경 너머의 그 어떤 기관으로부터도 간섭받지 않고 자신들의 일을 스스로 결정할 자유가 있는 국가라고 정의된다.

(C) 하지만 공간적 자유는 (그리고 영토 범위의 제한은) 단지 주권의 한 가지 특징일 뿐이다. 시간적 자유가 (그리고 시간적 범위에 대한 제한이) 마찬가지로 중요하며 어쩌면 더 근본적이다.

(B) 주권과 시민권은 최소한 동시대 권력으로부터의 자유만큼이나 과거로부터

의 자유를 필요로 한다. 국민들이 과거에 그들의 조상들에 의해 채택된 행동 방침을, 또는 한때 그들이 전념했던 행동 방침조차 바꿀 능력이 없다면 그 어떤 국가도 자주적일 수 없을 것이다.

(A) 공동체가 단절하기를 원할 수 있는 선조의 전통에 묶여 있는 한 어떤 시민도 그 공동체의 완전한 구성원이 될 수 없을 것인데, 이것은 Sophocles의 비극에서 Antigone의 문제이기도 하다. 따라서 주권과 시민권은 공간의 경계뿐만 아니라 시간의 경계 또한 필요로 한다.

Why? 왜 정답일까?

주권 국가는 국경 너머의 다른 기관으로부터 간섭받지 않을 자유를 지닌다는 내용의 주어진 글 뒤에는, 이러한 공간적 자유뿐 아니라 시간적 자유도 중요함을 언급하는 (C), 주권과 시민권을 실현하기 위해서는 과거로부터의 자유가 필요하다는 내용을 부연하는 (B), 과거에 묶여있는 한 어떤 시민도 공동체의 완전한 구성원이 될 수 없기에 시간의 경계가 중요하다는 결론을 강조하는 (A)가 차례로 이어져야 한다. 따라서 글의 순서로 가장 적절한 것은 ⑤ '(C) – (B) – (A)'이다.

- **interference** ⓝ 간섭, 개입
- **course of action** 행동 방침
- **characteristic** ⓝ 특징
- **agency** ⓝ 기관, 주체
- **commit oneself to** ~에 전념하다
- **fundamental** ⓐ 근본적인

구문 풀이

1행 A sovereign state is usually defined as <u>one</u> [whose citizens are free to determine their own affairs without interference from any agency beyond its territorial borders].
(동사구(~라고 정의되다) / 소유격 관계대명사 / 자유롭게 ~하는)

★★ 문제 해결 꿀~팁 ★★

▶ 많이 틀린 이유는?
오답이 ②, ③에 편중된 것으로 볼 때, 주어진 글에 바로 이어질 단락이 어느 단락인지를 정확히 파악하는 것이 풀이의 관건이다. 주어진 단락에서 주권 국가는 정해진 영토 범위에서 자결권을 갖는 국가임을 설명하므로, 이를 '공간적 자유'로 언급하며 시간적 자유 또한 마찬가지로 중요함을 언급하는 (C)가 바로 뒤따르는 것이 적절하다. (B)의 경우 첫 줄의 freedom from the past가 '시간적 자유'를 뜻하는데, 주어진 글에서는 시간과 관련된 내용이 언급되지 않았다. 따라서 (C)보다 (B)가 앞서 나오는 것은 적절하지 않다.

▶ 문제 해결 방법은?
But은 앞뒤 흐름을 반전할 때뿐 아니라 새로운 소재를 제시할 때 주의를 환기하며 이를 강조할 때에 쓰인다. (C)의 But 역시 주권 국가를 정의하는 데 있어 '시간적 자유' 개념을 처음 언급하며 이에 대한 독자의 주의를 환기하고 있다. 즉 (C)에서 이렇듯 주의를 환기한 뒤에야 비로소 시간적 자유에 대한 부연이 (B) – (A)에 걸쳐 이루어질 수 있는 것이다.

★★★ 1등급 대비 고난도 3점 문제

12 에너지 효율 증진 사업과 관련된 여러 가지 요소   정답률 42% | 정답 ⑤

주어진 글 다음에 이어질 글의 순서로 가장 적절한 것을 고르시오. [3점]

① (A) – (C) – (B)
② (B) – (A) – (C)
③ (B) – (C) – (A)
④ (C) – (A) – (B)
✓⑤ (C) – (B) – (A)

Experts have identified a large number of measures / that promote energy efficiency.
전문가들은 다수의 대책을 찾아냈다. / 에너지 효율을 증진하는

Unfortunately many of them are not cost effective.
유감스럽게도 그중 많은 수는 비용 효율적이지 않다.

This is a fundamental requirement for energy efficiency investment / from an economic perspective.
이것은 에너지 효율을 위한 투자에 근본적인 필요조건이다. / 경제적 관점에서

(C) However, / the calculation of such cost effectiveness is not easy: / it is not simply a case of looking at private costs / and comparing them to the reductions achieved.
그러나 / 그러한 비용 효율성의 산정은 쉽지 않은데, / 그것은 단순히 사적비용을 살펴보는 경우가 아니기 때문이다. / 그리고 달성한 절감액과 그것을 비교하는

(B) There are significant externalities to take into account / and there are also macroeconomic effects.
고려해야 할 상당한 외부 효과가 있고 / 거시 경제적 효과도 있다.

For instance, at the aggregate level, / improving the level of national energy

efficiency / has positive effects on macroeconomic issues / such as energy dependence, climate change, health, national competitiveness and reducing fuel poverty.
예를 들어 총체적 차원에서, / 국가의 에너지 효율 수준을 높이는 것은 / 거시 경제적 문제에 긍정적인 영향을 미친다. / 에너지 의존도, 기후 변화, 보건, 국가 경쟁력, 연료 빈곤을 줄이는 것과 같은

(A) And this has direct repercussions at the individual level: / households can reduce the cost of electricity and gas bills, / and improve their health and comfort, / while companies can increase their competitiveness and their productivity.
그리고 이것은 개인적 차원에서 직접적인 영향을 미치는데, / 즉 가정은 전기 비용과 가스 요금을 줄이고 / 그들의 건강과 안락함을 증진할 수 있다. / 기업들은 자체 경쟁력과 생산성을 증대시킬 수 있는 한편

Finally, / the market for energy efficiency / could contribute to the economy / through job and firms creation.
결국, / 에너지 효율 시장은 / 경제에 이바지할 수 있는 것이다. / 일자리와 기업 창출을 통해

전문가들은 에너지 효율을 증진하는 다수의 대책을 찾아냈다. 유감스럽게도 그중 많은 수는 비용 효율적이지 않다. 이것(비용 효율)은 경제적 관점에서 에너지 효율을 위한 투자에 근본적인 필요조건이다.

(C) 그러나 그러한 비용 효율성의 산정은 쉽지 않은데, 그것은 단순히 사적비용을 살펴보고 달성한 절감액과 비교하는 경우가 아니기 때문이다.

(B) 고려해야 할 상당한 외부 효과가 있고 거시 경제적 효과도 있다. 예를 들어 총체적 차원에서, 국가의 에너지 효율 수준을 높이는 것은 에너지 의존도, 기후 변화, 보건, 국가 경쟁력, 연료 빈곤을 줄이는 것과 같은 거시 경제적 문제에 긍정적인 영향을 미친다.

(A) 그리고 이것은 개인적 차원에서 직접적인 영향을 미치는데, 즉 가정은 전기 비용과 가스 요금을 줄이고 그들의 건강과 안락함을 증진할 수 있는 한편, 기업들은 자체 경쟁력과 생산성을 증대시킬 수 있다. 결국, 에너지 효율 시장은 일자리와 기업 창출을 통해 경제에 이바지할 수 있는 것이다.

Why? 왜 정답일까?

에너지 효율을 화제로 제시한 주어진 글 뒤에는, 에너지의 비용 효율을 산정하기 쉽지 않다는 점을 언급하며 에너지 효율을 따지는 것이 단순히 사적 비용을 고려하는 것과는 다르다고 설명하는 (C)가 먼저 이어진다. 이어서 (B)는 에너지 효율을 산정함에 있어 각종 외부 효과와 거시 경제적 효과를 고려해야 한다는 설명을, (A)는 에너지 효율 증진의 문제가 거시 경제뿐 아니라 개인 차원에도 영향을 미친다는 설명을 제시한다. 따라서 글의 순서로 가장 적절한 것은 ⑤ '(C) – (B) – (A)'이다.

- **cost effective** 비용 효율적인
- **requirement** ⓝ 필요조건, 요구사항
- **competitiveness** ⓝ 경쟁력
- **significant** ⓐ 상당한, 유의미한
- **take ~ into account** ~을 고려하다
- **calculation** ⓝ 산정, 계산
- **fundamental** ⓐ 근본적인
- **perspective** ⓝ 관점
- **productivity** ⓝ 생산성
- **externality** ⓝ 외부효과
- **macroeconomic** ⓐ 거시 경제의

구문 풀이

15행 For instance, at the aggregate level, improving the level of national energy efficiency has positive effects on macroeconomic issues such as energy dependence, climate change, health, national competitiveness and reducing fuel poverty.
(동명사구 주어(단수 취급) / 동사구(~에 영향을 미치다) / ~와 같은 / 명사1 / 명사2 / 명사3 / 명사4 / 명사5(동명사))

★★ 문제 해결 꿀~팁 ★★

▶ 많이 틀린 이유는?
처음에 이어질 단락을 잘 파악해야 하는 순서 문제이다. 주어진 글이 economic perspective로 끝나므로 macroeconomic effects를 언급하는 (B)가 바로 이어질 것이라고 생각하기 쉽다. 하지만 내용을 잘 읽어보면 주어진 글에서 가장 중요한 표현은 energy efficiency와 cost effective이므로, 이것을 such cost effectiveness로 받는 (C)가 주어진 글 뒤에 이어져야 한다.

▶ 문제 해결 방법은?
(C)를 처음에 배치하면 나머지는 비교적 쉽다. 먼저 (A)를 보면, (A)는 And로 시작하며 individual level을 언급하는데, (C)에는 이 말과 대구를 이룰 만한 표현이 없다. (B)를 보면, For instance 뒤로 individual level과 짝을 이루는 aggregate level이 언급되므로, (B) – (A)가 서로 연결되어야 적절하다.

DAY 13 　　글의 순서 03

01 ④	02 ②	03 ③	04 ②	05 ③
06 ②	07 ②	08 ②	09 ⑤	10 ④
11 ②	12 ⑤			

01 　고도로 복잡해진 소프트웨어와 그에 따른 부작용　　정답률 51% | 정답 ④

주어진 글 다음에 이어질 글의 순서로 가장 적절한 것을 고르시오.

① (A) − (C) − (B)
② (B) − (A) − (C)
③ (B) − (C) − (A)
✓④ (C) − (A) − (B)
⑤ (C) − (B) − (A)

The growing complexity of computer software / has direct implications for our global safety and security, / particularly as the physical objects upon which we depend / — things like cars, airplanes, bridges, tunnels, and implantable medical devices — / transform themselves into computer code.
컴퓨터 소프트웨어 복잡성의 증가 / 전 세계의 안전과 보안에 직접적인 영향을 주는데, / 특히 우리가 의존하는 물리적 대상이 / 즉 자동차, 비행기, 교량, 터널, 이식형 의료 기기와 같은 것들 / 컴퓨터 코드로 변해감에 따라 그렇다.

(C) Physical things are increasingly becoming information technologies.
물리적 사물은 점점 더 정보 기술이 되어가고 있다.

Cars are "computers we ride in," / and airplanes are nothing more than "flying Solaris boxes / attached to bucketfuls of industrial control systems."
자동차는 '우리가 타는 컴퓨터'이고, / 비행기는 '비행 솔라리스 박스'에 불과하다. / '수많은 산업 제어 시스템에 부착된'

(A) As all this code grows in size and complexity, / so too do the number of errors and software bugs.
이 모든 코드가 크기와 복잡성이 증가함에 따라, / 오류와 소프트웨어 버그 수 또한 증가한다.

According to a study by Carnegie Mellon University, / commercial software typically has twenty to thirty bugs / for every thousand lines of code / — 50 million lines of code means / 1 million to 1.5 million potential errors / to be exploited.
Carnegie Mellon 대학교의 연구에 따르면, / 상용 소프트웨어에는 보통 20~30개의 버그가 있어서, / 코드 1,000줄당 / 5천만 줄의 코드는 의미한다. / 1백만~150만 개의 잠재적 오류가 / 악의적으로 이용될 수 있다는 것을

(B) This is the basis for all malware attacks / that take advantage of these computer bugs / to get the code to do something / it was not originally intended to do.
이것이 바로 모든 악성 소프트웨어 공격의 근간이다. / 이 컴퓨터 버그를 이용하는 / 코드가 뭔가를 하게 하려고 / 그것이 원래 하도록 의도되지 않은

As computer code grows more elaborate, / software bugs flourish and security suffers, / with increasing consequences for society at large.
컴퓨터 코드가 더 정교해짐에 따라, / 소프트웨어 버그는 창궐하고 보안은 약화되어, / 사회 전반에 미치는 영향이 커진다.

컴퓨터 소프트웨어 복잡성의 증가는 전 세계의 안전과 보안에 직접적인 영향을 주는데, 우리가 의존하는 물리적 대상, 즉 자동차, 비행기, 교량, 터널, 이식형 의료 기기와 같은 것들이 컴퓨터 코드로 변해감에 따라 특히 그렇다.

(C) 물리적 사물은 점점 더 정보 기술이 되어가고 있다. 자동차는 '우리가 타는 컴퓨터'이고, 비행기는 '수많은 산업 제어 시스템에 부착된 비행 솔라리스 박스'에 불과하다.

(A) 이 모든 코드가 크기와 복잡성이 증가함에 따라, 오류와 소프트웨어 버그 수 또한 증가한다. Carnegie Mellon 대학교의 연구에 따르면, 상용 소프트웨어에는 보통 코드 1,000줄당 20~30개의 버그가 있어서, 5천만 줄의 코드는 1백만~150만 개의 잠재적 오류가 악의적으로 이용될 수 있다는 것을 의미한다.

(B) 이것이 바로 컴퓨터 버그를 이용해 코드가 원래 의도되지 않은 작업을 하게 하는 모든 악성 소프트웨어 공격의 근간이다. 컴퓨터 코드가 더 정교해짐에 따라, 소프트웨어 버그는 창궐하고 보안은 약화되어, 사회 전반에 미치는 영향이 커진다.

Why? 왜 정답일까?

주어진 글은 컴퓨터 소프트웨어의 복잡성에 관해 언급하며 물리적 대상이 컴퓨터 코드로 변해가고 있다고 이야기한다. (C)는 이 컴퓨터 코드를 '정보 기술'로 일반화하며, 자동차와 비행기의 변모를 예로 든다. 이어서 (A)는 코드의 복잡성 증가에 따라 오류의 수 또한

증가한다고 설명하고, (C)는 이런 점이 바로 악성 소프트웨어 공격으로 이어질 여지가 있다고 언급한다. 따라서 글의 순서로 가장 적절한 것은 ④ '(C) − (A) − (B)'이다.

- complexity ⓝ 복잡성
- physical ⓐ 물리적인
- medical device 의료 기기
- commercial ⓐ 상용의, 상업적인
- million ⓝ 100만
- take advantage of ~을 이용하다
- flourish ⓥ 번성하다
- nothing more than ~에 불과한
- bucketfuls of 수많은
- implication ⓝ 영향
- implantable ⓐ (체내에) 심을 수 있는
- software bug 소프트웨어 버그
- typically ⓐⓓ 보통
- exploit ⓥ 악용하다, 착취하다
- originally ⓐⓓ 원래
- at large 전체적인, 대체적인
- attached to ~에 부착된

구문 풀이

1행 The growing complexity of computer software has direct implications for our global safety and security, particularly as 〈접속사〉 the physical objects [upon which we depend] 〈주어〉 — (things like cars, 〈( ) : 삽입구〉 airplanes, bridges, tunnels, and implantable medical devices) — transform themselves into computer code. 〈동사(복수)〉

02 　인간을 만물의 척도로 보는 가정의 맹점　　정답률 50% | 정답 ②

주어진 글 다음에 이어질 글의 순서로 가장 적절한 것을 고르시오.

① (A) − (C) − (B)
✓② (B) − (A) − (C)
③ (B) − (C) − (A)
④ (C) − (A) − (B)
⑤ (C) − (B) − (A)

In the fifth century *B.C.E.*, / the Greek philosopher Protagoras pronounced, / "Man is the measure of all things."
기원전 5세기에, / 그리스의 철학자 Protagoras는 선언했다. / "인간이 만물의 척도이다."라고

In other words, / we feel entitled to ask the world, / "What good are you?"
다시 말해서, / 우리는 세상을 향해 물어볼 자격이 있다고 느낀다. / "당신은 무슨 쓸모가 있는가?"라고

(B) We assume / that we are the world's standard, / that all things should be compared to us.
우리는 추정한다 / 우리가 세상의 기준이라고 / 즉, 모든 것이 우리와 비교되어야 한다고

Such an assumption makes us overlook a lot.
그런 추정은 우리로 하여금 많은 것을 간과하게 한다.

(A) Abilities said to "make us human" / — empathy, communication, grief, toolmaking, and so on — / all exist to varying degrees / among other minds / sharing the world with us.
'우리를 인간답게 만들어 준다'고 일컬어지는 능력들, / 즉 공감, 의사소통, 슬픔, 도구 만들기 등은 / 다양한 정도로 다 존재한다. / 지력을 지닌 다른 존재들 사이에서도 / 우리와 세상을 공유하는

Animals with backbones (fishes, amphibians, reptiles, birds, and mammals) all / share the same basic skeleton, organs, nervous systems, hormones, and behaviors.
척추동물(어류, 양서류, 파충류, 조류, 포유류)은 모두 / 동일한 기본 골격, 장기, 신경계, 호르몬, 행동을 공유한다.

(C) Just as / different models of automobiles each / have an engine, drive train, four wheels, doors, and seats, / we differ / mainly in terms of our outside contours and a few internal tweaks.
~과 마찬가지로 / 다양한 자동차의 모델들이 각각 / 엔진, 동력 전달 체계, 네 바퀴, 문, 좌석을 가지고 있는 것 / 우리는 다르다. / 주로 우리의 외부 윤곽과 몇 가지 내부적인 조정 면에서

But like naive car buyers, / most people see only animals' varied exteriors.
하지만 순진한 자동차 구매자들처럼, / 대부분의 사람들은 오직 동물들의 다양한 겉모습만을 본다.

기원전 5세기에, 그리스의 철학자 Protagoras는 "인간이 만물의 척도이다."라고 선언했다. 다시 말해서, 우리는 세상을 향해 "당신은 무슨 쓸모가 있는가?"라고 물어볼 자격이 있다고 느낀다.

(B) 우리는 우리가 세상의 기준이라고, 즉 모든 것이 우리와 비교되어야 한다고 추정한다. 그런 추정은 우리로 하여금 많은 것을 간과하게 한다.

(A) '우리를 인간답게 만들어 준다'고 일컬어지는 능력들, 즉 공감, 의사소통, 슬픔, 도구 만들기 등은 모두 우리와 세상을 공유하는, 지력을 지닌 다른 존재들 사이에서도 다양한 정도로 다 존재한다. 척추동물(어류, 양서류, 파충류, 조류, 포유류)은 모두 동일한 기본 골격, 장기, 신경계, 호르몬, 행동을 공유한다.

(C) 다양한 자동차의 모델들이 각각 엔진, 동력 전달 체계, 네 바퀴, 문, 좌석을 가지고 있는 것과 마찬가지로, 우리는 주로 우리의 외부 윤곽과 몇 가

지 내부적인 조정 면에서 다르다. 하지만 순진한 자동차 구매자들처럼, 대부분의 사람들은 오직 동물들의 다양한 겉모습만을 본다.

Why? 왜 정답일까?

'인간은 만물의 척도'라는 가정을 제시하는 주어진 글 뒤에는, 이것이 곧 인간이 스스로를 만물에 대한 비교 기준으로 여기고 있음을 의미한다고 설명하는 (B), 이러한 인간 중심적 가정의 맹점을 지적하는 (A), 다른 동물들에 대한 우리의 태도를 자동차 구매자에 빗대어 지적하는 (C)가 차례로 연결되어야 한다. 따라서 글의 순서로 가장 적절한 것은 ② '(B) – (A) – (C)'이다.

- **philosopher** ⓝ 철학자
- **entitled** ⓐ 자격이 있는
- **grief** ⓝ 슬픔
- **reptile** ⓝ 파충류
- **overlook** ⓥ 간과하다, 무시하다
- **exterior** ⓝ 겉모습, 외부 ⓐ 외부의
- **pronounce** ⓥ 선언하다
- **empathy** ⓝ 공감, 감정 이입
- **amphibian** ⓝ 양서류
- **assumption** ⓝ 가정
- **naive** ⓐ 순진한, 세상을 잘 모르는

구문 풀이

12행 We assume that we are the world's standard, that all things
접속사1   접속사2(앞의 that절 동격)
should be compared to us.
조동사 수동태

03 동물과 여행 　　　　　　　정답률 64% | 정답 ③

주어진 글 다음에 이어질 글의 순서로 가장 적절한 것을 고르시오.

① (A) – (C) – (B)　　　　　② (B) – (A) – (C)
✔(B) – (C) – (A)　　　　　④ (C) – (A) – (B)
⑤ (C) – (B) – (A)

The desire to see and interact with animals, / shaped as it is by popular culture, / can be a motivating factor for travel, / but negative perceptions of certain animals / can perform an entirely opposite role / in discouraging people from visiting some destinations.
동물들을 보고 상호작용하려는 욕구는 / 대중문화에 의해 지금처럼 형성된 것으로, / 여행의 동기부여 요인이 될 수 있지만, / 특정 동물들에 대한 부정적인 인식은 / 완전히 정반대의 역할을 할 수 있다. / 사람들이 어떤 목적지들을 방문하는 것을 만류하는 데 있어

(B) The harmful effects of animals on tourism experiences / has been the subject of analysis / in a small number of studies, / but deaths or injuries caused by animals to tourists / are tiny in comparison to other causes / such as drowning and vehicular accidents.
동물이 관광 체험에 미치는 해로운 영향은 / 연구 주제가 되었다 / 소수의 연구에서 / 하지만 동물에 의해 관광객들에게 초래된 사망이나 부상은 / 다른 원인에 비해 미미하다. / 익사와 교통사고 등

(C) Nevertheless, / the possibility / that they might encounter a dangerous animal / such as shark or snake / or catch a disease such as malaria / is sufficient / to stop at least some tourists from visiting destinations / where such threats exist.
그럼에도 불구하고, / 가능성은 / 그들이 위험한 동물과 마주칠 수도 있다거나 / 상어나 뱀과 같은 / 말라리아와 같은 질병에 걸릴지도 모른다는 / 충분하다. / 적어도 일부 관광객들이 목적지들을 방문하지 않게 만들기에 / 그러한 위험이 존재하는

Sometimes / this fear is turned into a marketing opportunity.
때때로 / 이 두려움은 마케팅 기회로 전환된다.

(A) For example, / there are a variety of t-shirt and tea towel designs / which celebrate the dangerous animals / that can be encountered in Australia.
예를 들어, / 다양한 티셔츠와 행주 디자인들이 있다. / 위험한 동물들을 기념하는 / 호주에서 만나볼 수 있는

This is a whimsical reconfiguration of the perceived threat / that these animals pose to some tourists / considering travel to this country.
이것은 인식된 위험의 기발한 재구성이다. / 일부 관광객들에게 이 동물들이 제기하는 / 이 나라로의 여행을 고려하는

━━━━━━━━━━━━━━━━━

동물들을 보고 상호작용하려는 욕구는 대중문화에 의해 지금처럼 형성된 것으로, 여행의 동기부여 요인이 될 수 있지만, 특정 동물들에 대한 부정적인 인식은 사람들이 어떤 목적지들을 방문하는 것을 만류하는 완전히 정반대의 역할을 할 수 있다.

(B) 동물이 관광 체험에 미치는 해로운 영향은 소수의 연구에서 연구 주제가 되었는데, 동물이 관광객들에게 초래한 사망이나 부상은 익사와 교통사고 등 다른 원인에 비해 미미하다.

(C) 그럼에도 불구하고, 그들이 상어나 뱀과 같은 위험한 동물과 마주칠 수도 있다거나 말라리아와 같은 질병에 걸릴지도 모른다는 가능성은 적어도 일부 관광객들이 그러한 위협이 존재하는 목적지들을 방문하지 않게 만들기에 충분하다. 때때로 이 두려움은 마케팅 기회로 전환된다.

(A) 예를 들어, 호주에서 만나볼 수 있는 위험한 동물들을 기념하는 다양한 티셔츠와 행주 디자인들이 있다. 이것은 이 나라로의 여행을 고려하는 일부 관광객들에게 이 동물들이 제기하는 인식된 위협의 기발한 재구성이다.

Why? 왜 정답일까?

동물과 상호작용하려는 욕구는 여행을 촉진할 수도 있지만 막을 수도 있다는 주어진 글에 이어서, 우선 '부정적' 영향을 살펴보면 그렇게 영향력이 큰 것 같지는 않다고 언급하는 (B)가 연결된다. (C)는 Nevertheless로 글 흐름을 전환시키며, '그럼에도 불구하고' 실제로 여행을 단념시키는 사례가 있음을 설명하다가, 다시금 동물에 대한 두려움이 '기회'로 이어진다는 내용으로 전환된다. (A)는 동물에 대한 두려움이 여행을 촉진하는 마케팅과 연결되는 예시를 보여준다. 따라서 글의 순서로 가장 적절한 것은 ③ '(B) – (C) – (A)'이다.

- **interact with** ~와 상호작용하다
- **tea towel** 마른 행주
- **reconfiguration** ⓝ 재구성
- **injury** ⓝ 부상
- **vehicular** ⓐ 차량과 관련된
- **destination** ⓝ 목적지
- **whimsical** ⓐ 기발한
- **threat** ⓝ 위협
- **drowning** ⓝ 익사
- **sufficient** ⓐ 충분한

구문 풀이

1행 The desire to see and interact with animals, (shaped as it is
주어　　　　　　　　　　　수식
by popular culture), can be a motivating factor for travel, but negative
( ): 삽입구(주어 보충)　　동사
perceptions of certain animals can perform an entirely opposite role
in discouraging people from visiting some destinations.
「discourage+A+from+B : A가 B하지 못하게 낙담시키다」

04 도시의 생산성과 다양성 　　　　　정답률 48% | 정답 ②

주어진 글 다음에 이어질 글의 순서로 가장 적절한 것을 고르시오.

① (A) – (C) – (B)　　　　　✔(B) – (A) – (C)
③ (B) – (C) – (A)　　　　　④ (C) – (A) – (B)
⑤ (C) – (B) – (A)

What are some characteristics of cities / that must be maintained even if the population decreases?
도시의 몇 가지 특징들은 무엇인가? / 비록 인구가 줄어들더라도 반드시 유지되어야만 하는

If this question can be answered, / a new city model can be proposed / based on the concept.
만약 이 질문에 답할 수 있다면 / 새로운 도시 모델이 제안될 수 있다. / 그 개념에 근거하여

Here, we focus on productivity and diversity / as characteristics of cities.
여기서 우리는 생산성과 다양성에 초점을 맞춘다. / 도시의 특징들로

(B) This is because / ensuring productivity and diversity / is the driving force for sustainability.
이는 ~ 때문이다. / 생산성과 다양성을 보장하는 것이 / 지속 가능성을 위한 원동력이기

For example, / if there is a place to work, / people gather and work there, / and the population gradually accumulates to form a city.
예를 들어 / 만약 일할 장소가 있다면, / 사람들은 그곳에 모여 일을 하며 / 인구는 점차 축적되어 도시를 형성한다.

However, / the industrial structure / that depends on a single industry / is vulnerable to social changes.
그러나 / 산업 구조는 / 단일 산업에 의존하는 / 사회적 변화에 취약하다.

(A) Given / that gold mining cities and coal mining cities / have risen and fallen, / their vulnerability is obvious.
고려하면 / 금광 도시들과 탄광 도시들이 / 흥망성쇠해온 것을 / 그것들의 취약성은 분명하다.

A city where various people gather in various industries / is secure against social changes.
다양한 산업에 다양한 사람들이 모이는 도시는 / 사회적 변화에 안정적이다.

The same is true in the natural world, / and the importance of biodiversity is essential / for the sustainability of the species.
자연 세계에서도 마찬가지이며, / 생물 다양성의 중요성은 필수적이다. / 종의 지속 가능성에 있어서

(C) The same is true in cities.
도시에서도 마찬가지이다.

In a society / where people of all ages and income levels live together, / and diverse industries coexist / while depending on each other, / cities will continue to exist overcoming environmental changes / such as population decline.
사회에서 / 모든 연령대와 소득 수준의 사람들이 함께 살고, / 다양한 산업들이 공존하는 / 서로 의존하면서 / 도시들은 환경적 변화를 극복하면서 계속 존재할 것이다. / 인구 감소와 같은

━━━━━━━━━━━━━━━━━

비록 인구가 줄어들더라도 반드시 유지되어야만 하는 도시의 몇 가지 특징들은 무엇인가? 만약 이 질문에 답할 수 있다면 그 개념에 근거하여 새로운 도시

모델이 제안될 수 있다. 여기서 우리는 도시의 특징들로 생산성과 다양성에 초점을 맞춘다.

(B) 이는 생산성과 다양성을 보장하는 것이 지속 가능성을 위한 원동력이기 때문이다. 예를 들어 만약 일할 장소가 있다면, 사람들은 그곳에 모여 일을 하고 인구는 점차 축적되어 도시를 형성한다. 그러나 단일 산업에 의존하는 산업 구조는 사회적 변화에 취약하다.

(A) 금광 도시들과 탄광 도시들이 흥망성쇠를 겪은 것을 고려하면 그것들의 취약성은 분명하다. 다양한 산업으로 다양한 사람들이 모이는 도시는 사회적 변화에 안정적이다. 자연 세계에서도 마찬가지이며, 생물 다양성의 중요성은 종의 지속 가능성에 있어서 필수적이다.

(C) 도시에서도 마찬가지이다. 모든 연령대와 소득 수준의 사람들이 함께 살고, 다양한 산업들이 서로 의존하면서 공존하는 사회에서 도시는 인구 감소와 같은 환경적 변화를 극복하면서 계속 존재할 것이다.

Why? 왜 정답일까?

도시의 생산성과 다양성을 주요 화제로 언급하는 주어진 글 뒤로, 생산성에 관해 언급하며 단일 산업에만 의지하는 도시의 한계점을 지적하는 **(B)**가 이어진다. 뒤이어 **(A)**는 자연 세계에서도 생물 다양성이 중요하다는 보충 설명을 제시하고, **(C)**는 도시에서도 마찬가지라는 결론을 제시한다. 따라서 글의 순서로 가장 적절한 것은 ② '**(B) – (A) – (C)**'이다.

- propose ⓥ 제안하다
- productivity ⓝ 생산성
- gold mining 금 채굴, 금 채광
- vulnerability ⓝ 취약성
- gather ⓥ 모이다
- biodiversity ⓝ 생물의 다양성
- sustainability ⓝ 지속 가능성
- driving force 원동력
- overcome ⓥ 극복하다
- concept ⓝ 개념
- diversity ⓝ 다양성
- coal mining 채탄, 탄광업
- obvious ⓐ 명백한, 분명한
- secure ⓥ 안정성의
- essential ⓐ 필수적인
- ensure ⓥ 보장하다
- coexist ⓥ 공존하다
- environmental ⓐ 환경의

구문 풀이

6행 Given {that gold mining cities and coal mining cities have
분사구문(~을 고려하면)　　{ }: 명사절
risen and fallen}, their vulnerability is obvious.

05 잉여물의 거래　　정답률 61% | 정답 ③

주어진 글 다음에 이어질 글의 순서로 가장 적절한 것을 고르시오. [3점]
① (A) – (C) – (B)　　② (B) – (A) – (C)
✔③ (B) – (C) – (A)　　④ (C) – (A) – (B)
⑤ (C) – (B) – (A)

A classic positive-sum game in economic life / is the trading of surpluses.
경제생활에서 전형적인 포지티브섬 게임은 / 잉여물의 거래이다.

(B) If a farmer has more grain than he can eat, / and a herder has more milk than he can drink, / both of them come out ahead / if they trade some wheat for some milk.
농부가 자신이 먹을 수 있는 것보다 더 많은 곡식을 가지고 있고 / 목축업자가 자신이 마실 수 있는 양보다 더 많은 우유를 가지고 있을 경우, / 그들은 둘 다 결국 이득을 본다. / 그들이 약간의 밀과 약간의 우유를 교환한다면

As they say, everybody wins.
사람들이 말하는 것처럼, 모든 사람이 이긴다.

Of course, / an exchange at a single moment in time only pays / when there is a division of labor.
물론, / 한 시점에서의 교환은 오로지 이득이 된다. / 분업이 있을 때

(C) There would be no point in one farmer / giving a bushel of wheat to another farmer / and receiving a bushel of wheat in return.
한 농부에게 아무런 의미가 없을 것이다. / 다른 농부에게 1부셀의 밀을 주고 / 그 대가로 1부셀의 밀을 받는 것은

A fundamental insight of modern economics is / that the key to the creation of wealth is a division of labor, / in which specialists learn to produce a commodity / with increasing cost-effectiveness / and have the means / to exchange their specialized products efficiently.
현대 경제학의 근본적인 통찰은 / 부 창출의 핵심은 분업이라는 것이다. / 분업 안에서 전문가들은 상품을 생산하는 법을 배우고 / 비용 효율성을 늘리면서 / 수단을 갖는다. / 자신의 특화된 상품을 효율적으로 교환할 수 있는

(A) One infrastructure / that allows efficient exchange / is transportation, / which makes it possible / for producers to trade their surpluses / even when they are separated by distance.
한 가지 기반은 / 효율적인 교환을 가능하게 하는 / 운송이며, / 이는 가능하게 한다. / 생산자들이 자신의 잉여물을 교환하는 것을 / 그들이 거리상 떨어져 있을 때에도

Another is money, interest, and middlemen, / which allow producers to exchange many kinds of surpluses / with many other producers at many points in time.
또 다른 하나는 돈, 이자, 중간 상인인데, / 이것은 생산자들이 많은 종류의 잉여물들을 교환할 수 있게 해준다. / 여러 시점에서 많은 다른 생산자들과

경제생활에서 전형적인 포지티브섬 게임은 잉여물의 거래이다.

(B) 농부가 자신이 먹을 수 있는 것보다 더 많은 곡식을 가지고 있고 목축업자가 자신이 마실 수 있는 양보다 더 많은 우유를 가지고 있을 경우에, 그들이 약간의 밀과 약간의 우유를 교환한다면, 그들은 둘 다 결국 이득을 본다. 사람들이 말하는 것처럼, 모든 사람이 이긴다. 물론, 한 시점에서의 교환은 분업이 있을 때에만 이득이 된다.

(C) 한 농부가 다른 농부에게 1부셀의 밀을 주고 그 대가로 1부셀의 밀을 받는 것은 아무런 의미가 없을 것이다. 현대 경제학의 근본적인 통찰은 부 창출의 핵심은 분업이고, 분업 안에서 전문가들은 비용 효율성을 늘리면서 상품을 생산하는 법을 배우고 자신의 특화된 상품을 효율적으로 교환할 수 있는 수단을 갖는다는 것이다.

(A) 효율적인 교환을 가능하게 하는 한 가지 기반은 운송이며, 이는 생산자들이 거리상 떨어져 있을 때에도 자신들의 잉여물을 교환하는 것을 가능하게 한다. 또 다른 하나(기반)는 돈, 이자, 중간 상인인데, 이것은 생산자들이 여러 시점에서 많은 다른 생산자들과 많은 종류의 잉여물들을 교환할 수 있게 해준다.

Why? 왜 정답일까?

잉여물의 거래는 포지티섬 게임이라는 내용의 주어진 글 뒤에는 농부와 목축업자의 예를 들어 잉여물을 서로 거래하는 예시로 시작하는 **(B)**가 먼저 연결된다. 이어서 **(C)**는 교환은 결국 분업이 있을 때 이익이 된다는 **(B)** 후반부 내용에 대한 예를 제시한다. 마지막으로 **(A)**는 분업 안에서 각 상품의 전문가들은 자신의 특화 상품을 효율적으로 교환할 수단을 갖게 된다는 **(C)** 후반부 내용에 이어서 바로 그 한 가지 수단이 '운송'이라는 답을 제시한다. 따라서 글의 순서로 가장 적절한 것은 ③ '**(B) – (C) – (A)**'이다.

- surplus ⓝ 잉여(물)
- transportation ⓝ 운송, 수송
- division of labor 분업
- bushel ⓝ 부셸(곡물 또는 과일의 중량 단위로 8갤런에 해당함)
- fundamental ⓐ 근본적인
- specialist ⓝ 전문가, 전공자
- cost-effectiveness ⓝ 비용 효율성
- infrastructure ⓝ 기반 시설
- middleman ⓝ 중개인
- come out ahead 이득을 올리고 끝내다
- wealth ⓝ 부
- commodity ⓝ 상품

구문 풀이

3행 One infrastructure [that allows efficient exchange] is
　　주어　　　　　주격 관계대명사
transportation, which makes it possible for producers to trade their
선행사　　계속적 용법 5형식 동사　목적격 보어　의미상 주어　진목적어
surpluses even when they are separated by distance.
　　└ 가목적어

06 전통적 과학 사학자의 관점에 대한 비판　　정답률 50% | 정답 ②

주어진 글 다음에 이어질 글의 순서로 가장 적절한 것을 고르시오. [3점]
① (A) – (C) – (B)　　✔② (B) – (A) – (C)
③ (B) – (C) – (A)　　④ (C) – (A) – (B)
⑤ (C) – (B) – (A)

Traditionally, Kuhn claims, / the primary goal of historians of science / was 'to clarify and deepen an understanding / of *contemporary* scientific methods or concepts / by displaying their evolution'.
Kuhn이 주장하기를, 전통적으로 / 과학 사학자의 주요 목표는 / 이해를 분명히 하고 깊게 하는 것이다. / 당대의 과학적 방법이나 개념에 대한 / 그것의 점진적 발전을 보여 줌으로써

(B) This entailed relating the progressive accumulation / of breakthroughs and discoveries.
이것은 점진적인 축적을 거론하는 것을 수반했다. / 획기적 발전과 발견의

Only that which survived in some form in the present / was considered relevant.
현재에 어떤 형태로 살아남은 것만이 / 유의미한 것으로 여겨졌다.

In the mid-1950s, however, / a number of faults in this view of history / became apparent.
하지만 1950년대 중반에, / 역사에 대한 이러한 관점에서 많은 결함이 / 분명해졌다.

Closer analysis of scientific discoveries, for instance, / led historians to ask / whether the dates of discoveries and their discoverers can be identified precisely.

예를 들어, 과학적 발견에 대한 더 면밀한 분석은 / 역사가들로 하여금 묻게 했다. / 발견과 그러한 발견을 한 사람들이 정확하게 확인될 수 있는지를

(A) Some discoveries seem to entail numerous phases and discoverers, / none of which can be identified as definitive.

몇몇 발견은 무수한 단계와 발견자들을 수반하는 것처럼 보이는데, / 그중 어느 것도 확정적인 것으로 확인될 수 없다.

Furthermore, the evaluation of past discoveries and discoverers / according to present-day standards / does not allow us to see / how significant they may have been in their own day.

게다가, 과거의 발견과 발견자들을 평가하는 것은 / 현재의 기준에 따라 / 우리가 알 수 없게 한다. / 그것이 당시에 얼마나 중요했을지를

(C) Nor does the traditional view recognise the role / that non-intellectual factors, / especially institutional and socio-economic ones, / play in scientific developments.

전통적인 관점은 또한 역할을 인식하지 못한다. / 비지성적인 요인들, / 특히 제도적 요인과 사회경제적 요인이 / 과학 발전에서 하는

Most importantly, however, / the traditional historian of science seems blind to the fact / that the concepts, questions and standards / that they use to frame the past / are themselves subject to historical change.

하지만 가장 중요한 것은, / 전통적인 과학 사학자가 사실을 알지 못하는 것처럼 보인다는 것이다. / 개념, 질문, 기준 자체가 / 과거를 구상하기 위해 자신이 사용하는 / 역사적 변화의 영향 하에 있다는

Kuhn이 주장하기를, 전통적으로 과학 사학자의 주요 목표는 *당대*의 과학적 방법이나 개념의 점진적 발전을 보여 줌으로써 그것에 대한 이해를 분명히 하고 깊게 하는 것'이다.

(B) 이것은 획기적 발전과 발견의 점진적인 축적을 거론하는 것을 수반했다. 현재에 어떤 형태로 살아남은 것만이 유의미한 것으로 여겨졌다. 하지만 1950년대 중반에, 역사에 대한 이러한 관점에서 많은 결함이 분명해졌다. 예를 들어, 과학적 발견에 대한 더 면밀한 분석은 역사가들로 하여금 발견과 그러한 발견을 한 사람들이 정확하게 확인될 수 있는지를 묻게 했다.

(A) 몇몇 발견은 무수한 단계와 발견자들을 수반하는 것처럼 보이는데, 그중 어느 것도 확정적인 것으로 확인될 수 없다. 게다가, 현재의 기준에 따라 과거의 발견과 발견자들을 평가하는 것은 그것이 당시에 얼마나 중요했을지를 우리가 알 수 없게 한다.

(C) 전통적인 관점은 또한 비지성적인 요인들, 특히 제도적 요인과 사회경제적 요인이 과학 발전에서 하는 역할을 인식하지 못한다. 하지만 가장 중요한 것은, 전통적인 과학 사학자가 과거를 구상하기 위해 자신이 사용하는 개념, 질문, 기준 자체가 역사적 변화의 영향 하에 있다는 사실을 알지 못하는 것처럼 보인다는 것이다.

Why? 왜 정답일까?

전통적인 과학 사학자의 목표를 언급한 주어진 글 뒤에는, 이 목표의 내용을 This로 받으며 이것이 발전과 발견의 점진적 축적과 연관되어 있었다고 설명하는 **(B)**가 이어진다. 한편 **(B)**의 후반부에서는 이 전통적 관점에 결함이 있었음을 지적하며 예를 들고 뒤이어 **(A)**에서는 이 예시의 내용을 보충한다. 마지막으로 **(C)**는 전통적 관점의 가장 중대한 결함을 설명하며 글을 마무리한다. 따라서 글의 순서로 가장 적절한 것은 ② '**(B) – (A) – (C)**'이다.

- **clarify** ⓥ 명확하게 하다
- **contemporary** ⓐ 당대의, 현대의
- **significant** ⓐ 중요한
- **accumulation** ⓝ 축적
- **apparent** ⓐ 분명한
- **deepen** ⓥ 깊게 하다
- **definitive** ⓐ 확정적인
- **entail** ⓥ 수반하다
- **fault** ⓝ 잘못, 책임
- **institutional** ⓐ 제도적인

구문 풀이

19행 Nor does the traditional view recognise the role [that
　　　　「부정어구＋조동사＋주어＋동사원형」: 도치 구문」　선행사　목적격 관·대
non-intellectual factors, especially institutional (ones) and
　　　　　주어1　　　　　　주어1 동격
non-intellectual factors, especially institutional and socio-economic
　　　　　주어2　　　　　　　　　　주어2 동격
ones, play in scientific developments].
　　　동사(복수)

07　섭식 문제의 발생　　정답률 52% | 정답 ②

주어진 글 다음에 이어질 글의 순서로 가장 적절한 것을 고르시오. [3점]

① (A) – (C) – (B)　　✔ (B) – (A) – (C)
③ (B) – (C) – (A)　　④ (C) – (A) – (B)
⑤ (C) – (B) – (A)

Most of us have a general, rational sense / of what to eat and when / — there is no shortage of information on the subject.

우리 대부분은 일반적이고 합리적인 관념을 갖고 있으며, / 무엇을 먹을지, 그리고 언제 먹을지에 대한 / 그 문제에 관한 정보는 부족하지 않다.

(B) Yet there is often a disconnect / between what we know and what we do.

하지만 종종 단절이 존재한다. / 우리가 알고 있는 것과 우리가 행하는 것 사이에는

We may have the facts, / but decisions also involve our feelings.

우리가 사실을 알고 있을 수는 있지만, / 결정은 또한 우리의 감정을 수반한다.

Many people who struggle with difficult emotions / also struggle with eating problems.

힘겨운 감정과 씨름하는 많은 사람들은 / 또한 섭식 문제와 씨름한다.

(A) *Emotional eating* is a popular term / used to describe eating / that is influenced by emotions, / both positive and negative.

*감정적 식사*는 일반적인 용어이다. / 식사를 설명하기 위해 사용되는 / 영향 받는 / 긍정적 감정과 부정적 감정 모두에

Feelings may affect various aspects of your eating, / including your motivation to eat, / your food choices, / where and with whom you eat, / and the speed at which you eat.

감정은 식사의 여러 측면에 영향을 줄 수 있다. / 여러분의 식사 동기와 / 음식 선택, / 여러분이 어디서 누구와 식사할지, / 여러분이 식사하는 속도를 포함한

Most overeating is prompted / by feelings rather than physical hunger.

대부분의 과식은 유발된다. / 신체의 배고픔이 아니라 감정에 의해

(C) Individuals who struggle with obesity / tend to eat / in response to emotions.

비만과 씨름하는 사람들은 / 먹는 경향이 있다. / 감정에 반응하여

However, / people who eat for emotional reasons / are not necessarily overweight.

그러나 / 감정적인 이유로 먹는 사람이 / 반드시 과체중인 것은 아니다.

People of any size / may try to escape an emotional experience / by preoccupying themselves with eating / or by obsessing over their shape and weight.

신체 크기와 관계없이 사람들은 / 감정적인 경험에서 벗어나려고 할 수 있다. / 먹는 것에 몰두하거나 / 자기 몸매와 몸무게에 대해 강박감을 가짐으로써

우리 대부분은 무엇을 먹을지, 그리고 언제 먹을지에 대한 일반적이고 합리적인 관념을 갖고 있으며, 그 문제에 관한 정보는 부족하지 않다.

(B) 하지만 우리가 알고 있는 것과 우리가 행하는 것 사이에는 종종 단절이 존재한다. 우리가 사실을 알고 있을 수는 있지만, 결정은 또한 우리의 감정을 수반한다. 힘겨운 감정과 씨름하는 많은 사람들은 또한 섭식 문제와 씨름한다.

(A) *감정적 식사*는 긍정적 감정과 부정적 감정 모두에 영향 받는 식사를 설명하기 위해 사용되는 일반적인 용어이다. 감정은 여러분의 식사 동기와 음식 선택, 여러분이 어디서 누구와 식사할지, 여러분이 식사하는 속도를 포함한 식사의 여러 측면에 영향을 줄 수 있다. 대부분의 과식은 신체의 배고픔이 아니라 감정에 의해 유발된다.

(C) 비만과 씨름하는 사람들은 감정에 반응하여 먹는 경향이 있다. 그러나 감정적인 이유로 먹는 사람이 반드시 과체중인 것은 아니다. 신체 크기와 관계없이 사람들은 먹는 것에 몰두하거나 자기 몸매와 몸무게에 대해 강박감을 가짐으로써 감정적인 경험에서 벗어나려고 할 수 있다.

Why? 왜 정답일까?

사람들은 무엇을 언제 먹을지에 대한 합리적인 관념을 충분히 지니고 있다는 내용의 주어진 글 뒤에는, 앎과 행함 사이에 단절이 존재하므로 섭식 장애가 생겨난다는 내용의 **(B)**, '감정적 식사'를 예로 드는 **(A)**, 비만과 씨름하는 사람들의 예를 제시하며 감정적 식사의 내용을 설명하는 **(C)**가 차례로 이어지는 것이 자연스럽다. 따라서 글의 순서로 가장 적절한 것은 ② '**(B) – (A) – (C)**'이다.

- **rational** ⓐ 합리적인
- **term** ⓝ 용어
- **motivation** ⓝ 동기
- **hunger** ⓝ 배고픔
- **involve** ⓥ 수반하다
- **necessarily** ⓐⓓ 반드시, 필연적으로, 꼭
- **escape** ⓥ 벗어나다
- **shortage** ⓝ 부족
- **aspect** ⓝ 측면, 국면, 양상
- **overeat** ⓥ 과식하다
- **disconnect** ⓝ 단절, 분리
- **obesity** ⓝ 비만
- **overweight** ⓝ 과체중 ⓐ 과체중의
- **preoccupy** ⓥ 열중케 하다

구문 풀이

6행 Feelings may affect various aspects of your eating, including
your motivation to eat, your food choices, where and with whom you
목적어1(~하려는 동기)　　　　목적어2　　　　　목적어3(의문사절)
eat, and the speed [at which you eat].
목적어4

08 창작물에 대한 공로와 일체감을 인정받는 예술가 정답률 40% | 정답 ②

주어진 글 다음에 이어질 글의 순서로 가장 적절한 것을 고르시오. [3점]

① (A) − (C) − (B)　　　✔ (B) − (A) − (C)
③ (B) − (C) − (A)　　　④ (C) − (A) − (B)
⑤ (C) − (B) − (A)

Today the term artist is used to refer to a broad range of creative individuals / across the globe from both past and present.
오늘날 예술가라는 용어는 광범위한 창의적 개인을 지칭하는 데 사용된다. / 전 세계에 걸쳐 있는 과거와 현재의

This rather general usage erroneously suggests / that the concept or word "artist" existed in original contexts.
이런 다소 일반적인 사용은 잘못된 암시를 한다. / "예술가"라는 개념이나 말이 원래 맥락에 존재했다고

(B) In contrast to the diversity it is applied to, / the meaning of this term / continues to be mostly based on Western views and values.
이 용어가 적용되는 다양성과는 대조적으로, / 이것의 의미는 / 대체로 서양의 관점과 가치에 계속 기반을 두고 있다.

Since the fifteenth century, / this tradition has been concerned with recognizing individual achievements.
15세기 이래로 / 이 전통은 개인의 업적을 인정하는 것과 관련이 있었다.

(A) Inventions, ideas, and discoveries have been credited to the persons / who originated them.
발명품, 아이디어, 그리고 발견은 사람에게 공로가 있다고 여겨져 왔다. / 이를 처음 고안한

This view is also at the core of the definition of an "artist."
이 견해는 또한 "예술가"라는 정의의 핵심에 있다.

Artists are perceived to establish a strong bond with their art / to the point of combining into one "entity."
예술가는 예술품과 강한 유대감을 쌓아가게 된다고 여겨진다. / 자기 예술품과 하나의 "실체"로 합쳐지게 될 정도로

(C) Art history has reinforced this oneness:
예술사에서는 이 일체감을 강화해 왔다:

A painting by Pablo Picasso is called "a Picasso."
파블로 피카소가 그린 그림 한 점은 "a Picasso"라고 불린다.

This union between artists and their work / has determined the essential qualities of an artist: / originality, authorship, and authenticity.
예술가와 작품 간의 이러한 결합은 / 예술가의 필수 자질을 결정해 왔다. / 독창성, 원작자, 진정함이라는

오늘날 예술가라는 용어는 전 세계에 걸쳐 있는 과거와 현재의 광범위한 창의적 개인을 지칭하는 데 사용된다. 이런 다소 일반적인 사용은 "예술가"라는 개념이나 말이 원래 맥락에 존재했다고 잘못된 암시를 한다.

(B) 이 용어가 적용되는 다양성과는 대조적으로, 이것의 의미는 대체로 서양의 관점과 가치에 계속 기반을 두고 있다. 15세기 이래로 이 전통은 개인의 업적을 인정하는 것과 관련이 있었다.

(A) 발명품, 아이디어, 그리고 발견은 이를 처음 고안한 사람에게 공로가 있다고 여겨져 왔다. 이 견해는 또한 "예술가"라는 정의의 핵심에 있다. 예술가는 자기 예술품과 하나의 "실체"로 합쳐지게 될 정도로 예술품과 강한 유대감을 쌓아가게 된다고 여겨진다.

(C) 예술사에서는 이 일체감을 강화해 와서, 파블로 피카소가 그린 그림 한 점은 "a Picasso"라고 불린다. 예술가와 작품 간의 이러한 결합은 독창성, 원작자, 진정함이라는 예술가의 필수 자질을 결정해 왔다.

Why? 왜 정답일까?

오늘날 '예술가'라는 말이 상당히 넓게 쓰인다는 내용의 주어진 글 뒤로는, 본래 이 말의 의미는 창작자 개인의 공로를 인정하는 서양의 관점과 관련되어 있음을 설명하는 (B), 예술가는 자기 작품과 매우 밀접한 관련을 맺어 함께 하나의 실체로 여겨질 정도임을 설명하는 (A), 이 '일체감'을 피카소의 예로 설명하는 (C)가 차례로 이어지는 것이 자연스럽다. 따라서 글의 순서로 가장 적절한 것은 ② '(B) − (A) − (C)'이다.

- **refer to** ~을 가리키다, 지칭하다
- **erroneously** ad 잘못, 틀리게
- **to the point of** ~할 정도까지
- **in contrast to** ~와는 대조적으로
- **recognize** ⓥ 인정하다
- **reinforce** ⓥ 강화시키다
- **authorship** ⓝ 원작자, 작가

- **rather** ad 꽤, 다소
- **be credited to** ~의 공로이다
- **entity** ⓝ 실체, 독립체
- **be applied to** ~에 적용되다
- **achievement** ⓝ 업적, 성취
- **quality** ⓝ 자질
- **authenticity** ⓝ 진정함, 진짜임

구문 풀이

8행 Artists are perceived to establish a strong bond with their
　　　　　　　　　　~라고 여겨지다　　　　　　　~와의 유대감
art to the point of combining into one "entity."
　~할 정도까지　　~로 합쳐지다

---

09 친환경 제품에 대한 투자 결정에 수반되는 딜레마 정답률 34% | 정답 ⑤

주어진 글 다음에 이어질 글의 순서로 가장 적절한 것을 고르시오.

① (A) − (C) − (B)　　　② (B) − (A) − (C)
③ (B) − (C) − (A)　　　④ (C) − (A) − (B)
✔ (C) − (B) − (A)

Green products involve, / in many cases, / higher ingredient costs / than those of mainstream products.
친환경 제품은 수반한다. / 많은 경우, / 더 높은 원료비를 / 주류 제품의 원료비보다

(C) Furthermore, / the restrictive ingredient lists and design criteria / that are typical of such products / may make green products / inferior to mainstream products / on core performance dimensions / (e.g., less effective cleansers).
게다가 / 제한 성분 목록과 디자인 기준이 / 그런 제품에서 일반적인 / 친환경 제품을 만들 수 있다. / 주류 제품보다 더 열등하게 / 핵심 성능 측면에서 / (예를 들어, 성능이 덜 좋은 세척제)

In turn, / the higher costs and lower performance of some products / attract only a small portion of the customer base, / leading to lower economies of scale / in procurement, manufacturing, and distribution.
결과적으로, / 일부 제품의 더 높은 비용과 더 낮은 성능은 / 고객층의 오직 적은 부분만 유인해서, / 더 낮은 규모의 경제를 초래한다. / 조달, 제조, 유통에서

(B) Even if the green product succeeds, / it may cannibalize the company's higher-profit mainstream offerings.
친환경 제품이 성공하더라도 / 그것은 기업의 고수익 주류 제품을 잡아먹을 수 있다.

Given such downsides, / companies / serving mainstream consumers with successful mainstream products / face what seems like an obvious investment decision.
이런 부정적인 면을 고려하면, / 기업들은 / 성공적인 주류 제품으로 주류 소비자의 요구를 충족하는 / 마치 뻔한 투자 결정처럼 보이는 것에 직면한다.

(A) They'd rather put money and time / into known, profitable, high-volume products / that serve populous customer segments / than into risky, less-profitable, low-volume products / that may serve current noncustomers.
그들은 돈과 시간을 투자하고 싶어 한다. / 이미 알려져 있고 수익성이 있는 다량의 제품에 / 다수의 고객 계층의 요구를 충족하는, / 위험하고 수익성이 더 낮은 소량의 제품보다는, / 현재 고객이 아닌 사람들의 요구를 충족할 수 있는

Given that choice, / these companies may choose / to leave the green segment of the market / to small niche competitors.
그런 선택을 고려하면, / 이들 기업은 선택할 수 있다. / 시장의 친환경 부문을 남겨두기로 / 소규모 틈새 경쟁업체들에게

많은 경우, 친환경 제품은 주류 제품보다 더 높은 원료비를 수반한다.

(C) 게다가 그런 제품에서 일반적인 제한 성분 목록과 디자인 기준이 친환경 제품을 주류 제품보다 핵심 성능 측면(예를 들어, 성능이 덜 좋은 세척제)에서 더 열등하게 만들 수 있다. 결과적으로, 일부 제품의 더 높은 비용과 더 낮은 성능은 고객층의 오직 적은 부분만 유인해서, 조달, 제조, 유통에서 더 낮은 규모의 경제를 초래한다.

(B) 친환경 제품이 성공하더라도 기업의 고수익 주류 제품을 잡아먹을 수 있다. 이런 부정적인 면을 고려하면, 성공적인 주류 제품으로 주류 소비자의 요구를 충족하는 기업들은 마치 뻔한 투자 결정처럼 보이는 것에 직면한다.

(A) 그들은 현재 고객이 아닌 사람들의 요구를 충족할 수 있는 위험하고 수익성이 더 낮은 소량의 제품보다는, 다수의 고객 계층의 요구를 충족하는, 이미 알려져 있고 수익성이 있는 다량의 제품에 돈과 시간을 투자하고 싶어 한다. 그런 선택을 고려하면, 이들 기업은 소규모 틈새 경쟁업체들에게 시장의 친환경 부문을 남겨두기로 선택할 수 있다.

Why? 왜 정답일까?

주어진 글에서 친환경 제품은 주력 제품보다 보통 원료비가 더 높다고 언급한 데 이어, **Furthermore**로 연결되는 (C)는 친환경 제품이 기능 면에서도 부족할 수 있어 기업 입장에서 더 낮은 규모의 경제를 초래할 수 있다는 설명을 이어 간다. 다음으로 (B)는 친환경 제품이 성공하더라도 기업의 주력 제품을 잡아먹을 수 있기에 기업들은 '뻔한' 선택 상황에 놓인다고 언급한다. 이어서 (A)는 (B)에서 언급된 기업들을 **They**로 받으며, 이들이 수익성을 택하고 친환경을 다른 틈새 시장의 몫으로 '남겨둘' 수밖에 없다는 내용을 제시한다. 따라서 글의 순서로 가장 적절한 것은 ⑤ '(C) − (B) − (A)'이다.

- **profitable** ⓐ 수익성 있는
- **niche** ⓝ 틈새
- **obvious** ⓐ 명백한
- **ingredient** ⓝ 성분, 재료
- **be typical of** ~의 전형이다
- **manufacturing** ⓝ 제조

- **populous** ⓐ 인구가 많은
- **downside** ⓝ 부정적 측면
- **restrictive** ⓐ 제한적인
- **criterion** ⓝ 기준 (pl. criteria)
- **inferior to** ~보다 열등한
- **distribution** ⓝ 유통, 분배

구문 풀이

7행 Given such downsides, companies (serving mainstream
무인칭 독립분사구문(~을 고려하면)　주어　현재분사
consumers with successful mainstream products) face what seems
동사(복수)　관계대명사(~것)
like an obvious investment decision.

★★ 문제 해결 꿀~팁 ★★

▶ 많이 틀린 이유는?
주어진 글에서 Green products가 언급되므로, 마찬가지로 the green product
를 포함한 (B)가 주어진 글 뒤에 바로 연결되어야 하는 것처럼 보인다. 하지만 (B) –
(A)를 먼저 배치한 후 (C)를 연결할 경우, (C)의 such products가 지칭하는 대상
이 모호해진다. (A)에는 such products로 가리킬 만한 복수 명사가 구체적으로
언급되지 않는다.

▶ 문제 해결 방법은?
수능 순서 문제의 대명사와 지시사는 정답을 찾을 수 있게 해주는 가장 큰 힌트이다.
이때 대명사, 지시사의 '수'에도 각별한 주의를 기울여야 한다. 맥락상 친환경 제품을
가리키는 (C)의 such products가 복수 표현이므로, 바로 앞 단락에서 친환경 제
품이 복수 형태로 제시되어야 하는데, 실제로 친환경 제품을 Green products라는
복수 표현으로 언급한 단락은 주어진 글 뿐이다.

★★★ 1등급 대비 고난도 3점 문제

| 10 | 식민지화에 있어 '표현'의 힘 | 정답률 35% \| 정답 ④ |

주어진 글 다음에 이어질 글의 순서로 가장 적절한 것을 고르시오. [3점]

① (A) – (C) – (B)　② (B) – (A) – (C)
③ (B) – (C) – (A)　✓④ (C) – (A) – (B)
⑤ (C) – (B) – (A)

Representation is control.
표현은 지배력이다.
The power to represent the world / is the power / to represent us in it or it in
us, / for the final stage of representing merges the representor and the
represented into one.
세상을 표현하는 힘은 / 힘이다 / 세상 속 우리 또는 우리 안의 세상을 표현하는 / 왜냐하면 표현의 최종 단계는
표현하는 것과 표현되는 것을 하나로 합치기 때문이다.
Imperializing cultures produce great works of art (great representations) /
which can be put to work intellectually / as armies and trading houses work
militarily and economically.
제국주의화하는 문화는 훌륭한 예술 작품(위대한 표현)을 생산한다. / 지적으로 작동할 수 있는 / 군대와 무역
회사가 군사적, 경제적으로 작동하듯이
(C) Shakespeare, Jane Austen and maps / were as important to English
Imperial power / as was the East India Company, the British army and the
churches of England.
세익스피어와 제인 오스틴과 지도는 / 영국 제국의 힘에 중요했다. / 동인도 회사와 영국 군대와 영국 교회만큼
이나
It is no coincidence / that modern Europe, the Europe of colonization, / was
also the Europe of "great art," / and no coincidence either / that it was the
Europe of great map makers.
우연이 아니다 / 식민지화의 유럽인 현대 유럽이 / '위대한 예술'의 유럽이기도 했다는 것은 / 그리고 또한 우연
이 아니다 / 그것이 위대한 지도 제작자들의 유럽이었다는 것도
(A) That is because / unless we can control the world intellectually by maps
/ we cannot control it militarily or economically.
그것은 ~ 때문이다. / 우리가 지도로 세상을 지적으로 지배할 수 없다면 / 우리는 그것을 군사적으로나 경제적
으로 지배할 수 없기
Mercator, Molière, Columbus and Captain Cook / imperialized in different
ways, / but they all imperialized, / and ultimately the effectiveness of one /
depended upon and supported the effectiveness of all the others.
메르카토르, 몰리에르, 콜럼버스, 쿡 선장은 / 서로 다른 방식으로 제국주의화했지만, / 이들은 모두 제국주의화
했고, / 궁극적으로 하나의 유효성은 / 다른 모든 것들의 유효성에 의존하며 그것을 뒷받침해 주었다.
(B) Similarly / the US form of contemporary colonization, / which involves
occupying economies and political parties / rather than physical territories, /
is accompanied by the power of both Hollywood and the satellite / to
represent the world to and for the US.
마찬가지로, / 미국의 현대 식민지화 형태는 / 경제와 정당을 차지하는 것이 포함되는 / 물리적 영토보다는 /
할리우드의 힘과 인공위성의 힘을 둘 다 동반한다 / 세계를 미국에, 그리고 미국을 위해 표현하기 위해

―――――――――――――――――――――――――――
표현은 지배력이다. 세상을 표현하는 힘은 세상 속 우리 또는 우리 안의 세상
을 표현하는 힘인데, 왜냐하면 표현의 최종 단계는 표현하는 것과 표현되는 것

을 하나로 합치기 때문이다. 제국주의화하는 문화는 군대와 무역 회사가 군사
적, 경제적으로 작동하듯이 지적으로 작동할 수 있는 훌륭한 예술 작품(위대한
표현)을 생산한다.

(C) 세익스피어와 제인 오스틴과 지도는 동인도 회사와 영국 군대와 영국 교회
만큼이나 영국 제국의 힘에 중요했다. 식민지화의 유럽인 현대 유럽이 '위
대한 예술'의 유럽이기도 했다는 것은 우연이 아니며, 위대한 지도 제작자
들의 유럽이었다는 것도 우연이 아니다.

(A) 그것은 우리가 지도로 세상을 지적으로 지배할 수 없다면 군사적으로나
경제적으로 지배할 수 없기 때문이다. 메르카토르, 몰리에르, 콜럼버스,
쿡 선장은 서로 다른 방식으로 제국주의화했지만, 이들은 모두 제국주의
화했고, 하나의 유효성이 궁극적으로 다른 모든 것들의 유효성에 의존하
며 그것을 뒷받침해 주었다.

(B) 마찬가지로, 물리적 영토보다는 경제와 정당을 차지하는 것이 포함되는 미
국의 현대 식민지화 형태는 할리우드의 힘과 인공위성의 힘을 둘 다 동반
해 세계를 미국에, 그리고 미국을 위해 표현한다.

Why? 왜 정답일까?

문화 예술의 지배력을 설명하는 글이다. 먼저 주어진 글에서는 제국주의 문화권에서 군사
및 경제적 힘뿐 아니라 문화 예술적 우위를 지닌다는 것을 시사한다. 이어서 (C)는 영국
을 포함한 유럽의 예로 주어진 글을 뒷받침한 후 지도 제작 기술에 관해서도 언급하는데,
(A)는 바로 이 지도 제작 기술상의 우위가 왜 중요했는지를 설명하는 내용으로 시작된다.
마지막으로 (B)는 가장 최근인 현대 미국으로 넘어와, 미국의 할리우드와 인공위성 등
예술 · 과학 기술적 우위가 오늘날 미국의 지배력에 크게 기여하고 있다는 내용을 덧붙
인다. 따라서 글의 순서로 가장 적절한 것은 ④ '(C) – (A) – (B)'이다.

- merge ⓥ 합치다
- work of art 예술 작품
- militarily [ad] 군사적으로
- occupy ⓥ 차지하다
- accompany ⓥ 동반하다
- coincidence ⓝ 우연
- map maker 지도 제작자
- imperialize ⓥ 제국주의화하다
- intellectually [ad] 지적으로
- contemporary ⓐ 현대의
- territory ⓝ 영토
- imperial ⓐ 제국의
- colonization ⓝ 식민지화

구문 풀이

20행 Shakespeare, Jane Austen and maps were as important to
English Imperial power as was the East India Company, the British
「as(~만큼)+대동사+주어 : 도치 구문」
army and the churches of England.

★★ 문제 해결 꿀~팁 ★★

▶ 많이 틀린 이유는?
식민지화를 문화적 관점에서 설명하는 글로, 소재가 익숙하지 않아 내용을 파악하기 쉽
지 않다. 특히 ⑤를 고르지 않도록 주의해야 하는데, (C) – (B)가 Similarly를 사이
에 두고 마치 「예시1 – 예시2」로 연결되는 것처럼 보이기 때문이다. 하지만 (A)에서
(C)의 마지막 부분에 나온 '지도'를 연이어 다루기 때문에 (C) – (A)를 먼저 연결해
야 한다.

▶ 문제 해결 방법은?
(C)의 마지막 문장이 (A) 첫 문장의 That이다. 즉 (A)가 (C)의 사례인 '유럽'에 대한
보충 설명이므로, '미국'이라는 새로운 예를 제시하는 (B)는 흐름상 (A) 뒤에 와야 자
연스럽다.

★★★ 1등급 대비 고난도 3점 문제

| 11 | 인간의 직립 보행에 따른 이득 | 정답률 37% \| 정답 ② |

주어진 글 다음에 이어질 글의 순서로 가장 적절한 것을 고르시오. [3점]

① (A) – (C) – (B)　✓② (B) – (A) – (C)
③ (B) – (C) – (A)　④ (C) – (A) – (B)
⑤ (C) – (B) – (A)

Bipedalism, upright walking, / started a chain of enormous evolutionary
adjustments.
두 발 보행, 즉 직립 보행은 / 엄청난 진화적 조정을 연쇄적으로 시작하게 했다.
It liberated hominin arms / for carrying weapons / and for taking food to
group sites / instead of consuming it on the spot.
그것은 호미닌의 두 팔을 자유롭게 하여 / 무기를 휴대하고, / 음식을 집단이 있는 장소로 가져갈 수 있게 해 주
었다. / 그것을 즉석에서 먹는 대신

But bipedalism was necessary / to trigger hand dexterity and tool use.
그런데 두 발 보행은 필요했다. / 손재주와 도구 사용을 촉발하기 위해

(B) Hashimoto and co-workers concluded / that adaptations underlying tool use / evolved independently of those required for human bipedalism / because in both humans and monkeys, / each finger is represented separately in the primary sensorimotor cortex, / just as the fingers are physically separated in the hand.
Hashimoto와 동료들이 결론짓기로, / 도구 사용의 기초가 되는 적응이 / 인간의 두 발 보행에 필요한 적응과 독립적으로 진화했는데, / 왜냐하면 인간과 원숭이 모두에서 / 각 손가락이 1차 감각 운동피질에서 구분되어 나타나기 때문이다. / 손에 있는 손가락이 물리적으로 나뉘어 있는 것처럼

(A) This creates the ability / to use each digit independently / in the complex manipulations required for tool use.
이것은 능력을 만들어 낸다. / 각 손가락을 독립적으로 사용할 수 있는 / 도구 사용에 필요한 복잡한 조작에서

But without bipedalism / it would be impossible / to use the trunk for leverage / in accelerating the hand / during toolmaking and tool use.
그러나 두 발 보행이 없다면 / 불가능할 것이다. / 몸통을 지렛대 역할로 사용하는 것이 / 손놀림을 가속화할 때 / 도구 제작 및 도구 사용 중

(C) Bipedalism also freed the mouth and teeth / to develop a more complex call system / as the prerequisite of language.
두 발 보행은 또한 입과 치아를 자유롭게 하여 / 더 복잡한 소리 신호 체계를 발전시켰다. / 언어의 전제 조건인

These developments required larger brains / whose energy cost eventually reached three times the level for chimpanzees, / accounting for up to one-sixth of the total basal metabolic rate.
이러한 발전은 더 큰 두뇌를 필요로 했다. / 그 에너지 비용이 결국 침팬지의 3배 수준에 이르러 / 총 기초 대사율의 최대 6분의 1을 차지하는

두 발 보행, 즉 직립 보행은 엄청난 진화적 조정을 연쇄적으로 시작하게 했다. 그것은 호미닌의 두 팔을 자유롭게 하여 무기를 휴대하고, 음식을 즉석에서 먹는 대신 집단이 있는 장소로 가져갈 수 있게 해 주었다. 그런데 두 발 보행은 손재주와 도구 사용을 촉발하기 위해 필요했다.

(B) Hashimoto와 동료들이 결론짓기로, 도구 사용의 기초가 되는 적응이 인간의 두 발 보행에 필요한 적응과 독립적으로 진화했는데, 인간과 원숭이 모두에서 손에 있는 손가락이 물리적으로 나뉘어 있는 것처럼 각 손가락도 1차 감각 운동 피질에서 구분되어 나타나기 때문이다.

(A) 이것은 도구 사용에 필요한 복잡한 조작에서 각 손가락을 독립적으로 사용할 수 있는 능력을 만들어 낸다. 그러나 두 발 보행이 없다면 도구 제작 및 도구 사용 중 손놀림을 가속화할 때 몸통을 지렛대 역할로 사용하는 것이 불가능할 것이다.

(C) 두 발 보행은 또한 입과 치아를 자유롭게 하여 언어의 전제 조건인 더 복잡한 소리 신호 체계를 발전시켰다. 이러한 발전으로 인해 에너지 비용이 결국 침팬지의 3배 수준에 이르러 총 기초 대사율의 최대 6분의 1을 차지하는 더 큰 두뇌가 필요하게 되었다.

Why? 왜 정답일까?

두 발 보행이 손재주와 도구 사용을 촉발하기 위해 필요했다는 주어진 글 뒤로, 이를 뒷받침하는 연구를 언급하는 (B)가 먼저 연결된다. 뒤이어 (A)는 각 손가락이 1차 감각 운동 피질에서 구분된다는 (B) 후반부 내용에 연결되어, '이 사실' 덕분에 각 손가락이 따로 사용될 수 있기에 직립 보행과 더불어 인간의 도구 사용이 가능해졌다는 설명을 이어 간다. 마지막으로 (C)는 직립 보행으로 입과 치아가 자유로워지면서 인간의 언어 사용 또한 가능해졌다는 추가적 내용을 제시한다. 따라서 글의 순서로 가장 적절한 것은 ② '(B) – (A) – (C)'이다.

- **bipedalism** ⓝ 두 발 보행
- **enormous** ⓐ 거대한
- **hominin** ⓝ 호미닌(분류학상 인간의 조상으로 분류되는 종족)
- **weapon** ⓝ 무기
- **dexterity** ⓝ (손)재주
- **independently** ⓐⓓ 독립적으로
- **trunk** ⓝ (사람, 나무의) 몸통
- **underlying** ⓐ 기저의, 기초가 되는
- **separately** ⓐⓓ 따로
- **sensorimotor cortex** 감각 운동 피질
- **basal** ⓐ 기초의
- **upright walking** 직립 보행
- **liberate** ⓥ 해방시키다
- **on the spot** 즉석에서
- **digit** ⓝ 손가락, 숫자
- **manipulation** ⓝ 조작
- **leverage** ⓝ 지렛대
- **represent** ⓥ 나타나다
- **primary** ⓐ 1차의, 주요한
- **prerequisite** ⓝ 전제 조건
- **metabolic** ⓐ (신진)대사의

구문 풀이

20행 These developments required larger brains [whose energy
　　　　　　　　　　　　　　　　　　선행사　　소유격 관·대
cost eventually reached three times the level for chimpanzees],
　　　　　　　　　　　　　　　　　배수사
accounting for up to one-sixth of the total basal metabolic rate.
분사구문　　　분수(분자 - 분모 : 기수 - 서수)

★★ 문제 해결 꿀~팁 ★★

▶ 많이 틀린 이유는?
(B)와 (C) 중 어느 것을 먼저 배치할지가 관건이다. 주어진 글에서 직립 보행으로 '손과 도구 사용'이 자유로워졌다고 하는데, (B)는 이 '도구 사용'을 계속 언급하는 반면, (C)는 also와 함께 다른 내용(= 입과 치아의 자유)으로 넘어가고 있다. 따라서 소재가 동일한 (B)를 주어진 글에 이어 배치하는 것이 적절하다.

▶ 문제 해결 방법은?
also는 같은 주제에 대해 근거나 세부 사항을 '추가'할 때 쓴다. 따라서 앞에서 한 소재에 대한 내용이 다 마무리되어야 나올 수 있다.

★★★ 1등급 대비 고난도 3점 문제

12 도식이 야기하는 오류　　　정답률 34% | 정답 ⑤

주어진 글 다음에 이어질 글의 순서로 가장 적절한 것을 고르시오. [3점]

① (A) – (C) – (B)　　　　② (B) – (A) – (C)
③ (B) – (C) – (A)　　　　④ (C) – (A) – (B)
✔ ⑤ (C) – (B) – (A)

Clearly, / schematic knowledge helps you / — guiding your understanding / and enabling you to reconstruct things / you cannot remember.
분명히, / 도식적인 지식은 여러분에게 도움을 준다. / 여러분의 이해를 인도하고 / 것들을 재구성하게 하여 / 여러분이 기억할 수 없는

(C) But schematic knowledge can also hurt you, / promoting errors in perception and memory.
하지만 도식적인 지식은 또한 여러분에게 해를 끼칠 수 있다. / 인식과 기억에 오류를 조장하여

Moreover, / the types of errors / produced by schemata / are quite predictable:
게다가, / 오류의 '유형'은 / 도식에 의해서 발생하는 / 상당히 예측 가능하다.

Bear in mind / that schemata summarize the broad pattern of your experience, / and so they tell you, in essence, / what's typical or ordinary in a given situation.
명심하라. / 도식이 여러분의 경험의 광범위한 유형을 요약하며 / 그래서 그것이 본질적으로 여러분에게 말해 준다는 것을 / 주어진 상황에서 무엇이 전형적이거나 평범한 것인지

(B) Any reliance on schematic knowledge, therefore, / will be shaped by this information / about what's "normal."
따라서, 도식에 대한 어떠한 의존이라 하더라도, 그것은 / 이러한 정보에 의해 형성될 것이다. / 어떤 것이 '정상적'인 것인지에 대한

Thus, / if there are things you don't notice / while viewing a situation or event, / your schemata will lead you / to fill in these "gaps" with knowledge / about what's normally in place in that setting.
따라서 / 여러분이 알아차리지 못하는 것이 있으면, / 어떤 상황이나 사건을 보면서 / 여러분의 도식이 여러분을 이끌어줄 것이다. / 지식으로 이러한 '공백'을 채우도록 / 그 상황에서 일반적으로 무엇이 어울리는지에 관한

(A) Likewise, / if there are things you can't recall, / your schemata will fill in the gaps with knowledge / about what's typical in that situation.
마찬가지로, / 여러분이 기억할 수 없는 것이 있으면, / 여러분의 도식이 그 공백을 지식으로 채워 줄 것이다. / 그 상황에서 어떤 것이 일반적인 것인지에 대한

As a result, / a reliance on schemata / will inevitably make the world seem more "normal" / than it really is / and will make the past seem more "regular" / than it actually was.
결과적으로, / 도식에 의존하는 것은 / 불가피하게 세상을 더 '정상적'인 것으로 보이게 할 것이고, / 실제보다 / 과거를 더 '규칙적인' 것으로 보이게 할 것이다. / 실제보다

분명히, 도식적인 지식은 여러분의 이해를 인도하고 여러분이 기억할 수 없는 것들을 재구성하게 하여 여러분에게 도움을 준다.

(C) 하지만 도식적인 지식은 또한 인식과 기억에 오류를 조장하여 여러분에게 해를 끼칠 수 있다. 게다가, 도식에 의해서 발생하는 오류의 '유형'은 상당히 예측 가능하다. 도식이 여러분의 경험의 광범위한 유형을 요약하며 그래서 그것이 본질적으로 주어진 상황에서 무엇이 전형적이거나 평범한 것인지 여러분에게 말해 준다는 것을 명심하라.

(B) 따라서, 도식에 대한 어떠한 의존이라 하더라도, 그것은 어떤 것이 '정상적'인 것인지에 대한 이러한 정보에 의해 형성될 것이다. 따라서 어떤 상황이나 사건을 보면서 여러분이 알아차리지 못하는 것이 있으면, 여러분의 도식이 그 상황에서 일반적으로 무엇이 어울리는지에 관한 지식으로 이러한 '공백'을 채우도록 여러분을 이끌어줄 것이다.

(A) 마찬가지로, 여러분이 기억할 수 없는 것이 있으면, 여러분의 도식이 그 공백을 그 상황에서 어떤 것이 일반적인 것인지에 대한 지식으로 채워 줄 것이다. 결과적으로, 도식에 의존하는 것은 불가피하게 세상을 실제보다

더 '정상적인' 것으로 보이게 할 것이고, 과거를 실제보다 더 '규칙적인' 것으로 보이게 할 것이다.

Why? 왜 정답일까?

도식적 지식은 우리의 인지 작용에 도움을 주지만 한편으로 현상을 실제보다 단순화하여 보여주기 때문에 오류를 조장할 수 있다는 내용을 다룬 글이다. 도식적 지식이 기억과 이해에 유용하다는 내용의 주어진 글 뒤에는, 도식이 유발하는 오류를 지적하는 (C), 도식은 무엇이 정상적인가를 주로 취급한다는 내용의 (B), 그리하여 우리는 전형적이고 규칙적인 것 중심으로 세상을 이해하게 된다는 내용의 (A)가 차례로 이어지는 것이 자연스럽다. 따라서 주어진 글의 순서로 가장 적절한 것은 ⑤ '(C) – (B) – (A)'이다.

- schematic ⓐ 도식적인, 도식으로 나타낸
- recall ⓥ 기억하다, 회상하다
- promote ⓥ 조장하다, 장려하다
- predictable ⓐ 예측 가능한
- reconstruct ⓥ 재구성하다
- inevitably ⓐ🇩 불가피하게, 필연적으로
- perception ⓝ 인식, 인지
- in essence 본질적으로

구문 풀이

19행 Bear in mind {that schemata summarize the broad pattern
명령문(~을 명심하라)   주어1   동사1
of your experience, and so they tell you, in essence, what's typical
주어2 동사2 └→간접 목적어   직접 목적어(명사절)
or ordinary in a given situation}. { } : 목적어

★★ 문제 해결 꿀~팁 ★★

▶ 많이 틀린 이유는?
(C)의 마지막에서 도식은 무엇이 전형적인지를 알려준다고 하는데, (B)는 이를 'this information about "what's normal"'이라고 표현하고 있다. 즉 (C)의 후반부에 나온 화제가 (B)의 초반부에서 되풀이되며 (C) 뒤에 (B)가 이어진다는 단서를 준다.

▶ 문제 해결 방법은?
지시어와 더불어 연결어는 순서 문제에서 많은 힌트를 제공한다. 예컨대 (A)의 Likewise는 앞에서 한 주제에 대한 예를 하나 든 후 추가로 같은 주제에 대한 예를 이어갈 때 쓰는 말이다. 여기서도 (B)에서 if로 시작하는 예문이 나온 뒤 (A)의 초반부에서 또 다른 예문을 추가하기에 앞서 Likewise를 썼다.

---

01 ⑤	02 ②	03 ⑤	04 ②	05 ③
06 ②	07 ④	08 ⑤	09 ②	10 ⑤
11 ④	12 ④			

01 수위 차이가 있는 두 수역 간에 운하 건설하기   정답률 60% | 정답 ⑤

주어진 글 다음에 이어질 글의 순서로 가장 적절한 것을 고르시오.
① (A) – (C) – (B)   ② (B) – (A) – (C)
③ (B) – (C) – (A)   ④ (C) – (A) – (B)
✔ (C) – (B) – (A)

When two natural bodies of water stand at different levels, / building a canal between them / presents a complicated engineering problem.
두 곳의 자연 수역이 서로 수위가 다를 때, / 둘 사이에 운하를 건설하는 것은 / 복잡한 공학적 문제를 만들어 낸다.
(C) To make up for the difference in level, / engineers build one or more water "steps," / called locks, / that carry ships or boats up or down / between the two levels.
수위의 차이를 보전하기 위해 / 공학자들은 하나 이상의 물 '계단'을 만든다. / 로크라고 부르는 / 배나 보트를 위아래로 운반하는, / 두 수위 사이에서
A lock is an artificial water basin.
로크는 인공적인 물웅덩이이다.
It has a long rectangular shape / with concrete walls and a pair of gates at each end.
그것은 긴 직사각형 모양을 하고 있다. / 콘크리트 벽과 양 끝에 한 쌍의 문이 있는
(B) When a vessel is going upstream, / the upper gates stay closed / as the ship enters the lock at the lower water level.
선박이 상류로 올라가고 있을 때는, / 위쪽 문은 닫혀 있다. / 배가 더 낮은 수위에 있는 잠금장치에 들어서는 동안
The downstream gates are then closed / and more water is pumped into the basin.
그리고 나서 하류의 문이 닫히고 / 더 많은 물이 웅덩이 안으로 양수된다.
The rising water lifts the vessel / to the level of the upper body of water.
상승하는 물이 선박을 끌어올린다. / 위쪽의 물 높이 수준까지
(A) Then the upper gates open / and the ship passes through.
그러고 나면 위쪽 문이 열리고 / 배가 통과한다.
For downstream passage, / the process works the opposite way.
하류 통행의 경우, / 그 과정은 정반대로 작동한다.
The ship enters the lock from the upper level, / and water is pumped from the lock / until the ship is in line with the lower level.
배가 위쪽 수위의 로크로 들어오고, / 물이 로크로부터 양수된다. / 배가 더 낮은 수위와 일치할 때까지

두 곳의 자연 수역이 서로 수위가 다를 때, 둘 사이에 운하를 건설하는 것은 복잡한 공학적 문제를 만들어 낸다.

(C) 수위의 차이를 보전하기 위해 공학자들은 두 수위 사이에서 배나 보트를 위아래로 운반하는, 로크라고 부르는 하나 이상의 물 '계단'을 만든다. 로크는 인공적인 물웅덩이이다. 그것은 콘크리트 벽과 양 끝에 한 쌍의 문이 있는 긴 직사각형 모양을 하고 있다.

(B) 선박이 상류로 올라가고 있을 때는, 배가 더 낮은 수위에 있는 잠금장치에 들어서는 동안 위쪽 문은 닫혀 있다. 그러고 나서 하류의 문이 닫히고 더 많은 물이 웅덩이 안으로 양수된다. 상승하는 물이 선박을 위쪽의 물 높이 수준까지 끌어올린다.

(A) 그러고 나면 위쪽 문이 열리고 배가 통과한다. 하류 통행의 경우, 그 과정은 정반대로 작동한다. 배가 위쪽 수위의 로크로 들어오고, 배가 더 낮은 수위와 일치할 때까지 물이 로크로부터 양수된다.

Why? 왜 정답일까?

주어진 글은 수위가 다른 두 자연 수역 사이에 운하를 건설하는 것을 화제로 제시한다. 먼저 (C)는 '두 수역의 수위 차이'를 보전하기 위해 하나 이상의 물 계단인 '로크'가 만들어진다고 설명한다. 이어서 (B)는 선박이 상류로 올라갈 때를 예로 들어, 로크의 두 문이 어떻게 작용하는지 설명하기 시작한다. Then으로 시작하는 (A)는 (B)의 과정을 뒤이어 설명한다. 따라서 글의 순서로 가장 적절한 것은 ⑤ '(C) – (B) – (A)'이다.

- body of water 수역, 물줄기
- complicated ⓐ 복잡한
- canal ⓝ 운하
- engineering ⓝ 공학

- **downstream** ⓐ 하류의 ⓐⓓ 하류로
- **vessel** ⓝ 선박
- **basin** ⓝ 물웅덩이, 괸 물, (하천) 유역
- **make up for** ~을 보전하다, 보상하다
- **rectangular** ⓐ 직사각형의
- **in line with** ~에 맞춰서, ~와 함께
- **upstream** ⓐⓓ 상류로 ⓐ 상류의
- **lift** ⓥ 들어올리다
- **artificial** ⓐ 인공적인

15행 To make up for the difference in level, engineers build one
목적(~하기 위해)
or more water "steps," (called locks), that carry ships or boats up or
선행사 ( ): 과거분사구 →주격 관계대명사
down between the two levels.

---

02 과학에서의 결정론 정답률 58% | 정답 ②

주어진 글 다음에 이어질 글의 순서로 가장 적절한 것을 고르시오.
① (A) − (C) − (B) ✔(B) − (A) − (C)
③ (B) − (C) − (A) ④ (C) − (A) − (B)
⑤ (C) − (B) − (A)

Because a main goal of science is to discover lawful relationships, / science assumes that what is being investigated is lawful.
과학의 주요 목적은 법칙적인 관계를 발견하는 것이기 때문에, / 과학에서는 연구되고 있는 것이 법칙적이라고 가정한다.

For example, the chemist assumes that chemical reactions are lawful, / and the physicist assumes that the physical world is lawful.
예를 들어, 화학자는 화학 반응이 법칙적이라고 가정하고 / 물리학자는 물리적 세계가 법칙적이라고 가정한다.

(B) The assumption / that what is being studied can be understood / in terms of causal laws / is called determinism.
가정은 / 연구되고 있는 것이 이해될 수 있다는 / 인과 법칙의 관점에서 / 결정론이라고 불린다.

Richard Taylor defined determinism as the philosophical doctrine / that "states that for everything that ever happens / there are conditions / such that, given them, nothing else could happen."
Richard Taylor는 결정론을 철학적인 교리라고 정의한다 / '언제나 일어나는 모든 일에 대해서 / 조건이 있다고 말하는 / 그 조건이 주어지면 / 그 밖의 어떤 것도 일어날 수 없는 그런'이라고 말하는

(A) The determinist, then, assumes / that everything that occurs / is a function of a finite number of causes / and that, if these causes were known, / an event could be predicted with complete accuracy.
그래서 결정론자는 가정한다. / 일어나는 모든 일이 / 유한한 수의 원인들의 작용이고 / 이 원인들이 알려지면 / 사건은 완전히 정확하게 예측될 수 있다고

However, knowing *all* causes of an event / is not necessary; / the determinist simply assumes / that they exist / and that as more causes are known, / predictions become more accurate.
하지만 어떤 사건의 *모든* 원인을 아는 것은 / 필수가 아니며, / 결정론자는 그저 가정한다. / 원인들이 존재하고 / 더 많은 원인들이 알려질수록 / 예측은 더 정확해진다고

(C) For example, almost everyone would agree / that the weather is a function of a finite number of variables / such as sunspots, high-altitude jet streams, and barometric pressure; / yet weather forecasts are always probabilistic / because many of these variables change constantly, / and others are simply unknown.
예를 들어, 거의 모든 사람이 동의할 것이지만, / 날씨는 유한한 수의 변수들의 작용이라는 데 / 태양의 흑점, 높은 고도의 제트 기류, 그리고 기압과 같은 / 일기 예보는 늘 확률적인데 / 이 변수들 중 많은 것이 끊임없이 변하고 / 다른 변수들이 전혀 알려져 있지 않기 때문이다.

과학의 주요 목적은 법칙적인 관계를 발견하는 것이기 때문에, 과학에서는 연구되고 있는 것이 법칙적이라고 가정한다. 예를 들어, 화학자는 화학 반응이 법칙적이라고 가정하고 물리학자는 물리적 세계가 법칙적이라고 가정한다.

(B) 연구되고 있는 것이 인과 법칙의 관점에서 이해될 수 있다는 가정을 결정론이라고 한다. Richard Taylor는 결정론을 '언제나 일어나는 모든 일에 대해서 그 조건이 주어지면 그 밖의 어떤 것도 일어날 수 없는 그런 조건이 있다고 말하는' 철학적인 교리라고 정의한다.

(A) 그래서 결정론자는 일어나는 모든 일이 유한한 수의 원인들의 작용이고 이 원인들이 알려지면 사건은 완전히 정확하게 예측될 수 있다고 가정한다. 하지만 어떤 사건의 *모든* 원인을 아는 것은 필수가 아니며, 결정론자는 그저 원인들이 존재하고 더 많은 원인들이 알려질수록 예측은 더 정확해진다고 가정한다.

(C) 예를 들어, 날씨는 태양의 흑점, 높은 고도의 제트 기류, 그리고 기압과 같은 유한한 수의 변수들의 작용이라는 데 거의 모든 사람이 동의할 것이지만, 일기 예보는 늘 확률적인데 이 변수들 중 많은 것이 끊임없이 변하고 다른 변수들이 전혀 알려져 있지 않기 때문이다.

과학에서는 연구 대상이 법칙적이라고 가정한다는 내용의 주어진 글 뒤에는, 이것이 다른 말로 결정론이라고 불린다고 정리하는 (B), 결정론에 따르면 모든 사건은 유한한 원인들의 작용으로 발생하므로 원인이 더 많이 알려질수록 사건을 더 정확하게 예측할 수 있다고 상술하는 (A), 관련된 예를 드는 (C)가 차례로 이어져야 한다. 따라서 글의 순서로 가장 적절한 것은 ② '(B) − (A) − (C)'이다.

- **lawful** ⓐ 법칙적인, 합법적인
- **chemical reaction** 화학 반응
- **function** ⓝ 작용, 기능
- **accuracy** ⓝ 정확성
- **causal** ⓐ 인과 관계의
- **philosophical** ⓐ 철학적인
- **variable** ⓝ 변수
- **jet stream** 제트 기류
- **probabilistic** ⓐ 확률적인
- **investigate** ⓥ 연구하다
- **determinist** ⓝ 결정론자
- **finite** ⓐ 유한한, 한정된
- **prediction** ⓝ 예측
- **determinism** ⓝ 결정론
- **doctrine** ⓝ 교리, 주의
- **sunspot** ⓝ 태양의 흑점
- **forecast** ⓝ 예보

6행 The determinist, then, assumes that everything [that occurs]
동사 접속사1 주어
is a function of a finite number of causes / and that, if these causes
동사 접속사2 "if+주어+were ~.
were known, an event could be predicted with complete accuracy.
주어+ could+동사원형 : 가정법 과거"

---

03 미래가 있음을 알아도 제대로 대비할 수 없는 인간 정답률 42% | 정답 ⑤

주어진 글 다음에 이어질 글의 순서로 가장 적절한 것을 고르시오.
① (A) − (C) − (B) ② (B) − (A) − (C)
③ (B) − (C) − (A) ④ (C) − (A) − (B)
✔(C) − (B) − (A)

Humans are unique in the realm of living beings / in knowing there is a future.
인간은 생물의 영역에서 고유하다. / 미래가 있다는 것을 안다는 점에서

If people experience worry and hope, / it is because they realize the future exists, / that it can be better or worse, / and that the outcome depends to some extent on them.
사람들이 걱정과 희망을 경험한다면 / 그것은 사람들이 미래가 존재한다는 것을 깨닫기 때문이다. / 그것이 더 좋거나 나쁠 수 있다는 것을, / 그리고 그 결과가 어느 정도 자신에게 달려 있다는 것을

(C) But having this knowledge does not imply / that they know what to do with it.
하지만 이것을 알고 있는 것은 뜻하지 않는다. / 사람들이 이것을 가지고 뭘 해야 할지 알고 있다는 것을

People often repress their awareness of the future / because thinking about it distorts the comfort of the now, / which tends to be more powerful than the future / because it is present and because it is certain.
사람들은 미래에 대한 인식을 억누르는 경우가 많은데, / 왜냐하면 미래에 대해 생각하는 것이 현재의 안락함을 왜곡하기 때문이며, / 현재는 미래보다 더 강력한 경향이 있다. / 그것이 지금 존재하고 확실하다는 점에서

(B) The future, on the other hand, / must be imagined in advance / and, for that very reason, is always uncertain.
반면에 미래는 / 미리 상상되어야 하며, / 바로 그 이유로 항상 불확실하다.

Getting along with the future / is not an easy task, / nor is it one / in which instinct prevents us from blunders.
미래와 잘 지내는 것은 / 쉬운 일이 아니며, / 그런 일도 또한 아니다. / 본능이 우리가 큰 실수를 저지르지 않게 막아 주는

(A) That is why we so often have a poor relationship with the future / and are either more fearful than we need to be / or allow ourselves to hope against all evidence; / we worry excessively or not enough; / we fail to predict the future or to shape it / as much as we are able.
이 때문에 우리는 매우 자주 미래와 좋지 않은 관계를 가지게 되고, / 필요 이상으로 더 두려워하거나 / 우리 자신이 모든 증거에 반하여 희망을 갖게 한다 / 우리는 지나치게 또는 불충분하게 걱정하며, / 우리는 미래를 예측하거나 만들어 내지 못한다. / 우리가 할 수 있는 만큼

인간은 미래가 있다는 것을 안다는 점에서 생물의 영역에서 고유하다. 사람들이 걱정과 희망을 경험한다면 그것은 사람들이 미래가 존재하고, 그것이 더 좋거나 나쁠 수 있고, 그 결과가 어느 정도 자신에게 달려 있다는 것을 깨닫기 때문이다.

(C) 하지만 이것을 알고 있다고 해서 사람들이 이것을 가지고 뭘 해야 할지 알고 있다는 뜻은 아니다. 사람들은 미래에 대한 인식을 억누르는 경우가 많은데, 왜냐하면 미래에 대해 생각하는 것이 현재의 안락함을 왜곡하기 때문이며, 현재는 지금 존재하고 확실하다는 점에서 미래보다 더 강력한 경향이 있다.

(B) 반면에 미래는 미리 상상되어야 하며, 바로 그 이유로 항상 불확실하다. 미래와 잘 지내는 것은 쉬운 일이 아니며, 본능이 우리가 큰 실수를 저지르지 않게 막아 주는 그런 일도 아니다.

(A) 이 때문에 우리는 매우 자주 미래와 좋지 않은 관계를 가지게 되고, 필요 이상으로 더 두려워하거나 모든 증거에 반하여 희망을 갖게 된다. 우리는 지나치게 또는 불충분하게 걱정하며, 우리가 할 수 있는 만큼 미래를 예측하거나 만들어 내지 못한다.

Why? 왜 정답일까?

인간은 미래를 인지할 수 있다는 점에서 다른 동물과 구별된다는 주어진 글 뒤로, 그럼에도 불구하고 인간은 미래 대비를 잘하지 못하는데, 현재의 안락을 지키려는 마음 때문에 그렇다는 (C)가 먼저 연결된다. 이어서 (B)는 다시 미래 이야기로 흐름을 반전시키며, (A)는 최종 결론을 제시한다. 따라서 글의 순서로 가장 적절한 것은 ⑤ '(C) – (B) – (A)' 이다.

- unique ⓐ 고유한
- realize ⓥ 깨닫다
- to some extent 어느 정도는
- excessively ⓐⓓ 과도하게, 지나치게
- shape ⓥ 만들어내다, 영향을 주다
- in advance 미리, 사전에
- get along with ~와 어울리다
- prevent A from B A가 B하지 못하게 막다
- imply ⓥ 암시하다, 시사하다
- awareness ⓝ 인식, 앎
- comfort ⓝ 안락
- realm ⓝ 영역
- outcome ⓝ 결과
- fearful ⓐ 걱정하는, 염려하는
- fail to ~하지 못하다
- on the other hand 반면에
- uncertain ⓐ 불확실한
- instinct ⓝ 본능
- blunder ⓝ 큰 실수
- repress ⓥ 참다, 억누르다
- distort ⓥ 왜곡하다
- present ⓐ 현재의, 존재하는

구문 풀이

6행 **That is why we so often have a poor relationship with the future and are either more fearful than we need to be or allow ourselves to hope against all evidence; we worry excessively or not enough; we fail to predict the future or to shape it as much as we are able.**

그것은 ~한 이유이다(그래서 ~하다) 동사1 동사2-1 상관접속사(A 또는 B) 동사2-2 ~하지 못하다

04 물망초가 퍼지는 것을 돕는 개미들 정답률 70% | 정답 ②

주어진 글 다음에 이어질 글의 순서로 가장 적절한 것을 고르시오.

① (A) – (C) – (B) ✔② (B) – (A) – (C)
③ (B) – (C) – (A) ④ (C) – (A) – (B)
⑤ (C) – (B) – (A)

Forget-me-nots can conquer new territory / because they have an army of tiny allies: / ants.
물망초는 새로운 영역을 정복할 수 있다. / 그들이 작은 동맹군을 가지고 있기 때문에 / 개미라는

It's not that ants are particularly fond of flowers / — at least, they are not attracted by their aesthetic qualities.
개미가 특별히 꽃을 좋아하는 것은 아니다. / 즉, 적어도 그것이 꽃의 미적 가치들에 끌리는 것은 아니다.

(B) Ants are motivated by their desire to eat them, / and their interest is triggered / when forget-me-nots form their seeds.
개미는 그것을 먹고 싶은 욕망에 의해 동기 부여가 되며, / 그것의 관심은 촉발된다. / 물망초가 씨앗을 형성할 때

The seeds are designed to make an ant's mouth water, / for attached to the outside / is a structure called an elaiosome, / which looks like a tiny bit of cake.
그 씨앗은 개미의 입에 침이 고이도록 고안되었는데, / 왜냐하면 겉에 붙어 있기 때문이며 / 엘라이오솜이라고 불리는 구조물이 / 이것은 작은 케이크 조각처럼 보인다.

(A) This fat-and sugar-rich treat / is like chips and chocolate to an ant.
이 지방과 당분이 풍부한 맛있는 것 / 개미에게는 감자칩과 초콜릿과 같다.

The tiny creatures quickly carry the seeds back to their nest, / where the colony is waiting eagerly in the tunnels for the calorie boost.
그 작은 생명체는 그 씨앗을 자신의 둥지로 재빠르게 옮기는데 / 그곳에서는 군집이 굴 안에서 칼로리 상승을 간절하게 기다리고 있다.

The tasty treat is bitten off / and the seed itself is discarded.
그 맛있는 것은 뜯어 먹히고 / 씨앗 자체는 버려진다.

(C) Along come the trash collectors in the form of worker ants, / which dispose of the seeds in the neighborhood / — carrying them up to 200 feet away from home base.
일개미로 구성된 쓰레기 수거꾼이 따라와 / 그 씨앗을 인근에 버리는데, / 본거지로부터 200피트까지 떨어진 곳으로 그것을 옮겨놓는다.

Wild strawberries and other plants / also benefit from this distribution service: / ants are nature's gardeners, as it were.
야생 딸기와 다른 식물들도 / 역시 이 배포 서비스로부터 이득을 얻는다. / 개미는 말하자면 자연의 정원사이다.

물망초는 작은 동맹군인 개미를 가지고 있기 때문에 새로운 영역을 정복할 수 있다. 개미가 특별히 꽃을 좋아하는 것은 아니다. 즉, 적어도 개미들은 꽃의 미적 가치에 끌리지는 않는다.

(B) 개미는 그것을 먹고 싶은 욕망에 의해 동기 부여가 되며, 그것의 관심은 물망초가 씨앗을 형성할 때 촉발된다. 그 씨앗은 개미의 입에 침이 고이도록 고안되었는데, 왜냐하면 엘라이오솜이라고 불리는 구조물이 겉에 붙어 있기 때문이며 이것은 작은 케이크 조각처럼 보인다.

(A) 이 지방과 당분이 풍부한 맛있는 것은 개미에게는 감자칩과 초콜릿과 같다. 그 작은 생명체는 그 씨앗을 자신의 둥지로 재빠르게 옮기는데 그곳에서는 군집이 굴 안에서 칼로리 상승을 간절하게 기다리고 있다. 그 맛있는 것은 뜯어 먹히고 씨앗 자체는 버려진다.

(C) 일개미로 구성된 쓰레기 수거꾼이 따라 그 씨앗을 인근에 버리는데, 본 거지로부터 200피트까지 떨어진 곳으로 그것을 옮겨놓는다. 야생 딸기와 다른 식물들 역시 이 배포 서비스로부터 이득을 얻는다. 개미는 말하자면 자연의 정원사이다.

Why? 왜 정답일까?

주어진 글에서 물망초와 개미가 동맹 관계임을 언급한 데 이어, 본래 개미가 꽃에 끌리는 곤충은 아니라고 설명한다. 이어서 (B)는 주어진 글의 flowers를 them으로 받으며, 개미는 '꽃을' 먹고 싶어 하는 본능에 이끌리는 것이라고 보충 설명한다. 한편 (B)의 후반부에서 물망초의 씨앗에는 작은 케이크 조각처럼 생긴 엘라이오솜이 붙어 있다고 언급하는데, (A)는 이것을 This fat-and sugar-rich treat로 지칭하며 개미가 이것을 맛있게 뜯어먹고 씨앗은 버린다고 설명한다. 마지막으로 (C)는 이 씨앗이 일개미들에 의해 200피트까지 이동하게 되면서 물망초가 새로운 곳에 뿌리내리는 것이라는 결론을 제시한다. 따라서 글의 순서로 가장 적절한 것은 ② '(B) – (A) – (C)'이다.

- conquer ⓥ 정복하다
- be fond of ~을 좋아하다
- colony ⓝ (개미 등의) 거주지, 군집
- discard ⓥ 버리다
- benefit ⓝ 혜택, 이득
- nature ⓝ 자연, 천지 만물
- territory ⓝ 영역, 영토
- aesthetic ⓐ 미적인
- eagerly ⓐⓓ 간절히, 열망하여
- dispose of ~을 처분하다, 없애다
- distribution ⓝ 배포, 분배

구문 풀이

13행 **The seeds are designed to make an ant's mouth water, for attached to the outside is a structure called an elaiosome, which looks like a tiny bit of cake.**

주어1 동사1 부사적 용법(~하도록) 접속사(왜냐하면) 「보어 + 동사2 + 주어2 : 도치 구문」 선행사 계속적 용법

05 얼굴이 붉어지는 것의 사회적 의미 정답률 53% | 정답 ③

주어진 글 다음에 이어질 글의 순서로 가장 적절한 것을 고르시오. [3점]

① (A) – (C) – (B) ② (B) – (A) – (C)
✔③ (B) – (C) – (A) ④ (C) – (A) – (B)
⑤ (C) – (B) – (A)

Darwin saw blushing as uniquely human, / representing an involuntary physical reaction / caused by embarrassment and self-consciousness in a social environment.
다윈은 얼굴이 붉어지는 것을 특별나게 인간적인 것으로 여겼다. / 즉 무의식적인 신체 반응을 나타내는 것으로 / 사회적 환경에서 당혹감과 자의식에 의한

(B) If we feel awkward, embarrassed or ashamed / when we are alone, / we don't blush; / it seems to be caused by our concern / about what others are thinking of us.
우리가 어색하거나 부끄럽거나 창피하다고 느끼더라도 / 우리가 혼자 있을 때는 / 우리는 얼굴이 붉어지지 않는데, / 그것은 우리의 염려에 의해 생기는 것 같다. / 다른 사람들이 우리를 어떻게 생각할지에 대해

Studies have confirmed / that simply being told you are blushing / brings it on.
연구는 확인했다. / 단지 얼굴이 붉어진다는 말을 듣는 것만으로도 / 얼굴이 붉어진다는 것을

We feel / as though others can see through our skin and into our mind.
우리는 느낀다. / 다른 사람들이 우리 피부를 꿰뚫어 마음을 들여다볼 수 있는 것처럼

(C) However, / while we sometimes want to disappear / when we involuntarily go bright red, / psychologists argue / that blushing actually serves a positive social purpose.

그러나 / 우리가 때로 사라지고 싶어 하지만, / 자신도 모르는 사이에 얼굴이 새빨개질 때 / 심리학자들은 주장한다. / 얼굴이 붉어지는 것이 실제로는 긍정적인 사회적 목적에 부합한다고

When we blush, / it's a signal to others / that we recognize that a social norm has been broken; / it is an apology for a faux pas.
우리가 얼굴이 붉어질 때, / 그것은 다른 사람에게 알리는 신호이다 / 우리가 사회적 규범을 어겼음을 인정한다는 것을 / 그리고 그것은 실수에 대한 사과이다.

(A) Maybe / our brief loss of face / benefits the long-term cohesion of the group.
아마도 / 우리가 잠시 체면을 잃는 것이 / 집단의 장기적인 결속에 도움이 될 수 있을 것이다.

Interestingly, / if someone blushes after making a social mistake, / they are viewed in a more favourable light / than those who don't blush.
흥미롭게도 / 누군가가 사회적 실수를 저지른 후 얼굴을 붉히면, / 그 사람은 더 호의적인 시각으로 바라봐지게 된다. / 얼굴을 붉히지 않는 사람보다

다윈은 얼굴이 붉어지는 것을 특별나게 인간적인 것으로 여겨서, 사회적 환경에서 당혹감과 자의식에 의한 무의식적인 신체 반응을 나타내는 것으로 보았다.

(B) 우리가 혼자 있을 때는 어색하거나 부끄럽거나 창피하다고 느끼더라도 얼굴이 붉어지지 않는다. 얼굴이 붉어지는 것은 다른 사람이 우리를 어떻게 생각할지 우리가 염려하기 때문에 생기는 것 같다. 연구에 따르면 단지 얼굴이 붉어진다는 말을 듣는 것만으로도 얼굴이 붉어진다는 것이 확인되었다. 우리는 다른 사람들이 우리 피부를 꿰뚫어 마음을 들여다볼 수 있는 것처럼 느낀다.

(C) 그러나 우리가 때로 자신도 모르는 사이에 얼굴이 새빨개질 때 사라지고 싶어 하지만, 심리학자들은 얼굴이 붉어지는 것이 실제로는 긍정적인 사회적 목적에 부합한다고 주장한다. 얼굴이 붉어질 때, 그것은 우리가 사회적 규범을 어겼음을 인정한다는 것을 다른 사람에게 알리는 신호이자 실수에 대한 사과이다.

(A) 아마도 우리가 잠시 체면을 잃는 것이 집단의 장기적인 결속에 도움이 될 수 있을 것이다. 흥미롭게도 누군가가 사회적 실수를 저지른 후 얼굴을 붉히면, 우리는 그 사람을 얼굴을 붉히지 않는 사람보다 더 호의적인 시각으로 바라보게 된다.

Why? 왜 정답일까?

얼굴이 붉어지는 것을 핵심 소재로 언급하는 주어진 글 뒤로, 우리가 언제 얼굴을 붉히는지 예시를 들어 설명하는 (B)가 먼저 연결된다. 한편 (C)는 얼굴이 붉어지는 것이 긍정적 사회적 목적에 부합하는 것이라고 설명하고, (A)에서는 '긍정적 사회적 목적'이 바로 '집단 결속의 강화'임을 설명한다. 따라서 글의 순서로 가장 적절한 것은 ③ '(B) - (C) - (A)'이다.

- blushing ⓝ 얼굴을 붉힘
- involuntary ⓐ 자기도 모르게 하는
- embarrassment ⓝ 당황함
- brief ⓐ 짧은
- benefit ⓥ ~에 이득이 되다
- blush ⓥ 얼굴을 붉히다
- awkward ⓐ 어색한
- concern ⓝ 우려, 염려, 걱정
- bring on ~을 야기하다
- see through ~을 꿰뚫어보다
- signal ⓝ 신호 ⓥ 알리다
- faux pas 실수
- uniquely ⓐd 고유하게
- physical reaction 신체 반응
- self-consciousness ⓝ 자의식
- loss of face 체면 손상
- long-term ⓐ 장기적인
- favourable ⓐ 우호적인
- ashamed ⓐ 부끄러운, 창피한
- be told ~을 듣다
- as though ~인 것처럼
- serve a purpose 목적을 수행하다
- apology ⓝ 사과

구문 풀이

13행 Studies have confirmed that simply being told (that) you are
　　　　　　　　　접속사(~것)　　동명사구 주어　　being told의 목적절
blushing brings it on.
　　　구동사+목적어

---

06 진화를 하는 여러 가지 경우　　　　정답률 49% | 정답 ②

주어진 글 다음에 이어질 글의 순서로 가장 적절한 것을 고르시오. [3점]
① (A) - (C) - (B)　　　　☑ (B) - (A) - (C)
③ (B) - (C) - (A)　　　　④ (C) - (A) - (B)
⑤ (C) - (B) - (A)

Evolution works to maximize the number of descendants / that an animal leaves behind.
진화는 후손의 수를 최대화하기 위해 작용을 한다. / 동물이 남기는

Where the risk of death from fishing increases / as an animal grows, /

---

evolution favors those that grow slowly, / mature younger and smaller, / and reproduce earlier.
어로행위로 죽을 수 있는 위험이 증가하는 상황에서 / 동물이 성장할 때 / 진화는 천천히 성장하고, / 더 어린 나이에 그리고 더 작을 때에 성숙하고, / 더 일찍 번식하는 것을 선호한다.

(B) This is exactly what we now see in the wild.
이것은 정확하게 현재 우리가 야생에서 보는 것이다.

Cod in Canada's Gulf of St. Lawrence / begin to reproduce at around four today; / forty years ago they had to wait until six or seven / to reach maturity.
캐나다의 St. Lawrence 만에 사는 대구는 / 현재 네 살쯤 되었을 때 번식을 시작한다. / 40년 전에 그것은 6세나 7세가 될 때까지 기다려야 했다. / 성숙기에 도달하기 위해서는

Sole in the North Sea mature at half the body weight / they did in 1950.
북해의 가자미는 체중이 절반 정도만 되면 성숙한다. / 1950년에 비해

(A) Surely these adaptations are good news for species / hard-pressed by excessive fishing?
물론 이런 적응은 종들에게 좋은 소식일까? / 지나친 어로행위로 심한 압박을 받는

Not exactly.
꼭 그런 것은 아니다.

Young fish produce many fewer eggs than large-bodied animals, / and many industrial fisheries are now so intensive / that few animals survive more than a couple of years / beyond the age of maturity.
어린 물고기는 몸집이 큰 동물보다 훨씬 더 적은 수의 알을 생산하며, / 현재 많은 산업용 어업이 너무나 집약적이어서 / 2년 넘게 살아남는 동물은 거의 없다. / 성숙기의 연령을 지나서

(C) Together this means there are fewer eggs and larvae / to secure future generations.
동시에 이는 알이나 유충이 더 적어진다는 것을 의미한다. / 미래 세대를 보장하는

In some cases the amount of young produced today / is a hundred or even a thousand times less than in the past, / putting the survival of species, / and the fisheries dependent on them, / at grave risk.
오늘날 생산되는 어린 동물의 양이 / 과거보다 백 배나 천 배까지도 더 적어서, / 종의 생존이 처하게 되는 경우가 있다. / 그리고 그것에 의존하는 어업이 / 심각한 위기에

진화는 동물이 남기는 후손의 수를 최대화하기 위해 작용을 한다. 동물이 성장할 때 어로행위로 죽을 수 있는 위험이 증가하는 상황에서 진화는 천천히 성장하고, 더 어린 나이에 그리고 더 작을 때에 성숙하고, 더 일찍 번식하는 것을 선호한다.

(B) 이것은 정확하게 현재 우리가 야생에서 보는 것이다. 캐나다의 St. Lawrence 만에 사는 대구는 현재 네 살쯤 되었을 때 번식을 시작한다. 40년 전에 그것이 성숙기에 도달하기 위해서는 6세나 7세가 될 때까지 기다려야 했다. 북해의 가자미는 1950년에 비해 체중이 절반 정도만 되면 성숙한다.

(A) 물론 이런 적응은 지나친 어로행위로 심한 압박을 받는 종들에게 좋은 소식일까? 꼭 그런 것은 아니다. 어린 물고기는 몸집이 큰 동물보다 훨씬 더 적은 수의 알을 생산하며, 현재 많은 산업용 어업이 너무나 집약적이어서 성숙기의 연령을 지나서 2년 넘게 살아남는 동물은 거의 없다.

(C) 동시에 이는 미래 세대를 보장하는 알이나 유충이 더 적어진다는 것을 의미한다. 오늘날 생산되는 어린 동물의 양이 과거보다 백 배나 천 배까지도 더 적어서, 종의 생존, 그리고 그것에 의존하는 어업이 심각한 위기에 처하게 되는 경우가 있다.

Why? 왜 정답일까?

진화는 천천히 성장하고, 더 어리고 작을 때 성숙하고, 더 일찍 번식하는 것을 선호한다는 주어진 글 다음에, 대구와 가자미를 예로 들며 설명하는 (B)가 오고, 이런 식으로 진화하는 것이 바람직하지만은 않다고 하는 (A)가 이어진 후, 왜 바람직하지 않은지를 말하고 있는 (C)가 연결되는 것이 자연스럽다. 따라서 주어진 글 다음에 이어질 글의 순서로 가장 적절한 것은 ② '(B) - (A) - (C)'이다.

- evolution ⓝ 진화
- mature ⓥ 성숙해지다, 다 자라다
- hard-pressed 심한 압박을 받는
- intensive ⓐ 집중적인
- larvae ⓝ 유충(pl.; 단수형 larva)
- grave ⓐ 심각한
- descendant ⓝ 후손
- reproduce ⓥ 번식하다, 생식하다
- fishery ⓝ 어업
- maturity ⓝ 성숙
- secure ⓐ 안정된, 걱정 없는, 보장된

구문 풀이

19행 In some cases / the amount of young [produced today]
　　　　　　　　　　　　　　주어
is a hundred or even a thousand times less than in the past, /
동사
putting the survival of species, and the fisheries [dependent on
「put+A+at grave risk : A를 큰 위험에 처하게 하다」
them], at grave risk.

07 언어의 창의성 　정답률 54% | 정답 ④

주어진 글 다음에 이어질 글의 순서로 가장 적절한 것을 고르시오. [3점]

① (A) – (C) – (B)　② (B) – (A) – (C)
③ (B) – (C) – (A)　✔(C) – (A) – (B)
⑤ (C) – (B) – (A)

In the course of acquiring a language, / children are exposed / to only a finite set of utterances.
언어를 습득하는 과정에서 / 아이들은 접한다. / 유한한 발화만을

Yet they come to use and understand an infinite set of sentences.
하지만 그들은 무한한 문장들을 사용하고 이해하게 된다.

(C) This has been referred to / as the creative aspect of language use.
이것은 일컬어져 왔다. / 언어 사용의 창의적인 측면으로

This 'creativity' does not refer to the ability to write poetry or novels / but rather the ability to produce and understand an unlimited set of new sentences / never spoken or heard previously.
이 '창의성'은 시나 소설을 쓸 수 있는 능력을 일컫지 않는다 / 오히려 새로운 문장을 무한히 만들어내고 이해할 수 있는 능력을 일컫는다. / 이전에 결코 말하거나 듣지 못한

The precise linguistic input children receive / differs from child to child; / no two children are exposed / to exactly the same set of utterances.
아이들이 받는 정확한 언어 입력은 / 아이들마다 다르며, / 어떤 두 아이도 접하지 않는다. / 정확히 똑같은 발화를

(A) Yet, they all arrive at pretty much the same grammar.
하지만 그들은 모두 거의 동일한 문법에 도달한다.

The input that children get / is haphazard / in the sense that caretakers do not talk to their children / to illustrate a particular point of grammar.
아이들이 받는 입력은 / 무작위적이다. / 양육자들이 아이들에게 말을 하지는 않는다는 점에서 / 특정한 문법적 측면을 알려주려고

Yet, / all children develop systematic knowledge of a language.
하지만 / 모든 아이들은 언어에 대한 체계적인 지식을 발달시킨다.

(B) Thus, / despite the severe limitations and variation / in the input children receive, / and also in their personal circumstances, / they all develop a rich and uniform system of linguistic knowledge.
따라서, / 극심한 한계와 변동에도 불구하고, / 아이들이 받는 입력의 / 또한 개인적인 상황 속에서의 / 그들 모두는 언어 지식의 풍부하고 동일한 체계를 발달시킨다.

The knowledge attained / goes beyond the input in various ways.
습득된 지식은 / 다양한 방식으로 그 입력을 넘어선다.

언어를 습득하는 과정에서 아이들은 유한한 발화만을 접한다. 하지만 그들은 무한한 문장들을 사용하고 이해하게 된다.

(C) 이것은 언어 사용의 창의적인 측면으로 일컬어져 왔다. 이 '창의성'은 시나 소설을 쓸 수 있는 능력이라기보다는, 이전에 결코 말하거나 듣지 못한 새로운 문장을 무한히 만들어내고 이해할 수 있는 능력을 말한다. 아이들이 받는 정확한 언어 입력은 아이들마다 다르며, 어떤 두 아이도 정확히 똑같은 발화를 접하지 않는다.

(A) 하지만 그들은 모두 거의 동일한 문법에 도달한다. 양육자들이 아이들에게 특정한 문법적 측면을 알려주려고 말을 하지는 않는다는 점에서, 아이들이 받는 입력은 무작위적이다. 하지만 모든 아이들은 언어에 대한 체계적인 지식을 발달시킨다.

(B) 따라서, 아이들이 받는 입력과, 또한 개인적인 상황 속의 극심한 한계와 변동에도 불구하고, 그들 모두는 언어 지식의 풍부하고 동일한 체계를 발달시킨다. 습득된 지식은 다양한 방식으로 그 입력을 넘어선다.

Why? 왜 정답일까?

언어의 창의성 개념을 설명하는 글이다. 먼저 주어진 글은 아이들이 유한한 발화를 접하는데도 불구하고, 종국에는 무한한 발화를 이해하고 말할 수 있게 된다는 핵심 내용을 제시한다. (C)는 이 내용을 This라는 지시어로 받으며, 이것이 곧 '언어의 창의성'이라고 설명한 뒤, 그 어떤 아이도 동일한 입력에 노출되지는 않는다는 보충 설명을 시작한다. (A)는 Yet으로 주의를 환기하며, '그럼에도 불구하고' 아이들은 동일한 문법을 습득하고 언어에 대한 체계적 지식을 발전시킬 수 있다고 설명한다. Thus로 시작하는 (B)는 글의 전체적 결론을 요약 제시한다. 따라서 글의 순서로 가장 적절한 것은 ④ '(C) – (A) – (B)'이다.

- finite ⓐ 유한한
- input ⓝ 입력, 투입
- in the sense that ~한다는 점에서
- systematic ⓐ 체계적인
- attain ⓥ 달성하다
- poetry ⓝ 시
- unlimited ⓐ 무한한
- utterance ⓝ 발화
- haphazard ⓐ 무작위적인, 되는 대로의
- illustrate ⓥ 예를 들어 보여주다
- severe ⓐ 심각한
- be referred to as ~로 언급되다
- novel ⓝ 소설

---

08 미술 기록 보관에 관한 결정 　정답률 50% | 정답 ⑤

주어진 글 다음에 이어질 글의 순서로 가장 적절한 것을 고르시오. [3점]

① (A) – (C) – (B)　② (B) – (A) – (C)
③ (B) – (C) – (A)　④ (C) – (A) – (B)
✔(C) – (B) – (A)

It can be difficult / to decide the place of fine art, / such as oil paintings, watercolours, sketches or sculptures, / in an archival institution.
어려울 수 있다. / 순수 미술의 위치를 정하는 것은 / 유화, 수채화, 스케치, 또는 조각과 같은 / 기록 보관 기관에서

(C) Art can serve as documentary evidence, / especially when the items were produced / before photography became common.
미술은 기록 증거의 역할을 할 수 있다. / 특히 그 품목들이 생산되었을 때, / 사진 촬영이 보편화되기 전에

Sketches of soldiers on a battlefield, / paintings of English country villages / or portraits of Dutch townspeople / can provide the only visual evidence / of a long-ago place, person or time.
전쟁터에 있는 군인들의 스케치, / 영국 시골 마을의 그림 / 또는 네덜란드 시민들의 초상화는 / 유일한 시각적 증거를 제공할 수 있다. / 옛날의 장소, 사람 또는 시절의

(B) But art can also carry aesthetic value, / which elevates the job of evaluation into another realm.
그러나 미술은 또한 미적 가치를 지닐 수 있는데, / 그것은 (가치) 감정이라는 일을 다른 영역으로 격상시킨다.

Aesthetic value and the notion of artistic beauty / are important considerations, / but they are not what motivates archival preservation in the first instance.
미적 가치와 예술적 아름다움의 개념은 / 중요한 고려사항이지만, / 그것들은 기록 보존의 동기를 우선으로 부여하는 것은 아니다.

(A) The best archival decisions about art / do not focus on territoriality / (this object belongs in my institution / even though I do not have the resources to care for it) / or on questions of monetary value or prestige / (this object raises the cultural standing of my institution).
미술에 관한 최선의 기록 보관 결정은 / 영토권에 초점을 두지 않는다. / (이 물건은 내 기관에 속해 있다 / 내가 그것을 돌볼 자원이 없더라도) / 혹은 금전적 가치나 위신의 문제에 / (이 물건은 내 기관의 문화적 지위를 높인다)

The best decisions focus on / what evidential value exists / and what is best for the item.
최선의 결정은 초점을 맞춘다. / 어떤 증거 가치가 존재하고 / 그 품목에 무엇이 최선인지에

유화, 수채화, 스케치, 또는 조각과 같은 순수 미술의 위치를 기록 보관 기관에서 정하는 것은 어려울 수 있다.

(C) 미술은 특히 사진 촬영이 보편화되기 전에 그 품목들이 생산되었을 때 기록 증거의 역할을 할 수 있다. 전쟁터에 있는 군인들의 스케치, 영국 시골 마을의 그림 또는 네덜란드 시민들의 초상화는 옛날의 장소, 사람 또는 시절의 유일한 시각적 증거를 제공할 수 있다.

(B) 그러나 미술은 또한 미적 가치를 지닐 수 있는데, 그것은 (가치) 감정이라는 일을 다른 영역으로 격상시킨다. 미적 가치와 예술적 아름다움의 개념은 중요한 고려사항이지만, 그것들은 기록 보존의 동기를 우선으로 부여하는 것은 아니다.

(A) 미술에 관한 최선의 기록 보관 결정은 영토권(이 물건은 내가 그것을 돌볼 자원이 없더라도 내 기관에 속해 있다)이나 금전적 가치나 위신의 문제(이 물건은 내 기관의 문화적 지위를 높인다)에 초점을 두지 않는다. 최선의 결정은 어떤 증거 가치가 존재하고 그 품목에 무엇이 최선인지에 초점을 맞춘다.

Why? 왜 정답일까?

미술의 위치를 기록 보관 기관에서 결정하기는 어렵다는 일반론을 제시하는 주어진 글 뒤에는, 미술의 기록적 가치를 언급하는 (C), But으로 흐름을 뒤집으며 미술이 또한 미적 가치를 지니고 있지만 그러한 이유로 우선 보존 여부가 결정되지는 않는다고 설명하는 (B), 결론적으로 최선의 미술 기록 보관 결정은 증거 가치와 그 품목의 적절성 여부에 따라 내려지게 된다고 설명하는 (A)가 차례로 이어져야 한다. 따라서 글의 순서로 가장 적절한 것은 ⑤ '(C) – (B) – (A)'이다.

- fine art 미술
- watercolour ⓝ 수채화
- institution ⓝ 기관
- monetary ⓐ 금전적인
- aesthetic ⓐ 미적인
- preservation ⓝ 보존
- serve ⓥ 도움이 되다, 기여하다
- portrait ⓝ 초상화, 인물 사진
- oil painting 유화
- sculpture ⓝ 조각(품)
- territoriality ⓝ 영토권, 세력권
- evidential ⓐ 증거가 되는, 증거에 입각한
- elevate ⓥ 격상시키다, 높이다
- in the first instance 우선 먼저
- documentary ⓐ 기록의
- townspeople ⓝ 시민

4행 The best archival decisions about art do not focus
　　　　주어(복수)　　　　　　　　　　　동사
on territoriality (this object belongs in my institution even though
전명구1　　　　　　　　　　　　　　　　　양보 접속사(비록 ~이지만)
I do not have the resources to care for it) or on questions of monetary
　　　　　　　　　　　　　　　　　　전명구2
value or prestige (this object raises the cultural standing of my
institution).

★★★ 1등급 대비 고난도 2점 문제

09 단어의 언어적 '성별'에 따른 사물에 대한 인식 차이　정답률 50% | 정답 ②

주어진 글 다음에 이어질 글의 순서로 가장 적절한 것을 고르시오.

① (A) − (C) − (B)　　　　☑ (B) − (A) − (C)
③ (B) − (C) − (A)　　　　④ (C) − (A) − (B)
⑤ (C) − (B) − (A)

Shakespeare wrote, / "What's in a name? / That which we call a rose / by any other name / would smell as sweet."
셰익스피어는 썼다. / "이름이 뭐가 중요한가요? / 우리가 장미라고 부르는 것은 / 그 어떤 다른 이름으로 부르더라도 / 그만큼 달콤한 향이 날 거에요."라고

(B) According to Stanford University psychology professor Lera Boroditsky, / that's not necessarily so.
Stanford 대학교의 심리학 교수인 Lera Boroditsky에 따르면, / 그게 꼭 그렇지는 않다.

Focusing on the grammatical gender differences between German and Spanish, / Boroditsky's work indicates / that the gender our language assigns to a given noun / influences us to subconsciously give that noun / characteristics of the grammatical gender.
독일어와 스페인어 간의 문법적 성 차이에 초점을 맞춘 / Boroditsky의 연구에 따르면, / 우리의 언어가 특정 명사에 부여하는 성 / 우리가 무의식적으로 그 명사에 부여하도록 영향을 미친다. / 문법적 성의 특성을

(A) Take the word *bridge*.
*다리*라는 단어를 보자.

In German, *bridge* (die brücke) is a feminine noun; / in Spanish, *bridge* (el puente) is a masculine noun.
독일어로 *다리*(die brücke)는 여성 명사이지만, / 스페인어로 *다리*(el puente)는 남성 명사이다.

Boroditsky found / that when asked to describe a bridge, / native German speakers used words like *beautiful, elegant, slender*.
Boroditsky는 알아냈다. / 다리를 묘사하라는 요청을 받았을 때, / 독일어 원어민은 *아름다운, 우아한, 날씬한* 같은 단어를 사용한다는 사실을

When native Spanish speakers were asked the same question, / they used words like *strong, sturdy, towering*.
스페인어 원어민이 같은 질문을 받았을 때, / 그들은 *강한, 튼튼한, 우뚝 솟은* 같은 단어를 사용했다.

(C) This worked the other way around as well.
이것은 반대의 경우에도 마찬가지였다.

The word *key* is masculine in German and feminine in Spanish.
*열쇠*라는 단어는 독일어에서는 남성형이고 스페인어에서는 여성형이다.

When asked to describe a key, / native German speakers used words like *jagged, heavy, hard, metal*.
*열쇠*를 묘사하라는 요청을 받았을 때, / 독일어 원어민은 *뾰족뾰족한, 무거운, 단단한, 금속의* 같은 단어를 사용했다.

Spanish speakers used words like *intricate, golden, lovely*.
스페인어 사용자는 *정교한, 황금빛의, 사랑스러운* 같은 단어를 사용했다.

―――――――――――――――――――――

셰익스피어는 "이름이 뭐가 중요한가요? 우리가 장미라고 부르는 것은 그 어떤 다른 이름으로 부르더라도 똑같이 달콤한 향이 날 거예요."라고 썼다.

(B) Stanford 대학교의 심리학 교수인 Lera Boroditsky에 따르면, 그게 꼭 그렇지는 않다. 독일어와 스페인어 간의 문법적 성 차이에 초점을 맞춘 Boroditsky의 연구에 따르면, 우리의 언어가 특정 명사에 부여하는 성은 우리가 무의식적으로 그 명사에 문법적 성의 특성을 부여하도록 영향을 미친다.

(A) *다리*라는 단어를 보자. 독일어로 *다리*(die brücke)는 여성 명사이지만, 스페인어로 *다리*(el puente)는 남성 명사이다. Boroditsky는 독일어 원어민이 다리를 묘사하라는 요청을 받았을 때, *아름다운, 우아한, 날씬한* 같은 단어를 사용한다는 사실을 알아냈다. 같은 질문을 받았을 때, 스페인어 원어민은 *강한, 튼튼한, 우뚝 솟은* 같은 단어를 사용했다.

(C) 이것은 반대의 경우에도 마찬가지였다. *열쇠*라는 단어는 독일어에서는 남성형이고 스페인어에서는 여성형이다. 독일어 원어민이 열쇠를 묘사하라는 요청을 받았을 때, *뾰족뾰족한, 무거운, 단단한, 금속의* 같은 단어를 사용했다. 스페인어 사용자는 *정교한, 황금빛의, 사랑스러운* 같은 단어를 사용했다.

주어진 글에서 셰익스피어의 인용구를 들어 사물의 이름이 무엇이든 그 본질적 특성은 변하지 않을 것이라는 화제를 꺼낸다. (B)는 이를 반박하면서(that's not necessarily so) 실제로는 사물에 언어적으로 어떤 성을 부여했는가에 따라 사물에 대한 인식이 달라질 수 있다고 한다. (A)는 '다리'라는 단어를 놓고 독일어와 스페인어를 비교하고 있으며, (C)는 (A)와 대비되는 예시로 '열쇠'를 언급하고 있다. 따라서 글의 순서로 가장 적절한 것은 ② '(B) − (A) − (C)'이다.

● feminine ⓐ 여성의　　　　● masculine ⓐ 남성의
● slender ⓐ 날씬한　　　　　● sturdy ⓐ 튼튼한
● towering ⓐ 우뚝 솟은　　　● grammatical ⓐ 문법적인
● gender ⓝ 성별　　　　　　● indicate ⓥ 나타내다
● assign ⓥ 부여하다　　　　● given ⓐ 특정한
● subconsciously ⓐⓓ 무의식적으로　● characteristic ⓝ 특성
● the other way around 반대로, 거꾸로　● jagged ⓐ 뾰족뾰족한
● intricate ⓐ 정교한

1행 Shakespeare wrote, "What's in a name? That [which we call
　　　　　　　　　　　　　　　　　　대명사　목적격 관·대
a rose] (by any other name) would smell as sweet."
　　　부사구

★★ 문제 해결 꿀~팁 ★★

▶ 많이 틀린 이유는?
주어진 글이 (C)의 This로 이어지는 것처럼 보일 수도 있지만, '뭐가 반대로도 작용하는지'가 명확하지 않아 부자연스럽다.

▶ 문제 해결 방법은?
(C)의 the other way around as well 앞뒤로 (A)의 '다리', (C)의 '열쇠'가 서로 대비되는 사례로 연결되는 것임을 파악해야 한다. (B)는 일반적인 내용이므로, '일반적 진술 → 구체적 진술'의 흐름상 예시에 해당하는 (A) − (C)보다 앞에 와야 한다.

★★★ 1등급 대비 고난도 3점 문제

10 복수 균형의 예시　정답률 33% | 정답 ⑤

주어진 글 다음에 이어질 글의 순서로 가장 적절한 것을 고르시오. [3점]

① (A) − (C) − (B)　　　　② (B) − (A) − (C)
③ (B) − (C) − (A)　　　　④ (C) − (A) − (B)
☑ (C) − (B) − (A)

A firm is deciding whether to invest in shipbuilding.
한 회사가 조선업에 투자할지를 결정하고 있다.

If it can produce at sufficiently large scale, / it knows the venture will be profitable.
만약 충분히 대규모로 생산할 수 있다면, / 그것은 그 모험이 수익성이 있을 거라는 것을 알고 있다.

(C) But one key input is low-cost steel, / and it must be produced nearby.
하지만 한 가지 핵심 투입 요소는 저가의 강철이고, / 그것은 근처에서 생산되어야 한다.

The company's decision boils down to this: / if there is a steel factory close by, / invest in shipbuilding; / otherwise, don't invest.
그 회사의 결정은 결국 다음과 같다. / 만약 근처에 강철 공장이 있다면, / 조선업에 투자하고, / 그렇지 않으면 투자하지 말라.

Now consider the thinking of potential steel investors in the region.
이제 그 지역에 있는 잠재적 강철 투자자들의 생각을 고려해 보라.

(B) Assume / that shipyards are the only potential customers of steel.
가정하라. / 조선소가 유일한 잠재적 강철 소비자라고

Steel producers figure / they'll make money / if there's a shipyard to buy their steel, / but not otherwise.
강철 생산자들은 생각한다. / 자신이 돈을 벌 것이고, / 자신의 강철을 구매할 조선소가 있으면 / 그렇지 않으면 돈을 벌지 못하리라고

Now we have two possible outcomes / — what economists call "multiple equilibria."
이제 우리는 가능한 두 가지 결과를 갖게 된다 / 경제학자들이 '복수균형'이라고 부르는

(A) There is a "good" outcome, / in which both types of investments are made, / and both the shipyard and the steelmakers / end up profitable and happy.
'좋은' 결과가 있는데, / 그 결과 내에서는 두 가지 투자 형태가 모두 이루어지고, / 조선소와 제강업자 모두 / 결국 이득을 얻고 만족하게 된다.

Equilibrium is reached.
균형이 이루어지는 것이다.

Then there is a "bad" outcome, / in which neither type of investment is made.

그다음에 '나쁜' 결과가 있는데, / 그 결과 내에서는 (둘 중) 어떤 투자 형태도 이루어지지 않는다.
This second outcome also is an equilibrium / because the decisions not to invest reinforce each other.
이 두 번째 결과 또한 균형이 이루어진 것인데, / 왜냐하면 투자하지 않겠다는 결정이 서로를 강화하기 때문이다.

한 회사가 조선업에 투자할지를 결정하고 있다. 만약 충분히 대규모로 생산할 수 있다면, 그 (사업상의) 모험이 수익성이 있을 거라는 것을 알고 있다.

(C) 하지만 한 가지 핵심 투입 요소는 저가의 강철이고, 그것은 근처에서 생산되어야 한다. 그 회사의 결정은 결국 다음과 같다. 만약 근처에 강철 공장이 있다면 조선업에 투자하고, 그렇지 않으면 투자하지 말라는 것이다. 이제 그 지역에 있는 잠재적 강철 투자자들의 생각을 고려해 보라.

(B) 조선소가 유일한 잠재적 강철 소비자라고 가정하라. 강철 생산자들은 자신의 강철을 구매할 조선소가 있으면 자신이 돈을 벌 것이고, 그렇지 않으면 돈을 벌지 못하리라고 생각한다. 이제 우리는 경제학자들이 '복수균형'이라고 부르는 가능한 두 가지 결과를 갖게 된다.

(A) '좋은' 결과가 있는데, 그 결과 내에서는 두 가지 투자 형태가 모두 이루어지고, 조선소와 제강업자 모두 결국 이득을 얻고 만족하게 된다. 균형이 이루어지는 것이다. 그다음에 '나쁜' 결과가 있는데, 그 결과 내에서는 (둘 중) 어떤 투자 형태도 이루어지지 않는다. 이 두 번째 결과 또한 균형이 이루어진 것인데, 왜냐하면 투자하지 않겠다는 결정이 서로를 강화하기 때문이다.

Why? 왜 정답일까?

조선업 투자를 고민하고 있는 한 회사를 언급하는 주어진 글 뒤로, 투자 여부의 핵심 요소는 싼 강철을 근처에서 공급받을 수 있는지이기 때문에 주변에 강철 공장이 있는지에 따라 투자 여부가 결정될 것이라는 내용의 (C)가 먼저 연결된다. 한편 (C)의 마지막 문장은 이제 같은 지역의 강철 투자자들 입장을 생각해 보자는 내용인데, (B)의 첫 문장은 조선소가 이들의 유일한 소비자일 때를 가정해 보자고 언급하며 (C)와 자연스럽게 이어진다. 마지막으로 (A)는 (B)의 마지막 문장에서 언급된 '복수 균형'의 내용을 '좋은' 결과와 '나쁜' 결과로 나누어 설명한다. 따라서 글의 순서로 가장 적절한 것은 ⑤ '(C) – (B) – (A)'이다.

- shipbuilding ⓝ 조선(업)
- scale ⓝ 규모
- outcome ⓝ 결과
- shipyard ⓝ 조선소
- reinforce ⓥ 강화하다
- otherwise ⓐⓓ 그렇지 않으면
- investor ⓝ 투자자
- sufficiently ⓐⓓ 충분히
- profitable ⓐ 수익성 있는
- investment ⓝ 투자
- steelmaker ⓝ 제강업자
- assume ⓥ 가정하다
- boil down to 결국 ~이다, ~로 요약되다

구문 풀이

> **4행** There is a "good" outcome, in which both types of
> 　　　　선행사　　　계속적 용법(= where)　　주어1
> investments are made, and both the shipyard and the steelmakers
> 　　동사1　　　　주어2(both+A+and+B : A와 B 둘 다)
> end up profitable and happy.
> 「end up + 형 : 결국 ~한 상태가 되다」

★★ 문제 해결 꿀~팁 ★★

▶ 많이 틀린 이유는?
주어진 글에서 조선업을 시작할지 말지 결정하려는 회사에 관해 언급하고 있으므로, 뒤따르는 단락 또한 이 회사의 입장을 다뤄야 한다. (B)는 '조선소'를 언급하지만 자세히 보면 '강철 생산자'의 입장을 다루고 있으므로 주어진 글에 바로 연결되기에 적합하지 않다.

▶ 문제 해결 방법은?
(C)의 The company가 주어진 글에서 언급된 A firm을 가리키고, (C)의 마지막 문장에 언급된 potential steel investors가 (B)의 Steel producers로 이어진다는 점을 파악하면 (C) – (B)를 쉽게 연결할 수 있다.

★★★ 1등급 대비 고난도 3점 문제

| **11** 규범의 형성 | 정답률 34% \| 정답 ④ |

주어진 글 다음에 이어질 글의 순서로 가장 적절한 것을 고르시오. [3점]
① (A) – (C) – (B)
② (B) – (A) – (C)
③ (B) – (C) – (A)
✔ (C) – (A) – (B)
⑤ (C) – (B) – (A)

Norms emerge in groups / as a result of people conforming to the behavior of others.
규범은 집단에서 생겨난다. / 사람들이 다른 사람들의 행동에 순응하는 결과로
Thus, / the start of a norm occurs / when one person acts in a particular manner in a particular situation / because she thinks she ought to.
따라서 / 규범의 시작은 발생한다. / 한 사람이 특정 상황에서 특정 방식으로 행동할 때 / 자신이 그래야 한다고 생각하여
(C) Others may then conform to this behavior / for a number of reasons.
그런 다음 다른 사람들은 이 행동에 순응할 수도 있다. / 여러 가지 이유로
The person who performed the initial action / may think / that others ought to behave as she behaves / in situations of this sort.
최초의 행동을 한 사람은 / 생각할 수도 있다. / 다른 사람들이 자신이 행동하는 것처럼 행동해야 한다고 / 이런 종류의 상황에서
(A) Thus, / she may prescribe the behavior to them / by uttering the norm statement in a prescriptive manner.
따라서 / 그 사람은 그들에게 행동을 지시할 수도 있다. / 지시하는 방식으로 규범 진술을 말하여
Alternately, / she may communicate / that conformity is desired / in other ways, such as by gesturing.
아니면 / 그 사람은 전달할 수도 있다. / 순응이 요망된다는 것을 / 몸짓과 같은 다른 방식으로
In addition, / she may threaten to sanction them / for not behaving as she wishes.
게다가 / 그 사람은 그들에게 제재를 가하겠다고 위협할 수도 있다. / 자신이 원하는 대로 행동하지 않으면
This will cause some / to conform to her wishes / and act as she acts.
이것은 일부 사람들이 ~하게 한다. / 그 사람의 바람에 순응하고 / 그 사람이 행동하는 대로 행동하게
(B) But some others will not need / to have the behavior prescribed to them.
그러나 다른 일부 사람들은 필요 없을 것이다. / 자신한테 그 행동이 지시되게 할
They will observe the regularity of behavior / and decide on their own / that they ought to conform.
그들은 행동의 규칙성을 관찰하고 / 스스로 결정할 것이다. / 자신이 순응해야 한다고
They may do so / for either rational or moral reasons.
그들은 그렇게 할 수도 있다. / 이성적 또는 도덕적 이유로

규범은 사람들이 다른 사람들의 행동에 순응하는 결과로 집단에서 생겨난다. 따라서 규범의 시작은 한 사람이 특정 상황에서 자신이 그래야 한다고 생각하여 특정 방식으로 행동할 때 발생한다.

(C) 그런 다음 다른 사람들은 여러 가지 이유로 이 행동에 순응할 수도 있다. 최초의 행동을 한 사람은 다른 사람들이 이런 종류의 상황에서 자신이 행동하는 것처럼 행동해야 한다고 생각할 수도 있다.

(A) 따라서 그 사람은 지시하는 방식으로 규범 진술을 말하여 그들에게 행동을 지시할 수도 있다. 아니면 몸짓 같은 다른 방식으로 순응이 요망된다는 것을 전달할 수도 있다. 게다가 자신이 원하는 대로 행동하지 않으면 그들에게 제재를 가하겠다고 위협할 수도 있다. 이렇게 하면 일부 사람들은 그 사람의 바람에 순응하고 그 사람이 행동하는 대로 행동할 것이다.

(B) 그러나 다른 일부 사람들은 그 행동을 지시받을 필요가 없을 것이다. 그들은 행동의 규칙성을 관찰하고 순응해야 한다고 스스로 결정할 것이다. 그들은 이성적 또는 도덕적 이유로 그렇게 할 수도 있다.

Why? 왜 정답일까?

한 사람이 규범의 시작을 유도하는 상황을 언급한 주어진 글 뒤로, (C)는 다른 사람들이 '그런 다음' 여러 이유로 이 규범에 동참할 수 있다고 설명한다. (C) 후반부와 (A) 초반부에서 '최초의 사람'이 공통적으로 언급되므로, (C) 다음에 (A)가 온다는 것을 알 수 있는데, (A)는 이 사람이 타인에게 규범 진술이나 위협 등의 수단으로 순응을 요구할 수 있다고 설명한다. (B)는 (A)와는 상반되는 예시로 최초의 사람이 행동을 지시하지 않아도 되는 '다른' 사람들에 관해 언급한다. 따라서 글의 순서로 가장 적절한 것은 ④ '(C) – (A) – (B)'이다.

- norm ⓝ 규범
- conform to ~에 순응하다, ~을 따르다
- prescribe ⓥ 지시하다, 규정하다
- prescriptive ⓐ 지시하는
- conformity ⓝ 순응
- sanction ⓥ 제재를 가하다
- regularity ⓝ 규칙성
- moral ⓐ 도덕적인
- sort ⓝ 종류, 부류
- emerge ⓥ 생기다, 출현하다
- ought to ~해야 하다
- utter ⓥ 말하다, 발화하다
- alternately ⓐⓓ 그렇지 않으면
- threaten ⓥ 위협하다, 협박하다
- observe ⓥ 관찰하다
- rational ⓐ 이성적인, 합리적인
- initial ⓐ 최초의

구문 풀이

> **1행** Norms emerge in groups as a result of people conforming
> 　　　　　　　　　　　전치사　　　의미상 주어　　동명사
> to the behavior of others.

★★ 문제 해결 꿀~팁 ★★

▶ 많이 틀린 이유는?

(C) 후반부의 others가 (B)의 But some others와 대비되는 맥락처럼 보여 ⑤ '(C) – (B) – (A)'를 고르기 쉽다. 하지만 이 경우 (A)의 she가 누구인지 모호해 진다. 문맥상 이 she는 '규범을 처음 시행하는' 사람인데, (C)에서 이 최초 시행자가 언급된 후 (B)에서는 언급되지 않기 때문에, 대명사와 원래 명사의 거리가 너무 멀어 지기 때문이다.

▶ 문제 해결 방법은?

(B)에서 But some others로 화제를 전환하기 전에, '규범을 최초로 행한' 사람을 she로 받아 연속성 있게 설명하는 (C) – (A)가 서로 연결되어야 한다.

★★★ 1등급 대비 고난도 3점 문제

12 원시인들에게 있어 질병의 의미 정답률 31% | 정답 ④

주어진 글 다음에 이어질 글의 순서로 가장 적절한 것을 고르시오. [3점]

① (A) – (C) – (B)
② (B) – (A) – (C)
③ (B) – (C) – (A)
✔④(C) – (A) – (B)
⑤ (C) – (B) – (A)

To modern man / disease is a biological phenomenon / that concerns him only as an individual / and has no moral implications.
현대인에게 / 질병은 생물학적 현상이고 / 개인으로서만 관련 있는 / 어떤 도덕적 함의를 지니지 않는다.

When he contracts influenza, / he never attributes this event to his behavior / toward the tax collector or his mother-in-law.
개인은 인플루엔자에 걸렸을 때 / 이 사건을 결코 자신의 행동 탓으로 보지 않는다. / 세금 징수원 또는 장모에 대한

(C) Among primitives, because of their supernaturalistic theories, / the prevailing moral point of view / gives a deeper meaning to disease.
원시인들 사이에서는 그들의 초자연적인 생각 때문에 / 지배적인 도덕적 관념이 / 질병에 대해 더 깊은 의미를 제공한다.

The gods who send disease are usually angered / by the moral offences of the individual.
질병을 보내는 신들은 일반적으로 분노한다. / 개인의 도덕적 범죄에 대해

(A) Sometimes they may not strike the guilty person himself, / but rather one of his relatives or tribesmen, / to whom responsibility is extended.
때때로 그들은 죄가 있는 사람 본인이 아니라, / 대신에 친척이나 부족민 중 한 명을 공격할지도 모른다. / (죄의) 책임이 확장되는

Disease, action that might produce disease, and recovery from disease / are, therefore, of vital concern to the whole primitive community.
질병과, 질병을 일으켰을지도 모르는 행위, 질병으로부터의 회복은 / 따라서 전체 원시 사회에 매우 중요하다.

(B) Disease, as a sanction against social misbehavior, / becomes one of the most important pillars of order in such societies.
사회적 부정행위에 대한 제재로서의 질병은 / 그런 사회에서 질서의 가장 중요한 부분 중 하나가 되었다.

It takes over, in many cases, the role / played by policemen, judges, and priests in modern society.
많은 경우에 이는 역할을 떠안는다. / 현대 사회의 경찰관과 재판관, 사제가 행하는

현대인에게 질병은 개인으로서만 관련 있는 생물학적 현상이고 어떤 도덕적 함의를 지니지 않는다. 개인은 인플루엔자에 걸렸을 때 이 사건을 결코 세금 징수원 또는 장모에 대한 자신의 행동 탓으로 보지 않는다.

(C) 원시인들 사이에서는 그들의 초자연적인 생각 때문에 지배적인 도덕적 관념이 질병에 대해 더 깊은 의미를 제공한다. 질병을 보내는 신들은 일반적으로 개인의 도덕적 범죄에 대해 분노한다.

(A) 때때로 그들은 죄가 있는 사람 본인이 아니라, 대신에 (죄의) 책임이 확장되는 친척이나 부족민 중 한 명을 공격할지도 모른다. 따라서 질병과, 질병을 일으켰을지도 모르는 행위, 질병으로부터의 회복은 전체 원시 사회에 매우 중요하다.

(B) 사회적 부정행위에 대한 제재로서의 질병은 그런 사회에서 질서의 가장 중요한 부분 중 하나가 되었다. 많은 경우에 이는 현대 사회의 경찰관과 재판관, 사제가 행하는 역할을 떠안는다.

Why? 왜 정답일까?

현대인에게 질병은 도덕적인 의미를 갖는 현상이라기보다는 생물학적 현상으로 이해된 다는 내용의 주어진 글 뒤에는, 원시인들의 경우 질병을 도덕적인 범죄와 연결지어 생각 했다는 내용의 (C), 때때로 이 질병은 죄를 지은 사람 본인뿐 아니라 주변인으로도 확장 될 여지가 있다고 여겨졌기에 전체 사회에 중요한 의미를 가졌다는 내용의 (A), 그리하여

원시 사회의 질병은 사회적 제재로서의 기능을 담당했다는 내용의 (B)가 차례로 이어져 야 자연스럽다. 따라서 글의 순서로 가장 적절한 것은 ④ '(C) – (A) – (B)'이다.

- **phenomenon** ⓝ 현상
- **contract** ⓥ (병 등에) 걸리다
- **tribesman** ⓝ 부족 구성원
- **supernaturalistic** ⓐ 초자연적인
- **offence** ⓝ 범죄, 위법 행위
- **concern** ⓥ 관련시키다
- **attribute** ⓥ ~의 탓으로 돌리다
- **pillar** ⓝ (시스템·조직의) 기본적인 부분
- **prevailing** ⓐ 지배적인, 우세한

구문 풀이

6행 Sometimes they may not strike the guilty person himself, _{┌not A} but rather one of his relatives or tribesmen, [to whom responsibility is extended].
but (rather) B : A가 아니라 B / 「전치사 + 관계대명사」

★★ 문제 해결 꿀~팁 ★★

▶ 많이 틀린 이유는?

이 글은 '원시인의 질병에 대한 시각'을 설명하기 위해 '현대인의 시각'을 먼저 언급한 다. 주어진 글에서 현대인에게 질병은 생물학적으로 이해된다는 내용을 말한 뒤, (C) 에서는 'primitives'라는 주체를 처음 제시하며 '원시인의 경우 달랐다'는 내용을 설 명하고, (A) – (B)는 이 맥락을 이어간다. 최다 오답은 ②였는데 (B)는 'a sanction against social misbehavior', 즉 질병을 범죄 행위에 대한 처벌로서 보았던 원 시인들의 관점에 관해 흐름을 전환하는 연결어 없이 언급하고 있어 주어진 글에 연결 되기 적절하지 않다. 또한 주어진 글에서는 '현대 사회'에 대해서 말하고 있기 때문에 (B)를 여기 바로 연결할 경우 'such societies'가 '현대 사회'를 가리키게 되어 흐 름이 틀어진다.

▶ 문제 해결 방법은?

해석에만 의존하기보다 대명사, 지시사 등 분명한 단서에 근거하여 답안을 고르도록 한다.

DAY 15 　글의 순서 05

01 ②	02 ⑤	03 ⑤	04 ⑤	05 ④
06 ②	07 ③	08 ②	09 ③	10 ③
11 ⑤	12 ④			

01 　환경세 부과의 배경과 결과　정답률 66% | 정답 ②

주어진 글 다음에 이어질 글의 순서로 가장 적절한 것을 고르시오.
① (A) − (C) − (B)　　✔ ② (B) − (A) − (C)
③ (B) − (C) − (A)　　④ (C) − (A) − (B)
⑤ (C) − (B) − (A)

According to the market response model, / it is increasing prices / that drive providers to search for new sources, / innovators to substitute, / consumers to conserve, / and alternatives to emerge.
시장 반응 모형에 따르면, / 바로 가격의 인상이다. / 공급자가 새로운 공급원을 찾게 하고, / 혁신가가 대응하게 하고, / 소비자가 아껴 쓰게 하고, / 대안이 생기게 하는 것은

(B) Taxing certain goods or services, / and so increasing prices, / should result in either decreased use of these resources / or creative innovation of new sources or options.
특정 재화나 서비스에 과세하여 / 가격을 인상시키는 것은 / 이러한 자원의 사용이 줄어드는 결과를 낳을 것이다. / 혹은 새로운 공급원 또는 선택사항의 창조적 혁신을

The money raised through the tax / can be used directly by the government / either to supply services or to search for alternatives.
세금을 통해 조성된 돈은 / 정부에 의해 직접 사용될 수 있다. / 서비스를 공급하거나 대안을 모색하는 데

(A) Many examples of such "green taxes" exist.
그러한 '환경세'의 많은 예가 존재한다.

Facing landfill costs, / labor expenses, / and related costs in the provision of garbage disposal, / for example, / some cities have required households / to dispose of all waste in special trash bags, / purchased by consumers themselves, / and often costing a dollar or more each.
쓰레기 매립 비용에 직면한 / 인건비나 / 그리고 쓰레기 처리를 준비하는 데 관련된 비용에 / 예를 들어, / 일부 도시는 가정에 요구했는데, / 모든 폐기물을 특별 쓰레기 봉투에 담아서 처리하도록 / 이는 소비자가 직접 구입하는 것이며 / 한 장당 1달러 이상의 비용이 드는 것이었다.

(C) The results have been greatly increased recycling / and more careful attention by consumers to packaging and waste.
그 결과는 재활용을 크게 증가시켰다. / 그리고 포장과 폐기물에 대한 소비자의 더 세심한 주의(를 낳았다)

By internalizing the costs of trash to consumers, / there has been an observed decrease / in the flow of garbage from households.
소비자에게 쓰레기 비용을 자기 것으로 만들게 함으로써, / 감소가 관찰되었다. / 가정에서 나오는 쓰레기 흐름의

시장 반응 모형에 따르면, 공급자가 새로운 공급원을 찾게 하고, 혁신가가 대용하게 하고, 소비자가 아껴 쓰게 하고, 대안이 생기게 하는 것은 바로 가격의 인상이다.

(B) 특정 재화나 서비스에 과세하여 가격이 인상되면 이러한 자원의 사용이 줄거나 새로운 공급원 또는 선택사항의 창조적 혁신을 낳을 것이다. 세금을 통해 조성된 돈은 정부가 직접 서비스를 공급하거나 대안을 모색하는 데 사용할 수 있다.

(A) 그러한 '환경세'의 많은 예가 존재한다. 예를 들어, 쓰레기 매립 비용, 인건비, 쓰레기 처리를 준비하는 데 관련된 비용에 직면한 일부 도시는 가정이 모든 폐기물을 특별 쓰레기 봉투에 담아서 처리하도록 요구했는데, 이는 소비자가 직접 구입하는 것이며 한 장당 1달러 이상의 비용이 드는 것이었다.

(C) 그 결과 재활용이 크게 증가했고 소비자가 포장과 폐기물에 더 세심한 주의를 기울이게 되었다. 소비자에게 쓰레기 비용을 자기 것으로 만들게 함으로써, 가정에서 나오는 쓰레기 흐름의 감소가 관찰되었다.

Why? 왜 정답일까?

주어진 글에서 어떤 것을 아껴 쓰게 하거나 그 대안을 찾게 하려면 비용을 증가시키게 된다고 언급한 데 이어, **(B)**에서는 보다 구체적으로 특정 재화나 서비스에 '과세'를 하여 비용을 증가시키면 혁신이 일어날 수 있다고 설명한다. 이어서 **(A)**는 '환경세'의 다양한 예를 들고, **(C)**에서는 다양한 환경세를 부과한 결과 사람들이 재활용과 쓰레기 처리에 더 주의하는 결과가 나타났음을 제시한다. 따라서 글의 순서로 가장 적절한 것은 ② '**(B)** − **(A)** − **(C)**'이다.

● substitute ⓥ 대체하다　　● conserve ⓥ 아끼다, 보존하다

● emerge ⓥ 생겨나다, 나타나다　　● green tax ⓝ 환경세
● landfill ⓝ 쓰레기 매립지　　● expense ⓝ 비용
● provision ⓝ 제공, 공급　　● disposal ⓝ (없애기 위한) 처리
● result in ~을 초래하다　　● internalize ⓥ 내재화하다

구문 풀이

5행 Facing landfill costs, labor expenses, and related costs in
〔분사구문〕
the provision of garbage disposal, for example, some cities
　　　　　　　　　　　　　　　　　　　　〔주어〕
have required households to dispose of all waste in special trash bags,
〔5형식 동사〕　　〔목적어〕　　　〔목적격 보어〕　　　　　　〔선행사〕
(which are) purchased by consumers themselves, and often costing
〔생략(계속적 용법)〕　　〔보어1〕
a dollar or more each.
〔보어2〕

02 　정치에 대한 무지와 불합리　정답률 51% | 정답 ⑤

주어진 글 다음에 이어질 글의 순서로 가장 적절한 것을 고르시오.
① (A) − (C) − (B)　　② (B) − (A) − (C)
③ (B) − (C) − (A)　　④ (C) − (A) − (B)
✔ ⑤ (C) − (B) − (A)

Ever since the first scientific opinion polls revealed / that most Americans are at best poorly informed about politics, / analysts have asked / whether citizens are equipped to play the role / democracy assigns them.
최초의 과학적 여론 조사가 밝힌 이후에, / 대부분의 미국인들이 정치에 대해서 기껏해야 형편없이 알고 있다는 것을 / 분석가들은 물었다. / 시민들이 역할을 할 능력이 있는지 / 민주주의가 자신에게 부여한

(C) However, / there is something worse / than an inadequately informed public, / and that's a misinformed public.
그런데 / 더 해로운 것이 있는데, / 불충분하게 알고 있는 대중보다 / 그것은 잘못 알고 있는 대중이다.

It's one thing / when citizens don't know something, / and realize it, / which has always been a problem.
한 가지 경우인데, / 시민들이 어떤 것을 모르고 있다가 / 그것을 깨닫는 경우가 / 이는 늘 문제가 되어 온 것이다.

It's another thing / when citizens don't know something, / but think they know it, / which is the new problem.
또 다른 경우인데, / 시민들이 어떤 것을 알지 못하지만 / 그것을 알고 있다고 생각하는 경우는 / 이는 새로운 문제이다.

(B) It's the difference / between ignorance and irrationality.
그것은 차이이다. / 무지와 불합리 간의

Whatever else one might conclude about self-government, / it's at risk / when citizens don't know / what they're talking about.
자치에 관해 다른 어떤 것으로 결론을 내리든, / 위험하다. / 시민들이 모르는 경우는 / 스스로 무슨 말을 하고 있는지를

Our misinformation owes partly to psychological factors, / including our tendency to see the world / in ways that suit our desires.
우리가 잘못 아는 것은 부분적으로는 심리적 요인의 탓이다. / 우리가 세상을 바라보는 경향을 포함하는 / 자신의 갈망에 맞는 방식으로

(A) Such factors, however, / can explain only the misinformation / that has always been with us.
하지만 그런 요인들은 / 잘못된 앎만 설명할 수 있다. / 늘 우리와 함께 있어온

The sharp rise in misinformation in recent years / has a different source: / our media.
최근에 잘못된 앎의 급격한 증가에는 / 다른 원인이 있는데, / (그것은) 우리의 미디어이다.

"They are making us dumb," / says one observer.
"그들은 우리를 어리석게 만들고 있습니다."라고 / 한 논평자는 말한다.

When fact bends to fiction, / the predictable result is political distrust and polarization.
사실이 허구에 굴복하면, / 예견 가능한 결과는 정치적 불신과 대립이다.

최초의 과학적 여론 조사가 대부분의 미국인들이 정치에 대해서 기껏해야 형편없이 알고 있다는 것을 밝힌 이후에, 분석가들은 시민들이 민주주의가 자신들에게 부여한 역할을 할 능력이 있는지 물었다.

(C) 그런데 불충분하게 알고 있는 대중보다 더 해로운 것이 있는데, 그것은 잘못 알고 있는 대중이다. 시민들이 어떤 것을 모르고 있다가 그것을 깨닫는 경우가 한 가지 경우인데, 이는 늘 문제가 되어 온 것이다. 시민들이 어떤 것을 알지 못하지만 그것을 알고 있다고 생각하는 경우는 또 다른 경우인데, 이는 새로운 문제이다.

(B) 그것은 무지와 불합리 간의 차이이다. 자치에 관해 다른 어떤 것으로 결론을 내리든, 시민들이 스스로 무슨 말을 하고 있는지를 모르는 경우는 위험하다. 우리가 잘못 아는 것은 부분적으로는 우리가 자신의 갈망에 맞는 방식으로 세상을 바라보는 경향을 포함하는 심리적 요인의 탓이다.

(A) 하지만 그런 요인들은 늘 우리와 함께 있어온 잘못된 앎만 설명할 수 있다. 최근에 잘못된 앎의 급격한 증가에는 다른 원인이 있는데, (그것은) 우리의 미디어이다. "그들은 우리를 어리석게 만들고 있습니다."라고 한 논평자는 말한다. 사실이 허구에 굴복하면, 예견 가능한 결과는 정치적 불신과 대립이다.

Why? 왜 정답일까?

정치에 대한 미국인들의 무지를 언급하는 주어진 글 뒤에는, 무지보다 심각한 문제가 있음을 환기하는 (C), 무지와 불합리의 차이를 설명하는 (B), 미디어로 인해 정치에 대해 잘못 알게 되는 현상이 악화되고 있음을 지적하는 (A)가 차례로 이어지는 것이 자연스럽다. 따라서 글의 순서로 가장 적절한 것은 ⑤ 'C) – (B) – (A)'이다.

- **opinion poll** 여론 조사
- **at best** 기껏해야
- **bend** ⓥ 굴복하다, 구부러지다
- **polarization** ⓝ (정당·의견 등의) 대립
- **irrationality** ⓝ 불합리
- **suit** ⓥ (~에) 맞다, 좋다
- **reveal** ⓥ 밝히다, 드러내다
- **misinformation** ⓝ 잘못 알고 있음, 오보
- **distrust** ⓝ 불신
- **ignorance** ⓝ 무지, 무시
- **self-government** ⓝ 자치, 민주정치
- **inadequately** ⓐⓓ 부적당하게, 불충분하게

구문 풀이

> **1행** Ever since the first scientific opinion polls revealed that most
> ~ 이후로 줄곧   주어   과거동사
> Americans are at best poorly informed about politics, / analysts
>   기껏해야   주어
> have asked {whether citizens are equipped to play the role [democracy
> 현재완료 ~인지 아닌지   선행사
> assigns them]}.
> 4형식 동사 →간접 목적어

---

03 진화론을 뒷받침하고 검증하는 화석 기록 | 정답률 46% | 정답 ⑤

주어진 글 다음에 이어질 글의 순서로 가장 적절한 것을 고르시오.
① (A) – (C) – (B)
② (B) – (A) – (C)
③ (B) – (C) – (A)
④ (C) – (A) – (B)
✔ (C) – (B) – (A)

The fossil record provides evidence of evolution.
화석 기록은 진화의 증거를 제공한다.
The story the fossils tell / is one of change.
화석이 전하는 이야기는 / 변화에 관한 것이다.
Creatures existed in the past / that are no longer with us.
생물들이 과거에는 존재했다. / 더는 우리와 함께 하지 않는
Sequential changes are found in many fossils / showing the change of certain features over time from a common ancestor, / as in the case of the horse.
많은 화석에서 일련의 변화가 발견된다. / 시간이 지남에 따라 공통의 조상으로부터 특정 특징의 변화를 보여주는 / 말의 경우에서처럼
(C) Apart from demonstrating that evolution did occur, / the fossil record also provides tests of the predictions / made from evolutionary theory.
진화가 진짜 일어났다는 것을 증명하는 것 외에도, / 화석 기록은 또한 예측에 대한 테스트를 제공한다. / 진화론에서 만들어진
For example, / the theory predicts / that single-celled organisms evolved before multicelled organisms.
예를 들어, / 진화론은 예측한다. / 단세포 생물이 다세포 생물 이전에 진화했다고
(B) The fossil record supports this prediction / — multicelled organisms are found in layers of earth / millions of years after the first appearance of single-celled organisms.
화석 기록은 이 예측을 뒷받침하는데, / 다세포 생물은 지구 지층에서 발견된다. / 단세포 생물이 최초로 출현한 수백만 년 후
Note that the possibility always remains / that the opposite could be found.
가능성은 항상 남아 있다는 점에 주목하라. / 그 반대가 발견될 수 있는
(A) If multicelled organisms were indeed found / to have evolved before single-celled organisms, / then the theory of evolution would be rejected.
다세포 생물이 정말로 밝혀진다면, / 단세포 생물보다 먼저 진화한 것으로 / 진화론은 거부될 것이다.
A good scientific theory / always allows for the possibility of rejection.
좋은 과학 이론은 / 항상 거부의 가능성을 허용한다.
The fact that we have not found such a case / in countless examinations of the fossil record / strengthens the case for evolutionary theory.
그러한 경우를 발견하지 못했다는 사실은 / 화석 기록에 대한 수많은 조사에서 / 진화론을 위한 논거를 강화한다.

화석 기록은 진화의 증거를 제공한다. 화석이 전하는 이야기는 변화에 관한 것이다. 더는 우리와 함께하지 않는 생물들이 과거에는 존재했다. 말의 경우에서처럼, 시간이 지남에 따라 공통의 조상으로부터 특정 특징의 변화를 보여주는 많은 화석에서 일련의 변화가 발견된다.

(C) 진화가 진짜 일어났다는 것을 증명하는 것 외에도, 화석 기록은 또한 진화론에서 했던 예측에 대한 테스트를 제공한다. 예를 들어, 진화론은 단세포 생물이 다세포 생물 이전에 진화했다고 예측한다.

(B) 화석 기록은 이 예측을 뒷받침하는데, 다세포 생물은 단세포 생물이 최초로 출현한 수백만 년 후 지구 지층에서 발견된다. 그 반대가 발견될 수 있는 가능성은 항상 남아 있다는 점에 주목하라.

(A) 다세포 생물이 단세포 생물보다 먼저 진화한 것으로 정말로 밝혀진다면, 진화론은 거부될 것이다. 좋은 과학 이론은 항상 거부의 가능성을 허용한다. 화석 기록에 대한 수많은 조사에서 그러한 경우를 발견하지 못했다는 사실은 진화론을 위한 논거를 강화한다.

Why? 왜 정답일까?

화석 기록은 진화를 뒷받침한다는 주어진 글 뒤로, (C)는 '이외에도' 화석 기록이 진화론의 예측을 검증한다는 내용과 함께 단세포 생물이 다세포 생물에 선행했다는 예측을 예로 들기 시작한다. (B)는 (C)에서 언급한 예측을 this prediction으로 받으며, 화석 증거가 이를 뒷받침한다고 설명하고, (A)는 이것의 반론 가능성에 관해 언급한다. 따라서 글의 순서로 가장 적절한 것은 ⑤ 'C) – (B) – (A)'이다.

- **evidence** ⓝ 증거
- **ancestor** ⓝ 조상
- **single-celled organism** 단세포 생물
- **countless** ⓐ 수없이 많은
- **evolutionary** ⓐ 진화의
- **layer** ⓝ 지층
- **apart from** ~ 이외에도, ~와는 별개로
- **occur** ⓥ 일어나다, 발생하다
- **sequential** ⓐ 일련의, 연속적인
- **multicelled organism** 다세포 생물
- **reject** ⓥ 거부하다
- **examination** ⓝ 조사
- **prediction** ⓝ 예측
- **appearance** ⓝ 출현
- **demonstrate** ⓥ 입증하다

---

04 카본 싱크의 역할 | 정답률 57% | 정답 ⑤

주어진 글 다음에 이어질 글의 순서로 가장 적절한 것을 고르시오.
① (A) – (C) – (B)
② (B) – (A) – (C)
③ (B) – (C) – (A)
④ (C) – (A) – (B)
✔ (C) – (B) – (A)

A carbon sink is a natural feature / that absorbs or stores more carbon / than it releases.
카본 싱크(이산화탄소 흡수계)는 천연 지형이다. / 더 많은 탄소를 흡수하거나 저장하는 / 배출하는 양보다
(C) The value of carbon sinks is / that they can help create equilibrium in the atmosphere / by removing excess CO₂.
카본 싱크의 가치는 / 대기 안의 평형 상태를 만드는 데 도움을 줄 수 있다는 것이다. / 과다 이산화탄소를 제거하여
One example of a carbon sink / is a large forest.
카본 싱크의 한 예는 / 거대한 숲이다.
(B) Its mass of plants and other organic material / absorb and store tons of carbon.
그 안의 수많은 식물 및 다른 유기 물질은 / 많은 양의 탄소를 흡수하고 저장한다.
However, / the planet's major carbon sink / is its oceans.
하지만, / 지구의 주요 카본 싱크는 / 바다이다.
Since the Industrial Revolution began in the eighteenth century, / CO₂ released during industrial processes / has greatly increased the proportion of carbon in the atmosphere.
산업 혁명이 18세기에 시작된 이후로, / 산업 공정 중에 배출된 이산화탄소는 / 대기의 탄소 비율을 높게 증가시켰다.
(A) Carbon sinks have been able to absorb about half of this excess CO₂, / and the world's oceans have done the major part of that job.
카본 싱크는 이러한 이산화탄소 초과량의 절반을 흡수할 수 있었고, / 지구의 바다는 그 일에서 주된 역할을 해 왔다.
They absorb about one-fourth of humans' industrial carbon emissions, / doing half the work / of all Earth's carbon sinks combined.
바다는 인간의 산업으로 인한 탄소 배출물의 대략 4분의 1을 흡수하여, / 일의 절반을 한다. / 지구의 모든 카본 싱크를 합친 것이 하는

카본 싱크(이산화탄소 흡수계)는 배출하는 양보다 더 많은 탄소를 흡수하거나 저장하는 천연 지형이다.

(C) 카본 싱크의 가치는 과다 이산화탄소를 제거하여 대기 안의 평형 상태를 만드는 데 도움을 줄 수 있다는 것이다. 카본 싱크의 한 예는 거대한 숲이다.

(B) 그 안의 수많은 식물 및 다른 유기 물질은 많은 양의 탄소를 흡수하고 저장한다. 하지만, 지구의 주요 카본 싱크는 바다이다. 산업 혁명이 18세기에 시작된 이후로, 산업 공정 중에 배출된 이산화탄소는 대기의 탄소 비율을 높게 증가시켰다.

(A) 카본 싱크는 이러한 이산화탄소 초과량의 절반을 흡수할 수 있었고, 지구의 바다는 그 일에서 주된 역할을 해 왔다. 바다는 인간의 산업으로 인한 탄소 배출물의 대략 4분의 1을 흡수하여, 지구의 모든 카본 싱크를 합친 것이 하는 일의 절반을 한다.

Why? 왜 정답일까?

카본 싱크의 개념을 설명한 주어진 글 뒤에는, 카본 싱크의 가치를 언급하는 (C), (C)의 후반부에 이어 예시를 언급하는 (B), 카본 싱크의 역할을 정리하여 설명하는 (A)가 차례로 이어지는 것이 자연스럽다. 따라서 글의 순서로 가장 적절한 것은 ⑤ '(C) – (B) – (A)'이다.

- **feature** ⓝ 지형, 지세
- **release** ⓥ 배출하다
- **emission** ⓝ 배출물
- **mass** ⓐ 많은, 대량의
- **proportion** ⓝ 비율
- **absorb** ⓥ 흡수하다, 빨아들이다
- **excess** ⓐ 과다한, 초과한, 여분의
- **combined** ⓐ 합친
- **organic** ⓐ 유기체의
- **equilibrium** ⓝ 평형 상태, 균형

구문 풀이

> **11행** Since the Industrial Revolution began in the eighteenth
> 시간 접속사(~한 이래로)   과거동사
> century, CO₂ [released during industrial processes] has greatly
>   현재완료
> increased the proportion of carbon in the atmosphere.

---

05 주의 집중과 시선의 관계   정답률 59% | 정답 ④

주어진 글 다음에 이어질 글의 순서로 가장 적절한 것을 고르시오.

① (A) – (C) – (B)   ② (B) – (A) – (C)
③ (B) – (C) – (A)   ✔ (C) – (A) – (B)
⑤ (C) – (B) – (A)

It has been said / that eye movements are windows into the mind, / because where people look / reveals what environmental information / they are attending to.
이야기되어 왔다 / 눈의 움직임은 마음을 들여다보는 창이라고 / 사람들이 어디를 보는지는 / 어떤 환경적 정보인지를 드러내기 때문에, / 그들이 주목하고 있는

However, there is more to attention / than just moving the eyes to look at objects.
그러나 주의 집중의 전부인 것은 아니다. / 물체를 보려고 그저 눈을 움직이는 것이

(C) We can pay attention to things / that are not directly in our line of vision, / as evidenced by the basketball player / who dribbles down court / while paying attention to a teammate off to the side, / just before she throws a perfect pass without looking.
우리는 사물들에도 주목할 수 있는데, / 시선에 직접 들어와 있지 않은 / 농구 선수에 의해 입증되듯이 그렇다. / 코트를 드리블해 가는 / 한쪽에 떨어져 있는 팀 동료에게 신경을 쓰면서 / 보지 않고서도 완벽한 패스를 하기 직전에

We can also look directly at something / without paying attention to it.
우리는 또한 그것을 똑바로 바라볼 수 있다. / 무언가에 집중하지 않으면서도

(A) You may have had this experience / if you have been reading a book / and then suddenly become aware / that although you were moving your eyes across the page / and "reading" the words, / you had no idea what you had just read.
여러분은 이런 경험을 해 본 것일 수도 있다. / 여러분이 책을 읽고 있다가, / 문득 알아차린 적이 있다면 / 눈을 움직여 페이지를 누비며 / 단어들을 '읽고' 있었는데도 / 방금 무엇을 읽었는지 전혀 기억나지 않는다는 것을

(B) Even though you were *looking* at the words, / you apparently were not *paying attention*.
비록 여러분은 그 단어들을 *바라보고* 있었을지라도 / 명백히 *주의를 집중하고* 있지 않았다.

There is a mental aspect of attention / that involves processing / that can occur independently of eye movements.
주의 집중의 정신적 측면이 있다. / 처리 과정과 연관된, / 눈의 움직임과 독립적으로 일어날 수 있는

사람들이 어디를 보는지는 그들이 어떤 환경적 정보에 주목하고 있는지를 드러내기 때문에, 눈의 움직임은 마음을 들여다보는 창이라고들 말해 왔다. 그러나 물체를 보려고 그저 눈을 움직이는 것이 주의 집중의 전부인 것은 아니다.

(C) 우리는 시선에 직접 들어와 있지 않은 것들에도 주목할 수 있는데, 보지 않고서도 완벽한 패스를 하기 직전에 한쪽에 떨어져 있는 팀 동료에게 신경을 쓰면서 코트를 드리블해 가는 농구 선수에 의해 입증되듯이 그렇다. 우리는 또한 무언가에 집중하지 않으면서도 그것을 똑바로 바라볼 수 있다.

(A) 책을 읽고 있다가, 눈을 움직여 페이지를 누비며 단어들을 "읽고" 있었는데도 방금 무엇을 읽었는지 전혀 기억나지 않는다는 것을 문득 알아차린 적이 있다면 이런 경험을 해 본 것일 수도 있다.

(B) 비록 여러분은 그 단어들을 *바라보고* 있었을지라도 명백히 *주의를 집중하고* 있지 않았다. 눈의 움직임과 독립적으로 일어날 수 있는 처리 과정과 연관된, 주의 집중의 정신적 측면이 있다.

Why? 왜 정답일까?

보통 눈의 움직임은 집중의 방향과 연관되어 있다고 생각하지만 꼭 그런 것은 아니라는 내용의 주어진 글 뒤에는, 보지 않더라도 집중을 하는 경우가 있다며 농구선수의 예를 드는 (C), 역으로 집중을 하지 않더라도 보고만 있는 경우가 있을 수 있다며 독서하는 상황을 예로 드는 (A), 독서의 예에 대한 설명을 덧붙이며 글을 마무리하는 (B)가 차례로 이어지는 것이 자연스럽다. 따라서 글의 순서로 가장 적절한 것은 ④ '(C) – (A) – (B)'이다.

- **reveal** ⓥ 드러내다, 밝히다
- **attend to** ~에 주의를 기울이다
- **aspect** ⓝ 측면, 양상
- **independently of** ~와 관계없이
- **environmental** ⓐ 환경적인
- **apparently** ⓐⓓ 명백히
- **processing** ⓝ (정보 등의) 처리
- **evidence** ⓥ 입증하다, 증언하다

구문 풀이

> **6행** You may have had this experience / if you have been
> ~했을지도 모른다   접속사(~한다면)   동사1(현재완료 진행형)
> reading a book and then suddenly become aware [that (although
>   동사2(~을 알아차리다) 접속사(~것)
> you were moving your eyes across the page and "reading" the words),
> ( ) : 부사절   ] : become aware의 목적어
> you had no idea {what you had just read}].
> ~을 모르다   └ 관계대명사(~것)   { } : had no idea의 목적어

---

06 두려움을 중화시키는 전략   정답률 45% | 정답 ②

주어진 글 다음에 이어질 글의 순서로 가장 적절한 것을 고르시오. [3점]

① (A) – (C) – (B)   ✔ (B) – (A) – (C)
③ (B) – (C) – (A)   ④ (C) – (A) – (B)
⑤ (C) – (B) – (A)

When a young child sees clouds / moving across the sky, / the clouds may seem alive and independent, / perhaps dangerous.
어린아이가 구름을 보게 될 때, / 하늘을 가로질러 움직이는 / 구름은 살아 있고 독립적인 것처럼 보일 수도 있다. / 어쩌면 위험한

But if one sees clouds as fleecy lambs, / a metaphorical chain begins to neutralize the fear.
그러나 구름을 털이 많은 어린 양으로 본다면 / 은유의 사슬이 두려움을 중화하기 시작한다.

(B) The cloud may still be thought of as alive, / but it is no longer terrifying.
그 구름이 여전히 살아 있다고 생각될 수도 있지만, / 그것은 더는 무섭지 않다.

Repression and neutralization through metaphor / are possible strategies, / but there is another.
은유를 통한 억제와 중화도 / 가능한 전략이지만, / 또 한 가지 전략이 있다.

Faced with the moving clouds, / the child can theorize about their movement / in such a way that the clouds cease to be alive.
움직이는 구름을 마주쳤을 때 / 아이는 구름의 움직임에 대해 이론화할 수 있다. / 구름이 살아 있지 않다는 식으로

(A) "Cloud movement" becomes differentiated / from the kind of movement / that makes things alive, / because the clouds move / only if they are "pushed" by the wind, / and what can't move without a push from the outside / is not alive.
'구름의 움직임'은 차별화되는데, / 그런 종류의 움직임과는 / 어떤 것들을 살아 있게끔 해 주는 / 왜냐하면 구름은 움직이고, / 그것들이 바람에 의해 '밀려'야만 / 외부에서 밀지 않으면 움직일 수 없는 것은 / 살아 있지 않은 것이기 때문이다.

(C) Children develop theoretical constructs / that separate the motion of clouds / from the motion of people and animals / so that eventually the fear of living clouds disappears.
아이들은 이론적인 생각을 전개하고, / 구름의 움직임을 구분하는 / 사람 및 동물의 움직임으로부터 / 결국 살아 있는 구름에 대한 두려움은 사라진다.

If things seem uncomfortably on the border / between the alive and the not-alive, / use logic to redefine the boundaries / so that things fall more comfortably into place.
어떤 것들이 경계에 불편하게 걸쳐 있는 것으로 보인다면, / 살아 있는 것과 살아 있지 않은 것 사이의 / 그 경계선을 재정립하기 위해 논리를 이용하여 / 그것들이 더 편안하게 제 자리를 잡게 하라.

If it scares you, make a theory.
그것이 여러분을 무섭게 한다면, 이론을 세워 보라.

어린아이가 구름이 하늘을 가로질러 움직이는 것을 보게 될 때, 구름은 살아 있고 독립적이고 어쩌면 위험한 것처럼 보일 수도 있다. 그러나 구름을 털이 많은 어린 양으로 본다면 은유의 사슬이 두려움을 중화하기 시작한다.

(B) 그 구름이 여전히 살아 있다고 생각될 수도 있지만, 그것이 더는 무섭지 않다. 은유를 통한 억제와 중화도 가능한 전략이지만, 또 한 가지 전략이

있다. 움직이는 구름을 마주쳤을 때 아이는 구름이 살아 있지 않다는 식으로 구름의 움직임에 대해 이론화할 수 있다.

(A) '구름의 움직임'은 어떤 것들을 살아 있게끔 해 주는 그런 종류의 움직임과는 차별화되는데, 왜냐하면 구름은 바람에 의해 '밀려'야만 움직이고, 외부에서 밀지 않으면 움직일 수 없는 것은 살아 있지 않은 것이기 때문이다.

(C) 아이들은 구름의 움직임과 사람 및 동물의 움직임을 구분하는 이론적인 생각을 전개하고, 결국 살아 있는 구름에 대한 두려움은 사라진다. 어떤 것들이 살아 있는 것과 살아 있지 않은 것 사이의 경계에 불편하게 걸쳐 있는 것으로 보인다면, 논리를 이용해 그 경계선을 재정립하여 그것들이 더 편안하게 제 자리를 잡게 하라. 그것이 여러분을 무섭게 한다면, 이론을 세워 보라.

Why? 왜 정답일까?

어린아이가 구름을 '양' 같다고 보는 경우를 들어 은유가 두려움을 중화한다는 내용을 언급하는 주어진 글 뒤로, '또 다른 전략'에 관한 이야기를 꺼내는 (B)가 이어진다. 한편 (A)는 이 또 다른 전략이 곧 구름을 살아 있는 존재가 아니라고 여기는 것임을 설명하고, (C)는 이런 식의 이론화가 두려움을 중화하는 데 도움이 된다는 결론을 제시한다. 따라서 글의 순서로 가장 적절한 것은 ② '(B) - (A) - (C)'이다.

- **independent** ⓐ 독립된, 독립적인
- **lamb** ⓝ 어린 양
- **neutralize** ⓥ 중화하다
- **terrifying** ⓐ 무서운, 겁나게 하는
- **metaphor** ⓝ 은유
- **theorize** ⓥ 이론화하다
- **separate** ⓥ 구분하다, 구별하다
- **border** ⓝ 경계
- **redefine** ⓥ 재정립하다
- **comfortably** ⓐd 편안하게
- **fleecy** ⓐ 털이 많은
- **metaphorical** ⓐ 은유의
- **differentiate** ⓥ 차별화하다
- **repression** ⓝ 억제
- **strategy** ⓝ 전략
- **construct** ⓝ 생각, 구성 개념
- **eventually** ⓐd 결국
- **logic** ⓝ 논리
- **boundary** ⓝ 경계선
- **scare** ⓥ 무섭게 하다

구문 풀이

11행 The cloud may still be thought of as alive, but it is no longer 「A+be thought of as+B : A가 B라고 여겨지다」
terrifying. (현재분사(능동))

---

07 인간의 확장인 기술 정답률 50% | 정답 ③

주어진 글 다음에 이어질 글의 순서로 가장 적절한 것을 고르시오. [3점]

① (A) - (C) - (B)
② (B) - (A) - (C)
✓③ (B) - (C) - (A)
④ (C) - (A) - (B)
⑤ (C) - (B) - (A)

Marshall McLuhan, among others, / noted that clothes are people's extended skin, / wheels extended feet, / camera and telescopes extended eyes.
특히 Marshall McLuhan은 / 옷이 사람들의 확장된 피부이고, / 바퀴는 확장된 발이며, / 카메라와 망원경은 확장된 눈이라고 말했다.

Our technological creations are great extrapolations of the bodies / that our genes build.
우리의 기술적인 창조물들은 신체의 위대한 연장이다. / 우리의 유전자가 형성하는

(B) In this way, we can think of technology as our extended body.
이런 식으로, 우리는 기술을 우리의 확장된 신체라고 생각할 수 있다.

During the industrial age / it was easy to see the world this way.
산업 시대에는 / 세상을 이런 식으로 보는 것이 쉬웠다.

Steam-powered shovels, / locomotives, / television, / and the levers and gears of engineers / were a fabulous exoskeleton / that turned man into superman.
증기력으로 움직이는 동력삽, / 기관차, / 텔레비전, / 그리고 엔지니어의 지렛대와 톱니바퀴는 / 엄청난 외골격이었다. / 인간을 슈퍼맨으로 바꿔준

(C) A closer look reveals the flaw in this analogy:
더 자세히 살펴보면 이 비유의 결점이 드러난다.

The extended costume of animals is the result of their genes.
동물들의 확장된 의상은 그들의 유전자의 결과물이다.

They inherit the basic blueprints of what they make.
그들은 자신들이 만드는 것의 기본 청사진을 물려받는다.

Humans don't.
인간은 그렇지 않다.

(A) The blueprints for our shells spring from our minds, / which may spontaneously create something / none of our ancestors ever made or even imagined.
우리의 겉모습을 위한 청사진은 우리의 정신으로부터 나오는데, / 그것은 무언가를 자연스럽게 만들어 낼 수도 있다. / 우리 조상들 중 어느 누구도 만들어 내거나 심지어 상상하지도 못했던

If technology is an extension of humans, / it is not an extension of our genes but of our minds.
기술이 인간의 확장이라면, / 그것은 우리 유전자의 확장이 아니라 우리 정신의 확장이다.

Technology is therefore the extended body for ideas.
그러므로 기술은 아이디어를 위한 확장된 몸이다.

특히 Marshall McLuhan은 옷이 사람들의 확장된 피부이고, 바퀴는 확장된 발이며, 카메라와 망원경은 확장된 눈이라고 말했다. 우리의 기술적인 창조물들은 우리의 유전자가 형성하는 신체의 위대한 연장이다.

(B) 이런 식으로, 우리는 기술을 우리의 확장된 신체라고 생각할 수 있다. 산업 시대에는 세상을 이런 식으로 보는 것이 쉬웠다. 증기력으로 움직이는 동력삽, 기관차, 텔레비전, 그리고 엔지니어의 지렛대와 톱니바퀴는 인간을 슈퍼맨으로 바꿔준 엄청난 외골격이었다.

(C) 더 자세히 살펴보면 이 비유의 결점이 드러난다. 동물들의 확장된 의상은 그들의 유전자의 결과물이다. 그들은 자신들이 만드는 것의 기본 청사진을 물려받는다. 인간은 그렇지 않다.

(A) 우리의 겉모습을 위한 청사진은 우리의 정신으로부터 나오는데, 그것은 우리 조상들 중 어느 누구도 만들어 내거나 심지어 상상하지도 못했던 것을 자연스럽게 만들어 낼 수도 있다. 기술이 인간의 확장이라면, 그것은 우리 유전자의 확장이 아니라 우리 정신의 확장이다. 그러므로 기술은 아이디어를 위한 확장된 몸이다.

Why? 왜 정답일까?

기술을 신체의 확장으로 보는 비유가 있음을 언급하는 주어진 글 뒤에는, 산업 시대에는 이러한 비유가 적절했음을 설명하는 (B), 자세히 살펴보면 이 비유의 결점이 드러난다고 진술하는 (C), 기술은 인간의 신체보다는 정신의 확장이라는 결론을 제시하는 (A)가 차례로 이어져야 한다. 따라서 글의 순서로 가장 적절한 것은 ③ '(B) - (C) - (A)'이다.

- **extended** ⓐ 확장된
- **telescope** ⓝ 망원경
- **gene** ⓝ 유전자
- **shell** ⓝ 겉모습
- **spontaneously** ⓐd 자연스럽게
- **extension** ⓝ 확장
- **steam-powered** 증기력으로 움직이는
- **locomotive** ⓝ 기관차
- **gear** ⓝ 톱니바퀴
- **flaw** ⓝ 결함
- **costume** ⓝ 의상
- **wheel** ⓝ 바퀴
- **technological** ⓐ 기술적인
- **blueprint** ⓝ 청사진
- **spring from** ~에서부터 나오다[일어나다]
- **ancestor** ⓝ 조상
- **industrial** ⓐ 산업의
- **shovel** ⓝ 삽, 부삽
- **lever** ⓝ 지렛대
- **fabulous** ⓐ 기막히게 좋은
- **analogy** ⓝ 비유, 유추
- **inherit** ⓥ 물려받다

구문 풀이

6행 The blueprints for our shells spring from our minds, which
주어   자동사   선행사   계속적 용법
may spontaneously create something [(that) none of our ancestors
생략(목적격 관계대명사)
ever made or even imagined].

---

08 가정 도우미로 활약할 가능성이 있는 소셜 로봇 정답률 41% | 정답 ②

주어진 글 다음에 이어질 글의 순서로 가장 적절한 것을 고르시오. [3점]

① (A) - (C) - (B)
✓② (B) - (A) - (C)
③ (B) - (C) - (A)
④ (C) - (A) - (B)
⑤ (C) - (B) - (A)

Recently, / a number of commercial ventures / have been launched / that offer social robots as personal home assistants, / perhaps eventually to rival existing smart-home assistants.
최근에, / 많은 상업적인 벤처 기업들이 / 생겨났는데, / 소셜 로봇을 개인용 가정 도우미로 제공하는 / 아마도 결국 기존의 스마트홈 도우미와 경쟁하게 될 것이다.

(B) Personal robotic assistants are devices / that have no physical manipulation or locomotion capabilities.
개인용 로봇 도우미는 장치이다. / 신체 조작이나 이동 능력이 없는

Instead, / they have a distinct social presence / and have visual features / suggestive of their ability / to interact socially, / such as eyes, ears, or a mouth.
대신에, / 그것들에게는 뚜렷한 사회적 존재감이 있고 / 시각적 특징을 가지고 있다. / 능력을 암시하는 / 사회적 상호작용을 할 수 있는 / 눈, 귀 또는 입과 같은

(A) They might be motorized / and can track the user around the room, / giving the impression of being aware of the people in the environment.
그것들은 동력화될 수 있으며 / 실내에서 사용자를 추적할 수 있는데, / 환경 내의 사람들을 감지한다는 인상을 준다.

Although personal robotic assistants / provide services similar to those of smart-home assistants, / their social presence offers an opportunity / that is unique to social robots.
개인용 로봇 도우미는 / 스마트홈 도우미와 비슷한 서비스를 제공하긴 하지만, / 그들의 사회적 존재감은 기회를 제공한다. / 소셜 로봇에게만 특유한

(C) For instance, / in addition to playing music, / a social personal assistant robot / would express its engagement with the music / so that users would feel like / they are listening to the music together with the robot.
예를 들어, / 음악을 재생할 뿐만 아니라 / 소셜 개인용 도우미 로봇은 / 음악과의 교감을 표현한다. / 사용자가 느끼도록 / 그들이 로봇과 함께 그 음악을 듣는 것처럼

These robots can be used as surveillance devices, / act as communicative intermediates, / engage in richer games, / tell stories, / or be used to provide encouragement or incentives.
이들 로봇은 보안 감시 장치로 사용될 수 있거나, / 소통의 매개체 역할을 하거나, / 더 다채로운 게임에 참여하거나, / 이야기를 들려주거나, / 격려나 동기를 제공하는 데 사용될 수 있다.

최근에, 소셜 로봇을 개인용 가정 도우미로 제공하는 많은 상업적인 벤처 기업들이 생겨났는데, 아마도 결국 기존의 스마트홈 도우미와 경쟁하게 될 것이다.

(B) 개인용 로봇 도우미는 신체 조작이나 이동 능력이 없는 장치이다. 대신에, 그것들에게는 뚜렷한 사회적 존재감이 있고 눈, 귀 또는 입처럼 사회적 상호작용을 할 수 있는 능력을 암시하는 시각적 특징을 가지고 있다.

(A) 그것들은 동력화될 수 있으며 실내에서 사용자를 추적할 수 있는데, 환경 내의 사람들을 감지한다는 인상을 준다. 개인용 로봇 도우미는 스마트홈 도우미와 비슷한 서비스를 제공하긴 하지만, 그들의 사회적 존재감은 소셜 로봇 특유의 기회를 제공한다.

(C) 예를 들어, 소셜 개인용 도우미 로봇은 음악을 재생할 뿐만 아니라 사용자가 로봇과 함께 그 음악을 듣는 것처럼 느끼도록 음악과의 교감을 표현한다. 이들 로봇은 보안 감시 장치로 사용될 수 있거나, 소통의 매개체 역할을 하거나, 더 다채로운 게임에 참여하거나, 이야기를 들려주거나, 격려나 동기를 제공하는 데 사용될 수 있다.

Why? 왜 정답일까?

최근 소셜 로봇을 개인용 가정 도우미로 제공하는 업체가 생겨났다는 내용의 주어진 글 뒤로, 이들은 신체 조작이나 이동 능력이 없지만 사회적 존재감이 있다는 내용의 **(B)**, 이 것들은 환경 내 사람을 감지한다는 인상을 줄 수 있기에 다른 스마트홈 도우미와 차별화 된다는 내용의 **(A)**, 이러한 경우의 예를 드는 **(C)**가 차례로 이어져야 자연스럽다. 따라서 글의 순서로 가장 적절한 것은 ② '(B) – (A) – (C)'이다.

- **launch** ⓥ 시작하다, 진출하다, 출시하다
- **track** ⓥ 추적하다
- **distinct** ⓐ 독특한, 다른, 특유의
- **communicative** ⓐ 의사 전달의
- **encouragement** ⓝ 격려
- **motorize** ⓥ 동력화하다
- **manipulation** ⓝ 조작
- **suggestive of** ~을 암시하는
- **intermediate** ⓝ 매개체, 중간자
- **incentive** ⓝ 동기, 장려[우대]책

구문 풀이

1행 Recently, a number of commercial ventures have been
주어('a number of+복수 명사: 많은 ~」) 동사(현재완료 수동태)
launched [that offer social robots as personal home assistants],
[ ]: 주어 수식
perhaps eventually to rival existing smart-home assistants.

09 믿는 만큼 정교하지 않은 우리의 시각적 인식 정답률 58% | 정답 ③

주어진 글 다음에 이어질 글의 순서로 가장 적절한 것을 고르시오. [3점]
① (A) – (C) – (B)
② (B) – (A) – (C)
✔③ (B) – (C) – (A)
④ (C) – (A) – (B)
⑤ (C) – (B) – (A)

Our perception always involves some imagination.
우리의 인식은 항상 얼마간의 상상력을 수반한다.

It is more similar to painting than to photography.
그것은 사진보다는 그림과 더 비슷하다.

And, according to the confirmation effect, / we blindly trust the reality we construct.
그리고 확증 효과에 따르면, / 우리는 자신이 구축하는 현실을 맹목적으로 신뢰한다.

(B) This is best witnessed in visual illusions, / which we perceive with full confidence, / as if there were no doubt / that we are portraying reality faithfully.
이것은 시각적 착각들에서 가장 잘 목격되는데, / 우리는 그것을 온전히 자신 있게 인식한다. / 마치 의심의 여지가 없는 것처럼 / 우리가 현실을 충실하게 묘사하고 있다는 것에

One interesting way of discovering this / — in a simple game that can be played at any moment / — is the following.
이것을 발견하는 한 가지 흥미로운 방법은 / 언제든지 할 수 있는 간단한 게임에서 / 다음과 같다.

(C) Whenever you are with another person, / ask him or her to close their eyes, / and start asking questions about what is nearby / — not very particular details / but the most striking elements / of the scene.
여러분이 다른 사람과 함께 있을 때마다 / 그 사람에게 눈을 감으라고 요청하고, / 근처에 있는 것에 대해 질문하기 시작하라. / 즉 아주 구체적인 세부사항이 아니라 / 가장 눈에 띄는 요소들에 대해 / 그 현장의

What is the color of the wall? / Is there a table in the room? / Does that man have a beard?
벽의 색깔은 무엇인가? / 방에 테이블이 있는가? / 저 남자는 턱수염이 있는가?

(A) You will see / that the majority of us are quite ignorant / about what lies around us.
여러분은 / 우리 대다수가 상당히 무지하다는 것을 알게 될 것이다. / 우리 주변에 놓여 있는 것에 대해

This is not so puzzling.
이것은 그렇게 이해하기 어렵지 않다.

The most extraordinary fact is / that we completely disregard this ignorance.
가장 놀라운 사실은 ~이다. / 우리가 이 무지를 완전히 무시한다는 것

우리의 인식은 항상 얼마간의 상상력을 수반한다. 그것은 사진보다는 그림과 더 비슷하다. 그리고 확증 효과에 따르면, 우리는 자신이 구축하는 현실을 맹목적으로 신뢰한다.

(B) 이것은 시각적 착각들에서 가장 잘 목격되는데, 마치 우리가 현실을 충실하게 묘사하고 있다는 것에 의심의 여지가 없는 것처럼 우리는 그것을 온전히 자신 있게 인식한다. 언제든지 할 수 있는 간단한 게임에서 이것을 발견하는 한 가지 흥미로운 방법은 다음과 같다.

(C) 여러분이 다른 사람과 함께 있을 때마다 그 사람에게 눈을 감으라고 요청하고, 근처에 있는 것, 즉 그 현장의 아주 구체적인 세부사항이 아니라 가장 눈에 띄는 요소들에 대해 질문하기 시작하라. 벽의 색깔은 무엇인가? 방에 테이블이 있는가? 저 남자는 턱수염이 있는가?

(A) 여러분은 우리 대다수가 우리 주변에 놓여 있는 것에 대해 상당히 무지하다는 것을 알게 될 것이다. 이것은 그렇게 이해하기 어렵지 않다. 가장 놀라운 사실은 우리가 이 무지를 완전히 무시한다는 것이다.

Why? 왜 정답일까?

주어진 글에서 시각적 인식은 사진만큼 정확하기보다 그림처럼 상상력을 포함하기 마련 이지만, 우리는 우리 자신의 현실을 맹목적으로 신뢰하는 경향이 있다고 한다. **(B)**는 시 각적 착각을 살펴보면 이것을 잘 알 수 있다고 하고, **(C)**는 구체적으로 시각적 착각을 파 악할 수 있는 방법을 알려준다. **(A)**는 **(C)**에 제시된 방법대로 해보면 우리의 시각적 구성 에 허점이 많다는 것을 알 수 있다고 한다. 따라서 글의 순서로 가장 적절한 것은 ③ '(B) – (C) – (A)'이다.

- **confirmation** ⓝ 확증
- **construct** ⓥ 구성하다
- **extraordinary** ⓐ 놀라운, 특이한
- **illusion** ⓝ 환상
- **faithfully** ⓐ 충실하게
- **blindly** ⓐ 맹목적으로
- **puzzling** ⓐ 혼란스러운
- **disregard** ⓥ 무시하다
- **portray** ⓥ 묘사하다
- **striking** ⓐ 눈에 띄는, 현저한

구문 풀이

9행 This is best witnessed in visual illusions, which we perceive
선행사 목적격 관·대
with full confidence, as if there were no doubt [that we are portraying
「as if+주어+과거 동사: 실제 ~이지 않지만 마치 ~한 것처럼」
reality faithfully].
[ ]: doubt와 동격

★★★ 1등급 대비 고난도 2점 문제

10 열정 씨뿌리기의 과정 정답률 37% | 정답 ③

주어진 글 다음에 이어질 글의 순서로 가장 적절한 것을 고르시오.
① (A) – (C) – (B)
② (B) – (A) – (C)
✔③ (B) – (C) – (A)
④ (C) – (A) – (B)
⑤ (C) – (B) – (A)

In a process called *seeding*, / you need to have a time frame in mind.
씨뿌리기라고 불리는 과정에서, / 여러분은 마음속에 시간의 틀을 가질 필요가 있다.

Start telling your family / how you feel about your current job.
가족들에게 말하기 시작하라. / 여러분의 현재 직업에 대해 어떻게 느끼는지를

Tell them / how you get frustrated and bored with this job.
그들에게 이야기하라. / 이 직업에 대해 얼마나 좌절감을 느끼고 지루해 하는지를

(B) Discuss this almost twice a week.
거의 일주일에 두 번은 이것에 대해 논의하라.

Then start doing work related to your passion on the side / and let them see and experience / how happy you are while doing this.
그런 다음에 열정과 관련된 일을 추가로 하기 시작하고, / 그들이 보고 경험하게 하라. / 이 일을 하는 동안에 여러분이 얼마나 행복한지를

Find a way / to get your family and friends / involved in your passion.
방법을 찾아라. / 여러분의 가족과 친구들이 ~하게 할 / 여러분의 열정에 관여될

The more they see you doing your passion, / the more they connect with you emotionally.
여러분이 열정을 쏟는 것을 더 많이 볼수록, / 그들은 여러분과 감정적으로 더 많이 연결된다.

(C) Tell them stories / of how you are inspired by the passion / and how it makes a difference / not only to you but also to others.
그들에게 이야기하라. / 여러분이 그 열정에 어떻게 영감을 받고 / 어떻게 변화를 주는지에 대해 / 여러분뿐만 아니라 다른 사람들에게도

Give examples / of how someone living a similar passion started his or her life / and today how he or she is living happily.
예를 들어 주어라. / 비슷한 열정을 갖고 사는 사람이 어떻게 그 사람의 삶을 시작했는지 / 그리고 오늘날 그 사람이 어떻게 행복하게 살고 있는지

(A) These stories will make them realise / that you are meant to follow your passion.
이 이야기들은 그들이 깨닫게 해 줄 것이다. / 여러분이 열정을 따라야만 한다는 것을

At times they need to be surprised with your small achievements, / which could be some additional skills you acquired, / or some awards you won in your field of passion.
때때로 그들은 여러분의 작은 성과에 놀랄 필요가 있는데, / 그것은 여러분이 추가로 습득한 몇 가지 기술일 수도 있다. / 혹은 여러분이 열정을 쏟는 분야에서 받은 몇 개의 상일

*씨뿌리기*라고 불리는 과정에서, 여러분은 마음속에 시간의 틀을 가질 필요가 있다. 여러분의 현재 직업에 대해 어떻게 느끼는지를 가족들에게 말하기 시작하라. 이 직업에 대해 얼마나 좌절감을 느끼고 지루해 하는지를 그들에게 이야기하라.

(B) 거의 일주일에 두 번은 이것에 대해 논의하라. 그런 다음에 열정과 관련된 일을 추가로 하기 시작하고, 이 일을 하는 동안에 여러분이 얼마나 행복한지를 그들이 보고 경험하게 하라. 여러분의 가족과 친구들이 여러분의 열정에 관여하게 할 방법을 찾아라. 여러분이 열정을 쏟는 것을 더 많이 볼수록, 그들은 여러분과 감정적으로 더 많이 연결된다.

(C) 그 열정에 어떻게 영감을 받고 그것이 여러분뿐만 아니라 다른 사람들에게도 어떻게 변화를 주는지에 대해 그들에게 이야기하라. 비슷한 열정을 갖고 사는 사람이 어떻게 그 사람의 삶을 시작했으며 오늘날 그 사람이 어떻게 행복하게 살고 있는지 예를 들어 주어라.

(A) 이 이야기들은 여러분이 열정을 따라야만 한다는 것을 그들이 깨닫게 해 줄 것이다. 때때로 그들은 여러분의 작은 성과에 놀랄 필요가 있는데, 그것은 여러분이 추가로 습득한 몇 가지 기술이나 여러분이 열정을 쏟는 분야에서 받은 몇 개의 상일 수도 있다.

Why? 왜 정답일까?

자신의 열정에 대해 타인의 공감을 얻을 수 있는 방법인 '씨뿌리기' 과정을 설명한 글이다. 주어진 글에서 먼저 현재 하는 일에 대한 지루함을 다른 사람들에게 이야기할 것을 제시한 후, (B)에서는 거의 일주일에 두 번 이상 이렇게 이야기를 하고 나아가 자신이 지닌 열정에 관해서도 말하기 시작하라고 조언한다. (C)에서는 열정에 관해 어떻게 이야기해야 하는지 설명하고, 마지막으로 (A)에서는 (C)에서 언급한 방법으로 인해 다른 사람들이 열정에 공감해줄 수 있다는 결과가 제시되고 있다. 따라서 글의 순서로 가장 적절한 것은 ③ '(B) – (C) – (A)'이다.

- have in mind 염두에 두다
- passion ⑩ 열정
- additional @ 추가적인
- frustrated @ 좌절한
- achievement ⑩ 성취

구문 풀이

14행 The more **they see you doing your passion**, the more **they** connect with you emotionally.
「the+비교급 ~, the+비교급 … : ~할수록 더 …하다」

★★ 문제 해결 꿀~팁 ★★

▶ 많이 틀린 이유는?
주어진 글이 'Tell them ~'으로 끝나고 (C)의 첫 문장 또한 유사하게 'Tell them ~'으로 시작되므로 얼핏 보면 (C)가 세 단락 중 가장 먼저 나와야 할 것처럼 보인다. 하지만 (C) – (A)를 먼저 배치한 뒤 (B)를 이으면 (B) 첫 문장의 this가 가리키는 바가

모호해진다. (A)는 주변 사람들이 '나'의 열정을 알아주고 성취에 놀라는 상황을 언급하는데, 이 상황을 (B)의 this로 나타내기에는 부적절하다.

▶ 문제 해결 방법은?
주어진 글의 'Tell them how you get frustrated and bored with this job.'이 (B)의 this로 연결되고, 이어서 가까운 사람들에게 어떤 이야기를 더 할지 (C)에서 추가로 언급한 뒤, (C)의 stories와 examples를 (A)에서 These stories로 받아 마무리하는 흐름이 가장 적절하다.

★★★ 1등급 대비 고난도 3점 문제

11 과일의 숙성과 에틸렌   정답률 37% | 정답 ⑤

주어진 글 다음에 이어질 글의 순서로 가장 적절한 것을 고르시오. [3점]

① (A) – (C) – (B)   ② (B) – (A) – (C)
③ (B) – (C) – (A)   ④ (C) – (A) – (B)
✔ (C) – (B) – (A)

The fruit ripening process / brings about the softening of cell walls, sweetening and the production of chemicals / that give colour and flavour.
과일 숙성 과정은 / 세포벽의 연화, 감미, 화학 물질의 생산을 가져온다. / 색과 맛을 주는

The process is induced / by the production of a plant hormone called ethylene.
그 과정은 유도된다. / 에틸렌이라는 식물 호르몬의 생산에 의해

(C) The problem for growers and retailers is / that ripening is followed sometimes quite rapidly / by deterioration and decay / and the product becomes worthless.
재배자와 소매업자에게 문제는 / 숙성은 때로는 아주 빠르게 뒤따라서 / 품질 저하와 부패에 의해 / 제품이 가치 없게 된다는 것이다.

Tomatoes and other fruits / are, therefore, usually picked and transported / when they are unripe.
토마토와 다른 과일은 / 그러므로 일반적으로 수확되어 운송된다. / 그것들이 익지 않았을 때

(B) In some countries / they are then sprayed with ethylene / before sale to the consumer / to induce ripening.
일부 국가에서는 / 그런 다음 에틸렌을 그것들에 살포한다. / 소비자에게 판매하기 전에 / 숙성을 유도하기 위해

However, fruit picked before it is ripe / has less flavour than fruit picked ripe from the plant.
그러나 익기 전에 수확된 과일은 / 식물에 달려 익은 후 수확된 과일보다 맛이 덜하다.

Biotechnologists therefore saw an opportunity / in delaying the ripening and softening process in fruit.
따라서 생명공학자들은 기회를 엿보았다. / 과일의 숙성 및 연화 과정을 지연하는 데 있어서

(A) If ripening could be slowed down / by interfering with ethylene production / or with the processes that respond to ethylene, / fruit could be left on the plant / until it was ripe and full of flavour / but would still be in good condition / when it arrived at the supermarket shelf.
숙성이 늦춰질 수 있다면, / 에틸렌 생산을 방해하거나 / 에틸렌에 반응하는 과정을 방해함으로써 / 과일은 식물에 붙어 있을 수 있지만, / 그것이 익어서 맛이 풍부해질 때까지 / 여전히 좋은 상태를 유지할 것이다. / 그것이 슈퍼마켓 선반에 도착했을 때에도

과일 숙성 과정은 세포벽의 연화, 감미, 색과 맛을 주는 화학 물질의 생산을 가져온다. 그 과정은 에틸렌이라는 식물 호르몬의 생산에 의해 유도된다.

(C) 재배자와 소매업자에게 문제는 숙성 이후에 때로는 아주 빠르게 품질 저하와 부패가 뒤따라서 제품이 가치 없게 된다는 것이다. 그러므로 토마토와 다른 과일은 일반적으로 익지 않았을 때 수확되어 운송된다.

(B) 일부 국가에서는 그런 다음 숙성을 유도하기 위해 소비자에게 판매하기 전에 에틸렌을 그것들에 살포한다. 그러나 익기 전에 수확된 과일은 식물에 달려 익은 후 수확된 과일보다 맛이 덜하다. 따라서 생명공학자들은 과일의 숙성 및 연화 과정을 지연하는 데 있어서 기회를 엿보았다.

(A) 에틸렌 생산을 방해하거나 에틸렌에 반응하는 과정을 방해함으로써 숙성을 늦출 수 있다면, 과일은 익어서 맛이 풍부해질 때까지 식물에 붙어 있을 수 있지만, 슈퍼마켓 선반에 도착했을 때에도 여전히 좋은 상태를 유지할 것이다.

Why? 왜 정답일까?

과일 숙성 과정에 관여하는 에틸렌이라는 호르몬을 언급하는 주어진 글 뒤에는, 먼저 과일이 숙성되면 품질 저하나 부패가 뒤따르므로 토마토 등 과일들이 일반적으로 익기 전에 수확된다는 내용을 배경으로 제시하는 (C)가 먼저 연결된다. 이어서 (B)는 '그런 다음' 과일의 숙성을 유도하고자 에틸렌이 살포된다는 점과 에틸렌이 뿌려진 과일들이 일반적으로 다 익은 후 수확된 과일보다는 맛이 덜하다는 점을 차례로 언급한다. 마지막으로 (A)는 만일 (생명공학자들이) 에틸렌 생산 및 반응 과정을 더 잘 조작할 수 있다면 과일이

수확기까지 맛있게 익기를 기다렸다가 유통 또한 신선하게 할 수 있을 것이라는 전망을 제시한다. 따라서 글의 순서로 가장 적절한 것은 ⑤ '(C) − (B) − (A)'이다.

- ● ripening ⓝ 숙성, 성숙
- ● induce ⓥ 유도하다
- ● biotechnologist ⓝ 생명공학자
- ● transport ⓥ 운송하다
- ● flavour ⓝ 맛, 풍미
- ● interfere with ⓥ ~을 방해하다
- ● decay ⓝ 부패

★★ 문제 해결 꿀~팁 ★★

▶ 많이 틀린 이유는?

(B)의 초반부에 에틸렌이 분사되는 대상인 **they**가 나오는데, 주어진 글에는 **they**로 받을만한 복수 명사가 나오지 않는다. 맥락으로 보아 이 **they**는 (C)의 **Tomatoes and other fruits**를 가리키므로, 주어진 글 바로 뒤에 (C)가 연결되고, 나아가 (B)가 이어지는 구조임을 알 수 있다.

▶ 문제 해결 방법은?

주어진 글의 **ethylene**만 보고 바로 **(B)**를 연결시키지 말고, 지시어와 연결어가 제공하는 다른 힌트를 함께 적절히 활용하도록 한다.

★★★ 1등급 대비 고난도 3점 문제

12 승소 시 보수 약정의 관행 　　정답률 31% | 정답 ④

주어진 글 다음에 이어질 글의 순서로 가장 적절한 것을 고르시오. [3점]

① (A) − (C) − (B)
② (B) − (A) − (C)
③ (B) − (C) − (A)
④✓ (C) − (A) − (B)
⑤ (C) − (B) − (A)

The most commonly known form of results-based pricing / is a practice / called *contingency pricing*, / used by lawyers.
결과 기반 가격 책정 중 가장 일반적으로 알려진 형태는 / 관행이다. / 승소 시 보수 약정이라고 불리는 / 변호사가 사용하는

(C) Contingency pricing is the major way / that personal injury and certain consumer cases / are billed.
승소 시 보수 약정은 주요 방식이다. / 개인 상해 및 특정 소비자 소송이 / 비용 청구되는

In this approach, / lawyers do not receive fees or payment / until the case is settled, / when they are paid a percentage of the money / that the client receives.
이 방식에서 / 변호사는 수수료나 지불금을 받지 않고, / 소송이 해결될 때까지 / 그때 그들은 금액의 일정 비율을 받는다. / 의뢰인이 받는

(A) Therefore, / only an outcome in the client's favor / is compensated.
따라서 / 의뢰인에게 유리한 결과만 / 보수가 지불된다.

From the client's point of view, / the pricing makes sense / in part because most clients in these cases are unfamiliar with / and possibly intimidated by law firms.
의뢰인의 관점에서 보면 / 이 가격 책정은 타당한데, / 부분적으로 이러한 소송의 의뢰인 대부분이 (법률 사무소에) 익숙하지 않고 / 아마도 법률 사무소에 겁을 먹을 수 있다는 것 때문이다.

Their biggest fears are high fees for a case / that may take years to settle.
그들의 가장 큰 두려움은 소송에 대한 높은 수수료이다. / 해결하는 데 몇 년이 걸릴 수 있는

(B) By using contingency pricing, / clients are ensured / that they pay no fees / until they receive a settlement.
승소 시 보수 약정을 사용함으로써 / 의뢰인은 보장받는다. / 그들이 수수료를 지불하지 않도록 / 그들이 합의금을 받을 때까지

In these and other instances of contingency pricing, / the economic value of the service / is hard to determine before the service, / and providers develop a price / that allows them / to share the risks and rewards of delivering value to the buyer.
승소 시 보수 약정의 이런 비슷한 경우에서 / 서비스의 경제적 가치는 / 서비스 전에 결정하기 어렵고, / 공급자는 가격을 전달한다. / 그들이 ~할 수 있게 하는 / 구매자에게 가치를 전달하는 위험과 보상을 나눌 수 있게

────────────────────

결과 기반 가격 책정 중 가장 일반적으로 알려진 형태는 변호사가 사용하는 *승소 시 보수 약정*이라고 불리는 관행이다.

(C) 승소 시 보수 약정은 개인 상해 및 특정 소비자 소송에 대해 비용이 청구되는 주요 방식이다. 이 방식에서 변호사는 소송이 해결될 때까지 수수료나 지불금을 받지 않고, 해결 시에 그들은 의뢰인이 받는 금액의 일정 비율을 받는다.

(A) 따라서 의뢰인에게 유리한 결과만 보수가 지불된다. 의뢰인의 관점에서 보면 이 가격 책정은 타당한데, 이러한 소송의 의뢰인 대부분이 법률 사무소에 익숙하지 않고 아마도 겁을 먹을 수 있다는 것이 부분적인 이유다. 그들의 가장 큰 두려움은 해결하는 데 몇 년이 걸릴 수 있는 소송에 대한 높은 수수료이다.

(B) 승소 시 보수 약정을 사용함으로써 의뢰인은 합의금을 받을 때까지 수수료를 지불하지 않도록 보장받는다. 승소 시 보수 약정의 이런 비슷한 경우에서 서비스의 경제적 가치는 서비스 전에 결정하기 어렵고, 공급자는 그들이 구매자에게 가치를 전달하는 위험과 보상을 나눌 수 있게 하는 가격을 전달한다.

Why? 왜 정답일까?

'승소 시 보수 약정' 관행을 소재로 언급하는 주어진 글 뒤에는, 이 관행에 따를 때 변호사는 소송 종결 후 의뢰인이 (소송의 결과로) 받는 금액의 일정 비율을 가져간다고 보충 설명하는 (C)가 연결된다. 이어서 (A)는 '그래서' 의뢰인에게 유리한 결과가 나와야만 변호사에게 보수가 돌아간다고 설명하고, 의뢰인의 관점에서 이 관행이 타당한 이유를 설명한다. 마지막으로 (B)는 (A) 말미에 언급된 의뢰인의 '두려움'이 승소 시 보수 약정 관행을 통해 해결될 수 있다는 결론을 제시한다. 따라서 글의 순서로 가장 적절한 것은 ④ '(C) − (A) − (B)'이다.

- ● commonly ⓐⓓ 흔히, 공통적으로
- ● contingency pricing 승소 후 보수 약정
- ● outcome ⓝ 결과
- ● client ⓝ 고객, 의뢰인
- ● point of view 관점, 견해
- ● in part 부분적으로
- ● possibly ⓐⓓ 아마도
- ● fee ⓝ 요금
- ● settle ⓥ 해결하다, 합의하다
- ● determine ⓥ 결정하다
- ● reward ⓝ 보상
- ● injury ⓝ 상해, 부상
- ● practice ⓝ 관행
- ● lawyer ⓝ 변호사
- ● in one's favor ~에게 유리한
- ● compensate ⓥ 보상하다
- ● make sense 일리가 있다
- ● unfamiliar with ~에 익숙하지 않은
- ● intimidate ⓥ 위협하다
- ● case ⓝ 사례, 경우, 사건
- ● instance ⓝ 사례
- ● risk ⓝ 위험
- ● deliver ⓥ 전달하다
- ● bill ⓥ 청구하다 ⓝ 청구서, 계산서, 법안

구문 풀이

12행 In these and other instances of contingency pricing, the economic value of the service is hard to determine before the
　　　= it is hard to determine the economic value of the service
service, and providers develop a price that allows them to share the
　　　　　　　　　　　　　　　　　주격 관계대명사
risks and rewards of delivering value to the buyer.

★★ 문제 해결 꿀~팁 ★★

▶ 많이 틀린 이유는?

(C) − (B)는 크게 어색하지 않지만 (B) − (A)가 어색하므로 ⑤는 답이 될 수 없다. (B)의 마지막 부분은 승소 시 보수 약정에 대한 설명을 마무리하며 최종 결론을 제시하는데, (A)는 승소 시 보수 약정 관행이 이뤄지는 이유를 다루며 아직 부연 설명을 전개하는 중이다.

▶ 문제 해결 방법은?

(C)의 'when they are paid a percentage of the money that the client receives'와 (A)의 'only an outcome in the client's favor is compensated'는 사실상 의미가 같다. '의뢰인이 받는 돈의 일부를 받는다 = 의뢰인에게 돌아갈 이익이 있어야 돈을 받는다'이기 때문이다. 따라서 (C) − (A)가 인접함을 알 수 있다.

DAY 16 · 문장 삽입 01

01 ④	02 ⑤	03 ④	04 ④	05 ③
06 ④	07 ⑤	08 ⑤	09 ①	10 ②
11 ④	12 ⑤			

---

01 물질 이용의 확장   정답률 46% | 정답 ④

글의 흐름으로 보아, 주어진 문장이 들어가기에 가장 적절한 곳을 고르시오.

The earliest humans had access / to only a very limited number of materials, / those that occur naturally: / stone, wood, clay, skins, and so on.
초기 인류는 접근했다. / 매우 제한된 수의 물질에만 / 즉 자연적으로 존재하는 것들 / 돌, 나무, 찰흙, 가죽 등

① With time, / they discovered techniques for producing materials / that had properties / superior to those of the natural ones; / these new materials included pottery and various metals.
시간이 흐르면서 / 그들은 물질을 만들어 내는 기술을 발견했는데, / 특성을 가진 / 자연적인 특성의 물질보다 더 우수한 / 이 새로운 물질에는 도자기와 다양한 금속이 포함되었다.

② Furthermore, / it was discovered / that the properties of a material could be altered / by heat treatments / and by the addition of other substances.
게다가, / 발견되었다. / 물질의 특성이 바뀔 수 있다는 것이 / 열처리로 인해 / 그리고 여타 다른 물질의 첨가로 인해

③ At this point, / materials utilization was totally a selection process / that involved deciding / from a given, rather limited set of materials, / the one best suited for an application / based on its characteristics.
이 시기에, / 물질 이용은 전적으로 선택의 과정이었다. / 결정하는 것을 수반하는, / 상당히 제한된 특정 물질 집합 중에서 / 용도에 가장 적합한 물질을 / 물질의 특성에 근거하여

☑ It was not until relatively recent times / that scientists came to understand the relationships / between the structural elements of materials and their properties.
비교적 최근에 이르러서였다. / 과학자들이 비로소 관계를 이해하게 된 것은 / 물질의 구조적 요소와 물질 특성 사이의

This knowledge, / acquired over approximately the past 100 years, / has empowered them / to fashion, to a large degree, the characteristics of materials.
이 지식은 / 대략 지난 100년 동안 습득된 / 그들에게 힘을 주었다. / 상당한 정도로 물질의 특성을 형성할

⑤ Thus, / tens of thousands of different materials / have evolved / with rather specialized characteristics / that meet the needs of our modern and complex society, / including metals, plastics, glasses, and fibers.
따라서 / 수만 가지의 다양한 물질이 / 발전해 왔다. / 상당히 특화된 특성을 가진 / 복잡한 우리 현대 사회의 요구를 충족하는 / 금속, 플라스틱, 유리, 섬유를 포함하여

초기 인류는 매우 제한된 수의 물질, 즉 돌, 나무, 찰흙, 가죽 등 자연적으로 존재하는 물질에만 접근할 수 있었다. ① 시간이 흐르면서 그들은 자연적인 특성의 물질보다 더 우수한 특성을 가진 물질을 만들어 내는 기술을 발견했는데, 이 새로운 물질에는 도자기와 다양한 금속이 포함되었다. ② 게다가, 물질의 특성이 열처리와 여타 다른 물질의 첨가로 인해 바뀔 수 있다는 것이 발견되었다. ③ 이 시기에, 물질 이용은 상당히 제한된 특정 물질 집합 중에서 물질의 특성에 근거하여 용도에 가장 적합한 물질을 결정하는 것을 수반하는, 전적으로 선택의 과정이었다. ④ 과학자들이 물질의 구조적 요소와 물질 특성의 관계를 비로소 이해하게 된 것은 비교적 최근에 이르러서였다. 대략 지난 100년 동안 습득된 이 지식으로 그들은 상당한 정도로 물질의 특성을 형성할 수 있게 되었다. ⑤ 따라서 금속, 플라스틱, 유리, 섬유를 포함하여, 복잡한 우리 현대 사회의 요구를 충족하는 상당히 특화된 특성을 가진 수만 가지의 다양한 물질이 발전해왔다.

Why? 왜 정답일까?

인류가 이용하는 물질 범위가 확장된 과정에 관해 설명하는 글이다. ④ 앞까지 초기 인류는 자연적으로 존재하는 물질만 이용하다가, 열처리 등을 통해 물질 특성을 변화시킬 수 있다는 것을 알게 되면서 물질을 만들어낼 수 있게 되었는데, 이때 생성 가능한 물질 범위는 크게 제한되어 있었다는 내용이 전개된다. 여기에 이어 주어진 문장은 비교적 최근에 이르러서야 과학자들이 물질의 구조적 요소와 특성 사이의 관계를 알게 되었다고 언급한다. ④ 뒤의 문장은 이 관계에 관한 이해를 This knowledge로 받으며, 이를 바탕으로 많은 물질이 생성 가능해졌다는 내용을 제시한다. 따라서 주어진 문장이 들어가기에 가장 적절한 곳은 ④이다.

● relatively [ad] 비교적   ● structural @ 구조적인

● property ⓝ 특성, 속성
● clay ⓝ 찰흙
● pottery ⓝ 도자기
● heat treatment 열처리
● utilization ⓝ 이용, 활용
● characteristic ⓝ 특징
● fiber ⓝ 섬유
● have access to ~에 접근하다
● superior to ~보다 우수한
● alter ⓥ 바꾸다
● substance ⓝ 물질
● suited for ~에 적합한
● empower ⓥ 권한을 주다

구문 풀이

1행 It was not until **relatively recent times** that scientists came
「it is[was] not until ~ that : ~하고 나서야 비로소 …하다」
to understand the relationships between the structural elements of materials and their properties.

---

02 자연과 도시의 관계를 반영해 조성되는 공원   정답률 48% | 정답 ⑤

글의 흐름으로 보아, 주어진 문장이 들어가기에 가장 적절한 곳을 고르시오.

Parks take the shape / demanded by the cultural concerns of their time.
공원은 형태를 취한다. / 그것이 속한 시대의 문화적 관심사가 요구하는

Once parks are in place, / they are no inert stage / — their purposes and meanings are made and remade / by planners and by park users.
일단 공원이 마련되면, / 그것은 비활성화된 단계가 아니다. / 그것의 목적과 의미는 만들어지고 또 만들어진다. / 계획자와 공원 이용자에 의해

Moments of park creation are particularly telling, / however, / for they reveal and actualize ideas / about nature and its relationship to urban society.
공원을 조성하는 순간들은 특히 의미가 있는데, / 그러나 / 그것들이 생각을 드러내고 실현하기 때문이다. / 자연 그리고 자연과 도시 사회의 관계에 관한 (생각)

① Indeed, / what distinguishes a park from the broader category of public space / is the representation of nature / that parks are meant to embody.
실제로 / 공원을 더 넓은 범주의 공공 공간과 구별하는 것은 / 자연의 표현이다. / 공원이 구현하려는

② Public spaces include parks, concrete plazas, sidewalks, even indoor atriums.
공공 공간에는 포함된다. / 공원, 콘크리트 광장, 보도, 심지어 실내 아트리움도

③ Parks typically have trees, grass, and other plants / as their central features.
일반적으로 공원에는 나무, 풀, 그리고 다른 식물들이 있다. / 그들의 중심적인 특색으로

④ When entering a city park, / people often imagine a sharp separation / from streets, cars, and buildings.
도시 공원에 들어갈 때, / 사람들은 흔히 뚜렷한 분리를 상상한다. / 거리, 자동차, 그리고 건물과의

☑ There's a reason for that: / traditionally, / park designers attempted to create such a feeling / by planting tall trees at park boundaries, / building stone walls, / and constructing other means of partition.
거기에는 이유가 있는데, / 전통적으로 / 공원 설계자들은 그런 느낌을 만들어 내려고 했다. / 공원 경계에 키 큰 나무를 심고, / 돌담을 쌓고, / 다른 칸막이 수단을 세워

What's behind this idea is / not only landscape architects' desire / to design aesthetically suggestive park spaces, / but a much longer history of Western thought / that envisions cities and nature as antithetical spaces and oppositional forces.
이 생각의 배후에는 있다. / 조경가의 욕망뿐만 아니라 / 미적인 암시가 있는 공원 공간을 설계하려는 / 훨씬 더 오래된 서구 사상의 역사가 / 도시와 자연을 대조적인 공간과 반대 세력으로 상상하는

공원은 그것이 속한 시대의 문화적 관심사가 요구하는 형태를 취한다. 일단 공원이 마련되면, 그것은 비활성화된 단계가 아니다. 그것의 목적과 의미는 계획자와 공원 이용자에 의해 만들어지고 또 만들어진다. 그러나 공원을 조성하는 순간들은 특히 의미가 있는데, 자연 그리고 자연과 도시 사회의 관계에 관한 생각이 드러나고 실현되기 때문이다. ① 실제로 공원을 더 넓은 범주의 공공 공간과 구별하는 것은 공원이 구현하려는 자연의 표현이다. ② 공공 공간에는 공원, 콘크리트 광장, 보도, 심지어 실내 아트리움도 포함된다. ③ 일반적으로 공원에는 그들의 중심적인 특색으로 나무, 풀, 그리고 다른 식물들이 있다. ④ 도시 공원에 들어갈 때, 사람들은 흔히 거리, 자동차, 그리고 건물과의 뚜렷한 분리를 상상한다. ⑤ 거기에는 이유가 있는데, 전통적으로 공원 설계자들은 공원 경계에 키 큰 나무를 심고, 돌담을 쌓고, 다른 칸막이 수단을 세워 그런 느낌을 만들어 내려고 했다. 이 생각의 배후에는 미적인 암시가 있는 공원 공간을 설계하려는 조경가의 욕망뿐만 아니라 도시와 자연을 대조적인 공간과 반대 세력으로 상상하는 훨씬 더 오래된 서구 사상의 역사가 있다.

Why? 왜 정답일까?

⑤ 앞에서 도시 사람들은 공원에 들어갈 때 (도시의) 거리, 자동차, 건물 등과 뚜렷하게 분리되는 것을 상상한다고 언급한 데 이어, 주어진 문장에서는 그런 상상에 '이유'가 있다고 설명한다. ⑤ 뒤의 this idea는 주어진 문장에서 설명한 이유, 즉 '공원 설계자들이

공원 경계에 나무나 칸막이를 두어서 분리의 느낌을 내고자 했다는' 관념을 지칭하는 것이다. 따라서 주어진 문장이 들어가기에 가장 적절한 곳은 ⑤이다.

traditionally ⓐ 전통적으로	**attempt to** ~하려고 시도하다, 노력하다
plant ⓥ 심다	**boundary** ⓝ 경계
demand ⓥ 요구하다	**concern** ⓝ 관심사
in place 제자리에 있는, 준비가 되어 있는	**inert** ⓐ 비활성의
telling ⓐ 효과적인, 현저한, 보여주는	**reveal** ⓥ 드러내다
actualize ⓥ 실현하다	**relationship** ⓝ 관계
distinguish A from B A와 B를 구별하다	**representation** ⓝ 표현
be meant to ~하기로 되어 있다	**embody** ⓥ 구현하다
sidewalk ⓝ 인도	**atrium** ⓝ 아트리움
feature ⓝ 특색, 특징, 기능	**separation** ⓝ 분리
landscape ⓝ 조경	**aesthetically** ⓐⓓ 미적으로
suggestive ⓐ 암시하는	**envision** ⓥ 상상하다, 머릿속에 그리다
antithetical ⓐ 대조적인	**oppositional** ⓐ 반대의

구문 풀이

17행 When entering a city park, people often imagine a sharp
접속사 + 현재분사(~할 때)
separation from streets, cars, and buildings.

03 동물들의 신호 　　　　정답률 56% | 정답 ④

글의 흐름으로 보아, 주어진 문장이 들어가기에 가장 적절한 곳을 고르시오.

Many of the ritualized displays / performed by animals / look so bizarre to us / that we wonder how they came about.
의례화된 표현 중 많은 것이 / 동물들이 행하는 / 우리에게 너무 기이해 보여서, / 우리는 그런 표현이 어떻게 생겨났는지 궁금해한다.

① Most of the various forms of signaling / that are used by different species of animals / have not arisen afresh in each separate species.
다양한 신호 보내기 형식의 대부분은 / 여러 종의 동물에 의해 사용되는 / 각 개별 종에서 새로 생겨나지 않았다.

② As one species evolves into another, / particular forms of signaling may be passed on, / owing to the effects of both genes and learning or experience.
하나의 종이 다른 종으로 진화하면서, / 특정 신호 보내기 형식이 전달될 수도 있다. / 유전자 및 학습이나 경험 둘 다의 영향 때문에

③ Some signals have significance across many species, / and so remain much the same / over generations and in a number of species.
몇몇 신호는 여러 종에 걸쳐서 중요성을 지니며, / 그래서 거의 똑같이 남아 있다. / 세대를 넘어 많은 종에

✔But many signals, / as they are passed from generation to generation / by whatever means, / go through changes / that make them either more elaborate or simply different.
그러나 많은 신호가 / 그것이 대대로 전달될 때 / 어떤 방법에 의해서든 / 변화를 겪는다. / 그것을 더 정교하게, 또는 그저 다르게 만드는

If we examine closely related species, / we can often see slight variations in a particular display / and we can piece together an explanation / for the spread of the display across species.
우리가 밀접하게 관련된 종을 조사하면, / 우리는 하나의 특정한 표현에서 약간의 차이를 자주 볼 수 있고, / 우리는 설명을 종합할 수 있다. / 여러 종에 걸친 그 표현의 확산에 대한

⑤ Some very elaborate displays / may have begun / as simpler versions of the same behavioral pattern / that became more elaborate / as they developed and were passed on from generation to generation.
매우 정교한 몇몇 표현은 / 시작했을지도 모른다. / 똑같은 행동 양식의 더 단순한 형태로 / 더 정교해졌던, / 그것이 발전하고 대대로 전달되면서

동물들이 행하는 의례화된 표현 중에 많은 것이 우리에게 너무 기이해 보여서, 우리는 그런 표현이 어떻게 생겨났는지 궁금해한다. ① 여러 종의 동물들에 의해 사용되는 다양한 신호 보내기 형식의 대부분은 각 개별 종에서 새로 생겨나지 않았다. ② 하나의 종이 다른 종으로 진화하면서, 유전자 및 학습이나 경험 둘 다의 영향 때문에 특정 신호 보내기 형식이 전달될 수도 있다. ③ 몇몇 신호는 여러 종에 걸쳐서 중요성을 지니며, 그래서 세대를 넘어 많은 종에 거의 똑같이 남아 있다. ④ 그러나 많은 신호가 어떤 방법에 의해서든 대대로 전달될 때 그것을 더 정교하게, 또는 그저 다르게 만드는 변화를 겪는다. 밀접하게 관련된 종을 조사하면, 우리는 하나의 특정한 표현에서 약간의 차이를 자주 볼 수 있고, 여러 종에 걸친 그 표현의 확산에 대한 설명을 종합할 수 있다. ⑤ 매우 정교한 몇몇 표현은 그것이 발전하고 대대로 전달되면서 더 정교해졌던, 똑같은 행동 양식의 더 단순한 형태로 시작했을지도 모른다.

Why? 왜 정답일까?

동물의 신호에 관해 설명하는 글로, 몇몇 신호의 경우 세대와 종을 넘어 거의 똑같이 남아 있는 경우가 있다는 내용이 ④ 앞에서 언급된다. 한편 **But**으로 시작하는 주어진 문장은

어떤 형태로든 '전달'을 거치면 신호가 더 정교해지거나 달라지는 변화를 겪는 경우가 많다고 한다. 이어서 ④ 뒤에서는 주어진 문장의 결과로 밀접하게 연관된 종에서 나타나는 신호에 '차이'가 있다고 한다. 따라서 주어진 문장이 들어가기에 가장 적절한 곳은 ④이다.

generation ⓝ 세대	**means** ⓝ 방법, 수단
elaborate ⓐ 정교한	**ritualize** ⓥ 의례화하다
display ⓝ 표현, 전시	**bizarre** ⓐ 기이한, 특이한
come about 생겨나다, 발생하다	**arise** ⓥ 생기다, 발생하다
afresh ⓐⓓ 새롭게, 다시	**evolve** ⓥ 진화하다
particular ⓐ 특정한	**pass on** 전달하다, 전승하다
owing to ~ 때문에	**gene** ⓝ 유전자
significance ⓝ 중요성	**examine** ⓥ 조사하다, 검토하다
variation ⓝ 변화, 변형물	**behavioral** ⓐ 행동적인
piece together ~을 종합하다	

구문 풀이

5행 Many of the ritualized displays performed by animals look
　　　　주어(부분 + of + 전체)　　　과거분사구　　　동사(복수)
so bizarre to us that we wonder how they came about.
「so ~ that … : 너무 ~해서 …하다」

04 텃새의 서식지 선택 　　　　정답률 67% | 정답 ④

글의 흐름으로 보아, 주어진 문장이 들어가기에 가장 적절한 곳을 고르시오.

Resident-bird habitat selection / is seemingly a straightforward process / in which a young dispersing individual moves / until it finds a place / where it can compete successfully to satisfy its needs.
텃새들의 서식지 선택은 / 외견상 간단한 과정이다. / 흩어지는 어린 개체가 옮겨 다니는, / 그것이 장소를 찾을 때까지 / (생존을 위한) 필요를 충족시키기 위해 성공적으로 경쟁할 수 있는

① Initially, these needs include only food and shelter.
처음에는, 이러한 필요에 음식과 은신처만 포함된다.

② However, eventually, / the young must locate, identify, and settle in a habitat / that satisfies not only survivorship but reproductive needs as well.
그러나 궁극적으로, / 그 어린 새는 서식지를 찾고, 확인하고, 거기에 정착해야 한다. / 생존뿐만 아니라 번식을 위한 필요조건도 충족시켜 주는

③ In some cases, the habitat / that provides the best opportunity for survival / may not be the same habitat / as the one that provides for highest reproductive capacity / because of requirements specific to the reproductive period.
일부의 경우, 서식지가 / 생존을 위한 최고의 기회를 제공하는 / 동일한 곳이 아닐 수도 있다. / 최고의 번식 능력을 가능하게 해주는 서식지와 / 번식기에만 특별히 요구되는 조건들 때문에

✔Thus, individuals of many resident species, / confronted with the fitness benefits / of control over a productive breeding site, / may be forced to balance costs / in the form of lower nonbreeding survivorship / by remaining in the specific habitat / where highest breeding success occurs.
따라서 많은 텃새 종의 개체들은 / 합적성에서 오는 이득과 마주하면, / 다산에 유리한 번식지를 장악하는 것이 갖는 / 대가의 균형을 맞추도록 강요당할 수도 있다. / 더 낮은 비번식기 생존율의 형태로 / 특정 서식지에 머물러 있음으로써 / 가장 높은 번식 성공이 일어나는

Migrants, however, are free to choose the optimal habitat / for survival during the nonbreeding season / and for reproduction during the breeding season.
그러나 철새들은 최적의 서식지를 자유롭게 선택한다. / 번식기가 아닌 동안에는 생존을 위한 최적의 서식지를, / 번식기 동안에는 번식을 위한

⑤ Thus, habitat selection during these different periods / can be quite different for migrants / as opposed to residents, / even among closely related species.
이와 같이 서로 다른 시기 동안의 서식지 선택은, / 철새들에게 있어서 상당히 다를 수 있다. / 텃새들과는 달리 / 심지어 밀접하게 관련이 있는 종들 사이에서조차도,

텃새들의 서식지 선택은 흩어지는 어린 개체가 (생존을 위한) 필요를 충족시키기 위해 성공적으로 경쟁할 수 있는 장소를 찾을 때까지 옮겨 다니는, 외견상 간단한 과정이다. ① 처음에는, 이러한 필요에 음식과 은신처만 포함된다. ② 그러나 궁극적으로, 그 어린 새는 생존뿐만 아니라 번식을 위한 필요조건도 충족시켜 주는 서식지를 찾고, 확인하고, 거기에 정착해야 한다. ③ 일부의 경우, 번식기에만 특별히 요구되는 조건들 때문에, 생존을 위한 최고의 기회를 제공하는 서식지가 최고의 번식 능력을 가능하게 해주는 서식지와 동일한 곳이 아닐 수도 있다. ④ 따라서 많은 텃새 종의 개체들은 다산에 유리한 번식지를 장악하는 것이 갖는 합목적성에서 오는 이득과 마주하면, 가장 높은 번식 성공이 일어나는 특정 서식지에 머물러 있음으로써 더 낮은 비번식기 생존율의 형태로 대가의 균형을 맞추도록 강요당할 수도 있다. 그러나 철새들은 번식기가 아닌 동안에는 생존을 위한 최적의 서식지를, 번식기 동안에는 번식을 위한 최

적의 서식지를 자유롭게 선택한다. ⑤ 이와 같이 서로 다른 시기 동안의 서식지 선택은, 심지어 밀접하게 관련이 있는 종들 사이에서조차도, 텃새들과는 달리 철새들에게 있어서 상당히 다를 수 있다.

Why? 왜 정답일까?

텃새의 서식지 선택을 철새와 대비하여 설명한 글이다. ④ 앞에서 최적의 서식지와 최적의 번식지가 서로 다를 수 있음을 언급한 데 이어, **Thus**로 시작하는 주어진 문장은 그리하여 텃새가 번식에 적합한 장소에 살며 비번식기 생존율을 희생한다, 즉 평소 서식에 있어 희생을 감당한다는 결론을 제시하고 있다. ④ 뒤에서는 이러한 텃새의 선택을 철새의 경우와 대조하고 있다. 따라서 주어진 문장이 들어가기에 가장 적절한 곳은 ④이다.

- **confront** ⓥ 마주하다
- **straightforward** ⓐ 간단한, 쉬운, 솔직한
- **reproductive** ⓐ 번식의
- **specific** ⓐ 특별한
- **optimal** ⓐ 최적의, 최선의
- **selection** ⓝ 선별
- **compete** ⓥ 경쟁하다
- **capacity** ⓝ 능력
- **migrant** ⓝ 철새

구문 풀이

1행 Thus, individuals of many resident species, confronted with
〔주어〕 〔수동분사구문(~한 채로)〕
the fitness benefits of control over a productive breeding site,
may be forced to balance costs in the form of lower nonbreeding
〔동사(조동사 수동태)〕 〔보어〕
survivorship by remaining in the specific habitat [where highest
〔~함으로써〕 〔선행사〕
breeding success occurs].

---

05 기록으로 연구되는 역사 정답률 50% | 정답 ③

글의 흐름으로 보아, 주어진 문장이 들어가기에 가장 적절한 곳을 고르시오. [3점]

The evolutionary history of a species or a disease / is like any other kind of history.
어떤 종이나 질병의 진화 역사는 / 그 어떤 다른 종류의 역사와도 비슷하다.

① There is no experiment, / in the usual sense, / that we can do now / to decide how long ago our ancestors first started to use fires / for cooking or other purposes / and what subsequent evolutionary effects / that change may have had.
실험은 없다. / 일반적인 의미에서, / 우리가 지금 할 수 있는 / 우리 조상이 얼마나 오래전에 불을 처음 사용하기 시작했는지 파악하기 위해 / 요리나 다른 목적으로 / 그리고 이후의 어떤 진화적 영향 / 그 변화가 미쳤을 수도 있는지

② History can be investigated / only by examining the records it has left.
역사는 연구될 수 있다. / 역사가 남긴 기록들을 검사하는 것으로만

✔ Charred bones or even carbon deposits / from an ancient campfire / can be informative documents to people / who know how to read them.
까맣게 된 뼈나 심지어 탄소 퇴적물도 / 고대의 모닥불에서 나온 / 사람들에게는 유익한 정보를 주는 기록이 될 수 있다. / 그것들을 해독하는 법을 아는

Likewise, / the chemical structure of proteins and DNA / may be read / to reveal relationships among now strikingly different organisms.
마찬가지로 / 단백질과 DNA의 화학적 구조가 / 해독될 수도 있다. / 현재 현저히 다른 유기체들 사이의 관계를 밝히기 위해

④ Until a time machine is invented, / we will not be able to go back / and watch the evolution of major traits, / but we can nonetheless reconstruct prehistoric events / by the records they left / in fossils, carbon traces, structures, and behavioral tendencies, / as well as protein and DNA structures.
타임머신이 발명되기 전에는 / 우리가 과거로 가서 / 주요 특성들의 진화를 관찰할 수 없겠지만, / 그렇더라도 우리는 선사 시대의 사건들을 재구성할 수 있다. / 그것들이 남긴 기록으로 / 화석, 탄소 흔적, 구조물, 그리고 행동 성향에 / 단백질과 DNA 구조뿐만 아니라

⑤ Even when we cannot reconstruct the history of a trait, / we can often still be confident / that it was shaped by natural selection.
심지어 우리가 어떤 특성의 역사를 재구성할 수 없을 때도, / 우리는 흔히 여전히 확신할 수 있다. / 그것이 자연 선택으로 형성되었다고

어떤 종이나 질병의 진화 역사는 그 어떤 다른 종류의 역사와도 비슷하다. ① 일반적인 의미에서, 우리 조상이 얼마나 오래전에 요리나 다른 목적으로 불을 처음 사용하기 시작했는지, 그리고 그 변화가 이후의 어떤 진화적 영향을 미쳤을 수도 있는지 결정하기 위해 우리가 지금 할 수 있는 실험은 없다. ② 역사는 역사가 남긴 기록들을 검사하는 것으로만 연구될 수 있다. ③ 고대의 모닥불에서 나온 (탄화로) 까맣게 된 뼈나 심지어 탄소 퇴적물도 그것들을 해독하는 법을 아는 사람들에게는 유익한 정보를 주는 기록이 될 수 있다. 마찬가지로 현재 현저히 다른 유기체들 사이의 관계를 밝히기 위해 단백질과 DNA의 화학적 구조를 해독할 수도 있다. ④ 타임머신이 발명되기 전에는 우리가 과거로 가서

주요 특성들의 진화를 관찰할 수 없겠지만, 그렇더라도 우리는 단백질과 DNA 구조뿐만 아니라 화석, 탄소 흔적, 구조물, 그리고 행동 성향에 그것들이 남긴 기록으로 선사 시대의 사건들을 재구성할 수 있다. ⑤ 심지어 우리가 어떤 한 특성의 역사를 재구성할 수 없을 때도, 우리는 흔히 그것이 자연 선택으로 형성되었다고 여전히 확신할 수 있다.

Why? 왜 정답일까?

③ 앞에서 역사는 실험이 아닌 기록으로만 연구될 수 있다는 일반적인 내용만을 언급하는데, ③ 뒤의 문장은 하나의 주제에 대해 비슷한 사례를 연결할 때 쓰는 **Likewise**로 시작하며 구체적인 예를 언급한다. 즉, ③ 자리에 ③ 앞에 대한 예시가 하나 나오고, 이어서 ③ 뒤에서 또 다른 예를 열거하는 흐름이 적합하다. 따라서 주어진 문장이 들어가기에 가장 적절한 곳은 ③이다.

- **charred** ⓐ (탄화로) 까맣게 된
- **ancient** ⓐ 고대의
- **evolutionary** ⓐ 진화의
- **usual** ⓐ 일반적인, 통상적인
- **purpose** ⓝ 목적
- **investigate** ⓥ 조사하다, 연구하다
- **likewise** ⓐⓓ 마찬가지로
- **reveal** ⓥ 밝히다
- **organism** ⓝ 생물, 유기체
- **reconstruct** ⓥ 재구성하다
- **trace** ⓝ 흔적
- **tendency** ⓝ 경향
- **natural selection** 자연 선택
- **deposit** ⓝ 퇴적물
- **informative** ⓐ 정보를 주는
- **experiment** ⓝ 실험
- **ancestor** ⓝ 조상
- **subsequent** ⓐ 이후의
- **examine** ⓥ 조사하다, 검토하다
- **protein** ⓝ 단백질
- **strikingly** ⓐⓓ 현저히
- **nonetheless** ⓐⓓ 그럼에도 불구하고
- **fossil** ⓝ 화석
- **behavioral** ⓐ 행동의
- **confident** ⓐ 확신하는

구문 풀이

5행 There is no experiment, in the usual sense, [that we can do
[ ]: experiment 수식
now to decide {how long ago our ancestors first started to use fires
〔~하려고〕
for cooking or other purposes} and {what subsequent evolutionary
effects that change may have had}].
〔과거 추측(~했을지도 모른다)〕

---

06 책이나 서면의 오타와 생물의 돌연변이 비교 대조 정답률 53% | 정답 ④

글의 흐름으로 보아, 주어진 문장이 들어가기에 가장 적절한 곳을 고르시오. [3점]

Misprints in a book or in any written message / usually have a negative impact on the content, / sometimes (literally) fatally.
책이나 어떤 서면 메시지에서 오타가 발생하면 / 일반적으로 내용에 부정적인 영향을 미치며, / 때로는 (문자 그대로) 치명적이기도 하다.

① The displacement of a comma, / for instance, / may be a matter of life and death.
쉼표의 위치가 잘못 찍히는 것은 / 예를 들어, / 생사가 걸린 문제일 수 있다.

② Similarly most mutations have harmful consequences / for the organism in which they occur, / meaning that they reduce its reproductive fitness.
마찬가지로 대부분의 돌연변이는 해로운 결과를 가져오는데, / 그것이 발생하는 유기체에 / 그것들이 생식 적합성을 감소시킨다는 의미다.

③ Occasionally, however, / a mutation may occur / that increases the fitness of the organism, / just as an accidental failure to reproduce the text of the first edition / might provide more accurate or updated information.
그러나 때때로 / 돌연변이가 발생할 수 있다. / 유기체의 적합성을 상승시키는 / 우연히 초판의 텍스트를 복사하지 못한 것이 / 더 정확하거나 최신의 정보를 제공할 수도 있는 것과 꼭 마찬가지로

✔ At the next step in the argument, / however, / the analogy breaks down.
논거의 다음 단계에서는 / 그러나 / 그 유사성이 깨진다.

A favorable mutation is going to be more heavily represented in the next generation, / since the organism in which it occurred / will have more offspring / and mutations are transmitted to the offspring.
유리한 돌연변이는 다음 세대에 더 많이 나타날 것인데, / 그 돌연변이가 발생한 유기체는 / 더 많은 자손을 낳을 것이고 / 돌연변이가 자손에게 전달되기 때문이다.

⑤ By contrast, / there is no mechanism / by which a book that accidentally corrects the mistakes of the first edition / will tend to sell better.
대조적으로, / 메커니즘은 없다. / 우연히 초판의 오류를 바로잡은 책이 / 더 잘 팔리는 경향이 있을

책이나 어떤 서면 메시지에서 오타가 발생하면 일반적으로 내용에 부정적인 영향을 미치며, 때로는 (문자 그대로) 치명적이기도 하다. ① 예를 들어, 쉼표의 위치가 잘못 찍히는 것은 생사가 걸린 문제일 수 있다. ② 마찬가지로 대부분의 돌연변이는 그것이 발생하는 유기체에 해로운 결과를 가져오는데, 그것들이 생식 적합성을 감소시킨다는 의미다. ③ 그러나 때때로 유기체의 적합성을 상승시키는 돌연변이가 발생할 수 있는데, 이는 우연히 초판의 텍스트를 복사

DAY 16

하지 못한 것이 더 정확하거나 최신의 정보를 제공할 수도 있는 것과 꼭 마찬가지이다. ④ 그러나 논거의 다음 단계에서는 그 유사성이 깨진다. 유리한 돌연변이는 다음 세대에 더 많이 나타날 것인데, 그 돌연변이가 발생한 유기체는 더 많은 자손을 낳을 것이고 돌연변이가 자손에게 전달되기 때문이다. ⑤ 대조적으로, 우연히 초판의 오류를 바로잡은 책이 더 잘 팔리는 경향이 있을 메커니즘은 없다.

Why? 왜 정답일까?

책이나 서면의 오타와 생물의 돌연변이를 비교 대조하는 글로, ④ 앞에서는 오타와 돌연변이의 유사점을 주로 언급하지만, ④ 뒤의 두 문장은 둘의 차이점에 집중하고 있다. 따라서 주어진 문장이 들어가기에 가장 적절한 곳은 글의 흐름이 반전되는 지점인 ④이다.

- **analogy** ⓝ 유사
- **misprint** ⓝ 오타
- **literally** 〈ad〉 문자 그대로
- **displacement** ⓝ (제자리에서 쫓겨난) 이동
- **mutation** ⓝ 돌연변이
- **consequence** ⓝ 결과
- **reproductive** 〈a〉 생식의
- **accidental** 〈a〉 우연한
- **generation** ⓝ 세대
- **offspring** ⓝ 자손
- **by contrast** 대조적으로
- **break down** 무너지다
- **impact** ⓝ 영향
- **fatally** 〈ad〉 치명적으로
- **matter of life and death** 생사가 걸린 문제
- **harmful** 〈a〉 해로운
- **organism** ⓝ 유기체
- **fitness** ⓝ 적합성
- **edition** ⓝ (책 출간 횟수를 나타내는) 판
- **accurate** 〈a〉 정확한
- **transmit** 〈v〉 전달하다

구문 풀이

6행 Similarly most mutations have harmful consequences for the organism [in which they occur], meaning that they reduce its
선행사 「전치사＋관·대」 = which means(앞 문장 보충)
reproductive fitness.

---

07 렘수면 단계의 특징　　정답률 53% | 정답 ⑤

글의 흐름으로 보아, 주어진 문장이 들어가기에 가장 적절한 곳을 고르시오. [3점]

Most dreaming occurs during REM sleep.
대부분 꿈은 렘수면 동안에 발생한다.

① REM stands for Rapid Eye Movement, / a stage of sleep discovered by Professor Nathaniel Kleitman / at the University of Chicago / in 1958.
렘은 Rapid Eye Movement(급속 안구 운동)를 뜻한다. / Nathaniel Kleitman 교수에 의해 발견된 수면 단계인 / 시카고 대학의 / 1958년에

② Along with a medical student, Eugene Aserinsky, / he noted / that when people are sleeping, / they exhibit rapid eye movement, / as if they were "looking" at something.
의대생인 Eugene Aserinsky와 함께, / 그는 주목했다. / 사람들이 잠을 자고 있을 때, / 그들이 급속 안구 운동을 보인다는 데 / 그들이 마치 무엇인가를 '보고' 있는 것처럼

③ Ongoing research by Kleitman and Aserinsky concluded / that it was during this period of rapid eye movement / that people dream, / yet their minds are as active as someone who is awake.
Kleitman과 Aserinsky의 지속적인 연구는 결론을 내렸다. / 바로 이 급속 안구 운동 기간 중이라는 / 사람들이 꿈을 꾸는 / 하지만 정신은 깨어있는 사람만큼 활발한 것은

④ Interestingly enough, / studies have found / that along with rapid eye movement, / our heart rates increase and our respiration is also elevated / — yet our bodies do not move and are basically paralyzed / due to a nerve center in the brain / that keeps our bodies motionless / besides some occasional twitches and jerks.
흥미롭게도 / 연구에서 밝히기로는, / 급속 안구 운동과 함께, / 우리의 심장박동이 증가하고 호흡 또한 증가하지만 / 몸은 움직이지 않고 기본적으로 마비된다. / 뇌의 신경 중추 때문에 / 우리의 몸을 가만히 있게 유지하는 / 이따금의 씰룩거림과 홱 움직임 외에는

✔ This is why it is difficult / to wake up from or scream out during a nightmare.
이런 이유로 어려운 것이다. / 악몽에서 깨어나거나 악몽 중에 비명을 지르는 것이

To sum it up, / during the REM dream state, / your mind is busy but your body is at rest.
요약하면, / 렘 꿈 상태 동안에, / 여러분의 정신은 바쁘지만 몸은 움직이지 않는다.

대부분 꿈은 렘수면 동안에 발생한다. ① 렘은 1958년에 시카고 대학의 Nathaniel Kleitman 교수에 의해 발견된 수면 단계인 Rapid Eye Movement(급속 안구 운동)를 뜻한다. ② 의대생인 Eugene Aserinsky와 함께, 그는 사람들이 잠을 자고 있을 때, 그들이 마치 무엇인가를 '보고' 있는 것처럼 급속 안구 운동을 보인다는 데 주목했다. ③ Kleitman과 Aserinsky의 지속적인 연구는 사람들이 꿈을 꾸지만 정신은 깨어있는 사람만큼 활발할 때가 바로 이 급속 안구 운동 기간 중이라는 결론을 내렸다. ④ 흥미롭게도 연구에서 밝히기로는, 급속

안구 운동과 함께 우리의 심장박동이 증가하고 호흡 또한 증가하지만 몸은 이따금의 씰룩거림과 홱 움직이는 것 외에는 우리의 몸을 가만히 유지시키는 뇌의 신경 중추 때문에 움직이지 않고 기본적으로 마비된다. ⑤ 이런 이유로 악몽에서 깨어나거나 악몽 중에 비명을 지르는 것이 어려운 것이다. 요약하면, 렘 꿈 상태 동안에, 여러분의 정신은 바쁘지만 몸은 움직이지 않는다.

Why? 왜 정답일까?

⑤ 앞에서 연구 결과에 따르면 렘수면 중 우리는 심박수와 호흡이 증가하지만 몸은 기본적으로 마비되어 있다고 한다. 주어진 문장은 이 내용을 This로 가리키며 '이 이유로' 악몽에서 깨거나 악몽 중 비명을 지르기가 어려운 것이라고 보충 설명한다. ⑤ 뒤의 문장은 글의 내용을 요약 제시하며 마무리한다. 따라서 주어진 문장이 들어가기에 가장 적절한 곳은 ⑤이다.

- **nightmare** ⓝ 악몽
- **stage** ⓝ 단계
- **exhibit** 〈v〉 보이다
- **conclude** 〈v〉 결론을 내리다
- **respiration** ⓝ 호흡
- **basically** 〈ad〉 기본적으로
- **nerve center** 신경 중추
- **occasional** 〈a〉 이따금의
- **jerk** ⓝ (갑자기 날카롭게) 홱 움직임
- **at rest** 움직이지 않는
- **occur** 〈v〉 일어나다, 발생하다
- **along with** ~와 함께
- **ongoing** 〈a〉 진행 중인
- **period** ⓝ 기간, 시기
- **elevate** 〈v〉 증가하다, 높이다
- **paralyze** 〈v〉 마비시키다
- **motionless** 〈a〉 움직임이 없는
- **twitch** ⓝ 씰룩거림
- **state** ⓝ 상태

구문 풀이

6행 Along with a medical student, Eugene Aserinsky, he noted that when people are sleeping, they exhibit rapid eye movement,
접속사(~것)
as if they were "looking" at something.
「as if＋주어＋과거 동사 : (실제로 ~이지 않지만) 마치 ~인 것처럼」

★★★ 1등급 대비 고난도 2점 문제

08 소리의 디지털화가 음악 제작 방식에 끼친 변화　　정답률 20% | 정답 ⑤

글의 흐름으로 보아, 주어진 문장이 들어가기에 가장 적절한 곳을 고르시오.

The shift from analog to digital technology / significantly influenced how music was produced.
아날로그 기술에서 디지털 기술로의 전환은 / 음악이 제작되던 방식에 크게 영향을 미쳤다.

First and foremost, / the digitization of sounds / — that is, their conversion into numbers — / enabled music makers to undo what was done.
무엇보다도 / 소리의 디지털화, 즉 그것의 숫자로의 변환은 / 음악 제작자들이 기존의 작업을 되돌릴 수 있게 해 주었다.

① One could, in other words, / twist and bend sounds toward something new / without sacrificing the original version.
사람들은 다시 말해 / 소리를 비틀고 구부려 새로운 원가로 만들 수 있었다. / 원본을 희생하지 않으면서

② This "undo" ability made mistakes considerably less momentous, / sparking the creative process / and encouraging a generally more experimental mindset.
이러한 '되돌리기' 기능은 실수를 훨씬 덜 중대하게 만들어, / 창작 과정을 촉발하고 / 일반적으로 더 실험적인 사고방식을 장려했다.

③ In addition, / digitally converted sounds could be manipulated / simply by programming digital messages / rather than using physical tools, / simplifying the editing process significantly.
더구나, / 디지털로 변환된 소리는 조작될 수 있어서 / 단순히 디지털 메시지를 프로그래밍해서 / 물리적인 도구를 사용하기보다는 / 편집 과정을 크게 간소화했다.

④ For example, / while editing once involved razor blades / to physically cut and splice audiotapes, / it now involved the cursor and mouse-click of the computer-based sequencer program, / which was obviously less time consuming.
가령 / 한때는 편집에 면도기 칼날 사용이 수반됐지만, / 오디오 테이프를 물리적으로 자르고 합쳐 이으느라 / 이제 이것은 컴퓨터에 바탕을 둔 순서기 프로그램의 커서와 마우스 클릭을 수반해서, / 분명 시간을 덜 소모했다.

✔ Because the manipulation of digitally converted sounds / meant the reprogramming of binary information, / editing operations could be performed with millisecond precision.
디지털로 변환된 소리의 조작은 / 2진법의 정보를 다시 프로그래밍하는 것을 의미했으므로, / 편집 작업은 1,000분의 1초의 정밀도로 수행될 수 있었다.

This microlevel access at once made it easier / to conceal any traces of manipulations / (such as joining tracks in silent spots) / and introduced new possibilities / for manipulating sounds in audible and experimental ways.
이러한 매우 미시적인 접근은 그 즉시 더 쉽게 만들었고 / 조작의 흔적을 숨기는 것을 / (무음 지점에서 트랙을 결합하는 것과 같은) / 새로운 가능성을 내놓았다. / 들릴 수 있고 실험적인 방식으로 소리를 조작할

아날로그 기술에서 디지털 기술로의 전환은 음악이 제작되던 방식에 크게 영향을 미쳤다. 무엇보다도 소리의 디지털화, 즉 숫자로의 변환은 음악 제작자들이 기존의 작업을 되돌릴 수 있게 해 주었다. ① 다시 말해, 원본을 희생하지 않으면서 소리를 비틀고 구부려 새로운 뭔가로 만들 수 있었다. ② 이러한 '되돌리기' 기능은 실수를 훨씬 덜 중대하게 만들어, 창작 과정을 촉발하고 일반적으로 더 실험적인 사고방식을 장려했다. ③ 더구나, 디지털로 변환된 소리는 물리적인 도구를 사용하기보다는 단순히 디지털 메시지를 프로그래밍해 조작할 수 있어서, 편집 과정을 크게 간소화했다. ④ 가령 한때는 편집에 오디오 테이프를 물리적으로 자르고 합쳐 이으느라 면도기 칼날 사용이 수반됐지만, 이제 이것은 컴퓨터에 바탕을 둔 순서기 프로그램의 커서와 마우스 클릭을 수반해서, 분명 시간을 덜 소모했다. ⑤ 디지털로 변환된 소리의 조작은 2진법의 정보를 다시 프로그래밍하는 것을 의미했으므로, 편집 작업은 1,000분의 1초의 정밀도로 수행될 수 있었다. 이러한 매우 미시적인 접근은 그 즉시 (무음 지점에서 트랙을 결합하는 것 같은) 조작의 흔적을 숨기기 쉽게 했고, 들릴 수 있고 실험적인 방식으로 소리를 조작할 새로운 가능성을 내놓았다.

Why? 왜 정답일까?

⑤ 앞에서 디지털로 변화된 소리의 편집 과정이 물리적으로 자르고 오리는 과정에서 전자화되었다고 하는데, ⑤ 뒤에서는 갑자기 '이런 미세한 접근'을 언급한다. 이때 주어진 문장을 보면 '1,000분의 1초 단위의 정밀도'라는 표현이 있는데, 이것이 ⑤ 뒤의 This microlevel access로 연결된다. 따라서 주어진 문장이 들어가기에 가장 적절한 곳은 ⑤이다.

- **manipulation** ⓝ 조작
- **binary** ⓐ 2진법의
- **first and foremost** 무엇보다도
- **twist** ⓥ 뒤틀다
- **sacrifice** ⓥ 희생하다
- **momentous** ⓐ 중요한
- **simplify** ⓥ 간소화하다
- **splice** ⓥ 합쳐 잇다
- **time consuming** 시간이 많이 드는
- **conceal** ⓥ 숨기다
- **audible** ⓐ 들릴 수 있는
- **convert** ⓥ 변환하다, 전환하다
- **precision** ⓝ 정밀성
- **undo** ⓥ 되돌리다, 취소하다
- **bend** ⓥ 구부리다
- **considerably** ⓐ𝖽 상당히
- **spark** ⓥ 촉발하다
- **razor blade** 면도날
- **sequencer** ⓝ 순서기
- **microlevel** ⓐ 미시적인
- **trace** ⓝ 흔적

구문 풀이

21행 This microlevel access at once made it easier to conceal
　　　　　　　　　　　　　　　　동사1 → 형용사 진목적어 ← 가목적어
any traces of manipulations (such as joining tracks in silent spots)
and introduced new possibilities for manipulating sounds in audible
　　　동사2
and experimental ways.

★★ 문제 해결 꿀~팁 ★★

▶ 많이 틀린 이유는?
④ 뒤에서 갑자기 '면도날'이 언급되므로 어색해 보일 수 있지만, 앞뒤 흐름을 잘 봐야 한다. ④ 앞에서 음원의 디지털화 이후로 편집이 많이 간단해졌다고 하고, ④ 뒤에서는 디지털화 '이전'의 예시를 들어 예전에는 일일이 테이프를 자르고 붙이느라 시간이 많이 걸렸다고 부연하는 것이다. 즉 ④ 앞의 일반론을 ④ 뒤에서 대비되는 사례와 함께 보충 설명하는 흐름이 자연스럽기 때문에 문장을 추가할 필요가 없다.

▶ 문제 해결 방법은?
This microlevel access라는 지시어 힌트에 유의해야 한다. ⑤ 앞 문장에는 '미시적 접근'으로 요약할 만한 내용이 언급되지 않는다. 반면 주어진 문장에는 매우 세밀한 단위인 millisecond precision이 등장한다.

★★★ 1등급 대비 고난도 2점 문제

09 상상의 세계와 물리적 세계에 모두 속하는 관광　　정답률 33% | 정답 ①

글의 흐름으로 보아, 주어진 문장이 들어가기에 가장 적절한 곳을 고르시오.

Tourism takes place simultaneously / in the realm of the imagination / and that of the physical world.
관광은 동시에 발생한다. / 상상의 영역과 / 물리적인 세계의 영역에서

In contrast to literature or film, / it leads to 'real', tangible worlds, / while nevertheless remaining tied to the sphere / of fantasies, dreams, wishes — and myth.
문학이나 영화와는 달리, / 관광은 '실제적'이고 감지할 수 있는 세계로 이어지는데, / 그럼에도 불구하고 영역과 여전히 관련되어 있다. / 환상, 꿈, 소망, 그리고 신화의

It thereby allows the ritual enactment / of mythological ideas.

그렇기 때문에 관광은 의식으로 실행할 수 있게 한다. / 신화적인 개념

✔ There is a considerable difference / as to whether people watch a film / about the Himalayas on television / and become excited / by the 'untouched nature' of the majestic mountain peaks, / or whether they get up and go on a trek to Nepal.
상당한 차이가 있다. / 사람들이 영화를 시청하고 / 텔레비전에서 히말라야 산맥에 대한 / 흥분하는 것인지 / 장엄한 산봉우리의 '손대지 않은 자연'에 / 또는 일어나서 네팔로 긴 여행을 하는 것인지에 대해서는

Even in the latter case, / they remain, / at least partly, in an imaginary world.
심지어 후자의 경우에도, / 사람들은 머물러 있다. / 적어도 부분적으로는 상상 속의 세계에

② They experience moments / that they have already seen / at home in books, brochures and films.
그들은 순간을 경험한다. / 이미 보았던 / 집에서 책, 안내 책자 그리고 영화에서

③ Their notions / of untouched nature / and friendly, innocent indigenous people / will probably be confirmed.
그들의 개념은 / 손대지 않은 자연과 / 친절하고 순진한 토착민에 대한 / 아마도 확고해질 것이다.

④ But now / this confirmation is anchored / in a physical experience.
하지만 이제 / 이 확고함은 단단히 기반을 두고 있다. / 물리적인 경험에

⑤ The myth is thus transmitted / in a much more powerful way / than by television, movies or books.
따라서 신화는 전달된다. / 훨씬 더 강력한 방식으로 / 텔레비전, 영화, 또는 책에 의한 것보다

관광은 상상의 영역과 물리적인 세계의 영역에서 동시에 발생한다. 문학이나 영화와는 달리, 관광은 '실제적'이고 감지할 수 있는 세계로 이어지는데, 그럼에도 불구하고 환상, 꿈, 소망, 그리고 신화의 영역과 여전히 관련되어 있다. 그렇기 때문에 관광은 신화적인 개념을 의식으로 실행할 수 있게 한다. ① 사람들이 텔레비전에서 히말라야 산맥에 대한 영화를 시청하고 장엄한 산봉우리의 '손대지 않은 자연'에 흥분하는 것인지 또는 일어나서 네팔로 긴 여행을 하는 것인지에 대해서는 상당한 차이가 있다. 심지어 후자의 경우에도, 사람들은 적어도 부분적으로는 상상 속의 세계에 머물러 있다. ② 그들은 집에서 책, 안내 책자 그리고 영화에서 이미 보았던 순간을 경험한다. ③ 손대지 않은 자연과 친절하고 순진한 토착민에 대한 그들의 개념은 아마도 확고해질 것이다. ④ 하지만 이제 이 확고함은 물리적인 경험에 단단히 기반을 두고 있다. ⑤ 따라서 신화는 텔레비전, 영화, 또는 책에 의한 것보다 훨씬 더 강력한 방식으로 전달된다.

Why? 왜 정답일까?

문학·영화 등에서의 상상과 관광에서의 상상은 분명 상당한 차이점을 지니지만, 관광과 상상, 신화적 개념 등은 분명 연결고리를 지니며, 관광에서의 상상은 도리어 물리적 경험에 기반을 두기에 더 강력하게 전달될 수 있다는 내용을 담은 글이다. ① 앞에서 관광은 신화적인 개념을 의례로 실행할 수 있는 기회라는 내용을 제시한 데 이어, 주어진 문장은 '히말라야'라는 구체적 지명을 언급하며 어떤 장소를 영화 등을 통해 접하며 상상의 나라를 펼치는 것과 실제로 여행하는 것 사이에는 상당한 차이가 있다는 내용을 설명한다. ① 뒤의 문장에서는 이 중 '후자', 즉 실제 여행을 떠나는 경우'도 부분적으로는 상상의 세계에 속한다는 내용을 이어 간다. 따라서 주어진 문장이 들어가기에 가장 적절한 곳은 ①이다.

- **considerable** ⓐ (크기나 양이) 상당한
- **peak** ⓝ (산의) 봉우리[꼭대기 / 정상]
- **simultaneously** ⓐ𝖽 동시에
- **literature** ⓝ 문학
- **sphere** ⓝ (활동·영향·관심) 영역
- **thereby** ⓐ𝖽 그렇게 함으로써, 그것 때문에
- **enactment** ⓝ 실행
- **brochure** ⓝ (안내·광고용) 책자
- **innocent** ⓐ 순진한
- **be anchored in** ~에 단단히 기반을 두다
- **majestic** ⓐ 장엄한
- **take place** 발생하다, 일어나다
- **realm** ⓝ 영역
- **tangible** ⓐ 감지할 수 있는
- **myth** ⓝ 신화
- **ritual** ⓐ 의식적인, 의례적인
- **mythological** ⓐ (고대) 신화의
- **notion** ⓝ 개념, 관념, 생각
- **confirmation** ⓝ 확인
- **transmit** ⓥ 전달하다, 전송하다

구문 풀이

1행 There is a considerable difference as to {whether people
　　　　　　　　　　　　　　　　　　　　~에 관해서 ~인지 아닌지
watch a film about the Himalayas on television and become excited
　　　동사1　　　　　　　　　　　　　　　　　　　　　　동사2
by the 'untouched nature' of the majestic mountain peaks}, or {whether
they get up and go on a trek to Nepal}.　　{ } : as to의 목적어　~인지 아닌지

★★ 문제 해결 꿀~팁 ★★

▶ 많이 틀린 이유는?
내용이 추상적이고 흐름 반전의 포인트 대신 예시가 시작되는 부분에 주어진 문장을 넣어야 하기에 난이도가 높은 문제이다. ① 이하는 모두 주어진 문장의 예시를 부연한다.

DAY 16

▶ 문제 해결 방법은?
① 뒤의 'the latter'는 앞에서 두 가지 대상을 언급한 뒤 그 중 '나중에' 언급된 것을 가리킬 때 쓴다. 주어진 문장에서 '상상 속 관광 vs. 직접 관광'이라는 두 대상을 언급해야 '후자'의 의미를 파악할 수 있다.

★★★ 1등급 대비 고난도 3점 문제

10 나무의 성장   정답률 36% | 정답 ②

글의 흐름으로 보아, 주어진 문장이 들어가기에 가장 적절한 곳을 고르시오. [3점]

When trees grow together, / nutrients and water can be optimally divided among them all / so that each tree can grow into the best tree it can be.
나무가 함께 자랄 때는 / 영양분과 물이 그것들 모두 사이에서 최적으로 분배된다. / 각 나무가 최대한 좋은 나무로 성장할 수 있도록

If you "help" individual trees / by getting rid of their supposed competition, / the remaining trees are bereft.
만약 여러분이 개별 나무를 '도와주면' / 경쟁자로 여겨지는 나무를 제거해 / 나머지 나무를 잃게 된다.

They send messages out to their neighbors unsuccessfully, / because nothing remains but stumps.
이것들은 이웃 나무에 메시지를 보내더라도 소용이 없다. / 그루터기 외에는 무엇도 남아있지 않기 때문에

Every tree now grows on its own, / giving rise to great differences in productivity.
이제 모든 나무가 자기 나름대로 자라 / 생산성에 큰 차이가 생긴다.

① Some individuals photosynthesize like mad / until sugar positively bubbles along their trunk.
어떤 개체들은 미친 듯이 광합성을 한다. / 당분이 줄기를 따라 확연히 흘러넘칠 때까지

✔ As a result, / they are fit and grow better, / but they aren't particularly long-lived.
그 결과, / 그것들은 건강하고 더 잘 자라지만 / 그것들은 특별히 오래 살지는 못한다.

This is because a tree can be only as strong / as the forest that surrounds it.
이는 나무는 오로지 튼튼할 수 있기 때문이다. / 자신을 둘러싸고 있는 숲만큼만

③ And there are now a lot of losers in the forest.
그리고 지금 숲에는 많은 패자가 있다.

④ Weaker members, / who would once have been supported by the stronger ones, / suddenly fall behind.
더 연약한 구성원들이 / 한때는 더 튼튼한 구성원들의 지원을 받았을 / 갑자기 뒤처진다.

⑤ Whether the reason for their decline / is their location and lack of nutrients, / a passing sickness, / or genetic makeup, / they now fall prey to insects and fungi.
이들이 쇠락한 원인이 / 위치와 영양분 부족이든, / 일시적인 질병이든, / 혹은 유전적 구성이든, / 이제 그것들은 곤충과 균류의 먹이가 된다.

나무가 함께 자랄 때는 각 나무가 최대한 좋은 나무로 성장할 수 있도록 영양분과 물이 그것들 모두 사이에서 최적으로 분배된다. 만약 여러분이 경쟁자로 여겨지는 나무를 제거해 개별 나무를 '도와주면' 나머지 나무를 잃게 된다. 이것들은 그루터기 외에는 무엇도 남아있지 않기 때문에 이웃 나무들에 메시지를 보내더라도 소용이 없다. 이제 모든 나무가 자기 나름대로 자라 생산성에 큰 차이가 생긴다. ① 어떤 개체들은 당분이 줄기를 따라 확연히 흘러넘칠 때까지 미친 듯이 광합성을 한다. ② 그 결과, 그것들은 건강하고 더 잘 자라지만 특별히 오래 살지는 못한다. 이는 나무는 자신을 둘러싸고 있는 숲만큼만 튼튼할 수 있기 때문이다. ③ 그리고 지금 숲에는 많은 패자가 있다. ④ 한때는 튼튼한 구성원들의 지원을 받았을 연약한 구성원들이 갑자기 뒤처진다. ⑤ 이들이 쇠락한 원인이 위치와 영양분 부족이든, 일시적인 질병이든, 혹은 유전적 구성이든, 이제 그것들은 곤충과 균류의 먹이가 된다.

Why? 왜 정답일까?

나무의 성장을 돕기 위해 다른 나무를 베어냈을 때 생기는 예상치 못한 결과를 설명하는 글이다. ① 앞에서 나무 간 생산성에 차이가 생긴다고 언급한 후, ② 앞의 문장은 어떤 나무들이 열렬히 광합성을 한다고 설명한다. 하지만 ② 뒤는 나무가 자신이 자라는 숲만큼만 강할 수 있다는 동떨어진 내용이므로 흐름이 어색하게 끊긴다. 이때 주어진 문장을 보면, they가 ② 앞의 Some individuals을 가리켜, '광합성을 열심히 한 나무들'이 특별히 오래 살지는 못한다는 의미를 나타낸다. ② 뒤는 '오래 못 사는' 이유를 설명하는 것이다. 따라서 주어진 문장이 들어가기에 가장 적절한 곳은 ②이다.

● **long-lived** ⓐ 오래 사는	● **get rid of** ~을 제거하다
● **suppose** ⓥ 가정하다	● **remaining** ⓐ 남아 있는
● **bereft** ⓐ 잃은	● **unsuccessfully** ⓐⓓ 실패하여
● **stump** ⓝ 그루터기	● **give rise to** ~을 야기하다
● **photosynthesize** ⓥ 광합성하다	● **bubble** ⓥ (거품을 내며) 졸졸 흐르다

● **surround** ⓥ 둘러싸다, 에워싸다	● **fall behind** 뒤처지다
● **decline** ⓝ 쇠락, 감소	● **location** ⓝ 위치
● **genetic** ⓐ 유전적인	● **makeup** ⓝ 구성
● **fall prey to** ~의 먹이가 되다	● **fungus** (*pl.* fungi) ⓝ 균류

구문 풀이

16행 Whether the reason for their decline is their location and
「whether(부사절 접속사)+   A+
lack of nutrients, a passing sickness, or genetic makeup, they now
B+   or C : A이든 B이든 C이든 간에」
fall prey to insects and fungi.

★★ 문제 해결 꿀~팁 ★★

▶ 많이 틀린 이유는?
주어진 문장에서 나무들(they)이 특별히 오래 살지는 못한다고 하는데 ③ 뒤에서 losers를 언급하므로, 얼핏 보면 they가 losers로 연결되는 것처럼 보인다. 하지만 ③ 앞 문장과 주어진 문장이 As a result로 연결되지 않는다.

▶ 문제 해결 방법은?
주어진 문장의 they가 ② 앞에서 언급된, '남은 나무들 중 광합성을 많이 하는 나무들'임을 파악하는 것이 관건이다.

★★★ 1등급 대비 고난도 3점 문제

11 풀어진 예제 효과   정답률 51% | 정답 ④

글의 흐름으로 보아, 주어진 문장이 들어가기에 가장 적절한 곳을 고르시오. [3점]

How can we help students manage cognitive load / as they learn to perform complex tasks?
학생이 인지 부하를 관리하도록 어떻게 도와줄 수 있을까? / 그들이 복잡한 과제를 수행하는 것을 배울 때

One method that has proved effective in research studies / is to support some aspects of a complex task / while students perform the entire task.
조사 연구에서 효과적이라고 입증된 한 가지 방법은 / 복잡한 과제의 일부 측면을 지원하는 것이다. / 학생이 전체 과제를 수행할 때

① For example, / Swelter and Cooper demonstrated this / with students learning to solve problems / in a variety of quantitative fields from statistics to physics.
예를 들어, / Swelter와 Cooper는 이것을 보여주었다. / 문제를 푸는 법을 배우는 학생들을 통해 / 통계학에서 물리학까지 다양한 정량적 분야에서

② They found / that when students were given typical word problems, / it was possible for them to solve the problems / without actually learning much.
그들이 알아낸 바에 따르면, / 학생들에게 전형적인 문장제가 주어졌을 때, / 그들은 문제를 푸는 것이 가능했다. / 실제로는 많이 학습하지 않은 채로

③ This is because the problems themselves were sufficiently demanding / that students had no cognitive resources / available to learn from what they did.
이는 문제 자체가 충분히 어려워서 / 학생들이 인지적 자원을 갖고 있지 않았기 때문이다. / 자기가 해본 것에서 학습하는 데 이용할 수 있는

✔ But when students were given "worked-examples" / (such as pre-solved problems) / placed between problems to solve, / studying the worked-examples / freed up cognitive resources / that allowed students to see the key features of the problem / and to analyze the steps and reasons behind problem-solving moves.
하지만 학생들에게 '풀어진 예제들'이 주어지면, / (미리 풀어진 문제들과 같은) / 풀어야 할 문제들 사이에 있는 / 풀어진 예제들을 공부하는 것은 / 인지적 자원을 이용할 수 있게 했다. / 학생들이 문제의 주요 특징을 보고 / 문제 해결 조치의 이면에 있는 단계와 이유들을 분석하게 해 주는

The researchers found / this improved students' performance on subsequent problem solving.
연구자들이 알아낸 바에 따르면, / 이것은 차후 문제 풀이에서 학생들의 수행 능력을 향상시켰다.

⑤ This result, called the *worked-example effect*, / is one example of a process called *scaffolding*, / by which instructors temporarily relieve some of the cognitive load / so that students can focus on particular dimensions of learning.
*풀어진 예제 효과*라는 이런 결과는 / *발판 놓기*라는 과정의 한 사례이며, / 그것으로 교사는 인지 부하의 일부를 일시적으로 덜어 준다. / 학생이 학습의 특정 측면에 집중할 수 있도록

학생이 복잡한 과제를 수행하는 것을 배울 때 그들이 인지 부하를 관리하도록 어떻게 도와줄 수 있을까? 조사 연구에서 효과적이라고 입증된 한 가지 방법은 학생이 전체 과제를 수행할 때 복잡한 과제의 일부 측면을 지원하는 것이다. ① 예를 들어, Swelter와 Cooper는 통계학에서 물리학까지 다양한 정량적 분야에서 문제를 푸는 법을 배우는 학생들을 통해 이것을 보여주었다. ② 그들이

알아낸 바에 따르면, 학생들에게 전형적인 문장제가 주어졌을 때, 그들은 실제로는 많이 학습하지 못한 채로 문제를 푸는 것이 가능했다. ③ 이것은 문제 자체가 충분히 어려워서 학생들이 자기가 해본 것에서 학습하는 데 이용할 수 있는 인지적 자원을 갖고 있지 않았기 때문이다. ④ 하지만 학생들에게 풀어야 할 문제들 사이에 있는 (미리 풀어진 문제들과 같은) '풀어진 예제들'이 주어지면, 풀어진 예제들을 공부하는 것은 학생들이 문제의 주요 특징을 보고 문제 해결 조치의 이면에 있는 단계들과 이유들을 분석하게 해 주는 인지적 자원을 이용할 수 있게 했다. 연구자들이 알아낸 바에 따르면, 이것은 차후 문제 풀이에서 학생들의 수행 능력을 향상시켰다. ⑤ 풀어진 예제 효과라는 이런 결과는 *발판 놓기*라는 과정의 한 사례이며, 그것으로 교사는 학생이 학습의 특정 측면에 집중할 수 있도록 인지 부하의 일부를 일시적으로 덜어 준다.

Why? 왜 정답일까?

④ 앞에서 문장제 푸는 법을 배운 학생들의 사례를 들어, 이들이 문제를 풀어낼 수는 있었어도 학습 효과가 크지 않았던 이유를 설명하고 있다. 하지만 ④ 뒤는 갑자기 학생들의 문제 풀이 능력이 향상되었다는 내용이므로 흐름이 어색하게 끊긴다. 이때 주어진 문장을 보면, 미리 풀어진 예제를 제공하여 학생들의 학습을 도울 수 있었다는 내용을 But과 함께 제시하고 있다. 즉 '④ 앞: 얼마 배우지 못했다 → 주어진 문장: 하지만(But) 이미 풀어진 예제를 제공받으며 달랐다 → ④ 뒤: 실제로 수행이 향상됐다'는 흐름이므로, 주어진 문장이 들어가기에 가장 적절한 곳은 ④이다.

- **pre-solved** ⓐ 미리 해결된
- **analyze** ⓥ 분석하다
- **aspect** ⓝ 측면
- **statistics** ⓝ 통계
- **word problem** 문장제(이야기 형식으로 제시된 문제)
- **demanding** ⓐ 까다로운
- **scaffolding** ⓝ 발판 놓기
- **feature** ⓝ 특징
- **cognitive load** 인지적 부담
- **quantitative** ⓐ 정량적인, 양적인
- **physics** ⓝ 물리학
- **subsequent** ⓐ 이후의

구문 풀이

21행 This result, called the *worked-example effect*, is one example
of a process called *scaffolding*, by which instructors temporarily
(선행사) 「전치사＋관·대」
relieve some of the cognitive load so that students can focus on
목적(~하도록)
particular dimensions of learning.

★★ 문제 해결 꿀~팁 ★★

▶ 많이 틀린 이유는?
③ 앞의 문장과 주어진 문장이 But으로 자연스럽게 연결되어 보여 ③을 답으로 고를 수 있다. 하지만 주어진 문장과 ③ 뒤의 흐름이 어색하다.
▶ 문제 해결 방법은?
④ 뒷문장의 this에 주어진 문장의 'studying the worked-examples ~'를 넣어서 읽으면 흐름이 자연스럽다.

★★★ 1등급 대비 고난도 3점 문제

12 가르치려는 욕구의 실현 정답률 33% | 정답 ⑤

글의 흐름으로 보아, 주어진 문장이 들어가기에 가장 적절한 곳을 고르시오. [3점]

Erikson believes / that when we reach the adult years, / several physical,
social, and psychological stimuli trigger a sense of *generativity*.
Erikson은 믿는다. / 우리가 성년에 이를 때, / 몇 가지 신체적, 사회적, 그리고 심리적 자극이 생식성에 대한 인식을 촉발한다고

A central component of this attitude / is the desire to care for others.
이러한 태도의 한 가지 핵심 구성요소 / 다른 사람들을 돌보고자 하는 욕구이다.

① For the majority of people, / parenthood is perhaps the most obvious and
convenient opportunity / to fulfill this desire.
대다수 사람에게는 / 부모가 되는 것이 아마 가장 분명하고 편한 기회일 것이다. / 이러한 욕구를 충족할

② Erikson believes / that another distinguishing feature of adulthood / is the
emergence / of an inborn desire to teach.
Erikson은 믿는다. / 성인기의 또 다른 독특한 특징이 / 출현이라고 / 가르치고자 하는 타고난 욕구의

③ We become aware of this desire / when the event of being physically
capable of reproducing is joined / with the events of participating in a
committed relationship, / the establishment of an adult pattern of living, /
and the assumption of job responsibilities.
우리는 이 욕구를 인식하게 된다. / 신체적으로 자손을 퍼뜨리는 것이 가능해지는 일이 결합할 때 / 헌신적인 관계, / 성인 생활 패턴의 정착, / 그리고 업무 책임 떠맡기에 참여하는 일들과

④ According to Erikson, / by becoming parents / we learn that we have the

need to be needed by others / who depend on our knowledge, protection, and
guidance.
Erikson에 따르면, / 부모가 됨으로써 / 우리는 다른 사람들에게 필요해지고 싶은 욕구가 있다는 것을 알게 된다. / 우리의 지식, 보호, 그리고 지도에 의존하는

☑ We become entrusted / to teach culturally appropriate behaviors, values,
attitudes, skills, and information about the world.
우리는 위임받게 된다. / 문화적으로 적절한 행동, 가치, 태도, 기술, 그리고 세상에 대한 정보를 가르치는 일을

By assuming the responsibilities of being primary caregivers to children /
through their long years of physical and social growth, / we concretely
express / what Erikson believes / to be an inborn desire to teach.
일차적으로 돌봄을 제공하는 사람이 되는 책임을 떠맡음으로써, / 아이들이 신체적, 사회적으로 성장하는 긴 세월 동안 / 우리는 구체적으로 표현한다. / Erikson이 믿는 것을 / 가르치고자 하는 타고난 욕구라고

Erikson은 우리가 성년에 이를 때, 몇 가지 신체적, 사회적, 그리고 심리적 자극이 *생식성*에 대한 인식을 촉발한다고 믿는다. 이러한 태도의 한 가지 핵심 구성요소는 다른 사람들을 돌보고자 하는 욕구이다. ① 대다수 사람에게는 부모가 되는 것이 아마 이러한 욕구를 충족할 가장 분명하고 편한 기회일 것이다. ② Erikson은 성인기의 또 다른 독특한 특징이 가르치고자 하는 타고난 욕구의 출현이라고 믿는다. ③ 신체적으로 자손을 퍼뜨리는 것이 가능해지는 일이 헌신적인 관계, 성인 생활 패턴의 정착, 그리고 업무 책임 떠맡기에 참여하는 일들과 결합할 때 우리는 이 욕구를 인식하게 된다. ④ Erikson에 따르면, 부모가 됨으로써 우리는 우리의 지식, 보호, 그리고 지도에 의존하는 다른 사람들에게 필요해지고 싶은 욕구가 있다는 것을 알게 된다. ⑤ 우리는 문화적으로 적절한 행동, 가치, 태도, 기술, 그리고 세상에 대한 정보를 가르치는 일을 위임받게 된다. 아이들이 신체적, 사회적으로 성장하는 긴 세월 동안 일차적으로 돌봄을 제공하는 사람이 되는 책임을 떠맡음으로써, 우리는 가르치고자 하는 타고난 욕구라고 Erikson이 믿는 것을 구체적으로 표현한다.

Why? 왜 정답일까?

인간은 성인기에 타인을 가르치려는 욕구가 깨어나는데 이 욕구는 부모 역할을 통해 실현된다는 내용을 다룬 글이다. ⑤ 앞의 문장에서 우리는 부모가 되면서 누군가에게 '필요한' 사람이 되고 싶은 욕구를 자각하게 된다고 말한 데 이어, 주어진 문장에서는 우리가 부모로서 '가르치는' 역할을 떠맡게 된다는 내용을 이야기하고, ⑤ 뒤에서는 그리하여 가르치려는 욕구가 실현된다는 결론을 언급한다. 따라서 주어진 문장이 들어가기에 가장 적절한 곳은 ⑤이다.

- **entrust** ⓥ 위임하다, 맡기다
- **trigger** ⓥ 촉발시키다, 일으키다
- **fulfill** ⓥ 충족하다, 성취하다
- **inborn** ⓐ 타고난, 선천적인
- **committed** ⓐ 헌신적인, 열성적인
- **concretely** ⓐⓓ 구체적으로
- **appropriate** ⓐ 적절한
- **generativity** ⓝ 생식성
- **emergence** ⓝ 출현, 발생
- **reproduce** ⓥ 자손을 퍼뜨리다, 번식하다
- **assumption** ⓝ (책임, 역할의) 떠맡기

구문 풀이

19행 By assuming the responsibilities of being primary caregivers
~함으로써 전치사 동명사
to children through their long years of physical and social growth, /
we concretely express {what Erikson believes to be an inborn desire
관계대명사 주어 5형식 동사 목적격 보어
to teach}. { }: 명사절 목적어
형용사적 용법

★★ 문제 해결 꿀~팁 ★★

▶ 많이 틀린 이유는?
수험생으로서 생소한 '생식성'이라는 개념을 환기하며 타인을 가르치려는 인간의 선천적 욕구에 관해 설명한 지문이다. 지시사, 대명사 등 힌트에 주로 의존하여 기계적으로 풀기보다 글의 논리적인 흐름과 전개를 종합적으로 고려해야 한다는 점에서 난이도가 매우 높다.
▶ 문제 해결 방법은?
'부모가 되면서 우리는 타인에게 필요해지고 싶은 욕구가 있음을 깨닫게 되어 → 가르치는 행위를 맡게 되고 → 이를 통해 선천적인 욕구를 실현해나간다'는 논리적 흐름을 이해하도록 한다. 주어진 문장의 'become entrusted to teach ~'와 ⑤ 뒤의 'assuming the responsibilities of being primary caregivers ~'가 서로 같은 의미인 점도 참고한다.

DAY 16

DAY 17 　　문장 삽입 02

01 ⑤	02 ②	03 ④	04 ③	05 ④
06 ④	07 ④	08 ③	09 ⑤	10 ⑤
11 ③	12 ②			

01 　과학에서의 제도화　　정답률 46% | 정답 ⑤

글의 흐름으로 보아, 주어진 문장이 들어가기에 가장 적절한 곳을 고르시오.

As particular practices are repeated over time / and become more widely shared, / the values that they embody / are reinforced and reproduced / and we speak of them as becoming 'institutionalized'.
특정 관행이 오랜 기간 반복되고 / 더 널리 공유되면서 / 그 관행이 구현하는 가치는 / 강화되고 재생산되며, / 우리는 이것이 '제도화된' 것이라고 말한다.

① In some cases, / this institutionalization has a formal face to it, / with rules and protocols written down, / and specialized roles created / to ensure that procedures are followed correctly.
어떤 경우, / 이러한 제도화는 공식적인 면모를 갖추기도 하는데, / 규칙과 프로토콜이 문서화되고 / 전문화된 역할이 만들어진다. / 절차가 올바르게 지켜지도록 확실히 하기 위해

② The main institutions of state / — parliament, courts, police and so on — / along with certain of the professions, / exhibit this formal character.
국가의 주요 기관이 / 의회, 법원, 경찰 등 / 일부 전문직과 더불어 / 이러한 공식적 성격을 보여준다.

③ Other social institutions, / perhaps the majority, / are not like this; / science is an example.
다른 사회 기관들, / 아마도 대다수는 / 이와 같지 않을 것인데, / 과학이 그 예이다.

④ Although scientists are trained in the substantive content of their discipline, / they are not formally instructed / in 'how to be a good scientist'.
과학자들은 자기 학문의 실질적인 내용에 대해서는 훈련받겠지만, / 그들은 공식적으로 교육받지 않는다. / '좋은 과학자가 되는 방법'에 대해서는

✔ Instead, / much like the young child learning how to play 'nicely', / the apprentice scientist gains his or her understanding of the moral values / inherent in the role / by absorption from their colleagues / — socialization.
대신, / 마치 '착하게' 노는 법을 배우는 어린아이처럼 / 도제 과학자는 도덕적 가치에 대한 이해를 얻는다. / 그 역할에 내재한 / 동료들로부터의 흡수를 통해 / 즉 사회화

We think / that these values, / along with the values that inform many of the professions, / are under threat, / just as the value of the professions themselves / is under threat.
우리는 생각한다. / 이러한 가치가 / 그 전문직에 관한 많은 것을 알려주는 가치와 더불어, / 위협받고 있다고 / 마치 그 전문직 자체의 가치가 / 위협받고 있는 것과 마찬가지로

특정 관행이 오랜 기간 반복되고 더 널리 공유되면서 그 관행이 구현하는 가치는 강화되고 재생산되며, 우리는 이것이 '제도화된' 것이라고 말한다. ① 어떤 경우, 이러한 제도화는 공식적인 면모를 갖추기도 하는데, 규칙과 프로토콜이 문서화되고 절차가 올바르게 지켜지도록 확실히 하기 위해 전문화된 역할이 만들어진다. ② 의회, 법원, 경찰 등 국가의 주요 기관이 일부 전문직과 더불어 이러한 공식적 성격을 보여준다. ③ 다른 사회 기관들, 아마도 대다수는 이와 같지 않을 것인데, 과학이 그 예이다. ④ 과학자들은 자기 학문의 실질적인 내용에 대해서는 훈련받겠지만, '좋은 과학자가 되는 방법'에 대해서는 공식적으로 교육받지 않는다. ⑤ 대신, 마치 '착하게' 노는 법을 배우는 어린아이처럼 도제 과학자는 동료들로부터의 흡수, 즉 사회화를 통해 그 역할에 내재한 도덕적 가치에 대한 이해를 얻는다. 우리는 이러한 가치가 그 전문직에 관한 많은 것을 알려주는 가치와 더불어, 그 전문직 자체의 가치가 위협받고 있는 것과 마찬가지로 위협받고 있다고 생각한다.

Why? 왜 정답일까?

⑤ 앞에서 과학자는 학문의 실질적 내용은 배워도, '좋은 과학자가 되는 법'에 관해서는 교육받지 못한다고 언급하는데, ⑤ 뒤에서는 갑자기 '이러한 가치'를 언급한다. 즉 앞에서 언급되지 않은 내용을 가까운 대명사(these values)로 받아 흐름이 끊기는 상황이다. 이때 주어진 문장을 보면 the moral values가 언급된다. ⑤ 뒤의 these values는 바로 이 '도덕적 가치'를 가리키는 것이므로, 주어진 문장이 들어가기에 가장 적절한 곳은 ⑤이다.

- **apprentice** ⓝ 도제, 견습
- **absorption** ⓝ 흡수, 받아들임
- **repeat** ⓥ 반복하다
- **reinforce** ⓥ 강화하다
- **institutionalize** ⓥ 제도화하다
- **inherent** ⓐ 내재된
- **socialization** ⓝ 사회화
- **embody** ⓥ 구현하다
- **reproduce** ⓥ 재생산하다, 복제하다
- **institutionalization** ⓝ 제도화

- **protocol** ⓝ 프로토콜, 규약
- **procedure** ⓝ 절차
- **parliament** ⓝ 의회
- **profession** ⓝ 전문직
- **under threat** 위협받고 있는
- **ensure** ⓥ 보장하다, 반드시 ~하다
- **state** ⓝ 국가
- **court** ⓝ 법원
- **substantive** ⓐ 실질적인

구문 풀이

> **8행** In some cases, this institutionalization has a formal face to it, with rules and protocols written down, and specialized roles created 「with + 명사구1 + 과거분사1 + and + 명사구2 + 과거분사2 : 부대상황 분사구문(~이 …된 채로)」 to ensure that procedures are followed correctly.

02 　다면 평가의 시행 배경　　정답률 45% | 정답 ②

글의 흐름으로 보아, 주어진 문장이 들어가기에 가장 적절한 곳을 고르시오.

In most organizations, / the employee's immediate supervisor evaluates the employee's performance.
대부분의 조직에서 / 직원의 직속 상사는 그 직원의 성과를 평가한다.

① This is because / the supervisor is responsible for the employee's performance, / providing supervision, / handing out assignments, / and developing the employee.
이것은 ~이기 때문이다. / 그 관리자가 그 직원의 성과를 책임지기 / 감독을 제공하고, / 과업을 배정하며, / 그 직원을 계발하면서

✔ A problem, however, is / that supervisors often work in locations / apart from their employees / and therefore are not able to observe their subordinates' performance.
하지만 문제는 / 관리자가 흔히 장소에서 일하고 / 직원과 떨어진 / 그렇기 때문에 자신의 부하 직원들의 성과를 관찰할 수 없다는 것이다.

Should supervisors rate employees on performance dimensions / they cannot observe?
관리자는 성과 영역에 대해 직원들을 평가해야 하는가? / 자신이 관찰할 수 없는

③ To eliminate this dilemma, / more and more organizations are implementing assessments / referred to as *360-degree evaluations*.
이 딜레마를 없애기 위해, / 점점 더 많은 조직이 평가를 시행하고 있다. / *다면 평가*라고 불리는

④ Employees are rated / not only by their supervisors / but by coworkers, / clients or citizens, / professionals in other agencies with whom they work, / and subordinates.
직원들은 평가를 받는다. / 자신의 관리자에 의해서만이 아니라, / 동료, / 고객이나 시민, / 함께 일하는 다른 대행사의 전문가들, / 그리고 부하 직원들에 의해서도

⑤ The reason for this approach is / that often coworkers and clients or citizens / have a greater opportunity / to observe an employee's performance / and are in a better position / to evaluate many performance dimensions.
이 방법을 시행하는 이유는 / 동료와 고객이나 시민들이 흔히 / 더 많은 기회를 가지며, / 어떤 직원의 성과를 관찰할 / 더 나은 위치에 있기 때문이다. / 많은 평가 영역을 평가할 수 있는

대부분의 조직에서 직원의 직속 상사는 그 직원의 성과를 평가한다. ① 이것은 그 관리자가 (직원에게) 감독을 제공하고, 과업을 배정하며, 그 직원을 계발하면서, 그 직원의 성과를 책임지기 때문이다. ② 하지만 문제는 관리자가 흔히 직원과 떨어진 장소에서 일하기 때문에 자신의 부하 직원들의 성과를 관찰할 수 없다는 것이다. 관리자는 자신이 관찰할 수 없는 성과 영역에 대해 직원들을 평가해야 하는가? ③ 이 딜레마를 없애기 위해, 점점 더 많은 조직이 *다면 평가*라고 불리는 평가를 시행하고 있다. ④ 직원들은 자신의 관리자 뿐만 아니라 동료, 고객이나 시민, 함께 일하는 다른 대행사의 전문가들, 그리고 부하 직원들에 의해서도 평가를 받는다. ⑤ 이 방법을 시행하는 이유는 동료와 고객이나 시민들이 흔히 어떤 직원의 성과를 관찰할 더 많은 기회를 가지며, 많은 평가 영역을 평가할 수 있는 더 나은 위치에 있기 때문이다.

Why? 왜 정답일까?

② 앞에서 직속 상사는 직원의 성과를 책임지고 감독하는 입장에서 직원에 대한 성과 평가를 진행한다는 내용이 언급된다. 이어서 주어진 문장은 however로 흐름을 반전시키며, 관리자는 흔히 직원과 떨어져 있는 곳에서 일하기 때문에 부하 직원의 성과를 관찰하기 어렵다고 지적한다. ② 뒤의 문장은 이렇듯 관찰이 불가한 상황에서 직원들을 평가해야 하는지 의문을 제기한다. 따라서 주어진 문장이 들어가기에 가장 적절한 곳은 ②이다.

- **supervisor** ⓝ 상사
- **evaluate** ⓥ 평가하다
- **supervision** ⓝ 감독
- **assignment** ⓝ 과업, 과제
- **dimension** ⓝ 차원
- **implement** ⓥ 시행하다
- **degree** ⓝ (각도의 단위인) 도
- **observe** ⓥ 관찰하다
- **responsible for** ~에 책임이 있는
- **hand out** ~을 나눠주다
- **rate** ⓥ 평가하다
- **eliminate** ⓥ 제거하다
- **assessment** ⓝ 평가

1행 A problem, however, is that supervisors often work in
주어 　　　　　　 동사 　 접속사(~것) 　 주어 　　 동사1
locations apart from their employees and therefore are not able to
　　　　　　　　　　　　　　　　　　　　　　　　　　　 동사2
observe their subordinates' performance.

---

03 물 순환이 가능한 이유　　　　정답률 59% | 정답 ④

글의 흐름으로 보아, 주어진 문장이 들어가기에 가장 적절한 곳을 고르시오.

Water molecules circulate through the atmosphere / as a result of evaporation.
물 분자는 대기를 순환한다. / 증발의 결과로

① As water molecules rise high up in the atmosphere, / they may split up into their constituent chemical elements, / hydrogen and oxygen, / under the influence of sunlight.
물 분자가 대기 중으로 높이 상승하면, / 그것은 그것을 구성하는 화학 원소로 분해될 수도 있다. / 즉 수소와 산소 / 햇빛의 영향을 받아

② Whereas the much heavier oxygen either remains in the atmosphere / or is captured on the Earth's surface, / the hydrogen tends to escape into space, / because it is so light / that Earth's gravity cannot retain it.
훨씬 더 무거운 산소가 대기 중에 남아 있거나 / 그것이 지구 표면에 붙들리는 반면에, / 수소는 우주로 빠져나가는 경향이 있는데, / 수소가 너무 가벼워서 / 지구 중력이 그것을 붙잡아 둘 수 없기 때문이다.

③ As long as there was little or no free oxygen in the atmosphere / that could capture hydrogen / before it escaped into the cosmos, / this process would have continued unhindered.
유리 산소가 대기 중에 거의 없거나 전혀 없는 한, / 수소를 붙잡아 둘 수 있는 / 수소가 우주로 빠져나가기 전에 / 이 과정은 방해받지 않고 계속되었을 것이다.

☑ However, / after all the available materials on the Earth's surface, / mostly iron, / had combined with the free oxygen, / it began to appear in the atmosphere / in sizable quantities.
그러나 / 지구 표면의 이용 가능한 모든 물질이 / 대부분이 철인, / 유리 산소와 결합한 후, / 그것은 대기 중에 / 꽤 많은 양으로 모습을 드러내기 시작했다.

As soon as this happened, / the free oxygen would have captured most of the free hydrogen / by forming water molecules again, / thus slowing down the loss of hydrogen.
이런 일이 일어나자마자 / 유리 산소는 대부분의 유리 수소를 붙들어 두어 / 다시 물 분자를 형성함으로써 / 그 결과 수소 손실을 늦추었을 것이다.

⑤ Over the course of time, / this process would have helped to retain water on Earth, / while it also contributed to the emergence of oxygen in the atmosphere.
시간이 지남에 따라, / 이 과정은 지구에 물을 보유하는 데 도움을 주었을 것이고, / 동시에 대기 중 산소 발생에도 기여했다.

물 분자는 증발의 결과로 대기를 순환한다. ① 물 분자가 대기 중으로 높이 상승하면, 그것은 햇빛의 영향을 받아 그것을 구성하는 화학 원소인 수소와 산소로 분해될 수도 있다. ② 훨씬 더 무거운 산소가 대기 중에 남아 있거나 지구 표면에 붙들리는 반면에, 수소는 우주로 빠져나가는 경향이 있는데, 수소가 너무 가벼워서 지구 중력이 그것을 붙잡아 둘 수 없기 때문이다. ③ 수소가 우주로 빠져나가기 전에 수소를 붙잡아 둘 수 있는 유리 산소(화합물에서 떨어져 나온 산소)가 대기 중에 거의 없거나 전혀 없는 한, 이 과정은 방해받지 않고 계속되었을 것이다. ④ 그러나 대부분이 철인, 지구 표면의 이용 가능한 모든 물질이 유리 산소와 결합한 후, 그것은 대기 중에 꽤 많은 양으로 모습을 드러내기 시작했다. 이런 일이 일어나자마자 유리 산소는 다시 물 분자를 형성함으로써 대부분의 유리 수소를 붙들어 두어 그 결과 수소 손실을 늦추었을 것이다. ⑤ 시간이 지남에 따라, 이 과정은 지구에 물을 보유하는 데 도움을 주었을 것이고, 동시에 대기 중 산소 발생에도 기여했다.

Why? 왜 정답일까?

물 순환이 가능한 이유를 설명한 글이다. ④ 앞의 문장에서, 물 분자가 증발되어 대기로 올라가고 이것이 수소와 산소로 나누어졌을 때, 대기 중에 유리 산소가 만일 없다면 '수소가 계속 우주로 이탈하게' 되었을 것이라고 설명한다. 이때 주어진 문장은 However로 흐름을 반전시키며, 실제로는 지구 대기에 유리 산소가 다량 존재한다는 점을 언급한다. 이어서 ④ 뒤의 문장은 이 유리 산소가 분해되어 있는 수소와 다시 결합해 또 물 분자를 생성할 수 있어서 수소 손실이 늦춰질 수 있다는 보충 설명을 이어 간다. 따라서 주어진 문장이 들어가기에 가장 적절한 곳은 ④이다.

- available ⓐ 이용 가능한
- combine A with B A와 B를 결합하다
- as a result of ~의 결과로
- iron ⓝ 철
- atmosphere ⓝ 대기
- sizable ⓐ 꽤 많은, 꽤 큰

- molecule ⓝ 분자
- evaporation ⓝ 증발
- constituent ⓐ 구성하는
- hydrogen ⓝ 수소
- retain ⓥ 보유하다
- unhindered ⓐ 방해받지 않는
- slow down ~을 늦추다
- emergence ⓝ 발생, 출현
- circulate ⓥ 순환하다
- split up into ~로 쪼개지다
- under the influence of ~의 영향하에
- gravity ⓝ 중력
- cosmos ⓝ 우주
- form ⓥ 형성하다, 만들다
- over the course of time 시간이 지나면서

9행 Whereas the much heavier oxygen either remains in the
接续词(~한 반면에)　　　　　　　　　　　　　 「either+A or+B : A 또는 B」
atmosphere or is captured on the Earth's surface, the hydrogen tends
to escape into space, because it is so light that Earth's gravity cannot
　　　　　　　　　　　　　　　　　 「so ~ that … : 너무 ~해서 …하다」
retain it.

---

04 인쇄기의 발달과 정보 전파 속도의 향상　　　정답률 63% | 정답 ③

글의 흐름으로 보아, 주어진 문장이 들어가기에 가장 적절한 곳을 고르시오.

The printing press boosted the power / of ideas to copy themselves.
인쇄기는 능력을 신장시켰다. / 생각이 스스로를 복제하는

Prior to low-cost printing, / ideas could and did spread / by word of mouth.
비용이 적게 드는 인쇄술이 있기 전에, / 생각은 퍼져 나갈 수 있었고 실제로 그렇게 퍼져 나갔다. / 구전으로

While this was tremendously powerful, / ① it limited the complexity of the ideas / that could be propagated / to those that a single person could remember.
이것은 대단히 강력했지만, / 생각의 복잡성을 제한했다. / 전파될 수 있는 / 단 한 사람이 기억할 수 있는 것으로

It also added a certain amount of guaranteed error.
그것은 또한 일정량의 확실한 오류를 추가했다.

② The spread of ideas by word of mouth / was equivalent / to a game of telephone on a global scale.
구전에 의한 생각의 전파는 / 맞먹었다. / 전 세계적인 규모의 말 전하기 놀이와

☑ The advent of literacy / and the creation of handwritten scrolls / and, eventually, handwritten books / strengthened the ability / of large and complex ideas / to spread with high fidelity.
글을 읽고 쓸 줄 아는 능력의 출현과 / 손으로 쓴 두루마리와 / 궁극적으로 손으로 쓴 책의 탄생은 / 능력을 강화했다. / 크고 복잡한 생각이 / 매우 정확하게 퍼져 나가는

But the incredible amount of time / required to copy a scroll or book by hand / limited the speed / with which information could spread this way.
그러나 엄청난 양의 시간은 / 손으로 두루마리나 책을 복사하는 데 요구된 / 속도를 제한했다. / 이 방식으로 정보가 퍼져 나갈 수 있는

④ A well-trained monk / could transcribe around four pages of text / per day.
잘 훈련된 수도승은 / 약 4쪽의 문서를 필사할 수 있었다. / 하루에

⑤ A printing press could copy information / thousands of times faster, / allowing knowledge to spread / far more quickly, with full fidelity, than ever before.
인쇄기는 정보를 복사할 수 있었는데, / 수천 배 더 빠르게 / 그것은 지식이 퍼져 나갈 수 있게 하였다. / 이전 어느 때보다 훨씬 더 빠르고 최대한 정확하게

인쇄기는 생각이 스스로를 복제하는 능력을 신장시켰다. 비용이 적게 드는 인쇄술이 있기 전에, 생각은 구전으로 퍼져 나갈 수 있었고 실제로 그렇게 퍼져 나갔다. 이것은 대단히 강력했지만, 전파될 수 있는 생각의 복잡성을 단 한 사람이 기억할 수 있는 것으로 제한했다. ① 그것은 또한 일정량의 확실한 오류를 추가했다. ② 구전에 의한 생각의 전파는 전 세계적인 규모의 말 전하기 놀이와 맞먹었다. ③ 글을 읽고 쓸 줄 아는 능력의 출현과 손으로 쓴 두루마리와 궁극적으로 손으로 쓴 책의 탄생은 크고 복잡한 생각이 매우 정확하게 퍼져 나가는 능력을 강화했다. 그러나 손으로 두루마리나 책을 복사하는 데 요구된 엄청난 양의 시간은 이 방식으로 정보가 퍼져 나갈 수 있는 속도를 제한했다. ④ 잘 훈련된 수도승은 하루에 약 4쪽의 문서를 필사할 수 있었다. ⑤ 인쇄기는 정보를 수천 배 더 빠르게 복사할 수 있었는데, 그것은 지식이 이전 어느 때보다 훨씬 더 빠르고 최대한 정확하게 퍼져 나갈 수 있게 하였다.

Why? 왜 정답일까?

인쇄기의 발달로 인해 인간은 구전과 필사본을 통해 생각을 나누던 한계를 넘어 놀랍도록 빠르고 정확하게 정보를 공유할 수 있게 되었다는 내용을 다룬 글이다. ③ 앞에서 구전에 의한 정보 전파에 한계가 있었다는 내용을 언급한 데 이어, 주어진 문장은 손으로 책을 써서 생각을 전파했던 경우를 언급하는데, ③ 뒤에서는 이 또한 너무나 많은 노력을 요하여 정보 확산의 속도를 제한했다는 점을 지적한다. 따라서 주어진 문장이 들어가기에 가장 적절한 곳은 ③이다.

DAY 17

[문제편 p.110]

- **advent** ⓝ 출현, 도래
- **handwritten** ⓐ 손으로 쓴
- **strengthen** ⓥ 강화하다
- **printing press** 인쇄기
- **prior to** ~의 이전에
- **tremendously** ⓐⓓ 대단히, 엄청나게, 크게
- **propagate** ⓥ 전파하다
- **equivalent to** ~에 맞먹는, 동등한
- **incredible** ⓐ 엄청난
- **transcribe** ⓥ (생각이나 글을) 필사하다, 기록하다, 옮기다
- **literacy** ⓝ 글을 읽고 쓸 줄 아는 능력
- **scroll** ⓝ 두루마리
- **fidelity** ⓝ 충실함
- **boost** ⓥ 신장시키다
- **word of mouth** 구전
- **complexity** ⓝ 복잡성
- **guaranteed** ⓐ 확실한, 보장된
- **scale** ⓝ 규모, 범위
- **monk** ⓝ 수도승

구문 풀이

13행 But <u>the incredible amount of time</u> [required to copy a scroll
주어 ⸻⸻ 과거분사(~하는 데 요구된)
or book by hand] <u>limited</u> <u>the speed</u> [with which information could
동사 목적어(선행사) 「전치사＋관계대명사」
spread this way].

05 문제를 작게 쪼개는 전략 　정답률 53% | 정답 ④

글의 흐름으로 보아, 주어진 문장이 들어가기에 가장 적절한 곳을 고르시오. [3점]

Negotiators should try to find ways / to slice a large issue into smaller
pieces, / known as using *salami tactics*.
협상가들은 방법을 찾으려고 노력해야 하는데, / 큰 문제를 더 작은 조각으로 나누는 / 이것은 *살라미 전술*을 쓰는
것이라고 알려져 있다.

① Issues / that can be expressed in quantitative, measurable units / are easy
to slice.
문제는 / 정량적이고 측정 가능한 단위로 표현될 수 있는 / 쪼개기 쉽다.

② For example, / compensation demands can be divided into cents-per-hour
increments / or lease rates can be quoted as dollars per square foot.
예를 들어, / 보상 요구는 시간당 센트 증가로 나누거나 / 임대료는 평방 피트당 달러로 시세를 매길 수 있다.

③ When working to fractionate issues of principle or precedent, / parties
may use the time horizon / (when the principle goes into effect or how long
it will last) / as a way to fractionate the issue.
원칙이나 관례의 쟁점을 세분화하는 작업을 할 때, / 당사자들은 시간 지평을 사용할 수 있다. / (원칙이 효력을
발휘하거나 지속되는 기간) / 그 쟁점을 세분화하는 방법으로

✔ It may be easier / to reach an agreement / when settlement terms don't
have to be implemented / until months in the future.
아마도 더 쉬울 것이다. / 합의에 도달하기가 / 합의 조건이 이행될 필요가 없을 때 / 향후 몇 개월까지

Another approach is / to vary the number of ways / that the principle may be
applied.
또 다른 접근법은 ~이다. / 방법의 수를 다양화하는 것 / 원칙이 적용될 수 있는

⑤ For example, / a company may devise a family emergency leave plan /
that allows employees the opportunity / to be away from the company / for a
period of no longer than three hours, / and no more than once a month, / for
illness in the employee's immediate family.
예를 들어, / 회사는 가족 비상 휴가 계획을 고안할 수 있다. / 직원에게 기회를 제공하는 / 회사를 비울 / 3시간
이내의 기간으로 / 그리고 한 달에 한 번 이하로 / 직원의 직계 가족의 질병에 대해

협상가들은 큰 문제를 더 작은 조각으로 나누는 방법을 찾으려고 노력해야 하
는데, 이것은 *살라미 전술*을 쓰는 것이라고 알려져 있다. ① 정량적이고 측정
가능한 단위로 표현될 수 있는 문제는 쪼개기 쉽다. ② 예를 들어, 보상 요구는
시간당 센트 증가로 나누거나 임대료는 평방 피트당 달러로 시세를 매길 수 있
다. ③ 원칙이나 관례의 쟁점을 세분화하는 작업을 할 때, 당사자들은 그 쟁점
을 세분화하는 방법으로 시간 지평(원칙이 효력을 발휘하거나 지속되는 기간)
을 사용할 수 있다. ④ 합의 조건이 향후 몇 개월까지 이행될 필요가 없을 때
합의에 도달하기가 아마도 더 쉬울 것이다. 또 다른 접근법은 원칙이 적용될
수 있는 방법의 수를 다양화하는 것이다. ⑤ 예를 들어, 회사는 직원의 직계 가
족의 질병에 대해 직원에게 3시간 이내, 한 달에 한 번 이하로 회사를 비울 기
회를 제공하는 가족 비상 휴가 계획을 고안할 수 있다.

Why? 왜 정답일까?

① 뒤에서 정량적이고 측정 가능한 단위로 쪼갤 수 있는 문제는 쪼개기 쉽다는 일반론을
제시한 후, ④ 앞의 문장은 '시간' 지평을 사용하는 예시를 든다. 주어진 문장에도 시간과
관련된 표현(until months in the future)이 있는데, ④ 뒤의 문장은 Another
approach로 시작하며 다른 접근법으로 넘어가 버린다. 따라서 주어진 문장이 들어가
기에 가장 적절한 곳은 '다른 접근법'이 언급되기 전에 시간 지평에 관해 보충 설명할 수
있는 위치인 ④이다.

- **reach an agreement** 합의에 도달하다
- **term** ⓝ 조건, 용어
- **settlement** ⓝ 합의
- **negotiator** ⓝ 협상가

- **quantitative** ⓐ 양적인
- **increment** ⓝ 증가
- **rate** ⓝ 요금, 비율
- **square** ⓐ 제곱의, 평방의
- **principle** ⓝ 원칙
- **go into effect** 효력을 발휘하다
- **immediate** ⓐ 직계의, 아주 가까이에 (있는)
- **measurable** ⓐ 측정 가능한
- **lease** ⓝ 임대
- **quote** ⓥ 견적을 내다
- **fractionate** ⓥ 세분하다
- **precedent** ⓝ 관례, 선례
- **devise** ⓥ 고안하다

구문 풀이

15행 For example, a company may devise <u>a family emergency</u>
선행사
<u>leave plan</u> that allows employees the opportunity to be away from
주격 관·대 「allow＋목적어＋to부정사 : ~이 …할 수 있게 하다」
the company for a period of no longer than three hours, and no more
than once a month, for illness in the employee's immediate family.

06 영화 언어에 관한 규칙의 형성 　정답률 58% | 정답 ④

글의 흐름으로 보아, 주어진 문장이 들어가기에 가장 적절한 곳을 고르시오. [3점]

Film has no grammar.
영화에는 문법이 없다.

① There are, however, some vaguely defined rules / of usage in cinematic
language, / and the syntax of film — its systematic arrangement — / orders
these rules / and indicates relationships among them.
그러나 어렴풋이 정의된 몇 가지 규칙이 있고, / 영화 언어 사용에 관한 / 영화의 문법, 즉 그것의 체계적인 (처리)
방식은 / 이러한 규칙들을 정리하고 / 그것들 사이의 관계를 보여준다.

② As with written and spoken languages, / it is important to remember / that
the syntax of film is a result of its usage, / not a determinant of it.
문어와 구어에서와 마찬가지로, / 기억하는 것이 중요하다. / 영화의 문법은 그 사용의 결과물이지 / 그것의 결정
요인은 아니라는 것을

③ There is nothing preordained about film syntax.
영화 문법에 관해 미리 정해진 것은 아무것도 없다.

✔ Rather, / it evolved naturally / as certain devices were found in practice /
to be both workable and useful.
오히려, / 그것은 자연스럽게 발전했다. / 특정 방법이 실제로 밝혀지면서 / 운용할 수 있고 유용하다는 것이

Like the syntax of written and spoken language, / the syntax of film is an
organic development, / descriptive rather than prescriptive, / and it has
changed considerably over the years.
문어와 구어의 문법처럼, / 영화의 문법은 자연스럽게 성장한 것으로 / 규범적이지 않고 기술적이며 / 그것은 여러
해에 걸쳐 상당히 변화했다.

⑤ "Hollywood Grammar" may sound laughable now, / but during the
thirties, forties, and early fifties / it was an accurate model of the way /
Hollywood films were constructed.
'할리우드 문법'은 지금은 웃기는 것처럼 들릴지 모르지만, / 30년대, 40년대, 50년대 초반에는 / 방식의 정확
한 모델이었다. / 할리우드 영화가 제작되는

영화에는 문법이 없다. ① 그러나 영화 언어 사용에 관한 어렴풋이 정의된 몇
가지 규칙이 있고, 영화의 문법, 즉 그것의 체계적인 (처리) 방식은 이러한 규칙
들을 정리하고 그것들 사이의 관계를 보여준다. ② 문어와 구어에서와 마찬가지
로, 영화의 문법은 그 사용의 결과물이지 결정 요인은 아니라는 것을 기억하는
것이 중요하다. ③ 영화 문법에 관해 미리 정해진 것은 아무것도 없다. ④ 오히
려, 그것은 특정 방법이 실제로 운용할 수 있고 유용하다는 것이 밝혀지면서
자연스럽게 발전했다. 문어와 구어의 문법처럼, 영화의 문법은 자연스럽게 성
장한 것으로 규범적이지 않고 기술적이며, 여러 해에 걸쳐 상당히 변화했다.
⑤ '할리우드 문법'은 지금은 웃기는 것처럼 들릴지 모르지만, 30년대, 40년대,
50년대 초반에는 할리우드 영화의 제작 방식의 정확한 모델이었다.

Why? 왜 정답일까?

영화에는 미리 정해진 문법이 없지만 암시적으로 정해진 몇 가지 규칙이 있다는 내용의
글이다. ④ 앞에서 영화 문법에 미리 정해진 것이 아무것도 없다고 언급한 데 이어,
Rather로 시작하는 주어진 문장은 '오히려' 영화 문법이 실제 운용되며 유용성을 검증
받은 끝에 자연스럽게 발전하게 되었다고 설명한다. ④ 뒤의 문장은 주어진 문장에 이어
서 영화 문법이 '자연스럽게 성장한' 것임을 언급한다. 따라서 주어진 문장이 들어가기에
가장 적절한 곳은 ④이다.

- **workable** ⓐ 운용 가능한, 작동 가능한
- **cinematic** ⓐ 영화의
- **systematic** ⓐ 체계적인, 조직적인
- **order** ⓥ 정리하다
- **organic** ⓐ 저절로 생기는, 자연스러운
- **prescriptive** ⓐ 규범적인
- **accurate** ⓐ 정확한
- **vaguely** ⓐⓓ 어렴풋이, 희미하게
- **syntax** ⓝ 문법, 구문론
- **arrangement** ⓝ (처리) 방식, 준비, 마련
- **determinant** ⓝ 결정 요인
- **descriptive** ⓐ 기술적인
- **laughable** ⓐ 웃기는, 터무니없는

구문 풀이

14행 "Hollywood Grammar" may sound laughable now, but (during the thirties, forties, and early fifties) it was an accurate model of the way [Hollywood films were constructed].

---

07 광상의 활용   정답률 49% | 정답 ④

글의 흐름으로 보아, 주어진 문장이 들어가기에 가장 적절한 곳을 고르시오. [3점]

Ore deposits represent work / that nature does for us.
광상은 일을 나타낸다. / 자연이 우리를 위해 하는

① For instance, / Earth's crust contains an average of about 55 ppm (parts per million) of copper, / whereas copper ore deposits must contain about 5,000 ppm (0.5%) copper / before we can mine them.
예를 들어, / 지각(地殼)은 평균 약 55ppm(백만분율)의 구리를 포함하고, / 반면에 구리 광상은 약 5,000ppm (0.5%)의 구리를 포함해야만 한다. / 우리가 채굴할 수 있기 전에

② Thus, / geologic processes need to concentrate the average copper content of the crust / by about 100 times / to make a copper ore deposit that we can use.
따라서, / 지질 작용은 지각의 평균 구리 함유량을 농집시킬 필요가 있다. / 약 100배 / 우리가 사용할 수 있는 구리 광상을 만들기 위해

③ We then use industrial processes / to convert copper ore into pure copper metal, / an increase of about 200 times.
이후 우리는 산업 공정을 사용하는데, / 구리 광석을 순수 구리 금속으로 변환시키기 위해 / 이는 대략 200배의 증가이다.

✓By a fortunate coincidence, / elements and materials that we use in large amounts / need less natural concentration / than those that we use in small amounts.
운이 좋게도, / 우리가 다량으로 사용하는 원소들과 물질들은 / 더 낮은 자연 농집을 필요로 한다. / 우리가 소량으로 사용하는 것보다

Thus, / we are likely to have larger deposits of mineral commodities / that we use in large amounts.
따라서, / 우리는 광물 자원 광상을 더 많이 가질 확률이 높다. / 우리가 다량으로 사용하는

⑤ As long as energy costs remain high, / the relation / between work that we can afford to do / and work that we expect nature to do / will control the lower limit of natural concentrations / that we can exploit, / and this puts very real limits / on our global mineral resources.
에너지 비용이 높게 유지되는 한, / 관계는 / 우리가 할 수 있는 일과 / 우리가 자연이 할 것으로 기대하는 일 사이의 / 자연 농집의 하한선을 조절할 것이며, / 우리가 이용할 수 있는 / 이는 매우 현실적인 제한을 둔다. / 지구의 광물 자원에

광상은 자연이 우리를 위해 하는 일을 나타낸다. ① 예를 들어, 지각(地殼)은 평균 약 55ppm(백만분율)의 구리를 포함하고, 반면에 구리 광상은 우리가 채굴할 수 있기 전에 약 5,000ppm (0.5%)의 구리를 포함해야만 한다. ② 따라서 지질 작용은 우리가 사용할 수 있는 구리 광상을 만들기 위해 지각의 평균 구리 함유량을 약 100배 농집시킬 필요가 있다. ③ 이후 우리는 구리 광석을 순수 구리 금속으로 변환시키기 위해 산업 공정을 사용하는데, 이는 대략 200배의 증가이다. ④ 운이 좋게도 우리가 다량으로 사용하는 원소들과 물질들은 우리가 소량으로 사용하는 것보다 더 낮은 자연 농집을 필요로 한다. 따라서 우리는 우리가 다량으로 사용하는 광물 자원 광상을 더 많이 가질 확률이 높다. ⑤ 에너지 비용이 높게 유지되는 한, 우리가 할 수 있는 일과 자연이 할 것으로 기대하는 일 사이의 관계는 우리가 이용할 수 있는 자연 농집의 하한선을 조절할 것이며, 이는 지구의 광물 자원에 매우 현실적인 제한을 둔다.

Why? 왜 정답일까?

④ 앞에서 구리 광상을 예로 들어, 지질 작용을 통해 우리가 쓸 수 있는 만큼의 광상이 만들어지면, 우리는 산업 공정을 통해 이를 금속으로 변환시켜 사용한다는 것을 설명하고 있다. 이어서 주어진 문장은 '다행히도' 우리가 많이 사용하는 원소나 물질은 우리가 소량 사용하는 다른 원소나 물질에 비해 자연 농집이 덜 이뤄져도 된다는 내용을 제시한다. ④ 뒤의 문장은 '그 결과' 우리가 많이 사용하는 광물 자원의 광상이 더 많이 존재할 수 있다고 한다. 따라서 주어진 문장이 들어가기에 가장 적절한 곳은 ④이다.

- coincidence ⑩ 우연
- ore ⑩ 광석
- represent ⓥ 나타내다
- mine ⓥ 채굴하다
- content ⑩ 함유량
- commodity ⑩ 원자재, 상품
- mineral resources 광물 자원
- concentration ⑩ 농집, 농축
- deposit ⑩ 퇴적물, 광상(鑛床)
- copper ⑩ 구리, 동
- geologic ⓐ 지질의
- convert ⓥ 변환시키다
- exploit ⓥ 이용하다

구문 풀이

1행 By a fortunate coincidence, elements and materials [that we use in large amounts] need less natural concentration than those [that we use in small amounts].
= elements and materials

★★★ 1등급 대비 고난도 2점 문제

08 과학 대회를 '승자 독식'으로 보는 데 대한 반박   정답률 41% | 정답 ③

글의 흐름으로 보아, 주어진 문장이 들어가기에 가장 적절한 곳을 고르시오.

Science is sometimes described as a winner-take-all contest, / meaning that there are no rewards for being second or third.
과학은 때때로 승자 독식 대회로 묘사되는데, / 이는 2등이나 3등을 하는 데 대한 보상이 없다는 뜻이다.

This is an extreme view of the nature of scientific contests.
이는 과학 대회의 본질에 대한 극단적인 견해이다.

① Even those who describe scientific contests in such a way / note that it is a somewhat inaccurate description, / given that replication and verification have social value / and are common in science.
과학 대회를 그렇게 설명하는 사람들조차도 / 그것이 다소 부정확한 설명이라고 말하는데, / 반복과 입증이 사회적 가치를 지니고 있다는 걸 감안할 때 그렇다. / 그리고 과학에서 일반적이라는 것을

② It is also inaccurate / to the extent that it suggests / that only a handful of contests exist.
또한 그것은 부정확하다. / 그것이 보여주는 경우에 / 단지 소수의 대회만 존재한다는 것을

✓Yes, / some contests are seen as world class, / such as identification of the Higgs particle / or the development of high temperature superconductors.
물론, / 몇몇 대회는 세계적인 수준으로 여겨진다. / 힉스 입자의 확인 / 또는 고온 초전도체 개발과 같은

But many other contests have multiple parts, / and the number of such contests may be increasing.
하지만 다른 많은 대회에는 다양한 부문이 있고, / 그런 대회의 수는 증가하고 있을 것이다.

④ By way of example, / for many years / it was thought / that there would be "one" cure for cancer, / but it is now realized / that cancer takes multiple forms / and that multiple approaches are needed to provide a cure.
예를 들어, / 여러 해 동안 / 생각되었지만, / 암에 대해 '하나'의 치료법이 있다고 / 이제 인식된다. / 암은 여러 형태를 띠고 있으며 / 치료를 제공하기 위해 다양한 접근 방식이 필요하다고

⑤ There won't be one winner / — there will be many.
승자는 한 명이 아니라 / 다수 존재할 것이다.

과학은 때때로 승자 독식 대회로 묘사되는데, 이는 2등이나 3등을 하는 데 대한 보상이 없다는 뜻이다. 이는 과학 대회의 본질에 대한 극단적인 견해이다. ① 과학 대회를 그렇게 설명하는 사람들조차도 그것이 다소 부정확한 설명이라고 말하는데, 반복과 입증이 사회적 가치를 지니고 있으며 과학에서는 일반적이라는 것을 감안할 때 그렇다. ② 또한 그것은 단지 소수의 대회만 존재한다는 것을 보여주는 경우에 부정확하다. ③ 물론, 힉스 입자의 확인 또는 고온 초전도체 개발과 같은 몇몇 대회는 세계적인 수준으로 여겨진다. 하지만 다른 많은 대회에는 다양한 부문이 있고, 그런 대회의 수는 증가하고 있을 것이다. ④ 예를 들어, 여러 해 동안 암에 대해 '하나'의 치료법만 있다고 생각되었지만, 이제 암은 여러 형태를 띠고 있으며 치료를 제공하기 위해 다양한 접근 방식이 필요하다고 인식된다. ⑤ 승자는 한 명이 아니라 다수 존재할 것이다.

Why? 왜 정답일까?

③ 뒤에서 many other contests를 언급하는데, 이 other의 비교 대상이 ③ 앞에 언급되지 않으므로 글의 흐름이 단절된다. 이때 주어진 문장을 보면 some contests가 언급되는데, 이것이 many other contests와 대비 관계를 이룬다. 따라서 주어진 문장이 들어가기에 가장 적절한 곳은 ③이다.

- identification ⑩ 확인
- temperature ⑩ 온도, 체온
- winner-take-all ⓐ 승자독식의
- inaccurate ⓐ 부정확한
- verification ⑩ 입증
- a handful of 소수의
- by way of example 한 예를 들면
- particle ⑩ 입자
- superconductor ⑩ 초전도체
- nature ⑩ 특성, 본질
- replication ⑩ 반복
- to the extent that ~한 경우에
- exist ⓥ 존재하다
- cure ⑩ 치료법

구문 풀이

7행 Even those [who describe scientific contests in such a way] note that it is a somewhat inaccurate description, given that replication and verification have social value and are common in science.

DAY 17

▶ 많이 틀린 이유는?
보통 주어진 문장 넣기 문제에서는 주어진 문장에 흔히 역접어가 있는데, 이 문제의 주어진 문장은 오히려 긍정어(Yes)로 시작한다. 이 경우 높은 확률로 뒤에 역접어가 등장하고 이어서 앞과 상반된 내용이 전개된다.

▶ 문제 해결 방법은?
정답인 ④ 뒷 문장이 But으로 시작하면서 many other contests를 언급하는데, 어떤 대회와 비교했을 때 '다른' 것인지를 앞 내용만으로는 알 수 없다. 이렇게 '알 수 없는' 빈틈이 보이면 주어진 문장을 대입해 읽어보고, 자연스러운지 검토한다.

★★★ 1등급 대비 고난도 2점 문제

09 얼굴 표정과 연관된 두 가지 신경 체계 정답률 29% | 정답 ⑤

글의 흐름으로 보아, 주어진 문장이 들어가기에 가장 적절한 곳을 고르시오.

Humans can tell lies / with their faces.
사람은 거짓말을 할 수 있다. / 얼굴로
Although some are specifically trained / to detect lies from facial expressions, / the average person is often misled / into believing false and manipulated facial emotions.
비록 어떤 사람들은 특별히 훈련되어 있지만, / 얼굴 표정에서 거짓말을 탐지하도록 / 보통 사람은 흔히 현혹된다. / 거짓되고 조작된, 얼굴에 나타난 감정을 믿도록
One reason for this / is that we are "two-faced."
이것의 한 가지 이유는 / 우리가 '두 얼굴이기' 때문이다.
By this I mean / that we have two different neural systems / that manipulate our facial muscles.
이 말로써 내가 의미하는 것은 / 두 가지 서로 다른 신경 체계가 우리에게 있다는 것이다. / 얼굴 근육을 조종하는
① One neural system is under voluntary control / and the other works under involuntary control.
하나의 신경 체계는 자발적인 통제 하에 있고 / 다른 하나는 비자발적인 통제 하에서 작동한다.
② There are reported cases of individuals / who have damaged the neural system / that controls voluntary expressions.
사람들의 보고된 사례들이 있다. / 신경 체계가 손상된 / 자발적인 표정을 통제하는
③ They still have facial expressions, / but are incapable of producing deceitful ones.
그들은 여전히 얼굴 표정이 있지만, / 속이는 얼굴 표정을 지을 수는 없다.
④ The emotion that you see / is the emotion they are feeling, / since they have lost the needed voluntary control / to produce false facial expressions.
여러분이 보는 감정은 / 그들이 느끼고 있는 감정이다. / 그들은 필요한 자발적인 통제를 잃었으므로, / 거짓된 얼굴 표정을 짓기 위해
✔There are also clinical cases / that show the flip side of this coin.
임상 사례도 있다. / 그 동전의 반대쪽 면을 보여주는
These people have injured the system / that controls their involuntary expressions, / so that the only changes in their demeanor you will see / are actually willed expressions.
이 사람들은 시스템이 손상되었고, / 비자발적 표현을 통제하는 / 그래서 여러분이 보게 되는 그들의 유일한 표정 변화는 / 실제로 자발적인 표정이다.

사람은 얼굴로 거짓말을 할 수 있다. 비록 어떤 사람들은 얼굴 표정에서 거짓말을 탐지하도록 특별히 훈련되어 있지만, 보통 사람은 흔히 거짓되고 조작된, 얼굴에 나타난 감정을 믿도록 현혹된다. 이것의 한 가지 이유는 우리가 '두 얼굴이기' 때문이다. 이 말로써 내가 의미하는 것은 얼굴 근육을 조종하는 두 가지 서로 다른 신경 체계가 우리에게 있다는 것이다. ① 하나의 신경 체계는 자발적인 통제 하에 있고 다른 하나는 비자발적인 통제 하에서 작동한다. ② 자발적인 표정을 통제하는 신경 체계가 손상된 사람들의 보고된 사례들이 있다. ③ 그들은 여전히 얼굴 표정이 있지만, 속이는 얼굴 표정을 지을 수는 없다. ④ 그들은 거짓된 얼굴 표정을 짓기 위해 필요한 자발적인 통제를 잃었으므로, 여러분이 보는 감정은 그들이 느끼고 있는 감정이다. ⑤ 그 동전의 반대쪽 면을 보여주는 임상 사례도 있다. 이 사람들은 비자발적 표현을 통제하는 시스템이 손상되었고, 그래서 여러분이 보게 되는 그들의 유일한 표정 변화는 실제로 자발적인 표정이다.

Why? 왜 정답일까?

사람들은 보통 상대방의 '얼굴'을 보고 감정을 추론하는데 이는 사람의 표정을 조종하는 두 가지 상반된 체계 때문에 가능하다는 것을 설명한 글이다. ⑤ 앞의 두 문장에서는 '자발적인' 표현을 통제하는 체계가 손상되어 상대를 속이는 표정을 짓지 못하는 사람들에 관해 언급하는데, 주어진 문장은 '이와는 다른 사례'가 있음을 말하며 흐름을 전환하고 있다. ⑤ 뒤에서는 비자발적 표현을 통제하는 체계를 다친 사람들의 경우를 언급하고 있다. 따라서 주어진 문장이 들어가기에 가장 적절한 곳은 ⑤이다.

- clinical ⓐ (명사 앞에만 쓰여) 임상의
- manipulate ⓥ 조작하다
- deceitful ⓐ 속이는
- injure ⓥ 손상시키다, 다치게 하다
- specifically ⓐⓓ 특별히, 구체적으로
- neural ⓐ 신경의
- willed ⓐ 자발적인, 자신의 의지로 결정된

구문 풀이

17행 These people have injured the system [that controls their involuntary expressions], / so that the only changes in their demeanor [you will see] are actually willed expressions.

주격 관계대명사
결과의 부사절(~해서 …하다) 선행사 동사(단수)
주어(선행사) 동사

★★ 문제 해결 꿀~팁 ★★

▶ 많이 틀린 이유는?
서로 다른 두 대상을 대조하는 글로, '자발적인 vs. 비자발적인' 신경 체계가 손상된 사람들에 대한 설명이 나누어지는 부분을 찾아야 한다. 주어진 문장의 'the flip side of this coin'이라는 비유가 흐름을 반전시키는 어구임을 이해해야 한다.

▶ 문제 해결 방법은?
⑤ 뒤의 지시사가 답의 결정적인 힌트이다. 주어진 문장 없이 글을 읽으면 ⑤ 뒤의 These people은 ⑤ 앞에 이어서 '자발적 표정을 통제하는 신경 체계를 다친 사람'을 가리키는데, 이 경우 'have injured the system that controls their involuntary expressions, ~'와 의미상 충돌한다.

★★★ 1등급 대비 고난도 3점 문제

10 편의성과 귀찮음을 동시에 안겨주는 기술의 물결 정답률 34% | 정답 ⑤

글의 흐름으로 보아, 주어진 문장이 들어가기에 가장 적절한 곳을 고르시오. [3점]

Each new wave of technology / is intended to enhance user convenience, / as well as improve security, / but sometimes these do not necessarily go hand-in-hand.
매번의 새로운 기술의 물결은 / 사용자 편의성을 향상하려는 의도지만, / 보안을 향상시킬 뿐만 아니라, / 때때로 이것들이 반드시 함께 진행되지는 않는다.
For example, / the transition from magnetic stripe to embedded chip / slightly slowed down transactions, / sometimes frustrating customers in a hurry.
예를 들어 / 마그네틱 띠에서 내장형 칩으로의 전환은 / 거래를 약간 늦춰서, / 때로 바쁜 고객을 좌절시켰다.
① Make a service too burdensome, / and the potential customer will go elsewhere.
서비스를 너무 부담스럽게 만들라 / 그러면 잠재 고객은 다른 곳으로 갈 것이다.
② This obstacle applies at several levels.
이런 장벽은 여러 수준에서 적용된다.
③ Passwords, double-key identification, and biometrics / such as fingerprint-, iris-, and voice recognition / are all ways / of keeping the account details hidden from potential fraudsters, / of keeping your data dark.
비밀번호, 이중 키 확인, 그리고 생체 인식: 지문, 홍채 및 음성 인식과 같은 / 모두 방법이다. / 잠재적인 사기꾼으로부터 계정 세부 정보를 숨겨 주는, / 즉 여러분의 데이터를 비밀로 유지하는
④ But they all inevitably add a burden / to the use of the account.
하지만 그것들은 모두 불가피하게 부담을 가중한다. / 계좌 사용에
✔On top of the hurdles / introduced in accessing his or her money, / if a suspected fraud is detected, / the account holder has to deal with the phone call / asking if he or she made the suspicious transactions.
난관에 더해, / 자기 돈에 접근하는 데 도입된 / 만약 의심스러운 사기가 감지되면, / 예금주는 전화 통화를 응대해야 한다. / 본인이 그 의심스러운 거래를 했는지 묻는
This is all useful at some level / — indeed, it can be reassuring / knowing that your bank is keeping alert to protect you / — but it becomes tiresome / if too many such calls are received.
이것은 모두 어느 정도 도움이 된다 / 실제로 안심스러울 수 있다 / 여러분의 은행이 여러분을 보호하기 위해 경계를 늦추지 않고 있다는 것을 알게 되면 / 하지만 귀찮아진다. / 그러한 전화를 너무 많이 받으면

매번의 새로운 기술의 물결은 보안을 향상시킬 뿐만 아니라, 사용자 편의성을 향상하려는 의도지만, 때때로 이것들이 반드시 함께 진행되지는 않는다. 예를 들어 마그네틱 띠에서 내장형 칩으로의 전환은 거래(의 속도)를 약간 늦춰서, 때로 바쁜 고객을 좌절시켰다. ① 서비스를 너무 부담스럽게 만들면, 잠재 고객은 다른 곳으로 갈 것이다. ② 이런 장벽은 여러 수준에서 적용된다. ③ 비밀번호, 이중 키 확인, 지문, 홍채 및 음성 인식과 같은 생체 인식은 모두 잠재적인 사기꾼으로부터 계정 세부 정보를 숨겨 주는, 즉 여러분의 데이터를 비밀로 유지하는 방법이다. ④ 하지만 그것들은 모두 불가피하게 계좌 사용에 부담을 가중한다. ⑤ 자기 돈에 접근하는 데 도입된 난관에 더해, 만약 의심스러운 사

기가 감지되면, 예금주는 본인이 그 의심스러운 거래를 했는지 묻는 전화 통화를 응대해야만 한다. 이것은 모두 어느 정도 도움이 되지만 — 실제로 여러분의 은행이 여러분을 보호하기 위해 경계를 늦추지 않고 있다는 것을 알게 되면 안심스러울 수 있다 — 그러한 전화를 너무 많이 받으면 귀찮아진다.

Why? 왜 정답일까?

기술의 물결은 우리 생활에 더해질 때마다 우리 생활의 편의성을 향상해 주고자 하지만, 실제로 우리를 더 번거롭게 할 수도 있다는 내용의 글이다. ⑤ 앞의 두 문장에서 비밀번호나 각종 생체 인식은 오늘날 우리 데이터를 더 안전하게 지켜주지만, 계좌 사용에 더 많은 부담을 주기도 한다고 언급한다. 여기에 이어 주어진 문장은 '어떤 부담'이 가해지는지를 구체적으로 설명하고, ⑤ 뒤의 문장은 '그래서' 갖가지 기술 보안 장치가 유용하지만 한편으로 우리를 귀찮게 한다는 결론을 제시한다. 따라서 주어진 문장이 들어가기에 가장 적절한 곳은 ⑤이다.

● **hurdle** ⓝ 난관, 허들	● **access** ⓥ 접근하다, 이용하다
● **suspect** ⓥ 의심하다	● **fraud** ⓝ 사기
● **detect** ⓥ 감지하다, 탐지하다	● **account** ⓝ 계좌, 계정
● **deal with** ~을 대하다, 처리하다	● **suspicious** ⓐ 의심스러운
● **transaction** ⓝ 거래	● **wave of technology** 기술의 물결
● **convenience** ⓝ 편의성, 편리함	● **security** ⓝ 보안
● **go hand-in-hand** 함께 진행되다	● **transition** ⓝ 전환
● **slightly** ⓐⓓ 약간	● **slow down** ~을 느려지게 하다, 늦추다
● **frustrate** ⓥ 좌절시키다	● **burdensome** ⓐ 부담스러운
● **obstacle** ⓝ 장애물, 장벽	● **identification** ⓝ (신원) 확인, 식별
● **biometrics** ⓝ 생체 인식	● **fingerprint** ⓝ 지문
● **iris** ⓝ (눈의) 홍채	● **inevitably** ⓐⓓ 불가피하게
● **reassuring** ⓐ 안심시키는	● **alert** ⓐ 경계하는, 기민한
● **tiresome** ⓐ 귀찮은	

구문 풀이

18행 This is all useful at some level — (indeed, it can be reassuring
　　　　　　　　　　　　　　　　　가주어
knowing that your bank is keeping alert to protect you) — but it
진주어　　　　　　　　　　　　　　　　　　　( )：삽입절
becomes tiresome if too many such calls are received.

★★ 문제 해결 꿀~팁 ★★

▶ 많이 틀린 이유는?
'Make a service ~' 문장에서 서비스가 너무 복잡해지면 고객이 도망가는 결과가 생긴다고 했다. 이어서 ④ 앞에는 계좌 보안을 위한 다양한 기술을 예로 든다. 이 기술이 너무 복잡한 나머지, ④ 뒤에서는 계좌 사용에 '부담'이 가해졌다고 한다. 즉, ④ 앞 뒤는 '많은 서비스가 계좌주를 보호할 목적으로 도입됐다 → 그러나 실상은 부담이 더 늘어났다'는 의미로 자연스럽게 연결된다.

▶ 문제 해결 방법은?
⑤ 앞에서 계좌주를 보호할 다양한 보안 기술을 they로 가리켰는데, ⑤ 뒤에서는 갑자기 새로운 This를 언급한다. 문맥상 이 This는 주어진 문장 내용 전체로 봐야 자연스럽게 읽힌다.

★★★ 1등급 대비 고난도 3점 문제

11	텔레비전 시청자의 분열과 광고주들의 우려	정답률 37%	정답 ③

글의 흐름으로 보아, 주어진 문장이 들어가기에 가장 적절한 곳을 고르시오. [3점]

The fragmentation of television audiences during recent decades, / which has happened throughout the globe / as new channels have been launched everywhere, / has caused advertisers much concern.
최근 몇 십 년 동안 텔레비전 시청자의 분열은 / 전 세계적으로 일어난 / 도처에서 새로운 채널들이 생겨나면서 / 광고주들에게 많은 우려를 안겨주었다.

① Advertisers look back nostalgically to the years / when a single spot transmission would be seen / by the majority of the population at one fell swoop.
광고주들은 시절을 향수에 젖어 회상한다. / 한 군데에서 전송하는 것이 보아지곤 했던 / 대부분의 사람들에 의해 한 번에

② This made the television advertising of mass consumer products / relatively straightforward / — not to say easy — / whereas today it is necessary / for advertisers to build up coverage of their target markets over time, / by advertising on a host of channels with separate audiences.
이것은 대량 소비 제품의 텔레비전 광고를 만들어 주었는데, / 상대적으로 단순하게 — 쉬웠다고 말하는 것은 아니지만 / 반면에 오늘날에는 필요하다 / 광고주들이 자신의 목표 시장의 점유 범위를 시간을 두고 구축하는 것이 / 별도의 시청자가 있는 다수의 채널에 광고를 함으로써

✓ Still, it is arguable / that advertisers worry rather too much about this problem, / as advertising in other media has always been fragmented.
그렇다고 하더라도, 주장할 여지가 있다. / 광고주들이 이 문제에 대해 오히려 너무 많이 걱정하는 것일 수 있다고 / 다른 미디어를 이용한 광고들은 늘 단편적이었으므로

Moreover, advertisers gain considerable benefits / from the price competition / between the numerous broadcasting stations.
게다가, 광고주들은 상당한 이익을 얻는다. / 가격 경쟁으로부터 / 수많은 방송국들 간의

④ And television remains much the fastest way / to build up public awareness of a new brand or a new campaign.
그리고 텔레비전은 단연코 가장 빠른 방법으로 남아있다. / 새로운 브랜드나 새로운 캠페인에 대한 대중의 인식을 형성하는

⑤ Seldom does a new brand or new campaign / that solely uses other media, without using television, / reach high levels of public awareness very quickly.
새로운 브랜드나 새로운 캠페인은 거의 ~하지 못한다. / 텔레비전을 이용하지 않고, 다른 미디어만을 이용하는 / 아주 빠르게 높은 수준의 대중 인지도에 도달하지

최근 몇 십 년 동안 텔레비전 시청자의 분열은 도처에서 새로운 채널들이 생겨나면서 전 세계적으로 일어났는데, 이는 광고주들에게 많은 우려를 안겨주었다. ① 광고주들은 한 군데에서 전송하는 것을 대부분의 사람들이 한 번에 보곤 했던 시절을 향수에 젖어 회상한다. ② 이것은 대량 소비 제품의 텔레비전 광고를 상대적으로 단순하게 — 쉬웠다고 말하는 것은 아니지만 — 만들어 주었는데, 반면에 오늘날에는 광고주들이 별도의 시청자가 있는 다수의 채널에 광고를 함으로써, 자신들의 목표 시장의 점유 범위를 시간을 두고 구축하는 것이 필요하다. ③ 그렇다고 하더라도, 다른 미디어를 이용한 광고들은 늘 단편적이었으므로, 광고주들이 이 문제에 대해 오히려 너무 많이 걱정하는 것일 수 있다고 주장할 여지가 있다. 게다가, 광고주들은 수많은 방송국들 간의 가격 경쟁으로부터 상당한 이익을 얻는다. ④ 그리고 텔레비전은 새로운 브랜드나 새로운 캠페인에 대한 대중의 인식을 형성하는 단연코 가장 빠른 방법으로 남아있다. ⑤ 텔레비전을 이용하지 않고, 다른 미디어만을 이용하는 새로운 브랜드나 새로운 캠페인이 아주 빠르게 높은 수준의 대중 인지도에 도달하는 경우는 거의 없다.

Why? 왜 정답일까?

텔레비전 시청자가 분열되면서 광고주들이 품게 된 우려에 관해 설명한 글이다. ③ 앞에서는 과거의 경우 한 군데에서 광고를 전송하면 대부분의 시청자들에게 한 번에 전달되었지만, 오늘날에는 다수 채널에서 광고를 송출해야 하고, 목표 시장의 점유 범위를 구축하는 데 시간이 걸리게 되었다는 내용이 주로 제시된다. 주어진 문장은 Still로 이 흐름을 반전시키며, 그렇다고 하더라도 광고주들의 우려가 지나친 것일 수 있다는 점을 지적한다. ③ 뒤에서는 추가로 광고주들이 오히려 다수 방송국들 간의 가격 경쟁에서 이익을 취하고 있다는 점도 지적한다. 따라서 주어진 문장이 들어가기에 가장 적절한 곳은 ③이다.

● **arguable** ⓐ 논쟁의 소지가 있는	● **fragmentation** ⓝ 분열
● **recent** ⓐ 최근	● **globe** ⓝ 세계
● **launch** ⓥ 시작하다, 출범하다	● **nostalgically** ⓐⓓ 향수에 젖어
● **transmission** ⓝ 전송, 전달	● **majority** ⓝ 대다수
● **straightforward** ⓐ 간단한	● **build up** ⓥ 쌓아올리다
● **coverage** ⓝ 범위	● **separate** ⓐ 개별적인
● **broadcasting station** 방송국	● **public awareness** 대중 인지도
● **solely** ⓐⓓ 오로지	

구문 풀이

10행 This made the television advertising of mass consumer
　　　　　　5형식 동사　　　　　　　　　　　　　　　목적어
products relatively straightforward — not to say easy — / whereas
　　　　　　목적격 보어　　　　　　　　　　　　　접속사(~하는 반면에)
today it is necessary for advertisers to build up coverage of their
　　　　　가주어　　　　　　　　　의미상 주어　　　　진주어
target markets over time, by advertising on a host of channels with
　　　　　　　　　　　　　　　　　~함으로써
separate audiences.

★★ 문제 해결 꿀~팁 ★★

▶ 많이 틀린 이유는?
텔레비전 광고를 소재로 한 글로 문장이 대체로 길어 한눈에 읽기 어렵다. 특별히 두드러진 오답이 없다는 점에서 수험생들의 혼란이 엿보인다.

▶ 문제 해결 방법은?
③ 뒤의 연결어 Moreover는 앞 내용과 같은 맥락에서 부연 설명을 덧붙일 때 쓰는 말이다. 즉 Moreover 뒤로 광고주들이 이득을 본다는 말이 나오는 것으로 볼 때, 이 바로 앞 문장은 '텔레비전 시청자의 분열로 인해 광고주들이 꼭 어려움을 겪지만은 않으며, 그들의 걱정이 오히려 지나친 것일 수도 있다'는 내용이어야 적절하다.

★★★ 1등급 대비 고난도 3점 문제

12 지도자가 얻기 힘든 명료함 　　　　정답률 33% | 정답 ②

글의 흐름으로 보아, 주어진 문장이 들어가기에 가장 적절한 곳을 고르시오. [3점]

Clarity is often a difficult thing / for a leader to obtain.
명료함은 흔히 어려운 것이다. / 지도자가 얻기에

Concerns of the present tend to seem larger / than potentially greater concerns / that lie farther away.
현재의 우려는 더 커 보이는 경향이 있다. / 잠재적으로 더 큰 우려보다 / 더 멀리 떨어져 있는

① Some decisions by their nature / present great complexity, / whose many variables must come together a certain way / for the leader to succeed.
몇몇 결정은 그 본질상 / 엄청난 복잡성을 제시하는데, / 그것의 많은 변수들이 특정한 방식으로 합쳐져야 한다. / 지도자가 성공하기 위해서는

✓ Compounding the difficulty, now more than ever, / is what ergonomists call information overload, / where a leader is overrun with inputs / — via e-mails, meetings, and phone calls — / that only distract and confuse her thinking.
이제 그 어느 때보다도 어려움을 가중시키는 것은 / 인간 공학자들이 정보 과부하라고 부르는 것으로, / 그 경우 지도자는 조언에 압도당한다. / 이메일, 회의, 통화를 통한 / 자신의 생각을 흐트러뜨리고 혼란스럽게 할 뿐인

Alternatively, / the leader's information might be only fragmentary, / which might cause her to fill in the gaps with assumptions / — sometimes without recognizing them as such.
그게 아니면, / 지도자의 정보는 그저 단편적인 것일 수도 있으며, / 이는 지도자가 공백을 추정으로 채우게 하는데, / 때로는 그것을 추정으로 인식하지 못하면서 그렇게 할 수도 있다.

③ And the merits of a leader's most important decisions, / by their nature, / typically are not clear-cut.
그리고 지도자의 가장 중요한 결정의 가치는 / 그 본질상 / 보통 명확하지 않다.

④ Instead those decisions involve a process / of assigning weights to competing interests, / and then determining, based upon some criterion, / which one predominates.
그보다는 그러한 결정에는 과정이 포함된다. / 상충되는 이익에 중요성을 배정한 다음, / 어떤 기준에 따라 결정하는 / 어떤 것이 우위를 차지하는지

⑤ The result is one of judgment, of shades of gray; / like saying / that Beethoven is a better composer than Brahms.
그 결과는 판단에 따른 것, 회색의 미묘한 차이를 띤 것으로, / 말하는 것과 같다. / 베토벤이 브람스보다 더 훌륭한 작곡가라고

명료함은 지도자가 흔히 얻기 어려운 것이다. 현재의 우려는 더 멀리 떨어져 있는 잠재적으로 더 큰 우려보다 더 커 보이는 경향이 있다. ① 몇몇 결정은 그 본질상 엄청난 복잡성을 제시하는데, 지도자가 성공하기 위해서는 그것의 많은 변수들이 특정한 방식으로 합쳐져야 한다. ② 이제 그 어느 때보다도 어려움을 가중시키는 것은 인간 공학자들이 정보 과부하라고 부르는 것으로, 그 경우 지도자는 자신의 생각을 흐트러뜨리고 혼란스럽게 할 뿐인 이메일, 회의, 통화를 통한 조언에 압도당한다. 그게 아니면, 지도자의 정보는 그저 단편적인 것일 수도 있으며, 이는 지도자가 공백을 추정으로 채우게 하는데, 때로는 그것을 추정으로 인식하지 못하면서 그렇게 할 수도 있다. ③ 그리고 지도자의 가장 중요한 결정의 가치는 그 본질상 보통 명확하지 않다. ④ 그보다는 그러한 결정에는 상충되는 이익에 중요성을 배정한 다음, 어떤 기준에 따라 어떤 것이 우위를 차지하는지 결정하는 과정이 포함된다. ⑤ 그 결과는 판단에 따른 것, 회색의 미묘한 차이를 띤 것으로, 베토벤이 브람스보다 더 훌륭한 작곡가라고 말하는 것과 같다.

Why? 왜 정답일까?

② 앞에서 지도자의 결정에는 많은 변수가 개입한다고 언급하는데, 주어진 문장은 결정 과정을 어느 때보다도 어렵게 하는 요인이 정보 과부하, 즉 지도자에게 너무 많은 정보가 주어진다는 점임을 지적한다. ② 뒤에서는 **Alternatively**로 흐름을 반전시키며 정보 과부하와는 달리 정보가 너무 단편적으로만 주어지는 경우를 언급한다. 따라서 주어진 문장이 들어가기에 가장 적절한 곳은 ②이다.

- **compound** ⓥ 악화시키다
- **overrun** ⓥ 가득 차다, 급속히 들끓다
- **distract** ⓥ (주의를) 흩뜨리다
- **obtain** ⓥ 얻다
- **potentially** [ad] 잠재적으로
- **variable** ⓝ 변수
- **fragmentary** ⓐ 단편적인
- **clear-cut** ⓐ 명확한
- **competing** ⓐ 상충되는
- **predominate** ⓥ 우위를 차지하다
- **composer** ⓝ 작곡가
- **information overload** 정보 과부하
- **input** ⓝ 조언, 투입
- **clarity** ⓝ 명료함
- **concern** ⓝ 염려, 우려
- **farther** ⓐ 더 멀리
- **alternatively** [ad] 그 대신에
- **merit** ⓝ 가치, 장점
- **assign** ⓥ 배정하다, 할당하다
- **criterion** ⓝ 기준
- **shade** ⓝ (색조나 의미의) 미묘한 차이

구문 풀이

1행 Compounding the difficulty, now more than ever,
「주격 보어+
is what ergonomists call information overload, where a leader is
동사+주어(명사절) : 도치 구문」　　　　계속적 용법
overrun with inputs — via e-mails, meetings, and phone calls — that
선행사　　　　　　　　　　　　주격 관·대
only distract and confuse her thinking.

★★ 문제 해결 꿀~팁 ★★

▶ 많이 틀린 이유는?
④ 앞뒤의 문장은 decisions라는 단어를 반복하며 리더가 내리는 결정의 특성을 설명하고 있다. 두 문장은 같은 소재를 다루는 데다 내용상 상충하지도 않으므로, ④의 위치에는 주어진 문장이 들어가서 채워야 할 논리적 공백이 없다.

▶ 문제 해결 방법은?
Alternatively는 '그게 아니면, 그 대신에'라는 뜻으로 앞뒤 흐름을 반전시키는 연결어이다. 이 뒤로 지도자에게 너무 단편적인 정보만이 주어진 경우가 언급되는 것으로 보아, 앞에는 상반되게도 '정보가 너무 많은' 경우를 언급하는 문장이 연결되어야 한다.

DAY 18 문장 삽입 03

01 ④	02 ③	03 ④	04 ④	05 ③
06 ④	07 ④	08 ②	09 ⑤	10 ⑤
11 ④	12 ③			

---

01 살충제 사용에 관한 생각의 변화
정답률 50% | 정답 ④

글의 흐름으로 보아, 주어진 문장이 들어가기에 가장 적절한 곳을 고르시오.

Simply maintaining yields at current levels / often requires new cultivars and management methods, / since pests and diseases continue to evolve, / and aspects of the chemical, physical, and social environment / can change over several decades.
수확량을 단지 현재 수준으로 유지하는 것만 해도 / 보통 새로운 품종과 관리 기법을 필요로 하는데, / 해충과 질병이 계속 진화하고 있고 / 그리고 화학적, 물리적, 사회적 환경 양상은 / 수십 년에 걸쳐 변할 수 있기 때문이다.

① In the 1960s, / many people considered pesticides / to be mainly beneficial to mankind.
1960년대에 / 많은 사람은 살충제를 여겼다. / 사람들에게 대체로 유익한 것으로

② Developing new, broadly effective, and persistent pesticides / often was considered to be the best way / to control pests on crop plants.
새롭고 널리 효과를 거두고 지속하는 살충제를 개발하는 것은 / 흔히 최고의 방법으로 여겨졌다. / 농작물 해충을 통제하는

③ Since that time, / it has become apparent / that broadly effective pesticides / can have harmful effects on beneficial insects, / which can negate their effects in controlling pests, / and that persistent pesticides / can damage non-target organisms in the ecosystem, / such as birds and people.
그 이후로, / 분명해졌다. / 널리 효과를 거두는 살충제가 / 유익한 곤충에 해로운 영향을 미칠 수 있어서 / 해충 통제 효과를 무효화할 수 있으며, / 그 끈질긴 살충제가 / 생태계 속 목표 외 생물에게 해가 될 수 있다는 점이 / 새와 사람 같은

✔ Also, / it has become difficult for companies / to develop new pesticides, / even those / that can have major beneficial effects and few negative effects.
또한, / 기업들로서는 어려워졌다. / 새로운 살충제를 개발하는 것이 / 그것들조차 / 주된 이로운 효과가 있고 부작용이 거의 없는

Very high costs are involved in following all of the procedures / needed to gain government approval for new pesticides.
모든 절차를 따르는 데 아주 높은 비용이 수반된다. / 새로운 살충제에 정부 승인을 얻는 데 필요한

⑤ Consequently, / more consideration is being given / to other ways to manage pests, / such as incorporating greater resistance to pests into cultivars / by breeding and using other biological control methods.
결과적으로, / 더 많은 고려가 이루어지고 있다. / 해충을 관리하는 다른 방법들에 대해 / 품종에 더 강한 해충 내성을 포함시키는 것 같은 / 다른 생물학적 통제 기법을 개량해 사용하여

수확량을 단지 현재 수준으로 유지하는 것만 해도 보통 새로운 품종과 관리 기법을 필요로 하는데, 해충과 질병이 계속 진화하고 있고 화학적, 물리적, 사회적 환경 양상이 수십 년에 걸쳐 변할 수 있기 때문이다. ① 1960년대에 많은 사람은 살충제가 사람들에게 대체로 유익한 것으로 여겼다. ② 새롭고 널리 효과가 있고 지속하는 살충제를 개발하는 것은 흔히 농작물 해충을 통제하는 최고의 방법으로 여겨졌다. ③ 그 이후로, 널리 효과가 있는 살충제가 유익한 곤충에게 해로운 영향을 미칠 수 있어서 해충 통제 효과를 무효화할 수 있으며, 그 끈질긴 살충제가 새와 사람 등, 생태계 속 목표 외 생물에게 해가 될 수 있다는 점이 분명해졌다. ④ 또한, 기업들이 새로운 살충제를 개발하는 것이 어려워져서, 주된 이로운 효과가 있고 부작용이 거의 없는 것들조차 만들기 어렵게 되었다. 새로운 살충제에 정부 승인을 얻는 데 필요한 모든 절차를 따르는 데 아주 높은 비용이 수반된다. ⑤ 결과적으로, 해충을 관리하는 다른 방법들, 말하자면 다른 생물학적 통제 기법을 개량해 사용하여 (재배 중인) 품종에 더 강한 해충 내성을 포함시키는 것 등이 더 고려되고 있다.

Why? 왜 정답일까?
④ 앞에서 살충제는 1960년대만 해도 각광을 받았으나 이후 분명한 부작용이 밝혀졌음을 언급하고 있다. 이어서 Also로 연결되는 주어진 문장은 새로운 살충제를 기업에서 개발하기도 어려워졌음을 보태어 설명한다. ④ 뒤의 문장에서는 비용 문제가 따른다는 것을 언급하며 주어진 문장 내용을 뒷받침한다. 따라서 주어진 문장이 들어가기에 가장 적절한 곳은 ④이다.

- **pesticide** ⓝ 살충제
- **yield** ⓝ 수확량 ⓥ 산출하다
- **method** ⓝ 방법
- **beneficial** ⓐ 이로운
- **cultivar** ⓝ 품종
- **pest** ⓝ 해충

- **disease** ⓝ 질병
- **decade** ⓝ 십 년
- **broadly** ⓐⓓ 광범위하게
- **crop plant** 농작물
- **insect** ⓝ 곤충
- **non-target** 목표 외의
- **approval** ⓝ 승인
- **resistance** ⓝ 내성, 저항
- **aspect** ⓝ 양상
- **mankind** ⓝ 사람들
- **persistent** ⓐ 지속력 있는, 끈질긴
- **apparent** ⓐ 분명한
- **negate** ⓥ 무효화하다, 효력이 없게 만들다
- **procedure** ⓝ 과정, 절차
- **consequently** ⓐⓓ 결과적으로
- **breed** ⓥ 개량하다

구문 풀이

1행 Also, it has become difficult for companies to develop new
가주어 / 의미상 주어 / 진주어
pesticides, even those [that can have major beneficial effects and
대명사(= pesticides) / 주격 관·대
few negative effects].

---

02 인간 활동을 평가하는 기준이 되는 문화
정답률 59% | 정답 ③

글의 흐름으로 보아, 주어진 문장이 들어가기에 가장 적절한 곳을 고르시오.

If we look at contemporary British 'culture' / we will probably quickly conclude / that sport is an important part of the culture.
만약 우리가 현대 영국의 '문화'를 본다면 / 우리는 아마도 빠르게 결론지을 것이다. / 스포츠가 그 문화의 중요한 한 부분이라고

In other words, / it is something / that many people in the society share and value.
다시 말해서, / 그것은 어떤 대상이다. / 사회의 많은 사람이 공유하고 가치 있게 여기는

① In addition, / we would also probably conclude / that the most 'important' sport within British culture is football.
게다가, / 우리는 또한 아마도 결론 지을 수도 있다. / 영국 문화에서 가장 '중요한' 스포츠는 축구라고

② We would 'know' this from the evidence / that on a daily basis there is a significant amount of 'cultural' activity / all focused on football / in terms of the amount of people / who play it, watch it, read about it and talk about it.
증거로부터 우리는 이를 '알' 것이다. / 상당한 양의 문화적 활동이 매일 있다는 / 축구에 모든 초점이 맞춰진 / 사람 수로 볼 때, / 축구를 하고, 보고, 축구에 관해 읽고 이야기하는

✔ However, / within British society / not everybody would see football as 'their' game.
하지만, / 영국 사회 안에서 / 모든 사람이 축구를 '자기' 경기라고 여기지는 않을 것이다.

It could be argued / from looking at their 'cultural' activities and habits, / that people from a middle-class background seem to prefer rugby over football, / or that more women play netball than football.
주장할 수도 있을 것이다. / '문화적' 활동과 습관을 보건대, / 중산층 배경 출신의 사람들은 축구보다 럭비를 선호하는 것 같다거나, / 여자들은 축구보다 네트볼을 하는 사람이 더 많다고

④ Equally, / if you went to the USA and were talking about 'football', / most people would assume / you were talking about American football rather than soccer.
마찬가지로, / 만약 여러분이 미국에 가서 '축구'에 대해 이야기하고 있다면, / 사람들 대부분은 가정할 것이다. / 여러분이 축구보다는 미식축구에 관해 이야기하고 있다고

⑤ From this we can conclude / that different cultures produce different ways / of understanding, or evaluating, human activities such as sport.
이로부터 우리는 결론지을 수 있다. / 서로 다른 문화들이 서로 다른 방식들을 만들어낸다고 / 스포츠와 같은 인간 활동을 이해하거나 평가하는

만약 우리가 현대 영국의 '문화'를 본다면 우리는 아마도 스포츠가 그 문화의 중요한 한 부분이라고 빠르게 결론지을 것이다. 다시 말해서, 그것은 사회의 많은 사람이 공유하고 가치 있게 여기는 어떤 대상이다. 게다가, 우리는 또한 영국 문화에서 가장 '중요한' 스포츠는 축구라고 아마도 결론 지을 수도 있다. 축구를 하고, 보고, 축구에 관해 읽고 이야기하는 사람 수로 볼 때, 축구에 모든 초점이 맞춰진 상당한 양의 문화적 활동이 매일 있다는 증거로부터 우리는 이를 '알' 것이다. ③ 하지만 영국 사회 안에서 모든 사람이 축구를 '자기' 경기라고 여기지는 않을 것이다. '문화적' 활동과 습관을 보건대, 중산층 배경 출신의 사람들은 축구보다 럭비를 선호하는 것 같다거나, 여자들은 축구보다 네트볼을 하는 사람이 더 많다고 주장할 수도 있을 것이다. 마찬가지로, 만약 여러분이 미국에 가서 '축구'에 대해 이야기하고 있다면, 사람들 대부분은 여러분이 축구보다는 미식축구에 관해 이야기하고 있다고 가정할 것이다. 이로부터 서로 다른 문화들이 스포츠와 같은 인간 활동을 이해하거나 평가하는 서로 다른 방식들을 만들어낸다고 결론지을 수 있다.

Why? 왜 정답일까?
③ 앞은 영국 문화를 관찰하다 보면 축구가 가장 중요한 스포츠라고 여길 것이라는 내용인데, ③ 뒤에서는 다른 스포츠가 선호되거나 더 많이 경기되는 상황을 언급한다. 즉 ③ 앞 뒤로 흐름이 어색하게 끊긴다. 따라서 영국 사람들이 축구만 '자기 것'이라고 여기지는 않

는다고 설명하며 흐름을 전환시키는 주어진 문장이 들어가기에 가장 적절한 곳은 ③이다.

- **contemporary** ⓐ 현대의, 동시대의
- **evidence** ⓝ 증거
- **in terms of** ~의 관점에서
- **evaluate** ⓥ 평가하다
- **value** ⓥ 가치 있게 여기다
- **on a daily basis** 매일
- **middle-class** ⓐ 중산층의

구문 풀이

17행 Equally, if you went to the USA and were talking about
'if + 주어 + 과거 동사 ~'
'football', most people would assume you were talking about
주어 + 조동사 과거형 + 동사원형 : 가정법 과거
American football rather than soccer.
A + rather than + B : B라기보다 A인

---

03 풍향의 측정 　　　　　정답률 59% | 정답 ④

글의 흐름으로 보아, 주어진 문장이 들어가기에 가장 적절한 곳을 고르시오.

Wind direction is usually measured / through the use of a simple vane.
풍향은 보통 측정된다. / 단순한 풍향계를 사용하여

① This is simply a paddle of some sort / mounted on a spindle; / when it catches the wind, / it turns so that the wind passes by without obstruction.
이것은 단순히 일종의 노 모양의 물체로, / 회전축에 고정된 / 그것이 바람을 받으면 / 그것은 바람이 방해받지 않고 지나가도록 돌아간다.

② The direction is recorded, / but if you ever have a chance / to watch a wind vane on a breezy day, / you will notice / that there is a lot of variation in the direction of wind flow / — a lot!
방향은 기록되지만, / 만약 여러분이 기회가 있다면, / 산들바람이 부는 날에 바람 풍향계를 볼 / 여러분은 보게 될 것이다! / 바람의 흐름 방향에 많은 변화가 있다는 것을 / 아주 많은

③ Sometimes the wind can blow / from virtually every direction / within a minute or two.
때때로 바람은 불어올 수 있다. / 거의 모든 방향에서 / 1~2분 이내에

✔ In order to make some sense of this, / an average wind direction over an hour / is sometimes calculated, / or sometimes the direction / that the wind blew from the most during the hour / is recorded.
이것을 어느 정도 이해하기 위해, / 한 시간에 걸친 평균적인 풍향이 / 때때로 계산되거나, / 때때로 방향이 / 그 한 시간 동안 바람이 가장 많이 불어온 / 기록된다.

Either way, it is a generalization, / and it's important to remember / that there can be a lot of variation in the data.
어느 쪽이든, 그것은 일반화된 것이고, / 기억하는 것이 중요하다. / 데이터에는 많은 변화가 있을 수 있다는 것을

⑤ It's also important to remember / that the data recorded at a weather station / give an indication of conditions prevailing in an area / but will not be exactly the same / as the conditions at a landscape / some distance from the weather station.
기억하는 것도 중요하다. / 기상 관측소에서 기록되는 데이터는 / 한 지역에서 우세한 상태를 나타내지만 / 정확하게 같지는 않을 것임을 / 지형의 상태와 / 기상 관측소로부터 어느 정도 떨어진

풍향은 보통 단순한 풍향계를 사용하여 측정된다. ① 이것은 단순히 회전축에 고정된 일종의 노 모양의 물체로, 바람을 받으면 바람이 방해받지 않고 지나가도록 돌아간다. ② 방향은 기록되지만, 만약 여러분이 산들바람이 부는 날에 바람 풍향계를 볼 기회가 있다면, 여러분은 바람의 흐름 방향에 많은, 아주 많은 변화가 있다는 것을 보게 될 것이다! ③ 때때로 바람은 1~2분 이내에 거의 모든 방향에서 불어올 수 있다. ④ 이것을 어느 정도 이해하기 위해, 때때로 한 시간에 걸친 평균적인 풍향을 계산하거나, 때때로 그 한 시간 동안 바람이 가장 많이 불어온 방향을 기록한다. 어느 쪽이든, 그것은 일반화된 것이고, 데이터에는 많은 변화가 있을 수 있다는 것을 기억하는 것이 중요하다. ⑤ 기상 관측소에서 기록되는 데이터는 한 지역에서 우세한 상태를 나타내지만 기상 관측소로부터 어느 정도 떨어진 지형의 상태와 정확하게 같지는 않을 것임을 기억하는 것도 중요하다.

Why? 왜 정답일까?

④ 앞에서 간혹 바람은 1~2분만에 거의 모든 방향에서 불어올 수도 있다고 하는데, 주어진 문장은 이 경우(this) 풍향을 측정하려면 한 시간에 걸친 평균적 풍향을 계산하거나, 혹은 한 시간 동안 바람이 가장 많이 불어왔던 방향을 기록하는 방법을 취할 수 있다고 설명한다. ④ 뒤의 문장에서는 주어진 문장에서 언급한 두 방법 중 '어느 것을 취하든' 그 결과는 일반화된 것이므로 데이터상에는 변화가 많다는 점을 인지해야 한다고 언급한다. 따라서 주어진 문장이 들어가기에 가장 적절한 곳은 ④이다.

- **make sense of** ~을 이해하다
- **mount** ⓥ (무언가를 살펴보기 위해) 고정시키다, 끼우다
- **obstruction** ⓝ 방해
- **variation** ⓝ 변화, 차이
- **calculate** ⓥ 계산하다
- **breezy** ⓐ 산들바람이 부는
- **virtually** ⓐⓓ 거의, 사실상

- **generalization** ⓝ 일반화
- **prevailing** ⓐ 우세한
- **indication** ⓝ 지표, 암시, 조짐

구문 풀이

1행 In order to make some sense of this, an average wind direction
부사적 용법(~하기 위해서)　　　　　　　주어1
over an hour is sometimes calculated, or sometimes the direction
동사구1　　　　　　동사구2
[that the wind blew from the most during the hour] is recorded.
　　　　　　　　　　　　　　　　동사구2

---

04 사람과 쥐의 단것에 대한 선호와 섭식 행동 조정 　정답률 62% | 정답 ④

글의 흐름으로 보아, 주어진 문장이 들어가기에 가장 적절한 곳을 고르시오.

Both humans and rats / have evolved taste preferences for *sweet* foods, / which provide rich sources of calories.
사람과 쥐 모두 / 단 음식에 대한 맛의 선호를 진화시켜 왔는데, / 단 음식은 풍부한 열량의 원천을 제공한다.

A study of food preferences / among the Hadza hunter-gatherers of Tanzania / found that honey was the most highly preferred food item, / an item that has the highest caloric value.
음식 선호에 관한 연구에서는 / 탄자니아 Hadza 수렵 채집인의 / 꿀이 가장 많이 선호되는 식품이었음을 발견했다. / 가장 높은 열량 값을 가진 식품인

① Human newborn infants / also show a strong preference for sweet liquids.
인간 갓난아기는 / 또한 단 음료에 대한 강한 선호를 보인다.

② Both humans and rats dislike *bitter* and *sour* foods, / which tend to contain toxins.
사람과 쥐 모두 쓰고 신 음식을 싫어하는데, / 이는 독소를 포함하는 경향이 있다.

③ They also adaptively adjust their eating behavior / in response to deficits in water, calories, and salt.
그들은 또한 자신의 섭식 행동을 적절히 조정한다. / 물, 열량, 소금 부족에 대응하여

✔ Experiments show / that rats display an immediate liking for salt / the first time they experience a salt deficiency.
실험은 보여준다. / 쥐가 소금에 대한 즉각적인 선호를 보이는 것을 / 소금 결핍을 처음 경험할 때

They likewise increase their intake of sweets and water / when their energy and fluids become depleted.
마찬가지로 이들은 단것과 물 섭취를 늘린다. / 그들의 에너지와 체액이 고갈되면

⑤ These appear to be specific evolved mechanisms, / designed to deal with the adaptive problem of food selection, / and coordinate consumption patterns with physical needs.
이러한 것들은 특정한 진화된 기제처럼 보인다. / 음식 선택의 적응적 문제를 다루고 / 음식 섭취 방식을 신체적 욕구와 조화시키도록 고안된

사람과 쥐 모두 단 음식에 대한 맛의 선호를 진화시켜 왔는데, 단 음식은 풍부한 열량의 원천을 제공한다. 탄자니아 Hadza 수렵 채집인의 음식 선호에 관한 연구에서는 가장 높은 열량 값을 가진 식품인 꿀이 가장 많이 선호되는 식품이었음을 발견했다. ① 인간 갓난아기 또한 단 음료에 대한 강한 선호를 보인다. ② 사람과 쥐 모두 쓰고 신 음식을 싫어하는데, 이는 독소를 포함하는 경향이 있다. ③ 그들은 또한 자신의 섭식 행동을 물, 열량, 소금 부족에 대응하여 적절히 조정한다. ④ 실험에서는 쥐가 소금 결핍을 처음 경험할 때 소금에 대한 즉각적인 선호를 보이는 것으로 나타난다. 마찬가지로 이들은 에너지와 체액이 고갈되면 단것과 물 섭취를 늘린다. ⑤ 이러한 것들은 음식 선택의 적응적 문제를 다루고 음식 섭취 방식을 신체적 욕구와 조화시키도록 고안된, 특정한 진화된 기제처럼 보인다.

Why? 왜 정답일까?

④ 앞의 문장에서 인간과 쥐는 물, 열량, 소금의 부족 상황에 맞추어 섭식 행동을 조정한다고 하는데, 주어진 문장에서는 이에 대한 구체적인 예로서 쥐가 소금 결핍을 처음 경험할 때 소금에 대한 선호가 즉시 커진다는 실험 결과를 소개한다. ④ 뒤의 문장에서는 '마찬가지로' 에너지와 체액이 고갈되면 '쥐'가 단것과 물 섭취를 늘린다는 내용을 덧붙여 말한다. 따라서 주어진 문장이 들어가기에 가장 적절한 곳은 ④이다.

- **deficiency** ⓝ 결핍
- **infant** ⓝ 유아, 젖먹이
- **in response to** ~에 대응하여
- **specific** ⓐ 특정한, 구체적인
- **evolve** ⓥ 진화하다
- **toxin** ⓝ 독소
- **deficit** ⓝ 결손, 부족
- **adaptive** ⓐ 적응적인, 조정의

구문 풀이

16행 These appear to be specific evolved mechanisms, [designed
~인 것처럼 보이다　　　　　　　　　　　　과거분사
to deal with the adaptive problem of food selection, and coordinate
부정사1　　　　　　　　　　　　　　　(to 생략)　부정사2
consumption patterns with physical needs].

05 학습 행동의 질적 변화를 위한 수업 구성의 필요성　정답률 42% | 정답 ③

글의 흐름으로 보아, 주어진 문장이 들어가기에 가장 적절한 곳을 고르시오. [3점]

Carole Ames, / dean of the college of education at Michigan State University, / points out / that it isn't "quantitative changes in behavior" / (such as requiring students / to spend more hours in front of books or worksheets) / that help children to learn better.
Carole Ames는 / 미시간 주립 대학교의 사범대학장인 / 지적한다. / 바로 '행동의 양적 변화'가 아니라고 / (학생들에게 요구하는 이 같은 / 책이나 학습지 앞에서 더 많은 시간을 보내도록) / 아이들이 더 잘 배우도록 돕는 것은

① Rather, / it's "qualitative changes in the ways / students view themselves in relation to the task, / engage in the process of learning, / and then respond to the learning activities and situation."
오히려 / 바로 '방식에서의 질적 변화'이다. / '학생들이 과제와 관련하여 자신을 바라보는 / 학습 과정에 참여하며, / 그런 다음 활동과 상황에 대응하는'

② In turn, / these attitudes and responses / on the part of students / emerge from the way / teachers think about learning / and, as a result, / the ways they've organized their classrooms.
결국, / 이런 태도와 반응은 / 학생 쪽의 / 방식으로부터 생겨난다. / 교사가 학습에 대해 생각하는 / 그리고 그 결과로 / 그들이 자기 수업을 구성한 방식

☑ If the goal is to figure out / how best to cover a set curriculum / — to fill students with facts — / then it might seem appropriate / to try to maximize time on task, / such as by assigning homework.
만약 목표가 알아내는 것이라면, / 정해진 교육과정을 다루는 최선의 방법을 / 즉 학생들에게 사실을 채워줄 / 적절해 보일 수도 있다. / 과제에 들이는 시간을 최대화하려 애쓰는 게 / 숙제를 부여하는 것처럼

But that's unlikely / to have a positive effect on the critical variables / that Ames identifies.
하지만 그것은 ~할 것 같지 않다. / 중요한 변수에 긍정적인 영향을 미칠 / Ames가 밝히고 있는

④ Perhaps it makes sense to see education / as being less about how much the teacher covers / and more about what the students can be helped to discover.
아마도 교육을 보는 것이 타당할 것이다. / 교사가 얼마나 많은 부분을 다루는가와는 더 연관이 적고 / 학생들이 무엇을 발견하도록 도와줄 수 있을지와 더 관련이 있다고

⑤ More time won't do a thing / to bring about that shift.
더 많은 시간은 하나도 기여하지 못할 것이다. / 그런 변화를 야기하는 데

미시간 주립 대학교의 사범대학장 Carole Ames는 아이들이 더 잘 배우도록 돕는 것은 (학생들이 책이나 학습지 앞에서 더 많은 시간을 보내도록 요구하는 것 같은) '행동의 양적 변화'가 아니라고 지적한다. ① 오히려 (아이들이 더 잘 배우도록 돕는 것은) '학생들이 과제와 관련하여 자신을 바라보고 학습 과정에 참여하며, 그런 다음 활동과 상황에 대응하는 방식에서의 질적 변화'이다. ② 결국, 학생 쪽의 이런 태도와 반응은 교사가 학습에 대해 생각하는 방식과 그 결과로 교사들이 수업을 구성한 방식으로부터 생겨난다. ③ 만약 목표가 정해진 교육과정을 다루는, 즉 학생들에게 사실을 채워줄 최선의 방법을 알아내는 것이라면, 숙제를 부여하는 것처럼 과제에 들이는 시간을 최대화하려고 애쓰는 게 적절해 보일 수도 있다. 하지만 그것은 Ames가 밝히고 있는 중요한 변수에 긍정적인 영향을 미칠 것 같지 않다. ④ 아마도 교육은 교사가 얼마나 많은 부분을 다루는가와는 더 연관이 적고 학생들이 무엇을 발견하도록 도와줄 수 있을지와 더 관련이 있다고 보는 것이 타당할 것이다. ⑤ 더 많은 (학습) 시간을 들인다 해도 그런 변화는 하나도 일어나지 않을 것이다.

Why? 왜 정답일까?

③ 앞에서 학습에 진정 도움이 되는 것은 학습의 질적 변화로, 교사의 수업 구성 방식이 중요하다는 내용이 제시된다. 이에 이어 주어진 문장은 만일 교육의 목적이 정해진 교육과정을 그저 다루는 것이라면 공부 양을 늘려줄 수 있는 방법이 좋아보일 수도 있다고 언급한다. 한편, ③ 뒤에서는 흐름을 반전시키며(But) 학습 양보다는 학생들이 진정 도움받을 수 있는 부분을 고민하는 것이 교육의 본질적인 목표와 더 관련되어 있다는 주장을 다시금 전개한다. 따라서 주어진 문장이 들어가기에 가장 적절한 곳은 ③이다.

- figure out ~을 알아내다
- curriculum ⓝ 교육과정
- dean ⓝ 학장
- quantitative ⓐ 양적인
- in relation to ~와 관련되어
- emerge ⓥ 생겨나다, 출현하다
- identify ⓥ 밝히다, 확인하다
- cover ⓥ 다루다
- assign ⓥ 부여하다, 할당하다
- point out ~을 지적하다
- qualitative ⓐ 질적인
- engage in ~에 참여하다, 종사하다
- variable ⓝ 변수
- bring about ~을 야기하다

구문 풀이

1행 If the goal is to figure out {how best to cover a set curriculum
　　　　　　　　　　　　　　　　　　　　└ 명사구(to figure out의 목적어)
— to fill students with facts — } then it might seem appropriate
　　　　　　　　　　　　　　　　　　　가주어　　2형식 동사　　주격 보어
to try to maximize time on task, such as by assigning homework.
진주어(~것)　　　　　　　　　　　　　　　「by + 동명사 : ~함으로써」

06 속삭임의 회랑　정답률 47% | 정답 ④

글의 흐름으로 보아, 주어진 문장이 들어가기에 가장 적절한 곳을 고르시오. [3점]

Whispering galleries are remarkable acoustic spaces / found beneath certain domes or curved ceilings.
속삭임의 회랑은 놀라운 음향 공간이다. / 어떤 돔이나 곡면의 천장 아래에서 발견되는

A famous one is located outside a well-known restaurant / in New York City's Grand Central Station.
유명한 것 하나가 유명한 식당 밖에 있다. / 뉴욕시의 Grand Central 역에 있는

① It's a fun place to take a date: / the two of you can exchange romantic words / while you're forty feet apart and separated by a busy passageway.
그곳은 데이트하기에 재미있는 곳으로, / 여러분 두 사람은 낭만적인 말을 주고받을 수 있다. / 혼잡한 통로에 의해 분리되어 40피트 떨어져 있으면서도

② You'll hear each other clearly, / but the passersby won't hear a word you're saying.
여러분은 서로의 말을 분명하게 듣겠지만 / 지나가는 사람들에게는 여러분이 하는 말이 한마디도 들리지 않을 것이다.

③ To produce this effect, / the two of you should stand / at diagonally opposite corners of the space, / facing the wall.
이런 효과를 내기 위해 / 여러분 두 사람은 서 있어야 한다. / 그 공간의 대각선으로 맞은편의 구석에 / 벽을 바라보고

☑ That puts you each near a focus, a special point / at which the sound of your voice gets focused / as it reflects off the passageway's curved walls and ceiling.
그것은 여러분 각자를 특별한 지점인 초점 가까이 둔다. / 여러분의 목소리가 집중되는 / 그것이 통로의 곡면인 벽과 천장에서 반사될 때

Ordinarily, the sound waves you produce / travel in all directions / and bounce off the walls at different times and places, / scrambling them so much / that they are inaudible / when they arrive at the ear of a listener forty feet away.
보통 여러분이 만드는 음파는 / 모든 방향으로 이동하고 / 각기 다른 시간과 장소에서 벽에 반사되어 / 너무 많이 뒤섞이므로 / 들리지 않는다. / 그것들이 40피트 떨어져 있는 듣는 사람의 귀에 도달할 때는

⑤ But when you whisper at a *focus*, / the reflected waves all arrive at the *same* time at the other focus, / thus reinforcing one another / and allowing your words to be heard.
그러나 초점에서 속삭일 때, / 반사되는 음파는 전부 다른 초점에 동시에 도달하며, / 그리하여 서로를 강화하여 / 여러분의 말이 들리게 한다.

속삭임의 회랑은 어떤 돔이나 곡면의 천장 아래에서 발견되는 놀라운 음향 공간이다. 유명한 것 하나가 뉴욕시의 Grand Central 역에 있는 유명한 식당 밖에 있다. ① 그곳은 데이트하기에 재미있는 곳으로, 여러분 두 사람은 혼잡한 통로에 의해 분리되어 40피트 떨어져 있으면서도 낭만적인 말을 주고받을 수 있다. ② 여러분은 서로의 말을 분명하게 듣겠지만 지나가는 사람들에게는 여러분이 하는 말이 한마디도 들리지 않을 것이다. ③ 이런 효과를 내기 위해 여러분 두 사람은 그 공간의 대각선으로 맞은편의 구석에 벽을 바라보고 서 있어야 한다. ④ 그것은 여러분 각자를 여러분의 목소리가 통로의 곡면인 벽과 천장에서 반사될 때 집중되는 특별한 지점인 초점 가까이 둔다. 보통 여러분이 만드는 음파는 모든 방향으로 이동하고 각기 다른 시간과 장소에서 벽에 반사되어 너무 많이 뒤섞이므로 40피트 떨어져 있는 듣는 사람의 귀에 도달할 때는 들리지 않는다. ⑤ 그러나 초점에서 속삭일 때, 반사되는 음파는 전부 다른 초점에 동시에 도달하며, 그리하여 서로를 강화하여 여러분의 말이 들리게 한다.

Why? 왜 정답일까?

④ 앞에서 속삭임의 회랑 효과, 즉 멀리 떨어진 사람끼리 서로의 말을 선명히 들을 수 있는 효과를 내기 위해서는 두 사람이 대각선으로 맞은편 구석에 벽을 바라보고 서야 한다고 언급한 데 이어, 주어진 문장은 이 내용을 That으로 받으며 그렇게 하면 두 사람이 목소리 음파의 반사 초점 안에 들어오게 된다고 설명한다. ④ 뒤에서는 주어진 문장에 이어 두 사람이 만들어내는 음파를 언급하며, 이 음파는 본래 온갖 방향으로 반사되고 뒤섞여 들리지 않게 되지만 초점 안에서는 도리어 강화되어 들린다는 설명을 제시하고 있다. 따라서 주어진 문장이 들어가기에 가장 적절한 곳은 ④이다.

- reflect off 반사되다
- ceiling ⓝ 천장
- remarkable ⓐ 놀라운, 주목할 만한
- beneath ［prep］ 아래[밑]에
- apart ［ad］ (거리·공간·시간상으로) 떨어져
- diagonally ［ad］ 대각선으로
- ordinarily ［ad］ 보통은, 대개는, 정상적으로
- travel ⓥ 이동하다
- bounce off 튕기다
- inaudible ⓐ 들리지 않는
- passageway ⓝ 통로
- whispering ⓝ 속삭임, 소곤거림
- acoustic ⓐ 음향의, 청각의
- located ⓐ ~에 위치한
- passersby ⓝ 지나가는 사람들
- opposite ⓐ 맞은편의
- sound wave 음파
- direction ⓝ 방향
- scramble ⓥ 뒤죽박죽으로 만들다
- reinforce ⓥ 강화하다

구문 풀이

14행 Ordinarily, the sound waves [you produce] travel in all
directions and bounce off the walls at different times and places,
scrambling them so much that they are inaudible when they arrive
at the ear of a listener forty feet away.

주어 / 동사1 / 동사2 / 분사구문 / 「so ~ that … : 너무 ~해서 …하다」 / 시간 접속사

---

07 저작권의 보호 대상 　　　정답률 65% | 정답 ④

글의 흐름으로 보아, 주어진 문장이 들어가기에 가장 적절한 곳을 고르시오. [3점]

Designers draw on their experience of design / when approaching a new project.
디자이너는 자신의 디자인 경험을 이용한다. / 새로운 프로젝트에 접근할 때

This includes the use of previous designs / that they know work / — both designs that they have created themselves / and those that others have created.
이것에는 이전의 디자인을 활용하는 것이 포함된다. / 그들이 효과가 있다고 알고 있는 / 즉 그들이 직접 만들었던 디자인과 / 다른 사람들이 만들었던 디자인 둘 다

① Others' creations often spark inspiration / that also leads to new ideas and innovation.
다른 사람들의 창작물은 흔히 영감을 불러일으킨다. / 새로운 아이디어와 혁신으로도 이어지는

② This is well known and understood.
이는 잘 알려져 있고 이해되는 일이다.

③ However, / the expression of an idea is protected by copyright, / and people who infringe on that copyright / can be taken to court and prosecuted.
그러나 / 한 아이디어의 표현은 저작권에 의해 보호되며, / 그 저작권을 침해하는 사람들은 / 법정에 끌려가고 기소될 수 있다.

☑ Note / that copyright covers the expression of an idea / and not the idea itself.
유의하라. / 저작권은 아이디어의 표현을 다룬다는 점에 / 아이디어 그 자체가 아닌

This means, / for example, / that while there are numerous smartphones all with similar functionality, / this does not represent an infringement of copyright / as the idea has been expressed in different ways / and it is the expression that has been copyrighted.
이것은 의미한다. / 예컨대 / 모두 유사한 기능을 가진 많은 스마트폰이 있지만, / 이것이 저작권 침해를 나타내지 않는다는 것을 / 그 아이디어가 서로 다른 방식으로 표현되었고 / 저작권 보호를 받은 것은 그 표현이기 때문에

⑤ Copyright is free / and is automatically invested in the author, / for instance, the writer of a book or a programmer who develops a program, / unless they sign the copyright over to someone else.
저작권은 무료이며 / 저작자에게 자동으로 부여된다. / 가령 어떤 책의 저자나 프로그램을 개발하는 프로그래머에게 / 그 저작자가 저작권을 다른 누군가에게 양도하지 않는 한

디자이너는 새로운 프로젝트에 접근할 때 자신의 디자인 경험을 이용한다. 이것에는 그들이 효과가 있다고 알고 있는 이전의 디자인, 즉 그들이 직접 만들었던 디자인과 다른 사람들이 만들었던 디자인을 다 활용하는 것이 포함된다. ① 다른 사람들의 창작물은 흔히 새로운 아이디어와 혁신으로도 이어지는 영감을 불러일으킨다. ② 이는 잘 알려져 있고 이해되는 일이다. ③ 그러나 한 아이디어의 표현은 저작권에 의해 보호되며, 그 저작권을 침해하는 사람들은 법정에 끌려가고 기소될 수 있다. ④ 저작권은 아이디어 그 자체가 아닌 아이디어 표현을 다룬다는 점에 유의하라. 이것은 예컨대 모두 유사한 기능을 가진 많은 스마트폰이 있지만, 그 아이디어가 서로 다른 방식으로 표현되었고 저작권 보호를 받은 것은 그 표현이기 때문에 이것이 저작권 침해를 나타내지 않는다는 것을 의미한다. ⑤ 저작권은 무료이며 저작자, 가령 어떤 책의 저자나 프로그램을 개발하는 프로그래머가 저작권을 다른 누군가에게 양도하지 않는 한 그 저작자에게 자동으로 부여된다.

Why? 왜 정답일까?

저작권은 아이디어 자체가 아니라 아이디어를 구현한 개별의 창작물을 보호한다는 내용을 다룬 글이다. 먼저 ④ 앞의 문장에서 어떤 아이디어의 표현이 저작권에 의해 보호된다면 그 저작권을 침해하는 사람들은 처벌을 받게 된다고 언급한다. 이어서 주어진 문장은 이때 저작권의 범위가 아이디어 자체에 미치는 것은 아니고, 아이디어의 '표현'에 국한된다는 점을 상기시킨다. ④ 뒤의 문장은 같은 아이디어를 구현한 스마트폰이 아무리 많더라도 다 서로 다른 방식으로 표현된 이상 서로 저작권을 침해하지 않는 것이라는 예를 들어 주어진 문장을 뒷받침한다. 따라서 주어진 문장이 들어가기에 가장 적절한 곳은 ④이다.

- **copyright** ⓝ 저작권 ⓥ 저작권을 보호하다
- **previous** ⓐ 이전의, 먼젓번의
- **innovation** ⓝ 혁신, 쇄신
- **draw on** ~을 이용하다
- **inspiration** ⓝ 영감(靈感)
- **court** ⓝ 법정, 법원

- **numerous** ⓐ 많은
- **represent** ⓥ 대표하다, (~에) 해당하다
- **automatically** ⓐⓓ 자동으로
- **author** ⓝ 작가, 저자, 입안자
- **functionality** ⓝ 기능
- **infringement** ⓝ 위배, 위반
- **invest** ⓥ 부여하다, 투자하다
- **sign A over to B** B에게 A를 양도하다

구문 풀이

12행 This means, for example, that while there are numerous
smartphones all with similar functionality, this does not represent
an infringement of copyright as the idea has been expressed in
different ways and it is the expression that has been copyrighted.

접속사 / 접속사(~한 반면) / 주어 / 동사 / 목적어 / 접속사(이유) / 현재완료 수동태(~되어 왔다) / 「it is ~ that … 강조구문: …한 것은 바로 ~이다」

★★★ 1등급 대비 고난도 2점 문제

08 심리학에서 정의하는 '팀, 집단'의 개념 　　　정답률 33% | 정답 ②

글의 흐름으로 보아, 주어진 문장이 들어가기에 가장 적절한 곳을 고르시오.

In everyday life, / we tend to see any collection of people as a group.
일상생활에서 / 우리는 어떤 사람들의 무리라도 하나의 집단으로 보는 경향이 있다.

① However, / social psychologists use this term more precisely.
그러나 / 사회 심리학자들은 이 용어를 더 정확히 사용한다.

☑ In particular, / they define a group as two or more people / who interact with, / and exert mutual influences on, each other.
특히, / 그들은 둘 이상의 사람들로 집단을 정의한다. / (서로) 상호 작용하고 / 상호 영향력을 발휘하는

It is this sense of mutual interaction or inter-dependence / for a common purpose / which distinguishes the members of a group / from a mere aggregation of individuals.
바로 이런 서로의 상호 작용 또는 상호 의존감이다. / 공동의 목적을 위한 / 집단의 구성원들을 구별하는 것은 / 단순한 개인들의 집합으로부터

③ For example, / as Kenneth Hodge observed, / a collection of people / who happen to go for a swim after work on the same day each week / does not, strictly speaking, constitute a group / because these swimmers do not interact with each other in a structured manner.
예를 들어, / Kenneth Hodge가 진술한 바와 같이, / 사람들의 무리는 / 매주 같은 날에 일을 마치고 우연히 수영을 하러 가는 / 엄밀히 말하면 집단을 구성하지 않는데, / 이러한 수영하는 사람들은 구조적인 방식으로 상호 작용하지 않기 때문이다.

④ By contrast, / a squad of young competitive swimmers / who train every morning before going to school / is a group / because they not only share a common objective (training for competition) / but also interact with each other in formal ways / (e.g., by warming up together beforehand).
대조적으로, / 경쟁 관계의 어린 수영 선수들은 / 매일 아침 학교에 가기 전에 훈련하는 / 집단이 맞다. / 공동의 목표(경기를 위한 훈련)를 공유할 뿐만 아니라 / 공식적인 방식으로 상호 작용하기 때문에 / (예컨대, 미리 함께 몸 풀기)

⑤ It is this sense of people / coming together to achieve a common objective / that defines a "team".
바로 사람들의 이러한 생각이다. / 공동의 목표를 달성하기 위해 함께 모인다는 / '팀'을 정의하는 것은

일상생활에서 우리는 어떤 사람들의 무리라도 하나의 집단으로 보는 경향이 있다. ① 그러나 사회 심리학자들은 이 용어를 더 정확하게 사용한다. ② 특히, 그들은 서로 상호 작용하고 상호 영향력을 발휘하는 둘 이상의 사람들로 집단을 정의한다. 집단의 구성원들을 단순한 개인들의 집합으로부터 구별하는 것은 바로 공동의 목적을 위한 서로의 상호 작용 또는 상호 의존감이다. ③ 예를 들어, Kenneth Hodge가 진술한 바와 같이, 매주 같은 날에 일을 마치고 우연히 수영을 하러 가는 사람들의 무리는 엄밀히 말하면 집단을 구성하지 않는데, 이러한 수영하는 사람들은 구조적인 방식으로 상호 작용하지 않기 때문이다. ④ 대조적으로, 매일 아침 학교에 가기 전에 훈련하는 경쟁 관계의 어린 수영 선수들은 공동의 목표(경기를 위한 훈련)를 공유할 뿐만 아니라 공식적인 방식(예컨대, 미리 함께 몸 풀기)으로 상호 작용하기 때문에 집단이 맞다. ⑤ '팀'을 정의하는 것은 바로 공동의 목표를 달성하기 위해 사람들이 함께 모인다는 이러한 생각이다.

Why? 왜 정답일까?

② 앞에서 심리학자들은 집단을 더 정확하게 정의한다고 일반적으로 언급한 뒤, 주어진 문장은 '특히 심리학자들'의 정의를 구체적으로(In particular, ~) 설명하고 있다. ② 뒤의 문장은 주어진 문장에서 언급된 '구성원간의 상호 작용'이 '공동의 목적을 위한 상호 작용 또는 의존감'임을 보충 설명하고 있다. 따라서 주어진 문장이 들어가기에 가장 적절한 곳은 ②이다.

- **interact with** ~와 상호 작용하다
- **exert** ⓥ 발휘하다

- **mutual** ⓐ 상호의
- **term** ⓝ 용어
- **inter-dependence** ⓝ 상호 의존성
- **distinguish** ⓥ 구별하다
- **aggregation** ⓝ 집합
- **strictly speaking** 엄밀히 말하면
- **structure** ⓥ 구조화하다
- **competitive** ⓐ 경쟁하는, 경쟁력 있는
- **formal** ⓐ 공식적인
- **collection** ⓝ 모음, 수집
- **precisely** ⓐⓓ 정확히, 정밀하게
- **purpose** ⓝ 목적
- **mere** ⓐ 단순한
- **happen to** 우연히 ~하다
- **constitute** ⓥ 구성하다
- **squad** ⓝ 선수단, 분대
- **objective** ⓝ 목표
- **warm up** 몸을 풀다

구문 풀이

9행 For example, as Kenneth Hodge observed, a collection of
(주어)
people [who happen to go for a swim after work on the same day each
(우연히 ~하다)
week] does not, (strictly speaking), constitute a group because these
(동사구)   ( ): 삽입
swimmers do not interact with each other in a structured manner.

★★ 문제 해결 꿀~팁 ★★

▶ 많이 틀린 이유는?
③ 앞의 the members of a group이 주어진 문장의 they와 같은 집단을 가리킨다고 생각하면 함정에 빠지기 쉽다. 하지만 '집단 구성원들'보다는 '사회 심리학자들'이 집단을 규정 짓는 사람들이라고 보는 것이 타당하다.

▶ 문제 해결 방법은?
주어진 문장의 they가 문맥상 ② 앞의 social psychologists이다. 또한, 주어진 문장의 mutual influences가 ② 뒤에서 this sense of mutual interaction or inter-dependence로 이어진다.

★★★ 1등급 대비 고난도 2점 문제

09 네거티브 섬 경쟁의 개념과 예   정답률 35% | 정답 ⑤

글의 흐름으로 보아, 주어진 문장이 들어가기에 가장 적절한 곳을 고르시오.

In mature markets, / breakthroughs that lead / to a major change in competitive positions / and to the growth of the market / are rare.
성숙한 시장에서는 / 돌파구가 이끌어낼 수 있는 / 경쟁 위치의 변화와 / 시장 성장을 / 거의 없다.

① Because of this, / competition becomes a zero sum game / in which one organization can only win / at the expense of others.
이 때문에, / 경쟁은 제로섬 게임이 된다 / 한 조직이 승리를 거둘 수 있는 / 다른 조직이 희생되어야만

② However, / where the degree of competition is particularly intense / a zero sum game / can quickly become a negative sum game, / in that everyone in the market is faced with additional costs.
하지만, / 경쟁의 정도가 특히 심해지면 / 제로섬 게임은 / 급속히 네거티브 섬 게임으로 변할 수 있는데, / 그 시장에 있는 모두가 추가 비용에 직면한다는 점에서 그렇다.

③ As an example of this, / when one of the major high street banks in Britain / tried to gain a competitive advantage / by opening on Saturday mornings, / it attracted a number of new customers / who found the traditional Monday-Friday bank opening hours to be a constraint.
한 가지 예로, / 영국 중심가 은행 중 한 곳이 / 경쟁적 우위를 점하려고 했을 때, / 토요일 아침에 운영을 해서 / 이는 많은 새 고객을 유치했다. / 월요일─금요일 사이의 전통적 은행 영업시간이 제약이라고 생각하는

④ However, / faced with a loss of customers, / the competition responded / by opening on Saturdays as well.
하지만 / 고객을 잃을 위기에 처한 / 경쟁 은행은 이에 맞섰다. / 토요일에 문을 열어

✔ The net effect of this was / that, although customers benefited, / the banks lost out / as their costs increased / but the total number of customers stayed the same.
이 일의 실제 결과는, / 비록 고객들은 이득을 보긴 했어도 / 은행들은 손해를 보았다. / 비용이 증가했지만 / 총 고객 수는 그대로 유지되어서

In essence, / this proved to be a negative sum game.
본질적으로, / 이는 네거티브 섬 게임으로 판명되었다.

성숙한 시장에서는 경쟁 위치의 변화와 시장 성장을 이끌어낼 수 있는 돌파구가 거의 없다. ① 이 때문에, 경쟁은 다른 조직이 희생되어야만 한 조직이 승리를 거둘 수 있는 제로섬 게임이 된다. ② 하지만, 경쟁의 정도가 특히 심해지면 제로섬 게임은 급속히 네거티브 섬 게임으로 변할 수 있는데, 그 시장에 있는 모두가 추가 비용에 직면한다는 점에서 그렇다. ③ 한 가지 예로, 영국 중심가 은행 중 한 곳이 토요일 아침에 운영을 해서 경쟁적 우위를 점하려고 했을 때, 이는 월요일─금요일 사이의 전통적 은행 영업시간이 제약이라고 생각하는 많은 새 고객을 유치했다. ④ 하지만 고객을 잃을 위기에 처한 경쟁 은행도 토요일에 문을 열어 이에 맞섰다. ⑤ 이 일의 실제 결과는, 비록 고객들은 이득을

보긴 했어도 은행들은 비용이 증가했지만 총 고객 수는 그대로 유지되어서 손해를 보았다. 본질적으로, 이는 네거티브 섬 게임으로 판명되었다.

Why? 왜 정답일까?

이 글은 비용과 편익이 등가를 이루는 제로섬 게임이 네거티브 섬 게임, 즉 경쟁이 극심한 나머지 비용이 편익을 초과하여 모두에게 손해가 발생하는 상황으로 치닫는 과정을 설명한다. ③ 뒤부터 예시가 나오는데, 영국의 한 은행은 남들이 영업하지 않는 토요일에 문을 열어 추가적인 고객을 유치하려 하였다. 하지만 ⑤ 앞의 문장에 나오듯 경쟁 은행 쪽에서도 고객을 뺏기지 않으려고 토요일에 같이 문을 열기 시작하면서, 주어진 문장에서 말하듯이 결국 고객의 총 수는 이전과 별반 차이가 없는 채로 '주말에 문을 여는' 비용만이 추가되고 말았다. ⑤ 뒤의 문장에서는 바로 이 경우가 네거티브 섬 게임에 해당된다는 결론을 이야기한다. 따라서 주어진 문장이 들어가기에 가장 적절한 곳은 ⑤이다.

- **net effect** 실제 결과, 순효과
- **breakthrough** ⓝ 돌파구, 혁신적 발전
- **at the expense of** ~을 희생하여
- **constraint** ⓝ 제약, 제한
- **mature** ⓐ 성숙기의, 성숙한
- **zero sum** 제로섬 게임
- **negative sum** 네거티브 섬 게임
- **in essence** 본질적으로

구문 풀이

1행 The net effect of this was [that, (although customers
(주어)   (동사(단수))   (접속사(~것))   (접속사(비록 ~일지라도))
benefited), the banks lost out (as their costs increased but the total
(접속사(~하면서, ~함에 따라))
number of customers stayed the same)].

★★ 문제 해결 꿀~팁 ★★

▶ 많이 틀린 이유는?
주어진 문장의 지시대명사 'this'가 가리키는 바를 정확히 파악해야 수월하게 해결할 수 있는 문제였다. this는 하나의 단어나 짧은 구를 가리킬 수도 있지만 앞의 여러 문장에 걸쳐 설명된 내용을 포괄적으로 나타낼 수도 있다. 즉 여기서 this는 '한 은행이 토요일에 문을 열기 시작하자 다른 은행도 토요일에 같이 영업하기 시작한 것'이라는 상황을 폭넓게 나타내므로, 주어진 문장은 결국 예시를 마무리하는 부분에 삽입되어야 적절하다.

▶ 문제 해결 방법은?
주어진 문장에서 '은행'이라는 구체적인 대상을 언급하는데 ③ 앞에서는 은행에 대한 언급 없이 '네거티브 섬'이라는 일반적인 개념에 대한 설명만을 제시하므로, ①, ②, ③은 자연스럽게 정답 후보에서 제외된다. ④의 경우에도 However 앞뒤로 '한 은행만 문을 열었다 vs. 다른 은행도 따라 열었다'라는 내용이 적절히 대조되므로 사이에 논리적 공백이 있다고 보기 어렵다.

★★★ 1등급 대비 고난도 3점 문제

10 인간을 연구하는 데 있어 문화적 정보의 중요성   정답률 38% | 정답 ⑤

글의 흐름으로 보아, 주어진 문장이 들어가기에 가장 적절한 곳을 고르시오. [3점]

A meaningful level of complexity in our history / consists of culture: / information stored in nerve and brain cells / or in human records of various kinds.
우리의 역사에서 의미 있는 수준의 복잡성은 / 문화로 구성된다. / 즉 신경과 뇌세포에 저장된 정보 / 또는 다양한 종류의 인간 기록 안에

The species / that has developed this capacity the most / is, of course, humankind.
종은 / 이 능력을 가장 많이 발달시킨 / 물론 인간이다.

① In terms of total body weight, / our species currently makes up about 0.005 per cent of all planetary biomass.
총 무게 면에서 / 우리 인간은 현재 전체 지구 생물량의 약 0.005%를 차지한다.

② If all life combined were only a paint chip, / all human beings today / would jointly amount to no more than a tiny colony of bacteria / sitting on that flake.
모든 생명체를 합친 것이 벗겨진 페인트 조각에 불과하다면, / 오늘날의 모든 인간은 / 다 합쳐도 겨우 아주 작은 박테리아 군체에 해당할 것이다. / 그 조각 위에 놓여 있는

③ Yet through their combined efforts / humans have learned / to control a considerable portion of the terrestrial biomass, / today perhaps as much as between 25 and 40 per cent of it.
하지만 협력을 통해 / 인간은 ~하게 되었다. / 지구 생물량의 상당 부분을 통제하게 / 아마도 오늘날에는 그 중 25~40%나 되는

④ In other words, / thanks to its culture / this tiny colony of microorganisms / residing on a paint chip / has gained control over a considerable portion of that flake.
다시 말해서, / 자신들의 문화 덕분에 / 이 아주 작은 미생물 군체는 / 페인트 조각 위에 살고 있는 / 그 조각의 상당 부분에 대한 통제력을 얻었다.

✔️To understand how human societies operate, / it is therefore not sufficient / to only look at their DNA, / their molecular mechanisms / and the influences from the outside world.
따라서 인간 사회가 어떻게 작동하는지를 이해하려면, / 충분하지 않다. / 인간의 DNA를 보는 것만으로는 / 분자 메커니즘을 / 그리고 외부 세계로부터의 영향을

We also need to study the cultural information / that humans have been using / for shaping their own lives / as well as considerable portions of the rest of nature.
우리는 또한 문화적 정보를 연구할 필요가 있다. / 인간이 사용해 온 / 삶을 형성하기 위해 / 나머지 자연의 상당 부분뿐 아니라

우리의 역사에서 의미 있는 수준의 복잡성은 문화, 즉 신경과 뇌세포 또는 다양한 종류의 인간 기록 안에 저장된 정보로 구성된다. 이 능력을 가장 많이 발달시킨 좋은 물론 인간이다. ① 총 무게 면에서 우리 인간은 현재 전체 지구 생물량의 약 0.005%를 차지한다. ② 모든 생명체를 합친 것이 벗겨진 페인트 조각에 불과하다면, 오늘날의 모든 인간은 다 합쳐도 겨우 그 조각 위에 놓여 있는 아주 작은 박테리아 군체에 해당할 것이다. ③ 하지만 인간은 협력을 통해 지구 생물량의 상당 부분, 아마도 오늘날에는 그 중 25 ~ 40%나 되는 부분을 통제하게 되었다. ④ 다시 말해서, 자신들의 문화 덕분에 페인트 조각 위에 살고 있는 이 아주 작은 미생물 군체는 그 조각의 상당 부분에 대한 통제력을 얻었다. ⑤ 따라서 인간 사회가 어떻게 작동하는지를 이해하려면, 인간의 DNA와 분자 메커니즘, 그리고 외부 세계로부터의 영향을 보는 것만으로는 충분하지 않다. 인간이 삶뿐만 아니라 나머지 자연의 상당 부분을 형성하기 위해 사용해 온 문화적 정보 또한 우리는 연구할 필요가 있다.

Why? 왜 정답일까?

⑤ 앞까지 인간은 양적인 측면으로 보면 지구에서 매우 미미한 비중밖에 차지하지 않을지라도 특유의 '문화'로 인해 많은 부분에 대한 통제력을 얻을 수 있었다는 내용이 전개된다. 주어진 문장은 여기에 therefore로 연결되며, '그렇기 때문에' 인간 사회가 기능해온 방식을 살펴볼 때 생물학적 정보나 외부적 영향만을 검토해서는 불충분하다고 언급한다. ⑤ 뒤에서는 also와 함께 문화적 정보 '또한' 연구해야 한다는 내용을 제시하고 있다. 따라서 주어진 문장이 들어가기에 가장 적절한 곳은 ⑤이다.

- **sufficient** ⓐ 충분한
- **complexity** ⓝ 복잡성
- **amount to** (합계가) ~에 이르다
- **terrestrial** ⓐ 지구의
- **gain control over** ~에 대한 통제권을 얻다
- **molecular** ⓐ 분자의
- **jointly** ⓐd 공동으로, 합쳐서
- **considerable** ⓐ 상당한
- **biomass** ⓝ 생물량

구문 풀이

[11행] If all life combined were only a paint chip, all human beings
If + 주어 + 과거 동사 + 주어+
today would jointly amount to no more than a tiny colony of bacteria
조동사 과거형 + 동사원형: 가정법 과거」 단지 ~한
sitting on that flake.

★★ 문제 해결 꿀~팁 ★★

▶ 많이 틀린 이유는?
인류는 생물량 측면에서 보면 지구에서 아주 미미한 비중만을 차지하지만 '문화'로 인해 독보적인 위치를 차지하게 되었으므로 문화 연구가 그만큼 중요하다는 내용의 글이다. 최다 오답인 ④ 앞뒤로 논리적 공백이 있는지 살펴보면, 먼저 ④ 앞의 문장에서 인간은 양적으로 보면 박테리아 군체만큼 미미하지만 오늘날 지구의 25 ~ 40%에 달하는 부분을 통제하게 되었다고 언급한다. ④ 뒤의 문장은 여기에 In other words로 연결되며, 앞에 등장했던 비유를 이용해 ④ 앞 문장의 내용을 다시 설명한다. 즉 인간이라는 '미생물 군체'가 문화라는 요소 덕분에 25 ~ 40%나 되는 '상당 부분'에 대한 통제력을 갖게 되었다는 것이다. 이렇듯 ④ 앞뒤가 서로 같은 내용으로 잘 연결되므로 주어진 문장을 넣을 만한 논리적 공백이 ④에서 발생한다고 보기 어렵다.
▶ 문제 해결 방법은?
also가 있는 ⑤ 뒤의 문장은 우리가 인간 사회를 잘 알기 위해서는 문화적 정보 '또한' 살펴볼 필요가 있다는 내용이다. 즉 이 문장 앞에서는 문화적 정보 외에 인간 사회 연구에 도움이 되는 정보가 하나 미리 언급되어야 하는데, ⑤ 앞의 문장에 그러한 정보로 볼 수 있는 내용은 없다.

★★★ 1등급 대비 고난도 3점 문제

| 11 | 미적법 이후 수학의 발달 | 정답률 32% | 정답 ④ |

글의 흐름으로 보아, 주어진 문장이 들어가기에 가장 적절한 곳을 고르시오. [3점]

The era of unicellular life / lasted for about three and half billion years, / dominating most of the Earth's history.
단세포 생물의 시대는 / 약 35억 년간 지속되었으며 / 지구 역사의 대부분을 지배했다.

But around half a billion years ago, / during the Cambrian explosion, / a diversity of multicellular life including major animal groups / emerged in short period.
그러나 약 5억 년 전 / 캄브리아 폭발 동안 / 주요 동물군을 포함한 다양한 다세포 생물이 / 짧은 기간에 나타났다.

Similarly, / calculus was the Cambrian explosion for mathematics.
이와 비슷하게, / 미적법은 수학에 있어 캄브리아 폭발이었다.

① Once it arrived, / an amazing diversity of mathematical fields / began to evolve.
일단 그것이 도래하자 / 놀랍도록 다양한 수학 분야들이 / 진화하기 시작했다.

② Their lineage is visible in their calculus-based names, / in adjectives like *differential* and *integral* and *analytic*, / as in differential geometry, integral equations, and analytic number theory.
그것들의 계보는 미적법을 바탕으로 한 그것들의 이름에서 드러난다. / *미분의, 적분의, 해석적*과 같은 형용사에서 / 미분기하학, 적분방정식, 해석적 정수론에서처럼

③ These advanced branches of mathematics / are like the many branches and species of multicellular life.
이러한 진보된 수학 분야는 / 다세포 생물의 많은 계통들 및 종들과 같다.

✔️In this analogy, / the microbes of mathematics are the earliest topics: / numbers, shapes, and word problems.
이 비유에서, / 수학에서의 미생물들은 가장 초기의 주제들이다. / 수, 형태, 문장제

Like unicellular organisms, / they dominated the mathematical scene for most of its history.
단세포 생물처럼 / 그것들은 그 역사의 대부분 동안 수학의 장을 지배했다.

⑤ But after the Cambrian explosion of calculus / three hundred and fifty years ago, / new mathematical life forms began to flourish, / and they altered the landscape around them.
그러나 미적법의 캄브리아 폭발 후 / 350년 전 / 새로운 수학의 생명 형태들이 번성하기 시작했고 / 그것들은 그 주변의 경관을 바꾸었다.

단세포 생물의 시대는 약 35억 년간 지속되었으며 지구 역사의 대부분을 지배했다. 그러나 약 5억 년 전 캄브리아 폭발 동안 짧은 기간에 주요 동물군을 포함한 다양한 다세포 생물이 나타났다. 이와 비슷하게, 미적법은 수학에 있어 캄브리아 폭발이었다. ① 일단 그것이 도래하자 놀랍도록 다양한 수학 분야들이 진화하기 시작했다. ② 그것들의 계보는 미적법을 바탕으로 한 그것들의 이름인 미분기하학, 적분방정식, 해석적 정수론에서처럼 미분의, 적분의, 해석적과 같은 형용사에서 드러난다. ③ 이러한 진보된 수학 분야는 다세포 생물의 많은 계통들 및 종들과 같다. ④ 이 비유에서, 수학에서의 미생물들은 가장 초기의 주제들인 수, 형태, 문장제이다. 단세포 생물처럼 그것들은 그 역사의 대부분 동안 수학의 장을 지배했다. ⑤ 그러나 350년 전 미적법의 캄브리아 폭발 후 새로운 수학의 생명 형태들이 번성하기 시작했고 그 주변의 경관을 바꾸었다.

Why? 왜 정답일까?

단세포 생물의 시대가 캄브리아 폭발을 계기로 다세포 생물의 시대로 넘어갔듯이, 수학 또한 미적법의 출현 이후 다양한 분야의 발전을 맞이하게 되었다는 내용의 글이다. ④ 앞에서 미적법 이래 등장한 여러 세부 분야를 다세포 종에 비유할 수 있다고 한다. 이어서 주어진 문장은 '이러한 비유'에 따라 때 수학의 '미생물' 단계에는 수, 형태, 문장제가 있다고 언급한다. ④ 뒤의 두 문장에서는 이 세 가지 주제가 '단세포 생물처럼' 오래도록 수학을 지배했으나 미적법이라는 캄브리아 폭발 뒤로 수학의 생태계가 변화했다는 내용을 서술한다. 따라서 주어진 문장이 들어가기에 가장 적절한 곳은 ④이다.

- **analogy** ⓝ 비유, 유추
- **unicellular** ⓐ 단세포의
- **explosion** ⓝ 폭발
- **multicellular** ⓐ 다세포의
- **adjective** ⓝ 형용사
- **integral** ⓐ (수학) 적분의, 필수적인
- **flourish** ⓥ 번영하다
- **word problem** 문장제
- **dominate** ⓥ 지배하다
- **emerge** ⓥ 출현하다, 등장하다
- **visible** ⓐ 눈에 보이는
- **differential** ⓐ (수학) 미분의
- **analytic** ⓐ 분석적인
- **alter** ⓥ 바꾸다, 고치다

구문 풀이

부사(약, 대략)
[3행] The era of unicellular life lasted for about three and half
주어 자동사 전치사 기간 명사구
billion years, dominating most of the Earth's history.
분사구문(그리고 ~하다)

★★ 문제 해결 꿀~팁 ★★

▶ 많이 틀린 이유는?
③ 앞에서 'differential geometry, integral equations, and analytic number theory'와 같이 미적분학 이후 발달한 수학의 세부 분야를 열거하고, ③ 뒤

에서는 이들 분야를 These advanced branches로 언급하고 있다. 즉, ③ 앞뒤 는 적절한 지시대명사로 자연스럽게 연결된다.
▶ 문제 해결 방법은?
주어진 문장의 this analogy로 미루어 보아, 앞에 '비유'가 언급되고 뒤에 그 비유 를 해설하는 문장이 연결될 것임을 예측할 수 있다.

★★★ 1등급 대비 고난도 3점 문제

12 과학과 예술의 역할 분리　　　정답률 28% | 정답 ③

글의 흐름으로 보아, 주어진 문장이 들어가기에 가장 적절한 곳을 고르시오. [3점]

Representational theories of art / treat the work of the artist / as similar to that of the scientist.
예술 표상 이론은 / 예술가가 하는 일을 취급한다. / 과학자가 하는 일과 유사한 것으로

Both, so to speak, are involved / in describing the external world.
말하자면, 둘 다 관련이 있다. / 외부 세계를 묘사하는 것과

① But by the nineteenth century, / any comparison between the scientist and the artist / was bound to make the artist look like a poor relation / in terms of making discoveries about the world / or holding a mirror up to nature.
하지만 19세기 무렵에, / 과학자와 예술가 사이의 어떤 비교든 / 예술가를 천덕꾸러기처럼 보이게 하게 마련이었 다. / 세상에 관한 발견을 하거나 / 자연을 있는 그대로 묘사하는 것에 있어

② Here, science clearly had the edge.
여기서, 과학은 분명히 우세했다.

☑ So, there was a social pressure / for art to come up with some vocation / that both distinguished it from science / and, at the same time, made it equal in stature to science.
그래서 사회적 압력이 있었다. / 예술이 어떤 소명을 제시해야 한다 / 그것을 과학과 구별하는 / 동시에 과학과 동일한 수준으로 만드는

The notion that art specialized in the expression of the emotions / was particularly attractive in this light.
예술이 감정 표현을 전문으로 한다는 개념은 / 이런 관점에서 특히 매력적이었다.

④ It rendered unto science its own / — the exploration of the objective world — / while saving something comparably important for art to do — / to explore the inner world of feeling.
그것은 과학에 그 자체의 것을 주었고, / 즉 객관적 세계의 탐구를 / 동시에 예술이 해야 하는 마찬가지로 중요한 것을 남겨두었다. / 즉 감정이라는 내적 세계를 탐구하는 일

⑤ If science held the mirror up to nature, / art turned a mirror at the self and its experiences.
만약 과학이 자연을 있는 그대로 묘사했다면, / 예술은 거울의 방향을 자아와 그것의 경험으로 돌렸다.

예술 표상 이론은 예술가가 하는 일을 과학자가 하는 일과 유사한 것으로 취급 한다. 말하자면, 둘 다 외부 세계를 묘사하는 것과 관련이 있다. ① 하지만 19세기 무렵에, 과학자와 예술가 사이의 어떤 비교든 세상에 관한 발견을 하거 나 자연을 있는 그대로 묘사하는 것에 있어 예술가를 천덕꾸러기(과학자보다 열등한 것)처럼 보이게 하게 마련이었다. ② 여기서, 과학은 분명히 우세했다. ③ 그래서 예술이 그것(예술)을 과학과 구별하는 동시에 과학과 동일한 수준으로 만드는 어떤 소명을 제시해야 한다는 사회적 압력이 있었다. 예술이 감정 표현 을 전문으로 한다는 개념은 이런 관점에서 특히 매력적이었다. ④ 그것은 과학 에 그 자체의 것, 즉 객관적 세계의 탐구를 주었고, 동시에 예술이 해야 하는 마찬가지로 중요한 것, 즉 감정이라는 내적 세계를 탐구하는 일을 남겨두었다. ⑤ 만약 과학이 자연을 있는 그대로 묘사했다면, 예술은 거울의 방향을 자아와 그것의 경험으로 돌렸다.

Why? 왜 정답일까?

본래 예술은 과학과 마찬가지로 외부 세계를 묘사하는 데 주력하는 분야로 이해되었지만 19세기에 들어 과학과 구별되는 역할을 수행하기 시작했다는 내용을 다룬 글이다. ③ 앞 에서 과학이 현상을 있는 그대로 묘사하는 데 있어 예술보다 우위를 지녔다는 내용이 언 급된 데 이어, 주어진 문장은 '그리하여' 과학과 구별되는 예술만의 소명이 규명될 필요가 있었다는 내용을 제시한다. ③ 뒤에서는 이런 관점, 즉 예술만의 소명을 찾고자 하는 관 점에서 볼 때 예술의 감정 표현 기능이 주목받기 시작했다는 설명을 이어 간다. 따라서 주어진 문장이 들어가기에 가장 적절한 곳은 ③이다.

- come up with ～을 떠올리다
- equal ⓐ 동일한
- so to speak 말하자면
- comparison ⓝ 비교
- in terms of ～에 관하여
- have the edge 우세하다
- in this light 이러한 관점에서
- distinguish ⓥ 구별하다
- representational theory 표상 이론
- external ⓐ 외부의
- be bound to ～하게 마련이다
- hold a mirror up to ～을 그대로 보여주다
- specialize in ～을 전문으로 하다
- exploration ⓝ 탐구

구문 풀이

1행 So, there was **a social pressure** for **art** to come up with
　　　　　　　　주어　　　　　　　의미상 주어　　형용사적 용법
some vocation [that both distinguished it from science and, at the
선행사　　　주격 관·대　동사1「distinguish + A + from + B : A와 B를 구별하다」
same time, made it equal in stature to science].
동사2　=art

★★ 문제 해결 꿀~팁 ★★

▶ 많이 틀린 이유는?
과학과 예술의 기능 분화에 관해 설명하는 추상적인 글로, 주어진 문장이 But이나 However 등 역접의 연결어가 아닌 인과의 연결어인 So로 시작하고 있어 더욱 까 다롭다. 하지만 논리적 공백을 찾는 데 주력하면 어렵지 않게 답을 낼 수 있다. 최다 오답인 ④ 앞뒤는 '예술에는 자기표현 기능이 있으므로 → 과학과 구별되는 예술의 역할이 생겨나게 되었다'는 설명이 자연스럽게 이어진다. 따라서 맥락상 공백이 없어 주어진 문장이 필요하지 않다.
▶ 문제 해결 방법은?
③ 앞은 과학이 현실을 기술하는 데 있어 예술보다 우위를 지녔다는 내용이 주를 이루 고, ③ 뒤는 예술도 나름의 가치와 역할을 수행할 수 있게 되었다는 내용이 주를 이루 는 것으로 볼 때, ③에 논리적 공백이 있음을 파악할 수 있다.

DAY 18

DAY 19 　　　　문장 삽입 04

01 ④	02 ③	03 ⑤	04 ④	05 ③
06 ③	07 ③	08 ⑤	09 ②	10 ③
11 ⑤	12 ⑤			

01 시간 (부족)이 구매 결정에 미치는 영향　　정답률 62% | 정답 ④

글의 흐름으로 보아, 주어진 문장이 들어가기에 가장 적절한 곳을 고르시오.

Often time, or lack of time, / plays an important role / in the purchase of everyday products.
종종 시간 또는 시간 부족은 / 중요한 역할을 한다. / 일상 제품 구매에

Milica Milosavljevic and his coworkers / conducted an experiment / looking at the relationship / between visual salience and the decision to purchase.
Milica Milosavljevic과 그의 동료들은 / 실험을 수행했다. / 관계를 보는 / 시각적 두드러짐과 구매 결정 간의

① They showed subjects 15 different food items on fMRI, / such as those we find in a candy vending machine at the train station, / that is, bars, chips, fruity items, etc.
그들은 피실험자들에게 기능적 자기 공명 영상으로 15가지의 갖가지 음식 품목들을 보여주었다. / 우리가 기차역 사탕 과자 자판기에서 발견하는 것들인 / 즉 막대 과자, 감자칩, 과일 맛 상품 등등

② These were rated by the subjects on a scale of 1–15 / according to "favorite snack" to "don't like at all."
이것들은 피험자들에 의해 1~15점 척도로 등급이 매겨졌다. / '가장 좋아하는 간식'에서 '제일 좋아하지 않음'까지

③ They were then presented in varying brightness and time, / with subjects always having to make a choice between two products.
그리고 나서 그것들은 밝기와 시간을 달리하여 제시되었으며, / 피실험자들은 항상 두 제품 중 선택해야 했다.

☑The result was / that we don't always buy what we like best, / but when things have to happen quickly, / we tend to go for the product / that catches our eye the most.
결과는 ~이었다. / 우리가 항상 가장 좋아하는 것을 사지는 않지만, / 상황이 급할 때, / 우리는 제품을 선택하는 경향이 있다는 것 / 우리 눈에 가장 띄는

If we are also distracted / because we are talking to someone, / on the phone, / or our thoughts are elsewhere at the moment, / our actual preference for a product / falls further into the background / and visual conspicuousness comes to the fore.
또한 우리가 주의가 산만할 때 / 누군가와 이야기하고 있거나 / 통화 중이거나 / 그때 우리 생각이 딴 데 가 있어 / 어떤 제품에 대한 우리의 실제 선호는 / 더 뒷배경으로 물러나고, / 시각적으로 눈에 잘 띄는 것이 두드러진다.

⑤ Colors play an important role in this.
색깔은 여기에서 중요한 역할을 한다.

종종 시간 또는 시간 부족은 일상 제품 구매에 중요한 역할을 한다. Milica Milosavljevic과 그의 동료들은 시각적 두드러짐과 구매 결정 간의 관계를 보는 실험을 수행했다. ① 그들은 피실험자들에게 기능적 자기 공명 영상으로 우리가 기차역 사탕 과자 자판기에서 발견하는 것들인 막대 과자, 감자칩, 과일 맛 상품 등등 15가지의 갖가지 음식 품목들을 보여주었다. ② 이것들은 피험자들에 의해 '가장 좋아하는 간식'에서 '제일 좋아하지 않음'까지 1~15점 척도로 등급이 매겨졌다. ③ 그리고 나서 그것들은 밝기와 시간을 달리하여 제시되었으며, 피실험자들은 항상 두 제품 중 선택해야 했다. ④ 결과는 우리가 항상 가장 좋아하는 것을 사지는 않지만, 상황이 급할 때, 우리는 우리 눈에 가장 띄는 제품을 선택하는 경향이 있다는 것이었다. 또한 우리가 누군가와 이야기하고 있거나 통화 중이거나 그때 우리 생각이 딴 데 가 있어 주의가 산만할 때, 어떤 제품에 대한 우리의 실제 선호는 더 뒷배경으로 물러나고, 시각적으로 눈에 잘 띄는 것이 두드러진다. ⑤ 색깔은 여기에서 중요한 역할을 한다.

Why? 왜 정답일까?

④ 앞까지 실험 과정에 대한 설명이 나오고, 결과를 이야기하는 주어진 문장이 연결된 후, ④ 뒤에서 결과에 대한 보충 설명이 제시되는 흐름이 적합하다. 따라서 주어진 문장이 들어가기에 가장 적절한 곳은 ④이다.

- **catch one's eye** 시선을 끌다
- **fMRI** ⓝ 기능적 자기 공명 영상
- **fruity** ⓐ 과일 맛이 나는
- **distracted** ⓐ 정신이 산만해진
- **conspicuousness** ⓝ 눈에 잘 띔
- **salience** ⓝ 두드러짐
- **vending machine** 자판기
- **brightness** ⓝ 밝기
- **fall back into** ~로 물러나다
- **come to the fore** 전면에 나오다

13행 They were then presented in varying brightness and time, with subjects always having to make a choice between two products.
「with + 명사 + 분사 : 부대상황 분사구문(~이 …한 채로)」

02 숫자를 통한 상대적 크기 비교　　정답률 45% | 정답 ③

글의 흐름으로 보아, 주어진 문장이 들어가기에 가장 적절한 곳을 고르시오.

We sometimes solve number problems / almost without realizing it.
우리는 가끔 숫자 문제를 해결하기도 한다. / 그것을 거의 깨닫지도 못한 채

① For example, / suppose you are conducting a meeting / and you want to ensure / that everyone there has a copy of the agenda.
예를 들어, / 여러분이 회의를 진행하고 있다고 가정해 보라. / 그리고 여러분이 확실히 갖게 하고 싶어 한다고 / 그곳에 있는 모든 사람이 의제의 사본을

② You can deal with this / by labelling each copy of the handout in turn / with the initials of each of those present.
여러분은 이것을 처리할 수 있다. / 그 유인물의 각 사본에 차례대로 적음으로써 / 참석한 사람들 각각의 이름 첫 글자들을

☑As long as you do not run out of copies / before completing this process, / you will know / that you have a sufficient number to go around.
사본이 떨어지지 않는 한 / 이 과정을 완료하기 전에, / 여러분은 알 것이다. / (사람들에게) 돌아갈 충분한 수의 사본이 있다는 것을

You have then solved this problem / without resorting to arithmetic / and without explicit counting.
그렇다면 여러분은 이 문제를 해결한 것이다. / 산수에 의존하지 않고, / 그리고 명시적인 집계 없이

④ There are numbers at work for us here all the same / and they allow precise comparison of one collection with another, / even though the members that make up the collections / could have entirely different characters, / as is the case here, / where one set is a collection of people, / while the other consists of pieces of paper.
그래도 여기에는 우리에게 영향을 미치고 있는 숫자가 있고 / 그것(숫자)이 하나의 집합과 다른 집합을 정확히 비교할 수 있게 하는데, / 그 집합을 구성하는 것들이 / 완전히 다른 특징을 가질 수 있음에도 그러하다. / 여기서의 경우처럼 / 한 세트는 사람들의 집합인 / 다른 세트는 종이로 구성된 반면

⑤ What numbers allow us to do / is to compare the relative size of one set with another.
숫자가 우리로 하여금 할 수 있게 하는 것은 / 한 세트의 상대적인 크기를 다른 세트와 비교하는 것이다.

우리는 가끔 거의 깨닫지도 못한 채 숫자 문제를 해결하기도 한다. ① 예를 들어, 여러분이 회의를 진행하고 있고 그곳에 있는 모든 사람이 의제의 사본을 확실히 갖게 하고 싶어 한다고 가정해 보라. ② 여러분은 그 유인물의 각 사본에 참석한 사람들 각각의 이름 첫 글자들을 차례대로 적음으로써 이것을 처리할 수 있다. ③ 이 과정을 완료하기 전에 사본이 떨어지지 않는 한, 여러분은 사람들에게 돌아갈 충분한 수의 사본이 있다는 것을 알 것이다. 그렇다면 여러분은 산수에 의존하지 않고, 명시적인 집계 없이 이 문제를 해결한 것이다. ④ 그래도 여기에는 우리에게 영향을 미치고 있는 숫자가 있고 그것(숫자)이 하나의 집합과 다른 집합을 정확히 비교할 수 있게 하는데, 그 집합을 구성하는 것들이 이 경우처럼 한 세트는 사람들의 집합인 반면 다른 세트는 종이로 구성되어 완전히 다른 특징을 가질 수 있음에도 그러하다. ⑤ 숫자가 우리로 하여금 할 수 있게 하는 것은 한 세트의 상대적인 크기를 다른 세트와 비교하는 것이다.

Why? 왜 정답일까?

우리는 때로 명시적으로 수를 헤아리지 않아도 대략적으로 상대적인 크기를 비교하는 것으로 숫자 문제를 해결하기도 한다는 내용을 다룬 글이다. ③ 앞에서는 우리가 회의에서 유인물을 배부하기 앞서 종이에 사람들의 이름을 써보며 모든 구성원이 유인물을 받을 수 있는지를 따져보는 경우를 예로 드는데, 주어진 문장에서는 '이 과정'이 끝나기 전에 사본이 돌아나 않는다면 우리는 유인물이 충분함을 알 수 있게 된다고 말한다. then으로 이어지는 ③ 뒤의 문장에서는 이 경우 우리가 명시적 계산 없이도 숫자 문제를 해결한 것이라는 결론으로 나아간다. 따라서 주어진 문장이 들어가기에 가장 적절한 곳은 ③이다.

- **run out of** ~을 다 써버리다
- **go around** (사람들에게 몫이) 돌아가다
- **conduct a meeting** 회의를 진행하다
- **handout** ⓝ 유인물
- **resort to** ~을 이용하다
- **all the same** 그래도, 여전히
- **comparison** ⓝ 비교
- **entirely** ⓐⅆ 전적으로
- **as is the case** ~이 그렇듯이
- **consist of** ~으로 구성되다
- **sufficient** ⓐ 충분한
- **realize** ⓥ 깨닫다, 알아차리다
- **agenda** ⓝ 의제
- **initial** ⓝ 이름의 첫 글자[머리글자]
- **explicit** ⓐ 명시적인
- **precise** ⓐ 정확한, 정밀한
- **make up** ~을 구성하다
- **character** ⓝ 특징, 특성, 인격, 성격
- **collection** ⓝ (물건·사람들의) 무리, 더미

1행 As long as you do not run out of copies before completing
조건 접속사　　　　　　　　　　　　　전치사　　　동명사
this process, you will know that you have a sufficient number
주어　　동사(미래)　접속사(~것)
to go around.
형용사적 용법

---

03 불행 속에서 발견되는 더 강렬한 행복　　　정답률 46% | 정답 ⑤

글의 흐름으로 보아, 주어진 문장이 들어가기에 가장 적절한 곳을 고르시오.

We seek out feel-good experiences, / always on the lookout for the next holiday, purchase or culinary experience.
우리는 기분을 좋게 해 주는 경험을 찾아낸다. / 항상 다음 휴일, 구매, 또는 음식 체험이 있는지 살피면서

This approach to happiness is relatively recent; / it depends on our capacity / both to pad our lives with material pleasures / and to feel that we can control our suffering.
행복에 대한 이런 접근은 비교적 최근의 것인데, / 그것은 우리의 능력에 좌우된다. / 우리의 삶을 물질적으로 즐거움을 주는 것으로 채워 넣기도 하고 / 우리의 고통을 우리가 제어할 수 있다고 느끼기도 하는

① Painkillers, as we know them today, / are a relatively recent invention / and access to material comfort / is now within reach of a much larger proportion of the world's population.
오늘날 우리가 알고 있는 진통제는 / 비교적 최근의 발명품이며, / 물질적 안락에 대한 접근은 / 이제 훨씬 더 많은 전 세계 사람들의 손이 닿는 곳에 있다.

② These technological and economic advances / have had significant cultural implications, / leading us to see our negative experiences as a problem / and maximizing our positive experiences as the answer.
이런 과학 기술과 경제 발전은 / 문화적으로 상당한 영향을 미쳐서 / 우리가 우리의 부정적인 경험을 문제로 간주하게 하고 / 그 해결책으로 우리의 긍정적인 경험을 극대화하게 하였다.

③ Yet, through this / we have forgotten / that being happy in life is not just about pleasure.
하지만 이를 통해 / 우리는 잊게 되었다. / 인생에서 행복한 것이 단지 즐거움에 관련된 것만은 아니라는 것을

④ Comfort, contentment and satisfaction / have never been the elixir of happiness.
안락감, 만족감 그리고 충족감이 / 행복의 특효약이었던 적은 한 번도 없었다.

✔ Rather, happiness is often found / in those moments we are most vulnerable, alone or in pain.
오히려, 행복은 자주 발견된다. / 우리가 가장 상처받기 쉽거나 혼자이거나 고통을 겪는 그런 순간에

Happiness is there, on the edges of these experiences, / and when we get a glimpse of *that* kind of happiness / it is powerful, transcendent and compelling.
행복은 이런 경험의 가장자리에 있고, / 우리가 *그런* 종류의 행복을 언뜻 보게 될 때, / 그것은 강력하고 뛰어나며 강렬하다.

우리는 항상 다음 휴일, 구매, 또는 음식 체험이 있는지 살피면서 기분을 좋게 해 주는 경험을 찾아낸다. 행복에 대한 이런 접근은 비교적 최근의 것인데, 그것은 우리의 삶을 물질적으로 즐거움을 주는 것으로 채워 넣기도 하고 우리의 고통을 우리가 제어할 수 있다고 느끼기도 하는 우리의 능력에 좌우된다. ① 오늘날 우리가 알고 있는 진통제는 비교적 최근의 발명품이며, 물질적 안락에 대한 접근은 이제 훨씬 더 많은 전 세계 사람들의 손이 닿는 곳에 있다. ② 이런 과학 기술과 경제 발전은 문화적으로 상당한 영향을 미쳐서 우리가 우리의 부정적인 경험을 문제로 간주하게 하고 그 해결책으로 우리의 긍정적인 경험을 극대화하게 하였다. ③ 하지만 이를 통해 우리는 인생에서 행복한 것이 단지 즐거움에 관련된 것만은 아니라는 것을 잊게 되었다. ④ 안락감, 만족감 그리고 충족감이 행복의 특효약이었던 적은 한 번도 없었다. ⑤ 오히려, 행복은 우리가 가장 상처받기 쉽거나 혼자이거나 고통을 겪는 그런 순간에 자주 발견된다. 행복은 이런 경험의 가장자리에 있고, 우리가 *그런* 종류의 행복을 언뜻 보게 될 때, 그것은 강력하고 뛰어나며 강렬하다.

Why? 왜 정답일까?

우리는 부정적 경험을 줄이고 긍정적 경험을 늘려 행복을 추구하려 하지만 실은 불행 속에서의 행복이 더 강렬하며 쉽게 발견될 수도 있다는 내용을 다룬 글이다. ⑤ 앞에서 안락, 만족, 충족감 등은 행복의 특효약일 수 없다고 한 데 이어, Rather로 시작하는 문장은 '오히려' 행복이 고독과 고통 속에서 발견될 수 있음을 언급한다. ⑤ 뒤의 문장은 고독과 고통의 끝자락에서 발견되는 '그런' 행복이야말로 강력하고 뛰어나다는 결론을 내리고 있다. 따라서 주어진 문장이 들어가기에 가장 적절한 곳은 ⑤이다.

- **vulnerable** ⓐ 상처받기 쉬운, 연약한
- **seek out** ~을 찾아내다
- **culinary** ⓐ 요리의
- **in pain** 고통을 겪는
- **on the lookout for** ~을 찾아서, 살피며
- **relatively** [ad] 비교적

- **capacity** ⓝ 능력
- **suffering** ⓝ (육체적·정신적) 고통
- **invention** ⓝ 발명품
- **proportion** ⓝ 부분, 비율
- **implication** ⓝ 영향, 암시
- **elixir** ⓝ 특효약, 영약
- **transcendent** ⓐ 뛰어난, 탁월한
- **pad** ⓥ 채워 넣다, 메워 넣다
- **painkiller** ⓝ 진통제
- **within reach of** ~의 손이 닿는 곳에
- **significant** ⓐ 중요한, 유의미한
- **contentment** ⓝ 만족, 자족
- **get a glimpse of** ~을 언뜻 보다
- **compelling** ⓐ 강렬한

5행 This approach to happiness is relatively recent; / it depends
주어　　　　　　　　　　　　　　　　　　　동사
on our capacity both to pad our lives with material pleasures and
명사　　　　　　형용사적 용법1
to feel that we can control our suffering.
형용사적 용법2 └ 접속사(~것)

---

04 상업적 수은 방출 문제　　　정답률 52% | 정답 ④

글의 흐름으로 보아, 주어진 문장이 들어가기에 가장 적절한 곳을 고르시오.

An incident in Japan in the 1950s / alerted the world to the potential problems / of organic mercury in fish.
1950년대 일본에서 있었던 한 사건이 / 잠재적 문제에 대하여 전 세계에 경종을 울렸다. / 물고기에 들어 있는 유기 수은의

Factories were discharging mercury into the waters of Minamata Bay, / which also harbored a commercial fishing industry.
공장들이 미나마타 만의 수역에 수은을 방출하고 있었는데, / 이곳은 또한 상업적 어업이 이루어지는 곳이었다.

Mercury was being bioaccumulated in the fish tissue / and severe mercury poisoning occurred / in many people who consumed the fish.
물고기의 체내 조직에는 수은이 축적되고 있었으며 / 심한 수은 중독이 발생했다. / 그 물고기를 먹은 많은 사람들에게

① The disabling neurological symptoms / were subsequently called Minamata disease.
장애를 초래하는 이 신경학적 증상은 / 나중에 미나마타병으로 불렸다.

② Control over direct discharge of mercury from industrial operations / is clearly needed for prevention.
산업 활동으로 생기는 수은을 직접 방출하는 것에 대한 통제가 / 예방 위해서는 절실히 필요하다.

③ However, it is now recognized / that traces of mercury can appear in lakes / far removed from any such industrial discharge.
하지만 이제는 인식되고 있다. / 소량의 수은이 나타날 수 있다는 점이 / 그런 어떤 산업적 방출로부터 멀리 떨어진 호수에서도

✔ It is postulated / that such contamination may result from airborne transport / from remote power plants or municipal incinerators.
상정된다. / 그러한 오염은 공기 전파의 결과일 수 있다는 내용이 / 멀리 떨어진 발전소 또는 지방자치단체의 소각로로부터

Strictly controlled emission standards for such sources / are needed to minimize this problem.
그러한 오염원에 대해 엄격하게 통제된 배출 기준이 / 이 문제를 최소화하기 위해서 요구된다.

⑤ Fish advisories have been issued / for many lakes in the United States; / these recommend limits on the number of times / per month particular species of fish should be consumed.
물고기에 대한 권고안이 발표되었는데, / 미국의 많은 호수를 대상으로 / 이는 횟수에 대한 제한을 권고한다. / 한 달에 특정 종의 물고기를 먹어야 하는

1950년대 일본에서 있었던 한 사건이 물고기에 들어 있는 유기 수은의 잠재적 문제에 대하여 전 세계에 경종을 울렸다. 공장들이 미나마타 만의 수역에 수은을 방출하고 있었는데, 이곳은 또한 상업적 어업이 이루어지는 곳이었다. 물고기의 체내 조직에는 수은이 축적되고 있었으며 그 물고기를 먹은 많은 사람들에게 심한 수은 중독이 발생했다. ① 장애를 초래하는 이 신경학적 증상은 나중에 미나마타병으로 불렸다. ② 예방을 위해서는 산업 활동으로 생기는 수은을 직접 방출하는 것에 대한 통제가 절실히 필요하다. ③ 하지만 이제는 그런 어떤 산업적 방출로부터 멀리 떨어진 호수에서도 소량의 수은이 나타날 수 있다는 점이 인식되고 있다. ④ 그러한 오염은 멀리 떨어진 발전소 또는 지방자치단체의 소각로로부터 공기를 통해 전파된 결과일 수 있다는 내용이 상정된다. 이 문제를 최소화하기 위해서는 그러한 오염원에 대해 엄격하게 통제된 배출 기준이 요구된다. ⑤ 미국의 많은 호수를 대상으로 물고기에 대한 권고안이 발표되었는데, 이는 한 달에 특정 종의 물고기를 먹어야 하는 횟수에 대한 제한을 권고한다.

Why? 왜 정답일까?

공장에서 수은을 직접 방출한 행위가 초래한 악영향을 설명한 글이다. ④ 앞의 문장에서 방출지로부터 멀리 떨어진 곳 또한 수은 중독의 위기에서 안전할 수 없다고 말한 데 이어, 주어진 문장은 이런 오염이 공기를 통한 전파에 원인을 두고 있을 것이라는 추정이

DAY 19

있음을 이야기한다. ④ 뒤의 문장에서는 '이 문제'를 최소화하기 위해 오염원에 대한 엄격한 배출 기준이 있어야 할 것임을 설명한다. 따라서 주어진 문장이 들어가기에 가장 적절한 곳은 ④이다.

- contamination ⓝ 오염
- municipal ⓐ 지방자치제의, 시의
- disable ⓥ 장애를 초래하다, 불구로 만들다
- prevention ⓝ 예방
- minimize ⓥ 최소화하다
- result from ~에서 기인하다
- bioaccumulate ⓥ 생체 내에 축적되다
- subsequently ⓐd 나중에, 그 후
- emission ⓝ 방출, 배출물
- recommend ⓥ 권고하다, 추천하다

구문 풀이

1행 It is postulated [that such contamination may result from
가주어   수동태   접속사(~것)   ~에서 기인하다(뒤가 원인)
airborne transport from remote power plants or municipal incinerators].
[ ] : 진주어

---

05 예술 작품의 제작 이해 　　　정답률 39% | 정답 ③

글의 흐름으로 보아, 주어진 문장이 들어가기에 가장 적절한 곳을 고르시오. [3점]

Acknowledging the making of artworks / does not require a detailed, technical knowledge / of, say, how painters mix different kinds of paint, / or how an image editing tool works.
예술 작품의 제작을 인정하는 것은 / 자세하고 기술적인 지식이 필요하지 않다. / 예컨대 화가가 다양한 종류의 물감을 섞는 방법에 관한 / 혹은 이미지 편집 도구가 작동하는 방식 등에 관한

① All that is required is / a general sense of a significant difference / between working with paints and working with an imaging application.
필요한 것은 / 중대한 차이점에 대한 일반적인 인식뿐이다. / 물감 작업과 이미징 앱을 사용한 작업의

② This sense might involve / a basic familiarity with paints and paintbrushes / as well as a basic familiarity with how we use computers, / perhaps including how we use consumer imaging apps.
이러한 인식은 포함할 수도 있다. / 물감과 붓에 대한 기본적인 친숙함을 / 컴퓨터를 사용하는 방법에 대한 기본적인 친숙함뿐 아니라, / 아마도 소비자 이미징 앱의 사용법도 포함해서

☑ In the case of specialists such as art critics, / a deeper familiarity with materials and techniques / is often useful / in reaching an informed judgement about a work.
예술 비평가와 같은 전문가의 경우, / 재료와 기법에 대한 더 깊은 친숙함은 / 흔히 유용하다. / 작품에 대한 정통한 판단에 도달하는 데

This is because every kind of artistic material or tool comes / with its own challenges and affordances for artistic creation.
이것은 모든 종류의 예술 재료나 도구가 오기 때문이다. / 예술 창작에 있어 그것만의 도전과 행위유발성과 함께

④ Critics are often interested in the ways / artists exploit different kinds of materials and tools / for particular artistic effect.
비평가들은 흔히 방식에 관심이 있다. / 예술가들이 다양한 종류의 재료와 도구를 활용하는 / 특정한 예술적 효과를 위해

⑤ They are also interested in the success of an artist's attempt / — embodied in the artwork itself / — to push the limits of what can be achieved / with certain materials and tools.
또한 그들은 예술가의 시도 성공에 관심이 있다. / 예술 작품 그 자체로 구현된, / 달성될 수 있는 것의 한계를 뛰어넘으려는 / 특정 재료와 도구로

예술 작품의 제작을 인정하는 데는, 예컨대 화가가 다양한 종류의 물감을 섞는 방법이나 이미지 편집 도구가 작동하는 방식 등에 관한 자세하고 기술적인 지식이 필요하지 않다. ① 필요한 것은 물감 작업과 이미징 앱을 사용한 작업의 중대한 차이점에 대한 일반적인 인식뿐이다. ② 이러한 인식은 아마도 소비자 이미징 앱의 사용법도 포함해서 컴퓨터를 사용하는 방법에 대한 기본적인 친숙함뿐 아니라, 물감과 붓에 대한 기본적인 친숙함을 포함할 수도 있다. ③ 예술 비평가와 같은 전문가의 경우, 재료와 기법에 대한 더 깊은 친숙함은 작품에 대한 정통한 판단에 도달하는 데 흔히 유용하다. 이것은 모든 종류의 예술 재료나 도구가 예술 창작에 있어 그것만의(그 재료나 도구만의) 도전과 행위유발성을 동반하기 때문이다. ④ 비평가들은 흔히 예술가들이 특정한 예술적 효과를 위해 다양한 종류의 재료와 도구를 활용하는 방식에 관심이 있다. ⑤ 또한 그들은 예술 작품 그 자체로 구현된, 특정 재료와 도구로 달성할 수 있는 것의 한계를 뛰어넘으려는 예술가의 시도(가) 성공(했는지)에 관심이 있다.

Why? 왜 정답일까?

③ 앞은 재료나 소재에 대한 '기본적 친숙함'만 있어도 예술을 이해할 수 있다는 내용인데, 주어진 문장은 '예술 비평가' 같은 전문가들의 경우 재료와 소재를 '더 깊이' 이해하고 있어야 한다는 내용이어서 흐름이 반전된다. ③ 뒤는 주어진 문장을 **This**로 받아서, 왜 이들은 깊은 이해가 필요한 것인지 보충 설명한다. 따라서 주어진 문장이 들어가기에 가장 적절한 곳은 ③이다.

- familiarity ⓝ 친숙함
- acknowledge ⓥ 인정하다
- artistic ⓐ 예술적인
- embody ⓥ 구현하다
- informed ⓐ 정보에 근거한
- affordance ⓝ 행위유발성
- exploit ⓥ 활용하다

구문 풀이

5행 Acknowledging the making of artworks does not require a
　　　　　　동명사구 주어　　　　　　　　　　단수 동사
detailed, technical knowledge of, say, {how painters mix different
　　　　　　　　　　　　　　　　of의 목적어1
kinds of paint}, or {how an image editing tool works}.
　　　　　　　　of의 목적어2

---

06 인간 추론을 도울 수 있는 AI 도구들 　　정답률 40% | 정답 ③

글의 흐름으로 보아, 주어진 문장이 들어가기에 가장 적절한 곳을 고르시오. [3점]

Going beyond very simple algorithms, / some AI-based tools hold out the promise / of supporting better causal and probabilistic reasoning / in complex domains.
매우 간단한 알고리즘을 넘어선 / 몇몇 AI 기반 도구들은 가능성을 보인다. / 더 나은 인과적 추론과 확률적 추론을 지원할 / 복잡한 영역에서

① Humans have a natural ability / to build causal models of the world / — that is, to explain *why* things happen — / that AI systems still largely lack.
인간에게는 타고난 능력이 있다. / 세상에 관한 인과적 모형을 형성할 수 있는 / 다시 말해, 어떤 일이 *왜* 일어나는지를 설명하는 / AI는 대체로 아직 갖추고 있지 못한

② For example, / while a doctor can explain to a patient / why a treatment works, / referring to the changes it causes in the body, / a modern machine-learning system could only tell you / that patients who are given this treatment / tend, on average, to get better.
예를 들어, / 의사는 환자에게 설명할 수 있는 반면, / 그 치료가 왜 효과가 있는지를 / 어떤 치료가 몸에 끼치는 변화를 언급하면서 / 현대의 머신 러닝 체계는 여러분에게 말해줄 수 있을 뿐이다. / 이 치료를 받는 환자들이 / 평균적으로 더 나아지는 경향이 있다고

☑ However, / human reasoning is still notoriously prone to confusion and error / when causal questions become sufficiently complex, / such as when it comes to assessing the impact of policy interventions across society.
하지만 / 인간의 추론은 혼동하고 실수하기 쉬운 것으로 여전히 악명 높다. / 인과관계의 문제가 충분히 복잡해지면 / 정책 개입이 사회 전반에 끼치는 영향을 평가하는 경우처럼

In these cases, / supporting human reasoning with more structured AI-based tools / may be helpful.
이런 경우에는 / 더 체계화된 AI 기반 도구로 인간의 추론을 도와주는 것이 / 도움이 될 수 있다.

④ Researchers have been exploring the use of Bayesian Networks / — an AI technology / that can be used / to map out the causal relationships between events, / and to represent degrees of uncertainty around different areas — / for decision support, / such as to enable more accurate risk assessment.
연구자들은 Bayesian Networks 사용을 탐구해오고 있는데, / 이는 AI 기술이다. / 사용될 수 있는 / 사건 간의 인과관계를 정리하고 / 서로 다른 영역 주변의 불확실성 정도를 나타낼 목적으로 / 의사 결정을 도와주기 위해 / 더 정확한 위험 평가를 가능케 하는 등

⑤ These may be particularly useful / for assessing the threat of novel or rare threats, / where little historical data is available, / such as the risk of terrorist attacks and new ecological disasters.
이것들은 특히 유용할 수 있다. / 새롭거나 드문 위협들의 위험을 평가하는 데 / 이용할 수 있는 역사적 데이터가 거의 없는 / 테러 공격과 새로운 생태 재난의 위험과 같이

매우 간단한 알고리즘을 넘어선 몇몇 AI 기반 도구들은 복잡한 영역에서 더 나은 인과적 추론과 확률적 추론을 지원할 가능성을 보인다. ① 인간에게는 AI는 대체로 아직 갖추고 있지 못한, 세상에 관한 인과적 모형을 형성할 수 있는 — 다시 말해, 어떤 일이 왜 일어나는지를 설명하는 — 타고난 능력이 있다. ② 예를 들어, 의사는 환자에게 어떤 치료가 몸에 끼치는 변화를 언급하면서 그 치료가 왜 효과가 있는지를 설명할 수 있는 반면, 현대의 머신 러닝 체계는 여러분에게 이 치료를 받는 환자들이 평균적으로 더 나아지는 경향이 있다고 말해줄 수 있을 뿐이다. ③ 하지만 정책 개입이 사회 전반에 끼치는 영향을 평가하는 경우처럼, 인과관계의 문제가 충분히 복잡해지면 인간의 추론은 혼동하고 실수하기 쉬운 것으로 여전히 악명 높다. 이런 경우에는 더 체계화된 AI 기반 도구로 인간의 추론을 도와주는 것이 도움이 될 수 있다. ④ 연구자들은 더 정확한 위험 평가를 가능케 하는 등 의사 결정을 도와주기 위해 Bayesian Networks 사용을 탐구해오고 있는데, 이는 사건 간의 인과관계를 정리하고 서로 다른 영역 주변의 불확실성 정도를 나타낼 목적으로 사용될 수 있는 AI 기술이다. ⑤ 이것들은 테러 공격과 새로운 생태 재난의 위험과 같이, 이용할 수 있는 역사적 데이터가 거의 없는 새롭거나 드문 위협들의 위험을 평가하는 데 특히 유용할 수 있다.

단순 알고리즘을 넘어선 AI 기반 도구들은 인간 추론을 도와줄 수 있는 가능성이 있다는 내용으로, 첫 문장에 주제가 잘 제시된다. 특히 ①~③ 사이에서, 인간은 AI가 아직 갖추지 못한 타고난 추론 능력을 지니고 있어 사건의 인과적 연결고리를 형성하고 설명할 수 있다는 내용을 사례와 함께 말하고 있다. '하지만' 주어진 문장은 However로 흐름을 반전시키며, 인간의 이러한 추론 능력에는 한계가 있다는 점을 언급한다. ③ 뒤의 문장에서는 '이런 경우', 즉 인간의 추론 능력이 한계를 드러낼 수 있는 경우 AI 기반 도구가 개입하여 도움을 줄 수 있다는 핵심 내용을 제시한다. 따라서 주어진 문장이 들어가기에 가장 적절한 곳은 ③이다.

- **reasoning** ⓝ 추론
- **causal** ⓐ 인과관계의
- **intervention** ⓝ 개입
- **probabilistic** ⓐ 확률적인
- **patient** ⓝ 환자
- **refer to** ~을 언급하다
- **explore** ⓥ 탐구하다
- **represent** ⓥ 대표하다
- **threat** ⓝ 위협
- **notoriously** ⓐⓓ 악명 높게도
- **when it comes to** ~에 관해
- **hold out** (가능성이나 희망을) 보이다
- **largely** ⓐⓓ 주로, 대체로
- **treatment** ⓝ 치료
- **on average** 평균적으로
- **map out** 계획하다, 배치하다
- **enable** ⓥ 가능하게 하다
- **terrorist attack** 테러 공격

구문 풀이

18행 Researchers have been exploring the use of Bayesian
현재완료 진행(~해 오고 있었다)
Networks — an AI technology [that can be used to map out the
동격(= Bayesian Networks) 부사적 용법1
causal relationships between events, and to represent degrees of
부사적 용법2
uncertainty around different areas] — for decision support, such as
to enable more accurate risk assessment.

---

07 지식과 무지의 상호보완적 관계   정답률 54% | 정답 ③

글의 흐름으로 보아, 주어진 문장이 들어가기에 가장 적절한 곳을 고르시오. [3점]

Power and knowledge, as well as ignorance, / are interconnected in a productive and constitutive relationship.
무지뿐만 아니라 권력과 지식은 / 생산적이고 구성하는 관계에서 서로 연결되어 있다.

① Rulers know / that power cannot be executed without knowledge / — mortality tables, tax data, and the like / are crucial to running an effective public administration — / and conquerors have understood / that information is essential for dominating a territory.
통치자들은 알고 있고, / 권력이 지식 없이 이행될 수 없다는 것, / 즉 사망률 표, 세금 자료, 기타 등등이 / 효과적인 공공 행정을 운영하는 데 중요하다는 것을 / 정복자들은 이해해 왔다. / 정보가 영토를 지배하는 데 필수적이라는 것을

② Since the twentieth century, / Western societies have defined themselves / as knowledge societies, / where knowledge is essential for social organization and productivity.
20세기 이래로 / 서구 사회들은 정의되어 왔으며, / 지식 사회로 / 여기에서 지식은 사회 조직과 생산성에 필수적이다.

☑ At the same time, / the lack of knowledge proved to be important / for stabilizing political and social order.
동시에, / 지식의 부족은 중요한 것으로 판명되었다. / 정치적 및 사회적 질서를 안정시키는 데

For instance, / secrets were essential to creating legitimacy / in the early modern period, / when individuals believed / the world was created and ruled by divine power.
예를 들어, / 비밀은 정통성을 창조하는 데 필수적이었는데, / 초기 근대에 / 이때 개인들은 믿었다. / 세상이 신의 권능으로 창조되고 통치되었다고

④ By concealing the circumstances of their decisions, / rulers cultivated a special aura / that set them apart from ordinary people / and made them seem more like unknowable gods.
자신들의 결정 상황을 숨김으로써, / 통치자들은 특별한 분위기를 조성했다. / 자신들을 보통 사람들과 분리하고 / 알 수 없는 신처럼 더 보이게 만들었던

⑤ The complementary relationship between knowledge and ignorance / is perhaps most exposed in transitional societies / seeking to first disrupt and then stabilize social and political order.
지식과 무지 사이의 상호보완적 관계는 / 과도기 사회에서 아마도 가장 많이 드러난다. / 사회적 및 정치적 질서를 먼저 붕괴시킨 뒤 안정시키려는

무지뿐만 아니라 권력과 지식은 생산적이고 구성하는 관계에서 서로 연결되어 있다. ① 통치자들은 권력이 지식 없이 이행될 수 없다는 것, 즉 사망률 표, 세금 자료, 기타 등등이 효과적인 공공 행정을 운영하는 데 중요하다는 것을 알고 있고, 정복자들은 정보가 영토를 지배하는 데 필수적이라는 것을 이해해 왔

다. ② 20세기 이래로 서구 사회들은 지식 사회로 정의되어 왔으며, 여기에서 지식은 사회 조직과 생산성에 필수적이다. ③ 동시에, 지식의 부족은 정치적 및 사회적 질서를 안정시키는 데 중요한 것으로 판명되었다. 예를 들어 비밀은 초기 근대에 정통성을 창조하는 데 필수적이었는데, 이때 개인들은 세상이 신의 권능으로 창조되고 통치되었다고 믿었다. ④ 자신들의 결정 상황을 숨김으로써, 통치자들은 자신들을 보통 사람들과 분리하고 알 수 없는 신처럼 더 보이게 만들었던 특별한 분위기를 조성했다. ⑤ 지식과 무지 사이의 상호보완적 관계는 사회적 및 정치적 질서를 먼저 붕괴시킨 뒤 안정시키려는 과도기 사회에서 아마도 가장 많이 드러난다.

③ 앞은 지식이 권력과 지배에 필수적이라는 내용인데, ③ 뒤는 통치자들이 결정을 숨기고 사람들을 '무지'한 상태로 남겨두어 특별한 분위기를 조성했다는 내용이다. 즉 ③ 앞뒤로 지식이 중요한 상황과 비밀과 무지가 활용되는 상황이 대비되며 흐름이 끊기므로, 주어진 문장이 들어가기에 가장 적절한 곳은 ③이다.

- **lack** ⓝ 부족, 결핍
- **ignorance** ⓝ 무지
- **constitutive** ⓐ 구성하는
- **execute** ⓥ 실행하다
- **crucial** ⓐ 중요한
- **conqueror** ⓝ 정복자
- **social organization** 사회 조직
- **legitimacy** ⓝ 정통성, 타당성
- **circumstance** ⓝ 상황
- **set apart** 분리하다
- **unknowable** ⓐ 알 수 없는
- **transitional** ⓐ 과도기적인
- **social order** 사회 질서
- **interconnected** ⓐ 상호 연결된
- **ruler** ⓝ 통치자, 지배자
- **mortality** ⓝ 사망률
- **administration** ⓝ 행정
- **territory** ⓝ 영토
- **for instance** 예를 들어
- **divine** ⓐ 신성한
- **decision** ⓝ 결정, 판단
- **ordinary** ⓐ 보통의
- **complementary** ⓐ 상호 보완적인

구문 풀이

16행 By concealing the circumstances of their decisions, rulers
~함으로써
cultivated a special aura [that set them apart from ordinary people
선행사 주격 관·대 └ 동사1
and made them seem more like unknowable gods].
동사2 목적어 목적격 보어

★★★ 1등급 대비 고난도 2점 문제

08 로봇 도입에 대한 노동자의 두려움을 줄이는 방법   정답률 24% | 정답 ⑤

글의 흐름으로 보아, 주어진 문장이 들어가기에 가장 적절한 곳을 고르시오.

Introduction of robots into factories, / while employment of human workers is being reduced, / creates worry and fear.
공장에 로봇을 도입하는 것은 / 인간 노동자의 고용이 줄어들며 / 걱정과 두려움을 불러일으킨다.

① It is the responsibility of management / to prevent or, at least, to ease these fears.
경영진의 책임이다. / 이러한 두려움을 예방하거나 최소한 완화하는 것은

② For example, / robots could be introduced only in new plants / rather than replacing humans in existing assembly lines.
예를 들어, / 로봇은 새로운 공장에만 도입될 수 있다. / 기존 조립 라인에서 인간을 대체하는 대신

③ Workers should be included / in the planning for new factories / or the introduction of robots into existing plants, / so they can participate in the process.
노동자는 포함되어야 하는데, / 새로운 공장을 계획하거나 기존의 공장에 로봇을 도입하는 데 / 그렇게 하여 그들은 그 과정에 참여할 수 있다.

④ It may be that robots are needed / to reduce manufacturing costs / so that the company remains competitive, / but planning for such cost reductions / should be done jointly by labor and management.
로봇이 필요할 수도 있지만, / 제조원가를 낮추기 위해 / 회사가 경쟁력을 유지하도록 / 그러한 원가절감을 위한 계획은 / 노사가 함께해야 한다.

☑ Retraining current employees / for new positions within the company / will also greatly reduce their fear of being laid off.
현재 직원을 재교육하는 것은 / 회사 내 새로운 직책을 위해 / 또한 해고에 대한 그들의 두려움을 크게 줄일 것이다.

Since robots are particularly good / at highly repetitive simple motions, / the replaced human workers should be moved to positions / where judgment and decisions beyond the abilities of robots are required.
로봇은 특히 능하기 때문에 / 매우 반복적인 단순 동작에 / 교체된 인간 노동자는 위치로 옮겨져야 한다. / 로봇의 능력을 넘어선 판단과 결정이 필요한

공장에 로봇을 도입하는 것은 인간 노동자의 고용이 줄어들며 걱정과 두려움을 불러일으킨다. ① 이러한 두려움을 예방하거나 최소한 완화하는 것은 경영

진의 책임이다. ② 예를 들어 로봇은 기존 조립 라인에서 인간을 대체하는 대신 새로운 공장에만 도입될 수 있다. ③ 노동자는 새로운 공장을 계획하거나 기존의 공장에 로봇을 도입하는 데 포함되어야 하는데, 그렇게 하여 그들은 그 과정에 참여할 수 있다. ④ 회사가 경쟁력을 유지하도록 제조원가를 낮추기 위해 로봇이 필요할 수도 있지만, 그러한 원가절감을 위한 계획은 노사가 함께해야 한다. ⑤ 또한 회사 내 새로운 직책을 위해 현재 직원을 재교육하면 해고에 대한 두려움도 크게 줄어들 것이다. 로봇은 특히 매우 반복적인 단순 동작을 잘하기 때문에 교체된 인간 노동자는 로봇의 능력을 넘어선 판단과 결정이 필요한 위치로 옮겨져야 한다.

Why? 왜 정답일까?

공장에 로봇을 도입할 때 노동자가 불안을 덜 느끼도록 경영진이 신경 써야 한다는 내용의 글이다. For example로 시작하는 문장에서 불안을 줄일 방법의 예로 로봇을 새로운 공장에만 우선 도입해볼 수 있다고 언급한 후, 도입을 결정할 때 노사가 함께해야 한다는 내용이 ⑤ 앞까지 제시된다. 이어서 also를 포함한 주어진 문장은 기존 직원을 재교육하여 새로운 직책의 기회를 열어주면 불안을 줄일 수 있을 것이라는 또 다른 해결책을 언급한다. ⑤ 뒤에서는 로봇이 단순 노동을 대신해주면 기존에 있던 직원에게 다른 업무가 주어져야 한다는 설명으로 주어진 문장의 내용을 뒷받침한다. 따라서 주어진 문장이 들어가기에 가장 적절한 곳은 ⑤이다.

- **be laid off** 해고되다, 실직되다
- **ease** ⓥ (고통·괴로움 등을) 완화시키다
- **assembly** ⓝ 조립
- **competitive** ⓐ 경쟁력 있는
- **repetitive** ⓐ 반복적인
- **management** ⓝ (사업체·조직의) 경영
- **replace** ⓥ 대체하다
- **manufacturing** ⓝ 제조
- **jointly** ⓐⓓ 합동으로

구문 풀이

4행 Introduction of robots into factories, (while employment of
　　　 주어　　　　　　　　　　　　　　　　( )：삽입
human workers is being reduced), creates worry and fear.
　　　　　현재진행 수동태(~되고 있다) 동사(단수)

★★ 문제 해결 꿀~팁 ★★

▶ 많이 틀린 이유는?
④ 앞까지 비용에 대한 언급이 없다가 갑자기 ④ 뒤에서 '비용(costs)'이 등장하므로, 글을 주의 깊게 읽지 않으면 ④에서 흐름이 끊긴다고 오해하기 쉽다. 하지만 비용은 부차적인 소재이고, ④ 앞뒤로 '계획에 노동자 참여가 필요하다(Workers should be included in the planning)', '계획에 노사가 함께해야 한다(planning ~ should be done jointly by labor and management)'라는 표현이 반복된다는 점에 주목해야 한다. 같은 이야기를 하는 두 문장 사이에 논리적 공백은 발생하지 않는다.

▶ 문제 해결 방법은?
주어진 문장에서 also와 함께 '직원의 재교육과 재배치'를 언급하므로, 이 문장 앞에서는 재교육과 재배치를 언급하지 않아야 하고, 뒤에서는 반드시 재교육과 재배치에 관한 내용을 다뤄야 한다. 이 점을 염두에 두고 독해해보면, 정답인 ⑤ 앞까지는 내용 흐름을 보면 로봇 도입을 '계획'하는 내용, 이 과정에서 기업의 경쟁력이나 비용을 생각하는 내용 등이 주를 이룬다. 하지만 ⑤ 뒤에서는 갑자기 노동자를 옮기는(moved to positions), 즉 재배치하는 상황을 이야기하고 있다. 즉 ⑤를 기점으로 글의 세부적인 키워드가 달라진다는 점을 파악할 수 있다.

★★★ 1등급 대비 고난도 2펨 문제

09 인간와 동물의 관습적 구별　　　　　정답률 41% | 정답 ②

글의 흐름으로 보아, 주어진 문장이 들어가기에 가장 적절한 곳을 고르시오.

Language, and the word "animal," / deceives us.
언어, 그중에서도 '동물'이라는 단어는 / 우리를 속인다.

The word "animal" categorizes all non-human animals / and distances
humans from other animals.
'동물'이라는 단어는 인간이 아닌 모든 동물을 분류하고 / 인간을 다른 동물로부터 떼어 놓는다.

① Seeing all other animals as one group / in contrast to humans / reinforces
anthropocentrism, / which contributes to the legitimization of practices / in
which other animals are used for human benefit.
모든 다른 동물을 한 집단으로 보는 것은 / 인간과 대조되는 / 인간 중심주의를 강화하는데, / 이는 관행의 정당화에 기여한다. / 다른 동물이 인간의 이득을 위해 이용되는

☑Jacques Derrida argues / that instead of one line / between Man on the
one side and Animal on the other, / there is a multiple and heterogeneous

border; / beyond the edge of the "so-called human," / we find a
heterogeneous plurality of the living.
Jacques Derrida는 주장한다. / 선이 하나 있는 대신 / 한쪽에 있는 '인간'과 그 상대편에 있는 '동물' 사이에 / 복합적이고 이질적인 경계가 있다고 / '소위 인간'이라는 가장자리 너머에서 / 우리는 살아 있는 것들의 이질적인 복수성을 발견한다.

To account for this multitude, / using the word "animot" has been
proposed.
이 다양성을 설명하기 위해, / 'animot'이라는 단어를 사용하는 것이 제안되었다.

③ In speech it refers to the plural, the multiplicity of animals, / which is
necessary / because there is no one "animal."
언어에서 이것은 복수, 즉 동물의 다양성을 가리키는데, / 이는 필요하다. / 하나의 '동물'만 있지는 않기 때문에

④ The "mot" in "animot" / refers to the act of naming / and the risks
involved in drawing a distinction between human and animal / by the
human.
'animot'의 'mot'은 / 명명하는 행위를 나타낸다. / 그리고 인간과 동물 사이를 구분하는 행위에 수반되는 위험을 / 인간에 의해

⑤ It reminds us of the fact / that it is a word for animals, / not a reference to
an existing group of animals.
이것은 우리에게 사실을 상기시킨다. / 이 단어가 동물들을 위한 단어이지 / 기존의 동물 집단을 지칭하는 것이 아니라는

언어, 그중에서도 '동물'이라는 단어는 우리를 속인다. '동물'이라는 단어는 인간이 아닌 모든 동물을 분류하고 인간을 다른 동물로부터 떼어 놓는다. ① 모든 다른 동물을 인간과 대조되는 한 집단으로 보는 것은 인간 중심주의를 강화하는데, 이는 다른 동물이 인간의 이득을 위해 이용되는 관행의 정당화에 기여한다. ② Jacques Derrida는 한쪽에 있는 '인간'과 그 상대편에 있는 '동물' 사이에 선이 하나 있는 대신 복합적이고 이질적인 경계가 있다고 주장한다. '소위 인간'이라는 가장자리 너머에서 우리는 살아 있는 것들의 이질적인 복수성을 발견한다. 이 다양성을 설명하기 위해, 'animot'이라는 단어의 사용이 제안되었다. ③ 언어에서 이것은 복수, 즉 동물의 다양성을 가리키는데, 이는 하나의 '동물'만 있지는 않기 때문에 필요하다. ④ 'animot'의 'mot'은 명명하는 행위와 인간이 인간과 동물 사이를 구분하는 행위에 수반되는 위험을 나타낸다. ⑤ 이것은 우리에게 이 단어가 동물들을 위한 단어이지 (사람을 제외한) 기존의 동물 집단을 지칭하는 것이 아니라는 사실을 상기시킨다.

Why? 왜 정답일까?

② 앞은 '동물'이라는 단어가 인간 중심주의를 강화하는 단어임을 지적하는데, ② 뒤에서는 갑자기 '다양성'을 언급하므로 글의 흐름이 어색하게 끊긴다. 이때 주어진 문장을 보면, 인간과 동물은 명확히 한 가지 선으로 구별되지 않고, 복잡하고 이질적인 경계에 의해 구별된다는 내용이다. 이 복잡한 경계와 이질적 복수성을 '다양성'으로 볼 수 있다는 점에서, 주어진 문장이 들어가기에 가장 적절한 곳은 ②이다.

- **heterogeneous** ⓐ 여러 다른 종류로 이뤄진, 이질적인, 다차원적인
- **so-called** ⓐ 소위 말하는
- **deceive** ⓥ 속이다
- **reinforce** ⓥ 강화하다
- **legitimization** ⓝ 정당화
- **multiplicity** ⓝ 다수, 다양성
- **plurality** ⓝ 복수성
- **distance A from B** A와 B를 떼어놓다
- **anthropocentrism** ⓝ 인간 중심주의
- **account for** ~을 설명하다
- **draw a distinction** 구별하다

구문 풀이

12행 To account for this multitude, using the word "animot"
　　　　　목적(~하려면)　　　　　　　　주어(동명사구)
has been proposed.
현재완료 수동태(has : 단수)

★★ 문제 해결 꿀~팁 ★★

▶ 많이 틀린 이유는?
①, ④, ⑤가 비교적 명백한 오답이어서 ③이 혼동을 유발할 수 있다. 하지만 ③ 앞뒤가 모두 '다양성'에 관해 언급하고, ③ 앞의 "animot"이 ③ 뒤에서 그대로 it으로 이어지는 것으로 보아 주어진 문장을 넣을 만한 논리적 공백이 발생하지 않는다.

▶ 문제 해결 방법은?
② 앞뒤는 '동물이라는 단어에 한계가 있다 → 그렇기에 새로운 단어가 필요하다'는 자연스러운 흐름처럼 보인다. 하지만, this multitude를 잘 봐야 한다. ② 앞에는 '이 다양성'이라는 말로 가리킬 만한 내용이 나오지 않는다.

★★★ 1등급 대비 고난도 3펨 문제

10 집단적 탐지 역학　　　　　정답률 38% | 정답 ③

글의 흐름으로 보아, 주어진 문장이 들어가기에 가장 적절한 곳을 고르시오. [3점]

The dynamics of collective detection have an interesting feature.
집단적 탐지의 역학은 흥미로운 특징이 있다.

Which cue(s) do individuals use as evidence of predator attack?
개체들은 어떤 단서를 포식자 공격의 증거로 사용하는가?

In some cases, / when an individual detects a predator, / its best response is to seek shelter.
어떤 경우, / 개체가 포식자를 탐지할 때 최선의 반응은 피신처를 찾는 것이다.

① Departure from the group / may signal danger to nonvigilant animals / and cause what appears to be a coordinated flushing of prey from the area.
무리로부터의 이탈은 / 경계하지 않는 동물들에게 위험 신호를 보내서 / 먹잇감 동물이 그 구역에서 조직화되어 날아오르는 것처럼 보이는 행위를 일으킬 수도 있다.

② Studies on dark-eyed juncos (a type of bird) / support the view / that nonvigilant animals attend to departures of individual group mates / but that the departure of multiple individuals / causes a greater escape response in the nonvigilant individuals.
(새의 한 종류인) 검은 눈 검은방울새에 관한 연구는 / 견해를 뒷받침해준다. / 경계하지 않는 동물들이 무리 친구들의 개별적 이탈에 주목한다는 / 하지만 여러 개체의 이탈이 / 경계하지 않는 동물에게 더 큰 도망 반응을 일으킬 수 있다는

☑ This makes sense / from the perspective of information reliability.
이것은 이치에 맞는다. / 정보 신뢰성의 관점에서

If one group member departs, / it might have done so for a number of reasons / that have little to do with predation threat.
무리 구성원 하나가 이탈하는 경우, / 그것은 여러 이유로 그렇게 했을 수 있다. / 포식 위험과 관계가 거의 없는

④ If nonvigilant animals escaped / each time a single member left the group, / they would frequently respond / when there was no predator (a false alarm).
경계하지 않는 동물들이 도망한다면, / 단 하나의 구성원이 무리를 떠날 때마다 / 이들은 자주 반응할 것이다. / 포식자가 전혀 없는 (가짜 경보인) 때에도

⑤ On the other hand, / when several individuals depart the group at the same time, / a true threat is much more likely to be present.
반면에 / 여러 개체가 동시에 무리를 이탈할 때, / 진짜 위험이 존재할 가능성이 훨씬 더 크다.

집단적 탐지의 역학은 흥미로운 특징이 있다. 개체들은 어떤 단서를 포식자 공격의 증거로 사용하는가? 어떤 경우, 개체가 포식자를 탐지할 때 최선의 반응은 피신처를 찾는 것이다. ① 무리로부터의 이탈은 경계하지 않는 동물들에게 위험 신호를 보내서 먹잇감 동물이 그 구역에서 조직화되어 날아오르는 것처럼 보이는 행위를 일으킬 수도 있다. ② (새의 한 종류인) 검은 눈 검은방울새에 관한 연구는 경계하지 않는 동물들이 무리 친구들의 개별적 이탈에 주목하기는 하지만, 여러 개체의 이탈은 경계하지 않는 동물에게 더 큰 도망 반응을 일으킬 수 있다는 견해를 뒷받침해준다. ③ 이것은 정보 신뢰성의 관점에서 이치에 맞는다. 무리 구성원 하나가 이탈하는 경우, 그것은 포식 위험과 관계가 거의 없는 여러 이유로 그렇게 했을 수 있다. ④ 경계하지 않는 동물들이 단 하나의 구성원이 무리를 떠날 때마다 도망한다면, 이들은 포식자가 전혀 없는 (가짜 경보인) 때에도 자주 반응할 것이다. ⑤ 반면에 여러 개체가 동시에 무리를 이탈할 때, 진짜 위험이 존재할 가능성이 훨씬 더 크다.

Why? 왜 정답일까?

③ 앞에서 새에 관한 연구를 근거로 들어, 개체가 개별적으로 도망갈 때보다 여럿이 도망갈 때 더 큰 도망 반응을 일으킬 수 있음을 언급하고 있다. 주어진 문장은 이 내용을 This로 받으며, 정보 신뢰성의 관점에서 봤을 때 '이러한 사실'이 이치에 맞는다는 일반론을 제시한다. 이어서 ③ 뒤부터는 하나의 개체가 도망갔을 때와 여러 개체가 도망갔을 때를 나누어, 후자일 때 실제로 위험이 있을 가능성이 더 크기에 도망 신호가 더 신뢰할 만하다는 점을 설명한다. 따라서 주어진 문장이 들어가기에 가장 적절한 곳은 ③이다.

- **make sense** 이치에 맞다, 타당하다
- **dynamics** ⓝ 역학
- **detection** ⓝ 탐지, 간파
- **predator** ⓝ 포식자
- **departure** ⓝ 이탈, 떠남, 출발
- **signal** ⓥ 알리다, 신호를 보내다
- **flushing** ⓝ 날아오름
- **attend to** ~에 주의를 기울이다
- **have little to do with** ~과 관계가 거의 없다
- **predation** ⓝ (동물의) 포식
- **frequently** ⓐⓓ 자주, 빈번히

- **reliability** ⓝ 신뢰성
- **collective** ⓐ 집단적인, 집단의
- **feature** ⓝ 특징
- **seek shelter** 피난하다
- **junco** ⓝ 검은방울새(의 일종)
- **vigilant** ⓐ 경계하는
- **prey** ⓝ 먹이
- **depart** ⓥ 떠나다
- **threat** ⓝ 위험

구문 풀이

> **10행** Studies on dark-eyed juncos (a type of bird) support the view {that nonvigilant animals attend to departures of individual group mates} but {that the departure of multiple individuals causes a greater escape response in the nonvigilant individuals}.
> { }: 동격 명사절(the view 보충 설명)

★★★ 1등급 대비 고난도 3점 문제

11 과거보다 더 세분화된 식품 소비자 집단   정답률 26% | 정답 ⑤

글의 흐름으로 보아, 주어진 문장이 들어가기에 가장 적절한 곳을 고르시오. [3점]

The growing complexity of the social dynamics / determining food choices / makes the job of marketers and advertisers / increasingly more difficult.
사회적 역학의 증가하는 복잡성은 / 식품 선택을 결정하는 / 마케팅 담당자와 광고주의 업무를 만든다. / 점점 더 어렵게

① In the past, / mass production allowed for accessibility and affordability of products, / as well as their wide distribution, / and was accepted as a sign of progress.
과거에 / 대량 생산은 제품의 입수 가능성과 (가격의) 적정성을 허용했으며, / 제품의 광범위한 유통뿐 아니라 / 발전의 신호로 받아들여졌다.

② Nowadays it is increasingly replaced / by the fragmentation of consumers / among smaller and smaller segments / that are supposed to reflect personal preferences.
요즘 그것은 점점 더 대체되고 있다. / 소비자 단편화에 의해 / 점점 더 작은 규모의 부문 사이에서 / 개인의 선호를 반영해야 하는

③ Everybody feels different and special / and expects products serving his or her inclinations.
모든 사람은 각기 다르고 특별하다고 느끼고, / 자신의 기호를 만족시키는 제품을 기대한다.

④ In reality, / these supposedly individual preferences / end up overlapping / with emerging, temporary, always changing, almost tribal formations / solidifying around cultural sensibilities, / social identifications, / political sensibilities, / and dietary and health concerns.
현실에서, / 개인적 선호라고 생각되는 이런 것들은 / 겹쳐지게 된다. / 최근에 생겨나고 일시적이며 항상 바뀌고 거의 부족적인 형성물과 / 결국 문화적 감성을 중심으로 확고해지는 / 사회 정체성, / 정치적 감성, / 그리고 식생활과 건강에 관한 관심

☑ Personal stories connect with larger narratives / to generate new identities.
개인의 이야기는 더 큰 이야기와 연결된다. / 새로운 정체성을 생성하며

These consumer communities go beyond national boundaries, / feeding on global and widely shared repositories / of ideas, images, and practices.
이들 소비자 집단은 국경을 넘어 / 세계적으로 널리 공유되는 저장소로 인해 더 강화된다. / 개념, 이미지, 관습의

식품 선택을 결정하는 사회적 역학이 점점 복잡해지면서 마케팅 담당자와 광고주의 업무가 점점 더 어려워지고 있다. ① 과거에 대량 생산은 제품을 광범위하게 유통하게 할 뿐만 아니라 제품을 입수하고 구매 비용을 감당할 수 있게 했으며, 발전의 신호로 받아들여졌다. ② 요즘 그것은 개인의 선호를 반영해야 하는 점점 더 작은 규모의 부문 사이에서 소비자 단편화에 의해 점점 더 대체되고 있다. ③ 모든 사람은 각기 다르고 특별하다고 느끼고, 자신의 기호를 만족시키는 제품을 기대한다. ④ 현실에서, 개인적 선호라고 생각되는 이런 것들은 결국 문화적 감성, 사회 정체성, 정치적 감성, 식생활과 건강에 관한 관심을 중심으로 확고해지는, 최근에 생겨나고 일시적이며 항상 바뀌고 거의 부족적인 형성물과 겹쳐지게 된다. ⑤ 개인의 이야기는 새로운 정체성을 생성하며 더 큰 이야기와 연결된다. 이들 소비자 집단은 국경을 넘어 세계적으로 널리 공유되는 개념, 이미지, 관습의 저장소로 인해 더 강화된다.

Why? 왜 정답일까?

대량 생산이 주로 이루어지던 과거와는 달리 오늘날은 소비자의 개성이 중시되면서 고객층이 단편화되고 있고, 이에 따라 마케팅도 복잡해지고 있다는 내용의 글이다. ②와 ④ 사이에서 소비자의 단편화에 관해 설명한 데 이어, ⑤ 앞의 문장은 사실 개인의 선호처럼 보이는 것들이 사회문화적 특성과 연관되어 확고해지는 '부족적' 형성물과 겹쳐진다는 점을 언급한다. 여기에 이어 주어진 문장은 결국 개인의 이야기가 개인 너머의 '더 큰' 이야기와 연결되는 것이라고 설명한다. ⑤ 뒤의 문장 또한 소비자 집단이 국경을 초월하여 그 특성을 강화시킬 수 있다는 내용으로 마무리된다. 따라서 주어진 문장이 들어가기에 가장 적절한 곳은 ⑤이다.

- **generate** ⓥ 만들어내다, 생성하다
- **mass production** 대량 생산
- **complexity** ⓝ 복잡성
- **accessibility** ⓝ 입수할 수 있음

DAY 19

- **affordability** ⓝ 적당한 가격으로 구입할 수 있는 것
- **distribution** ⓝ 유통, 분배
- **inclination** ⓝ 성향, 경향
- **overlap with** ~와 겹치다
- **solidify** ⓥ 강화하다
- **identification** ⓝ 정체성, 신원
- **segment** ⓝ 부문
- **supposedly** ⓐⓓ 아마도, 추정컨대
- **tribal** ⓐ 부족적인
- **sensibility** ⓝ 감성
- **feed on** ~로 인해 더 강해지다

13행 In reality, these supposedly individual preferences
　　　　　　　　　　　　　　　　　　　　　주어
end up overlapping with emerging, temporary, always changing,
「end up+동명사 : 결국 ~하게 되다」
almost tribal formations (solidifying around cultural sensibilities,
　　　　　　　　　　　　　　　　　　현재분사
social identifications, political sensibilities, and dietary and health
concerns).

★★ 문제 해결 꿀~팁 ★★

▶ 많이 틀린 이유는?
식품 소비자 집단의 단편화를 설명한 글이다. 오늘날 식품 소비자들은 '소비자'라는 하나의 큰 집단 안에 획일적으로 포괄되기보다 각자 뚜렷한 개성을 지니고 있으며, 이 개성에 따라 작은 집단으로 나뉘게 된다는 것이다. 최다 오답인 ④ 앞뒤를 살펴보면, 먼저 ④ 앞은 오늘날 개인 소비자들은 각자 자신을 특별하게 여겨서 자신만의 성향을 반영한 제품을 기대한다는 내용이다. 한편 ④ 뒤는 이렇듯 개인적인 것처럼 보이는 선호 사항이 실제로는(In reality) 조금씩 서로 겹친다는 내용이다. 즉 In reality 앞뒤로 흐름이 반전되며 개인의 선호가 '특별하다 vs. 겹친다'라는 내용이 알맞게 대비되므로, ④ 자리에는 주어진 문장이 들어갈 만한 논리적 공백이 없다.

▶ 문제 해결 방법은?
⑤ 앞에서 개인적이고 특별해 보이는 선호가 서로 겹치면서 문화적으로 일종의 '부족(tribal)'처럼 연결될 수 있다고 했다. 주어진 문장이 이 내용을 간략히 정리하여 결국 개인의 이야기가 더 큰 '새로운 정체성(new identities)'으로 연결되는 것이라고 했다. 그리고 ⑤ 뒤의 문장은 주어진 문장의 '새로운 정체성'을 더 명확한 말로 '소비자 집단(These consumer communities)'이라고 묘사하였다. 즉 ⑤ 앞, 주어진 문장, ⑤ 뒤 순서로 단편화된 소비자 집단을 가리키는 말이 단계적으로 구체화된다.

★★★ 1등급 대비 고난도 3점 문제

12 작곡가의 재빠른 작업 속도	정답률 36% | 정답 ⑤

글의 흐름으로 보아, 주어진 문장이 들어가기에 가장 적절한 곳을 고르시오. [3점]

There are many instances of rapid work / on the part of the great composers; / and their facility and quickness of composition / causes great wonder and admiration.
재빨리 작업한 예들은 많이 있는데 / 위대한 작곡가들이 / 이들이 작곡을 하는 솜씨와 신속함은 / 커다란 경이로움과 감탄을 불러일으킨다.

① But our admiration is often misdirected.
그러나 우리의 감탄은 흔히 그 방향이 잘못되어 있다.

② When we hear of some of the speedy writing of great works / by Mozart or Mendelssohn, / we might think / that this speed was of the composing power as well as of pen, / but, in fact, such was seldom the case.
우리가 위대한 작품들을 빠르게 써낸 것에 관한 이야기를 얼마간 들을 때 / 모차르트나 멘델스존이 / 우리는 생각할 수 있지만, / 이 속도가 펜을 움직이는 속도뿐 아니라 작곡을 하는 능력의 속도라고 / 실제로 이는 거의 사실이 아니었다.

③ These great musicians generally did their composition mentally / without reference to pen or piano, / and simply postponed the unpleasant manual labor / of committing their music to paper / until it became absolutely necessary.
이 위대한 음악가들은 마음속으로 작곡을 하였으며, / 보통 펜이나 피아노와는 상관없이 / 즐겁지 않은 육체노동을 그저 미루어 두었다. / 음악을 종이에 옮기는, / 그것이 절대적으로 필요하게 될 때까지

④ Then they got credit for incredible rapidity of composition.
그런 다음 그들은 놀라운 작곡 속도에 대해 칭찬을 받게 되었다.

✔ But it is no light matter / to quickly and correctly pen a long and complicated composition.
그러나 결코 쉬운 문제가 아니다. / 길고 복잡한 작품을 빠르고 정확하게 써내는 것은

One has only to copy a piece of music / or to try to put into notes some piece of music previously memorized, / to realize this.
우리는 그저 한 곡의 음악을 그대로 옮겨 써보거나 / 전에 기억해 둔 어떤 음악을 음표로 옮기려고 해 보면 된다. / 이를 깨닫기 위해서는

위대한 작곡가들이 재빨리 작업한 예들은 많이 있는데 이들이 작곡을 하는 솜씨와 신속함은 커다란 경이로움과 감탄을 불러일으킨다. ① 그러나 우리의 감

탄은 흔히 그 방향이 잘못되어 있다. ② 모차르트나 멘델스존이 위대한 작품들을 빠르게 써낸 것에 관한 이야기를 얼마간 들을 때 우리는 이 속도가 펜을 움직이는 속도뿐 아니라 작곡을 하는 능력의 속도라고 생각할 수 있지만, 실제로 이는 거의 사실이 아니었다. ③ 이 위대한 음악가들은 보통 펜이나 피아노와는 상관없이 마음속으로 작곡을 하였으며, 절대적으로 필요하게 될 때까지 음악을 종이에 옮기는, 즐겁지 않은 육체노동을 그저 미루어 두었다. ④ 그런 다음 그들은 놀라운 작곡 속도에 대해 칭찬을 받게 되었다. ⑤ 그러나 길고 복잡한 작품을 빠르고 정확하게 써내는 것은 결코 쉬운 문제가 아니다. 이를 깨닫기 위해서는 그저 한 곡의 음악을 그대로 옮겨 써보거나 전에 기억해 둔 어떤 음악을 음표로 옮기려고 해 보면 된다.

Why? 왜 정답일까?

⑤ 앞에서 위대한 작곡가들은 악보에 쓰면서 작곡을 한 것이 아니라 머릿속으로 다 작곡을 해놓고 나중에 옮기는 방식으로 작업을 했고, 이로 인해 엄청난 작곡 속도를 지닌 것으로 칭찬을 받게 되었음을 이야기하는데, 주어진 문장은 But으로 주의를 환기하며 길고 복잡한 작품을 그저 펜으로 빠르게 정확하게 써내는 것도 쉽지는 않다는 것을 언급한다. ⑤ 뒤에서는 '이 사실'을 깨달으려면 음악을 외워서 써 보거나 이미 알고 있는 음악을 음표로 옮겨보면 된다는 것을 이야기한다. 따라서 주어진 문장이 들어가기에 가장 적절한 곳은 ⑤이다.

- **composition** ⓝ 작곡
- **complicated** ⓐ 복잡한
- **facility** ⓝ (타고난) 재능, 솜씨
- **without reference to** ~와 관계없이
- **commit to paper** ~에 적어두다
- **get credit for** ~로 칭찬받다
- **correctly** ⓐⓓ 정확하게, 바르게
- **instance** ⓝ 사례, 예시
- **misdirect** ⓥ 엉뚱한 방향으로 보내다
- **postpone** ⓥ 미루다, 연기하다
- **absolutely** ⓐⓓ 절대적으로
- **previously** ⓐⓓ 사전에, 이전에

10행 These great musicians generally did their composition
　　　　　　　　　　　　　　　　　　　　　　동사1
mentally without reference to pen or piano, / and simply postponed
　　　　　　　~와 관련없이　　　　　　　　　　　　　　　동사2
the unpleasant manual labor of committing their music to paper
　　　　　　　　　　　　　　　동격(~라는)←┘　　　　~을 종이에 적다
until it became absolutely necessary.
접속사(~까지)

★★ 문제 해결 꿀~팁 ★★

▶ 많이 틀린 이유는?
최다 오답은 ④인데 ④ 뒤의 문장까지는 '작곡가들이 머릿속으로 작곡을 했다가 나중에 펜으로 적는 작업만 했기 때문에 적는 것만 보는 사람들 입장에서는 작곡가들이 매우 빠르게 작곡을 한다고 생각했다'는 내용을 일관되게 다루므로 반전의 포인트가 없다.

▶ 문제 해결 방법은?
주어진 문장의 내용을 먼저 정확히 파악하도록 한다. 이는 '이미 머릿속에서 끝난 작곡이더라도 그 길고 복잡한 곡을 펜으로 옮기는 작업 자체가 빨리 이루어지기 쉬운 일은 아니다'라는 뜻이다. ⑤ 뒤의 문장에서는 이 전체 내용을 맨 마지막에 나온 대명사 'this'로 받으며 '한 번 이미 머릿속으로 알고 있는 음악을 쓰는 작업만 해 본다면 펜으로 옮기는 작업의 어려움을 알 수 있을 것'이라는 내용을 다루고 있다.

DAY 20   문장 삽입 05

01 ④	02 ⑤	03 ④	04 ④	05 ④
06 ③	07 ④	08 ④	09 ④	10 ⑤
11 ⑤	12 ③			

---

01   공리주의 윤리와 쾌락   정답률 63% | 정답 ④

글의 흐름으로 보아, 주어진 문장이 들어가기에 가장 적절한 곳을 고르시오.

Utilitarian ethics argues / that all action should be directed / toward achieving the greatest total amount of happiness / for the largest number of people.
공리주의 윤리는 주장한다. / 모든 행동은 지향해야 한다고 / 최대 행복을 달성하는 쪽을 / 최대 다수의 사람들을 위한

① Utilitarian ethics assumes / that all actions can be evaluated in terms of their moral worth, / and so the desirability of an action is determined / by its resulting hedonistic consequences.
공리주의 윤리는 가정한다. / 모든 행동이 도덕적 가치의 관점에서 평가될 수 있으며, / 따라서 어떤 행동의 바람직함은 결정된다고 / 그 행동이 초래하는 쾌락적인 결과에 의해

② This is a consequentialist creed, / assuming / that the moral value and desirability of an action / can be determined from its likely outcomes.
이것은 결과주의의 신조인데, / 가정한다. / 어떤 행동의 도덕적 가치와 바람직함은 / 그것이 가져올 결과로부터 결정될 수 있다고

③ Jeremy Bentham suggested / that the value of hedonistic outcomes can be quantitatively assessed, / so that the value of consequent pleasure can be derived / by multiplying its intensity and its duration.
Jeremy Bentham은 말했다. / 쾌락적인 결과의 가치는 정량적으로 평가될 수 있으며, / 따라서 결과적 쾌락의 가치가 도출될 수 있다고 / 그것의 강도와 지속성을 곱하여

✔ In contrast, / the other major advocate of utilitarianism, John Stuart Mill, / argued for a more qualitative approach, / assuming that there can be different subjective levels of pleasure.
그와 대조적으로, / 공리주의의 다른 주요 옹호자인 John Stuart Mill은 / 보다 질적인 접근 방식을 찬성하는 주장을 했다. / 여러 주관적인 차원의 쾌락이 있을 수 있다고 가정하고

Higher-quality pleasures are more desirable than lower-quality pleasures.
질 높은 수준의 쾌락이 질 낮은 수준의 쾌락보다 더 바람직하다.

⑤ Less sophisticated creatures (like pigs!) / have an easier access to the simpler pleasures, / but more sophisticated creatures like humans / have the capacity to access higher pleasures / and should be motivated to seek those.
덜 고상한 생명체(돼지처럼!)는 / 더 단순한 쾌락에 더 쉽게 접근할 수 있지만, / 인간처럼 더 고상한 생명체는 / 더 질 높은 쾌락에 접근할 수 있는 능력을 지녔으며, / 그것을 추구하도록 동기를 부여받아야 한다.

공리주의 윤리는 모든 행동은 최대 다수의 최대 행복 달성을 지향해야 한다고 주장한다. ① 공리주의 윤리는 모든 행동이 도덕적 가치의 관점에서 평가될 수 있으며, 따라서 어떤 행동의 바람직함은 그 행동이 초래하는 쾌락적인 결과에 의해 결정된다고 가정한다. ② 이것은 결과주의의 신조인데, 어떤 행동의 도덕적 가치와 바람직함은 그것이 가져올 결과로부터 결정될 수 있다고 가정한다. ③ Jeremy Bentham은 쾌락적인 결과의 가치는 정량적으로 평가될 수 있으며, 따라서 결과적 쾌락의 가치가 그것의 강도와 지속성을 곱하여 도출될 수 있다고 말했다. ④ 그와 대조적으로 공리주의의 다른 주요 옹호자인 John Stuart Mill은 여러 주관적인 차원의 쾌락이 있을 수 있다고 가정하고 보다 질적인 접근 방식을 찬성하는 주장을 했다. 질 높은 수준의 쾌락이 질 낮은 수준의 쾌락보다 더 바람직하다. ⑤ 덜 고상한 생명체(돼지처럼!)는 더 단순한 쾌락에 더 쉽게 접근할 수 있지만, 인간처럼 더 고상한 생명체는 더 질 높은 쾌락에 접근할 수 있는 능력을 지녔으며, 그것을 추구하도록 동기를 부여받아야 한다.

Why? 왜 정답일까?

④ 앞에서 쾌락적 결과는 정량적으로 평가할 수 있다고 설명하는데, ④ 뒤에서는 쾌락의 양이 아닌 '수준'을 언급하고 있다. 즉 ④ 앞뒤로 글의 흐름이 반전되는데 적절한 역접어가 없는 상황이다. 이때 주어진 문장을 보면, **In contrast**라는 연결어로 논리적 공백을 적절히 메우면서, 쾌락의 양이 아닌 질, 즉 주관적 '수준'에 대해서도 논해볼 수 있다는 의미이다. 따라서 주어진 문장이 들어가기에 가장 적절한 곳은 ④이다.

- **advocate** ⑩ 옹호자
- **qualitative** ⑧ 질적인
- **subjective** ⑧ 주관적인
- **desirability** ⑩ 바람직함
- **consequence** ⑩ 결과, 영향
- **utilitarianism** ⑩ 공리주의
- **assume** ⑨ 가정하다
- **evaluate** ⑨ 평가하다
- **hedonistic** ⑧ 쾌락적인
- **creed** ⑩ 신조

- **likely** ⑧ 가능한
- **assess** ⑨ 평가하다, 측정하다
- **sophisticated** ⑧ 교양 있는, 세련된
- **quantitatively** [ad] 정량적으로
- **derive** ⑨ 도출하다

구문 풀이

19행 Less sophisticated creatures (like pigs!) have an easier access to the simpler pleasures, but more sophisticated creatures 전치사(~에) like humans have the capacity to access higher pleasures and 전치사(~처럼) 형용사적 용법 should be motivated to seek those. 대명사(= higher pleasures)

---

02   반딧불이가 빛을 내는 이유   정답률 43% | 정답 ⑤

글의 흐름으로 보아, 주어진 문장이 들어가기에 가장 적절한 곳을 고르시오.

Fireflies don't just light up their behinds / to attract mates, / they also glow to tell bats not to eat them.
반딧불이는 단지 꽁무니에 불을 밝히는 것이 아니라, / 짝의 주의를 끌기 위해서 / 박쥐에게 자기들을 먹지 말라고 말하기 위해 빛을 내기도 한다.

This twist in the tale of the trait / that gives fireflies their name / was discovered by Jesse Barber and his colleagues.
특성에 대한 이야기의 이 반전은 / 반딧불이의 이름을 지어주는 / Jesse Barber와 그의 동료들에 의해 발견되었다.

The glow's warning role benefits both fireflies and bats, / because these insects taste disgusting to the mammals.
빛이 하는 경고 역할은 반딧불이와 박쥐 모두에게 유익한데, / 왜냐하면 이 곤충이 그 포유동물(박쥐)에게는 역겨운 맛이 나기 때문이다.

① When swallowed, / chemicals released by fireflies / cause bats to throw them back up.
(반딧불이가) 삼켜지면, / 반딧불이가 배출하는 화학 물질은 / 박쥐가 그것을 다시 토해내게 만든다.

② The team placed eight bats in a dark room / with three or four fireflies / plus three times as many tasty insects, / including beetles and moths, / for four days.
연구팀은 여덟 마리의 박쥐를 어두운 방에 두었다. / 서너 마리의 반딧불이와, / 그보다 수가 세 배가 많은 맛 좋은 곤충들과 함께 / 딱정벌레와 나방을 포함해서 / 나흘 동안

③ During the first night, / all the bats captured at least one firefly.
첫날 밤 동안에, / 모든 박쥐는 적어도 한 마리의 반딧불이를 잡았다.

④ But by the fourth night, / most bats had learned to avoid fireflies / and catch all the other prey instead.
그러나 네 번째 밤에 이르러서는, / 대부분의 박쥐는 반딧불이를 피하고 / 대신 다른 모든 먹이를 잡는 법을 배웠다.

✔ When the team painted fireflies' light organs dark, / a new set of bats took twice / as long to learn to avoid them.
그 팀이 반딧불이에서 빛이 나는 기관을 어둡게 칠했을 때, / 새로운 한 무리의 박쥐는 두 배의 시간이 걸렸다. / 그것들을 피하는 법을 배우는 데

It had long been thought / that firefly bioluminescence mainly acted as a mating signal, / but the new finding explains / why firefly larvae also glow / despite being immature for mating.
오랫동안 생각되었지만, / 반딧불이의 생물 발광(發光)은 주로 짝짓기 신호의 역할을 한다고 / 새로운 연구 결과는 설명해 준다. / 반딧불이 애벌레 역시 빛을 내는 이유를 / 짝짓기를 하기에 미숙함에도 불구하고

반딧불이는 단지 짝의 주의를 끌기 위해서 꽁무니에 불을 밝히는 것이 아니라, 박쥐에게 자기들을 먹지 말라고 말하기 위해 빛을 내기도 한다. 반딧불이의 이름을 지어주는 특성에 대한 이야기의 이 반전은 Jesse Barber와 그의 동료들에 의해 발견되었다. 빛이 하는 경고 역할은 반딧불이와 박쥐 모두에게 유익한데, 왜냐하면 이 곤충이 그 포유동물(박쥐)에게는 역겨운 맛이 나기 때문이다. ① 반딧불이를 삼키면, 반딧불이가 배출하는 화학 물질 때문에 박쥐가 그것을 다시 토해내게 된다. ② 연구팀은 여덟 마리의 박쥐를 서너 마리의 반딧불이와, 딱정벌레와 나방을 포함해서 그보다 수가 세 배가 많은 맛 좋은 곤충들과 함께 어두운 방에 나흘 동안 두었다. ③ 첫날 밤 동안에, 모든 박쥐는 적어도 한 마리의 반딧불이를 잡았다. ④ 그러나 네 번째 밤에 이르러서는, 대부분의 박쥐는 반딧불이를 피하고 대신 다른 모든 먹이를 잡는 법을 배웠다. ⑤ 그 팀이 반딧불이에서 빛이 나는 기관을 어둡게 칠했을 때, 새로운 한 무리의 박쥐는 그것들을 피하는 법을 배우는 데 두 배의 시간이 걸렸다. 오랫동안 반딧불이의 생물 발광(發光)은 주로 짝짓기 신호의 역할을 한다고 생각되었지만, 새로운 연구 결과는 짝짓기를 하기에 미숙함에도 불구하고 반딧불이 애벌레 역시 빛을 내는 이유를 설명해 준다.

Why? 왜 정답일까?

반딧불이가 박쥐에게 먹히지 않기 위해 빛을 낸다는 사실을 실험의 예로 설명하고 있는 글이다. ⑤ 앞에서 실험이 시작된 후 나흘째 밤이 되자 박쥐가 반딧불이를 피하고 다른

먹이만을 잡았다고 언급하는데, 주어진 문장에서는 이어서 연구자들이 반딧불이의 몸에서 빛이 나는 기관을 까맣게 칠하자 박쥐가 반딧불이를 피하기까지 두 배의 시간이 들었다고 서술한다. ⑤ 뒤에서는 주어진 문장까지의 내용을 바탕으로 반딧불이가 짝짓기 목적만이 아닌, 추가적인 이유로 빛을 내는 것이라는 결론을 도출한다. 따라서 주어진 문장이 들어가기에 가장 적절한 곳은 ⑤이다.

- glow ⓥ 빛나다 ⓝ 빛
- disgusting ⓐ 역겨운
- prey ⓝ 먹잇감
- immature ⓐ 미숙한
- trait ⓝ 특성
- throw up ⓥ 토하다
- act as ⓥ ~의 역할을 하다

구문 풀이

10행 When swallowed, chemicals released by fireflies cause bats
접속사 / 분사구문 / 주어 ↖ 과거분사 「cause+목적어+
to throw them back up.
to부정사: ~이 …하게 야기하다」

---

03 인권에 관한 이상과 현실 사이의 격차 정답률 51% | 정답 ④

글의 흐름으로 보아, 주어진 문장이 들어가기에 가장 적절한 곳을 고르시오.

There is obviously a wide gap / between the promises of the Universal Declaration of Human Rights in 1948 / and the real world of human-rights violations.
분명히 큰 격차가 있다. / 1948년 세계 인권 선언의 약속과 / 인권 침해의 현실 세계 사이에는

In so far as we sympathize with the victims, / we may criticize the UN and its member governments / for failing to keep their promises.
우리가 피해자들과 공감하는 한, / 우리는 유엔과 그 회원국 정부들을 비난할 수도 있을 것이다. / 자신들의 약속을 지키지 못한 것에 대해

① However, we cannot understand the gap / between human-rights ideals and the real world of human-rights violations / by sympathy or by legal analysis.
그러나 우리는 격차를 이해할 수는 없다. / 인권의 이상과 인권 침해의 현실 세계 사이의 / 공감이나 법률적 분석을 통해

② Rather, it requires investigation by the various social sciences / of the causes of social conflict and political oppression, / and of the interaction between national and international politics.
오히려 그것은 다양한 사회과학의 연구를 필요로 한다. / 사회 갈등과 정치 억압의 원인과 / 국내 정치와 국제 정치 사이의 상호 작용에 대한

③ The UN introduced the concept of human rights / into international law and politics.
유엔은 인권이라는 개념을 도입했다. / 국제법과 국제 정치에

☑ The field of international politics / is, however, dominated by states and other powerful actors / (such as multinational corporations) / that have priorities other than human rights.
국제 정치 분야는 / 그러나 국가 및 기타 강력한 행위자에 의해 지배되고 있다. / (다국적 기업과 같은) / 인권 외에 다른 우선순위 사항을 가진

It is a leading feature of the human-rights field / that the governments of the world proclaim human rights / but have a highly variable record of implementing them.
인권 분야의 주된 특징이다. / 세계 각국 정부가 인권을 선언하고 있지만 / 그것을 시행하는 데 매우 가변적인 기록을 갖고 있다는 것이

⑤ We must understand why this is so.
우리는 이것이 왜 그런지를 이해해야 한다.

1948년 세계 인권 선언의 약속과 인권 침해의 현실 세계 사이에는 분명히 큰 격차가 있다. 우리가 피해자들과 공감하는 한, 우리는 유엔과 그 회원국 정부들이 자신들의 약속을 지키지 못한 것에 대해 비난할 수도 있을 것이다. ① 그러나 우리는 공감이나 법률적 분석을 통해 인권의 이상과 인권 침해의 현실 세계 사이의 격차를 이해할 수는 없다. ② 오히려 그것은 사회 갈등과 정치 억압의 원인과 국내 정치와 국제 정치 사이의 상호 작용에 대한 다양한 사회과학의 연구를 필요로 한다. ③ 유엔은 국제법과 국제 정치에 인권이라는 개념을 도입했다. ④ 그러나 국제 정치 분야는 인권 외에 다른 우선순위 사항을 가진 국가 및 (다국적 기업과 같은) 기타 강력한 행위자에 의해 지배되고 있다. 세계 각국 정부가 인권을 선언하고 있지만 그것을 시행하는 데 매우 가변적인 기록을 갖고 있다는 것이 인권 분야의 주된 특징이다. ⑤ 우리는 이것이 왜 그런지를 이해해야 한다.

Why? 왜 정답일까?

인권 실현에 관하여 이상과 현실의 격차가 있음을 설명한 글이다. ④ 앞의 문장에서 국제법과 국제 정치에 인권이 도입되었다고 언급한 후, however를 포함한 주어진 문장에서는 '그러나' 국제 정치 분야가 인권 외에 다른 것들을 우선시하는 국가들 혹은 다른 강력

한 행위자에 의해 지배된다는 점을 지적한다. ④ 뒤의 문장에서는 그리하여 각국이 인권을 선언하고 있다 해도 실행이 균일하게 이루어지지 않고 있다는 내용을 부연한다. 따라서 주어진 문장이 들어가기에 가장 적절한 곳은 ④이다.

- international politics 국제 정치
- multinational corporation 다국적 기업
- violation ⓝ 침해
- analysis ⓝ 분석
- variable ⓐ 가변적인, 변동이 심한
- state ⓝ 국가
- human right 인권
- sympathize with ~와 공감하다
- investigation ⓝ 연구, 조사
- implement ⓥ 시행하다

구문 풀이

7행 In so far as we sympathize with the victims, we may criticize
~하는 한 / ~와 공감하다 / ↖criticize+
the UN and its member governments for failing to keep their promises.
A+ / for+B : B에 대해 A를 비난하다」

---

04 재정 적자 및 연방 정부 부채 증가의 원인 정답률 74% | 정답 ④

글의 흐름으로 보아, 주어진 문장이 들어가기에 가장 적절한 곳을 고르시오.

Both the budget deficit and federal debt / have soared / during the recent financial crisis and recession.
재정 적자와 연방 정부의 부채가 모두 / 치솟았다. / 최근의 재정 위기와 경기 침체 동안에

① During 2009 – 2010, / nearly 40 percent of federal expenditures / were financed by borrowing.
2009년 ~ 2010년 동안에 / 연방 정부 지출의 거의 40퍼센트가 / 대출로 자금이 충당되었다.

② The huge recent federal deficits / have pushed the federal debt / to levels not seen / since the years immediately following World War II.
최근의 막대한 연방 재정 적자는 / 연방 정부의 부채를 밀어 올렸다. / 본 적이 없었던 수준으로 / 제2차 세계대전 직후의 기간 이후로

③ The rapid growth of baby-boomer retirees / in the decade immediately ahead / will mean higher spending levels and larger and larger deficits / for both Social Security and Medicare.
베이비붐 세대 퇴직자의 빠른 증가는 / 바로 이어질 향후 10년 동안 / 더 높은 지출 수준과 적자의 점진적인 증가를 의미할 것이다. / 사회 보장 연금과 노인 의료 보험 제도의

☑ Moreover, / more than half of Americans age 18 and older / derive benefits from various transfer programs, / while paying little or no personal income tax.
더욱이, / 18세 이상의 미국인들 중 절반이 넘는 사람들이 / 다양한 (소득) 이전 지원 프로그램으로부터 보조금을 얻어낸다. / 개인 소득세를 거의 혹은 전혀 내지 않으면서

All of these factors / are going to make it extremely difficult / to slow the growth of federal spending / and keep the debt from ballooning out of control.
이러한 모든 요인들은, / 대단히 어렵게 만들 것이다. / 연방 정부의 재정 지출 증가를 늦추고 / 부채가 통제 불능 상태로 불어나지 않도록 막는 것을

⑤ Projections indicate / that the net federal debt will rise / to 90 percent of GDP by 2019, / and many believe / it will be even higher / unless constructive action is taken soon.
예측들이 보여주고 있으며, / 연방 정부의 순 부채가 증가하리라는 것을 / 2019년쯤에는 국내 총생산의 90퍼센트까지 / 많은 사람들은 믿고 있다. / 그것이 훨씬 더 높아질 것이라고 / 곧 건설적인 조치가 취해지지 않으면

최근의 재정 위기와 경기 침체 동안에 재정 적자와 연방 정부의 부채가 모두 치솟았다. ① 2009년 ~ 2010년 동안에 연방 정부 지출의 거의 40퍼센트가 대출로 자금이 충당되었다. ② 최근의 막대한 연방 재정 적자는 제2차 세계대전 직후의 기간 이후로 본 적이 없었던 수준으로 연방 정부의 부채를 밀어 올렸다. ③ 바로 이어질 향후 10년 동안 베이비붐 세대 퇴직자의 빠른 증가는 사회 보장 연금과 노인 의료 보험 제도의 더 높은 지출 수준과 적자의 점진적인 증가를 의미할 것이다. ④ 더욱이, 18세 이상의 미국인들 중 절반이 넘는 사람들이 개인 소득세를 거의 혹은 전혀 내지 않으면서 다양한 (소득) 이전 지원 프로그램으로부터 보조금을 얻어낸다. 이러한 모든 요인들은, 연방 정부의 재정 지출 증가를 늦추고 부채가 통제 불능 상태로 불어나지 않도록 막는 것을 대단히 어렵게 만들 것이다. ⑤ 2019년쯤에는 연방 정부의 순 부채가 국내 총생산의 90퍼센트까지 증가하리라는 것을 예측들이 보여주고 있으며, 많은 사람들은 곧 건설적인 조치가 취해지지 않으면 그것이 훨씬 더 높아질 것이라고 믿고 있다.

Why? 왜 정답일까?

미국에서 재정 적자와 연방 정부의 부채 증가가 문제시됨을 언급하며 그 원인을 진단한 글이다. ④ 앞의 문장에서 베이비붐 세대의 은퇴가 국가의 재정 부담을 키우고 있다고 말한 데 이어, 주어진 문장은 18세 이상의 미국인 중 절반 이상이 보조금을 타고 있음을 언급하고, ④ 뒤에서는 '이러한 요인들'이 문제 해결을 지연시키고 있다는 결론을 제시한다. 따라서 주어진 문장이 들어가기에 가장 적절한 곳은 ④이다.

- derive A from B A를 B로부터 얻다, 끌어내다
- recession ⓝ 침체
- retiree ⓝ 퇴직자, 은퇴자
- constructive ⓐ 건설적인
- expenditure ⓝ 지출, 비용, 경비
- balloon ⓥ 부풀다, 커지다

- representation ⓝ 묘사, 표현
- entirely ⓐd 전적으로
- delivery ⓝ 전달
- come into play 작용하기 시작하다
- theorist ⓝ 이론가
- do nothing but 오로지 ~할 뿐이다
- essence ⓝ 본질
- coincide ⓥ 일치하다

구문 풀이

14행 All of these factors are going to make it extremely difficult
「make + 가목적어 + 형용사 + 진목적어1 + 진목적어2 : 5형식 가목적어 구문」
to slow the growth of federal spending and (to) keep the debt from
「keep + A + from + 동명사 : A가 ~하지 못하게 막다」
ballooning out of control.

구문 풀이

4행 Cinema is valuable not {for its ability to make visible the
「not + (A) +
hidden outlines of our reality}, but {for its ability to reveal what
but + (B) : (A)가 아니라 (B)인」
reality itself veils — the dimension of fantasy}.

---

05 환상적 예술로서의 영화 　　정답률 45% | 정답 ④

글의 흐름으로 보아, 주어진 문장이 들어가기에 가장 적절한 곳을 고르시오. [3점]

Cinema is valuable / not for its ability / to make visible the hidden outlines of our reality, / but for its ability / to reveal what reality itself veils / — the dimension of fantasy.
영화는 가치가 있다. / 능력 때문이 아니라 / 우리 현실의 숨겨진 윤곽을 보이게 만드는 / 능력 때문에 / 현실 자체가 가리고 있는 것을 드러내는 / 즉 환상의 차원을

① This is why, to a person, / the first great theorists of film / decried the introduction / of sound and other technical innovations (such as color) / that pushed film in the direction of realism.
이것이 어떤 사람에게는 이유이다. / 최초의 위대한 영화 이론가들은 / 도입을 공공연히 비난했던 / 소리와 (색채와 같은) 다른 기술 혁신의 / 영화를 사실주의 쪽으로 밀어붙였던

② Since cinema was an entirely fantasmatic art, / these innovations were completely unnecessary.
영화는 전적으로 환상적인 예술이었기 때문에 / 이러한 혁신은 완전히 불필요했다.

③ And what's worse, / they could do nothing but turn filmmakers and audiences away / from the fantasmatic dimension of cinema, / potentially transforming film / into a mere delivery device for representations of reality.
그리고 설상가상으로 / 그것들은 영화 제작자와 관객을 멀어지게 할 수 있을 뿐이었다. / 영화의 환상적인 차원에서 / 잠재적으로 영화를 변형시키면서, / 현실의 묘사를 위한 단순한 전달 장치로

☑ As long as the irrealism of the silent black and white film predominated, / one could not take filmic fantasies / for representations of reality.
무성 흑백 영화의 비현실주의가 지배하는 동안은 / 사람들은 영화적 환상을 착각할 수 없었다. / 현실에 대한 묘사로

But sound and color threatened to create just such an illusion, / thereby destroying the very essence of film art.
그러나 소리와 색채는 바로 그러한 착각을 만들겠다고 위협하여 / 영화 예술의 바로 그 본질을 파괴했다.

⑤ As Rudolf Arnheim puts it, / "The creative power of the artist / can only come into play / where reality and the medium of representation do not coincide."
Rudolf Arnheim이 표현한 것처럼 / "예술가의 창의적 힘은 / 오로지 발휘될 수 있다 / 현실과 묘사의 매체가 일치하지 않는 곳에서만"

영화는 우리 현실의 숨겨진 윤곽을 보이게 만드는 능력 때문이 아니라 현실 자체가 가리고 있는 것, 즉 환상의 차원을 드러내는 능력 때문에 가치가 있다. ① 이 때문에 최초의 위대한 영화 이론가들은 영화를 사실주의 쪽으로 밀어붙였던 소리와 (색채와 같은) 다른 기술 혁신의 도입을 공공연히 비난했다. ② 영화는 전적으로 환상적인 예술이었기 때문에 이러한 혁신은 완전히 불필요했다. ③ 그리고 설상가상으로 그것들은 잠재적으로 영화를 현실의 묘사를 위한 단순한 전달 장치로 변형시키면서, 영화 제작자와 관객을 영화의 환상적인 차원에서 멀어지게 할 수 있을 뿐이었다. ④ 무성 흑백 영화의 비현실주의가 지배하는 동안은 영화적 환상을 현실에 대한 묘사로 착각할 수 없었다. 그러나 소리와 색채는 바로 그러한 착각을 만들겠다고 위협하여 영화 예술의 바로 그 본질을 파괴했다. ⑤ Rudolf Arnheim이 표현한 것처럼 "예술가의 창의적 힘은 현실과 묘사의 매체가 일치하지 않는 곳에서만 발휘될 수 있다."

Why? 왜 정답일까?

영화는 현실 너머의 환상을 보여준다는 점에서 가치가 있기에, 영화 이론가들은 영화에 소리와 색을 입혀 보다 '사실주의'적으로 만들고자 하는 시도를 반대했다는 내용의 글이다. ④ 앞의 문장에서 영화에 소리와 색을 도입하려는 시도는 영화를 환상적 예술에서 현실 반영의 수단으로 전락시키고 말 것이라는 우려가 있었음을 시사한다. 주어진 문장은 영화에 소리도 없고 색도 없던 시대에는 영화를 현실에 대한 묘사로 착각할 수 없었다는 설명으로 ④ 앞의 내용을 뒷받침한다. 이어서 But으로 시작하는 ④ 뒤의 문장은 '그러나' 소리와 색채가 영화는 현실의 묘사라는 착각을 만들어내며 영화 예술의 본질, 즉 환상적 측면을 파괴했다고 설명한다. 따라서 주어진 문장이 들어가기에 가장 적절한 곳은 ④이다.

- irrealism ⓝ 비현실주의
- predominate ⓥ 지배하다

---

06 과학적 관측에 대한 시각 　　정답률 43% | 정답 ③

글의 흐름으로 보아, 주어진 문장이 들어가기에 가장 적절한 곳을 고르시오. [3점]

Babylonian astronomers created detailed records of celestial movements in the heavens, / using the resulting tables to sieve out irregularities / and, with them, the favour of the gods.
바빌로니아의 천문학자들은 하늘에서의 천체 운동에 대한 자세한 기록을 만들어, / 그 결과표를 사용해 불규칙성을 살펴보고, / 그것을 가지고 신의 은총을 가려냈다.

① This was the seed / of what we now call the scientific method / — a demonstration / that accurate observations of the world could be used / to forecast its future.
이것이 씨앗이다. / 우리가 현재 과학적인 방법이라고 부르는 것의 / 즉 보여 주는 것 / 세상에 대한 정확한 관측이 이용될 수 있다는 것을 / 미래를 예측하기 위해

② The importance of measurement / in this sort of cosmic comprehension / did not develop smoothly over the centuries.
측정의 중요성은 / 이런 식의 우주 이해에 있어 / 수 세기 동안 원활하게 발전하지는 않았다.

☑ Indeed, in the Middle Ages in Europe, / calculating by hand and eye / was sometimes seen / as producing a rather shabby sort of knowledge, / inferior to that of abstract thought.
사실, 유럽의 중세 시대에는 / 손과 눈으로 측정하는 것은 / 때때로 여겨졌다. / 다소 터무니없는 종류의 지식을 만들어낸다고 / 추상적인 사고가 만들어낸 지식보다 열등한

The suspicion was / due to the influence of ancient Greeks in the era's scholasticism, / particularly Plato and Aristotle, / who stressed / that the material world was one of unceasing change and instability.
그 의심은 ~이었다. / 당대 스콜라 철학의 고대 그리스인들의 영향 때문 / 특히 플라톤과 아리스토텔레스 / 이들은 강조했던 / 물질 세계는 끊임없는 변화와 불안정의 하나라고

④ They emphasized / that reality was best understood / by reference to immaterial qualities, / be they Platonic forms or Aristotelian causes.
그들은 강조했다. / 현실이 가장 잘 이해된다고 / 비물질적인 자질을 참조해 / 플라톤적인 형태이든 아리스토텔레스적인 원인이든

⑤ It would take the revelations of the scientific revolution / to fully displace these instincts, / with observations of the night sky once again proving decisive.
과학적인 혁명이라는 뜻밖의 새로운 발견이 필요했을 것이고, / 이러한 직관을 완전히 대체하려면 / 밤하늘의 관찰이 결정적이라는 것이 다시금 입증되었다.

바빌로니아의 천문학자들은 하늘에서의 천체 운동에 대한 자세한 기록을 만들어, 그 결과표를 사용해 불규칙성을 살펴보고, 그것으로 신의 은총을 가려냈다. ① 이것이 우리가 현재 과학적인 방법이라고 부르는 것, 즉 세상에 대한 정확한 관측이 미래를 예측하기 위해 이용될 수 있다는 것을 보여 주는 씨앗이었다. ② 이런 식의 우주의 이해에 있어 측정의 중요성은 수 세기 동안 원활하게 발전하지는 않았다. ③ 사실, 유럽의 중세 시대에는 손과 눈으로 측정하는 것은 다소 터무니없는 종류의 지식, 즉 추상적인 사고가 만들어낸 지식보다 열등한 지식을 만들어 낸다고 때때로 여겨졌다. 그 의심은 당대 스콜라 철학의 고대 그리스인들, 특히 물질 세계는 끊임없는 변화와 불안정의 하나라고 강조했던 플라톤과 아리스토텔레스의 영향 때문이었다. ④ 그들은 현실이 플라톤적인 형태이든 아리스토텔레스적인 원인이든 비물질적인 자질을 참조해 가장 잘 이해된다고 강조했다. ⑤ 이러한 직관을 완전히 대체하려면 과학적인 혁명이라는 뜻밖의 새로운 발견이 필요했을 것이고, 밤하늘의 관찰이 결정적이라는 것이 다시금 입증되었다.

Why? 왜 정답일까?

③ 앞에서는 우주 이해에 있어 측정의 중요성이 고대 이후 몇 세기 동안 제대로 발전하지 못했다고 한다. 이어서 ③ 뒤는 갑자기 '의심'을 언급하므로 흐름이 어색하게 끊긴다. 이때 주어진 문장을 보면, ③ 앞의 '바빌로니아 시대 이후' 몇 세기에 해당하는 '유럽의 중세'를 언급하며, 이 시대에는 관측보다도 추상적 사고가 더 중요하게 여겨졌다고 설명한다. 이렇듯 관측의 효과를 열등하게 보는 시각을 ③ 뒤에서 '의심'으로 언급하는 것이다. 따라서 주어진 문장이 들어가기에 가장 적절한 곳은 ③이다.

- **Middle Ages** (유럽) 중세
- **inferior to** ~보다 열등한
- **celestial** ⓐ 천체의
- **irregularity** ⓝ 불규칙성
- **comprehension** ⓝ 이해
- **suspicion** ⓝ 의심
- **scholasticism** ⓝ 스콜라 철학
- **instability** ⓝ 불안정성
- **immaterial** ⓐ 비물질적인
- **displace** ⓥ 대체하다
- **shabby** ⓐ 부당한, 터무니없는
- **astronomer** ⓝ 천문학자
- **sieve out** ~을 잘 살펴보다
- **cosmic** ⓐ 우주의
- **smoothly** ⓐⓓ 부드럽게, 원활히
- **era** ⓝ 시대
- **unceasing** ⓐ 끝없는
- **emphasize** ⓥ 강조하다
- **revelation** ⓝ 발견, 폭로

- **squeeze** ⓥ 짜내다, 짜다
- **confusion** ⓝ 혼동, 혼란
- **thread** ⓝ 실
- **harden** ⓥ 굳히다, 단단하게 하다
- **twist** ⓥ 꼬다, 비틀다

구문 풀이

5행 One is the formation of individual fibers / by squeezing a liquid
　　　　　　　　　　　　　　　　　　　　　　　by + 동명사1
(through one or more small openings in a nozzle called a spinneret)
전치사(~을 통하여)　　　　　　　　　　　　　　과거분사구
and letting it harden.
동명사2(~함으로써)　└→ letting의 목적격 보어(원형부정사)

★★★ 1등급 대비 고난도 2점 문제

08 언어의 의미　　　　　　　　　　　정답률 35% | 정답 ④

글의 흐름으로 보아, 주어진 문장이 들어가기에 가장 적절한 곳을 고르시오.

The linguistic resources we choose to use / do not come to us as empty forms / ready to be filled with our personal intentions; / rather, / they come to us / with meanings already embedded within them.
우리가 사용하기로 선택하는 언어 자원들은 / 텅 빈 형태로 우리에게 오는 것이 아니다. / 우리의 개인적인 의도로 채워질 준비가 된 / 오히려, / 그것들은 우리에게 온다, / 그 안에 이미 뿌리 박힌 의미들과 함께

① These meanings, however, / are not derived / from some universal, logical set of principles; / rather, as with their shapes, / they are built up over time / from their past uses in particular contexts / by particular groups of participants / in the accomplishment of particular goals / that, in turn, are shaped by myriad cultural, historical and institutional forces.
그런데 이런 의미들은 / 나오지 않는다. / 어떤 보편적이고 논리적인 일련의 원리에서 / 오히려, 형태에서도 그렇듯, / 그것들은 오랜 기간에 걸쳐 쌓인다. / 이전에 특정 상황에서 사용한 것에서 / 특정 집단 사람들에 의해 / 특정한 목적 달성에 관여하는 / 결국 무수히 많은 문화, 역사, 그리고 제도적 힘으로 형성된

② The linguistic resources / we choose to use at particular communicative moments / come to these moments / with their conventionalized histories of meaning.
언어 자원들은 / 특정한 의사소통의 순간들에 우리가 사용하기로 선택하는 / 이런 순간에 나타난다. / 관습화된 의미의 역사를 지닌 채

③ It is their conventionality / that binds us to some degree / to particular ways of realizing our collective history.
바로 이러한 관습성이다. / 우리를 어느 정도 속박시키는 것은 / 우리의 집단적 역사를 실현하는 특정한 방식에

✔ However, / while our resources come with histories of meanings, / *how they come to mean* at a particular communicative moment / is always open to negotiation.
하지만 / 우리의 자원들이 의미의 역사를 지닌 채 오더라도, / 특정한 의사소통 순간에 *그것이 어떤 의미를 갖는 가는* / 항상 협상의 여지가 있다.

Thus, / in our individual uses of our linguistic resources / we accomplish two actions simultaneously.
그래서, / 우리의 언어 자원을 우리가 개별적으로 사용할 때 / 우리는 두 가지 행위를 동시에 달성한다.

⑤ We create their typical — historical — contexts of use / and at the same time we position ourselves / in relation to these contexts.
우리는 그것들의 전형적인, 즉 역사적인 사용의 맥락을 만들고 / 동시에 우리는 우리만의 입장을 취한다. / 이런 맥락에 관해

구문 풀이

17행 They emphasized that reality was best understood by reference to immaterial qualities, be they Platonic forms or Aristotelian causes.
　　　　be (it / they) A or B : 이든 B이든 간에

07 방적의 두 가지 방식　　　　　정답률 57% | 정답 ④

글의 흐름으로 보아, 주어진 문장이 들어가기에 가장 적절한 곳을 고르시오. [3점]

In fiber processing / the word 'spinning' means two quite different things.
섬유 가공에서 / '방적'은 상당히 다른 두 가지 의미이다.

① One is the formation of individual fibers / by squeezing a liquid / through one or more small openings in a nozzle / called a spinneret / and letting it harden.
하나는 개개의 섬유를 형성하는 것이다. / 액체를 짜내고 / 노즐 속의 하나 혹은 그 이상의 구멍을 통해서 / 방사 노즐이라고 불리는 / 그것을 굳혀서

② Spiders and silkworms / have been spinning fibers / in this way for millions of years, / but chemists and engineers / learned the procedure from them / only about a century ago.
거미와 누에는 / 섬유를 뽑아내 오고 있지만 / 몇 백만 년 간 이런 식으로 / 화학자 및 공학자들은 / 그들에게서 이 방법을 배웠다. / 고작 약 한 세기 전에야

③ In the other kind of spinning / — sometimes called throwing / to prevent confusion with the first kind — / two or more fibers are twisted together / to form a thread.
다른 종류의 방사는, / 간혹 꼬기라고도 불리는데, / 첫 번째와의 혼동을 막기 위해 / 둘 또는 그 이상의 섬유를 함께 꼬는 것이다. / 한 가닥의 실을 만들기 위하여

✔ Human beings discovered this art / thousands of years ago, / and they have invented several devices / to make it easier and faster.
사람들은 이 기술을 발견했고 / 수천 년 전에 / 몇 가지 장치를 발명했다. / 이를 더 쉽고 빠르게 하기 위해서

The ancient distaff and spindle are examples / that were replaced by the spinning wheel / in the Middle Ages.
고대의 실을 감는 막대와 추는 예이다. / 물레로 대체된 / 중세에

⑤ Later came / the spinning jenny, the water frame, and Crompton's mule / — spinning machines / that became symbols of the Industrial Revolution.
이후에 출현했는데, / 다축 방적기, 수력 방적기, Crompton의 뮬 정방기(실을 탄력 있게 만들고자 잡아당겨 늘이면서 꼬임을 주는 데 쓰는 기계) / 이것들은 방적기들이었다. / 산업혁명 시대의 상징이 된

섬유 가공에서 '방적'은 상당히 다른 두 가지 의미이다. ① 하나는 방사 노즐이라고 불리는 노즐 속의 하나 혹은 그 이상의 구멍을 통해서 액체를 짜내고 그것을 굳혀서 개개의 섬유를 형성하는 것이다. ② 거미와 누에는 몇 백만 년 간 이런 식으로 섬유를 뽑아내 오고 있지만 화학자 및 공학자들은 고작 약 한 세기 전에야 그들에게서 이 방법을 배웠다. ③ 다른 종류의 방사는, 간혹 첫 번째와의 혼동을 막기 위해 꼬기라고도 불리는데, 한 가닥의 실을 만들기 위하여 둘 또는 그 이상의 섬유를 함께 꼬는 것이다. ④ 사람들은 수천 년 전에 이 기술을 발견했고 이를 더 쉽고 빠르게 하기 위해 몇 가지 장치를 발명했다. 고대의 실을 감는 막대와 추는 중세에 물레로 대체된 예이다. ⑤ 이후에 다축 방적기, 수력 방적기, Crompton의 뮬 정방기(실을 탄력 있게 만들고자 잡아당겨 늘이면서 꼬임을 주는 데 쓰는 기계)가 출현했는데, 이것들은 산업혁명 시대의 상징이 된 방적기들이었다.

Why? 왜 정답일까?

이 글은 방적의 두 가지 주된 방식을 설명한다. 방사 노즐 구멍을 통해 액체를 짜내고 이를 굳혀서 실을 만드는 첫 번째 방식을 설명한 데 이어, ④ 앞의 문장은 일명 '꼬기'라고도 불리는 두 번째 방식도 있음을 소개하는데, 주어진 문장에서는 이 '꼬기' 방식을 'this art, it' 등으로 나타내며 사람들이 이 방식을 이미 수천 년 전에 발명하였고 이 과정을 쉽게 하고자 다양한 장치도 개발하였음을 이야기한다. ④ 뒤의 문장에서는 그 예로 고대의 실을 감는 막대와 추, 물레 등을 언급한다. 따라서 주어진 문장이 들어가기에 가장 적절한 곳은 ④이다.

- **processing** ⓝ 가공
- **formation** ⓝ 형성

우리가 사용하기로 선택하는 언어 자원들은 우리의 개인적인 의도로 채워질 준비가 된 텅 빈 형태로 우리에게 오는 것이 아니다. 오히려, 그 안에 이미 뿌리 박힌 의미들과 함께 우리에게 온다. ① 그런데 이런 의미들은 어떤 보편적이고 논리적인 일련의 원리에서 나오지 않는다. 오히려, 형태에서도 그렇듯, 그것들은 결국 무수히 많은 문화, 역사, 그리고 제도적 힘으로 형성된 특정한 목적 달성에 관여하는 특정 집단이 특정 상황에서 이전에 오랜 기간 사용한 것에서 비롯된다. ② 특정한 의사소통의 순간들에 우리가 사용하기로 선택하는 언어 자원들은 관습화된 의미의 역사를 지닌 채 이런 순간에 나타난다. ③ 바로 이러한 관습성이 우리를 우리의 집단적 역사를 실현하는 특정한 방식에 어느 정도 속박시킨다. ④ 하지만 우리의 자원들이 의미의 역사를 지닌 채 오더라도, 특정한 의사소통 순간에 그것이 어떤 의미를 갖는가는 항상 협상의 여지가 있다. 그래서, 우리의 언어 자원을 우리가 개별적으로 사용할 때 우리는 두 가지 행위를 동시에 달성한다. ⑤ 우리는 그것들의 전형적인, 즉 역사적인 사용의 맥락을 만드는 동시에 이런 맥락에 관해 우리만의 입장을 취한다.

Why? 왜 정답일까?

언어의 의미는 오랜 세월 축적된 '관습'처럼 결정되지만, 동시에 사용자의 '현재' 문맥에 따라 새롭게 만들어질 여지도 있다는 내용이다. ④ 앞에서는 언어 의미의 관습성을 주로 언급하며, 우리가 이러한 관습과 방식에 어느 정도는 '속박된다'고 설명한다. 한편, **However**로 시작하는 주어진 문장은 언어 자원이 이렇듯 의미의 '역사'와 함께 오더라도 의사소통 '당시'에 어떤 의미를 띨 것인가에 관해 협상의 여지가 있다고 반박한다. 이

어서 ④ 뒤는 그렇기에(Thus) 우리는 언어 자원을 사용할 때 관습을 따르는 동시에 관습을 만들어 나가기도 한다는 결론을 제시한다. 따라서 주어진 문장이 들어가기에 가장 적절한 곳은 ④이다.

- **negotiation** ⓝ 협상
- **embed** ⓥ (단단히) 끼워 넣다
- **institutional** ⓐ 기관의
- **bind** ⓥ 속박하다, 묶다
- **linguistic** ⓐ 언어적인
- **myriad** ⓐ 무수히 많은
- **conventionality** ⓝ 관습성
- **simultaneously** ⓐⓓ 동시에

구문 풀이

4행 The linguistic resources we choose to use do not come to
us as empty forms ready to be filled with our personal intentions;
rather, they come to us with meanings already embedded within them.
(but) rather+B : A가 아니라 오히려 B인, 　　　　　과거분사구
not+A+ 　　형용사구

★★ 문제 해결 꿀~팁 ★★

▶ 많이 틀린 이유는?
③ 앞의 their conventionalized histories of meaning은 ③ 뒤의 their conventionality로 바로 연결된다. 즉 ③ 앞뒤로 논리적 공백은 발생하지 않는다.

▶ 문제 해결 방법은?
④ 앞에서는 언어의 의미와 관련해 '관습성'을 주로 언급하는데, ④ 뒤의 두 문장은 '그래서' 우리가 언어 자원을 사용할 때 '두 가지' 행위, 즉 관습적 맥락을 그대로 형성하는 한편 우리 자신만의 입장도 형성하게 된다고 한다. 이렇게 '두 가지' 행위를 정리하려면, 관습성 외 다른 내용이 ④ 자리에 언급되어야 하는데, 그 내용이 바로 주어진 문장의 '협상'이다.

★★★ 1등급 대비 고난도 2점 문제

| **09** | 단어의 사용과 발화의 의미 | 정답률 47% | 정답 ④ |

글의 흐름으로 보아, 주어진 문장이 들어가기에 가장 적절한 곳을 고르시오.

Imagine I tell you that Maddy is bad.
내가 여러분에게 Maddy가 나쁘다고 말한다고 생각해 보라.

Perhaps you infer from my intonation, / or the context in which we are talking, / that I mean morally bad.
아마 여러분은 나의 억양으로부터 추론한다. / 혹은 우리가 말하고 있는 맥락으로 보아 / 내가 도덕적으로 나쁘다는 뜻을 의도하고 있음을

Additionally, / you will probably infer / that I am disapproving of Maddy, / or saying that I think you should disapprove of her, or similar, / given typical linguistic conventions / and assuming I am sincere.
게다가 / 여러분은 아마도 추론할 것이다. / 내가 Maddy를 못마땅해하고 있다고, / 또는 내 생각에 여러분이 그녀를 못마땅하든지 해야 한다고 말하고 있는 것이라고 / 일반적인 언어 관행을 고려하고 / 내가 진심이라고 상정한다면

① However, / you might not get a more detailed sense of the particular sorts of way / in which Maddy is bad, / her typical character traits, and the like, / since people can be bad in many ways.
하지만 / 여러분은 어떤 특정한 방식에 대해서 더 자세하게 인식하지 못할 수도 있는데, / Maddy가 나쁜 / 그리고 그녀의 일반적인 성격 특성 등등에 대해서는 / 사람들은 여러 방면에서 나쁠 수 있기 때문이다.

② In contrast, if I say that Maddy is wicked, / then you get more of a sense / of her typical actions and attitudes to others.
그에 반해서, 만일 내가 Maddy는 사악하다고 말한다면, / 여러분은 더 알게 된다. / 다른 사람들에 대한 그녀의 일반적인 행동과 태도에 관해

③ The word 'wicked' is more specific than 'bad'.
'사악한'이라는 낱말은 '나쁜'보다 더 구체적이다.

☑ I have still not exactly pinpointed Maddy's character / since wickedness takes many forms.
나는 여전히 Maddy의 성격을 정확하게 지적하지 않았다. / 사악함은 많은 형태를 띤다는 점에서

But there is more detail nevertheless, / perhaps a stronger connotation of the sort of person Maddy is.
하지만 그럼에도 불구하고 더 많은 세부 사항이 있다. / 아마도 Maddy가 어떤 사람인지에 관한 더 강한 함축적 의미가

⑤ In addition, and again assuming typical linguistic conventions, / you should also get a sense / that I am disapproving of Maddy, / or saying that you should disapprove of her, or similar, / assuming that we are still discussing her moral character.
게다가 다시 한번 일반적인 언어 관행을 상정하면, / 여러분은 또한 파악할 것이다. / 내가 Maddy를 못마땅해하고 있거나 / 여러분이 그녀를 못마땅하든지 해야 한다고 말하고 있는 것임을 / 우리가 여전히 그녀의 도덕적 성격을 논하고 있다고 가정하며

내가 여러분에게 Maddy가 나쁘다고 말한다고 생각해 보라. 아마 여러분은 나

의 억양이나 우리가 말하고 있는 맥락으로 보아 내가 도덕적으로 나쁘다는 뜻을 의도하고 있음을 추론한다. 게다가 일반적인 언어 관행을 고려하고 내가 진심이라고 상정한다면, 여러분은 내가 Maddy를 못마땅해하고 있다고, 또는 내 생각에 여러분이 그녀를 못마땅하든 해야 한다고 말하고 있는 것이라고 아마도 추론할 것이다. ① 하지만 여러분은 Maddy가 어떤 식으로 특정하게 나쁜 것인지와 그녀의 일반적인 성격 특성 등등에 대해서는 더 자세하게 인식하지 못할 수도 있는데, 사람들은 여러 방면에서 나쁠 수 있기 때문이다. ② 그에 반해서, 만일 내가 Maddy는 사악하다고 말한다면, 여러분은 다른 사람들에 대한 그녀의 일반적인 행동과 태도를 더 알게 된다. ③ '사악한'이라는 낱말은 '나쁜'보다 더 구체적이다. ④ 사악함은 많은 형태를 띤다는 점에서 나는 여전히 Maddy의 성격을 정확하게 지적하지 않았다. 하지만 그럼에도 불구하고 더 많은 세부 사항, 아마도 Maddy가 어떤 사람인지에 관한 더 강한 함축적 의미가 있다. ⑤ 게다가 다시 한번 일반적인 언어 관행을 상정하면, 우리가 여전히 그녀의 도덕적 성격을 논하고 있다고 가정하며, 여러분은 내가 Maddy를 못마땅해하고 있거나 여러분이 그녀를 못마땅해하든지 해야 한다고 말하고 있는 것임을 또한 파악할 것이다.

Why? 왜 정답일까?

어떤 사람을 '나쁘다'는 말과 '사악하다'라는 말로 묘사했을 때 이 말을 듣는 상대방이 어떤 식으로 화자의 의도와 발화의 의미를 파악해 가는지 설명한 글이다. In contrast 앞에서 '나쁘다'라는 다소 일반적인 단어로 어떤 사람을 묘사하는 경우를 언급한 뒤, In contrast 이후로는 '사악하다'라는 단어를 사용한 경우에 관해 서술하고 있다. ④ 앞의 문장에서 '사악하다'라는 단어는 '나쁘다'는 말에 비해 더 구체적이라고 언급한 데 이어, 주어진 문장은 그래도 여전히(still) 화자가 성격에 관해 아주 정확하게 꼬집지는 않았다는 점을 제시한다. 이어서 ④ 뒤의 문장은 그렇다고 하더라도(nevertheless) '사악하다'라는 말 속에 훨씬 강한 함의가 내포되어 있어 묘사되는 사람이 어떤 사람인지를 대략 파악할 수 있다고 설명한다. 따라서 주어진 문장이 들어가기에 가장 적절한 곳은 ④이다.

- **pinpoint** ⓥ 정확하게 지적하다
- **wickedness** ⓝ 사악함
- **disapprove of** ~을 못마땅해하다
- **linguistic** ⓐ 언어적인
- **trait** ⓝ 특성
- **nevertheless** ⓐⓓ 그럼에도 불구하고
- **character** ⓝ 성격, 성품
- **intonation** ⓝ 억양
- **given** prep ~을 고려할 때
- **convention** ⓝ 관행
- **specific** ⓐ 구체적인

구문 풀이

18행 In addition, and again assuming typical linguistic conventions,
　　　　　　　　　　　　　　　　　　　분사구문
you should also get a sense that I am disapproving of Maddy, or
주어　　동사　　목적어　동격└→주어　동사1
(am) saying that you should disapprove of her, or similar, assuming
동사2　　접속사(~것)　　　　　　　　　　　　　분사구문
that we are still discussing her moral character.
접속사(~것)

★★ 문제 해결 꿀~팁 ★★

▶ 많이 틀린 이유는?
③ 앞에서 wicked를 쓰면 bad를 썼을 때보다 '더 많은' 정보를 얻을 수 있다고 했는데, ③ 뒤에서는 그 이유로 wicked라는 단어가 더 구체적이기 때문임을 언급하고 있다. 따라서 ③ 앞뒤는 논리적으로 자연스럽게 연결된다. 또한, ⑤ 앞에서 wicked라는 단어는 bad에 비해 더 강한 의미가 실려 있다고 언급한 데 이어, ⑤ 뒤에서는 이 단어를 들은 청자가 그 뜻과 대화 규범에 기반하여 화자의 의도를 추론해나가는 과정을 서술하고 있다. 따라서 ⑤ 앞뒤 또한 맥락에 어긋남 없이 연결된다.

▶ 문제 해결 방법은?
④ 앞에서 wicked는 bad보다 더 구체적(more specific)이라고 언급하고 있다. 이때 ④ 뒤의 문장이 But으로 시작하므로, 만일 ④ 앞뒤에 논리적 공백이 없다면 ④ 뒤에는 wicked가 bad보다 '구체적이지 않다'는 반박이 이어져야 한다. 하지만 ④ 뒤에 더 구체적이라는(more detail) 설명이 그대로 이어지는 것으로 볼 때, ④ 자리에는 들어가야 하는데 빠진 내용이 있다. 따라서 ④에 주어진 문장을 넣어야만 한다.

★★★ 1등급 대비 고난도 2점 문제

| **10** | 고전 시대 음악이 자유롭게 공유되었던 이유 | 정답률 31% | 정답 ⑤ |

글의 흐름으로 보아, 주어진 문장이 들어가기에 가장 적절한 곳을 고르시오.

In the classical period of European music, / much musical material was *de facto* considered common property.

DAY 20

유럽 음악의 고전 시대에는 / 많은 음악 자료가 사실상 공유물이라고 여겨졌다.

① When Antonio Vivaldi presented in Venice his opera *Rosmira fedele*, / the score was actually a pastiche / in which, among his own ideas, / musicologists later identified ideas / by George Frederic Handel, Giovanni Battista Pergolesi and Johann Adolph Hasse, / among others.

Antonio Vivaldi가 베네치아에서 그의 오페라인 *Rosmira fedele*를 공연했을 때, / 그 악보는 실제로는 혼성곡이었다. / 그만의 악상들 사이에서 / 음악학 연구가들이 나중에 악상들이라고 확인했던 / George Frederic Handel, Giovanni Battista Pergolesi, Johann Adolph Hasse에 의한 / 다른 음악가들 중

② As far as recycling of segments of music / initially written for other occasions / into new pieces / is concerned, / it needs to be observed / how today composers are discouraged from doing so for a number of reasons.

음악의 일부를 다시 이용하는 것이 / 당초 다른 행사들을 위해 쓰여진 / 새로운 작품으로 / 관련한 한, / 주목될 필요가 있다. / 어떻게 오늘날 작곡가들은 많은 이유로 인해 그렇게 못하는지

③ A practical one is / that each new piece is sure to remain available, / in score or as an audio file.

한 가지 실질적인 이유는 / 각각의 새로운 작품이 확실히 이용 가능한 채 남아 있다는 것이다. / 악보나 오디오 파일로

④ In the 18th century, on the contrary, / once the particular occasion for performing a new piece was over, / it became almost impossible / to ever hear it again.

대조적으로, 18세기에는 / 일단 하나의 새로운 작품을 공연하기 위한 특정 행사가 끝나면 / 거의 불가능해졌다. / 그것을 다시 듣는 것이

☑ Under such circumstances, / recycling previously composed music / was the only way to make it more durable.

그러한 상황에서는 / 이전에 작곡된 음악을 다시 이용하는 것이 / 그것을 더 오래가게 하는 유일한 방법이었다.

And if new pieces also contained ideas from other composers, / that would re-enforce European musical traditions / by increasing the circulation of melodies and harmonic patterns / people loved to hear.

그리고 만약 새로운 작품들이 또한 다른 작곡가들의 악상들을 포함한다면, / 그것은 유럽 음악의 전통들을 강화했을 것이다. / 선율과 화음 패턴의 순환을 증가시킴으로써 / 사람들이 듣고 싶어 했던

유럽 음악의 고전 시대에는 많은 음악 자료가 *사실상* 공유물이라고 여겨졌다. ① Antonio Vivaldi가 베네치아에서 그의 오페라인 *Rosmira fedele*를 공연했을 때, 그 악보는 실제로는 Vivaldi의 악상들 사이에서 음악학 연구가들이 나중에 다른 음악가들 중 George Frederic Handel, Giovanni Battista Pergolesi, Johann Adolph Hasse의 악상들이라고 확인했던 혼성곡이었다. ② 당초 다른 행사들을 위해 쓰여진 음악의 일부를 새로운 작품으로 다시 이용하는 것에 관해서, 어떻게 오늘날 작곡가들은 많은 이유로 인해 그렇게 못하는지 주목될 필요가 있다. ③ 한 가지 실질적인 이유는 각각의 새로운 작품이 악보나 오디오 파일로 확실히 이용 가능한 채 남아 있다는 것이다. ④ 대조적으로, 18세기에는 일단 하나의 새로운 작품을 공연하기 위한 특정 행사가 끝나면 그것을 다시금 듣는 것이 거의 불가능해졌다. ⑤ 그러한 상황에서는 이전에 작곡된 음악을 다시 이용하는 것이 그것을 더 오래가게 하는 유일한 방법이었다. 그리고 만약 새로운 작품들이 또한 다른 작곡가들의 악상들을 포함했다면, 그것은 사람들이 듣고 싶어 했던 선율과 화음 패턴의 순환을 증가시킴으로써 유럽 음악의 전통들을 강화했을 것이다.

Why? 왜 정답일까?

오늘날과는 달리 과거 고전 시대 음악이 거의 공유물처럼 자유롭게 이용되었던 이유를 설명하는 글이다. ⑤ 앞의 두 문장에서 오늘날 음악 작품은 악보나 오디오 파일 형태로 존재하는 반면, 18세기에는 한 번 음악이 공연되고 나면 보존하여 다시 듣기가 어려운 형편이었다고 언급한다. 주어진 문장은 이러한 18세기의 상황을 such circumstances로 받으며, 그렇기에 이전에 작곡한 음악을 다시 새로운 곡에 이용하는 것이 그 음악을 보존하는 유일한 방법이었다고 설명한다. ⑤ 뒤의 문장에서는 이렇듯 새로운 곡이 이전의 악상을 포함한 형태로 작곡되면서 특유의 음악적 양식이 강화되었을 것이라는 내용을 서술한다. 따라서 주어진 문장이 들어가기에 가장 적절한 곳은 ⑤이다.

- **circumstances** ⑩ 상황, 환경
- **durable** ⓐ 오래 가는, 내구성 있는
- **musicologist** ⑩ 음악학 연구가
- **initially** ⓐⓓ 처음에
- **discourage** ⓥ 저지하다, 말리다
- **score** ⑩ 악보
- **previously** ⓐⓓ 이전에
- **common property** 공유 재산
- **identify** ⓥ 확인하다
- **occasion** ⑩ 행사, 경우
- **practical** ⓐ 실질적인
- **circulation** ⑩ 순환

구문 풀이

11행 As far as recycling of segments of music initially written for
　　　 ┌── as far as ──┐ 주어 +
other occasions into new pieces is concerned, it needs to be observed
　　　　　　　　　　 is concerned : ~에 관한 한, └→ 가주어
{how today composers are discouraged from doing so for a number
　　　{ } : 진주어
of reasons}.

▶ 많이 틀린 이유는?

음악의 재사용에 관한 과거와 오늘날의 관행을 대조하는 글이다. 먼저 ② 앞에서 과거 상황을 언급한 후, ② 뒤의 문장에서는 음악의 재사용에 관한 과거와 오늘날의 관행에 왜 차이가 있는지를 알기 위해서는 오늘날 왜 재사용이 금지되는지부터(a number of reasons) 파악해야 한다고 설명한다. ③ 뒤의 문장에서는 '한 가지 실질적 이유로(A practical one)' 오늘날에는 과거와 달리 음악이 음원이나 악보로 잘 보존된다는 점을 생각해볼 수 있다고 언급한다. 즉 ②, ③ 앞뒤 문장은 모두 논리적 공백 없이 흐름상 자연스럽게 연결된다.

▶ 문제 해결 방법은?

주어진 문장의 such circumstances는 '이전에 썼던 음악을 재활용하는 것이 그 음악을 보존하는 유일한 수단인' 상황이다. 즉 음원이나 악보로 음악이 쉽게 보존되는 오늘날의 상황과는 달리, '음악을 한 번 연주하면 다시 듣기 어려운' 상황이어야 음악의 재활용이 곧 음악의 보존 수단 역할을 할 수 있게 되는 것이다.

---

11 진화에 있어서 잠이 하는 역할 　　　 정답률 34% | 정답 ⑤

글의 흐름으로 보아, 주어진 문장이 들어가기에 가장 적절한 곳을 고르시오. [3점]

The role that sleep plays in evolution / is still under study.

진화에 있어서 잠이 하는 역할은 / 여전히 연구 중이다.

① One possibility is / that it is an advantageous adaptive state of decreased metabolism for an animal / when there are no more pressing activities.

한 가지 가능성은 / 잠이 신진대사를 줄이는, 동물에게 유리한 적응적 상태라는 것이다. / 더 이상 긴급한 활동이 없을 때

② This seems true for deeper states of inactivity / such as hibernation during the winter / when there are few food supplies, / and a high metabolic cost to maintaining adequate temperature.

이것은 더 깊은 무활동 상태의 경우에 해당하는 것처럼 보인다. / 겨울 동안의 겨울잠과 같은, / 먹을 것이 거의 없고 / 적정한 체온을 유지하는 데 높은 신진대사 비용이 드는

③ It may be true in daily situations as well, / for instance for a prey species / to avoid predators after dark.

그것은 일상 상황에도 해당될지도 모른다. / 예컨대 먹잇감이 되는 동물이 / 어두워진 이후에 포식자를 피하려는 상황 같은

④ On the other hand, / the apparent universality of sleep, / and the observation / that mammals such as cetaceans / have developed such highly complex mechanisms / to preserve sleep on at least one side of the brain at a time, / suggests / that sleep additionally provides some vital service(s) for the organism.

다른 한편으로는, / 잠의 분명한 보편성, / 그리고 관찰 결과는 / 고래목의 동물들과 같은 포유동물들이 / 매우 고도로 복잡한 기제를 발전시켰다는 / 한 번에 적어도 뇌의 한쪽에서는 잠을 유지하는 / 보여 준다. / 잠이 생명체에게 생명 유지와 관련된 어떤 도움(들)을 추가로 제공한다는 것을

☑ This is particularly true / since one aspect of sleep / is decreased responsiveness to the environment.

이것은 특히 그러하다. / 잠의 한 가지 측면은 / 환경에 대한 반응성이 감소하는 것이라는 점에서

If sleep is universal / even when this potential price must be paid, / the implication may be / that it has important functions / that cannot be obtained just by quiet, wakeful resting.

잠이 보편적으로 나타난다면, / 이러한 잠재적인 대가가 처러져야 할 때조차도 / 함의는 ~일 수도 있다. / 잠이 중요한 기능을 갖고 있다는 것일 / 조용하고 깨어 있는 상태의 휴식만으로는 얻을 수 없는

진화에 있어서 잠이 하는 역할은 여전히 연구 중이다. ① 한 가지 가능성은 잠이 더 이상 긴급한 활동이 없을 때 신진대사를 줄이는, 동물에게 유리한 적응적 상태라는 것이다. ② 이것은 먹을 것이 거의 없고 적정한 체온을 유지하는 데 높은 신진대사 비용이 드는 겨울 동안의 겨울잠과 같은, 더 깊은 무활동 상태의 경우에 해당하는 것처럼 보인다. ③ 그것은 예컨대 먹잇감이 되는 동물이 어두워진 이후에 포식자를 피하려는 상황 같은, 일상 상황에도 해당될지도 모른다. ④ 다른 한편으로는, 잠의 분명한 보편성 그리고 고래목의 동물들과 같은 포유동물들이 한 번에 적어도 뇌의 한쪽에서는 잠을 유지하는 매우 고도로 복잡한 기제를 발전시켰다는 관찰 결과는 잠이 생명체에게 생명 유지와 관련된 어떤 도움(들)을 추가로 제공한다는 것을 보여 준다. ⑤ 잠의 한 가지 측면은 환경에 대한 반응성이 감소하는 것이라는 점에서 이것은 특히 그러하다. 이러한 잠재적인 대가가 처러져야 할 때조차도 잠이 보편적으로 나타난다면, 그것이 갖는 함의는 조용하고 깨어 있는 상태의 휴식만으로는 얻을 수 없는 중요한 기능을 잠이 갖고 있다는 것일 수도 있다.

Why? 왜 정답일까?

⑤ 앞의 문장에서 잠의 보편성이나 여러 고래들이 활동 중에도 한쪽 뇌를 재우는 기제를

발달시켰다는 점 등을 고려하면 잠이 생명 유지에 추가적으로 도움을 주는 것일 수 있다고 설명한다. 이어서 주어진 문장은 잠을 자면 환경에 대한 반응성이 감소한다는 사실을 고려할 때 이것(This), 즉 ⑤ 앞의 문장 내용은 특히 사실이라고 언급한다. ⑤ 뒤의 문장에서는 주어진 문장에서 언급한 '환경에 대한 반응성 감소'를 '잠재적 대가(this potential price)'라는 말로 가리킨다. 따라서 주어진 문장이 들어가기에 가장 적절한 곳은 ⑤이다.

- **responsiveness** ⓝ 반응성
- **adaptive** ⓐ 적응적인
- **inactivity** ⓝ 무활동, 휴지
- **adequate** ⓐ 적절한
- **apparent** ⓐ 명백한
- **additionally** ⓐⓓ 추가적으로
- **implication** ⓝ 함의, 함축, 암시
- **advantageous** ⓐ 유리한
- **pressing** ⓐ 긴급한, 무시하기 힘든
- **hibernation** ⓝ 겨울잠, 동면
- **predator** ⓝ 포식자
- **universality** ⓝ 보편성
- **vital** ⓐ 생명 (유지)과 관련된, 필수적인

구문 풀이

11행 On the other hand, the <u>apparent universality of sleep</u>, and (주어1)
<u>the observation</u> {that mammals such as cetaceans have developed (주어2)
such highly complex mechanisms to preserve sleep on at least one
side of the brain at a time}, suggests that sleep additionally provides
{ }: 동격(=the observation)   동사   접속사(~것)
some vital service(s) for the organism.

★★ 문제 해결 꿀~팁 ★★

▶ 많이 틀린 이유는?
최다 오답인 ④ 앞뒤 흐름을 보면, ④ 앞은 생명체가 긴급한 활동이 없을 때 신진대사를 줄이기 좋도록 잠을 선택한다는 내용이고, ④ 뒤는 '추가적으로' 잠이 생명 유지 관점에서 주는 이득이 있음을 시사하는 관찰 결과가 있다는 내용이다. 즉 앞에서 언급된 이점 외에 잠에 추가적인 이점이 있을 것으로 여겨진다는 내용이 서로 자연스럽게 연결된다.

▶ 문제 해결 방법은?
⑤ 뒤의 문장의 this potential price가 가리키는 내용에 주목해야 한다. ⑤ 앞의 문장에서 잠의 이득(service(s))만을 언급하므로, ⑤ 앞뒤 문장이 바로 이어지면 this potential price가 무엇을 가리키는지가 애매해진다.
이때 주어진 문장에는 잠자는 동안 환경에 대한 반응이 줄어든다(decreased responsiveness)는 언급이 있으므로, 이것이 잠재적으로 생존에 위협이 될 수 있다는 의미를 나타내기 위해 potential price라는 표현이 쓰인 것임을 알 수 있다.

★★★ 1등급 대비 고난도 3점 문제

12 등고선을 이용한 지형 묘사   정답률 35% | 정답 ③

글의 흐름으로 보아, 주어진 문장이 들어가기에 가장 적절한 곳을 고르시오. [3점]

A major challenge for map-makers / is the depiction / of hills and valleys, slopes and flatlands / collectively called the *topography*.
지도 제작자들의 커다란 도전은 / 묘사이다. / 언덕과 계곡, 경사지와 평지의 / 집합적으로 *지형*이라고 불리는

This can be done in various ways.
이것은 여러 방법으로 할 수 있다.

One is to create an image of sunlight and shadow / so that wrinkles of the topography are alternately lit and shaded, / creating a visual representation of the shape of the land.
한 가지 방법은 빛과 그림자의 이미지를 만들어 내는 것이다. / 지형의 주름이 번갈아 빛이 비치고 그늘지게 만들어, / 땅의 모양을 시각적으로 표현하는 것을

① Another, technically more accurate way / is to draw contour lines.
기술적으로 더 정확한 또 다른 방법은 / 등고선을 그리는 것이다.

② A contour line connects all points / that lie at the same elevation.
등고선은 모든 점을 연결한다. / 동일한 고도에 있는

☑ A round hill rising above a plain, / therefore, / would appear on the map / as a set of concentric circles, / the largest at the base and the smallest near the top.
평야 위로 솟은 둥그런 산은 / 따라서 / 지도에 나타날 것이다. / 일련의 동심원으로 / 가장 큰 동심원이 맨 아랫부분 그리고 가장 작은 동심원은 꼭대기 근처에 있는

When the contour lines are positioned closely together, / the hill's slope is steep; / if they lie farther apart, / the slope is gentler.
등고선이 서로 가깝게 배치되면 / 산의 경사가 가파르고, / 등고선이 더 멀리 떨어져 있으면 / 기울기가 더 완만하다.

④ Contour lines can represent / scarps, hollows, and valleys of the local topography.
등고선은 나타낼 수 있다. / 지역 지형의 가파른 비탈, 분지, 계곡을

⑤ At a glance, / they reveal / whether the relief in the mapped area is great or small: / a "busy" contour map means lots of high relief.
한눈에, / 그것들은 드러내는데, / 지도로 그려진 지역의 고저가 큰지 작은지를 / '복잡한' 등고선 지도는 많은 높은 기복을 의미한다.

지도 제작자들의 커다란 도전은 집합적으로 *지형*이라고 불리는 언덕과 계곡, 경사지와 평지의 묘사이다. 이것은 여러 방법으로 할 수 있다. 한 가지 방법은 지형의 주름이 번갈아 빛이 비치고 그늘지게 빛과 그림자의 이미지를 만들어, 땅의 모양을 시각적으로 표현하는 것을 만들어 내는 것이다. ① 기술적으로 더 정확한 또 다른 방법은 등고선을 그리는 것이다. ② 등고선은 동일한 고도에 있는 모든 점을 연결한다. ③ 따라서 평야 위로 솟은 둥그런 산은 가장 큰 동심원이 맨 아랫부분에 그리고 가장 작은 동심원은 꼭대기 근처에 있는 일련의 동심원으로 지도에 나타날 것이다. 등고선이 서로 가깝게 배치되면 산의 경사가 가파르고, 등고선이 더 멀리 떨어져 있으면 기울기가 더 완만하다. ④ 등고선은 지역 지형의 가파른 비탈, 분지, 계곡을 나타낼 수 있다. ⑤ 한눈에, 그것들은 지도로 그려진 지역의 고저가 큰지 작은지를 드러내는데, '복잡한' 등고선 지도는 많은 높은 기복을 의미한다.

Why? 왜 정답일까?

지도 제작자들은 평면으로 된 지도에 다양한 지형을 묘사하기 위해 등고선을 이용한다는 내용을 다룬 글이다. ③ 앞에서 등고선은 동일한 고도에 있는 점을 연결한 것임을 설명한 데 이어, 주어진 문장은 '따라서' 산을 지도에 그리면 여러 개의 동심원 형태로 나타난다고 설명한다. ③ 뒤에는 산을 묘사하는 경우에 대한 추가적인 설명으로서 등고선이 서로 가까우면 가파른 경사를, 서로 멀면 완만한 경사를 나타낸다는 내용이 나온다. 따라서 주어진 문장이 들어가기에 가장 적절한 곳은 ③이다.

- **depiction** ⓝ 묘사, 그림, 서술
- **representation** ⓝ 표현, 묘사
- **accurate** ⓐ 정확한
- **elevation** ⓝ 고도, 해발 높이
- **hollow** ⓝ 분지, 우묵한 땅
- **topography** ⓝ 지형, 지형학
- **technically** ⓐⓓ 기술적으로
- **contour** ⓝ 등고선, 윤곽
- **steep** ⓐ 가파른

구문 풀이

7행 One is to create an image of sunlight and shadow so that
주격 보어(명사구)   ~하도록(목적)
wrinkles of the topography are alternately lit and shaded, creating a
주어   동사   과거분사구(수동태)   분사 구문
visual representation of the shape of the land.

★★ 문제 해결 꿀~팁 ★★

▶ 많이 틀린 이유는?
문장 삽입 문제는 선택지 앞뒤로 논리적 공백이 있는 부분을 찾는 것이 포인트이다. 최다 오답인 ④ 앞뒤로는 등고선을 활용하여 경사가 있는 다양한 지역, 즉 산, 비탈, 분지, 계곡 등을 묘사할 수 있다는 설명이 자연스럽게 이어지므로, 이 사이에 주어진 문장이 들어갈 만한 논리적 공백이 있다고 보기 어렵다.

▶ 문제 해결 방법은?
'③ 앞 : 등고선의 의미 소개 → 주어진 문장 : 등고선으로 산 나타내기 → ③ 뒤 : 등고선을 활용한 산의 경사 표현'이라는 도식을 통해 글에서 논리가 발전되는 과정을 이해하도록 한다.

MEMO

수능 1등급 완벽 대비 수능기출

20일 완성 영어독해

빈칸순서삽입

실전

The Real series ipsifly provide
questions in previous real test and you can
practice as real college scholastic ability test.

하루 20분! 20일 완성!

영어 독해
빈칸·순서·삽입
기본

영어 독해
빈칸·순서·삽입
완성

영어 독해
빈칸·순서·삽입
실전

**Believe in
yourself and
show us what
you can do!**

자신을 믿고 자신의 능력을 당당히 보여주자.

리얼 오리지널 하루 20분 20일 완성 | 영어 독해 | 빈칸·순서·삽입 [실전]

발행처 수능 모의고사 전문 출판 입시플라이 **발행일** 2024년 6월 1일 **등록번호** 제 2017-22호
홈페이지 www.ipsifly.com **대표전화** 02-433-9979 **구입문의** 02-433-9975 **팩스** 02-6305-9907
발행인 조용규 **편집책임** 양창열 김유 이혜민 임명선 김선영 **물류관리** 김소희 이혜리 **주소** 서울특별시 중랑구 용마산로 615 정민빌딩 3층

※ 페이지가 누락되었거나 파손된 교재는 구입하신 곳에서 교환해 드립니다. ※ 발간 이후 발견되는 오류는 입시플라이 홈페이지 정오표를 통해서 알려드립니다.